Sunset
Western
Garden Book

*By the Editors of Sunset Magazine
and Sunset Books*

Lane Publishing Co. • Menlo Park, California

Editor, Sunset Books: David E. Clark

Fifteenth Printing January 1977

Foreword

We who put this book together look upon gardening as the most satisfying and enjoyable of hobbies — or pursuits — or chores — classify it as you will. Gardening offers a rare combination of satisfactions — it is recreation, relaxation, exercise, with the gardener setting the pace; it offers esthetic delights for the gardener and also for his friends and his family.

This book is written to serve the thousands and thousands who plant, maintain, and enjoy gardens in the Western United States — all the way from the eastern borders of Idaho, Utah, and Arizona through the mountains, deserts, hills, and valleys to the Pacific beaches.

It describes several thousand plants we can grow in widely separated, greatly varied Western climates and it tells how to take care of them.

It assigns these plants to the Western garden climates in which they grow best. There are 24 of these climates — you'll find them distributed over just about every square mile of the West in the maps on the following pages.

The book further recognizes that our climates allow us to do more in our gardens than can be done in most other parts of the world. In the special green-paper section you'll find a plant-use guide for 36 different landscaping problems.

We dedicate this book to Western gardeners of every degree of skill and interest. At one end of the spectrum we see the willing or unwilling beginner-novice standing trowel in hand, wondering just what to do with that flat of pansies or that canned camellia or that baby pine tree. At the other extreme we see the all-out expert who may pick up this book to find out, let's say, what distinguishes *Sasa pygmaea* 'Variegated' from other dwarf bamboos. In between, of course, are the thousands of post-novice and pre-expert gardeners who are most of us.

Whatever gardening means to you, we hope that this book will make it even more enjoyable.

JOSEPH F. WILLIAMSON
GARDEN EDITOR, SUNSET MAGAZINE

EDITORIAL DIRECTOR: JOSEPH F. WILLIAMSON, GARDEN EDITOR, SUNSET MAGAZINE

*

BOOK EDITOR: John R. Dunmire
SUPERVISING EDITOR: David E. Clark

STAFF EDITORS: Paul C. Johnson, Roy Krell, William R. Marken,
Donald E. Erskine, Elton Welke, Marion Baldwin

*

SPECIAL CONSULTANTS: Walter L. Doty, Elsa Uppman Knoll

*

ILLUSTRATIONS: E. D. Bills
CLIMATE MAPS: Joe Seney
LAYOUT ASSISTANT: William Gibson
FRONT COVER ILLUSTRATIONS: JANE TEIKO OKA
STAFF BOTANIST: Beryl Jespersen
GLOSSARY SKETCHES: Kelly Solis-Navarro
EDITORIAL ASSISTANTS: Marian May, Sherry Gellner, Lynne Meyer,
Virginia Bickford, Audra Terry, Dagny Janss

Consultants

PACIFIC NORTHWEST

NOBLE BASHOR, Rosarian, Salem
DONALD W. BERRY, County Agricultural Agent,
Medford, Ore.
WILBUR L. BLUHM, County Agricultural Agent, Salem
LLOYD BOND, Landscape Architect, Eugene
J. HAROLD CLARKE, Nurseryman, Long Beach, Wash.
JAN DE GRAAFF, Bulb Grower and Hybridist,
Gresham, Ore.
FRED L. DELKIN, Bulb Grower, Bellevue, Wash.
ANDREW A. DUNCAN, Extension Vegetable Specialist,
O.S.U., Corvallis
CHANDLER D. FAIRBANK, Landscape Architect, Portland
JAMES GOSSLER, Horticulturist, Springfield, Ore.
JEANNETTE GROSSMAN, Horticulturist, Portland
L. KEITH HELLSTROM, Landscape Architect, Spokane
HAROLD T. HOPKINS, Nurseryman, Bothell, Wash.
ANTON S. HORN, Horticulturist, Boise
HUNTINGTON AND ROTH, Landscape Architects, Portland
RUDY KALMBACH, Rosarian, Portland
CHARLES A. KREMENAK, Rosarian, Lewiston, Idaho
RAY A. MCNEILAN, County Agricultural Agent,
Gresham, Ore.
GRANT E. MITSCH, Bulb Grower and Hybridist,
Canby, Ore.
EARL L. PHILLIPS, Climatologist, Seattle

WALLACE M. RUFF, Professor of Landscape Architecture,
U. of O., Eugene
GEORGE SCHENK, Nurseryman, Bothell, Wash.
R. M. SNODGRASS, Nurseryman, Portland
GILBERT STERNES, Climatologist, Portland
D. J. STEVLINGSON, Climatologist, Boise
DONALD W. STRYKER, Nurseryman, Langlois, Ore.
CHARLES THURMAN, Horticulturist, Spokane
PAUL VAN ALLEN, Nurseryman, Portland
TED VAN VEEN, Nurseryman, Portland
MARY WHITELEY, Rhododendron Expert, Seattle
JOSEPH A. WITT, Horticulturist, U. of W. Arboretum,
Seattle
HARRIETT G. ZORNER, Nurserywoman, Portland

NORTHERN CALIFORNIA, NEVADA, UTAH

WORTH BROWN, Bulb Grower, Capitola, Calif.
P. H. BRYDON, Horticulturist, Strybing Arboretum, San
Francisco
CHARLES BURR, Nurseryman, Palo Alto, Calif.
DONALD F. DILLON, Nurseryman, Fremont, Calif.
ECKBO, DEAN, AUSTIN, AND WILLIAMS, Landscape
Architects, San Francisco
JOHN EDWARDS, Nurseryman, Palo Alto, Calif.
CLYDE ELMORE, Extension Technologist, U.C., Davis
DAVID FEATHERS, Camellia Specialist, Lafayette, Calif.

ROXANA FERRIS, Botanist Emeritus, Stanford
BRYAN FEWER, Arborist, San Francisco
LEON FREHNER, Landscape Architect, Salt Lake City
BURR GARMAN, Landscape Architect, Fresno
DEWAYNE E. GILBERT, Extension Bioclimatologist, U.C., Davis
J. DUNCAN GRAHAM, Eucalyptus Expert, Benicia, Calif.
GEORGE HAIGHT, Nurseryman, San Jose
WILLIAM A. HARVEY, Extension Weed Control Specialist, U.C., Davis
WILLIAM H. HENDERSON, Nurseryman, Clovis, Calif.
COLIN JACKSON, Arborist, Sunnyvale, Calif.
WILLIAM LOUIS KAPRANOS, Landscape Architect, San Rafael, Calif.
MASARU KIMURA, Landscape Architect, Palo Alto, Calif.
ANNA KLINE, Horticulturist, Palo Alto, Calif.
ANDREW T. LEISER, Professor of Horticulture, U.C., Davis
PETER J. LERT, County Farm Advisor, San Jose
LOUIS LEVALLEY, Professor of Horticulture, Fresno State College
W. M. LOCKHART, Meteorologist, Menlo Park, Calif.
ROBERT LUDEKENS, Nurseryman, Visalia, Calif.
BARBARA LYNCH, Horticulturist, Santa Clara, Calif.
HENRY R. MARTIN, Nurseryman, Sebastopol, Calif.
ARTHUR H. McCAIN, Extension Plant Pathologist, U.C., Berkeley
ELIZABETH McCLINTOCK, Botanist, Cal. Acad. of Sciences, San Francisco
ROD McLELLAN, Nurseryman, Colma, Calif.
WOODBRIDGE METCALF, Extension Forester (ret.), U.C., Berkeley
RAY MILLER, Landscape Architect, Santa Cruz, Calif.
DENNISON MOREY, Plant Breeder, Santa Rosa, Calif.
JAY E. MORING, Landscape Architect, Visalia, Calif.
HAROLD PRICKETT, Nurseryman, Santa Rosa, Calif.
ERNEST F. REIMSCHUSSEL, Professor of Horticulture, B.Y.U., Provo, Utah
VICTOR REITER, JR., Nurseryman, San Francisco
WAYNE RODERICK, Horticulturist, U.C., Berkeley
ROYSTON, HANAMOTO, BECK, AND ABEY, Landscape Architects, San Francisco.
ROBERT H. RUF, Horticulturist, University of Nevada, Reno
ROY RYDELL, Landscape Architect, Santa Cruz, Calif.
SARATOGA HORTICULTURAL FOUNDATION, Saratoga, Calif.
WILLIAM E. SCHMIDT, Nurseryman, Palo Alto, Calif.
JACK SCHNEIDER, Nurseryman, Lafayette, Calif.
R. H. SCIARONI, County Farm Advisor, Half Moon Bay, Calif.
DOROTHY STEMLER, Rose Grower, Watsonville, Calif.
PETER SUGAWARA, Nurseryman, Los Altos, Calif.
MARGARET TRUAX, Nurserywoman, Carmel, Calif.
ELMER TWEDT, Seedsman, San Juan Bautista, Calif.
MAX WATSON, Eucalyptus Expert, San Jose
ADRIAN WILSON, Book Designer, San Francisco
JAMES WILSON, Seedsman, Mountain View, Calif.

SOUTHERN CALIFORNIA AND ARIZONA

WILLIAM APLIN, Horticulturist, Ventura, Calif.
DAVID ARMSTRONG, Nurseryman, Ontario, Calif.
ARMSTRONG AND SHARFMAN, Landscape Architects, Los Angeles

ROBERT BODDY, Nurseryman, Chino, Calif.
JOHN BOETHING, Nurseryman, Woodland Hills, Calif.
PHILIP E. CHANDLER, Horticultural Consultant, Santa Monica
FRANCIS CHING, Horticulturist, L.A. State and County Arboretum, Arcadia
CLIFFORD COMSTOCK, Nurseryman, Azusa, Calif.
AL CONDIT, Seedsman, Santa Paula, Calif.
IRA J. CONDIT, Professor of Horticulture, Emeritus, U.C., Riverside
ANDRE CUENOUD, Landscape Architect, Scottsdale, Ariz.
A. G. DAVIDS, Bulb Grower, Los Angeles
MILDRED DAVIS, Landscape Architect, Santa Monica
JOCELYN DOMELA, Landscape Architect, Los Angeles
KEN DYO, Landscape Gardener, Pasadena
MORGAN EVANS, Landscape Architect, Los Angeles
PERCY C. EVERETT, Horticulturist, Rancho Santa Ana Bot. Gdn., Claremont, Calif.
JOSEPH E. FOLKNER, Landscape Architect, Tucson
TOKUJI FURUTA, Extension Ornamental Horticulturist, U.C., Riverside
J. N. GIRIDLIAN, Nurseryman, Arcadia, Calif.
SVEND GOTTSCHALK, Nurseryman, Brea, Calif.
ERNEST HETHERINGTON, Nurseryman, San Gabriel, Calif.
BARBARA JOE HOSHIZAKI, Botanist, L. A. City College
DORIS JAMES, Nurserywoman, Douglas, Ariz.
ERIC JOHNSON, Landscape Designer, Duarte, Calif.
WARREN JONES, Landscape Architect, La Habra, Calif.
MARSTON H. KIMBALL, Extension Bioclimatologist (ret.), Alhambra, Calif.
MYRON W. KIMNACH, Botanist, Huntington Bot. Gdn., San Marino, Calif.
FREDERICK M. LANG, Landscape Architect, South Laguna, Calif.
RALPH G. LA RUE, Agriculturist, South Pasadena, Calif.
WALTER LEE, Nurseryman, Azusa, Calif.
JAMES M. LYONS, Professor of Vegetable Crops, U.C., Riverside
MARK MARKO, Nurseryman, Azusa, Calif.
OTTO MARTENS, Nurseryman, Monrovia, Calif.
MILDRED MATHIAS, Botanist, U.C.L.A.
RALPH D. McPHEETERS, Nurseryman, Tucson
ARTHUR OTIS, Garden Writer, San Diego
JAMES C. PERRY, Nurseryman, La Puente , Calif.
ROBERT G. PLATT, Extension Citrus Specialist, U.C., Riverside
R. W. RAGLAND, Camellia Specialist, Los Angeles
DAVID R. ROBERTS, Nurseryman, Balboa Park, San Diego
GEORGE HARMON SCOTT, Nurseryman, Pasadena
L. K. SMITH, Landscape Architect, Thousand Oaks, Calif.
HAROLD SWANTON, Horticulturist, Northridge, Calif.
SOIL AND PLANT LABORATORY, INC., Orange, Calif.
VERNON T. STOUTEMYER, Professor of Ornamental Horticulture, U.C.L.A.
HARVEY F. TATE, Extension Horticulturist, U.A., Tucson
RICHARD B. TAYLOR, Landscape Architect, Santa Barbara
JOHN VAN BARNEVELD, Rosarian, Whittier, Calif.
RICHARD D. WESTCOTT, Nurseryman, Los Angeles
JAMES K. WHEAT, Nurseryman, Phoenix
HARRIETT WIMMER AND JOSEPH YAMADA, Landscape Architects, San Diego
DONALD P. WOOLLEY, Horticulturist, South Coast Bot. Gdn., Palos Verdes, Calif.

Table of Contents

More than 5,000 plants, listed alphabetically according to botanical names.
Common names are also listed for easy cross-reference.

The West's 24 Climate Zones

In this book's Western Plant Encyclopedia (pages 168 to 445) and in the Plant Selection Guide (pages 98 to 160) you will find climate zones assigned to every listed plant (except annuals and house plants).

If you've been gardening for any time at all, you know why such climate assignments are necessary. The plants we grow in Western gardens come from all parts of the world. Because of their greatly varied backgrounds, they differ immensely in their response to the different climates of the West. Many can't live through a cold winter. Others must have cold winters. Some can't perform well in

coastal humidity; others depend on damp air. And so it goes: Many factors combine and interplay to establish plant climates. These factors combine in so many ways in the West that in this book we have identified two dozen different plant climates.

A plant climate is an area in which a common set of temperature ranges, humidity patterns, and other geographic and seasonal characteristics combine to allow certain plants to succeed and cause others to fail.

Remember, there's a difference between *weather* and *climate*. Weather is what is going on in the atmosphere outside your window at the moment you read this. Climate is the all-seasons accumulation of the effect of the weather that comes to your area.

Six important factors combine to make up Western plant climates. Here they are:

1. Distance from the equator (latitude). Generally, the farther a spot is from the equator, the longer and colder are its winters. The number of hours of daylight increases in summer and decreases in winter as you progress from the equator toward the pole.

2. Elevation. High elevations mean longer and colder winters, and comparatively lower night temperatures all through the year.

3. Influence of the Pacific Ocean. Weather in Western United States comes almost completely from two sources, and the Pacific Ocean is one of them. The more an area is dominated by the Pacific Ocean's weather, the moister is its atmosphere at all seasons, the milder its winters, the cooler its summers, and the more is its rainfall limited to fall, winter, and spring.

4. Influence of the continental air mass. This is the other major source of our weather in the West. The more an area is influenced by the continental air mass, the colder are its winters, the hotter and drier are its summers, and the more likely is its precipitation to come at any time of the year.

5. Mountains and hills. Our systems of hills and mountains act as barriers that determine whether areas beyond them will be influenced mostly by marine air or mostly by continental air — or, as happens in some places, by some of each. The Coast Ranges take some of the marine influence out of air that passes west-to-east across them. And the marine influence that the Coast Ranges don't take out is effectively weakened or stopped by the lofty second line of defense — the Sierra-Cascades and southern California's interior mountains. In exactly the opposite order, first the interior ranges and then the Coast Ranges lessen or eliminate the westward influence of the continental air mass.

6. Local terrain. The five factors mentioned above operate at all seasons. Local terrain has its major effect on the cold air and frosts of fall, winter, and spring.

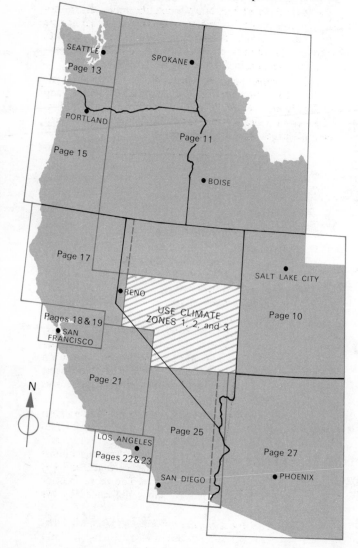

Warm air rises. Cold air sinks. Experienced gardeners understand the practical applications of this physical fact; they know that cold air flows (or moves or slides) downhill. If yours is a sidehill garden or even if your entire community is on a slanting plain that ultimately leads to lower ground in the next county, your garden will never be quite as cold in winter as will the gardens at the base of the hill, along the distant river, or at the lowest end of the sloping plain. The bands of a hillside or tilted valley floor from which cold air flows downhill are called *thermal belts*. The lowlands, valley centers, and river bottoms into which the cold air flows are called *cold-air basins*. Above the thermal belt, winter air can be so cold (because of the elevation influence mentioned above) that the temperature can be as low as in the cold basin at the base of the thermal belt, or even lower.

The 24 plant climate zones used in this book were mapped by drawing lines at certain latitudes (distance from equator), drawing other lines representing the typical penetrations of marine and interior air, and drawing still other lines for elevations and the big, significant thermal belts and cold basins. The result was to define climate areas that are relatively constant within their boundaries.

In many cases, the lines that delineate the climates were plotted according to the success-failure records of certain indicator plants. Where such a plant succeeds regularly in one area and fails regularly in a nearby area, the climate line was drawn to separate the two.

Do not consider the lines on the maps as rigid. Only in a very few places in the West are the climate controlling factors so consistent that we can draw a line controlling on the ground with a stick and say "on this side of the line is climate X and on the other side climate Y." Mostly, such a line would be nonsense. As the strengths of the controlling factors rise or fall, the lines shift gradually back and forth.

If your garden is well inside a climate zone's mapped boundaries, you can rest assured that your garden is in that zone without much qualification. But if you live near a dividing line, your climate can occasionally resemble the climate across the line.

Another point to consider is that conditions in your garden or neighborhood can create microclimates (little climates a few feet or a few hundred feet wide) that will be somewhat different from the general climate of your area. For example, a solid fence or row of dense evergreen trees at the bottom of a slope can trap cold air and cause colder night temperatures there. A south-facing wall will accumulate heat, creating a warm microclimate.

Also, there are many little thermal belts, hilltops, swales, canyons, and fog belt fingers that are too small to register on the maps. In such a location your climate may be *slightly* milder or *slightly* more severe than that of your neighbors half a mile away. But usually the change is no greater than to an adjacent climate.

Here is how to find the mapped climate zone for your area. First, look at the locator map on the opposite page. It tells you the page on which your state or your part of your state is mapped. Then turn to that page and on its map you will find your climate zone number.

The reference guides are county lines (dashed lines), state borders, and dots representing cities and towns. In larger towns and cities, the dot represents the city hall. The Los Angeles area map on pages 22 and 23, where county lines are few and cities are big, is further oriented by freeway routes. Communities shown on the maps are not necessarily the largest or most important. Many smaller towns are included because they happen to be on or near a transition line from one zone to another.

Descriptions of the 24 plant climate zones follow. In the Encyclopedia and Plant Selection Guide, climate adaptability is repeatedly indicated by two zone numbers connected by a dash (as Zones 4-9). This means that the plant is recommended for all the zones indicated from first to second number inclusive. In the descriptions that follow, temperatures are in degrees Fahrenheit.

SPECIAL ACKNOWLEDGMENT

The publishers of this book thank the many climatologists, bioclimatologists, meteorologists, and horticulturists who gave valuable assistance in making these climate maps. These experts are listed by name in the acknowledgments section in the opening pages of this book.

Special thanks go to the University of California Agricultural Extension Service for making available the map in *California's Plantclimates* (a publication released in 1967) from which most of the California climates shown on these pages were originally derived.

ZONE 1 *Coldest Winters in the West*

Zones 1, 2, and 3 are the snowy parts of the West — the regions where snow falls and stays on the ground (a day, a week, or all winter) every winter. Of the three snowy-winter climates, this is the coldest.

The extreme winter cold of Zone 1 can be caused by any or all of the three factors that can make cold winters: latitude (the farther north, the colder); influence of continental air mass (the more of it, the colder); and elevation (the higher, the colder). Most of Zone 1 in the Northwest and in Utah does indeed get its cold winter temperatures from all three contributing factors.

The Zone 1 areas of western Oregon and Washington get their climate features from only two of the three factors — northerly latitude and elevation. In California and Arizona, those Zone 1 areas that exist are due almost exclusively to elevation — you will notice that Zone 1 is all in high mountains in those areas. The more interior of these Zone 1 areas are also partly influenced by the continental air mass.

In this zone, the typical growing season (period between last frost in springtime and first frost in fall) lasts for not much longer than 100 days — although it may average as high as 180 days in some parts. In most Zone 1 places, frosts can occur on any day of the year.

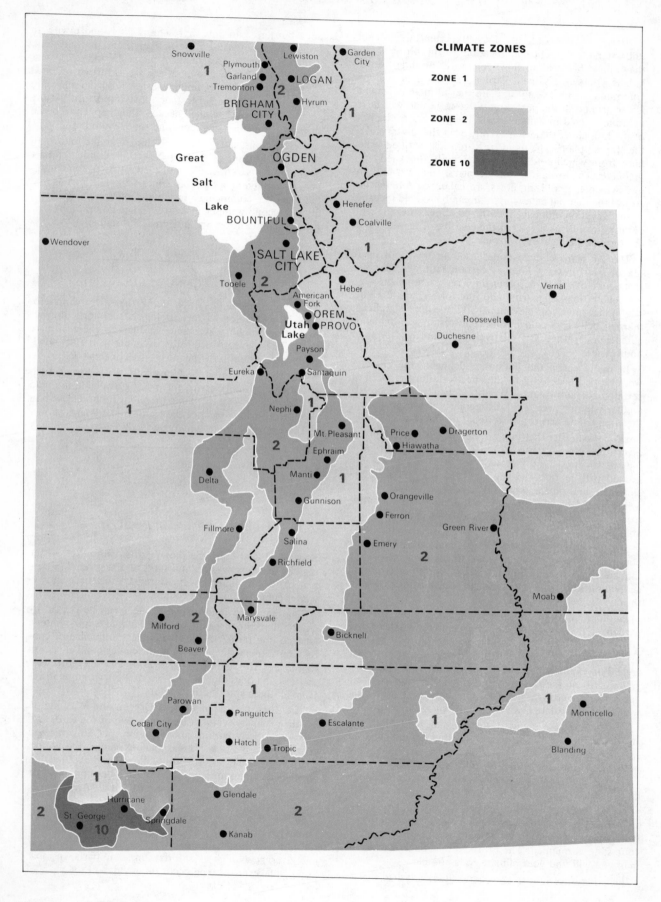

CLIMATE ZONES

ZONE 1

ZONE 2

ZONE 10

Snowville
Lewiston
Garden City
Plymouth
1
Garland
Tremonton
LOGAN
2
Hyrum
BRIGHAM CITY
1
Great Salt Lake
OGDEN
Henefer
Coalville
BOUNTIFUL
Wendover
SALT LAKE CITY
1
Tooele
2
Heber
Vernal
American Fork
OREM PROVO
Roosevelt
Utah Lake
Payson
Duchesne
Eureka
Santaquin
1
Nephi
1
Mt. Pleasant
1
Price
Dragerton
Ephraim
Hiawatha
2
Manti
1
Delta
Gunnison
Orangeville
Ferron
Fillmore
Salina
Emery
Green River
2
Richfield
Moab
1
2
Marysvale
Milford
Bicknell
Beaver
1
Parowan
Panguitch
1
Cedar City
Escalante
Monticello
1
Hatch
Tropic
Blanding
1
Glendale
Hurricane
2
St. George
Springdale
2
10
Kanab

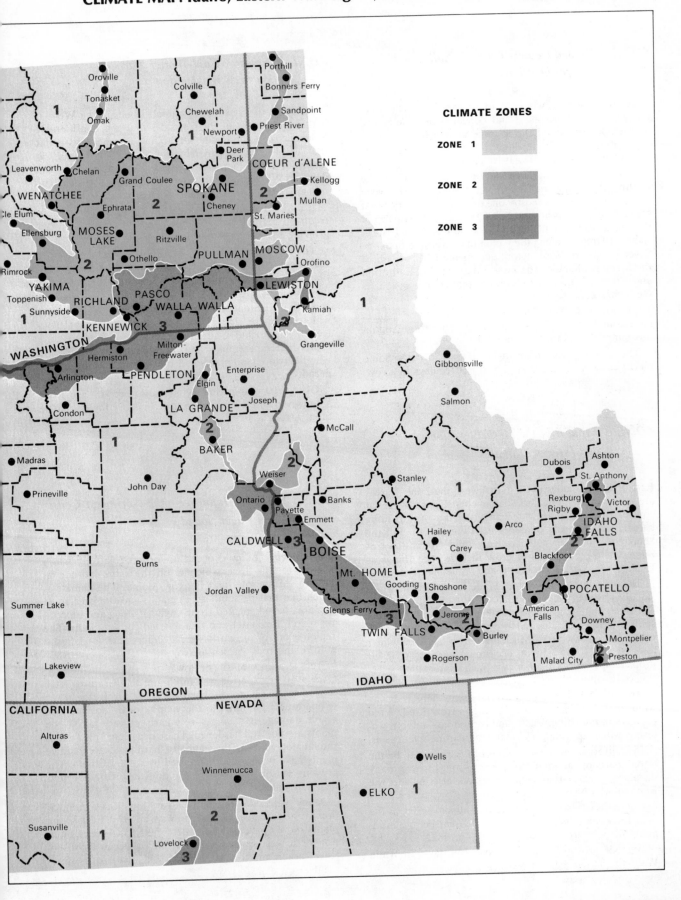

CLIMATE ZONES

ZONE 1

ZONE 2

ZONE 3

ZONE 2 Second Coldest Climate, Soil Freezes in Winter

Here, too, snow in winter is to be expected. The chief difference between Zone 2 and Zone 1 is that the record low temperatures and the average annual low temperatures are not as low as in Zone 1. And this makes a difference with many desirable garden plants.

In the northerly latitudes and interior areas where the continental air mass rules supreme, the difference between Zone 2 and Zone 1 is mostly one of elevation. Notice that some Zone 2 exists around Salt Lake City, along parts of the Snake River of Idaho, the Grande Ronde and Burnt rivers of Oregon, along the Columbia River and Spokane River in eastern Washington, and in the lakes region of the Idaho panhandle. The Zone 2 that exists in California and Arizona is in higher elevations that are not as cold as the higher Zone 1.

According to Weather Bureau records, temperatures have gone below $-30°$. During a 10 year period, annual low temperatures ranged from $-8°$ to $-29°$.

The growing season averages about 150 days. Some places can count on almost 200 frost-free days in a row.

ZONE 3 Mildest of the High-Elevation and Interior Climates

East of the Cascades in the Northwest, the Zone 3 areas are the ones that get called "banana belts" most often. Of course, the only place you can grow the real, fruiting banana satisfactorily outdoors is in the tropics. But the "bananas" that the comparatively mild winter lows of Zone 3 allow gardeners to grow include such things as English boxwood, Irish heath, and winter jasmine.

The portion of Zone 3 from Hood River to Lewiston is slightly lower in elevation than the surrounding Zone 2. This fact, combined with the influence of Pacific air that spills over the Cascades and through the Columbia Gorge, moderates most winters. Much planting is based on winter lows of 10° to 15°. In an occasional winter, arctic air drops temperatures much lower. Such winters limit selection of broad-leafed evergreens.

Absolute cold is not so much the enemy here as drying winds that dehydrate plants growing in frozen soil. Wind protection, mulching, shade, and careful late autumn watering will help you grow many borderline evergreens.

In California the Zone 3 areas often happen to be the lowest parts of the high mountains — areas where many people keep gardens at cabins. The zone also includes the Reno area in Nevada.

Coldest recorded temperatures are almost as low as the ones for Zone 2, below $-30°$. In a 10 year period, minimum temperatures ranged from $-9°$ to $-22°$.

Average growing season is about 160 days. In Walla Walla the season lasts almost 220 days.

ZONE 4 Interior, Cold-Winter Parts of Western Washington

This is one of the smallest climate zones in the West. It is the region west of the Cascades that gets considerable influence from the Pacific Ocean and Puget Sound — but that also is affected either by the continental air mass at times, or by higher elevation, or both. It touches salt water in Whatcom County and nowhere else, but in some higher spots it is in distant view of the ocean or the sound.

It differs from neighboring Zone 5 principally in more frequent extreme low winter temperatures, a shorter growing season, and considerably more rainfall.

The two Puget Sound climates (Zones 4 and 5) can be found in the same neighborhood, and their presence is behind much of the familiar Northwestern talk about warm or cold gardens.

Some of the tenderer rhododendrons that Seattle grows will freeze here, as will some of the rarer shrubs from New Zealand and Chile. On the other hand, no zone grows better perennials and bulbs than Zone 4. People who like woodland plants and rock plants find this area a paradise.

Over a 10-year period, winter lows here ranged from 5° down to $-2°$; in all of recorded history the lows have ranged from 0° to $-5°$.

ZONE 5 Marine Influence—the Northwest Coast and Puget Sound

The influence of mild ocean air brings relatively warm winters to this area, which is on the same latitude as Duluth, Minnesota, and Bangor, Maine. The climate is much like that of southern England, and the gardens in this area have benefited from England's long and successful search for better and more varied garden plants. The region is one of the world's great centers of rhododendron culture and rock gardening.

Temperatures of 0° or lower are quite uncommon. Over a 10-year period, the minimum temperatures have ranged from 13° to 3°. The occasional big freeze when temperatures plummet to the vicinity of 0° does considerable damage if it comes very early or very late, when plants are not well hardened. These occasional big freezes should not serve as the gauge of hardiness; even native plants have been killed or injured by some of them. The growing season may run to 250 days in favored regions near salt water.

Many waterside areas show a very low heat accumulation in the summer. Those who want to grow heat-loving plants should pick out the hottest spots for them; a south wall or a west wall sheltered from cold winds will do. Select peach and tomato varieties with low heat requirements.

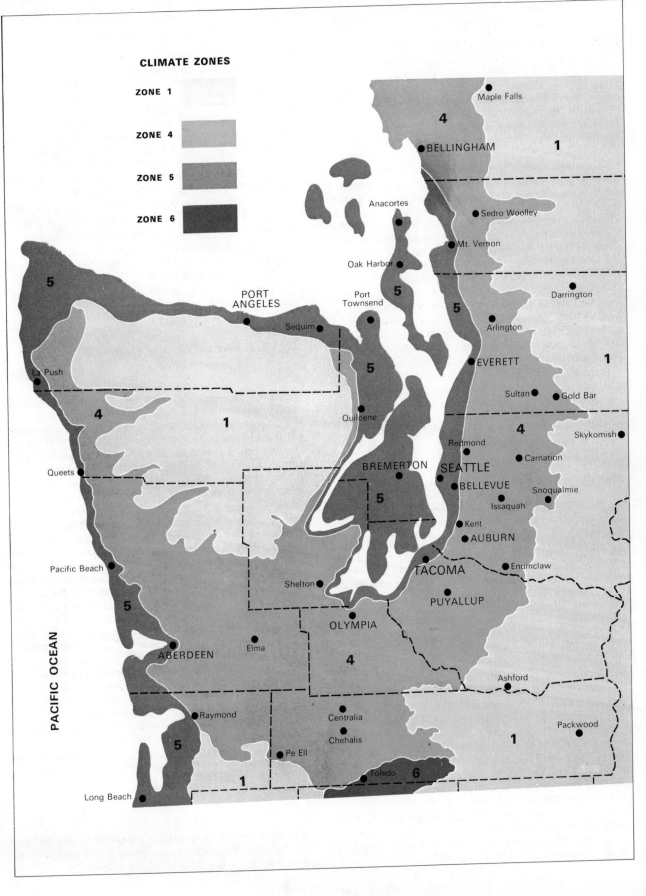

CLIMATE ZONES

ZONE 1

ZONE 4

ZONE 5

ZONE 6

Maple Falls

4

BELLINGHAM

1

Anacortes

Sedro Woolley

Mt. Vernon

Oak Harbor

5

5

Darrington

PORT ANGELES

Port Townsend

Arlington

5

Sequim

EVERETT

La Push

5

5

Sultan

Gold Bar

4

Quilcene

1

Redmond

4

Skykomish

Queets

BREMERTON

SEATTLE

Carnation

BELLEVUE

Snoqualmie

5

Issaquah

Kent

Pacific Beach

AUBURN

5

TACOMA

Enumclaw

Shelton

PUYALLUP

OLYMPIA

PACIFIC OCEAN

ABERDEEN

Elma

4

Ashford

Raymond

Centralia

Packwood

5

Chehalis

1

Pe Ell

Toledo

6

1

Long Beach

4

Port Angeles

ZONE 6 *Willamette Valley—Partly Marine Influence, Partly Interior*

A somewhat longer growing season and warmer summers set the Willamette Valley climate off from the coast - Puget Sound climate. The Coast Range tempers the coastal winds and somewhat reduces the rainfall, but the climate of the valley is still essentially maritime much of the year, hence getting much less winter cold and less summer heat than areas east of the Cascades.

Average lows are similar to those of the coast - Puget Sound zone — even slightly colder in some places — but summer high temperatures average 5° to 8° warmer, warm enough to put sugar in the Elberta peaches and to speed growth of such evergreens as abelia and nandina. The long, mild growing season has made the Willamette Valley one of the West's great growing areas for nursery stock. Many of the West's (and the nation's) fruit and shade trees, deciduous shrubs, and broad-leafed evergreens started life here.

Any mention of the Willamette Valley must include roses and rhododendrons, both of which attain near-perfection here. Broad-leafed evergreens generally are at their clean, green best; choice rhododendrons, azaleas, and pieris grow with sufficient ease to qualify as basic landscaping shrubs.

Here, as further north, local microclimates are important, especially to the successful blooming of early flowering material. Avoid cold-air pockets when setting out apricots, figs, deciduous magnolias, and the earliest rhododendrons.

ZONE 7 *Oregon's Rogue River Valley and California's Digger Pine Belt*

Zone 7 appears over quite a few thousand square miles in the regions west of the Sierra-Cascades. Because of the influence of latitude, this climate of similar character is found at low elevations in a valley in Oregon (the Rogue Valley) but at middle elevations in California (the low mountains, most of which can be identified by native Digger pines).

Hot summers and mild but pronounced winters give this area sharply defined seasons without severe winter cold or enervating humidity. The climate pleases the plants that require a marked seasonal pattern to do well —peony, iris, lilac, flowering cherry. Deciduous fruits that require a marked seasonal pattern do well; the region is noted for its pears, apples, peaches, and cherries.

Gardeners in a few spots in the Coast Ranges near San Francisco Bay will be surprised to find their gardens mapped in Zone 7, even though there isn't a Digger pine in miles. These are hilltop and ridge-top areas that are too high (and hence too cold in winter) to be included with milder Zones 15 and 16.

For such a big area, it is of course impossible to state exact low temperatures. But at weather-recording stations in the Zone 7 area, the typical winter lows range from 23° to 9°, the record lows from 15° to −1°.

ZONE 8 *Cold-Air Basins (Low Spots) of California's Central Valley*

Only a shade of difference exists between Zone 8 and Zone 9, but it's an important difference — critical in some cases. Zone 9 is a thermal belt, meaning that cold air can flow from it to lower ground — and the lower ground is here in Zone 8. Citrus furnish the most meaningful illustration. Lemons, oranges, and grapefruit cannot be grown commercially in Zone 8 because winter nights can frequently be cold enough to injure or even kill the trees and the trees would need heating regularly. The same winter cold can damage many garden plants.

Zone 8 differs from Zone 14, which it joins near the latitudes of North Sacramento and Modesto, in that Zone 14 occasionally gets some marine weather influence.

Low temperatures in Zone 8 over a 10-year period have ranged from 22° to 14°. In all of recorded history, lows here have ranged from 18° to 13°.

Certain features that Zone 8 and 9 share in common are described under Zone 9.

ZONE 9 *Thermal Belts of California's Central Valley*

Repeating the example cited for Zone 8, the biggest readily apparent difference between 8 and 9 is that Zone 9 is a safer citrus climate. Most of the Valley's commercial citrus crops are grown in Zone 9. The same distinction, thermal belt versus cold basin, is reflected in this book for certain species and varieties of hibiscus, melaleuca, pittosporum, and other plants — recommended for Zone 9 but not for Zone 8.

Zones 8 and 9 have these features in common: summer daytime temperatures are high, sunshine is almost constant during the growing season, and growing seasons are long. Deciduous fruits and vegetables of nearly every kind thrive in these long, hot summers; winter cold is just adequate to satisfy dormancy requirements of the fruit trees. Fiercely cold, piercing north winds blow for several days at a time in winter — more distressing really to gardeners than to garden plants. Tule fogs (dense fogs that rise from the ground under certain peculiar weather conditions) come and stay for hours or days during winter. The fogs usually hug the ground at night and rise to 800 to 1,000 feet by afternoon. Heat-loving plants such as oleander and crape myrtle perform at their peak in Zones 8 and 9 (and 14). Plants that like summer coolness and humidity demand some fussing; careful gardeners accommodate them by providing shade and frequent sprinkling or misting.

In Zone 9, winter lows over a 10-year period have ranged from 24° to 18°. Record lows have ranged from 21° to 15°.

ZONES 10-13 These four zones are found mostly on the last two maps (pages 25 and 27) and so are described at the end of this chapter on page 26.

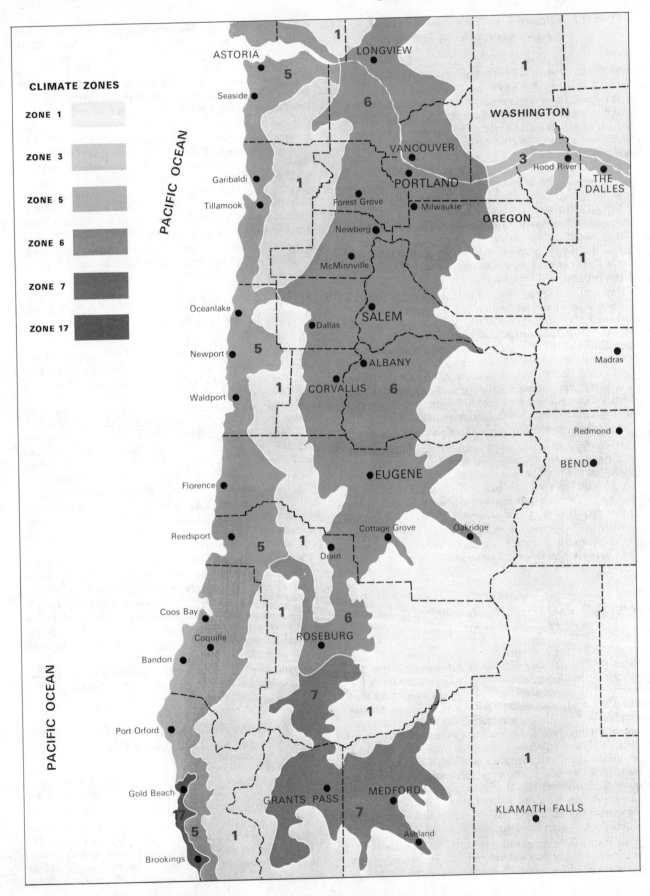

CLIMATE ZONES

ZONE 1

ZONE 3

ZONE 5

ZONE 6

ZONE 7

ZONE 17

ZONE 14 Northern California's Inland Areas with Occasional Ocean Influence

This designation is used for similar climates that come about in two different ways:

(1) Zone 14 in some cases illustrates the moderating effect of marine air on inland areas that otherwise would be colder in winter and hotter in summer. The gap in northern California's Coast Ranges created by the Golden Gate and San Francisco and San Pablo bays allows considerable marine air to spill much farther inland than it can anywhere else. The same thing happens, but the penetration is not as deep, in the Salinas Valley.

(2) Zone 14 is also used to designate the cold-winter valley floors, canyons, and land-troughs in the Coast Ranges — all the way from Solvang and Santa Ynez in Santa Barbara County to Willow Creek in Humboldt County. These pockets are colder than the surrounding areas because cold air sinks.

These two kinds of Zone 14 are quite similar in maximum and minimum temperatures. The one measurement on which they differ a bit is humidity. A good example can be seen in the lowland parts of Contra Costa County that lie east of the Oakland - Berkeley - El Cerrito hills as compared with Stockton and Sacramento on the floor of the Central Valley. Both areas are in Zone 14. In Stockton and Sacramento crape myrtles perform mightily. In the Contra Costa section they grow all right, but they suffer mildew because there is more moisture in the atmosphere.

Are you in a dryer or the moister part of Zone 14?

If on the map your closest neighboring climate is one of the summer-dry ones — 7, 8, 9, or 18 — you can conclude that yours is the dryer kind of Zone 14. But if Zone 15, 16, or 17 is your nearest neighbor, you are in one of the moister sections where crape myrtles and some other plants would be inclined to mildew.

Over a 10-year period, this area has had lows ranging from 26° to 16° Weather Bureau records show all-time lows here ranging from 22° down to 11°.

ZONE 15 Cold-Winter Portions of Northern California's Coastal Climate

"Coastal climate" as used here means the areas that are influenced by the ocean approximately 85 per cent of the time and by inland air 15 per cent of the time. Note that Zone 16 is also within the northern California coastal climate, but its winters are more mild because the areas are in thermal belts, as explained in the introduction on page 9. The cold-winter areas that make up Zone 15 are either in cold-air basins, or on hilltops above the thermal belts, or — as is the case north of Petaluma — in such northerly latitudes that plant performance dictates they be designated Zone 15. In Contra Costa, Napa, and Sonoma counties, Zone 15 exists on hills above the colder valley floors which are designated Zone 14.

In Zone 15 the finest climate for fuchsias begins. Lantanas may freeze but will recover quickly. Many plants recommended for Zone 15 are not suggested for 14 be-cause they must have the moister atmosphere, the cooler summers, the milder winters, or all three. Such plants include azara, canary bird flower (Crotalaria), Brunfelsia calycina, and leptospermum. On the other hand, Zone 15 also gets enough winter chilling to favor some of the cold-winter specialties such as herbaceous peonies (not recommended for milder-winter Zones 16 and 17).

Most of this zone, like 16 and 17, gets a regular afternoon wind in summer. It blows from early afternoon until shortly before sunset. Trees and dense shrubs planted on the windward side of a garden can disperse this nagging wind, making the garden more comfortable for plants and people. A neighborhood full of trees can successfully keep the wind above the rooftops. The wind is natural to coastal regions and will surely blow across the ground again if and when such windbreak plants are removed.

Low temperatures over a 10-year period here range from 28° to 21° and record lows from 26° to 16°.

ZONE 16 Thermal Belts of Northern California's Coastal Climate

Here's a much-favored climate that exists in patches and strips along the Coast Ranges from western Santa Barbara County north to northern Marin County. It's one of northern California's finest horticultural climates — especially for subtropical plants. The reason is that this climate consists of the thermal belts (slopes from which cold air drains) in the coastal area (dominated by ocean weather about 85 per cent of the time and by inland weather about 15 per cent). This climate gets more heat than maritime-dominated Zone 17 and has warmer winters than Zone 15. That's a happy combination.

Favored here but not favored in Zone 15 are such subtropical delights as princess flower (Tibouchina), lemon-scented gum (Eucalyptus citriodora), the hardiest avocados, and Natal plum (Carissa).

Some of the more favored portions of Zone 16, such as the hills of Oakland and Berkeley, practically never see a white frost. Very few weather recording stations are placed squarely within the indefinite borders of Zone 16. Those that do exist there show a typical range of winter lows over a 10-year period of 32° to 24°. The lowest recorded temperatures in history at points within the zone range from 25° to 18°.

A summer afternoon wind is an integral part of this climate. Read about it under the Zone 15 heading.

ZONE 17 Marine Influence—Northern California and Southern Oregon Coast

This climate is dominated by the ocean about 98 per cent of the time. In most cases you can see salt water from Zone 17; if you can't you can probably hear the foghorns.

Garden plants here seldom suffer a frost of any consequence—in some areas of the zone frosts are unknown. The climatic features are cool, wet winters, and cool summers with frequent fog or wind. On most days and in most places the fog is not the sort that creeps across the

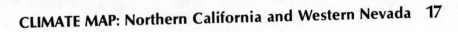

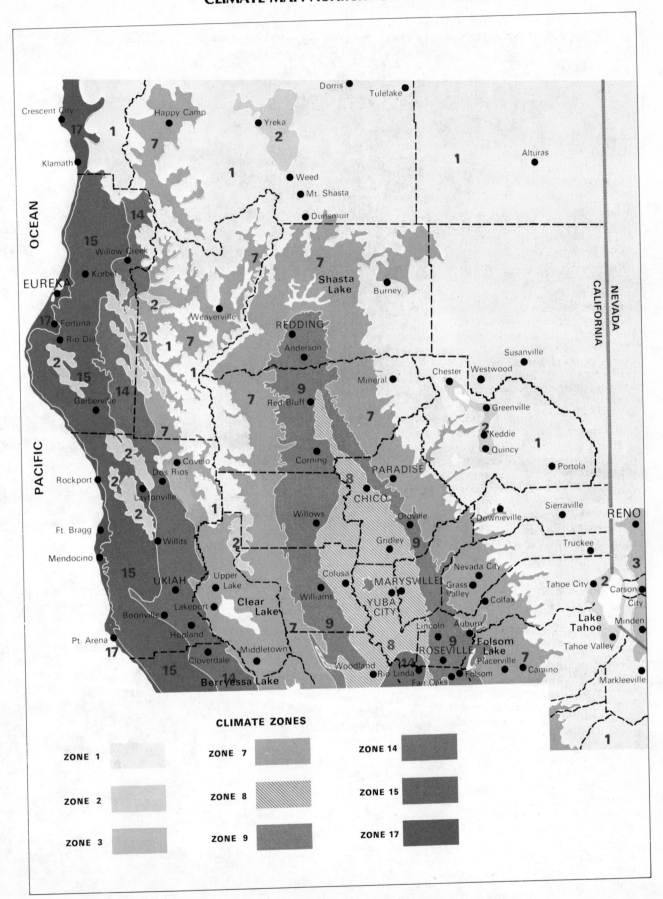

CLIMATE ZONES

ZONE 1	ZONE 7	ZONE 14
ZONE 2	ZONE 8	ZONE 15
ZONE 3	ZONE 9	ZONE 17

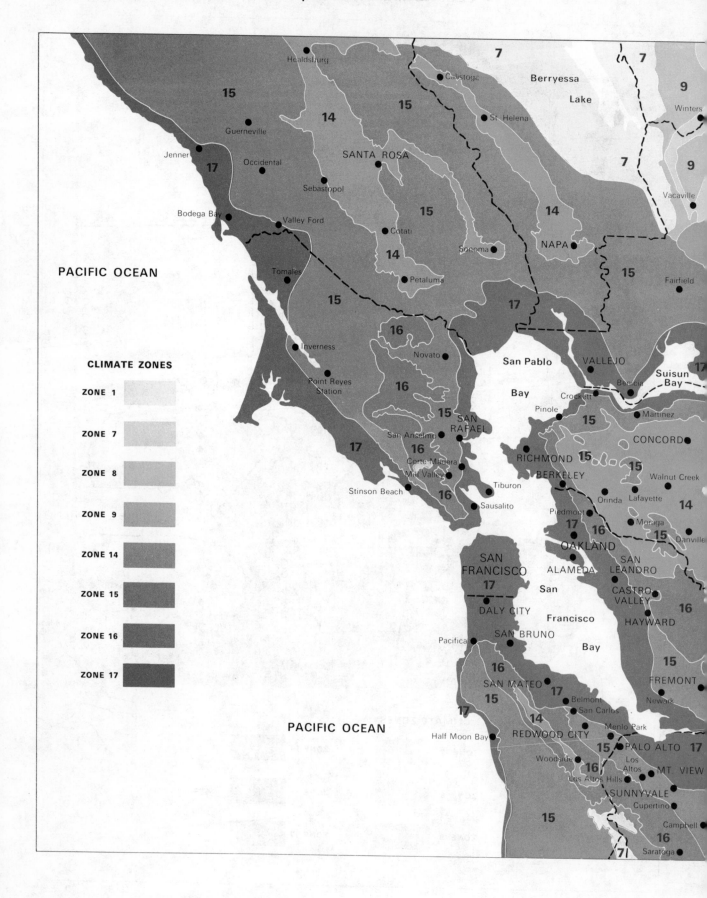

PACIFIC OCEAN

CLIMATE ZONES

ZONE 1
ZONE 7
ZONE 8
ZONE 9
ZONE 14
ZONE 15
ZONE 16
ZONE 17

PACIFIC OCEAN

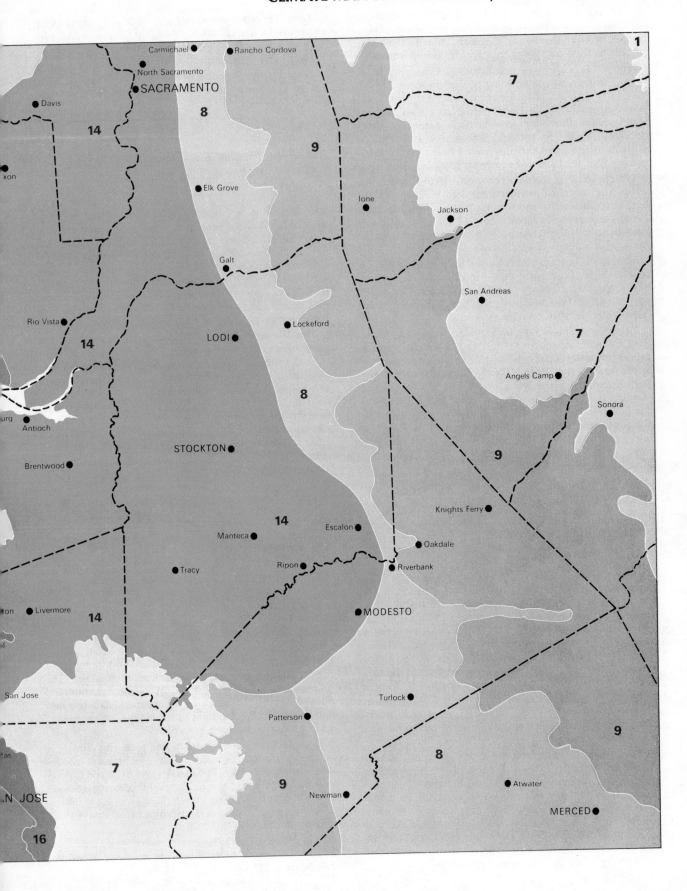

ground and blots visibility; it tends, rather, to come in high and fast, interposing a cooling and humidifying blanket between the sun and the earth, reducing the intensity of the light and the percentage of possible sunshine.

The result is a climate that favors fuchsias, rhododendrons, azaleas, hydrangeas, ferns, and begonias. Many plants that require shade elsewhere grow well here in full sun. Some heat-loving plants refuse to bloom because heat accumulation is too low (hibiscus, gardenia); many deciduous fruits do not find sufficient winter chill to set fruit; many citrus varieties cannot bear sweet or satisfactory fruit for lack of the necessary heat.

Unless local features offer shelter from prevailing winds, the shoreline itself and the area immediately behind it are too gusty and too much subject to salt spray for any except the toughest, most tolerant plants. Beach gardens usually need all the help you can give them in the way of screens or windbreaks.

Behind the beaches and sea cliffs, local geography may reduce the fog cover, lessen the winds, and boost summer heat enough to create "banana belts" — areas in which you can grow the subtropicals that ordinarily sulk or decline under the cool overcast.

In a 10-year period the lowest winter temperatures in Zone 17 may range from 36° to 24°. The lowest temperatures on record range from 30° to 20°. Of further interest in this heat-starved climate are the highs of summer. The normal summer highs are in the 60° to 75° range. The average highest temperature on record of 12 weather stations in Zone 17 is only 97°. In all the other northern California climates, average highest temperatures on record are in the 104° to 116° range.

ZONE 18 *Above and Below Thermal Belts in Southern California's Interior Valleys*

Zones 18 and 19 are classified as interior climates. The major climate influence is that of the continental air mass; the ocean determines the climate no more than 15 per cent of the time. The difference between 18 and 19 is that winters are colder in Zone 18 than in Zone 19 because the latter is favorably situated on slopes and hillsides where cold air drains off on winter nights. Zone 18 represents the cold-air basins beneath the air-drained thermal belts and the hilltops that stand above them.

The high and low deserts of southern California are something else — see Zones 11 and 13. Zone 18 is generally west of the low deserts and lower in elevation than the high deserts.

Historically, many of the valley-floor parts of Zone 18 were once apricot, peach, apple, and walnut regions. The orchards have given way to homes, but the climate remains one that supplies enough winter chill for some plants that need it while not becoming too cold for many of the hardier subtropicals. It is too hot, too cold, and too dry for fuchsias; but, on the other hand, cold enough for tree peonies and many apple varieties, and mild enough for a number of avocado varieties.

Zone 18 never amounted to much for commercial citrus production (frosty nights called for too much heating) but citrus can be grown here, either by choosing the hardier kinds or by protecting plants from frosts.

Over a 10-year period, winter lows have ranged from 22° to 17°. The all-time lows recorded in Zone 18 range from 22° to 7°.

ZONE 19 *Thermal Belts Around Southern California's Interior Valleys*

This climate is as little influenced by the ocean as Zone 18, making it also a poor climate for such plants as fuchsias, rhododendrons, and tuberous begonias. But air-drainage on winter nights generally takes away enough cold air to make winter lows much less severe here. Many sections of Zone 19 have always been prime citrus country — especially for those kinds that need extra summer heat in order to grow sweet fruit. Likewise, most avocado varieties can be grown here, and so can macadamia nuts.

The Western Plant Encyclopedia in this book cites many ornamental plants for Zone 19 (but not for 18) for reasons of the milder winters in Zone 19. Bougainvillea, bouvardia, bromelia, calocephalus, cape chestnut (*Calodendrum*), chorizema, several kinds of coral tree (*Erythrina*), leucocoryne, livistona palms, giant Burmese honeysuckle, myoporum, several of the more tender pittosporums, lady palm (*Rhapis excelsa*), and rondeletia are a few of them.

Winter lows over a 10-year period have ranged from 27° to 23°, and the all-time lows from 23° to 17°. These are considerably higher than in neighboring Zone 18, and that fact is what makes the big difference.

ZONE 20 *Cold Winters in Southern California's Sections of Occasional Ocean Influence*

In Zones 20 and 21 the same relative pattern prevails as in Zones 18 and 19, in that the even-numbered zone is the climate made up of cold-air basins and hilltops and the odd-numbered one is the air-drained thermal belt. The difference is that Zones 20 and 21 get both coastal and interior weather. In these transitional areas, climate boundaries often move 20 miles in 24 hours with the movement of marine or interior weather.

Because of the greater ocean influence, this climate is better for plants that need moisture — fuchsias, rhododendrons, and the like. The Los Angeles State and County Arboretum at Arcadia is in Zone 20 (bordering on Zone 21). The array of plants grown there gives some indication of the great choice in landscaping plants that is available to gardeners in this zone.

Winter lows over a 10-year period have ranged from 28° to 23°. In all of recorded history, lows here have ranged from 21° to 14°.

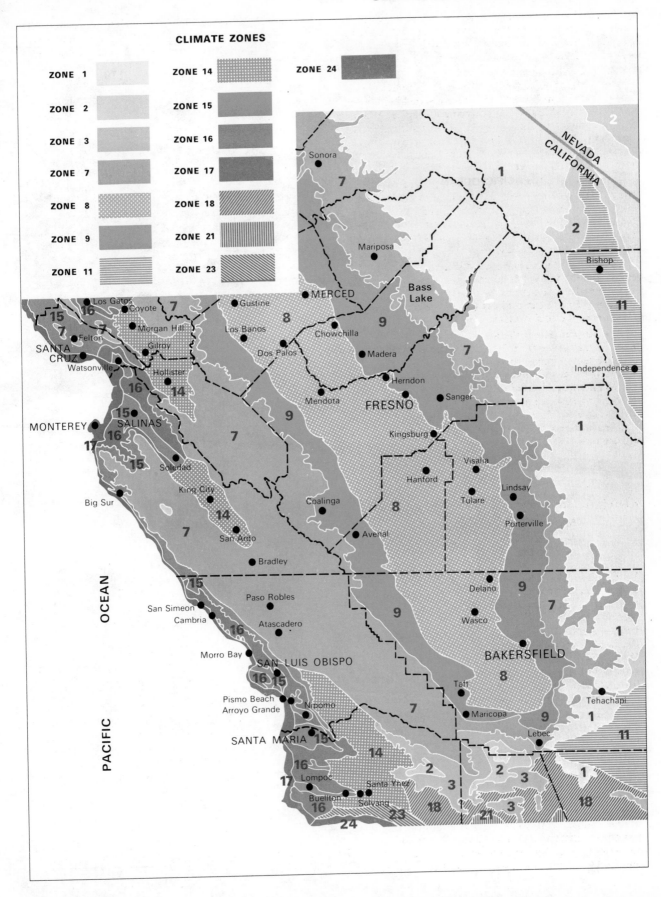

CLIMATE ZONES

ZONE 1   ZONE 14   ZONE 24

ZONE 2   ZONE 15

ZONE 3   ZONE 16

ZONE 7   ZONE 17

ZONE 8   ZONE 18

ZONE 9   ZONE 21

ZONE 11   ZONE 23

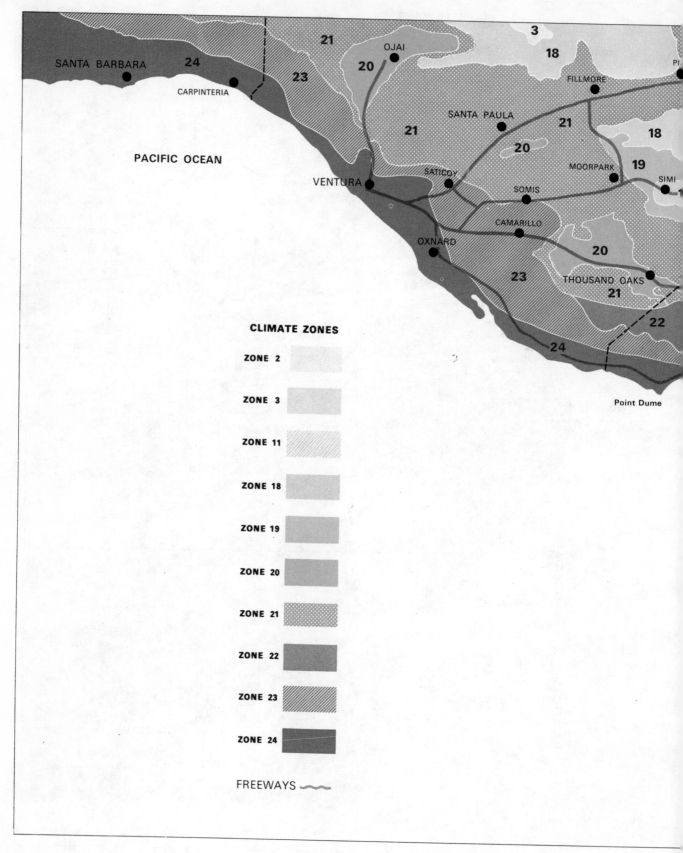

SANTA BARBARA

CARPINTERIA

PACIFIC OCEAN

OJAI

20

24

23

21

3

18

FILLMORE

PI

SANTA PAULA

21

20

MOORPARK

18

19

SIMI

VENTURA

SATICOY

SOMIS

CAMARILLO

OXNARD

23

20

THOUSAND OAKS

21

22

24

Point Dume

CLIMATE ZONES

ZONE 2

ZONE 3

ZONE 11

ZONE 18

ZONE 19

ZONE 20

ZONE 21

ZONE 22

ZONE 23

ZONE 24

FREEWAYS

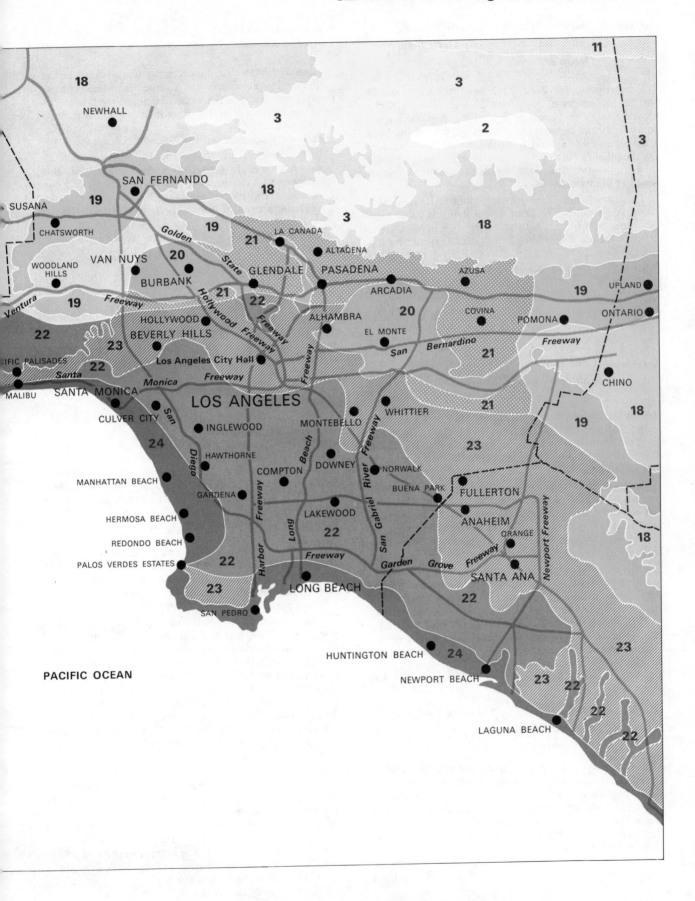

PACIFIC OCEAN

ZONE 21 Thermal Belts in Southern California's Sections of Occasional Ocean Influence

The description for Zone 20 tells of the interplay of weather influences in both Zone 20 and Zone 21. Your garden can be in ocean air or under a high ocean fog for one day and experience a mass of interior air (perhaps a drying santa-ana wind from the desert) the next day. On the other hand, this Zone 21 is a thermal belt: Cold air of winter nights drains off, making it possible to grow tenderer plants here.

This area is fine citrus-growing country. Its mild winters favor a number of other tender items, because temperatures never dip very far below 30° here. Over a 10-year period, winter lows at the weather-recording stations in Zone 21 ranged from 27° to 23°. In all of recorded history, lows have ranged from 27° to 17°.

This is the mildest zone (highest number) that gets adequate winter chilling for some plants (most forms of lilac, for instance).

ZONE 22 Cold-Winter Portions of Southern California's Coastal Climate

This is the climate that is influenced by the ocean approximately 85 per cent of the time, and further is either a cold-air basin in winter or a hilltop above the air-drained slopes. It gets lower winter temperatures than the neighboring Zone 23.

Actually, the winters are so mild here that winter lows are not of much significance, seldom below 28°. The coldest temperatures generally are experienced in canyons and near canyon mouths where considerable cold air drainage may cause fairly heavy frost damage. The winter lows in all of recorded history range from 21° to 24°.

Gardeners who take advantage of building overhangs or the protection of tree branches can grow an impressive variety of subtropical plants — bananas, gingers, tree ferns, and the like. The lack of a pronounced chilling period during the winter limits the use of such deciduous woody plants as flowering cherry and lilac. Many herbaceous perennials from colder regions fail to thrive without their winter dormancy.

ZONE 23 Thermal Belts of Southern California's Coastal Climate

This is one of the most favored gardening climates in North America for the growing of subtropical plants. It could be called the avocado belt, for this has always been southern California's best strip for growing that crop. Frosts don't amount to much (it's an air-drained thermal belt) and most of the time (approximately 85 per cent) it is under the influence of the Pacific Ocean; only 15 per cent of the time is the determining influence from the interior. A notorious portion of this 15 per cent is on those days when hot and extremely drying santa-ana winds blow down the hills and canyons from the mountains and deserts.

Zone 23 lacks either the necessary summer heat or the winter cold to grow successfully some items such as pears, most apples, most peaches. On the other hand, it enjoys more heat than the neighboring maritime climate, Zone 24. As an example of that difference, gardenias and oleanders are recommended for Zone 23 but not Zone 24.

In the temperature records books, most of Zone 23 fares pretty well as far as mildness is concerned. But severe winters have descended on some sections of Zone 23 at times, and the net result of this has been to make a surprising spread of low temperatures. Over a 10-year period, lows have ranged from 32° to 23°. In all of recorded history, the lows have ranged from 28° to 23°.

ZONE 24 Marine Influence— Southern California Coast

This is the climate along southern California's beaches that is almost completely dominated by the ocean. Where the beach runs along the base of high cliffs or palisades, Zone 24 extends only to the base of the precipice. But where hills are low or nonexistent, it runs inland several miles.

This is a mild marine climate (milder than northern California's maritime Zone 17) because below Point Conception the Pacific is comparatively warm. The winters are mild, the summers are cool and often of limited sunshine because of daily high fogs, and the air is seldom really dry. This is southern California's best fuchsia and tuberous begonia climate. Scores of less well known plants from Chile, New Zealand, the Canary Islands, and the moister parts of South Africa do well here for the same reason — *Leucadendron argenteum* and *Corynocarpus laevigata* are examples. Very tender plants find a good home here, but they must be able to get along with only moderate summer heat. It's a climate in which gardens planted with certain kinds of plants can become jungles in a few years.

Areas of Zone 24 that are close to the mouths of canyons can suffer in winter from cold air that comes down the canyons on some winter nights. Several such canyons are big enough to be shown on the map — you will see them on the map along the coast south of Laguna Beach. Partly because of the unusually low temperatures created by this canyon action, the scope of winter lows in Zone 24 is broader than you might think. In a 10-year period, lows have ranged from 35° to 24°. The all-time record lows range from 33° to 20°. As you can see, there are some weather stations in Zone 24 that have never recorded a freezing temperature (32° or below).

The all-time high temperatures here are interesting in that they help define the total climate, but they aren't greatly significant in terms of plant growth. Average all-time high of weather stations in Zone 24 is 105°. Compare this to northern California's marine climate Zone 17 which averages 97°, and to the average in some of southern California's inland climates — Zone 22 at 111°, Zone 20 at 114°, and Zone 18 at 115°.

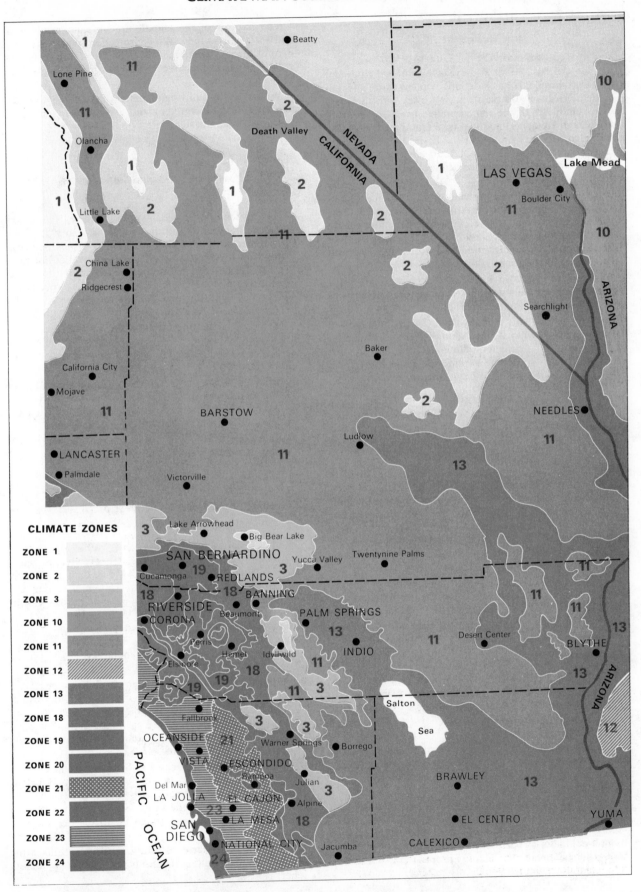

CLIMATE ZONES

ZONE 1
ZONE 2
ZONE 3
ZONE 10
ZONE 11
ZONE 12
ZONE 13
ZONE 18
ZONE 19
ZONE 20
ZONE 21
ZONE 22
ZONE 23
ZONE 24

ZONE 10 Arizona's High Desert

This zone consists mostly of the 3,300 to 4,500 foot elevation parts of Arizona. It also exists in southern Utah and southern Nevada. It has a definite winter season — from 75 to more than 100 nights each winter with temperatures below 32°. In the representative towns of Benson, Bowie, and Douglas, minimum temperatures average 28° in December, 30° in January, 31° in February. Late frosts, with lows of 25° to 22°, are expected in April. Lowest temperatures recorded are around 6°.

Here the low winter temperatures give necessary chilling to make possible the growing of all of the deciduous fruits and the perennials that thrive in the coldest climates — lilacs, spiraea, and the like. The definite winter season calls for spring planting, followed by a spring-summer growing season (in neighboring Zones 12 and 13, most planting should be done in fall).

Temperatures are high enough for olives and crape myrtle, and summers are mild enough to allow annuals and perennials to flourish through the summer.

Distinguishing this climate from Zone 11 are more rainfall and less wind. Annual rainfall averages 12 inches, with half of that amount falling in July and August. Many plants of borderline hardiness in Zone 11 perform well here — star jasmine and xylosma, for example.

ZONE 11 California's Medium to High Desert

Exactly where the high desert becomes the intermediate desert can't be marked on the map. In varying degrees, this climate zone borrows from two extremes — the winter-cold Zones 1, 2, and 3, and the subtropical desert, Zone 13. For example, Twentynine Palms to the south has a winter climate not much colder than that of the low desert, while Bishop to the north takes on the minus zero temperatures of the intermountain deserts.

In this zone we take as typical the climates of Victorville, Palmdale, Lancaster, Mojave, California City, and China Lake.

This climate is characterized by wide swings in temperature, both between summer and winter and between day and night. Winter lows of 6° to 0° have occurred throughout the area, but the mean daily minimums range from 32° to 28° from December through February. Highest summer temperatures recorded range from 114° to 117°. On the average, there are 110 days with temperatures above 90°, to 80 and 85 nights with temperatures below 32°.

Unlike the low desert, the hot summer days are followed by cool nights; and unlike the cold-winter zones, the freezing nights are followed by days of 60° mean temperatures.

The adaptation of plants reflects the extremes. Deciduous flowering shrubs (forsythia, spiraea, lilacs) and deciduous fruits (especially apples and pears) that require winter cold flourish here. At the same time the heat-loving crape myrtle, pomegranate, and European grapes find this climate to their liking.

The hazards of the climate are the late spring frosts and the desert winds. Wind protection, whether by the natural terrain, windbreaks, or the clustering of homes, greatly increases the chance of plant survival and the rate of plant growth.

Winter winds and bright sunlight may combine to kill normally hardy evergreen plants by desiccation, if winter soil moisture is not adequate.

ZONE 12 Arizona's Intermediate Desert

This is Arizona's intermediate desert climate. The critical difference between it and the low desert (Zone 13) is in the number of days of killing frost. The mean number of nights with temperatures below 32° in localities of Zone 12 are: Tucson 22, Wickenburg 65. Extreme low temperatures of 6° have been recorded. The mean maximum temperatures in July and August are 5° or 6° cooler than the highs of Zone 13.

Many of the subtropicals that do well in Zone 13 are not reliably hardy here. However, the average winter temperatures are high enough to encourage growing of many, with protection in extreme winters.

Although winter temperatures are lower than in Zone 13, the total hours of cold are not enough to provide sufficient winter chilling for some of the deciduous fruits and deciduous flowering shrubs.

As in Zone 13, the growing season starts in September-October (the best planting season for most plants).

ZONE 13 Low Desert—Mildest of Desert Winters

The low desert, from below sea level in the Imperial Valley to 1,100 feet elevation in the Phoenix area, is rightly classified as subtropical desert. Mean daily maximum temperatures in the hottest month (July) range from 106° to 108°. The winters are short and mild. Frosts can be expected from December 1 to February 15 but they are of short duration. There are rarely more than 6 to 10 nights with temperatures below 32°. The average minimum temperature in the winter months is 37°. However, lows of 19° to 13° have been recorded.

Winter lows and summer highs exclude some of the subtropicals grown in southern California's mild-winter Zones 22 to 24. However, numerous subtropicals with high heat requirements thrive in this climate. Some examples are dates, grapefruit, bauhinia, beaumontia, many cassias, thevetia, jacaranda.

The gardening year begins in September and October for most vegetables and annual flowers (corn and melons are planted in late winter). Growth of the fall-planted plants is slow through the short winter, picks up speed in mid-February and races through the increasing temperatures of March and April.

The lack of winter cold rules out fruits and flowering fruits with high chilling requirements, such as apples and cherries.

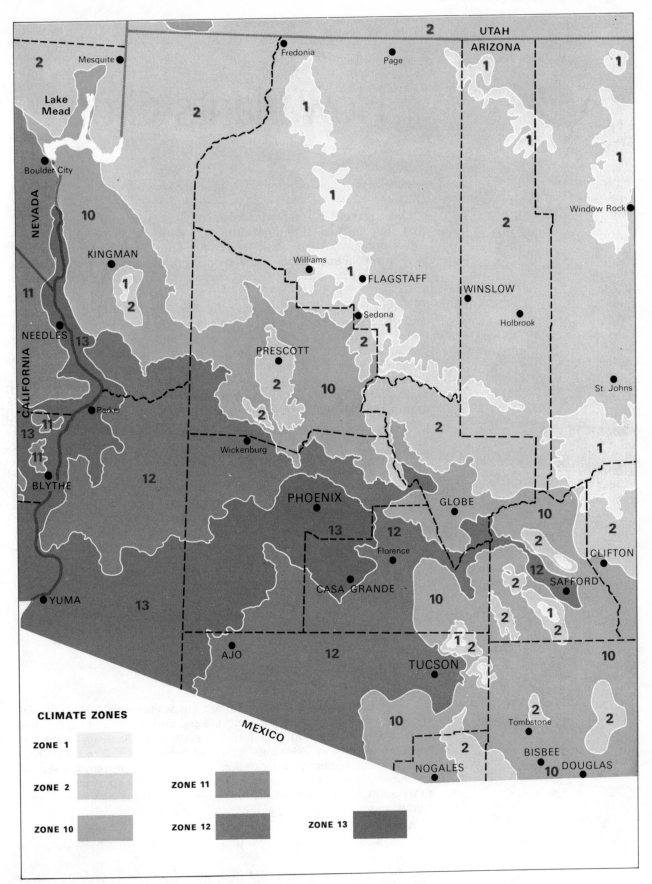

CLIMATE ZONES

ZONE 1

ZONE 2

ZONE 10

ZONE 11

ZONE 12

ZONE 13

How Plants Grow

A knowledge of how plants grow is one of the keys to becoming a successful gardener.

Green plants that grow on land share certain characteristics with animals; both are composed of protoplasm (largely water and proteins); both have tissues of various kinds which serve various functions; both consume and store energy; both are capable of reproducing themselves. The main difference is that green plants are able to manufacture their own food from inorganic materials.

Follow a plant through its life cycle. Typically this cycle begins with a seed. (Exception: Ferns and certain garden nuisances like mosses, fungus, and algae develop from spores.) Depending on its kind, a seed may be very large or of dustlike smallness, but each contains inside its protective coating an embryo plant and a supply of stored food (starch, proteins, oils) to start the embryo on its way. It is these stored foods that we eat in grains, peas, beans, and nuts. They are usually sufficient to launch the embryo plant into growth and sustain it until it is capable of manufacturing its own food.

Seeds sprout when given favorable conditions. These include moisture and a certain amount of warmth. Some seeds have other special requirements: light or absence of light; a period of dormancy for after-ripening; very high or very low temperatures; softening and cracking of the seed coat by weathering, exposure to acids, or grinding. When germination occurs, the coating splits; a rootlet starts downward, and a sprout carrying the seed leaves makes its way toward the surface. Most garden plants have two seed leaves; familiar exceptions are the grasses, iris, lilies, and others which have one; and conifers, which have many. Seed leaves are usually different in appearance from the mature leaves of a plant.

Hypocotyl is an embryo plant; the cotyledons help maintain it.

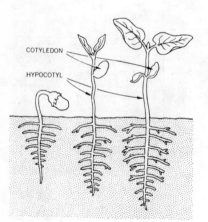

When true leaves and roots appear, plantlet is on its own.

The Roots

The single root begins to branch out into tiny white rootlets which draw in chemical substances needed for plant life and also the water to carry these substances to the rest of the plant. If no water is available to any of a plant's roots, the plant dies. As plants grow and branch, they take on different functions and a different appearance. The older portions grow a skinlike covering somewhat similar to bark. These larger, older roots act as vessels to transport water and nutrients to the rest of the plant, and sometimes as storage vessels for food. The entire root system anchors the plant in the soil.

Always at the ends are tender root tips. These contain a growing point which continually produces elongating cells that push the roots deeper or farther out in moist soil.

Immediately behind the root tip (or cap) is a zone of cells that produce single-celled root hairs. These perform the actual absorption of water and nutrients. These hairs are very delicate; exposed to sunshine or dry air they shrivel and die very quickly. This is why gardeners transplant swiftly and without exposing roots any more than is necessary. It is the loss of these hairs that causes wilting in a new transplant; until it grows a new set, it cannot meet the needs for water and food set up by the leaves.

The Stem

Between the seed leaves (or enfolded within the single seed leaf) is the growth tip which eventually elongates to form the stem. Buds develop along the stem and they open to produce the first true leaves. The stem continues to elongate, producing additional buds. The end bud, also called the terminal bud, carries the growth upward. Side buds (lateral buds) develop into leaves or, as the plant becomes larger, into branches.

The gardener's art of "pinching" is the manipulation of growth by nipping off selected buds; pinching side buds channels energy into terminal growth, while pinching terminal buds speeds up growth of side buds, making for denser, bushier plants. In some plants the buds may lie dormant in stem or bark for many years (latent buds), starting into growth only after pruning or injury removes the damaged upper growth. These latent buds account for the sprouting of shrubs and trees from stumps.

A primary function of the stem is to transmit water and nutrients from the root hairs to the growing points (buds, leaves, flowers) and to return to the roots the food (sugars) manufactured in the leaves. This exchange is carried on by a complex duct system that begins in the roots and leads to the growing points. In the stems of most trees, shrubs, and herbaceous (soft-wooded) plants, the tissues that make up the duct system are concentrated on either side of (or very near) the cambium—which is a layer of cells often located just inside of the bark or "skin." This layer of cells maintains the duct system as well as adding tissue that increases the girth of the plant. If labels or plant ties become too tight, they not only cut off the plant's circulation system but also interfere with the cambium layer that produces new girth cells. Unless these ties are loosened, the plant may be severely damaged or may die. This type of damage (often referred to as girdling) can also be caused by insects, fungus attack, or gnawing by animals.

Another primary function of the stem is supporting the plant. Stems of many plants are quite rigid because the walls of their cells are stiffened by cellulose, lignin, and similar substances. In trees and shrubs, the interior dense heartwood serves solely as support, having outlived the function of supplying conductive or storage tissue. Some stems are too long and thin to be held erect even by woody tissue. So it is that vines have developed twining stems, tendrils, coiled leaf stalks, or adhesive disks to carry leaves and flowers up into the sunlight. And so it is also that some annuals and perennials must be staked to be kept vertical—the stems don't form enough woody tissue to stand as upright as you would like.

Many stems or modified stems such as bulbs, rhizomes, corms, tubers, store food to tide the plant through dormancy, start its growth in spring, or bring forth its flowers and seeds.

When food moves through the plant from the leaves, it is in the form of sugars. When stored, it is converted into starch. When it is ready to move again in spring for the plant's use, it changes back to sugar.

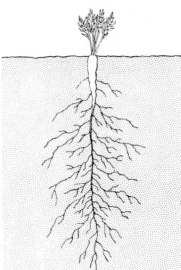

Root system of carrot can be much deeper than top is tall.

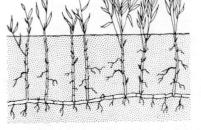

Rhizome (underground stem), running bamboo. Aerial stems above.

Leaves

As soon as true leaves expand, the plant begins to function as a mature plant. The basic function of leaves is the manufacture of sugars and other carbohydrates. This manufacture is carried out by the green material known as chlorophyll, which converts carbon dioxide, water, and the energy from sunlight into carbohydrates and oxygen.

This process (photosynthesis) requires large quantities of water, which is drawn up through the stem from the roots and into the leaf tissue. Here it encounters carbon dioxide in the air which passes into the leaf through minute breathing pores (stomata). Since the interior of the leaf must be moist and since the outside air is frequently dry, the pores are able to close when necessary to prevent dehydration. The leaf is further protected against drying by an outer coat (epidermis) which may be waxy, resinous, hairy, or scaly.

The pores taking the inflow of carbon dioxide from the air also permit the outflow of excess water vapor and waste oxygen.

The manufacture of carbohydrates stops in deciduous plants during the dormant season, and slows down greatly in evergreen plants during their modified dormancy in cold weather. Simultaneously, of course, the requirement for water drops, and roots no longer strain to keep up with the demands of the leaf system's manufacturing process. As a consequence, we are able to dig plants up and move them with moderate safety during the dormant season (late fall to early spring).

Fertilizers are necessary because the soil does not supply dependably enough all the essential nutrients the plant needs to synthesize the chlorophyll that manufactures the essential carbohydrates. Most important of the fertilizer elements is nitrogen, a major element in proteins.

Anything that interferes with photosynthesis and subsequent transfer of carbohydrates throughout the plant can have harmful consequences. Insect or fungus disease attacks which reduce leaf area not only slow growth but also interfere with the plant's accumulation of winter food storage. Soot, grime, and dust can interfere with free air circulation through pores or reduce available light to the leaves. A smothering mat of leaves on a lawn can halt the production of chlorophyll and cause leaves to yellow and growth to cease.

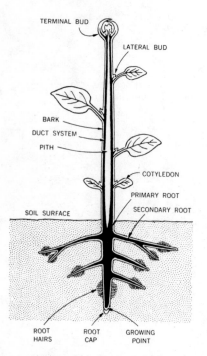

Terminal and lateral buds, root tips are principal growth areas.

Flowers and Fruit

All garden plants form flowers if permitted to do so, but not all flowers are noticeable. Some are green and scarcely distinguishable from leaves without close inspection; others are hidden by leaves or are so small that they escape detection. The flower contains within itself female parts that, when fertilized by male sexual cells (pollen), produce seeds. And, the seeds reproduce the plant. The various flower parts and their functions are diagrammed and explained on page 163. The different ways that fertilization takes place in the flower are explained under *Pollination* on page 165.

In nature, the seedlings of any single kind of plant tend to vary rather widely. Isolation or carefully controlled breeding can assure uniform seedlings. Such work is done for you by growers when they select the seed that goes into seed packets or select the seed from which nursery plants are grown.

Propagation by Means Other than Seeds

Although producing seeds is the normal method by which plants start, some plants can be propagated by other methods—see pages 87 to 91.

Under some conditions certain plant tissues in the areas of growth (the tip and side shoots, and the cambium layer of stems, branches, and trunks), are able to develop into roots rather than forming other kinds of tissues. Some plants can even develop roots from leaf tissues, leaf stalks, or veins. Gardeners take advantage of this power by rooting cuttings or by grafting parts of one plant onto another by matching cambium layers. Many plants produce buds and aerial parts on underground stems or even on roots; these plants are easy to multiply by breaking plants apart and resetting divisions, or by making root cuttings. In any of these forms of asexual reproduction, the newly propagated plant will be identical with the plant from which the plant tissue came.

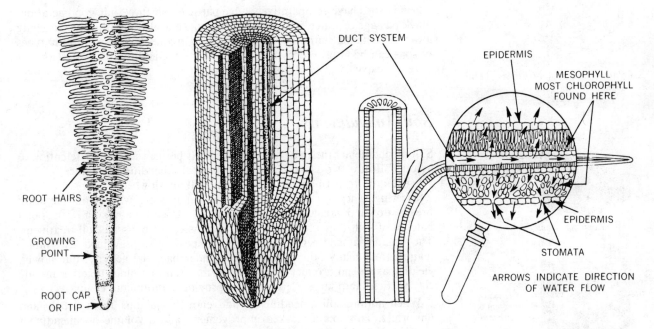

Root elongates just behind the cap; hairs absorb water, nutrients. Duct system of plant extends from root hairs to leaf tissue.

Soils and Planting Mixes

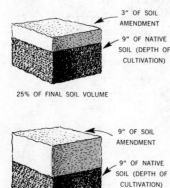

CLAY
LESS THAN 1/12500"

SILT
UP TO 1/500"

FINE SAND
UP TO 1/250"

MEDIUM SAND
UP TO 1/60"

LARGEST SAND
PARTICLES—1/12"

Relative sizes of soil particles. Blend determines soil texture.

3" OF SOIL
AMENDMENT

9" OF NATIVE
SOIL (DEPTH OF
CULTIVATION)

25% OF FINAL SOIL VOLUME

9" OF SOIL
AMENDMENT

9" OF NATIVE
SOIL (DEPTH OF
CULTIVATION)

50% OF FINAL SOIL VOLUME

Soil amendments should total at least 25 per cent of final volume.

Of all the many aspects of gardening, an understanding of your soil is probably the most important. Read these pages on soil (and the related pages on fertilizers and watering) carefully; a working knowledge of them should become second nature. Such a knowledge, refined almost to the point of intuition, is what is commonly called a green thumb.

Soil is a mass of mineral particles mixed with living and dead organic matter and incorporating quantities of air and water. Size of mineral particles determines the texture of the soil. Clay or adobe is composed of microscopically small particles, fine and coarse sandy soil of increasingly larger particles. Small, flat particles of clay fit closely together, with little air space between them. When clay soils get wet, they dry out slowly because downward movement of water (drainage) is slow. Since air content is limited, root growth is inhibited. Clay soils warm up slowly in spring and delay plant growth. On the other hand, the small particles of clay may be well supplied with nutrients, and the slow drainage prevents the loss of these nutrients by leaching.

Sandy soils have comparatively huge particles which permit good aeration, quick passage of water, and quick warming. They also permit rapid leaching away of valuable nutrients under necessary frequent watering. Both types of soils can be improved by the same means—the addition of materials that have the capacity to hold both air and water.

Soil Amendments

Soil amendments, the materials that can add both air and water-retention to a soil, fall into two classes: the first, mineral amendments (pumice, perlite, vermiculite) are permanent in the soil, breaking down only very slowly by weathering. They are especially useful in sandy soils, where good aeration breaks down organic amendments quickly. Useful in mixing with small batches of soil, they are typically too expensive for big-scale soil treatment. The organic amendments (ground bark, peat moss, sawdust, leaf mold, manure, and many others) decompose under bacterial activity, but slowly, yielding as an end product humus, a soft material that binds together minute clay particles into larger "crumbs", improving aeration and drainage.

When adding soil amendments, add enough and mix them deeply and uniformly. To make a marked improvement, add a volume of amendment equal to 25 to 50 per cent of the total soil volume in the cultivated area. Mix in thoroughly, either by spading and respading or by rotary tilling; the physical mixing will add some air to the soil, and the amendment will help to keep it there.

Organic Amendments—Some Cautions

Organic material is broken down by organisms that require nitrogen; if these organisms cannot get sufficient nitrogen from the organic material itself, they will get it from the soil, robbing roots of whatever nitrogen is available. Any organic material that contains at least 1.5 per cent nitrogen has enough to take care of its own decomposition needs. Leaves and leaf mold, peat moss, garden compost, and manure usually contain sufficient nitrogen (but manure may also contain salts). Thoroughly composted sawdust or ground bark, or these materials specially fortified with nitrogen, will cause no nitrogen depletion. Raw shavings, ground bark, and straw decompose relatively slowly, but require additional nitrogen; for each 1,000 square feet of these materials, laid 3 inches deep, mix in 55 pounds of ammonium sulfate or 35 pounds of ammonium nitrate.

In addition to light, air, water, and root room, growing plants need a supply of nutrients — elements necessary to carrying out of their life processes. Some of these, the so-called trace elements, are needed only in infinitesimal quantities and are usually present in most soils, but three major nutrient elements, nitrogen, phosphorus, and potassium, have to be supplied. Phosphorus and potassium are present in the mineral particles in most soils, but they become available to plants so slowly that supplementary feedings are often advisable. In unimproved soils, nitrogen comes from decomposing organic material, which is generally in very short supply in Western soils, especially in drier regions. Nitrogen is used in large quantities by plants; it is also easily lost by leaching action of rainfall or irrigation or used up by soil organisms. As a result, nitrogen must be added from time to time (usually at least twice a year) if good growth is expected.

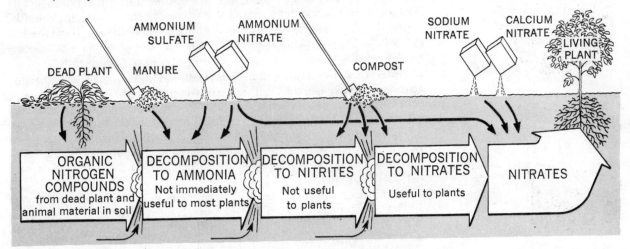

Nitrogen from decaying organic material is not directly available to plants. It must be converted by soil organisms (fungi, molds, bacteria) first into ammonia, then into nitrites, and finally into nitrates which are taken up by plant roots. These micro-organisms, being plants themselves, need a certain amount of warmth, air, water, and nitrogen to do their job. Any soil amendments which improve aeration and water penetration will also improve the efficiency of the soil organisms at their vital job of making nitrogen available.

Soil Problems

Entirely satisfactory garden soils are rare indeed, and when they exist they usually represent careful preparation and careful management over a period of years. Some soil problems are quite obvious; others may require the assistance of professional help.

Alkalinity. Alkaline soil, common in light-rainfall areas, is soil that is high in calcium carbonate (lime) and certain other minerals. Many plants

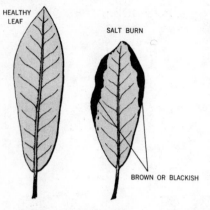

HEALTHY LEAF

SALT BURN

BROWN OR BLACKISH

Blackened areas on older leaves may mean salt burn.

grow well in moderately alkaline soil; others, notably camellias, rhododendrons, and azaleas, will not thrive there. Large-scale chemical treatment of highly alkaline soil is expensive and complex. A better bet is to plant in raised beds and containers, using a good prepared soil mix. Soils that are only slightly alkaline or nearly neutral will support many garden plants; they can be made to grow acid soil plants with liberal additions of peat moss, ground bark or sawdust and fertilizing with acid-type fertilizers.

Liberal watering can help lessen alkalinity, so take all possible precautions to keep soil well drained.

Salinity. An excess of salts in the soil is a widespread problem in arid parts of the West. These salts may come from water (especially softened water, which has a high sodium content), from fertilizers and chemical amendments, and from manures with high salt content. Where these salts are not leached through the soil by high rainfall or deep irrigation, they reach high concentration in the root zone, where they inhibit germination of seeds, stunt growth, and cause leaves to scorch and turn yellow or leaf margins to brown and wither (salt burn). Periodic and thorough leaching will lessen the salts content. To carry out this leaching, drainage must be good.

Acidity. Acid soil is at the opposite end of the scale from alkaline soil. It is most common in areas of heavy rainfall and is often associated with sandy soil. Most plants grow well under mildly acid soil conditions, but intensely acid soils are undesirable. Such soils are uncommon in the West; adding lime to the soil (a common treatment in some eastern states) should not be undertaken here unless a soil test indicates it to be necessary. If acidity is a problem and lime is used to correct it, be sure to use fertilizers which do not have an acid reaction.

Nutrient deficiency. If soil drains well, has ample water, is neither too acid nor too alkaline, and still fails to sustain plant growth well, it may be deficient in nutrients, most likely in nitrogen. Fertilizers are the quickest and easiest answer. Many complete fertilizers are available, and there are also formulations of nitrogen, phosphorus, and potassium compounds that provide these single nutrients. Manure and compost yield small quantities of nutrients, but are effective principally in building up the supply of organic material in the soil.

Soil analysis will reveal nutrient deficiencies as well as excess acidity or alkalinity. Commercial laboratories can perform such analyses. In some Western states the agricultural extension service can analyze soil. Check with your county agent.

Chlorosis. Chlorosis, a condition in which leaves turn yellow, is usually caused by a deficiency of iron (rarely it results from lack of another mineral such as zinc). If the deficiency is mild, areas of yellow show up between the veins of the leaves, which remain a dark green. In severe or long-continued cases, the entire leaf (except the veins) turns yellow. Iron deficiency is only occasionally the result of a lack of iron in the soil; more frequently it is the result of some other substance (usually lime) making the iron unavailable to the plant. To correct chlorosis, treat the soil with iron sulfate or with iron chelates; the latter has the important ability to hold iron in a form that is available to plants. Follow label instructions carefully and avoid overdosing. Plants with serious iron shortages can also be treated with foliar sprays of iron.

Shallow soil (hardpan). A tight, impervious layer of soil can give trouble if it lies at or near the surface. Such a layer can be a natural formation, but often it is man-made. Commonest kind occurs when builders spread out excavated subsoil over the surface, then compact it by driving trucks or other heavy equipment over it. If the subsoil has a clay content and is damp while construction is going on, it can take on bricklike hardness when it dries. A thin layer of topsoil conceals the problem without solving it. Roots

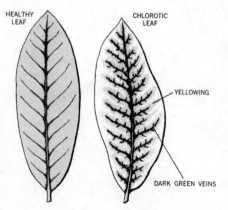

HEALTHY LEAF

CHLOROTIC LEAF

YELLOWING

DARK GREEN VEINS

Yellowing leaves with dark green veins usually mean chlorosis.

cannot penetrate the hard layer, and water cannot drain through it. Planting holes become water tanks, and plants fail to grow. They may even die.

If the hardpan layer is thin, drill through it with a soil auger when planting. If it is too thick, a landscape architect can help you with a drainage system. Or you can switch to raised bed and container gardening. For special planting techniques in soil that doesn't drain, see page 43. If you want to improve the soil over large planting areas, scarify the area to a depth of 18 inches or so with heavy equipment, then add soil amendments and thoroughly mix them in. As a beneficial extra step, you can then grow a crop of some heavy-rooting grass, and, after it grows up, rotary till it into the soil to add organic material to it.

When one kind of soil overlies another, water movement across the dividing line (called an interface) is slowed or stopped. Water also fails to move upward across the interface by capillary action. If you must bring in additional soil to fill in low spots or to raise the entire level of your soil, don't add it as one single layer. Instead, add half the required new soil and mix it in thoroughly with existing soil by spading or rotary tilling. Then add the rest of the new soil to bring level up to desired height.

If you purchase topsoil, look for crumbly texture and try to determine whether or not it is saline (it shouldn't be). If it comes from good crop land, you can assume that salinity is low enough. Very fine textured soils (clays and silts) should be avoided, as should soils that grew noxious weeds (Bermuda, wild morning glory, quack grass, etc.).

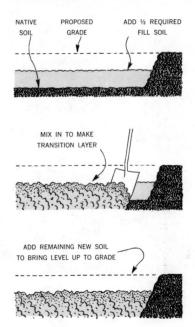

To avoid an interface, blend in new topsoil with old soil.

Soil Sampling Tube

The easiest and most efficient way to acquaint yourself with your soil is to use a soil sampling tube, illustrated here. This implement is sold by firms that offer scientific apparatus and greenskeeper's equipment. You just push the tube into the ground—in a lawn, flower bed, shrubbery bed, orchard, anywhere. When it's at the depth to which you want to explore, twist it and pull it out. The tube will remove a column of soil which you can easily read. You can test water penetration and retention. Damp soil in the column represents an area that provides plenty of moisture for roots. A muddy foul-smelling soil is holding too much water. A powdery-dry soil is unlikely to support most garden plants.

You can also learn the nature of your soil. A clay or sandy layer shows that such strata exist at corresponding depths in the soil. You can tell how deep and how uniformly a bed has been conditioned with ground bark or peat moss. Often you can see how deep roots grow. You can look for root insects such as soil mealybugs. The best way to take soil samples for analysis at a laboratory is with a soil sampling tube.

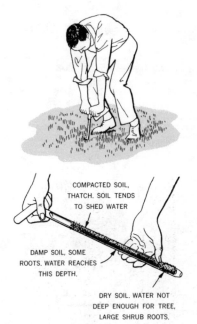

To see what actually happens in the soil, use a sampling tube.

Raised Beds

If drainage is really bad, consider building a raised bed, in which you can tailor exactly a well-aerated rooting bed. Even if your soil is good you may find that the raised bed will highlight a spectacular planting, bring plants up to eye level, supply built-in seating, or interrupt the monotony of a flat garden or paved area. Walls may be of wood or masonry.

Soil for Pots, Containers, Raised Beds

Ready-to-use planting mixes are available at many nurseries, but you may prefer to mix your own, especially if you need large quantities. A good potting soil should contain sufficient nutrients for healthy plant growth; it should be easy for roots to penetrate; it should drain well, yet retain sufficient moisture to keep the plant well supplied with water. A popular basic mix consists of 2 parts of good garden soil, 1 part sand, and 1 part peat moss or the equivalent. Some gardeners add bonemeal or other fertilizers. The formula can be varied; if your garden soil is sandy, omit the sand and use 3 parts soil. If you wish to grow plants that need acid soil—azaleas or rhododendrons—use a mix that contains at least 50 per cent organic material such as finely ground bark, peat moss, or leaf mold. Never use a clay soil in a container mix.

Commercial growers who need a uniform and predictable mix don't rely on garden soil for growing container plants. They use an artificial soil known as U.C. Mix. The basis for this mix is a combination of fine sand or perlite with peat moss, sawdust, or ground bark. In addition, fertilizers are blended into the mix to form a growing medium of uniform and known quality. This mix gives excellent aeration and drainage, good water availability, and easy leaching. The ingredients are free of soil-borne disease-producing fungi (those growers who modify the mix by adding soil always sterilize the soil carefully).

Home gardeners can use this mix if they are careful with watering and feeding. Since the material leaches quickly, it is necessary to feed regularly and frequently, and to water carefully. Gardeners who wish to use the U.C. Systems should refer to University of California Manual 23.

Compost

Well-aged compost is a soft, crumbly brownish or blackish substance resulting from the thorough decay of vegetable refuse. It has some limited value as plant food and much greater value as a source of moisture-holding humus. Composting takes time, effort, and a certain amount of space. A poorly maintained compost pile breeds enormous quantities of flies (more so in California than in the Northwest and interior) and it has an obnoxious odor.

In its simplest form, composting consists of piling up grass clippings, leaves and other garden refuse, plus certain kitchen refuse (coffee grounds, vegetable parts) and permitting it to decompose. In three to six months (depending on temperature and humidity) you spade it back into the garden, thus adding humus and some nutrients to the soil. A better way is to stack the debris 4 to 6 feet high inside a bin with slatted sides (air spaces between slats). There should be water close by with which to sprinkle the mass from time to time during dry seasons; it should be about as wet as a squeezed sponge. Turn the heap every week (or oftener) with a spading fork to put air into the center and to relocate material in various processes of decomposition.

Don't add large, coarse pieces which decompose slowly; break or chop them into walnut-size or smaller. Don't add diseased material. Decomposition will go on faster if you add a few handfuls of high-nitrogen fertilizer with every load of raw material.

The ideal bin will have three receptacles, one for incoming material, one for working material, and one for the finished product. The finished product can be screened or sifted; a 1/2-inch screen will give compost fine enough for potting mixes or lawn dressing. A 1-inch screen will give compost fine enough for general garden use. Material too coarse to pass the 1-inch screen can go back into the bin for further decomposition.

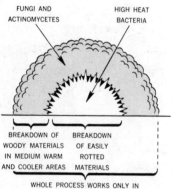

FUNGI AND ACTINOMYCETES   HIGH HEAT BACTERIA

BREAKDOWN OF WOODY MATERIALS IN MEDIUM WARM AND COOLER AREAS   BREAKDOWN OF EASILY ROTTED MATERIALS

WHOLE PROCESS WORKS ONLY IN PRESENCE OF AIR AND MOISTURE

Turn compost pile often to keep materials moist, bacteria active.

Planting Techniques

Seeds in the Open Ground

Native wildflowers will make a reasonably good show if they are sown where they are to grow in time to catch fall rains, but they will do better if sown in prepared ground from which weeds and grasses have been cleared. Most garden annuals and vegetables can also be sown in place, but they will need more attention. Prepare the seedbed with care; moisten it well a few days before planting if rains haven't done the job. Fork, spade, or rotary till the area, working in soil amendments and a complete fertilizer (read label to find how much per 100 or 1,000 square feet). Rake smooth. If you plan to grow vegetables or annuals in rows, hold back the fertilizer and apply it instead at seeding time in furrows 1 inch deeper than the seed and 2 inches on either side of the seed row (again, follow label instructions for amount per foot of row).

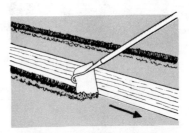

Board makes a good straightedge.

Orient rows to take advantage of the sun's path; a north-south direction will give equal sunlight on both sides of the row. If you intend planting flowers in drifts or patches, outline areas with gypsum or sand. If planting in rows, follow seed packet instructions for spacing the rows, and lay out rows with string stretched between two stakes. Make furrows with hoe or rake, using the edge of a plank as a straightedge if necessary. To sow seeds in furrows, tap carefully from an opened corner of the packet or pour a small quantity of seed into your hand, then lift pinches between fingers and scatter in the furrow. Cover to the depth indicated on seed packet. If soil is heavy, crumble or sift soil over seeds. Firm soil around seeds with back of the hoe or by pressing with a plank or block of wood. Water thoroughly but gently to avoid washing out seed.

Sow seed carefully in the furrow.

If you are broadcasting seed in drifts or patterned plantings, or if you wish to sow a broad area with tough, easy plants such as sweet alyssum or California poppies, you can get a more even distribution by mixing the seed with several times its bulk of fine sand. If possible, cover freshly planted seeds with a very thin mulch to prevent crusting of soil. On small areas you can use strips of burlap over the furrows; be sure to remove it as soon as germination begins. Take care that soil around the seedlings doesn't dry out.

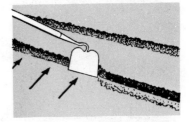

Cover seed; see packet for depth.

When seedlings appear, thin them out—remove excess seedlings so that those left standing are spaced the distance apart that is recommended on the seed packet. If you wait too long to thin the seedlings, plants will develop poorly and will be more difficult to remove ultimately. Also, weeds will sprout and come up with the seedlings—pull them at the same time as you thin. Some helpful seed packets show pictures of the seedlings that will grow from the seeds, helping you to distinguish them from the weeds. If you want to expand your planting and if you work carefully, you can use thinnings from one area to plant in another.

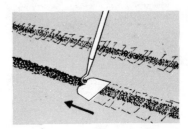

Tamp soil into contact with seed.

Seeds in Flats, Pots

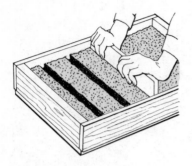

Mark drills for sowing the seeds.

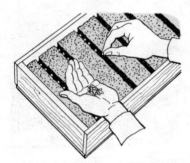

Sow seeds in drills at right depth.

Carefully sift covering over seed.

Press mix firmly with flat board.

Many plants get off to a better start if sown in containers and transplanted into place later. Starting seedlings indoors or in a greenhouse or other sheltered location can give you a jump on the season.

For large-scale production, a standard nursery flat is desirable, but for smaller quantities of plants use half-flats, small low-sided boxes (with drainage holes drilled in the bottoms), clay pots or pans (shallow pots). If you need to grow only a few tomato, pepper, or melon plants, use sturdy paper cups or cut-off pint milk cartons, perforated on the bottom for drainage.

Before filling containers with soil and sowing seeds, make sure that the containers are clean. If they have been used before, avoid risk of damping-off fungi or insect pests by giving them a thorough cleaning. Vigorous scrubbing followed by a few days in the sun are usually sufficient.

Be sure that containers have provision for drainage. Line flats with newspaper to prevent soil washing through between boards, then slash the newspaper in a few places to permit water to pass through.

Mix approximately equal parts of topsoil, sand, and peat moss or ground bark. If you have any reason to believe that the soil may contain weed seeds or disease organisms, you can sterilize the mix by baking it in an oven at 160° to 180° for two hours. The baking process gives off a terrible, permeating smell. Or, you can fumigate the soil with Mylone or Vapam, following label instructions. Or, buy a prepared potting mix.

Sift the mixture through a 1/4-inch screen into the flat or container. With a flat board, level the mix to about 3/4-inch from top of the flat or rim of the pot. Carefully press mix down into edges and corners with fingers.

When the dry surface is ready, sow the seeds (which may be treated with a seed disinfectant first, if desired). Very fine seed can be broadcast over the surface. Larger seeds can be planted in shallow furrows called "drills". These will vary in depth with the size of the seed. Label the flats; if several varieties are sown in one flat, label each drill. Cover seeds by sifting through a fine sifter (window screen is good) a mixture of half sand, half peat moss or ground bark. Barely cover the seeds. Shake or tap sifter carefully to disperse just the right amount. A good general rule is to cover seed to a depth equal to twice their diameter. Press down surface gently but firmly with a flat board. Water gently with watering can or fine mist from hose. Do not disturb seeds. If you have a tub or sink, put 1 to 2 inches of water in it and place the seed flat in it to soak the needed water up from the bottom.

Cover flat or pot with a sheet of newspaper and a pane of glass; place in a warm, protected spot out of direct sunlight. Keep the seeding mixture moist but not soaking wet. As soon as the first seedlings begin to appear, remove the covering and give full light, but not direct sun.

A good trick with slow-sprouting seed or with plants whose seedlings develop slowly is to sow seeds in pots, cover, then tie a clear plastic bag around the pot. Air can get through the plastic, but water vapor cannot; seedlings will have enough water to reach transplant stage without need for further watering. If you use this technique, be sure that your seeding soil mix is sterile.

Transplant flat. As soon as possible after plants have formed the second set of true leaves, transplant to another flat or pot, giving seedlings space for development. Work quickly and carefully, in a shaded, wind-free location. Lift a small block of seedlings with a pointed stick, fork, or knife blade; go deep enough to avoid root damage (roots are often much longer than plants are tall). Separate individual seedlings by gently disentangling each one from its neighbors; handle plants by leaves to avoid injury to tender stems. If roots are tangled, soak root ball in water.

The transplant flat should have a richer soil than the seedling flat, because the plants are going to do a lot of growing in the next few weeks. Use two parts top soil, and one part each of sand and peat moss or ground bark. Punch a hole in the seed-bed deep enough to accommodate roots without crowding; space holes about 2 inches apart each way. Insert roots of seedling, then firm soil around them. Use your finger or a small stick for digging and firming. Water the flat thoroughly but gently. Shade seedlings and keep out of drafts until they are over transplant shock and growing well. Expose them to increasing amounts of light and air.

Lift seedlings; handle by leaves.

Planting from Flats

Most busy gardeners forego the pleasures of seeding nowadays and buy their bedding plants at the nursery, which has or can get for you a wide variety of annuals and vegetables, and even some perennials, ground covers, and hedge plants in flats.

In planting from flats, prepare the garden soil as for sowing seed, adding amendments and fertilizer, tilling or spading, then smoothing with a rake. Be sure that your plants don't dry out in flats (or, if you have bought only a dozen or so plants, in the cardboard or other containers). With putty knife or spatula, separate plants in the flat by cutting straight down around each one. Some gardeners prefer to tear individual plants out of flats with fingers; you lose some soil this way, but you keep more roots on the plant, and if you work quickly plants are not injured. Dig generous holes large enough to accommodate root mass of plant without squeezing it in. Lift plant carefully, place in hole, and firm the soil around the root mass. Set so that top of root ball is slightly lower than surface of soil, and make a small basin around plant for watering. Mulch after watering to conserve water, inhibit weed growth, prevent soil caking and water runoff.

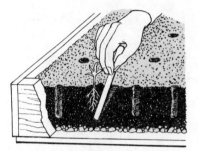

Firm soil around roots with stick.

When you set out plants in peat pots, make sure that they are moist and permeable; a dry peat pot takes up moisture slowly, and roots may be slow in breaking through the soil. If your plants are growing in plant bands, slip them out before planting.

Planting Balled and Burlapped Shrubs, Trees

Balled and burlapped plants (often referred to as B and B) are dug from the ground with a ball of soil around the roots. This ball is wrapped in burlap and tied up with twine to keep it intact. Plants sold this way include such evergreen shrubs as rhododendron and azalea, conifers, and certain deciduous shrubs that don't survive bare-root transplanting (dogwood, liquidambar, some oaks). Planting season varies by locality; appearance of plants at the local nursery signifies that planting season is here. Handle plants carefully; don't use the trunk as a handle, and don't drop them. Cradle the root ball well, with one hand supporting the bottom. If plant is too heavy to carry to planting site, get a friend to help you carry it in a sling of canvas or stout burlap. Planting hole should be about twice the width of the root ball, and at least half again as deep as the height of the root ball. Mix the excavated soil with soil amendments, and place in the bottom of the hole enough improved soil so that the top of the root ball is slightly higher than surrounding soil when plant is placed in the hole (soil will settle when wet, and ball will sink somewhat). Before filling the hole, check plant to find its "best side," and position the plant accordingly by rotating root ball. Fill hole half-full with amended soil, firming with stick. If a stake is needed, put it in now so that you don't damage root ball.

Place ball on improved soil mix.

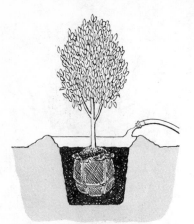

Make basin, irrigate thoroughly.

PREVAILING WINDS

1. DIG HOLE 1½-2 TIMES SIZE OF ROOT SYSTEM

2. LINE HOLE WITH 4"-6" OF "TRANSITION ZONE" SOIL

3. DRIVE STAKE (6'-8' LONG, 1¼"-2" DIA.) IN DIRECTION OF PREVAILING WINDS

4. ADD "ROOT ZONE" SOIL TO FORM A CONE

5. SPREAD ROOTS OVER CONE — PRUNE OUT BROKEN ROOTS (YOU'LL NEED HELP TO KEEP TREE STRAIGHT)

NATIVE SOIL

Planting bare-root trees is easier if you have a helper.

6. ADD MORE "ROOT ZONE" SOIL UNTIL ROOT ZONE IS ⅔ FULL—CAREFULLY WORK IN AROUND ROOTS

7. ADJUST TREE SO THAT NURSERY SOIL LINE IS AT GRADE LEVEL

8. WATER TO SETTLE SOIL AROUND ROOTS. IF TREE OR SOIL SETTLES, MAKE ADJUSTMENT (SEE 7)

9. TIE SECURELY IN 2 OR 3 PLACES WITH PLASTIC, CLOTH, OR RUBBER TIES (FORMING FIGURE 8)

10. ADD "ROOT ZONE" SOIL TO LEVEL OF SURROUNDING GRADE. WATER AGAIN.

NATIVE SOIL

Thorough watering at planting is a must for all plants.

Loosen twine and burlap at top of ball; fill hole to top with soil. Build water basin by hoeing up a circle of soil. Soak well, filling basin two or three times. *This is important;* if the soil ball has a clay content, and if it dries out, the ball will shrink, harden, and shed water. If you plant during the rainy season (which is likely), knock down the basin after plant is thoroughly soaked. Rebuild it when irrigating time comes around again.

If you are planting shallow-rooted plants that prefer acid soil, you should make the planting hole wider and backfill with an acid soil mix (see *Camellia, Rhododendron*).

Planting Bare-Root

In winter and early spring you can find bare-root plants for sale in many nurseries. Deciduous fruit and shade trees, flowering shrubs, roses, cane fruits, strawberries, and some perennials are among the plants most commonly sold bare-root.

There are two very valid reasons for getting out in the cold and wet of winter to buy and set out bare-root plants—rather than waiting until spring, summer, or fall and planting the same plants from containers:

(1) You save money. Typically, a bare-root plant costs only 40 to 70 per cent of what the same plant will cost later in the year in the container.

(2) The manner in which a bare-root plant is planted makes it easier to maintain and often makes it healthier and more vigorous than it would be if set out later in the year from a container.

When you plant a bare-root tree, you can refill the entire hole with one uniform soil mix (the root zone soil). By contrast, when you plant a container plant, you actually put two different soils in the hole—the soil mix that is in the container root ball, and the other soil mix with which you refill the hole around the root ball. Seldom can you make the backfill soil identical to the container soil. With two different kinds of soil, it is difficult to get uniform water penetration into the total rooting area. This may cause slow root growth from the container soil into the backfill soil. In other words, a deciduous plant from a container root ball may take longer to establish itself than it would from bare roots.

For bare-root planting to be successful, the roots should be fresh, not half-dead, and plump, not dry and withered. If you have any doubt at all about the freshness and plumpness of the roots, soak them overnight in a bucket of water before planting.

In many cases the roots and tops should be pruned in a certain fashion, depending on the kind of plant. An experienced nurseryman knows how to prune various kinds of deciduous trees, shrubs, and vines—and which ones to leave alone. He will be pleased to do whatever pruning is necessary for the plants you buy.

Dig the planting hole large enough to accommodate roots without cramping, bending, or cutting them. If it's a tree, vine, or large shrub, drive the training stake in the center of the hole. Place the plant next to the stake on the leeward side. Adjust depth so that the old soil line, visible at base of trunk, is at grade level. Refill the hole, working soil around all the roots. For very heavy soil, mix ground bark or other soil conditioner into the backfill soil. Tie tree or plant securely to the stake in two or three places with cloth, plastic, or rubber ties. Form watering basin around the plant and soak the hole thoroughly.

Grape vines and rose plants each require their own special kinds of bare-root planting—read the planting sections under *Grape* and *Rosa*.

Water bare-root plantings conservatively; dormant plants need less water than actively growing ones, and if you keep the soil too wet new feeder roots will not form. Water by inspection; check soil for moisture by using a trowel, soil sampling tube, or any pointed instrument. If soil is damp, the plant doesn't need water. When growth becomes active and weather turns warm, build an irrigating basin. Extend this basin every year to keep roots moving outward. And be patient; some bare-root trees and shrubs are slow to leaf out. Many will not do so until a few really warm days break their dormancy.

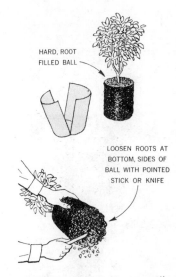

HARD, ROOT FILLED BALL

LOOSEN ROOTS AT BOTTOM, SIDES OF BALL WITH POINTED STICK OR KNIFE

Loosening can-bound roots will give faster, better rooting out.

Planting from Cans and Containers

Plants grown in containers are popular for many reasons: they are available at all seasons for planting when the gardener is ready to use them; they come in a variety of sizes and prices; and they are easy to transport and store. You can buy a container plant in bloom or in fruit and know exactly what color you're getting. In shopping for container-grown plants, look for a generally healthy, vigorous appearance and good foliage. The root system should be unencumbered, and not tangled or constricted by the plant's own roots. As evidence of a rootbound condition, look for roots above the soil level or growing through the can's drainage holes. Avoid such plants. And, further, look for symptoms of crowded roots: tops unusually large, trunks or stems unusually leggy, dead twigs or branches.

Best time to cut cans is just before you plant, but you may prefer to have cans cut at the nursery before taking plants home. If planting is delayed, keep such plants in a cool place and water occasionally to keep roots moist; water gently so that you don't wash out soil.

Dig holes twice the size of the container. It's especially important in planting container stock to add soil amendments. Many container plants are grown in a light, loose, fast draining mix that favors quick, even root development. If set into small holes in dense, impervious soil roots will be reluctant to move outward and downward. The result will be shallow rooted, slow-growing plants that are highly subject to drying out.

The basic planting process is very similar to that used in planting balled and burlapped material. There is one important difference: in removing the plant from the container you get a look at the outside of the root system. If roots there are crowded or coiled, you can straighten and loosen them with a pointed stick or knife just before covering the ball with earth. Or you can score the root ball lightly with a knife. If you plant during dry weather, don't forget a watering basin.

If you don't have cans cut for you, you can cut them at home with a patented can cutter (you can rent them from equipment rental firms, some nurseries), tin snips, or a screwdriver notched on the side near the tip. Wear stout gloves; cut edges are sharp, and chances for infection high. If can or container is tapered, you can usually tap out the plant as you would from a pot; if the plant won't slide out, cut the can. If you don't, you may disturb the root system by shaking off a lot of dirt.

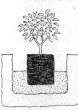

FILL PLANTING HOLE WITH WATER THEN LET IT DRAIN AWAY

SET PLANT IN HOLE FILL HALF WAY WITH SOIL. ADJUST PLANT TO GRADE. WATER.

FINISH ADDING SOIL. MAKE WATERING BASIN WATER AGAIN

Container plants do best if you follow these three steps.

Moving a Shrub or Small Tree

A time may come when it is desirable or necessary to move a shrub or small tree from one place to another. With expert care you can do this at any time of year, but you'll reduce your chance of losses if you do it in cool weather while the plant is dormant or semi-dormant. Some loss of roots at this time is not critical. If you have time enough, you can prepare the plant for moving several months ahead of actual moving. Shorten outer roots by cutting vertically with a spade in a circle around the plant, preferably near the drip

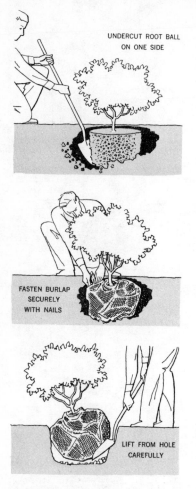

UNDERCUT ROOT BALL ON ONE SIDE

FASTEN BURLAP SECURELY WITH NAILS

LIFT FROM HOLE CAREFULLY

In transplanting, make root ball large, keep it intact.

line. The plant will grow a more compact set of feeder roots after this operation. Two to three days before moving, soak the root mass thoroughly so that it will hold together. Dig the new hole and prepare soil mix as described under PLANTING BALLED AND BURLAPPED SHRUBS, TREES. The faster you make the move, the less shock to the plant. As a further safeguard, you can spray the shrub or tree with an antidesiccant spray to cut down its water loss during the period while new roots are forming.

Decide on size of root ball which will sever fewest roots, then dig a trench around the root ball. Shape the ball with light cuts with spade or back of shovel. Heavy soil will allow a larger root ball than sandy soil. Cut down sides of trench to make room for wrapping and undercutting. Cut half way under root ball at one side. Be careful not to crumble root ball. Wrap burlap sacking around root ball as tightly as possible; pin burlap together with large nails; roll it underneath cut half of ball. Undercut other side of ball and lift plant from hole carefully, using the shovel as a lever. Be careful not to break the root ball at this stage. Set plant on open sack beside hole, tip ball slightly, remove shovel, give plant final wrapping with sack. Pin with nails and tie firmly with twine. Replant as described for balled and burlapped plants. If the plant and soil ball are small, and if the soil ball holds together well, you may be able to bypass the burlapping process. It's a risky operation and should be attempted only in cool weather. You'll have to work quickly and carefully to bring it off.

Planting Bulbs in Open Ground

First, prepare ground as you would for planting vegetables or annuals, incorporating amendments and fertilizer by spading or tilling. For planting a single bulb, dig a hole about 3 times the greatest diameter of the bulb. Loosen soil at bottom of hole. Many gardeners like to put a tablespoonful of bonemeal into the bottom of the hole at this point. Whether or not this traditional rite is worthwhile is a topic of continual debate. One thing is sure: It doesn't do any harm. Put a one-inch layer of sand on the bottom of the hole, set in the bulb, and cover with soil.

To plant many bulbs in the same bed, dig a trench to the required depth, spread a one-inch layer of sand, set the bulbs on the sand, and cover with soil. Set large bulbs five or six inches apart, smaller bulbs two to four inches apart. Be sure that all bulbs of a given kind are planted at a uniform depth. In most climates you won't have to water at all, or at least not until flower buds appear, but if you live in an arid climate or have an unusually dry winter you may have to give the bed an occasional soaking. Summer flowering bulbs will, of course, require irrigation.

Transplanting Bulbs and Perennials

Keep foliage on bulbs green as long as possible after bloom; those green leaves may not fit in with your garden plans, but they build up stored food in the bulb for next year's blooms. Cutting off green foliage may sacrifice next year's flowers. If you must transplant bulbs while foliage is green, perhaps to make room for other plants, take plenty of soil with the roots and heel them in in some out of the way corner of the garden. Keep plants watered until foliage ripens naturally. To make the yellowing foliage inconspicuous, you can bind it neatly with a rubber band, or pin it flat to the ground with a hairpin-shaped piece of wire. Yellowing foliage can be concealed by a covering of some quick growing annual, planted between the bulbs after bloom or sown directly above the bulbs in fall.

Timing and immediate transplanting are important factors in moving and replanting perennials. Dig and move spring and early summer flowering kinds in early fall. Transplant late blooming kinds like chrysanthemum and Michaelmas daisies in early winter (if you live in a mild climate) or in spring (if you live where winters are cold). Work quickly in moving perennials so that roots won't dry out. If you can't replant immediately, heel in the plants, cover with wet burlap, or wrap in polyethylene. Moving is a good time to divide; for instructions, see the propagating chapter.

When a Planting Hole Won't Drain

If a planting hole won't drain, it will act as a tank, keeping soil in the root zone saturated, and shutting off air, which is necessary to root growth in most plants. Without air, molds and rot take over. Even if the plant survives these, it will have to cope with a concentration of soluble salts left behind when excess water evaporates. Tight soil prevents excess water from leaching these salts on through the root zone; stunted growth and chlorosis are result.

With luck, you may be able to penetrate the tight layer to a more permeable one with spade, shovel, or post-hole digger. If the tight layer isn't too thick, dig or drill the planting hole full width clear through to the porous layer. Otherwise, drill a chimney a foot across from the bottom of your full-width hole until it reaches the porous stratum. Fill this with fine sand, peat moss, ground bark, or a mixture of half existing soil, half peat moss or bark. *Do not* put coarse gravel or rock in the chimney; it will interfere with free movement of water downward, not aid it.

Make the planting hole generous; suggested sizes: for large trees, 6 feet wide, 3 feet deep; small trees, 5 feet wide, 3 feet deep; large shrubs, 4 feet wide, 3 feet deep; small shrubs, 2 feet wide, 2 feet deep; flower borders, 18 inches wide and deep. In planting, backfill the hole with a mixture of 1/2 to 2/3 soil from the hole, and the rest coarse organic amendment. If you use raw sawdust or ground bark not already stabilized with nitrogen, add 1/2 cup ammonium sulfate or 3/4 cup of ammonium nitrate for every five cubic feet of organic material. It's also a good idea to add either superphosphate or a complete fertilizer. Iron sulfate added now will prevent chlorosis, and soil sulfur will reduce soil alkalinity, both conditions frequently associated with impermeable soil. Mix all ingredients thoroughly.

If you can't bore through to a porous layer, you may still succeed in growing a plant in the hole. Make the holes large, as mentioned above. Plant high, so that roots will be just that much above standing water. Rough up the sides of the hole; loosen soil in the bottom and mix it with backfill mixture to aid penetration by roots. Put edging boards around the shoulders of the planting hole. Mulch heavily, and irrigate lightly and frequently during dry weather. An occasional long, slow soaking will dissolve and overflow accumulated salts to a surface runoff point.

Bottom or side sumps may be the answer to desperate problems. To build the former, dig a hole three times the diameter of the root ball and 24 inches deep in the bottom of the planting hole. Pour in fine sand or other porous material (not rock or gravel) to the depth of a foot. Cover with a fiberglass pad 1/2 inch thick (to prevent fine material from washing into and filling the hole), add backfill and plant. For a side sump, dig a hole three or four feet wide and four to five feet deep about a foot away from the planting hole. Connect the two holes with a drain extending downward from a corner of the planting hole to the bottom of the sump. Fill the bottom of the planting hole, the drain line, and two feet of the sump with sand, cover with fiberglass pads, and fill the rest of the sump with native soil.

Another way out is to switch to raised beds or containers filled with a custom-made planting mix. With careful planning you can make such raised beds a positive asset to the landscape.

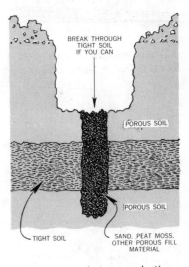

BREAK THROUGH TIGHT SOIL IF YOU CAN

POROUS SOIL

POROUS SOIL

TIGHT SOIL

SAND, PEAT MOSS, OTHER POROUS FILL MATERIAL

"Chimney" technique works if you can dig to porous layer.

Watering Your Garden

"How often shall I water it?" is perhaps the question most frequently asked by the novice gardener. No question is quite so difficult to answer. The variable factors involved are many and complex: the needs of the particular plant, its age, the season, the weather (temperature, humidity, and amount of wind), the nature of the soil (and the water), the method of application. To ignore these factors and water by calendar and clock may subject your garden to drought or drowning. To say "Give a plant as much water as it needs for healthy growth" is not really an answer. But this much we can say: frequent light sprinkling and frequent heavy soaking alike are bad. Water thoroughly —and infrequently.

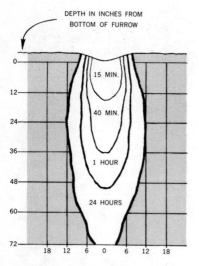

Note that water moves down in the soil. Little lateral movement.

Water Thoroughly

A little water wets only a little soil. You can't dampen soil to any depth by watering it lightly. You can have a damp soil only by wetting it thoroughly, then letting it partially dry out. Water moves down through the soil by progressively wetting soil particles. When every particle in the top inch has acquired its clinging film of water, every additional drop becomes "free" water, free to move down and wet lower particles. And it does move *down;* there is very little lateral movement of water within the soil. It is important to wet the entire root zone. Keep this in mind when building basins or ditches. A small basin around the trunk of a tree will tend to keep the roots inside a small area. Water put into a ditch 6 inches or more from a row of plants will not water the entire root area. Soak every square inch of root area.

Shallow Watering—Shallow Roots

Roots develop and grow only in the presence of water, soil, air, and nutrients. Except for a few naturally shallow-rooted plants, most plants will root throughout the depth at which these four essentials are to be found. If only the top foot of soil is kept well watered, roots will develop in the top foot. Even lawn grasses, generally considered shallow rooted, will run roots from 10 to 36 inches deep. If shallow watering keeps the roots near the surface, plants will be open to severe damage if you go away for a long weekend and weather turns hot; there will be no deep reserves of water to tap, and no roots to tap them.

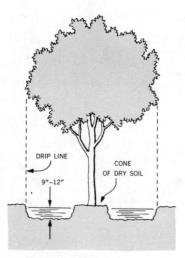

Watering basin should provide for plant's entire rooting area.

Water Infrequently

"Infrequently" is a relative term. What it means is that deep waterings should not be performed too often. When free water reaches the point where it fills the interspaces between soil particles, the supply of oxygen to the roots is cut off and they begin to "drown." Root elongation stops and nutrient absorption is hindered. If the soil continues low in oxygen long enough, harmful organisms thrive, producing toxic substances. Beneficial bacteria are killed off. Roots become susceptible to fungus diseases. Plants vary in their ability to resist these conditions, but many of our choicest plants absolutely require air in the soil.

Where water goes, air must follow. When you soak your soil, you are wetting each layer of soil, as the water drains through it, to a condition known as field capacity. In this condition, each soil particle holds the maximum amount of water it can against the pull of gravity. Air space in the soil is at its lowest percentage. As plant roots and evaporation draw water from the soil, the films of water become thinner, and more space is gained for soil air and oxygen. When the film becomes so thin that its molecular attraction to the soil particle is stronger than the root tips' ability to extract it, the plant will wilt, even though there is still some water in the soil. During all the stages in which soil dries from field capacity to wilting point the plant has sufficient water for healthy growth. To maintain a desirable air-water ratio, you should not keep your garden constantly at field capacity.

The rate of water use by plants depends on light intensity, temperature, humidity, and wind. It is influenced by competition with roots of other trees, shrubs, grasses, and weeds. Field capacity varies by soil type; clay soils with many fine particles hold more water than sandy soils with fewer, coarser particles. Loamy soils, with a mixture of particle sizes, have an intermediate field capacity.

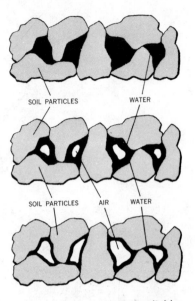

Upper sketch shows soil at field capacity; little air in soil.

How Many Days Between Watering?

In time you can answer this question best by your own observations in your own garden or, if you are a perfectionist, you can use a soil sampling tube, a device described in the soils chapter, which enables you to see and feel how much water there is underground. Or, you can install a tensiometer, an instrument that will give a precise measurement of water in the soil. We can give you some guidelines, based on University of California observations on average gardens in full growth.

Days between waterings

	SANDY	LOAM	CLAY
Shallow-rooted	4-6	7-10	10-12
Medium-rooted	7-10	10-15	15-20
Deep-rooted	15-20	20-30	30 or more

The rate of use of water in the soil reservoir by lawns in the various climates of the West is estimated as follows:

Water use by lawn per week (in inches)

California:		Oregon-Washington:	
Dry desert areas	2.5	Cool	1.0
San Joaquin Valley	2.1	Moderate	1.4
Sacramento Valley	1.8	Hot	1.8
Inland coastal areas	1.5		
Coastal slopes	1.0		

If the *use* of 1 inch per week is charted against root depth of grasses in lawns, you get this picture:

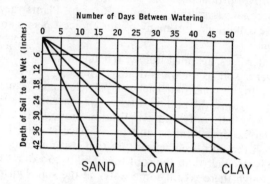

Number of Days Between Watering

How to read chart: If you are watering a lawn where rate of use averages 1 inch per week and root depth is 12 inches and soil is loam, follow the 12-inch line across the chart to the loam diagonal where you read off approximately 7 days. If your soil is in the clay class, the chart says that for a 12-inch depth the interval could be 14 days. Since this figure is based on cool climates (1 inch used per week), the interval would be cut to 7 days in hot climates (2 inches per week).

If you are now watering every other day, you will insist that the chart is good theory "but they don't know my lawn."

It is very true that you can't change from an every-other-day interval to a twice-a-month interval in one jump. As a matter of fact, *the time to make the switch is right at the end of the rainy season.* Start right out watering very deep at your maximum interval, and stick with the schedule through the dry season. If water penetration and drainage are good, you can get subsoil moisture by increasing the length of each irrigation.

How Much Water to Apply?

Assuming that you want to encourage deep rooting by deep watering, your next question undoubtedly is: How much water does it take to irrigate to the 2-foot level?

The answer depends on the soil. Some soils absorb water rapidly and yield it up rapidly; others absorb water very slowly and hold it for a long period of time. Clay, with its many microscopic particles, is slow to take up water; each particle in the top layer must become wet before water will drop to the lower levels. Sand, with its relatively few particles, presents a much smaller area of surfaces to be wetted. It takes 3/4 inch of rain to wet sand to a depth of 1 foot; it takes 2-1/2 inches of rain to wet clay to the same depth.

In practical terms, if you wish to soak a 100-square-foot garden bed to a depth of 2 feet, you would need to apply 125 gallons to a sandy soil, 190 gallons to a loamy soil, and 330 gallons to clay. If you were applying water from a hose under normal volume (about 5 gallons a minute), you would need about 25 minutes to soak the sandy bed, 38 minutes for the loamy one, and an hour and 5 minutes for the clay. Actually the clay would take longer; it absorbs water so slowly that water would very likely puddle and run off if you tried to apply it all at one watering session.

This does not mean that your water bills will be less if you have a sandy soil. The clay, once wet, will hold the water for a long time, and will not have to be watered nearly so often as the sand.

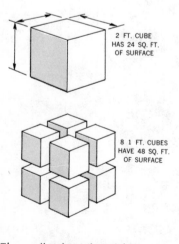

2 FT. CUBE HAS 24 SQ. FT. OF SURFACE

8 1 FT. CUBES HAVE 48 SQ. FT. OF SURFACE

The smaller the soil particles are, the larger their total surface.

How Long to Run the Sprinklers?

If you are using a sprinkler to apply the water—as on a lawn—you can easily compute the amount to apply and figure how long you should let the sprinkler run.

Start with the fact that 1 inch of rain will penetrate 12 inches in sandy soil, about 7 inches in loam, and 4 to 5 inches in clay. Thus, if a lawn is to be watered to 12 inches, it would need 1 inch of rain if planted in sandy soil and 2-1/2 inches if in clay.

Next question in the formula is how much "rain" your sprinkler produces. This is easy to determine. Place a number of coffee cans spaced at regular intervals in a line running out from the sprinkler. Turn on the water and note the time it takes to fill the cans to 1 inch. (This experiment may also provide you with revealing information about the efficiency of your sprinkler. Many sprinklers do not put down a uniform distribution of water.)

When you know how long it takes your sprinkler to rain an inch, you can then multiply this interval by the number of inches required and then determine just how long you should leave the sprinkler turned on.

Ordinarily, conscientious watering by clock and calendar should guarantee adequate irrigation for your garden. Weather conditions, however, are likely to upset such a schedule.

Under the influence of a hot, dry wind, the rate of water use by plants is so rapid that shallow-rooted plants sometimes cannot carry water fast enough to prevent wilting.

Thus, in periods of cool, humid weather, less frequent watering may be required than in intervals of hot, dry weather.

There is one watering test that can be applied safely to all types of soils and climates. This guide is provided by testing the soil before you water. If you cannot easily insert a trowel, spade, or sharpened stick more than 3 or 4 inches into the soil, watering is necessary. The soil sampling tube gives a more revealing and detailed reading.

If subsoil is dry despite adequate amounts of water, you may have a run-off problem. On a heavy soil, the penetration of water can be so slow that more than 50 per cent of the water is lost by run-off if there is the slightest slope. In other words, you could easily sprinkle on 6 inches of water and get only 3 inches into the soil.

There are several ways to overcome this condition. You can have the soil aerated with an aerator that *removes plugs of soil*. Spiking soil is generally not desirable because the spikes are likely to compact the soil around the holes they drive.

Or, adjust your sprinkling procedure. For one thing, you can slow down the delivery rate so that the soil absorbs the delivered water. The other choice is to run the sprinklers at full rate until run-off starts, then shut them off for a half hour, then repeat the process.

The ideal solution to this dilemma is to remove the plants from the bed (or tear out the old lawn) and condition the soil to a 9-inch depth (or as deep as you can make a rotary tiller penetrate). Thoroughly incorporate into the soil an amendment of a volume equal to 25 to 50 per cent of the total volume of soil being treated. This method is described in the soils chapter under *Soil Amendments* and is discussed again under subsequent heading in that chapter. A clay soil conditioned in this fashion will take water much faster than it did before it was conditioned and it will hold it longer, all the while keeping more soil air around the roots. After the conditioning job is completed, replace the plants or plant a new lawn.

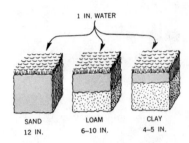

Water is slower in penetrating clay than sand or loam.

Test the "rainfall" from sprinkler by this simple scheme.

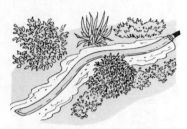

Canvas soaker waters long beds without washing soil.

Water bubbler breaks force of flow without decreasing volume.

Subsoil irrigator puts water right where roots can use it.

Flooding and Soaking

Flooding or soaking is a most effective way to water large shrubs or trees. Surround each plant with a depression extending a short distance beyond the drip line, or make a basin by drawing up earth into a circular dike several inches high. If plants are shallow rooted (azaleas, camellias, and many other shade plants), surround the watering area with a low ridge or dike, but don't draw away surface soil from the roots of the plants. Fill the basin slowly with water until it no longer sinks in. Basins around large, deep-rooted trees should be 9 to 12 inches deep. To prevent irrigation water from wetting the bases of sensitive trees such as citrus or walnut, build a cone of dry soil around the base of the trunk.

For soaking smaller plants, tie a piece of burlap over the end of a hose or attach a manufactured water bubbler or force-breaker, turn on the hose and let the water flow out gently. Move the hose end from place to place as soil becomes thoroughly wet. To soak large areas, use a canvas or plastic soaker that permits water to escape slowly along its entire length.

To water single shrubs in the ground or in containers, use a watering stick —a long aluminum tube with a device at the end to break the force of the water without diminishing the flow.

If you grow vegetables or flowers for cutting in rows, the furrow substitutes for the basin. Scoop out furrows between rows with shovel or hoe. Broad, shallow furrows are generally preferable; there is less danger to roots in preparing such furrows, and less likelihood that roots will be exposed by a strong flow of water. Moreover, the wide furrow will assure soaking of a wider root area. Ideally, furrowing should be done before root systems of plants have developed and spread to a point where they might be injured by furrowing.

A device that puts water right down to the deep roots of large shrubs and trees is the subsoil irrigator, a sharpened, perforated pipe that you attach to the end of a hose. The most useful models are equipped with a valve. You insert the pointed pipe into the soil to the desired depth, turn on the valve, and water passes down through the pipe and out into the soil. The channels left by the irrigator also afford a path for air to get into the soil—a useful by-product. A refinement of the subsoil irrigator mixes fertilizer from a cartridge with the water.

Sprinkling

The best way to apply water evenly over a large surface is by sprinkling. One disadvantage of sprinkling is that in areas where humidity is high, mildew, rust, and other diseases are encouraged. This drawback can be overcome to a degree by sprinkling early in the morning, so that plants will be dry by nightfall, when humidity is highest. Another disadvantage is that some plants with weak stems and heavy flowers will bend, and possibly break under a load of water from a sprinkler.

Many plants, especially the shade-loving ones that prefer acid soil, do better with overhead sprinkling. Plants benefit by the rinsing that washes dust from the leaves, and certain pests, especially spider mites, are discouraged by sprinkling.

Portable sprinklers that you attach to the end of a hose are handy and quite serviceable. But a permanent underground sprinkling system is far more efficient and timesaving. These can be manually controlled or they can be installed with clock-activated devices that turn them on and off at a set time.

Fertilizing Your Garden

Complete fertilizer. Any fertilizer that contains all three of the primary nutrient elements—nitrogen, phosphorus, and potassium—is known as a complete fertilizer.

Fertilizer men talk of the elements nitrogen, phosphorus, and potassium by their chemical symbols N, P, and K respectively. Gardeners and farmers use another shortened term—three numbers in a row representing the percentages of N, P, and K.

Some fertilizer manufacturers put their analysis percentages in big numbers on the label, right under the product name, like this: 10-8-6. Without looking at the fine print under *Guaranteed Analysis*, you can tell that the fertilizer contains 10 per cent total nitrogen, 8 per cent phosphoric acid, and 6 per cent water-soluble potash.

Actually, there are many different analyses; however, even when the analysis is the same on two different products, the formula or "recipe" by which one manufacturer arrived at his analysis can differ from the others.

Special purpose plant foods. At the stores and nurseries you will find fertilizers packaged for certain uses, such as "Camellia Food," "Rhododendron Food," or "Rose Food." The camellia and rhododendron foods belong to an old established group—the acid plant foods. Some of the compounds used in these fertilizers are chosen because they have an acid reaction. Many other fertilizers packaged for certain plants do not have quite as valid a background.

Another special category is the controlled or timed release fertilizer. In various complete formulations, these fertilizers are processed so that their nutrients will be made available over extended periods of time—from several months to several years.

A third special kind of fertilizer, sometimes not truly a complete fertilizer, is the low-nitrogen or no-nitrogen type—used on certain plants to encourage bloom or induce maturity without stimulating further growth.

True organic fertilizers. Cottonseed meal, blood meal, bonemeal, and similar organic fertilizers have their NPK ratios stated on the labels. Most are high in just one of the three elements, low or zero in the other two. But they are useful for specific purposes.

Manure is a complete fertilizer, but weak when judged on NPK standards. Manures vary in their nutrient content according to the animal and what the animal had been eating. But an NPK ratio of approximately 1-1-1 is typical. Manure never registers as high as the mildest of complete chemical fertilizers, but under certain circumstances, it may still be a useful mulch or soil conditioner.

Timing a Feeding

When you realize what can happen in 12 months to the fertilizer you apply at any one time, you see why one feeding is seldom adequate. The nitrogen

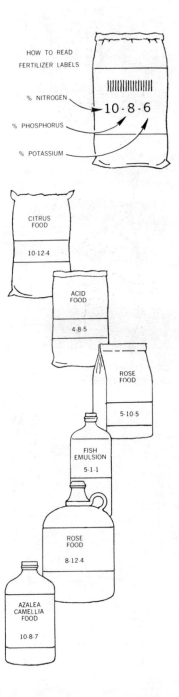

HOW TO READ FERTILIZER LABELS

% NITROGEN
% PHOSPHORUS
% POTASSIUM

10-8-6

CITRUS FOOD
10-12-4

ACID FOOD
4-8-5

ROSE FOOD
5-10-5

FISH EMULSION
5-1-1

ROSE FOOD
8-12-4

AZALEA CAMELLIA FOOD
10-8-7

Holes-around-the-dripline feeding good for older trees.

Surface feeding near dripline is satisfactory for younger trees.

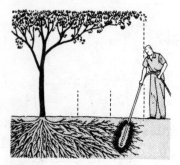

Liquid food applied by root-zone applicator works fast.

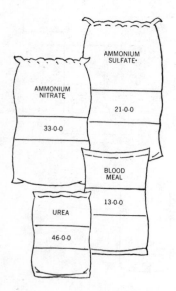

that isn't used by plants can be leached out by watering and used up by soil organisms. The phosphorus may have been just enough to satisfy the hungry minerals that "fix" it (see next page), leaving the roots to get what soil phosphorus they can. The soluble potassium may be used up rapidly, creating a hard pull on what exchangeable potassium (see page 52) exists in the soil.

If your fertilizer carries no instructions on it for repeating application, use these suggestions as a general guide:

Feed roses with label-recommended amounts as new year's growth begins and subsequently as each bloom period comes to an end.

Feed rhododendrons, azaleas, and camellias immediately after bloom, and again monthly until August.

Feed fuchsias, begonias, and other lush, verdant, summertime flower producers every month with label-recommended doses, or once every 10 days to 2 weeks with light doses.

Fruit trees can take nutrients almost any time, but the time of greatest need is about 2 or 3 weeks before blossoming. Big, old garden trees can be fed by the holes-around-the-drip-line method once a year if you think they need it. This method works best in areas of moderate rainfall and mild climate. Fertilizer placed this way must have sufficient water to make it available to nearby roots, yet not so much as to leach it out of the root area.

Use an auger to drill holes in a circle just inside the drip line. Make holes 18 to 24 inches apart (the sandier the soil, the closer the holes, since follow-up watering in sandy soil will distribute nutrients *downward* quite rapidly but laterally not very far.) Don't drill down too far—just to the surface root zone.

Use a complete fertilizer, carefully following package directions as to the amount to be used and dividing by the number of holes you are going to fill. Before inserting in holes, mix the fertilizer with an equal amount of sand. Irrigate immediately and thoroughly; otherwise you'll burn the roots.

Young trees and fast-growing, surface-rooting trees like willows can be fed on the surface, as the labels suggest for shrubs.

Most annual crops—vegetables and flowers—benefit from a starter fertilizer at planting time. In addition, give them additional nitrogen (or complete fertilizer if it's handier) after they are well started. For anything else, feed when you see growth starting, again in summer, and—in mild climates or with definitely hardy plants—feed once more in the fall.

Nitrogen

In the natural course of events (with no fertilizer added), nitrogen that comes into the soil as dead plant or animal material must undergo several chemical changes before it becomes available to plants' roots. See *Organic Amendments*, pages 32-33.

Most of the nitrogen in complete fertilizers is in the organic form, either natural or synthetic. A good number of complete fertilizers contain nitrogen in the ammonia form. A few contain nitrogen in the nitrate form.

If a fertilizer's label says that all or most of the nitrogen contained is in the nitrate (or nitric) form, you know it will be fast acting. On the other hand, if it's mostly ammonic or organic, the response will be not quite as fast, but it should be more sustained once it starts. The ammonic nitrogen should cause a faster response than organic nitrogen.

The fast response is much more noticeable and significant in lawns than in plants and trees, though it applies to all. It's also easy to burn a lawn by putting on too much nitrogen, since grass is made up of thousands of tiny plants growing together. Shrub roots grow deep and wide and have more soil around them to act as a buffer.

Not a mineral. Nitrogen is not present in the minute particles of mineral soil from which plants get their phosphorus, potassium, and the other mineral elements. All nitrogen must come from the air (some of which gets into soil via rainfall and some of which is extracted from soil air by specialized bacteria), from organic matter, or from fertilizers. As a fertilizer, nitrogen (the nitrate form) leaches through the root area quickly.

Carbon-nitrogen ratio. If organic matter that you add to the soil is high in carbon compared to nitrogen, soil organisms working to digest the high carbon material may compete with the crops for nitrogen. For this reason, you should do one of the following two things when using sawdust, shavings, ground bark, or straw as a soil conditioner. One choice is to shop for and buy those materials in fortified form (nitrogen already added to the high-carbon material). Or, get untreated material and mix nitrogen fertilizer with it. For each 1,000 square feet of the material, laid 3 inches deep, mix in 55 pounds of ammonium sulfate or 35 pounds of ammonium nitrate. The supplementary nitrogen keeps the carbon-nitrogen ratio in balance.

What nitrogen does. The nitrogen in soil regulates a plant's ability to make proteins that are vital to formation of new protoplasm in the cells. Nitrogen is most active in the young, tender parts of plant tissues, such as tips of shoots, buds, and opening leaves. If there's a deficiency, only the growing tips will function properly. Older cells may turn yellow, and old leaves may die and drop off.

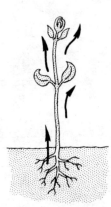

Nitrogen speeds vegetative growth, gives rich green leaf color.

Phosphorus

The mineral or clay soil particles that contain phosphorus ions give them up reluctantly to the microscopic film of water (soil solution) that surrounds the particles. As the root tips grow into contact with the soil solution, they absorb the phosphorus that the solution is holding in available form. This reduces the concentration of phosphorus ions in the soil solution around the root tips, and the phosphorus becomes insufficient to meet the plant's needs. Then, more phosphorus is released from the particle to the solution surrounding it, and the root takes it up.

The root grows on to fresh areas of soil solution, repeating the process. During periods of rapid growth, the phosphorus absorption and renewal cycle around a soil particle takes place constantly, if the soil is fertile. If the concentration of phosphorus in the soil solution is too low, or if the rate of renewal is too slow, plant growth is retarded.

Why phosphorus moves slowly. The phosphoric acid from fertilizer ionizes in the soil to form other phosphate compounds, some of which plants can use, some of which are so insoluble that plants cannot use them. This is called "fixation," and it is more of a problem in definitely acid soils than in neutral or alkaline soils. If yours is an acid soil, you should raise your soil's available phosphorus level to a point where the fixing power has been satisfied and there are no longer many "hungry" minerals to combine with the phosphate ions.

The least effective ways of applying a fertilizer containing phosphorus are to broadcast and mix it lightly into the surface or to spray a solution on the soil surface. Most effective way is to concentrate the phosphates where roots can get at them. In practical terms this means banding fertilizer beside seed rows—a few inches to one side and a few inches below the seed level (following label directions for amounts per foot of row). When you plant a new tree or shrub, mix superphosphate or a complete fertilizer into the backfill (the soil that goes into the hole). Or, spade it in, mixing it thoroughly into what you estimate will be the root area for a few years to come.

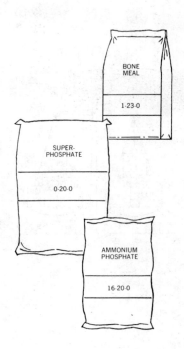

BONE MEAL 1-23-0

SUPER-PHOSPHATE 0-20-0

AMMONIUM PHOSPHATE 16-20-0

What phosphorus does. Phosphorus is necessary for the process of photosynthesis and it provides the mechanism by which energy is transferred within a plant. It is present in all living tissue.

Potassium

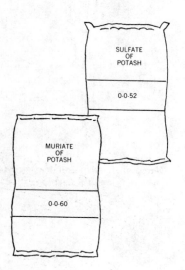

Usually, the last percentage listed in the label's analysis is potassium. It's said in different ways on different labels: "available or soluble potash," "water soluble potash," "water soluble potash from muriate or tankage."

Plants remove from the soil more potassium than any other nutrients except nitrogen and calcium. Potassium in the soil exists in several forms. One form is soluble in water; other forms are insoluble; some are insoluble even in strong acids. Most of the natural soil potassium is not available to plants even though plants have been growing in the soil for years.

Little made available. About 1 per cent of the total soil potassium is an important reservoir. It's what is called exchangeable potassium. It may be derived from minerals or fertilizers or crop residues. It is not soluble or free to move with soil water unless it is replaced or undergoes a slow weathering process. However, roots can pick up exchangeable potassium from the clay or humus particle without that element actually entering the soil solution.

When you add fertilizer containing soluble potassium to the soil, a transfer occurs from solution to exchangeable potassium. An equilibrium is re-established at a higher potassium level.

What potassium does. Potassium is essential to the life processes of a plant, including manufacture and movement of sugars and starch, and normal growth by cell division.

Sulfur, Magnesium, Calcium

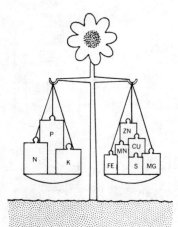

Some fertilizers contain these elements, others do not. Actually, it makes little difference; these elements, while important, are usually present in the soil in good supply. Also, calcium and sulfur get into the soil in other kinds of garden products: lime (calcium), lime-sulfur fungicides and soil conditioners (calcium and sulfur), gypsum (calcium and sulfur), superphosphate (some sulfur in addition to the phosphates), and soil sulfur used for acidifying alkaline soils.

What they do. Calcium is a highly essential plant nutrient. It plays a fundamental part in cell manufacture and growth. Most roots must have some calcium right at the growing tips. In the cells of green leaves every chlorophyll molecule has an atom of magnesium as its central part.

Sulfur acts hand-in-hand with nitrogen in making new protoplasm for plant cells; it therefore is just as essential as nitrogen, but its deficiency in the soil is not so prevalent.

Iron, Zinc, Manganese

If a soil is quite alkaline, as some soils are in low-rainfall areas, plants may not be able to absorb enough iron, zinc, and manganese. If you live in such an area, you probably know of the need for these minor elements (see *Chlorosis,* page 34).

Nurseries and garden stores sell products you can put on the soil or spray on the leaves to correct the problem. Some such soil products are chelated, meaning that the iron, zinc, or manganese is in a form that should remain available to roots and not be susceptible to the fixing or locking that makes the native iron, zinc, or manganese unavailable.

What they do. Iron is essential to chlorophyll formation. Manganese and zinc seem to function as catalysts in the utilization of other nutrients.

Biological Pest Control

For many years, most gardeners took it for granted that regular spraying was a prerequisite for an attractive garden. Now, much evidence against this habit has been gathered. Studies show that constant and/or heavy spraying often creates more problems than it solves. Beneficial insects are killed along with the pests, and the ecological balance of the garden (and the community) is thrown out of kilter.

When the ecological balance in a garden is upset — by killing both pests and beneficial insects (predators and parasites) for example — a secondary pest outbreak can occur. A brand-new population of some other pest develops. These secondary pests can do more damage to the garden than the original pest did — and the spraying leaves few, if any, beneficial insects in the garden who can stop the new pest invasion. If the gardener sprays again, the vicious circle will continue.

The discovery that certain pesticides can harm the environment has helped to make biological control increasingly popular. Biological control (often called biocontrol), a practice which began in China several centuries ago, is a pest control system that avoids the use of chemicals. Instead, natural enemies of garden pests are used to control the problem insects. You won't get results as quickly as you would with chemicals, but control will last much longer.

How Biocontrol Works

Pest outbreaks occur when predators or parasites aren't around to keep tiny invaders under control. Insects accidentally imported into the United States from foreign countries often cause the most trouble because they have no natural enemies here; these foreign pest populations can increase nearly unchecked. In contrast, native American pests are usually kept under control by predators that have developed along with the pests.

Scientists often search a pest's homeland for its natural enemies. If a natural predator is found, it is carefully observed to be sure it will be beneficial *only;* then it is raised in great numbers in an insectary (a hatchery for keeping and breeding live insects). The predators are then ready to be sold for release in home gardens. If you can't bear the thought of releasing insects in your garden, consider this: There are over one million different types of insects on earth, only a very small number of which are capable of causing people discomfort. Insects are not as frightening as we've been brought up to believe.

An insect pest population may continue to increase for a time even after predators have been released, until the predators can become established. The introduced insects will multiply and probably either feed on the pests or parasitize them (lay eggs in their eggs) — for example, lacewing larva eating aphids, or *Trichogramma* wasps depositing eggs within moth eggs. When the biocontrol system is working, the pest and predator populations are interdependent.

The Pluses and the Minuses

The greatest advantage of biocontrol is that the system can continue indefinitely in your garden — that means you may not have to spray again. It is not necessary to eliminate the pest population. In fact, you should never kill all the pests; the beneficial insects will not have anything to feed on, and they will not stay in the area — they'll either leave or die of starvation. With the predators gone, there will be nothing to restrain the pests when they return to your garden.

The major drawback of biological control is the time it takes for the system to begin working. During the interim your garden may suffer some damage, and you'll have to cope with the frustration that comes from breaking the old habit of spraying at the first sign of trouble.

Never demand (or even expect) total eradication of a pest population. If you have a low tolerance for insect damage in your garden, you may have to learn to accept a little more — it is not hard to do, and well worth the effort. Minor damage to plants will not cause you any real trouble.

Give biological control a try in your garden. If you are patient, and don't seek total elimination of pests, you will be pleased with this environmentally safe pest control system. You will be able to avoid contact with potentially dangerous substances; beneficial insects will keep pest populations at low levels; and biocontrol will be less expensive than chemicals in the long run.

These Sprays are Safe

Here are two sprays that won't hurt plants, people, or the environment.

Water jet. This method works well against aphids, spider mites and other free-moving pests. An adjustable hose nozzle, or a pistol type that delivers sudden, sharp blasts of water, works best against these pests.

Where aphids are very dense, loosen them with your fingers as you blast them with water. Aphids rarely return to plants after being knocked off. Spider mites love to hide in dust on the undersides of leaves. If these tiny creatures are on your plants, clean the foliage by turning the hose nozzle up and spraying upward from the base of the plant.

Bacillus thuringiensis. This substance, a bacteria commonly referred to as B.t., is deadly to many types of moth and butterfly larvae (the lepidoptera group). B.t. contains a spore and a crystal that combine to destroy caterpillars' digestive systems. *Bacillus thuringiensis* is a safe, efficient control for pesty foliate feeders — and an excellent alternative to chemicals. B.t. is available as a powder or a liquid; it is sold under the names Biotrol, Dipel, and Thuricide. Caterpillars have to ingest B.t. before it will affect them, so spray it on the foliage where they're feeding. Once the bacteria are inside the larvae, they multiply and kill the host caterpillars.

MANY PLANT PESTS ARE FOUND UNDERNEATH THE LEAVES— SPRAYING LEAF SURFACES MAY NOT GET THEM

SO DIRECT SPRAYS **UP**

To get best results from sprays, spray whole plant thoroughly.

Do-It-Yourself Methods

If you don't mind stalking garden pests, hand methods and traps are successful controls; if you are consistent, pest populations do not have a chance to reach damaging numbers.

Hand picking. Though not for the squeamish, this method can be a great success — it gives you the satisfaction of knowing just what you've captured. You will be happier if you wear gloves to squash snails, slugs, and pesty bugs. If the direct approach doesn't appeal to you, try putting your collection of pests in a bag and burning it. Or, put pests in a jar full of water, cap it, and dump it the next day. Night hunts with a flashlight are successful against snails and slugs.

You can get rid of tent caterpillars by cutting off the branch (just below the tent) and burning it.

Adhesive barriers. You can buy these sticky substances in nurseries, or use petroleum jelly if the plant you're protecting does not get much hot sunlight. These barriers are great for keeping crawling insects, like ants, out of trees. Check the stickiness frequently; long exposure to the atmosphere can make adhesive barriers ineffective.

Seedling protectors. You can keep cutworms away from young plants by placing a can (first, remove both ends) over each seedling. Spread a mulch of dry sawdust or shavings around seedlings to thwart snails and slugs.

Traps. Rolled newspapers, placed about your garden, will draw earwigs to their dark folds. Throw away or burn the papers to get rid of the earwigs. Small boards or upside down flower pots, placed on damp ground, will attract snails and slugs who wish to hide — so you can squash them conveniently.

Helpful accessories for hand picking.

Introducing Some Helpful Friends

Some insects and small mammals readily kill plant damaging pests. Though there is no guarantee that they will help, you should learn which garden creatures to protect and encourage to stay in the area. Here is a group of the most helpful garden inhabitants.

Amphibians, Lizards

Toads, frogs, and salamanders are included in this group. They all feed on insects and certain other garden pests. If you do not have one of these helpers in your garden, try to get one from a friend or a pet shop; then release it. Be sure there is water available at all times or these creatures could die.

Bats

These small mammals are among the garden-insect-eating champions. Though they're rarely visible during the day, you can often see bats darting about the sky at dusk. A word of caution: Never try to touch a bat or examine a sick one, they can carry rabies.

(Continued on next page)

Birds

Many birds are insect and grub eaters (some eats plants too). You can encourage your favorite birds to stay around by putting out food for them. Most birds like suet and bird seed. Hummingbirds, who eat many small insects, are attracted by sugar water in special feeders.

Flower Fly

This is a large group of very common flies that are usually found hovering around flowers. Many are brightly colored, and their bodies may be smooth or covered with tiny hairs; they often resemble bees, but are slightly smaller. They do not bite or sting. Their larvae feed on aphids.

Ground Beetles

These nocturnal, shiny black beetles are among the most beneficial garden insects. They consume some of our worst pests, including cutworms and other larvae, and they frequently climb trees in search of prey. They can produce a foul odor when handled. Don't kill them.

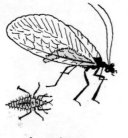

Lacewings

You are fortunate if there are green lacewings in your garden. If not, you can buy and release them. The larvae, commonly known as "aphid lions," consume large quantities of aphids; they're also fond of mealybugs and spider mites. The delicate looking adult females lay their eggs at the ends of hairlike stalks, so don't disturb them if you find any.

Ladybird Beetles

Also known as ladybugs, this large group contains many predators. The larvae (and the adults to some extent) feed on aphids, scale insects, and mites. Beware of most ladybugs sold commercially. After release, they must fly to burn off winter fat deposits before they can feed and lay eggs—so they probably won't stay in your garden.

Shrews

These tiny, above-ground relatives of the mole are excellent insect eaters. They feed constantly and occasionally attack creatures bigger than themselves. You will probably never see a shrew; but you should hope that they are in your garden.

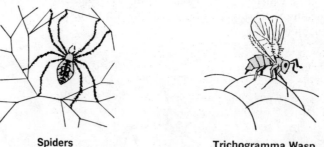

Spiders

Spiders eat lots of insects and mites and, since some are nocturnal, they can work in your garden day and night. Some spiders trap their prey in webs, while others hunt or wait for unsuspecting insects.

Trichogramma Wasp

You might want to introduce this tiny (less than 1mm long), helpful wasp to your garden. Just buy the eggs (advertised in many regional garden magazines), and place them in your garden; they hatch by themselves. The adult wasps can kill over 200 different pest insects, including codling moths, cabbage loopers, and cutworms. The wasps do this by laying their eggs in the pests' eggs—the wasp larvae hatch inside the pests' eggs and kill them.

Integrated Pest Control

The previous chapter describes biological control. Biocontrol is an important aspect in all types of pest control; it plays such a large and influential role in integrated control that it deserves a proper introduction. Biological control is basically nature balancing herself. Fortunately, man is becoming more aware of how he can benefit from this natural balance, and how he can combine it with other techniques to develop highly efficient pest control methods.

Integrated control is a pest management system that stops plant damagers in several ways. These methods can be divided into three parts: physical control, biological control, and chemical control. Think of integrated control as a total approach to preventing pest damage in your garden.

The goal of integrated control, as with biological control, is to keep pest damage at tolerable levels. The principles are the same too: Never expect to eliminate all the pests; know who the culprit doing the damage is; always use the weakest control first — if hand picking and beneficial insects can keep pest populations controlled, chemicals are not necessary.

Physical control. Your first safeguard against plant damagers is careful garden planning. Mix different kinds of plants together, as much as possible, in your garden. And, plant disease resistant varieties, such as VFN tomatoes, if you can get them. Expanses of one kind of plant invite attacks by organisms that thrive on that plant. Furthermore, if you select only one plant for your garden, that plant may not be able to sustain beneficial insects. The plants in your garden should be varied, so they will provide homes for many different insects who can keep each other in check.

Preventive garden maintenance will help thwart pest invasions too. Keep the ground surface around plants clean by digging in or removing fallen leaves and fruit. Layers of debris — when not disturbed for long periods — become breeding and hiding places for insect pests. Always remove infested, damaged, or weak plants, and annuals that have passed their prime; they all harbor pests.

Chemical control. The integrated control philosophy opposes preventive spraying. You should not spray until pests are doing intolerable damage to your plants, and then only if other methods have been unable to control the pests.

Deciding if and when insecticides are truly needed is tricky. Rare is the gardener who has not had to spray infested plants from time-to-time. If you must spray to save a certain kind of plant, try to time the application to stop pests while their numbers are growing. Once a pest population reaches its maximum size, it will decline by itself — predators will overcome the pests or a food shortage will cause some pests to starve to death.

You will find many insecticides in your local nursery or garden center; some are safer to use than others. Petroleum oils and products containing sulfur or copper are less hazardous to nontarget organisms (creatures you are not trying to kill) than are most chemical formulations. Others, such as pyrethrum and rotenone, are made from the leaves and roots of certain plants. They are fairly safe to use since they break down rapidly in the presence of sunlight — and these two won't harm plants. Limit your use of any of these chemicals to afflicted plants only, and use the correct chemical on the pest you are trying to eradicate.

To apply chemicals, a small, portable, pressurized tank sprayer is easier to handle and less wasteful than the extremely fast hose-end sprayers. The

READ **ALL** THE LABEL BEFORE YOU BUY OR USE

WHAT THE SPRAY CONTROLS

DIRECTIONS, DILUTION AND ADDITIONAL INFORMATION

WHAT IT CONTAINS

WARNINGS CAUTIONS

Read directions, follow them, and follow to the letter.

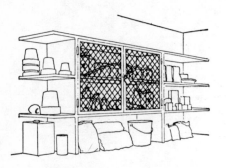

A locked cabinet for garden sprays, dusts, can save lives.

tank holds just enough mixture for small jobs; you won't be tempted to spray other plants with the leftover spray. Always follow label directions precisely when mixing chemicals — a little may be good, but more is definitely not better. Store pesticides outside your house, preferably in a locked cabinet where children cannot get at them. Be sure to wash your hands and, if the pesticide label recommends it, change and wash your clothes after spraying.

The Pluses and the Minuses

Since integrated control is like biological control, but with more dimensions (physical and chemical), it has many of the same advantages. Natural predators can perpetually keep pest levels low. You, the gardener, can help the predators with their biological control by implementing physical controls. If biocontrol and physical control combined can't hold pest populations in check, you still have a stopgap measure remaining, chemical control.

Integrated control deals with the causes (conditions responsible for pest invasion) of garden problems through preventive maintenance. In contrast, a system that involves the use of chemicals alone treats symptoms (only the pests themselves). The cause, for example, debris such as dead plants that harbor pests, remains to hide new pests after chemicals are applied. If plant damagers continually invade your garden, this is a sign that there is not a natural balance between the pests and their predators. But, when dead plants are removed the pests, left without places to hide, are at a disadvantage; then the predators can do their job of controlling the invaders.

CONTROLS

Recommendations are for ornamental plants only. Follow label directions carefully for how and when to apply chemicals, and which ones to use on vegetables and fruits. List of chemicals includes those sold by name and in multipurpose formulations. (Certain products may contain three of them.)

1. **Adhesive barriers**
2. **Bacillus thuringiensis**
3. **Hand picking**
4. **Lacewings**
5. **Sulfur**
6. **Trichogramma wasp**
7. **Water jet**
8. **Bait containing baygon**
9. **Diazinon**
10. **Dibrom**
11. **Di-syston granules***
12. **Malathion**
13. **Meta-systox***
14. **Methoxychlor**
15. **Nicotine sulfate**
16. **Petroleum oils**
17. **Pyrethrins**
18. **Rotenone**
19. **Sevin** (Kills honeybees)

*Systemics. These products poison the plant's juices, killing sucking insects. Never use them on any type of food crop. Follow label directions exactly.

INSECT CONTROL CHART

Aphids

Control: 3, 4, 7, 9-12, 13

Tiny green, black, yellow or pink insects; sometimes winged. Live and feed in colonies; stunt plant growth. Some excrete honeydew. Some spread diseases.

Cabbage looper

Control: 2-4, 6, 12, 17, 18

Larval form is a striped measuring worm, adult is a gray-brown moth. Feeds on many different vegetables from spring through summer. Larvae leave green droppings on leaves.

Cabbage worm

Control: 2-4, 6, 9, 10, 17-19

Larva is velvety green, fat and bristly, has dark stripe down back. Adult is a white butterfly; lays yellowish eggs on outer leaves. Feeds on cabbage and its relatives, can do a lot of damage.

Corn earworm, Geranium budworm

Control: 3, 4, 6, 9, 19

These two pests are close relatives. The geranium budworm is also "that little green worm that eats petunias" during the summer. Once these caterpillars get into corn ears or geranium buds it is difficult to control them.

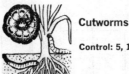

Cutworms

Control: 5, 11

Hairless moth caterpillars; common leaf-eating pests that feed at night. Often cut off seedlings at ground level. Some hide in soil during the day.

Dichondra flea beetle

Control: 9

Shiny, black, pinhead size adults rasp soft leaf tissue on dichondra; makes lawns brown and withered. Young (larvae) feed underground on dichondra roots, cause collapse of plants. No known biological controls.

Earwigs

Control: 3, 8

Ugly night feeding insects. Feed on other insects as well as flowers and leaves. Hide in soil and other close, dark places by day.

Leaf Miners

Control: 9-12, 14, 18

Insects lay eggs on leaf surfaces. Tiny larvae enter leaves; feeding results in unsightly serpentine effect. Spray to kill adults before they lay eggs, or as larvae enters leaf.

Mealybugs

Control: 3, 4, 9-11, 15-17

Small, waxy white nearly immobile insects that form colonies at stem joints or toward base of leaves (usually the underside). Soil mealybugs feed on roots.

Mites

Control: 4, 5, 7, 9-12, 16

To the naked eye, mites look like specks of red, yellow, or green dust. They cause stippled leaves with silvery webs on underside. One common kind is known as red spider mite.

Oak Moths

Control: 2, 4, 10

Common pest of California native oaks, particularly in the coast ranges. Two broods each year—spring and summer. During heavy infestations, larvae strip trees of all leaves.

Scale

Control: 5, 9-12, 15, 16

Small insects that attach themselves to stems and leaves; generally covered with protective shell; form colonies. Many kinds secrete honeydew that attracts ants.

Tent caterpillars

Control: 2, 3, 18, 19

These black and orange worms grow in an expanding tentlike web from March to June. The caterpillars move out from tents to feed on foliage—they can do a lot of damage. You can cut off the branch below the tent; destroy by burning it.

Thrips

Control: 9-12, 13, 15-18

Tiny, fast moving insects that damage plant tissue by rasping surface cells. Feed inside flower buds, distort them, so they seldom open. Also feed on and distort foliage.

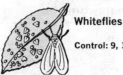

Whiteflies

Control: 9, 12, 13, 17

These tiny, white insects fly up when disturbed. Non-flying forms live on leaf backs. Other insects keep whiteflies in check; don't spray unless whiteflies are doing damage.

(More pests on the following page)

Some Occasional "Bad Actors"

The pests in the list below are either less common or less damaging than the ones on page 59—but they can still be bothersome.

Controls for many of the pests on the list are the same as those mentioned for pests in the illustrated chart. You should not use chemicals unless the pests are becoming a major problem. If you do have to spray, follow label directions exactly, and spray infested plants only.

	ADHESIVE BARRIERS	BACILLUS THURINGIENSIS	HAND PICKING	WATER JET	DIAZINON	DIBROM	DI-SYSTON GRANULES	MALATHION	META-SYSTOX	METALDEHYDE	METHOXYCHLOR	NICOTINE SULFATE	PYRETHRINS	ROTENONE
Ants	•			•	•	•		•						
Borers					•									
Codling moths					•						•			
Diabrotica			•		•	•		•			•			
Grasshoppers			•		•	•								
Lawn moths					•	•							•	•
Leafhoppers					•	•	•	•	•			•	•	•
Soil mealybugs					•		•	•	•					
Snails, Slugs			•							•				
Strawberry root weevil					NO AVAILABLE CONTROL									
Symphilids					•									
Tomato hornworm		•	•											
Wireworms					•									

Plant Diseases

Knowing about plant diseases helps not only to recognize them but also points the way to their control. Some plant diseases are caused by the deficiency of one or more essential nutrients, by the inability of plants to utilize such nutrients, by poor drainage, or by excess salts in the soil. Most diseases, however, are caused by bacteria, viruses, or fungi.

Bacterial Diseases

Bacteria are microscopic single-celled plants that are unable to manufacture their own food, as do green plants; those which cause plant diseases must obtain their nutrients from other plants. Fireblight of pears and blight (dead bud) of flowering cherries are examples of their work.

Fireblight. This disease is caused by bacteria that survive in blighted twigs and cankers. When a flowering shoot of a pear, apple, crabapple, pyracantha, cotoneaster, quince, hawthorn, or toyon suddenly wilts and looks as though it was scorched by fire, it has fireblight. During moist weather in early spring the bacteria are carried to the blossoms by bees, flies, and other insects. The infection progresses down the shoot into the bark of larger limbs where dark sunken cankers form.

There are two steps to control. Protect blossoms from infection by spraying at 4 or 5-day intervals through the blossoming period with a weak Bordeaux spray or fixed copper spray. Also, prune out and burn the diseased twigs and branches. Make cuts at least 6 inches below the infected area. After each cut, sterilize the pruning tools and the cut surface with disinfectant. A 5 per cent solution of a household bleach may be used.

Cherry "dead bud." This bacterial blight disfigures both the fruiting and flowering cherry in the Northwest. First symptom is dying buds on spurs in early spring. Disease starts in lower limbs and moves up. Both flower buds and leaf buds are affected. Spray once in October and again as soon as possible after January. Use Bordeaux, fixed copper, or streptomycin sprays.

Virus Diseases

The ultra-microscopic virus particles are capable of infecting plants and reproducing in them at the expense of the host. Insects and man carry viruses from plant to plant.

Virus diseases are a serious threat to many agricultural crops such as tomatoes, sugar beets, beans, citrus, and sugar cane. In the home garden, virus damage is seen in many forms. In some cases, such as rose mosaic, it does not reduce the growth of the plant. The most common symptom is a mottled area on leaves or a stunting and general yellowing of the foliage. Viruses produce abnormalities in growth, variegation, or "breaking" of blossom color.

At this time there is no cure for a virus-infected plant. However, you can reduce chances of its entry into the plant by controlling the insects that

Scorched look, sudden decline are signs the plant has fireblight.

carry the virus. Aphids are most efficient in spreading different kinds of viruses; leafhoppers, thrips, and whiteflies can be culprits too. Also, man does a fair job of spreading these diseases by propagating infected plants from cuttings, by budding or grafting, and by pruning and pinching diseased plants.

Fungus Diseases

Certain many-celled, branching, threadlike plants called fungi obtain their food parasitically from green plants, causing diseases in the process. Many of these fungi produce great numbers of tiny reproductive bodies called spores. These can be carried by wind or water to other plants where they germinate to produce another group of fungus threads. Fungus diseases are among the most widespread of plant diseases; fortunately most are controllable by sanitation, dusts, and sprays.

Powdery mildew. This disease appears as a white or gray, powdery or mealy coating on leaves, tender stems, and flower buds. Powdery mildew spores are unique in that they can cause infection in the absence of free moisture. Plants are most susceptible under conditions of high humidity, crowding, poor circulation, and more shade (less sun) than the plant needs. Powdery mildew occurs even in desert climates because of an increase in humidity (and lower temperature) at night — especially when air circulation is poor.

Rust. This disease usually appears first on the underside of leaves. The yellow-orange colored pustules or wartlike formations which eventually burst. Spores are spread by wind and splashing water. Upper leaf surfaces may show mottled and yellowish areas in corresponding position to the rust pustules. Generally the development of rusts is favored by moisture (rain, dew, or fog), cool nights, and fairly warm days. Rust survives the winter on living plants and on dead leaves. Winter cleanup will reduce infestation.

Leaf spot, leaf blight, scab, anthracnose, shot hole. Red, brown, or yellow spots on leaves and stems are common on a number of plants. In some cases the spots drop out leaving a "shot hole" condition. The spores of fungi causing these diseases are airborne or waterborne. The source of the disease is generally in plant refuse, dead leaves, or fruit. Thorough garden cleanup is important in order to avoid infection.

The fungi flourish in a wet rainy spring with warm temperatures and also in rainy summer weather. Therefore, these diseases are far less serious in the low rainfall areas than in the Northwest and the moist areas of the California coast. Black spot on roses, for example, is practically unknown in areas of limited rainfall.

Recommended sprayings for scab in heavy rainfall areas: Just before the buds open, spray with dormant spray of lime sulfur. Then spray with wettable sulfur when blossoms show pink and again when ¾ of blossom petals have fallen.

The anthracnose fungus infects leaves and tender shoots as they emerge in the spring. On older leaves the infection produces large irregular brown blotches, and leaves fall earlier than they should. This fungus also causes a twig die-back and canker on small branches. These blighted twigs and cankers are the source of infection the following spring. Spread of fungus spores depends on rain or dripping fogs. Disease is most severe in wet springs and is checked by dry weather. To control, prune infected twigs and branches; also, see chart for correct sprays to use.

Peach leaf curl. This disease also infects nectarines and almonds. The disease is easily recognized when new leaves thicken and pucker along the

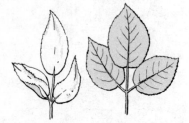

White powdery or mealy growth and distortion—signs of mildew.

Lower surface of snapdragon leaf (right) shows rust symptoms.

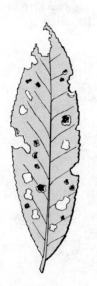

Shot hole fungus has left its very distinctive marks on this leaf.

midrib, causing curling. The curled leaves may be tinged with red or yellow, and they fall prematurely. New leaves then arise from dormant buds.

The fungus overwinters on the bark of dormant trees, and develops most rapidly during cool, moist spring weather. You can control peach leaf curl by spraying the entire tree with lime sulfur or Bordeaux mixture after leaves drop in the fall and again just before buds open in the spring.

Dutch elm disease. Though the United States has had a quarantine for years against this disease, it managed to slip into the country. It slowly spread across the continent and now, unfortunately, dutch elm disease (DED) has reached the West.

DED is spread by the elm bark beetle. Beetle larvae overwinter in dead and dying elm trees, and as young beetles emerge in the spring the sticky disease spores attach to their bodies.

The beetles spread the disease when they migrate to healthy elms to feed. The fungus spores are deposited in feeding wounds where some begin to grow, and others spread throughout the tree and clog conductive tissues as they grow. First, the foliage on infected trees wilts due to lack of water. Next, leaves turn yellow from lack of nutrients (a condition called chlorosis). The leaves eventually fall off, and finally the tree dies.

If you have an elm and suspect that it has DED, call your county agriculture department and report the symptoms. Someone there will advise you on the best control method.

Peach leaf curl disfigures leaves, can weaken tree.

Soil-Borne Diseases

These infect plants through roots, which are often severely damaged before symptoms show on upper portions of plant.

Verticillium wilt. This is one of the most widespread and destructive plant diseases — especially in California. The fungus that causes the diseases can survive in the soil for years. Rotation (the growing of nonsusceptible plants on the infected soil for long periods) will not starve out this fungus, but will reduce disease losses.

The fungus invades and plugs the water-conducting tissues in the roots. The common symptoms are a wilt on one side of the plant. The leaves yellow, brown, and die upward from the base of the plant or branch. The affected branches of woody plants die. The sapwood (outer layer or tissue in a stem or branch) is usually discolored — frequently olive green, dark brown, or black. The development of the fungus is favored by a cool moist soil in spring. Wilting of foliage may not show until days are sunny and warm and the plant is under water stress.

No spray is effective since the fungus attacks through the root system. The disease can be controlled for shallow-rooted plants by having a professional fumigate the soil with chloropicrin (tear gas) or methyl bromide before planting or replanting (don't handle this toxic material yourself). However, fumigation has not been successful with deep-rooted shrubs and trees. Planting wilt resistant varieties will help reduce infection too.

Mildly affected plants often recover from an attack. You can aid recovery by deep but infrequent irrigation. If plant has been neglected, add fertilizer to stimulate new root growth. Shrubs and trees in lush vegetative growth should not be fertilized after disease appears. A soil on which highly susceptible crops have been grown, such as tomatoes, potatoes, cotton, strawberries, and various melons, is frequently infected.

Resistant or immune plants: Apple, *Arctostaphylos* (manzanita), *Asparagus,* bamboo, beans, *Buxus* (boxwood), *Ceanothus, Citrus,* conifers, corn, *Eucalyptus,* ferns, fig, grasses, *Liquidambar, Morus* (mulberry), *Nerium*

Verticillium wilt causes tomato plant to die from base upward.

(oleander), pear, *Pyracantha, Quercus* (oak), strawberries (certain varieties), tomatoes (certain varieties — see Tomato in encyclopedia section), *Umbellularia californica,* walnut.

Texas root rot. Damaging and widespread disease in the semi-arid Southwest, it is known to occur also in the Imperial and Coachella valleys in California. It is caused by a fungus that destroys the outer portions of the roots, thus cutting off the water supply to the upper parts of the plant. The first sign of the disease is a sudden wilting of the leaves. When this happens at least 50 per cent of the root system has been damaged.

This fungus is favored by a highly alkaline soil that contains very little organic matter. Fortunately the fungus does not compete well with other soil inhabiting organisms. Therefore, control measures are aimed at lessening alkalinity by adding sulfur and at increasing the population of organisms that are antagonistic to the fungus by adding organic matter that decomposes rapidly, such as manure and fir sawdust.

You can attempt to save a damaged tree this way: drill holes 2 to 3 feet deep and spaced 3 feet apart in a wide band around the drip line of the tree. Fill holes with a mix of organic matter (manure or sawdust and soil). If using manure only, don't go higher than 10 per cent of the mix. If you use sawdust, make a mix of 1 to 5. To a yard of mix add 5 lbs. of sulfur and 1 lb. of ammonium sulfate. You'll get quicker action in lowering the *p*H by using iron sulfate or combining 4 lbs. of sulfur and 2 lbs. of iron sulfate. Blend the mix well and fill holes. Water deeply.

Since the root system is damaged, decrease the above ground growth by pruning back and thinning to remove half the foliage.

When setting out shrubs, dig a broad deep hole and backfill around the roots with a mix of about 20 per cent organic matter (10 per cent if it's manure) and 80 per cent soil. Add sulfur, iron, and ammonium sulfate.

Root rots — water molds. The diseases caused by the water mold fungi are so much a part of Western gardening that they are seldom mentioned as diseases. However, they are indirectly referred to in practically all of the advice given on soil preparation and watering. When we talk about *touchy plants, infrequent but deep watering, sharp drainage, well drained soil, good aeration, keeping a plant on the dry side,* we often mean water molds.

Free water (excess water that fills all the air spaces in the soil) causes death to plant roots by suffocation. But water can pass through the soil continuously without root damage if it carries air with it. The damage from "overwatering" is, in almost all cases, not caused by water itself but by the destruction of roots by water molds.

How to live with water molds? To lessen root damage and prevent fatalities, take seriously all advice on improving soil drainage. See pages 32-36.

Damping off. The most conspicuous type of "damping off" is that seen when seedlings develop a stem rot near the soil surface and fall over. Another type rots the seedling before it merges from the soil, or causes seed to decay before sprouting. A third (often called sore shin) girdles the seedling, which may remain alive and standing for a while. These damping off diseases are most serious in nursery operations, agriculture, and floriculture, but they can plague home gardeners too. Professional horticulturists practice careful sanitation and sterilize their soil mixes. Here are two things the home gardener can do to reduce the occurrence of damping off: 1) Buy seeds that have been treated with a fungicide or dust them with captan before planting. 2) Use an inert material rather than garden soil to sow seeds or root cuttings; sphagnum moss, vermiculite, perlite, pumice, sand and sterilized commercial mix are all possibilities. These are safe, at least the first time they are used.

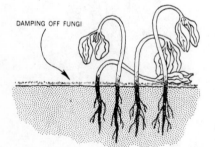

DAMPING OFF FUNGI

"Sore shin" is one common kind of damping off disease.

Control for Leaf and Stem Diseases

Of the three kinds of diseases of leaves, stems, and flowers discussed on pages 61-64, the fungi are the most controllable. Fireblight, a bacterial disease, is controllable by chemicals and it, too, is charted with the fungus diseases.

All of the chemicals listed in the chart should be available, individually or in mixtures, in small packages in your nursery or garden center. Always follow label directions for mixing and applying the chemicals. Also, use a product only on the plants mentioned on the label.

COMMON OR COINED NAME OF ACTIVE INGREDIENT	FORMULATION	Anthracnose	Damping off	Fireblight	Leaf spot	Peach leaf curl	Powdery mildew	Scab	Shot hole	Rust
Acti-dione (Cycloheximide)	wettable powder						•			•
Benomyl	wettable powder	•			•		•		•	
Bordeaux	water suspension of copper and lime	•		•	•	•		•	•	
Captan	dust or wettable powder	•	•		•			•	•	
Fixed copper	dust or liquid	•		•	•			•	•	
Folpet (Phaltan)	dust or wettable powder	•			•		•	•		•
Lime sulfur	liquid	•			•	•	•	•	•	
Karathane	dust, liquid, or wettable powder						•			
Sulfur	dust or wettable powder				•		•	•		
Thiram	dust or wettable powder	•	•		•					
Zineb (Dithane Z-78)	dust or wettable powder	•	•	•		•			•	•

Gophers, Deer, and Other Plant Damagers

Damage done by creatures other than insects is one of the most frustrating things a gardener has to deal with. After you've worked hard to get your garden in shape, and you've nurtured plants from tiny seeds to giant, gorgeous specimens, it's disheartening to find that all or part of them have been eaten or trampled. A number of animals and birds can cause damage in your garden. Fortunately there are some things you can do to foil them.

Gophers

Gophers are serious garden pests in many areas of the West. They feed on roots and bulbs from an elaborate system of tunnels usually 6 to 18 inches below the surface. First sign of their presence is usually a mound of fresh, finely pulverized soil in lawn or flower bed. This soil is a by-product of burrowing operations, and it is brought to the surface through short side runs opening off the main burrow. You may find a hole in this mound, or (more often) you will find a plug of loose earth blocking the exit.

Trapping is the most widely used and generally most successful control method. Avoid the temptation to place a single trap down a hole you can see from the surface. Instead dig down to the main horizontal runway from which the surface hole comes. If you are using the Macabee trap (most popular), place two of them in each runway, one on either side of your excavation. Attach each trap to a stake on the surface with chain or wire.

Plug the hole with folded carrot tops, fresh green grass, or some other fresh, tender greens; their scent attracts the gophers. Next, place dirt over the greens and the top of the hole to block all light. Check traps frequently and clear tunnels if the gopher has pushed dirt into the traps. Be persistent; a wily gopher may avoid getting trapped on your first tries.

Poisoned baits dropped into the burrow may be effective. Probe for the runway and insert the poisoned material there, as described on the next page for moles.

If you live near orchards or open fields and suffer frequent invasions by gophers, protect your young plants by lining planting holes with chicken wire or other fine-meshed (one-inch or smaller) hardware cloth.

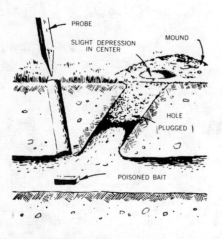

Two Macabee traps in the main run are still best gopher control.

PROBE

SLIGHT DEPRESSION IN CENTER

MOUND

HOLE PLUGGED

POISONED BAIT

In probing for run, a yielding of pressure means you have it.

Moles

Some moles are insectivorous; others eat plants as well as bugs and worms. Regardless of their feeding habits, their tunnels cause trouble, disfiguring lawns, heaving up seedlings, and severing tender roots. Evidences are ridges of raised and cracked soil above feeder runs and little conical mounds of dirt pushed up from below.

Again, trapping is the most efficient control method. Set traps carefully. The harpoon-type trap is the easiest to set because you don't have to dig into the runway, the trap is positioned above the soil.

Poison bait is sometimes effective too. Probe for the deep burrows with a metal rod or sharpened stick, then insert bait and gently close the hole.

Voles, field mice

These small rodents multiply with astonishing rapidity when not controlled by their natural predators — owls, snakes, weasels, cats — and can become serious pests. Though they live in abandoned gopher and mole burrows they feed principally on above-ground portions of plants.

Some people have succeeded in trapping voles and field mice in mouse traps, rat traps, and box traps. Try baiting traps with walnut meats securely attached with thread or a rubber band. In general, these animals' skill at concealment and rapid breeding make control difficult. An adept professional exterminator can quickly wipe them out.

Birds

Most gardeners consider birds as friends rather than enemies, but certain birds at certain times can be nuisances, eating tender seedlings, transplants, fruits, nuts, and berries. Reflectors and fluttering objects may reduce damage. However, the only across-the-board solution to garden-plundering birds is screen or netting. You can buy nylon netting in rolls from 4½ to 13 feet wide and up to 200 feet long.

Broad-mesh netting (¾ inch) is the most popular for trees, since it lets air, water, and sunlight in easily. Enclose fruit trees with nets two or three weeks before fruits ripen. Tie nets off where the lowest branches leave the trunk. Remove net permanently at harvest time.

Fine-mesh screen and nylon netting are the most popular for covering rows of sprouting seedlings and maturing vegetables — birds can't get their beaks through them. Tent the material over the rows with stakes and string for support.

Deer

Though they're nice to see, deer can ruin the looks of a garden in a very short time. If you're worried about deer eating part of your garden try putting chicken wire cages around young plants; these cages will keep other nibblers away too. For more control measures and a list of deer-proof plants turn to page 133.

Mole creates unsightly ridges in lawns and flower beds.

Weed Control

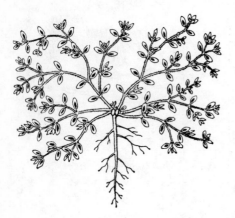

Weed control is more than mere garden housekeeping. A weed-free garden is not only more attractive than a weedy one, but healthier as well. Weeds compete with garden plants for water, nutrients, and space. Control consists basically of preventing weed growth, mechanical destruction of weeds, or killing them by chemical means.

Home gardeners can plant ground covers, annuals, and vegetables close together to shade out weeds, thereby preventing the weeds from growing at all. Most mulches retard weed growth, too. If some weeds do come up you can pull, hoe, or cultivate; many people prefer these methods for the exercise they get.

Hand pulling (the most primitive kind of control) is sometimes necessary, as when weeds are growing among choice, shallow-rooted plants such as cyclamen, rhododendrons, and azaleas. Hoeing and cultivating give good control and, in roughing up the soil surface and breaking the crust, give better aeration and water penetration. Many tools are available for various types of weeds and plantings; common garden hoes and cultivating forks in a variety of sizes are useful for working among row crops, little garden plants, and shrubs. Scuffle hoes (flat-bladed, disk type, or U-shaped) are easier to use in close quarters or under spreading plants. You push and pull them, and they cut weeds on either kind of stroke without digging into roots of desirable plants (see pages 92-93).

For larger areas (orchards, roadsides, vacant lots), rotary tilling or disking is effective, especially where there are no summer rains to germinate late weed crops. They not only knock down weeds but incorporate them into the soil, where they decay to form humus.

If you keep an eye out for small weeds, and uproot them when you first see them, your garden should be neat, and you'll never have to struggle with large weeds. So, become acquainted with the wide variety of hoes and culti-vators your garden center carries; many of them are fun to use and the end result, a weed-free garden, is always satisfying.

Chemical weed killers come into our lives mostly as overflow from agri-culture and institutional landscape maintenance work. In those endeavors, these chemicals are used mostly to reduce labor costs (hoeing, hand pull-ing, or cultivating). As home gardeners you don't need the chemicals for those reasons; and you run the risk of the spray drifting onto and damaging valuable plants.

If you feel you must use chemical weed killers, the list on the next page contains some of the least dangerous. Always follow label directions exactly, and be careful not to let the chemicals come in contact with anything but the weeds you're trying to kill. (If you use a sprayer to apply weed killers, *never* use the same sprayer to spray any other substance on garden plants.)

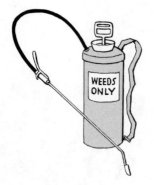

A tank sprayer marked this way can avoid damage to garden plants.

WEED CONTROL CHART

CHEMICAL	EFFECT IT HAS	COMMENTS
AMINO TRIAZOLE	Kills poison oak and other woody perennials; annuals.	Will also kill or damage desirable grasses and ornamentals.
AMMATE	Kills annual and woody vegetation (poison oak).	Respraying probably necessary. Clean sprayer thoroughly after use.
CACODYLIC ACID	Kills all top growth. Best on young weeds.	Won't kill perennial plants.
CASORON	Kills weeds around roses and other selected woody ornamentals.	Work into soil.
CYANAMID	Temporary soil sterilant (used before turf is planted).	After application wait 24 to 30 days before planting turf.
DACTHAL	Kills grass in established plants.	Destroys germinating seeds.
DALAPON	Controls grasses.	Don't irrigate for 24 hours after applying.
DIPHENAMID	Grass control in ground covers.	Work into soil.
EPTC	Grass control around shrubs and trees.	Work into soil.
FORTIFIED DIESEL, STOVE, OR WEED OILS	Destroys top growth of all the vegetation it contacts.	May smell oily for several days after application.
TRIFLURALIN	Controls annual weeds in established plantings.	Work into soil.
2,4-D	Kills broad-leafed weeds in established turf grass.	Use only in low dosages on bent grasses.
2,4,5-TP (SILVEX)	Kills broad-leafed weeds in established turf grass.	Especially useful against mouse-ear chickweed and oxalis.
VAPAM	A soil fumigant that kills many seeds before they sprout.	Don't breathe fumes or get the material on your shoes.

Vegetable Garden Calendar

Bok choy ?

Plant these vegetables for SUMMER-FALL harvest

Plant	How Planted	Climate Zones									Approximate day to Harvest
		1-3	4-7	8-9	10&11	12&13	14-17	18-19	20-21	22-24	
Beans (Lima)	seeds*	June	May-June	Apr.-June	May-July	July-Aug.	Apr.-July	Mar.-Aug.	Mar.-Aug.	Mar.-Aug.	65-95 days**
Beans (Snap)	seeds*	June	May-June	Apr.-June	May-June	July-Aug.	Apr.-July	Mar.-Aug.	Mar.-Aug.	Mar.-Aug.	50-70 days**
Beets	seeds*	May-June	Apr.-June	Apr.-June	Mar.-May	Sept.	Apr.-Sept.	Apr.-Sept.	Apr.-Sept.	Apr.-Sept.	46-65 days
Broccoli	plants	Apr.-June	Apr.-May	Mar. & Aug.	Apr.-July	Sept.	Mar. & Aug.				50-90 days
Brussels sprouts	plants	May-June	Mar.-May	Aug.	July-Aug.						80-90 days
Cabbage	plants	May-June	Mar.-May		Mar.-May	Sept.					60-120 days
Carrots	seeds	May-July	May-July	May-June	Mar.-May Aug.-Sept.	Sept.	Mar.-Apr. Sept.	Mar.-Aug.	Mar.-Aug.	Mar.-Aug.	65-75 days
Cauliflower	plants	May-June	Mar.-May		Mar.-May	Sept.					60-100 days
Celery	plants	June-July	May		May-June						100-135 days
Chard	seeds	Mar.-June	Mar.-June	Mar.-Apr. Aug.	July-Sept.	Sept.	Aug.-Sept.	Aug.-Oct.	Aug.-Oct.	Aug.-Oct.	45-60 days
Corn	seeds	June	May-June	May-June	May-July	Mar.-Apr.	Mar.-July	Mar.-July	Mar.-July	Mar.-July	60-90 days**
Cucumbers	seeds	mid May-June	May-June	May-June	May-June	Aug.-Sept.	Apr.-June	Mar.-July	Mar.-July	Mar.-July	55-65 days
Eggplant	plants	mid May-June	May-June	May-June	May-June	Apr.-May	Apr.-June	Mar.-June	Mar.-June	Mar.-June	65-80 days
Endive	seeds	Apr.-June	Apr.-May	Apr.-May		Sept.	Mar.-Apr.	Apr.-June	Apr.-June	Apr.-June	65-90 days
Kohlrabi	seeds	Apr.-May	Apr.-May	Apr.-May		Sept.	Mar.-Apr.				55-65 days
Lettuce	seeds*	Mar.-Aug.	Mar.-Apr. Aug.	Mar.-Apr. Aug.	July-Aug.	Sept.	Mar. Aug.-Sept.	Sept.	Sept.	Apr. & Sept.	40-95 days**
Melons	seeds	May-June	May-June	May-June	May-June	Apr.-June	Apr.-June	Apr.-July	Apr.-July	June-July	80-95 days
Onions (Bunching)	seeds*	Apr.-May	Apr.-May	Mar.-Apr. Sept.	Apr.	Sept.	Mar.-Apr. Sept.				60-75 days
Onions (Bulbing)	sets	Apr.-May	Mar.-May	Feb.-Apr.		Oct.-Apr.	Oct.-Apr.	Oct.-Apr.	Oct.-Apr.	Oct.-Apr.	100-120 days

* For continuous crop, sow seeds at 2-3 week intervals.

** Depends on variety planted.

Plant	How Planted	Climate Zones 1-3	4-7	8-9	10&11	12&13	14-17	18-19	20-21	22-24	Approximate days to Harvest
Parsley	seeds	Apr.-May	Apr.-May	Apr.-May	May-June		Apr.-June	Apr.-June	Apr.-June	Apr.-June	70-90 days
Parsnip	seeds	Apr.-May	Apr.-May	Apr.-May	Mar.-Apr.		Apr.-May	Mar.-May	Mar.-May	Mar.-May	100-120 days
Peas	seeds	Mid Feb.-May	Mid Feb.-May	Feb.-Apr. & Sept.	July-Aug.	Aug.-Sept.	Mar.-Apr. Sept.	Sept.	Sept.	Sept.	60-70 days
Peppers	plants	May	May	May-June	May-June	Mar.-May	Mar.-June	Mar.-July	Mar.-July	June-July	60-80 days
Potatoes	sets	May	Apr.-May	Mar.-Apr. & Sept.	Mar.-July	Mar.-Apr.	Mar. & Sept.	Mar.-Apr.	Mar.-Apr.	Mar.-Apr.	90-105 days
Pumpkins	seeds	June	June	Apr.-June	May-June	Apr.-Aug.	Apr.-June	Apr.-June	Apr.-June	Apr.-June	100-120 days
Radishes	seeds*	Apr.-June-	Apr.-June	Mar.-May Sept.-Oct.	July-Sept.	Sept.-Oct.	Mar.-May Sept.-Oct.	May-Oct.	May-Oct.	May-Oct.	20-50 days**
Rutabagas	seeds	Apr.-May	Mar.	Mar.	Mar.		Mar.				90 days
Spinach	seeds*	Apr.-May	Apr.-May	Apr.-May	July-Aug.	Sept.-Oct.	May	Sept.	Sept.	Sept.	40-50 days
Squash	seeds	May-June	Apr.-June	Mar.-June	May-July	May-Aug.	Mar.-June	Mar.-July	Mar.-July	Mar.-July	50-60 days
Tomatoes	plants	May-early June	May-June	Apr.-July	May-June	Apr.	Apr.-July	Apr.-July	Apr.-July	June-July	55-90 days**
Turnips	seeds*	Apr.-May	Mar.-May	Mar.-May		Aug.-Sept.	Mar.-Apr.	Apr.-Sept.	Apr.-Sept.	Apr.-Sept.	35-60 days

Plant these vegetables for WINTER-SPRING harvest

Plant	How Planted	Climate Zones 1-3	4-7	8-9	10&11	12&13	14-17	18-19	20-21	22-24	Approximate days to Harvest
Artichokes	Plants or roots			Sept.-May			Sept.-May	Sept.-May	Sept.-May	Sept.-May	1 year
Asparagus	roots	Apr.-May	Apr.	Nov.-Mar.	Feb.-Apr.		Nov.-Mar.	Oct.-Feb.	Oct.-Feb.	Oct.-Feb.	2 years
Beets	seeds*					Oct.-Mar.		Oct.-Mar.	Oct.-Mar.	Oct.-Mar.	46-65 days
Broccoli	plants					Oct.-Dec.	Sept.-Feb.	Oct.-Feb.	Oct.-Feb.	Oct.-Feb.	50-90 days
Brussels sprouts	plants					Sept.-Dec.	Sept.-Oct.	Oct.-Feb.	Oct.-Feb.	Oct.-Feb.	80-90 days
Cabbage	plants					Oct.-Dec.	Sept.-Oct.	Oct.-Jan.	Oct.-Jan.	Oct.-Jan.	60-120 days
Carrots	seeds*					Oct.-Mar.	Oct.-Mar.-June	Sept.-Feb.	Sept.-Feb.	Sept.-Feb.	65-75 days
Cauliflower	plants					Oct.-Dec.	Sept.-Oct.	Sept.-Feb.	Sept.-Feb.	Sept.-Feb.	60-100 days

*For continuous crop, sow seeds at 2-3 week intervals.

**Depends on variety planted.

(Continued on next page)

Winter-Spring Harvest (cont'd.)

Plant	How Planted	Climate Zones									Approximate days to Harvest
		1-3	4-7	8-9	10-11	12&13	14-17	18-19	20-21	22-24	
Celery	seeds					Aug.-Oct.	Sept.	Aug.-Oct.	Aug.-Oct.	Aug.-Oct.	100-135 days
Chard	seeds				Feb.-Apr.	Oct.-Mar.	Mar.	Oct.-Mar.	Oct.-Mar.	Oct.-Mar.	45-60 days
Cucumbers	seeds					Dec.-Mar.					55-65 days
Eggplant	plants					Feb.-Mar.					65-80 days
Endive	seeds				Feb.-Mar.	Oct.-Feb.		Oct.-Jan.	Oct.-Jan.	Oct.-Jan.	65-90 days
Kohlrabi	seeds				Feb.-Mar.	Oct.-Feb.		Oct.-Jan.	Oct.-Jan.	Oct.-Jan.	55-65 days
Lettuce	seeds*				Feb.-Mar.	Oct.-Apr.	Sept.-Mar.	Oct.-Mar.	Oct.-Mar.	Oct.-Mar.	40-95 days**
Melons	seeds					Feb.-Mar.					80-95 days
Onions (Bunching)	seeds				Feb.-Mar.	Oct.-Feb.	Oct.-Feb.	Oct.-Jan.	Oct.-Jan.	Oct.-Jan.	60-75 days
Onions (Bulbing)	sets				Nov.-Apr.	Nov.-Feb.					100-120 days
Parsley	seeds					Sept.-Jan.		Oct.-Jan.	Oct.-Jan.	Oct.-Jan.	70-90 days
Parsnip	seeds					Sept.-Jan.		Jan.	Jan.	Jan.	100-120 days
Peas	seeds				Feb.-Mar.	Oct.-Mar.	Oct.	Oct.-Jan.	Oct.-Jan.	Oct.-Jan.	60-70 days
Peppers	plants					Feb.					60-80 days
Potato	sets					Sept.-Feb.	Feb.-Mar.	Dec.-Feb.	Dec.-Feb.	Dec.-Feb.	90-105 days
Radishes	seeds*			Mar.-Apr.	Mar.-Apr.	Nov.-Apr.	Mar.-Apr.	Nov.-Apr.	Nov.-Apr.	Nov.-Apr.	20-50 days**
Rhubarb	root	Mar.-Apr.	Mar.-Apr.		Mar.-Apr.		Jan.	Nov.-Feb.	Nov.-Feb.	Nov.-Feb.	1 year
Rutabagas	seeds					Sept.-Feb.	Sept.-Oct.	Oct.-Nov.	Oct.-Nov.	Oct.-Nov.	90 days
Spinach	seeds*				Feb.-Mar.	Nov.-Mar.	Sept.-Nov.	Oct.-Feb.	Oct.-Feb.	Oct.-Feb.	40-50 days
Squash	seeds					Dec.-Mar.					50-60 days
Tomatoes	plants					Jan.-Mar.					55-90 days
Turnips	seeds*				Mar.	Oct.-Mar.	Sept.-Oct.	Oct.-Mar.	Oct.-Mar.	Oct.-Mar.	35-60 days

* For continuous crop, sow seeds at 2-3 week intervals.

** Depends on variety planted.

Pruning Techniques

Of all the many gardening techniques, pruning stands alone as the most misunderstood—and most frequently neglected—of them all. The truth of the matter is that by understanding a few basic pruning fundamentals you can be well on your way to becoming a truly effective director of plant growth.

Why is Pruning Important?

General objectives of pruning have to do with modifying the growth of the plant to adjust it to the conditions of the garden. Some plants require considerable pruning, others may need little or none.

Specifically, you should prune to maintain plant health by cutting out dead, diseased, or injured wood; to control growth when an unshapely shrub or tree might result; and to increase the quality and yield of flowers or fruit.

Importance of Terminal Buds

To understand the "why" of pruning, it is highly important that you learn about terminal buds. These are the growing buds on the ends of all branches and branchlets. During the season of active growth, these tip buds draw plant energy to themselves and grow, adding length to the stems. But if any growing terminal bud is cut or nipped off, growth ceases at that part of the plant and the growth energy which would have gone to that bud goes instead to other buds.

The flow of plant energy to a terminal bud is caused by hormones or auxins produced within the bud. When you remove the bud, one of the buds below will begin to produce auxin and will take over and draw plant energy to it.

The practical application of this lesson is that by pinching or pruning out buds you can make many plants—especially small ones—behave the way you want.

Supposing you want a fuchsia plant to get denser. Pinch out all the terminal buds on every branch. This will force growth into all buds that are at the leaf stem bases along the stems. You will make perhaps two, three, or four new side branches where you had one lengthening branch before. When you make this happen all over the plant, you get all-over bushiness.

You make a young zinnia or chrysanthemum form several main stems instead of one by pinching out the tip of the single stem when the plant is young.

Supposing one main trunk begins to dominate an erect shrub or tree that is supposed to have many approximately equal-length main trunks. Cut back the terminal bud on the dominant trunk (if the resulting bushiness below the cut won't hurt the appearance) or cut out the dominant trunk altogether. One way or the other, you will be channeling growth energy into the terminal buds that were lagging.

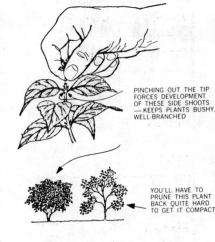

PINCHING OUT THE TIP FORCES DEVELOPMENT OF THESE SIDE SHOOTS — KEEPS PLANTS BUSHY, WELL-BRANCHED

YOU'LL HAVE TO PRUNE THIS PLANT BACK QUITE HARD TO GET IT COMPACT

Frequent tip-pinching when plants are young saves pruning later.

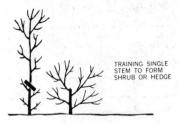

TRAINING SINGLE STEM TO FORM SHRUB OR HEDGE

Removing lead shoot forces growth of lateral shoots, twigs.

Pruning to a side shoot; damage soon concealed by new growth.

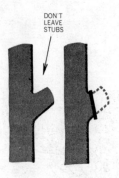

Stub looks ugly; more important, it can result in decay.

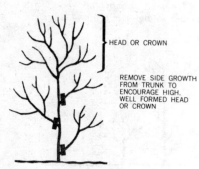

Prune this way to give tree a head you can walk or mow under.

Supposing a plant that should be growing vertically takes a notion to throw most of its growth into an errant side branch instead of the main vertical trunk or leader. Nip back the tip of the side branch (if you will accept the resulting bushiness at the tip) or cut it out.

Where to Make Cuts

Whenever you approach a plant that you are going to prune for any reason— to take its flowers, to improve its shape, to make it bushier, or to make it more open—remember this: Make your cuts only above a bud, a small side branch, a main branch, or even the ground level (in which case the growing point is the very base of the stem).

Some smart person once coined a fine phrase for this advice and it's been picked up in horticultural literature a thousand times since: "Never leave a stub that you can hang your hat on." If it's a bud that you are cutting above, make sure you won't be able to hang your hat on the stub after the bud elongates.

You see, among other things, a stem or branch is a sort of conveying tube. If you cut a branch some distance above its uppermost growing part, you leave nothing in the stub itself to maintain growth and there is no reason for water and nutrients to enter it. The stub is no longer a part of the plant's active metabolism, so it withers and dies. Decay and insects can work into the plant through the dead stub.

If you have a choice of which bud or side branch to cut back to, choose the one that points in the direction you'd like new growth to take. And, if you, yourself, have no personal preference for the branch's direction, remember that generally it's better for the plant if the new branch can grow toward an open space rather than toward another branch. Crossing branches are troublesome. They rub against each other and they spoil a plant's looks. You get them frequently enough by accident without encouraging them by pruning.

The only situation where pruning to a growing point does not apply is in shearing. In this case you are cutting such small, twiggy growth that the dead stubs are of no consequence.

Pruning to Shape

If you want a tree to branch sufficiently high so that traffic can circulate under it, stake the leading shoot and permit it to grow. Shorten branches that form below the desired branching point. (You don't remove them at once because their leaves will manufacture food that speeds the growth of the leading shoot.) When the branching point is reached, permit side branches to develop. Keep lower branches short, and remove them when the crown of branches is well enough developed to keep the tree nourished and the trunk shaded from sunburn. Then remove lower branches right back to the trunk, and rub out buds that form along trunk.

If a tree or shrub has a picturesque branching habit or handsome bark, trim away enough twiggy growth to show. If a tree or large shrub shows promise of being a good-looking multiple-trunk tree, select well-placed large branches and stake them to assume angles that will give the desired grace and spread. Keep on the lookout for particularly shapely specimens of trees or shrubs you're interested in (live plants or pictures of them) and try to determine what you like about them, then prune to get that effect. In Japanese maple, for instance, you may have seen a plant with heavy, horizontal tiers of branches at different levels (a typical growth pattern in this plant). To get the same effect, stake up a leading shoot and permit large branches to appear at intervals; suppress other branches until your plant is as tall as you want it to be.

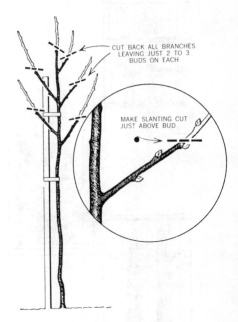

Shortening branches at planting time will make for stronger structure.

Prune to Strengthen Trunk and Branches

Some trees can grow too fast for their own good, producing long, soft, brittle growth that's easily damaged by wind and the weight of water on the leaves. Eucalyptus and silk oak are two examples. Cut them back hard, preferably after tree has been in the ground for at least a year and has a sturdy root system. If you can, cut to a side branch or a bud; if you can't find any low enough, cut right into bare wood. New buds will form and branches will grow from them. Do this between March and August to allow growing time before freezes. Later go back and take out all except one (or several) branches.

A few trees (fruitless mulberry is an example) make long branches that droop with their own weight, interfering with circulation underneath them and creating danger of breakage. Such branches can be cut back to an upward-growing branchlet. The parent branch will thicken and the secondary branch will elongate to take the place of the branch that was removed. The process can be repeated until a sturdy system of scaffold branches has been developed.

To avoid splitting wood and tearing bark when a heavy limb falls, make preliminary cut as shown.

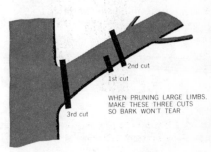

To prevent tearing bark, split in trunk, cut limb as shown.

Pruning and Supporting Vines

Some vines (wisteria and grape) flower and bear well only when carefully pruned to get renewal wood for bearing. Their pruning is described under the appropriate entry in the encyclopedia section. But all vines require some kind of support, and most require some pruning to prevent tangling and to get good coverage for the area on which they are grown (many vines will go straight up toward sunlight and bear leaves or flowers only at the top). Type of support depends on the kind of vine and the area to be covered. Some (ivy, Boston ivy) have holdfasts and will cling to any reasonably rough surface (a boon on masonry, but a problem on wood or shingles that require painting or staining). Others have tendrils and require trellis, frame, strings, or wires. Twining vines (both those with twining stems and those with twining leaf stalks) require similar support. Some vines and shrubs grown as vines have no special means of support; these must be tied or stapled to the surface they cover. In any case, make sure that the support or the fastening devices (staples, eye bolts, screw eyes, or adhesive discs) are strong enough for the job. Fully grown vines can be very heavy.

To get better coverage of the surface, fan out branches of vines toward the horizontal. You'll accomplish several things: in the first place, you're likely to stimulate a number of lateral branches. These will cover the surface better and, since laterals often bear flowers, you'll get heavier bloom. You'll avoid tangling (a serious problem with rank-growing vines). Finally, you'll avoid the topheavy effect so often seen in which the vine is bare at the bottom, brushy at the top. But even this effect can be controlled and turned to advantage; use a vine for an "eyebrow" effect along eaves or fence top by letting one or several stems go right to the top, then training them laterally.

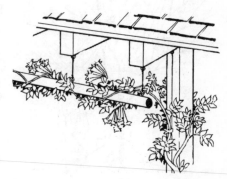

Vines that make much top growth are good "eyebrows" on eaves.

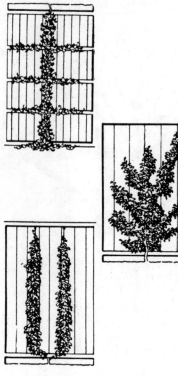

Here are three of the many ways to shape an espaliered shrub, tree.

Pruning for Specific Landscape Uses

Many plants are adaptable enough to do landscape jobs not conventionally associated with them. Many sprawling shrubs or vines, for instance (climbing roses, bougainvillea, xylosma) can easily be made into good ground covers by suppressing vertical growth and pegging down horizontal branches (use pieces of wire bent into hairpin shapes). California pepper, ordinarily considered a tree, makes a very fine clipped hedge. Sturdily upright Japanese black pine may be trained to cascade.

If your planting space is narrow, consider espaliers. Originally developed to conserve space and to gain reflected heat for ripening fruit, espaliers are used in the West largely to adorn walls and fences. A host of plants can be used for espaliering; among the most popular are pyracantha, citrus, evergreen magnolia, certain bottlebrushes, and, of course, deciduous fruit trees. Like vines, espaliers need sturdy supports and faithful attention to tying, pinching, and pruning. The essential operations are leading branches where you want them and suppressing other branches that interfere with the desired effect. Treatment can be rambling and informal, or stylized and formal, with fan or grid patterns popular.

Pruning Fruit Trees

The business of making a fruit tree grow to your eye's satisfaction, while still getting a good crop of fruit, is mostly a matter of knowing how the tree grows by nature, then pruning every year (when the tree is bare) to direct this natural growth as well as you can.

You can afford to be bold when you go about the job. A few wrong cuts can't kill a tree. The tree's growth in spring and summer will hide or correct most of the mistakes. It is usually better to prune a fruit tree and take the risk of making a few mistakes than not to prune at all.

The aim of all fruit tree pruning is to make or keep good tree structure and to force more growth into fewer buds, thereby making bigger fruit.

Peach and nectarine. These are the most vigorous growing fruit trees. The voluminous new growth of long, willowy shoots bears fruit the following summer. The new growth bears only once. You should prune hard to encourage new growth; otherwise, fruit will be produced farther and farther out on the branches year by year. The general rule is to remove 2/3 of last year's growth.

Apricot and plum. These make almost as much growth as the peach, and need almost as much pruning. Although these trees grow fruit-producing shoots almost as abundantly as the peach, they also form fruit spurs (stubby fruit-bearing twigs up to 3 inches long). The spurs on apricot and Japanese plums grow very slightly each year and are usually productive for only about 3 to 5 years. By the time a spur-carrying branch is that age, a new branch should be selected to replace the old one.

Slow growers. These include apple, pear, cherry, prune, and almond. Comparatively little new fruit-bearing wood is produced each year.

Pears, apples, and cherries grow so slowly that conventional pruning consists mostly of cutting out the dead, twiggy, and misplaced branches, and encouraging new branches. The fruits grow on long-lived spurs. Cut the vegetative growth back a little if it's getting away from you.

On almond trees, remove small branches to stimulate growth of new spurs and shoots, which bear the almonds.

Prune fruit trees to control size, stimulate fruit bud production.

Pruning Tools and How to Use Them

A thumb and forefinger, diligently used, can save wear and tear on your other pruning tools. As you walk around the garden, keep an eye open for lanky shoots that may spoil the symmetry of your perennials or shrubs and pinch them back. Rub out unwanted buds along the stems of standard roses or other plants trained into tree form. Snap off faded blooms or seed pods.

Pruning shears and pruning saws come in many different forms because there are many kinds of cuts to be made and each implement is designed to do certain kinds of cutting. If you use one kind of pruning implement for many kinds of plant cutting, you will probably make bad cuts at times—occasionally damaging both the plants and the overextended or misused tools. Illustrated here are the seven basic kinds of pruning devices, in a total of 20 different models. In the descriptions that follow, numbers in parentheses refer to numbers on the tools in the illustrations.

Border shears (1). With this tool, you can stand up to cut the edges of lawns (you can cut right into the sod) and the edges of thick, spreading ground covers such as ivy and vinca.

Grass shears (2, 3 and 4). These tools are meant only for shearing grass and will not do a satisfactory cutting job on garden plants. They cut grass by action of one steel blade slicing across another. Number 2 operates by vertical squeezing action; one handle is over the other. (There is another form, in which one blade remains in a fixed position while the other slices across it. The harder you squeeze on its vertical handles the more tension you apply to its blades, thereby forcing a cut through tough grass stems and stolons.)

Number 3 operates by horizontal action; handles are on the same plane as the blades, but offset so you don't bruise your knuckles.

Number 4 has grass shears on wheels at base of a 3-foot handle, so you can wheel it along, squeezing the handle to clip grass from a stand-up position.

Lopping shears (5 and 6). Use these wherever added leverage of long handles will give you more cutting strength than you get from one-hand shears and wherever the long handles can help you reach farther.

Number 5 is the hook and blade style. The hook holds the branch while the blade slices through it. Number 6 is the blade and anvil type. A sharp steel blade cuts against a flat plate or anvil of brass.

Pruning shears (7, 8, 9, 10, 11, 12 and 13). One or more of these shears is an essential part of any gardener's tool kit.

Numbers 7 and 8 are the most basic of all pruning tools. They are one-hand pruning shears to use for countless light pruning jobs. Number 7 cuts with a steel blade against a brass anvil. Number 8 cuts with a hook and blade. Many gardeners use both and find it hard to see any difference in the kind of cuts made.

Number 9 comes from Japan. Its Japanese name is *masakuni*. When it cuts a branch at the base, it leaves a concave depression, rather than a flush cut or a stub. Such a cut can heal very fast. Bonsai experts like to prune their plants with masakuni.

Number 10, a pair of flower shears, has blades designed to cut and hold flower stems.

Number 11 comes in many models. These are fruit shears, used commonly to cut stems of fruits that don't break off—such as lemons and grapes. Sharp blade crosses over sharp blade. The same cutting method is employed in other one-hand specialty pruning shears that look like this one.

Number 12 is a leather scabbard with belt slots in the top flap. You can hang one of them on your hip, put your pruning shears in it.

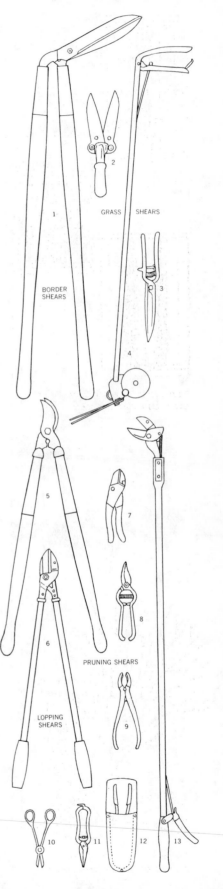

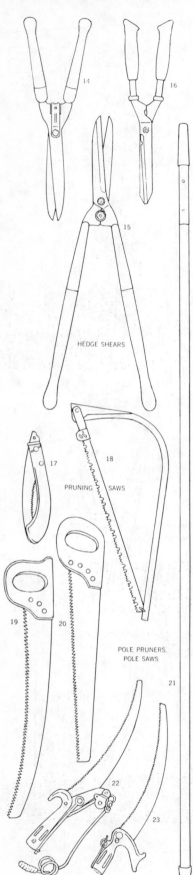

HEDGE SHEARS

PRUNING SAWS

POLE PRUNERS, POLE SAWS

Number 13 is an extension pruner with blade and anvil cutter at one end of a 4-foot, lightweight pole, and a squeeze handle to work it on the other end. Use it for cutting flowers and doing other light pruning beyond arm's reach.

Hedge shears (14, 15 and 16). Hand-operated hedge shears are used by gardeners with not enough hedge to make an electric trimmer worthwhile and by others who believe that they can do a better job manually than with an electric trimmer.

Numbers 14 and 16 are similar except that number 14 has a shock absorber between the blade butts to absorb the jar when the blades come together.

Number 15 has longer handles (20 inches long instead of 10 inches) for trimming tall hedges. If you are 5 feet, 5 inches tall you can clip as high as 8½ feet with this one.

Most hedge shears have one blade serrated and notched. The notch holds bigger twigs for non-slip slicing.

Pruning saws (17, 18, 19 and 20). You should never try to force pruning shears through a branch. If shears won't cut a branch easily, use a pruning saw.

Pruning saws are designed to cut quickly through fresh, green, wet wood. Many of them, such as the curved types represented by numbers 17 and 19, are also designed to fit into close quarters. Curved pruning saws have teeth made in such a way that they cut on the pull stroke. Straight ones cut on the push stroke. This makes the curved ones especially useful for doing overhead work. The curved blade on saw number 17 folds into the handle for carrying and storage. A hole at the base of the blade, exposed when folded, makes it possible to hang the saw, with a clip, from your belt. The curved blade on saw number 19 is broader and has fewer points to the inch, suiting it to heavier work than number 17.

Number 20, a straight saw, has 6 points to the inch (more than number 19 and fewer than number 17), and it's designed for the heaviest pruning work. Saw number 18 is one of several utility saws for pruning and for cutting up logs. Some have a full bow as a frame. This model has a triangular frame. The acute-angled end goes away from you, and it pushes overhanging branches out of the way as you cut.

Pole pruners and pole saws (21, 22 and 23). You need one of these devices to cut or saw branches high overhead.

Number 21 is a telescoping lightweight metal tube that can be extended from 6 to 12 feet (and, with an extra unit, to 18 feet). To the wooden cap at the upper end you can attach either of the pruning units 22 or 23.

Number 22 is a combination pruning saw and cord-operated cutting shears (the shears are inside the beaklike hook). You place the hook over a branch and pull the cord to draw the blade through the branch. Wrap the cord a turn or two around the pole so the pole won't bow out when you pull the cord. The saw attached to number 22 is a regular draw-cut curved pruning saw.

Number 23, another attachment for the telescoping pole, is just a saw. The hook at the base of the saw is for pulling off dead branches. The little horn on the outer end of the hook is for pushing branches and raising ropes.

Similar units use a series of wooden poles that lock together to make any length up to 18 feet, instead of a telescoping metal tube. If, in your pruning, there is any chance whatsoever of contacting electric lines overhead, the wooden units offer the only safe choice.

Planting a Lawn

Installing a lawn the right way is neither easy nor cheap, but every hour and every dollar you spend at the outset will save you time and money later. The most important factor is furnishing a good environment for roots. This environment will be neither very acid nor very alkaline, will be well furnished with nutrients and air, and will be easily permeable by water and grass roots. It should be uniform to a depth of 8 to 12 inches or more.

If you're replacing a poor lawn, remove the old sod with a power sod cutter or spade. Digging existing sod into the soil makes for poor rooting, erratic water penetration, and irregular settling. If you must add topsoil to raise the grade, buy the best you can find and blend it carefully with existing soil to avoid an "interface," a plane where two unlike soils meet. Before tampering with the acidity or alkalinity of your soil, get a soil test. County agricultural agents can recommend laboratories; in some areas they themselves will do soil tests. If pH is below 5.5, add lime (calcium carbonate is best) at the rate of 50 to 75 pounds per 1,000 square feet; apply with a spreader to dry soil, being careful to keep lime away from roots of acid-loving plants. If the pH is above 8.0 (highly alkaline), add iron sulfate at 20 pounds per 1,000 square feet or soil sulfur at 10 pounds per 1,000 square feet. Incorporate material into the surface 6 inches. Iron sulfate is fast acting and will supply iron which is a necessary nutrient. A pH higher than 8.5 may indicate an alkaline soil problem caused by excessive sodium. Consult your County Agricultural Agent or a commercial soil laboratory for assistance in correction of this type of soil problem.

1 Add materials necessary to correct pH, soil amendments.

Mix Nutrients into Rooting Area. Although you can't possibly add enough nitrogen to last the life of your lawn, you should add enough to sustain the grass right after it sprouts. This can be added along with organic materials, or it can be spread on the finished seedbed. You should add phosphorus during the preparatory stages; tilling it in is the only way to get it into the rooting area. Before cultivating, add 40 pounds of single superphosphate. In some areas of the West, especially where rainfall is high, you might need potash. Check with your county agricultural agent or other local expert. If you need it, cultivate in 10 pounds of muriate of potash per 1,000 square feet. If you plan to add large quantities of sawdust, add iron in the form of sulfate or chelate to avoid symptoms of chlorosis. Use 5 to 10 pounds of iron sulfate per 1,000 square feet, being careful to avoid staining concrete. Follow label directions for chelates.

2 Incorporate amendments, nutrients into soil. Mix thoroughly.

Organic Soil Amendments. Few soils are naturally capable of taking up water easily (no runoff) and holding it so that watering intervals can be lengthened during a long dry season. To get this kind of soil, add and blend in a bold quantity of porous soil amendment to supply air spaces in the soil and improve water penetration.

Nitrogen stabilized soil amendments derived from sawdust and ground bark are available at most garden supply stores. These products are the simplest and safest to use, although more costly than untreated raw materials. Use plenty—30 to 50 percent by volume. Three inches of amendment mixed with the top six inches of soil makes a 33 percent mix. If you use raw sawdust or bark, provide extra nitrogen to take care of the needs of soil organisms that work to decompose them. Mix in 55 pounds of ammonium sulfate or 35 pounds of ammonium nitrate for each 1,000 square feet of sawdust or bark laid 3 inches deep. Or use calcium cyanamid (25 pounds per 1,000 square feet) before blending in amendments. This material will kill weed seeds during its decomposition and will leave behind suffi-

3 Pick out weeds, stones, sticks, old grass clumps, other refuse.

cient nitrogen to feed the soil organisms and the young grass. If you use cyanamid at this stage, be sure to follow it up with another application to the finished seedbed. When adding nitrogen to raw materials to hasten their breakdown it is necessary to keep the seedbed moist for at least 30 days prior to seeding. Failure to do so will produce a temporary salinity which could be harmful to germination and subsequent growth.

Blend in the amendment and nutrients thoroughly with rotary tiller, making repeated passes until the mixture is completely uniform.

Smoothing the Seedbed. Rake and drag the seedbed until it is smooth and flat, free of clods, high and low spots. Usually you'll have to conform to surrounding paving, but if you have a choice, try to have a slight pitch, a fall of 6 to 12 inches per 100 square feet for better drainage. After raking and leveling, firm the seedbed with a full roller, making passes in two directions. If rolling turns up low spots, rake or drag and roll again. If you're using cyanamid, spread 35 pounds per 1,000 square feet evenly over the finished surface. Rake it lightly into the top $\frac{1}{4}$ to $\frac{1}{2}$ inch of seedbed, where most of the weed seeds are. Soak the area and keep it moist (sprinkle daily) for 24 to 30 days. In warm weather you may not have to wait so long; sow a few radish seeds, which will sprout in a few days. If they begin to form true leaves, soil is safe for grass seed.

Sowing the Seed. Cool-season grasses may be sown almost any month of the year in mild climates and from spring through fall in colder areas, but fall and spring are usually best. Fall seeding reduces danger of heat injury, but allow 6 weeks of 50° to 70° weather for grass to get a good start before heavy frosts come and soils turn cold. Spring seeding gives grass a long growing season in which to get established, but summer heat and weeds may cause problems.

Pick a windless day for sowing, and sow seed as evenly as possible. A spreader or mechanical seeder will help here. After sowing, rake in seed very lightly to insure contact with seedbed. If you expect hot, dry weather or drying winds, it's a good idea to put down a thin, moisture-holding mulch. Use $\frac{1}{8}$ to 3/16 inch of peat moss or screened, aged sawdust. To keep peat moss from blowing away (and to overcome its reluctance, when dry, to take up water), soak, knead, and pulverize it. After mulching, roll with an empty roller to press seed into contact with soil.

Water thoroughly, taking care not to wash out seed, then keep seedbed dark with moisture until all the grass is up. This may mean half an hour each day (sometimes 2 or 3 times a day) for up to three weeks if your seed mixture contains slow-germinating varieties. Hand sprinkling is best, although a well-designed underground system may do the job without flooding or washouts. Mow for the first time when blades are about two inches high, or when they begin to take on a noticeable curvature. Mow bent grasses when they reach one inch. Be sure mower blades are sharp, and let sod dry out enough so that mower wheels will not skid or tear.

Sodding, Sprigging, Stolons, Plugs. Western turf farms offer ready-made (almost) lawns in the form of sod. It's expensive compared with seeding, but the labor involved is much less and the saving in time is considerable. Prepare a seedbed as previously described, but work for a surface about $\frac{3}{4}$ inch lower than the surrounding paving. Spread a layer of complete fertilizer (same amount as label calls for on new lawns), then unroll delivered sod on prepared seedbed. Lay strips parallel with strip ends staggered as in a bricklayer's running bond pattern. Press end of each strip closely against the end of the last strip laid. Roll with a half-full roller, then water carefully until roots have penetrated deeply into the prepared seedbed.

In sprigging (widely used to establish hybrid Bermudas and some bents), prepare seedbed as for sowing. Pre-soak seedbed so that it will be damp

4 *Drag the seedbed to establish level, reveal high and low spots.*

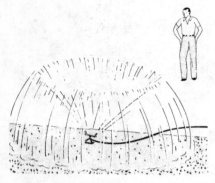

5 *Water seedbed thoroughly to settle soil, further reveal low spots.*

6 *Pull any weeds brought up by first watering; fill in low spots.*

when you plant sprigs, then let it dry out to good working consistency. Make a series of parallel trenches 3 inches deep and 10 inches apart. Plant sprigs or stolons (either from plastic bags or freshly torn from flats or sod) vertically in trenches and press soil back into trenches. Keep moist until sprigs root and begin to grow.

You can broadcast stolons over prepared seedbed at the rate of 3 to 5 bushels per 1,000 square feet. Roll with a half-filled roller, then mulch with ½ inch of top-grade topsoil, peat moss, sawdust, or ground bark. Roll again, water thoroughly, and keep moist until grass takes root and begins to grow. Or you can cut and lift plugs from flats of grass with a special plugging tool. Plant these in holes in the seedbed prepared by the same planting tool. Space 12 to 15 inches apart.

Cool-Season Grasses

Seeds of grasses described below are sold either singly or in blends. The former perform well enough by themselves to make a good stand alone. Lawns made of a single grass type will be uniform and will give you just what you want, whether it be toughness or fine texture. Such lawns could be wiped out if your one grass succumbed to a pest, disease, or environmental condition to which it was susceptible. A blend of 3 or 4 kinds of grasses is safer; even though the make-up of the established lawn may dwindle to 1, 2 or 3 kinds, these will be the kinds that do best under your lawn's conditions of soil, climate, and maintenance practices. Buy your seed first on the basis of the kind of lawn you want, next on the cost required to cover your area—not the cost per pound. Choice, fine-leafed blends have many more seeds per pound than coarse, fast growing blends and cover a much greater area per pound. Above all, remember that good seed will germinate and come true to name; whether or not it makes a good lawn depends entirely upon the environment as you make it or keep it.

Bent. All bent grasses are high-maintenance grasses requiring careful attention to mowing, feeding, watering, and disease control. All have fine leaves and spread by stolons (surface runners). With frequent, close mowing they make picture book lawns during cool weather. During hot weather they are subject to disease attack. Without care in thatch removal and close mowing, stolons override each other, make untidy mats. Bents can become weeds in bluegrass lawns, especially if they are mown too close. They begin as dollar-sized infestations and, if not dug out (there is no chemical control) will in a few seasons spread and merge to take over the entire lawn. All kinds of bent grass take sun or part shade. No deep shade.

Kinds can be classified as Colonial bents and creeping bents. The former are more erect than the latter, will withstand more neglect than creeping kinds, but still need considerable care to look their best. Best known kinds are Astoria and Highland, with the latter being tougher, hardier, more disease-tolerant. It is grayish green, while Astoria varies from dull to light green. Mow at ¾ inch.

Creeping bents need lower (½-inch) cutting. Seaside, grown from seed, gives plants of varying quality, but all will have fine, flat, narrow, blue-green leaves. Penncross is healthier, more disease-resistant than Seaside. Congressional and Old Orchard, premium bents, are available only as stolons (sprigs of surface runners) or as sod.

Fine Fescues. All these have fine, rolled leaves like tiny soft needles. Along with Kentucky bluegrass, they make up the bulk of most fine-textured lawn mixtures. Fescues are supposedly less particular about soil conditions than either bent or bluegrass; they are fairly drought-tolerant and will take some shade (more than most lawn grasses—Creeping Red is supposed to be the

7 Give seedbed a final rolling with a light roller to make it level.

8 Spread commercial fertilizer over area according to label directions.

9 Sow seed, by hand or spreader; if by hand, choose a still day.

best fescue for shade). Fine fescues should not be used alone; they get too clumpy. Mow them at 1½ to 2 inches. Popular kinds are Creeping Red, Illahee, Rainier, and Chewings.

Bluegrasses. Kentucky bluegrass is what most people think of as the ideal lawn grass. Actually, Kentucky bluegrass is not a pure strain; it is a mixture of many types which are distinct to a turf expert. All have dark green leaves, make dense sod, and grow best in cooler weather, slowing down in summer and going dormant in mid-winter with sustained freezing. All are susceptible to a number of insects and diseases (some being more resistant to some diseases than others), but are easier to manage than bents. All prefer sun, will take light shade only in hot summer areas. Kentucky bluegrass should be cut at 1½ inches; selections can be cut as low as ¾ inch, but are better at 1½ inches.

10 Rake in seed lightly to insure good contact with the seedbed.

11 Apply mulch of damp peat moss or sawdust. Make it 1/8-3/16 inch deep.

12 Roll mulch over seeds with light roller. Not essential; nice extra.

CHOICE OF GRASS DEPENDS ON CLIMATE

Although there are a few broad-leafed plants (not grasses) that can be used as lawns, only dichondra (see page 84) is widely used, and its use is confined to California and Arizona. Most lawns over most of the West are made of grasses planted either singly or in a number of combinations. The two basic kinds of grasses are cool-season and subtropical, and each has its own part of the West. The latter, which thrive in hot weather and go dormant or freeze out in cold or frosty weather, are best adapted in the Southwest and in other climates with hot summers and mild winters. Cool-season grasses withstand winter cold but languish in hot, dry summers; they are best adapted to the Northwest and to regions where marine influence tempers summer heat.

Merion, Newport or C-1, Windsor, Delta, Prado, and Campus are selections that are offered separately or in mixtures with other bluegrasses and fine fescues. Park, a mixture of several selected varieties, starts fast and has high seedling vigor.

Poa trivialis. This is one bluegrass that does well in shade. In fact, no other grass does so well in damp, shady places. It is fine-textured, apple green in color, and should be cut 1½ inches tall, although it will survive at ¾ inch. In hot summers will survive only with shade and abundant water.

Rye Grasses. Perennial rye is a major constituent of inexpensive lawn grass mixes. It's medium-coarse in texture with a waxy sheen on the rather sparsely set leaves. Easy to grow in a wide variety of climates, but is too rough and bunchy to make a "perfect green carpet". Hard to mow in summer when wiry seed stalks tend to lie down under mower. Cut at 1½ inches. Will take some light shade.

Annual rye, coarser in texture than the perennial kind, grows fast and is used for quick cover, for erosion control, and for winter grass on Bermuda lawns. Most of it dies out in a year's time. Mow at 1½ inches.

Redtop. Similar to Astoria bent, but coarser in texture. Quick growing in wet or dry soils, in shade or sun. Gets clumpy with time. Mow at ¾ to 1 inch. Used primarily as temporary "nurse grass", in mixes for neglected areas that need cover, and for over-seeding Bermuda.

Coarse Fescues. All are wide-bladed, clumping, very tough and wear-resistant, useful only in football fields or lawns that get very rough treatment. Sow thickly to minimize clumpy appearance, and sow alone. In mix with fine-bladed grasses, the coarse fescues stand out as weeds. One of them, meadow fescue, is better than rye for quick cover and will take difficult conditions, including some shade. Alta or Kentucky 31 and Goars (an improved Alta) are wear-resistant, drought-resistant, and long lived. Mow at ¾ to 2 inches.

Clover. Not a grass, but often planted with lawn grasses. Three-parted leaves are dark green, soft, lush. Forms patches in lawns, and stains clothing badly. Gets lanky in shade. High mowing encourages it, low mowing discourages it. Under right conditions, it manufactures its own nitrogen, so that a grass and clover lawn needs less feeding.

Subtropical Grasses

These, unlike the cool-season grasses, grow vigorously during hot weather and go dormant in cool or cold winters. But even in their brown or straw-colored winter phase they keep up a thick carpet that keeps mud from being tracked into the house. And they can either be dyed green in winter or over-seeded with annual rye, redtop, bents, fine fescues, or bluegrass.

The better subtropical grasses are grown from stolons, sprigs, plugs, or sod. Common Bermuda, U-3 Bermuda, and *Zoysia japonica* are available in seed form, but seeding is unsatisfactory and the seeds are not widely offered. The hybrid Bermudas cover quickly from runners, while the zoysias are relatively slow. All can crowd out broad-leafed weeds. On the other hand, the hybrid Bermudas require frequent, close mowing, and frequent attention to thatch removal.

Zoysia Grasses. When zoysias first came on the market they suffered from irresponsible advertising. They are not perfect, being slow to establish and cover, and (generally) having a long dormant season; nevertheless, once established, they make an outstanding fine-textured turf with no Bermuda, weeds, diseases, or pests. A single edging board will contain them, and they can even take some shade in areas where summer nights are warm.

Zoysia japonica. Comparatively coarse-bladed. Best cut at 1½ inches.

Meyer zoysia. Established turf looks like good bluegrass. Very hardy to winter cold, very wear-resistant. Slow to establish and has a long, brown dormant season. Drought and weed-resistant. Mow at ½ inch.

Z. matrella. Medium fine texture, similar to bluegrass in appearance. Easy to maintain, and holds color better than Meyer; may hold fair color in mild winter. Produces some seed that may not come true. Mow at ½ inch.

Emerald. Wiry, dark green, prickly-looking turf. Slow. Dense, wiry blades hard to cut. More frost-tolerant than other zoysias and Bermudas. Stays green in frost-free areas.

St. Augustine Grass. Coarse-textured, with very wide blades of dark green. Planted away from other grasses so that you can't notice its coarse texture, it makes a serviceable lawn which is pest-free and salt-tolerant. Coarse texture makes power mowing necessary. Although it creeps into flower beds, shallow rooting makes it easy to control there. Turns brown with frost, but has comparatively short dormant season. Will take shade. Cut ½ to 1½ inches high.

Bermuda Grasses. These fine-bladed grasses spread aggressively and knit tenaciously into soil by surface runners and rhizomes. All brown out during a frosty winter, but some stay green longer than others. All require sun and should be cut as low as possible—½ inch if possible. They look their best only if you are careful about removing thatch, a matted layer of old stems and stolons beneath the green blades.

Common Bermuda. Coarsest of the Bermudas, but pretty enough if fertilized regularly. Bronzy seed spikes, free seeding habit, and invasive roots keep it from being a first-rate lawn. Can be grown from seed (hulled) or sprigs.

13 *Keep mulch or seedbed dark with moisture until grass is up.*

14 *A week after grass is up, you can pull weeds; no weed sprays yet.*

NO FOOT TRAFFIC WHILE GRASS "KNITS" . . .   EIGHT WEEKS AFTER THE FIRST MOWING . . .

15 *Keep barrier around area until 8 weeks after first mowing.*

Lay sod strips so joints at ends of strips will not be continuous.

Hybrid Bermudas. New ones appear from time to time, and each is an improvement over its predecessors in one respect or another. All are finer in texture than common Bermuda and have better color. They will crowd out common Bermuda in time, but are harder to overseed with rye, bluegrass, or red fescue. Help them stay green in winter by fertilizing in September and October, and by removing thatch, which insulates grass from warm soil. Among varieties recommended for areas with short dormant season are:

Santa Ana. Deep green, medium to coarse textured with upright growth. Holds color long into cold weather. Good for lawns under heavy use. Tends to build up thatch.

Tifgreen. Fine-textured, deep blue green, dense. Fewer seed spikes than most Bermudas, sterile seeds. Takes very close mowing and is preferred for putting greens. Outstanding hybrid for home lawns in general.

Tifway. Prostrate growth, fine texture, stiff blades, dark green color. Dense and wear-resistant. Is slower than other hybrids to establish and tends to grow in whorls. Sterile (no seeds).

Tifdwarf. Extremely low and dense; takes very close mowing. Slower to establish than others, but slower to spread into places where it's not wanted.

U-3. Finer-textured than common Bermuda, but with seed spikes just as obvious and unattractive. Very tough. Grow from sprigs; not dependable from seed, tending to revert to a mixture of many types. Not up to the other Bermudas in quality.

The Dichondra Lawn

Dichondra (*Dichondra carolinensis*) is a ground-hugging plant that spreads by rooting surface runners to cover the ground with a mat of small, round leaves that resemble miniature waterlily pads. It grows best in areas where winter temperatures don't drop below 25°, but it has been grown successfully in colder areas.

Once grown only from plugs (and still offered in flats for plugging), dichondra is now widely grown from seed. The amount you plant determines how quickly you get coverage. Two pounds to 1,000 square feet (sown in March to May) will give you a lawn in 5 weeks. One pound will give you a lawn in 6 to 7 weeks. One ounce will give you coverage in several years, but remember that the longer you have bare ground, the greater your weed problem will be. Planting early will give sturdy root systems that can take midsummer heat and water stress. You can plant in midsummer; germination is quickest then, but you'll have to water more carefully. Seedbed preparation is the same as for grasses.

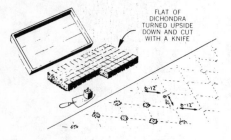

FLAT OF DICHONDRA TURNED UPSIDE DOWN AND CUT WITH A KNIFE

Dichondra is easier to cut into strips when turned out of flat.

To plant from plugs, prepare the seedbed as for sowing. Then turn dichondra out of flats upside down and cut plugs or strips with a knife. Plugs should be at least an inch square, and 2 inches is better. Place plugs in soil at 6 to 12 inch intervals, making sure that runners on plug are at soil level or below, then press plug firmly into soil. High planting will make for a lumpy, irregular surface. Water regularly and deeply to encourage deep rooting, and feed frequently but lightly. If you use selective weed killers in dichondra lawns, *follow label instructions to the letter.*

Dichondra planted in areas that get regular heavy traffic will naturally grow low and tight. Grown in shade, or with little traffic, and with much fertilizer it can grow as high as 6 inches with a lush but uneven look. Mowing is required more often in the shaded, low-traffic areas if you are to maintain an even quality without a scalped look after mowing. Where dichondra grows low and dense, mowing is required less often.

Container Gardening

Consider the varied reasons for growing plants in containers: If you have a sunny garden with alkaline soil, you may be able to grow shade loving, acid-soil plants only in a container of peaty mix in a shaded, paved breezeway or entryway. If drainage is poor, container (or raised bed) culture is the easiest way out. If plants need a little extra protection from frost, growing them in containers makes it easy to bring them under cover of porch roof or garage. This portability brings other benefits. If you grow flowering plants in containers, you can put them on display at the peak of their form, then haul them away when flowers have faded and replace them with other container-grown plants. A garden that has many container plants may require a lot of attention but it also can be unusually dramatic and attractive.

There are some places, of course, where you just can't grow plants any other way—indoors, on paved areas, roofs, or decks. But there's good reason for growing plants in containers even if you don't have to. The decorative value of a good-looking plant well matched to a good-looking container is reason enough.

Kinds of containers. These may be clay pots, boxes, barrels, tubs, window boxes, or custom-made containers of considerable sophistication. Principal requirements are that they be well drained and that they be appropriate to the plant and to the garden situation. Most pots have adequate drainage holes; with boxes, barrels, and tubs you'll have to make sure; try to have at least 2 good-sized drainage holes for every square foot of bottom, and space them well. More will be desirable. (Some undrained "planters" are made, and some people grow plants in them successfully by using charcoal in the bottom to lessen soil souring, but you'll have a much easier time with drained containers.)

Soil mix. Use a fast-draining, porous soil mix. Avoid clay and heavy soils. Prepared mixes are sold at many nurseries and garden supply stores. Or, you can mix your own. The U.C. mixes are excellent, having been developed specifically for container culture. For plants that do best in acid soil, increase the peat moss or ground bark component. For succulents and cacti, use more sand.

Watering. Water by inspection of the soil rather than by schedule. Plants in containers can't develop a deep root system; water must be there; and, since well-grown container plants have a root system that nearly fills the container, they use water fast. In hot, dry, windy weather actively growing plants may need water 2 or 3 times daily. If weather is cool, still, or overcast, or if plants are semi-dormant, watering can be far less frequent. Test soil with your fingers: if it's dry beneath the surface, it's time to water. And water until you see water coming out the drainage holes. (If it comes out too fast, your plant may be in trouble. If the root ball becomes too dry, it may shrink away from the sides of the container. If it does, water will run around, not through the ball. If this should happen, soak the plant and container in a tub or bucket until bubbles stop rising, or cork the drainage holes and water. Remove corks after soil is soaked.)

Heavy watering leaches out plant nutrients, so regular feeding is a necessity with container plants. Either liquid or dry fertilizer will do. Light and frequent

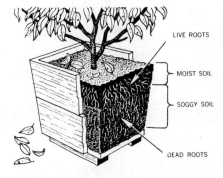

LIVE ROOTS
MOIST SOIL
SOGGY SOIL
DEAD ROOTS

Water-logged roots at bottom of the container are dead or dying.

Strong jets can wash soil from the container; use bubbler.

If dry root ball shrinks away from container, water escapes around it.

Firm fresh soil around plant; stick is convenient, handy tool.

Shaving away an inch of old root permits use of old tub, new soil.

feeding is usually the best pattern. Again, let the plant, not a schedule, be your guide. Study its color, its growth rate, its bloom, and fertilize accordingly.

Transplanting. Move plants to larger containers as their root systems fill pots or containers. Generally speaking, pot plants should be moved on when their roots fill the pot, and they should be moved to the next size pot, not to a very large one. With fast-growing plants you can skip a size, or you can put several small plants into a large pot. The object is to keep the soil mass fairly well filled with roots. When moving up plants in larger containers, select a new container that will allow an inch or two of fresh mix on all sides of the root mass. Old plants in very large containers can be turned out and an inch of the outer root mass shaved off with a knife, then replanted in the same container with fresh mix around the outside.

A trip to a nursery will show you that there are very few plants that can't be grown in containers for a considerable time.

House Plants

In general, plants kept indoors are handled just like other container plants. Give them good light, but not searing sun in a hot west window. Plants that make a big flower display generally require more light than foliage plants. Low humidity is the bane of most house plants, and low humidity goes with high heat. Cooler spots around the house are best for plants, and sites near hot air registers should be avoided at all costs. High humidity in bathrooms and kitchens favors plant growth. Avoid softened water; the sodium content may rise dangerously high and cause scorching or blackening of leaf edges. If the municipal water in your area is softened, give the plant a thorough leaching by setting it in the sink and letting a trickle of water run through it.

Indoor-Outdoor Plants

If you move indoor plants outside for the summer, make the move on a day when temperature contrasts are not too strong, and set the plant in light very little stronger than that in which it grew before. If indoor plants grow too tall and lanky (philodendrons and dieffenbachia are notorious examples), you have several choices. Re-root tops by air-layering; replant in a larger container, adding smaller plants to conceal bare stems; cut back plant to near the base and let it sprout a fresh stem; or (this isn't done often enough) throw it out and get another plant.

Bonsai

In bonsai the container plant transcends horticulture and becomes a fine art. The selection of proper plants and appropriate containers, the matching of a plant to a style of training, the careful wiring, pruning, and pinching can easily become a passion. It is simple in essence. It consists in dwarfing trees, shrubs, or vines and keeping them small while maintaining carefully controlled shape and proportion through pruning of roots and tops. It can be as complicated in execution as you have time for.

Propagating Techniques

The advantage of vegetative propagation is that the plants you propagate will be identical with the parent plant, whereas seedlings may vary considerably. Many gardeners have rooted geranium or fuchsia cuttings and most have divided bulbs, tubers, or perennials; comparatively few have tried to grow shrubs from cuttings, or have grafted or budded fruit trees, which involves more complicated procedures.

Perennials that make runners can usually be picked apart easily

Division

If you grow perennials, bulbs, or plants with rhizomes or tubers, you're bound to get involved with propagation sooner or later. To keep these plants healthy and vigorous, it's necessary to divide them occasionally. Each year the typical perennial gains in girth by growing new roots and stems, usually around the outer perimeter of the previous year's growth. Eventually (usually in 2 or 3 years) these clumps get too big for their space. Or perhaps growth has become weakened due to competition and crowding. Then it's time to divide the plant.

Each root segment or division is actually a plant in itself or is capable of becoming a new plant. Divide an overgrown clump into separate parts and you get many new plants. It's a fast and inexpensive way of increasing your supply of favorite perennials.

Divide in autumn or early spring, when plants are dormant. Fall is generally the best time to divide perennials that bloom in spring or early summer (in cold winter regions, this must be done in *early* fall). After dividing, keep roots moist and plant as soon as possible.

Deciduous and semi-deciduous perennials may be cut back to about 4 inches from the ground when you divide and transplant. Young, healthy foliage of evergreen perennials should not be cut back, but dead leaves should be removed. Perennials that form a tap root and a single crown are best propagated by making cuttings of side branches or by seeds.

Use trowel, knife, or spade to cut tough rootstocks of perennials.

Those bulbs that live over from year to year should be left undivided until flower production starts to fall off. Then dig (after foliage is thoroughly ripened) and pull the bulbs apart. Replant in well prepared soil, or store until appropriate planting time. Gladiolus, dahlias, and other similar plants are customarily dug up every year, divided, and stored until it's time to replant.

Softwood and Semihardwood Cuttings

The terms softwood, semihardwood, hardwood refer to the maturity of the wood; softwood cuttings, which can be taken any time in spring or early summer during the active growing season, are the easiest and quickest rooting of the three types, and so are probably the best for the beginner to start with. Softwood cuttings can be taken from deciduous or evergreen shrubs or trees, or from herbaceous or evergreen perennials. Semihard cuttings are taken in summer or fall, just at the point where growth is firm enough to snap when twig is bent sharply. If wood bends, cutting is too old for satisfactory rooting. Other than that, the methods and considerations with semihardwood cuttings are the same as with softwood cuttings, as follows:

TAKE FUCHSIA CUTTINGS WHEN NEW SHOOTS ARE 2" TO 3" LONG

STRIP OFF LOWER LEAVES THAT MAY TOUCH ROOTING MEDIUM

Softwood cuttings can be taken from tips or side shoots of plants.

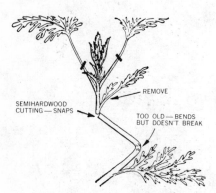

Semihardwood cutting is ready to take if twig snaps when bent.

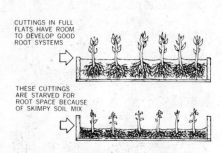

Sturdier, healthier plants result from deep rooting medium.

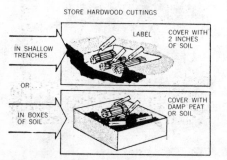

Store hardwood cuttings so that they will callus before planting.

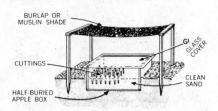

Here is an easy frame for rooting a few hardwood cuttings.

Side branches that have formed after the growing tip of the main stem of a plant has been pinched off generally make good cuttings. Avoid abnormal growth, including weak shoots from the center of the plant.

If leaves are quite large, it may be necessary to cut back part of the leaf surface to lessen water loss and to reduce the space required by the cutting in the propagating box. But where possible, retain as much of the foliage as you can.

You have a choice of good rooting mixtures: coarse river sand; a mixture of half sand and half peat moss; half sand and half perlite; or vermiculite. The sand and peat moss mix is best for acid-loving plants such as azaleas. Vermiculite has a tendency to stay quite moist, so use it with caution. If you are rooting a large number of cuttings, a nursery flat makes a good propagating bed. For just a few, use a clay pan or one-pound coffee can. If you want to avoid damaging young, tender roots, root cuttings individually in peat pots or small clay pots.

Rooting of softwood and semihardwood cuttings can be greatly speeded by treating the base of the cutting with a rooting hormone. Speed is important, because the quicker the cutting takes up water the less chance it will wilt. Follow directions on the label, and don't expect the hormone to make up for any mistakes you may make in watering, shading, or sanitation.

When plants are rooted (this may take from two weeks to several months, depending on the kind of plant) you still don't necessarily achieve success. Lift and repot rooted cuttings with extreme care, shade new transplants, and keep them out of drafts until roots are established and new growth begins.

Root rot and wilting are the principle reasons why cuttings may not grow. Prevent root rot by planting the cutting in a well aerated mix (described above), and by watering carefully. Wilting can be prevented by keeping the humidity high; either grow cuttings in a coldframe, or cover containers with glass or polyethylene.

Hardwood Cuttings

You can increase your supply of certain deciduous shrubs and trees by making hardwood cuttings in late fall to early spring when plants are dormant—after leaves have fallen. Patience is the byword if you intend to propagate by this method, since most hardwood cuttings are slow in getting established (sometimes as long as a year).

Hardwood cuttings can be made of deutzia, forsythia, grapes, kolkwitzia, philadelphus, and weigela, to name just a few examples.

The following, however, do not root satisfactorily from hardwood cuttings and are normally propagated from seed, grafting, or budding: fruit trees, most nut trees, maple, oak, birch, linden, and beech trees.

Cut the tip of the branch back to where wood is about the size of a lead pencil. Make the cuttings 6 to 9 inches long; include at least two leaf joints. Make the bottom cut a slanting one at, or just below, a leaf joint. Tie the cuttings of each kind together in a bundle, and attach a label marked with the name of the plant and date of cutting.

Dig a shallow trench in well drained soil. Put in the cuttings; cover them with about 2 inches of soil. In regions where the ground freezes, add enough mulch to keep the cuttings free from frosts.

You may, if you wish, store the cuttings in boxes of soil. If you do this, keep the soil moist through the winter. Cuttings stored in the garden get enough moisture from the soil to keep their tissues from drying out.

By the time weather warms up in spring the cuttings will have formed calluses or roots, and they can be set in an open cutting bed.

Root Cuttings

Cuttings can be taken from the roots of any plant that produces sprouts from the roots. Actually, the roots you plant will show no visible growth buds; the buds develop after the root cutting is planted. Plants which may be propagated from root cuttings include: Japanese anemone, Oriental poppy, trumpet creeper, blackberry, and raspberry. To make root cuttings, select roots 3/16 to 3/8 inch in diameter from vigorous plants. Cut roots into pieces 1 to 3 inches long. Fill a box or flat to within about 1 inch of the top with light garden loam; place cuttings 2 inches apart in a horizontal position on top of the soil. Cover with about ½ inch of additional soil, and water thoroughly. Cover with glass or newspaper and place in the shade. If you wish to root only a few cuttings, place them upright around the edge of a pot, being sure that the thickest end is upright. Top should be just at soil level.

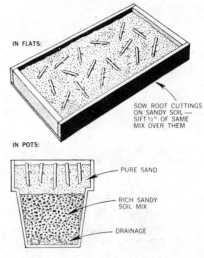

Root cuttings are easy, reliable with the right plants.

Ground Layering

Ground layering is a simple method of plant propagation in which branches are notched and brought into contact with the soil to make them take root while still attached to the parent plant. Once they've formed roots, they can be detached and planted, thus becoming new plants.

Select a low-growing branch that can be bent down to the ground. Mark a point about 12 inches from the end of the branch and just below a joint. Directly underneath dig a hole in the soil 4 inches deep and line it with a good planting mix. On underside of branch at selected point, make a slanting cut halfway through the branch; wedge it open with a pebble or peg. Bend branch into hole, placing cut at center and well toward bottom. Anchor it with a heavy wire loop, fill the hole with good soil mix, firm mix, and place a brick or stone directly above the cut to anchor branch, and conserve moisture. Protect with a mulch in winter. In nine months or a year dig down carefully to see if rooting has taken place. If it has, sever from parent branch, lift carefully, and replant. If rooting has not taken place, put back soil mix and wait; some plants may take two years or more to root.

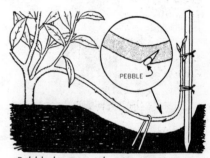

Pebble keeps notch open; roots are more likely to form near wound.

Sever rooted layer carefully; roots are tender, easily torn.

Air Layering

Air layering is an ancient, well proved, and highly interesting technique. It is an excellent method for increasing choice shrubs and trees, as it often works on plants which are difficult or impossible to root by other methods. Polyethylene plastic material makes the process quite simple. Here's how:

Select a branch from pencil size up to an inch in diameter. Below a joint either make a slanting cut 1/3 through the stem, inserting a piece of matchstick to keep it spread apart, or remove a ring of bark about ¾ inch wide, scraping it down to the heartwood (the hard core of wood at the center of a stem or branch).

Dust the cut lightly with rooting hormone powder, wrap the area with a generous handful of damp sphagnum moss, and enclose it in polyethylene. Bind it securely above and below the cut with string or wire ties.

This procedure is well worth trying on choice plants such as deciduous magnolias. Philodendrons also take well to this process. If it works, you'll see roots appearing in the sphagnum moss in a month or two. Then you can separate the youngster from the mother plant. If it doesn't root, the branch will callus, new bark will eventually grow over the cut area, and you're no worse off than before.

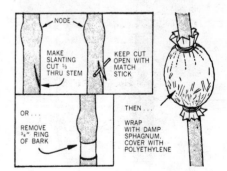

Air layering is fun; and it's a good way to rejuvenate house plants.

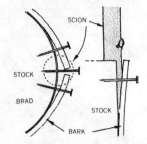

Bark grafting is good method for novices; good on older trees.

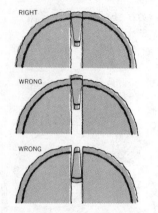

It is essential to match cambium layers if you want graft to take.

Saw kerf graft fits scions into saw kerfs in the stock plant.

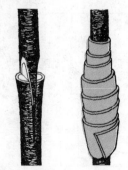

Wedge graft is used on small stocks and scions; easy for novice.

Grafting

On these pages you will find illustrated the wondrous and ancient horticultural practice called grafting—the operation of inserting a short piece of stem bearing one or more growth buds from one plant into another plant to form a union that grows together. If the graft succeeds, a branch grows from it and carries the flowers and fruits of the plant from which the piece of stem was taken; the rest of the plant will continue to carry its own flowers and fruits.

Many a home gardener has tried his hand at grafting, as much for the satisfaction of doing it and seeing the graft grow as for any practical purpose (such as adding another variety to a pear tree or to a camellia bush). It is a test of skill as well as a practical accomplishment.

Anyone interested in learning the art should first introduce two important words into his vocabulary: *stock* and *scion* (SIGH-un). Stock is the name for the plant onto which you graft. The scion is the piece of stem, containing one or more growth buds, that you insert in the stock. Nature doesn't allow you to graft a scion from any plant onto any other plant. For a graft to work, the scion and stock plants must be close botanical relations. But even some close relations are not reliable candidates. By reading books on propagation in your local libraries, you can come up with a list of compatible plants with which to try your grafting experiments. Here's a sample of what you could try: pear on hawthorn; peach on plum and vice versa; apricots on peach, plum, or prune; sweet cherry on sour cherry.

Of course, your safest first try would be to graft one variety on another variety of the same kind—peach on peach, camellia on camellia, wisteria on wisteria. Once you've become skillful and successful with these grafts, you can start trying other combinations of closely related plants.

The next word for a novice grafter to learn: *cambium*. It is the soft layer of tissue in a stem (or root) that lies between the bark and the wood. When you peel bark off a tree it comes loose at the cambium layer. Through cell division, this layer gives rise to new bark tissue on the outside and new wood tissue on the inside. In other words, it is the place from which growth on the mature part of a stem or branch originates.

The crucial point of grafting is to align a section of the cambium layer of the scion with the cambium layer of the stock, as completely as possible, and then bind the stock and scion together so that a union takes place between the two cambium layers. A graft can succeed only if you line up the cambium layers—in some places, if not completely. The illustrations show how to accomplish this crucial alignment.

The knives that you use should be high-quality steel, kept very sharp. A sharp tool makes a clean slice, thereby insuring maximum contact of cambium layers.

There's a way to cut scions without cutting yourself (if you do it wrong, injury is quite likely): Sit down and hold scion horizontally against your chest, with end to be cut at your right (left if you're left-handed). Hold knife securely in the other hand with blade on one side of the scion and thumb, in a parallel position, on the other. Pull to right to make cuts, *moving thumb with knife.* You may court trouble if you slide knife in front of a thumb held rigidly.

All grafting methods shown here, except one, call for sawing branch or trunk back to a stub. Cut the stub cleanly and smoothly. If the branch is heavy or horizontal, pre-cut as shown on page 75 in the pruning chapter.

In all grafting methods, the tight union between stock and scion must be sealed off from air with some kind of sealing agent. Probably easiest for a novice is the manufactured tree sealing compound (water base asphalt emulsion) that comes in cans. If it rains during first 24 hours after applying, examine for wash-off; you may need to apply more.

Graft deciduous trees and shrubs any time during the dormant season. Usually it's most satisfactory if done before buds begin to swell in late winter or early spring. Evergreens can be grafted in early spring, just before plants begin to grow actively.

Budding

In summer and early fall comes the season for the kind of propagating that professionals call "summer budding."

You insert a growth bud from one plant under the bark of a plant of a related variety. If the two plants are compatible and if you are skillful (or lucky), the bud and the plant will unite. Through the fall and winter, the live, plump bud remains dormant. In spring, when the surge of growth comes to all the buds on the plant, the implanted bud also starts to grow and you cut back to just above it.

All the growth from the implanted bud—flowers, fruits, and leaves—will have the characteristics of the plant from which you took the bud.

Budding accomplishes the same end result as grafting, but it differs in that it is considerably easier to do. If it doesn't take, the plant is not disfigured as with an unsuccessful grafting operation. You get the journeyman's satisfaction that comes with mastering a new skill; and you can convert a plant to a better variety or add another variety to an existing plant, for novelty or for some practical purpose such as furnishing a pollinating variety within a fruit tree's structure. Nurserymen use summer budding to convert easily grown seedling bushes or tree saplings to varieties that people want but that cannot be grown easily from seed. They place the bud in the bottom 3 or 4 inches of the seedling.

The plant and the section of branch into which you place the bud is called the *stock*. The buds come from the *budstick*, a length of branch containing several buds which you cut from the introduced variety. It should not differ greatly in size from the section of stock, and it should be fresh. Also, it should bear vegetative buds, not flowering buds.

To implant a bud into the upper branches of a big tree or older shrub, choose a branch of one to two-year-old wood, remove foliage that would interfere with the budding operation, and proceed as shown in either of the two methods above.

Usually, you will find the buds on the budstick at the base of leaf stalks. Remove the leaf, but don't cut off the leaf stalk. Use it as a handle and also as an indicator: If, when it withers a week or two after budding, the bud remains plump and green, then the operation is a success. But if the entire bud shield or patch (bark, bud, and leaf stalk) withers or turns dark, the operation has failed.

In a few weeks cut off the tying material if it appears to be constricting the stock. Late the following winter, cut off the old stock above the bud and it will grow into a flourishing stem.

The illustrated T-bud method is the easiest one for a novice, and is the most widely used. Use patch budding with plants that have thick bark, such as walnuts, pecans, and avocados. Double-bladed tools for patch budding, as shown in the picture at right, have been manufactured but are not always widely sold. You can make one with two knife blades mounted on a block so that they will be 1¼ inches apart. Knives for any kind of budding should be kept very sharp.

Both methods work only if bark pulls away from the wood easily.

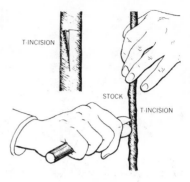

Making T-incision in the stock; works when bark pulls away easily.

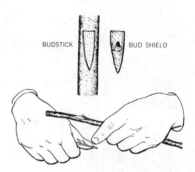

Cutting out bud shield from the budstick. Use sharp knife.

Here bud shield is inserted in the T-incision. Now wrap and tie.

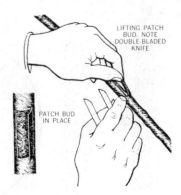

Patch bud shown here is used with thick-barked plants.

Garden Maintenance

Garden maintenance can be pleasant exercise or sheer drudgery; which it is depends to a large degree on whether you use the right or the wrong tools or equipment for the job at hand.

Gloves. Unless your hands are well hardened, you should wear gloves if you are going to handle soil or rocks, pull many weeds, grasp tool handles for long periods, or work among thorny plants. Work gloves of cloth, plastic, or leather are all useful; use the ones that feel best on your hands. (You may find that leather gives the best protection if you're pruning thorny plants.)

Shovels, spades, trowels. Shovels are designed for scooping, lifting, digging, and mixing. Shovel (A) is most useful for digging, mixing, and moving soil. Square-bladed shovel (B) is best for moving loose soil or other bulky materials, mixing concrete, cleaning up around paved surfaces. Small trench spade (C) is handy for digging in close quarters. Standard spade (D) is designed for digging and turning soil, incorporating soil amendments, digging trenches and planting holes, and pruning roots. Some gardeners learn to use it for weeding (sliding it along parallel to the ground with a slicing motion) or breaking up soil crust (quick, shallow, closely-spaced vertical slices). Narrow spade (E) (often called a "sharp-shooter") is used for digging ditches and post holes and for balling plants for transplanting. Small spade (F) is for transplanting small shrubs, perennials, and the like.

To use a spade properly, drive the blade straight down with your foot, rock the handle back, lift the soil and turn it on its side—not upside down. Blade will work more easily in clay soil if kept clean, oiled, and rust-free. Use a file to center the cutting edge, but don't sharpen too thin. Choice of long handle or short, D-handle is a personal one; use the one that feels best.

Trowels are designed for planting bulbs, annuals, and seedlings, but they can also be used to dig an occasional weed or to make a short furrow. Styles and construction details differ, but essentially they are either scoops (A, B, C) or spatulas (D). The latter type is used for lifting seedlings out of a flat. Pick a trowel that fits your hand and feels balanced. Buy a sturdy one. Working in hard soil will bend the shanks on all except the best trowels.

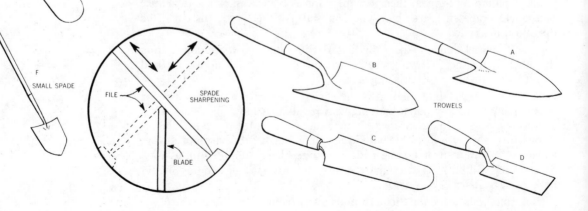

A ROUND-POINT SHOVEL

B SQUARE-BLADED SHOVEL

C TRENCH SPADE

D SPADE

E NARROW SPADE

F SMALL SPADE

FILE — SPADE SHARPENING

BLADE

TROWELS

Hoes. Use these to cultivate (break up crusted soil), dig furrows, and to destroy weeds. Standard hoe (A) comes in heavy or light weight models; use it for weeding, for making furrows, or for rearranging loose soil. Wide-bladed hoe (B) is useful for light cultivation and for working under low plants. Useful for the same purpose is the scuffle hoe (C), which cuts with either edge and is used by pushing it back and forth at or just under the soil surface. Variations have disk-shaped blades or a hinged, rocker-type blade. Warren hoe (D) is designed for weeding, furrowing, hilling. You make the furrow with the pointed end, seed, then turn the hoe over and use the "ears" to pull the soil over the seed. Two-pronged weeding hoe (E) is made to up-root big weeds with pronged side, chop or scrape small weeds with the flat side.

In hoeing weeds, advance toward the unhoed weeds as you go, rather than backing into them and trampling them under foot. Hold the standard hoe so that the blade is at about a 30-degree angle. Hoe with a smooth, horizontal movement, drawing back toward you so that weeds are deposited in a straight line. Do not chop downward—chopping with a hoe jars your arms and shoulders needlessly, makes an uneven surface, and may cut roots of desirable plants. To sharpen, draw file across blade as illustrated.

Rakes and cultivators. Use rakes to break up spaded soil, smooth seedbeds, gather up debris, renew lawns. Commonest are the level-headed rake (A) and the bow rake (B). Bow rake is springy, best for working in lighter soils; sturdy level-headed rake is best for heavy clay soils. Self-cleaning rake (C) sometimes called a Bermuda rake, is heavier than other types, but it does one certain job. You don't lift it from the ground. The pull stroke gathers debris toward the operator; the push stroke clears material from the blades. This rake is especially useful in clearing out lawn thatch and severing long surface runners of certain lawn grasses.

Leaf or grass rakes (D) sweep leaves or lawn clippings from lawns, paths, or garden beds. Both steel and bamboo are built to be light in weight, springy, gentle on surface that's being raked. Steel is longer-lasting, but bamboo is cheaper and many gardeners prefer its feel. In addition to standard widths, bamboo is also available in a very wide style and in a very narrow, short-handled style for raking up in close quarters under and between plants in beds. The latter is often called a shrub rake.

Small, 3-pronged cultivator (E) is used to break up soil crust and for light weeding and cultivating jobs. Use the heavier type (F) (sometimes called a potato hook) for heavier cultivating jobs. Used with a chopping, pulling, raking action in moderately soft soil it can do a quick job of preparing a seed bed. Spading fork (G) does many of the jobs of a spade and is also useful in digging bulbs, rhizomes, and tubers. Penetration is easier than with a spade, especially in heavy or stony soils, and the fork tends to break clods as it turns over the soil. A sharp tap with the back of the fork will break up any which don't fall apart. (Caution: Don't dig or cultivate wet soils, especially

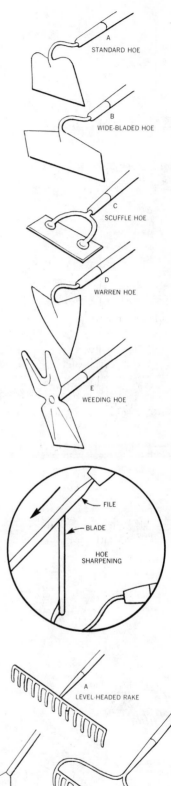

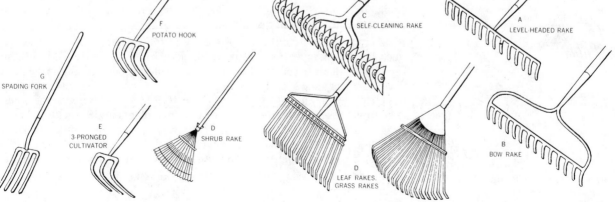

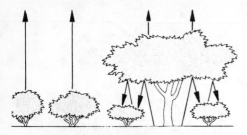

Arrows represent heat loss. Plants exposed to open sky—especially north sky—are more subject to frost damage than are plants grown under trees.

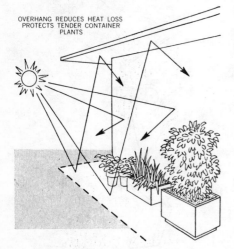

OVERHANG REDUCES HEAT LOSS PROTECTS TENDER CONTAINER PLANTS

South or west wall with overhang is safest place against frosts.

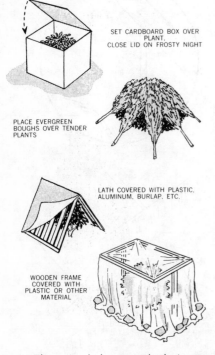

SET CARDBOARD BOX OVER PLANT. CLOSE LID ON FROSTY NIGHT

PLACE EVERGREEN BOUGHS OVER TENDER PLANTS

LATH COVERED WITH PLASTIC, ALUMINUM, BURLAP, ETC.

WOODEN FRAME COVERED WITH PLASTIC OR OTHER MATERIAL

These simple home-made devices can save a choice plant from frost.

wet clays; you'll compact the soil into dense, airless clods that only weathering will break up. Soil should be damp enough to penetrate with spade, fork, or cultivator, but it should be dry enough to crumble.)

An easy way to maintain all soil-working tools is to scrape off all dirt with a flat stick or putty knife as soon as you've finished working with them, then work the tool up and down in a bucket of oiled sand to remove remaining dirt and put on a rust-resisting film of oil.

Frost Protection

Protecting plants from cold weather is second nature to gardeners in regions where winter means snow and zero weather. Roses and other plants that can't take the cold are bundled up or buried under piles of leaves or straw. Container plants are moved to sheltered locations. In mild-winter regions where frosts and occasional hard freezes occur, gardeners are not so winter-conscious. They grow many semi-hardy and tender plants, and frequently several winters will pass with no damage. Then along comes a winter with temperatures a few degrees lower, and those tender plants are killed—unless they are protected.

There are a number of things you can do to minimize frost and freeze damage. First, build your basic landscaping—shade trees, screening and foundation plantings, hedges—with thoroughly hardy plants. Use more tender plants as fillers, as summertime display plants, in borders, or in areas of secondary interest; or plant them in sheltered sites (entryways, courtyards); or grow them in containers and move them to sheltered sites.

Next, learn your garden microclimates; find which areas are warm, which cool. Most dangerous to tender plants are stretches of open ground exposed to the sky on all sides, particularly to the *north* sky. Plants in hollows or in low enclosed areas where cold air is held motionless are also in danger. Safest areas for tender plants are under overhanging eaves (best protection), lath structures, or tree branches. Slopes from which cold air drains freely are safer than valley or canyon floors. South-facing walls absorb much heat during the day and radiate it at night, warming nearby plants. Warmest location of all is a south-facing wall with an overhang. Not only does it give maximum protection against frost, in cool-summer climates it also supplies the heat necessary to stimulate bud, blossom, and fruit in heat-loving plants such as bougainvillea, hibiscus, fig, and evergreen magnolia.

Condition plants and soil for frosts. Feed and water while plants are growing fastest in late spring, early summer, but taper off nitrogen feeding in late summer, early fall to slow growth, permit wood to ripen and harden. Plants in active growth are less hardy to cold than dormant or semi-dormant plants. Reducing water will help harden growth, but soil around plants should be moist at the onset of the frost season; moist soil holds and releases more heat than dry soil.

Be especially watchful for frosts early in fall or late in spring; these are much more damaging than frosts which come while plants are semi-dormant. The signs: still air (tree branches motionless, smoke goes straight up); absence of cloud cover (stars easily visible, very bright); low humidity (windshield, grass dry); low temperature (45° or less at 10 P.M.). If you notice these signs at bedtime, take steps to get tender container plants under shelter of porch roof, eaves, or garage, or to erect shelters over tender plants. Burlap or plastic film over stakes or frames will do the job. Make sure that the covering material does not touch the plant, and uncover the plant during daytime.

If plants have been damaged by frost, don't hurry to prune them. Premature trimming may stimulate new, tender growth that will be nipped by later frosts. Wait until new growth begins in spring, then remove only wood which is clearly dead.

Some hardy plants have early blossoms which are damaged by spring frosts. Try to delay bloom of deciduous magnolias, some early rhododendrons beyond the time of heavy frosts by giving plants a cool, shaded north slope, north exposure, or shade of high-branching deciduous trees.

Where Winters Are Really Cold

In intermountain and mountain areas where soil freezes hard and temperatures drop below zero gardeners grow few tender or semi-hardy plants, but most do grow roses and a few attempt broad-leafed evergreens—boxwood, euonymus, holly, rhododendrons, pieris. With roses, the problem is simply one of preserving live roots and canes for next spring's growth and bloom. Mound soil or mulching material around base of plants, or use wire cylinders to hold mulching material. For tree or climbing roses, tie cornstalks or straw around plants, or dig around base of plants, lay them down, and protect with soil, leaves, or other mulching material.

Broad-leafed evergreens may be hardy to cold, but they suffer from windburn and sunburn when low temperatures, strong sun, and cold, drying winds combine forces. Protect with burlap or lath shelters or evergreen boughs stuck in the ground to windward, and plant (if possible) on north side of house or wall where bright sun will not strike frozen plants. Above all, keep soil moist and keep moisture available by means of an effective mulch. Greatest damage comes when plants transpire water through the leaves and can't replace it because soil is frozen.

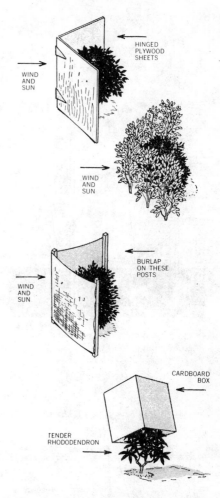

Keep freezing wind, drying sun from evergreens with such shelters.

Heat, Shade, Humidity

These three subjects are bound together very closely. In plant descriptions, you frequently see such recommendations as "Grow in sun near coast, part or full shade inland." This tells what to do for shade-loving plants. These plants, mostly native to forest floors, have shallow roots that seldom penetrate beneath the surface layer of leaf mold. They use much water during growth and bloom (tuberous begonias, fuchsias, azaleas), but their leaves are not adapted to store water (as succulent plants do) or to resist evaporation in warm, dry, windy weather (as many waxy- or leathery-leafed plants do). In hot sun, in very dry weather, or in warm windy weather, they lose water faster than they can take it up; sunburn, wilting, or withering result.

To grow shade plants successfully, keep direct sunlight down, humidity up. If you live near the ocean, a fog cover and natural humidity may be enough (but even here you'll need to furnish shelter against strong, constant winds). Further inland place your shade plants under shelter of high-branching trees, under lath structures, or on the north or east sides of buildings, walls, or fences. Protect from drying winds by fences, louvers, windbreak plantings. Keep humidity high by reducing air motion, by mulching (a coarse, moist mulch will evaporate a considerable amount of water into the air), and by watering often. When temperatures are really high or humidity exceptionally low, water with special diligence and supplement surface irrigation with sprinkling or misting. (This last may not be practical where water contains large amounts of salts.)

Protect newly-set plants with temporary shelters from strong sun and wind. These can be as simple as shingle lean-tos placed on the sunny side of

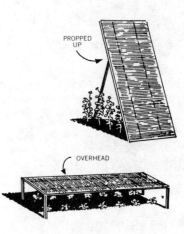

Frame covered with bamboo blind is easy, adaptable sun screen.

the plant or small newspaper pup tents held down at the edges by a few handfuls of soil. Or they can be as elaborate as lath or burlap panels supported above the plants on low stakes. The object is to keep strong sun and wind from the young plants until the roots are able to do an efficient job of taking water from the soil to meet the plant's needs.

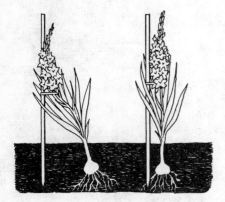

Stake plants before, and not after, they show need for support.

Staking, Tying

Keep a supply of stakes and ties on hand so that you can use them when they are needed. It's discouraging to try to stake up a tall, slender, flowering stem that has fallen over of its own weight or as the result of wind and water. At best you get a lopsided, awkwardly curving bloom cluster. At the worst, you may break the stem. The time to stake and tie is before an accident happens. Stake flowers that need staking as soon as flower spikes begin to lengthen; put supports around peonies, carnations, and other spreading or floppy perennials before stems start to bend or sprawl. And make sure that stakes are tall and stout enough, and that ties are secure without being tight enough to constrict the stem.

Be especially careful with newly set trees. The stake that came with the tree (if any) may be long enough and stout enough, but then again it may not. It's better to have the stake too large than too small. A two-inch stake is generally safe for a six-foot tree. The stake should penetrate deeper than the root ball of the newly set tree. If it does not, the stake, tree, and root ball may all fall over together when high winds combine with wet soil.

Prepare trees for autumn storms by checking stakes and ties. Replace stakes that are undersized or rotted at the soil level. Check ties to see that they are secure but not so tight as to cut into the wood. Densely foliaged broad leafed evergreen trees should be opened up so that they offer lessened resistance to the wind ("putting holes in the sail"). Young or newly set trees of considerable size may require guying rather than staking. Use three guy wires attached to rubber-covered tree ties made snug around the trunk. Fasten the ends of the wires to 2 by 4-inch stakes driven 2 feet into the ground. Make sure the pull of the wires is against the 4-inch side. Use turnbuckles to equalize and maintain tautness of wires.

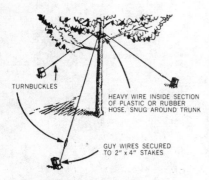

TURNBUCKLES

HEAVY WIRE INSIDE SECTION OF PLASTIC OR RUBBER HOSE, SNUG AROUND TRUNK

GUY WIRES SECURED TO 2" x 4" STAKES

Guy wires necessary with newly set large trees, big shrubs.

Garden Sanitation

Occasional cleanups keep a garden healthy as well as attractive. Vegetable trash around the garden affords damp, cool breeding grounds for slugs, snails, and insects. Lumber stacked on the ground also affords feeding grounds to termites; try to keep it on racks against a seldom-seen stretch of fence or outbuilding wall.

If you keep pots and other plant containers on bare ground, move them occasionally, so you can look for and exterminate slugs, snails, and their pearly eggs that might be hiding there. At the same time, probe the container drainage holes for more eggs and creatures.

Occasionally, when you go out to look around the garden, carry a bucket, pruning shears (a scabbard is handy for this), and tying materials. Cut off dead wood, spent flowers, developing seed clusters or fruits of ornamentals (unless you wish to save them for some particular purpose). Tie up any plants that need it, and cut off withered foliage and stalks of spent annuals, bulbs, and perennials. Drop all the removed plant parts in the bucket and, when you are through, put the contents in the garbage. Performing a few of these chores several times a week will save you major cleanups later.

PLANT SELECTION GUIDE

The thousands of different plants that we grow in the West include an almost infinite variety of sizes, shapes, textures, colors, and degrees of seasonal impact. The best way to design a garden and make it interesting each season is to consider these thousands of shapes, colors, and textures as available units with which you can put together the permanent framework of your garden and stage the seasonal shows you'd like to have take place. This chapter helps you select the plants to do these jobs.

Here we list, compare, and evaluate garden plants for many different landscape uses. The charts and lists which follow give limited information for each plant. For more complete information, consult the Western Plant Encyclopedia.

Plants are listed in the use charts by botanical names, occasionally with helpful common names in parentheses. Two climate zone numbers joined by a dash (as 8–24) mean that a plant is recommended for all zones between the two numbers, inclusive. Climate zone numbers are mapped and explained on pages 8 to 27.

This section of the book is divided as follows: Basic Landscaping Situations, pages 98 to 110; Special Landscaping Situations, pages 111 to 133; Garden Color, pages 134 to 147; Special Effects, pages 148 to 154; Problem Areas, pages 155 to 160.

PARKING STRIPS

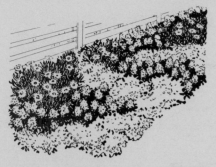

A parking strip is the soil area between street and sidewalk, or immediately adjacent to the street. It's sometimes called a boulevard strip. Plants that grow here must stay attractive all year and ask for little maintenance because the strip is difficult to water and a nuisance to weed or spray. Here are some suggestions. Those classified as vines are used in parking strips as rambling ground covers.

CONSISTENT PERFORMERS, EASY, NEAT

NAME OF PLANT	KIND	CLIMATE ZONES
Arctostaphylos uva-ursi	Shrub	1-9, 14-24
Hedera (ivy)		
Hedera canariensis	Vine	8, 9, 12-24
H. helix	Vine	All Zones
H. h. 'Hahn's Self-branch-ing	Vine	All Zones
Juniperus (juniper)		
Juniperus chinensis 'San Jose'	Shrub	All Zones
J. c. sargentii	Shrub	All Zones
J. conferta (shore juniper)	Shrub	All Zones
J. horizontalis (creeping juniper)	Shrub	All Zones
J. h. 'Bar Harbor'	Shrub	All Zones
J. h. 'Douglasii'	Shrub	All Zones
J. h. 'Plumosa'	Shrub	All Zones
J. h. 'Webberi'	Shrub	All Zones
Vinca minor or V. major	Perennial	All Zones

CHOICE, NEED SOME EXTRA ATTENTION

NAME OF PLANT	KIND	CLIMATE ZONES
Ajuga reptans	Perennial	All Zones
Carissa grandiflora	Shrub	13, 16-24
Ceanothus gloriosus	Ground cover	5-9, 14-24
Euonymus fortunei 'Vegeta'	Shrub	1-17
Fragaria chiloensis (wild strawberry)	Ground cover	4-6, 15-17, 20-24
Mahonia aquifolium 'Compacta' (Oregon grape)	Shrub	1-10, 14-21
Rosmarinus officinalis 'Prostratus' (rosemary)	Shrub	4-24
Trachelospermum jasminoides (star jasmine)	Vine	8-24

WALK-ON GROUND COVERS

NAME OF PLANT	KIND	CLIMATE ZONES
Phyla nodiflora	Perennial	8-24
Zoysia tenuifolia	Grass	8-24

SHOWY FLOWERS IN SEASON

NAME OF PLANT	KIND	CLIMATE ZONES
Agapanthus africanus	Perennial	8, 9, 12-24
Gazania	Perennial	8-24
Iris	Bulb	All Zones
Lantana	Shrub	12, 13, 15-23
Pelargonium peltatum	Perennial	15-17, 20-24
Verbena peruviana	Perennial	8-24

FOR SHADY PARKING STRIPS

NAME OF PLANT	KIND	CLIMATE ZONES
Asarum caudatum	Perennial	4-6, 15-17, 21
Pachysandra terminalis	Subshrub	1-10, 14-21
Viburnum davidii	Shrub	4-9, 14-24

PATTERN PLANTINGS AND NARROW STRIPS

NAME OF PLANT	KIND	CLIMATE ZONES
Festuca ovina 'Glauca'	Grass	All Zones
Irish moss and Scotch moss	Ground cover	All Zones
Juniperus procumbens 'Nana' (juniper)	Shrub	All Zones
Potentilla verna	Perennial	All Zones
Sedum (many kinds)	Succulent	Vary by kind
Teucrium chamaedrys 'Prostratum'	Shrub	All Zones
Thymus serpyllum (thyme)	Ground cover	All Zones

RUGGED GROWERS, INFORMAL, TAKE POOR SOIL

NAME OF PLANT	KIND	CLIMATE ZONES
Baccharis pilularis	Shrub	7-24
Cistus hybridus (rockrose)	Shrub	7-9, 14-24
Hypericum calycinum	Shrub	2-24

PLANTS TO DISCOURAGE CROSS TRAFFIC

NAME OF PLANT	KIND	CLIMATE ZONES
Berberis verruculosa	Shrub	4-6, 15-17
Cotoneaster dammeri	Shrub	All Zones
Pyracantha 'Santa Cruz'	Shrub	4-24

LAWN SUBSTITUTES

The home lawn is here to stay—a panel of green grass or dichondra makes a pretty setting for the house, looks cool, and is wonderful to play on. But there are many good ground covers and low shrubs that can be used in combination with a lawn or even as a substitute for a lawn. For the most part, these plants require less maintenance than grass or dichondra and still give the general visual impression of a lawn.

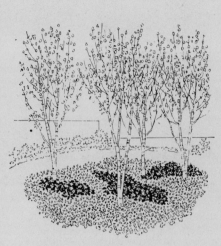

Most flat-growing ground covers will take some foot traffic—enough so that you can walk across them to weed, cut back, or rake off leaves. But they usually cannot stand up under children's play. If you have to walk regularly through a lawn substitute planting, place some stepping stones in it.

Shrubby-type ground covers are fairly permanent, and once planted will continue to serve for many years. In time the plants may mound up too high or grow too far out over walks. When that begins to happen, thin out and cut back the excess growth.

Since ground cover plants eventually put a solid layer of branches and leaves over the soil, and since it's next to impossible to do much cultivating when this happens, it's important to prepare the soil before planting as if you were putting in a lawn. Cultivate, remove rocks, incorporate soil conditioner and fertilizer, then rake level and plant.

SUBSTANTIAL COVERS FREQUENTLY USED IN LARGE AREAS:

NAME OF PLANT	KIND	CLIMATE ZONES
Carissa grandiflora 'Tuttle'	Shrub	13, 16-24
Ceanothus gloriosus	Shrub	5-9, 14-24
Ceanothus griseus horizontalis	Shrub	5-9, 14-24
Cotoneaster dammeri	Shrub	All Zones
Cotoneaster 'Lowfast'	Shrub	4-13
Euonymus fortunei 'Azusa'	Shrub	1-17
Euonymus fortunei radicans	Shrub	1-17

NAME OF PLANT	KIND	CLIMATE ZONES
Euonymus fortunei 'Colorata'	Shrub	1-17
Euonymus fortunei 'Vegeta'	Shrub	1-17
Hedera (ivy)	Vine	Vary by kind
Hypericum calycinum	Shrub	2-24
Juniperus	Ground cover	Vary by kind
Lonicera japonica 'Halliana'	Vine	2-24
Pachysandra terminalis	Shrub	1-10, 14-21
Pyracantha 'Santa Cruz'	Shrub	4-24
Pyracantha 'Walderi'	Shrub	4-24
Trachelospermum jasminoides (star jasmine)	Shrub	8-24
Vinca minor	Perennial	All Zones

NOT AS SUBSTANTIAL AS ABOVE BUT ATTRACTIVE LOW COVER WHEN PROPERLY CARED FOR:

NAME OF PLANT	KIND	CLIMATE ZONES
Ajuga	Perennial	All Zones
Fragaria chiloensis	Ground cover	4-24
Delosperma 'Alba' (see ice plant)	Succulent perennial	12-24
Drosanthemum floribundum (see ice plant)	Succulent perennial	14-24
Malephora (see ice plant)	Perennial	Vary by kind
Ophiopogon (see Liriope and Ophiopogon)	Perennial	5-9, 14-24
Pelargonium peltatum	Perennial	8, 9, 12-17, 22-24

USE IN SMALL AREAS AS A SUBSTITUTE FOR LAWN; GREEN CARPETS YOU CAN WALK ON.

NAME OF PLANT	KIND	CLIMATE ZONES
Anthemis nobilis	Perennial	All Zones
Irish moss, Scotch moss	Perennial	All Zones
Mentha requienii	Perennial	5-9, 12-24
Phyla nodiflora	Perennial	8-24
Thymus (thyme)	Ground cover	All Zones

PLANTING NEAR HOUSE OR FENCE

Some plants grow best on the north side of a wall or fence, where it's shady much of the day, and others grow on the south side where it is sunny and often hot. The lists on this page name plants that are notable for growing well in each of the four different exposures. Some of the plants can be espaliered, a few are vines that will climb on the wall, but most are meant to stand free, near the base of the wall. In this use, several plants of just one kind will be much more effective than a mixture of many different kinds.

FOR A WEST-FACING WALL

NAME OF PLANT	KIND	CLIMATE ZONES
Bamboo	Grass	Vary by kind
Bougainvillea	Vine	12, 13, 15-17, 19, 21-24
Callistemon (bottlebrush)	Shrub	8, 9, 12-24
Cotoneaster horizontalis perpusilla	Shrub	All Zones
Elaeagnus pungens	Shrub	4-24
Elaeagnus macrophylla 'Ebbingi'	Shrub	5-24
Fig	Tree	4-9, 12-24
Grewia caffra	Shrub	8, 9, 14-24
Hibbertia scandens	Vine	16, 17, 21-24
Photinia fraseri	Shrub	4-24
Pittosporum	Shrub	Vary by kind
Pyracantha	Shrub	Vary by kind
Rose, climbing	Shrub	Vary by kind
Solandra hartwegii	Vine	15-24
Wisteria	Vine	All Zones
Xylosma congestum	Shrub	8-24

FOR AN EAST-FACING WALL

Almost all west wall plants, plus these:

NAME OF PLANT	KIND	CLIMATE ZONES
Beaumontia grandiflora	Vine	13, 21-24
Camellia	Shrub	4-6, 8, 9, 14-24
Cocculus laurifolius	Shrub	7-9, 12-24
Eriobotrya (loquat)	Tree	Vary by kind
Escallonia	Shrub	4-9, 14-17, 20-24
Hibiscus rosa-sinensis	Shrub	9, 14-16, 19-24
Magnolia grandiflora	Tree	4-12, 14-24
Mahonia lomariifolia	Shrub	6-9, 14-24
Osmanthus delavayi	Shrub	4-9, 14-21
Osmanthus fragrans	Shrub	8, 9, 12-24
Podocarpus gracilior	Tree	8, 9, 13-24
Pyrus kawakamii	Tree	8, 9, 12-24
Trachelospermum (star jasmine)	Vine	Vary by kind
Viburnum japonicum	Shrub	5-9, 14-24
Viburnum suspensum	Shrub	8-24

FOR A SOUTH-FACING WALL

All of the above west-wall plants, plus these:

NAME OF PLANT	KIND	CLIMATE ZONES
Apple	Tree	Vary by kind
Beaumontia grandiflora	Vine	13, 21-24
Calliandra inaequilatera	Shrub	22-24
Citrus	Tree	8, 9, 12-24
Coprosma repens	Shrub	8, 9, 14-17, 21-24
Eriobotrya japonica (loquat)	Tree	4-24
Hibiscus rosa-sinensis	Shrub	9, 14-16, 19-24
Ilex cornuta 'Burfordii' (holly)	Shrub	4-24
Lonicera hildebrandiana (honeysuckle)	Vine	9, 14-17, 19-24
Magnolia grandiflora	Tree	4-12, 14-24
Parthenocissus tricuspidata (Boston ivy)	Vine	All Zones
Pear	Tree	Vary by kind
Phaedranthus buccinatorius	Vine	8, 9, 14-24
Pyrus kawakamii	Tree	8, 9, 12-24
Thunbergia grandiflora	Vine	16, 21-24
Viburnum rhytidophyllum	Shrub	2-9, 14-24

FOR A NORTH-FACING WALL

NAME OF PLANT	KIND	CLIMATE ZONES
Abutilon	Shrub	15-24
Azara microphylla	Shrub	15-24
Camellia	Shrub	4-6, 8, 9, 14-24
Clytostoma callistegiodes	Vine	9, 13-24
Euonymus fortunei 'Vegeta'	Shrub-vine	1-17
Fatshedera lizei	Shrub-vine	4-9, 14-24
Fatsia japonica	Shrub	4-9, 14-24
Ficus pumila	Vine	8-24
Fuchsia hybrids	Shrub	4-6, 15-17, 21-24
Griselinia lucida	Shrub	9, 14-17, 20-24
Hedera helix 'Baltica' (ivy)	Vine	All Zones
Hydrangea anomala petiolaris	Shrub-vine	1-21
Magnolia grandiflora espalier	Tree	4-12, 14-24
Osmanthus delavayi	Shrub	4-9, 14-21
Parthenocissus	Vine	All Zones
Photinia fraseri	Shrub	4-24
Pittosporum tobira	Shrub	8-24
Podocarpus	Tree-shrub	Vary by kind
Raphiolepis indica	Shrub	8-10, 14-24
Rhododendron (azalea)	Shrub	Vary by kind
Taxus baccata	Tree-shrub	1-9, 14-24
Ternstroemia gymnanthera	Shrub	4-9, 12-24

HEDGES AND SCREENS

Plants brought together in this group function in various ways. Some make low, trimmed hedges to border flower beds or walks. Some can serve as trimmed hedges three to six feet high to divide your property from street or adjoining property or to screen garden areas. A third use is as tall screens for privacy, sun or wind control.

NAME OF PLANT	CLIMATE ZONES	EVERGREEN	DECIDUOUS	LOW UNDER 18 INCHES	MEDIUM 1½ TO 5 FEET	TALL 5 TO 10 FT. AND MORE	SHEARED	NATURAL
Abelia	Vary by kind	●		●	●		●	●
Acacia	Vary by kind	●				●		●
Atriplex, tall-growing kinds	Vary by kind	●	●		●	●	●	●
Bamboo	Vary by kind	●		●	●	●		●
Berberis (barberry)	Vary by kind	●	●	●	●	●	●	●
Buxus (boxwood)	Vary by kind	●		●	●	●	●	●
Calocedrus decurrens (incense cedar)	1-12, 14-24	●				●	●	●
Camellia japonica	4-6, 8, 9, 14-24	●			●	●		●
Carissa grandiflora (Natal plum)	13, 16-24	●		●	●		●	●
Ceanothus	Vary by kind	●			●	●		●
Cephalotaxus harringtonia	4-6, 15-17	●				●		●
Chaenomeles (flowering quince)	1-21		●		●	●		●
Choisya ternata (Mexican orange)	4-9, 12-17	●			●	●		●
Cocculus laurifolius	7-9, 12-24	●			●	●		●
Coprosma repens (mirror plant)	8, 9, 14-17, 21-24	●			●	●	●	●
Cotoneaster	Vary by kind	●	●		●	●	●	●
Diosma (see page 235)	7-9, 14-24	●			●			●
Duranta	Vary by kind	●				●		●
Elaeagnus pungens	4-24	●			●	●	●	●
Erica arborea (see page 292)	4-6, 15-17, 21-24	●			●	●		●
Escallonia	7-9, 14-17, 20-24	●			●		●	●
Eucalyptus	Vary by kind	●				●	●	●
Euonymus	Vary by kind	●	●	●	●	●	●	●
Feijoa sellowiana (pineapple guava)	8, 9, 12-24	●			●	●	●	●
Gardenia	Vary by kind	●		●	●			●
Garrya elliptica	6-9, 14-21	●			●	●		●
Hakea	9, 12-17, 19-24	●				●		●
Hebe	14-24	●		●	●	●		●
Ilex aquifolium (English holly)	4-9, 15-17	●				●	●	●
Ilex cornuta (Chinese holly)	8, 9, 14-16, 18-21	●			●	●		●
Ilex crenata (Japanese holly)	2-9, 14-24	●		●	●	●	●	●

(Continued on next page)

Hedges and screens (cont'd.)

NAME OF PLANT	CLIMATE ZONES	EVERGREEN	DECIDUOUS	LOW UNDER 18 INCHES	MEDIUM 1½ TO 5 FEET	TALL 5 TO 10 FT. AND MORE	SHEARED	NATURAL
Itea ilicifolia	4-24	•				•		•
Larrea divaricata (creosote bush)	10-13, 19	•			•	•	•	•
Laurus nobilis (Grecian laurel)	6-10, 12-24	•				•	•	•
Lavandula (lavender)	Vary by kind	•		•	•		•	•
Leptospermum	15-24	•			•	•	•	•
Ligustrum (privet)	Vary by kind	•	•		•	•	•	•
Mahonia aquifolium (Oregon grape)	1-21	•			•	•		•
Myrica californica (Pacific wax myrtle)	4-6, 14-17, 20-24	•				•	•	•
Myrsine africana	8, 9, 14-24	•			•		•	•
Myrtus (myrtle)	Vary by kind	•		•	•	•	•	•
Nerium oleander (oleander)	8-16, 18-23	•			•	•		•
Olmediella betschleriana (Guatemalan holly)	9, 14-24	•				•	•	•
Osmanthus	Vary by kind	•			•	•	•	•
Pachistima myrsinites	1-10, 14-21	•		•	•		•	•
Photinia	Vary by kind	•	•			•		•
Pieris japonica	1-9, 14-17	•			•	•		•
Pittosporum	Vary by kind	•			•	•	•	•
Podocarpus	Vary by kind	•			•	•	•	•
Prunus caroliniana (Carolina laurel cherry)	7-24	•				•	•	•
Prunus ilicifolia (hollyleaf cherry)	7-9, 12-24	•			•	•	•	•
Prunus laurocerasus (English laurel)	4-9, 14-24	•				•	•	•
Prunus lyonii (Catalina cherry)	7-9, 12-24	•			•	•	•	•
Pseudotsuga menziesii (Douglas fir)	1-10, 14-17	•				•	•	
Psidium cattleianum (strawberry guava)	9, 14-24	•				•		•
Punica granatum 'Nana' (dwarf pomegranate)	5-24		•	•	•			•
Raphiolepis indica (India hawthorn)	8-10, 14-24	•			•			•
Rhamnus alaternus	4-24	•				•	•	•
Rhododendron	Vary by kind	•			•	•		•
Rhus lancea	8, 9, 12-24	•				•	•	•
Rosa (rose)	Vary by kind		•		•	•		•
Rosmarinus (rosemary)	4-24	•		•	•		•	•
Salix purpurea	All Zones		•			•	•	
Santolina	All Zones	•		•			•	•
Schinus molle (pepper tree)	8, 9, 12-24	•				•	•	
Sequoia sempervirens (coast redwood)	4-9, 14-24	•				•	•	•
Serenoa repens	7-9, 12-24	•			•			•
Syzygium paniculatum	16, 17, 19-24	•				•	•	•
Tamarix	Vary by kind	•	•			•	•	•
Taxus (yew)	1-9, 14-24	•			•	•	•	•
Teucrium chamaedrys	All Zones	•		•			•	•
Teucrium fruticans	4-24	•			•	•	•	•

Hedges and screens (cont'd.)

NAME OF PLANT	CLIMATE ZONES	EVERGREEN	DECIDUOUS	LOW UNDER 18 INCHES	MEDIUM 1½ TO 5 FEET	TALL 5 TO 10 FT. AND MORE	SHEARED	NATURAL
Thevetia	Vary by kind	●				●	●	●
Thuja occidentalis 'Fastigiata'	1-9, 15-17, 21-24	●				●	●	●
Thuja plicata (Western red cedar)	1-9, 14-24	●				●	●	●
Tsuga canadensis (Canada hemlock)	1-7, 14-17	●				●	●	●
Tsuga heterophylla (Western hemlock)	1-7, 14-17	●				●	●	●
Vaccinium ovatum (evergreen huckleberry)	4-7, 14-17	●			●	●	●	●
Viburnum	Vary by kind	●				●		●
Xylosma congestum	8-24	●				●	●	●

BACKGROUND PLANTS

These are the evergreen shrubs and trees often used to enclose a garden. For the most part they are large plants with foliage from the ground up. Flowering plants show off well against them. They give greater privacy than a six-foot fence and can screen out views of surrounding rooftops. Many of the shrubs eventually attain treelike proportions. Hedge plants (the preceding category) are usually sheared. These, on the other hand, are typically left alone to take their own form.

NAME OF PLANT	KIND	CLIMATE ZONES
Acacia longifolia	Shrub	8, 9, 14-24
Arbutus unedo	Shrub-tree	4-24
Bamboo	Grass	Vary by kind
Cocculus laurifolius	Shrub-tree	7-9, 12-24
Cotoneaster franchetii	Shrub	4-13
Cotoneaster pannosa	Shrub	4-24
Cotoneaster parneyi	Shrub	4-24
Cupressus glabra (cypress)	Tree	8-24
Dodonaea viscosa	Shrub	7-9, 12-24
Elaeagnus pungens	Shrub	4-24
Escallonia rubra	Shrub	4-9, 14-17, 20-24
Feijoa sellowiana	Shrub-tree	8, 9, 12-24
Ficus retusa nitida	Tree	9, 13-24
Griselinia littoralis	Shrub	9, 14-17, 20-24
Hakea suaveolens	Shrub	9, 12-17, 19-24
Itea ilicifolia	Shrub	4-24
Leptospermum laevigatum	Shrub-tree	14-24
Ligustrum (privet)		
Ligustrum japonicum	Shrub	4-24
Ligustrum japonicum 'Texanum'	Shrub	4-24
Ligustrum lucidum	Tree	5, 6, 8-24
Myrica californica	Shrub	4-6, 14-17, 20-24
Myrtus communis (myrtle)	Shrub	8-24
Nerium oleander	Shrub	8-16, 18-23
Osmanthus fragrans	Shrub	8, 9, 12-24
Osmanthus heterophyllus 'Ilicifolius'	Shrub	3-10, 14-24
Photinia fraseri	Shrub	4-24
Photinia serrulata	Shrub-tree	4-16, 18-22

NAME OF PLANT	KIND	CLIMATE ZONES
Pinus (pine)		
Pinus canariensis	Tree	8-11, 14-24
Pinus halepensis	Tree	8-24
Pinus muricata	Tree	8, 9, 14, 17, 22-24
Pinus nigra	Tree	1-12, 14-17
Pinus radiata	Tree	8, 9, 14-24
Pinus sylvestris	Tree	1-9, 14-17
Pittosporum crassifolium	Shrub-tree	9, 14-17, 19-24
Pittosporum eugenioides	Shrub-tree	9, 14-17, 19-22
Pittosporum tenuifolium	Shrub-tree	9, 14-17, 19-24
Pittosporum tobira	Shrub	8-24
Pittosporum undulatum	Shrub-tree	16, 17, 21-24
Podocarpus gracilior	Tree	8, 9, 13-24
Podocarpus macrophyllus	Shrub-tree	4-9, 12-24
Prunus caroliniana	Shrub-tree	7-24
Prunus ilicifolia	Shrub-tree	7-9, 12-24
Prunus laurocerasus	Shrub-tree	4-9, 14-24
Prunus lusitanica	Shrub-tree	4-9, 14-24
Pyracantha	Shrub	4-24
Rhamnus alaternus	Shrub-tree	4-24
Schinus polygamus (pepper tree)	Tree	8-24
Schinus terebinthifolius	Tree	15-17, 19-24
Sequoia sempervirens (coast redwood)	Tree	4-9, 14-24
Taxus baccata 'Stricta'	Shrub	1-9, 14-24
Viburnum cinnamomifolium	Shrub	5-9, 14-24
Viburnum japonicum	Shrub-tree	5-9, 14-24
Viburnum suspensum	Shrub	8-24
Xylosma congestum	Shrub-tree	8-24

STREET TREES AND SHADE TREES

Here are trees for your street or to give shade elsewhere. The encyclopedia gives sizes and habits. Your city may plant your street trees or tell you which trees you can plant here. If the city list disagrees with this list, the city is right. Special conditions rule out some fine trees. Trees that reach into the sky—too tall for a place under wires—become the community's treasured skyline when planted under open sky.

CLIMATE ZONES

★ = Star performer in zone indicated
● = Frequently recommended for zones indicated

NAME OF PLANT	E/D	1	2	3	4	5	6	7	8	9	10	11	12	13	14	15	16	17	18	19	20	21	22	23	24
Acer platanoides (Norway maple)	D	★	★	★	★	★	★	★	●	●															
Acer rubrum (scarlet maple)	D	★	★	★	★	★	★	●	●																
Acer saccharum (sugar maple)	D	●	●	●	●	★	★	●	●	●	●														
Aesculus carnea (red horsechestnut)	D	●	●	●	●	●	★	★	●						●	★	★	●							
Agonis flexuosa	E																					●	★	★	★
Albizia julibrissin (silk tree)	D							●	●	●	●	★	★	●	★	●	★	★	★	●	●	●	●	●	
Brachychiton acerifolium (flame tree)	E																		●	●		●			
Brachychiton discolor (pink flame tree)	E																		●		●	●			
Brachychiton populneum (bottle tree)	E													★	●	●	●		●	●	●	●			
Callistemon citrinus (lemon bottlebrush)	E								●	●			●	●	●	●	●	●	★	★	★	★	★	★	★
Callistemon viminalis (weeping bottlebrush)	E								●	●			●	●	●	●	●	●	★	★	★	●	●	●	●
Carpinus betulus (European hornbeam)	D	★	★	★	★	★	★	●	●						●	●	●								
Carpinus caroliniana (American hornbeam)	D							●	●	●					●	●	●								
Celtis australis (European hackberry)	D								★	★	●	●			★										
Celtis sinensis (Chinese hackberry)	D								★	★	●	●	●		★	●									
Ceratonia siliqua (carob)	E													●	●	●	●		★	★	★	★			
Cinnamomum camphora (camphor tree)	E													●	★	★		★	★	★	★	●			
Cornus florida (flowering dogwood)	D		★	★	●	●	●	●	●							●	●								
Crataegus lavallei (Carriere hawthorn)	D			●	★	★	★	●							●	●	●								
Crataegus oxyacantha (English hawthorn)	D	●	●	●	●	★	★	★	●						●	●	●								
Crataegus phaenopyrum (Washington thorn)	D	●	★	★	★	★	★	★	●						★	★	★								
Cupaniopsis anacardioides	E																			●	●	●	★	★	★
Dodonaea viscosa 'Purpurea'	E																		●	●	●	●	●	●	●
Erythea armata (Mexican blue palm)	E																		★	★	●	●	●	●	
Erythrina caffra	D																					●	★	★	★
Erythrina coralloides	D																				●	●	★	★	★
Eucalyptus camaldulensis	E								★	★	●	●	●	●	★				★	★	★	●	●	●	●
Eucalyptus citriodora (lemon-scented gum)	E																		●	●	●	●	★	★	★
Eucalyptus ficifolia (red-flowering gum)	E															●	★						★	★	★
Eucalyptus lehmannii	E																		●	●		●	●	★	★

Street trees and shade trees (cont'd.)

CLIMATE ZONES

★ = Star performer in zone indicated
● = Frequently recommended for zones indicated

NAME OF PLANT	EVERGREEN (E) / DECIDUOUS (D)	1	2	3	4	5	6	7	8	9	10	11	12	13	14	15	16	17	18	19	20	21	22	23	24
Eucalyptus leucoxylon macrocarpa 'Rosea'	E															●	●	●	●	●	●	●	●	●	●
Eucalyptus linearis (white peppermint)	E															●	★	●	●	●	●	★	★	●	●
Eucalyptus maculata	E																	●	●		●	●	●		
Eucalyptus melliodora	E															★	★	●			●	●			
Eucalyptus nicholii	E															●	●	●			●	●	●		
Eucalyptus polyanthemos (silver dollar gum)	E								●	★						★	★	★	★	★	★	★	★	●	●
Eucalyptus robusta (swamp mahogany)	E								●	●			●	●	●	●			●	●	●	●	●	●	●
Eucalyptus rudis	E								★	★				●	●	★	●		●	●	●	●	●	●	●
Eucalyptus sideroxylon (red ironbark)	E									●						●	★	★	●						
Fagus sylvatica (European beech)	D		●	●	●	★	★	●	●																
Ficus macrophylla (Moreton Bay fig)	E																	●			●	●	●	●	
Ficus retusa (and *F. r. nitida*)	E																●	★			●	●	●	●	
Ficus rubiginosa	E																				●	●	●	●	●
Fraxinus uhdei (evergreen ash)	E																		★	★	★	★	●	●	●
Fraxinus velutina (Arizona ash)	D										★	★	●	●	●	●	●				●	●	●		
Fraxinus velutina 'Modesto' (Modesto ash)	D								●	★	★	★	★	●	●	●	●				●	●	●		
Ginkgo biloba	D	●	●	●	●	●	●	●	●	●	●				●	★	★	●		●	●	●	●		
Gleditsia tricanthos inermis (thornless honey locust)	D	★	★	★	●	●	●	●	★	●	●	●	★						●	●					
Hakea laurina	E															●	●	●			●	●	●	●	
Harpephyllum caffrum	E																	●				●	●	●	●
Ilex altaclarensis 'Wilsonii' (Wilson holly)	E															●	●	●	●		●	●	●	●	●
Jacaranda acutifolia	D													●							●	●	★	★	●
Lagerstroemia indica (crape myrtle)	D								●	★	★		●	●	★				★	★	★	★			
Lagunaria patersonii	E																●	●			●	●	●	●	●
Laurus nobilis (Grecian laurel)	E								●	●	●					●	●	●	★						
Ligustrum lucidum (glossy privet)	E									●	●		●	●	●	●	●	●			●	●			
Liquidambar styraciflua	D	●	●	●	●	●	●	●	★	★	★				●	★	★	●		★	★	★	★	●	
Liriodendron tulipifera (tulip tree)	D	●	●	●	●	●	●	★	●	●						●	●	●		●	●				
Magnolia grandiflora	E				●	●	●	●	●	●						●	★	★		★	★	★	★	●	●
Malus (crabapple)	D	●	●	●	●	●	●	●	●							●	●	●							
Maytenus boaria (mayten tree)	E								★	★						★	★	★	★	●	●				
Melaleuca quinquenervia	E																				●	●		★	★
Metrosideros excelsa	E																	★						★	★
Morus alba (white mulberry)	D								●	●	●	★	★	★	●	●	●	●		●	●	●			
Myoporum laetum	E																	★	★					★	★
Nerium oleander (oleander)	E								●	●		●	●	●	●	●	●			★	★	★	★	★	★
Olmediella betschleriana (Guatemalan holly)	E																				●	●	●		
Persea borbonia	E																●	●			●	●	●	●	
Persea indica	E																	●	●			●	●	●	●

(Continued on next page)

Street trees and shade trees (cont'd.)

CLIMATE ZONES

★ = Star performer in zone indicated
● = Frequently recommended for zones indicated

NAME OF PLANT	E/D	1	2	3	4	5	6	7	8	9	10	11	12	13	14	15	16	17	18	19	20	21	22	23	24
Phoenix canariensis (Canary Island date palm)	E												●	●		●	●		●	●	●	●	●	●	●
Pinus canariensis (Canary Island pine)	E								●	●				●	●	●			★	★	★	★	●	●	
Pinus densiflora (Japanese red pine)	E				●	●	●																		
Pinus halepensis (Aleppo pine)	E								●	●	★	★	★	★	●				★	★	★	★	★	★	●
Pinus pinea (Italian stone pine)	E								●	●				●	★	★	●		★	★	★	★	●		
Pistacia chinensis (Chinese pistache)	D								★	★	●	●	●	●	●	★	★	★		★	★	★	★		
Pittosporum rhombifolium	E															●	●	●	●	●		●		●	●
Pittosporum undulatum	E																●	●					●	●	●
Pittosporum viridiflorum	E																					●	●	★	★
Platanus acerifolia (London plane tree)	D	●	●	●	●	●	●	●	●	●	●		●		●	●	●	★	●	●	●	●	●	●	●
Podocarpus gracilior	E								●	●					●	●	●								
Podocarpus macrophyllus	E								●	●					●	●	●	●	●	●	●	●			
Prunus blireiana (flowering plum)	D		●	●	●	●	●	●	●	●	●				●	●	●			●					
Prunus caroliniana (Carolina laurel cherry)	E							●	●	●			●	●	●	●			●	●	●	●	●	●	●
Prunus cerasifera 'Atropurpurea' (purple-leaf plum)	D		●	●	●	●	●	★	●	●					●	●	●								
Prunus lyonii (Catalina cherry)	E														●	●	●		●	●	●	●	●	●	●
Prunus sargentii (Sargent cherry)	D	●	●	●	●	●	●	●							●	●									
Prunus serrulata 'Sekiyama'	D		●	●	●	●	●	●	●	●					●	●	●								
Pyrus kawakamii (evergreen pear)	E														●	●	●				●	●	●		
Quercus agrifolia (coast live oak)	E								●	●					●	●	●		●	●	●	●	●	●	●
Quercus alba (white oak)	D	●	●	●	●	●	●	●																	
Quercus coccinea (scarlet oak)	D	●	●	●	●	●				●					●										
Quercus ilex (holly oak)	E								●	●					●	●	●	●		●	●	●	★	★	★
Quercus palustris (pin oak)	D	●	●	●	●	●	●	●	●	●					●	●	●								
Quercus rubra (red oak)	D	●	●	●	●	●		●	●										●	●	●				
Quercus suber (cork oak)	E								●	●					●				●	●	●				
Quercus virginiana (southern live oak)	E																		●	●	●				
Rhus lancea (African sumac)	E										★	★	●						●	●					
Schinus terebinthifolius (Brazilian pepper)	E													●	●	★		●	●	●		●	●	●	●
Sequoia sempervirens (coast redwood)	E														●	●		●	●	●	●	●	●	●	●
Sorbus aucuparia (European mountain ash)	D	●	●	●	●	●	●																		
Tilia americana (American linden)	D	●	●	●	●	●	●	●	●	●															
Tilia cordata (little-leaf linden)	D	●	●	●	●	●	●	●	●	●					●	●	●								
Tilia euchlora (Crimean linden)	D	●	●	●	●		●																		
Tristania conferta (Brisbane box)	E															●	●				●	●	●	★	★
Vitex lucens	E																						●	●	●
Washingtonia filifera (California fan palm)	E								●	●		★	★	●	●			★	★	●	●	●	●	●	●
Washingtonia robusta (Mexican fan palm)	E								●	●		★	★	●	●			★	★	★	★	★	★	★	★
Zelkova serrata	D	●	●	●	●	●	●	●	●	●					●	●	●								

TREES FOR GARDEN AND PATIO

This tree-finder chart can help you find a tree for a special purpose. To the right of each tree's name you'll find the climate zones in which it will grow. In the columns to the right of the zone numbers are characteristics that may distinguish the tree. Two of the columns indicate the tree's use in the garden—*patio tree* if it's a small tree that gives a nice display, *shade tree* if it casts a big pool of shade; sometimes both. If you want a flowering tree for the patio that will give summer shade and also let winter sun come through, look down the columns headed Deciduous, Patio Tree, Flowers, and Shade Tree. After finding a tree with all four characteristics, see if your zone number is listed for it. If it is, consider the tree as a candidate. For flower colors, tree size, growth habit, see the encyclopedia section.

NAME OF PLANT	CLIMATE ZONES	EVERGREEN	DECIDUOUS	PATIO TREE	DISTINCTIVE FOLIAGE	DISTINCTIVE BARK	DISTINCTIVE FORM	FLOWERS OR FRUITS	SHADE TREE
Acacia baileyana	8, 9, 13-24	●			●			●	
Acacia farnesiana	8, 9, 12-24	●						●	
Acacia pendula	13-24	●					●		
Acacia retinodes	8, 9, 13-24	●						●	
Acer (maple) Acer circinatum	1-6, 15-17		●				●		
Acer davidii	1-6, 15-17, 20, 21		●			●	●		●
Acer ginnala	1-9, 14-16		●				●		
Acer japonicum	1-6, 14-16		●				●		
Acer palmatum	1-9, 14-24		●	●					
Acmena smithii	15-17, 19-24	●			●			●	
Agonis flexuosa	15-17, 20-24	●				●	●		
Albizia julibrissin (silk tree)	2-23		●	●				●	●
Arbutus unedo	4-24	●					●	●	
Bauhinia variegata	13, 18-23	●		●				●	●
Bauhinia variegata candida	13, 18-23	●		●				●	●
Betula (birch) Betula nigra	All Zones		●			●	●		
Betula verrucosa	1-11, 14-24		●			●	●		
Betula verrucosa 'Dalecarlica'	1-11, 14-24		●			●	●		
Callistemon citrinus (lemon bottlebrush)	8, 9, 12-24	●						●	
Callistemon viminalis (weeping bottlebrush)	8, 9, 12-24	●					●	●	
Calodendrum capense	19, 21-24	●						●	
Ceanothus arboreus	5-9, 15-24	●						●	

(Continued on next page)

Trees for garden and patio (cont'd.)

NAME OF PLANT	CLIMATE ZONES	EVERGREEN	DECIDUOUS	PATIO TREE	DISTINCTIVE FOLIAGE	DISTINCTIVE BARK	DISTINCTIVE FORM	FLOWERS OR FRUITS	SHADE TREE
Cercidiphyllum japonicum	4-6		•		•		•		
Cercidium floridum (palo verde)	11-13, 18-20	•		•		•	•	•	•
Cercis canadensis (eastern redbud)	1-3, 7-9, 14-20		•	•			•	•	•
Cercis occidentalis (Western redbud)	2-9, 14-24		•					•	
Chionanthus virginicus (fringe tree)	1-6, 15-17		•					•	
Citrus, dwarf forms	8, 9, 12-24	•			•				
Clethra arborea	15-17, 21-24	•		•				•	
Cocculus laurifolius	7-9, 12-24	•			•				
Cornus florida (flowering dogwood)	1-9, 14-16		•	•			•	•	
Cornus nuttallii (Western dogwood)	2-9, 14-20		•				•	•	
Corynocarpus laevigatus (New Zealand laurel)	16, 17, 23, 24	•			•				
Cotinus coggygria	All Zones		•		•			•	
Crataegus (hawthorn)									
Crataegus 'Autumn Glory'	1-11, 14-17		•					•	
Crataegus lavallei	1-11, 14-17		•					•	
Crataegus oxyacantha	1-11, 14-17		•					•	
Crataegus phaenopyrum	1-11, 14-17		•					•	
Crinodendron patagua	14-24	•		•				•	
Cupaniopsis anacardioides	16, 17, 19-24	•		•	•				•
Dodonaea viscosa 'Purpurea'	7-9, 12-24	•		•	•				
Drimys winteri	8, 9, 14-24	•			•		•	•	
Eriobotrya deflexa (bronze loquat)	8, 9, 14-24	•		•	•				
Eriobotrya japonica (loquat)	4-24	•		•	•			•	
Erythrina (coral tree)									
Erythrina americana	12, 13, 19-24		•				•	•	
Erythrina bidwillii	8, 9, 12-24		•					•	
Erythrina coralloides	12, 13, 19-24		•				•	•	
Erythrina humeana	12, 13, 20-24		•					•	
Erythrina ovalifolia	12, 13, 19-24	•						•	
Eucalyptus									
E. caesia	15-17, 19-24	•				•		•	
E. cornuta	15-17, 19-24	•					•	•	•
E. erythrocorys	19-24	•						•	
E. erythronema	15-17, 19-24	•				•		•	
E. ficifolia	15-17, 22-24	•		•				•	
E. forrestiana	16, 17, 21-24	•		•			•	•	
E. lehmannii	16, 17, 21-24	•						•	•
E. leucoxylon macrocarpa 'Rosea'	8, 9, 12-24	•				•	•	•	

Trees for garden and patio (cont'd.)

NAME OF PLANT	CLIMATE ZONES	EVERGREEN	DECIDUOUS	PATIO TREE	DISTINCTIVE FOLIAGE	DISTINCTIVE BARK	DISTINCTIVE FORM	FLOWERS OR FRUITS	SHADE TREE
E. linearis	8, 9, 14-24	•		•	•		•		•
E. macrandra	8-24	•					•		
E. maculata	9, 14-24	•			•	•	•		
E. maculosa	15-17, 19-24	•		•		•	•		
E. microtheca	8-24	•		•	•		•		
E. nicholii	8-24	•		•			•		
E. pauciflora	8-24	•				•	•		
E. polyanthemos	8, 9, 12-24	•		•	•		•		•
E. pulverulenta	8, 9, 14-24	•			•				
E. sideroxylon	9, 14-17, 19-24	•		•	•			•	
E. stellulata	8-24	•		•	•	•	•		•
E. torquata	16, 17, 21-24	•		•			•	•	
Feijoa sellowiana (pineapple guava)	8, 9, 12-24	•					•	•	
Ficus retusa (and *F. r. nitida*)	9, 13-24	•		•	•				•
Hakea laurina	9, 12-17, 19-24	•		•	•			•	•
Harpephyllum caffrum	17, 19, 21-24	•		•	•				•
Heteromeles arbutifolia (toyon)	5-24	•						•	
Ilex altaclarensis 'Wilsonii' (Wilson holly)	3-24	•				•		•	
Jacaranda acutifolia	9, 13-24		•	•				•	•
Juniperus chinensis 'Torulosa' (Hollywood juniper)	All Zones	•					•		
Koelreuteria henryi (Chinese flame tree)	8-24			•				•	•
Koelreuteria paniculata (goldenrain tree)	2-21			•				•	•
Laburnum (goldenchain tree)	1-10, 14-17			•			•	•	
Lagerstroemia indica (crape myrtle)	1-9, 12-14, 18-21		•	•		•		•	
Laurus nobilis (Grecian laurel)	6-10, 12-24	•			•				
Leptospermum laevigatum (Australian tea tree)	15-24	•		•	•	•	•		
Ligustrum lucidum (glossy privet)	5, 6, 8-24	•		•	•				•
Liquidambar formosana	8, 9, 14-24		•		•		•		
Liquidambar styraciflua	1-9, 14-24		•		•		•		
Magnolia grandiflora	4-12, 14-24	•			•			•	•
Magnolia grandiflora 'Exoniensis'	4-12, 14-24	•		•	•			•	•
Magnolia grandiflora 'St. Mary'	4-12, 14-24	•		•	•			•	•
Magnolia kobus stellata	1-9, 14-24			•			•	•	
Malus (flowering crabapple)	1-11, 14-21			•			•	•	
Maytenus boaria (mayten tree)	8, 9, 14-21	•		•	•		•		•
Melaleuca ericifolia	9, 12-24	•				•			
Melaleuca hypericifolia	9, 12-24	•						•	
Melaleuca quinquenervia	9, 13, 16, 17, 20-24	•				•	•		•

(Continued on next page)

Trees for garden and patio (cont'd.)

NAME OF PLANT	CLIMATE ZONES	EVERGREEN	DECIDUOUS	PATIO TREE	DISTINCTIVE FOLIAGE	DISTINCTIVE BARK	DISTINCTIVE FORM	FLOWERS OR FRUITS	SHADE TREE
Myrica california (Pacific wax myrtle)	4-6, 14-17, 20-24	•			•				
Nerium oleander (oleander)	8-16, 18-23	•						•	
Olea europaea (olive)	7-24	•		•			•	•	•
Olmediella betschleriana (Guatemalan holly)	9, 14-24	•			•				
Persea indica	16, 17, 20-24	•		•	•				•
Pinus (pine)	Vary by kind	•					•		
Pistacia chinensis (Chinese pistache)	8-16, 18-23		•	•	•		•		•
Pittosporum crassifolium	9, 14-17, 19-24	•		•	•				•
Pittosporum phillyraeoides	9, 13-24	•		•	•		•		
Pittosporum rhombifolium	14-24	•		•	•				•
Pittosporum tobira	8-24	•		•	•				
Pittosporum undulatum	16, 17, 21-24	•		•	•				•
Pittosporum viridiflorum	15-17, 20-24	•			•				•
Poinciana gilliesii	8, 9, 12-16, 18-23		•					•	
Prunus blireiana (flowering plum)	2-12, 14-20		•	•	•			•	
Prunus caroliniana (Carolina laurel cherry)	7-24	•		•	•				•
Prunus cerasifera 'Atropurpurea' (purple-leaf plum)	2-20		•		•			•	
Prunus lyonii (Catalina cherry)	7-9, 12-24	•		•	•				
Prunus serrulata 'Beni Hoshi'	2-7, 14-20		•	•			•	•	
Prunus serrulata 'Sekiyama'	2-7, 14-20		•	•			•	•	
Prunus serrulata 'Shirofugen'	2-7, 14-20		•	•			•	•	
Prunus subhirtella autumnalis	2-7, 14-20		•	•			•	•	
Prunus yedoensis 'Akebono'	2-7, 14-20		•	•			•	•	
Punica granatum (pomegranate)	5-24		•					•	
Pyrus kawakamii (evergreen pear)	8, 9, 12-24	•		•				•	
Robinia pseudoacacia 'Decaisneana' (pink flowering locust)	All Zones		•					•	•
Schinus terebinthifolius (Brazilian pepper)	15-17, 19-24	•		•			•	•	•
Sophora secundiflora	8-16, 18-24	•		•				•	•
Sorbus aucuparia (European mountain ash)	1-6, 15-17		•					•	
Stenocarpus sinuatus (firewheel tree)	16, 17, 20-24	•						•	
Stewartia koreana	4-6, 14-17, 20, 21		•				•	•	
Styrax japonica	1-10, 12-21		•	•			•	•	
Styrax obassia	1-10, 12-21		•				•	•	
Tipuana tipu	14-16, 18-24		•	•				•	
Tristania conferta (Brisbane box)	15-24	•				•	•		
Vitex lucens	16, 17, 22-24	•					•	•	
Xylosma congestum	8-24	•		•					•

PLANTING AROUND A POOL

The first list is of plants to grow around swimming pools. They should be as litter-free as possible and lack bristles or thorns. There are no *trees* listed for Zones 1 to 3. The reason is that broad-leafed evergreens are best for this purpose (deciduous leaf fall and conifer needles make too much mess) and there are no trees of this type for the cold-winter areas.

The second list is of plants for small garden pools. Choose plants from this list if the pool is watertight. But, if the soil around the pool is always wet, select from the Wet Places list, page 158.

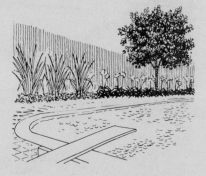

SWIMMING POOLS

TREES

NAME OF PLANT	CLIMATE ZONES
Callistemon citrinus	8, 9, 12-24
Chamaerops humilis	5-24
Cordyline australis	8-11, 14-24
Ficus	Vary by kind
Magnolia grandiflora	4-12, 14-24
Yucca elephantipes	16, 17, 19-24

LOW BORDER PLANT OR TALL GROUND COVER (TO 3 FEET)

NAME OF PLANT	CLIMATE ZONES
Agapanthus	8, 9, 12-24
Ferns	Vary by kind
Juniperus (juniper)	All Zones
Moraea iridioides	8-24
Pyracantha	Vary by kind
Rosmarinus officinalis 'Lockwood de Forest'	4-24
Viburnum davidii	4-9, 14-24

TALL BACKGROUND OR SCREENING PLANTS (6 FEET AND OVER)

NAME OF PLANT	CLIMATE ZONES
Camellias	4-6, 8, 9, 14-24
Carissa grandiflora	13, 16-24
Griselinia	9, 14-17, 20-24
Ilex (holly)	Vary by kind
Juniperus	All Zones
Ligustrum japonicum	4-24
Ligustrum lucidum	5, 6, 8-24
Nandina domestica	5-24
Phormium tenax	7-24
Pittosporum	Vary by kind
Rhododendrons	Vary by kind
Ternstroemia gymnanthera	4-9, 12-24
Viburnum tinus	4-12, 14-23

MEDIUM-SIZED SHRUBS (4 TO 5 FEET)

NAME OF PLANT	CLIMATE ZONES
Carissa grandiflora 'Tuttle'	13, 16-24
Ilex (holly)	Vary by kind
Juniperus	All Zones
Pinus mugo mughus	1-11, 14-24
Pinus thunbergiana	1-12, 14-24
Pittosporum	Vary by kind
Pyracantha	Vary by kind
Raphiolepis	8-10, 14-24
Rosmarinus officinalis	4-24
Strelitzia reginae	9, 12-24
Xylosma congestum	8-24
Yucca gloriosa	7-24

VINES

NAME OF PLANT	CLIMATE ZONES
Cissus	Vary by kind
Ficus pumila	8-24

SMALL GARDEN POOLS AND PONDS

PLANTS THAT PROVIDE COLORFUL FLOWERS AND/OR FRUITS

NAME OF PLANT	KIND	CLIMATE ZONES
Ajuga	Perennial	All Zones
Astilbe	Perennial	2-9, 14-24
Azalea (see page 395)	Shrub	Vary by kind
Canna	Bulb	All Zones
Cornus (dogwood)	Shrub, tree	Vary by kind
Dierama	Bulb	4-24
Erythronium	Bulb	1-7, 15-17
Hemerocallis (daylily)	Perennial	All Zones
Iris kaempferi	Bulb	All Zones
Lythrum salicaria	Perennial	All Zones
Mahonia	Shrub	Vary by kind
Moraea iridioides	Bulb	8-24

INTERESTING FOLIAGE PATTERNS

NAME OF PLANT	KIND	CLIMATE ZONES
Acer circinatum	Shrub	1-6, 15-17
Acer palmatum	Shrub	1-9, 14-24
Chamaerops humilis	Tree	5-24
Cornus (dogwood)	Shrub, tree	Vary by kind
Cyperus alternifolius	Perennial	8, 9, 12-24
Cyperus papyrus	Perennial	8, 9, 12-24
Dierama	Bulb	4-24
Erythronium	Bulb	1-7, 15-17
Liriope and Ophiopogon japonicus	Perennial	5-9, 14-24
Philodendron selloum	Shrub	8, 9, 12-24
Phoenix reclinata	Palm	23, 24
Pittosporum phillyraeoides	Shrub	9, 13-24
Salix (willow)	Shrub	Vary by kind

WINDBREAKS

The need for a windbreak exists chiefly in those climates where a wind blows from a predictable direction daily or almost daily all through certain seasons. The best plan is to lift the wind gradually. If you have space, do it with as many as five rows of shrubs and trees with rows 16 feet apart. If space is limited, use a row of shrubs on the windward side and trees inside. Even if space allows only one row, some bushy trees will do the job adequately.

NAME OF PLANT	KIND	CLIMATE ZONES	EVERGREEN	DECIDUOUS	COASTAL WINDS	INTERIOR WINDS	FREEZING WINDS
Acacia cyclops	Shrub	8, 9, 13-24	•		•		
Acacia longifolia	Shrub	8, 9, 14-24	•		•	•	
Acacia melanoxylon	Tree	8, 9, 13-24	•		•	•	
Acacia verticillata	Shrub	14-24	•		•		
Bambusa oldhamii (see page 194)	Bamboo	16-24	•			•	
Calocedrus decurrens (incense cedar)	Tree	1-12, 14-24	•			•	•
Caragana arborescens	Shrub-tree	1-21		•		•	•
Casuarina stricta	Tree	7-9, 11-24	•		•	•	
Cortaderia selloana (pampas grass)	Grass	4-24	•		•	•	
Cupressus glabra (cypress)	Tree	8-24	•			•	•
Cupressus macrocarpa	Tree	17	•		•		
Dodonaea viscosa	Shrub	7-9, 12-24	•			•	
Elaeagnus angustifolia	Tree	1-3, 7-14, 18, 19		•		•	•
Elaeagnus pungens	Shrub	4-24	•		•	•	
Escallonia	Shrub	4-9, 14-17, 20-24	•		•	•	
Eucalyptus E. camaldulensis	Tree	8, 9, 12-24	•			•	
E. cladocalyx	Tree	15-17, 19-24	•		•		
E. cornuta	Tree	15-17, 19-24	•		•		
E. globulus	Tree	15-17, 19-24	•		•		
E. globulus 'Compacta'	Tree	15-17, 19-24	•		•		
E. grossa	Shrub	15-17, 19-24	•		•		
E. gunnii	Tree	5, 6, 8, 9, 14-24	•		•	•	
E. lehmannii	Tree	16, 17, 21-24	•		•		
E. melliodora	Tree	15-24	•		•	•	
E. microtheca	Tree	8-24	•			•	
E. platypus	Shrub-tree	15-17, 19-24	•		•		
E. robusta	Tree	8, 9, 12-24	•		•	•	
E. rudis	Tree	8, 9, 12-24	•		•	•	
E. spathulata	Tree	15-17, 19-24	•		•	•	

NAME OF PLANT	KIND	CLIMATE ZONES	EVERGREEN	DECIDUOUS	COASTAL WINDS	INTERIOR WINDS	FREEZING WINDS
Hakea suaveolens	Shrub-tree	9, 12-17, 19-24	•		•	•	
Juniperus scopulorum (juniper)	Shrub-tree	All Zones	•			•	•
Juniperus virginiana	Shrub-tree	All Zones	•			•	•
Lagunaria patersonii	Tree	13, 15-24	•		•		
Leptospermum laevigatum	Shrub-tree	15-24	•		•		
Ligustrum japonicum 'Texanum' (privet)	Shrub	4-24	•		•	•	
Ligustrum lucidum	Tree	5, 6, 8-24	•		•	•	
Lonicera tatarica (honeysuckle)	Shrub	1-21		•			•
Myoporum laetum	Shrub-tree	8, 9, 14-17, 19-24	•		•		
Nerium oleander (oleander)	Shrub	8-16, 18-23	•			•	
Picea abies (spruce)	Tree	1-6, 15-17	•				•
Pinus (pine)							
Pinus canariensis	Tree	8-11, 14-24	•		•	•	
Pinus contorta	Tree	4-6, 14-17	•		•		
Pinus halepensis	Tree	8-24	•			•	
Pinus muricata	Tree	8, 9, 14-17, 22-24	•		•		
Pinus nigra	Tree	1-12, 14-17	•				•
Pinus ponderosa	Tree	1-12, 14-17	•			•	
Pinus radiata	Tree	8, 9, 14-24	•		•		
Pinus sylvestris	Tree	1-9, 14-17	•				•
Pittosporum crassifolium	Shrub	9, 14-17, 19-24	•		•	•	
Pittosporum undulatum	Shrub-tree	16, 17, 21-24	•		•		
Populus nigra 'Italica' (Lombardy poplar)	Tree	All Zones		•	•	•	•
Prunus caroliniana	Shrub-tree	7-24	•		•	•	
Prunus lyonii	Shrub-tree	7-9, 12-24	•		•		
Pseudotsuga menziesii (Douglas fir)	Tree	1-10, 14-17	•		•		
Pyracantha (tall growing)	Shrub	Vary by kind	•		•	•	
Rhamnus alaternus	Shrub	4-24	•		•	•	
Robinia (locust) Robinia 'Idaho'	Tree	All Zones		•		•	•
Robinia pseudoacacia	Tree	All Zones		•		•	•
Robinia pseudoacacia 'Decaisneana'	Tree	All Zones		•		•	•
Sequoia sempervirens (coast redwood)	Tree	4-9, 14-24	•		•		
Syringa vulgaris	Shrub	1-11, 14-16, 18-22		•			•
Tamarix aphylla	Tree	10-13	•			•	
Taxus (yew) Taxus baccata 'Stricta'	Shrub-tree	1-9, 14-24	•			•	
Taxus cuspidata	Shrub-tree	1-9, 14-24	•		•		
Taxus media	Shrub-tree	1-9, 14-24	•		•		
Thuja occidentalis (arborvitae)	Shrub-tree	1-9, 15-17, 21-24	•		•	•	•
Thuja plicata	Tree	1-9, 14-24	•		•		•

FAST-GROWING PLANTS

Here are the plants that grow fast. In the case of a shrub, tree or vine, "fast" means that it will grow rapidly enough (upwards and sideways) to begin assuming its mature role in the landscape in one to four years. In the case of an annual or perennial, "fast" means that it will reach an impressive size within a year.

The way things often work out, you may have to accept some other less desirable attributes along with the fast growth you seek. The price you have to pay could be weediness, an unkempt quality, or overgrowth. In a few cases you have a lifetime garden guest, less and less welcome, that you cannot eradicate short of using dynamite. That's why the right-hand column of the chart answers the question: Are there any faults that offset the speed advantage? If there are no such faults, that column either tells you so or just mentions some of the plant's favorable attributes.

As a double-check on possible surprises (good or bad) that any one of the fast growers may hold in store for you, read thoroughly the description of the plant in the Western Plant Encyclopedia. Some plants simply grow fast under almost any conditions. Others definitely need a certain environment and culture to grow with racehorse speed.

NAME OF PLANT	KIND	CLIMATE ZONES	ANY FAULTS THAT OFFSET THE SPEED ADVANTAGE?
Abutilon	Shrub	15-24	Unless you pinch branch tips regularly, plants can become coarse and rangy.
Acacia			Many kinds grow fast and begin to play their parts in the landscape within 2 or 3 years. But many get rangy. Most are short-lived. To select the fastest for your purpose, see pages 169 to 171.
Acanthus mollis	Perennial	4-24	Large, glossy leaves in attractive pattern. Can be difficult to eradicate.
Ailanthus altissima	Tree	All Zones	Beautiful and fast but suckers profusely.
Ajuga reptans	Perennial	All Zones	Fast-growing, blue-flowered ground cover with no real faults at all.
Albizia distachya	Tree	15-17, 22-24	Best for temporary screening.
Alnus rhombifolia (alder)	Tree	1-9, 14-21	Fast with ample water.
Betula verrucosa (birch)	Tree	1-11, 14-24	Handsome tree with good manners. Not as fast as some of the trees charted here.
Buddleia davidii	Shrub	1-9, 12-24	Grows like a weed. Has pretty flowers. If not maintained, can look like a big weed with pretty flowers.
Ceanothus			Most kinds of ceanothus grow very fast and fulfill landscaping roles quickly. But they are relatively short-lived. Choose the fast one you want on pages 217 to 219.
Celastrus scandens	Vine	1-7	With support, makes vigorous, twining screen.
Choisya ternata (Mexican orange)	Shrub	7-9, 12-24	Fast, with fragrant white flowers. But it's touchy about soil conditions and gets many pests.
Chrysanthemum frutescens (marguerite)	Perennial	14-24	Small plants set out in spring will be 4 feet wide by summer. Many flowers. Short-lived.
Cistus (rockrose)	Shrub	4-9, 12-15, 18-22	Fast, even in poor soil. Showy flowers. No bad habits.
Clematis armandii	Vine	4-9, 12-24	Fast when established. White flowers. Evergreen. Jungle thicket in few years unless pruned carefully.

Fast-growing plants (cont'd.)

NAME OF PLANT	KIND	CLIMATE ZONES	ANY FAULTS THAT OFFSET THE SPEED ADVANTAGE?
Colocasia esculenta	Perennial	All Zones	Huge leaves give lush tropical effect.
Cornus stolonifera (dogwood)	Shrub	1-9, 14-21	Rank growing to 15 feet. Multi-stemmed. Deciduous.
Cortaderia selloana (pampas grass)	Grass	4-24	May grow 8 feet in 1 year. Attractive flower plumes.
Cotoneaster lactea	Shrub	4-24	Handsome, upright. Red berries. Evergreen.
Crotalaria agatiflora	Shrub	13, 15-24	Unique, birdlike flowers. Evergreen. Fast. Needs pruning 2 or 3 times a year.
Cyperus papyrus	Perennial	8, 9, 12-24	Moisture-loving. Attractive form.
Cytisus (broom)	Shrub	Vary by kind	Vigorous and quick but can become weedy.
Daubentonia tripetii	Shrub	7-9, 12-16, 18-23	Fast growing but not long lived. Showy flowers. Deciduous.
Dodonaea viscosa	Shrub	7-9, 12-24	Quickly makes a dense shrub. Evergreen.
Dombeya	Shrub	21-24	Large, tropical looking leaves. Pink to red flowers in winter. Evergreen.
Elaeagnus	Shrub	Vary by kind	All kinds grow fast. and abundantly. Not showy but serviceable.
Eriobotrya deflexa (loquat)	Tree	8, 9, 14-24	Makes a handsome display of foliage in a hurry.
Escallonia	Shrub	4-9, 14-17, 20-24	Becomes big mass of foliage quickly. Nice flowers, too.
Eucalyptus	Most kinds grow fast and begin to fulfill their appointed roles in the landscape in 1 to 3 years. See pages 263 to 271.		
Fatshedera lizei	Shrubby vine	4-9, 14-24	Polished leaves on fast-growing stems. Train it or it becomes a puzzle.
Fatsia japonica	Shrub	4-9, 14-24	Glossy, fanlike leaves. Needs some pest control.
Felicia amelloides	Perennial	8, 9, 13-24	Profusion of blue flowers. Needs regular pruning or cutting back to avoid ragged look.
Forsythia intermedia	Shrub	1-11, 14-16	Masses of yellow flowers in early spring. Needs pruning, little else.
Fraxinus uhdei (ash)	Tree	9, 12-24	Fast growing, with no serious faults in its best climates.
Fuchsia hybrida	Shrub	2-9, 14-17, 20-24	Needs much care but repays in vigorous growth, great show of flowers.
Gleditsia triacanthos (honey locust)	Tree	1-13, 18-20	Some kinds have grown 8 feet a year. Some have messy pods, pavement-cracking roots, thorns.
Grevillea robusta (silk oak)	Tree	8, 9, 12-24	Fast under tough conditions but also somewhat messy and brittle.
Hakea suaveolens	Shrub	9, 12-17, 19-24	Useful screen plant with fragrant white flowers.
Hedera (ivy)	Vine	Vary by kind	Slow to start, fast after established.
Hydrangea	Shrub	Vary by kind	Fast and floriferous if given conditions it needs. If not, it sits and sulks.
Hypericum calycinum	Shrub	2-24	Tough but may become invasive unless confined. Yellow flowers.
Lavatera trimestris	Annual	All Zones	Grows 3 to 6 feet from seed in one year. Colorful flowers.
Ligustrum lucidum (privet)	Tree	5, 6, 8-24	Glossy leaves. Becomes a tree quickly and has few faults.
Lonicera hildebrandiana (honeysuckle)	Vine	9, 14-17, 19-24	Heavy ropelike branches need strong support. Many fragrant flowers.

(Continued on next page)

Fast-growing plants (cont'd.)

NAME OF PLANT	KIND	CLIMATE ZONES	ANY FAULTS THAT OFFSET THE SPEED ADVANTAGE?
Magnolia veitchii	Tree	4-9, 14-24	Very fast. Branches are brittle. Needs wind protection.
Morus alba, fruitless forms (mulberry)	Tree	All Zones	Grows fast and full under many conditions but needs pruning to shape up well.
Myoporum laetum	Shrub-tree	8, 9, 14-17, 19-24	Excellent for beach plantings. Dark green, shiny leaves.
Myrica californica	Shrub-tree	4-6, 14-17, 20-24	Clean looking, glossy foliage all year.
Parthenocissus quinquefolia (Virginia creeper)	Vine	All Zones	Ground cover or clinging vine. Dependable fall color.
Paulownia tomentosa	Tree	All Zones	A surface-rooting litter-maker but with nice flowers and foliage.
Philadelphus (mock orange)	Shrub	Vary by kind	Large, vigorous, deciduous shrubs with many white flowers. Need annual pruning.
Philodendron	Vine or shrub	Vary by kind	Leathery, glossy, evergreen leaves. Vine types get leggy in due time.
Phyllostachys bambusoides (see page 193)	Bamboo	4-24	Bold and handsome but must be curbed or will invade all around.
Phormium tenax (New Zealand flax)	Perennial	5-24	Swordlike leaves in fan pattern. Tall flower stalks. No major shortcomings.
Pinus (pine)			Many pines grow fast and begin to carry full weight in landscape in just a few years. Choose a fast grower from the many charted on pages 368 to 373.
Pistacia chinensis	Tree	8-16, 18-23	Noted for beautiful fall colors. Prune young trees to shape.
Platanus (plane tree, sycamore)	Tree	Vary by kind	Tolerant of many environmental conditions but subject in some areas to diseases. Ask locally.
Populus (poplar, cottonwood, aspen)	Tree	Vary by kind	Fast, tough, hardy, and easy, but roots are extremely invasive. Many form root suckers.
Prunus laurocerasus (English laurel)	Shrub	4-9, 14-24	Well known, popular hedge plant. Leathery, glossy leaves. Greedy and difficult to garden under.
Pyracantha coccinea	Shrub	All Zones	Vigorous, tall shrub with decorative berries. Needs thoughtful annual pruning to make best display.
Rhus (sumac)	Shrub	Vary by kind	Some kinds sucker, others need good drainage. Variously known for handsome foliage, decorative fruits.
Ricinus communis (castor bean)	Annual	All Zones	Can grow 6 to 15 feet in one season. Leafy background in a hurry. Poisonous seeds.
Romneya coulteri	Perennial	5-10, 12-24	Spectacular white flowers. Gray-green leaves. Invasive.
Salix (willow)			Most willows grow very fast, need plenty of water, have invasive roots, are hard to garden under. The kinds are described on page 410.
Sequoia sempervirens (coast redwood)	Tree	4-9, 14-24	The famous redwood grows fast (3 to 5 feet a year) and high. Easy to live with.
Sparmannia africana	Shrub-tree	17, 21-24	Fast; needs water, feeding, some pest control, pruning.
Tipuana tipu	Tree	14-16, 18-24	Broad, flattened crown. Showy flowers. Fast with no notable bad habits.
Ulmus parvifolia (Chinese elm)	Tree	8, 9, 12-24	Very fast. The price: variable form, aggressive and competitive roots, need for thinning and pruning.
Wigandia caracasana	Treelike perennial	17, 22-24	Coarse-appearing plant with large leaves. Early spring flowers. Prickly.
Wisteria	Vine	All Zones	Fast, long-lived, beautiful, dependable—but you must train it and prune it to live with it.

PLANTS THAT ARE EASY TO GROW

Plants on the following lists are easy to grow, relatively free of pests and diseases, and useful in many landscape situations. They will give maximum performance with minimum effort on the gardener's part. The lists cover shrubs, perennials, annuals, bulbs, vines, and Western native plants (mostly shrubs). Trees are not listed here; they are covered in other lists. Native plants are separated from common garden plants primarily because they are easy only with reservations. They are easy in the regions where they grow wild or in gardens where they can be given conditions approximating those in their native sites. A garden of native plants can be an easy-to-grow garden with planning; without planning it may be a high-mortality garden.

SHRUBS

NAME OF PLANT	CLIMATE ZONES	QUALITIES	USES
Abelia 'Edward Goucher'	5-24	Lilac-pink flowers over long season, lacy texture. Evergreen to partly deciduous.	Shrub gardens, foundation plantings, low dividers.
Abelia grandiflora	5-24	White, pink-tinged flowers, long bloom season. Evergreen to partly deciduous.	Shrub borders, screen, tall foundation plantings.
Arbutus unedo	4-24	Handsome form, bark, leaves. White flowers, red fruits. Evergreen.	Screen or background. Can be pruned into multiple-trunk tree.
Aucuba	4-11, 14-23	Big, leathery leaves, often variegated. Red fruit. Evergreen.	One of most reliable shade plants for open ground or container.
Callistemon citrinus (bottlebrush)	8, 9, 12-24	Coppery new growth, bright red flowers over long season. Evergreen.	Screen, hedge, big shrub, espalier, small tree (trained).
Carissa grandiflora	13, 16-24	Glossy foliage, showy white flowers, edible red fruits. Evergreen.	Many kinds in sizes suitable for ground cover, screens, espaliers.
Chaenomeles (flowering quince)	1-21	Picturesque form, bright flowers, shiny leaves. Deciduous.	Border, espalier, container. Tall and low kinds available.
Elaeagnus pungens	4-24	Strongly angular outline, olive-drab foliage color. Evergreen.	Screen, container. Takes heat, wind, dryish soil.
Fatsia japonica (Japanese aralia)	4-9, 14-24	Big, bold dark green leaves with tropical look. Evergeen.	Massed or single for silhouette. Containers.
Feijoa sellowiana (pineapple guava)	8, 9, 14-24	Glossy foliage with gray tone, showy flowers, edible fruit. Evergreen.	Espalier, screen, hedge, or (trained) small tree.
Juniperus, shrubby kinds (junipers)	All Zones	Green, grayish, bluish, or golden foliage, neat growth. Evergreen.	Ground cover, bank cover, screen, hedge, foundation plantings.
Ligustrum japonicum 'Texanum' (privet)	4-24	Compact growth habit, glossy green leaves. Evergreen.	Hedge, screen, shaped plants, small standard trees, containers.
Mahonia aquifolium (Oregon grape)	1-21	Leathery, handsome leaves. Bronzy new growth. Yellow flowers, blue fruits. Evergreen.	Foundation plantings, woodland gardens, low screen, in containers.
Myrtus communis 'Compacta' (myrtle)	8-24	Densely-set small leaves. Compact growth habit. Evergreen.	Low edging, low hedge, foundation planting.
Nandina domestica	5-24	Erect stems, airy foliage, red winter color, red fruits. Evergreen.	Use for airy, vertical effect. Screen, tub plant.
Nerium oleander (oleander)	8-16, 18-24	Narrow, dark green leaves, showy flowers in white, pink, red. Evergreen.	Screens, borders, backgrounds, small trees.

(Continued on next page)

Plants that are easy to grow . . . shrubs (cont'd.)

NAME OF PLANT	CLIMATE ZONES	QUALITIES	USES
Pittosporum tobira	8-24	Clean-looking foliage, fragrant flowers, showy seed capsules. Evergreen.	Screens, massing, trained as small, crooked-stemmed tree.
Podocarpus gracilior	8, 9, 13-24	Billowy masses of soft-looking foliage. Highly trainable. Evergreen.	Espalier, vine, tree, shrub, hedge, container plant, indoor plant.
Podocarpus macrophyllus	4-9, 12-24	Rich, bright green foliage. Takes wide range of conditions. Evergreen.	Big shrub, tree, espalier. Container plant indoors or out.
Raphiolepis indica	8-10, 14-24	Leathery leaves, bronzy new growth, profuse bloom, blue fruits. Evergreen.	Background, ground cover, informal hedge, low divider.
Rosmarinus officinalis 'Prostratus' (rosemary)	4-24	Aromatic gray and green foliage, light lavender-blue flowers. Evergreen.	Ground cover, trailing over wall or raised bed.
Sarcococca ruscifolia	4-9, 14-24	Deep green leaves, orderly growth, fragrant flowers. Evergreen.	Shade plant for containers, raised beds, open ground, espalier.
Xylosma congestum	8-24	Shiny, clean, yellow-green foliage, graceful habit. Evergreen.	Ground cover, espalier, hedge, single or multiple trunk tree.

PERENNIALS

Agapanthus africanus	8, 9, 12-24	Rich green foliage, blue or white flowers. Evergreen.	Borders, containers.
Hemerocallis (daylily)	All Zones	Sword-shaped leaves, bright flowers in wide color range. Evergreen or deciduous.	Borders, massing, bank plantings, ground cover, cut flowers.
Iris, Tall Bearded	All Zones	Sword-shaped leaves, bright flowers in many colors. Evergreen.	Borders, massing, cutting.

ANNUALS

Begonia semperflorens	All Zones	Waxy green to reddish leaves, profusion of flowers over long season. Evergreen mildest climates; grow as annual elsewhere.	Mass plantings, edgings, containers. Sun near coast, part shade elsewhere.
Lobularia maritima (sweet alyssum)	All Zones	Low, compact masses of flower color. Quick, dependable.	Carpeting, edging, bulb cover, temporary filler, between flagstones, containers.
Petunia hybrida (petunia)	All Zones	Profusion of large, fragrant flowers in many colors. Perennial grown as annual.	Buy in flats for quick, long-lasting show of flowers.
Tagetes (marigold)	All Zones	Bright flowers over a long season.	Flower beds, edging, containers, cutting.

BULBS

Narcissus (daffodil)	All Zones	Yellow, white, orange, bicolor flowers. Deciduous.	Under trees and shrubs, in borders, containers, for cutting.

VINES

Hedera canariensis (Algerian ivy)	8, 9, 12-24	Large, lush, glossy leaves in green or green and white. Evergreen.	Ground cover, bank cover, erosion control, vine.
Hedera helix (English ivy)	All Zones	Dark leaves with paler veins. Many varieties with different leaf shapes. Evergreen.	Ground cover, bank cover, vine, house plant, formal sheared plant.
Parthenocissus (Boston ivy and Virginia creeper)	All Zones	Deciduous. Vines cling to walls. Dependable fall leaf color.	Dense, even wall cover, or bank cover.
Trachelospermum jasminoides (star jasmine)	8-24	Lustrous, dark green leaves, fragrant white flowers. Evergreen.	Vine, ground cover, raised beds, edging.

Plants that are easy to grow (cont'd.)

NATIVE PLANTS

NAME OF PLANT	CLIMATE ZONES	QUALITIES	USES
Acer circinatum (vine maple)	1-6, 15-17	Picturesque habit, fall foliage color. Deciduous.	Woodland garden with ferns, shade plants. Espaliers.
Arctostaphylos columbiana (hairy manzanita)	4-6, 15-17	Picturesque branches, bark. Gray-green foliage, white flowers.	Highway plantings, roadside, bank cover.
Arctostaphylos densiflora 'Howard McMinn'	7-9, 14-21	Dense, spreading growth. Whitish pink flowers.	Ground or bank cover.
Arctostaphylos hookeri (Monterey manzanita)	6-9, 14-24	Low, dense growth, bright green foliage.	Ground and bank cover.
Arctostaphylos uva-ursi (bearberry, kinnikinnick)	1-9, 14-21	Flat, spreading growth, glossy leaves, red berries.	Ground or bank cover, trailing over walls.
Baccharis pilularis	7-24	Dense growth. Tolerates varying conditions.	Ground and bank cover.
Ceanothus gloriosus	5-9, 14-24	Dense growth, handsome leaves, garden tolerant.	Ground cover, bank cover in sun.
Ceanothus griseus horizontalis	5-9, 14-24	Glossy leaves, blue flowers.	Bank and ground cover in sun.
Ceanothus griseus horizontalis 'Yankee Point'	5-9, 14-24	Bright blue flowers, excellent garden tolerance.	Bank and ground cover in sun.
Garrya elliptica (coast silktassel)	6-9, 14-21	Good green foliage, interesting flower catkins, fruit.	Screen, informal hedge, display shrub.
Gaultheria shallon (salal)	4-7, 14-17	Glossy leaves, bell-shaped flowers, blue-black fruit. Graceful.	Woodland plantings, informal ground cover, cut branches for arrangements.
Heteromeles arbutifolia (toyon)	5-24	Dark green leaves, bright red fruits.	Screen, bank planting, erosion control. Trimmed to tree form.
Holodiscus discolor	1-7, 16, 17	Creamy white flower clusters. Adaptable. Deciduous.	Screens, woodland garden, background, borders.
Mahonia aquifolium (Oregon grape)	1-21	Handsome leaves, flowers, fruit. Adaptable.	Massing, foundations, low screen, woodland garden, tubs.
Mahonia nervosa	2-9, 14-17	Low grower, exceptionally handsome foliage.	Woodland, low ground cover in shade.
Myrica californica	4-6, 14-17, 20-24	Clean looking foliage, dense habit.	Screen, informal hedge, clipped hedge.
Prunus ilicifolia	7-9, 12-24	Deep, rich green leaves.	Small tree, tall screen, clipped hedge.
Prunus lyonii	7-9, 12-24	Handsome dark green foliage.	Screen, hedge, tree.
Rhus glabra (smooth sumac)	1-9, 14-17	Brilliant fall foliage color, red fruits, good winter silhouette.	Plant where fall leaves can contrast with evergreens.
Rhus integrifolia	15-17, 20-24	Leathery leaves, white or pinkish flowers. Tolerates salt winds.	Ground cover, screen, background, hedge, espalier.
Rhus ovata	8, 9, 11-24	Leathery leaves; white to pinkish flowers; small, reddish, hairy fruit.	Same uses as above. Plant is hardier.
Ribes sanguineum	4-9, 14-24	Pink to red flowers, good foliage. Deciduous.	Screen, background, woodland gardens.
Ribes viburnifolium	8, 9, 14-24	Fragrant, dark green leaves on wine red stems. Low growing.	Ground cover, bank cover.
Vaccinium ovatum	4-7, 14-17	Lustrous foliage, bronzy new growth, black fruits.	Woodland gardens.

ARBORS, TRELLISES, ESPALIERS

Because of the way they grow, many plants lend themselves happily to being trained as part of garden structures—arbors, trellises, and espaliers. The branches on the plants grow strong but are quite tractable and easy to train when young. The fruits and flowers form dependably even though certain portions of twigs and branches may have to be pruned annually. The magic combination of plants and structures makes structures more pleasant to look at and makes the plants useful and often more interesting than they would be otherwise.

NAME OF PLANT	KIND	CLIMATE ZONES	HOW TO TRAIN, WHAT TO EXPECT
Actinidia chinensis	Vine	4-6, 15-17	Twining vine. Loose, open growth. Guide and tie as necessary.
Actinidia kolomikta	Vine	4-6, 15-17	More dense than A. chinensis; needs same training.
Akebia quinata	Vine	All Zones	Moderately dense foliage. Needs regular pruning and control.
Ampelopsis brevipedunculata	Vine	All Zones	Strong rampant climber, twining tendrils. Needs strong support.
Apple	Tree	Vary by kind	Espalier on stout framework.
Beaumontia grandiflora	Vine	13, 21-24	Semi-twining climber, good for arbors Give it sturdy support.
Bougainvillea	Vine	12, 13, 15-17, 19-24	Many colors available. Need sturdy support.
Camellia sasanqua	Shrub	4-6, 8, 9, 14-24	Limber branches can be trained up on trellis or frame.
Callistemon viminalis (bottle brush)	Shrub	8, 9, 12-24	Fast-growing shrub with pendulous branches that can be espaliered on an arbor.
Campsis radicans	Vine	1-21	Heavy, vigorous vine; fast growing. Funnel-shaped, deep orange-red flowers.
Celastrus scandens (bittersweet)	Vine	All Zones	Vigorous, twining. Needs support. Becomes tangled mass unless pruned.
Cissus antarctica	Vine	13, 16-24	Fast grower with evergreen foliage. Climbs by tendrils.
Cissus rhombifolia	Vine	13, 15, 16, 21-24	Evergreen, dark green, divided leaves with bronzy tint; interesting pattern.
Clematis armandii	Vine	4-9, 12-24	Densely foliaged vine with sprays of white blossoms. Good along eaves. Needs regular pruning and thinning.
Clematis jackmanii	Vine	1-6, 15-17	Many varieties with very showy blossoms. Grow it over a doorway or along porch eave.
Clematis montana	Vine	1-6, 15-17	Vigorous climber; with white or pinkish blooms.
Clytostoma callistegioides	Vine	9, 13-24	Heavy vine needs strong support. Climbs by tendrils. Large violet or purple trumpets in early summer.
Cocculus laurifolius	Shrub	7-9, 12-24	Slender pliable branches can be trained against trellises. Glossy green leaves.
Doxantha unguis-cati	Vine	8-24	Rampant grower in hot locations. Will cling to any support. Yellow blossoms, early summer.
Fatshedera lizei	Vine	4-9, 14-24	Polished leaves like giant ivy make bold patterns. Guide and tie young stems into place.
Fuchsia	Shrub	15-17, 22-24	Some kinds can be trained to make interesting trellis plants.
Gelsemium sempervirens	Vine	8-24	Light texture, good for growing along eaves. Fragrant yellow flowers.

Arbors, trellises, espaliers (cont'd.)

NAME OF PLANT	KIND	CLIMATE ZONES	HOW TO TRAIN, WHAT TO EXPECT
Grape	Vine	Vary by kind	Effective vine for covering large arbors; deciduous. Train by tying.
Hardenbergia comptoniana	Vine	15-24	Open growing vine. Climbs by twining stems. Needs annual pruning. Violet-blue flowers.
Hedera (ivy)	Vine	Vary by kind	Choose a kind with leaf size, color, or markings to fit the design you have in mind. Will cling to rough or stone walls.
Hibbertia scandens	Vine	16, 17, 21-24	Fast-growing, shrubby vine with yellow flowers. For trellis or low fence.
Hoya carnosa	Vine	15-24	A little vine for post or trellis. Thick, succulent leaves. Fragrant, pink, waxy flowers.
Hydrangea anomala petiolaris	Vine	1-21	Clings to rough surfaces. White flowers in large showy clusters.
Jasminum nudiflorum	Shrub	3-21	Arbors or trellises. Slender branches covered with yellow flowers late winter.
Jasminum officinale	Vine	12-24	Rapid growing vine. White summer flowers.
Kadsura japonica	Vine	7-9, 14-22	Evergreen, woody, twining climber for posts. Decorative scarlet fruits in autumn.
Lonicera hildebrandiana (honeysuckle)	Vine	9, 14-17, 19-24	Fast growing, tall. Needs tying when young. Long, tubular flowers.
Lonicera japonica 'Halliana'	Vine	2-24	Fast growing, dense vine. Needs severe annual pruning.
Mandevilla 'Alice du Pont'	Vine	21-24	Shrubby climber (twining stems) with pink flowers.
Mandevilla laxa	Vine	4-9, 14-21	Deciduous vine. Very fragrant large flowers. Twining.
Muehlenbeckia complexa	Vine	8, 9, 14-24	Fast-growing vine forms mattress-like mat of wiry stems with small leaves.
Parthenocissus quinquefolia (Virginia creeper) and P. tricuspidata (Boston ivy)	Vines	All Zones	Graceful, cling to walls. Handsome fall color.
Passiflora alato-caerulea	Vine	5-9, 12-24	Lush tangling growth. Large white shaded pink and lavender blossoms.
Pears	Tree	Vary by kind	Espalier on stout framework.
Phaedranthus buccinatorius	Vine	8, 9, 14-24	Evergreen strong climber (tendrils). Clusters of blood red blossoms.
Plumbago auriculata	Shrub	8, 9, 12-24	Shrubby. Tie up to trellises or arbors. Attractive blue summer flowers.
Podocarpus gracilior	Tree	8, 9, 13-24	Evergreen. Tie pendulous branches to trellises or fences.
Polygonum aubertii	Vine	All Zones	Vigorous grower. Foamy masses of white summer flowers.
Pyracantha	Shrub	Vary by kind	Branches can be tied up on trellises. Decorative winter berries. Prune regularly.
Rhododendron 'Fragrantissimum'	Shrub	5, 6, 14-17 21-24	Train up as espalier or trellis plant. Fragrant white and pink flowers.
Rhoicissus capensis	Vine	16, 17, 21-24	Climbs by tendrils. Needs strong support. Guide branches in right direction. Thin and pinch often.
Rose	Shrub, climbing forms	Vary by kind	For arbor or trellis training, see *Rosa* in encyclopedia section.
Schizophragma hydrangeoides	Vine	4-10, 14-22	Clings to rough surfaces. White flowers in showy clusters.
Solandra hartwegii	Vine	15-24	Fast, rampant vine, must be tied to support. Large, golden yellow blossoms.

(Continued on next page)

Arbors, trellises, espaliers (cont'd.)

NAME OF PLANT	KIND	CLIMATE ZONES	HOW TO TRAIN, WHAT TO EXPECT
Sollya fusiformis	Shrub-vine	8, 9, 14-24	Shrublike but can be tied up to cover small trellis. Brilliant blue summer flowers.
Tecomaria capensis	Vine	12, 13, 16, 18-24	Brilliant orange-red blossoms, fall and winter. Must be tied to support. Can be espaliered.
Tetrastigma voinierianum	Vine	13, 17, 20-24	Climbs by tendrils. Leaves glossy, dark green.
Thunbergia grandiflora	Perennial	16, 21-24	Vigorous twiner. Use to cover arbor or fence. Profuse show of sky blue flowers in summer.
Trachelospermum asiaticum	Vine	6-24	Twining vine with dense, lustrous foliage. Fragrant yellowish white flowers.
Trachelospermum jasminoides	Vine	8-24	Widely used twining vines with fragrant flowers. Good on posts, walls, fences, trellises.
Viburnum plicatum	Shrub	1-9, 14-24	Vigorous grower. Can be espaliered, or tied against large arbor. White flowers in big clusters.
Wisteria	Vine	All Zones	Woody vines useful for overhead arbor or trellis. Long clusters of fragrant violet-blue flowers. Other colors.

PLANTS FOR BARRIERS

Some of the prettiest garden plants happen to have formidable stickers or thorns on them. This limits the scope of their normal landscape use. But here is a prime use for these attractive but thorny plants: Put them at a corner to discourage unwanted foot traffic or prevent shortcuts. Or, plant them along a property line to act as an effective barrier against trespassing.

EVERGREEN

NAME OF PLANT	KIND	CLIMATE ZONES
Acacia armata	Shrub	13-24
Acacia cultriformis	Shrub	13-24
Acacia verticillata	Shrub	14-24
Atriplex lentiformis breweri	Shrub	8, 9, 14-24
Berberis gagnepainii	Shrub	4-6, 15-17
Berberis julianae	Shrub	4-6, 15-17
Berberis triacanthophora	Shrub	4-6, 15-17
Berberis wilsonae	Shrub	4-6, 15-17
Bougainvillea 'Barbara Karst'	Vine	12, 13, 15-24
Bougainvillea 'San Diego Red'	Vine	12, 13, 15-24
Carissa grandiflora	Shrub	13, 16-24
Citrus	Shrub-tree	8, 9, 12-24
Cortaderia selloana (pampas grass)	Ornamental grass	4-24
Dovyalis caffra	Shrub	21-24
Duranta erecta	Shrub	13, 16, 17, 21-24
Elaeagnus angustifolia	Tree	1-3, 7-14, 18, 19
Elaeagnus pungens	Shrub	4-24
Fouquieria splendens	Shrub	10-13, 18-20
Hakea suaveolens	Shrub	9, 12-17, 19-24
Ilex aquifolium (holly)	Shrub-tree	4-9, 15-17
Ilex cornuta	Shrub	8, 9, 14-16, 18-21
Itea ilicifolia	Shrub	4-24
Juniperus chinensis 'Pfitzeriana' (juniper)	Shrub	All Zones

NAME OF PLANT	KIND	CLIMATE ZONES
Mahonia aquifolium (Oregon grape)	Shrub	1-21
Mahonia bealei	Shrub	All Zones
Mahonia lomariifolia	Shrub	6-9, 14-24
Opuntia bigelovii	Cactus	11-24
Osmanthus heterophyllus	Shrub	3-10, 14-24
Phormium tenax (New Zealand flax)	Perennial	7-24
Serenoa repens	Palm	7-9, 12-24
Yucca	Shrub-tree	Vary by kind

DECIDUOUS

NAME OF PLANT	KIND	CLIMATE ZONES
Acacia farnesiana	Shrub	8, 9, 12-24
Berberis thunbergii	Shrub	All Zones
Berberis wilsonae	Shrub	4-6, 15-17
Blackberry	Shrub	Vary by kind
Chaenomeles (flowering quina)	Shrub	1-21
Parkinsonia aculeata	Tree	11-24
Punica granatum (pomegranate)	Tree	7-24
Ribes speciosum	Shrub	8, 9, 14-24
Rosa multiflora (rose)	Shrub	All Zones
Rosa 'Mermaid'	Shrub	All Zones

PLANTS TO CASCADE OVER A WALL

The first list, the spillers and drapers, consists of normally wide-spreading plants that, when planted near the top of a wall, will drape down over the face of the wall. The second list is of vines that will perform in the same fashion. The third list, flowery cascades, are plants (chiefly perennials) that are noted for their flower display and that will drape down a wall.

SPILLERS AND DRAPERS

NAME OF PLANT	KIND	CLIMATE ZONES
Arctostaphylos uva-ursi	Shrub	1-9, 14-24
Asparagus sprengeri	Perennial	15-24
Carissa	Shrub	13, 16-24
Ceanothus gloriosus	Ground cover	5-9, 14-24
Ceanothus 'Joyce Coulter'	Shrub	15-17, 21-24
Ceanothus griseus horizontalis	Ground cover	5-9, 14-24
Chorizema varium	Shrub	15-17, 19-24
Cistus hybridus (rockrose)	Shrub	4-9, 12-15, 18-22
Cotoneaster adpressa	Shrub	All Zones
Cotoneaster apiculata	Shrub	All Zones
Cotoneaster dammeri	Shrub	All Zones
Cotoneaster horizontalis	Shrub	All Zones
Cotoneaster 'Lowfast'	Shrub	4-13
Cotoneaster pannosa 'Nana'	Shrub	4-24
Daphne cneorum	Shrub	2-9, 14-17
Erica carnea (see page 291)	Shrub	2-9, 14-24
Erica purpurascens 'Darleyensis' (see page 291)	Shrub	4-9, 14-24
Euonymus fortunei 'Azusa'	Shrub	1-17

NAME OF PLANT	KIND	CLIMATE ZONES
Euonymus fortunei 'Vegeta'	Shrub	1-17
Fuchsia	Shrub	Vary by kind
Gaultheria shallon	Shrub	4-7, 14-17
Graptopetalum	Succulent	8-24
Juniperus conferta	Shrub	All Zones
Juniperus horizontalis	Shrub	All Zones
Juniperus horizontalis 'Douglasii'	Shrub	All Zones
Juniperus procumbens 'Nana'	Shrub	All Zones
Kleinia	Succulent	Vary by kind
Lantana	Shrub	12, 13, 15-24,
Lotus berthelotii	Perennial	9, 13-24
Plumbago auriculata	Shrub	8, 9, 12-24
Pyracantha 'Santa Cruz'	Shrub	4-24
Ribes viburnifolium	Shrub	8, 9, 14-24
Rosmarinus officinalis 'Prostratus'	Shrub	4-24
Sollya fusiformis	Shrub	8, 9, 14-24
Taxus baccata 'Repandens'	Shrub	1-9, 14-24
Vinca minor	Perennial	All Zones
Xylosma congestum	Shrub	8-24

VINES TO SPILL OVER A WALL

NAME OF PLANT	KIND	CLIMATE ZONES
Beaumontia grandiflora	Vine	13, 21-24
Bougainvillea	Vine	12, 13, 15-17, 19, 21-24
Cissus rhombifolia	Vine	13, 15, 16, 21-24
Gelsemium sempervirens	Vine	8-24
Hedera (ivy)	Vine	Vary by kind
Jasminum mesnyi (jasmine)	Shrub	4-24

NAME OF PLANT	KIND	CLIMATE ZONES
Jasminum nitidum	Vine	12, 13, 16, 19-21
Jasminum nudiflorum	Vine	3-21
Lonicera (honeysuckle)	Vine	Vary by kind
Polygonum aubertii	Vine	1-9, 12-24
Rosa 'Mermaid' (rose)	Shrub	4-24
Solanum rantonnetii	Vine	15-24
Thunbergia gibsonii	Vine	All Zones
Trachelospermum jasminoides (star jasmine)	Vine	8-24
Wisteria	Vine	All Zones

FLOWERY CASCADES

NAME OF PLANT	KIND	CLIMATE ZONES
Alyssum saxatile	Perennial	All Zones
Arabis	Perennial	Vary by kind
Aubrieta deltoidea	Perennial	1-9, 14-21
Campanula	Perennial	Vary by kind
Campanula isophylla	Perennial	All Zones
Campanula portenschlagiana	Perennial	All Zones
Cerastium tomentosum	Perennial	All Zones
Gazania	Perennial	8-24

NAME OF PLANT	KIND	CLIMATE ZONES
Iberis (candytuft)	Annual-Perennial	Vary by kind
Lobelia	Annual-Perennial	Vary by kind
Pelargonium peltatum	Perennial	8, 9, 12-24
Pelargonium tomentosum	Perennial	8, 9, 12-24
Petunia hybrida	Annual	All Zones
Phlox subulata	Perennial	1-17
Tropaeolum majus (nasturtium)	Annual	All Zones
Verbena peruviana	Perennial	8-24
Zauschneria	Perennial	4-9, 14-24

CONTAINER PLANTS

There is a chapter in this book on growing plants in containers. It begins on page 85. You can read there about the reasons for growing plants in containers, the kinds of containers, watering, feeding, and transplanting. On page 36, you will find instructions for making container soil mixes. On these six pages are some of the best plants to grow and display in different size containers and in special-purpose containers.

LARGE SIZE CONTAINERS

(14 inches and up)

NAME OF PLANT	KIND	CLIMATE ZONES	SUN OR SHADE	REASONS FOR GROWING IN CONTAINERS
Abies nordmanniana	Tree	1-11, 14-24	Sun	Some plants have handsome, twisted growth habit.
Acer circinatum	Tree	1-6, 15-17	Sun	Blazing autumn color.
Agapanthus orientalis	Perennial	8, 9, 12-24	Sun, part shade	Summer flower display. Grow in groups of 3 or 5 in large tubs.
Agave attenuata	Succulent	20-24	Part shade	Will thrive for years in a large tub.
Alsophila cooperi	Fern	15-17 21-24	Sun, part shade	Redwood tubs complement tree fern color, texture.
Araucaria heterophylla	Tree	17, 21-24	Sun	Dark green horizontal branches, symmetrically arranged.
Butia capitata	Palm	7-9, 13-24	Sun	Always attractive and formal looking.
Chrysalidocarpus lutescens	Palm	24	Shade	Graceful, smooth trunk; best grown in clumps.
Crataegus oxyacantha 'Paul's Scarlet'	Tree	1-11, 14-17	Sun	Pretty red spring flowers, thorny branches.
Crataegus phaenopyrum	Tree	1-11, 14-17	Sun	White flowers, fall leaf color, red winter berries.
Fagus sylvatica (European beech)	Tree	1-9, 14-24	Sun, part Shade	Smooth bark; clean, lustrous leaves.
Fagus sylvatica 'Purpureo-pendula'	Tree	1-9, 14-24	Sun	Dramatic weeping beech. Holds for years in big pots.
Ficus benjamina	Tree	13, 23, 24	Sun, shade	Use as focal point of patio, courtyard.
Ginkgo biloba	Tree	1-9, 14-24	Sun	Leaves brilliant yellow in fall.
Laurus nobilis	Tree	6-10, 12-24	Part shade	Can be clipped to formal topiary shapes.
Ligustrum lucidum (privet)	Tree	5, 6, 8-24	Sun	Leathery leaves, feathery flowers.
Lime, Rangpur (See Sour Acid Mandarin Orange, page 232)	Tree	8, 9, 12-24	Sun, part shade	Dense growth; decorated with fruit all year.
Osmanthus fragrans	Shrub	8, 9, 12-24	Part shade	Use by entrance to give fragrance.
Peach and nectarine, dwarf kinds	Tree	7-9, 14-16, 18-21	Sun	Dwarf kinds bear standard-size fruit when grown in 18- to 24-inch tubs.
Phormium tenax	Shrub	5-24	Sun, part shade	Grows to large size; withstands neglect.
Phyllostachys nigra (see page 193)	Bamboo	5-24	Sun, part shade	Unsurpassed for Oriental motif. Green and black stems.

Container plants . . . large containers (cont'd.)

NAME OF PLANT	KIND	CLIMATE ZONES	SUN OR SHADE	REASONS FOR GROWING IN CONTAINERS
Phyllostachys viridis (see page 193)	Bamboo	4-24	Sun, part shade	Striking yellow stems.
Pittosporum undulatum	Shrub	16, 17, 21-24	Sun, part shade	Train to single stem to form small tree. Fragrant blooms.
Prunus blireiana (flowering plum)	Tree	2-12, 14-20	Sun	Colorful red-purple foliage.
Prunus serrulata (flowering cherry)	Tree	2-7, 14-20	Sun	Incomparable spring blossoms.
Rosa (rose)	Shrub	All Zones	Sun	Rose roots should not be cramped—use large earthen pots or wooden tubs.
Trachycarpus fortunei	Palm	4-24	Sun, shade	Thick trunk covered with hairy fiber. Fan-type leaves.
Tsuga canadensis 'Pendula'	Tree	1-7, 14-17	Part shade	Pendulous branches. Slow growing in large box.
Tupidanthus calyptratus	Shrub	19-24	Sun, part shade	Leathery, bright green leaves. Prune to shape.

MEDIUM CONTAINERS

(8 to 14 inches inside diameter)

NAME OF PLANT	KIND	CLIMATE ZONES	SUN OR SHADE	REASONS FOR GROWING IN CONTAINERS
Aeonium arboreum	Succulent	15-24	Sun	Decorative leaf rosettes. Will grow in shallow containers.
Agathis robusta	Tree	15, 16, 20-23	Sun	Handsome, glossy leaves. Use young plants.
Aloe arborescens	Succulent	8, 9, 12-24	Part shade	Spiny-edged leaves. Showy winter bloom.
Arbutus unedo	Shrub	4-24	Part shade	Allow multiple trunks to form; prune to shape.
Aucuba japonica	Shrub	4-11, 14-23	Shade	Dense, shiny foliage effective near doorway.
Azalea, Kurume (see page 395)	Shrub	4-9, 14-24	Part shade	Profusion of blooms; handsome, dense foliage.
Bambusa (see page 193)	Bamboo	Vary by kind	Sun	Leaf pattern, variations in stem color. Grow head-high.
Beleperone guttata	Shrub	16, 17, 21-24	Part shade	Unusual shrimplike flower clusters. Prune to shape.
Brunfelsia calycina floribunda	Shrub	13, 15-17, 20-24	Part shade	Blossoms change color from day to day.
Buxus microphylla japonica (boxwood)	Shrub	8, 9, 12-24	Sun, shade	Use at entries, balconies. Shear in formal shapes.
Buxus sempervirens	Shrub	3-6, 15-17	Sun, shade	Dense foliage, lustrous dark green leaves. Shear in formal shapes.
Camellia japonica	Shrub	4-6, 8, 9, 14-24	Part shade	One of best plants for containers. Leaves attractive even when plant is out of bloom.
Camellia sasanqua	Shrub	4-6, 8, 9, 14-24	Part shade	Easily trained. Blooms heavily in autumn.
Cedrus deodara	Tree	4-12, 14-24	Sun	Use as Christmas tree. Put casters under tub for easy moving.
Chaenomeles 'Contorta'	Shrub	1-21	Sun	Interesting branching pattern. Blooms early spring.
Chamaedorea elegans	Palm	16, 17, 22-24	Shade	Plant 3 per pot. Feather-type leaves.
Clivia miniata	Bulb	15-17, 19-24	Shade	Brilliant orange late winter blooms; red berries follow.
Crassula argentea	Succulent	16, 17, 22-24	Sun, shade	Plant sturdy jade plant in shallow containers.

(Continued on next page)

Container plants . . . medium containers (cont'd.)

NAME OF PLANT	KIND	CLIMATE ZONES	SUN OR SHADE	REASONS FOR GROWING IN CONTAINERS
Daphne	Shrub	Vary by kind	Part shade	Containers fulfill the need for perfect drainage.
Dioon edule	Cycad	13, 17, 19-24	Part shade	Feathery, arching leaves; heat resistant.
Dracaena deremensis 'Warneckii'	Tree	24	Part shade	Long green leaves, striped gray and white.
Elaeagnus pungens	Shrub	4-24	Sun	Shear to shape. Takes reflected heat.
Enkianthus	Shrub	2, 9, 14-21	Part shade	Pendulous flowers. Good fall leaf color.
Fatshedera lizei	Vine	4-9, 14-24	Shade	Polished leaves look like giant ivy.
Fatsia japonica 'Moseri'	Shrub	4-9, 14-24	Shade	Bold leaves attractive in entryway containers.
Gardenia jasminoides	Shrub	8, 9, 12-16, 18-23	Sun, part shade	Tubs can be moved to satisfy gardenias' need for warmth.
Griselinia lucida	Shrub	14-17, 20-24	Part shade	Polished evergreen leaves; upright growth.
Hosta	Perennial	1-10, 12-21	Sun, shade	Try groups in 12-inch pots under trees; handsome foliage.
Howeia	Palm	17, 23, 24	Part shade	Slow growing; clean trunks; arching feather-type leaves.
Hydrangea macrophylla	Shrub	2-24	Part shade	The French hybrids adapt easily to tubs.
Ilex cornuta 'Burfordii Nana' (holly)	Shrub	4-24	Part shade	Glossy leaves, berries show off well in redwood tubs.
Juniperus chinensis 'Torulosa' (juniper)	Shrub	All Zones	Sun, part shade	Twisted, wind-blown look. Try concrete aggregate container.
Kumquat, Nagami dwarf (see page 232)	Shrub	8, 9, 12-24	Sun, part shade	Slow growing, profuse small, orange winter fruit.
Leptospermum scoparium varieties	Shrub	14-24	Sun	Display of showy little flowers. Group tubs with plants of different sizes.
Leucadendron argenteum	Tree	17, 20-24	Sun	Silvery bark and leaves. Dramatic in black box.
Lilium (lily)	Bulb	All Zones	Part shade	Wide variety of flower colors.
Mahonia lomariifolia	Shrub	6-9, 14-24	Shade	Unusual shaped leaves are showy. Yellow flowers.
Myrsine africana	Shrub	8, 9, 14-24	Sun	Allow it to grow informally or shear to shape.
Nandina domestica	Shrub	5-24	Sun, part shade	Attractive evergreen with lacy foliage pattern.
Nerium oleander (oleander)	Shrub	8-16, 18-23	Sun	Excellent in tubs in hot, dry locations.
Orange, dwarf kinds (see citrus)	Tree	8, 9, 12-24	Sun, part shade	Show off dark green foliage in white tubs.
Philodendron selloum	Shrub	8, 9, 12-24	Part shade	Needs no support for tall stems, large leaves.
Picea glauca 'Conica' (dwarf Alberta spruce)	Tree	1-6, 15-17	Part shade	Symmetrical, compact; good outdoor Christmas tree.
Pieris japonica	Shrub	1-9, 14-17	Part shade	Year-round beauty; attractive drooping flower clusters.
Pinus thunbergiana (pine)	Tree	1-12, 14-24	Sun	Slow growing, upright, uneven branching.
Pittosporum phillyraeoides	Shrub	9, 13-24	Sun	Unusual weeping habit. Withstands heat.
Podocarpus gracilior	Tree	8, 9, 13-24	Sun, part shade	Choice, clean entryway plant.
Podocarpus macrophyllus maki	Shrub	4-9, 12-24	Sun, part shade	Pliable branches can be espaliered or pinned down.
Rhapis excelsa	Palm	14-17, 19-24	Part shade	Choice; grows in clumps. Fan-type leaves.

Container plants ... medium containers (cont'd.)

NAME OF PLANT	KIND	CLIMATE ZONES	SUN OR SHADE	REASONS FOR GROWING IN CONTAINERS
Rhododendron 'Bric-a-Brac'	Shrub	5-9, 14-17	Shade	Low growing; white winter blossoms.
Sasa palmata (see page 193)	Bamboo	4-24	Sun, shade	Neat and hardy. Leaves divided into fingerlike leaflets.
Strelitzia reginae (bird of paradise)	Perennial	9, 12-24	Part shade	Exotic flowers outstanding. Blooms best with crowding.
Ternstroemia gymnanthera	Shrub	4-9, 12-24	Sun, shade	Handsome foliage plant. Green in shade, bronzy to red in sun.
Vallota speciosa	Bulb	16, 17, 23, 24	Part shade	Rich orange-colored flowers in summer.
Yucca recurvifolia	Shrub	7-24	Sun	Grow in tubs on warm patios. Striking bloom.

SMALL CONTAINERS

(6 to 8 inches inside diameter)

NAME OF PLANT	KIND	CLIMATE ZONES	SUN OR SHADE	REASONS FOR GROWING IN CONTAINERS
Adiantum pedatum	Fern	1-9, 14-21	Shade	Airy foliage.
Asparagus plumosus, dwarf kinds	Perennial	15-24	Part shade	Lacy, fernlike foliage.
Asplenium nidus	Fern	House plant	Shade	Nestlike cluster of tender, undivided fronds.
Azalea, Macrantha (see page 395)	Shrub	4-9, 14-24	Part shade	Compact, excellent foliage; generous spring bloom.
Begonia semperflorens	Perennial	1-9, 14-24	Sun, part shade	Group for color spots in pots, window boxes.
Chrysanthemum frutescens (marguerite)	Perennial	All Zones	Sun	Excellent for quick effect.
Echeveria setosa	Succulent	17, 23, 24	Part shade	Rosette of furry leaves; red and yellow blooms.
Fuchsias, erect kinds	Shrub	2-9, 14-17, 20-24	Part shade	Popular and showy. Pinch to shape.
Haemanthus katherinae	Bulb	14-24	Part shade	Long leaves obscure pot; clusters of salmon red blooms.
Kalanchoe beharensis	Succulent	21-24	Sun, part shade	Arrow-shaped leaves are crimped, velvety.
Narcissus (daffodils)	Bulb	All Zones	Sun, part shade	Mix early, midseason, and late-blooming kinds for longer flowering season.
Nephrolepis cordifolia	Fern	16, 17, 19-24	Shade	Tough, easy-to-grow fern for garden or house.
Pelargonium hortorum	Perennial	8, 9, 12-24	Sun	Live for years in same container.
Pellaea rotundifolia	Fern	14-17, 19-24	Part shade	Pretty little fern to display in pots.
Pinus mugo mughus	Shrub	1-11, 14-24	Sun	Low-growing, shrubby pine popular for containers.
Portulacaria afra	Succulent	8, 9, 12-24	Sun	Allow to grow informally or train to tree shape. Small, fleshy leaves.
Roses, miniature kinds	Shrub	All Zones	Sun	Slender canes; small leaves and blooms. Do well in pots.
Salvia officinalis (sage)	Perennial	All Zones	Sun	Mass in pots for late summer, fall color.
Sempervivum	Succulent	All Zones	Sun	Group several in Mexican pots.

(Continued on next page)

Container plants (cont'd.)

HANGING BASKETS

(Includes plants for all sizes of hanging containers)

NAME OF PLANT	KIND	CLIMATE ZONES	SUN OR SHADE	REASONS FOR GROWING IN CONTAINERS
Abelia floribunda	Shrub	8, 9, 12-24	Sun	Descending branches carry reddish purple blooms.
Abutilon megapotamicum	Shrub	15-24	Part shade	Vinelike growth, lantern-shaped bellflowers.
Asparagus sprengeri	Perennial	15-24	Sun	Light green foliage on graceful arching branches. Red berries.
Begonia tuberhybrida 'Pendula'	Bulb	1-9, 14-24	Shade	Vivid blooms in cascading sprays brighten shady spots.
Browallia speciosa	Annual	All Zones	Part shade	Trailing vines bloom all summer in considerable heat.
Campanula fragilis	Perennial	All Zones	Part shade	One of best for hanging baskets; blue flowers.
Campanula isophylla	Perennial	All Zones	Part shade	Trails vigorously to 2 ft. Blue, white blooms.
Cotoneaster dammeri	Shrub	All Zones	Sun, part shade	Trailing mat with red berries in winter.
Fuchsia, trailing kinds	Shrub	2-9, 14-17, 20-24	Part shade	Select pendulous, branching kinds.
Hedera (ivy)	Vine	All Zones	Sun, shade	Makes pretty, all green (or green and white) foliage mass.
Lantana montevidensis	Shrub	8, 9, 12-24	Sun	Good for hot locations; long bloom season.
Lobelia erinus, trailing kinds	Annual	All Zones	Part shade	Plant several lobelias alone or with campanula.
Lotus berthelotii	Perennial	9, 13-24	Sun, part shade	Gray foliage on trailing branches. Attractive in earth-colored containers.
Lysimachia nummularia	Perennial	1-9, 14-24	Shade	Use to cover the ground around shrubs in large containers.
Pelargonium peltatum	Perennial	8, 9, 12-24	Sun	Try in three Mexican pots hung at different heights.
Petunia, Cascade series	Annual	All Zones	Sun	Large-flowered; branches trail to 2 ft., arch upward.
Rosmarinus officinalis 'Prostratus' (rosemary)	Shrub	4-24	Sun	Use to cascade over rim of pot holding larger plant.
Sedum morganianum	Succulent	13-24	Part shade	Overlapping leaves give pendulous stems a "donkey tail" look.
Sedum sieboldii	Succulent	All Zones	Part shade	Trailing stems to 9 in. with round, blue-gray leaves.
Sollya fusiformis	Shrub	8, 9, 14-24	Part shade	Use for brilliant blue blooms.
Tropaeolum majus (nasturtium)	Annual	All Zones	Sun	Trail or climb with support.

BONSAI

Acer buergerianum

Acer palmatum

Azalea, Kurume (see page 395)

Camellia sasanqua

Chaenomeles 'Contorta' (flowering quince)

Chamaecyparis, many kinds

Cotoneaster conspicua

Cotoneaster dammeri

Cotoneaster microphylla

Fagus sylvatica (European beech)

Ginkgo biloba

Hebe cupressoides 'Nana'

Juniperus chinensis sargentii

Juniperus scopulorum

Juniperus virginiana

Nandina domestica

Pinus bungeana

Pinus thunbergiana

Psidium cattleianum

Punica granatum 'Nana'

Pyracantha coccinea

Pyracantha fortuneana

Sciadopitys verticillata

Sequoia sempervirens (coast redwood)

Wisteria floribunda

Wisteria sinensis

Zelkova serrata

Container plants (cont'd.)

HOUSE PLANTS

NAME OF PLANT	REASONS FOR GROWING
Aglaonema	Ornamental foliage; flowers like tiny green callas.
Anthurium	Lacquered-looking flower bracts. Attractive foliage.
Asparagus sprengeri	Long, arching stems. Pink, fragrant flowers.
Asplenium nidus	Fern with apple green, 4-foot-long fronds.
Aucuba japonica 'Crotonifolia'	Leaves splashed with white and gold.
Aucuba japonica 'Variegata'	Dark green leaves spotted with yellow.
Cattleya	Most popular of the orchids, very showy.
Chamaedorea elegans	Best indoor chamaedorea palm. Tolerates poor light.
Cissus antarctica	Easy-to-grow, graceful vine.
Cissus rhombifolia	Bronzy green leaves. Takes low light intensity.
Coffea arabica	Shining leaves, fragrant flowers; red fruits contain coffee beans.
Coleus blumei	Brilliantly colored leaves. Requires sun.
Cypripedium	North window exposure best for lady slipper orchids.
Dieffenbachia amoena	White stripes on 18-inch-long leaves.
Dieffenbachia picta	Plant singly for best foliage effect.
Dizygotheca elegantissima	Unusual lacy leaf pattern. Give ample light.
Dracaena deremensis 'Warneckii'	Most decorative dracaena. Striped leaves.
Dracaena fragrans 'Massangeana'	Tolerates darker location than other dracaenas.
Dracaena sanderiana	Neat, upright plant with white-striped leaves.
Epidendrum	Clusters of miniature cattleya-type flowers.
Fatsia japonica	Bold leaf pattern. Needs a cool room.
Ficus benjamina	Leathery leaves; excellent indoor plant.
Ficus diversifolia	Interesting open, twisted branch pattern.
Ficus elastica (rubber plant)	One of the most foolproof indoor plants.
Ficus lyrata	Dramatic, huge fiddle-shaped leaves.
Fittonia verschaffeltii	Low evergreen. Useful in terrariums.
Hedera helix, small-leafed kinds (ivy)	Use as ground cover with other potted plants.

NAME OF PLANT	REASONS FOR GROWING
Howeia belmoreana	Feather palm; withstands water neglect, dust, drafts.
Hoya carnosa	Vine with waxy flowers and leaves. Grow in sunny window.
Lithops	Showy flower grows from fissure in succulent that looks like "living rock."
Maranta leuconeura	New leaves spotted with brown, look like "rabbit tracks."
Monstera deliciosa	Vine with big, leathery, dark green leaves deeply split or perforated.
Nephrolepis exaltata 'Bostoniense'	Classic parlor fern; arching, graceful.
Odontoglossum crispum	White flowers. Requires a northern exposure.
Odontoglossum grande	Tiger-striped blooms make good cut flowers.
Oncidium	Fine cut flowers. Need considerable light, good air circulation.
Pelargonium (geranium)	There are kinds with fancy leaves, fragrant foliage, also flowers in many colors.
Peperomia	Foliage plants; some upright, some drooping. Good in dish gardens.
Philodendron	Vines and shrubby kinds; tough, adaptable. Well known house plants.
Phoenix roebelenii	Feather-type palm; needs constant moisture.
Rhaphidophora aurea	Climbing plant with variegated leaves. Good in window boxes, planters.
Rhipsalidopsis gaertneri	Drooping branches bear many showy blooms in shades of pink or red.
Rhoeo spathacea	Dark green leaves, purple underneath. Plant takes low light intensity.
Saintpaulia ionantha (African violet)	Flowers generously. Many varieties. Popular for window gardens.
Sansevieria	Thick swordlike leaves in basal clumps. Variegated kinds most popular. Withstands neglect.
Saxifraga stolonifera	Shows off white-veined leaves if planted in hanging pots.
Spathiphyllum	Grows and blooms readily indoors; has white flower bracts.
Syngonium podophyllum	Vining plant with arrow-shaped, sometimes lobed leaves. Good in terrariums, dish gardens.
Tillandsia lindeniana	Large flower spike of crimson bracts, small purplish flowers, above cluster of 1-foot leaves.
Tolmiea menziesii	Abundant attractive leaves. Forms new plantlets in interesting way.
Tradescantia fluminensis	Trailing plant for pots, window boxes; will even grow in water.

PLANTS IN AND AROUND PAVED AREAS

The landscaping idea illustrated at left can do wonderful things for an expanse of paving. It softens the look of it, of course, but it also interrupts the flatness and gives a third dimension. And anyway, shouldn't garden paving have some garden in it? Listed below are some of the best plants to use for this purpose. A planting panel in paving can also be the spot in which to grow a patio tree (see page 107).

LOW-GROWING, MATLIKE (WITH SEASONAL COLOR) FOR PLANT POCKETS OR SMALL PANELS

NAME OF PLANT	KIND	CLIMATE ZONES
Ajuga	Perennial	All Zones
Alyssum saxatile	Perennial	All Zones

NAME OF PLANT	KIND	CLIMATE ZONES
Arabis caucasica	Perennial	All Zones
Aubrieta deltoidea	Perennial	1-9, 14-21
Bellis perennis	Perennial	All Zones
Gazania	Perennial	8-24
Helianthemum nummularium	Shrublet	All Zones
Iberis sempervirens	Perennial	All Zones
Nierembergia repens	Perennial	5-9, 14-17
Phlox subulata	Perennial	1-17

SPREADERS THAT WILL FEATHER OUT OVER PAVING—IF YOU ALLOW THEM TO HAVE THEIR WAY

NAME OF PLANT	KIND	CLIMATE ZONES
Arctostaphylos uva-ursi	Shrub	1-9, 14-24
Carissa	Shrub	13, 16-21, 22-24

NAME OF PLANT	KIND	CLIMATE ZONES
Cotoneaster dammeri	Shrub	All Zones
Juniperus (juniper)	Shrub	All Zones
Pelargonium peltatum	Perennial	8, 9, 12-17, 22-24
Pyracantha 'Santa Cruz'	Shrub	4-24
Pyracantha 'Walderi'	Shrub	4-24
Rosmarinus officinalis 'Prostratus'	Shrub	4-24
Vinca minor	Perennial	All Zones

IN CRACKS BETWEEN FLAGSTONES AND IN PLANTING POCKETS OR SMALL PANELS FOR A CARPET OF GREEN OR GRAY

NAME OF PLANT	KIND	CLIMATE ZONES
Anthemis nobilis	Perennial	All Zones
Arenaria	Perennial	2-9, 14-24

NAME OF PLANT	KIND	CLIMATE ZONES
Erodium chamaedryoides	Perennial	7-9, 14-24
Mazus	Perennial	1-7, 14-24
Mentha requienii (mint)	Perennial	5-9, 12-24
Moss, Irish or Scotch	Perennial	All Zones
Raoulia australis	Perennial	7-9, 13-24
Sedum	Succulent	Vary by kind
Thymus serpyllum (thyme)	Ground cover	All Zones

PATTERN MAKERS, TUFTLIKE GROWERS

NAME OF PLANT	KIND	CLIMATE ZONES
Dianthus (pink)	Perennial	All Zones
Echeveria	Succulent	Vary by kind
Festuca ovina 'Glauca'	Ornamental grass	All Zones
Liriope and Ophiopogon	Perennial	5-9, 14-24
Sempervivum	Succulent	All Zones

LOW TO MEDIUM GROWERS THAT MASS WELL

NAME OF PLANT	KIND	CLIMATE ZONES
Berberis buxifolia 'Nana'	Shrub	4-6, 15-17
Calluna vulgaris (see page 291)	Shrub	2-6, 17
Erica carnea (see page 291)	Shrub	2-9, 14-24
Lavandula spica 'Munstead'	Shrub	All Zones
Santolina	Perennial	All Zones
Sasa pygmaea	Bamboo	4-24

VEGETABLES BY SEASONS

Cool-season vegetables make best growth before (or after) summer temperatures peak. Where winters are cold and summers are hot, plant them as soon as soil can be worked so that they might mature before midsummer heat arrives. Or plant in midsummer so that the plants can make maximum growth in fall (when days are warm but nights are cool) and ripen the crop harvest sometime between late fall and early spring.

Where summers are cool and winters mild, some of the cool-season vegetables may be planted and brought to harvest stage at any time the year around.

Warm-season vegetables make best growth and mature their crops only when temperatures are high. Plant when frost danger has passed. Start indoors in advance of planting time if it is necessary to stretch a short growing season. Another way to condense the growing season is to buy started plants at the nursery and plant them.

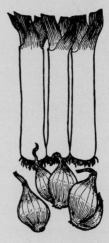

Some vegetables are pretty enough to do duty as ornamental plants, either in containers or in the open ground as edgings, informal hedges, or as bedding plants. These are especially useful where garden space is limited.

A few vegetables are perennials which, once established, will yield crops for many years. Fortunately these include some of the handsomest plants among vegetables.

Instructions for sowing seeds in open ground, sowing in flats, and planting seedlings from flats will be found on pages 37 to 39.

COOL-SEASON VEGETABLES

Artichoke
Asparagus
Bean, broad
Beet
Broccoli
Brussels sprouts
Cabbage
Carrots
Cauliflower
Celery
Chinese cabbage
Chives
Dandelion
Endive
Garlic
Kale
Kohlrabi
Leek
Lettuce
Mustard
Onion
Parsnip
Pea
Potato
Radish
Rhubarb
Salsify
Shallots
Spinach
Turnip, rutabaga

WARM-SEASON VEGETABLES

Beans
Chayote
Collards
Corn
Cucumber
Eggplant
Melon, muskmelon, cantaloupe
New Zealand spinach
Okra
Peppers
Squash
Sweet potato
Swiss chard
Tomato

PERENNIAL VEGETABLES

Artichoke
Asparagus
Chayote
Rhubarb

ORNAMENTAL VEGETABLES

Artichoke
Asparagus
Bean, scarlet runner
Kale

Lettuce
Pepper
Rhubarb
Swiss chard

PLANTS THAT ATTRACT BIRDS

You can use this list in two ways. If you like to have birds in your garden, you can include some of these plants in your landscaping. Remember, though, that if your plot succeeds, you probably won't get full enjoyment from any fruits that these plants produce. Birds eat them just when they become colorful and tasty.

The other way to use the list is negative. If birds are already numerous in your neighborhood, you might want to avoid using these plants because fruit-eating birds are too likely to diminish your enjoyment of the plants' full seasonal display.

Most of the plants whose flowers are listed as attractants are ones that hummingbirds visit in their search for flower nectar.

When birds spend long periods of time hopping about in a tree or shrub that is not carrying fruits, they probably are eating insects.

SHRUBS

NAME OF PLANT	CLIMATE ZONES	WHAT ATTRACTS THEM
Amelanchier	1-3	Fruit
Arbutus	4-24	Fruit
Arctostaphylos	Vary by kind	Fruit
Berberis (barberry)	Vary by kind	Fruit
Callistemon	8, 9, 12-24	Flowers
Carissa	22-24	Fruit
Cotoneaster	Vary by kind	Fruit
Elaeagnus	Vary by kind	Fruit
Eriobotrya japonica	4-24	Fruit
Feijoa	8, 9, 12-24	Flowers, fruit
Fremontodendron californica	7-24	Flowers
Fuchsia	16, 17, 22-24	Flowers
Garrya	6-9, 14-21	Fruit
Heteromeles arbutifolia	5-24	Fruit
Ilex	Vary by kind	Fruit
Lantana	13, 17, 23, 24	Flowers, fruit
Ligustrum	Vary by kind	Fruit
Mahonia	Vary by kind	Fruit
Myrica california	4-6, 14-17	Fruit
Pernettya mucronata	4-7, 14-17	Fruit
Photinia	Vary by kind	Fruit
Prunus,	Vary by kind	Fruit
Pyracantha	Vary by kind	Fruit
Rhus	Vary by kind	Fruit
Ribes	Vary by kind	Fruit
Rosa multiflora	All Zones	Fruit
Sambucus	Vary by kind	Fruit
Stranvaesia davidiana	4-11, 14-17	Fruit
Symphoricarpos	Vary by kind	Fruit

TREES

NAME OF PLANT	CLIMATE ZONES	WHAT ATTRACTS THEM
Albizia julibrissin	2-23	Flowers
Alnus (alder)	Vary by kind	Cones
Betula (birch)	Vary by kind	Conelike fruit
Cornus (dogwood)	Vary by kind	Fruit
Crataegus (hawthorn)	1-11, 14-17	Fruit
Edible fruits (soft-skinned orchard-type fruits that people like to eat)		
Malus	1-11, 14-21	Fruit
Melia azedarach	6, 8-24	Fruit
Morus alba (mulberry)	All Zones	Fruit
Platanus (plane, sycamore)	Vary by kind	Seed clusters
Quercus (oak)	Vary by kind	Acorns
Sorbus aucuparia (European mountain ash)	1-6, 15-17	Fruit

VINES

NAME OF PLANT	CLIMATE ZONES	WHAT ATTRACTS THEM
Actinidia	4-6, 15-17	Fruit
Hedera (ivy)	Vary by kind	Fruit
Lonicera hildebrandiana (honeysuckle)	9, 14-17	Flowers, fruit
Parthenocissus quinquefolia (Virginia creeper)	All Zones	Fruit

ANNUALS AND OTHERS

NAME OF PLANT	CLIMATE ZONES	WHAT ATTRACTS THEM
Duchesnea indica	All Zones	Fruit
Helianthus	Vary by kind	Seeds
Tagetes (marigold)	All Zones	Seeds
Tropaeolum (nasturtium)	All Zones	Seeds

DEER-PROOF (OR CLOSE TO IT)

Browsing deer can do a lot of damage in country and suburban places. Commercial repellents work *if* you spray frequently enough to keep new growth well covered and to replace what rains or sprinklings remove. Some people have success repelling deer with blood meal; they sprinkle it on the ground around plantings or hang little cloth bags filled with it around the garden. Advantages: it often works, and it furnishes fertilizer to the garden as it dissolves; disadvantages: it smells bad when wet, and dogs sometimes invade the garden to get at it. Dogs, lights, noisemakers, and scarecrows may or may not work. Six-foot fences usually keep deer out on level ground, but some deer can clear seven or even eight feet. A horizontal outrigger extension on a deer fence makes it harder for a deer to jump it.

Following is a list of plants that deer usually shun. In each category the least palatable (from the deer's point of view) are listed first.

SHRUBS & GROUND COVERS

Nerium oleander

Rhododendron
(not azaleas)

Cistus (rockrose)

Rosmarinus (rosemary)

Juniperus (juniper)

Bamboo

Mahonia

Ilex (holly)

Daphne

Romneya

Ferns

Lantana

Arbutus unedo

Hypericum

Ricinus (castor bean)

BULBS

Iris

Narcissus (daffodil)

Tulipa

FRUITS & VEGETABLES

Artichoke

Fig

Squash

TREES

Eucalyptus

Abies (fir)

Cedrus (cedar)

ANNUALS & PERENNIALS

Zinnia

Papaver rhoeas, P. orientalis
(Shirley and Oriental Poppies)

Digitalis (foxglove)

Calendula

Chrysanthemum frutescens (marguerite)

Rudbeckia hirta (gloriosa daisy)

THESE PLANTS DRAW BEES *Butterflies? Moths?*

For moth try Nicotiana (p. 347)
Petunias (p. 362)
Oenothera (p. 348)
Matthiola (p. 339) (Stocks)

Some flowers draw bees abundantly. Whether this is a blessing or a nuisance depends on your point of view. The following are notorious bee plants.

* For butterflies
* Asclepias
* Asters

Abelia

Acacia

Arenaria verna
caespitosa (see page 308)

Artemisia

Avocado

* Buddleia

Callistemon citrinus
(bottlebrush)

Calluna (see page 291)

Ceanothus

Choisya ternata
(Mexican orange)

Citrus

Clover

Cotoneaster

Crataegus (hawthorn)

Echium

Erica (see page 291)

Eriogonum

Escallonia

Eucalyptus (especially
E. ficifolia & E. melliodora)

Feijoa

Gleditsia

Heteromeles

Iceplant

Ligustrum (privet)

Lonicera japonica
'Halliana' (honeysuckle)

Murraya paniculata

Phyla nodiflora

Polygonum capitatum

Pyracantha

Rosmarinus officinalis
(rosemary)

Sorbus aucuparia
(European mountain ash)

Syzygium

Teucrium chamaedrys

Thymus (thyme)

Trachelospermum
jasminoides (star jasmine)

Salvia (sage)

Wisteria

* Lavandula (p. 318)

FLOWER COLOR BY SEASONS

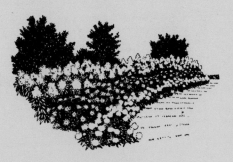

Here is the guide to garden showmanship. The garden showman always thinks ahead. In one season, while enjoying the flowers of the moment, he plans and plants for seasons to come. The next ten pages list the outstanding and dependable suppliers of seasonal flower color—by season from spring around the calendar to winter.

Several important facts are given for each plant on the lists: best time to plant (cues for the director of garden showmanship), duration of bloom ("long" is three to six months, "medium" one to three months, "short" two weeks to a month), and flower colors available. See encyclopedia section for the kinds that supply the different available colors.

SPRING FLOWER COLOR

ANNUALS

NAME OF PLANT	CLIMATE ZONES	BEST TIME TO PLANT	DURATION OF BLOOM	YELLOW	ORANGE	RED	PINK	LAVENDER	PURPLE OR VIOLET	BLUE	WHITE	MULTI-COLORS
Antirrhinum majus (snapdragon)	All Zones	Early fall to early spring	Medium	•	•	•	•	•	•		•	•
Calendula officinalis	All Zones	Fall or spring	Long	•	•							
Centaurea cyanus (bachelor button)	All Zones	Fall or early spring	Medium			•	•	•		•	•	
Clarkia (includes Godetia)	All Zones	Fall or spring	Medium	•	•	•	•	•	•		•	
Delphinium ajacis (larkspur)	All Zones	Fall or early spring	Medium			•	•	•	•	•	•	•
Dianthus barbatus (sweet William)	All Zones	Late spring (for bloom next spring)	Long			•	•		•		•	•
Dianthus chinensis (pink)	All Zones	Fall or early spring	Long			•	•	•			•	•
Eschscholzia californica (California poppy)	All Zones	Fall	Medium	•	•	•	•				•	•
Lathyrus odoratus (sweet pea)	All Zones	Early fall, winter, or early spring	Medium			•	•	•	•	•	•	
Linaria maroccana	All Zones	Spring or fall	Medium	•			•	•	•	•		•
Lobularia maritima (sweet alyssum)	All Zones	Spring to fall	Long					•	•		•	•
Lupinus nanus	All Zones	Fall or winter	Medium							•		
Matthiola incana (stock)	All Zones	Early fall or early spring	Medium	•		•	•	•	•	•	•	

Spring flower color . . . annuals (cont'd.)

NAME OF PLANT	CLIMATE ZONES	BEST TIME TO PLANT	DURATION OF BLOOM	YELLOW	ORANGE	RED	PINK	LAVENDER	PURPLE OR VIOLET	BLUE	WHITE	MULTI-COLORS
Myosotis sylvatica (forget-me-not)	All Zones	Fall or early spring	Long							•	•	•
Nemesia strumosa	All Zones	Fall or spring	Medium	•	•	•	•	•	•	•	•	•
Papaver rhoeas (Shirley poppy)	All Zones	Spring and summer	Short		•	•	•				•	•
Viola tricolor hortensis (pansy)	All Zones	Summer, fall or spring	Long	•	•	•	•	•	•	•	•	•

BULBS AND BULBLIKE PLANTS

NAME OF PLANT	CLIMATE ZONES	BEST TIME TO PLANT	DURATION OF BLOOM	YELLOW	ORANGE	RED	PINK	LAVENDER	PURPLE OR VIOLET	BLUE	WHITE	MULTI-COLORS
Anemone coronaria	All Zones	Late fall or spring	Medium			•	•	•	•	•	•	•
Calochortus	All Zones	Fall	Medium	•				•	•	•	•	
Clivia miniata	15-17, 19-24	Early fall	Medium	•	•	•					•	
Crocus	All Zones	Summer or fall	Medium	•	•		•	•	•	•	•	•
Erythronium	1-7, 15-17	Fall	Short	•			•	•		•	•	
Freesia	8, 9, 12-24	Summer or fall	Medium	•	•	•	•	•	•	•	•	•
Fritillaria	1-7, 15-17	Fall	Short	•	•	•			•		•	
Hyacinthus orientalis	All Zones	Early fall	Short	•	•	•	•	•	•	•	•	
Iris, Bearded	All Zones	Late summer	Medium	•	•	•	•	•	•	•	•	
Iris, Dutch	All Zones	Fall	Medium	•	•				•	•	•	
Muscari	All Zones	Fall	Medium						•	•	•	
Narcissus (daffodil)	All Zones	Early fall	Short	•	•						•	•
Ranunculus asiaticus	All Zones	Fall or early spring	Medium	•	•	•	•				•	•
Scilla hispanica	All Zones	Fall	Short				•			•	•	
Sparaxis tricolor	9, 13-24	Fall	Medium	•		•			•	•	•	•
Tulipa (tulip)	All Zones	Fall to early winter	Medium	•	•	•	•	•	•		•	•
Watsonia	All Zones	Late summer or early fall	Short			•	•	•			•	
Zantedeschia (calla)	5, 6, 8, 9, 14-24	Fall	Short	•	•	•	•				•	•

VINES

NAME OF PLANT	CLIMATE ZONES	BEST TIME TO PLANT	DURATION OF BLOOM	YELLOW	ORANGE	RED	PINK	LAVENDER	PURPLE OR VIOLET	BLUE	WHITE	MULTI-COLORS
Bougainvillea	12, 13, 15-17, 19, 21-24	Early spring	Long	•	•	•	•		•		•	
Wisteria	All Zones	Winter	Medium				•	•	•		•	

(Continued on next page)

Spring flower color (cont'd.)

PERENNIALS AND BIENNIALS

NAME OF PLANT	CLIMATE ZONES	BEST TIME TO PLANT	DURATION OF BLOOM	YELLOW	ORANGE	RED	PINK	LAVENDER	PURPLE OR VIOLET	BLUE	WHITE	MULTI-COLORS
Aethionema	1-9	Fall	Medium				●	●			●	
Alyssum saxatile	All Zones	Fall or early spring	Medium	●								
Aquilegia (columbine)	All Zones	Fall or early spring	Medium	●		●	●	●	●	●	●	●
Arabis	Vary by kind	Fall	Medium				●		●		●	
Aubrieta deltoidea	1-9, 14-21	Late spring (seeds) or fall (plants)	Medium			●	●	●	●	●		
Bellis perennis	All Zones	Fall	Long			●	●				●	
Billbergia	16-24	Late fall	Medium			●				●		●
Convallaria majalis (lily-of-the-valley)	1-7	Fall	Short								●	
Cynoglossum amabile	All Zones	Fall or early spring	Medium				●			●	●	
Delphinium, Pacific strain	1-9, 14-24	Fall or spring	Medium				●	●	●	●	●	●
Dianthus (carnation, pink)	All Zones	Late spring (seeds) or fall (plants)	Medium	●	●	●	●	●	●		●	●
Dicentra spectabilis (bleeding heart)	1-9, 14-24	Fall or early spring	Medium				●					
Digitalis purpurea (foxglove)	All Zones	Fall or spring	Long	●		●	●	●	●			●
Heliotropium arborescens	8-24	Early spring	Long					●	●	●		
Helleborus	All Zones	Spring to fall	Long				●		●		●	●
Heuchera sanguinea (coral bells)	All Zones	Fall or spring	Long			●	●				●	
Iberis sempervirens (evergreen candytuft)	All Zones	Fall or spring	Long								●	
Phlox subulata	1-17	Fall	Short			●	●	●		●	●	
Primula malacoides (fairy primrose)	14-24	Fall	Medium			●	●	●			●	
Primula polyantha (polyanthus primrose)	1-9, 14-24	Fall to spring	Medium	●	●	●	●	●	●	●	●	●
Saxifraga	1-7 14-24	Fall to spring	Long	●		●	●				●	
Senecio cruentus (cineraria)	15-24	Fall or spring	Long			●	●	●	●	●	●	●
Viola cornuta (viola)	All Zones	Late summer–early spring	Medium	●	●	●			●	●	●	
Viola odorata (sweet violet)	All Zones	Late summer, fall, or early spring	Medium				●		●		●	

Spring flower color (cont'd.)

SHRUBS

NAME OF PLANT	CLIMATE ZONES	BEST TIME TO PLANT	DURATION OF BLOOM	YELLOW	ORANGE	RED	PINK	LAVENDER	PURPLE OR VIOLET	BLUE	WHITE	MULTI-COLORS
Azalea (see page 395)	Vary by kind	Late fall or spring	Medium	•	•	•	•	•	•		•	•
Callistemon (bottlebrush)	8, 9, 12-24	Fall or spring	Long	•		•	•	•	•			
Choisya ternata (Mexican orange)	7-9, 12-24	Early spring	Long								•	
Cleyera japonica	4-6, 8, 9, 14-24	Fall or spring	Medium								•	
Gamolepis chrysanthemoides	8, 9, 13-24	Fall or spring	Medium	•								
Melaleuca	Vary by kind	Fall or spring	Long			•	•	•	•		•	
Raphiolepis	4-10, 14-24	Fall or spring	Long			•	•				•	
Rosa (rose)	All Zones	Winter, early spring, or fall	Long	•	•	•	•	•			•	•
Syringa vulgaris (lilac)	1-11	Spring	Medium			•	•	•	•	•	•	•

TREES

NAME OF PLANT	CLIMATE ZONES	BEST TIME TO PLANT	DURATION OF BLOOM	YELLOW	ORANGE	RED	PINK	LAVENDER	PURPLE OR VIOLET	BLUE	WHITE	MULTI-COLORS
Aesculus carnea	1-9, 14-17	Winter, spring	Medium			•	•					
Bauhinia	Vary by kind	Spring	Long			•	•		•		•	•
Cherry, Flowering (see page 384)	4-6, 15-17	Winter	Short	•			•				•	
Cornus florida	1-9, 14-16	Winter	Short			•	•				•	
Erythrina coralloides	12, 13, 19-24	Fall to spring	Medium			•						
Laburnum watereri	1-10, 14-17	Winter or early spring	Short	•								
Magnolia soulangiana	1-10, 14-24	Late winter or early spring	Medium			•	•				•	
Paulownia tomentosa	All Zones	Fall or spring	Short							•		
Peach, Flowering (see page 384)	2-24	Winter	Short			•	•				•	•
Plum, Flowering (see page 384)	2-20	Winter	Short				•				•	
Tabebuia chrysotricha	15, 16, 20-24	Fall to early spring	Medium	•								

(Continued on next page)

SUMMER FLOWER COLOR

ANNUALS

NAME OF PLANT	CLIMATE ZONES	BEST TIME TO PLANT	DURATION OF BLOOM	YELLOW	ORANGE	RED	PINK	LAVENDER	PURPLE OR VIOLET	BLUE	WHITE	MULTI-COLORS
Ageratum houstonianum	All Zones	Late spring	Long				•	•		•	•	
Amaranthus	All Zones	Late spring-summer	Medium			•						
Browallia americana	All Zones	Early spring	Long						•	•		
Callistephus chinensis (China aster)	All Zones	Spring	Medium			•	•	•	•	•	•	
Celosia	All Zones	Late spring	Long	•	•	•	•					
Convolvulus tricolor (dwarf morning glory)	All Zones	Spring	Long			•				•		•
Coreopsis tinctoria	All Zones	Spring	Long	•	•	•						
Cosmos	All Zones	Spring to summer	Long	•	•	•	•	•	•		•	•
Gaillardia pulchella	All Zones	Spring	Long	•	•	•						
Gypsophila elegans	All Zones	Spring into summer	Short				•				•	
Helianthus annuus (sunflower)	All Zones	Spring	Long	•	•							
Helichrysum bracteatum (strawflower)	All Zones	Late spring or early summer	Long	•	•	•	•				•	
Impatiens holstii	All Zones	Spring	Long		•	•	•				•	
Ipomoea (morning glory)	All Zones	Spring	Long				•	•	•	•	•	•
Limonium	All Zones	Spring	Long	•			•	•				
Linum grandiflorum 'Rubrum'	All Zones	Fall or early spring	Long			•						
Lobelia erinus	All Zones	Late winter or early spring	Long				•		•	•	•	•
Mimulus tigrinus	All Zones	Spring	Medium	•								•
Nicotiana	All Zones	Early spring	Long	•		•					•	
Petunia hybrida	All Zones	Early spring	Long	•		•	•	•	•	•	•	•
Phlox drummondii	All Zones	Fall or spring	Long			•	•	•	•		•	•
Portulaca	All Zones	Spring	Long	•	•	•	•	•			•	
Quamoclit pennata	All Zones	Spring	Long		•	•					•	
Salvia splendens (scarlet sage)	All Zones	Early spring	Long			•	•	•				
Scabiosa atropurpurea	All Zones	Spring	Long				•	•			•	
Tagetes (marigold)	All Zones	Spring to summer	Long	•	•							
Thunbergia alata	All Zones	Early spring	Long	•	•						•	•
Torenia fournieri	All Zones	Spring	Long							•	•	•
Tropaeolum majus (nasturtium)	All Zones	Early spring	Medium	•	•	•	•				•	•
Verbena hybrida	All Zones	Spring	Long			•	•		•	•		•
Zinnia	All Zones	Spring to summer	Long	•	•	•	•	•	•		•	•

Summer flower color (cont'd.)

BULBS AND BULBLIKE PLANTS

NAME OF PLANT	CLIMATE ZONES	BEST TIME TO PLANT	DURATION OF BLOOM	YELLOW	ORANGE	RED	PINK	LAVENDER	PURPLE OR VIOLET	BLUE	WHITE	MULTI-COLORS
Agapanthus	8, 9, 12-24	Spring	Medium						•	•	•	
Amaryllis belladonna	4-24	Early fall	Short				•					
Begonia, Tuberous Rooted	1-9, 14-24	Spring	Long	•	•	•	•				•	•
Canna	All Zones	Spring	Long	•	•	•	•				•	•
Dahlia	All Zones	Spring	Long	•	•	•	•	•	•		•	•
Gladiolus	All Zones	Early winter to late spring	Short	•	•	•	•	•	•	•	•	•
Hemerocallis (daylily)	All Zones	Spring or late fall	Medium	•	•	•	•				•	•
Hippeastrum (amaryllis)	19, 21-24	Winter to early spring	Medium		•	•	•				•	•
Iris kaempferi (Japanese iris)	All Zones	Fall or spring	Medium			•	•	•	•		•	
Lilium (lily)	All Zones	Fall	Medium	•	•	•	•	•	•		•	•
Moraea	8-24	Fall	Long	•						•	•	•
Nymphaea (water lily)	All Zones	Early spring to summer	Medium	•	•	•	•		•	•	•	
Tigridia pavonia	All Zones	Spring	Medium	•	•	•	•				•	•

PERENNIALS

NAME OF PLANT	CLIMATE ZONES	BEST TIME TO PLANT	DURATION OF BLOOM	YELLOW	ORANGE	RED	PINK	LAVENDER	PURPLE OR VIOLET	BLUE	WHITE	MULTI-COLORS
Achillea (yarrow)	All Zones	Fall	Long	•		•					•	
Aster	All Zones	Fall	Medium			•	•	•	•	•	•	
Astilbe	2-9, 14-17	Fall	Long			•	•				•	
Begonia, Fibrous Rooted	1-9, 14-24	Early spring to early summer	Long			•	•				•	
Calceolaria integrifolia	15-24	Spring	Long	•	•	•						
Campanula	Vary by kind	Fall or spring	Medium				•	•	•	•	•	
Catharanthus roseus (Vinca rosea)	All Zones	Spring	Long			•	•				•	•
Ceratostigma plumbaginoides	2-9, 14-24	Fall	Medium							•		
Chrysanthemum maximum (Shasta daisy)	All Zones	Fall	Medium	•							•	
Coreopsis grandiflora	All Zones	Fall	Long	•								
Gaillardia grandiflora	All Zones	Fall	Long	•		•						
Gazania	8-24	Fall or early spring	Long	•	•	•	•				•	•
Gerbera jamesonii	8, 9, 12-24	Spring	Long	•	•	•						•

(Continued on next page)

Summer flower color . . . perennials (cont'd.)

NAME OF PLANT	CLIMATE ZONES	BEST TIME TO PLANT	DURATION OF BLOOM	YELLOW	ORANGE	RED	PINK	LAVENDER	PURPLE OR VIOLET	BLUE	WHITE	MULTI-COLORS
Heliopsis scabra 'Incomparabilis'	1-16	Fall or spring	Long	•								
Hosta	1-10, 12-21	Early spring	Medium					•		•	•	
Hunnemannia fumariaefolia	All Zones	Spring	Long	•								
Kniphofia uvaria	1-9, 14-24	Fall or spring	Long	•	•	•					•	•
Limonium	Vary by kind	Fall or spring	Long				•		•	•	•	•
Lobelia cardinalis	1-7, 14-17	Fall or spring	Medium			•						
Mirabilis jalapa (Four o'clock)	All Zones	Spring	Long	•	•	•					•	
Paeonia, herbaceous (peony)	1-11, 14, 15	Early fall	Medium	•		•	•				•	
Papaver orientale (Oriental poppy)	1-17	Fall or spring	Medium		•						•	
Pelargonium domesticum (Martha Washington geranium)	8, 9, 12-24	Spring	Long			•	•	•	•		•	•
Pelargonium hortorum	8, 9, 12-24	Spring	Long		•	•	•	•				•
Penstemon gloxinioides	All Zones	Fall or early spring	Medium		•	•	•	•	•		•	
Phlox paniculata	1-14, 18-21	Fall or early spring	Long			•	•	•			•	•
Platycodon grandiflorum	All Zones	Fall or spring	Medium					•	•	•	•	
Romneya coulteri (Matilija poppy)	5-10, 12-24	Fall	Medium								•	
Rudbeckia hirta (Gloriosa daisy)	All Zones	Spring	Long	•	•							
Tithonia rotundifolia	All Zones	Spring	Long		•	•						

SHRUBS

NAME OF PLANT	CLIMATE ZONES	BEST TIME TO PLANT	DURATION OF BLOOM	YELLOW	ORANGE	RED	PINK	LAVENDER	PURPLE OR VIOLET	BLUE	WHITE	MULTI-COLORS
Abutilon	15-24	Fall or spring	Medium	•	•	•	•	•		•	•	
Bouvardia	13, 16, 17, 19-24	Fall	Long			•	•				•	
Brunfelsia	13, 15-17, 20-24	Spring	Long					•	•		•	
Datura	16-24	Spring	Long			•					•	
Daubentonia tripetii	7-9, 12-16, 18-23	Spring	Long		•							
Erythrina bidwillii	8, 9, 12-24	Fall to spring	Long			•						
Fuchsia	2-9, 14-17, 20-24	Spring	Long		•	•	•	•	•		•	•

Summer flower color . . . shrubs (cont'd.)

NAME OF PLANT	CLIMATE ZONES	BEST TIME TO PLANT	DURATION OF BLOOM	YELLOW	ORANGE	RED	PINK	LAVENDER	PURPLE OR VIOLET	BLUE	WHITE	MULTI-COLORS
Hibiscus rosa-sinensis	9, 14-16, 19-24	Spring	Long	•	•	•	•				•	•
Hibiscus syriacus	1-21	Fall or spring	Medium			•	•	•	•	•	•	•
Hydrangea macrophylla	2-24	Fall or spring	Long			•	•			•	•	
Jacobinia carnea	6-9, 13-24	Spring	Medium			•	•					
Nerium oleander	8-16, 18-23	Fall or spring	Long	•		•	•				•	
Tibouchina semidecandra	16, 17, 21-24	Spring	Long						•			

TREES

NAME OF PLANT	CLIMATE ZONES	BEST TIME TO PLANT	DURATION OF BLOOM	YELLOW	ORANGE	RED	PINK	LAVENDER	PURPLE OR VIOLET	BLUE	WHITE	MULTI-COLORS
Calodendrum capense	19, 21-24	Spring	Medium					•				
Eucalyptus ficifolia	15-17, 22-24	Spring	Long		•	•	•					
Jacaranda acutifolia	9, 13-24	Spring	Medium				•	•		•	•	
Lagerstroemia indica (crape myrtle)	7-9, 12-14, 18-21	Fall or spring	Medium			•	•	•	•			
Magnolia grandiflora	4-12, 14-24	Late winter, early spring	Long								•	
Magnolia macrophylla	2-9, 14-21	Late winter, early spring	Medium								•	

VINES

NAME OF PLANT	CLIMATE ZONES	BEST TIME TO PLANT	DURATION OF BLOOM	YELLOW	ORANGE	RED	PINK	LAVENDER	PURPLE OR VIOLET	BLUE	WHITE	MULTI-COLORS
Antigonon leptopus	12, 13, 18-21	Early spring	Long				•					
Bean, scarlet runner	All Zones	Late spring	Long			•						
Calonyction aculeatum	All Zones	Spring	Long								•	
Cobaea scandens	All Zones	Spring	Long						•		•	
Dolichos lablab	All Zones	Spring	Long						•		•	
Dolichos lignosus	16, 17, 21-24	Spring	Long						•		•	
Phaedranthus buccinatorius	8, 9, 14-24	Fall or spring	Long			•						
Trachelospermum jasminoides (star jasmine)	8-24	Fall or spring	Medium								•	

(Continued on next page)

FALL FLOWER COLOR

BULBS AND BULBLIKE PLANTS

NAME OF PLANT	CLIMATE ZONES	BEST TIME TO PLANT	DURATION OF BLOOM	YELLOW	ORANGE	RED	PINK	LAVENDER	PURPLE OR VIOLET	BLUE	WHITE	MULTI-COLORS
Colchicum autumnale	All Zones	Summer	Short				•	•	•		•	
Cyclamen, hardy	1-9, 14-17	Summer	Medium			•	•				•	•
Lycoris	4-9, 12-24	Summer	Medium	•		•	•				•	•
Schizostylis coccinea	5-9, 14-24	Spring or fall	Medium			•	•					
Zephyranthes	All Zones	Late summer-early fall	Long	•		•	•				•	•

PERENNIALS

NAME OF PLANT	CLIMATE ZONES	BEST TIME TO PLANT	DURATION OF BLOOM	YELLOW	ORANGE	RED	PINK	LAVENDER	PURPLE OR VIOLET	BLUE	WHITE	MULTI-COLORS
Anemone hupehensis japonica	All Zones	Spring	Short			•	•				•	
Anthemis tinctoria	All Zones	Late fall or spring	Long	•								
Arctotis	7-9, 12-24	Late spring	Long	•	•		•		•		•	•
Begonia, Fibrous Rooted	1-9, 14-24	Spring to fall	Long			•	•				•	
Ceratostigma plumbaginoides	2-9, 14-24	Fall	Medium							•		
Chrysanthemum morifolium	All Zones	Spring	Medium	•	•	•	•	•	•		•	•
Chrysanthemum frutescens (marguerite)	All Zones	Spring	Long	•			•				•	
Echinops exaltatus	All Zones	Late fall or spring	Long							•		
Francoa ramosa	All Zones	Late fall or spring	Long				•				•	
Gerbera jamesonii	8, 9, 12-24	Spring	Long	•	•	•						•
Helenium autumnale	All Zones	Late fall or spring	Medium	•	•	•						
Rehmannia angulata	7-10, 12-24	Spring	Long				•		•		•	
Sedum spectabile	All Zones	Early spring	Medium			•	•					
Stokesia laevis	1-9, 12-24	Fall or spring	Medium						•	•	•	

WINTER FLOWER COLOR

BULBS AND BULBLIKE PLANTS

NAME OF PLANT	CLIMATE ZONES	BEST TIME TO PLANT	DURATION OF BLOOM	YELLOW	ORANGE	RED	PINK	LAVENDER	PURPLE OR VIOLET	BLUE	WHITE	MULTI-COLORS
Clivia miniata	15-17, 19-24	Fall	Long	•	•	•					•	
Cyclamen persicum	16-24	Summer or fall	Long			•	•	•	•		•	•
Eranthis hyemalis	1-9, 15-17	Summer or early fall	Short	•								
Iris, Dutch	All Zones	Fall	Medium	•	•			•	•	•	•	
Iris unguicularis	5-24	Spring or early fall	Medium							•		

Winter flower color (cont'd.)

ANNUALS

NAME OF PLANT	CLIMATE ZONES	BEST TIME TO PLANT	DURATION OF BLOOM	YELLOW	ORANGE	RED	PINK	LAVENDER	PURPLE OR VIOLET	BLUE	WHITE	MULTI-COLORS
Calendula officinalis	All Zones	Early Fall	Medium	•	•							
Dimorphotheca (Cape marigold, African daisy)	All Zones	Late summer-early fall	Medium	•	•				•		•	•
Iberis (candy tuft)	All Zones	Fall	Long			•	•	•			•	
Lathyrus odoratus (early-flowering sweet pea)	13, 17, 21-24	Late summer or early fall	Medium			•	•	•	•	•	•	
Lobularia maritima (sweet alyssum)	All Zones	Fall	Long				•	•	•		•	
Matthiola incana (stock)	8, 9, 12-24	Early Fall	Long	•		•	•	•	•	•	•	
Papaver nudicaule (Iceland poppy)	All Zones	Fall	Long	•	•		•				•	
Primula malacoides (primrose)	14-24	Fall	Long			•	•	•			•	
Viola cornuta (viola)	All Zones	Late summer or fall	Long	•	•	•			•	•	•	
Viola tricolor hortensis (pansy)	All Zones	Fall	Long	•	•	•	•	•	•	•	•	•

PERENNIALS

NAME OF PLANT	CLIMATE ZONES	BEST TIME TO PLANT	DURATION OF BLOOM	YELLOW	ORANGE	RED	PINK	LAVENDER	PURPLE OR VIOLET	BLUE	WHITE	MULTI-COLORS
Bergenia crassifolia	1-9, 14-24	Summer or fall	Medium				•	•	•			
Bulbinella robusta	14-24	Spring	Medium	•								
Helleborus	All Zones	Summer or fall	Long				•		•		•	•
Iberis sempervirens (candytuft)	All Zones	Fall	Long								•	
Lampranthus (see page 303)	15-24	Summer or fall	Long	•	•	•	•		•			
Senecio cruentus (cineraria)	15-24	Spring or fall	Long				•	•	•	•	•	•
Strelitzia reginae (bird of paradise)	9, 12-24	Spring or fall	Long		•					•		•
Tulbaghia fragrans	14-24	Spring	Long				•	•				

SHRUBS

NAME OF PLANT	CLIMATE ZONES	BEST TIME TO PLANT	DURATION OF BLOOM	YELLOW	ORANGE	RED	PINK	LAVENDER	PURPLE OR VIOLET	BLUE	WHITE	MULTI-COLORS
Camellia japonica	4-6, 8, 9, 14-24	Fall to spring	Medium			•	•				•	•
Euphorbia pulcherrima (poinsettia)	16-24	Summer	Long	•		•	•				•	
Jasminum mesnyi	4-24	Spring or fall	Long	•								

TREES

NAME OF PLANT	CLIMATE ZONES	BEST TIME TO PLANT	DURATION OF BLOOM	YELLOW	ORANGE	RED	PINK	LAVENDER	PURPLE OR VIOLET	BLUE	WHITE	MULTI-COLORS
Acacia baileyana	8, 9, 13-24	Spring or fall	Medium	•								
Erythrina caffra	21-24	Spring or fall	Medium			•						

PLANTS WITH GRAY FOLIAGE

There are plants with foliage in almost every shade of gray, including blue-gray, green-gray, pinkish gray, and silvery gray, or almost white. There are also interesting textures in gray foliage: some are velvety, others are lacy, feathery, or fernlike. Soft, subtle grays can tone down harsh or brilliant colors and create harmonious transitions. The monotony of a predominantly green garden can be relieved with silvery or gray-white foliage. Some gray plants have a luminosity that brightens a garden on a dark day or shines magically in the moonlight.

In the following list are plants with foliage in many different shades of gray. (The encylopedia section describes their shades.)

LOW-GROWING (TO 1 FT.)

NAME OF PLANT	KIND	CLIMATE ZONES	NAME OF PLANT	KIND	CLIMATE ZONES
Achillea clavennae argentea	Perennial	All Zones	Euphorbia myrsinites	Perennial	All Zones
Alyssum saxatile	Perennial	All Zones	Festuca ovina 'Glauca'	Grass	All Zones
Arabis alpina	Perennial	All Zones	Helianthemum nummula-	Shrublet	All Zones
Arabis caucasica	Perennial	All Zones	rium (some varieties)		
Artemisia frigida	Perennial	All Zones	Sedum brevifolium	Succulent	8, 9, 14-24
Artemisia schmidtiana 'Nana'	Perennial	All Zones	Sedum oaxacanum	Succulent	8-24
Centaurea cineraria	Perennial	8-24	Sedum sieboldii	Succulent	All Zones
(dusty miller)			Sempervivum arachnoideum	Succulent	All Zones
Cerastium tomentosum	Perennial	All Zones	Sempervivum tectorum	Succulent	All Zones
			Thymus lanuginosus (thyme)	Ground cover	All Zones

MEDIUM HEIGHT (1 to 3 FT.)

NAME OF PLANT	KIND	CLIMATE ZONES	NAME OF PLANT	KIND	CLIMATE ZONES
Artemisia albula 'Silver Queen'	Perennial	All Zones	Lotus berthelotii	Perennial	9, 13-24
			Lychnis coronaria	Annual	All Zones
Catananche coerulea	Perennial	All Zones	Nepeta mussinii	Perennial	All Zones
Centaurea gymnocarpa	Perennial	8-24	Salvia officinalis (sage)	Herb	All Zones
Convolvulus cneorum	Shrub	5-9, 12-24	Santolina chamaecyparissus	Subshrub	All Zones
Dianthus 'Allwoodii' (pink)	Perennial	All Zones	Sedum sediforme	Succulent	8-24
Dianthus caryophyllus (carnation)	Perennial	All Zones	Senecio cineraria (dusty miller)	Perennial	All Zones
Helichrysum petiolatum	Perennial	17, 22-24	Stachys olympica	Perennial	1-9, 12-24
			Zauschneria californica	Subshrub	4-9, 14-24

TALL GROWING (3 FT. AND OVER)

NAME OF PLANT	KIND	CLIMATE ZONES	NAME OF PLANT	KIND	CLIMATE ZONES
Artemisia pontica	Shrub	All Zones	Eriogonum arborescens	Shrub	14-24
Artichoke	Vegetable	8, 9, 14-24	Eriogonum giganteum	Shrub	14-24
Cytisus battandieri	Shrub	5, 6	Lavandula spica (lavender)	Shrub	All Zones
Echinops exaltatus 'Taplow Blue'	Perennial	All Zones	Phlomis fruticosa	Perennial	All Zones
			Romneya coulteri	Perennial	5-10
			Senecio greyii	Shrub	5-9, 14-24
			Senecio leucostachys	Perennial	All Zones
			Teucrium fruticans	Shrub	4-24

SHOWY FRUITS AND BERRIES

There are some plants that earn their place in Western gardens not so much for their flowers as for their colorful or otherwise attractive display of fruits.

Listed on these pages are 54 such plants, the climate zones in which they grow best, and brief descriptions of what their fruits look like. You'll find more details about the fruits that grow on these plants in the plant description in this book's Western Plant Encyclopedia. And you will also find many of these same plants listed under Plants that Attract Birds, page 132.

Notice that many of these plants have edible fruits. But not all edible attractive fruits—such as citrus, eggplant, cherry—are listed.

SHRUBS

NAME OF PLANT	CLIMATE ZONES	WHAT FRUITS LOOK LIKE
Acmena smithii	15-17, 19-24	Edible, mainly lavender berries in winter
Acokanthera	21, 23, 24	Very poisonous black, olive-sized fruits
Arbutus unedo	4-24	Strawberrylike winter fruit, edible but mealy
Arctostaphylos uva-ursi	1-9, 14-24	Bright red or pinkish fruit. Prostrate ground cover
Aronia arbutifolia	1-7	Long fall season of bright red foliage, fruit
Berberis	4-6, 15-17	Shiny berries are dark blue or black
Carissa grandiflora	13, 16-21	Edible, red plum-shaped fruits follow fragrant white flowers
Cornus mas	1-6	Clusters of edible scarlet fruit in September
Cotoneaster	Vary by kind	Produces more berries in poor soil
Euonymus fortunei 'Vegeta'	1-17	Attractive fruit—orange seeds in "hat boxes"
Euonymus kiautschovica	4-13	Showy pinkish fruit with red seeds
Feijoa sellowiana (pineapple guava)	8, 9, 12-24	Bland, pineapple-flavored, gray-green fruit
Heteromeles arbutifolia	5-24	Bright red clustered berries in winter
Ilex (holly)	Vary by kind	Berries are red, orange, yellow, or black
Ligustrum (privet)	Vary by kind	Small, blue-black fruits conspicuous on unpruned plants
Mahonia	Vary by kind	Yellow flowers precede blue-black berries

NAME OF PLANT	CLIMATE ZONES	WHAT FRUITS LOOK LIKE
Nandina domestica	5-24	Single plants seldom fruit heavily
Pernettya mucronata	4-7, 14-17	Half-inch berries with metallic sheen
Photinia	Vary by kind	Attractive foliage and fruit color
Pittosporum rhombifolium	14-24	Yellow, orange fruit contrasts with glossy leaves
Psidium cattleianum	9, 14-24	Tart-sweet edible fruit, usually dark red
Punica granatum 'Nana' (dwarf pomegranate)	5-24	Small, dry red fruits
Pyracantha coccinea	All Zones	Popular for bright berries, evergreen foliage
Raphiolepis	4-10, 14-24	Dark blue berries follow profusion of blooms
Rhamnus californica	4-24	Large berries change from green to red to black
Rhus, shrubby kinds	Vary by kind	White or reddish fruits, sometimes furry
Skimmia	4-9, 14-22	Red hollylike fruit through December
Solanum pseudocapsicum	23, 24	Fruits like tiny tomatoes; may be poisonous
Stranvaesia	4-11, 14-17	Red berry clusters against bronzy foliage
Syzygium jambos	18-24	Small, greenish yellow fruit; sweet flavor
Ugni molinae	14-24	Flavorsome fruits useful in jellies
Vaccinium (huckleberry, lingonberry)	Vary by kind	Tasty red or black berries
Viburnum	Vary by kind	Many kinds have showy fruit.

Showy fruits and berries (cont'd.)

TREES

NAME OF PLANT	CLIMATE ZONES	WHAT FRUITS LOOK LIKE
Arbutus menziesii (madrone)	1-7, 14-19	Orange and red wrinkly berries in fall
Avocado	9, 16-24	Green to purplish edible fruit. Dense shade tree
Cornus nuttallii	2-9, 14-20	Decorative buttonlike fruit clusters in fall
Crataegus (hawthorn)	1-11, 14-17	Showy fruits in summer and fall
Eriobotrya japonica (loquat)	4-24	Aromatic, sweet, edible fruit, large smooth seeds
Macadamia ternifolia	9, 16, 17, 19-24	Winter clusters of hard-shelled delicious nuts
Malus (crabapple)	1-11, 14-21	Colorful little apples follow handsome flowers
Olea europaea (olive)	7-24	Green fruit, turning black. Must be processed to be edible
Persimmon	Vary by kind	Orangey edible fruit with outstanding ornamental qualities
Punica granatum 'Wonderful'	5-24	Best known fruiting pomegranate, red flowers

NAME OF PLANT	CLIMATE ZONES	WHAT FRUITS LOOK LIKE
Schinus molle (California pepper tree)	8, 9, 12-24	Clusters of tiny rose-colored berries; fall, winter
Schinus terebinthifolius	15-17, 19-24	Bright red berries very showy in winter
Sorbus aucuparia	1-6, 15-17	Midsummer bright orange-red berries hang on until midwinter
Syzygium paniculatum	16, 17, 19-24	Showy, rosy fruit, edible but insipid
Zizyphus jujuba	4-16, 18-24	Shiny, reddish brown datelike fruits in fall

VINES

NAME OF PLANT	CLIMATE ZONES	WHAT FRUITS LOOK LIKE
Actinidia chinensis	4-6, 15-17	Gooseberry-flavored fall fruit
Celastrus (bittersweet)	All Zones	Orangey capsules split, show red seeds
Grape	All Zones	For best fruit, choose kind for your climate
Passiflora edulis	16, 17, 21-24	Passion fruits are delicious and fragrant

AUTUMN FOLIAGE COLOR

Many plants change their leaf color in fall when air begins to get cold. They do it in varying degrees depending on the nature of the plant and the kind of climate they grow in (generally, in mild-winter areas the change is less noticeable than in cold-winter areas). In some cases, the color change is simply to a dull tone before leaves fall, or, in the case of evergreens, before the new crop of leaves forms. The plants listed below make an autumnal foliage color change worthy of notice. They are plants that you can put in a garden just for this particular contribution.

TREES

NAME OF TREE	CLIMATE ZONES	COLOR OF AUTUMN LEAVES
Acer davidii	1-6, 15	Bright yellow, red-orange, purple
Acer macrophyllum	4-17	Spectacular yellow
Acer negundo	1-9, 12-20	Yellow
Acer platanoides	1-9, 14, 15	Yellow
Acer rubrum	1-6, 14-16	Brilliant scarlet

NAME OF TREE	CLIMATE ZONES	COLOR OF AUTUMN LEAVES
Acer saccharum	1-9, 14, 15	Scarlet-orange, yellow
Cercidiphyllum japonicum	4-6, 14-16, 18-20	Brilliant red or yellow
Cornus (dogwood)	1-9, 14-16	Reds and yellows
Cotinus coggygria	1-11, 14-16	Yellow to orange-red
Crataegus lavallei	1-11, 14-16	Bronze red

Autumn foliage color (cont'd.)

NAME OF TREE	CLIMATE ZONES	COLOR OF AUTUMN LEAVES
Crataegus phaenopyrum	1-11, 14-16	Orange and red
Cryptomeria japonica 'Elegans'	4-6, 8, 9, 14-20	Coppery red or purplish
Fagus sylvatica	1-9, 14-16	Red-brown
Franklinia alatamaha	2-6, 14-17	Scarlet
Fraxinus ornus (ash)	1-9, 14-17	Soft lavender and yellow
Fraxinus velutina 'Modesto'	8, 9, 13-24	Bright yellow
Ginkgo biloba	1-9, 14-24	Gold
Gleditsia triacanthos 'Shademaster'	1-13, 18-20	Yellow
Koelreuteria henryi	8-16	Yellow
Koelreuteria paniculata	2-16	Yellow
Lagerstroemia	7-9, 14, 15, 18-21	Yellow or orange to red
Larix (larch)	Vary by kind	Bright yellow and orange
Liquidambar styraciflua	1-9, 14-24	Purple, yellow, or red
Liriodendron tulipifera	1-10, 14-23	Yellow or yellow and brown
Nyssa sylvatica	1-10, 14-21	Coppery red

NAME OF TREE	CLIMATE ZONES	COLOR OF AUTUMN LEAVES
Oxydendrum arboreum	1-9, 14-16	Orange and scarlet
Parrotia persica	4-6, 15-17	Yellow to orange to scarlet
Persimmon, Japanese	7-9, 14-16, 18-23	Yellow, orange or scarlet
Pistacia chinensis	8-16, 18-23	Scarlet, crimson, orange, yellow
Populus fremontii	7-11	Bright lemon yellow
Populus nigra 'Italica'	1-11, 14-21	Golden yellow
Populus tremuloides	1-7	Brilliant golden yellow
Prunus cerasifera 'Atropurpurea' (see page 387)	2-20	Purplish red
Prunus sargentii (see page 386)	1-7, 14-16	Yellow and red
Punica granatum	7-24	Brilliant yellow
Quercus coccinea	1-16	Bright scarlet
Quercus palustris	1-16	Yellow, red, and brown
Quercus rubra	1-16	Dark red, brown, or orange
Salix babylonica	All Zones	Yellow
Sapium sebiferum	8, 9, 14-16, 18-21	Bright red, plum purple, or yellow orange
Sorbus aucuparia	1-6, 14, 15	Yellow or rusty yellow
Stewartia	4-6, 14-16	Orange or red

SHRUBS

NAME OF SHRUB	CLIMATE ZONES	COLOR OF AUTUMN LEAVES
Acer circinatum	1-6, 15	Orange-scarlet or yellow
Acer ginnala	1-9, 14-16	Striking red
Acer palmatum	1-9, 14-15	Red, yellow, or rose
Amelanchier	1-3	Yellow to red
Berberis thunbergii	1-11, 14-20	Yellow, orange, and red
Cercis occidentalis	2-9, 14-24	Light yellow or red
Cotinus coggygria	1-11, 14-16	Yellow to orange-red
Cotoneaster horizontalis	1-11, 14-16	Orange and red
Enkianthus	2-9, 14-16	Orange and red
Euonymus alata	1-9, 14-16	Rose red
Fothergilla	2-9, 14-17	Red or orange to purplish red
Hydrangea quercifolia	1-16	Bronze or crimson
Lagerstroemia	7-9, 14, 15, 18-21	Yellow or orange to red
Lindera benzoin	1-7	Bright yellow

NAME OF SHRUB	CLIMATE ZONES	COLOR OF AUTUMN LEAVES
Nandina	5-16, 18-20	Purplish and bronzy green to red
Pernettya mucronata	4-7, 14-17	Red or bronzy
Photinia serrulata	4-16, 18-22	Scattered crimson
Rhus glabra (sumac)	1-9, 14-17	Brilliant scarlet
Rhus typhina	1-9, 14-16	Rich red
Viburnum opulus	1-11, 14-16	Red
Viburnum plicatum tomentosum	1-11, 14-16	Purplish red

OTHER PLANTS FOR FALL COLOR

NAME OF PLANT	CLIMATE ZONES	COLOR OF AUTUMN LEAVES
Kochia scoparia 'Culta' (annual)	All Zones	Red
Parthenocissus species (vine)	All Zones	Orange to scarlet

FRAGRANCE IN THE GARDEN

Here are plants of all kinds that can perfume garden air in one way or another—most with flowers, some by way of moistened or crushed leaves. Fragrant plants represent such a variety of landscape uses that you should turn to other lists in this chapter and to the encyclopedia section to find how to use them.

NAME OF PLANT	KIND	CLIMATE ZONES	THE KIND OF FRAGRANCE
Aloysia triphylla (lemon verbena)	Shrub	9, 10, 14-24	Lemon-scented leaves; use to flavor iced drinks.
Amaryllis belladonna (naked lady)	Bulb	4-24	Heavily scented rosy pink flowers.
Anthemis nobilis (chamomile)	Perennial	All Zones	Bruised leaves have pleasant scent.
Artemisia	Shrub	All Zones	Sagebrush-scented silvery foliage.
Boronia megastigma	Shrub	17	Heady bouquet like orange blossoms.
Bouvardia longiflora 'Albatross'	Shrub	13, 16, 17, 19-24	Heavily fragrant tubular flowers.
Calocedrus decurrens (incense cedar)	Tree	1-12, 14-24	Pungent fragrance in warm weather.
Carissa grandiflora	Shrub	13, 16-24	Large white flowers nearly as fragrant as star jasmine.
Cedrus atlantica	Tree	4-16, 18-23	"Christmas tree" scent, especially after rain.
Cestrum nocturnum (night jessamine)	Shrub	13, 16-24	Penetrating fragrance. At best on summer nights.
Cestrum parqui	Shrub	13-24	Its perfume is potent.
Chimonanthus praecox	Shrub	4-9, 14-17	Spicy fragrance in late winter.
Choiysa ternata (Mexican orange)	Shrub	4-9, 12-24	Delicate orange blossom fragrance.
Citrus	Tree	8, 9, 12-24	Subtle fragrance doesn't become tiresome.
Clematis armandii	Vine	4-9, 12-17	Glistening white fragrant flowers.
Coleonema album	Shrub	7-9, 14-24	Foliage has a piny fragrance.
Convallaria majalis (lily-of-the-valley)	Perennial	1-7	Small bouquet will perfume a room.
Cupressus (cypress)	Tree	Vary by kind	Sweet fragrance for Christmas decorations.
Daphne	Shrub	Vary by kind	Fragrance pervades even on cool days.
Datura candida	Shrub	16-24	Heavy, musky night fragrance.
Dianthus (pink, carnation)	Perennial	All Zones	Clove or cinnamon scented flowers.
Eucalyptus citriodora	Tree	16, 17, 19-24	Foliage lemon-scented when crushed.
Freesia	Bulb	8, 9, 12-24	Sweetly perfumed, long lasting spring favorite.
Gardenia	Shrub	Vary by kind	Unmistakable, unique sweetness.
Hamamelis mollis (Chinese witch hazel)	Shrub	4-7, 15-17	Fragrant yellow flowers with narrow crumpled petals.
Hedychium	Perennial	17, 22-24	Rich, ginger-scented flowers in dense spikes.
Heliotropium arborescens	Perennial	All Zones	Flowers have fruity cherry-pie fragrance.
Hyacinthus (hyacinth)	Bulb	All Zones	Very fragrant, early spring blooms.
Hymenocallis	Bulb	5, 6, 8, 9, 14-24	Huge white flowers. Fragrant in clusters.

PLANTS THAT ARE FRAGRANT (cont.)

NAME OF PLANT	KIND	CLIMATE ZONES	THE KIND OF FRAGRANCE
Hymenosporum flavum	Tree	8, 9, 14-16, 18-23	Orange-blossom honey fragrance.
Jasminum grandiflorum	Shrub	9, 12-24	Fragrant, as are most of the evergreen types.
Laurus nobilis	Tree	6-10, 12-24	Leaves aromatic.
Lavandula spica (English lavender)	Shrub	All Zones	Fresh or dried, English lavender gives nostalgic fragrance.
Lilium (lily)	Bulb	All Zones	Notably fragrant in summer.
Lobularia maritima (sweet alyssum)	Annual	All Zones	Sweetly fragrant during cool seasons.
Lonicera (honeysuckle)	Shrub-Vine	Vary by kind	Most species valued for hauntingly sweet fragrance.
Magnolia grandiflora	Tree	4-12, 14-24	Heavy, very sweet scent.
Mandevilla laxa	Vine	4-9, 14-21	White trumpets have intense aroma.
Matthiola (stock)	Annual	All Zones	Cut stock holds its heavy spicy perfume for days.
Michelia figo	Shrub	9, 14-24	Creamy yellow blooms release a banana fragrance.
Myrtus communis (myrtle)	Shrub	8-24	Leaves give off pleasant aroma when brushed against.
Narcissus, Jonquilla hybrids	Bulb	All Zones	Very fragrant yellow, orange, ivory white flowers.
Nicotiana	Annual	All Zones	Sweet perfume as blossoms open at evening.
Osmanthus	Shrub	Vary by kind	Flowers sweeten the summer air day and night.
Philadelphus coronarius (sweet mock orange)	Shrub	1-17	Intense fragrance, somewhat like citrus.
Pittosporum tobira	Shrub	4-24	Faint orange blossom fragrance, night and day.
Plumeria rubra	Shrub	21-24	Very fragrant frangipani blossoms when limbs are bare.
Polianthes tuberosa (tuberose)	Bulb	24	Powerful, intoxicating fragrance.
Prunus 'Alma Stultz' (see page 385)	Tree	4-6, 15-17	Flowers are deliciously fragrant.
Reseda odorata (mignonette)	Annual	All Zones	Plant in masses for full effect of fragrance.
Rhododendron 'Fragrantissimum'	Shrub	4-6, 15-17	Powerfully fragrant large, white flowers.
Robinia pseudoacacia (black locust)	Tree	All Zones	Pendulous clusters have clean sweet fragrance.
Rosa (rose)	Shrub	All Zones	Fragrance is lacking in some roses, intense in others.
Rosmarinus officinalis (rosemary)	Shrub	4-24	Resinous odor from foliage.
Sarcococca humilis	Shrub	4-9, 14-24	Fragrance carries even on cold days.
Sarcococca ruscifolia	Shrub	4-9, 14-24	Noticeably fragrant flowers nearly hidden in foliage.
Stephanotis floribunda	Vine	23, 24	One of the most enjoyable floral fragrances.
Syringa vulgaris (lilac)	Shrub	1-11	Fragrance is legendary.
Thymus (thyme)	Ground	All Zones	Herbal smell when trod upon.
Trachelospermum jasminoides (star jasmine)	Vine	8-24	Perhaps the most fragrant vine.
Viburnum	Shrub	Vary by kind	Several deciduous species are grown for fragrant flowers.
Viola odorata (violet)	Perennial	All Zones	Several of the large flowered named varieties are just as sweet as the old fashioned violet.
Wisteria	Vine	All Zones	Drooping flower strands give delicate odor.

INTERESTING WINTER EFFECTS

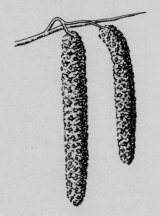

A sensitive or practiced eye can take great joy from some of the most subtle of seasonal performances by plants. This is one of those subleties. Once you open your eyes to the wintertime delights described here you can find regular enjoyment in them. You may even find a way to incorporate these plants' into your garden for the special effects that they give in winter.

Or, you might grow some of these in containers that you can move close by a window so you can enjoy them from inside. Or light them. Midwinter days are short, so they can be illuminated early in the evening. At Christmas time you can hang them with decorations. Most of the year leaves clothe deciduous plants. In winter, instead, you see twigs, bark, and fruits.

TREES

NAME	CLIMATE ZONES	WINTER FEATURES
Acer davidii	1-6, 15-17, 20, 21	Bark green striped with white
Acer rubrum	1-6, 14-17	Red twigs and branchlets
Aesculus californica	4-7, 14-19	Silvery trunk, branches, branchlets
Alnus rhombifolia	1-9, 14-21	Small woody cones
Betula (birch)	Vary by kind	Flaky bark. Conelike fruit
Crataegus lavallei (hawthorn)	1-11, 14-17	Very large orange to red fruits
Crataegus phaenopyrum	1-11, 14-17	Chinese red fruits
Dalea spinosa	11-13	Network of grey branches
Erythrina caffra	21-24	Angular branch structure
Fagus sylvatica 'Pendula'	1-9, 14-24	Irregular form, weeping branches
Fig	4-9, 12-24	Gnarled trunk. Picturesque silhouette

NAME	CLIMATE ZONES	WINTER FEATURES
Hamamelis mollis	4-7, 15-17	Zigzag branch pattern
Koelreuteria paniculata	2-21	Fruits buff to brown
Liquidambar styraciflua	1-9, 14-24	Branch pattern, furrowed bark, hanging fruits
Persimmon, Oriental	4-16, 18-23	Orange-scarlet fruit. Picturesque branches
Platanus (plane, sycamore)	Vary by kind	Interesting bark, seed clusters
Platanus racemosa	4-24	Twisted smooth branches
Quercus alba	All Zones	Gray bark. Rugged framework
Quercus kelloggii	5-7, 15, 16	Interesting trunk and branch pattern
Salix alba 'Tristis'	All Zones	Bright yellow twigs
Sorbus aucuparia	1-6, 15-17	Orange-red fruit
Stewartia monadelpha	4-6, 14-17, 20, 21	Distinctive branch pattern. Flaking bark
Ziziphus jujuba	7-16, 18-24	Attractive silhouette

SHRUBS

NAME	CLIMATE ZONES	WINTER FEATURES
Acer circinatum	1-6, 15-17	Contorted branch pattern
Acer palmatum	1-9, 14-24	Green and red branch pattern
Acer palmatum 'Sangokaku'	Same as above	Twigs, young branches red
Amelanchier	1-3	Attractive branch and twig pattern
Cercis occidentalis	2-9, 14-24	Picturesque branch pattern
Chaenomeles (flowering quince)	1-21	Flowers on angular, picturesque, bare branches

NAME	CLIMATE ZONES	WINTER FEATURES
Cornus alba 'Sibirica'	1-9, 14-24	Coral red branches
Cornus stolonifera	1-9, 14-21	Bright red twigs
Corylopsis pauciflora	4-7, 15-17	Open, delicate branching pattern
Cotoneaster	Vary by kind	Berries
Kerria japonica	1-21	Green branches
Koelreuteria paniculata	2-21	Fruits buff to brown
Lagerstroemia indica	1-9, 12-14, 18-21	Attractive bark. Interesting branch pattern
Rhus typhina	1-9, 14-17	Fuzzy crimson fruit
Salix magnifica	4-6, 14-17	Red shoots
Salix purpurea	All Zones	Purple branches

DRAMATIC LEAVES

A quick way to add drama to a garden is to use plants with big, bold leaves. In containers they can add a tropical feeling to a patio or court, even though the plants may be completely hardy, even deciduous. Rain or sprinkler water that splashes on big leaves gives you the rare opportunity to *hear* your garden.

Big-leafed plants give bold shadow patterns against a wall, fence, or when seen through a translucent plastic panel, and for this reason are favorite subjects for garden lighting. Wind tends to shred and tear most large leaves, so use them in protected locations. They also show up damage done by chewing critters more readily than smaller-leafed plants.

Another group of plants have sword-shaped leaves. These give a very strong design element to their area of the garden.

BIG, BOLD LEAVES

NAME OF PLANT	KIND	CLIMATE ZONES
Acanthus	Perennial	4-24
Alocasia macrorhiza	Perennial	22-24
Alpinia speciosa	Perennial	15-17, 22-24
Aralia chinensis	Tree	2-24
Aralia spinosa	Tree	2-24
Asarum caudatum	Perennial	4-6, 15-17, 21
Aucuba	Shrub	4-11, 14-23
Banana	Perennial	See Musa, Ensete
Beaumontia grandiflora	Vine	13, 21-24
Bergenia	Perennial	1-9, 14-24
Brassaia actinophylla	Shrub, tree	21-24
Caladium bicolor	Perennial	23, 24
Canna	Bulb	All Zones
Catalpa	Tree	All Zones
Clerodendrum trichotomum	Shrub, tree	5, 6, 15-17, 20-24
Colocasia esculenta	Perennial	16-24
Dombeya wallichii	Shrub	21-24
Eriobotrya	Tree, shrub	8, 9, 14-24
Fatshedera lizei	Shrub, vine	4-9, 14-24
Fatsia japonica	Shrub	4-9, 14-24
Ferns, certain kinds		Vary by kind
Ficus (ornamental)	Tree, vine	Vary by kind
Fig	Tree	Vary by kind
Firmiana platanifolia	Tree	5, 6, 8, 9, 12-24
Gunnera chilensis	Perennial	4-6, 14-17, 20-24
Gunnera manicata	Perennial	4-6, 14-17, 20-24

NAME OF PLANT	KIND	CLIMATE ZONES
Helleborus	Perennial	All Zones
Hosta	Perennial	1-10, 12-21
Hydrangea	Shrub, vine	1-22
Magnolia acuminata	Tree	1-9, 14-21
Magnolia campbellii	Tree	4-9, 14-21
Magnolia grandiflora	Tree	4-24
Magnolia macrophylla	Tree	2-9, 14-21
Mahonia lomariifolia	Shrub	6-9, 14-24
Melianthus major	Shrub	8, 9, 12-24
Monstera deliciosa	Vine	21-24
Nymphaea	Water plant	All Zones
Paulownia tomentosa	Tree	All Zones
Persea	Tree	Vary by kind
Philodendron selloum	Shrub	8, 9, 12-24
Plumeria	Shrub	21-24
Rauwolfia samarensis	Tree	22-24
Rhododendron, some kinds	Shrub	Vary by kind
Rhoicissus capensis	Vine	16, 17, 21-24
Rhubarb	Vegetable	1-11
Ricinus communis	Annual	All Zones
Solandra	Vine	15-24
Sparmannia africana	Shrub, tree	16-24
Strelitzia	Perennial	Vary by kind
Tetrapanax papyriferus	Shrub	15-24
Tupidanthus calyptratus	Shrub, tree	19-24
Viburnum cinnamomifolium	Shrub	5-9, 14-24
Viburnum davidii	Shrub	4-9, 14-24
Viburnum rhytidophyllum	Shrub	2-9, 14-24
Wigandia caracasana	Perennial	17, 22-24
Zantedeschia	Bulb	5, 6, 8, 9, 14-24

PLANTS WITH DECORATIVE, SWORD-SHAPED LEAVES

NAME OF PLANT	KIND	CLIMATE ZONES
Agapanthus	Perennial	8, 9, 12-24
Agave	Succulent	12-24
Aloe	Succulent	8, 9, 12-24

NAME OF PLANT	KIND	CLIMATE ZONES
Cordyline australis	Tree	8-11, 14-24
Doryanthes palmeri	Succulent	15-17, 19-24
Dracaena draco	Tree	17, 23, 24
Iris	Bulb	All Zones
Moraea	Bulb	8-24
Palms	Tree	Vary by kind
Phormium tenax	Perennial	Vary by kind
Yucca	Shrub, tree	Vary by kind

GOOD CHOICES FOR ROCK GARDENS

Gathered together here are plants frequently seen in association with rocks. Some are rock plants in the classic tradition of the English rock garden. Far more are plants used effectively in a variety of rock situations. Many popular rock plants of the Pacific Northwest are used as ground covers in southern California.

TOUGHEST, EASIEST ROCK GARDEN PLANTS
All take sun

NAME OF PLANT	KIND	CLIMATE ZONES
Alyssum saxatile	Perennial	All Zones
Arabis	Perennial	Vary by kind
Aubrieta deltoidea	Perennial	1-9, 14-21
Calluna vulgaris (see page 291)	Shrub	2-6, 17
Carissa grandiflora	Shrub	13, 16-24
Cerastium tomentosum	Perennial	All Zones
Erica arborea (see page 291)	Shrub	4-6, 15-17, 21-24
Festuca ovina 'Glauca'	Ornamental grass	All Zones
Iberis sempervirens	Perennial	All Zones
Juniperus	Shrub	All Zones
Lotus	Shrub	Vary by kind
Nepeta mussinii	Perennial	All Zones
Oscularia deltoides (see page 303)	Shrub	15-24
Phlox subulata	Perennial	1-17
Potentilla verna	Perennial	All Zones
Sedum acre	Succulent	All Zones
Sedum amecamecanum	Succulent	8, 9, 14-24
Sedum brevifolium	Succulent	8, 9, 14-24
Sedum dendroideum	Succulent	8, 9, 14-24
Sedum lineare	Succulent	All Zones
Teucrium chamaedrys	Shrub	All Zones
Thymus (thyme)	Ground cover	All Zones
Verbena peruviana	Perennial	8-24

PLANTS WITH ROCKS IN PARTIAL SHADE

NAME OF PLANT	KIND	CLIMATE ZONES
Adiantum pedatum	Fern	1-9, 14-21
Andromeda polifolia	Shrub	All Zones
Aquilegia (columbine)	Perennial	All Zones
Ardisia japonica	Shrub	5, 6, 15-17
Asplenium trichomanes	Fern	All Zones
Azalea, low growers (see page 395)	Shrub	Vary by kind
Bergenia cordifolia	Perennial	1-9, 14-24
Blechnum spicant	Fern	1-9, 14-24
Campanula portenschlagiana	Perennial	1-9, 14-24
Daphne cneorum	Shrub	2-9, 14-17
Helleborus	Fern	All Zones
Irish moss, Scotch moss	Fern	4-9, 14-24
Ophiopogon japonicum (see page 325)	Perennial	All Zones
Oxalis	Perennial	All Zones
Polystichum munitum	Perennial	5-9, 14-24
Soleirolia soleirolii	Perennial	Vary by kind
Viola	Perennial	8-21
Woodwardia fimbriata	Perennial	Vary by kind

CHOICE PLANTS FOR THE TRADITIONAL ROCK GARDEN

NAME OF PLANT	KIND	CLIMATE ZONES
Achillea (yarrow)	Perennial	1-24
Aethionema	Perennial	1-9
Anemone pulsatilla	Perennial	1-6
Cornus canadensis	Ground cover	1-6
Draba olympica	Perennial	1-6
Dryas octopetala	Perennial	1-6
Epimedium	Perennial	1-9, 14-17
Erysimum kotschyanum	Perennial	1-11, 14-21
Gentiana	Perennial	1-6, 14-17
Hebe, lower kinds	Shrub	Vary by kind
Iris cristata	Bulb	1-24
Linum perenne	Perennial	All Zones
Lithodora diffusa	Perennial	5-7, 14-17
Menziesia purpurea	Shrub	4-7, 14-17
Oxalis adenophylla	Perennial	4-9, 14-24
Penstemon rupicola	Shrub	1-7
Pimelea coarctata	Shrub	4-7, 14-17
Veronica	Perennial	All Zones

PLANTS TO GO WITH LARGE ROCKS

Maybe one rock with one plant and ground cover, or plants in rock outcroppings, or in rocky meadow.

NAME OF PLANT	KIND	CLIMATE ZONES
Agapanthus	Perennial	8, 9, 12-24
Agave attenuata	Succulent	20-24
Aloe striata	Succulent	8, 9, 12-24
Bamboo	Grass	Vary by kind
Cistus	Shrub	4-6, 7-9, 12-24
Cordyline indivisa	Shrub	16, 17, 20-24
Crassula falcata	Succulent	8, 9, 12-21
Crassula multicava	Succulent	8, 9, 12-21
Felicia amelloides	Perennial	8, 9, 13-24
Mahonia aquifolium	Shrub	1-21
Mahonia bealei	Shrub	All Zones
Mahonia lomariifolia	Shrub	6-9, 14-24
Moraea iridioides	Bulb	8-24
Nandina domestica	Shrub	5-24
Pennisetum setaceum	Perennial	All Zones
Phormium tenax	Perennial	5-24
Pinus mugo mughus	Shrub	1-11, 14-24
Pinus thunbergiana	Tree	1-12, 14-24
Taxus baccata 'Repandens'	Shrub	1-9, 14-24
Yucca recurvifolia	Perennial	7-24

STANDARDS

The Gardeners' Language section in this book defines a standard as "A plant that does not naturally grow as a tree, trained into a small treelike form with a single, upright trunk and rounded crown. The tree rose is the most familiar example."

The plants listed here lend themselves to this kind of training. Many of them are sold by nurseries as ready-trained standards. Or, you can train any of them in that fashion, yourself. First, select a vigorous, upright stem. Cut out other upright stems if there are any, and also remove side branches on the selected stem. Tie the selected stem to a stake and, as it grows, continue to tie new growth into the vertical position. After the tip passes the point where you want it to branch, cut the top off. Branches will form beneath the cut. Save them but remove side branches on the trunk.

NAME OF PLANT	KIND	CLIMATE ZONES
Acmena smithii	Shrub	15-17, 19-24
Arbutus unedo	Shrub	4-24
Azalea, Southern Indica (see page 398)	Shrub	8, 9, 14-24
Buxus sempervirens (boxwood)	Shrub	3-6, 15-17
Calliandra inaequilatera	Shrub	22-24
Callistemon citrinus	Shrub	8, 9, 12-24
Callistemon viminalis	Shrub	8, 9, 12-24
Camellia japonica	Shrub	4-6, 8, 9, 14-24
Carissa edulis	Shrub	13, 16-24
Cedrus atlantica	Tree	4-16, 18-23
Cestrum purpureum	Shrub	13, 17, 19-24
Citrus	Tree	8, 9, 12-24
Cotoneaster parneyi	Shrub	4-24
Cotoneaster 'Pendula'	Shrub	4-24
Cupressus glabra	Tree	8-24
Datura suaveolens	Shrub	16-24
Dodonaea viscosa	Shrub	7-9, 12-24
Duranta stenostachya	Shrub	13, 16, 17, 21-24
Eriobotrya japonica (loquat)	Tree	4-24
Eucalyptus ficifolia	Tree	15-17, 22-24
Eugenia uniflora	Shrub	21-24
Fatsia japonica	Shrub	4-9, 14-24
Feijoa sellowiana	Shrub	8, 9, 12-24
Ficus benjamina	Tree	13, 23, 24
Ficus retusa	Tree	9, 13-24
Fuchsia	Shrub	Vary by kind
Gardenia thunbergia	Shrub	16, 17, 21-24
Griselinia lucida	Shrub	9, 14-17, 20-24
Heteromeles arbutifolia (toyon)	Shrub	5-24
Hibiscus rosa-sinensis	Shrub	9, 14-16, 19-24
Hibiscus syriacus	Shrub	1-21
Hydrangea paniculata 'Grandiflora'	Shrub	1-21
Ilex altaclarensis 'Wilsonii'	Shrub	3-24
Jasminum nudiflorum	Shrub	3-21
Lagerstroemia indica	Tree	1-9, 12-14, 18-21
Lantana montevidensis	Shrub	12-24
Laurus nobilis (sweet bay)	Tree	6-10, 12-24
Ligustrum lucidum (privet)	Shrub	5, 6, 8-24
Macadamia ternifolia	Tree	9, 16, 17, 19-24
Magnolia grandiflora 'Majestic Beauty'	Tree	4-12, 14-24
Magnolia grandiflora 'St. Mary'	Tree	4-12, 14-24
Magnolia kobus stellata	Shrub	1-9, 14-24
Magnolia liliflora	Shrub	2-9, 14-24
Maytenus boaria	Tree	8, 9, 14-21
Metrosideros excelsa	Tree	17, 23, 24
Murraya paniculata	Shrub	21-24
Myrica californica	Shrub	4-6, 14-17, 20-24
Myrtus communis (myrtle)	Shrub	8-24
Nerium oleander	Shrub	8-16, 18-23
Olea europaea (olive)	Tree	7-24
Osmanthus fragrans	Shrub	8, 9, 12-24
Pelargonium (geranium)	Perennial	8, 9, 12-24
Photinia fraseri	Shrub	4-24
Photinia serrulata	Shrub	4-16, 18-22
Pittosporum crassifolium	Shrub	9, 14-17, 19-24
Pittosporum rhombifolium	Shrub	14-24
Pittosporum tobira	Shrub	4-24
Pittosporum undulatum	Shrub	16, 17, 21-24
Prunus caroliniana	Shrub	7-24
Prunus laurocerasus	Shrub	4-9, 14-24
Psidium cattleianum	Shrub	9, 14-24
Pyracantha coccinea 'Government Red'	Shrub	All Zones
Pyrus kawakamii	Shrub	8, 9, 12-24
Raphiolepis indica	Shrub	8-10, 14-24
Rhododendron 'Bow Bells'	Shrub	4-9, 14-24
Rosa (rose)	Shrub	All Zones
Solanum rantonnetii	Shrub	15-24
Sophora secundiflora	Shrub	8-16, 18-24
Stenocarpus sinuatus	Tree	16, 17, 20-24
Syzygium paniculatum	Shrub	16, 17, 19-24
Ternstroemia gymnanthera	Shrub	4-9, 12-24
Umbellularia californica	Tree	4-10, 12-24
Viburnum japonicum	Shrub	5-9, 14-24
Viburnum odoratissimum	Shrub	5-9, 14-24
Viburnum tinus 'Robustum'	Shrub	4-9, 14-24
Wisteria floribunda	Vine	All Zones
Wisteria sinensis	Vine	All Zones
Xylosma congestum	Shrub	8-24

PLANTS THAT HAVE MANY TRUNKS

The 76 plants listed here have one thing in common—they all can have multiple trunks. This gives them a special usefulness. A tree or shrub with many trunks spreads wide. It puts emphasis on trunks and plant form. A few of them give the impression of a grove.

SHRUBS

NAME OF PLANT	EVERGREEN OR DECIDUOUS	CLIMATE ZONES
Eucalyptus grossa	Evergreen	16, 17, 20-24
Ligustrum japonicum	Evergreen	4-24
Magnolia soulangiana	Deciduous	1-10, 14-24
Myrica californica	Evergreen	4-6, 14-17, 20-24
Nandina domestica	Evergreen or semi-deciduous	5-24
Tetrapanax papyriferus	Evergreen	15-24
Yucca gloriosa	Evergreen	7-24

TREES

NAME OF PLANT	EVERGREEN OR DECIDUOUS	CLIMATE ZONES
Agonis flexuosa	Evergreen	15-17, 20-24
Albizia julibrissin	Deciduous	2-23
Alnus glutinosa	Deciduous	All Zones
Betula verrucosa (birch)	Deciduous	1-11, 14-24
Cercidiphyllum japonicum	Deciduous	4-6, 14-16, 18-20
Cordyline australis	Evergreen	8-11, 14-24
Cornus (dogwood)		
Cornus florida	Deciduous	1-9, 14-16
Cornus nuttallii	Deciduous	2-9, 14-20
Cupaniopsis anacardioides	Evergreen	16, 17, 19-24
Drimys winteri	Evergreen	8, 9, 14-24
Eriobotrya japonica	Evergreen	4-24
Erythrina caffra	Briefly deciduous	21-24
Eucalyptus polyanthemos	Evergreen	8-24
Eucalyptus spathulata	Evergreen	15-17, 19-24
Ficus retusa	Evergreen	9, 13-24
Ficus rubiginosa	Evergreen	18-24
Harpephyllum caffrum	Evergreen	17, 19, 21-24
Jacaranda acutifolia	Deciduous to semi-evergreen	9, 13-24
Ligustrum lucidum	Evergreen	5, 6, 8-24
Maytenus boaria	Evergreen	8, 9, 14-21
Olea europaea (olive)	Evergreen	7-24
Pinus bungeana	Evergreen	1-9, 14-21
Pittosporum undulatum	Evergreen	16, 17, 21-24
Platanus acerifolia	Deciduous	All Zones
Platanus racemosa	Deciduous	4-24
Podocarpus gracilior	Evergreen	8, 9, 13-24
Pseudopanax lessonii	Evergreen	17, 20-24
Rhus lancea	Evergreen	8, 9, 12-24
Schinus terebinthifolius	Evergreen	15-17, 19-24
Umbellularia californica	Evergreen	4-10, 12-24
Yucca elephantipes	Evergreen	16, 17, 19-24

SHRUB-TREES

NAME OF PLANT	EVERGREEN OR DECIDUOUS	CLIMATE ZONES
Acer (maple)		
Acer circinatum	Deciduous	1-6, 15-17
Acer ginnala	Deciduous	1-9, 14-16
Acer palmatum	Deciduous	1-9, 14-24
Aesculus californica	Deciduous	4-7, 14-19
Amelanchier, certain kinds	Deciduous	1-3
Arbutus unedo	Evergreen	4-24
Calycanthus occidentalis	Deciduous	4-9, 14-22
Ceratonia siliqua	Evergreen	9, 13-16, 18-23
Cercis occidentalis	Deciduous	2-9, 14-24
Cocculus laurifolius	Evergreen	7-9, 12-24
Cornus kousa	Deciduous	3-9, 14, 15, 18, 19
Erythrina crista-galli	Deciduous	7-9, 12-17, 19-24
Escallonia montevidensis	Evergreen	4-9, 14-17, 20-24
Eucalyptus caesia	Evergreen	15-17, 19-24
Eucalyptus eremophila	Evergreen	20-24
Eucalyptus erythrocorys	Evergreen	19-24
Eucalyptus preissiana	Evergreen	17, 22-24
Exochorda racemosa	Deciduous	1-9, 14-18
Feijoa sellowiana	Evergreen	8, 9, 12-24
Heteromeles arbutifolia	Evergreen	5-24
Lagerstroemia indica	Deciduous	7-14, 18-21
Laurus nobilis	Evergreen	6-10, 12-24
Leptospermum laevigatum	Evergreen	15-24
Melaleuca	Evergreen	Vary by kind
Myoporum laetum	Evergreen	8, 9, 14-17, 19-24
Parrotia persica	Deciduous	4-6, 15-17
Pinus densiflora 'Umbraculifera'	Evergreen	1-9, 14-17
Prunus caroliniana	Evergreen	7-24
Psidium cattleianum	Evergreen	9, 14-24
Pyrus kawakamii	Evergreen	8, 9, 12-24
Trochodendron aralioides	Evergreen	4-7, 14-17
Tupidanthus calyptratus	Evergreen	19-24
Xanthoceras sorbifolium	Deciduous	1-10, 14-17

FIVE MORE FAVORITES—ALL EVERGREEN

NAME OF PLANT	KIND	CLIMATE ZONES
Bamboo	Grass	Vary by kind
Chamaerops humilis	Palm	5-24
Echium fastuosum	Perennial	7-9, 14-24
Phoenix reclinata	Palm	23, 24
Rhapis	Palm	Vary by kind

HILLSIDE LOCATIONS

Here, and on page 156, are lists of shrubs, vines, grasses, and succulents that grow well and serve well on hillsides in the climate zones indicated.

Those plants marked have the dense, strong roots, a suitable branching habit, and the rugged constitutions to cover and hold soil in a way that can effectively reduce soil erosion.

SHRUBS

NAME OF PLANT	EROSION CONTROL	CLIMATE ZONES
Acacia cyanophylla		13-24
Acacia longifolia		8, 9, 14-24
Arctostaphylos (manzanita)		
Arctostaphylos densiflora		7-9, 14-21
Arctostaphylos edmundsii		6-9, 14-24
Arctostaphylos hookeri		6-9, 14-24
Arctostaphylos uva-ursi		1-9, 14-24
Baccharis pilularis		7-24
Calluna vulgaris 'Mrs. Ronald Gray' (see page 291)		2-6, 17
Calluna vulgaris 'Mullion' (see page 291)		2-6, 17
Carissa grandiflora 'Green Carpet'		13, 16-24
Carissa grandiflora 'Prostrata'		13, 16-24
Carissa grandiflora 'Tuttle'		13, 16-24
Ceanothus gloriosus	★	5-9, 14-24
Ceanothus griseus	★	7-9, 14-24
Ceanothus griseus horizontalis	★	5-9, 14-24
Ceanothus 'Joyce Coulter'	★	15-17, 21-24
Cercis occidentalis		2-9, 14-24
Cistus (rockrose)	★	Vary by kind
Coleonema and Diosma		7-9, 14-24
Convolvulus cneorum		7-9, 12-24
Coprosma kirkii	★	8, 9, 14-17, 21-24
Correa		Vary by kind
Cotoneaster, low-growing	★	Vary by kind
Cytisus kewensis (broom)		4-6, 16, 17
Echium fastuosum	★	7-9, 14-24
Erica carnea (see page 291)		2-9, 14-24
Erica cinerea (see page 291)		4-6, 15-17
Erica 'Dawn' (see page 291)		4-9, 14-24
Eriogonum fasciculatum	★	14-24
Fallugia paradoxa	★	8, 9, 11-23
Forsythia		1-11, 14-16
Gaultheria shallon		4-7, 14-17
Grevillea lanigera		15-24
Holmskioldia sanguinea		13, 17, 22, 23
Hypericum calycinum	★	2-24
Jasminum mesnyi (jasmine)	★	4-24
Juniperus, low-growing kinds	★	All Zones
Lantana montevidensis	★	8-24
Lonicera pileata (honeysuckle)		2-9, 14-24
Mahonia repens	★	1-21
Myoporum debile		15-17, 19-24
Olearia haastii		4-6, 14-17
Osteospermum	★	8, 9, 14-24
Philadelphus mexicanus		8, 9, 14-24
Plumbago auriculata		8, 9, 12-24

SHRUBS (cont'd)

NAME OF PLANT	EROSION CONTROL	CLIMATE ZONES
Prunus laurocerasus 'Zabeliana'		3-9, 14-21
Pyracantha 'Santa Cruz'		4-24
Pyracantha 'Walderi'		4-24
Rhamnus crocea ilicifolia	★	7-16, 18-21
Rhus integrifolia (sumac)	★	15-17, 20-24
Ribes viburnifolium	★	8, 9, 14-24
Rosa (rose)		
Rosa banksiae	★	4-9, 12-24
Rosa bracteata 'Mermaid'	★	4-24
Rosa roxburghii	★	2-24
Rosmarinus officinalis (rosemary)	★	4-24
Santolina	★	All Zones
Sophora secundiflora		8-16, 18-24
Spartium junceum (see page 248)	★	5-9, 11-24
Symphoricarpos	★	Vary by kind
Taxus baccata 'Repandens' (yew)		1-9, 14-24
Westringia rosmariniformis		15-17, 19-24
Xylosma congestum		8-24

VINES

NAME OF PLANT	EROSION CONTROL	CLIMATE ZONES
Bougainvillea		12-17, 19-24
Cissus antarctica	★	13, 16-24
Cissus hypoglauca	★	13, 19-24
Euonymus fortunei 'Azusa'	★	1-17
Hedera (ivy)	★	Vary by kind
Lonicera henryi	★	2-24
Lonicera japonica 'Halliana'	★	2-24
Parthenocissus quinquefolia (Virginia creeper)	★	All Zones
Passiflora jamesonii	★	14-24
Plumbago auriculata		8, 9, 12-24
Rhoicissus capensis	★	16, 17, 21-24
Solandra hartwegii	★	17, 21-24
Tecomaria capensis		12, 13, 16, 18-24
Tetrastigma	★	13, 17, 20-24
Trachelospermum jasminoides (star jasmine)	★	8-24

(Continued on next page)

Hillside locations (cont'd.)

GRASSES

NAME OF PLANT	EROSION CONTROL	CLIMATE ZONES
Bamboo, Group I	★	Vary by kind
Bermuda, Hybrid (see Lawn Chapter)	★	8, 9, 12-14, 18-24
Cortaderia selloana (pampas grass)	★	4-24
Zoysia tenuifolia	★	8-24

SUCCULENTS

NAME OF PLANT	EROSION CONTROL	CLIMATE ZONES
Delosperma 'Alba'	★	12-24
Drosanthemum (see page 303)	★	14-24
Lampranthus aurantiacus	★	14-24
Lampranthus filicaulis	★	14-24
Malephora crocea	★	11-24
Sedum	★	Vary by kind

SOIL WITH OAK ROOT FUNGUS

Oak root fungus (*Armillaria*) infects the soil in many parts of the world, but for various reasons it is more of a problem in California than elsewhere in the West. The fungus organism sustains itself on buried wood, mostly dead roots, but it also gets into the tissues of living plants and often it kills them. Some plants resist armillaria infection. Gardeners in armillaria-infested neighborhoods can do their basic permanent landscaping with these resistant plants if they wish to play safe.

TREES:

NAME OF PLANT	CLIMATE ZONES
Abies concolor	1-9, 14-24
Acacia longifolia	8, 9, 14-24
Acer macrophyllum	4-17
Acer palmatum	1-9, 14-24
Ailanthus altissima	All Zones
Arbutus menziesii	1-7, 14-19
Avocado	Vary by kind
Brachychiton populneum	13-24
Broussonetia papyrifera	3-24
Calocedrus decurrens	1-12, 14-24
Carya illinoinensis (pecan)	7-9, 12-16, 18-23
Castanea dentata (chestnut)	1-9, 14-17
Castanea sativa	1-9, 14-17
Catalpa bignonioides	All Zones
Celtis occidentalis	All Zones
Ceratonia siliqua	9, 13-16, 18-23
Cercis occidentalis	2-9, 14-24
Cercis saliquastrum	2-19
Crabapple	1-9, 11-21
Cryptomeria japonica	4-6, 8, 9, 14-20
Elaeagnus angustifolia	1-3, 7-14, 18, 19
Eucalyptus camaldulensis	8-24
Fig, 'Kadota'	4-9, 12-24
Fig, 'Mission'	4-9, 12-24
Fraxinus uhdei	9, 12-24
Fraxinus veluteina 'Modesto'	7-11, 13-24
Ginkgo biloba	1-9, 14-24
Ilex aquifolium (holly)	4-9, 14-24

NAME OF PLANT	CLIMATE ZONES
Ilex opaca	2-9, 15, 16, 19-23
Jacaranda acutifolia	9, 13-24
Liquidambar orientalis	5-9, 14-24
Liquidambar styraciflua	1-9, 14-24
Liriodendron tulipifera	1-10, 14-23
Maclura pomifera	All Zones
Magnolia grandiflora	4-12, 14-24
Maytenus boaria	8, 9, 14-21
Melaleuca styphelioides	9, 13-24
Metasequoia glyptostroboides	3-24
Pear	1-11, 14-16, 18
Persea indica	16, 17, 20-24
Persimmon, American	2-9, 14-16, 18-23
Persimmon, Oriental	7-9, 14-16, 18-23
Phellodendron amurense	1-17
Pinus canariensis	5-24
Pinus nigra	All Zones
Pinus patula	5-24
Pinus radiata	7-9, 14-24
Pinus torreyana	5-24
Pistacia chinensis	8-16, 18-23
Pittosporum rhombifolium	12-24
Plum, Japanese	Vary by kind
Prunus cerasifera	2-20
Pyrus calleryana	2-9, 14-21
Quillaja saponaria	8, 9, 14-24
Sapium sebiferum	8, 9, 14-16, 18-21
Sequoia sempervirens	4-9, 14-24
Sophora japonica	All Zones
Ulmus parvifolia	8, 9, 12-24
Walnut, California black	5-9, 14-20

SHRUBS:

NAME OF PLANT	CLIMATE ZONES
Abutilon vitifolium	15-24
Acacia verticillata	14-24
Buxus sempervirens	3-6, 15-17
Calycanthus occidentalis	4-9, 14-22
Carpenteria californica	5-9, 14-24
Clerodendrum bungei	5-9, 12-24
Cotinus coggygria	All Zones
Datura suaveolens	16-24
Erica arborea	15-17, 21-24
Exochorda racemosa	1-6
Hibiscus syriacus	1 21
Ilex aquipernyi	4-9, 14-24
Lonicera nitida	4-9, 14-24
Mahonia aquifolium	1-21
Mahonia nevinii	8-24
Myrica pensylvanica	4-7
Nandina domestica	5-24
Phlomis fruticosa	All Zones
Prunus caroliniana	7-24
Prunus ilicifolia	7-9, 12-24
Prunus lyonii	7-9, 12-24
Psidium cattleianum	9, 14-24
Vitex agnus-castus	4-24

SHADY PLACES

Shade in a covered, north-facing entryway is so dark that very few flowering plants will grow there. But shade under a fine-textured, open-branched tree differs only a little from the open sun light nearby. Here and on page 158 are garden plants that will grow well at most light levels between the two extremes.

GROUND COVERS (UNDER 1 FOOT)

Attractive foliage pattern

NAME OF PLANT	KIND	CLIMATE ZONES
Asarum caudatum	Perennial	4, 6, 15-17, 21
Asparagus falcatus	Perennial	15-24
Asperula odorata	Perennial	1-6, 15-17

NAME OF PLANT	KIND	CLIMATE ZONES
Hedera helix (ivy)	Vine	All Zones
Hedera canariensis	Vine	All Zones
Ophiopogon japonicus (see page 325)	Perennial	1-10, 14-23
Pachysandra terminalis	Shrub	1-10, 14-21
Rhoicissus capensis	Vine	16, 17, 21-24
Soleirolia soleirolii	Perennial	8-24

Colorful flowers or fruits

NAME OF PLANT	KIND	CLIMATE ZONES
Epimedium grandiflorum	Perennial	1-9, 14-17
Erythronium	Bulb	1-7, 15-17
Hepatica	Perennial	1-11, 14-16
Linnaea borealis	Perennial	1-7, 14-17
Polemonium caeruleum	Perennial	1-11 ,14-17

NAME OF PLANT	KIND	CLIMATE ZONES
Primula (primrose)		
Primula malacoides	Annual	All Zones
P. obconica	Perennial	15-24
P. polyantha	Perennial	1-9, 14-24
Ramonda myconi	Perennial	1-6, 17
Schizocentron elegans	Perennial	15-24
Vinca	Perennial	Vary by kind
Viola odorata (sweet violet)	Perennial	All Zones

PLANTS FROM 1 TO 3 FEET HIGH

Attractive foliage pattern

NAME OF PLANT	KIND	CLIMATE ZONES
Ardisia japonica	Shrub	5, 6, 15-17
Aspidistra elatior	Perennial	4-9, 12-24
Caladium	Perennial	12, 13, 17, 21-24

NAME OF PLANT	KIND	CLIMATE ZONES
Farfugium japonicum 'Aureo-maculatum'	Perennial	4-10, 14-24
Fern (hardy and tropical kinds)	Fern	Vary by kind
Hosta	Perennial	1-10, 12-21

Colorful flowers or fruits

NAME OF PLANT	KIND	CLIMATE ZONES
Acanthus mollis	Perennial	4-24
Bergenia	Perennial	1-9, 14-24
Clivia	Perennial	15-17, 19-24
Dicentra (bleeding heart)	Perennial	1-9, 14-24
Francoa ramosa	Perennial	All Zones
Helleborus	Perennial	All Zones

NAME OF PLANT	KIND	CLIMATE ZONES
Impatiens holstii	Perennial	All Zones
Mertensia	Perennial	1-21
Rehmannia angulata	Perennial	7-10, 12-24
Sarcococca humilis	Shrub	4-9, 14-24
Smilacina racemosa	Perennial	1-7, 15-17
Tradescantia virginiana	Perennial	All Zones
Trillium	Perennial	Vary by kind
Trollius	Perennial	All Zones
Vancouveria	Perennial	4-6, 14-17

BACKGROUND PLANTS (3 TO 6 FEET OR MORE)

Attractive foliage pattern

NAME OF PLANT	KIND	CLIMATE ZONES
Acer circinatum (maple)	Shrub	1-6, 15-17
Fatshedera lizei	Vine	4-9, 14-24
Fatsia japonica	Shrub	4-9, 14-24
Ficus benjamina	Tree	13, 23, 24
Ficus elastica	Shrub	16, 17, 19-24
Ficus elastica 'Decora'	Shrub	16, 17, 19-24

NAME OF PLANT	KIND	CLIMATE ZONES
Griselinia lucida	Shrub	9, 14-17, 20-24
Howeia	Palm	17, 23, 24
Hydrangea anomala petiolaris	Vine	1-21
Philodendron	Vine	21-24
Podocarpus	Tree-shrub	Vary by kind
Rhapis	Palm	Vary by kind
Rhopalostylis	Palm	17, 23, 24
Fern, tree	Fern	Vary by kind

(Continued on next page)

Shady places ... background plants 3 to 6 feet or more (cont'd.)

Colorful flowers or fruits

NAME OF PLANT	KIND	CLIMATE ZONES
Aucuba japonica	Shrub	4-11, 14-24
Brunfelsia calycina floribunda	Shrub	13, 15-17, 20-24
Fuchsia hybrida	Shrub	4-6, 15-17, 22-24
Gaultheria shallon	Shrub	4-7, 14-17

NAME OF PLANT	KIND	CLIMATE ZONES
Hoya carnosa	Vine	15-24
Mahonia	Shrub	Vary by kind
Osmanthus	Shrub	Vary by kind
Sarcococca ruscifolia	Shrub	4-9, 14-24
Skimmia japonica	Shrub	4-9, 14-22
Tetrapanax papyriferus	Shrub	15-24
Thalictrum	Perennial	All Zones
Umbellularia californica	Tree	4-10, 12-24

WET PLACES

Water must pass through the root area quickly or the plants will suffer from lack of oxygen. Even so, some plants grow very well in wet places—in soils where excess water limits but does not exclude oxygen. Such plants are listed below. Don't expect heroic swamp tolerance; *Nymphaea* is the only true water plant on the list, and a few others such as *Cyperus* are bog plants. Most of the plants simply offer better than average performance under poor drainage conditions. Look in the encyclopedia section for degree of moisture tolerance.

TREES AND SHRUBS

NAME OF PLANT	KIND	CLIMATE ZONES
Abutilon	Shrub	15-24
Acer rubrum	Tree	1-6, 14-17
Alnus rhombifolia	Tree	1-9, 14-21
Aronia arbutifolia	Shrub	1-7
Betula nigra	Tree	All Zones
Chaenomeles	Shrub	1-21
Cornus stolonifera	Shrub	1-9, 14-21
Fraxinus latifolia	Tree	4-24

NAME OF PLANT	KIND	CLIMATE ZONES
Kalmia polifolia	Shrub	1-9, 14-17
Leucothoe davisiae	Shrub	4-7, 14-17
Ligustrum (privet)	Shrub	Vary by kind
Nerium oleander	Shrub	8-16, 18-23
Nyssa sylvatica (sour gum)	Tree	1-10, 14-21
Salix (willow)	Tree	Vary by kind
Sequoia sempervirens	Tree	4-9, 14-24
Spiraea douglasii	Shrub	1-11, 14-17
Taxodium distichum	Tree	1-9, 14-24
Tetrapanax papyriferus	Shrub	15-24
Yucca recurvifolia	Tree	7-24

PERENNIALS, BULBS, OTHERS

NAME OF PLANT	KIND	CLIMATE ZONES
Acanthus mollis	Perennial	4-24
Aconitum	Perennial	1-9, 14-21
Adiantum pedatum	Fern	1-9, 14-21
Alocasia	Perennial	All Zones
Arundo donax	Perennial	All Zones
Bamboo	Grass	Vary by kind
Caltha palustris	Perennial	All Zones
Camassia	Bulb	1-9, 14-17
Clivia miniata	Perennial	15-17, 19-24
Colocasia esculenta	Perennial	All Zones
Cortaderia selloana	Grass	4-24
Cyperus papyrus	Perennial	8, 9, 12-24
Equisetum hyemale	Perennial	All Zones
Erythronium	Bulb	1-7, 15-17
Iris douglasiana	Bulb	All Zones

NAME OF PLANT	KIND	CLIMATE ZONES
Iris kaempferi	Bulb	1-9, 14-24
Iris sibirica	Bulb	All Zones
Iris unguicularis	Bulb	5-24
Lobelia cardinalis	Perennial	1-7, 14-17
Lonicera japonica 'Halliana'	Vine	2-24
Mentha requienii	Perennial	5-9, 12-24
Mimulus tigrinus	Perennial	All Zones
Nymphaea (water lily)	Water plant	All Zones
Oxalis oregana	Perennial	4-9, 14-24
Phormium tenax	Perennial	7-24
Scirpus cernuus	Perennial	7-24
Solandra hartwegii	Vine	15-24
Soleirolia soleirolii	Perennial	8-24
Tradescantia virginiana	Perennial	All Zones
Trollius	Perennial	All Zones
Vinca	Perennial	Vary by kind
Watercress	Perennial	All Zones
Woodwardia fimbriata	Fern	4-9, 14-24
Zantedeschia (calla)	Bulb	5, 6, 8, 9, 14-24

DRY PLACES

Most parts of the West have a long dry season, so a dry place here is most often simply a spot that doesn't get any irrigation during the rainless season. The plants on this page will grow in those spots. Plant early in the rainy season. Try to water the trees or shrubs two or three times during the first two summers. Keep weeds out from under them (spray, hoe, or cultivate).

TREES AND SHRUBS

NAME OF PLANT	KIND	CLIMATE ZONES
Acacia	Shrub	Vary by kind
Arbutus unedo	Shrub	4-24
Arctostaphylos (manzanita)	Shrub	Vary by kind
Artemisia	Shrub	All Zones
*Atriplex canescens (saltbush)	Shrub	2-24
*Atriplex halimus	Shrub	12-24
*Atriplex lentiformis breweri	Shrub	8, 9, 14-24
*Atriplex semibaccata	Shrub	8, 9, 12-24
*Baccharis pilularis	Shrub	7-24
Berberis mentorensis	Shrub	All Zones
Buddleia alternifolia	Shrub	2-24
Buxus microphylla japonica	Shrub	8, 9, 12-24
Callistemon citrinus	Shrub	8, 9, 12-24
Callistemon rigidus	Shrub	8, 9, 12-24
Caragana arborescens	Shrub	1-21
Cassia artemisioides	Shrub	8, 9, 12-24
Catha edulis	Shrub	13, 16-24
Ceanothus crassifolius	Shrub	18-24
Ceanothus megacarpus	Shrub	16, 17, 21-24
Cercis occidentalis (red bud)	Shrub	2-9, 14-24
Chamaelaucium uncinatum	Shrub	8, 9, 12-24
*Cistus ladaniferus maculatus	Shrub	4-9, 12-24
*Cistus villosus	Shrub	4-9, 12-24
Cotinus coggygria	Tree	All Zones
Cotoneaster	Shrub	Vary by kind
Cupressus glabra	Tree	All Zones
Cytisus (broom)	Shrub	Vary by kind
Dalea spinosa	Tree	11-13
Dendromecon	Shrub	5-8, 14-24
Diplopappus filifolius	Shrub	8, 9, 14-24
Dodonaea viscosa	Shrub	7-9, 12-24
Elaeagnus angustifolia	Tree	1-3, 7-14, 18, 19

NAME OF PLANT	KIND	CLIMATE ZONES
Eriogonum	Shrub	14-24
Eucalyptus	Tree	8-24
Fremontodendron	Shrub	7-24
Garrya	Shrub	Vary by kind
Grevillea rosmarinifolia	Shrub	8, 9, 12-24
Hakea suaveolens	Shrub	9, 12-17, 19-24
*Helianthemum nummularium	Shrub	All Zones
Heteromeles arbutifolia (toyon)	Shrub	5-24
Hypericum calycinum	Shrub	4-24
Juniperus	Shrub	All Zones
Lagerstroemia indica	Shrub	1-9, 12-24
Lantana	Shrub	8, 9, 12-24
Lavandula spica	Shrub	All Zones
Leptospermum	Shrub	14-24
Mahonia aquifolium	Shrub	1-21
Melaleuca armillaris	Shrub	9, 12-24
Nerium oleander	Shrub	8-16, 18-23
Olea europaea (olive)	Tree	7-24
Pinus (pine)	Tree	Vary by kind
Prunus caroliniana	Shrub	7-24
Prunus ilicifolia	Shrub	7-9, 12-24
Prunus lyonii	Shrub	7-9, 12-24
Pyracantha	Shrub	Vary by kind
Quercus suber	Tree	8-16, 18-23
Rhamnus alaternus	Shrub	4-24
Rhus integrifolia	Shrub	15-17, 20-24
Rhus ovata	Shrub	8, 9, 11-24
Robinia pseudoacacia (locust)	Tree	All Zones
*Rosmarinus officinalis	Shrub	4-24
*Rosmarinus officinalis 'Prostratus'	Shrub	4-24
*Santolina	Shrub	All Zones
Schinus molle (pepper tree)	Tree	8, 9, 12-24
Sorbus aucuparia	Tree	1-6, 15-17
Xylosma congestum	Shrub	8-24

PERENNIALS, BULBS, OTHERS

NAME OF PLANT	KIND	CLIMATE ZONES
*Achillea tomentosa (yarrow)	Perennial	All Zones
*Aeonium decorum	Succulent	15-24
Anacyclus depressus	Perennial	All Zones
*Artemisia pycnocephala	Perennial	All Zones
Cerastium tomentosum	Perennial	All Zones
Chamaerops humilis	Palm	5-24
Cleome spinosa	Annual	All Zones
Cortaderia selloana	Grass	4-24
Dorotheanthus bellidiformis (see page 303)	Succulent	All Zones
Echium	Perennial	Vary by kind
Gazania	Perennial	8-24
*Hedera canariensis	Vine	8, 9, 12-24

NAME OF PLANT	KIND	CLIMATE ZONES
*Hedera helix	Vine	All Zones
*Helichrysum petiolatum	Perennial	17, 22-24
Linaria dalmatica	Perennial	All Zones
*Lotus berthelotii	Perennial	13-24
Oenothera speciosa childsii	Perennial	All Zones
Pennisetum setaceum	Grass	All Zones
Phormium	Perennial	5-24
Polygonum cuspidatum compactum	Perennial	8, 9, 12-24
Portulaca grandiflora	Annual	All Zones
*Portulacaria afra	Succulent	8, 9, 12-17, 22-24
Raoulia australis	Perennial	7-9, 13-24
Thymus (thyme)	Perennial	All Zones
Veronica	Perennial	All Zones
Vinca	Perennial	Vary by kind
Yucca	Perennial	Vary by kind
Zauschneria	Perennial	4-9, 14-24

*Indicates fire resistant plants.

WINDY PLACES

Native plants in windy locations survive because they adapt their growing habit to offer minimum resistance to the wind. This can give you a clue. Plants in windy places should not require staking and should not have long, heavy branches. Begin with small plants; they usually get off to a faster start and grow into their peculiar environment.

PERENNIALS OR SHRUBBY PERENNIALS

NAME OF PLANT	CLIMATE ZONES
Agapanthus africanus	8, 9, 12-24
Aloe	8, 9, 12-24
Artemisia pycnocephala	All Zones
Echium fastuosum	7-9, 14-24
Impatiens oliveri	15-17, 21-24
Moraea iridioides	8-24
Pelargonium hortorum	8, 9, 12-24
Santolina chamaecyparissus	All Zones
Yucca whipplei	5-24

VINES AND GROUND COVERS

NAME OF PLANT	CLIMATE ZONES
Arctostaphylos (manzanita)	
A. densiflora	7-9, 14-24
A. edmundsii	6-9, 14-24
A. hookeri	6-9, 14-24
A. pumila	14-24
A. uva-ursi	1-9, 14-24
Asparagus sprengeri	15-24
Baccharis pilularis	7-24
Carissa grandiflora (low growing)	22-24
Ceanothus gloriosus	5-9, 14-24
Ceanothus griseus horizontalis	5, 6, 7-9, 14-24
Fragaria chiloensis	4-24
Hedera canariensis	8, 9, 12-24
Hedera helix	All Zones
Ice plant	Vary by kind
Juniperus (ground cover forms)	All Zones
Lonicera japonica 'Halliana'	2-24
Muehlenbeckia axillaris	4-9, 14-24
Muehlenbeckia complexa	8, 9, 14-24
Pelargonium peltatum	8, 9, 12-24
Quamoclit pennata	All Zones
Ribes viburnifolium	8, 9, 14-24
Sedum spathulifolium	All Zones
Solandra hartwegii	15-24
Tecomaria capensis	12, 13, 16, 18-24
Vinca major	5-24
Vinca minor	All Zones

SHRUBS AND SHRUB-TREES

NAME OF PLANT	CLIMATE ZONES	NAME OF PLANT	CLIMATE ZONES
Abelia grandiflora	5-24	Ilex aquifolium (holly)	4-9, 14-24
Acacia armata	13-24	Juniperus (juniper)	All Zones
Acacia longifolia	8, 9, 14-24	Lavatera assurgentiflora	14-24
Acacia verticillata	14-24		
Acokanthera	21, 23, 24	Leptospermum laevigatum	15-24
Arctostaphylos (manzanita)			
A. columbiana	4-6, 15-17	Leptospermum scoparium	15-24
A. insularis	8, 9, 14-24		
A. manzanita	4-9, 14-24	Leucophyllum frutescens	7-24
Atriplex lentiformis	7-14	Ligustrum (privet)	Vary by kind
Atriplex lentiformis breweri	8, 9, 14-24	Mahonia aquifolium	1-21
Aucuba japonica	4-11, 14-23	Mahonia aquifolium 'Compacta'	1-21
Berberis darwinii	4-6, 15-17	Melaleuca ericifolia	9, 12-24
Buxus sempervirens	3-6, 15-17	Melaleuca hypericifolia	9, 12-24
Callistemon citrinus	8, 9, 12-24		
Candollea cuneiformis	13, 15-24	Melaleuca nesophila	9, 13, 16-24
Caragana arborescens	1-21	Melaleuca styphelioides	9, 13-24
Carissa grandiflora	22-24		
Cassia artemisioides	8, 9, 12-24	Myrica californica	4-6, 14-17, 20-24
Ceanothus arboreus	5, 6, 7-9, 15-24		
Ceanothus thyrsiflorus	5, 6, 16, 17, 23, 24	Myrsine africana	8, 9, 14-24
		Myrtus communis	8-24
Chamaecyparis lawsoniana	2-9, 14, 15-21	Nerium oleander	8-16, 18-23
		Olearia haastii	4-6, 14-17
Cistus (rockrose)	4-9, 12-24	Phormium tenax	7-24
Coprosma kirkii	8, 9, 14-17, 21-24	Pittosporum crassifolium	9, 14-17, 19-24
Coprosma repens	8, 9, 14-17, 21-24	Pittosporum eugenioides	9, 14-17, 19-22
Cortaderia selloana	4-24	Pittosporum tobira	8-24
Cotoneaster	Vary by kind	Pittosporum undulatum	16, 17, 21-24
Cytisus (broom)	Vary by kind		
Dodonaea viscosa	7-9, 14-24	Prunus ilicifolia	7-9, 12-24
Dodonaea viscosa 'Purpurea'	7-9, 14-24	Prunus laurocerasus	4-9, 14-24
		Prunus lusitanica	4-9, 14-24
Elaeagnus angustifolia	1-3, 7-14, 18, 19	Prunus lyonii	7-9, 12-24
Elaeagnus pungens	4-24	Pseudopanax lessonii	17, 20-24
Eriogonum arborescens	14-24	Pyracantha	Vary by kind
Eriogonum giganteum	14-24	Raphiolepis	8-10, 14-24
Escallonia	4-9, 14-17, 20-24	Rhamnus alaternus	4-24
		Rhamnus californica	4-24
Euonymus japonica	4-13, 18-20	Rhododendron occidentale	4-24
Garrya elliptica	6-9, 14-21		
Gaultheria shallon	4-7, 14-17	Rhus integrifolia	15-17, 20-24
Griselinia littoralis	9, 14-17, 20-24	Rhus ovata (sumac)	8, 9, 11-24
Griselinia lucida	9, 14-17, 20-24	Rosmarinus officinalis	4-24
		Sambucus callicarpa	4-7, 14-17
Hakea laurina	9, 12-17, 19-24	Senecio greyii	5-9, 14-24
Hakea suaveolens	9, 12-17, 19-24	Tamarix	Vary by kind
Hebe	14-24	Vaccinium ovatum	4-7, 14-17
Holodiscus discolor	1-7, 16, 17	Viburnum suspensum	8-24
		Xylosma congestum	8-24

Gardeners' Language

To describe the thousands of Western garden plants in the plant encyclopedia, pages 167 to 445, it was often necessary to use special gardening terms. These somewhat technical words, known to most experienced gardeners, must be explained to novices. That's what you find on the next six pages—a gardening and landscaping glossary.

In addition to these gardening terms, certain other words describe specific large groups of plants—bamboo, bromeliads, cycads, cactus, ferns, herbs, orchids, palms, succulents. These words are defined in their alphabetical place in the encyclopedia.

ACID SOIL, ALKALINE SOIL. There's no way to avoid technical words when defining these terms. Acidity and alkalinity describe an aspect of the soil's chemical reaction: the concentration of hydrogen ions (an ion is an electrically charged atom or molecule). The relative concentration of hydrogen ions is represented by a mathematical symbol called *p*H. A *p*H of 7 means the soil is neutral, neither acid nor alkaline. Below 7 means soil is acid, above 7 it's alkaline.

Soils in areas with high rainfall tend to be acid. Areas with light rainfall tend to have alkaline soil. Adding peat moss, ground bark, or sawdust to the soil increases acidity. Adding lime increases alkalinity.

ACTUAL (as in *actual* nitrogen). Farmers and soil scientists use this term most, but it is useful in everyday gardening. It means the portion of a manufactured fertilizer (or any product containing several ingredients) that supplies a specific needed element. A 25-pound bag of fertilizer containing 22 percent nitrogen will yield 5½ pounds actual nitrogen (25 pounds x .22 = 5.5 pounds).

ANNUAL. A plant that completes its life cycle in a year or less. Seed germinates and the plant grows, blooms, sets seed, and dies—all in one growing season. Examples: marigolds, sweet alyssum, zinnias. The expression "grow as an annual" or "treat as an annual" means to plant an item (shrub or whatever) in spring after the last frost, enjoy it from spring through fall, and pull it out or let the frosts kill it at the end of the year.

BALLED AND BURLAPPED (sometimes abbreviated B and B). A nurseryman's term. From late fall to early spring, shrubs and trees are dug from fields with a *ball* of dirt around the roots; the ball is wrapped in *burlap* to hold it together and the plant is sold that way.

BARE ROOT. Another nurseryman's term. In winter and early spring many deciduous plants are sold with their roots bare. Dormant plants are dug from fields; roots are trimmed, cleaned, and kept from drying out until planting time.

BIENNIAL. A plant whose life cycle is completed in its second year. Typical pattern: sow seed in June; set plants out in October; plants bloom the following spring, then set seed and die. Examples: foxgloves, sweet Williams.

BONSAI. Japanese term for one of the garden fine arts: growing dwarfed, carefully trained plants in containers designed to harmonize with the plants. The bonsai craftsman meticulously wires and prunes branches and trims roots to get the desired effect: the character of an ancient weathered tree, on a miniature scale.

BRACTS. See FLOWER PARTS.

BROAD-LEAFED. Used in the sense of "broad-leafed evergreen" it refers to a plant that is evergreen but not an evergreen conifer with needlelike leaves. Used in connection with weeds, it means any weeds that are not grasses.

BUDDING. In basic principle it's similar to grafting. A bud of one plant is inserted in the bark of another plant (called the *stock*). If all goes well, the bud and stock unite; the bud will then develop the characteristics of the plant it came from, while the stock supplies it with water and nutrients.

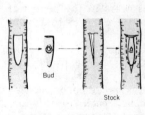

BULB. In everyday conversation, any thickened underground stem usually is referred to as a *bulb*. But, precisely, a bulb is only one type of thickened underground stem; other types are called rhizomes, corms, tubers, tuberous roots. A "true" bulb is more or less rounded, made up of fleshy leaves (or scales) that store food and protect the developing plant inside (slice an onion to see the scales) and its outer scales dry to form a papery covering.

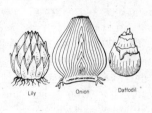

Lily   Onion   Daffodil

CALYX. See *Sepal* under FLOWER PARTS.

CAMBIUM LAYER. See GRAFTING.

CATKIN. The slender, spikelike, often drooping flower cluster of such plants as willow, alder, birch, poplar. Catkins may be either male or female, the male catkins borne on one tree, the female on another (willows, cottonwoods); or both may be on same tree (alder, birch).

CHILLING REQUIREMENTS. Many deciduous shrubs and trees (fruiting types in particular) and perennials need certain amounts of cold weather in winter to blossom and develop leaves properly in spring. Where winters are mild, certain plants don't get the necessary cold weather, so gardeners there must choose plants with low chilling requirements (not needing much winter cold) and avoid types that need high chilling.

CHLOROSIS. When a leaf looks yellower than it should (especially between the leaf veins), it often is chlorotic or suffering from *chlorosis.* Frequently chlorosis is caused by a plant's inability to obtain the iron it needs to produce green coloring. For one way to correct this condition, see IRON CHELATE.

COMPLETE FERTILIZER. Not as vague or promotional as it sounds. To be "complete" a plant food has to contain all three of the primary nutrient elements: nitrogen, phosphorus, potassium.

COMPOSITE (COMPOSITAE) FAMILY. Often called the daisy, sunflower, or aster family. The flower structure is a composite of many flowers tightly grouped into a head and surrounded by bracts that form a cup (involucre). Several kinds of flowers are found in the composite head: *Disk flowers* are small tubular flowers in the center of most composite flower heads. They usually form a compact cushionlike center. Some plants have disk flowers only. *Ray flowers,* often erroneously called petals, usually surround a center of many disk flowers as in marguerites, dahlias, marigolds.

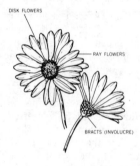

DISK FLOWERS

RAY FLOWERS

BRACTS (INVOLUCRE)

CONIFER. A more precise word for what many people call "evergreens," such as junipers, cypress, pines, and cedars. Leaves on most kinds are narrow and needlelike. Not all conifers are evergreen, but all bear naked seeds in cones or conelike structures.

CONSERVATORY. A fancy word for greenhouse. Often it is a fancy greenhouse.

CORM. A short, fat underground portion of a stem often called a bulb. Technically, it differs from a true bulb in that food is stored in the solid center tissue, not in the scales.

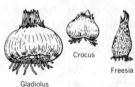

Crocus

Freesia

Gladiolus

CUTTINGS. Some gardeners use the word "slips" to describe this method of propagating plants. The method involves cutting or breaking off part of a branch or root and planting it in rooting medium (or even water) so that it can grow roots and eventually develop into a plant just like the one it came from.

Hardwood cuttings are taken from the mature wood of deciduous (and occasionally evergreen) plants during their dormant season—late fall to early spring.

Softwood cuttings are taken from evergreen or deciduous plants during spring or early summer, when plants are growing actively and wood is limber and soft.

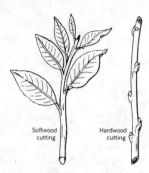

Softwood cutting

Hardwood cutting

Semihardwood cuttings are taken in summer or fall, after growth has slowed and wood has begun to harden.

DAISY FLOWER. See COMPOSITE FAMILY.

DAMPING OFF. This plant disease, caused by fungus in the soil, makes tiny seedlings quickly rot, wilt, or fall over and die just before or soon after they break through the soil.

DECIDUOUS. A plant that sheds all of its leaves at one time annually is *deciduous.*

DISK FLOWER. See COMPOSITE FAMILY.

DIVIDING. The easiest way to increase perennials, bulbs, and other plants that spread by developing roots and top growth in clumps—for example, daylilies, coral bells, dahlias, iris. To divide, dig up all or part of the plant and break apart the independently rooted sections. Plant these sections ("divisions") to get new plants.

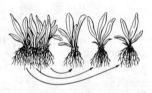

DOUBLE FLOWER. A flower with an indefinite number of petals that usually obscure the stamens and pistils. Petals, stamens, pistils defined under FLOWER PARTS.

DRAINAGE. "Good drainage," "bad drainage," "slow drainage," "fast drainage," "well drained"—all of these terms refer to the speed with which water passes through the root area, and water must pass through if most plants are to grow. It's not the standing water that hurts plants directly; it is the fact that the water excludes oxygen and most roots can't live long without oxygen. Drainage is fast (soil is "well drained") if water disappears from a shrub or tree planting hole in 10 minutes or less. It is slow if water is still standing in the hole after an hour.

DRIP LINE. The line you would draw on the soil around a tree directly under its outermost branch tips. Rainwater tends to drip from the tree at this point. The term is used in connection with feeding, watering, and grading around existing trees and shrubs.

DUST (noun or verb). Several insecticides and fungicides are manufactured as powders so finely ground that they are dusts. You put the dust into a special applicator (sometimes the container is the applicator) and poof it onto the plants. If you do this early in the morning when air is still, it makes a huge cloud—the particles slowly settle as a thin, even coating over everything. The advantage over spraying is convenience—you can dust in two minutes while wearing your Sunday best.

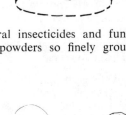

EPIPHYTE. A plant that grows on another plant but doesn't receive any nourishment from it.

ESPALIER. A tree or shrub with its branches trained to grow in a flat pattern, as on a fence or trellis.

EVERGREEN. A plant that never loses all its leaves at the same time. For what many people call evergreens, see Conifer.

EVERLASTINGS. Flowers that hold their shape and color when dried.

EYE. An undeveloped growth bud which ultimately produces a new plant or new growth. For example an "eye" on a potato (tuber) will, when planted, produce a new plant. "Eyes" at joints of a rooted cutting will produce new growth.

FAMILY. See PLANT CLASSIFICATION.

FIREBLIGHT. A highly infectious (it spreads like fire) bacterial disease that causes blossoms, young fruits, foliage, and branches to shrivel and blacken. The affected parts look as if they've been scorched by fire. Apples, pears, pyracantha, and other members of the rose family are most susceptible.

FLOWER PARTS. Following are the parts of a flower, starting from the outside and moving toward the center.

Bracts. Modified leaflike structures that grow in a flower cluster or around a flower.

Sepals. The flower parts that make up the outer circle. Usually these are green, but they can be brightly colored. When sepals are united, the whole structure is called a *calyx.*

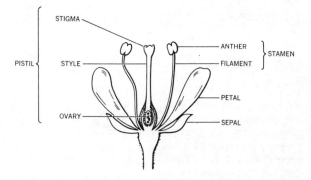

Petals. The second circle of flower parts. When the petals are united the structure is called a corolla; this can be of different shapes—flared as in petunias, bell-shaped as in campanulas, or tubular. Petals are not necessarily uniform in shape.

Segments. Lilies and tulips show no difference between sepals and petals; in such a case, they are called segments.

Spurs. Short, saclike or long, tubular projections from the flower. They can arise from sepals or petals.

Stamens. Typically they consist of a stalk, called a filament, topped by an anther. The anther (most often yellow) contains the dustlike pollen—the male element needed in the fertilization process to produce the fruit. Some flowers have only stamens.

Pistils. They're in the center of the flower. Usually each one consists of a swollen portion at the base called an ovary which contains the part that will eventually bear fruit after pollination. From the ovary arises a stalklike tube called the style, topped by a stigma. The position of the ovary varies. The pistil is the female structure of the flower, and some flowers have only one or more pistils (no stamens).

FORCING. Hastening a plant along to maturity (or to some usable state), usually by growing it under glass or other shelter for added heat. Off-season chrysanthemums are forced by controlling amount of light.

FOUNDATION PLANT. Originally, this term referred to a plant used to hide the foundation of a house. Today's houses rarely have visible foundations but the term lives on—referring to the shrubs that you plant next to house walls.

FRONDS. In the strictest sense, it refers to the foliage of ferns, but the word is sometimes used to designate any foliage that looks fernlike, and also to the featherlike leaves of many palms.

GENUS. See PLANT CLASSIFICATION.

GRAFTING. A method of propagating plants. A section from one plant *(scion)* is inserted into a branch of another plant *(stock).* The graft works—the two grow together as one plant— only if the *cambium layers* of both scion and stock make contact. (The cambium is the thin layer of tissue between the bark and wood.) If the graft takes, the scion develops foliage, flowers, and fruits just like the plant it came from; the stock supplies water and nutrients as before.

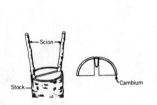

HARDY. When used in connection with plants, this word means frost or freeze-tolerant. It does not mean tough, pest-resistant, or disease-resistant.

HEADING BACK. A pruning term for cutting a branch back to a bud or side branch to increase the number of shoots, or make the plant bushier. For a method that produces roughly the opposite effect, see THINNING OUT.

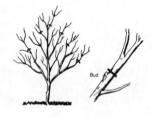

HEAVY SOIL. This rather imprecise term really means dense soil—made up of extremely fine particles (clay particles are especially fine), packed closely together.

HEELING IN. Temporarily storing plants by covering or burying their roots with soil, sawdust, or similar material. You heel in fruit trees before planting to keep the bare roots from drying out; you heel in bulbs after digging if their leaves are still green but flowers have faded.

HERBACEOUS. The word has two uses. It designates a soft plant (annual, perennial, or bulb) as opposed to a woody plant (shrub or tree). Or it is used in such phrases as "herbaceous perennial", meaning a perennial that dies to the ground each year and regrows its top the succeeding year—as compared to an "evergreen perennial" which is leafy all year.

HONEYDEW DRIP. The sticky mess you find on your windshield when you park your car under a birch tree. It's not the fault of the birch (it can happen under other trees) but of the aphids feeding in the tree. Aphids, as well as several other sucking insects, secrete a sticky substance called *honeydew*. Certain ants and fungus feed on honeydew, adding to the mess.

HUMUS. A soft brown or black substance formed in the last stages of the decomposition of animal or vegetable matter. Common usage has made the term mean practically all humus-making materials—forest duff, sawdust, and such—in all stages of decomposition.

HYBRID. See PLANT CLASSIFICATION.

IRON CHELATE (pronounced *key*-late). A chemical you add to the soil to treat plants with iron chlorosis (see CHLOROSIS). It is a combination of iron and a complex organic substance that makes the iron already in the soil more available to roots.

LATH. In gardening this word is used to designate any overhead plant-protecting structure (as a roof of spaced laths) to reduce the amount of sunlight that shines on the plants below it or to protect them from frost.

LAYERING. A method of propagating plants, especially useful with some that are hard to root otherwise.

Ground layering: Bend a limber branch; remove a circle of bark or cut a slit in it (keep the slit open with a rock or peg); bury the cut part. After it roots, separate it from the parent plant.

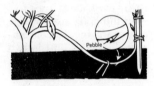

Air layering: Similar to ground layering but done above ground. Surround the cut branch with wet sphagnum moss or something else that holds moisture well; wrap in tight polyethylene. After roots form, cut the branch off, and plant.

LEACHING. Think of brewing tea or coffee. When you pour hot water through tea leaves or ground coffee, you are *leaching.* You leach soil with water when you want to remove excess salts (see SALINITY) or other impurities from the topsoil. In humid areas, rainwater leaches good as well as bad substances from the soil.

LEAFLET. Many leaves are simple in form, but some are divided into *leaflets.* Leaves may be divided featherwise (as at left) or fanwise (at right).

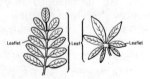

MULCH (noun or verb). Any loose material placed over the soil, such as peat moss, sawdust, straw, or leaves. A mulch can serve any of several purposes: reduce evaporation of moisture from soil; prevent mud from splashing onto foliage and other surfaces; reduce or prevent weed growth; protect falling fruit from injury; make a garden bed look neat; or insulate soil from extremes or rapid changes of temperature.

NODE. A joint in a stem; the point where a leaf starts to grow. The part between joints is called the internode.

OFFSET. Think of hen and chickens *(Sempervivum)* and hen and chicks *(Echeveria)*—the chickens or chicks are the offsets. This is one of the ways in which plants reproduce themselves, sending out a short stem that produces a new plant next to the parent plant.

ORGANIC MATTER. Applied to home gardening in the West, this term usually means a bulky soil conditioner of organic origin such as leaf mold, peat moss, ground bark, or manure.

PERENNIAL. A plant that lives more than two years. Generally the word is used to mean a plant whose top growth dies down each winter and regrows the following spring. But some perennials keep leaves all year.

PERLITE. A mineral expanded by heating to form white, very light kernels useful in lightening soil.

PETALS. See FLOWER PARTS.

PINCHING BACK. Using thumb and forefinger to nip tips of branches to force side growth and make plant bushier.

PISTILS. See FLOWER PARTS.

PLANT CLASSIFICATION. Botanists have classified plants into an orderly, ranked system that reflects the similarities among the world's plant life. The plant kingdom, the most inclusive group, is broken down into groups that are less and less inclusive: division, class, order, and then the groups defined below—which are the ones of most significance to gardeners.

Family. Each plant belongs to a family. All members of a certain family share certain characteristics—good examples are explained under the heading COMPOSITE FAMILY. Although family names—rose family (Rosaceae), lily family (Liliaceae)—aren't as important to gardeners as the groups into which the families are divided, sometimes they help to understand a plant's cultural requirements.

Genus. A plant family is divided into groups of more closely related plants called genera (plural of genus). The first word in a plant's botanical name is the name of the genus to which the plant belongs: for example, *Sequoia, Liquidambar, Primula.*

Species. A genus may include one or a great number of species. Each species is a particular kind of plant: *Sequoia sempervirens, Liquidambar styraciflua, Primula malacoides.* The second word in a plant's botanical name designates the species, distinguishing it from other plants in the same genus (plants with the same first name). Species in the same genus share many common features, but differ in one or more characteristics.

Variety. A third word in a botanical name indicates a variety (or subspecies): *Juniperus communis saxatilis.* Growing wild or in the garden, varieties retain most characteristics of the species, while differing in some way—such as flower color or leaf size.

Horticultural variety (clone). These are varieties that have been developed in nurseries—not in the wild. Such plants are given a variety name added onto the rest of the plant name and set off by single quotation marks: *Liquidambar styraciflua* 'Palo Alto'.

Hybrid. A result of a cross between two species or varieties or strains—or even between two plants belonging to different genera.

Strain. This word is usually applied to mixtures or color blends. These plants have many similar characteristics, but they are not sufficiently distinct to be separated out and given a name as a horticultural variety.

PLEACHING. A method of training plant growth. Branches are interwoven and plaited together to form a hedge or arbor. The only pruning that's done is to keep a neat, rather formal pattern.

POLLARDING. Tree tops are drastically sheared each year. Eventually form large knobby stubs from which long shoots grow each spring. London plane tree is most often subjected to this treatment—often erroneously called pleaching.

POLLINATION. The fertilization of plants by transfer of pollen from stamens to pistils. (See FLOWER PARTS for definition of stamens and pistils.) After fertilization takes place, fruit or seed begins to develop. Certain species bear male flowers (stamens only) and female flowers (pistils only) on separate plants; to get fruit on the female plant, you need to plant a male plant nearby.

A number of plants that have both stamens and pistils will not set many fruits when they are planted singly. A group of several such plants give better cross pollination, and thus more fruit.

With certain fruit trees you need to plant two varieties to get fruit. This is necessary in cases where pollen of a variety is not ripe at the time the pistil of the same variety is ready for fertilization or vice versa. So you plant a variety whose pollen will ripen when the pistil of the other variety is ready.

RAY FLOWER. See COMPOSITE FAMILY.

RHIZOME. A thickened underground stem that spreads by creeping. Rhizomes may be long and slender, as in lawn grasses, or thick and fleshy, as in iris.

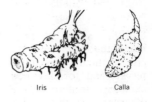

Iris   Calla

ROOTBOUND (or POTBOUND). The disastrous condition that occurs when a plant grows for too long in its container—tangled, matted roots with no room for additional growth go around in circles. Rootbound plants placed in the ground often never outgrow their choked roots and suffer from the constriction later on.

ROSETTE. A cluster of leaves arranged in a circular and overlapping pattern, somewhat like the petals of a rose. The term should be limited to small clusters.

RUST. A large group of fungus infecting certain garden plants such as roses and snapdragons. You can recognize rust by round pustules on the leaves filled with many yellowish or reddish spores.

SALINITY. Western gardeners use this word when talking of an excess of salts in the soil. Frequently excess soil salinity results from continued light irrigations with domestic tap water in semi-arid regions. Gardeners in such regions must wash accumulated salts out of the plant root zone by periodic leaching. High salinity stunts plant growth, causes leaves to scorch and turn yellow, and in general does great harm to many but not all plants.

SCREE. Fragmented rocks and pebbles usually found in nature at the base of a cliff or boulder. Many gardeners create their own scree as a place for growing alpine plants.

SEGMENTS. See FLOWER PARTS.

SEMI-DOUBLE FLOWER. A flower with a few more than the normal number of petals—but not so many that the stamens and pistils are hidden. Petals, stamens, and pistils are defined under FLOWER PARTS.

SEPALS. See FLOWER PARTS.

SINGLE FLOWER. When a flower has the normal number of petals—3, 4, or 5 depending on the kind—it is a single flower. (See FLOWER PARTS for definition of petals.)

SPECIES. See PLANT CLASSIFICATION.

SPHAGNUM. A group of mosses native to bogs. Much of the peat moss sold in the West is formed partly or wholly of these mosses in a decomposed state. They also are collected and packaged in whole pieces, fresh or dried; pieces of sphagnum moss are good to use for air layering or lining wire baskets.

SPORE. A simple type of reproductive cell that is capable of producing a new plant. Certain kinds of plants (such as algae, fungus, mosses, and ferns) reproduce by spores.

SPURS. See FLOWER PARTS.

STAMENS. See FLOWER PARTS.

STANDARD. A plant that does not naturally grow as a tree trained into a small treelike form with a single, upright trunk and rounded crown. The tree rose is the most familiar example.

STOLON. A stem that creeps along the surface of the ground, taking root at intervals and forming new plants where it roots. Another word for this is "runner." Bermuda grass spreads by stolons.

STRAIN. See PLANT CLASSIFICATION.

SUBSHRUB. A plant, usually under 3 feet high and with more or less woody stems and branches, that is some-

times grown and used as a perennial, sometimes grown and used as a shrub.

SUCKER. Any unwanted shoot—it may come up from underground, the lower part of a plant, or even on the trunk or large branches (in which case it's called a water sprout).

SYSTEMIC. Anything that is introduced into a plant's system. There are systemic insecticides and weed killers.

TAPROOT. A main fleshy root that grows straight down, like the root of a carrot or dandelion. In dry areas some plants have very deep taproots in order to get their water from a water table which is very far down in the soil.

TENDER. Use just the reverse of the way you use the word hardy; to denote lack of tolerance for cold weather.

TENDRIL. A twisting threadlike projection found on many vines which enables them to cling and climb on their supports.

THINNING OUT. In pruning, this term means removing entire branches—large or small ones—clear back to the main trunk or side branch. The object is to give the plant a more open growth pattern.

In growing plants from seed, it means removing excess seedlings so that those remaining are spaced the distance apart that is recommended on the seed packet label.

TOPIARY. Topiary pruning is the technique of shaping shrubs and trees into unnatural, formalized shapes resembling such things as animals and geometrical figures. Sometimes called "poodle pruning" but that term is inadequate because it limits the pruning only to puffs as on a trimmed poodle.

TRUSS. A cluster of flowers, usually rather compact, at the end of a stem, branch, or stalk.

TUBER. The world's most famous tuber is the potato. A tuber is a fat underground stem, similar to a rhizome, but usually shorter and thicker.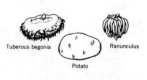

TUBEROUS ROOT. A thickened underground food storage structure that is actually a root—not a stem. Growth buds are in the old stems at the base of the plant.

U. C. MIX. A lightweight, porous, disease-free soil mix formulated by University of California soil scientists. The basic ingredients are fine sand or perlite combined with peat moss or sawdust or ground bark. Proportions of each ingredient vary, depending mainly on type of plant that will grow in the mix. Since the mix is unfertile, fertilizers must be incorporated or added according to directions (in U. C. Manual 23).

VARIETY. See PLANT CLASSIFICATION.

VERMICULITE. A mineral that's heated and popped to form spongelike, light-weight kernels, useful in conditioning soils and as a medium in which to root cuttings.

WETTABLE POWDER. A finely ground pesticide that can be mixed in water and sprayed on plants. Some kinds also can be dusted on, as described under DUST.

WHORLS. Three or more leaves, branches, or flowers that grow in a circle from a joint (node) on a stem or trunk.

WESTERN PLANT ENCYCLOPEDIA

The plant descriptions in this encyclopedia appear in alphabetical order under each plant's scientific name, except for fruits and vegetables, which are described under common names (apple, tomato). If you know only a plant's common name, you will find it in its alphabetical place with a cross-reference to the scientific name.

At the head of a description, a plant's common name appears in lighter typeface than its scientific name. Directly after the common name (if there is one), you find a word or two telling what the plant is—evergreen, tree, bulb, perennial, whatever.

A statement of climate adaptability is given for each plant except annuals and some house plants. "All Zones" means the plant is recommended for the entire West. Other than that, zones are indicated by numbers, which are explained and mapped on pages 8 to 27. Where two zone numbers are joined by a dash, as in "Zones 1-6, 15-17", the plant is recommended for all the zones between the joined numbers, inclusive.

Occasionally, technical words are used—they are defined in the Gardeners' Language section, pages 161 to 166.

Climate Zone maps pages 8-27

AARON'S BEARD. See Hypericum calycinum

ABELIA. Evergreen, partially evergreen, or deciduous shrubs. Graceful arching branches densely clothed with oval leaves about ½-1½ in. long, usually quite glossy; the new growth bronzy. Tubular or bell-like flowers in clusters at ends of branches or among the leaves; blossoms small but generous enough to be showy mostly during the summer and early fall months. When blooms drop, they usually leave purplish or copper-colored sepals which continue color into the fall months. Leaves also may take on bronzy tints during autumn.

To keep abelias' graceful form, prune them selectively; don't shear. The more stems you cut to the ground in winter or early spring, the more open and arching will be next year's growth. Plants grow and flower best in sun, but they will take some shade. Abelias are adaptable and useful in shrub borders, as space dividers and visual barriers, near house walls; lower kinds are good bank or ground covers.

A. 'Edward Goucher' (*A. gaucheri*). Evergreen to almost deciduous at 15°. Zones 5-24. Hybrid between *A. grandiflora* and *A. schumanii*. Lower-growing (to 3-5 ft.), lacier texture than *A. grandiflora*. At 0° both freeze to the ground, but usually recover to bloom the same year on new wood. In these areas, they make graceful little border plants 10-15 in. high. Small lilac pink tubular flowers with orange throats make showy display June to October.

A. floribunda. MEXICAN ABELIA. Evergreen. Zones 8, 9, 12-24. Severely damaged at 20°. Usually 3-6 ft. tall, sometimes 10 ft. Arching stems are reddish and downy hairy. Pendulous tubular flowers, 1½ in. long, reddish purple, singly or in clusters of 3. Usually summer blooming, but often in full bloom in January. Partial shade in hot-summer areas.

A. grandiflora. GLOSSY ABELIA. Evergreen to partially deciduous. Zones 5-24. Hybrid of two species from China. Best known and most popular of the abelias. Grows to 8 ft. or more high. Spreads to 5 ft. or more. Flowers white or faintly tinged pink June-October.

A. g. 'Prostrata'. Occasionally partially deciduous even in mildest climates. Low-growing (1½-2 ft.), spreading variety useful as ground cover, bank planting, low foundation shrub. For massing, set 3-4 ft. apart.

A. g. 'Sherwoodii'. Smaller than *A. grandiflora*, more spreading; grows 3-4 ft. tall, 5 ft. wide.

A. schumannii. Deciduous or partially evergreen. Zones 5-21. Native to China. Slender shrub to 5-8 ft. tall. Flowers lavender-pink; profuse, June-August.

ABELIOPHYLLUM distichum. WHITE FORSYTHIA. Deciduous shrub. Native to Korea. Best adapted Zones 2-6, often freezes back in Zone 1. Not a forsythia but resembles it in growth habit and profusion of bloom in February—but in dazzling white. Lower and slower growing than most forsythias, to 3-4 ft. and as wide. Leaves bluish green, opposite, 1-2 in. long. Attractive purple buds in fall and winter set on brown or black new wood. Buds open pink, flowers quickly turn white. Fragrant. Budded branches will

bloom in winter when brought indoors. Easy to grow in sun or light shade. Routine garden care. Prune in bloom or immediately after. Cut some oldest branches at base to keep new flowering wood coming.

ABERIA. See Dovyalis

ABIES. FIR. Evergreen trees. In nature tall erect, symmetrical trees with uniformly spaced branch whorls. Look for large cones held erect; they shatter after ripening, leaving a spiky stalk. Most (but not all) native firs are high mountain plants which grow best in or near their natural environment. They grow slowly if at all in hot, dry, windy areas at low elevations.

Christmas tree farms grow native firs for cutting and nurseries in the Northwest and northern California grow a few species for the living Christmas tree trade. Licensed collectors in the Northwest dig picturesque, contorted firs at high elevations near timberline and market them through nurseries as "alpine conifers." Use these in rock gardens; small specimens are good container or bonsai subjects.

Firs from some other parts of the world do well in warm, dry climates.

Firs are not ordinarily bothered by pests, but watch out for spider mites and spray to control them.

A. amabilis. SILVER FIR, CASCADE FIR. Zones 1-7, 15-17. Native to southern Alaska south through Coast Ranges and Cascades of Washington and Oregon. Tall tree in the wilds, smaller (20 to 50 ft.) in lowland gardens in the Pacific Northwest. Dark green leaves, silvery beneath, curve upward along the branches. Give it room to grow.

A. balsamea. BALSAM FIR. Zones 1-7, 15-17. Native to eastern American mountains. Only the dwarf variety 'Nana' is occasionally sold in the West. Interesting rock garden subject. Slow growing, dense, dark green cushion. Give it partial shade, ample water.

A. bracteata (*A. venusta*). SANTA LUCIA FIR, BRISTLECONE FIR. Zones 8, 9, 14-21. From steep, rocky slopes on the seaward side of the Santa Lucia Mountains, Monterey County, California. A tall tree (70 ft. in 50 years), with spreading (15 to 20 ft.) lower branches, and a slender steeplelike crown. Its stiff needles, 1½ to 2½ in. long, have unusually sharp points; dark green above, white lines beneath. Roundish cones are unique—about 4 in. long, with a long, slender, pointed bract on each cone scale.

A. concolor. WHITE FIR. Zones 1-9, 14-24. Native to mountains of southern Oregon, California, southern Rocky Mountains, Lower California. One of the big five in timber belt of the Sierra Nevada, along with ponderosa pine, sugar pine, incense cedar, and Douglas fir. It's one of the popular Christmas trees, and one of the most commonly grown native firs in Western gardens.

Large, very symmetrical tree in its native range and in the Northwest. Slower growing in California gardens; best as a container plant in southern California. Bluish green, 1-2-in.-long needles.

A. grandis. LOWLAND FIR, GRAND FIR. Zones 1-9, 14-17. From British Columbia, inland to Montana, southward to Sonoma County, California. In California it grows near the ocean along Highway 1.

Under this fir, many Northwest gardeners live and garden successfully; they prune it high. It's one of the largest firs, reaching to 300 feet; lower in cultivation. Handsome, deep green, 1-1½-in.-long needles, glossy above, white lines beneath; in two rows along the branches.

A. lasiocarpa. ALPINE FIR. Zones 1-9, 14-17. Native to Alaska, south through the high Cascades of Washington and Oregon; nearly throughout the Rocky Mountains. Narrow, steeple-shaped tree 60-90 ft. in good soil in moist areas. Bluish green, 1 to 1½-in.-long needles.

Best known in gardens as an "alpine conifer" dug near timberline and sold in nurseries. Extremely slow growing in California gardens. Allow 15 to 20-ft. spread in Northwest gardens as it usually doesn't hold its narrow shape in cultivation.

A. l. arizonica. CORK FIR. Zones 1-9, 14-17. Native to San Francisco Peaks, Arizona, at 8,500 ft. elevation. Has interesting creamy white, thick, corky bark. Very handsome as a youngster.

A. magnifica. RED FIR. Zones 1-7. Native to the mountains of southern Oregon; California's Sierra Nevada south to Kern County, and the Coast Ranges south to Lake County. Tall stately tree with symmetrical, horizontal, rather short branches. New growth silvery gray. Mature, 1-in.-long needles blue-green, curve upward on upper limbs, in two rows on lower branches.

The "silver tip" of California cut Christmas tree trade is red fir. Hard to grow at low elevations.

A. nordmanniana. NORDMANN FIR. Zones 1-11, 14-24. Native to the Caucasus, Asia Minor, Greece. Vigorous, densely foliaged fir 30-50 ft. tall in cultivation and 20 ft. wide. Shining dark green, ¾-1½-in.-long needles, with whitish bands beneath, densely cover branches.

More adaptable to California gardens than native firs. Give it adequate water. Will submit to container growing for a long period.

A. pinsapo. SPANISH FIR. Zones 5-11, 14-24. Native to Spain. A fine tree that deserves wider use in warm dry areas. Very slow growing to 25 ft. in 40 years. In southern California, good dwarf effect for years, extremely slow. Dense symmetrical form; it's sometimes taken for a spruce. Stiff, deep green, ½-¾-in.-long needles uniformly around branches. There is a blue-gray foliage variety 'Glauca'.

A. procera (*A. nobilis*). NOBLE FIR. Zones 1-7, 15-17. Native to the Siskiyou Mountains of California, north in the mountains of Oregon and Washington. Grown in Northwest nurseries as live Christmas trees. Similar to California's red fir in appearance. Grows 90 to 200 ft. high in wilds, almost as high in Northwest gardens. Short stiff branches, blue-green, 1-in.-long needles.

ABRONIA. SAND VERBENA. Perennial. Zones 5, 17, 24. Not a true verbena. Oval to roundish, very thick, fleshy leaves. Small, tubular, fragrant flowers in headlike clusters. The following two species are naturally suited for holding sand in beach gardens. They are not hardy in severe climates.

A. latifolia. YELLOW SAND VERBENA. Native to seacoast, British Columbia to Santa Barbara. Under ideal conditions plants form

Climate Zone maps pages 8-27

leafy mats up to 3 ft. across. Thick leaves 1½ in. long and as wide. The whole plant is gummy enough so that it may become incrusted with sand or dust. Bright yellow flowers from May to October. Sow seed in flats, pots, or in light well drained sandy soil. Scraping or peeling off the papery covering that encloses the seed should facilitate germination.

A. umbellata. Pink sand verbena. Native to coasts, British Columbia to Baja California. Creeping, rather slender, fleshy, often reddish stems 1 ft. or more long. Leaves 1-2 in. long, not quite as wide. Flowers rosy pink, bloom almost throughout year. Grow as *A. latifolia*.

ABUTILON. Flowering maple, Chinese bellflower, Chinese lantern. Evergreen viny shrubs. Zones 15-24. Mostly native to South America. Rapid growing; planted primarily for the pleasure provided by the flowers. The coarse and rangy growth can be avoided by pinching out branch tips often.

Can be trained as standards or espaliers, but best as loose, informal espalier. Abutilons enjoy moist soil. Partial shade inland, full sun on coast. Will not bloom in deep shade. In cold climates it can be used as container plant indoors in winter; out on terrace in summer. Gets whitefly and scale insects. Control both with malathion or light oil spray.

A. hybridum. Upright arching growth to 8-10 ft., and spreading as wide. Broad maple-like leaves. Drooping bell-like flowers in white, yellow, pink, and red. Main blooming season from April-June. White and yellow forms seem to bloom almost continuously. The best-known flowering maple.

A. megapotamicum. Vigorous, growth to 10 ft. and as wide. Leaves are arrowlike, 1½-3-in.-long. Flowers like red and yellow lanterns gaily decorate the long rangy branches from May to September. This vine-shrub is more graceful in detail than in entirety, but can be trained to an interesting pattern. Good hanging basket plant.

A. striatum thompsonii. Similar to *A. hybridum*, but foliage strikingly variegated with creamy yellow. Pale orange bells veined with red.

A. vitifolium. Grows quickly to 8-12 ft. or more. Large 3-5-lobed leaves 4-6 in. across, soft velvety, hairy beneath. Showy clusters of 2-3-in. lavender-blue (rarely white) flowers in May-June. Best in areas with cool summers.

ACACIA. Evergreen shrubs and trees. Native to tropics, and warm temperate regions all over the world, particularly Australia.

The first acacias came into California gardens a few years after the discovery of gold. More than 80 species have been tested in the past 100 years. Of these, some 20

ACACIA

NAME	ZONES	HEIGHT	SPREAD	LEAVES	FLOWERS	COMMENTS
ACACIA armata KANGAROO THORN	13-24	10-15 ft.	10-12 ft.	Light green, waxy, 1-in.-long leaves on thorny branches.	Yellow, single ¼-in.-wide balls. Feb.-Mar.	Blooms when young. Used as a pot plant in cold areas. Grown as shrub barrier in California. Thorniness makes it real barrier to man and boy.
A. baileyana BAILEY ACACIA (Often called mimosa as cut flowers.)	7-9, 13-24 Borderline Zone 6.	20-30 ft.	20-40 ft.	Feathery, finely cut, blue-gray.	Yellow, in clusters. Profuse in Jan.-Feb. Fragrant.	Most commonly planted and one of hardiest. Wonderful tree on banks when grown as a multiple trunked tree-shrub.
A. b. 'Purpurea' PURPLE-LEAF ACACIA	8, 9, 14-24	20-30 ft.	20-30 ft.	Same, except for lavender to purple new growth.	Same.	Cut back to encourage new growth, prolong foliage color.
A. cultriformis KNIFE ACACIA	13-24	10-15 ft.	10-15 ft.	Silvery gray, shaped like 1-in.-long paring knife blades stuck into stems.	Yellow, in clusters. Mar.	Naturally a multiple stemmed tree. Barrier or screen. Useful on banks, slopes.
A. cyanophylla BLUE-LEAF WATTLE	13-24	20-30 ft.	15-20 ft.	Narrow, 6-12 in. long, bluish.	Nearly orange balls in clusters. Heavy bloom in Mar., Apr.	Screen for privacy against wind, dust. Multiple trunked tree-shrub on banks, hillsides. Long branches droop gracefully when laden with flowers.
A. cyclops	8, 9, 13-24	10-15 ft.	15-20 ft.	Dark green, rather narrow, to 3½ in. long.	Bright yellow, single or clustered; rather inconspicuous. Spring.	Screening plant along highways. Very drought resistant. Good for hedges. Unusual seeds—black with red rings.
A. decora GRACEFUL WATTLE	13-24	6-8 ft.	6-8 ft.	Rather narrow, 2 in. long, curved, bluish.	Yellow balls in 2-in.-long clusters. Mass display in spring.	Screening. Can be used as trimmed hedge 5 ft. high. Drought resistant.
A. decurrens GREEN WATTLE	8, 9, 14-24 Borderline Zone 6.	To 50 ft.	40-50 ft.	Feathery, dark green.	Yellow, in clusters. Feb.-Mar.	Longer lived than *A. baileyana*; takes more wind and water. Leaves larger, but still finely cut. Looks almost pinelike in groves.
A. d. dealbata	8, 9, 14-24 Borderline Zone 6.	Same	Same	Feathery, silvery gray.	Same. Fragrant.	Twigs and young branches also silvery gray; very attractive. Very fast growing.

(Continued on next page)

A

Climate Zone maps pages 8-27

NAME	ZONES	HEIGHT	SPREAD	LEAVES	FLOWERS	COMMENTS
A. elata CEDAR WATTLE	14-24	To 90 ft.	60-70 ft.	Leaves divided into 2-in.-long, dark green leaflets.	Yellow, in 6-in.-clusters. Often blooms twice a year.	One of the most beautiful acacias. Long-lived but fast-growing—as much as 25 ft. in 3 years.
A. farnesiana SWEET ACACIA	8, 9, 12-24	To 20 ft.	15-25 ft.	Deciduous. Feathery, finely divided. Branches thorny.	Deep yellow, fragrant, single balls. Jan.-Apr., and longer.	Does well in alkaline soils of low and high deserts where temperatures do not drop below 15°. A valuable tree or screen in Arizona.
A. glandulicarpa	14-24	7-8 ft.	7-8 ft.	Tiny, waxy green.	Yellow, very profuse, in puff-ball form. Spring bloom.	Compact shrub, low branching, with fragrant flowers.
A. longifolia (Often sold as *A. latifolia*) SYDNEY GOLDEN WATTLE	8, 9, 14-24	To 20 ft.	To 20 ft.	Bright green, 3-6 in. long.	Golden yellow in loose 2½-in.-long spikes along branches in summer.	Usually big, rounded, billowy shrub. Very fast growing; very tolerant. Used as road screening against dust, headlights. Good soil binder near beach (winds make it prostrate).
A. melanoxylon BLACKWOOD ACACIA, BLACK ACACIA	8, 9, 13-24	To 40 ft.	To 20 ft.	Dark green, 2-4 in.-long.	Creamy to straw color, in short clusters. Mar.-Apr.	Fast upright grower. The one acacia that always succeeds in California's Central Valley. A trouble-maker in confined situations.
A. pendula WEEPING ACACIA, WEEPING MYALL	13-24	To 25 ft.	To 15 ft.	Blue-gray, to 4 in. long, on long weeping branches.	Yellow, in pairs or clusters. Blooms erratically in Apr., May.	Beautiful weeping tree. Perfect for cascading from behind wall. Interesting structural form as mature individual. Makes graceful espalier.
A. podalyriaefolia PEARL ACACIA	8, 9, 13-24	10-20 ft.	12-15 ft.	Roundish, 1½ in. long, silvery gray, soft and satiny to touch.	Light yellow, fluffy, in long clusters. Nov.-Mar.	Shrub or can be trained as rounded, open-headed tree. Excellent for patio use. Good winter color; earliest to bloom (November in San Diego).
A. pruinosa FROSTY ACACIA	13-24	To 60 ft.	To 40 ft.	Light green, divided into ¾-in.-long leaflets. New growth in copper shades.	Cream and yellow, in clusters; fragrant. June to Sept.	Another large, dense, spreading, beautiful acacia. Longer lived than most where soil and water suits.
A. pycnantha GOLDEN WATTLE	13-24	To 25 ft.	To 15 ft.	Lime green, 6 in. long, very broad, curved.	Golden yellow, large balls in clusters; fragrant. Profuse bloom in March.	Erect tree or large spreading shrub. Stems of new growth golden; older stems shade to plum red. Has short but brilliant life.
A. retinodes (Often sold as *A. floribunda*.) WATER WATTLE, FLORIBUNDA ACACIA	8, 9, 13-24 Borderline Zones 5, 6	To 20 ft.	To 20 ft.	Yellow-green, to 5 in. long.	Yellow, small heads in clusters. Blooms most of year near coast.	Quick screen. Less dense than *A. longifolia*. Tends to get leggy. The only acacia with chance of survival in Seattle if mild winters come four in a row.
A. saligna WILLOW ACACIA	14-24	10-20 ft.	15-25 ft.	Dark green, to 8 in. long.	Yellow, showy, large, in clusters. Profuse in Mar.	Graceful weeping habit. Fast growth. Reaches good flowering size in 3 to 4 years from seed.
A. verticillata	14-24	To 15 ft.	To 15 ft.	Dark green, needle-like leaves, ¾ in. long, in whorls. Looks like an airy conifer.	Pale yellow in 1-in.-long spikes. Apr. to May.	Good low hedge in wind. Unpruned, it develops open form with many spreading, twisting trunks. Sheared, it grows dense and full. One of the best plants at the beach.

Climate
Zone maps
pages 8-27

species now serve, beautifully and functionally, in California and Arizona landscape. Several are fountains of clear yellow flowers in January and February. Some are quite fragrant when in bloom. Many decorate and protect hillsides, banks, freeway landscapes. Some serve well in beach plantings.

The acacias differ widely in foliage and growth habit. Some have feathery, much divided leaves; others have flattened leaf stalks that fulfill the function of leaves.

Whether the acacia is a shrub or tree depends on how it is pruned in youth. Remove the lead shoot and it grows as a shrub. Remove the lower branches and it grows treelike. Stake the tree types until they are deeply anchored. Deep infrequent watering will discourage surface rooting and give plants better anchorage.

Prune large trees to open interiors reducing dieback of shaded branches and preventing damage by wind. Thin by removing branches entirely to the trunk.

All acacias are relatively shortlived—20 to 30 years. But if a tree grows to 20 ft. high in 3 years, the short life can be accepted.

Many acacias become chlorotic where water is bad and salts accumulate. as do many other plants in such soil.

The blackwood acacia (*A. melanoxylon*) has aggressive roots, lifts sidewalks, splits easily, suckers. In shallow soil or where roots compete, it is a bad actor. Yet in the right place it is a well behaved, beautiful tree. It is vigorous and dependable under difficult conditions or poor soil, wind, and drought.

ACAENA. SHEEP BUR. Perennials. Zones 4-9, 14-24. The two New Zealand natives described below are plants that form large loose mats of attractive gray-green or pale green leaves that are divided into leaflets. Grow from seed or divisions in spring. Rather slow to establish. Plant 6-12 in. apart in sun or part shade. Burn in hot sun. Need ample water. Use in areas where a gray-green, loose, fine-textured mat is wanted—beside paths, under trees where not too shady, or in rock gardens. Take only occasional foot traffic. Remove burs, which look messy and stick to clothing or to coats of pets.

A. buchananii. Has densely silky, whitish green, round, small leaflets with scallop-toothed edges.

A. microphylla. NEW ZEALAND BUR. Has 7-13 pale green leaflets that are similar to the above, but larger and almost without hairs.

ACALYPHA. Evergreen tropical shrubs. Zones 21-23. Both species described below are quite tender. One of them can be used as an annual.

A. hispida. CHENILLE PLANT. Native to the East Indies. Needs tropical climate. Best grown in plastic-covered outdoor rooms. Control size by pinching and pruning; can grow to a bulky 10 ft. Leaves, heavy, broad to 8 in., rich green. Flowers hang in 18-in.-long clusters resembling tassels of crimson chenille. Blooms most heavily in June; scattered bloom throughout year. With heavy pruning, a good house plant

A. wilkesiana (*A. tricolor*). COPPER LEAF. Native to South Pacific islands. Foliage more colorful than many flowers. Used

as an annual in Disneyland plantings as a substitute for flowers from September to frost. Leaves, to 8 in., bronzy green mottled with shades of red and purple; or red with crimson and bronze; or green, edged with crimson, stippled with orange and red. In a warm, sheltered spot, it can grow as a shrub to 6 ft. or more if winter appearance is not important. Best in container with fast-draining soil mix, kept slightly dry through winter.

ACANTHOPANAX sieboldianus (*Aralia pentaphylla*). Deciduous shrub. Zones 1-17. Native to Japan, China. Not showy or pushy, just quietly handsome foliage. Glossy, rich green leaves divided fanwise into 5-7, 2-in.-long, toothed leaflets. Carried on upright to arching branches to 10 ft. Accepts any soil—cold, damp, shaded situations. Prune by thinning out some of the oldest stems each year.

ACANTHUS mollis. BEAR'S BREECH. Perennial. Zones 4-24. Native to southern Europe. Spreading plant with basal clusters of handsome, deeply lobed and cut, shining, dark green leaves to 2 ft. long. Rigid 1½-ft. spikes of tubular whitish, lilac, or rose flowers with green or purplish spiny bracts top 2-3-ft. stems. Blooms early summer. Variety 'Latifolius' has larger leaves and is hardier.

Requires shade but will take sun in coastal areas. Wash leaves with hose in summer. Cut back after flowering. If you grow it for the foliage alone, cut off flower stalks before they bloom. Bait for slugs and snails. Divide clumps between October and March. Plant where it can be confined. Roots travel underground, make plant difficult to eradicate. Effective with bamboo, large-leafed ferns. Best in moist shady situations, but will also grow in dry, sunny areas, even succeeding in parking strips.

ACER. MAPLE. Deciduous or evergreen trees or large shrubs. When you talk of maples, you're talking about many trees—large and medium-sized deciduous shade trees, smaller evergreen and deciduous trees, and dainty, picturesque shrub-trees. In general, maples are highly favored in the Pacific Northwest, in the intermountain areas, and to a lesser extent in northern California, and but, with a few exceptions are not adapted to southern California or the Southwest desert areas. Practically all maples in southern California show marginal leaf burn after mid-June, and lack the fall color common to maples in colder areas.

The larger maples have extensive fibrous root systems that make heavy demands on the soil. The great canopy of leaves calls for a steady, constant supply of water, not necessarily frequent watering, but constantly available water throughout the root zone. Ample deep watering and periodic feeding will help keep roots down.

A. buergerianum. TRIDENT MAPLE. Deciduous tree. Zones 4-9, 14-17, 20, 21. Native to China, Japan. Grows 20-25 ft. high. Roundish crown of 3-in.-wide, glossy, 3-lobed leaves that are pale beneath. Fall color usually red, varies to orange or yellow. Low spreading growth; stake and prune to make it branch high. A decorative useful patio tree. A favorite bonsai subject.

A. campestre. HEDGE MAPLE. Deciduous tree. Zones 1-9, 14. Native to Europe, western Asia. Slow growing to 70 feet, seldom over 30 feet in cultivation. Forms especially dense, compact, rounded head in the Northwest, thinner in California. Leaves 3-5-lobed, 2-4 in. wide, dull green above; turn yellow in fall. Rated very high in the Northwest.

A. cappadocicum. COLISEUM MAPLE. Deciduous tree. Zones 1-6. Native to western Asia. Known here in its variety 'Rubrum', RED COLISEUM MAPLE. Grows to 35 ft.; forms compact rounded crown. Leaves 5-7-lobed, 5½ in. wide. Bright red spring foliage turns rich, dark green.

Upper left is a leaf of vine maple. At lower right is a leaf of trident maple.

A. circinatum. VINE MAPLE. Deciduous shrub or small tree. Zones 1-6, 14-17. Native to moist woods, stream banks in coastal mountains of British Columbia south to northern California. Crooked, sprawling and vinelike in the forest shade, with many stems from the base, or single trunked small tree 5-35 ft. high in full sun. Leaves 5-11-lobed, 2-6 in. wide and as long; light green turning orange-scarlet or yellow in the fall; new spring foliage usually has reddish tints. Tiny reddish purple flowers in clusters, April-May, followed by paired winged fruits which look like little red bow ties among the green leaves. One of the most airy and delicate Western natives.

Let it go untrimmed to make natural bowers, ideal settings for ferns and woodland flowers. Use under a canopy of tall conifers where its blazing fall color is brilliant contrast. Can be espaliered against shady side of a wall. Its contorted leafless branches make an interesting pattern in winter. Loses its vinelike characteristics in open situations. Select in fall to get best forms for autumn color.

A. davidii. DAVID'S MAPLE. Deciduous tree. Zones 1-6, 15-17, 20, 21. Native to central China. This 20-35-ft.-high maple is distinctive on several counts. Bark is shining green striped with silvery white, particularly effective in winter. Leaves are glossy green, heart-shaped, 2-7 in. long, 1½-4 in. wide, each embossed with deep veins. New foliage bronze tinted turning to bright yellow, red-orange, and purple in fall. Greenish yellow flowers, in clusters, showy in April or May.

Climate Zone maps pages 8-27

A. ginnala. AMUR MAPLE. Deciduous shrub or small tree. Zones 1-9, 14-16. Native to Manchuria, north China, Japan. To 20 ft. high. Three-lobed, toothed leaves to 3 in. long, 2 in. wide. Striking red fall color. Clusters of small yellowish flowers fragrant in early spring; followed by handsome bright red, winged fruits. Comes into its own in the coldest areas of the West. Grown as a staked, trained single tree or a multiple trunked tall shrub.

A. griseum. PAPERBARK MAPLE. Deciduous tree. Zones 1-9, 14-21. Native to China. Grows to 25 ft. with narrow to rounded crown. In winter it makes a striking silhouette with bare branches angling out and up from main trunk and reddish bark peeling away in paper thin sheets. Late to leaf out in spring, leaves are divided into 3 coarsely toothed leaflets 1½ to 2½ in. long, dark green above, silvery below. Inconspicuous red flowers in spring develop into showy winged seeds. Foliage turns brilliant red in fall.

Leaf of Amur maple, right. The other two are forms of Acer oblongum.

A. japonicum. FULLMOON MAPLE. Deciduous shrub. Zones 1-6, 14-16. Native to Japan. Small tree to 20-30 ft. Nearly round 2-5-in.-long leaves cut into 7-11 lobes. Practically unknown, but two varieties are obtainable. Both are small, slow-growing, best placed as shrubs.

A. j. 'Aconitifolium'. FERNLEAF FULLMOON MAPLE. Has leaves deeply cut, almost to the leaf stalk, with each lobe cut and toothed. Fine fall color where adapted.

A. j. 'Aureum'. GOLDEN FULLMOON MAPLE. Leaves open pale gold in spring and remain a pale chartreuse yellow all summer.

A. macrophyllum. BIGLEAF MAPLE. Deciduous tree. Zones 4-17. Native to streambanks, moist canyons, Alaska to foothills of California. Broad-topped, dense shade tree 30-95 ft. high—too big for a small garden or a street tree. Large 3-5-lobed leaves, 6-15 in. wide; sometimes bigger on young, vigorous sapling growth; medium green turning yellow in fall. Small greenish yellow flowers in drooping clusters, April-May. Fo'lowed by clusters of paired winged seeds which look rather like tawny drooping butterflies. Yellow fall color spectacular in cool areas.

A. negundo. BOX ELDER. Deciduous tree. Zones 1-9, 12-24. Native to eastern U.S. Where you can grow maples of your choice this is a weed tree of many faults—seeds readily, hosts box elder bugs, suckers badly, subject to breakage. Fast-growing

to 60 ft., usually less. Leaves divided into 3-5 (or 7-9), oval, 2-5-in.-long leaflets with toothed margins; turn yellow in fall.

Two varieties are native to the West. *A. n. californicum* grows nearly throughout the foothills and valleys of California. *A. n. interius* ranges from Alberta to Arizona. Both have leaves with three leaflets.

A. n. 'Variegatum'. VARIEGATED BOX ELDER. Not as large or weedy as the species. Combination of green and creamy white leaves stands out in any situation. Highly regarded in the Northwest; occasionally planted in northern California.

A. oblongum. EVERGREEN MAPLE. Evergreen or partially evergreen tree. Zones 8, 9, 14-24. Native to the Himalayas and China. To 20-25 ft. high, spreads almost as wide; branches tend to sweep outward and upward. Slender, shiny, deep green leaves, no lobes. New growth attractive bronzy pink in spring. Loses all leaves in sharp cold.

A. o. biauritum. (Usually sold as *A. paxii*.) Denser habit and slower than evergreen maple. Leaves usually three-lobed but occasionally oval or mitten-shaped.

A. palmatum. JAPANESE MAPLE. Deciduous shrub or tree. Zones 1-9, 14-24. Native to Japan and Korea. Slow growing to 20 ft. Normally many stemmed. Most airy and delicate of all maples. Leaves 2-4 in. long, deeply cut into 5-9 toothed lobes. All year interest: young spring growth is glowing red; summer's leaves are soft green; foliage turns scarlet in fall months; slender leafless branches in greens and reds provide winter pattern.

Grafted garden varieties are popular (see below) but even common seedlings have uncommon grace and usefulness. They are more rugged, faster, and stand more sun and wind than named forms. They thrive everywhere in the Northwest (where they make good small street trees). They can be grown with success in California, if given shelter from hot, dry, or constant winds. Filtered shade is best. In California consider the local soil and water; wherever azaleas are difficult and suffer from salt buildup in the soil, Japanese maple will

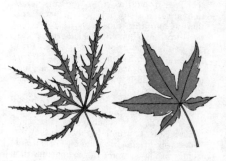

Seedling Japanese maple (right) and red laceleaf maple show varied leaf shapes.

show burn on leaf edges. Give same watering treatment as azaleas—flood occasionally to leach out salt accumulation.

Used effectively on north and east walls, in patios and entryways, as small lawn tree. Attractive in groves (like birches) as woodland planting; set out plants of different sizes and spacings for natural effects.

Seen under oaks, as background for ferns and azaleas, alongside pools. Invaluable in tubs and for bonsai. Since it is inclined to grow in planed surfaces, pruning to accentuate this growth habit is easy. Prune to plane downward when given a water foreground.

The grafted garden forms are smaller than seedlings, more weeping and spreading, brighter in foliage color, and more finely cut in leaf. In California it seems that the finer the cut leaf the greater the leaf burn problem. Since these kinds make good tub plants, it's easy to give them special placement and watering attention. Some of the best are:

'Atropurpureum'. RED JAPANESE MAPLE. Purplish or bronze to bronzy green leaves, brighter in sun. Holds color all summer.

'Bonfire'. Brilliant orange-pink spring and fall foliage. Picturesque habit, with twisted trunk, short branches, drooping branchlets.

'Burgundy Lace'. Leaves more deeply lobed than 'Atropurpureum'. Branchlets bright green.

'Dissectum'. LACELEAF JAPANESE MAPLE. Leaves finely cut into threadlike segments, bright green. Mounded form, weeping branches.

'Ornatum' ('Dissectum Atropurpureum'). RED LACELEAF JAPANESE MAPLE. Like the last, but with red leaves.

'Oshio Beni'. Similar to variety 'Atropurpureum' but more vigorous; makes long, arching branches.

'Sangokaku'. More treelike than most named forms. Fall foliage yellow, tinted rose. Winter twigs, young branches striking red.

A. platanoides. NORWAY MAPLE. Deciduous tree. Zones 1-9, 14-17. Native to Europe, western Asia. Broad-crowned, densely-foliaged tree to 50-60 ft. Leaves 5-lobed, 3-5 in. wide, deep green above, paler beneath; turn yellow in fall. Showy clusters of small, greenish yellow flowers in early spring. Very adaptable, tolerating many soil and climate conditions. Forget it in southern California and desert. Once a widely recommended street tree but now objected to where aphids cause honeydew drip and sooty mold. Voracious root system deep down and at surface also a problem. Among the horticultural varieties here are some of the best (purple-leafed forms perform poorly in alkaline soils unless soil is conditioned):

'Columnare'. PYRAMIDAL NORWAY MAPLE. Slower in growth and narrower in habit.

'Crimson King'. Holds purple foliage color until leaf drop. Slower growing than the species. Fine in Northwest and foothill California.

'Drummondii'. Has its leaves edged with silvery white; unusual, striking.

'Faassen's Black'. Pyramidal in shape, and has dark purple leaves.

'Royal Red Leaf'. Another purple-leafed form.

'Schwedleri'. Has purplish red leaves in spring; these later turn to dark bronzy green, then to gold in the autumn.

A. pseudo-platanus. SYCAMORE MAPLE. Deciduous tree. Zones 1-9, 14-20. Native to Europe, western Asia. Moderate growth to 40 ft. or more. Leaves 3-5 in. wide, 5-lobed, thick, prominently veined, dark green above, pale below. No particular fall color. The variety 'Atropurpureum' has leaves that are rich purple underneath.

A. rubrum. SCARLET MAPLE, RED MAPLE. Deciduous tree. Zones 1-7, 14-17. Native to eastern U.S. Fairly fast growth to 40 ft. or more with 20-ft. spread. Faster than Norway or sycamore maples. It is red in twigs, branchlets, buds, and quite showy flowers. Fruits dull red. Leaves 2-4 in. long, 3-5-lobed, shining green above, pale beneath, furnish brilliant scarlet in frosty areas. Rates high in Pacific Northwest where several selected forms are available. Needs ample moisture in Zone 14.

A. rufinerve. REDVEIN MAPLE. Deciduous tree. Zones 1-9, 14-21. Native to Japan. Bark on this 40-ft. maple is distinctive feature: green with prominent gray streaks. Leaves are 3-lobed, to 5 in. long and broad, turn bright crimson in fall.

A. saccharinum. SILVER MAPLE. Deciduous tree. Zones 1-9, 14-17. Native to eastern U.S. Grows fast to 40-100 ft. with equal spread. Open form, with semi-pendulous branches; casts fairly open shade. Bark silvery gray except on oldest wood. Leaves 3-6 in. wide, 5-lobed, light green above, silvery beneath. In Northwest, fall color is a mixture of scarlet-orange and yellow—often in same leaf.

You pay a penalty for the advantage of fast growth. Weak wood and narrow crotch angles make it subject to breakage. Many rate it least desirable of maples. Unusually susceptible to aphids and cottony scale. Suffers from chlorosis in alkaline soils.

A. s. 'Laciniatum' (*A. s.* 'Wieri'). WIER MAPLE, CUTLEAF SILVER MAPLE. Same as species except leaves are much more finely cut, makes open shade.

Top, leaf of Acer truncatum. Center, silver maple. At bottom, sugar maple.

A. saccharum. SUGAR MAPLE. Deciduous tree. Zones 1-9, 14-20. From eastern U.S.; in the Northeast it's source of maple sugar. Moderate growth to 60 ft. and more. Stout branches with upward sweep form fairly compact crown. Leaves 3-6 in. wide, 3-5 lobed, green above, pale below. Spectacular fall color in cold-winter areas—yellow and orange to deep red and scarlet.

A. truncatum. Deciduous tree. Zones 1, 4-9, 14-23. Native to China. Grows fairly rapidly to 25 ft. Like a small Norway maple

with more deeply lobed leaves to 4 in. wide. Expanding leaves a purplish red, summer leaves green, autumn leaves dark purplish red. A good lawn or patio tree.

ACHILLEA. YARROW. Perennial. All Zones. Yarrows are among the most care-free and generous blooming perennials for summer and early fall, several being equally useful in the garden or as cut flowers. Leaves are gray or green, bitter-aromatic, usually finely divided, some with toothed edges. Flower heads usually in flattish clusters. Yarrows thrive in sun, need only routine care — moderate watering, cutting back after bloom, dividing when clumps get crowded.

A. ageratifolia. GREEK YARROW. Native to Balkan region. Low mats of silvery leaves, nearly smooth-edged to slightly lobed. White flower clusters ½-1 in. across on stems 4-10 in. tall. Variety *aizoon* (often sold as *Anthemis aizoon*) similar to above, but leaves typically don't have toothed edges.

A. clavennae argentea (*A. argentea*). SILVERY YARROW. Mats of silvery gray, silky leaves that are lobed somewhat like chrysanthemum leaves. Flat-topped loose clusters of ½-¾-in.-wide flower heads on 5-10 in.-high stems. Combines beautifully with *Festuca ovina* 'Glauca', yellow sunroses (*Helianthemum*), creeping yellow-flowered sedums.

A. filipendulina. FERNLEAF YARROW. Native to the Orient. Tall erect plants 4-5 ft. high with deep green, fernlike leaves. Chrome yellow flower heads in large flat-topped clusters. Dry or fresh, they are good for flower arrangements. Several horticultural varieties available: 'Gold Plate', a tall plant, has flower clusters up to 6 in. wide; and 'Coronation Gold', to about 3 ft., also with large flower clusters. Combine these tall yarrows in borders with clumps of delphiniums, red-hot poker, and Shasta daisies.

A. millefolium. COMMON YARROW, MILFOIL. Native to Europe and Asia. Naturalized in North America where it is often considered a weed. It may spread a bit or grow erect to 3 ft. Narrow, fernlike leaves on 3-ft.-high stems are green or gray-green. White flower clusters grow on long stems. One of the more successful garden varieties is 'Fire King'. It grows to about 3 ft., has gray foliage and dark reddish flowers, and is good for dry, hot situations. 'Cerise Queen' has brighter red flowers.

A. nana. Native to southern Europe. Woolly-leafed plants spreading by underground stems. Leaves much divided into short, sharp segments. White flower heads in dense flat clusters on stems 2-8 in. high.

A. ptarmica. Erect plant up to 2 ft. high. Narrow leaves with finely toothed edges. White flower heads in rather open, flattish clusters. Several varieties are available in nurseries: 'The Pearl' and 'Perry's White' both have double flowers, those of the latter larger (1 in. across). 'Boule de Neige', ('Snowball') is a semi-dwarf variety 14 in. high.

A. taygetea. Native to Levant. Grows to 18 in. Gray-green divided leaves 3-4 in. long. Dense clusters of bright yellow flower heads fade to primrose yellow—excellent

contrast in color shades until time to shear off the old stalks. Good cut flowers.

A. tomentosa. WOOLLY YARROW. Native to Europe and the Orient. Makes a flat spreading mat of fernlike, deep green, hairy leaves. Golden flower heads in flat clusters top 6-10-in. stems in summer. A good edging and a neat ground cover for sunny or partly shaded small areas; used in rock gardens. Shear off dead flowers to leave attractive green mat.

ACHIMENES. Tender perennial with very small, irregular, conelike rhizomes. Related to African violet and gloxinia, requires similar treatment. Plants 12-24 in. high, some trailing. Slender stems; roundish, crisp, bright to dark green, hairy leaves. Flaring tubular flowers 1-3 in. across, pink, blue, lavender, orchid, purple.

Grow as house plant, in greenhouse or lathhouse, or in patio protected from direct sun and wind. Plant rhizomes March-April, placing ½-1 in. deep in moist peat moss and sand. Keep in light shade at 60°, with even moisture. When 3 in. high, set 6-12 plants in 6-7-in. fern pot or hanging basket. Soil mix: equal parts peat moss, perlite, leaf mold. In fall, cure and dry rhizomes, store in cool dry place over winter; repot in spring.

ACIDANTHERA bicolor. ABYSSINIAN SWORD LILY. Corm. Native to tropical Africa. Closely related to gladiolus. In appearance, halfway between gladiolus and ixia. Growth habit similar to gladiolus but leaves are smaller and less stiff. To 2-3 ft. tall. Flowers 2-3 in. across, 4-5 in. long, fragrant, creamy white blotched brown in loose spikelike clusters. Bloom late summer and fall. Variety 'Murieliae' (*Gladiolus murieliae*) has heavily-scented flowers of same form and coloring, grows to 3 ft. or more. Makes long-lasting, fragrant cut flower.

Plant in spring in full sun. In colder areas, start in pots indoors, plant out after

On 2-3-ft. stems, acidanthera forms these creamy white and brown flowers.

frost. Set corms 3-4 in. deep, 4-6 in. apart. Lift corms after first frost, dry immediately, store in cool, dry place in same way as gladiolus.

Climate Zone maps pages 8-27

ACMENA smithii (*Eugenia smithii*). LILLY-PILLY TREE. Evergreen large shrub or small tree. Zones 15-17, 19-24. Australia. Big feature is its dramatic show of clusters of white, lavender, or lavender-pink ¼-½-in.-wide, edible berries in winter; they last a long time. If trained, can make tree to 10-25 ft. high. Awkward in growth unless trained. Shiny, pinkish green to green, 3-in.-long leaves. Many small white flowers in clusters at branch tips. Takes normal good garden care.

ACOELORRHAPHE wrightii (*Paurotis wrightii*). Palm. Outdoors Zones 19-24, house plant anywhere. Native to Florida, West Indies. Fan palm with several trunks growing stiffly and slowly to 10-15 ft. Leaves 2-3 ft. across, green above, silvery below. Very hardy (to 20°) but difficult to establish; needs lots of water.

ACOKANTHERA. Evergreen shrub. Zones 21, 23, 24. Native of South Africa. Distinguished, rather slow growing, to 10 ft. and as wide (keep them smaller and more dense by cutting back long branches and removing weak ones). Most admired for leaf color—glossy dark green to deep plum purple—against a very dark brown framework of stems and branches. Flowers, white or tinged pink and very fragrant, appear throughout the year with the big show in early spring. They are followed by

Acokantheras give all-year performance. Spring flowers white, tinged pink.

blackish purple, olive-size fruits which are very poisonous (fruits can be avoided by removing flowers as they fade or by picking when young).

Especially tolerant of wind and salt. Best in full sun. Needs plenty of water in summer. Useful in hedges, foundation plantings, and as an espalier. For color complement, use ground covers like *Polygonum capitatum* and *Kleinia repens*.

A. spectabilis (*Carissa spectabilis*). AFRICAN WINTERSWEET. Narrow leaves, 3-5 in. long. Flowers about 1 in. long. Many plants sold under this name belong to the next species.

A. venenata (*Carissa acokanthera*). BUSHMAN'S POISON. Flowers smaller than above. Leaves broader, relatively shorter, tinged red, purplish, or bronze.

ACONITE, WINTER. See Eranthis

ACONITUM. MONKSHOOD, ACONITE. Perennial. Zones 1-9, 14-21. Entirely different from delphiniums, despite some resemblance. Leaves in basal clusters usually divided into lobes. Flowers shaped like hoods or helmets, along tall spikes. Caution: all parts of the plant are poisonous. Monkshood has a definite place in rich soil under trees, or at the back of flower beds or even at the edge of a shaded bog garden. Substitute for delphinium in shade. Combines effectively with ferns, thalictrum, Japanese anemone, astilbe, hosta, and francoa.

Difficult to establish in warm, dry climates. Needs ample moisture; should never dry out. Sow seeds in spring, or late summer and early fall, for bloom the following year. Divide clumps in early spring or late fall, or leave undivided for years. Goes completely dormant in winter; mark site to avoid losing plants.

A. carmichaelii (*A. fischeri*). Native to central China. Densely leafy stems 2-4 ft. high. Leaves leathery, dark green, lobed and coarsely toothed. Deep purple-blue flowers form in dense branching clusters 4-8 in. long. Blooms in fall. Variety 'Wilsonii' grows 6-8 ft. high, has more open flower cluster 10-18 in. long.

A. napellus. ENGLISH MONKSHOOD. Native to Europe. Upright leafy plants 2-5 ft. high. Leaves 2-5 in. wide, divided into narrow lobes. Flowers usually blue or violet, in spikelike clusters.

ACROCARPUS fraxinifolius. Deciduous to almost evergreen tree. Zones 21-24. Native to India. Along the southern California coast, in Pasadena, and Fullerton, it fills a definite need for a tall-growing slender tree; has a clean green trunk. Striking foliage—large 2-ft.-wide leaves, divided into many leaflets, are red as they expand, later green. Small scarlet blossoms in dense clusters bloom in great profusion on bare branches in late winter, early spring. Performs best in wind-protected sites.

ACROCOMIA. GRUGRU PALM. Slow-growing feather palms from Mexico, West Indies, South America. Long, black spines grow on the single or multiple trunks. Fruit sweet and edible.

A. mexicana. Zone 24. Mexican palm 15-20 ft. tall, with olive to dark green 8-12-ft. feather leaves on mature plants. Takes little or no frost.

A. totai. Zones 23, 24. Native to Paraguay, Argentina. To 20 ft., with 6-9-ft.-long, medium to dark green feather leaves. Hardier than the former; has gone through several winters at Disneyland and has survived 22° in Florida.

ACTINIDIA. Deciduous vines. Native to east Asia. Handsome foliage. Plant in rich soil. Give ample water and feeding. Supply sturdy supports for them to twine upon—such as a trellis, arbor, or patio overhead. Or you can train them to cover walls and fences; guide and tie vines to the support as necessary. Thin occasionally to shape or to control pattern.

A. chinensis. KIWI, KIWI VINE, YANGTAO, CHINESE GOOSEBERRY. Zones 4-9, 14-24. Twines and leans to 30 ft. if not curbed.

Leaves 5-8 in. long, roundish, rich dark green above, white velvety below. New growth often has rich red fuzz. Flowers (May) 1-1½ in. wide, opening creamy and fading buff. Fruits egg-sized, roughly egg-shaped, covered with stiff brown fuzz. Pale green flesh edible and delicious, with hints of melon, strawberry, banana. You need a male and a female plant for fruit—but single plants are ornamental.

A. kolomikta. Zones 4-6, 15-17. Rapid growth to 15 ft. or more to produce a wondrous foliage mass made up of heart-shaped, 3-5-in.-long, variegated leaves. Some leaves all white, some green splashed with white, others have rose, pink, or even red variegation. Both male and female plants show variegation, but the male plants have the most reliably colorful leaves.

ACTINOPHLOEUS. See Ptychosperma

ADAM'S NEEDLE. See Yucca filamentosa

ADIANTUM. MAIDENHAIR FERN. Mostly native to tropics; some are Western natives. Stems are thin, wiry, and dark. Fronds finely cut, the leaflets mostly fan-shaped, bright green, thin-textured. Plants need shade, steady moisture, and a soil rich in organic matter. Leaves die back in hard frosts. Bait for snails and slugs.

A. capillus-veneris. SOUTHERN MAIDENHAIR. Zones 5-9, 14-24. Native to southern North America; found in California. To 18 in. tall, fronds twice-divided but not forked. Needs leaf mold or peat moss.

A. jordani. CALIFORNIA MAIDENHAIR. Zones 5-9, 14-24. Native to California Coast Ranges, Sierra Nevada, southern Oregon. Resembles *A. raddianum* but the fertile leaflets are roundish or half-moon-shaped. Difficult to grow. Best on steep, shady banks, where it cascades.

A. pedatum. FIVE-FINGER FERN, WESTERN MAIDENHAIR. Zones 1-9, 14-21. Western North America. Fronds fork to make a fingerlike pattern atop slender 1-2½-ft. stems. General effect airy and fresh; excellent in containers or shaded ground beds.

A. raddianum (*A. cuneatum*). Brazil. Tender fern for house or greenhouse. Fronds cut 3-4 times, 15-18 in. long. Many named varieties differing in texture and compactness. Grow in pots; move outdoors to a sheltered, shaded patio in summer.

AECHMEA. Bromeliads (see page 204). Outdoors Zones 22-24. Elsewhere, greenhouse or indoor plants. In the frost-free areas, grow in pots, hanging baskets, or in moss fastened in crotches of trees—always in shaded places with good air circulation. Indoors or outdoors, soil should be fast-draining but moisture-retentive. Apply water every week or two into cups within leaves. Put water on soil when it's really dry to the touch.

A. fasciata. Gray-green leaves, cross banded with silvery white. From the center grows a cluster of rosy pink flower bracts in which nestle pale blue flowers that change to deep rose.

A. fulgens. Green leaves, dusted with gray, 12-16 in. long, 2-3 in. wide. Flower cluster usually above the leaves; blossoms red, blue, and blue-violet. Variety *discolor* has brownish red or violet-red leaves, usually faintly striped. Many hybrids.

A. 'Foster's Favorite'. Hybrid with bright wine red, lacquered leaves about 1 ft. long. Drooping spikelike clusters of coral red and blue flowers. 'Royal Wine', another hybrid, forms an open rosette of somewhat leathery, glossy, light green leaves, burgundy red beneath. Orange to blue flowers in drooping clusters.

AEGOPODIUM podagraria. BISHOP'S WEED, GOUT-WEED. Deciduous perennial. Zones 1-7. A very vigorous ground cover best in semi-shade or shade. The many light green, divided leaves make a low (6 in.) dense mass; leaflets are ½-3 in. long. To keep it low and even, mow it 2 or 3 times a year. Spreads by creeping, underground rootstocks, may become invasive; best if contained behind an underground barrier of wood, metal, concrete, or heavy tar paper.

A. p. variegatum. The most widely planted form; leaflets are edged white.

AEONIUM. Succulents. Zones 15-24. Among the most useful succulents for decorative effects, in pots or in the ground. Especially good near the ocean or in milder inland gardens.

A. arboreum. Branched stems to 3 ft. tall, each branch with a 6-8-in.-wide rosette of light green, lightly fringed, fleshy leaves. Yellow flowers in long clusters. Variety 'Atropurpureum' has dark purple rosettes, is more striking and more widely grown than the green one.

A. decorum. Bushy rounded plants to 10 in., the many branches ending in 2-in. rosettes. Fleshy leaves tinted reddish, and with red edges. Neat and compact. Flowers soft pink.

A. haworthii. Free-branching, shrubby, to 2 ft., with blue-green, red-edged rosettes 2-3 in. wide. White flowers.

A. holochrysum. Branching, with 15-18-in.-wide, densely-packed leaf rosettes of shiny green. Tall clusters of soft yellow flowers in May. Best in some afternoon shade.

A. simsii (*A. caespitosum*). Low, dense, spreading, very leafy. Bright green rosettes of leaves. Forms a cushion 6 in. tall. Yellow flowers. A hybrid of this and *A. spathulatum,* similar in appearance, is somewhat smaller, with variegated leaves and flowers of much deeper yellow. Widely sold.

AESCHYNANTHUS (*Trichosporum*). Trailing house plants and greenhouse plants. Related to African violets but you wouldn't guess it. Shining leaves usually in pairs along stems. Bright tubular flowers. Good in hanging pots. Need high temperatures, high humidity, and much light. Plant in loose, open, fibrous potting mix.

A. lobbianus. LIPSTICK PLANT. Tubular red flowers, 2 in. long, emerge from the calyces like lipsticks from their cases.

A. marmoratus. Grown for its green leaves mottled maroon rather than for its green flowers.

A. speciosus. Bright yellow and orange flowers up to 4 in. long.

AESCULUS. Deciduous trees or large shrubs. Leaves are divided fanwise into large toothed leaflets. Flowers in long, dense, showy clusters at the ends of branches. Fruit is a leathery capsule enclosing glossy seeds.

A. californica. CALIFORNIA BUCKEYE. Zones 4-7, 14-19. Native to dry slopes and canyons below 4,000 ft. elevation in Coast Ranges and Sierra Nevada foothills. Shrublike or small tree, often with several stems to 10-20 ft. or more high. New foliage pale apple green; mature leaves have 5-7 rich green, 3-6-in.-long leaflets. Striking sight in April or May when fragrant, creamy flower plumes make it a giant candelabrum. Large, pear-shaped fruits, with green covering splitting to reveal large, brown, shiny seeds, are favorites for fall flower arrangements.

In drought conditions it drops its leaves very early—by July, but if given plenty of water will hold them until fall. After leaf drop presents interesting silhouette—silvery trunk, branches, branchlets. Needs room; it's very wide-spreading.

A. carnea. RED HORSECHESTNUT. Zones 1-9, 14-17. Origin: Hybrid between *A. hippocastanum* and *A. pavia.* Has same limited adaptability as the common horsechestnut. Smaller growing to 40 ft. with 30-ft. spread. Round-headed with large dark green leaves divided fanwise into 5 leaflets; casts dense shade. In April-May the tree wears hundreds of 8-in.-long plumes of soft pink to red flowers. *A. c.* 'Briotii' has rosy crimson flowers. These smaller horsechestnuts are easy to handle in small gardens.

A. hippocastanum. COMMON HORSECHESTNUT. Zones 1-9, 14-17. Grows to 60 ft. with a 40-ft. spread; bulky, densely-foliaged tree giving heavy shade. Leaves divided fanwise into 5-7, toothed, 4-10-in.-long leaflets. Spectacular in spring with its ivory flowers with pink markings in 12-in.-long plumes.

AETHIONEMA. STONECRESS. Perennial. Zones 1-9. Native to Mediterranean region and Asia Minor. Choice little shrublets, attractive in or out of bloom, best adapted to colder climates, and a favorite among rock gardeners. Need full sun, grow best in a light porous soil with considerable lime. Bloom late spring to summer.

A. cordifolium. LEBANON STONECRESS. Rather thick unbranched stems 4-10 in. high, with blue-green, narrow, ⅓-⅔-in.-long leaves. Flowers pink or rosy lilac in dense clusters. Often confused with *A. pulchellum.*

A. grandiflorum. PERSIAN STONECRESS. The tallest one, erect stems 12-18 in. tall; leaves ⅝-1½ in. long. Flowers large, rose-colored, in spikelike clusters to 3 in. long and 1 in. wide.

A. iberideum. Cushion plant. Short slanting stems 6 in. high. White flowers in short clusters.

A. pulchellum. Trailing stems, branched at ends. Rosy pink flowers in dense clusters.

A. schistosum. Erect, unbranched stems 5-10 in. high, densely clothed with narrow, slate blue, ½ in.-long leaves. Flowers rose, petals about ¼ in. long, fragrant.

A. 'Warley Rose'. A hybrid, forms a neat, compact plant to 8 in. high. Pink flowers in dense clusters. Widely used; only aethionema planted to any extent in warmer climates.

AFRICAN BOXWOOD. See Myrsine

AGAPANTHUS. LILY-OF-THE-NILE. Evergreen or deciduous perennials with thick rootstocks and fleshy roots. Outdoor plants in Zones 7-9, 12-24; indoor-outdoor tub or pot plants where winters are cold.

Grow in sun except in warm inland sections where partial shade keeps leaves from burning, flowers from fading. Best in loamy soil but will grow in heavy soils. Thrives with ample water during growing season. Divide infrequently; every 5 or 6 years is usually sufficient. In cold-winter areas lift and store over winter, replant in spring. Superb container plant.

A. africanus. (Often sold as *A. umbellatus*). Evergreen. Leaves shorter, narrower than those of *A. orientalis;* flower stalks shorter (to 1½ ft. tall), fewer-flowered (20-50 to the cluster). Blue flowers midsummer to early fall.

Agapanthus has flowers in blue, purple, white. Dwarf 'Peter Pan' (right) foreground.

A. 'Dwarf White'. Evergreen. Foliage clump 1-1½ ft. tall; clusters of white flowers on stalks 1½-2 ft. tall.

A. inapertus. Deciduous. Deep blue tubular flowers droop from a 4-5 ft. stalk.

A. orientalis. (Often sold as *A. africanus, A. umbellatus*). Evergreen. Most commonly planted. Broad, arching leaves in big clumps. Stems to 4-5 ft. tall bear up to 100 blue flowers. There are white, double blue, and giant blue varieties.

A. 'Peter Pan'. Evergreen. Outstanding free-blooming dwarf variety. Foliage clumps are 8-12 in. tall; clustered blue flowers top 12-18-in. stems.

AGATHAEA coelestis. See Felicia

AGATHIS robusta. QUEENSLAND KAURI. Evergreen tree. Zones 15, 16, 20-23. Here's a dramatic strong skyline tree. Handsome in youth in containers. Moderate growth to an eventual 75 ft. in 80 years. Typically narrow and columnar. Open spaces between clumped branches present a striking layered effect. Leaves, light green to pinkish copper in new growth, then dark green, are broad, leathery, 2-4 in. long, and exceptionally glossy. The foliage mass shines in the sun, sparkles in the rain, and ripples brightly in the breeze. A moisture-loving tree—be generous with water and fertilizer.

AGAVE. Succulents, mostly gigantic, with large clumps of fleshy, strap-shaped leaves. The flower clusters are big, but not colorful. After flowering, which may take years, the foliage clump dies, usually leaving behind suckers which make new plants.

Climate Zone maps pages 8-27

A. americana. CENTURY PLANT. Zones 12-24. Leaves to 6 ft. long, with hooked spines along the edge and a wicked spine at the tip, blue-green in color. Be sure you really want one before planting it. The bulk and spines make it formidable to remove. After 10 years or more the plant makes a branched flower stalk 15-40 ft. high with yellowish green flowers. There are several varieties with yellow or white striped leaves.

A. attenuata. Zones 20-24. Leaves 2½ ft. long, soft green or gray-green, fleshy, somewhat translucent, no spines. Makes clumps to 5 ft. across; older plants develop a stout trunk to 5 ft. tall. Greenish yellow flowers dense on arching spikes, to 12-14 ft. long. Will take poor soil but is best in rich soil with ample water. Protect from frost and hot sun. Statuesque container plant.

A. victoriae-reginae. Zones 21-24. Clumps only a foot or so across. The many dark green leaves are 6 in. long, 2 in. wide, stiff, thick, with narrow white lines. Slow growing, it will stand in pot or ground 20 years before flowering (greenish flowers on tall stalks) and dying.

AGERATUM houstonianum. FLOSS FLOWER. Annual. Reliable favorite for summer and fall color in borders and containers. The lavender-blue-flowered varieties combine with flowers of almost any color or shape. Leaves roundish, usually heart-shaped at the base, soft green, and hairy. Tiny lavender-blue, white, or pink flowers in dense tassel-like clusters. Dwarf varieties make excellent edgings, or pattern plantings with other low-growing annuals.

Plant in sun except in hot summer climates where filtered shade is beneficial. Rich, moist soil best. In mild-winter areas, plant in late summer for fall color. Easy to transplant, even when in bloom. Effective combinations: Lavender-blue ageratum with salmon pink annual phlox, Madagascar periwinkle (Catharanthus) 'Little Pinkie', or dwarf yellow marigolds.

'Blue Mink' is superior to other lavender-blue varieties, forming more uniform plants 6-12 in. high and 12 in. across, with larger flower clusters. 'Midget Blue' is an older dwarf (4-6-in.-high) variety. Also available are dwarf varieties 'Blue Mist', 'Blue Bedder', and 'Fairy Pink', a lavender-pink that combines nicely with blue varieties. White varieties are not popular because the flowers tend to look dirty.

AGLAOMORPHA. See Polypodium coronans

AGLAONEMA. Perennials. Tropical plants valued mostly for their ornamental foliage, and usually grown in greenhouses or as house plants. Flowers resemble small, greenish white callas. Among the best plants for poorly lighted situations. Need a rich, porous potting mix; thrive with lots of water but will get along with small amounts. Will grow a long time in a glass of plain water. Exudation from leaf tips, especially of *A. modestum*, spots wood finishes, as on table tops.

A. commutatum. Grows to 2 ft. Leaves to 6 in. long, 2 in. across, deep green, marked on veins with pale green. Flowers followed by inch-long clusters of yellow to red berries.

A. modestum (*A. simplex*). CHINESE EVERGREEN. A serviceable, easily grown plant, in time forming substantial clumps with several stems 2-3 ft. high. Leaves shiny dark green, to 18 in. long, 5 in. across.

A. roebelinii. Robust plant with coarse leathery leaves 10 in. long, 5 in. wide, marked with pale green.

AGONIS. Evergreen tree. Zones 15-17, 20-24. Native to Australia.

A. flexuosa. PEPPERMINT TREE, AUSTRALIAN WILLOW MYRTLE. One of the best small trees for California gardens where temperatures stay above 27°. Will freeze to the ground at 25°; in the Sacramento Valley, it has come back from the stump. Spreading, medium fast-growing to 25-35 ft., or a big shrub. Narrow, willowlike leaves to 6 in. long, are conspicuously copper edged, and densely clothe the weeping branches. Leaves smell like peppermint when crushed. Small white flowers carried abundantly in June. Use it in a lawn, trained as an espalier, or as a tub plant. Very tolerant as to soil.

A. juniperina. JUNIPER MYRTLE. More open, finer-textured than *A. flexuosa*, but grows to about the same height. Narrow, ¼-½-in.-long leaves are soft green. Bears fluffy white flower clusters, summer to November. Same climate adaptability as *A. flexuosa*. Especially lovely with junipers and other needle-leafed plants.

AILANTHUS altissima (*A. glandulosa*). TREE-OF-HEAVEN. Deciduous tree. All Zones. Native to China. Planted a century ago in California's gold country where it now runs wild. Fast growth to 50 ft. One to 3-ft.-long leaves are divided into 13 to 25 3-5-in.-long leaflets. Inconspicuous greenish flowers are usually followed by handsome clusters of red-brown, winged fruits in late summer and fall; great for dried arrangements. Often condemned as a weed tree because it suckers profusely, but it must be praised for its ability to create beauty and shade under adverse conditions—drought, hot winds, and every type of difficult soil.

AIR PLANT. See Kalanchoe pinnata

AJUGA. CARPET BUGLE. Perennial. All Zones. One species is a rock garden plant; the others, better known, are ground covers.

A. genevensis. Rock garden plant 5-14 in. high, no runners. Grayish hairy stems and coarse-toothed leaves to 3-in. long. Flowers in blue spikes; there are rose and white forms. Full sun.

A. pyramidalis. Erect plants 2-10 in. high; do not spread by runners. Stems, with long grayish hairs, have many roundish 1½-4-in.-long leaves. Violet-blue flowers are not obvious among the large leaves. Variety 'Metallica-crispa' has reddish brown leaves with a metallic glint.

A. reptans. The popular ground cover ajuga. It always spreads by runners and makes a mat of dark green leaves that grow 2-3 in. wide in full sun, 3-4 in. wide in part shade. Bears mostly blue flowers in 4-6-in.-high spikes. Many varieties are available; some are sold under several names.

All the varieties of *A. reptans* (listed below) make thick carpets of lustrous leaves,

enhanced from spring to early summer with spikes of showy flowers. Plant in spring or early fall 6-12 in. apart, 18-in. for the big ones. Full sun to part shade; those with bronze or metallic tints keep color best in full sun. Feed in spring or late summer. Water every 7-10 days in summer. Mow or trim off old flower spikes. Subject to root-knot nematodes; also to rot and fungus diseases where drainage is poor.

The first four varieties are known as the giant and jungle ajugas. The green forms are often sold under the variety name 'Crispa'. The purplish or bronze-leafed varieties are often sold under the name of 'Metallica-crispa' (they are not the same as *A. pyramidalis* 'Metallica-crispa'). All have blue flowers.

'Giant Bronze'. Deep metallic bronze leaves larger, more vigorous, and crisper than those of *A. reptans*. To 6 in. in sun, 9 in. in shade.

'Giant Green.' Like 'Giant Bronze' except leaves are bright green.

'Jungle Bronze'. Large, rounded, wavy-edged leaves of bronzy tone, in clumps; tall growing; flowers on 8-10-in.-high spikes.

'Jungle Green'. Largest-leafed ajuga—rounded, crisp-edged, and green. Less mounding than 'Jungle Bronze'.

'Purpurea'. (Often sold as 'Atropurpurea'.) Similar to *A. reptans* but with bronze or purple tint in leaves. Leaves often slightly larger.

'Variegata'. Leaves edged and splotched with creamy yellow. Flowers blue.

AKEBIA quinata. FIVELEAF AKEBIA. Deciduous vine, evergreen in mild winters. All Zones. Native to Japan, China, and Korea. Twines to 15-20 ft. Grows fast in mild regions, slower where winters are cold. Dainty leaves on 3-5-in. stalks, each divided into 5 deep green leaflets 2-3 in. long, notched at tip. Its clusters of quaint dull purple flowers in spring are more a surprise than a show. The edible fruit, if produced, looks like a thick, 2½-4-in.-long, purplish sausage. Plant in sun or shade.

You can see why it's called fiveleaf akebia. And, the flowers are dull purple.

Give it support to climb on and keep it under control. Benefits from annual pruning. Recovers quickly when cut to the ground. When grown on post or column, and you want a tracery effect, prune out all but 2 or 3 basal stems.

ALBIZIA (formerly *Albizzia*). Deciduous to semi-evergreen trees. Two species grow in Western gardens.

Climate
Zone maps
pages 8-27

A. distachya (*A. lophantha*). PLUME ALBIZIA. Semi-evergreen. Zones 15-17, 22-24. Native to Australia. Not as hardy as the better-known *A. julibrissin*. In California coastal areas it often naturalizes. Will grow in pure sand at beach. Many mass plantings in Golden Gate Park, San Francisco. Fast growing to 20 ft. Foliage is dark velvety green compared to the light yellowish green of *A. julibrissin*, but also fernlike. The flowers in late spring are greenish yellow in fluffy, 2-in.-long spikes. Best as a temporary screening at beach while slower permanent planting develops. Gets tacky looking inland.

Flowers of silk tree are bonus on one of best spreading shade trees for patio.

A. julibrissin. SILK TREE (this is the mimosa of eastern U.S.). Deciduous. Zones 2-23. Native to Asia from Iran to Japan. Rapid growth to 40 ft. with wider spread. Can be headed back to make a 10-20-ft. umbrella. Pink fluffy flowers, like pincushions on ferny-leafed branches in summer. Light-sensitive leaves fold at night. The variety 'Rosea' has richer pink flowers and is considered hardier.

Does best with high summer heat. One of the three best sellers in inland valleys of southern California. Attractive in both high and low deserts of the Southwest. It's sufficiently hardy in the mild areas of the Pacific Northwest where it appreciates the extra heat from a wall.

It's an excellent small shade tree with unique flat-topped shape making a true canopy for a patio. Because of its undulating form and flowers held above the foliage, silk tree is especially beautiful when viewed from above—from a deck or hilltop. Somewhat of a problem to get started as a high-headed tree. Must be staked and trained by rubbing out any buds which start too low. Best planted from containers established at least one year.

It is most attractive in its natural growth habit—a multiple stemmed tree. Filtered shade permits growth of lawn and shrubs beneath it. However, litter of fallen leaves, flowers, and pods must be considered.

ALDER. See Alnus

ALDER, AFRICAN RED. See Cunonia

ALLAMANDA cathartica. Evergreen viny shrub or shrubby vine. Zones 23, 24. From Brazil. For only sunny spots or plastic-

covered outdoor room in the warmest, most frost-free areas of southern California. Elsewhere, a greenhouse plant. Give it rich soil, ample feeding, and pinching to control growth and shape. Climbs to 10 ft., or spreads as a shrub, depending on pruning. Dense foliage of dark green, rather thick, roundish oval, 6-in.-long leaves. Flowers in loose, few-flowered clusters are golden yellow tubes flaring to 3 in. wide, with white mark in throat. June. Variety 'Hendersonii' has glossier leaves and larger flowers (to 5 in. wide).

ALLIUM. ORNAMENTAL ALLIUM. Bulb. About 500 species, all from the northern hemisphere, many from mountains of the West. Relatives of the edible onion, peerless as cut flowers (fresh or dried) and useful in borders; smaller kinds are effective in rock gardens. Most ornamental alliums are hardy, sun-loving, easy to grow. Thrive in deep, rich, sandy loam; need ample moisture when growing. Plant bulbs in fall. Lift and divide only after they become crowded.

Alliums bear small flowers in compact or loose roundish clusters at ends of leafless stems 6 in. to 5 ft. or more tall. Many are delightfully fragrant; those with onion odor must be bruised or cut to give it off. Flowers in shades of pink, rose, violet, red, blue, yellow, to white. Bloom from late spring through summer. Leaves grow from the ground.

A. ascalonicum. See Shallot

A. albopilosum (*A. christophii*). STAR OF PERSIA. Distinct, with very large clusters, to 1 ft. across, of lavender to deep lilac, starlike flowers with metallic sheen; June bloom. Stems 12-15 in. tall. Leaves to 18 in. long, white-hairy beneath. Dried flower cluster looks like an elegant ornament.

A. caeruleum (*A. azureum*). BLUE ALLIUM. Cornflower blue flowers in dense round clusters 2 in. across on 1 ft. stems. June bloom.

A. cepa. See Onion

A. christophii. See *A. albopilosum*

A. giganteum. GIANT ALLIUM. Spectacular ball-like clusters of bright lilac flowers on stems 5 ft. or more tall. Leaves 1½ ft. long, 2 in. wide. July bloom.

A. karataviense. TURKESTAN ALLIUM. Large, dense, round flower clusters vary from pinkish to beige to reddish lilac, bloom in May. Broad, flat, recurving leaves, 2-5 in. across.

A. moly. GOLDEN GARLIC. Bright, shining yellow flowers in open clusters on 1½-ft.-high stems; June bloom. Flat leaves 2 in. wide, almost as long as flower stems.

A. neapolitanum. Spreading clusters of large white flowers on 12-in. stems; bloom in May. Leaves 1 in. wide. Variety 'Grandiflorum' is larger and earlier. A form of 'Grandiflorum' listed as 'Cowanii' is considered superior. Grown commercially as cut flowers; pot plant in cold climates.

A. ostrowskianum. Large, loose clusters of rose-colored flowers in June on 8-12 in. stems; 2-3 narrow, gray-green, somewhat limp leaves. Variety 'Zwanenburg' has deep carmine red flowers; 6-in. stems. Rock gardens, cutting.

A. porrum. See Leek

A. sativum. See Garlic

A. schoenoprasum. See Chives

A. tuberosum. See Chives, Garlic

A. unifolium. California native with extremely handsome, satiny lavender-pink flowers on 1-2-ft. stems; June bloom.

ALLSPICE, CAROLINA. See Calycanthus floridus

ALMOND. Deciduous tree. Zones 8-10, 14-16, 19-21. Almonds as trees are nearly as hardy as peaches but as nut producers they

Harvest almonds when hulls split open. Tap branches with pole to bring them down.

are far more exacting in climate adaptation. Zones listed are for best nut production. Frost during their early blooming period cuts the crop, and if they escape that a late (April) frost will destroy small fruits that are forming. Nuts will not develop properly in areas with cool summers and high humidity. To experiment in areas where frost is a hazard, choose late-blooming varieties.

Tree grows to 20-30 ft. high, erect when young, spreading and dome-shaped in age. Leaves 3-5 in. long, pale green with gray tinge. Flowers 1-2 in. across, palest pink or white. Fruit looks like a leathery, flattened, dwarf green peach. The hull splits to reveal the pit which is the almond that you harvest.

Almonds do well on any type of soil except heavy, poorly drained soil, where it is subject to root rot. Need deep soil—at least 6 ft. Will exist on less water than most fruit trees. Water deeply but infrequently. They need spraying to control mites which cause premature yellowing and falling of leaves. Trees can be weakened or eventually killed by mites. Brown rot makes fruit rot and harden; it also attacks twigs, killing them back, and forming cankers on main trunk and branches.

Two varieties must be planted for pollination. (If you don't have room, plant 2 or 3 in one hole.) These are the varieties you may find in nurseries:

'Davey'. Important commercially as pollinator for 'Nonpareil.' Harder to train, requires more pruning than other almonds.

'Jordanola'. High quality nut, but is susceptible to a disease that makes buds fail to open.

'Kapareil'. New variety with small kernels. Good pollenizer for 'Nonpareil'.

'Mission' ('Texas'). Small, semi-hard-shelled nut. Regular heavy producer. Late blooming, it is the variety for cold-winter,

Climate Zone maps pages 8-27

late-frost areas. Use 'Nonpareil' as a pollenizer.

'Ne Plus Ultra'. Large nuts in attractive soft shell. A good pollenizer for 'Nonpareil'.

'Nonpareil'. Best all around variety. Easily shelled by hand. Widely adapted.

ALMOND, DWARF FLOWERING. See Prunus glandulosa

ALMOND, FLOWERING. See Prunus triloba

ALNUS. ALDER. Deciduous trees. Moisture-loving, of remarkably rapid growth. All give interesting display of tassel-like greenish yellow male flower catkins (in clusters) before leaves. Female flowers develop into small woody cones that decorate bare branches in winter; these delight flower arrangers. Roots are invasive—less troublesome if deep watering practices are followed.

A. cordata. ITALIAN ALDER. Zones 8, 9, 12-24. Native to Italy, Corsica. Young growth vertical; older trees to 40 ft., spreading to 25 ft. Heart-shaped, 4-in. leaves, glossy rich green above, paler beneath. Short deciduous period. More restrained than *A. rhombifolia*. Favored in Southwest, except high desert.

A. glutinosa. BLACK ALDER. All Zones. Native to Europe, North Africa, Asia. Not as fast as *A. rhombifolia*. Probably best as multiple stemmed tree. Grows to 70 ft. Roundish, 2-4-in., coarsely toothed leaves, dark lustrous green. Makes a dense mass from ground up. Good for screen.

A. oregona (*A. rubra*). RED ALDER. Zones 4-6, 15-17. Native to stream banks and marshy places. The most common alder of the lowlands in the Pacific Northwest. Ranges from Alaska south to Santa Cruz County, California; rarely found more than 10 miles from the coast in California. Grows to 90 ft. high but usually 45-50 ft. Attractive light gray, smooth bark. Dark green, 2-4-in. leaves, rusty hairy beneath, the coarsely toothed margins are rolled under. Can take a surprising amount of brackish water and is useful wherever underground water may be somewhat saline. Generally disliked in Northwest because it's a favorite of the tent caterpillar.

A. rhombifolia. WHITE ALDER. Zones 1-9, 14-21. Native along streams throughout most of California's foothills except along coast; mountains of Oregon, Washington, north to British Columbia, east to Idaho. Very fast growing to 50-90 ft., with a 40-ft. spread. Spreading or ascending branches often pendulous at tips. Coarsely toothed, 2½-4½-in. leaves dark green above, paler green beneath. In its native areas, it's susceptible to tent caterpillar.

ALOCASIA. Perennial. Outdoors in Zones 22-24; indoor-outdoor plants anywhere. Native to tropical Asia. Handsome, lush plants for tropical effects. Often referred to as elephant's ear. Flowers resemble those of calla (*Zantedeschia*). Plant in filtered sunlight in wind-protected places. Provide ample organic matter in soil, lots of water, light frequent feedings.

A. macrorrhiza. Evergreen at 29°; loses leaves at lower temperatures but comes back in spring if frosts not too severe.

Large arrow-shaped leaves to 2 ft. or longer on stalks to 5 ft. tall. Makes dome-shaped plant 4 ft. across. Tiny flowers on spike surrounded by a greenish white bract. Reddish fruits form on spike much like corn on the cob.

A. odora. Similar to above, but not quite so hardy. Flowers fragrant.

ALOE. Succulents of lily family. Zones 8, 9, 12-24. Form clumps of fleshy pointed leaves and branched or unbranched clusters of orange, yellow, or red flowers. Most are South African. Showy and easy, they rate among southern California's most valuable ornamentals. Some species in bloom every month of the year. Biggest show February-September. Range from 6-in. miniatures to trees. Leaves may be green or gray-green, and are often strikingly banded or streaked with contrasting colors. Aloes grow easily in well drained soil in reasonably frost-free areas. Where winters are cooler, grow in pots and shelter from frost.

A. arborescens. TREE ALOE. Older clumps may reach 18 ft. Branching stems carry big clumps of gray-green, spine-edged leaves. Flowers (December-February) in

For striking color in winter on a huge interesting plant, try 18-ft. tree aloe.

long, spiky clusters, bright vermilion to clear yellow. Stands drought, sun, salt spray. Tolerates shade. Foliage damaged at 29°, but plants have survived 17°.

A. aristata. Dwarf species for pots, edging, ground covers. Reaches 8-12 in. height and spread. Rosettes densely packed with 4-in.-long, ⅜-in.-wide leaves ending in whip-like threads. Flowers orange-red in 12-18 in.-tall clusters, winter.

A. brevifolia. Makes low clumps of blunt, thick, gray-green, spine-edged leaves 3 in. long. Clusters of red flowers, 20 in. tall, intermittent all year.

A. ciliaris. Climbing, sprawling with pencil-thick stems to 10 ft. long. Leaves small, thick, soft green. Long-stalked 3-6-in. flower clusters with 20-30 scarlet, green or yellow-tipped flowers, intermittent all year. Takes some shade. Little frost.

A. ferox. Tree type. Thick, 15-ft. trunk carries rosettes of very spiny, dull green, 2½-ft.-long leaves. Glowing scarlet flower clusters like large candelabra.

A. marlothii. When small, use in pots or dish gardens. Mature, a tree type with 2½-ft.-long, spiny leaves and red flowers in large candelabra.

A. nobilis. Rosettes to 12 in. across and about as tall. Dark green leaves edged with small hooked teeth. Clustered orange-red flowers appear on 2 ft. stalks in June, last for six weeks. Good container subject—takes limited root space.

A. saponaria. Short-stemmed, broad clumps. Broad, thick, 8-in.-long leaves variegated with white spots. Branched flower clusters 18-30 in. tall. Orange-red to shrimp pink flowers over long period.

Aloe saponaria is showy in large rock gardens. It's 1/8 the size of tree aloe.

A. striata. CORAL ALOE. Rosettes 2 ft. wide on short trunk. Leaves broad 20-in. long, spineless, gray-green, with a narrow pinkish red edge. Brilliant coral-pink to orange flowers in branched clusters February-May. Handsome, tailored plant. Keep it from the hottest sun in desert areas.

A. variegata. PARTRIDGE-BREAST OR TIGER ALOE. Foot-high triangular rosette of fleshy, triangular, dark green, 5-in.-long leaves

Partridge-breast aloe is an easy house plant in colder areas; needs good light.

strikingly banded and edged with white. Loose flower clusters of pink to dull red flowers, intermittent all year.

ALOYSIA triphylla (*Lippia citriodora*). LEMON VERBENA. Deciduous or partially evergreen herb-shrub. Zones 9, 10, 14-24. Borderline hardy as far north as Seattle if planted against warm wall. The herb that grew like a gangling shrub in grandmother's garden. Prized for its lemon-scented leaves. Used in potpourri, iced drinks; a leaf in bottom of jar when making apple jelly. Legginess is natural state of this plant ranging up to 6 ft. or more. Narrow leaves to

Climate
Zone maps
pages 8-27

3 in. long are arranged in whorls of 3 or 4 along the branches. Bears open clusters of very small lilac or whitish flowers in summer. By pinch-pruning you can shape to give an interesting tracery against a wall. Or let it grow out of lower growing plants to hide its legginess. Full sun.

Lemon verbena has flowers but plant is favored for scent of dull green leaves.

ALPINIA speciosa (*A. nutans*). SHELL FLOWER, PORCELAIN GINGER. Perennial with rhizomes. Evergreen in Zones 22-24, dies down in winter Zones 15-17. Root hardy to about 15°. Native to tropical Asia and Polynesia. Grandest of gingers, best all-year appearance. To 8-9 ft. tall, distinguished from all other California-grown gingers by leaf sheaths; entire stem maroon at maturity. Leaves shiny, 2 ft. long, 5 in. wide, with distinct parallel veins. Waxy white or pinkish, shell-like, fragrant flowers marked red, purple, brown, in pendant clusters on arching stems.

Give lightly shaded, wind-free exposure, good soil. In order to bloom, must be established at least 2 years, have lots of water. Each year, remove canes that have flowered.

ALSOPHILA cooperi (*A. australis*). AUSTRALIAN TREE FERN. Zones 15-24. The fastest growing of the fairly hardy tree ferns. Eventually 20 ft. tall, the broad, arching fronds finely cut, bright green, to 12 in. long. Chaffy scales on trunk. Hardy

Australian tree fern is good choice for a dominant position near an entryway.

to 30°, but reasonably safe in sheltered places along the coast and in warm coastal valleys. Established plants will take full sun in the coastal fog belt, part shade elsewhere.

ALSTONIA scholaris. See Rauwolfia

ALSTROEMERIA. Perennial. Zones 5-9, 14-24. South American natives. Leafy stems 2-5 ft. tall topped with broad loose clusters of azalealike flowers in beautiful colors—orange, yellow, shades of pink, rose, red, lilac, creamy white to white; many are streaked and speckled with darker colors. Masses of color in borders from May to midsummer. Long-lasting cut flowers.

Nurseries differ as to what names they sell them by but you're sure to get vibrant colors whether you buy them as the Chilean hybrids, Ligtu hybrids, or just plain alstroemeria. A few nurseries offer the 3-4-ft.-high Peruvian lily (*A. aurantiaca*) which has orange-yellow flowers spotted with brown, and its pure yellow form—variety 'Lutea'. Also somewhat available is lily of Lima. (*A. pelegrina*); grows to 2 ft., and has lilac flowers streaked with maroon. Its variety 'Alba' has pure white flowers. This species (and its variety) not hardy in colder climates.

Best in cool, moist, deep, sandy to medium loam. Plant roots in fall; if you buy alstroemeria in gallon cans, you can plant it out anytime in mild-winter climates. Set roots 6-8 in. deep, 12 in. apart; handle the brittle roots gently. Leave clumps undisturbed for many years because they reestablish slowly after transplanting. With the above noted exception, all are hardy in cold-winter climates if planted to the proper depth and kept mulched in winter. Give them ample water in spring and summer; taper off in late summer, fall. Partial shade in warm-summer areas; sun along coast.

ALTERNANTHERA bettzickiana. Perennial usually grown as an annual. Native to Brazil. Grows to 16 in. high, with spoon-shaped leaves ½-1½ in. long, colored in many shades ranging from creamy yellow to red. Similar in effect to coleus, which is more widely available. Plant in sun. In cold-winter climate, set outside only after weather is warm. Keep low and compact by shearing. Grow from cuttings, divisions.

ALTHAEA rosea. HOLLYHOCK. Biennial or short-lived perennial. All Zones. In days past, no garden was complete without hollyhocks. Although rarely seen now, they have their place against a fence or wall, or in back of wide borders. Stems up to 9 ft.; large, rough, roundish heart-shaped leaves with 5-7 lobes; single or double flowers 3 in. or more across, in long wandlike spikes. Many colors—pinks, rose, red, yellow, apricot, and white. Bloom in summer. Powder Puffs, is a more refined strain, 4 ft. high, with very full double flowers in a range of clear bright colors. Leaves subject to rust; destroy infected leaves as soon as disease appears. Bait to protect from snails, slugs.

ALTHAEA, SHRUBBY. See Hibiscus syriacus

ALUMINUM PLANT. See Pilea

ALUM-ROOT. See Heuchera

ALYSSUM. Perennials. All Zones. Mostly native to Mediterranean region. Mounding plants or shrublets that brighten spring borders and rock gardens with their cheerful bloom.

A. montanum. Stems up to 8 in. high; leaves gray, hairy (denser on underside); flowers yellow, in dense short clusters.

A. saxatile. BASKET-OF-GOLD, GOLDEN TUFT. Stems 8-12 in. high; leaves gray, 2-5 in. long. Dense clusters of tiny golden yellow flowers in spring and early summer. Variety 'Compactum', dwarf, dense growing; 'Luteum' (often sold as 'Citrinum') has pale yellow flowers. Shear lightly (not more than half) after blooming. Generally hardy. Plants may be killed in extremely severe winters. Self-sow readily.

A. spinosum. A dense, spiny, rock garden shrublet 4-6 in. high. Silvery leaves ½-2 in. long. Flowers white to pinkish, fragrant, in short clusters. Variety 'Roseum' has deep rose-colored blooms.

ALYSSUM, SWEET. See Lobularia

AMARACUS dictamnus. CRETE DITTANY. Perennial. Zones 8-24. Native to Mediterranean area. Aromatic herb with slender, arching stems to 1 ft. long. Thick roundish leaves to ¾ in. long, white-woolly and somewhat mottled. Flowers pink to purplish, ½ in. long; rose-purple fruits in hoplike heads. Blooms summer to fall. Shows up best when planted individually—as in a rock garden—or in a container; good in hanging basket. Thrives in full sun, ordinary soil.

AMARANTHUS. AMARANTH. Annual. Coarse, sometimes weedy plants, a few ornamental kinds grown for their brightly colored foliage or flowers.

A. caudatus. LOVE-LIES-BLEEDING, TASSEL FLOWER. Sturdy, branching plant 3-8 ft. high; leaves 2-10 in. long, ½-4 in. wide; flowers red, in drooping, tassel-like clusters. A curiosity, rather than a pretty plant.

A. hybridus hypochondriacus. PRINCE'S FEATHER. To 5 ft. high with leaves 1-6 in. long, ½-3 in. wide, usually reddish. Flowers red or brownish red in many-branched clusters.

A. tricolor. JOSEPH'S COAT. Branching plant 1-4 ft. high. Leaves 2½-6 in. long, 2-4 in. wide, blotched in shades of red and green. Small round clusters of red flowers among leaves and at top of stems.

AMARCRINUM 'Howardii'. Bulb. Hybrid between *Crinum moorei* and belladonna lily (*Amaryllis belladonna*). Blooms outdoors in summer and fall in California; also a pot plant. Flowering stems to 4 ft. carry very large clusters of soft pink, funnel-shaped, very fragrant, long-lasting flowers resembling the belladonna lily.

AMARYLLIS belladonna (*Brunsvigia rosea*). BELLADONNA LILY, NAKED LADY. Bulb. Zones 4-24. Hardy in mild-winter areas; needs protected south exposure and warm, dry summer to bloom in western Oregon and Washington. Native to South Africa. Bold straplike leaves in clumps 2-3 ft. across in fall and winter; dormant late spring and early summer. In August, clusters of 4-12 trumpet-shaped, rosy pink, fragrant flowers bloom on top of bare, reddish brown stalks 2-3 ft. tall. Will grow

Climate
Zone maps
pages 8-27

in almost any soil; drought resistant. Plant right after bloom; set bulb top even with ground level. Lift and divide clumps infrequently; may not bloom for several years if disturbed at wrong time.

AMARYLLIS, GIANT or ROYAL DUTCH. See Hippeastrum

AMARYLLIS hallii. See Lycoris squamigera

AMELANCHIER. SHADBLOW, SHADBUSH, SERVICE BERRY (often pronounced "sarvis berry"). Deciduous shrubs or small trees. Valued in Zones 1-3. All-season performance: very showy clusters of white flowers precede the leaves in early spring; small edible fruits in summer, much loved by birds; colorful autumn foliage; and a most attractive winter branch and twig pattern. Good trees to garden under; roots not invasive, shade not heavy. Use against dark background to emphasize delicate values of flowers, foliage, and winter form.

A. alnifolia. WESTERN OR SASKATOON SERVICE BERRY. Native to mountains of California from near sea level to sub-alpine in Oregon and Washington, and east to Rocky Mountains. Shrublike growth to 12-15 ft. Clusters of pure white flowers in early spring. Small 1-2-in.-long leaves open a bronzy red, change to dark to pale green in summer, then to yellow and dusty red in autumn. Tiny, ¼-inch, bluish fruits in June-July.

A. canadensis. SHADBLOW SERVICE BERRY. Slender tree of slow growth to 30 ft. or more, but often shrubby. New foliage pinkish, leaves more rounded than *A. alnifolia*, flowers white, fruits dark red, autumn foliage yellow to red.

A. grandiflora. Hybrid between *A. canadensis* and *A. laevis*. Large flowers. There's a pink-flowered variety, 'Rubescens'.

A. laevis. SHADBUSH. Tree to 30-35 ft., sometimes a shrub. Young foliage purplish, white flowers in long, drooping clusters.

A. stolonifera. Upright, dense, twiggy shrub to 4 ft., spreading by underground roots to form thickets. Small purplish black fruits in late summer.

AMETHYST FLOWER. See Browallia

AMPELOPSIS brevipedunculata. BLUE-BERRY CLIMBER. Deciduous vine. All Zones. Strong rampant climber, with twining tendrils. To 20 ft. Large, handsome, 3-lobed, 2½-5-in.-wide leaves are dark green. In warm climates it turns red and partially drops its leaves; more leaves come out and redden and drop all winter. Many clusters of small grapelike berries turn from greenish ivory to brilliant metallic blue in late summer and fall. Sun or shade. Needs strong support. Superb on concrete and rock walls, or to shade arbors.

Boston ivy and Virginia creeper, formerly included in the genus *Ampelopsis* are now placed under the genus *Parthenocissus* because, unlike *Ampelopsis*, both have disks at the ends of their tendrils.

ANACYCLUS depressus. Perennial. All Zones. Forms a dense, spreading mat somewhat like chamomile. Leaves finely divided; single daisylike flowers to 2 in. across; white ray-petals red on reverse side; yellow

center discs. Blossoms in summer. Good in dry, hot rock gardens. Generally hardy, but may freeze in extremely severe winters.

ANAGALLIS. PIMPERNEL. Annual, biennial, or perennial. Although two species are ornamental, the best known is the annual spring weed called scarlet pimpernel (*A. arvensis*), also called poor man's weatherglass because the flowers close with approach of bad weather. Its ¼-in.-wide flowers are pale scarlet or salmon-colored; there's also a blue-flowered form (variety *caerulea*), pretty but also a weed.

Sow seeds of the cultivated kinds in a sunny location after weather warms in spring. Slow to germinate. Blue-flowered species effective in rock gardens and on banks with yellow, white, or pink sunroses (*Helianthemum*), low-growing sedums, or snow-in-summer (*Cerastium*). Can grow either kind in pots.

A. linifolia. (*A. grandiflora, A. grandiflora caerulea*). Perennial or biennial, often grown as an annual. Has square stems, somewhat woody at base, to 18 in. high. Narrow, 1-in.-long leaves, often with inrolled edges. Flowers saucer-shaped, blue, reddish tinged beneath, ¾ in. wide, on slim stalks 2-4 times the leaf length. There's a form (variety *monellii*) with broader leaves.

A. tenella. BOG PIMPERNEL. Annual. Grows to 6 in. high. Leaves roundish oval, ½ in. long. Flowers bell-shaped, ½ in. wide, red.

ANCHUSA. Annual, biennial, or perennial. Related to forget-me-not (*Myosotis*), but larger and showier, anchusas are worth growing for vibrant blue color.

A. azurea (*A. italica*). Perennial. All Zones. Coarse, loose-spreading 3-5 ft. tall. Leaves 6 in. or more long, covered with stiff bristly hairs. Clusters of bright blue blossoms ½-¾ in. across bloom in summer and fall. Horticultural forms include 'Dropmore', gentian blue; 'Opal', sky blue; and 'Loddon Royalist', more recent, bearing rich blue flowers. Plant in sun. Not for small areas. Once established, difficult to eradicate.

A. capensis. CAPE FORGET-ME-NOT, SUMMER FORGET-ME-NOT. Native of South Africa. Hairy biennial 1½ ft. high; leaves narrow, to 5 in. long, ½ in. wide. Flowers bright blue, white-throated, ¼ in. across, in clusters 2 in. long. Use for vivid clean blue in summer borders with marigolds, petunias.

Cape forget-me-not flowers contain a rich, pure blue—rare in bedding plants.

A. myosotidiflora. See Brunnera macrophylla

ANDROMEDA polifolia. BOG ROSEMARY. Evergreen shrublet. Hardy all zones. Not adapted in areas with alkaline soil or water. Grows to 12 in., spreading by creeping rootstocks. Leathery narrow leaves, somewhat like rosemary, 1½-in. long, gray-green above, gray beneath. Bears attractive clusters of pale pink, ¼-in. globe-shaped flowers at tip of branches in April. Sun or part shade. Choice rock garden plant in Zones 4-6 where it combines well with other acid-loving plants. Inconsistent in northern California. Varieties 'Nana' and 'Nana Compacta' are lower growing and more compact.

A. floribunda. A. japonica. See Pieris floribunda, P. japonica

A. speciosa. See Zenobia

ANDROSACE. ROCK-JASMINE. Perennial. Most used Zones 1-6, 17. Choice rock garden miniatures grown mostly by alpine plant specialists. All types require perfect drainage, best adapted to gravelly banks in rock gardens. Protect from more aggressive rockery plants such as alyssum, arabis, aubrieta. Rarely succeed in warm-winter areas.

A. lanuginosa. Trailing plant forms mats 3 ft. across. Silvery leaves to ¾ in. long, covered with silky white hairs. Pink flowers in dense clusters on 2-in. stems. Variety 'Leichtlinii' has white flowers with a crimson eye.

A. primuloides. Trailing, forms 4-in.-long runners. Leaves ½-2 in. long in rosettes covered with silvery hairs. Flowers pink, to ½ in. across, in clusters on 5-in. stems.

A. sarmentosa. Spreads by runners. Leaves to 1½ in. long, in rosettes, covered with silvery hairs when young. Flowers rose-colored, ¼ in. across, in clusters on stems 5 in. tall. Variety *chumbyi* forms dense clump, has woolly leaves.

ANEMONE. WINDFLOWER, ANEMONE. Perennials with tuberous or fibrous roots. A rich and varied group of plants ranging in size from alpine rock garden miniatures to tall Japanese anemones grown in borders; bloom extends from very early spring to fall, depending on species. The first three species described below (*A. blanda, A. coronaria, A. fulgens*) happen to be anemones that you can grow from tubers. Directions for planting all of them are given in the three paragraphs that follow the description of *A. fulgens*. The other two species at the end are treated as hardy perennials.

A. blanda. SAPPHIRE ANEMONE. The stems rise 2-8 in. high from tuberous roots. Finely divided leaves covered with soft hairs. One sky blue flower 1-1½ in. across on each stem. Often confused with *A. apennina*, which has more pointed leaf segments. For best display, plant in open situation, away from larger plants. Associate with miniature daffodils, tulips, scillas; or grow in pots.

A. coronaria. POPPY-FLOWERED ANEMONE. The common large-flowered, showy anemone valued for cutting and for spectacular color in spring borders. Finely divided green leaves. Flowers red, blue, and

Climate
Zone maps
pages 8-27

white, 1½-2½ in. across, borne singly on
6-18-in. stems. Tuberous rooted. Popular
strains include: De Caen, with single
flowers in mixed colors, also named varieties in separate colors; St. Brigid, with
double or semi-double flowers in mixed and
separate colors.

*Flower and tuber of poppy-flowered anemone.
Plant with old stem scar up.*

A. fulgens. SCARLET WINDFLOWER. To 1
ft. from tuberous roots. Leaves entire or
slightly divided. Flowers 2½ in. across, brilliant scarlet with black stamens. St. Bavo
strain comes in an unusual color range that
includes pink. Effective in rock garden
pockets, borders, containers, and for cut
flowers.

Plant *A. coronaria* and *A. fulgens* in full
sun, *A. blanda* in light shade. Set out tubers
October to November.

In cold-winter areas, wait until spring
to set out *A. coronaria* and *A. fulgens;* or
if planted in November, mulch with 6-8 in.
of leaf mold or peat moss after the first
hard frost. Rake off thick mulches after
hard frosts have passed.

Plant 1-2 in. deep, 8-12 in. apart, in rich,
light, well drained garden loam, or start in
flats of damp sand, set out in garden when
leaves are few inches tall. Protect from
birds until leaves toughen. In warmer climates, some soak tubers of poppy-flowered
anemones for few hours before planting. In
high-rainfall areas excess moisture induces
rot.

A. hupehensis japonica (*A. japonica*).
JAPANESE ANEMONE. All Zones. A long-
lived, fibrous-rooted perennial indispensable
for fall color in partial shade. Graceful
branching stems 2-4 ft. high rise from clump
of dark green, soft-hairy, 3-5-lobed leaves.
Flowers semi-double, white, silvery pink, or
rose. Many named varieties available. Slow
to establish, but once started spreads readily if roots not disturbed. Mulch in fall
where winters are extremely severe. Increase
by divisions in fall or early spring, or root
cuttings in spring. Effective in clumps in
front of tall shrubbery, along fences or
walls, or under high-branching trees.

A. pulsatilla. EUROPEAN PASQUE FLOWER.
Zones 1-6. Attractive alpine plant forming
clumps, 9-12 in. high. Fernlike silky-hairy
leaves, 4-6 in. long, appearing after flowers.
Blossoms bell-shaped, to 2½ in. across, blue
to reddish purple, with golden stamens, appearing in April and May. Handsome seed
clusters like feathery, smoky gray pompons.
This hardy plant best adapted to cool, moist
climates, rarely succeeds in warm dry areas.
Sun or partial shade. Sow seeds or make
divisions in spring. Choice and distinctive
in foreground of border or in rock garden.

ANEMONE, BUSH. See Carpenteria

ANEMOPAEGMA chamberlaynii (*Bignonia
chamberlaynii*). YELLOW TRUMPET VINE.
Evergreen vine. Zones 15-17, 19, 21-24.
Climbs by unbranched tendrils. Leaves
divided into two leaflets to 7 in. long.
Flowers yellow, trumpet-shaped, 3 in. long,
in clusters longer than the leaves. Summer-
blooming. Often confused with *Doxantha
unguis-cati*.

ANETHUM graveolens. DILL. Annual herb.
To 3-4 ft. Soft, feathery leaves; umbrellalike 6-in.-wide clusters of small yellow flowers. Seeds and leaves have pungent fragrance. Sow seed where plants are to be
grown, in full sun. Thin seedlings to 18 in.
apart. Sow seed several times during spring
and summer for constant supply. Use the
seeds in pickling and vinegar; fresh or dried
leaves in salads, on lamb chops, stews,
sauces.

ANGELICA archangelica. ANGELICA. Biennial. To 6 ft. Tropical looking plant with
divided and toothed, yellow-green leaves
2-3 ft. long. Greenish white flowers in large
umbrellalike clusters. Grow in moist, rich,
slightly acid soil in part shade. Cut flowers
before buds open to prolong plant's life.
Propagate from seed sown as soon as ripe
in fall. Use to flavor wines; hollow stems
may be candied.

ANGELICA TREE. See Aralia

**ANGEL'S HAIR. See Artemisia schmidti-
ana**

**ANGEL'S TEARS. See Narcissus triandrus,
Soleirolia**

ANGOPHORA lanceolata. GUM MYRTLE.
Evergreen tree. Zones 16, 17, 21-24. Native
to eastern Australia. Highly praised by
those who have used it and seen it. Mature
tree in Pasadena 40-50 ft. high and almost
as broad.

Beautiful smooth trunk in tones of
cream, rose, and mauve. Has thick, glossy,
3-5-in.-long, eucalyptuslike leaves with a
prominent midrib. New growth is shiny red
turning to rich green. White flowers are carried in clusters at branch ends in summer
followed by fruits with spiny prickles. Appears to adapt to a variety of soils and
watering treatments. Probably as tough and
tolerant as its eucalyptus relatives. A skyline tree and a tree to live with where it
has room.

ANIGOZANTHUS. KANGAROO PAW. Evergreen perennial. Zones 15-24. Hardy to
about 25°. Native to open eucalyptus forests
in Western Australia. From thick rootstocks
grow clumps of dark green, smooth, swordlike leaves to 3 ft. or taller. Striking tubular
flowers curved at tips like kangaroo paws
(tips split into 6 segments) in red, purple,
green, or yellow in woolly one-sided spikes
on 3-6-ft. stems. Intriguing in flower, otherwise not outstanding. Bloom from late
spring to fall if spent flowering spikes cut
to ground. Light, sandy soil, or heavier
soil with good drainage; sunny exposure.

A. flavida. Branching stems to 5 ft.
Tubular, curved, hairy flowers 1-1½ in.
long, yellow-green tinged with red.

A. manglesii. Unbranched green stems
to 3 ft., thickly covered with red hairs.

Flowers deep green, red at base, woolly on
outside, 3 in. long.

ANISACANTHUS thurberi. DESERT HONEY-
SUCKLE. Evergreen or deciduous shrub.
Zones 8-13, 18, 19. Native to Arizona, New
Mexico, Texas, northern Mexico. In mild-
winter areas grows to 3-5 ft. with stout
branches. Looks best when treated as a perennial, cut to the ground in winter either by
frost, or by pruning shears. Valued for its
long season of color—spring and summer.
Tubular, 1½-in.-long yellow-orange flowers
in spikes; light green 1½-2-in.-long leaves.

ANISE. See Pimpinella

ANNONA cherimola. CHERIMOYA. Briefly
deciduous large shrub or small tree. Zones
21-24. Hardy to about 25°. Grows fast first
3-4 years, then slows to make a 15-ft. tree
with a 15-20-ft. spread. After tree has developed for 4 or 5 years, prune annually
to produce bearing wood. Leaves dull green
above, velvety-hairy beneath, 4-10 in. long,
drop in late spring. Thick, fleshy, 1-in.,
brownish or yellow-hairy flowers begin
opening about the time of leaf fall and
continue forming for 3-4 months, give a
fruity fragrance, pleasant near terrace.

Large green fruits weigh ½-1½ lbs. Skin
of most varieties looks like short overlapping leaves; some show knobby warts. Pick
when fruit turns to yellowish green, then
store in refrigerator until skin turns brownish green to brown. Creamy white flesh contains large black seeds. Flesh is almost
custardlike; you eat it with a spoon. Flavor
is bland, with a suggestion of bananas, pineapples, or nectarines. Serve chilled.

ANREDERA cordifolia (*Boussingaultia bas-
elloides, B. gracilis pseudo-baselloides*).
MADEIRA VINE. Perennial vine. Zones 4-24.
In Zones 4-12, treat as you would dahlias:
Dig in fall and store tubers over winter.
Heart shaped green leaves 1-3 in. long.
Fragrant white flowers in foot-long spikes
late summer, fall. Climbs with tendrils, may
reach 20 ft. in one season. Sun. Small tubers
form where leaves join stems.

**ANTHEMIS aizoon. See Achillea agerati-
folia aizoon**

ANTHEMIS. Evergreen perennials. All Zones.
Aromatic foliage, especially when it's
bruised. Leaves divided into many segments. Flowers daisylike or buttonlike.

A. nobilis. CHAMOMILE. Forms a soft-
textured, spreading, 3-12-in. mat of light
bright green, finely cut, aromatic leaves.
Most commonly grown form has summer-
blooming flower heads resembling small
yellow buttons; some forms have little
daisylike flower heads. Makes a lawn substitute if mowed or sheared occasionally.
Also used between stepping stones. Plant
divisions 12 in. apart in full sun or very
light shade. Water moderately. Chamomile
tea is made from the dried flower heads.

A. tinctoria. GOLDEN MARGUERITE. Erect,
shrubby. Grows to 2-3 ft. Angular stems.
Light green leaves with broader divisions
than *A. nobilis*. Golden yellow, daisylike
flowers to 2 in. across bloom in summer
and fall. Plant in full sun. Grow from
seed, stem cuttings, or divisions in fall or
spring. Summer border plant. Variety
'Moonlight' has pale yellow flowers; 'Gral-
lagh Gold', deep golden yellow flowers.

Climate Zone maps pages 8-27

ANTHRISCUS cerefolium. CHERVIL. Annual culinary herb. Grows 1-2 ft. Finely cut, fernlike leaves resembling parsley; white flowers. Use fresh or dried same as parsley. Flavor milder than parsley. Grow from seed in raised bed near kitchen door, in box near barbecue, or in vegetable garden. Part shade best, ordinary garden soil, moisture. Goes to seed quickly in hot weather. Keep flower clusters cut to encourage vegetative growth.

ANTHURIUM. Perennial greenhouse or house plant. Native to tropical American jungles. Exotic anthuriums with lustrous flower bracts in vivid red, luscious pinks, or white, and handsome dark green leaves are no more difficult to grow as house plants than are some orchids.

The higher the humidity, the better. Anthurium leaves lose shiny texture and may die if humidity drops below 50 per cent for more than a few days. Keep pots on trays of moist gravel, in bathroom, or under polyethylene cover. Sponge or spray leaves several times daily. For good bloom plant by window with good light but no direct sun. Generally grow best in 80°-90° temperatures, but will get along in normal house temperature (low 70's). Growth stops below 65°, damaged below 50°. Protect from drafts. Pot anthuriums in a coarse porous mix of leaf mold, sandy soil, and shredded osmunda. Give a mild feeding every 4 weeks.

A. andraeanum. Dark green oblong leaves to 1 ft. long and 6 in. wide, heart-shaped at base. Flower bracts spreading, heart-shaped to 6 in. long, surrounding yellow, callalike flower spike. Flower bracts in shades of red, rose, pink, and white shine as though lacquered. Bloom more or less continuously—plant may have 4 to 6 flowers during the year. Flowers last 6 weeks on plant—4 weeks after cut.

A. scherzerianum. Slow-growing, compact plant to 2 ft. Dark green leaves 8 in. long, 2 in. wide. Flower bracts broad, 3 in. long, deep red varying to rose, salmon, white. Yellow flower spikes spirally coiled.

ANTIGONON leptopus. ROSA DE MONTANA, QUEEN'S WREATH, CORAL VINE (must have been loved by many to earn so many nice common names). Deciduous vine, evergreen in warmest winter areas. Zones 12, 13, 18-21. Native to Mexico. Revels in high summer heat. Fast growing, climbing by tendrils to 40 ft. Foliage, of dark green, 3-5-in.-long, heart-shaped or arrow-shaped leaves, is open and airy. Small rose pink flowers to 1½ in. long are carried in long trailing sprays from midsummer to fall. In cold winters leaves fall and most of top dies. Recovers quickly. Treat as a perennial. Where winter temperatures drop below 25° protect roots with a mulch.

A wonderful vine in the low deserts of California and Arizona. Elsewhere give it hottest spot in the garden. Let it shade patio or terrace; drape its foliage and blossom sprays along eaves, fence, or garden wall.

ANTIRRHINUM majus. SNAPDRAGON. Perennial usually treated as an annual. Among the best flowers for borders and cutting, reaching greatest perfection in spring and early summer. Individual flowers that make the "dragon's jaws" are really tubes flaring into 5 unequal lobes. These flowers in white

and many bright and pastel colors grow in upright spikes, the length of which varies in different types. Dark green 3-in. leaves densely clothe the base of the plant.

There are tall snaps 2½-4 ft. high (Rocket, Sentinel, Super Tetra, Supreme, and other strains), intermediates 15-18 in., and dwarf forms 6-9 in. The Bellflower strain, with round open flowers that scarcely resemble snapdragons, grows 18 inches high.

Sow seed in flats from late summer to early spring for later transplanting, or buy flat-grown plants at nursery. Set out plants

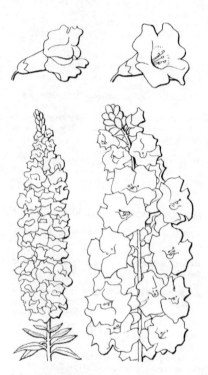

Common snapdragons at left show jaws; Bellflower strain has open flowers.

in early fall in mild-winter areas, spring in colder sections. If snapdragons set out in early fall reach bud stage before night temperatures drop below 50°, they will start blooming in winter and continue until the weather gets hot. Rust is most serious handicap; plants in vigorous growth, watered and fed regularly, most likely to resist attacks. Avoid overhead watering, which helps spread rust spores.

Valuable cut flowers. Tall and intermediate forms splendid vertical accents in borders with delphinium, iris, daylily, peach-leafed bluebell, Oriental poppy. Dwarf kinds effective as edgings, in rock gardens, raised beds, or pots.

APHELANDRA squarrosa. Evergreen house plant. Native to Mexico, South America. Popular for two good reasons: Large, 8-12-in.-long, dark green leaves strikingly veined with white. The yellow flowers, tipped with green, and waxy, golden yellow flower bracts make colorful upright spikes at tips of the stems. Variety 'Louisae' is best known, but

newer varieties are more compact and show more white venation. To make plants bushy, cut stems back to one or two pairs of leaves after flowering. Give plant routine house-plant culture. Place it where it gets morning (or filtered) sun. Occasionally used outdoors in protected spots in southern California gardens.

APPLE. Deciduous fruit tree. Most widely adapted deciduous fruit. It is grown in every Western climate except the low deserts of California and Arizona. The mild winters of the low desert and the marine and coastal climates of southern California do not provide enough winter cold for most standard varieties. Since nursery customers often insist on the most popular varieties they see on the fruit stand, varieties are sold in areas unfavorable to best performance. Often, in southern California, Phoenix, Tucson, nurseries offer varieties for customers who live in nearby higher elevations. For this reason, the apple chart indicates where some varieties perform best, as well as where they are sold.

Varieties that need a pollenizer to set fruit are noted on the chart. All others are self-fruitful or partially self-fruitful. If a pollenizing variety grows in your neighborhood, you need not plant one yourself.

If you have a tree that is not bearing, graft a branch of another variety onto it; or place fresh flower bouquets from another variety (in a can of water) in or at the base of the tree. Don't use 'Gravenstein' or 'Winesap' to pollinate other self-unfruitful varieties. The apple needs sun. Don't crowd it into partially shaded places. The wish for more than one variety in limited space can be solved by buying multiple variety trees or dwarf trees.

Dwarf apple trees—standard varieties grown on dwarfing rootstock — can be used in almost any kind and size of garden. Grow them as a hedge, supported by posts and wire. Train them as a formal espalier or informally against fence or wall. The true dwarf tree will not exceed 5-6 ft. in height and spread. The semi-dwarf will grow to 10-15 ft. with a more treelike structure. Other advantages: fruit production starts in first or second year; pest control is mostly at waist height. Disadvantages: root systems are shallow; trees should be given support; young trees must be consistently pruned to get a compact form. Since it grows in the top few feet of soil, it must be watered and fertilized oftener than standard trees.

In selecting varieties remember that all good apples are not red. Skin color is not an indicator of quality or taste. Red varieties are widely sold only because red apples have sales appeal. Make sure that eye appeal alone or a slight preference of taste or name doesn't dictate your selection of a difficult-to-grow variety. For example: if to your taste 'Golden Delicious' and 'Red Delicious' are nearly equal, consider the differences in growing them. 'Yellow Delicious' produces fruit without a pollenizer. It comes into bearing earlier. It keeps well, while the 'Red Delicious' becomes mealy if not stored at 50° or lower. And, it can be used for cooking while 'Red Delicious' is strictly an eating apple.

The apple tree will need much care if you want perfect fruit. However, as an ornamental tree it has more character, better

APPLE

VARIETY	CLIMATE ADAPTATION	RIPENING DATE	FRUIT	REMARKS
'Arkansas Black'	Zones 1-3, 10-11	Late	Medium size. Dark, dark red. Hard-crisp.	Winter apple. Ripens in December.
'Astrachan' ('Red Astrachan')	Zones 7-9, 14-22	Early July	Medium size, irregular in shape. Red-striped or yellow. Juicy and tart. Good eating, excellent cooking.	Early ripening makes a good variety in California's interior valleys. There's more red in 'Red Astrachan'.
'Bellflower'	Best in 14-16, 18-22	September	Medium to large. Greenish to yellow. Semi-firm, fine texture. Good quality.	Big, spreading tree, makes good shade tree.
'Beverly Hills'	Zones 18-24. One of the best for southern California.	Early	Small to medium, yellow, splashed and striped red. Tender, somewhat tart. Excellent quality. Somewhat resembles a 'McIntosh'.	Definitely for cool areas. Will not develop good quality in hot interiors.
'Buckley Giant'	Zones 4-6	Midseason	Medium to large, yellow with red striping. Moderately firm, fleshy, fine texture. Not juicy.	Like a 'Gravenstein' but lacking the flavor. Not susceptible to many diseases. Bears well.
'Cortland'	Zones 1-6	Fall	Medium size, pale red, fine texture, mild flavor.	Related to 'McIntosh'. Fruit can be too soft when ripe.
'Delicious' ('Red Delicious')	Sold everywhere apple trees are bought. Best in Zones 2-7.	Midseason to late.	The glamorous variety everyone knows. See text. The only difference between 'Delicious' and 'Red Delicious' is skin color.	'Starking' and 'Richared' are redder sports of the original. *Needs a pollenizer.*
'Golden Delicious'	Most widely adapted variety. Try it anywhere except Zones 12, 13.	Midseason to late.	Clear yellow similar in shape to 'Delicious' with less prominent knobs. Highly aromatic, crisp. Excellent eating and cooking.	Not a yellow-colored 'Red Delicious'. Different in taste and growth habit.
'Gravenstein'	Widely sold, Zones 4-11, 14-24. Best in 15-17.	Early to midseason	Brilliantly red-striped over deep yellow. Crisp, aromatic, juicy. Excellent eating; applesauce with character.	Justly famous variety of California's north coast apple district. *Needs a pollenizer.*
'Holland'	Sold in Southern California. Zones not tested.	Early	Very large. Dark-strawberry-red skin. Firm, smooth, juicy.	Bears fruit at early age. Recent introduction.
'Jonathan'	Sold everywhere. Best, Zones 2-7.	Midseason. Early fall.	Medium to large. Round-oblong. High-colored red. Juicy, moderately tart, sprightly, crackling crisp.	An all-purpose apple. 'Jonared' and 'Blackjon' are deeper and more uniformly red.
'King'	Zones 4, 5	Midseason to late.	Large, waxy yellow with red striping. Crisp and sweet. Excellent eating and baking.	Large sturdy tree to 30-35 ft. *Needs a pollenizer.*
'Lodi'	Zones 1-6	Early	Large, yellow. Crisp and tart.	Resembles 'Transparent'.
'McIntosh' ('Red McIntosh')	Zones 4, 6, 11-12.	Late midseason.	Medium to large. Bright red. Nearly round. Snow-white, tender flesh. Tart, excellent.	Excellent apple for garden if good care given. 'Early McIntosh', cross between 'Yellow Transparent' and 'McIntosh,' resembles 'McIntosh'.
'Milton'	Zones 4-6	Midseason	Large, pinkish red. Crisp. Good sprightly flavor.	Related to 'McIntosh'.
'Newtown Pippin' ('Yellow Pippin')	Zones 1-11, 13-22.	Late	Large, green. Crisp and tart. Fair for eating, excellent cooking.	Large, vigorous tree.
'Northern Spy' ('Red Spy')	Zones 1-3, 6. Best in cold winter areas.	Late	Large, red. Tender, fine-grained flesh. Apple epicure's delight for sprightly flavor.	Slow to reach bearing age. *Needs a pollenizer.*

(Continued on next page)

A

Climate Zone maps pages 8-27

VARIETY	CLIMATE ADAPTATION	RIPENING DATE	FRUIT	REMARKS
'Pacific Pride'	Zones 4-6	Midseason. Earlier than 'King'.	Large. Striped red over yellow. Juicy, firm, crisp and tart. A high quality apple for eating and cooking.	Vigorous and productive. Resembles 'King' and 'Gravenstein'.
'Red June'	Zones 5-7. High elevations in California	Early	Medium sized, red. Tender flesh, tart, sprightly. For fresh use.	Attractive summer apple.
'Red Melba'	Zones 1-6	Early August	Medium size, greenish white with red blush. Medium fine texture. Mild flavor.	Bears well. Very hardy. Rather disease-free.
'Rome Beauty' ('Red Rome')	Sold everywhere. Best, cold-winter areas—Zones 3-7, 10, 11	Late midseason	Large, smooth and round. Greenish white flesh. Mediocre fresh. Outstanding baking apple.	Early bearer. 'Red Rome' is the red-skinned sport most frequently sold.
'Spitzenberg'	Zones 1-3, 6. High elevations of California	Late	Medium to large red, dotted yellow. Crisp, fine-grained, tangy and spicy.	An old favorite. Best in winter-cold areas.
'Stayman Winesap' (and 'Winesap')	Sold widely, best in Zones 1-7, 10, 11	Latest	Medium to large. Round. Lively flavor. Fine-grained, firm, juicy. 'Stayman Winesap' is large, red with green and russet dots. 'Winesap' is smaller, all red.	An old, old timer that remains a top favorite. Most 'Winesap' trees sold at nurseries are really 'Stayman Winesap'.
'Transparent' ('Yellow Transparent')	Sold and good in Zones 1-9, 14, 15, 19, 20	Early	Medium to large greenish or whitish yellow, lightly blushed one side. Tender and tart; good quality for cooking.	Ripens mid-June to mid-July in Sacramento Valley.
'White Pearmain' ('White Winter Pearmain')	Sold and best Zones 20-24.	Midseason	Medium to large. Pale greenish-yellow skin with pink blush. Excellent flavor, tender flesh, fine-grained. All purpose.	Will perform better than standard cold-winter varieties in Southern California. *Needs a pollenizer.*
'Winesap'. See 'Stayman Winesap'				
'Winter Banana'	Zones 4-9, 14-24.	Midseason	Large, of fragile beauty. Pale, blushed pink, waxy finish. Tender, tangy, with distinctive aroma.	One of few standard varieties that will accept mild winters. *Needs a pollenizer.*

form, and longer life than most deciduous fruit trees. It does best in deep soil but gets by in many imperfect situations, including heavy soils with poor drainage. To prevent wormy apples and other damage from insects and disease it is generally necessary to follow a spray program. Your county agent or farm advisor has pamphlet instructions for timing in your area.

Apples produce fruit from short fruit spurs which may remain productive for up to 20 years. Pruning consists of removal of weak, dead, and poorly placed branches, twigs; this will encourage development of strong new growth.

APRICOT. Deciduous fruit tree. Apricots can be grown throughout the West, with these limitations: because they bloom early in the season they will not fruit in regions with late frosts; in cool, humid coastal areas, tree and fruit are unusually subject to brown rot and blight; in mild-winter areas of southern California, choose varieties with low chilling requirements. Apricots are good choice as a dual-purpose fruit and shade tree. Easy to maintain. If you have moved into a house with an apricot in the lawn

area, water deeply once a month in summer in addition to regular lawn watering. Your county agent or farm advisor can give you a local timetable and directions for spraying apricots. Essential dates: during dormant season; and before and after flowering. To get big apricots do this: in mid-spring, thin excess fruits off branches to leave 2-4 in. between individual apricots.

Apricots bear most fruit on short fruit spurs which form on last year's growth and remain fruitful for about 4 years. Pruning should be directed toward conserving enough new growth (which will produce spurs) to replace old, exhausted spurs which should be cut out.

Here's a list of the varieties sold at nurseries. Some varieties need a pollenizer.

'Blenril'. Zones 2, 3, 5, 6. Equal to 'Royal' in fruit quality. Needs pollenizing (any variety except seldom-sold 'Riland').

'Chinese' ('Mormon'). Zones 1-3, 5, 6. Good production in late-frost areas.

'Earliril'. Zones 2, 3, 5, 6. Similar to 'Blenril' and with same pollenizing requirement.

'Moorpark'. Zones 2, 3, 5-11, 14-16. Very large, excellent flavor. Ripens unevenly. Not a good canner.

'Newcastle'. Zones 10, 11, 20-23. Developed for mild-winter areas of southern California. Little winter chilling needed.

'Nugget'. Zones 18-23. Another with low winter chilling requirement. Ripens early to escape early summer heat.

'Perfection' ('Goldbeck'). Zones 2, 3, 5-9, 12-16, 19-23. Low chilling requirement. Unusually large fruit. Needs pollenizer (any variety except 'Reeves').

'Redsweet'. Zones 12-16, 18-23. Very early. Fruit ripens before extreme heat. Needs a pollenizer (another early-blooming variety — 'Nugget' or 'Perfection').

'Reeves'. Zones 12, 13, 18-24. Medium sized, yellow-orange, flavorful fruit. Ripens early. Needs pollenizer.

'Royal' and 'Blenheim'. Zones 2, 3, 5-16, 18-23. Regardless of how labeled in nursery these are either two identical varieties or one variety under two names. Standard variety in California's commercial apricot regions.

'Tilton'. Zones 1-3, 5-8, 10, 11, 18, 20. Higher chilling requirements than 'Royal' but less subject to brown rot and sunburn.

'Wenatchee Moorpark' ('Wenatchee'). Zones 2 3, 5-6. Large fruit; excellent flavor.

APRICOT, JAPANESE FLOWERING. See Prunus mume

AQUILEGIA. COLUMBINE. Perennials. All Zones. Columbines have a fairylike, woodland quality with their lacy foliage and beautifully posed flowers in exquisite pastels, deeper shades, or white. Erect, branching, from 2 in. to 4 ft. high. Fresh green divided leaves reminiscent of maidenhair fern. Bloom in spring and early summer. Flowers to 3 in. across; erect or nodding, often with sepals and petals in contrasting colors; usually have backward-projecting, nectar-bearing spurs. Some kinds have large flowers and very long spurs. The long-spurred hybrids easily grown from seed include Dobbie's Imperial Giants, McKana's Giants, Mrs. Scott Elliott hybrids. Named varieties in separate colors are available.

All columbines are hardy and tolerant of filtered shade but will take full sunlight, especially along coast. Cut back old stems for second crop of flowers; leave some seed if you want plants to self-sow. All kinds of columbines attract hummingbirds. Subject to leaf miners, aphids, and red spider mites but usually require only routine care. Replace old plants about every 3 years.

A. alpina. ALPINE COLUMBINE. Native of the Alps. Plant to 12 in. high. Flowers blue, to 2 in. across, with straight or curved spurs 1 in. long.

A. caerulea. ROCKY MOUNTAIN COLUMBINE. Plants 1½-3 ft. Flowers erect, 2 in. or more across, blue and white. Spurs straight or spreading, to 2 in. long. This species hybridized with A. chrysantha and others to produce the many long-spurred hybrids.

A. chrysantha. GOLDEN or GOLDEN-SPURRED COLUMBINE. Native to Rocky Mt. region and Texas. Large, much branched plant to 3-4 ft. One of the showiest species. Leaflets densely covered with soft hairs beneath. Flowers erect, 1½-3 in. across, clear yellow; spurs slender, 2-2½ in. long.

A. formosa. WESTERN COLUMBINE. Native Utah and California to Alaska. Plant 1½-3 ft. high. Flowers nodding, 1½-2 in.

Western columbine's red and yellow flowers bloom in summer. Gray-green leaves.

across, red and yellow; spurs stout and straight, red. Good in woodland garden; allow to set seeds which are relished by song sparrows, juncos, and other small birds.

A. longissima. Native to southwest Texas and northern Mexico. Plant 2½-3 ft. tall. Similar to A. chrysantha. Flowers numerous, erect, pale yellow, spurs very narrow, drooping, 4-6 in. long.

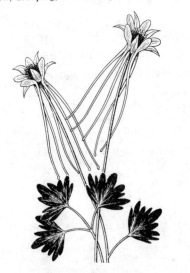

Flowers of Aquilegia longissima—very long spurs, pale yellow, July-October.

A. vulgaris. EUROPEAN COLUMBINE. Naturalized in eastern U.S. Plant to 1-2½ ft. Flowers nodding, 2 in. or less across, blue, purple, or white; short, knobby spurs about ¾ in. long.

ARABIS. ROCKCRESS. Perennial. Low growing, spreading plants for edgings, rock gardens, ground covers, pattern plantings. All kinds have attractive year-around foliage, and clusters of white, pink, or rose-purple flowers in spring.

A. alpina. MOUNTAIN ROCKCRESS. Zones 1-7. Low tufted plant, rough-hairy, with leafy stems 4-10 in. high and basal leaves in clusters. White flowers in dense, short clusters. Variety 'Rosea', 6 in. high, has pink flowers; 'Variegata' has variegated leaves. Quite often plants sold as A. alpina really are A. caucasica.

A. blepharophylla. CALIFORNIA ROCKCRESS, ROSE CRESS. Zones 5, 6, 15-17. Native to rocky hillsides and ridges near sea, Marin County to Monterey County, California. A tufted perennial 4-8 in. high. Basal leaves 1-2¾ in. long. Rose-purple flowers, fragrant, ½-¾ in. wide, in short dense clusters. Blooms March and April. A rock plant in nature, equally adapted to a well drained spot in a rock garden.

A. caucasica (A. albida). WALL ROCKCRESS. All Zones. Native Mediterranean region to Iran. A dependable old favorite. Forms mat of gray leaves to 6 in. high. White ½-in. flowers almost cover plants in early spring. Excellent ground cover and base plantings for spring-flowering bulbs such as daffodils and paper white narcissus. Companion for Alyssum saxatile and aubrieta.

A. c. 'Variegata'. Has gray leaves with creamy white margins. 'Flore-pleno' has double flowers; 'Rosabella' and 'Pink Charm' have pink blooms. The latter two are popular rock garden plants in colder climates. Start plants from cuttings or sow seeds in spring or fall. Provide some shade in hot dry areas. Short-lived where winters are warm.

ARALIA. Deciduous shrub-trees. Zones 2-24. Striking bold-leafed plants that may eventually grow to 25-30 ft. under ideal conditions. Often shrublike, especially in colder areas where it may grow as a multi-stemmed (because of suckering habit) shrub to 10 ft. Branches are nearly vertical or slightly spreading, usually very spiny. Huge leaves, clustered at ends of branches, divided into many leaflets; have effective pattern value. White flowers may be small but in such large, branched clusters they are showy in midsummer, followed by black berrylike fruits.

Not good near swimming pools because of spines; even the leaf stalks are sometimes prickly. Protect plants from wind to avoid burning foliage.

A. chinensis. CHINESE ANGELICA. Less prickly than A. spinosa. Leaves 2-3 ft. long, divided into 2-6-in.-long, toothed leaflets without stalks. Flower clusters 1-2 ft. long.

A. elata. JAPANESE ANGELICA TREE. Native to northeast Asia. Similar to A. chinensis but leaflets are narrower, have fewer teeth.

A. elegantissima. See Dizygotheca

A. papyrifera. See Tetrapanax

A. pentaphylla. See Acanthopanax

A. sieboldii. JAPANESE ARALIA. **See Fatsia**

A. spinosa. DEVIL'S WALKING STICK, HERCULES CLUB, ANGELICA TREE. Native to eastern U.S. Like the other two aralias, but much more spiny, branches look more clublike. Leaves 3-4 ft. long, divided into 2-3-in.long, stalked, finely toothed leaflets. Branched flower clusters—huge—3-4 ft. long.

ARALIA, THREADLEAF FALSE. See Dizygotheca

ARAUCARIA. Evergreen trees. These strange looking conifers provide a definite silhouette with their evenly spread tiers of stiff branches. Prominent skyline trees in many parks and old estates in California. Most have stiff, closely overlapping, dark to bright green leaves. In age they bear large, heavy, 10-15-lb. cones that fall with a crash — not a tree to sit under.

All do well in a wide range of soils with adequate drainage and an abundance of moisture. They become so towering that they should be given park space. Can serve well as skyline trees. They thrive in containers for several years, even in desert areas.

A. araucana (A. imbricata). MONKEY PUZZLE TREE. Zones 4-9, 14-24. Native to Chile. An arboreal oddity with heavy, spreading branches and tangled, ropelike branchlets closely set with sharp-pointed dark green leaves. Hardiest of the araucarias. Slow growing in youth, it eventually reaches 70-90 ft. Hardy west of the Cascades in the Northwest.

Climate Zone maps pages 8-27

A. bidwillii. BUNYA-BUNYA. Zones 7-9, 14-24. Native to Australia. Probably most widely planted Araucaria both in coastal and valley areas of California. Moderate growth to 80 ft.; broadly rounded crown supplies dense shade. Two kinds of leaves: juvenile — glossy, rather narrow; ¾-2 in. long, stiff, more or less spreading in 2 rows; mature leaves—oval, ½-in. long, rather woody, spirally arranged and overlapping along branches.

A. cunninghamii. HOOP PINE. Zones 17, 21-24. Native to Australia. Unusual silhouette of long horizontal or upswept branches with foliage tufted at the tips. Eventual height 100 ft. Juvenile leaves needlelike and flattened, ½ in. long, with spiny recurved points; adult leaves broader, overlapping, and the points incurved.

A. heterophylla (*A. excelsa*). NORFOLK ISLAND PINE. Zones 17, 21-24. Moderate growth rate to 100 ft., of pyramid shape. Juvenile leaves rather narrow, ½ in. long, curved and with sharp point; mature leaves somewhat triangular and densely overlapping. Can be held in containers for many

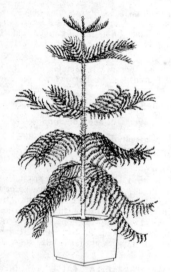

Tubbed Norfolk Island pine invites decoration with formal, elegant ornaments.

years—outdoors in mild climates, a house plant in colder climates. In containers can be used as indoor Christmas tree.

ARAUJIA sericofera. WHITE BLADDER FLOWER. Evergreen or partially deciduous

Araujia has puffy white flowers, June to frost, glossy leaves, vining growth.

vine. Zones 8, 9, 14-24. Native to Brazil. Woody vine that sometimes pops up spontaneously in gardens from wind-borne, silky-tufted seeds. Becomes a weedy, massive tangle in a year or two. Leaves tend to drop at base. Twines to 20-30 ft. in one season. Leaves 2-4 in. long, glossy dark green above, whitish beneath. White or pinkish flowers, bell-shaped, 1-1½ in. wide, followed by long, flat, leathery fruits. Not a first-class vine. Used for quick temporary screen in poor soil, windy places.

ARBORVITAE. See Thuja

ARBORVITAE, FALSE. See Thujopsis

ARBORVITAE, ORIENTAL. See Platycladus

ARBUTUS. Evergreen tree and shrub-tree. One is a Western native, the other a Mediterranean shrub-tree of wide adaptability.

A. menziesii. MADRONE, MADRONA. Evergreen tree or large shrub. Zones 3-7, 14-19. Native from British Columbia to southern California in Coast Ranges, occasionally in middle elevations of Sierra Nevada. Mature height varies—20-100 ft. Forms a broad, round head almost as wide as tall. In groves, grows more slender.

Main feature is smooth reddish brown bark that peels in thin flakes. Leathery 3-6-in.-long leaves are shiny dark green on top, dull gray-green beneath. In spring, large clusters of white to pinkish, bellshaped flowers at branch ends. These are followed in early fall by clusters of brilliant red and orange wrinkly berries that remain on tree most of winter if birds don't get them first.

If you live in madrone country and have a tree in your garden, treasure it. It is exacting in requirements in gardens outside of its native area. Must have fast drainage and non-alkaline water. Water just enough to keep plants going until they are established, and then only infrequent and deep watering. Beautiful and distinguished in the right place, but constant dropping of leaves, fruit, and bark rule it out for some uses.

A. unedo. STRAWBERRY TREE. Evergreen shrub-tree. Zones 4-24. Native to southern Europe, Ireland. Damaged in severe winters in Zones 4-7, but worth the risk. Remarkably good performance in both climate and soil extremes from desert (in shade) to seashore.

Slow to moderate growth to 8-35 ft. with equal spread. Normally has basal suckers, stem sprouts. Can be pruned, not sheared to make an open-crowned tree. Or, plant several and leave unpruned to make a screen. Trunk and branches have rich red-brown, shreddy bark; tend to become somewhat twisted and gnarled in age. Dark green, handsome, red-stemmed leaves are oblong and 2-3 in. long. Clusters of small white or greenish white, urn-shaped flowers and red and yellow, ¾-in. round fruit, somewhat strawberrylike in texture, appear at the same time in fall and winter; fruits edible but mealy.

Spray for aphids everywhere, a die-back and leafminers in the Northwest, thrips in southern California.

ARBUTUS, TRAILING. See Epigaea repens

ARCHONTOPHOENIX. Palm. Outdoors in Zones 21-24, house plant anywhere. Called bangalow or piccabeen palms in Australia.

They grow to 50 ft. or more, with a 10-15-ft. spread. Handsome, stately, difficult to transplant when large. Where winds are strong, plant in lee of buildings to prevent damage. Young trees can't take frost; mature plants may stand 28°. They tolerate

Clean, stately Alexandra palm is magnificent tree in mildest coastal climates.

shade and can grow many years grouped under tall trees. Old leaves shed cleanly, leaving smooth green trunks. Feathery leaves on mature trees 8-10 ft. long, green above, gray-green beneath.

A. alexandrae. ALEXANDRA PALM. Trunk enlarged toward base.

A. cunninghamiana. (Often sold as *Seaforthia elegans*.) Commoner than the above. Trunk not prominently enlarged at base. Clustered amethyst flowers are handsome. Highly recommended for nearly frost-free areas.

ARCTOSTAPHYLOS. MANZANITA. Evergreen shrubs. Large group of Western natives ranging in size from creepers to full-size shrubs to small trees. Waxy bell-like flowers and fruits like tiny apples. Most are characterized by (and admired for) crooked branches with smooth red to purple bark.

The low-growing ground cover manzanitas do best in loose soils that drain rapidly. They tolerate heavier soils. Taller ground covers, especially those that spread by rooting branches, and most of the shrub and tree forms, *must* have a loose, well drained soil.

Although manzanitas live in the wild without much summer water, they generally need summer water in the garden for normal growth and attractive foliage. The first summer after planting, water every 4-7 days, depending on weather. Established plants in warm-summer areas generally thrive on once-a-month watering in well drained soil; less frequently in heavy soils. You may be able to stretch intervals to once or twice a summer. Control growth by frequent pinching during the growing season.

Blooming season is not noted in the following list unless it differs from the general February-March-April sequence.

Climate Zone maps pages 8-27

A. columbiana. HAIRY MANZANITA. Zones 4-6, 15-17. Native to low coastal mountains, central California to British Columbia. Open growing, strongly branched, varying from 3-15 ft. tall. Bark red-brown to purplish red. Branches with long white hairs. Gray-green, hairy, 3-in., oval leaves contrast with red bark, and red-cheeked fruit in summer. Flowers white. Northwest nurseries offer plants from a selected manzanita and sold as 'Oregon Hybrid'. Has all the good qualities of *A. columbiana* but is far more compact. A useful manzanita; has done well in highway plantings.

A. densiflora. VINE HILL MANZANITA. Zones 7-9, 14-21. Native to Sonoma County, California. All varieties except 'Sentinel' grow low and spreading, outer branches take root when they touch the soil. Main stems slender and crooked. Bark of trunks and branches smooth, reddish black. Leaves, light or dark green, glossy, small, in the ½-1 in. range. Flowers white or pink. In bank planting, the low types do best on east or northeast facing slopes, loose soil, good drainage.

A. d. 'Howard McMinn'. Grows to a mounding 30 in. and spreads as much as 7 ft. in 5 years. If tip-pruned after flowering, plant becomes as dense as a sheared Kurume azalea. (Don't prune tips of prostrate branches.) Flowers whitish pink.

A. d. 'James West'. Lower growing than 'Howard McMinn'.

A. d. 'Sentinel'. A rigidly upright form to 6 ft. or more and spreading to 8 ft. Light green, downy leaves. Full sun. Can be trained as a small tree by selecting dominant stem or stems and removing others.

A. edmundsii. LITTLE SUR MANZANITA. Zones 6-9, 14-24. Native to Hurricane Point area, Monterey County. Grows 4-24 in. high and more than 12 ft. wide. Can be used for border and massed ground cover in full shade, semi-shade, full sun, in sharply drained rocky loam, and in tight clay. Where surface drainage is slow, mound soil slightly for quick runoff. Roundish leaves are light green, 1 in. long, on red stems. December-January show of pink flowers.

A. hookeri. MONTEREY MANZANITA. Zones 6-9, 14-24. Native to Monterey Peninsula. Slow growing to form dense mounds 1½-4 ft. high, spreading to 6 ft. and more. Oval, ¾-in.-long, bright green, glossy leaves. Flowers white to pinkish. Fruit bright red, shiny. Bark red-brown, smooth.

A. h. 'Monterey Carpet'. Compact growth to make a 12-in.-high ground cover spreading by rooting branches to 12 ft.

A. h. 'Wayside'. Taller growing to 3 ft. while spreading to 8 ft. and more. Trailing branches take root. May be slow to fill in.

A. insularis. ISLAND MANZANITA. Zones 8, 9, 14-24. To 8 ft. tall, spreading habit. Dark red bark. Leaves bright green, oval, 1-2 in. long. Flowers white, in spreading clusters. Fruit yellowish-brown. Takes moderate summer watering and is considered one of the easier manzanitas.

A. manzanita. COMMON MANZANITA. Tall shrub or treelike shrub. Zones 4-9, 14-24. Native to inner Coast Ranges, Sierra Nevada foothills. Widely adapted. Grows 6-20 ft. high, spreads 4-10 ft. wide. Crooked picturesque branching habit; purplish red bark. Shiny bright green to dull green,

broadly oval leaves, ¾-1½ in. long. Flowers white to pink in open drooping clusters. Fruit white turning to deep red.

A. media. Zones 4-9, 14-24. May be a natural hybrid of *A. uva-ursi* and *A. columbiana*. As far as the gardener is concerned it's a higher-growing *A. uva-ursi* (to 2 ft.) with brighter red branches and leathery dark green leaves. Spreads faster than *A. uva-ursi*.

A. obispoensis. SERPENTINE MANZANITA. Zones 15-17, 22-24. Native to serpentine formations in Monterey and San Luis Obispo county. Has classic manzanita look. Erect growth to 9 ft.; twisted branch pattern; dark purplish red bark in contrast with distinctly gray foliage; white-pink flowers in upright clusters; fruit pale orange-brown to red-brown.

A. pumila. DUNE MANZANITA. Zones 14-24. Native to dunes around Monterey Bay, California. Spreading, prostrate habit, to 1-2½ ft. high. Roots freely where branches touch ground. Leaves dull green, narrowish, ½-1 in. long. Short dense clusters of small white to pink flowers. Good ground cover in sandy or well-drained soil.

A. stanfordiana. STANFORD MANZANITA. Zones 4-9, 14-17. Native to California's Lake, Mendocino, Napa, and Sonoma counties. Wide climate range. Soil adaptation not so good. Must have rapid drainage to avoid root rot. Spreading shrub to 3-7 ft. with smooth reddish brown bark, glossy deep green leaves 1-1¾ in. long. Flowers pink in open clusters. Fruit red to red-brown. A relaxed and graceful manzanita. Selected forms, propagated by cuttings, are:

A. s. 'Fred Oehler'. Parent plant is 4 ft. high, 6 ft. wide. Produces a good crop of pink flowers in pendulous clusters.

A. s. 'Louis Edmunds'. (May be sold as *A. s. bakeri* 'Louis Edmunds'.) Erect upright growth to 5-6 ft. Flowers pink in drooping clusters. Similar in appearance to *A. stanfordiana* but root system tolerates garden conditions better.

A. s. 'Trinity'. Similar to *A. stanfordiana* but has reddish purple flowers.

A. uva-ursi. BEARBERRY, KINNIKINNICK. Zones 1-9, 14-24. Native from San Mateo County, California, north to Alaska. Thence wide-spread in northern latitudes. Long a popular ground cover in Pacific Northwest and intermountain areas. Prostrate spreading and rooting as it creeps to 15 ft.;

Kinnikinnick branches with springtime flowers (¼ in.), red berries that follow.

bright glossy green, leathery leaves to 1 in., turning red in winter. Flowers white or pinkish. Fruits bright red or pink. A most useful plant in the Northwest: for slopes too steep for lawn, a trailing mat atop a wall, combining with mugho pines, yews. Slowness in starting causes weed problems. Mulch with peat moss or sawdust to keep down weeds, and keep soil moist for root growth and rooting of branches.

A. u. 'Point Reyes'. Leaves, dark green, are close-set along branches.

A. u. 'Radiant'. Leaves lighter green, more widely spaced along stems. Heavy crop of large bright red fruits in autumn, lasting into winter.

ARCTOTHECA calendula. CAPE WEED. Evergreen perennial. Zones 8, 9, 14-24. Rapid-running ground cover, less than 1 ft. tall, with yellow daisies most abundant in spring. Gray-green, deeply divided leaves. Full sun. Space 12-18 in. apart.

ARCTOTIS. AFRICAN DAISY. Annual and perennials. Zones 7-9, 12-24. Mostly native to South Africa. Colorful sun-loving plants with abundant daisy flowers that bloom from fall to early summer in mild-winter sections of the West. Any of the kinds make gay splashy masses of color when used as ground covers.

A. acaulis. Perennial. Makes widespreading stemless clump of divided or lobed leaves, 6-8 in. long, green and rough (or hairy) above, white-woolly beneath. Flowers (on long stalks) 3 in. wide, rays yellow, (purplish underneath) surround purple-black center. Hybrids in many colors—violet, purple, yellow, orange, pink.

A. breviscapa. Annual. Divided 6-in.-long leaves somewhat like those of above species. Flowers 2 in. wide, at top of 6-18-in.-high stems; rays orange-yellow, brown or bluish at base, dark brown at center.

A. stoechadifolia. AFRICAN DAISY. Perennial. Bushy, to 2½ ft., with leafy stems. Leaves lobed, somewhat toothed, white woolly when young, to 4 in. long. Flowers to 3 in. wide, on long stalks above leaves; rays white, violet beneath, purplish center. Variety *grandis*, grown as annual, has leaves to 6 in. long, and 6-12 in. long stems. Flowers apricot yellow, terra cotta, white, with dark centers. Sow the seed where the plants are to bloom, in a sunny place. Plants need plenty of room.

ARDISIA. Evergreen shrubs or shrublets.

A. crenata (*A. crenulata, A. crispa*). Usually grown indoors. Most familiar as an 18-inch, single-stemmed pot plant. In a large tub it can reach 4 ft. with nearly equal spread. In spring, spirelike clusters of tiny (¼ in.) white or pinkish flowers are carried above shiny, wavy-edged, 3-in.-long leaves. Flowers are followed by brilliant scarlet fruits in autumn and usually through winter.

A. japonica. Zones 5, 6, 15-17. Low shrub that spreads as a ground cover by rhizomes to produce a succession of upright branches 6-18 in. high. Leathery, bright green leaves (4 in. long) are clustered at the tips of the branches. White, ¼-in. flowers, 2-6 in a cluster, appear in fall, followed by small (¼ in.), round, bright red fruits that last into the winter. Makes a quality ground cover in the shade.

Climate Zone maps pages 8-27

ARECA lutescens. See Chrysalidocarpus

ARECASTRUM romanzoffianum. (Often sold as *Cocos plumosa.*) QUEEN PALM. Zones 15-17, 19-24. S. America. Exceptionally straight trunk to 50 ft. tall, arching, bright green, glossy feather-type leaves 10-15 ft. long are subject to breakage in high

Use handsome, clean-cut queen palm in avenue planting or beside a pool.

wind. Fast grower, responding quickly to water and fertilizer. Damaged at 28°, but has recovered from a 20° freeze.

ARENARIA. SANDWORT. Perennial ground covers. Zones 2-9, 14-24. Low evergreen plants carpet the ground with dense mats of moss-like foliage, have small white flowers in late spring and summer. They are often used as lawn substitutes, between stepping stones, or for velvety green patches in rock gardens.

A. balearica. CORSICAN SANDWORT. Forms a dense mat to 3 in. high. Leaves oval, thick, glossy, to ⅛ in. long. Grows best in shade with lots of water. Adapted to planting in small areas such as a carpet at base of a container-grown tree.

A. montana. It grows 2-4 in. high with weak stems up to 1 ft. long usually covered with soft hairs. Leaves grayish, ½-¾ in. long. White flowers 1 in. across profuse in June. A good plant to let trail over a sunny rock or tumble over a low wall.

A. verna caespitosa. See Irish Moss, Scotch Moss

ARENGA engleri. Palm. Zones 23, 24. Slow growing feather palm from Formosa, southern Japan. Makes a many-stemmed clump seldom over 8 ft. tall. Stands full sun near coast; has a better green in part shade inland. Has taken 26° with only moderate damage.

ARGEMONE. PRICKLY POPPY. Annual or biennial. Prickly-leafed plants with large, showy poppy flowers. Native to desert or dry areas Wyoming to Mexico and west to California. Grow easily from seed sown where plants are to bloom, or from seed sown in pots for gentle transplanting. Need sun and good drainage. Bloom mostly in summer. To 3 ft.

A. intermedia. White flowers.
A. mexicana. Yellow to orange flowers.
A. platyceras. White flowers. Commonest kind.

ARISTOLOCHIA. Deciduous vines. Curiously shaped flowers in rather sober colors resemble curved pipes with flared bowls.

A. californica. CALIFORNIA DUTCHMAN'S PIPE. Zones 7-9, 13-24. Native to Coast Ranges and Sierra Nevada foothills of northern California. Will cover an 8 by 12-ft. screen with some training, or climb by long thin shoots 10-16 ft. into a tree. Flower display before leaves, late January to April. Pendulous, 1-in.-long flowers are cream-colored with red-purple veins at maturity. Bright green, heart-shaped leaves to 5 in. long. Grow from seed or from rooted shoots around base of vine. Interesting and useful where many less hardy vines would freeze. Accepts any soil, but needs partial shade and ample moisture.

A. durior. DUTCHMAN'S PIPE. Perennial treated as annual in mild climates. All Zones. Native to eastern United States. Will cover 15 by 20 ft. in one season. Easily grown from seed. Large, 6-14-in.-long, kidney-shaped, deep green, glossy leaves are carried in shinglelike pattern to form a dense cover on trellis. Flowers, with yellowish green, 3-in. curved tube, flare into 3 brownish purple lobes about 1 in. wide. Bloom in June and July, almost hidden by the leaves. No special care. Generous feeding and watering will speed growth. Cut back in winter if too heavy. Short-lived in warm-winter areas. Will not stand strong winds.

ARISTOTELIA racemosa. NEW ZEALAND WINEBERRY. Evergreen shrub or small tree. Zones 15-20. Usually fast growing to 20 ft.

Reddish tints on twigs, lower leaf surfaces of Aristotelia. Tiny red flowers in May.

Rather airy growth with quite flexible branches. Bark of young trees red, turning black with age. Foliage an unusual two-tone, with leaves 3-5 in. long, glossy green above and rich reddish brown beneath. In May produces a profusion of graceful plumes of tiny rose to wine-colored (sometimes white) blossoms. Fruits, pea-sized, red to almost black, will not appear unless both male and female trees are planted (difficult because trees sold are usually seedlings with sex unknown). It's choice without fruit.

A most versatile tree. Attractive in large containers on patio or terrace. Casting open shade, deep rooting, it's a tree to garden under. Give it full sun, fast drainage, ample moisture.

ARMERIA. THRIFT, SEA PINK. Hardy evergreen perennials. All Zones. Narrow stiff leaves grow in compact tufts or basal rosettes; small white, pink, rose or red flowers in dense globular heads from early spring to late fall. Sturdy, dependable plants for edging walks or borders, for tidy mounds in rock gardens, raised beds, and attractive in containers. Need full sun and fast drainage. Shear flowers after bloom. Feed once a year with slow acting fertilizer. Propagate from seeds in spring or fall, or by divisions.

A. juniperifolia (*A. caespitosa*). Native to mountains of Spain. Stiff, needle-shaped leaves ½ in. long in low, extremely compact rosettes. Flowers rose-pink, in dense round clusters on 2-in. stems. This little mountain native is very touchy about drainage; apply mulch of fine gravel around plants to prevent basal stem rot, especially in summer.

A. maritima (*Statice armeria, Armeria vulgaris*). COMMON THRIFT. Tufted mounds spreading to 1 ft. with 6-in.-long stiff, grasslike leaves. Small white to rose-pink flowers in tight round clusters at top of 6-10-in. stalks. Blooms almost all year along coast; flowers profusely in spring in other areas.

ARNICA cordifolia. WOODLAND DAISY, ARNICA. Perennial. Zones 1-6, 15-17. Native to mountains, California to Alaska and east to the Rockies. Spreads from long rhizomes. Forms clumps of heart-shaped leaves 1-4 in. long. Stems, with smaller leaves, ½-2 ft. high. Daisylike flowers yellow, borne individually or 2-3 in a cluster. Good for naturalizing in woodland areas.

ARONIA arbutifolia. RED CHOKEBERRY. Deciduous shrub. Zones 1-7. Native to eastern United States. Hardy to —10°. Noteworthy for long season of bright red foliage and fruit in autumn. Large, openly branched, upright to 6-10 ft. or more. Leaves, narrow ovals generally about 3 in. long and half as wide, are dark green above, gray feltlike beneath. Small ½-in. flowers, white

Fall-winter fruits for which red chokeberry is named. White spring flowers.

or pink tinged, in 2-in. clusters, April or May. Followed by clusters of brilliant red, ¼-in. berrylike fruits. They ripen to blend with red foliage in September and hang on after leaves have fallen. Variety 'Erecta'

Climate
Zone maps
pages 8-27

is a narrow-growing from to 5-6 ft. Variety 'Brilliantissima' has exceptionally good fall color.

Any soil. Tolerates heavy clay. Grows in swamps in native area. Use in shrubbery border, at edge of woodland. Good combination: with staghorn sumac, Michaelmas daisies in foreground.

ARTEMISIA. Evergreen or deciduous shrubs or woody perennials. All Zones. Several species are valuable for interesting leaf patterns and silvery gray or white aromatic foliage; others are aromatic herbs. Plant in full sun. Drought resistant. Keep on dry side. Divide in spring and fall. Most kinds excellent for use in mixed border where the white or silvery leaves soften harsh reds or oranges, and blend beautifully with blues, lavenders, and pinks.

A. abrotanum. SOUTHERNWOOD, OLD MAN. Woody shrub. To 3-5 ft. Beautiful lemon scented, green, feathery foliage; yellowish white flower heads. Use for pleasantly scented foliage in shrub border. Hang sprigs in closet to discourage moths. Burn a few leaves on stove to kill cooking odors.

A. absinthium. COMMON WORMWOOD. Woody shrub. To 2-4 ft. Silvery gray, finely divided leaves with bitter taste but pungent odor. Minute yellow flowers. Keep pruned to get better shaped plant. Divide every 3 years. Background shrub. Good gray feature in flower border, particularly fine with delphiniums. Leaves used to flavor wine, season poultry, also for medicinal uses.

A. albula. SILVER KING ARTEMISIA. Bushy perennial. To 2-3½ ft., with slender spreading branches, silvery white 2-in. leaves, the lower ones with 3-5 lobes, upper ones narrow and unlobed. 'Silver Queen' is improved variety with more silvery foliage. Cut foliage, fresh or dried, useful in arrangements.

A. dracunculus. FRENCH TARRAGON, TRUE TARRAGON. Perennial. To 1-2 ft.; spreads slowly by creeping rhizomes. Creeping habit. Shiny, dark green, narrow leaves—very aromatic. Woody stems. Flowers greenish white in branched clusters. Dies to ground in winter. Divide every 3 to 4 years. Attractive container plant. Cut sprigs in June for seasoning vinegar. Use fresh or dried leaves to season salads, egg and cheese dishes, fish.

A. frigida. FRINGED WORMWOOD. Perennial. To 1-1½ ft. with white, finely cut leaves. Young plants compact. Cut back when they start to become rangy.

A. lactiflora. WHITE MUGWORT. Border perennial. Tall straight column to 4-5 ft. One of the few artemisias with attractive flowers: creamy white in large, branched, 18-in. sprays, August-Stepember. Leaves dark green, with broad, toothed-edged lobes.

A. pontica. ROMAN WORMWOOD. Shrub. To 4 ft. Feathery, silver-gray leaves. Heads of whitish yellow nodding flowers in long, open, branched clusters. Leaves used in sachets. Medicinal uses.

A. pycnocephala. SANDHILL SAGE. Shrubby perennial. Native to beaches of northern California. Erect, rounded, somewhat spreading 1-2 ft. tall. Soft, silvery white or gray leaves, crowded, divided into narrow lobes. Remove flower spikes as they open to keep plants compact. Becomes unkempt with age. Replace every 2 years.

A. schmidtiana. ANGEL'S HAIR. Woody perennial. Forms 2 ft. high, 1 ft. wide dome of woolly, silvery-white, finely-cut leaves. Variety 'Silver Mound' is 12 in. high. Variety 'Nana' only 2 in. high.

A. stelleriana. BEACH WORMWOOD, OLD WOMAN, DUSTY MILLER. Woody perennial. Dense, silvery-gray plant to 2½ ft. with 1-4 in. lobed leaves. Hardier than *Senecio cineraria* (another dusty miller), this artemisia is often used in its place in colder climates. Yellow flowers in spikelike clusters.

A. tridentata. BIG SAGEBRUSH. Evergreen shrub. Native to Great Basin region of the West. Grows 1½-15 ft. high. Many branches. Hairy gray leaves about ¾ in. long. Narrow, usually 3-toothed at tip, very aromatic. This is the sagebrush that gives the pungent sage fragrance for which the Western deserts are known. Of limited landscape use, but grows easily in any sunny, well drained situation.

ARTICHOKE. Perennial vegetable with landscape value. Zones 8, 9, 14-24. A big ferny-looking plant with an irregular, somewhat fountainlike form—to 4 ft. high, 6-8 ft. wide. Leaves are silvery green. Big flower buds form at tops of stalks; they are the artichokes you cook and eat. If not cut, the buds open into spectacular purple-blue, 6-in. thistlelike flowers which can be cut for fresh or dry arrangements.

In California's cool-summer coast (Zone 17), where it is grown commercially, the artichoke can be both a handsome ornamental plant and a producer of fine, tender artichokes from September to May or all year. In climate Zones 8, 9, 14-16, 18-24 the plant grows luxuriantly at least from spring through fall, and edible buds come as an extra dividend in early summer only. In the colder winter climates the artichoke is a rarity and must be protected through winter to keep roots and shoots alive.

Plant dormant roots or plants from containers in winter or early spring, setting root shanks vertically with buds or shoots just above soil line. Space plants 4-6 ft.

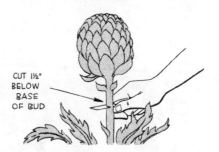

CUT 1½"
BELOW
BASE
OF BUD

Cut like this, while bud is tight and plump. Top one on stem always biggest.

apart. After growth starts, water thoroughly once a week, wetting entire root system. Spray to control aphids; after buds start to form use just strong jet sprays of water to blast off aphids (no insecticides then). Bait to control snails and slugs. Harvest buds while they are still tight and plump. Cut off old stalks near ground level when leaves begin to yellow. In cold-winter areas, cut tops to 12 in. in fall, tie them over the root crown, and mulch heavily.

ARTICHOKE, JERUSALEM. See Helianthus tuberosus

ARTILLERY PLANT. See Pilea microphylla

ARUM. Perennials with tuberous roots. Zones 8-24. Arrow-shaped or heart-shaped leaves. Curious callalike blossoms on short stalks. Flower bract half encloses thick fleshy spike which bears the tiny flowers. Require shade, rich soil, ample moisture. Use in flower borders where hardy; as indoor plants in cold-winter climates.

A. cornutum. See Sauromatum

A. italicum. ITALIAN ARUM. Arrow-shaped leaves 8 in. long and broad, veined with white. Very short stem; white or greenish-white (sometimes purple-spotted) flower bract first erect then folds over and conceals short yellow spike; spring and early summer. Dense clusters of bright red fruits follow.

A. palaestinum. BLACK CALLA, JERUSALEM ARUM. Leaves 6-8 in. long, also arrow-shaped flower bract about same length, greenish outside, black-purple within, curved back, revealing the black-purple spike; spring and early summer.

A. pictum. Light green, heart-shaped, 10-in.-long leaves on 10-in. stalks appear in spring. Flower bract is violet, green at base. Spike purplish-black.

ARUNDINARIA. See Bamboo

ARUNDO donax. GIANT REED. Perennial. All Zones. One of the largest grasses, planted for bold effects in garden fringe areas, or by watersides. Often called a bamboo. Strong somewhat woody stems, 6-20 ft. high. Leaves to 2 ft. long, flat, 3 in. wide. Flowers in rather narrow, erect clusters to 2 ft. high. *A. d.* 'Versicolor' (*A. d.* 'Variegata') has white or yellowish-striped leaves. Needs rich moist soil. Protect roots with a mulch in cold-winter areas. Cut out dead stems and thin occasionally to get look-through quality. Extremely invasive; plant only where you can control it.

ASARUM caudatum. WILD GINGER. Perennial. Zones 4-6, 15-17, 21. Native to woods of Coast Range, mainly in redwood belt from Santa Cruz Mts. to Del Norte County, north to British Columbia. Remarkably handsome ground cover for shade, forming a lush, lustrous, dark green carpet of heart-shaped leaves 2-7 in. across, 7-10 in. high. Flowers reddish brown, bell-shaped with long tails, produced close to ground under leaves; bloom in spring.

Grows in average soil with heavy watering, but spreads faster, is more luxuriant in rich soil with ample humus. Start from divisions or from container-grown plants.

ASH. See Fraxinus

ASH, EUROPEAN MOUNTAIN. See Sorbus aucuparia

ASPARAGUS, EDIBLE. Perennial vegetable. All Zones. One of the most permanent and dependable of home garden vegetables. Plants take 2-3 years to come into full production, but then furnish delicious spears every spring for 10-15 years. They take up considerable space, but do so in the grand manner, the tall, feathery, graceful plants being highly ornamental. Use asparagus along a sunny fence or as background for flowers or vegetables.

Seeds grow into strong young plants in one season (sow in spring), but roots are

Climate Zone maps pages 8-27

far more widely used. Set out seedlings or roots (not wilted, no smaller than a man's hand) in fall or winter (mild climates), or early spring (cold winters). Make trenches 1 ft. wide and 8-10 in. deep. Space trenches 4-6 ft. apart. Heap loose, manure-enriched soil at bottom of trenches and soak. Set roots so that tops are 6-8 in. below surface. Space them 12 in. apart. Spread roots out evenly. Cover with 2 in. of soil and water again.

As young plants grow, gradually fill in the trench, taking care not to cover the growing tips. Soak deeply whenever soil begins to dry out at root depth. Don't harvest any spears the first year; the object at this time is to build a big root mass. When plants turn brown in late fall or early winter, cut stems to the ground. In cold-winter areas permit dead stalks to stand until spring; they will help trap and hold snow, which will furnish protection to the root crowns.

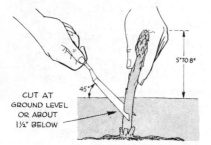

Cut asparagus carefully; avoid damaging root crown. Cut at surface or 1 1/2 in. below.

The following spring you can cut your first spears; cut only for 4-6 weeks, or until appearance of thin spears indicates that roots are nearing exhaustion. Then permit plants to grow. Cultivate, feed, and irrigate heavily. The third year you should be able to cut spears for 8-10 weeks. Spears are ready to cut when they are 5-8 in. long. Thrust the knife down at a 45° angle to the soil; flat cutting may injure adjacent developing spears. If asparagus beetle appears during cutting season, control with rotenone or (carefully noting label precautions) malathion. After cutting season spray with any all-purpose insecticide. Use bait to control snails and slugs; sevin, dibrom, or diazinon for earwigs or cutworms.

ASPARAGUS, ORNAMENTAL. Perennials. Outdoors in Zones 15-24, house plant anywhere. There are about 150 kinds of asparagus besides the edible one—all members of the lily family. Best known of ornamental kinds is the fern asparagus (*A. plumosus*), which is not a fern. Although valued mostly for their handsome foliage of unusual texture quality, some have small but fragrant flowers and colorful berries. Green foliage sprays are made up of what looks like leaves (needle-like or broader). Actually they are short branches called cladodes. The true leaves are inconspicuous dry scales.

Most ornamental asparagus look greenest in part shade, but thrive in sun near coast. Leaves turn yellow in dense shade. Plant in well drained soil to which peat moss or ground bark have been added. Because of fleshy roots, can withstand some drought, but grow better with ample water. Feed in

spring with complete fertilizer. Trim out old shoots to make room for new growth. Will survive light frosts but may be killed to ground by severe cold. Frosted plants often come back from roots.

A. asparagoides. SMILAX ASPARAGUS. Much branched vine with spineless stems to 20 ft. or more. Leaves to 1 in. long, sharp-pointed, stiffish, glossy, grass green.

Smilax asparagus will cascade nicely from pot. Leaves are rather triangular.

Small fragrant white flowers in spring, followed by blue berries. Often seen in older gardens, foliage sprays prized for table decoration. If it gets little water, plant dies back in summer, coming back from roots with fall rains. Self-sows readily. Becomes tangled mass unless trained. Variety 'Myrtifolius,' commonly called baby smilax, is more graceful form, with smaller leaves.

A. crispus (*A. scandens* 'Deflexus'). BASKET ASPARAGUS. Airy, graceful plant for hanging baskets. Drooping, zigzag stems have bright green, 3-angled leaves in whorls of three.

A. densiflorus 'Myeri' (*A. meyeri*). MYERS ASPARAGUS. Plants send up several to many stiffly upright stems to 2 ft. or more—they are densely clothed with needle-like, deep green leaves. Plants have a fluffy look. Good in containrs. A little less hardy than Sprenger asparagus.

A. d. 'Sprengeri' (*A. sprengeri*). SPRENGER ASPARAGUS. Arching or drooping stems 3-6 ft. long. Shiny bright green needlelike leaves 1 in. long, in bundles. Bright red berries. Popular for hanging baskets or containers, indoors and out.

Sprenger asparagus widely used as ground cover, for spilling from pots, over walls.

Train on trellis; climbs by means of small hooked prickles. Used as a billowy ground cover where temperatures stay above 24°. Takes full sun as well as part shade; grows in ordinary soil—even poor soil.

A. falcatus. SICKLE-THORN ASPARAGUS. Derives common name from curved thorns along stems by which it climbs to 40 ft. in its native area (in gardens usually grows to 10 ft.). Leaves 2-3 in. long in clusters of

Sickle-thorn asparagus, normally a vine, can, with tip-pinching, be a shrub.

3-5 at ends of branches. Tiny, white, fragrant flowers in loose clusters. Brown berries. Rapid growing. Excellent foliage mass to cover fence or wall, or provide shade for a pergola or lathhouse. Foliage resembles that of *Podocarpus macrophyllus*.

A. meyeri. See **A. densiflorus 'Myeri'**

A. officinalis altilis. See **Asparagus, edible**

A. plumosus. See *A. setaceus*

A. retrofractus. Erect, shrubby, slightly climbing, very tender. Slender, zigzag, silvery gray stems grow slowly to 8-10 ft. high. Leaves threadlike, 1-in. long, in fluffy, rich green tufts. Clusters of small white flowers. Handsome in containers; useful in flower arrangements. Cut foliage lasts 10 days out of water, several weeks in water.

A. scandens. BASKET ASPARAGUS. Slender branching vine climbing to 6 ft. Deep green needlelike leaves on zigzag drooping stems. Greenish white flowers 1/8 in. long. Scarlet berries.

A. scandens 'Deflexus'. See *A. crispus*

A. setaceus (*A. plumosus*). FERN ASPARAGUS. Sometimes called emerald feather. Branching woody vine climbing by wiry, spiny stems to 10-20 ft. Tiny, threadlike

Asparagus setaceus. Foliage extremely fine-textured, yet amazingly durable.

leaves in dark-green feathery sprays that resemble fern fronds. Tiny white flowers. Berries purple-black. Dense, fine-textured foliage mass useful as a screen against walls, fences. Florists use foliage as fillers in bouquets; holds up better than delicate ferns. Dwarf varieties good for containers.

A. sprengeri. See **A. densiflorus 'Sprengeri'**

A. virgatus. Bushy, with many stiff upright branches toward the top. Usually

Climate
Zone maps
pages 8-27

grows to 2 ft., may reach 3-5 ft. Leaves ¾ in. long, slender, producing a wispy fragile quality. Greenish white flowers; orange-red berries. Effective grown against a white wall.

ASPEN. See Populus

ASPERULA odorata. SWEET WOODRUFF. Perennial. All Zones, best in Zones 1-6, 15-17. Attractive, low-spreading perennial that is reminiscent of deep shaded woods. Slender square stems 6-12 in. high, encircled every inch or so by whorls of 6-8 aromatic, bristle-tipped leaves. Clusters of tiny white flowers show above foliage in late spring and summer. Leaves and stems give off fragrant, haylike odor when dried; used for making May wine.

In the garden sweet woodruff's best use is as a ground cover or edging along a path in a shaded location. Will spread rapidly in rich soil with abundant moisture. Self-sows freely. Can increase by root division in fall or spring.

ASPIDISTRA elatior (A. lurida). CAST-IRON PLANT. Evergreen perennial. Zones 4-9, 12-24, also house plant. A sturdy, long-lived foliage plant remarkable for its ability to thrive under conditions unacceptable to most kinds of plants. Leaf blades 1-2½ ft. long, 3-4 in. wide, tough, glossy, dark green arching, with distinct parallel veins—each blade supported by a 6-8 in.-long grooved leaf stalk. Inconspicuous brownish flowers bloom in spring close to the ground. Although extremely tolerant, requiring minimum care, aspidistra grows best in porous soil enriched with organic matter, and responds to feeding in spring and summer. Will grow in dark shaded areas (under decks or stairs) as well as in filtered sun. Keep leaves dust-free and glossy by hosing them off, or clean with a soft brush or cloth.

The variegated form (A. elatior 'Variegata') has leaves striped with white, loses its variegation if planted in too rich soil.

ASPIDUM capense. See Rumohra

ASPLENIUM. Fern. A widespread and variable group.

A. bulbiferum. MOTHER FERN. Outdoors Zones 17, 20-24, house plant elsewhere. From New Zealand. Graceful, very finely cut light green fronds to 4 ft. tall. Fronds produce plantlets which can be removed and planted. Heavy or medium shade. Hardy to 26°. Watch for snails and slugs.

A. nidus (A. nidus-avis). BIRD'S-NEST FERN. House plant. Tender fern with showy apple green, undivided fronds to 4 ft. long, 8 in. wide, growing upright in a cluster. Striking foliage plant; best as a container plant to be grown indoors in winter, on a shady patio in summer. One snail or slug can ruin a frond.

A. trichomanes. MAIDENHAIR SPLEENWORT. All Zones. Dainty, hardy, evergreen fern with 8-in.-long fronds, dark brown, shiny stems. Good-looking in the shady rock garden or wild garden.

ASTER. Perennials. All Zones. (For the common annual or China aster, sold in flats at nurseries, see Callistephus). There are over 600 species of true asters ranging from alpine kinds forming compact mounds 6 in. high to open branching plants 6 ft. tall.

Flowers white or in shades of blue, red, or purple, mostly with yellow centers. Most asters bloom in summer and fall; some hybrids start flowering in spring. Taller asters are invaluable for abundant color in large borders or among shrubs. Large sprays effective in arrangements. Compact dwarf or cushion types make tidy edgings, mounds of color in rock gardens, good container plants.

Plant in full sun. Adapted to most soils, need routine care, although more luxuriant in fertile soil, with regular watering. Resistant to insects and diseases, except for mildew on leaves in late fall. Strong growing asters have invasive roots, need control. Divide clumps yearly in late fall or early spring. Replant vigorous young divisions from outside of clump; discard old center. Divide smaller, tufted, less vigorous growing kinds every 2 years.

A. alpinus. ROCK ASTER, ALPINE DAISY. Mounding plant 6-12 in. Leaves ½-5 in. long, mostly in basal tuft. Several stems grow from basal clump and each carries one violet-blue flower 1½-2 in. across; May-June bloom. Best in cold-winter areas.

A. amellus. ITALIAN ASTER. Sturdy, drought resistant, hairy plant to 2 ft. Branching stems with violet, yellow-centered flowers 2 in. across. Many varieties.

A. dumosus. BUSHY ASTER. To 2-3 ft. Narrow leaves 3 in. long. Blue or white flowers ½ in. across. Widely used in developing lower-growing varieties, commonly called dwarf Michaelmas daisies, invaluable as low border plants.

A. ericoides. HEATH ASTER. Much branched, usually growing 2-3 ft. in gardens, natively to 7 ft. Narrow leaves ½-1 in. long. Tiny white or pinkish flowers in dome-shaped clusters. Dainty, effective with larger, bright colored asters.

A. frikartii. One of the finest, most useful and widely adapted perennials introduced in the last few decades. Hybrids between A. amellus (see above) and A. thomsonii, a hairy-leafed, lilac-flowered, 3-ft.

Aster frikartii *flowers and how they grow. Lavender-blue with yellow centers.*

species native to the Himalayas. Abundant, single, lavender to violet-blue, fragrant flowers, 2½ in. across. Open spreading growth to 2 ft. high. Blooms May to October — almost all year in mild-winter areas if dead flowers are removed regularly. Two varieties are 'Wonder of Stafa' (best known), and 'Jungfrau'.

A. fruticosus. See Diplopappus

A. novae-angliae. NEW ENGLAND ASTER. Stout-stemmed plant to 3-5 ft. with hairy leaves to 5 in. long. Flowers deep purple, 2 in. across.

A. novi-belgii. NEW YORK ASTER. To 3 ft., similar to New England aster, but with smooth leaves. Full clusters of bright blue-violet flowers.

Michaelmas daisy is the name applied to hybrids of A. novae-angliae and A. novi-belgii. They are tall (3-4 ft.), graceful, branching plants. Many horticultural varieties with flowers in white, pale to deep pink, rose, red, and many shades of blue, violet, and purple.

Oregon-Pacific asters, hybrids between a dwarf species native to the West and some well-known Michaelmas daisies, are splendid garden plants. Dwarf, intermediate, taller forms ranging in height from under 12 in. to 30 in. Compact, floriferous, blooming late spring to fall. Many named varieties available in white, blue, lavender, purple, rose, pink, cream.

A. yunnanensis 'Napsbury'. An improved garden variety of this Chinese species. Leaves dark green in basal tufts. Stems to 18 in., each bearing a single lavender-blue, orange-centered flower. Blooms in summer.

ASTER, BEACH. See Erigeron glaucus

ASTER, CHINA. See Callistephus

ASTER, SHRUB. See Diplopappus

ASTER, STOKES. See Stokesia

ASTILBE. FALSE SPIRAEA, MEADOW SWEET. Perennial. Zones 2-7, 14-17 (treat as annual in Zones 8, 9, 18-24). Valued for the light airy quality of plumelike flower clusters and attractive foliage, ability to provide color from May through July. Leaves divided, with toothed or cut leaflets; leaves in some species simply lobed with cut margins. Small white, pink, or red flowers in graceful branching clusters held on slender, wiry stems from 6 in.-3 ft. or higher.

Most astilbes sold in nurseries are hybrids developed from several species. Among those available are: 'Crispa', 6-10 in., pink flowers; 'Deutschland', to 2 ft., creamy white flowers; 'Fanal', to 2 ft., bronze foliage and garnet-red flowers; 'Peach Blossom', 2½ ft., shell pink flowers.

Plant in sun or shade depending on light intensity. Needs a cool, moist soil, rich in humus. Cut back after flowering. Divide

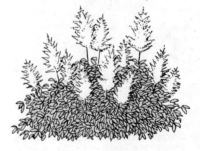

May to July, *typical astilbe is 2-3-ft. mass of pink, white, or rose plumes.*

Climate
Zone maps
pages 8-27

clumps every 4-5 years. Combine in shade gardens with columbine, meadow rue, plantain lily, bergenia, in sunnier situations with peonies, delphinium, iris. Often planted at edge of pools. Good in pots and tubs.

ATHEL TREE. See Tamarix aphylla

ATHYRIUM filix-foemina. LADY FERN. All Zones. Grows to 4 ft. or more in rich, damp soil in shade. Rootstock rises up to make a short trunk in older plants. Vertical effect, narrow at bottom, spreading broadly at the top. Thin fronds, very finely cut, bright green, semi-evergreen in the mildest areas but deciduous with repeated frosts. Good choice for woodland or streamside garden. Shelter it from strong winds that might break the brittle stems. Fanciers may find named garden forms with crested or forked fronds.

ATRIPLEX. SALTBUSH. Evergreen or deciduous shrubs. Unusually tolerant of direct seashore conditions or highly alkaline desert soils. Saltbushes are mostly grown for their gray or silvery foliage; flowers and fruits unimportant. Many species useful as fire-resistant plants on arid hillsides of California. Plants char but come back.

A. canescens. FOUR-WING SALTBUSH. Evergreen. Zones 2-24. Native throughout much of the arid section of the West. Fire-resistant. Dense growth 3-6 ft., spreading to 4-8 ft. Narrow gray leaves ½-2 in. long. Mass plantings, clipped and unclipped hedges. Space plants 4 ft. apart.

A. halimus. MEDITERRANEAN SALTBUSH. Semi-evergreen. Zones 12-24. Native to southern Europe. Fire resistant. Deep rooted, dense growing to 6 ft. and as wide. Roundish leaves, silvery gray, ½-2 in. long. Mass plantings, clipped and unclipped hedges. Space 4-6 ft. apart.

A. hymenelytra. DESERT HOLLY. Evergreen (everwhitish). Zones 3, 7-14, 18, 19. Native to deserts of southern California, western Arizona, southern Nevada, southwestern Utah. Compact shrub 1-3 ft. high with whitish branches and silvery, deeply toothed, roundish leaves, to 1½ in. long. Has the Christmas holly look — in white. Much used for decorations. Outside its native range, soil drainage must be very fast. Water heavily only during blooming period —February-May; some summer water if drainage fast. Short-lived.

A. lentiformis. QUAIL BUSH. Deciduous. Zones 7-14, 18, 19. Native to alkali wastes in California valleys and deserts and east to Nevada, Utah, and New Mexico. Densely branched, sometimes spiny shrub, 3-10 ft. high, 6-12 ft. wide. Oval, bluish gray leaves ½-2 in. long. Useful as hedge or windbreak where salt-tolerant plants are needed.

A. l. breweri. BREWER SALTBUSH. Almost evergreen. Zones 8, 9, 14-24. Native to California coast south of San Francisco Bay, inland to Riverside County. Fire resistant. Like quail bush but not spiny. Grows 5-7 ft. high, 6-8 ft. wide; can be hedge sheared. Useful gray plant on ocean front. Will grow in reclaimed marine soil. Plant 4-6 ft. apart for solid cover.

A. semibaccata. AUSTRALIAN SALTBUSH. Evergreen. Zones 8, 9, 12-24. Fire resistant. Excellent gray-green ground cover to 12 in., spreading to 1-6 ft. and more. Forms dense mat of ½-1½-in.-long leaves. Deep rooted. Plant 3 ft. apart for solid cover.

AUBRIETA deltoidea. COMMON AUBRIETA. Perennial. Zones 1-9, 14-21. Native from east Mediterranean region to Iran. Low spreading mat-forming perennial — a familiar sight in Northwest rock gardens where it is often seen in bloom in early spring, with basket-of-gold alyssum, rockcress (*Arabis*), perennial candytuft (*Iberis*), and *Phlox subulata*. Plant 2-6 in. high, 12-18 in. across. Small, gray-green leaves with a few teeth at the top. Tiny rose to deep red, pale to deep lilac, or purple flowers.

Plant in full sun except in hot sections, where light shade is recommended. After bloom shear off flowers before they set seed. Don't cut back more than half — always keep some foliage. After trimming, topdress with mixture of gritty soil and bonemeal. Sow seeds in late spring for blooms the following spring. Difficult to divide clumps; make cuttings late summer.

AUCUBA japonica. JAPANESE AUCUBA. Evergreen shrub. Zones 4-11, 14-23. Native from Himalayas to Japan. Important shrub to Western gardeners. Performs well in deep shade. Seedlings vary in leaf form and variegations; many varieties offered. The standard green-leafed aucuba grows at moderate rate to 6-10 (sometimes 15) ft. and almost as wide. Can be kept lower by pruning. A buxom shrub densely clothed with polished, dark green leaves 3-8 in. long, 1½-3 in. wide, edges toothed.

Minute, dark maroon flowers in March are followed by clusters of bright red, ¾-in. berries from October to February. Both sexes must be planted to insure fruit crop. The green-leafed varieties are: 'Longifolia' ('Salicifolia'), narrow willowlike leaves (female); 'Nana', dwarf female form to about 3 ft.; 'Serratifolia', long leaves coarsely toothed edges (female).

The variegated-leafed varieties (usually slower growing) are: 'Crotonifolia' (male), leaves heavily spotted or splashed with white and gold; 'Fructo-albo' (female), leaves variegated with white, berries pale pinkish buff; 'Picturata' ('Aureo-maculata') (female), leaves centered with golden yellow, edged with dark green dotted yellow; 'Sulphur', green leaves with broad yellow edge; 'Variegata', or gold dust plant (male or female), dark green leaves spotted with yellow (best known aucuba).

Tolerant of wide range of soil, but will grow better and look better if poor or heavy soils are improved. Needs ample water. Requires shade from hot sun; accepts deep shade. Gets mealybug, scale insects. Keep leaves clean with frequent water spray. Prune to control height or form by cutting back to a leaf joint (node).

All aucubas make choice tub plants for shady patios or in the house. Use variegated forms to light up dark corners. Associate with ferns, hydrangeas.

AURICULA. See Primula auricula

AVOCADO. Evergreen tree. Two races of avocados are grown in California — Mexican and Guatemalan. (Widely planted 'Fuerte' is thought to be a hybrid of the two.) Guatemalan varieties find ideal climate protected from direct wind in Zones 19, 21, 23, and 24. Mexican varieties — smaller and less attractive fruits — are hardier and grow in Zones 9, 16-24. Although avocados are hardy to 20°-24°, flowers form in win-

ter and temperatures much below freezing destroy the crop.

Avocados tend to bear crops in cycles, producing a heavy crop one year and a light one the next. (The light crop is generally enough for the home owner.) Consistent bearing varieties are noted below.

When using in landscape, remember that most varieties will grow to 30 ft., and spread wider (tree size can be controlled by pruning). Tree should have best of protection from winds. It drops leaves quite heavily all year. The wide-spreading branches with heavy foliage make dense shade beneath — a good garden area for potted plants that need shade. St. Augustine grass will grow beneath avocado trees.

The all-important factor in growing avocados is good drainage. A high water table in the winter rainy season is often fatal, even in well drained soils. Build a wide basin for watering, let fallen leaves build up there to provide a mulch. Most of the roots are in the top 2 ft. of soil. So water lightly and frequently enough to keep that layer moist but not wet (fast drainage is important). Give a heavy irrigation every third or fourth time to wash out any excess accumulated salts. This will minimize salt burn. Fertilize lightly. Control chlorosis with iron sulfate or iron chelate.

Fruits of all varieties on the following list have thin, pliable, smooth skin—except those otherwise noted.

'Bacon'. Mexican. Zones 19-24. Upright grower. Medium-sized green fruit of good quality, November-March. Regular annual crop. Produces when young.

'Duke'. Mexican. Zones 16-22. Large tree. Medium to large green fruit, September-November.

'Fuerte'. Hybrid. Zones 20-24. Large tree; the best known avocado. Early flowers subject to frost in borderline areas. Medium green fruit of high quality, November-June.

'Hass'. Guatemalan. Zones 21, 23, 24. Large spreading tree. Medium to large dark purple (almost black) fruit, April-October. Pebbly skin, thick but pliable.

'Jalna'. Mexican. Zones 9, 16-24. One of the hardiest. Upright, vigorous tree. Consistent, heavy bearer. Medium-sized green fruit, November-December.

'Mexicola'. Mexican. Zones 9, 16-22. A good garden avocado but fruit too small for commercial market. Probably the hardiest. Consistent bearer of small, dark purple fruit with thin, tender skin, and outstanding nutty flavor, August-October.

'Rincon'. Guatemalan. Zones 19-24. Low-growing tree. Small, green fruit with large seed. Ripens January-April. Smooth skin, medium-thick, pliable.

'Zutano'. Mexican. Zone 9, 19-24. Upright grower. Pear-shaped fruits, 'Fuerte' size, green, good quality, October-February. In southern California, tends to get "end spot" (brown scaly area at tip of fruit).

AZALEA. See Rhododendron

AZALEA, WESTERN. See Rhododendron occidentale

AZARA. Evergreen shrub. Most appreciated in Zones 15-17. Best known species is *A. microphylla*. Its flat branching habit, and neatly arranged leaves make it a natural for espaliers or as free-standing silhouettes against walls. The other two species are quite different. But all three have sweetly fragrant yellow flowers that smell like chocolate to some, vanilla to others.

All azaras need protection from hot afternoon sun. All need fast-draining soil, ample water, and regular fertilizing.

Boxleaf azara is especially effective as silhouette against wall or frame.

A. lanceolata. LANCELEAF AZARA. Zones 15-17. Large spreading shrub to 20 ft. Equal to *A. microphylla* in pattern value but with much larger leaves, more lush effect. Leaves, mostly 2½ in. long, rather narrow. Foliage bright yellowish green. April flowers pale yellow, in short clusters.

A. microphylla. BOXLEAF AZARA. Zones 7-9, 14-24. Slow growing when small, fast when established; to 12-18 ft., spreading 8-12 ft. When old, treelike to 30 ft.

Arching branches spread fanlike to give a definite two-dimensional effect. May become leggy and awkward unless controlled by tipping young branches. Shiny dark green leaves, roundish, ½-¾ in. long. Flowers yellow, fragrant, in short clusters in February to March.

A. petiolaris (*A. gilliesii*). Zones 15-17. Large shrub to 15-20 ft., but easily trained into a single-stemmed tree. Deep green, lustrous, oval to roundish leaves, 1½-3 in. long, look somewhat like holly leaves and hang from the branches like aspen. Nodding, 1-in.-long clusters of bright yellow, tiny flowers February-March.

BABIANA. BABOON FLOWER. Corm. Half-hardy; outdoors in Zones 4-24. Native to South Africa. Spikes of freesialike flowers in blue, lavender, red, cream, and white; bloom in May and June. Leaves are strongly ribbed, usually hairy, set edgewise to stem. Full sun or very light shade. Plant corms 4 in. deep, 3 in. apart. Plant along border edge, paths, in rock gardens; also in deep pots. Ample water during growth, less after leaves turn yellow. In mild climates leave in ground several years, but never in cold, wet, heavy ground. In coldest areas, lift, store corms like gladiolus.

B. plicata. Spikes to 6 in. with lavender, white-marked flowers, carnation-scented.

B. stricta. Very attractive. Royal blue flowers on 1 ft. stems. Leaves 6 in. high. Varieties in blue and red, pale yellow, white, and blue and white.

BABOON FLOWER. See Babiana

BABY-BLUE-EYES. See Nemophila menziesii

BABY'S BREATH. See Gypsophila paniculata

BABY'S TEARS. See Soleirolia

BACCHARIS pilularis. DWARF COYOTE BRUSH, DWARF CHAPARRAL BROOM. Evergreen shrub. Zones 7-24. Native to California coast, Sonoma to Monterey counties. Remarkable climate and soil adaptation. Thriving in almost swampy situation or

without summer water along coast. Most dependable of all ground covers in California's high desert.

Makes a dense, rather billowy mat of bright green, 8-24 in. high and spreading to 6 ft. or more. The small, ½-in., toothed leaves are closely set on the many branches. A very valuable, very dependable bank cover for minimum maintenance areas. Needs pruning once a year before new growth starts. Cut out old arching branches, and thin to rejuvenate. Flowers are of no interest, male and female borne on different plants. Female plants produce cottony seeds which can make a mess as they blow about. Plants available in most nurseries are cutting-grown from male plants.

BACHELOR'S BUTTON. See Centaurea cyanus

BACULARIA. See Linospadix

BALLOON FLOWER. See Platycodon

BALM, LEMON. See Melissa

BALM, SWEET. See Melissa

BALM OF GILEAD. See Populus candicans

BALSAM. See Impatiens balsamina

BAMBOO. Giant grasses with woody stems divided into sections called internodes by obvious joints called nodes. Upper nodes produce buds which develop into branches; these, in the larger bamboos, divide into secondary branches which bear the leaves. Bamboos spread by underground stems (rhizomes) which, like the above-ground stems, are jointed and carry buds. The manner in which the rhizomes grow explains the difference between the running and the clump bamboos.

BAMBOO

NAME	SYNONYMS	CONTROLLED HEIGHT (UNCONTROLLED HEIGHT)	STEM DIAMETER	HARDI-NESS	GROWTH HABIT (I, II, III, IV —SEE TEXT, END OF CHART). CHARACTERISTICS AND USES
ARUNDINARIA variegata DWARF WHITESTRIPE BAMBOO	*Sasa variegata*	1-2 ft. (2-3 ft.) Running	¼ in.	0°	I. Fast spreader. Curb the rhizomes. Use in tubs or as deep ground cover.
BAMBUSA beecheyana BEECHEY BAMBOO	*Sinocalamus beecheyanus*	12-20 ft. (20-40 ft.) Clump	4 in.	20°	IV. Stems arch strongly, giving a broad, graceful head. Scarce.
B. multiplex HEDGE BAMBOO	*B. argentea*	8-10 ft. (15-25 ft.) Clump	1½ in.	15°	II. Branches from base to top. Many branches at nodes. Dense.
B. m. 'Alphonse Karr'	*B. verticillata*	10-15 ft. (15-30 ft.) Clump	½-¾ in.	15°	II. Young stem sheaths striped pink and green, stems yellow, with green stripes of varying width. Handsome.
B. m. 'Fernleaf' FERNLEAF HEDGE BAMBOO	*B. nana B. disticha B. falcata*	6-10 ft. (10-20 ft.) Clump	½ in.	15°	II. Solid stem. Closely spaced leaves, 10-20 to a twig. Loses ferny quality with rich soil, ample water, or unrestrained root room.

(Continued on next page)

B

NAME	SYNONYMS	CONTROLLED HEIGHT (UNCONTROLLED HEIGHT)	STEM DIAMETER	HARDINESS	GROWTH HABIT (I, II, III, IV —SEE TEXT, END OF CHART). CHARACTERISTICS AND USES
B. m. 'Golden Goddess'		6-8 ft. (6-10 ft.) Clump	½ in.	15°	II. Graceful dense growth. Larger leaves than above. Needs width to show off grace.
B. m. riviereorum CHINESE GODDESS BAMBOO	*B. argentea nana, Pleioblastus distichus*	4-6 ft. (5-8 ft.) Clump	½ in.	15°	II. Solid stems. Graceful growth and predictably dwarf in habit. Tiny leaves in ferny sprays.
B. m. 'Stripestem Fernleaf'		10-15 ft. (25-30 ft.) Clump	½ in.	15°	II. Solid stems like 'Fernleaf' but with more green stripes on stems and more upright and vigorous. Scarce.
B. oldhamii OLDHAM BAMBOO, CLUMP GIANT TIMBER BAMBOO	*Sinocalamus oldhamii.* Often sold as *Dendrocalamus latiflorus*	15-25 ft. (20-40 ft.) Clump	3 in.	20°	IV. Densely foliaged, erect clumps make it good plant for big, dense screens. Or use single plant for mass.
B. tuldoides PUNTING POLE BAMBOO	Sometimes sold as *B. thouarsii*	15-20 ft. (20-40 ft.) Clump	2 in.	20°	IV. Prolific producer of slender erect stems. Best as a single specimen. Scarce.
B. ventricosa BUDDHA'S BELLY BAMBOO		3-6 ft. (15-30 ft.) Clump	2 in.	20°	II-IV. Produces swollen internodes that give it its name only when confined in tubs or grown in poor, dryish soil. Otherwise a giant bamboo with straight internodes.
CHIMONOBAMBUSA marmorea MARBLED BAMBOO	*Arundinaria marmorea.* Sometimes sold as "dwarf black bamboo"	2-4 ft. (4-6 ft.) Running	¼ in.	20°	III. New stem sheaths marbled cream and purplish; older stems nearly black. Densely leafy. First-class hedge plant if rhizomes curbed.
C. quadrangularis SQUARE-STEM BAMBOO	*Bambusa quadrangularis*	10-15 ft. (15-20 ft.) Running	1½ in.	20°	III. Handsome, erect, squarish stems; very prominent nodes. Dense foliage.
PHYLLOSTACHYS aurea GOLDEN BAMBOO		6-10 ft. (10-20 ft.) Running	2 in.	0°	III. Erect, stiff stems, usually with crowded nodes near base—a good identifying mark. Dense foliage. Needs frequent watering to keep foliage attractive, but takes some drought. Good in tubs.
P. aureosulcata YELLOW GROOVE BAMBOO		12-15 ft. (15-25 ft.) Running	1½ in.	—20°	III. Like a more slender, more open golden bamboo. Young stems green, showing a pronounced yellowish groove. Hardiest bamboo.
P. bambusoides GIANT TIMBER BAMBOO, JAPANESE TIMBER BAMBOO	*P. reticulata*	15-35 ft. (25-45 ft.) Running	6 in.	0°	IV. Commonest of the large, hardy timber bamboos. Keep thinned for grove effect. Clean small branches from lower part of stems to show their beauty.
P. b. 'Castillon'		10-15 ft. (15-20 ft.) Running	2 in.	0°	III. Bright yellow stems marked with bright green vertical bands above each branch cluster. Many plants have flowers, a problem. See text.
P. meyeri		10-20 ft. (20-30 ft.) Running	2 in.	0°	III. Resembles golden bamboo, but lacks crowded basal internodes.
P. nigra BLACK BAMBOO		4-8 ft. (10-15 ft.) Running	1½ in.	5°	III. Stems vary from pure black to olive dotted black. Does best in afternoon shade where summers are hot.

NAME	SYNONYMS	CONTROLLED HEIGHT (UNCONTROLLED HEIGHT)	STEM DIAMETER	HARDI-NESS	GROWTH HABIT (I, II, III, IV —SEE TEXT, END OF CHART). CHARACTERISTICS AND USES
P. pubescens MOSO BAMBOO	*P. edulis*	20-40 ft. (40-60 ft.) Running	8 in.	5°	IV. Largest of the running timber bamboos. Gray-green, heavy stems; small, feathery leaves.
P. viridis	*P. mitis,* *P. sulphurea* *viridis*	15-20 ft. (20-30 ft.) Running	1 in.	—10°	IV. More plentiful in Northwest than in California. Beautiful curving stem with ferny growth at base. Used in containers in entryways.
P. v. 'Robert Young'		15-20 ft. (20-30 ft.) Running	2 in.	—10°	IV. Growth less arching, more stiff. Yellow stems have green stripes and a green ring at each node.
PSEUDOSASA japonica METAKE, ARROW BAMBOO	*Arundinaria* *japonica*	6-10 ft. (10-20 ft.) Running	³/₄ in.	0°	III. Stiffly erect stems bear one branch at each node. Leaves large, with long, tail-like point. Rampant thick hedge; good on hillsides for erosion control.
SASA disticha DWARF FERNLEAF BAMBOO	*Pleioblastus* *distichus*	1-2 ft. (2-3 ft.) Running	¹/₈ in.	10°	I. Delicate in appearance. Tiny, two-ranked, ferny leaves. Rampant, cut back to ground when too stemmy or woody.
S. humilis LOW BAMBOO		1-3 ft. Running	¹/₈ in.	0°	I. Graceful, arching stems. Aggressive. Good erosion control.
S. palmata PALMATE BAMBOO	*Sasa senanensis,* *Sasa paniculata*	4-5 ft. (8-12 ft.) Running	³/₈ in.	0°	In a class by itself. Grow bigger in Zones 4-6, and 15-17 than in 18-24. Broad, handsome leaves (to 15 in. long by 4 in. wide) spread finger-like from stem and branch tips. Most unbamboolike appearance. Rampant spreader.
S. pygmaea DWARF BAMBOO	*Pleioblastus* *viridi-striatus* *vagans*	¹/₂-1 ft. (1-1¹/₂ ft.) Running	¹/₈ in.	**0°**	I. Aggressive spreader. Semi-deciduous in cold winters. Naturalizes. Good erosion control.
S. p. 'Variegated' VARIEGATED DWARF BAMBOO		¹/₂-1 ft. (1-1¹/₂ ft.) Running	¹/₈ in.	0°	I. Foliage variegated with white. Same growth characteristics as *S. pygmaea.*

In running bamboos, the underground stems grow rapidly to varying distances from the parent plant before giving rise to new vertical stems. These bamboos eventually form groves of considerable size unless the rhizomes are curbed.

In clump bamboos the underground stems make very little horizontal growth. Although the plant expands in diameter, it does so slowly and makes a tight clump, not a grove.

Plant bamboos from containers at any time of the year. Best time to divide clump bamboos is in spring when side stems are 6-12 in. tall and starting to make obviously fast growth. Cut or saw out at least three stems with attached roots. Divide running kinds early spring to late fall. There's less wilting in early spring or late fall.

Don't expect bamboos to grow phenomenally fast the first year after planting. Giant timber bamboo, for example, needs 3-5 years to build up a root system capable of producing 3-in. stems that push up several feet a day. The thickness of stem never exceeds that of shoot as it breaks through

the soil. First year's stems of the giants may be less than ½ in. thick, 6 ft. tall.

Disregard rule of never buying root-bound plant in case of bamboo. The more crowded it is in the container, the faster its growth when planted out. Running and clump types grow equally well when roots are confined. Spread of running kinds can

be controlled by planting in boxes, above or in the ground. In large areas, control with soil barriers of 18-in.-deep strips of galvanized sheet metal or poured concrete. You can limit lateral spread by running a spade to its full depth around the circumference of the clump. New shoots are tender, break off easily, and do not resprout.

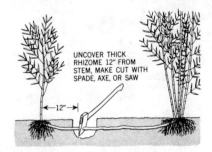

To divide running bamboo, cut rhizome, dig plant with ball of soil around roots.

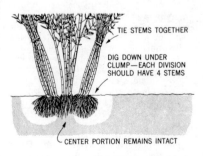

Clump bamboo: tie stems together, sever roots with axe or spade, dig divisions.

Climate Zone maps pages 8-27

If you want fast growth, treat these giant grasses as lawn grass, watering once a week and feeding once a month. Roots will not grow into dry soil or into water. To restrain growth, confine roots, keep on dry side, don't feed. As you can see in the accompanying chart, each bamboo has two height ranges, depending on how it is grown.

The chart classes each bamboo by habit of growth, which, of course, determines its use in the garden. In Group I are the dwarf or low-growing ground cover types.

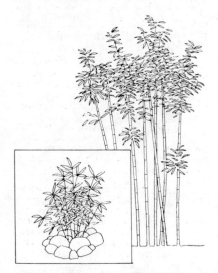

Timber bamboos can reach to 72 ft. Dwarf kinds (shown in inset) grow 1-3 ft. tall.

These can be used for erosion control or (carefully confined in a length of flue tile) as small clumps for border or rock garden. Group II includes clump bamboos with a fountainlike habit of growth. These have the widest use in landscaping. They require no more space than average strong-growing shrub. Clipped, they make hedges or screens that won't spread much into surrounding soil; unclipped, they may be lined up as informal screens or grown singly to show off their graceful form.

Bamboos in Group III are running bamboos of moderate size and more or less vertical growth. Use them as screens, hedges, or (curbed) alone. Group IV includes the giants. Use the running kinds for groves, Oriental effects on grand scale. Clumping kinds have a tropical look, especially if used with broad-leafed tropical plants. All may be thinned and clipped to show off stems. Thin clumps or groves by cutting out old or dead stems at the base.

Bamboo seldom flowers. Some species have never bloomed in cultivation, and others are on a 30-60-year cycle. When they bloom they die or are set back drastically. Castillon bamboo has flowered in a number of Western gardens. In most cases it recovers and regains its vigor in 3-5 years if watered and fertilized.

Not recommended for year-round indoor culture, but container-grown plants can spend extended periods indoors in cool, bright rooms. Revive plants by taking them outdoors, but avoid too-sudden changes in temperature, light.

BAMBOO, HEAVENLY. See Nandina

BAMBOO, SACRED. See Nandina

BAMBURANTA. See Ctenanthe, Hybophrynium

BAMBUSA. See Bamboo

BANANA. See Musa, Ensete

BANANA SHRUB. See Michelia figo

BANYAN, WEEPING CHINESE. See Ficus benjamina

BAPTISIA australis. FALSE INDIGO, WILD INDIGO. Perennial. All Zones. Native to eastern and southern U.S. Somewhat like bush lupine in habit, 3-6 ft. tall, with bluish-green, deeply cut leaves. Spikes of small, indigo blue, sweet pea-shaped blooms in early summer, followed by inflated seed pods — both interesting in arrangements. Full sun, ordinary soil. Tap-rooted, stands drought. Cut back spent flowers for repeat bloom. Specialists carry seed.

BARBADOS PRIDE. See Poinciana pulcherrima

BARBERRY. See Berberis

BASEBALL PLANT. See Euphorbia obesa

BASIL. See Ocimum

BASKET FLOWER. See Hymenocallis calathina

BASKET-OF-GOLD. See Alyssum saxatile

BASSWOOD. See Tilia americana

BAUHINIA. Evergreen or deciduous trees or half-climbing shrubs. These flamboyant flowering plants have a very special place in Hawaii, mild-winter areas of California, and Arizona. They vary greatly by species and climate vagaries. Common to all bauhinias are the twin "leaves" (actually twin lobes).

B. blakeana. HONG KONG ORCHID TREE. Partially deciduous for short period. Zones 19, 21, 23. Native to southern China. Its flowers, shaped like some orchids, range from cranberry maroon through rose, purple, to orchid pink, often in the same blossoms. They are much larger (5½-6 in. wide) than those of the other bauhinias; unlike the others, they appear in autumn and early winter. Gray-green leaves tend to drop off around bloom time but not completely. Umbrella type growth habit, to 20 ft.

B. forficata. (Often sold as *B. corniculata* or *B. candicans.*) Evergreen to deciduous large shrub or tree. Zones 9, 13-23. Native to Brazil. Probably hardiest bauhinia. Creamy white flowers to 3 in. wide, with narrow petals in spring and through the summer. Deep green leaves, more pointed lobes than others. Grows to 20 ft., often with twisting, leaning trunk, picturesque angled branches. Short sharp thorns at branch joints. Good canopy patio tree.

B. galpinii. RED BAUHINIA. Evergreen to semi-deciduous shrub. Zones 13, 18-23. Native to South and tropical Africa. Brick red to orange flowers, spectacular as bougainvillea where adapted. Sprawling, half-climbing with a 15-ft. spread. Best as espalier on a warm wall.

B. variegata. (Commonly sold as *B. purpurea.*) PURPLE ORCHID TREE. Partially to wholly deciduous. Zones 13, 18-23. Native

to India, China. Most frequently planted. Hardy to 22°. Spectacular street trees where spring weather is warm and stays warm. Wonderful show of light pink to orchid purple, broad petaled, 2-3-in.-wide flowers usually January to April. Light green, broadly lobed leaves generally drop in midwinter. Inclined to grow as a shrub with multiple stems. Staked and pruned it becomes an attractive tree 20-35 ft. high.

B. v. candida. WHITE ORCHID TREE. Has white flowers.

BAY, CALIFORNIA. See Umbellularia

BAY, SWEET. See Laurus

BAYBERRY. See Myrica pensylvanica

BEAD PLANT. See Nertera

BEAN, BROAD. Also called "fava" or "horse bean". This bean was known in ancient and medieval times; it is a Mediterranean plant, while all other beans are New World plants. It is an annual of bushy growth to 2-4 ft. You can cook and eat immature pods like sugar-podded peas; prepare immature and mature seeds the same way as green or dry limas.

Unlike the true beans, this is a cool-season plant. In cold-winter areas plant as early in spring as soil can be worked. In mild coastal climates, plant in fall for late winter or early spring ripening. Matures in 120-150 days, depending on temperature. Plant seeds 1 in. deep at 4-5-in. intervals, and thin to 8-10 in. apart in rows. Space rows 18-30 in. apart. Spray or dust for aphids.

BEAN, DRY. Same culture as bush form of snap bean. Let beans remain on bush until pods turn dry or begin to shatter, thresh them from hulls, dry, store to be soaked and cooked later. 'Pinto', 'Red Kidney', and 'White Marrowfat' are this kind.

BEAN, HYACINTH. See Dolichos lablab

BEAN, LIMA. Like snap or string beans, limas come either in bush or vine (pole) form. They develop slower than string beans, the bush types requiring 65-75 days, the pole kinds 78-95 days; and they do not produce as reliably in extremely dry, hot weather. They must be shelled before cooking — a tedious chore, but worth it if you like fresh limas. Among bush types 'Burpee's Improved Bush', 'Henderson Bush', and 'Fordhook 242' are outstanding; the last two are especially useful in hot-summer areas. 'Prizetaker' and 'King of the Garden' are fine large-seeded climbing forms; 'Small White Lima' or 'Sieva' is usually grown for drying, but it gives heavy yields of green shelled beans. Culture is same as for snap beans.

BEAN, SCARLET RUNNER. Annual twining vine. Showy and ornamental with bright scarlet flowers in slender clusters, and with bright green leaves divided into 3 roundish, 3-5-in.-long leaflets. Use to cover fences, arbors, outbuildings; for quick shade on porches, summer cottages.

Flowers are followed by flattened, very dark green pods which are edible and tasty when young, but which toughen as they reach full size. Beans can be shelled from older pods for cooking like green limas. Culture is same as for snap beans.

BEAN, SNAP. The snap (or string, or green) bean is the most widely planted and most useful for home gardens of all the kinds of beans. These have tender, fleshy pods with little fiber. They may be green, yellow (wax beans), or purple ('Blue Coco', 'Royalty'). The purple kinds turn green in cooking. The plants grow as self-supporting bushes or as climbing vines (pole beans). Bush types bear earlier, but vines are more productive. Varieties are too numerous to discuss.

Plant seeds as soon as the soil is warm, in full sun and good soil. These seeds must push heavy seed-leaves through the soil, so see that it is reasonably loose and open. Plant seeds of bush types an inch deep and 1-3 in. apart in rows, with 2-3 ft. between rows. Pole beans can be managed in a number of ways: 3 or 4 poles can be set in the ground and tied together at the top in wigwam fashion; or set single poles 3 or 4 ft. apart and sow 6 or 8 beans around each, thinning to the 3 or 4 strongest seedlings; or insert poles 1 or 2 ft. apart in rows and sow seeds as you would bush beans; or sow along a sunny wall, fence, or trellis and train the vines on a web of light string supported by wire or heavy twine. Moisten ground thoroughly before planting; do not water again until seedlings have emerged.

Once growth starts, keep soil moist. Occasional deep soaking is preferable to frequent light sprinklings which may encourage mildew. Feed after plants are in active growth and again when pods start to form. Pods are ready in 50-70 days, according to variety. Pick every 5-7 days; if pods mature the plants will stop bearing. Control aphids and diabrotica (spotted cucumber beetle) with rotenone or an all-purpose vegetable garden dust. Check whiteflies with a malathion spray, following precautions on the label concerning harvest date.

BEARBERRY. See Arctostaphylos uva-ursi

BEARD TONGUE. See Penstemon

BEAR'S BREECH. See Acanthus

BEAUFORTIA sparsa. GRAVEL BOTTLE-BRUSH. Evergreen shrub. Zones 17, 19-24. Native to Western Australia. Very open, almost gaunt habit of growth to 4-8 ft. tall. Leaves small, narrow ovals of dark green. Bottlebrush-shaped clusters of long-stamened brilliant salmon scarlet flowers appear from time to time following spurts of new growth. Worthwhile for its color in garden situations where its gawkiness will not be too obtrusive when it is out of bloom. Best in full sun, constant moisture but no standing water.

BEAUMONTIA grandiflora. HERALD'S TRUMPET, EASTER LILY VINE. Evergreen vine. Zones 13, 21-24. Climbs by arching, semi-twining branches to as much as 30 ft., and spreads as wide. Large, dark green, 6-9-in., oval to roundish leaves, smooth and shiny above, slightly downy beneath, furnish a lush tropical look. From April until September it carries fragrant, trumpet-shaped, 5-in.-long, white, green-veined flowers which look like Easter lilies.

Needs deep, rich soil, ample water, and heavy feeding. Prune after flowering to keep it in scale, but preserve a good proportion of 2 and 3-year-old wood. Flowers are not borne on new growth. Makes a big espalier on a warm wall, sheltered from wind. Or train along eaves of house; give it a sturdy support. Hardy to 28°.

BEAUTY BERRY. See Callicarpa.

BEAUTY BUSH. See Kolkwitzia

BEE BALM. See Monarda

BEECH. See Fagus

BEEFWOOD. See Casuarina

BEET. As early in spring as possible, plant a 10-ft. row in soil that won't crust and that doesn't contain rocks, keep soil moist, and in some 60 days you'll get 50 delicious, tender, small beets (tenderest at 1½-2 in. diameter). Meanwhile, when plants are 5 in. high, begin pulling out excess so that by the time the remaining plants are 60 days old (harvest time) they will be 4 in. apart. The thinnings (tiny beets and the tops) can be cooked as very good greens. If you follow up with similar plantings every week or two, you can extend the harvest season. In hot-summer areas, do not plant in late spring or summer. Best varieties are the early 'Crosby's Egyptian' and the large 'Detroit Dark Red'.

BEGONIA. Perennials, a few becoming shrubby, a few others treated as annuals. Tuberous, rhizomatous, or fibrous-rooted. Native to moist tropical countries and good anywhere as indoor, or cool or warm greenhouse plants. Some adapted to outdoor use as indicated below, generally best in cool summer climates near the sea.

All kinds generally best in filtered shade with rich, porous, fast-draining, slightly acid soil, perfect drainage, ample moisture, consistent feeding.

There are hundreds of begonia species and varieties; there is also a special language for describing and classifying them. Here is a brief dictionary of kinds and terms.

Angel-wing begonias. Many cane-stemmed kinds are called angel-wing begonias because leaves, having one lobe at stem end higher than the other, resemble wings in flight.

Cane-stemmed begonias. Fibrous-rooted begonias with jointed stems having prominent bamboolike joints. Plants erect or spreading, some vinelike. Includes angel-wing begonias.

B. 'Corallina de Lucerna' ('Lucerna'). Tall, sturdy angel-wing begonia with silver-spotted leaves (red underneath) and big clusters of coral flowers.

B. digswelliana. Fibrous-rooted begonia of open, erect growth to 2 ft. Reddish stems; leaves fleshy, glossy dark green. Drooping clusters of rosy scarlet flowers fading almost to white in deep shade.

Elatior begonias. House plants. Strain resulting from crossing tuberous begonias with a winter-blooming bulbous begonia. Flowers are smaller (2 in. wide) than those of tuberous begonias, far more numerous, appear over a long season, mostly in winter (but florists can force bloom at any season). Single ('Schwabenland') kinds come in red, red-orange, and pink on upright plants. Double ('Aphrodite') kinds are red, rose, or pink and plants are sprawly. The related 'Bernsteins Gelbe' has single yellow flowers.

Give plenty of light in winter (but not hot sunlight); in summer put plants where they won't be exposed to hot noonday sun. Water thoroughly when top inch of soil dries out. Keep water off leaves. Cut back to 4-in. stubs when plants get rangy.

B. 'Erythrophylla' (B. 'Feastii'). BEEF-STEAK BEGONIA. Easy-to-grow rhizomatous begonia. Masses of thick, juicy, round 2-3-in. leaves, dark green above, deep red underneath. Showers of pink blooms on stems that top the leaves. Fine house plant.

Fibrous-rooted begonias. Begonias that grow from masses of fibrous roots rather than from bulbs, tubers, or rhizomes. Includes many species and hybrids, most of them easy to grow.

B. fuchsioides. Fibrous-rooted, shrubby-stemmed begonia 2-5 ft. tall with erect stems arching at tips. Profusion of small, shiny bright green leaves and drooping clusters of ½-¾-in. flowers of pink or red.

House plant or indoor-outdoor plant. Used for hedges in its native Mexico.

B. masoniana. IRON CROSS BEGONIA. Rhizomatous begonia with big, rough, chartreuse-green leaves centered with a brown replica of a Maltese or German iron cross. White flowers with dark bristles less important than hand-sized leaves.

B. 'Pink Rubra' ('Pink Shasta'). Cane-stem begonia with bright green, smooth angel-wing leaves and slender stems. Arching or vining in growth; makes a good trellis or hanging basket plant. Nearly continuous production of big pure pink flower clusters.

B. rex-cultorum. REX BEGONIA. Outdoors in Zones 23, 24; greenhouse or indoor plant anywhere. Many named varieties with magnificently colored shieldlike leaves available from specialists. Selected seedlings may be nearly as good as plants propagated by leaf cuttings. Leaf colors include maroon, lilac, rose, light and dark green, silvery gray, and any combinations of these. See Rhizomatous begonias for culture.

Rhizomatous begonias. Begonias that form a rhizome—a thick, short stem, usually creeping, sometimes underground.

Don't overwater or overfeed; the rhizome is a sort of emergency canteen that takes plants through adversity. Give good light (but not hot sun) in winter, filtered shade in summer. Some kinds go nearly dormant in winter; keep these on the dry side until new growth resumes.

B. 'Richmondensis.' Fibrous-rooted begonia to 2 ft. or more with arching stems, crisp-looking shiny leaves, deep green above, red beneath. Salmon pink flowers from darker buds give a two-tone effect. Filtered shade or considerable sun where

B

*Climate
Zone maps
pages 8-27*

summers are cool; more colorful in sun. Big and sturdy enough to plant outdoors (outdoor-indoor plant where frosts are severe). Excellent hanging basket plant.

B. semperflorens. BEDDING BEGONIA. Also called wax begonia. Many varieties; ranks among the most useful and free-flowering plants for summer and fall color in Western gardens. Often grown as annuals in colder areas. Dwarf (4-6 in.), intermediate (8-10 in.), and tall (12-18 in.) varieties. Leaves bright green, bronzy, or reddish, often with red-tinged ribs. Flowers single or double, in white, red, rose, or pink shades, borne in clusters among the leaves. Bloom early summer to fall, almost all year in mild winters. Thrive in full sun along coast; shade in interior but can take sun if well watered. Varieties with darker colored leaves and flowers take sun best. Splendid for mass planting, edgings, containers.

Calla lily begonias are a special kind of *B. semperflorens* characterized by having some leaves heavily variegated with white; occasional leaves or shoots are completely white. There are many varieties, all rather delicate and used as house plants. Give them cool, bright, humid conditions and avoid overwatering.

B. tuberhybrida. TUBEROUS BEGONIA. These are the well-known tuberous begonias widely grown in Western gardens for summer and fall flowers. Growth habit varies from upright and little branching to low-branching and spreading. The variety 'Pendula' has graceful pendulous branches. Flowers of tuberous begonias have always been spectacular, but those of modern varieties are remarkable for size, beauty, and diversity of color and form, firm substance, elegant texture. Mostly double, with plain, ruffled, or frilled petals, some with contrasting colors on edges. Flower forms usually designated in catalogs as ruffled, rose, picotee, and carnation-flowered. Colors include practically every shade of pink, red, rose, orange, yellow, salmon; also white. Cut flowers keep well, may be floated in bowls of water, or worn as corsages.

Start from tubers, seed, or nursery transplants. To start tubers, place them (when pink buds show) in flats of coarse leaf mold, ground bark, or similar material. Cover tubers with ½ in. of the material—encourage roots over entire surface. Place flat in well-lighted area, not in direct sunlight; keep rooting mixture damp, not wet. When tubers have produced 2 leaves, pot plants; set out in garden after frosts are past.

Seed is extremely fine; sow thinly and evenly on finely screened leaf mold, ground bark, peat moss, or sphagnum moss. Do not cover. Water with mist spray or by soaking container from below. Cover seed container with glass or plastic to maintain humidity. When seedlings appear, admit air, but take care not to let dry out. Transplant into another flat in about 8 weeks. Set out plants when weather has warmed.

Plant in partial shade; shelter from wind. Mix existing soil with ½ ground bark, leaf mold, or peat moss; or plant in pure leaves, leaf mold, or ground bark. When potting, allow 2 in. between sides of tuber and pot;

put 2-in.-wide tuber in 6-in. pot. Large tubers may need 12-in. pot.

Water regularly, but do not let soil get soggy. In warm dry areas, spray overhead with fog nozzle to cool and humidify air. Feed monthly with complete fertilizer when plants are few inches high; stop 6 weeks before anticipated first frost. Withhold water when leaves start to turn yellow. After foliage is completely yellow, dig tubers, wash off soil, remove stems, cure tubers in sun for several days. Store in cool, dry, frost-free place until time to start growth again.

Control snails and slugs. Control mildew on leaves with one of the fungicides on page 63.

Multiflora begonias. The plants grow bushy, compact, 12-18 in. tall. Profusely covered all summer with single or semi-double flowers in carmine, scarlet, orange, yellow, apricot, salmon, and pink. Unsurpassed for mass color in garden beds, as edgings, in pots, window boxes, raised beds. More sun, less water than most begonias.

BEILSCHMIEDIA miersii (*Cryptocarya miersii*). Evergreen tree. Zones 14-17, 20-24. Native to Chile. Moderate growth to 30-40 ft.; crown eventually dense, giving deep shade. Leaves roundish, 2-3 in. long, thin-textured, shining dark green above with prominent veins beneath. New growth slightly tinged red. Beautiful mature trees occasionally seen near coast, or in coastal and intermediate valleys in California.

BELAMCANDA chinensis. BLACKBERRY LILY. Perennial with rhizome. All Zones. Common name derives from cluster of shining black seeds exposed when capsules split. Sword-shaped, irislike leaves 1 in. wide. Flowers 1½-2 in. across, orange dotted with red, on 2-3-ft. branching stems; bloom over long period in August, September. Sun or part shade. Plant rhizomes 1 in. deep in porous soil. Effective in clumps in border, as container plant. Seed capsules make unique arrangements.

BELLFLOWER. See Campanula

BELLFLOWER, CHILEAN. See Lapageria

BELLFLOWER, CHINESE. See Abutilon

BELL-FRUITED MALLEE. See Eucalyptus preissiana

BELLIS perennis. ENGLISH DAISY. Perennial, often treated as an annual. All Zones. Native to Europe and Mediterranean region. The original English daisies are the kind you often see growing in lawns. Plump, fully double ones sold in nurseries are horticultural varieties. Rosettes of dark green leaves 1-2 in. long. Pink, rose, red, or white double flowers on 3-6-in. stems, in spring, early summer. A meadow plant, needs good soil, much moisture, light shade in warm areas; full sun near coast. Edging or low bedding plant; effective with spring bulbs.

BELLS OF IRELAND. See Molucella

BELOPERONE. Evergreen or deciduous shrubs. The attention-grabbing shrimp

plant and a little-known desert native represent the beloperones in Western gardens.

Overlapping bracts, not the flowers, give shrimp plant its distinctive appearance.

B. californica. CHUPAROSA, CALIFORNIA BELOPERONE. Deciduous. Zones 10-13. Native to edges of Colorado Desert to Arizona and northern Mexico. A low gray-green shrub 2-5 ft. high, spreading to 4 ft. Arching branches appear almost leafless. Small, roundish, ¼-in. leaves. Tubular, bright red flowers, 1½ in. long in clusters, give a good show of color in April-May.

B. guttata (*B. tomentosa*). SHRIMP PLANT. Evergreen. Native to Mexico. Zones 16, 17, 21-24, and anywhere as an indoor-outdoor plant, or an annual. Will grow to a 3 by 4-ft. mound but can be kept much lower. Leaves egg-shaped, to 2½ in. long, apple green, often dropping in cold weather or in soil too wet or too dry. Tubular flowers white, spotted purple, enclosed in coppery bronze, overlapping bracts forming compact, drooping spikes 3 in. long (lengthening to 6-7 in. if allowed to remain on plant). In total, the spike formation somewhat resembles a large shrimp.

Will take sun but bracts and foliage fade unless grown in partial shade. A variety called 'Chartreuse' has spikes of chartreuse yellow which sunburn more easily than those of the coppery kind. To shape plant, pinch continuously in early growth until compact mound of foliage is obtained and then let bloom. To encourage continued bushiness, cut back stems when flower bracts turn black. Good for pot or tub, for close-up planting near terraces, patios, entryways.

BENT GRASS. See Lawn Chapter

BERBERIS. BARBERRY. Deciduous and evergreen shrubs. The evergreen forms are at their best in Zones 4-6 and 15-17. Approximate hardiness for each species, deciduous and evergreen, is given in the descriptions below. The ability of barberries, especially the deciduous species, to take punishment in climate and soil extremes makes them worth attention in all "hard" climates. Barberries require no more than ordinary garden care. Vigorous growers can take a lot of cutting back for growth renewal. Left to their own ways, some of the inner branches die and the plant becomes ratty.

In the list below, details on time of bloom, flower color, and spines are omitted unless the plant differs from the typical — yellow flowers in spring, and spiny branches.

B. buxifolia. MAGELLAN BARBERRY. Evergreen. Hardy to 0°. Rather rigid upright growth to 6 ft., and as wide. Leaves small, leathery, to 1 in. long. Flowers orange-yellow. Berries dark purple.

B. b. 'Nana'. To 1½ ft. high, and 2 ft. wide. Use as traffic regulator or where yellow bloom in an evergreen is important. (There is an even lower-growing variety, 'Pygmaea'.)

B. darwinii. DARWIN BARBERRY. Evergreen. Hardy to 10°. Showiest barberry. Fountainlike growth to 5-10 ft. high and 4-7 ft. wide. Leaves, small (1 in.), crisp, dark green, hollylike. Orange-yellow flowers are so thick along the branches that it's difficult to see the foliage. Wonderful as a background for Oregon grape *(Mahonia aquifolium)*. Spreads by underground runners.

B. gagnepainii. BLACK BARBERRY. Evergreen. Hardy to 10°. Open rangy growth to 6 ft. Leaves narrow, to 3 in. long, dark green, spiny-toothed. Berries black with blue-gray cast. Spines long and sharp. Use as rough barrier hedge.

B. irwinii *(B. stenophylla irwinii)*. Hybrid. Evergreen. Hardy to 0°. Graceful fountainlike growth habit to 18 in. high. Attractive dark green foliage of narrow 1-in.-long leaves.

B. julianae. WINTERGREEN BARBERRY. Evergreen or semi-deciduous. Hardy to 0°, but foliage burns in winter cold. Dense, upright, to 6 ft., with slightly angled branches. Very leathery, spiny-toothed, 3-in.-long, dark green leaves. Fruits bluish black. Reddish fall color. One of thorniest. Formidable as barrier hedge.

B. mentorensis. Hybrid. Evergreen to about —5°. Semi-deciduous to deciduous in colder weather. Hardy to —20°. Stands hot, dry weather. Rather compact growth to 7 ft. and as wide. Easy to maintain as hedge at any height. Leaves dark green, 1 in. long. Berries dull dark red.

B. sargentiana. SARGENT BARBERRY. Hardy to 5°. A 6-ft.-high evergreen. Dark green, 4-in.-long, spiny-toothed leaves. Flowers in clusters followed by black fruits. Long spines.

B. stenophylla. ROSEMARY BARBERRY. Evergreen. Hybrid. Hardy to 0°. Grows 3-9 ft. high with slender arching branches. Leaves rather narrow, ½-1 in. long, with inrolled edges and spiny tip, dark green above, pale beneath. Flowers in nodding clusters. Fruit black. Among the named varieties selected for grace and flower display are:

B. s. 'Corallina Compacta'. CORAL BARBERRY. An 18-in. dwarf. Orange flowers. Useful in foreground plantings, rock gardens, or as low space divider.

B. s. 'Gracilis'. Fountainlike growth to 3-4 ft.

B. thunbergii. JAPANESE BARBERRY. Deciduous. Hardy to —20°. Graceful growth habit with slender, arching, spiny branches, usually to 4-6 ft. tall with an equal spread. if not sheared. Densely foliaged with roundish, ½-1½-in.-long leaves, deep green above, paler beneath, turning to yellow, orange,

and red before they fall. Beadlike, bright red berries stud branches in fall and through winter. Hedge, barrier planting, or single shrub.

B. t. 'Atropurpurea'. RED-LEAF JAPANESE BARBERRY. Foliage bronzy red to purplish red all summer. Must have sun to develop color.

B. t. 'Crimson Pygmy' (*B. t.* 'Atropurpurea Nana'). Hardy to 0°. Selected miniature form, generally less than 1½ ft. high and 2½ ft. wide as 10-yr.-old. Mature leaves bronzy blood red, new leaves bright red. Must have sun to develop color.

B. triacanthophora. THREE-SPINE BARBERRY. Evergreen shrub to 5 ft. tall, equally broad. Narrow 1-2-in.-long leaves, bright green above, somewhat grayish green beneath, with spiny-toothed edges. Clusters of whitish flowers tinged red in spring. Blue-black berries. Slender spines discourage intruders; they discourage pruning, too, so grow as a 5-ft.-tall, 5-ft.-wide unclipped barrier hedge. Hardy to 0°.

B. verruculosa. WARTY BARBERRY. Evergreen. Hardy to 0°. Neat, tailored shrub with informal elegance. Can reach 3-4 ft. tall, but can be held to 18 in. without becoming clumpy. Perky, glossy dark green, 1-in.-long leaves are whitish beneath. In fall and winter a red leaf develops as a highlight here and there in the green foliage. Berries black with purplish bloom. Very choice and easy to use on banks, in the foreground of shrubbery, or in front of leggy rhododendrons or azaleas.

B. wilsonae. WILSON BARBERRY. Deciduous to nearly evergreen in mild climates. Hardy to 5°. Moderate growth to 6 ft. high and as wide, but can be held to a 3-4 ft. hedge. Fine-textured foliage, with light green, roundish, ½-1 in. leaves. Small yellow flowers in dense clusters. Beautiful coral to salmon red berries. A handsome barrier hedge.

BERGENIA. Perennial, evergreen except in coldest areas. Zones 1-9, 14-24. Member of saxifrage family, native to Himalayas and mountains of China. Thick rootstocks; large, glossy green leaves. Thick leafless stalks, 12-18 in. high, bear graceful nodding clusters of small white, pink, or rose flowers. Ornamental foliage an all-year asset. Strong, substantial textural quality in borders, under trees, as a bold-patterned ground cover. Effective with ferns, hellebores, hostas, as foreground planting for *Fatsia japonica*, aucubas, rhododendrons.

Best performance in partial shade but will take full sun in cool coastal climates. *B. cordifolia* and *B. crassifolia* endure neglect, poor soil, cold, but respond to good soil, regular watering, grooming. Cut back yearly to prevent legginess. Divide crowded clumps; replant vigorous divisions. Bait for snails and slugs.

B. cordifolia. HEARTLEAF BERGENIA. Leaves glossy, roundish, heart-shaped at base, with wavy-toothed edges. Spring-blooming rose or lilac flowers in pendulous clusters partially hidden by large leaves. Plant grows to 20 in.

B. crassifolia. WINTER-BLOOMING BERGENIA. Best known. Leaves dark green, 8 in. or more across, slightly toothed, and wavy on edges. Flowers rose, lilac, or purple, in dense clusters on erect stems

standing well above leaves. Plants 20 in. high. Bloom January, February.

B. ligulata. Choicest, most elegant. To 1 ft. Lustrous, light green leaves to 12 in. long and wide; smooth on edges but fringed with soft hairs; young leaves bronzy. Flowers white, rose, or purplish, bloom late spring, summer. Slightly tender; leaves burn in severe frost.

BERMUDA GRASS. See Lawn Chapter

BETULA. BIRCH. Deciduous trees. When you talk about a birch tree, most people picture the light, graceful European white birch. All birches need ample water at all times and a regular feeding program. All are susceptible to aphids that drip honeydew.

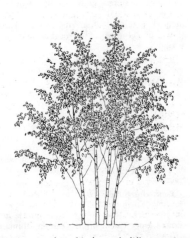

European white birches of different sizes spaced to make natural-looking grove.

Not a tree for a patio or to park a car under. Spray with aphid or all-purpose spray as leaves unfold in spring and repeat in two weeks. On all birches, small conelike fruits hang on branches through the winter.

B. maximowicziana. MONARCH BIRCH. Zones 4-24. Native to Japan. Fast growing, somewhat stiffer in structure than most birches, to as high as 80 ft. Flaky orange-brown bark, eventually becoming gray or whitish. Leaves large, 3-6 in. long, turn golden yellow in the fall, even in southern California.

B. nigra. RIVER BIRCH, RED BIRCH. All Zones. Native to eastern half of the United States. Very fast growth in first years. Eventually to 50-90 ft. Pyramidal form. Trunk often forks near the ground, but tree can be trained to single stem. Young bark is pinkish, very smooth, and shining. On older trees it flakes and curls in cinnamon brown to blackish sheets. Diamond-shaped leaves 1-3 in. long, are bright glossy green above, silvery below. Needs ample moisture.

B. papyrifera. CANOE BIRCH, PAPER BIRCH. Zones 1-6. Native to northern part of North America. Similar to European white birch but tree is more open, less weeping. Trunk creamy white. Bark peels off in papery layers. Leaves are larger (to 4 in. long), more sparsely borne.

B. verrucosa. (Usually sold as *B. alba* or *B. pendula*.) EUROPEAN WHITE BIRCH. Zones 1-11, 14-24. Native from Europe to

Climate Zone maps pages 8-27

Asia Minor. Probably the most frequently planted deciduous tree in the West. Delicate and lacy. Upright branching with weeping side branches. Average mature tree 30-40 ft. high, spreading to half its height. Bark on twigs and young branches is golden brown. Bark on trunk and main limbs becomes white, marked with black clefts; oldest bark at base is blackish gray. Rich green, glossy leaves to 2½ in. long, diamond-shaped, with slender tapered point. Often sold as weeping birch, although trees vary somewhat in habit, and young trees show little inclination to weep.

European white birch has many uses. Its form and color are enhanced by a dark background of pines. Dramatic when night lighted. Lends itself to planting in grove formation, some single, some grouped. Trees of unequal sizes and planted with unequal spacing look more natural. Trees grown in clumps of several trunks are available.

B. v. 'Dalecarlica' (*B. pendula* 'Laciniata', *B. alba* 'Laciniata'). CUTLEAF WEEPING BIRCH. Leaves deeply cut. Branches strongly weeping; graceful open tree. Weeping forms are more affected by dry hot weather than species. Foliage shows stress by late summer.

B. v. 'Fastigiata' (*B. pendula* 'Fastigiata', *B. alba* 'Fastigiata'). PYRAMIDAL WHITE BIRCH. Branches upright; habit somewhat like Lombardy poplar. Excellent screening tree.

B. v. 'Purpurea' (*B. pendula* 'Purpurea', *B. alba* 'Purpurea'). PURPLE BIRCH. Twigs purple-black. New foliage rich purple-maroon, fading to purplish green in summer; striking effect against white bark. Best in cool to cold climates.

B. v. 'Youngii' (*B. pendula* 'Youngii'). YOUNG'S WEEPING BIRCH. Slender branches hang straight down. Form like weeping mulberry, but tree is more graceful. Decorative display tree. Trunk must be staked to desired height. Same climate limitations as *B. v.* 'Dalecarlica'.

BIGNONIA. TRUMPET VINE. Botanists have reclassified plants formerly called *Bignonia*, so that the trumpet vines you knew as *Bignonia* are now placed under other names. Many are still sold under the old names. Since most gardeners still compare one "bignonia" with another when making their selections, we list them below and give the names under which they are described:

B. chamberlaynii. See Anemopaegma

B. cherere. See Phaedranthus

B. chinensis. See Campsis grandiflora

B. jasminoides. See Pandorea

B. radicans. See Campsis radicans

B. speciosa. See Clytostoma

B. tweediana. See Doxantha

B. venusta. See Pyrostegia

B. violacea. See Clytostoma

BIG TREE. See Sequoiadendron

BILLBERGIA. Evergreen perennial. Zones 16-24. Indoor-outdoor plants anywhere. Relative of the pineapple, native to Brazil, where the plants grow as epiphytes on trees. Stiff, spiny-toothed leaves in basal clusters. Showy bracts and tubular flowers in drooping clusters. Usually grown in containers for display indoors or in patios. In southern California, often grown on limbs of trees or on bark slabs, with roots wrapped in sphagnum moss and leaf mold; as an easy ground cover under trees; or in borders. Excellent cut flowers.

Best in filtered shade. Pot in light porous mixture of sand, ground bark, or leaf mold. Need little water in winter when growth is slow, large amounts during active growth in warm weather. Usually hold water in funnel-like center of leaf rosette which acts as a reservoir. When grown as house plants give plenty of light, and sun. Increase by cutting off suckers from base of plant.

B. nutans. QUEEN'S TEARS. Most commonly grown. Spiny green leaves to 1½ ft. long. Long spikes of rosy red bracts and drooping flowers with green petals edged deep blue. Vigorous, easy to grow.

B. pyramidalis. Leaves to 3 ft. long, 2½ in. wide, with spiny-toothed margins. Flowers with red, violet-tipped petals and bright red bracts in dense spikes 4 in. long.

B. sanderiana. Leaves leathery, to 1 ft. long, spiny-toothed, dotted with white. Loose, nodding, 10-in.-long clusters of flowers with blue petals, yellowish green at the base; sepals tipped with blue, bracts rose-colored.

BIRCH. See Betula

BIRD OF PARADISE. See Strelitzia

BIRD OF PARADISE BUSH. See Poinciana gilliesii

BIRD'S-EYE BUSH. See Ochna

BIRD'S EYES. See Gilia tricolor

BIRDSFOOT TREFOIL. See Lotus corniculatus

BISHOP'S HAT. See Epimedium

BISHOPS'S WEED. See Aegopodium

BITTERROOT. See Lewisia rediviva

BITTERSWEET. See Celastrus

BLACKBERRY. The West has its own special kinds of blackberries. Most are trailing types as compared to the hardy, upright, stiff-caned kinds of the Midwest and East. The wild blackberry of the Pacific Northwest and northern California has contributed its rich, sprightly flavor to several varieties. Each has its own pattern of climate adaptation.

All blackberries require a deep soil, full sun, and ample water through growing season. Trailing types are best grown on some kind of a trellis. See illustration below.

Pruning must follow growth habit. Roots are perennial but the canes are biennial, appearing and growing one year, flowering and fruiting the second. Where grown on a trellis, train only the 1-year-old canes on the trellis, and remove all canes that have fruited in August after harvest (cut canes to the ground). Train canes of the current season (growing beneath the trellis) on the trellis and prune to 6-8 feet. Thin out all but 12 to 16 canes. These will produce side branches during remainder of growing season. Cut side branches back to 12 inches in early spring. With the new spring growth, small branches grow from the side branches. These will carry the fruits.

Thin out semi-upright varieties to 4 to 8 canes, prune at 5-6 feet, and spread fanwise on the trellis. Upright varieties need no trellis but are easier to handle tied to a wire about 2½ feet above the ground. Select 3 or 4 canes and tip them at 2½ to 3 feet to force side growth. Tie where the canes cross the wire.

Red-berry mite (mostly in the 'Himalaya' and 'Evergreen' varieties), spider mites, and whitefly are sometimes a problem. To control, spray in winter and again as buds are about to break with a dormant spray containing lime sulfur. Spray as leaves unfold and again a month later with malathion.

Fertilize established plantings with commercial fertilizer according to manufacturer's label. In Northwest, feed at blossom time. Best results in California if you split yearly amount into 3 applications: before new growth starts, again in midspring, and again in midsummer. Keep down weeds. Pull out suckers. Above all, don't let plants get away from you.

These varieties are available in Western nurseries (all are trailing types except where noted otherwise):

'Aurora'. Recommended for Zones 4-6 only. Has failed in California. A very early variety with large (1¼ in. long, ¾ in. thick) berries that taste like a blend of 'Logan' and 'Cascade'.

'Boysen' and 'Thornless Boysen'. All Zones. Not reliably hardy in Zone 1 but comes through the winter if canes are left on ground and covered by snow or with straw mulch. Popular for high yield and

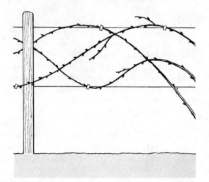

Trailing blackberries do best on trellis; two-wire type (wires at 3 and 5 ft.) easy. Weave canes on trellis (right); don't bend too sharply. Or tie to wires (left).

flavor—eaten fresh, cooked, or frozen. Berries are reddish, large (1¼ in. long, 1 in. thick), soft, sweet-tart, delightful aroma. Berries carry dusty bloom, are not shiny.

'Cascade'. Best in Zones 4-6, 16, 17. Some grown 20-24. Not adapted 9-13. Not reliably hardy Zones 1-3. Berries bright, deep red, almost black (cook red), about 1 in. long, ½ in. thick, with classic wild blackberry flavor. Tender and very juicy; a poor shipper but an excellent garden variety.

'Evergreen' and 'Thornless Evergreen'. Strong canes, semi-erect growth. This is *the* commercial blackberry in Zones 4-6. Not reliably hardy Zones 1-3. Grown in Zones 15-17 where quantity is important. Bushes vigorous with heavy crops of large (1½ in. long, ¾ in. thick), exceptionally firm, black, sweet berries. Seeds large.

'Himalaya'. Seldom sold but has escaped and grows wild wherever adapted. Can be a prodigious, spreading pest. Grown in Zones 14-17 for long harvest season—mid-July to October. Extremely vigorous, semierect, canes grow 20-30 feet in one season. Berries shiny jet-black, medium (1 in. long, ¾ in. thick). Seeds medium large.

'Logan' and 'Thornless Logan'. Same climate adaptation as 'Boysen' berry. Berries (1¼ in. long, ¾ in. thick) are light reddish, not darkening when ripe, with fine hairs that dull its color. Flavor tarter than 'Boysen'; excellent for canning and pies.

'Marion'. Similar to 'Olallie' in berry size and quality but better adapted Zones 4-6. Climate adaptation same as 'Cascade'.

'Nectar'. Identical to 'Boysen'.

'Olallie'. Better adapted in California than in its Oregon homeland. Zones 7-9, 14-24. Berries large (1½ in. long, ¾ in. thick), shiny black, firm, sweeter than 'Cascade' but with some wild blackberry sprightliness.

'Texas Wonder'. A hardy upright type with strong canes. Will take temperature extremes. Sold in Zones 10-13. Berries almost as large as 'Boysen' berry, but black and shiny.

'Young' and 'Thornless Young'. Climate adaptation similar to 'Boysen' berry, but not as productive in all climates. Berry same size and color as 'Boysen' but shiny and somewhat sweeter.

BLACKBOY. See Xanthorrhea preissii

BLACK-EYED SUSAN. See Rudbeckia hirta

BLACK-EYED SUSAN VINE. See Thunbergia alata

BLACK SALLY. See Eucalyptus stellulata

BLADDER FLOWER, WHITE. See Araujia

BLANKET FLOWER. See Gaillardia

BLECHNUM (*Lomaria*). Evergreen ferns of a symmetrical, formal appearance.

B. brasiliense. Zones 19, 21-24. Dwarf tree fern reaching only 4 ft. in height. Nearly erect fronds in compact clusters. The variety 'Crispum' has elegantly ruffled fronds, reddish when young.

B. gibbum. Zones 19, 21-24. Dwarf tree fern with a wide-spreading crown of fronds atop a slender trunk eventually 3 ft. high. 'Moorei' has wider, more leathery leaflets, is more attractive in winter. Needs moist soil and shade, but avoid overhead water.

B. spicant. DEER FERN, DEER TONGUE FERN. Zones 1-9, 14-24. Native to northern California and the Northwest. Produces fronds of 2 kinds: the sterile fronds narrow, dark glossy green, spreading or angled, 1-3 ft. tall; fertile fronds stiffly erect, very narrow; with narrow, widely spaced leaflets. Deep shade, moisture, woodsy soil. Difficult in southern California.

BLEEDING HEART. See Dicentra

BLETILLA striata (*B. hyacinthina*). CHINESE GROUND ORCHID. A terrestrial orchid native to China and Japan. Lavender, cattleya-shaped, 1-2-in. flowers produced up to a dozen on a 1½-2-ft. stem, for about 6 weeks beginning in June. Pale green, plaited leaves 3-6 to a plant. *B. s.* 'Alba' is a white flowered form.

Plant the tuberlike roots outdoors in fall in all but the coldest areas of the West for spring and early summer bloom. Hardy to about 20°. Dies back to ground each winter.

These little (1-2-in.), lavender flowers form on Bletilla striata, early summer.

Mulch with straw in cold climates. In time will develop large clumps if grown in light shade and in a moist soil, rich in humus. Can be divided in early spring before growth starts, but don't do it too often; they bloom best when crowded.

Locate plants (potted or in ground) under high branching trees or under lath.

BLIGHIA sapida. See Cupaniopsis

BLISTERCRESS. See Erysimum

BLOOD-LEAF. See Iresine

BLOODROOT. See Sanguinaria

BLUE BEARD. See Caryopteris

BLUEBELL. See Scilla

BLUEBELL CREEPER, AUSTRALIAN. See Sollya

BLUEBELL OF SCOTLAND. See Campanula rotundifolia

BLUEBELL, PEACH-LEAFED. See Campanula persicifolia

BLUEBELLS, VIRGINIA. See Mertensia

BLUEBERRY. Deciduous shrub. Best in Zones 4-6. Hardy in Zones 2, 3 but needs special acid soil preparation there. Grown successfully in northern California coastal area (Zone 17) and by gardeners willing to give them special attention in Zones 7-9, 14-16. Native to eastern U.S. Blueberries thrive under conditions that suit rhododendrons and azaleas, to which they are related. They need cool, moist, acid soil that drains well. In California if soil is at all alkaline grow them in straight peat moss or ground bark.

Blueberries contribute more than fruit to the garden. They are handsome plants for a hedge or shrub border. Most varieties are upright growers to 6 ft. or more; a few are rather sprawling and under 5 ft. Leaves, to 3 in. long, bronze in new growth, then dark green, turning scarlet or yellow in fall. Flowers, tiny, white to pinkish, urn-shaped, in spring. Fruits highly decorative through summer. Plant 3 ft. apart as an informal hedge; in larger plantings, as shrubs, space 4-5 ft. apart.

Plant two varieties for better pollination. Shallow roots benefit from a 4-6-in.-thick mulch of sawdust, ground bark, or the like. Water frequently. Use acid-forming fertilizers. In California you may need to use iron sulfate or iron chelate to correct chlorosis.

Prune to prevent overbearing. Plants shape themselves, but often produce so many fruit buds that fruits are undersized

Climate Zone maps pages 8-27

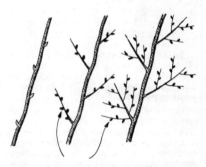

Second-year branch (center) with fruit bud; cut 3rd-year branch after fruiting.

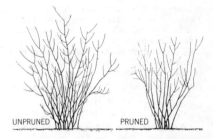

Upright blueberry needs thinning; cut out oldest branches, top taller ones (right).

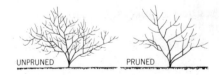

Spreading blueberry seldom makes multiple stems; thin wood, tip new branches.

Climate
Zone maps
pages 8-27

and growth of plants slows down. Keep first-year plants from bearing by stripping off flowers. On older plants cut back ends of twigs to a point where fruit buds are widely spaced. Or, simply remove some of the oldest branches each year. Remove all weak shoots.

The following varieties have proved themselves in home gardens. Choose for long harvest season. Plant at least 2 for each season ("early" means ripening early to mid-June; "mid-season" means early to mid-July; "late" means late July into August). Allow 2 plants for each member of your family. Although all varieties are sold in Northwest and northern California, growers especially recommend for California: 'Berkeley', 'Bluecrop', 'Dixi', 'Earliblue', 'Jersey'.

'Atlantic'. Late. Sprawling habit. Light blue, large berry.

'Berkeley'. Midseason to late. Open, spreading, tall. Very large light blue berries.

'Bluecrop'. Midseason. Erect, tall growth. Large berries. Excellent flavor. Attractive shrub.

'Blueray'. Midseason. Vigorous, tall. Large, highly flavored crisp berries. Attractive shrub.

'Coville'. Late. Tall, open, spreading. Unusually large leaves. Very attractive. Long clusters of very large light blue berries.

'Concord'. Midseason. Upright to spreading growth. Attractive. Large berry of tart flavor until fully ripe.

'Dixi'. Late. Not an attractive plant—tall and open. Needs heavy pruning. Berries, among the largest and tastiest, are medium blue, firm and sweet.

'Earliblue'. Early to midseason. Tall, erect. Large heavy leaves. Large berries of excellent flavor.

'Ivanhoe'. Early to midseason. Very large dark blue berries—firm, crisp, tart.

'Jersey'. Midseason to late. Tall, erect growing. Large, light blue berries. Very bland. Yellow fall and winter color.

'Pemberton'. Very vigorous, tall. Berries large, dark blue, of good dessert quality.

'Rancocas'. Early to midseason. Tall, erect, open arching habit. Excellent shrub. Leaves smaller than most. Needs heavy pruning. Berries mild and sweet. Dependable old-timer.

'Rubel'. Early to late. Erect tall growth. Berries firm and tart. Needs pruning to produce large berries.

'Stanley'. Early to midseason. Erect medium tall. Attractive foliage. One of the tastiest—firm, aromatic berries with spicy flavor.

'Weymouth'. Very early. Ripens all berries quickly. Erect, medium height. Large dark blue berries of fair quality. Lack aroma.

BLUEBERRY CLIMBER. See Ampelopsis brevipedunculata

BLUE BLOSSOM. See Ceanothus thyrsiflorus

BLUE DAWN FLOWER. See Ipomoea leari

BLUE DICKS. See Brodiaea pulchella

BLUE-EYED GRASS. See Sisyrinchium bellum

BLUE GRASS. See Lawn Chapter

BLUE GUM. See Eucalyptus globulus

BLUE LACE FLOWER. See Trachymene

BLUE MIST. See Caryopteris clandonensis

BOLTONIA. Perennials. All Zones. Tall, branching plants with clusters of dainty flowers like small Michaelmas daisies in late summer and fall. Useful as a filler in large mixed borders, contrasted with coarser-flowered perennials. Plant in sun. Routine care. Roots are invasive; avoid planting near choice material unless carefully controlled. Divide clumps yearly. Grows readily from seed.

B. asteroides. To 8 ft. high. Narrow, 2-5-in.-long leaves. Flower head to ¾ in. wide, rays white to violet and purple; yellow centers. 'Snowbank', a white variety growing to 4 ft., is a better size for average garden.

B. latisquama. Flower heads larger (1 in. or more) than above, blue-violet with yellow centers. Variety 'Nana' grows 2-3 ft.; rays pale pink.

BORAGO officinalis. BORAGE. Annual herb. Grows 1-3 ft. high. Leaves bristly, gray-green to as long as 4-6 in.; edible, taste like cucumbers. Blue, saucer-shaped, nodding flowers in leafy clusters on branched stems. Sun or shade, poor soil, medium watering. Grows large, needs lots of room. Seeds itself freely but doesn't transplant easily. Good drought-resistant ground cover, soil binder. Use small tender leaves in salads, pickling, or cooked as greens. Flowers attractive garnish, also good cut flower.

BORONIA megastigma. BROWN BORONIA. Evergreen short-lived shrub. Zone 17. To 2 ft. with leaves divided into 3-5 narrow leaflets. Flowers, small, ½-in.-wide, nodding, open bells, are brownish maroon outside, chartreuse or yellow within; February to March. As a provider of fragrance—a blend of all flowers and orange blossoms—it is the greatest. Excellent cut flowers; very long lasting. Must have acid, peaty, sandy soil that drains perfectly but never goes dry. Sun or light shade. Seldom offered by nurseries. Grow from seed, cuttings.

BOTTLEBRUSH. See Callistemon, Melaleuca

BOTTLEBRUSH, GRAVEL. See Beaufortia

BOTTLE TREE. See Brachychiton populneum

BOUGAINVILLEA. Evergreen shrubby vines. Reliably hardy in the nearest thing we have to a tropical climate—Zones 22-24. Yet widely and satisfyingly grown in Zones 12, 13, 15-17, 19, 21. Low-growing shrubby types in full bloom in a gallon can and adaptable to container growing, have widened their use even into Zones 5, 6 of the Northwest. There it is used on terrace or patio as a summer annual or moved into protected area over winter. Where frost is expected, the vine should be given a protected warm wall or the warmest spot in the garden. If the vine gets by the first winter or two it will be big enough to take winter damage and recover. In any case, flower production comes so quickly that replacement is not a real deterrent.

Bougainvillea's vibrant color comes not from the small inconspicuous flowers, but from the 3 large bracts that surround them. Vine makes dense cover of medium-size, medium-green leaves. Vigor and growth habit varies by species and variety. Plant in sun, or light shade in hottest areas. Plant in early spring (after frosts) to give longest possible growing season before next frost.

Caution: Bougainvilleas must be planted with care. Roots don't knit soil together in firm root ball. If you remove them from the can in usual fashion you may disturb them fatally. Place can in hole, slit sides to bottom in 4 to 6 places, pull can sides away from root ball and fill in with soil mix. Or, cut out bottom of can, leaving sides intact. Or poke 6 to 8 holes in sides and bottom of can before setting it in hole. Can metal will rust away.

Supply sturdy supports and keep shoots tied up so that they won't whip in the wind, and so strong gusts won't shred leaves against the sharp thorns along stems.

Fertilize in spring and summer. Water normally while plants are growing fast, then ease off temporarily in midsummer to promote better flowering. Don't be afraid to prune—to renew plant, shape, or direct growth. Prune heavily in spring after frost. On wall-grown plants, nip back long stems during growing season to produce more flowering wood. Shrubby kinds or heavily-pruned plants make good self-supporting container shrubs for terrace or patio. Without support and with token corrective pruning bougainvillea can make a broad, sprawling shrub or bank and ground cover.

All of the following are tall-growing vines except those noted as shrubs.

'Afterglow'. Yellow-orange; heavy bloom. Open growth, sparse foliage.

'Barbara Karst'. Bright red in sun, bluish crimson in shade; blooms young and for long period. Vigorous growth. Likes heat of desert. Fast comeback after frost.

'Betty Hendry' ('Indian Maid'). Basically red, but with touches of yellow and purple. Blooms young and for a long period.

B. brasiliensis. See B. spectabilis

'California Gold'. The closest to pale yellow. Blooms young.

'Carmencita'. Bright red, double. Long blooming season, medium growing.

'Convent' ('Panama Queen'). Low, shrublike. Big clusters of magenta-purple bracts over a long season.

'Crimson Jewel'. Shrubby, sprawly plant. Vigorous. Good in containers or as shrub. Effective cover for sunny bank. Lower growth, better color than 'Temple Fire'. Heavy bloom, long season.

'Crimson Lake'. See 'Mrs. Butt'.

'Jamaica White'. White, veined light green. Blooms young. Moderately vigorous.

'La Jolla'. Bright red, compact, shrubby. Good in containers or in shrub border.

'Mrs. Butt'. (Usually sold as 'Crimson Lake'.) Old-fashioned variety with good crimson color. Needs lots of heat for bloom. Moderately vigorous.

'Orange King'. Bronzy orange. Open growth. Needs long summer, no frost.

'Pink Tiara'. Delicate pink to rose. Long flowering season.

'San Diego Red' ('San Diego', 'American Red', 'Scarlet O'Hara'). One of the best on all counts: large, deep green leaves that hold well in cold winters; deep red bracts over a long season; hardiness equal to the old-fashioned purple kind. Vigorous, high climbing. Train to tree form by staking and pruning.

B. spectabilis (*B. brasiliensis*). Very hardy and vigorous. Blooms creditably in cool summers. Best for Zones 16, 17.

'Temple Fire'. Shrublike growth to 4 ft. high, 6 ft. wide. Partially deciduous. Bronze red.

'Texas Dawn'. Best of the pinks. Vigorous. Purplish pink bracts in large sprays.

BOUSSINGAULTIA. See Anredera

BOUVARDIA. Evergreen shrubs. Zones 13, 16, 17, 19-24. Native to Mexico and Central America. Loose, often straggling growth habit. Showy clusters of tubular flowers (fragrant in one species). The fragrant one is the most tender and looks poorest after flowers are gone. The non-fragrant red-flowered types are hardier, easier.

B. leiantha. Open growth to 5-6 ft.; leaves, 1-3 in., in whorls of 3-4; large clusters of deep red ½-in. flowers at end of stems. An improved form is 'Fire Chief'.

B. longiflora 'Albatross' (*B. humboldtii* 'Albatross'). The fragrant one. Snow white, 3-in.-long tubular flowers in loose clusters on a weak-stemmed shrub, 2-3 ft. high. They appear at almost any time. Pinch out stem tips to make bushier. Cut back flowering branches from time to time to stimulate new growth. Grow in tubs or boxes in rich fast-draining soil mix.

B. ternifolia (*B. jacquinii*). A 6-ft.-tall shrub with 2-in. leaves in whorls of 3 or 4. Red, 1-in.-long, tubular flowers in loose clusters at the ends of the branches. Selected forms are pink, rose, coral, red.

BOWER VINE. See Pandorea jasminoides

BOX, BOXWOOD. See Buxus

BOX ELDER. See Acer negundo

BOX, VICTORIAN. See Pittosporum undulatum

BOXWOOD, AFRICAN. See Myrsine

BOXWOOD, OREGON. See Pachistima myrsinites

BRASS BUTTONS, NEW ZEALAND. See Cotula

BRACHYCHITON (*Sterculia*). Evergreen to partly or wholly deciduous trees. Native to Australia. Four quite different trees come under this name. All have woody, canoe-shaped fruits that delight flower arrangers, but are merely litter to some gardeners.

B. acerifolium (*Sterculia acerifolia*). FLAME TREE, AUSTRALIAN FLAME TREE. Deciduous for brief period. Zones 16-21, 23. When at its best, a most spectacular red-flowering tree. Hardy to 25°. To 60 ft. or more. Strong, heavy, smooth trunk, usually green. Leaves are handsome, glossy, bright green 10-in.-wide fans, deeply lobed. Showiest flowering season usually May to June. Tree wholly or partially covered with great clusters of small, ¾-in., tubular, red or orange-red bells. Leaves drop before flowers appear in portion of tree that blooms.

B. bidwillii (*Sterculia bidwillii*). Almost evergreen. Similar to above, but smaller

(to 20 ft.), with a more slender trunk, and round-headed crown. Three-lobed leaves. Brownish red flowers.

B. discolor (*Sterculia discolor*). QUEENSLAND LACEBARK, PINK FLAME TREE. Deciduous for brief period. Zones 19, 21, 23. Similar in growth habit to *B. acerifolium* but often taller, to 90 ft. Leaves differ from *B. acerifolium* by being shallowly lobed, only 6 inches wide, and blue-green instead of bright green, and the undersides are whitish. Bell-like, deep rose pink flowers, although not as many, are much larger. Flowers and fruits densely covered with rusty wool on outside. Same erratic blooming habit and leaf drop as *B. acerifolium*, but it's summer blooming.

B. populneum (*Sterculia diversifolia*). BOTTLE TREE. Evergreen. Zones 13-24. Moderate growth to 30-50 ft., 30-ft. spread. Common name from very heavy trunk, broad at base, tapering quickly. Leaves (2-3 in. long) give general effect of poplar. They shimmer in breeze like aspen's. Clusters of small, bell-shaped, white flowers in May and June noticeable close up. The 2½-3-in. woody fruits that follow are noticeable in litter they produce. Appreciated in low desert, where frequently used as screens or high, wide windbreaks.

BRACHYCOME iberidifolia. SWAN RIVER DAISY. Annual. Native to Western Australia. Charming plant producing myriad daisy-like flowers, 1 in. across, in blue, rose, white, and bicolors. Bloom in late spring and early summer. Small, narrow, divided leaves. Sow seed in broad masses where plants are to grow. Sun. Effective under light foliaged deciduous trees, as a ground cover in bulb beds, or in rock gardens.

BRACHYSEMA lanceolatum. SCIMITAR SHRUB, SWAN RIVER PEA SHRUB. Evergreen. Zones 8, 9, 13-24. Earns its common names and place in gardens by its unusual flowers. They are bright red, sweet pea-shaped, but with inch-long pairs of petals (keels) shaped like a scimitar. Never makes a great show of flowers, but it's rarely out of bloom. To 3 ft. or more, loosely formed, erect in growth, spreading in age. Leaves narrow, to 4 in. long, dark green above, silvery beneath. Prune by thinning out old straggly stems. Does best in full sun and with fast drainage in sandy soil. Don't pamper. Go light with fertilizers.

BRACKEN. See Pteridium

BRAKE. See Pteris

BRASSAIA actinophylla (*Schefflera actinophylla*). QUEENSLAND UMBRELLA TREE, OCTOPUS TREE. Evergreen house plant; outdoor shrub/tree in Zones 21-24. As a garden plant, grows fast to 20 ft. The "umbrella" name comes from way giant leaves are held. Horizontal tiers of long-stalked leaves, divided into 7-16 large (12 in.) leaflets that radiate outward like the ribs of an umbrella. The "octopus" comes from the curious arrangement of flowers in narrow clusters to 3 ft. long that spread horizontally. Color changes with age from greenish yellow to pink to dark red. Tiny dark purple fruits.

Striking plant for tropical effects, for silhouette, and for foliage contrast with ferns and other foliage plants. Cut out tips occasionally to keep from becoming leggy. Leggy stems can be cut almost to ground;

they will branch and make better shaped plant. Takes full sun or deep shade. Requires good drainage. For fast growth, plant in rich soil, water heavily, feed frequently. For closely related plants see *Schefflera*.

Almost always sold as schefflera, Brassaia is a most desirable tubbed foliage plant.

BRASSAVOLA. Epiphytic orchids native to tropical America. Large spiderlike, white or greenish-white flowers with narrow sepals and petals and large lip. The flowers grow singly or in short-stemmed clusters. Tough leathery leaves grow from small pseudobulbs. Plants similar to laelias. Grow in any orchid soil mix. Need 60° to 65° night temperature, 5° to 10° higher in day. Water liberally and give plenty of sun during growing season. Reduce humidity during dormant period.

B. cucullata. Fragrant, 2-in. flowers in summer or fall. Grasslike leaves to 12 in. long with pseudobulb included. Unlike many orchids this one will produce flower stems from the same pseudobulb for several years in succession. Hardy enough to grow outdoors through winter in warm climate areas of southern California.

B. nodosa. LADY-OF-THE-NIGHT. In fall 3-in. flowers appear, 2-6 on a stem; sweetly fragrant at night. Fleshy, 6-in.-long leaves. Hardy outdoors in winter where temperatures are mild. Grows best in hanging containers.

BREATH OF HEAVEN. See Coleonema

BRIDAL WREATH. See Spiraea

BRISBANE BOX. See Tristania conferta

BRIZA maxima. RATTLESNAKE GRASS, QUAKING GRASS. Annual. Native to Mediterranean region. Ornamental grass of delicate, graceful form used effectively in dry arrangements and bouquets. Grows 1-2 ft. high. Leaves to 6 in. long, 1/4 in. wide. Clusters of nodding, seed-bearing spikelets ½ in. or more long, papery and straw-colored when dry, dangle on threadlike stems. Spikelets resemble rattlesnake rattles. Broadcast seed where plants are to grow; thin seedlings to 1 ft. apart. Often grows wild along roadsides, in fields.

Climate Zone maps pages 8-27

BROCCOLI. Best all-around cole crop (cabbage and its close relatives) for the home gardener; bears over a long season, is not difficult to grow. Grows to 4 ft. and has a branching habit; the central stalk bears a cluster of green flower buds that may reach 6 in. in diameter. When this is removed, side branches will lengthen and produce smaller clusters. Good varieties are 'Waltham', 'De Cicco', 'Green Mountain', and 'Number Five'.

It's a cool-season plant which tends to bolt into flower when temperatures are high. Plant it to mature during cool weather. In mild climates plant in late summer, fall, or winter for winter or early spring crops. In cold-winter areas set out young plants in late winter or early spring, about 2 weeks before the last frost.

Young plants resist frost, but not hard freezing. A good guide to planting time is the appearance of young plants in nurseries. You can raise young plants from seed sown 4 or 6 weeks ahead of planting time, but even one pack of seed will produce far more plants than even the largest home garden could handle, so save surplus seed for later plantings. A dozen plants at each planting will supply a family.

Sun. Space plants 18-24 in. apart in rows and leave 3 ft. between rows. Keep plants growing vigorously with regular deep irrigation and one or two feedings of commercial fertilizer before heads start to form. Cut heads before clustered buds begin to open. Include 5 or 6 in. of edible stalk and leaves. Control aphids and cabbage worm with malathion *before heads form*, or use all-purpose vegetable dust.

BRODIAEA. Corm. All Zones. Many are natives of the Pacific Coast where they bloom in fields and meadows, spring and early summer. Few grasslike leaves, and clusters of funnel-shaped or tubular, ½-2-in.-long flowers atop the stem. In nature often found in adobe soil, where it rains heavily in winter and early spring, and corms completely dry out in summer. Best with similar conditions in gardens (no dry-season watering). Where plants must take summer watering, plant in sandy or gritty soil. Plant corms 2-3 in. deep. In cold-winter areas, grow in containers or protect from freezing and thawing by a mulch.

B. elegans. HARVEST BRODIAEA. Open clusters of 3 to 10 violet-purple flowers, 1¼-1¾ in. long, on 18-in. stems. Blooms in early summer after field grass has started to turn brown.

B. hyacinthina. WHITE BRODIAEA. Clusters of 10 to 40 bell-shaped, white, purple-tinged flowers with greenish veins, somewhat papery in texture. Stems 1-1¾ ft. high. Blooms in June, July.

B. ida-maia. FIRECRACKER FLOWER. Clusters of 6-23 pendulous, tubular, scarlet flowers tipped with green. Blooms May-July.

B. laxa. ITHURIEL'S SPEAR, GRASS NUT. A very beautiful species resembling the harvest brodiaea but growing 1-2¼ ft. high on stout rigid stems and blooming earlier—April to June. Clusters of 8-48 violet-purple flowers. Adapted to adobe soils.

B. lutea. GOLDEN BRODIAEA, PRETTY FACE. Open clusters of 16-40 golden yellow, ¾-in. long funnel-shaped flowers with conspicuous black-purple veins on outside. Blooms May to August.

B. pulchella. BLUE DICKS, WILD HYACINTH. Deep blue or violet-blue flowers in a tight headlike cluster surrounded by metallic purple bracts. Blooms from March to May.

B. uniflora. See Ipheion

BROMELIAD. Any plant belonging to the bromelia or pineapple family (Bromeliaceae) is a bromeliad. Most bromeliads are stemless perennials with clustered leaves and with showy flowers in simple or branched clusters. Leaves of many kinds are handsomely marked, and the flower clusters gain beauty from colorful bracts.

In most areas of the West bromeliads are considered choice house plants. Kinds most often grown indoors were, in their native homes, epiphytes, plants that perch on trees or rocks and gain their sustenance from rain and from whatever leaf mold gathers around their roots. These often have cupped leaf bases that hold water between rains. In the mildest areas of the West many of these epiphytes grow well in sheltered places out of doors.

A few bromeliads (*Puya*, for instance) are desert-dwelling plants that resemble yuccas.

BROMELIA balansae. HEART OF FLAME. Bromeliad. Zones 19-24. Pineapple relative. Forms impressive cluster of 30-50 arching leaves, saw-toothed, glossy dark green above, whitish beneath. To 4 ft. tall, 4-6 ft. across. Center leaves turn bright scarlet in spring or early summer. From this center rises a stalk bearing spike of rose-colored flowers margined with white. Needs warm nights to perform satisfactorily. Almost any soil if drainage is good. Grows best in porous soil with plenty of organic matter. Water occasionally, feed lightly once or twice in summer.

BROOM. See Cytisus

BROOM, SPANISH. See Spartium under Cytisus

BROUSSONETIA papyrifera. (Has been sold as *Morus papyrifera*.) PAPER MULBERRY. Deciduous tree. Zones 3-24. Valuable as shade tree where soil and climate limit choice. Takes alkaline soils, strong winds, desert heat. Hardy in all but coldest areas. Moderate growth to 50 ft. with dense, broad crown to 40 ft. across. Smooth gray bark. Heart-shaped, 4-8-in., rough leaves, gray hairy beneath; edges toothed, often lobed when young. Suckering habit can be problem in highly cultivated gardens. Seldom suckers in desert. Good in rough bank plantings.

BROWALLIA. AMETHYST FLOWER. Annual, sometimes living over as perennial. Choice plant for connoisseur of blue flowers. Bears one-sided clusters of lobelia-like blooms ½-2 in. long and wide in brilliant blue, violet, or white; the blue flowers more striking because of contrasting white eye or throat. Free flowering in warm shade or filtered sunlight. Graceful in hanging basket or pots. Fine cut flower.

Sow seeds in early spring for summer bloom; in fall for winter color indoors or in greenhouses. Plants need warmth, regular moisture. Can lift vigorous plants in fall, cut back and pot; new growth will produce flowers through winter in warm

location. Rarely sold as plants in nurseries; seeds from specialists.

B. americana. Branching, 1-2 ft. high, roundish leaves. Violet or blue flowers ½ in. long and wide, borne among the leaves. 'Sapphire', dwarf compact variety, dark blue with white eye, very free blooming. This species and its variety often listed in catalogs as *B. elata* and *B. elata* 'Sapphire'.

B. speciosa. Lives over as perennial in mild-winter climates. Sprawling, to 1-2 ft. high. Flowers dark purple above, pale lilac beneath, 1½-2 in. across.

BRUNFELSIA calycina. BRAZIL RAINTREE. Evergreen shrub. Zones 13, 15-17, 20-24. In all but the warmest locations they will lose most of their foliage for a short period. Upright or spreading, to about 3 ft. Oval, 3-4-in.-long leaves dark green above, pale green below. Tubular, rich dark purple flowers flare to 2 in. wide, several in a cluster spring, early summer.

The handsome brunfelsias deserve extra attention. Give them a soil mix that's rich, well drained, on acid side. Protect from full sun for very best in foliage and flower. Needs constant supply of water and food through the growing season. Prune in spring to remove scraggly growth and to shape. Use where you can admire spectacular flower show. Grow well in containers.

B. c. eximia. FADING BRAZIL RAINTREE. This is a somewhat dwarfed, compact version of the following, more widely planted variety. Flowers are a bit smaller but more generously produced.

B. c. floribunda. YESTERDAY-TODAY-AND-TOMORROW. Earns its common name by quick color change of blossoms — purple ("yesterday"), lavender ("today"), white ("tomorrow"). Flowers profusely displayed all over plant. In partial shade, will reach 10 ft. or more with several stems from base. (May be held to 3 ft. by pruning.)

B. c. macrantha (*B. floribunda* 'Lindeniana', *B. grandiflora*). Differs markedly from above. The most tender. More slender growing; larger leaves, often 8 in. long, 2½ in. wide. Flowers 2-4 in. across, are deep purple with lavender zone bordering white throat. Lack marked change of color.

BRUNNERA macrophylla. BRUNNERA. Perennial. All Zones. Charming in filtered shade in warm areas, sun or light shade on coast. In spring, airy clusters of tiny, clear blue forget-me-not flowers with yellow center. Dark green, heart-shaped leaves 3-6 in. across. To 18-in. high. Uses: informal ground cover under high branching deciduous trees; among spring-flowering shrubs such as forsythia, deciduous magnolias; filler between newly planted evergreen shrubs. Once established, self-sows freely. Planted seeds often difficult to germinate (try freezing them in freezer before sowing). Increase by dividing clumps in fall.

BRUNSVIGIA rosea. See Amaryllis belladonna

BRUSSELS SPROUTS. A cabbage relative of unusual appearance. A mature plant has a crown of fairly large leaves and its tall stem is completely covered with tiny sprouts. Fairly easy to grow where summers are not too hot, long, or dry. 'Jade Cross Hybrid' is easiest to grow and most heat-tolerant; 'Long Island Improved' ('Catskill') is the

Climate
Zone maps
pages 8-27

standard market variety. You may have to grow your own from seed. Sow outdoors or in flats in April, transplant young plants in June or early July to the place where they will grow and bear in fall. In mild climates plant in fall or winter for winter and spring use.

Treat it the same as broccoli. When big leaves start to turn yellow, begin picking. Snap off little sprouts from bottom first—best when slightly smaller than a golf ball. Leave little sprouts on upper stem to mature. After picking remove only the leaves below harvested sprouts. They continue to produce over a long period; a single plant will yield from 50 to 100 sprouts.

BUCKEYE. See Aesculus

BUCKTHORN, ITALIAN. See Rhamnus alaternus

BUCKWHEAT. See Eriogonum

BUDDLEIA. BUTTERFLY BUSH. Evergreen or deciduous shrub or small tree. Many species known; all have some charm either of flower color or fragrance, but only two species are readily available.

B. alternifolia. FOUNTAIN BUTTERFLY BUSH. Deciduous shrub or small tree. Zones 2-24. It can reach 12 ft. or more, with arching, willowlike branches rather thinly clothed with 1-4-in.-long leaves, dark dull green above, gray hairy beneath. Blooms in spring from the previous year's growth, the small clusters of mildly fragrant lilac-purple flowers carried in profusion to make sweeping wands of color. Tolerant of many soils, doing especially well in poor, dry gravels. Prune after bloom by removing some of the oldest wood down to within a few inches of the ground. Or train up into a small single or multiple-trunked tree.

B. davidii. COMMON BUTTERFLY BUSH, SUMMER LILAC. Deciduous or semi-evergreen shrub. Zones 1-9, 12-24. Makes fast, rank growth each spring and summer to 3, 4, or even 10 ft. Leaves tapering, 4-12 in. long, dark green above, white felted beneath. In midsummer small fragrant flowers (lilac with orange eye) appear in dense, arching, spikelike, slender clusters 6-12 in. or more long, at branch ends. Smaller clusters appear at ends of side branches. Butterflies often visit flowers.

Vigorous and grows like a weed. Needs good drainage and enough water to maintain growth, but little else. In cold climates the soft wood freezes nearly to the ground but roots hardy. Whether plants are deciduous in cold-winter areas or semi-evergreen in mild winters, for best appearance cut plants back to within a few inches of the ground—do this after fall flowering in Zones 4-9, 12-24; or in spring in Zones 1-3, 10, 11. Susceptible to pests, especially red spider mites in hot dry areas.

Many varieties are obtainable, differing mostly in flower color: 'Charming' and 'Fascinating' are pink; 'Fortune' is lilac, and has 18-in.-long flower clusters; 'Empire Blue' is medium blue; 'Peace' and 'White Profusion' are white; 'Purple Prince', 'Black Knight', 'Dubonnet', and 'Flaming Violet' are purples.

Collectors might look for *B. asiatica*, ASIAN BUTTERFLY BUSH, a tender, evergreen, white-flowering shrub with delightful fragrance; *B. globosa*. GLOBE BUTTERFLY BUSH

evergreen to semi-evergreen shrub with ball-shaped clusters of orange flowers; and *B. salvifolia*, a powerfully fragrant creamy white-flowering semi-evergreen shrub. The latter two should prove hardy Zones 5-9, 14-24. All are rare.

BUGBANE. See Cimicifuga

BULBINELLA robusta (*B. setosa*). Perennial, tuberous rootstock. Zones 14-24. Native to South Africa. Valuable for winter color, forming large clump of 20-26-in., narrow, floppy leaves topped in January-February with 4-in.-long spikes of clear yellow flowers. Similar to poker plant (*Kniphofia*) but spikes are shorter, less pointed, and individual flowers are bell-shaped, not tubular. Splendid cut flower. Low-maintenance

Bulbinella — yellow flowers in winter. Leaves dry in spring, regrow in fall.

borders. Sun; part shade in hot-summer areas. Any soil, if well drained. Ample water in winter, spring; keep on dry side in summer. Pull off old dry foliage after bloom. Divide crowded clumps. Easy from seed sown in spring.

BULRUSH, LOW. See Scirpus

BUNCHBERRY. See Cornus canadensis

BUNYA-BUNYA. See Araucaria bidwillii

BURNET, SALAD. See Sanguisorba

BURNET, SMALL. See Sanguisorba

BURNING BUSH. See Kochia scoparia 'Culta'

BURRO TAIL. See Sedum morganianum

BUSHMAN'S POISON. See Acokanthera venenata

BUSHY YATE. See Eucalyptus lehmannii

BUSY LIZZIE. See Impatiens walleriana

BUTCHER'S BROOM. See Ruscus aculeatus

BUTCHER'S BROOM, CLIMBING. See Semele

BUTIA capitata. PINDO PALM. Zones 7-9, 13-24. Native to Brazil, Uruguay, Argentina. Slow growing, very hardy palm to 10-20 ft. Trunk heavy, strongly patterned with stubs of old leaves: attractive if these are trimmed to the same length. Feather leaves—gray-green, arching. Hardy to 15°. Slow growth.

BUTTERCUP, CREEPING. See Ranunculus repens pleniflorus

BUTTERFLY BUSH. See Buddleia

BUTTERFLY FLOWER. See Schizanthus

BUTTONWOOD. See Platanus occidentalis

BUXUS. BOXWOOD, BOX. Evergreen shrubs, small trees. Widely used for edging and hedging. When not clipped, most grow soft and billowing. All grow in full sun or shade. All are easy where adapted and therefore often neglected. Extra care with watering, feeding, and spraying in summer for mites and scale will pay off in better color and greater vigor.

B. harlandii. Zones 8, 9, 12-24. The boxwood sold by this name in California and commonly called Korean boxwood does not fit the description of the true species *B. harlandii* and differs from both the Japanese boxwood and the true Korean boxwood. Leaves are narrower and brighter green than those of Japanese boxwood and the plant appears better suited to the colder areas of California, with greener winter color.

B. microphylla. This species is rarely planted. Its varieties are:

B. m. japonica. JAPANESE BOXWOOD. Zones 8, 9, 12-24. Hardy to 0° but poor winter appearance in cold areas. It takes California's dry heat and alkaline soil that rule out English boxwood. Compact foliage (small, ⅛-1 in. round-tipped leaves) is lively bright green in summer, turns brown or bronze in winter in many areas. Grows slowly to 4-6 ft. if not pruned, and then a pleasing informal green shrub. Most often clipped as low or medium hedge or shaped into globes, tiers, pyramids in containers.

B. m. koreana. KOREAN BOXWOOD. All Zones. Hardy to –18°. Slower and lower growing than Japanese boxwood. Leaves smaller, ¼-½ in. This should not be confused with the "Korean boxwood" or "*Buxus harlandii*" commonly sold in California. *B. m. koreana* is noted for its hardiness and will live where others freeze out. It is slower growing, and smaller in leaf than the plant sold as *B. harlandii*.

B. m. 'Richardii'. Hardy to 0°. Zones 4-24. Tall growing, more vigorous than Japanese boxwood. Leaves deeper green, larger, and usually notched at the tip.

B. sempervirens. COMMON BOXWOOD, ENGLISH BOXWOOD. Zones 3-6, 15-17. Dies out in alkaline soils, hot-summer areas. The dwarf form *B. s.* 'Suffruticosa' is best known; the taller-growing varieties are used in the Northwest. The species will grow to a height of 15-20 ft. with an equal spread. Dense foliage of medium-sized, lustrous, dark green, oval leaves.

B. s. arborescens. Slow. Becomes beautiful small tree to 18 ft. More open than species.

B. s. 'Aureo-variegata'. Leaves yellow or marked with yellow.

B. s. 'Handsworthii'. Erect, densely bushy, to 8 ft. with large broad leaves.

B. s. 'Suffruticosa'. TRUE DWARF BOXWOOD. Slower growing than species, to 4-5 ft. but generally clipped lower. Small leaves, dense form and texture. There's a silver-edged variegated form.

Climate
Zone maps
pages 8-27

CABBAGE. There are early varieties that take 2-3 months to mature and should be spaced 9-12 in. apart, and late varieties that mature in 3-4 months and need 18-30 in. spacing. Ask your nurseryman which kind you are buying, or read the descriptions on the seed packets. To avoid over-production, set out a few plants every week or two or plant both early and late kinds. Time plantings so heads will form either before or after the hot summer months. In cold-winter areas, set out late varieties in midsummer for late fall and early winter crops. In mild-winter areas plant in fall or winter.

Set plants in rich, moist soil, deeply and firmly so heavy heads won't lean or blow over. As plants grow, mound soil around stems to support tops. Additional roots will grow from covered stems. Never let plants wilt, especially after heads start to form. Control aphids and cabbageworm as suggested for broccoli. Prevent cabbage maggot damage to roots by spraying around young seedlings with sevin or diazinon (use only in seedling stage).

CABBAGE TREE, SPIKED. See Cussonia

CACTUS. Large family of succulent plants. (See Succulents.) Generally leafless, they have stems modified into cylinders, pads, or joints which store water in times of drought. A thick skin reduces evaporation, and most species have spines to protect plants against browsing animals. Flowers are usually large and brightly colored; fruits may also be colorful, and a few are edible.

All (with one doubtful exception) are native to the Americas. Here they grow from Canada to Argentina, from sea level into high mountains, in deserts or in dripping jungles. Many are native to drier parts of the West.

They range in height from a few inches to 50 ft. Larger species are used to create desert landscapes. Smaller species are grown in pots or, if sufficiently hardy, in rock gardens. Many are easy, showy house or

To handle cactus painlessly, use a paper collar to protect fingers from spines.

greenhouse plants. Large cactus for landscaping require full sun, well-drained soil. Water newly-planted cactus very little; roots are subject to rot at this stage. In 4-6 weeks, when new roots are active, water thoroughly, then let soil dry before watering again. Reduce watering in fall to allow plants to go dormant. Feed monthly in spring, summer. For some of the larger kinds for garden use see: *Carnegiea, Cephalocereus, Cereus, Echinocactus, Espostoa, Ferocactus, Lemaireocereus, Opuntia.*

Smaller cactus for pot or rock garden culture usually have interesting form and brightly colored flowers. Feed and water plants well during warm weather for a good display; taper off on fertilizer to encourage winter dormancy. Use a fast-draining mix. See *Chamaecereus, Coryphantha, Echinopsis, Lobivia, Lobivopsis, Mammillaria.*

Showiest in flower are the jungle cactus that grow as epiphytes on trees or rocks. These need rich soil with much vegetable matter, frequent feeding and watering, partial shade, and protection from frost. Grow in lath house or greenhouse, or handle as outdoor-indoor plants. See *Epiphyllum, Rhipsalidopsis, Schlumbergera, Zygocactus.*

CACTUS, BARREL. See Echinocactus, Ferocactus

CACTUS, CHRISTMAS. See Schlumbergera bridgesii

CACTUS, EASTER. See Rhipsalidopsis

CACTUS, EASTER LILY. See Echinopsis

CACTUS, CRAB. See Schlumbergera truncata

CACTUS, INDIAN FIG. See Opuntia ficus-indica

CACTUS, OLD MAN. See Cephalocereus

CACTUS, ORCHID. See Epiphyllum

CACTUS, ORGANPIPE. See Lemairecereus

CACTUS, PERUVIAN OLD MAN. See Espostoa

CACTUS, SEA URCHIN. See Echinopsis

CACTUS, TEDDYBEAR. See Opuntia bigelovii

CAESALPINIA. See Poinciana

CAJEPUT TREE. See Melaleuca quinquenervia

CALADIUM bicolor. FANCY-LEAFED CALADIUM. Tuberous-rooted perennial. Best adapted Zones 23, 24; in protected gardens Zones 12, 13, 16, 17, 21, 22; elsewhere as indoor or greenhouse plant in winter, outdoors in summer. Native to tropical America.

Not grown for flowers. Instead, entire show comes from large arrow-shaped, long-stalked, almost translucent leaves colored in bands and blotches of red, rose, pink, white, silver, bronze, and green. Most varieties sold in nurseries derived from *C. bicolor*, 2 ft., occasionally to 4 ft. Because caladiums need warm shade, daytime temperature of 70°, best adapted as summer pot plant in sheltered patios, or plunged in borders. Combine with ferns, coleus, alocasias, colocasias, and tuberous begonias.

Same pot culture as tuberous begonias. Start tubers indoors in March, outdoors in May. Pot in mix of equal parts coarse sand, leaf mold, ground bark or peat moss. Use 5-in. pot for 2½-in. tuber, 7-in. pot for 1 larger or 2 smaller tubers. Fill pot half-way with mix, stir in heaping teaspoon of fish meal. Add 1 in. mix, set tuber with knobby side up, cover with 2 in. of mix. Water thoroughly.

To plant in ground, replace top 6 in. of existing soil with same mix as for pots. Place 1 tablespoon of fish meal in bottom of each hole, proceed as described above. Keep soil moist, not wet. Provide more moisture as leaves develop. Syringe overhead every day or two during active growth. Feed with liquid fish fertilizer once a week, starting when leaves appear. Bait for slugs and snails. Gradually withhold water when leaves start to die down. In about a month, lift tubers, remove most of soil, dry in semi-shade for 10 days. Dust tubers with insecticide-fungicide preparation; store for winter in dry peat moss or vermiculite at temperature between 50-60°.

C. esculentum. See Colocasia

CALAMONDIN. See Citrus

CALATHEA. Indoor or greenhouse plants. Native to tropical America or Africa. Calatheas are usually called marantas, to which they are closely related and from which they differ only in technical aspects. Interesting plants for indoor decoration in winter, outdoor use in summer. Ornamental leaves, beautifully marked in various shades of green, white, and pink, arranged in basal tufts. Flowers inconspicuous and of no consequence. Need warm, moist atmosphere (not under 55°) and shade, although good light necessary for rich leaf color. Porous soil mix, perfect drainage; stagnant conditions harmful. Wet leaves frequently. Repot as often as necessary to avoid root-bound condition.

C. insignis. Striking, 3-7 ft. in native jungle, lower in cultivation, with 12-18-in.-long, yellow-green leaves striped olive green.

C. makoyana. Showy, 2-4 ft. high. Leaves with areas of olive green or cream above; pink blotches beneath. Silver featherings on rest of upper surface, with corresponding area underneath cream-colored.

C. ornata. Sturdy, 1½-3 ft. high. Leaves 2-3 ft. long, rich green above, purplish red beneath. Juvenile leaves usually pink-striped between veins, intermediate foliage striped white. Variety 'Rosea Lineata' has pink and white stripes at angle to midrib. Variety 'Sanderiana' is compact, leaves regularly marked with fine white lines.

C. zebrina. ZEBRA PLANT. Compact, 1-3 ft. high. Elliptic leaves 1-2 ft. long, almost half as wide, velvety green with alternating bars of pale yellow-green and olive green extending outward from midrib; purplish red underneath.

CALCEOLARIA. Perennials. Native Mexico to Chile. Loose clusters of small pouchlike or slipperlike flowers, usually yellow, sometimes red-bronze, or spotted with red or orange-brown, in spring and summer. Plants much-branched, often woody-stemmed and shrubby, 8 in. to 6 ft. high, with dark green, crinkly leaves.

Cheerful color in sun or filtered shade; also in pots or hanging baskets. Some sold in pots or cans. For others, sow seed in spring or summer in flats or pots of light porous soil. Grow shrubby kinds from cuttings. Keep in cool, airy, shaded place at temperature of 60°. In fall transplant into pots.

C. crenatiflora. Zones 17, 19-24. Calceolaria of the florists. To 2½ ft. Coarsely toothed, soft-hairy leaves 4-8 in. long. Drooping flowers 1 in. long, yellow, with orange-red spots on inflated lower lip. Numerous strains with many color variations. Best in cool greenhouse, in cool, shady places. Sometimes used as bedding plants.

C. integrifolia. Zones 15-24. Shrubby plant 1½-6 ft. high. Leaves about 3 in. long and 1 in. wide. Clusters of yellow to red-brown, unspotted flowers ½ in. across. Will grow in full sun, take heat, light frost. Borders, pots, hanging baskets. Best bloom where root-bound. Good cut flower. Variety 'Golden Nugget' most commonly sold: vigorous, 18-24 in., clear golden yellow flowers from spring to fall.

C. 'John Innes'. All Zones. Bedding and rock garden plant to 8 in. high, with 3-in.-long leaves and large, golden yellow, purple-spotted flowers in June, July. Spreading growth habit in some instances; stems tend to take root in contact with soil. Needs rich, moist soil and shade.

CALENDULA officinalis. CALENDULA, POT MARIGOLD. Annual. Sure, easy color from late fall through spring in mild-winter areas; spring to midsummer in colder climates. Besides the familiar orange and bright yellow double, daisylike blooms 2½-4½ in. across, calendulas come in more subtle shades of apricot, persimmon, cream, and soft yellow. Pacific Beauty strain one of the best. Plants somewhat branching, 1-2 ft. high. Leaves are long, narrow, round on the ends, and slightly sticky. Plants effective in masses of single colors in borders, parking strips, along drives, in containers. Long-lasting cut flowers.

Sow seed in place or in flats in late summer or early fall in mild-winter climates; spring elsewhere. Or buy seedlings at nurseries. Adapts to most soils, ample or little water, if drainage is fast. Remove spent flowers to prolong bloom.

CALICO BUSH. See Kalmia latifolia

CALIFORNIA POPPY. See Eschscholzia

CALLA. See Zantedeschia

CALLA, BLACK. See Arum palaestinum

CALLIANDRA. Evergreen shrub. A group of 250 or more species represented here by a flame bush, a pink powder puff, and a fairy duster. All are showy, spreading shrubs that need sun and warmth.

C. eriophylla. FAIRY DUSTER, FALSE MESQUITE. Zones 10-13. Native to Imperial and eastern San Diego counties, California, east to Texas; and Baja California. Open growing to 3 ft., spreading 4-5 ft. Leaves finely cut into tiny leaflets. Flower clusters show pink to red stamens in fluffy balls to 1½ in. across, February or March.

C. inaequilatera. PINK POWDER PUFF. Zones 22-24. Native to Bolivia. Grows fast to 10 ft. or more, equal spread. Its beauty

has carried it into less kind areas than Zones 22-24: into 13, 16-21 where it is given special protection of overhang or warm sunny wall. (In form, it's a natural espalier.) Foliage not as feathery as *C. tweedii*. Leaflets longer, broader and darker green; glossy copper when new, turning to a dark metallic green. Big powder puffs (2-3 in. across) of silky stamens, watermelon pink, are produced October-March. Needs plenty of water and a fast-draining light soil.

C. tweedii (*C. guildingi*). TRINIDAD FLAME BUSH, BRAZILIAN FLAME BUSH. Best in Zones 22-24; satisfactory 15-21; freezes back but recovers in Zones 7-9, 12-14. Graceful picturesque structure to 6-8 ft. tall, 5-8 ft. wide. Leaves, lacy and fernlike, divided into many tiny leaflets, scarcely hide the branches. At branch ends flower clusters show as bright crimson pompons, February to fall. Not fussy about soil. Once established it's quite drought resistant. Prune to thin and also to retain the interesting branch pattern.

CALLICARPA. BEAUTY BERRY. Deciduous shrubs. Zones 1-6. Grown in cold-winter areas for many showy pea-sized fruits in clusters close to stem from October until birds strip them. Freezes to ground in severe winter, comes back quickly from stump sprouts.

C. bodinieri giraldii (*C. giraldiana*). To 6-10 ft. with gracefully recurving branches. Leaves narrow, 4 in. long, somewhat resemble peach leaves, turn pink or purple before dropping. Small lilac flowers in 1-in.-wide clusters followed by violet-purple fruits. Makes a good deciduous hedge plant.

C. dichotoma. Upright growth to 6 ft. Leaves (1½-3 in. long) and stems turn purplish in autumn. Tiny pink flowers in ½-in.-wide clusters followed by pinkish violet fruits.

CALLIOPSIS. See Coreopsis tinctoria

CALLISTEMON. BOTTLEBRUSH. Evergreen shrubs or trees. Zones 8, 9, 12-24, but borderline and severely damaged at 20°. Native to Australia. Colorful flowers in dense spikes or round clusters consisting principally of long, threadlike stamens—hence the name bottlebrush. Flowers followed by woody capsules that persist for years and sometimes look like bands of beads pressed into bark. Thrive in full sun. Drought tolerant but grow best in moist, well drained soils. Generally tolerant of saline-alkaline soils but sometimes suffer from chlorosis. Fast growing, easy to train. Quick wall cover as informal espaliers. Several can be trained as small trees. Some can be used in formal clipped hedges or as informal screens or windbreaks. A few can be trained as ground covers.

Many kinds are being sold under names whose identification is uncertain. Closely related to *Melaleuca*, and some plants sold as *Callistemon* may be melaleucas.

C. brachyandrus. PRICKLY BOTTLEBRUSH. Slender shrub 4-6 ft. high. Sparsely foliaged with stiff, narrow, sharp-pointed, gray-green leaves that look like inch-long pine needles. Flowers in 3-in.-long clusters, dark red or purplish.

C. citrinus (*C. lanceolatus*). LEMON BOTTLEBRUSH. Best-selling bottlebrush, most

tolerant of heat, cold, adverse soils. A massive shrub to 10-15 ft., but with staking and pruning in youth easily trained into a narrowish, round-headed 20-25-ft. tree. Nurseries offer it as shrub, espalier, or tree. Narrow, 3-in.-long leaves coppery colored in new growth, then vivid green. Bright red, 6-in.-long brushes appear in cycles throughout the year.

A variable plant when grown from seed. Cutting-grown selections with good flower size and color are *C. c.* 'Improved' and *C. c.* 'Splendens'. *C. c.* 'Compacta' is smaller (4 ft. by 4 ft. at 3 years), with smaller spikes.

C. cupressifolius. The plant sold under this name may be a melaleuca or a variety of some other species of *Callistemon*. Shrubby, 4-5 ft. high, 4-6 ft. wide. Habit spreading, with drooping branchlets. Foliage gray-green; new foliage pink. Red flower clusters to 3 in. long in June-July.

C. 'Jeffersii'. The plant sold under this name may be a form of *C. citrinus*. It's shrubby, to 6 ft. tall, 4 ft. wide, stiffer in habit, with narrower and smaller leaves than lemon bottlebrush. Flowers reddish purple fading lavender.

C. lilacinus. (Often sold as *C. violaceus*.) Dense, rounded shrub. 10 ft. high (sometimes taller). Branches more spreading than *C. citrinus*. Light green leaves. Deep red, 2-in.-long flower brushes; blooms in cycles, peak in spring.

C. linearis. NARROW-LEAFED BOTTLEBRUSH. Shrubby, 6-8 ft. tall (sometimes to 15 ft.), 5 ft. wide, with narrow, 2-5-in.-long leaves. Bright crimson brushes 5 in. long in summer. *C. l.* 'Pumila' reaches 3-6 ft. Has loose, airy growth habit. New growth has silky sheen, turns purplish at maturity.

C. phoeniceus. FIERY BOTTLEBRUSH. Shrub 6-8 ft. high, similar to *C. citrinus*, but stiffer growing, more densely foliaged. Light green to gray leaves 4 in. long. Flower brushes to 4 in. long, rich red; blooms in spring, again in fall. Variety 'Prostrata' is a sprawling shrub to 5-6 ft. Useful as bank cover.

C. pinifolius. Shrub 6-7 ft. high with airy open growth. Narrow leaves like 4-in. pine needles. Flower spikes 6 in. long, yellowish to green. Summer bloom.

C. rigidus. STIFF BOTTLEBRUSH. Erect, sparse, rigid shrub or small tree to 20 ft. with 10-ft. spread. Leaves sharp-pointed, gray-green (sometimes purplish). Red flower brushes 2½-4½ in. long, spring and summer. Seed capsules prominent. Least graceful bottlebrush, but drought tolerant.

C. 'Rosea'. Plants sold under this name are similar to *C.* 'Jeffersii' but taller, and have rose-pink flowers.

C. salignus. WHITE BOTTLEBRUSH. Shrub or tree to 20-25 ft. Dense crown of foliage. New growth bright pink to copper. Willowy leaves 2-3 in. long. Flowers pale yellow to creamy, in 1½-3-in. clusters. Train as small shade tree or plant 4-5 ft. apart as a hedge.

C. viminalis. WEEPING BOTTLEBRUSH. Shrub or small tree with pendulous branches. Fast growing to 20-30 ft. with 15-ft. spread. Leaves narrow, light green, 6 in. long. Bright red brushes May-July, and scattered bloom throughout year. Needs ample water. Not for windy, dry areas. As

Climate
Zone maps
pages 8-27

a tree, it needs staking, thinning of surplus branches to prevent tangled, topheavy growth. Inclined toward sparseness because leaves tend to grow only at ends of long, hanging branchlets. *C. v.* 'McCaskillii' is more vigorous, denser in habit, better in flower color and form. A variety sold as 'Dwarf' resembles variety 'McCaskillii'.

CALLISTEPHUS chinensis. CHINA ASTER. Annual. A splendid cut flower and effective bedding plant when well grown and free of disease. Plants 1-3 ft. high, some kinds branching, others (developed mainly for florists) with strong stems and no side-shoots. Leaves deeply toothed or lobed. Summer is the bloom season. Many different flower forms: quilled, curled, incurved, ribbonlike, or interlaced rays; some with crested centers; varieties offered as pompon, peony-flowered, anemone-flowered, ostrich feather. Colors range from white to pastel pinks, rose-pink, lavender, lavender-blue, violet, purple, crimson, wine, and scarlet.

Plant in rich loamy or sandy soil in full sun. Sow seed in place after frosts or set out plants from flats. Keep growth steady; sudden checks in growth are harmful. Subject to aster yellows, a virus disease carried by leafhoppers. Remove and burn infected plants. Spray or dust to control leafhoppers. Control of aster wilt or stem rot, caused by parasitic fungus which lives in soil and is transmitted through roots into plants, is possible only through use of wilt-resistant types. Overwatering produces ideal condition for diseases, especially in heavy soil. Never plant in same location in successive years.

CALLUNA. See Heaths and Heathers

CALOCEDRUS decurrens (*Libocedrus decurrens*). INCENSE CEDAR. Evergreen tree. Zones 1-12, 14-24. Native to mountains of southern Oregon, California, western Nevada; northern Baja California. Unlike its native associates—white fir, Douglas fir, ponderosa pine, sugar pine—it adapts to many Western climates. Symmetrical tree to 75-90 ft. with dense, narrow, pyramidal crown; trunk with reddish brown bark. Rich green foliage in flat sprays. Tree gives pungent fragrance to garden in warm weather. Small, yellowish brown to reddish brown cones which, when open, look like ducks' bills.

Although slow growing at first, once established it may grow 2 ft. per year. Deep but infrequent watering in youth will make it unusually drought tolerant when mature. Good tree to make a green wall, high screen, windbreak.

CALOCEPHALUS brownii. CUSHION BUSH. Evergreen shrubby perennial. Zones 16, 17, 19, 21-24. Best adapted Zones 17, 24. Native to Australia, Tasmania. An unusual mounding plant, silvery white throughout, at its best when buffeted by winds and exposed to salt air and spray. Wiry branching stems, tiny, threadlike leaves, ⅛ in. long, pressed tightly against slender stems. Flower heads button-shaped, ½ in. across, in clusters. Stunning high ground cover or rock garden plant. Effective in large planters with succulents. Fresh or dried foliage attractive in arrangements. Full sun, sandy or gravelly soil, fast drainage. Sensitive to excess water,

severe cold. Cut out dead wood on older plants.

CALOCHORTUS. Corms. All Zones. Western natives, numerous in California. Of most interest to hobbyists willing to devote more than ordinary care to a beautiful group of plants. It's best to plant kinds native to your area or a similar climate. All kinds should be kept moist in spring, allowed to go dry in summer. Can grow in cans or boxes; plunge in garden in fall, lift after bloom to dry out in summer. In colder

Cat's ears (note hairy flower segments); not showiest Calochortus, but appealing.

climates, mulch plantings to protect from alternate freezing and thawing, remove mulch in spring; or grow indoors in pots. Flower forms divide into 3 groups:

GLOBE TULIPS, FAIRY LANTERNS

Each stalk bears 2-5 nodding flowers; petals turn inward to form a globe.

C. albus. WHITE GLOBE LILY, FAIRY LANTERN. Sierra foothills, north Coast Ranges. Slender 2-ft. stems; white 1¼-inch flowers March-May.

C. amabilis. GOLDEN FAIRY LANTERN. North Coast Ranges. Stems 15 in. tall; flowers 1¼ in. long, deep yellow often tinged brown, March-May.

C. amoenus. PURPLE GLOBE TULIP. Sierra foothills. Rosy purple lanterns 1¼-in. long; 8-16-in. stems; April-June.

STAR TULIPS, CAT'S EARS

Erect, cup-shaped flowers, often with tips of petals rolled outwards. Those with long, straight hairs on inner surfaces of blooms called cat's ears.

C. coeruleus. CAT'S EARS. Sierra Nevada. Bluish flowers ½ in. long, 1 in. wide, on 3-6-in. stems in March-April.

C. uniflorus (*C. lilacinus*). STAR TULIP. Northern California coast and northern Coast Ranges. Lilac flowers 1 in. long, 1½ in. wide, 10-in. stems, April-June.

MARIPOSA LILIES

Most striking. Erect branching stems 10-24 in. tall. Big, colorful, cup-shaped flowers.

C. clavatus. Dry Sierra Nevada foothills. Clear yellow flowers, sometimes marked brownish red, 2-3 in. wide; stems to 3 ft., April-June.

C. kennedyi. Arizona, California, Nevada deserts. Yellow, orange, vermilion flowers, 2-3 in. wide, April-June.

C. macrocarpus. GREEN-BANDED MARIPOSA LILY. British Columbia, Montana south to northeastern California. Purple flowers 2-4 in. wide, green stripe down middle of each petal, often deep purple center; stems 2 ft., July-August.

C. nuttallii. SEGO LILY. Washington to northern California, east and south to New Mexico. State flower of Utah. Flowers white, marked lilac or purple, 2-3 in. wide; stems 1½ ft. tall. Early summer bloom.

C. venustus. WHITE MARIPOSA LILY. Central, southern California Coast Ranges, Sierra Nevada foothills. Flowers 3-3½ in. wide, white or yellow to purple, dark red, often with peacock eye at base of petals. Stems 10 in. or more. Blooms May-July.

CALODENDRUM capense. CAPE CHESTNUT. Briefly deciduous tree. Zones 19, 21-24. Native to South Africa. Broad-crowned, 25-40 ft., noteworthy for profuse display of spikes of rosy lilac, 1½-in.-long flowers, the whole cluster measuring 10-12 in. high by as much across, and extending well above foliage like candelabra. Blooms generally from May into July. Seldom flowers when young. Slow growing. Leaves are light to medium green, oval-shaped, to 6 in. Time of flowering and deciduous period varies by location and season. Plant it out of prevailing wind.

CALONYCTION aculeatum. MOONFLOWER. Perennial vine usually treated as annual. Greenhouse plant in coldest climates. Fast-growing (20-30 ft. in a season) shade for arbor, trellis, or fence in summer. Effective combined with annual 'Heavenly Blue' morning glory. Luxuriant leaves, 3-8 in. long, heart-shaped, closely spaced on stems. Flowers fragrant, white, rarely lavender-pink, often banded with green, 6 in. long and across. Theoretically flowers open only after sundown, but they stay open on dull days. Seeds very hard; file, or soak 1-2 days for faster sprouting.

CALOTHAMNUS. NET BUSH. Evergreen shrubs. Native to Western Australia. Related to bottle brush (*Callistemon*) and probably adapted to same climates. Fairly drought resistant, take sun, heat, wind, salt breeze, and poor soil if it drains well (expect root rot if drainage is poor). Needlelike leaves densely clothe the rather spreading branches. Flowers, somewhat resembling bottlebrushes, grow along the branches, rather close to the wood. Bloom sporadic throughout the year.

Prune hard after flowering to keep plants from getting straggly. Generally not attractive in age, showing more wood than foliage.

A number of species were introduced into California in the 1920's. The following are being grown by nurseries:

C. quadrifidus. Grows to 6-8 ft. high. Dark green leaves, ½-1 in. long. Short clusters of dark red flowers.

C. rupestris. Grows to 5 ft. Short, curved leaves. Short clusters of crimson flowers.

C. villosus. To 4 ft. Soft-hairy, ½-in.-long leaves. Long, deep red flower clusters.

CALTHA palustris. MARSH-MARIGOLD. Perennial. All Zones. Native to eastern U. S. A bog or marsh plant well adapted to edges of pools, ponds, streams, other moist situations. With sufficient water, can be grown in borders, but must not dry out in summer. Good with bog irises, moisture-loving ferns. To 2 ft., lush green leaves 2-7 in. across; vivid yellow flowers 2 in. across, in clusters. Increase by divisions or sow seed in boggy soil.

CALYCANTHUS. SWEET SHRUB. Deciduous shrubs. Represented in western gardens by a western and eastern native.

C. floridus. CAROLINA ALLSPICE. Hardy Zones 1-9, 14-22. Native Virginia to Florida. Grows to 10 ft., spreading 5-8 ft., stiffly branched. Leaves oval to 5 in., glossy dark green above, grayish green beneath. Flowers, 2 in. wide, maroon brown, with strawberry-like fragrance, carried at ends of leafy branchlets in May to July, depending on climate and exposure. They are followed by brownish pear-shaped capsules fragrant when crushed. Grows in shade or sun, any soil.

C. occidentalis. SPICE BUSH. Zones 4-9, 14-22. Native along streams, moist slopes, California Coast Ranges, Sierra Nevada foothills. To 4-12 ft. high. Leaves 2-6 in. long, 1-2 in. wide, bright green, turning yellow in fall. Flowers reddish brown to 2 in. across, like small water lilies, appear April-August depending on climate. Both flowers and bruised leaves have the fragrance of an old wine barrel. Takes sun or part shade and ordinary garden care. Can be trained into a multi-stemmed small tree.

CALYPSO bulbosa. Terrestrial orchid. Zones 4-6, 15-17. Native to the northern hemisphere and fairly common in heavily forested areas of the Northwest, where they grow on decayed logs or in leaf mold.

Solitary, pendant, pink flowers an inch or more across with brown spots in lines, and purple and yellow markings in the pouchlike lip. Grow them in leaf mold or forest duff and protect from birds and slugs. Will take sub-zero temperatures.

CAMASSIA. CAMASS. Bulbs. Zones 1-9, 14-17. Most species native to moist meadows, marshes, fields in northern California and the Northwest. Plant in moist situation, fairly heavy soil, where bulbs can remain undisturbed for many years. Set bulbs 4 in. deep, 6 in. apart. To avoid premature rooting, plant after weather cools in fall. Need lots of water while growing. The grasslike basal leaves dry quickly after late spring-early summer bloom.

C. cusickii. Dense clusters of pale blue flowers on stems 3-4 ft. tall.

C. howellii. Pale blue flowers in full clusters on 18-in. stems.

C. leichtlinii. Large handsome clusters of deep blue-violet to bright blue (sometimes white) flowers on stems 2-4 ft. tall.

C. quamash. Loose clusters of deep blue-violet flowers on 3 ft. stems.

CAMELLIA. Evergreen shrubs. Most favored in Zones 4-9, 14-24. Native to eastern and southern Asia. There are over 3,000 named kinds, and the range in color, size, and form is remarkable. But camellia breeding is still in its infancy, and what is yet to come stirs the imagination—blue and purple camellias, yellow and orange camellias, fragrant camellias, all are possible and all will come.

In these few pages we treat briefly the cultural requirements of camellias and describe some of the lesser known species as well as the widely distributed old favorites and new varieties. Where a certain type of camellia has a specific cultural need, that need is given in the description.

Camellias need a well drained soil rich in organic material. If drainage is slow, or if the soil is highly alkaline, plant in raised beds or in containers. Fill with a U.C.-type mix with perhaps 50 per cent or more organic material. Never plant camellias so that trunk base is below soil line, and never permit soil to wash over and cover this base. Keep roots cool with a 2-in.-thick mulch.

Keep soil moist, not wet. Don't forget to water plants under roof overhangs during rainy seasons. In hot, dry spells sprinkle the foliage, but don't make this a substitute for regular watering. Where water is high in salts, leach accumulated salts by an extra deep soaking—twice in summer—to carry excess salts below the root zone.

Fertilize with a commercial acid plant food. Generally, the time to feed is in the weeks and months following bloom; read fertilizer label for complete instructions. Don't use more than called for. Better to cut amounts in half and feed twice as frequently. Don't feed a sick plant. Poor drainage, water or soil with excess salts are the main trouble causers. Best cure is to move plant into above-ground bed of straight ground bark or peat moss until it recovers.

Scorched or yellowed areas in the center of leaves are usually due to sunburn. Burned leaf edges, excessive leaf drop, or corky spots usually indicate over-fertilizing. Yellow leaves with green veins are signs of chlorosis. Check drainage, leach, treat with iron or iron chelates.

One disease may be serious: camellia petal blight. Flowers rapidly turn an ugly brown. Browning at the edges of petals (especially whites and pale pinks) may be caused by sun or wind, but if brown rapidly runs into center of flower, suspect petal blight. Pick up and burn (or place in a covered garbage can) all fallen flowers and petals, and pick off all infected flowers from the plants. Remove mulch (if you use one), haul it away, and replace with a fresh one. Spray the ground under plants with PCNB several weeks before flowers begin to open.

Generally, camellias are remarkably pest free. Occasionally they may be bothered by aphids, scale, spider mites, slugs or snails. If leaf edges are chewed or notched, check for brachyrhinus or similar weevils, treat soil for them if they are present.

Some flower bud dropping may be a natural phenomenon; many camellias set more buds than they can open. Some bud drop can be caused by overwatering, more by underwatering, especially during summer.

Some varieties bear too many flowers. To get nicest display from them, disbud in midsummer like this: From branch-end clusters, remove all but one or two round flower buds (leaf buds are slender). Along stems, remove enough to leave a single flower bud for each 2-4 in. of branch.

Prune right after flowering or during summer and fall. Remove dead or weak wood and thin when growth is so dense that flowers have no room to open properly. Prune at will to get the form you want. Shorten lower branches to encourage upright growth. Lanky shrubs can be fattened by cutting back top growth. Make cut just above the scar that terminates the previous year's growth; it is usually a slightly thickened, somewhat rough area where bark texture and color change slightly. A cut just above this point will usually force 3 or 4 dormant buds into growth.

C. granthamiana. Many plants are rare in nature. This one is as rare as can be; only one specimen has ever been found in the wilds, and that not until 1955. Its offspring are now growing in a number of Western nurseries and gardens in several of California's camellia climates.

It promises to be a big shrub or small tree of rather open growth with leathery, heavily veined and crinkled glossy leaves 2-6 in. long. Flowers large (to 6 in. or more across), white, single, often with

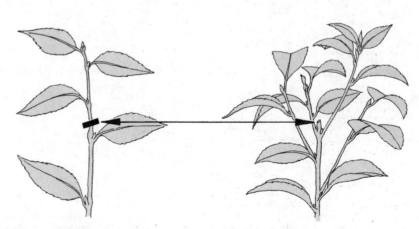

To prune camellias for bushiness, make cuts just above scar at point where one year's growth stopped and next began (left). Several branches will grow beneath cut (right).

Climate Zone maps pages 8-27

fluted or folded ("rabbit-ear") petals, and centered with a heavy tuft of bright yellow stamens. Flowers open in October, November, and December from large, brown, scaly, silky-haired buds. Blooms sensational on young plants in 1-gallon cans. A plant for fanciers and for hybridists, who hope to breed its unusual foliage and early bloom into other species.

C. hiemalis. Includes a number of varieties formerly listed as Sasanquas. They were segregated because of their later and longer bloom and heavier-textured flowers. Three good examples:

'Shishi-Gashira'. One of the most useful and ornamental shrubs. Low growing with arching branches that in time pile up tier on tier to make a compact, dark green, glossy-leafed plant. Leaves rather small for a camellia, giving a medium-fine foliage texture. Flowers rose red, semi-double to double, 2-2½ in. wide, heavily borne over a long season—October to March in a good year. Full sun or shade.

'Showa-No-Sakae'. Faster growing, more open than 'Shishi-Gashira'; willowy, arching branches. Semi-double to double flowers of soft pink, occasionally marked with white. Try this as an espalier or in a hanging basket.

'Showa Supreme' is very similar, but has somewhat larger flowers of peony form.

C. japonica. This to most gardeners is *the* camellia. Naturally a large shrub or small tree, but variable in size, growth rate, and habit. Hundred-year-old plants in California are over 20 ft. high and equally wide, and larger plants exist, but most gardeners can consider camellias 6-12-ft. shrubs, and many varieties are lower growing.

Here is a selection of 20 varieties that are old standbys with Western gardeners. Easily obtainable, inexpensive, and handsome even in comparison with some of the newest introductions, they are plants for the beginner—but not only for the beginner.

In the list, season of bloom is noted by "E", "M", or "L". In California "early" means October to January; "midseason", January to March; "late", March to May. In the Northwest, it's December to February for "early"; March and April, "midseason"; May, "late".

Also, flower size is noted for each variety. A "very large" flower is over 5 in. across. "Large" is 4-5 in., "medium large" 3½-4 in., "medium" 3-3½ in., "small" 2½-3 in., "miniature" 2½ in. or less.

'Adolphe Audusson'. M. Very large, dark red, semi-double flowers, heavily borne on a medium-sized, symmetrical, vigorous shrub. Hardy. 'Adolphe Audusson Variegated' is identical, but heavily marbled white on red.

'Alba Plena'. E. Brought from China in 1792, and still a favorite large, white, formal, double. Slow bushy growth. Early bloom a disadvantage in cold or rainy areas. Protect flowers from rain and wind.

'Berenice Boddy'. M. Medium semi-double, light pink with deeper shading. Vigorous, upright growth. One of the most cold-hardy of camellias.

'Daikagura'. E. Large, deep rose pink, peony-form flowers marbled white. Begins flowering with the earliest and blooms until the season ends. Not at its best in cold regions. Slow, compact grower. Several closely related varieties are identical except for color: 'Daikagura Red', solid red; 'High Hat', pale pink; 'Conrad Hilton', eggshell white.

'Debutante'. E-M. Medium large, peony-form flowers of light pink. Free-blooming. Vigorous upright growth.

'Donckelarii'. M. Red marbled white; amount of marbling varies, even on the same plant. Large semi-double flowers. Slow, bushy growth. Hardy.

'Dr. Tinsley'. M. Medium semi-double of wild rose form. Blooms very pale pink shading deeper pink at petal edge. Compact, upright plant of good cold resistance.

'Elegans (Chandler)'. (Also known as 'Chandleri Elegans' and 'Francine'). E-M. Very large anemone-form camellia with rose pink petals and smaller petals called petaloids, the latter often marked white. Slow growth and spreading, arching branches make it a natural for espalier. Stake to provide height, and don't remove the main shoot; it may be very slow to resume upward growth. A hundred-year-old-plus variety that remains a favorite. Its offspring resemble it in every way except flower color: 'C. M. Wilson', pale pink; 'Shiro Chan', white, sometimes faintly marked with pink; and 'Elegans (Chandler) Variegated', heavily marbled rose pink and white.

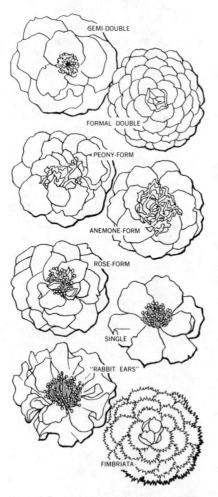

SEMI-DOUBLE

FORMAL DOUBLE

PEONY-FORM

ANEMONE-FORM

ROSE-FORM

SINGLE

"RABBIT EARS"

FIMBRIATA

Varied flower forms of Camellia japonica; flower size ranges from 2 to more than 5 in.

'Finlandia'. E-M. Medium large semi-double with swirled and fluted petals. Medium, compact growth. Similar are 'Finlandia Blush', with pale pink flowers; 'Finlandia Red', a salmon red; and 'Finlandia Variegated', with white flowers streaked crimson. All free blooming.

'Glen 40'. ('Coquetti'). M-L. Large formal double of deep red. One of the best reds for corsages. Slow, compact, upright growth. Handsome even out of flower. Hardy. Plant very good in containers.

'Herme'. ('Jordan's Pride'). M. Medium large, semi-double flowers are pink, irregularly bordered white and streaked deep pink. Sometimes has all solid pink flowers on certain branches. Free-blooming, dependable.

'Kumasaka'. M-L. Medium large, rose-form to peony-form rose pink. Vigorous, compact, upright growth and remarkably heavy flower production make it a choice landscape plant. Hardy. Takes morning sun.

'Lady Clare'. E-M. Large, semi-double rose pink, saucer-shaped blooms. Not long lasting but drop cleanly. Vigorous, spreading, willowy. Ideally adapted as espalier.

'Magnoliaeflora'. M. Medium semi-double flowers of pale pink. Free blooming and a good cut flower. Medium grower of compact yet spreading form. Hardy.

'Mathotiana'. M-L. Very large rose-form to formal double of deep crimson, sometimes with a purplish cast. Vigorous, upright grower. Takes cold and stands up well in hot summer areas. Not too good on southern California coast.

'Mrs. Charles Cobb'. M. Large semi-double to peony-form flowers in deep red. Free flowering. Compact plant with dense foliage. Best in warmer areas.

'Mrs. Nellie Eastman'. M. White striped and streaked red. Large peony-form to rose-form double. Medium growth rate, upright habit.

'Prince Eugene Napoleon'. ('Pope Pius IX'). M. A cherry red, medium large formal double. Medium, compact, upright growth.

'Purity'. L. White, medium size rose-form to formal double, usually showing a few stamens. Vigorous, upright plant. Late bloom often escapes rain damage.

'Ville de Nantes'. M-L. Large semi-double flowers of deep red blotched white. Petals pleated and fringed. Slow, bushy growth.

Every year new introductions bid for a place on the list of favorites. Of the newer varieties these are choice:

'Betty Sheffield Supreme'. M. Unique flower markings: petals white with a deep pink to red border. Form variable, from semi-double through peony-form to formal double. Large flowers on a medium, compact shrub.

'Carter's Sunburst'. E-L. Large to very large pale pink flowers striped deeper pink. Semi-double to peony-form to formal double flowers on a medium, compact plant.

'Drama Girl'. M. Huge, semi-double flowers of deep salmon rose pink. Vigorous, open, pendulous growth.

'Guilio Nuccio'. M. Coral rose, very large semi-double flowers with inner petals fluted in "rabbit-ear" effect. Unusual depth and substance. Vigorous, upright growth. Only variety to win the Royal Horticultural

C

Climate Zone maps pages 8-27

Society's Award of Merit, it may well be the world's greatest camellia. Variegated, fringed forms are available.

'Kramer's Supreme'. M. Very large, deep peony-form full flowers of deep clear red. Slightly fragrant. Unusually vigorous, compact, and upright. Takes some sun.

'Mrs. D. W. Davis'. M. Spectacular, very large, somewhat cup-shaped flowers of palest blush pink open from egg-sized buds. Vigorous, upright, compact plant with very handsome broad leaves.

'Reg Ragland'. E-L. Large, semi-double red flowers with smaller, upright center petals surrounding a mass of yellow stamens. Medium, compact growth.

'Tiffany'. M-L. Very large, warm pink flowers. Rose-form to loose, irregular semi-double. Vigorous, upright shrub.

'Tomorrow'. E-M. Very large semi-double to peony-form flower of strawberry red. Vigorous, open, somewhat pendulous growth.

'White Nun'. M. Very large, semi-double flowers on vigorous, upright shrub. A fine pure white.

C. reticulata. Some of the biggest and most spectacular camellia flowers occur in this species, and likely as not they appear on some of the lankiest and least graceful plants.

The plant varies somewhat according to variety, but generally speaking, it is a rather gaunt and open shrub which eventually becomes a tree of considerable size—possibly 35 or 50 ft. tall. For gardens, consider it a 10-ft.-tall shrub, 8 ft. wide. Leaves also variable, tend to be dull green, leathery, and strongly net-veined.

Culture is quite similar to that of other camellias, except that the plants seem intolerant of heavy pruning. This, added to their natural lankiness and size, makes them difficult to place in the garden. They are at their best in the light shade of old oaks, where they should stand alone with plenty of room to develop. They are good container subjects while young, but are not handsome out of bloom. They develop better form and heavier foliage in the open ground. In Zones 4-6 grow them in containers so you can move them into winter protection.

Best known varieties have very large, semi-double flowers with the inner petals deeply fluted and curled. These inner petals give great depth to the flower. All bloom from January to May in California, March through May in the Northwest. Best varieties for garden use are these:

'Buddha'. Rose pink flower of very large size, the inner petals unusually erect and wavy. Gaunt, open; fast growth.

'Butterfly Wings'. Loose, semi-double, of great size (reported up to 9 in. across), rose pink; petals broad and wavy. Growth open, rather narrow.

'Captain Rawes'. Reddish rose pink semi-double flowers of large size. Vigorous, bushy plant with good foliage. Hardiest of the Reticulatas.

'Chang's Temple'. Pink, heavily variegated with white. Large, deep, irregular peony-form flowers with wavy petals. Vigorous plant with big leaves usually marked with white. May be same as the variety 'Cornelian'.

'Crimson Robe'. Very large, bright red, semi-double flowers. Petals firm-textured and wavy. Vigorous plant of better appearance than most Reticulatas.

'Lion Head'. Very large red flowers heavily variegated with white. Irregular semi-double to peony-form. Petals wavy, curled, often arched over the flower center. Vigorous grower.

'Noble Pearl'. Very large, deep red-pink flowers of loose semi-double form with heavily crinkled petals. Plant form and foliage very good.

'Purple Gown'. Large purplish red, peony-form to formal double flowers. Compact plant with best growth habit and foliage in the group.

'Shot Silk'. Large, loose, semi-double flowers of brilliant pink with an iridescent finish that sparkles in the sunlight. Fast, rather open growth.

C. saluenensis. Shrub of densely leafy habit to 10-15 ft. tall. Leaves elliptic, rather narrow, pointed, thick-textured, 1½-2½ in. long and half as wide. The flowers bell-shaped, rather small, and vary in color from white to fairly deep pink. Flowering is in early spring. Not of great value in itself, it has brought floriferousness, hardiness, and graceful appearance to a large group of its hybrids.

C. sasanqua. The Sasanquas are useful broad-leafed evergreens for espaliers, ground covers, informal hedges, screening, containers, and bonsai. They vary in habit from upright and densely bushy to spreading and vinelike. Leaves dark green, shiny, 1½-3½ in. long, a third as wide. Flowers very heavily produced in autumn and early winter, short-lived, rather flimsy, but so numerous that plants make a show for months. Some are lightly fragrant.

Most Sasanquas tolerate much sun, and some thrive in full hot sun if soil is right and watering ample. The Sasanquas are perfectly hardy in the camellia areas of the Pacific Northwest, but flowers are too often damaged by fall and winter rains and frost to call them successful.

'Cleopatra'. Rose pink, semi-double, with narrow, curving petals. Growth is erect, fairly compact. Takes clipping well.

'Hugh Evans'. Small to medium, pink flowers very heavily produced on upright, bushy shrub with weeping branches. Quite sun-tolerant. Effective as screen or informal hedge.

'Jean May'. Large double shell pink. Compact, upright grower with exceptionally glossy foliage.

'Mine-No-Yuki'. ('White Doves'). Large, white, peony-form double. Drops many buds. Spreading, willowy growth; effective espalier.

'Rosea'. Medium, single, rose pink with considerable fragrance. Upright growth. Hardy.

'Setsugekka'. Large white semi-double flowers with fluted petals. Considerable substance to flowers; cut sprays hold well in water. Upright, rather bushy growth.

'Shichi-Fukujin'. Very large, semi-double rose pink with deeper edge. Petals crimped. Upright growth.

'Sparkling Burgundy'. Large peony-form flowers of ruby rose. Vigorous, upright growth. Excellent espalier.

'Tanya'. Deep rose pink single flowers. Spreading growth with excellent foliage and high heat and sun resistance. A fine ground cover.

'White Frills'. Semi-double, frilled white flowers on a spreading, willowy plant. Outstanding in Zones 23, 24.

C. sinensis (*Thea sinensis*). TEA. Here the tea plant grows as a dense, round shrub to 15 ft. with leathery, dull dark green leaves to 5 in. long. Flowers are white, small (1½ in. across), and fragrant; autumn. Takes well to pruning. Tea can be grown in California but has never been a major crop for economic reasons.

C. vernalis. Certain camellias once classed as Sasanquas have been placed here because they bloom later than Sasanquas, are denser in growth, shinier in leaf, and have firmer-textured flowers. They are generally sold as Sasanquas. The best known varieties are:

'Dawn'. Single to semi-double small white flowers blushed pink. Dense, upright shrub of unusual hardiness.

'Hiryu'. Deep red, small, rose-form, double. Dense, upright plant.

Hybrid camellias. The term as used here refers to camellias which are the hybrids between two or more species. At present we have at least a hundred hybrids in the nursery trade, most involving *C. japonica* and *C. saluenensis*, as parents. Many are rare, but these are available and choice (the flowering-time code letters E, M, and L are explained under *C. japonica*).

'Bonnie Marie'. E-L. Large, semi-double to anemone-form, phlox pink flowers with fluted petals. Bloom in mass display. Upright, compact growth. Stands full sun except in very hot, dry areas.

'Brigadoon'. M. Medium, semi-double flowers of fuchsia pink. Blooms heavily and flowers drop cleanly. Compact, upright growth. Best in part shade.

'Donation'. M. Large, semi-double flowers of orchid pink borne all along the stems. Blooms young and heavily on a vigorous, upright, compact plant with slightly pendulous branches. Quite cold and sun-resistant. Appreciates a little shade in hot, dry areas. There is a variegated form.

'E. G. Waterhouse'. M-L. Medium, full formal double of excellent form. Light pink flowers heavily produced on vigorous, upright shrub.

'Flirtation'. E-M. Medium-sized, light silvery pink, single flowers on a vigorous, upright shrub. Takes full sun. Excellent for shrub border, hedge.

'Howard Asper'. M-L. Very large, peony-form, salmon pink bloom with loose, upright petals. Vigorous, upright, spreading, with unusually rich, heavy foliage. Shows good qualities of its *C. reticulata—C. japonica* parents.

'J. C. Williams'. E-L. Medium-sized, single, cup-shaped flowers of phlox pink over a very long season. Vigorous, upright shrub with rather pendulous branches.

'Robbie'. M. Very large, orchid pink, semi-double flowers. Slow, compact, upright growth.

CAMPANULA. BELLFLOWER. Mostly perennial, some biennial, a few annual. All Zones. Majority best adapted in Zones 1-7, but several thrive in Zones 8, 9, 14-24. A vast and varied group (nearly 300 species) including creeping or tufted miniatures, trailers, and erect kinds 1-6 ft. tall. Flowers generally bell-shaped, but some star-shaped, cup-shaped, or round and flat. Usually blue,

CAMPANULA

C

Climate Zone maps pages 8-27

NAME	GROWTH HABIT, SIZE	FOLIAGE	FLOWERS	USES-REMARKS
CAMPANULA barbata Short-lived perennial or biennial	Clumps of erect stems 4-18 in. high.	Leaves mostly at base of stem, 2-5 in. long, narrow, hairy.	Bell-shaped, lilac-blue, bearded inside, 1 in. long, nodding, few near top of each stem. Summer.	Foreground in borders, rock gardens. Tap-rooted and needs good drainage. White forms may appear from seed.
C. carpatica TUSSOCK BELLFLOWER Perennial	Compact, leafy tufts, stems branching and spreading. Usually about 8 in. tall, may reach 12-18 in.	Leaves smooth, bright green, wavy, toothed, 1-1½ in. long.	Open bell or cup-shaped, blue, or white, 1-2 in. across, single and erect on stems above foliage. Blooms late spring.	Rock garden, foreground in borders, edging. Variable in flower size and color. 'Blue Carpet' and 'White Carpet' good dwarf varieties. Easy from seed; increase named varieties from cuttings.
C. elatines garganica (*C. garganica*) Perennial	Low (3-6 in. high) with outward spreading stems.	Small, gray or green sharply toothed, heart-shaped leaves.	Flat, star-shaped, violet-blue, borne few or singly at tops of stems. June to fall.	Rock gardens. Usually sold as *C. garganica*. Somewhat like a miniature, prostrate *C. poscharskyana*.
C. fragilis Perennial	Vine-like trailing stems 12-16 in. long.	Glossy oval leaves 1 in. across.	Star-shaped, blue with white centers, 1½ in. across, in leaf joints at ends of branches. Late summer and fall.	Choice spots in rock gardens or walls. Hanging containers. A plant for collectors, specialists.
C. glomerata Perennial	Upright, with erect side branches to 1-2 ft.	Basal leaves broad, wavy-edged. Stem leaves broad, toothed. Both somewhat hairy.	Narrow, bell-shaped, flaring at the mouth, 1 in. long, blue-violet, tightly clustered at tops of stems. June-July.	For shaded borders or large rock gardens. Plants have proportionately more foliage than flowers.
C. isophylla ITALIAN BELLFLOWER, STAR OF BETHLEHEM Perennial	Trailing or hanging stems to 2 ft. long.	Leaves heart-shaped, light green, toothed, 1-1½ in. long and wide.	Pale blue, star-shaped, 1 in. wide, profuse in late summer and fall. Variety 'Alba' most popular, has white flowers, larger than the above. Variety 'Mayi', gray, soft hairy leaves, large lavender blue flowers.	Hanging baskets, wall pots, on top of walls, rock garden. Choice ground cover for small areas on slopes, in mild-winter climates. Filtered shade. Hardy San Francisco and south; indoor-outdoor plant in cold-winter areas.
C. lactiflora Perennial	Erect, branching, leafy 3½-5 ft. tall.	Oblong, pointed, toothed leaves 2-3 in. long.	Broadly bell-shaped to star-shaped, 1 in. long, white to pale blue in drooping clusters at ends of branches, June-September.	Rear of borders in sun or partial shade. Quite drought resistant. Endures even dry shade and is long-lived.
C. medium CANTERBURY BELL Biennial or annual	Sturdy, hairy, leafy, with erect stems 2½-4 ft. tall.	Basal leaves 6-10 in. long, stem leaves 3-5 in., wavy-margined.	Bell-shaped, urn-shaped, 1-2 in across, single or double, held upright in long, loose open clusters. Purple, violet, blue, lavender, pink, white, May-July.	Sow seed in May-June for bloom next year, or set out plants from nursery 15-18 in. apart. Good for cutting. 'Calycanthema', commonly called cup-and-saucer flower, very popular. Annual variety with bell-shaped flowers (not cup-and-saucer) blooms in 6 months from seed.
C. persicifolia PEACH LEAFED BLUEBELL Perennial	Strong growing, slender, erect stems 2-3 ft. tall. Plants leafy at base.	Basal leaves smooth-edged, green, 4-8 in. long. Stem leaves 2-4 in. long, shaped like leaves of peach tree.	Open, cup-shaped, about 1 in. across, held erect on short side shoots on sturdy stems. Blue, pink, or white. June-Aug.	Choice plant for borders. Easy from seed sown in late spring. 'Telham Beauty', old but still popular, has 3-in. blue flowers. 'Blue Gardenia' and 'White Pearl' have double flowers.

NAME	GROWTH HABIT, SIZE	FOLIAGE	FLOWERS	USES-REMARKS
C. portenschlagiana *(C. muralis)* DALMATIAN BELLFLOWER Perennial	Low, leafy, mounding mats 4-7 in. high.	Roundish, heart-shaped, deep-green leaves with deeply toothed, slightly wavy edges.	Flaring bell-shaped, to 1 in. long, violet-blue, 2-3 flowers on each semi-erect stem. May-August, sometimes blooming again in fall.	Fine plant for edging or as small-scale ground cover. In warm regions best in partial shade. Spreads moderately fast, is sturdy, permanent, and not invasive. Easily increased by dividing.
C. poscharskyana SERBIAN BELLFLOWER Perennial	Spreading, much branching, leafy, with semi-upright flowering stems 1 or more ft. tall.	Long heart-shaped, irregularly-toothed, slightly hairy leaves 1-3½ in. long, ¾-3 in. wide.	Star-shaped, ½-1 in. across, blue-lilac or lavender, spring to early summer.	Very vigorous. Shaded border near pools, shaded rock gardens, with fuchsias and begonias. Stands some drought; takes sun near coast.
C. pyramidalis CHIMNEY BELLFLOWER Biennial or short-lived perennial	Sturdy, upright stems, unbranched or branched at the base, 4-5 ft. tall.	Leaves nearly heart-shaped, about 2 in. long, with long stalks.	Flat, saucer-shaped blue or white flowers, over 1 in. long, in dense spikes. July-September.	For back of perennial borders or for bays in big shrubbery borders, or in containers. Stake early to keep stems straight. In cold-winter climates, mulch around plants.
C. rotundifolia BLUEBELL OF SCOTLAND, HAREBELL Perennial	Upright or spreading, simple or much branched, 6-20 in. tall.	Leaves green or sometimes slightly grayish. Basal leaves roundish, long-stalked, 1 in. across. Stem leaves grass-like, 2-3 in. long. May dry up before blooming time.	Broad bell-shaped, bright blue, 1 in. across, 1 or a few nodding in open clusters. July-August.	Flower color variable, sometimes in lavender, purple, or white shades. Rock gardens, borders, naturalized under deciduous trees. Self-sows in favorable situations.

Climate Zone maps pages 8-27

lavender, violet, purple, or white; some pinks, and few rare yellows. Bloom period from spring to fall, according to species.

Uses for campanulas are as varied as the plants. Gemlike miniatures deserve special settings—close-up situations in rock gardens, niches in dry walls, in raised beds, or containers. Trailing kinds are ideal for hanging pots or baskets, wall crevices; vigorous, spreading growers serve well as ground covers. Upright growers are valuable in borders, for cutting, occasionally in containers.

In general, campanulas grow best in good, readily drained soil; filtered shade in warmer climates, full sun near coast. Exceptions are noted in chart. Most species

Campanula glomerata *differs from most campanulas, has tightly clustered blooms.*

fairly easy to grow from seed sown in flats in spring and early summer, transplanted to garden in fall for bloom the following year; also increased by cuttings or divisions. Divide clumps in fall every 3-4 years; some may need yearly division. Low growing kinds especially attractive to snails, slugs.

CAMPHOR TREE. See Cinnamomum

CAMPSIS. TRUMPET CREEPER, TRUMPET VINE. Deciduous vine. Vigorous climbers that cling to wood, brick, and stucco surfaces with aerial rootlets. Old plants sometimes become topheavy and pull away from supporting surface unless thinned. Will spread through garden and into neighbor's by suckering root. If you dig it out, a piece of roots left will grow another plant. Can be trained as big shrub, flowering hedge if branches are shortened after first year's growth. Use for large-scale effects—a quick summer screen. All produce open arching sprays of trumpet-shaped flowers in August-September.

C. grandiflora *(Bignonia chinensis).* CHINESE TRUMPET CREEPER. Zones 2-9, 11, 14-21. Not as vigorous, large, or hardy as the American native, but with slightly larger scarlet flowers. Leaves divided into 7-9 2½-in.-long leaflets.

C. radicans *(Bignonia radicans).* COMMON TRUMPET CREEPER. Zones 1-21. Native to eastern United States. Most used in cold-winter areas. A deep freeze will kill to the ground but new stems grow quickly. Leaves divided into 9-11, 2½-in.-long, toothed leaflets. Flowers are 3-in.-long orange tubes with scarlet lobes that flare to 2 in. wide, grow 6-12 in a cluster. Grows fast to 40 ft. or more, bursting with health and vigor.

C. tagliabuana. All Zones. Hybrid between the two first named species. 'Mme. Galen', the best known variety, has attractive salmon red flowers.

CANARY BIRD BUSH. See Crotalaria

CANARY-BIRD FLOWER. See Tropaeolum peregrinum

CANDLE BUSH. See Cassia alata

CANDOLLEA cuneiformis. Evergreen shrub. Zones 13, 15-24. Native to Australia. Pleasing appearance and substance, to 4 ft. and somewhat broader. Small, 1-in.-long, polished green leaves tapered at base, and toothed at tip. Flowers, like clear yellow wild roses, are carried all along the new growth March-June. Prune after flowering to control outline. Needs food and water in average amounts but exceptionally fast drainage. Resists wind well. Associate with rockroses (*Cistus*), sunroses (*Helianthemum*), and *Aster frikartii.*

CANDYTUFT. See Iberis

CANDYTUFT, EVERGREEN. See Iberis sempervirens

CANNA. Tuberous rootstock. All Zones, but lifted and stored over winter in colder climates. Best adapted to warm-summer climates. Native to tropics and subtropics. An old favorite that can add a tropical touch in right place. Large, rich green to bronzy red leaves resemble those of banana or ti plants. Flowers reminiscent of ginger lilies (*Hedychium*) bloom on 3-6-ft. stalks in summer, fall. A dozen or more varieties available, in varying sizes and shapes in white, ivory, shades of yellow, orange, pink, apricot, coral, salmon, and red. Bicolors also available. The Pfitzer Dwarf cannas are only 30-36 in. tall.

Most effective in groups of single colors

Climate Zone maps pages 8-27

against plain background. Grow in borders, near poolside (with good drainage); in large pots or tubs on terrace or patio. Leaves useful in arrangements; cut flowers do not keep well. Plant rootstocks in spring, after frosts, in rich loose soil in full sun. Set 5 in. deep, 10 in. apart. Water heavily during flowering season; remove faded flowers after bloom. After all flower clusters have bloomed, cut stalk to ground.

CANTALOUPE. See Melon

CANTERBURY BELL. See Campanula medium

CANTUA buxifolia. MAGIC FLOWER, SACRED FLOWER OF THE INCAS. Evergreen shrub. Zones 16-24. Native of Peru, Bolivia and northern Chile. Scraggly open growth to 6-10 ft. Small leaves 1-in. or less in length. Magnificent blossoms. Sporadically through the year, 4-in. tubular rose or cerise red flowers (tubes striped yellow), appear in terminal clusters arching the branches with their weight.

Give it light soil in part shade. Needs support of stake or trellis. Young plants effective in hanging baskets. Or grow in a tub and hide the plant when it's out of bloom. Prune after flowering. Spray for red spider mites.

CAPE COWSLIP. See Lachenalia

CARAGANA arborescens. SIBERIAN PEA-SHRUB. Deciduous shrub or small tree. Zones 1-21. Native to Siberia, Manchuria. Fast growing to 20 ft., with 15-ft. spread, often with spiny twigs. Flowers in spring resemble yellow sweet peas. Fragrant. Leaves 1½ to 3 in. long, divided into 4-6 pairs of roundish, bright green, ½-inch leaflets. Useful where choice is limited by extremes in cold or heat and by poor soil. Nearly indestructible in mountains or desert. Use as windbreak, clipped hedge, cover for wild life, attractive small tree.

CARAWAY. See Carum

CARDINAL CLIMBER. See Quamoclit pennata

CARDINAL FLOWER. See Lobelia cardinalis

CARICA. Evergreen. One papaya is a relatively hardy (to 28°) ornamental plant or tree; the other is the typical fruiting tree.

C. candamarcensis. MOUNTAIN PAPAYA. Zones 21-24. Native to mountains of Colombia and Ecuador. Generally grown as a shrub though it resembles a many-trunked, upright tree to 10-12 ft. Foliage borne in dense clusters at tops of trunks. Elaborately lobed, 12-13-in.-wide leaves are fanlike, veined, sandpapery, dark green above, lighter below. Fruits are small (3-4 in.) but edible in exotic preserves.

C. papaya. PAPAYA. Outdoors in Zones 21, 23, 24; or a greenhouse plant. Native to tropical America. Key to success is to live in the right place—where there's soil warmth in winter. More are lost to damping off in late winter and spring than to frosts. Grow on south slope or south side of house where winter sun hits soil—and the more reflected heat at that season the better.

Grow 3 to 5 in a group. Need male and female trees for fruit production. Papaya grows as a straight trunk, topped by crown of broad (to 2 ft.) fanlike, deeply lobed leaves on 2-ft.-long stems. To get the most fun and fruit, don't attempt to grow it as a permanent tree. It bears fruit when young. Keep a few plants coming along each year and destroy old ones. Give plants ample water and fertilizer in warm weather.

CARISSA. Evergreen shrubs. Its rightful climates are Zones 22-24; however so many find carissa appealing that it is being grown far beyond its safe limits (Zones 13, 16-21). Excellent in ocean wind, salt spray. Easy to grow. Accepts variety of soils, exposures. Bloom and fruit best in full sun but will take fairly heavy shade. Prune to control erratic growth.

C. acokanthera. See Acokanthera venenata

C. edulis. Native to Egypt. Differs from widely grown *C. grandiflora* in several ways. Shrubby or somewhat vinelike to 10 ft. (Will grow to 30 ft. high and as wide.) Foliage of small (to 2-in.) glossy, bright green, red-tinged leaves. Bears large clusters of pure white fragrant flowers, opening from pink buds. Cherry-size fruit changes from green to red to purplish black as it ripens.

C. grandiflora. NATAL PLUM. Native to South Africa. Fast-growing, strong, upright, rounding shrub of rather loose habit, 5-7 ft. (Occasionally to 18 ft.) Lustrous, leathery, rich green, 3-in., oval leaves. Spines along branches and at end of each twig. White flowers, almost as fragrant as star jasmine and of same 5-petal star shape but larger (to 2-in. wide), appear throughout year, followed by red plum-shaped (1-2 in.) fruits. Flowers, green and ripe fruit often appear together. Fruits vary in sweetness, but generally have quality of rather sweet cranberry and make good sauce. Use as screen or hedge. Prune heavily for formal hedges, lightly for an informal screen. Strong growth and spines discourage trespassers.

If you grow Natal plum outside Zones 22-24, give it the same favorite spot you'd give bougainvillea—a warm south or west facing wall, preferably with an overhang to keep off frost.

C. g. 'Boxwood Beauty'. Exceptionally compact growth to 2 ft. and as wide. Deep green leaves, like a large-leafed boxwood. Excellent for hedging and shaping. No thorns.

C. g. 'Fancy'. Upright grower to 6 ft. Unusually large fruits, good show of flowers. Use as lightly pruned screen.

C. g. 'Green Carpet'. Low growing to 1-1½ ft. and flat spreading to 4 ft. and more. Leaves smaller than species. Excellent ground cover.

C. g. 'Horizontalis'. To 1½-2 ft., spreading, trailing. Dense foliage.

C. g 'Minima'. To 1-1½ ft. high, 2 ft. wide. Leaves, flowers unusually small. Not vigorous. Interesting in containers.

C. g. 'Prostrata'. Vigorous, to about 2 ft. and spreading. Good ground cover. Prune out any growth that tends toward upright. Can be trained as espalier.

C. g. 'Ruby Point'. Upright grower to 6 ft. New leaves hold their red coloring through the growing season.

C. g. 'Tomlinson'. Dwarf compact growth to 2-2½ ft. high, 3 ft. wide. Shiny, mahogany-tinted foliage, large flowers, wine-colored fruits. No thorns. Slow growing. Tub plant, foundation plantings.

C. g. 'Tuttle' (*C. g.* 'Nana Compacta Tuttlei'). To 2-3 ft. high, 3-5 ft. wide. Compact, dense foliage. Heavy producer of flowers and fruit. Used as ground cover.

C. spectabilis. See Acokanthera spectabilis

CARMEL CREEPER. See Ceanothus griseus horizontalis

CARNATION. See Dianthus caryophyllus

CARNEGIEA gigantea. SAGUARO. Giant cactus. Zones 12, 13, 18-21. Native to northern Mexico, Arizona, California. Columnar and branching, with prominent ribs that give it a fluted appearance. It grows very slowly to 50 ft. Spines light brown, ½-3 in. long. Flowers on mature plants only, white, 4-5 in. long, May. Night blooming. State flower of Arizona. Oval, edible fruits split open to show red pulp within; sometimes mistaken for flowers. Slow enough to stay pot-size or garden-size for many years.

CAROB. See Ceratonia

CARPENTERIA californica. BUSH ANEMONE. Evergreen shrub. Zones 5-9, 14-24. Native to California, localized in Sierra Nevada foothills between Kings and San Joaquin rivers in Fresno County. Slow growing to 3-6 ft. with many stems arising from the base. Older bark light colored and peeling, new shoots purplish. Leaves thick, narrow, dark green above and whitish beneath, 2-4½ in. long. Flowers, white, anemonelike, 1½-3 in. wide, opening May-August, are slightly and pleasantly fragrant.

This attractive native with a rather formal look accepts ordinary garden conditions. Grows in shade or sun, but looks best in light shade. Unusually susceptible to aphids that roll leaves, disfigure plant. Spray as new leaves form. Prune after flowering to restrain growth or shape.

CARPET BUGLE. See Ajuga

CARPINUS. HORNBEAM. Deciduous trees. Zones 2-9, 14-17. Hardy, well-behaved, relatively small shade trees. Long life and good habits as street trees (not recommended for southern California and desert). Retain leaves well into winter. Fruits, small hard nutlets in leaflike bracts, are carried in attractive, drooping clusters.

C. betulus. EUROPEAN HORNBEAM. Moderate growth to 40 ft. Dense pyramidal form, eventually becoming broad with drooping outer branches. Dark green leaves, 2-5 in. long and toothed. Fall color yellow in cold winters. Fruit cluster to 5 in. long. Subject to scale insect infestations. Can be clipped into hedge or screen. Variety 'Fastigiata' is a dense, narrow column.

C. caroliniana. AMERICAN HORNBEAM. Native from Florida to Texas, north to Virginia, southern Illinois. Moderate growth to 25-30 ft., round-headed. Bark is smooth and gray. Dark green leaves, 1-3 in. long, edges toothed. In fall leaves turn a mottled yellow and red. Fruit cluster 1½-4 in. long.

ARPOBROTUS. See Ice plant

ION FLOWER. See Stapelia

The variety to plant depends on ...dition: carrots reach smooth ... good-textured soil free ... the long market ... of

plant... ...

climates ... ...st sowing 70 days before anticipated killing frost. When tops are 2 in. high thin plants to 1½ in. apart, and thin again if roots begin to crowd. Tiny carrots removed in thinnings are good butter-steamed. After the first thinning, apply a thin band of commercial fertilizer 2 in. out from the row. Begin harvest when carrots reach finger size. Diseases and pests not a problem in most home gardens.

CARROT WOOD. See Cupaniopsis

CARTHAMUS tinctorius. SAFFLOWER, FALSE SAFFRON. Annual. A relative of the thistles that is ornamental as well as economically useful. Erect spiny-leafed stems, 1-3 ft. tall, branching above, bearing orange-yellow flower heads above leafy bracts; the inner bracts are spiny. Durable cut flower, fresh or dried. (An ornamental spineless safflower is also available.) Grown commercially for oil extracted from the seeds. The dried flowers from the flower heads have been used for seasoning in place of the true saffron, which they strongly resemble in color and flavor. Sow seeds in place in spring after frosts, in full sun. Once established, plants need little water.

CARUM carvi. CARAWAY. Biennial herb. Mound of carrotlike leaves, 1-2 ft. high, first year. Umbrellalike clusters of white flowers rise above foliage second year. Plant dies after seeds ripen in midsummer. Start from seed sown in fall or spring where to be grown. Thrives in well drained soil in full sun. Thin seedlings to 18 in. Use dried seeds for flavoring pickles, vegetables, cookies, rye bread.

CARYA illinoinensis (*Carya pecan*). PECAN. Deciduous tree. Zones 7-9, 12-16, 18-23 as ornamental; Zones 8-9, 12-14, 18-20 to produce good nut crop. Native to southern and central U.S. Graceful, shapely tree to 70 ft. tall and wide. Foliage like English walnut but prettier, with more (11 to 17) leaflets that are narrower and longer (4-7 in.); foliage pattern finer textured, shade lighter.

Needs deep (6-10 ft.), well drained soils. Won't stand salinity. Prune to shape or to remove dead wood. Select varieties by climate: 'F. W. Anderson' (self-fertile) good for San Joaquin Valley; 'Mahan' (self-fertile) thrives in low desert; 'Western Schley' fruits over wide range of climates,

needs a pollenizer. 'Wichita' is good pollenizer for 'Western Schley,' bears good nuts very young. 'Barton,' 'Burkett,' 'Choctaw,' 'Stuart,' 'Success' also sold. 'Burkett' needs pollenizer.

CARYOPTERIS. BLUEBEARD. Deciduous shrubs. Zones 1-7, 14-17. Valued for contribution of cool blue to the flower border ... frost. Generally grown as ... ... than above, to 3-4 ft., with lavender-blue flowers.

CARYOTA. FISHTAIL PALM. Outdoors in Zones 23, 24, house plant anywhere. Feather palms with finely divided leaves, the leaflets flattened and split at the tips like fish tails. Tender. Come from southeast Asia, where they grow in full sun. In California they need partial shade and a protected site.

C. mitis. CLUSTERED FISHTAIL PALM. Slow grower to 20-25 ft. Basal offshoots eventually form clustered trunks. Foliage light green. Very tender, and thrives only in an ideal environment. Not for novices.

C. ochlandra. CANTON FISHTAIL PALM. Probably eventually 25 ft. tall. Medium dark green leaves. Hardiest of the caryotas, it has survived temperatures of 26°.

Canton fishtail palm has leaflets like fishtails. Stem bases, lower trunk.

C. urens. FISHTAIL WINE PALM. Single-stemmed palm to 100 ft. in Asia, to 15-20 ft. here with careful protection. If temperatures go below 32°, it's certain to die. Dark green leaves.

CASCARA SAGRADA. See Rhamnus purshiana

CASHMERE BOUQUET. See Clerodendrum bungei

CASIMIROA edulis. WHITE SAPOTE. Evergreen, or erratically briefly deciduous tree.

Zones 15, 16, 22-24. A beautiful tropical tree that will withstand more cold than most avocados, and seems to do well wherever lemons are grown. To 50 ft. Keep it to almost any height by pinching out terminal bud if wide umbrella type is wanted. Prune off lower branches. Luxuriant glossy green leaves divided fanwise into 3-7 oval, 3-5-in.-long leaflets.

Tree bears a heavy crop of 3-4-in., round fruits, pale green to yellow. Flavor ... in many ways—similar to ... ...d, a banana only ... syrup, custard ... nsistency of a ...st through November ... becomes slightly ... ipe; allow yellowish ... low and sweet. A mature... produce several hundred ... fruit, far more than any one family can use. Cleanup becomes a chore. Plant where dropping fruits can be raked up, or get lost in a ground cover. Goes deciduous for a short time, when hit by frost or in June when the tree "moults" or becomes completely bare for a brief period.

Not particular about soil; needs ample water and consistent feeding. Budded trees give best fruit, and are grown in limited quantities. 'Coleman', 'Pike', 'Wilson', and 'Suebelle' are all good varieties.

CASSIA. SENNA. Evergreen, partially evergreen, or deciduous shrubs, trees. For southern California and Arizona, a great reservoir of landscaping materials from many lands. Yellow or golden are the words for cassia. Flowers on the different kinds are yellow, egg-yolk yellow, bright yellow, deep yellow, gold. As a group, cassias bloom better and live longer in fast draining soil with infrequent but deep watering. Some of the tree forms, *C. excelsa* and *C. leptophylla,* grow in lawns where drainage is fast.

In the following list of kinds, flowering dates are approximate. Many will bloom almost any time or scatter bloom over a long period.

C. alata. CANDLE BUSH. Deciduous shrub 8-12 ft., and spreading wider. Zone 23. Native to tropics. Golden yellow flowers (1 in. wide) in big spikelike clusters, November-January. Leaves of 12-28 2½-in. leaflets. Prune hard after bloom.

C. artemisioides. FEATHERY .CASSIA. Evergreen shrub. Zones 8, 9, 12-24. Native to Australia. Attractive, light and airy structure to 3-5 ft. Leaves divided into 6-8 gray, 1-in.-long, needlelike leaflets. Flowers (¾ in.) sulfur yellow, 5-8 in a cluster, January-April, often into summer. Prune lightly after flowering.

C. bicapsularis. Evergreen shrub to 10 ft. Zones 13, 22-24. Native to the tropics. Recovers after killed to the ground by frost. Yellow (½ in. wide) flowers in spikelike clusters, from October to February if not cut short by frost. Prune hard after flowering. Leaflets roundish, rather thick, 6-10 to a leaf.

C. corymbosa. FLOWERY SENNA. Large evergreen shrub to 10 ft. Zones 13, 21-24; naturalized here and there in Santa Barbara. Native to Argentina. Yellow flowers in rounded clusters, spring to fall. Dark green leaves with 6 narrow, oblong, 1-2 in.

C

Climate
Zone maps
pages 8-27

leaflets. Prune hard after flowering. (For the small garden the less rank-growing *C. tomentosa* or *C. glauca* are better.)

C. didymobotrya. (Also sold as *C. nairobensis.*) Evergreen shrub. Zones 13, 22-24; often escapes, naturalizes. Native to east Africa. Rangy grower to 10 ft. Leaflets 2 in. long, 8-16 pairs per leaf. Yellow, 1½-in.-wide flowers in upright, dense clusters (to 12 in.), December-April. Thrives in heat. Stands some drought when established.

C. excelsa (*C. carnaval*). CROWN OF GOLD TREE. Partially evergreen tree. Zones 12, 13, 19-24 (borderline Zone 21). Native to Argentina. Grows fast to 25-30 ft. Leaves divided into 10-20 pairs of 1-in.-long leaflets. Large bright yellow flowers in 12-16-in.-long clusters, late summer, early fall. Prune hard after flowering. Needs moisture in growing season.

C. fistula. GOLDEN SHOWER TREE. Deciduous tree. Native to India, spectacular in Hawaii. Has long tempted gardeners in most protected locations Zone 23. A few have succeeded—between "unusually cold" years. To 30 ft. Leaves of 8-16, oval, 2½-in.-long leaflets. Orange-yellow flowers in clusters a foot or more long.

C. leptocarpa. Evergreen subshrub. Valuable addition in Zones 12, 13. Native New Mexico, southern Arizona, to South America. Grows to 3-5 ft. and spreads as wide. Flowers bright yellow in large branched clusters at ends of branches, July to September. Leaves of 4-8 pairs, a little over ½ in. long. Foliage ill smelling.

C. leptophylla. GOLD MEDALLION TREE. Near-evergreen tree. Zones 21-24. Native to Brazil. Most shapely and graceful of the cassias. Fast growing to 20-25 ft.; open headed, low spreading, tending to weep. Deep yellow flowers to 3 in. wide, in 6-8-in.-long spikes through July-August with scattered blooms April-May.

C. multijuga. Evergreen tree. Zones 22-24. Native to Brazil. Heavy foliaged, much branched tree to 15-20 ft. Somewhat brittle. Yellow, 2-in.-wide flowers in clusters in late summer and fall. The leaves have 18-40 pairs of rather narrow, ¾-in.-long leaflets.

C. splendida. GOLDEN WONDER SENNA. Evergreen shrub. Zones 12, 13, 21-24. Native to Brazil. This name has been applied to a number of cassias of varying growth habits. Those in Los Angeles State and County Arboretum are 10 to 12 ft. high, and about as wide. Orange-yellow flowers (1½-in. wide) in loose clusters, at branch ends November-January. Other plantings of cassias with this name, with bright yellow flowers, are strongly horizontal in branch pattern, 5-8 ft. high, spreading to 12 ft. wide. All need to be hard pruned after flowering.

C. surattensis (*C. glauca*). Evergreen shrub. Zones 19-24. Grows fast to 6-8 ft., and spreads wider. Bright yellow flowers (¾ in. wide) in small clusters at branch ends, nearly the year around. Roundish, 1½-in.-long leaflets, 12-20 to each leaf. Does not need to be pruned heavily. One of best for small gardens.

C. tomentosa. WOOLLY SENNA. Evergreen shrub. Zones 13, 17, 22-24. Native to Mexico and South America. Vigorous, rank growth to 8 ft. (or 12-15 ft.). Leaves divided into 12-16 leaflets 2½ in. long that are green above, white-hairy beneath. Deep yellow flowers in upright clusters at ends of branches in winter, early spring. Prune hard after flowering.

CASTANEA. CHESTNUT. Deciduous trees. Zones 1-9, 14-17. The American chestnut (*C. dentata*) is nearing extinction as a result of a fungus disease. However, two other chestnuts are available in the West. They have handsome dark to bright green foliage. Creamy white, small flowers in long (about 8-10 in.) slim catkins make quite a display in June or July. The large edible nuts are enclosed in a prickly bur. Wonderful dense shade trees where there is space to accommodate them, such as large country places.

C. mollissima. CHINESE CHESTNUT. Native to China, Korea. Grows to 60 ft. with rounded crown that may spread to 40 ft. Leaves 3-7 in. long, with coarsely toothed edges. Most nursery trees are grown from seeds, hence the nuts are variable, but generally of good quality. Single trees bear lightly or not at all. Plant two or more to insure cross pollination and you'll get a substantial crop. Intolerant of alkaline soil conditions.

C. sativa. SPANISH CHESTNUT. Native to southern Europe, north Africa, western Asia. Larger, broader tree than Chinese chestnut. Can reach 100 ft. in height with greater spread, but usually a 40-60-ft. tree in gardens. Leaves 4-9 in. long, with sharply toothed edges. Produces large chestnuts of excellent quality; these are the ones usually sold in markets. Size, litter, and disagreeable odor of pollen make it a tree for wide open spaces.

CASTANOPSIS. CHINQUAPIN. Evergreen trees and shrubs. Western natives with attractive foliage. Slow growing. Thrive in sunny locations, poor dry soil, little care after established. Fruits look like clusters of small chestnut burs.

C. chrysophylla. GIANT CHINQUAPIN. Zones 4-7, 16, 17. Tree to 75 ft. or shrubby tree to 20-25 ft. Native to coastal northern California, Oregon, rare in Washington. Heavily ridged bark, spreading branches. Handsome tapered leaves 3-6 in. long, glossy dark green above with golden felt-like hairs beneath. Showy summer bloom of small creamy white flowers in fluffy spikes.

C. c. minor. GOLDEN CHINQUAPIN. Zones 4-7, 16, 17. Usually shrubby, to 3-15 ft. Native to northern California Coast Ranges. Leaves more troughlike than species, smaller (to 3 in.), darker green above, and deep gold beneath. Makes a dense hedge. Good contrast in planting of pines.

C. sempervirens. BUSH CHINQUAPIN, SIERRA CHINQUAPIN. Zones 1-7. Shrub to 8 ft. Native to mountains of California and southwestern Oregon. Stands up well under winter cover of snow. Useful as a low ground covering shrub; grows naturally in thickets. Can be kept under 8 ft. by pruning. Makes a spreading rounded mass of 1-3-in.-long leaves, grayish green to yellowish green above, golden or rusty-hairy beneath.

CASTANOSPERMUM australe. MORETON BAY CHESTNUT. Evergreen tree. Zones 18-22. Native to Australia. Beautiful in foliage; spectacular in flower. Large leaves,

dark shiny green, are divided into 11 to 15 leaflets about 1½ by 5 in. Flowers are bright red and yellow, produced in stiff spikes about 8 in. long. They grow from twigs, branches, and main trunk in summer. Seeds like a chestnut are edible when roasted, and palatable to the aborigines of Australia.

CAST-IRON PLANT. See Aspidistra

CASTOR BEAN. See Ricinus

CASUARINA. BEEFWOOD, SHE-OAK. Evergreen trees. Zones 7-9, 11-24. Native mostly to Australia. Sometimes called Australian pine. Slight resemblance to a pine, and the fruits look like woody cones, but it's not a pine. Long, thin, jointed, green branches with inconspicuous true leaves look like long pine needles. Tolerates many tough conditions, dry or wet soil, heat, wind. Particularly useful in desert areas. Hardy to 15°. In desert, it is often confused with Athel tamarisk (*Tamarix aphylla*) because of similar foliage. Distinctive difference: casuarinas produce woody, conelike fruits.

C. cunninghamiana. RIVER SHE-OAK. Tallest and largest. To 70 ft. Finest texture, with dark green branches.

C. equisetifolia. HORSETAIL TREE. Fast grower to 40-60 ft., 20-ft. wide. Has pendulous gray-green branches. Plant sold under this name may be *C. cunninghamiana* or a hybrid between it and *C. glauca*.

C. stricta. MOUNTAIN OR DROOPING SHE-OAK, COAST BEEFWOOD. Fast grower to 20-35 ft. Darkest green foliage and largest cones (1 in.) Makes beautiful silhouette against sky. Properly watered and shaped, makes a most attractive street tree.

CATALINA PERFUME. See Ribes viburnifolium

CATALPA. Deciduous tree. All Zones. One of the few truly hardy deciduous trees that can compete in flower and leaf with the subtropicals of southern California. Large upright clusters of trumpet-shaped, 2-in.-wide flowers, pure white, striped and marked with yellow and soft brown, displayed in late spring and summer above bold, large heart-shaped leaves. Flowers are followed by long, bean-shaped seed capsules sometimes called Indian beans or Indian stogies.

Unusually well adapted to extremes of heat and cold, and to soils throughout the West. Where winds are strong, should be planted in lee of taller trees or buildings to protect leaves from wind damage. Some gardeners object to litter of fallen flowers in summer, and seed capsules in autumn.

C. bignonioides. COMMON CATALPA, INDIAN BEAN. Native to southeastern United States. Generally smaller than *C. speciosa*, 20-50 ft. according to climate or soil, with somewhat smaller spread. Leaves 5-8 in. long, often in whorls, odd odor when crushed.

C. b. 'Nana'. (Almost always sold as *C. bungei*.) UMBRELLA CATALPA. A dense globe form usually grafted high on the species. It never blooms. Cut it back to keep it in scale.

C. speciosa. WESTERN CATALPA. Native southern Illinois to Arkansas. A round-headed, 40-70-ft. tree. Leaves 6-12 in. long; no odor when crushed. Flowers fewer in cluster than *C. bignonioides*. Most widely distributed in the West. Early training and pruning will give a tall trunk and umbrella-shaped crown.

CATANANCHE caerulea. CUPID'S DART. Perennial. All Zones. Sturdy, free-flowering plant for summer borders and arrangements. Leaves gray-green, 8-12 in. long, mostly at base of stem. Lavender-blue 2-in. flower heads reminiscent of cornflowers are surrounded by strawlike shining bracts. Stems 2 ft. tall. Flowers may be dried for use in bouquets. Remove faded flowers to prolong bloom. Plant in full sun; drought resistant. 'Alba' is a white variety.

CATHA edulis. KHAT. Evergreen shrub. Zones 13, 16-24. Valued for all-year foliage beauty. Bronzy green, shiny, oval, 2-4-in.-long, slightly toothed leaves take on reddish tints through fall and winter. Grown as a spreading shrub to 8 ft. Old plants in parks more than 20 ft. Pinch or prune to keep compact. Effective as an espalier. Red stems and bark add interest. Medium-sized leaves make good transition between large leaves such as loquat and small-scale foliage. Needs fast drainage but not rich soil. Does well in poor soil, dry situations, and great heat.

CATHARANTHUS roseus (*Vinca rosea*). MADAGASCAR PERIWINKLE. Perennial, usually grown as an annual. Invaluable for summer-fall color in hot climates. Showiest summer flower in desert gardens. Glossy, leaves 1-3 in. long cover bushy plant 1-2 ft. high. Phloxlike flowers 1½ in. wide in pure white, white with a rose or red eye, blush pink, or bright rose. Popular varieties include: 'Bright Eyes', dwarf white with red eye; 'Coquette', dwarf rose. Will bloom first season from seed sown early indoors, in greenhouse or coldframe. Nurseries sell plants in flats in late spring. Plant in full sun or partial shade. Ordinary soil, but needs much moisture. Self-sows readily.

Continues to flower after zinnias and marigolds have gone, up until Thanksgiving if weather stays mild. Lives over in frostless areas, but may look ragged in winter. In coastal areas, blooms in late summer after heat builds up.

CATMINT. See Nepeta mussinii

CATNIP. See Nepeta

CAT'S CLAW VINE. See Doxantha

CAT'S EARS. See Calochortus coeruleus

CATTLEYA. Epiphytic orchids. Native to tropical America. Most popular and best known of orchids. For house and greenhouse primarily. Showy flowers are used extensively for corsages.

Species, varieties, and hybrids are too numerous to list here. All have pseudobulbs bearing 1-3 thick leathery leaves, and flowers 1-4 or more on a stem. Commercial growers offer plants with a wide range of flower colors: lavender and purple; white; semi-albas (white with colored lip); novelties—yellow, orange, red, green, bronze—many of which are crosses between *Cattleya* and other genera. Newest hybrid forms are the miniature cattleyas and the bifoliates or multifloras. The latter are standard-sized plants, with leaves in pairs. These plants produce large clusters of 3-5-in. flowers, and, best of all, many bloom more than once a year.

All cattleyas grow best in a greenhouse where temperature, humidity, and light can be readily controlled. However, you can also grow them as house plants. Main requirements: (1) warm temperature (60° at night, 10° or more higher during the day); (2) relatively high humidity—50-60 per cent or better; (3) good light—20-40 per cent of outside light with protection from hot midday sun. (Color of orchid foliage should be light green and leaves should be erect. When light intensity is too low leaves turn dark green and new growth becomes soft.)

Potting medium: osmunda fiber, hapuu (tree fern stem), or ground bark. Most popular now is bark, which is readily available, easy to handle, and fairly inexpensive. Use fine grade for small pots 3 in. or less, medium grade for 4-in. pots and larger. It's sensible to use ready-made mixes sold by orchid growers; these are generally blended for proper texture and acidity.

Water plants about once a week—when mix dries out and becomes light weight. Feed plants with a commercial water-soluble orchid fertilizer about once every two weeks during the growing season. To provide humidity for plants in house, fill a waterproof metal or plastic tray with gravel and add enough water so gravel is just above it. Stretch hardware cloth over top of pan, leaving about an inch between gravel and wire for air circulation. Set pots on top. Maintain water level.

Pests: Mainly thrips and scale insects. Control by spraying with malathion or sevin. Use ant cups to control ants. Spray or bait regularly for snails and slugs.

CAULIFLOWER. Related to broccoli and cabbage, and similar in cultural requirements, but more difficult to grow. Easy in cool, humid coastal regions, but where summers are dry and hot, grow it to harvest well before or well after midsummer. Home gardeners usually plant one of the several 'Snowball' varieties, and 'Burpee's Dry Weather'. An unusual variety is 'Purple Head', which has large plants with heads of deep purple color, turning green in cooking; and a flavor somewhat intermediate between cauliflower and broccoli.

Grow cauliflower like broccoli. Start with small plants. Space them 18-20 in. apart in rows 36 in. apart. Be sure to keep plants actively growing; any check in transplanting or later growth is likely to cause premature setting of undersized heads. When heads first appear, tie up the large leaves around them to keep them white. 'Purple Head' does not need this treatment. Harvest as soon as it reaches full size.

CEANOTHUS. WILD LILAC. Mostly evergreen shrubs, small trees, or ground covers (a few deciduous, and they are indicated on list that follows). Some species grow in eastern U. S., the intermountain area, and the Northwest, but most are native to California. They range in flower color from white through all shades of blue to deep violet-blue and almost pink. They all flower in spring, mostly in March or April. In the descriptions that follow, time of flowering is not indicated unless it is unusual.

Ceanothus sometimes get aphids and whitefly, but these are easy to control. As a group ceanothus are short-lived.

Almost all ceanothus can succumb to root rots caused by water mold organisms. In the wild, this doesn't happen because the plants generally go without water all summer. But in the garden it's a major factor. You should locate a ceanothus in the garden according to how much water you can give it in summer. Put most susceptible types where they can be watered infrequently but deeply, allowing the soil to dry out between waterings. (Keep in mind that as drought-tolerant shrubs, this group will never appear lush in summer.) Put kinds with fair to good garden tolerance where they can receive water as frequently as every 2 weeks, if drainage is fast. Plants of excellent garden tolerance can be watered as often as the average shrubs in the garden. The garden tolerance of each kind is noted in the descriptions below.

C. arboreus. FELTLEAF CEANOTHUS. Large shrub or small tree to 25 ft. Borderline Zones 5, 6, grown in 7-9, best in 15-24. Oval leaves 2-3 in. long, dark green above, white-hairy beneath. Flowers usually pale blue in branched clusters 2-6 in. long. February to May. Good garden tolerance. Prune lightly but frequently to shape.

C. a. 'Ray Hartman'. Big shrub or small tree. Borderline in Zones 5, 6; grows in 7-9; best in 15-24. Grows 10-15 ft. tall, 12-15 ft. wide. Large, dark green leaves, gray-hairy beneath. Bright blue flowers in 3-5-in. open clusters, March to May and sometimes again in late summer. Easily shaped into single-stemmed or multi-stemmed tree. Good garden tolerance.

C. 'Concha'. Shrub. Zones 15-24. To 6 ft. high. Very dark blue flowers in round tight clusters. Dark green, wrinkled, semi-glossy leaves. Good garden tolerance.

C. cordulatus. SNOW BUSH, MOUNTAIN WHITETHORN. Shrub. Zones 1, 7, 10. Native to mountains from Oregon to Baja California. Very spiny, 2-5 ft. high, may spread to 12 ft. Oval gray-green leaves, 1 in. long. Masses of white flowers in 1½-in. clusters, May to July, resemble patches of snow. Attractive garden shrub with good garden tolerance in its native range.

C. crassifolius. HOARYLEAF CEANOTHUS. Shrub or tree. Zones 18-24. Native to dry mountains of southern California, Baja California. To 15 ft. high. Small, thick, leathery leaves coated with white felt on undersides. Roundish clusters of white flowers, January to April. Very drought resistant. Good garden tolerance.

C. cyaneus. SAN DIEGO CEANOTHUS. Shrub. Zones 7-9, 14-24. Native to dry slopes in mountains of San Diego County. Grows fast to 10 ft. or more but best as 5-6-ft. dense and bushy shrub. Leaves 1-2 in. long, glossy, medium green. Flowers violet-blue in 6-to-12-in. clusters. One of the showiest, but short-lived and of poor garden tolerance.

C. c. 'Sierra Blue'. Shrub. Zones 5, 6 with protection; 7-9, 14-24. Erect, to 6-12 ft. high, densely foliaged to the base with medium-sized, dark green leaves. Flowers deep pure blue in great profusion. Can be sheared into a tall hedge or shaped lightly into an attractive informal screen. Good garden tolerance.

C. delilianus. Deciduous shrub. Zones 4-6. Hybrid between a hardy, white-flowered

Zone maps
pages 8-27

...species and a tender, blue-...ican one. There are several ...ties. The best known is 'Gloire ...les', an upright shrub 8-12 ft. tall ...dark green oval, 2-3-in.-long leaves ...and 4-6-in.-long clusters of fragrant lilac blue flowers, June to late fall. Because it flowers on new wood, it looks best with heavy annual pruning (late winter or early spring); shorten main branches to 12-18 in. and cut secondary branches to 2-6 buds. Good garden tolerance.

C. 'Far Horizon'. Shrub. Zones 15-24. Compact growth to 4-5 ft. Prolific display of dark blue flowers in small round clusters. Leaves very small and dull green. Fair garden tolerance.

C. foliosus. WAVYLEAF CEANOTHUS. Low shrub. Zones 15-17, 19-24. Native to Coast Ranges, northern California, Cuyamaca Mts. of San Diego County. To 2-3 ft. high, sometimes higher. Wavy-edged leaves, about ½ in. long, glossy dark green above, whitish beneath. Pale to dark blue flowers in 1-in.-long dense clusters. Fair garden tolerance.

C. gloriosus. POINT REYES CEANOTHUS. Ground cover. Zones 5-9, 14-24. Native to coast, Marin to Mendocino counties in northern California. Low, dense growth, 4-24 in. high, spreading to 5 ft. Leaves leathery, roundish, dark green, ½-1½ in. long, with spiny-toothed edges. Lavender-blue flowers in rounded clusters, March to May. Excellent garden tolerance (can even take lawn sprinkling).

C. g. 'Bamico'. Ground cover. Zones 5-9, 14-24. Leaves are lighter green than the species and plant grows slightly higher (2-3 ft.). It fills in well and has a good spreading habit. Excellent garden tolerance.

C. g. exaltatus. NAVARRO CEANOTHUS. Shrub or high ground cover. Zones 5-9, 14-24. Grows much taller (2-12 ft.) and wider (to 10 ft.) than Point Reyes ceanothus. Flowers are deep lavender-blue. Good garden tolerance.

C. g. e. 'Emily Brown'. Ground cover. Zones 5-9, 14-24. Fast-growing to 2-3 ft. high, spreading by rooting branches to 8-12 ft. Small, thick, dark green, glossy, spiny toothed leaves. Many violet-blue flowers in short clusters, March-April. Good garden tolerance.

C. g. 'Tuttle'. Ground cover. Zones 5-9, 14-24. Known for its very wrinkled, holly-like leaves. Light blue flowers. Otherwise, same as C. gloriosus. Good garden tolerance in most soils.

C. griseus. CARMEL CEANOTHUS. Ground cover, shrub. Borderline in Zones 5, 6; best in 7-9, 14-24. Native to Monterey Peninsula and other parts of coast. Varies in growth habit from low and spreading to upright and 8 ft. high. Leaves dark green, 1-2 in., gray-hairy beneath. Violet-blue flowers in dense 1-2-in.-long clusters. Fair to good garden tolerance.

C. g. 'Louis Edmunds'. Shrub. Zones 7-9, 14-24. To 4-5 ft. high, up to 12 ft. wide. Good garden tolerance. Otherwise, same as C. griseus.

C. g. 'Santa Ana'. Shrub. Zones 7-9, 14-24. To 4-8 ft. high, up to 20 ft. wide. Pruning will limit its spread. Flowers rich pure blue. Excellent garden tolerance. Otherwise, same as C. griseus.

C. g. horizontalis. CARMEL CREEPER.

Ground cover. Zones 5-9, 14-24. Native to coastal Monterey County, California. Usually low and creeping but varies from 18-30 in. high and 5-15-ft. spread. Leaves are deep green, glossy, oval, 1-2 in. Blue flowers in dense clusters. Good garden tolerance.

C. g. h. 'Compacta'. Ground cover. Zones 5-9, 14-24. To 12 in. high, 3 ft. wide, compact and very solid habit (a ball of green). Small leaves, dark glossy green. Small blue flowers. Good garden tolerance.

C. g. h. 'Hurricane Point'. Ground cover. Zones 5-9, 14-24. Fast growing to 24 in. high, spreading to 36 ft. wide; may spread to 4 ft. in a single season. Light blue flowers sparsely produced. Good garden tolerance.

C. g. h. 'Yankee Point'. Ground cover. Zones 5-9, 14-24. Grows 2-3 ft. high, 8 ft. wide. Well-foliaged with dark, glossy green leaves and profuse clusters of bright blue flowers. Excellent garden tolerance.

C. impressus. SANTA BARBARA CEANOTHUS. Shrub. Zones 5-9, 14-24. Native to limited area in Santa Barbara and San Luis Obispo counties. Fast growing to 4-10 ft. or more, wider than high. Branching pattern dense. Leaves small (¼-1 in. long), dark green, and wrinkled. Many deep blue flowers in ½-1-in. clusters. February to April. Pinch growing tips to induce bushiness. Good garden tolerance.

C. i. 'Mountain Haze'. Shrub. Zones 5-9, 14-24. Similar to C. impressus. Grows to 2-4 ft. in drought conditions; to 12 ft. or more with abundant water. Seems to have exceptional garden tolerance and takes normal watering.

C. i. 'Puget Blue'. Shrub. Zones 5, 6. Erect, densely branched; grows rapidly to 8-10 ft. Dark green, wrinkled and furrowed leaves ¼-½ in. long. Deep blue flowers in ½-1-in.-long clusters. Fair garden tolerance.

C. integerrimus. DEER BRUSH. Deciduous to semi-deciduous shrub. Zones 1-7. Native to middle elevations, mountains of California; in the Cascades in Washington and Oregon. Open, spreading, 3-10 ft. high. Dark to medium green, thin, 1-3-in.-long leaves. Flowers white to pale or dark blue, rarely pink, in spikelike clusters, May to July. Low maintenance plant for homes in its native range. Poor garden tolerance elsewhere. Prune occasionally for more compact growth.

C. 'Joyce Coulter'. Shrub. Zones 15-17, 21-24. A hybrid, its leaves and flowers resemble C. papillosus. Vigorous, extremely wide spreading to 3 ft. high, 12-20 ft. wide. Excellent bank or ground cover. Good garden tolerance.

C. 'Julia Phelps'. Shrub. Zones 5-9, 14-24. To 6-8 ft. high by 8-10 ft. wide. Rich cobalt blue, small flowers in clusters. Pinch and prune to shape when young. Stunning as big screen planting, or as a single shrub. Much like its parent C. impressus, but more garden tolerant.

C. maritimus. MARITIME CEANOTHUS. Ground cover. Zones 21-24. Native to coastal bluffs, San Luis Obispo County. This one really hugs the ground. Rounded leaves, dark green above, white-hairy beneath. Light to deep blue flowers, January to March. Fair garden tolerance.

C. 'Mary Lake'. High ground cover. Zones 15-17. Moderate to rapid growth to 2-3 ft., spreads to 10 ft. Trailing branches

take root. Dark green, small leaves with wavy margins. Blue flowers in rounded clusters. Good garden tolerance.

C. megacarpus. BIG-POD CEANOTHUS. Shrub. Zones 16, 17, 21-24. Chaparral plant from southern California Coast Ranges. To 5-12 ft. high, sometimes treelike with trunk. Furrowed bark. Dark green, wedge-shaped leaves, ½-1 in. long. Profusion of white flowers. Drought-resistant shrub for no-maintenance areas, poor garden tolerance.

C. papillosus. WARTLEAF CEANOTHUS. Shrub. Zones 15-17, 21-24. Native to Coast Ranges, San Mateo to San Luis Obispo counties. Variable. 4-15 ft. high, with spread to 15 ft. or more. Leaves narrow, gummy, ½-2 in. long, very warty and shiny dark green above, gray feltlike beneath. Deep blue flowers in dense ½-2-in.-long clusters. Fair garden tolerance.

C. p. roweanus. MT. TRANQUILLON CEANOTHUS. Shrub or high ground cover. Zones 15-17, 21-24. Low-spreading, 1-4 ft. high, twice as wide. Leaves usually longer and narrower than wartleaf ceanothus. Flowers same, but bloom February to June. Fair garden tolerance.

C. prostratus. SQUAW CARPET, MAHALA MAT. Ground cover. Zones 1-7. From 3,000 to 6,500-ft. levels, north Coast Ranges, Sierra Nevada of California, north to Washington. Forms dense mat that spreads by rooting branches to 2 in. high, 8 ft. wide. Thick, leathery, deep green, ¼-1-in.-long, wedge-shaped leaves with spiny edges. Flowers deep to light blue in small rounded clusters. If this grows on your summer home property, cherish it. Good garden tolerance in its native range.

C. purpureus. HOLLYLEAF CEANOTHUS. Shrub. Zones 5-9, 14-24. Native to Napa County, California. Erect, 2-4 ft. high, with spreading, red-brown branches closely set with small hollylike leaves, ½-¾-in.-long, dark green above, grayish beneath. Bluish purple flowers in roundish clusters. Fair to poor garden tolerance.

C. rigidus 'Snowball'. Shrub. Zones 15-24. Distinct roundish white flower clusters grow along rigid, open, spreading branches. To 4-5 ft. Leaves very small, light green, slightly wrinkled. Fair garden tolerance.

C. thyrsiflorus. BLUE BLOSSOM. Shrub or small tree. Zones 5, 6, 16, 17, 23, 24. Native to outer Coast Ranges, Santa Barbara to southern Oregon. Extremely variable in growth, usually 4-8 ft. tall, sometimes to 20 ft. Glossy dark green leaves, 1-2 in. long. Flowers from deep to washed-out blue, in 1-3-in. dense clusters. Fair garden tolerance.

C. t. repens. CREEPING BLUE BLOSSOM. Zones 5, 6, 16, 17, 23, 24. Resembles C. thyrsiflorus in every way except habit. It is a creeping plant a few inches high which makes mats many feet wide.

C. tomentosus olivaceus. WOOLLY-LEAF CEANOTHUS. Shrub. Zones 7-9, 14-24. Native to southern California, Redlands through San Diego County. To 6-8 ft. high, open habit. Leaves dark green above, white or brownish-hairy beneath, with toothed edges. Light blue flowers in 1-2-in. clusters. Magnificent in natural stands but useful on property chiefly as tough, durable, no-maintenance filler. Poor garden tolerance.

C. veitchianus. VEITCH CEANOTHUS. Shrub. Best proved in Zones 4-6, possible in 7-9, 14-24. Probably a hybrid. Open growth habit to 8-12 feet. Glossy, roundish leaves, ½-1 in. long. Bright blue flowers in dense 1-2-in. clusters on 1-2 in. stems. May and June. Good garden tolerance.

C. velutinus. TOBACCO BRUSH, VARNISH-LEAF CEANOTHUS. Shrub. Zones 1-7. Native to mountains of northern California, north to British Columbia, east to Rockies. Rounded growth, 2-5 ft. high. Leathery round leaves, 1½-2 in., dark green, varnished on top, velvety gray beneath; smell like balsam when crushed. Creamy white flowers in dense conical clusters 2-4 in. long, May to August. Good around mountain cabins. Good garden tolerance.

C. v. laevigatus. Shrub or small tree. Zones 4-6. Native to coastal areas northern California north to British Columbia. Taller growing than *C. velutinus*, almost treelike, 6-20 ft. high. Leaves smooth and light green beneath. Good garden tolerance.

CEDAR, ALASKA YELLOW. See Chamaecyparis nootkatensis

CEDAR, ATLAS. See Cedrus atlantica

CEDAR, DEERHORN. See Thujopsis

CEDAR, DEODAR. See Cedrus deodara

CEDAR, HIBA. See Thujopsis

CEDAR, INCENSE. See Calocedrus

CEDAR OF LEBANON. See Cedrus libani

CEDAR, PLUME. See Cryptomeria japonica 'Elegans'

CEDAR, PORT ORFORD. See Chamaecyparis lawsoniana

CEDAR, SALT. See Tamarix pentandra

CEDAR, WESTERN RED. See Thuja plicata

CEDRELA. Deciduous or evergreen trees. Flower in spring. Leaves divided into many leaflets, somewhat like the tree of heaven (*Ailanthus*).

C. fissilis. Evergreen in tropical areas, deciduous in mildest California climates. Zones 16, 17, 22-24. Native to Central and South America. Grows to a clean-trunked, round-headed tree to 50 ft. or more. Beautiful old street trees in Santa Barbara. Yellowish, velvety flowers in dense drooping clusters followed by star-shaped woody capsules containing winged seeds; much prized for dry arrangements.

C. sinensis. Deciduous. Zones 2-9, 14-24. Native to China. Slow to medium growth to 50 ft. White flowers in long, pendulous clusters, April and May, followed by capsules similar to above. Prized for beauty of new growth—tinted in shades of cream, soft pink, and rose.

CEDRUS. CEDAR. Evergreen trees. These conifers are the true cedars, and among the most widely grown conifers in the West. Cedars bear needles in tufted clusters. Cone scales are deciduous, like those of firs. Male catkins produce prodigious amounts of pollen that may cover you with yellow dust on a windy day.

C. atlantica. ATLAS CEDAR. Zones 4-16, 18-23. Native to Algeria. Slow to moderate growth to 60 ft. and more. Open, angular growth in youth. Branches usually get too long and heavy on young trees unless tips are pinched out or cut back. Growth naturally less open with age. Less spreading than other true cedars, but still needs a 30-ft. circle. Needles, less than 1 in. long, are bluish green. Varieties: *C. a.* 'Aurea', leaves with yellowish tint; *C. a.* 'Glauca', silvery blue; *C. a.* 'Pendula', branches droop vertically. Untrained, spreading, informally branching plants are sold as "rustics".

Stiffer branches, angular look distinguish Atlas cedar (left) from deodar cedar.

C. deodara. DEODAR CEDAR. Zones 4-12, 14-24. Native to the Himalayas. Fast growing to 80 ft. with 40-ft. spread at ground level. Lower branches sweep down to the ground then upwards. Upper branches openly spaced, graceful. Nodding tip identifies it in skyline. Softer, lighter texture than other cedars. Planted as a living Christmas tree in a small lawn, it soon overpowers the area. However, you can control spread of the tree by cutting new growth of side branches halfway back in late spring. This pruning also makes the tree more dense.

Although the deodars sold by the nurseries are very similar in form, many variations occur in a group of seedlings—from scarecrows to compact low shrubs. Two have been propagated: *C. d.* 'Prostrata' grows flat on the ground or will hang over a wall; *C. d.* 'Repandens' grows shorter, stiffer, with horizontal branches that spread stiffly over the ground. Deodar cedar can be pruned to grow as a spreading low or high shrub. Annual late spring pruning will keep it in the shape you want.

C. libani. CEDAR OF LEBANON. All Zones. Native to Asia Minor. To 80 ft., but slow growing—to 15 ft. in 15 years. Variable in growth habit. Usually a dense narrow pyramid in youth. Needles less than 1 in. long are brightest green of the cedars in young trees, dark gray-green in old trees. Spreads picturesquely as it matures to become a majestic skyline tree with long horizontal arms and irregular crown. Rather scarce and expensive because of time to reach salable size. Routine garden care. Infrequent, but deep watering. No pruning needed.

CELASTRUS. BITTERSWEET. Deciduous vines. Hardy all Zones, adapted only where winters are cold. Grown principally for clusters of handsome fruits, yellow to orange capsules which split open to display brilliant red-coated seeds inside. Branches bearing fruits are much prized for indoor arrangements. Birds seem not to be interested in the fruit, which prolongs its display into winter.

Vigorous and twining, with ropelike branches. Needs support. Will become a tangled mass of intertwining branches unless pruned continuously. Cut out fruiting branches in winter; pinch out tips of vigorous branches in summer.

C. angulatus. To 20 ft. with angular branchlets. Leaves oval to 7 in. long, shiny, bright green. Fruits, decorative in winter, are partially obscured by leaves in fall.

C. loeseneri. CHINESE BITTERSWEET. To 20 ft. with dark green, oval leaves to 5 in. long. Fruits heavily borne all along the branches.

C. orbiculatus. To 30-40 ft. Leaves roundish, toothed, to 4 in. Fruits on short side shoots are partially obscured until leaves fall.

C. scandens. AMERICAN BITTERSWEET. Native to eastern U.S. To 10-20 ft. Leaves very light green, oval, toothed, to 4 in. Fruits in scattered dense clusters are held above the leaves and showy before foliage falls. Male and female flowers on different plants. To get fruits plant one male plant with the female plants.

CELERIAC. A form of celery grown for its large, rounded, edible roots rather than for its leaf stalks. Usually displayed in markets as "celery root". These roots are peeled and cooked or used raw in salads. Growth requirements are same as for celery. Plants should grow 6-8 in. apart in rows spaced 18-24 in. apart. Harvest when roots are 3 in. across or larger—in about 120 days. 'Giant Prague' is the recommended variety.

CELERY. Difficult to grow. Plant seeds in flats in early spring. Where winters are mild, start in summer and grow as winter crop. Seedlings are slow to reach planting size (save time by purchasing seedlings). Plant seedlings 6 in. apart in rows 24 in. apart. Enrich planting soil with fertilizer. Sandy soil best. Soak ground around plants thoroughly and often. Every 2 or 3 weeks, apply liquid fertilizer with irrigation water. Work some soil up around plants as they grow to keep them upright and whiten the stalks. Control aphids with rotenone or malathion, but not within 2 weeks of harvest.

CELOSIA. COCKSCOMB, CHINESE WOOL-FLOWER. Annuals. Grow best in hot-summer climates, including desert. Richly colored tropical plants, some with flower clusters in bizarre shapes. Although attractive in cut arrangements with other flowers, in gardens celosias are most effective by themselves. Cut blooms can be dried for winter bouquets. Sow seed in place in late spring or set out plants from flats. Most successful in rich soil, with ample water.

Cockscombs are derived from a silvery white-flowered species, *C. argentea*, which has narrow leaves 2 in. or more long. There are two kinds. One group has plumy flower clusters (plume cockscomb), often sold as *C.* 'Plumosa'. Some of these, like Chinese woolflower (sometimes sold as *C.* 'Childsii') have plumy flower clusters that look like tangled masses of yarn. Flowers come in brilliant colors of pink, orange-red, crimson, gold. You can get forms that grow

C

Climate Zone maps pages 8-27

2½-3 ft. high or dwarf, more compact varieties. The latter, with their heavily branched plumes, grow to about 1 ft. high.

The other group is the crested cockscombs (often sold as *C.* 'Cristata')—velvety fan-shaped flower clusters, often much contorted and fluted. Flowers are yellow, orange, crimson, purple, and red. There are tall kinds to 3 ft. and dwarf varieties to 10 in. high.

CELTIS. HACKBERRY. Deciduous trees. Related to elm and similar to them in most details, but smaller. All have virtue of deep rooting; old trees in narrow planting strips expand in trunk diameter and nearly fill the strips—but without a surface root or any sign of heaving the sidewalk or curb. Bareroot plants, especially in larger sizes, sometimes fail to leaf out. Safer to buy in containers. Or try for small size bare-root trees with big root systems. Stake well in windy locations, at least until tree is well established. When established will take desert heat, wind, much drought, and alkaline soil.

Street or lawn trees, overhead shade, even near buildings or paving. Especially good in windy places. Only pest of note seems to be aphids occasionally. In Arizona, insects cause leaf gall on hackberry trees.

C. australis. EUROPEAN HACKBERRY. Zones 8-16, 18-20. A moderate grower to 40 ft. in 14-15 years. In youth, branches are more upright than other hackberries. Never as wide-spreading as common hackberry. Dark green leaves 2-5 in. long, more coarsely toothed and more sharply pointed than common hackberry. Has shorter deciduous period than common hackberry.

C. douglasii (*C. laevigata reticulata*). WESTERN HACKBERRY. Zones 1-3, 10-12. Native to eastern Washington and through intermountain area to Utah, and in the desert mountains of Arizona and southern California. A worthwhile ornamental tree in that area. Grows to 25-30 ft. high with a similar spread. Has somewhat pendulous branches. Oval leaves to 4 in. long, margins toothed, pale beneath, strongly veined.

C. laevigata. MISSISSIPPI HACKBERRY, SUGARBERRY. Zones 1-3, 10-12. Native to eastern U.S. Grows to 100 ft. where native, but a 30-50-ft. tree in California deserts. Spreading, broad, open crown with branches more or less pendulous. Leaves to 4 in. long, long pointed, thin, usually with smooth edges.

C. occidentalis. COMMON HACKBERRY. All Zones. Native to eastern U.S. Grows to form a rounded crown 50 ft. or more high, and nearly as wide. Branches are spreading and sometimes pendulous. Leaves oval, bright green, 2-5 in. long, finely toothed on the edges. Tree does not leaf out until April or later. In Zones 10-13, it lives longer than and is superior to the commonly planted so-called Chinese elm (correctly the Siberian elm—*Ulmus pumila*).

C. sinensis. CHINESE HACKBERRY, YUNNAN HACKBERRY. Zones 8-16, 18-20. Similar in growth habit to common hackberry, but smaller. Leaves to 4 in. long, smoother and glossier than other hackberries, and have scallop-toothed edges.

CENTAUREA. Annuals and perennials. Perennial kinds hardy Zones 8-24. Out of some 500 species, only a dozen or so widely cultivated. Of these, annuals (cornflower and sweet sultan) grown mainly for cut flowers; perennial kinds used principally for soft, silvery white or gray foliage. All centaureas relatively easy to grow, need full sun, perform best in light, neutral soils; add lime to acid soils. Sow seed of annuals in spring or fall. Set out plants of perennial kinds from cans or flats any time, preferably spring or fall; also sow seed, make cuttings in summer.

C. cineraria (*C. candidissima*). DUSTY MILLER. (This common name applied to many plants with whitish foliage. Also see *Senecio cineraria*.) Compact perennial to 1 ft. or more, velvety white leaves, strap-shaped, with broad, roundish lobes, mostly in basal clump. Solitary 1-in. flower heads (purple, occasionally yellow) in summer. Trim back after flowering. Most popular of dusty millers in California.

C. cyanus. CORNFLOWER, BACHELOR'S BUTTON. Annual, 1-2½ ft., branching if given sufficient space. Narrow, gray-green leaves, 2-3 in. long. Flower heads 1-1½ in. across, blue, pink, rose, wine red, and white. Blue varieties are traditional favorites for boutonnieres. 'Jubilee Gem', bushy, compact, 1-ft. tall, deep blue flowers; Pink Julep strain has pink or white to wine red shades. Sow seed in early spring in cold-winter areas, late summer-fall where winters are mild. Spray for aphids in spring.

C. gymnocarpa. VELVET CENTAUREA. (Often called dusty miller.) Perennial. 1-3-ft., white feltlike leaves, somewhat resembling *C. cineraria* but leaves more finely divided. Usually 2 or 3 purple flower heads at ends of leafy branches. Trim plants after bloom.

C. moschata. SWEET SULTAN. Annual. Erect, branching at base, to 2 ft. Green, deeply toothed leaves; thistlelike, 2-in. flower heads mostly in shades of lilac through rose, sometimes white or yellow; musklike fragrance. Sow seed directly on the soil in spring or set out as transplants. Needs lots of heat; no overhead water. Splendid cut flower.

CENTIPEDE PLANT. See Homalocladium

CENTURY PLANT. See Agave

CENTRANTHUS ruber (*Valeriana rubra*). JUPITER'S BEARD, RED VALERIAN. Perennial. Rank, invasive, and much maligned. Used correctly, hard to beat for long, showy bloom in difficult situations. Bushy, to 3 ft. high. Bluish green leaves 4 in. long. Small deep crimson to pale red flowers about ½ in. long, in dense terminal clusters. Blooms late spring, early summer. Variety 'Albus' white.

Use in fringe areas of garden, on rough slopes. Naturalized in many parts of West. White variety especially attractive with large beds of daylilies. Good cut flower. Plant in sun or partial shade. Will grow in poor, dry soil, accepts almost any condition except damp shade. Self-sows prolifically because of small dandelionlike parachutes on seeds. Cut off old flowering stems to shape plant and prolong bloom.

CEPHALOCEREUS senilis. OLD MAN CACTUS. Zones 21-24. Native to Mexico. Slender, columnar cactus of slow growth to an eventual 40 ft., usually much less. Covered with long, grayish white hairs. Yellow, 1½ in. spines. Old plants have 2-in.-long, rose-colored flowers in April. Night blooming. Protect from hard frosts. Good pot plant; older plants striking in cactus garden.

CEPHALOPHYLLUM. See Ice Plant

CEPHALOTAXUS harringtonia. KOREAN YEW. Evergreen tree. Zones 4-6, 15-17. Shrubby conifer of slow growth to 10-12 ft. in height, with equal spread. Rather broad, soft, 2-in.-long needles resemble true yew but are brighter green. Grow it in acid or neutral soil, and give it partial shade in hot regions. Useful screen; distinguished hedge, but expensive because of rarity and slow growth; good in containers for many years. Variety 'Fastigiata' is narrow and upright, resembling Irish yew but slower in growth, livelier in color, somewhat larger in leaf. Good shrub for narrow vertical effect in limited space.

CERASTIUM tomentosum. SNOW-IN-SUMMER. Perennial. All Zones. Low-growing plant that performs equally well in mild and cold climates, coastal or desert areas. Spreading, dense, tufty mats of silvery gray, ¾-in.-long leaves. Snowy white masses of flowers, ½-¾ in. across, in early summer. Plant grows to about 6-8 in. high, spreads 2-3 ft. in 1 year.

Use as ground cover on sunny bank or on level ground. (Avoid extensive planting in prominent situations, not as long-lived as some ground covers.) Effective in patterns with other low perennials; in rock gardens; cascading from top of walls; edging paths or driveways; between stepping stones or bulbs; as filler between low shrubs.

Plant in full sun, or light shade in warmest areas. Any soil as long as drainage is good; standing water causes root rot. Set divisions or plants 12-18 in. apart, or sow seeds. Once established, needs only occasional watering; for fast growth, water regularly and feed 2 or 3 times a year. Shear off faded flower clusters. May look a bit shabby in cold winters, but revives rapidly in spring. Divide in fall or early spring.

CERATONIA siliqua. CAROB, ST. JOHN'S BREAD. Evergreen large shrub or tree. Zones 9, 13-16, 18-23. Native to the eastern Mediterranean region. Allowed to grow naturally it maintains a bushy form with branches to the ground, often multi-stemmed. Use this way as a big hedge, informal or trimmed. Trained as a tree, with lower branches removed, it grows at a moderate rate to become dense, round-headed, to 30-40 ft., and as wide. Will reach 20 ft. in 10 years. As a street tree, it needs more than normal space as roots will break sidewalks.

Foliage is unusually dense, dark green with a sparkle. Individual leaves are divided into 4-10 round leaflets averaging about 2 in. long. Flowers of male trees give off a strong pungent odor. Female trees offer problem of pod pick-up. The flattened, dark brown, leathery pods, 1 ft. long, grow abundantly. Rich in sugar, the pods are milled to a fine powder and sold in health food stores as a substitute for chocolate.

Give young trees winter protection the first year or two. Hardy to 18°. Although often given summer watering, the carob is subject to root crown rot and should be watered infrequently and deeply.

CERATOSTIGMA. Technically evergreen or semi-evergreen subshrubs or perennials, but

C

*Climate
Zone maps
pages 8-27*

all best treated as perennials, cutting back each winter regardless of frost. Valued for rich deep blue, phloxlike flowers, in clusters, summer to late fall when garden needs cool blues. Tolerant of varying soils, water schedules, sun or part shade.

C. griffithii. BURMESE PLUMBAGO. Similar to *C. willmottianum* (see below), but more compact and lower growing (2½-3 ft.). Displays its brilliant blue flowers somewhat later, from July into late fall.

C. plumbaginoides. (Often sold as *Plumbago larpentae*.) DWARF PLUMBAGO. Zones 2-9, 14-24. A perennial wiry-stemmed ground cover 6-12 in. high. In loose soil and where growing season is long, spreads rapidly by underground stems, eventually covering large areas. Bronzy green to dark green leaves, 3 in. long, turn red-brown with frosts. Intense blue (½-in.-wide) flowers from July until first frosts. When plants show signs of aging, remove old crowns, replace with rooted stems.

C. willmottianum. CHINESE PLUMBAGO. Zones 4-9, 14-24. Grows as an airy mass of wiry stems to 2-4 ft. high and equally wide. Deep green leaves, roundish to oval, 2 in. long; turn yellow or red and drop quickly after frost. Bright blue, ½-in. wide flower, June-November.

For the pale blue-flowered Cape plumbago, see *Plumbago auriculata*.

CERATOZAMIA mexicana. Cycad. Zones 21-24. Related to *Cycas revoluta*, similar in appearance. Trunk usually a foot high, 4-6 ft. in great age, a foot thick. Very slow in growth. Leaves in a whorl, 3-6 ft. long, divided featherwise into 15-20 pairs of foot-long, inch-wide leaflets. Striking in containers or protected place in open ground. Part shade. Protect from frosts.

CERCIDIPHYLLUM japonicum. KATSURA TREE. Deciduous tree. Zones 4-6; under high branching trees in Zones 14-16, 18-20. Native to Japan. A tree of many virtues where adapted. A light and dainty branch and leaf pattern. Foliage, always fresh looking, shows tints of red throughout the growing season, beautifully colored in brilliant red or yellow in the fall, especially if watered less at the end of summer.

Rather slow growing, eventually to 40 ft. or more. Varying growth habits: some have single trunk; most have multiple trunks angled upward and outward. Nearly round, 2-4-in. leaves neatly spaced in pairs along arching branches. Mature leaves are dark blue-green above, grayish beneath.

Needs special protection from hot sun and dry winds.

C. j. magnificum. Has larger leaves and grows faster.

CERCIDIUM. PALO VERDE. Deciduous trees. Zones 10-13, 18-20. The common name palo verde covers three trees in the desert—Mexican palo verde (see *Parkinsonia*), blue palo verde, and littleleaf palo verde.

C. floridum (*C. torreyanum*). BLUE PALO VERDE. Native to deserts of southern California, Arizona, Sonora, Baja California. It belongs to and beautifies the desert and the garden oases that have been planted there. In gardens, grows fast to 25 ft. and as wide. In spring, 2-4½-in.-long clusters of small bright yellow flowers almost hide the branches. When out of bloom, an intricate

pattern of blue-green, spiny branches, branchlets, and leaf stalks. Leaves have 1-3 pairs of smooth, tiny leaflets, are shed early, leaving bluish green leaf stalks for lightly filtered shade.

Will survive much drought, but is denser, more attractive, and grows faster with water and fertilizer.

C. microphyllum. LITTLELEAF PALO VERDE. Native to eastern San Bernardino County, California; Arizona; Sonora; Baja California. Similar to blue palo verde, except bark and leaves (with 4-12 pairs of hairy leaflets) yellowish green, and the flowers paler yellow in 1-in.-long clusters.

CERCIS. REDBUD. Deciduous shrubs or trees. Four redbuds are grown in the West: a Western native, an Eastern native, one from Europe, one from China. Early spring flowers are sweet pea-shaped, small, in clusters, and where adapted, borne in great profusion on bare twigs, branches, sometimes even on main trunk. Attractive broad, rounded leaves are heart-shaped at base. All give fall color with first frosts. Flowers are followed by clusters of flat pods.

C. canadensis. EASTERN REDBUD. Zones 1-3, 7-9, 14-20. Native of eastern U.S. Largest and fastest of available species where adapted. To 25-35 ft. tall. Most apt to take tree form. Round-headed but with horizontally tiered branches in age. Rich green 3-6-in.-long leaves have pointed tips. Small (½-in.-long) rosy pink flowers clothe bare brown branches in early spring.

Garden varieties include: 'Alba' ('White Texas'), white flowers, choice; 'Forest Pansy', purple foliage and reddish branches; 'Oklahoma', wine red flowers; 'Plena' ('Flame'), double flowers like rosebuds.

C. chinensis. CHINESE REDBUD. Zones 4-20. Native to China, Japan. Seen mostly as a light, open shrub to 10-12 ft. Clusters (3-5 in. long) are a deep rose, almost rosy purple. Leaves perhaps glossier and brighter green than *C. canadensis*, with a transparent line around the edge. Spectacular in high deserts of Arizona.

C. occidentalis. WESTERN REDBUD. Zones 2-9, 14-24. Native to California, Arizona, Utah, but predominantly in California foothills below 4,000 ft., inner Coast Ranges (Humboldt to Solano counties), Sierra foothills (Shasta to Tulare counties), desert slopes of Laguna and Cuyamaca Mts. in southern California.

A shrub or small tree 10-18 ft. in height and spread. Usually grows several trunks from base. All-year interest. In spring it delivers a 3-week brilliant display of magenta flowers, ½ in. long. Summer foliage of handsome blue-green, 3-in. leaves, notched or rounded at tip; interspersed are brilliant magenta newly forming seed pods. In fall whole plant turns light yellow or red. In winter, bare branches in picturesque pattern hold reddish brown seed pods.

Excellent for dry, seldom-watered banks. Use with *Ceanothus griseus* for deep blue color complement. Water regularly in first year or two to speed growth. Profuse flower production only where winter temperatures drop to 28° or lower.

C. siliquastrum. JUDAS TREE. Zones 2-19. Native to Europe and western Asia. Generally of shrubby habit to 25 ft., occasionally a taller, slender tree with single trunk. Flowers are purplish rose, ½ in. long. Large

3-5-in. leaves, deeply heart-shaped at base, rounded or notched at the tip. Occasionally damaged by late frosts in Northwest. Legend has this as the tree upon which Judas hanged himself after the betrayal.

CERCOCARPUS. MOUNTAIN-MAHOGANY. Evergreen or partially deciduous tall shrubs or small trees. Natives of our mountains and foothills, worth appraisal as garden plants. Several have a most attractive open structure and branching pattern. Distinguished in fall by long-lasting small fruits topped by a long twisted, feathery, tail-like plume that sparkles in the sunlight. About 20 kinds are native to the West, but these two are most widespread:

C. betuloides. Zones 6-24. Native to dry slopes and foothills, below 6,000 ft. elevation, southwestern Oregon, California, northern Baja California. Called hardtack, mountain ironwood, sweet brush. Generally a shrub 5-12 ft. high. Can form small tree to 20 ft. with wide-spreading crown of arching branches. Wedge-shaped, ½-1-inch leaves clustered on short spurs; dark green above, pale beneath, feather veined with toothed edges.

C. ledifolius. CURL-LEAF MOUNTAIN-MAHOGANY. All Zones. Native to dry mountain slopes, 4,000 to 9,000 ft. elevation, throughout the Western states east of Sierra-Cascades and in desert mountains of southern California and eastward. About same height as *C. betuloides*, but eventually to 30 ft. with spreading, open crown of stout, intricately twisted branches. Leathery, ½-1-inch-long leaves, resinous, dark green above, white hairy beneath, with inrolled edges.

CEREUS peruvianus. Cactus. Zones 16, 17, 21-24. Tall, branching treelike cactus eventually reaching 30-50 ft. Striking bluish green, especially when young, ribbed, with scattered spines. Flowers white, 6-7 in. long, 5 in. across, in June. Night blooming. Variety 'Monstrosus' is smaller, slower growing, with ribs irregularly broken up into knobs and crests. Striking outline; effective in large containers. Protect from hard frosts.

CEROPEGIA woodii. ROSARY VINE. Succulent. Outdoors in Zones 21-24, house plant anywhere. From South Africa. Little vine with hanging or trailing thin stems growing from a tuberous base. Leaves in pairs, heart-shaped, thick and succulent, ⅔ in. long, dark green marbled white. Little tubers that form on stems can be used to start new plants. Flowers small, dull pink or purplish, not showy but interesting in structure. Best in pots; stems may trail in a thin curtain or be trained on a small trellis. Give some shade and regular watering.

Other ceropegias are available from specialists: some are shrubby, some vining, some stiffly succulent, but all have similarly fascinating flower structure.

CESTRUM. Evergreen shrubs. Native to American tropics. All the kinds have showy, tubular flowers. Fast growth, inclined to be rangy and topheavy unless consistently pruned. Best in warm sheltered spot in part shade. Feed and water generously. Add organic soil amendments before planting. Nip back consistently for compactness and

C

Climate Zone maps pages 8-27

cut back severely after flowering or fruiting. In climates specified below, plants may freeze back in heavy frosts but recover quickly.

C. aurantiacum. ORANGE CESTRUM. Zones 21-24. Native to Guatemala. Rare and handsome. To 8 ft. Brilliant show: clusters of 1-in.-long orange flowers late spring, summer, followed by white berries. Deep green, oval, 4-in. leaves. Tall growing, it is best used as vine or espalier.

C. fasciculatum. Zones 13, 16-24. To 10 or more ft. tall, arching and half-climbing, with broad oval 2-in.-long leaves and clusters of purple-red flowers in spring or summer, followed by red berries. Big background shrub or espalier.

C. nocturnum. NIGHT JESSAMINE. Zones 13, 16-24. Native to West Indies. Evergreen shrub to 12 ft. with 4-8-in.-long leaves and clusters of creamy white flowers in summer, white berries. Powerfully fragrant at night. Too powerful for some people.

C. parqui. WILLOW-LEAFED JESSAMINE. Zones 13-24. Native to Chile. To 6-10 ft. tall with many branches from the base. Dense foliage of willowlike leaves, 3-6 in. long. Flowers, greenish yellow, 1 in. long, in clusters, summer. Berries dark violet-brown. Not as attractive as other species in form, flowers, or fruit but its perfume is potent. Leaves blacken in light frost. Best used where winter appearance is unimportant. In cold-winter areas, protect roots with mulch and use as perennial.

C. purpureum (*C. elegans*). RED CESTRUM. Zones 13, 17, 19-24. Shrub or semi-climber to 10 ft. high or higher, with arching branches, deep green, 4-in. leaves. Masses of purplish red, 1-in.-long flowers in spring and summer; scattered bloom throughout the year; followed by red berries. Good espalier.

CHAENOMELES. (Some formerly called *Cydonia.*) FLOWERING QUINCE. Deciduous shrubs. Zones 1-21. Flowering quinces are among the first shrubs to bloom each year. As early as January you can take a budded stem or two indoors, place it in water in a warm window and watch the buds break

into bloom. The plants, themselves, are picturesque, practically indestructible shrubs of varying growth habit. Leaves shiny green, red-tinged when young. Branches are attractive when out of leaf—strong in line with an Oriental feeling. Some grow to 10 ft. and spread wider; some are compact and low growing; most are thorny; a few are thornless. Some of them bear small quince-like fruits.

All are easy to grow. Tolerant of extremes in cold and heat, light to heavy soil. May suffer from chlorosis in alkaline soils (use iron chelate or iron sulfate). May bloom reluctantly in warm-winter areas. Prune any time to shape, limit growth, or gain special effects. Good time to prune is in bud and bloom season. (Use cut branches for indoor arrangements.) The new growth that follows will bear next year's flowers.

Since in addition to *C. speciosa*, 4 hybrid species are involved in the parentage of many of the named varieties, and rarely included on the label, the variety (or hybrid) name is the only guide. In the following list of choice varieties we have noted, in addition to color, the height. Those noted as tall are in the 6-ft. and more class; the low varieties are in the 2-3-ft. range.

'Afterglow'. Tall. Large, double, white bud opens to soft rose.
'Apple Blossom'. Tall. White and pink.
'Cameo'. Low, compact. Double, soft apricot pink.
'Candida'. Tall. White, cup-shaped.
'Cardinal'. Tall. Deep red, massed toward ends of long slim side branches.
'Clarke's Giant Red'. Tall. Bright red.
'Contorta'. Low. White to pink; twisted branches. Good as bonsai.
'Corallina'. ('Coral Glow'). Tall. Reddish orange.
'Coral Sea'. Tall. Large, coral pink.
'Enchantress'. Tall. Large, shell pink.
'Falconet Charlot'. Tall, thornless. Double salmon pink.
'Jet Trail'. Low. Pure white.
'Knap Hill'. Low. Vermilion-red.
'Nivalis'. Tall. Large, pure white.
'Pink Beauty'. Tall. Purplish pink.
'Red Rufflles'. Tall. Almost thornless.

Large, ruffled, red.
'Rowallane'. Low, compact. Vivid red.
'Simoni'. Low. Deep blood red.
'Snow'. Tall. Large, pure white.
'Stanford Red'. Low, almost thornless. Tomato red.
'Texas Scarlet'. Low. Tomato red.
'Toyo Nishiki'. Tall. Pink, white, pink and white, solid red all on same branch.

CHAMAECEREUS silvestri. PEANUT CACTUS. Zones 16, 17, 19-24. Native to Argentina. Dwarf cactus with cylindrical, ribbed, spiny, 2-3-in. joints that fall off easily and root just as easily. Free blooming in spring and early summer; even tiny rooted joints bloom. Flowers bright scarlet, almost 3 in. long. Great favorite with children.

CHAMAECYPARIS. FALSE CYPRESS. Evergreen trees, shrubs, and shrublets.
Many varieties, but all sold are forms of five kinds—three Western natives, and two from Japan. These are the basic five (they and their many varieties are charted for size, shape, texture, and performance):

C. lawsoniana. An important timber tree in coastal Oregon (also native to extreme northern California). It and its varieties are probably the most adaptable in mild Western climates. Its yellow-leafed varieties seem to burn in California. Best in Zones 4-6. Foliage burns in dry cold or hot sun in Zones 2, 3. Good performance in Zones 15-17 and poor to satisfactory in Zones 7-9, 14, 18-21 (best in partial shade there).

C. nidifera. Natural hybrid between *C. lawsoniana* and *C. nootkatensis*.

C. nootkatensis. The hardy timber tree of Alaska and mountains of Oregon and Washington. It and its varieties do not thrive in climates of cold dry winds and summer heat. Use in Zones 4-6, 15-17.

Of the two Japanese species, *C. pisifera* is hardier than *C. obtusa* contrary to published reports. *C. pisifera* is grown to some extent in Zones 1-3. Both Japanese species and their varieties are best adapted in Zones 4-6, and 15-17.

Chamaecyparis is a rich source of bonsai material—many interesting dwarf forms

CHAMAECYPARIS

SPECIES OR VARIETY	HEIGHT	SPREAD	COLOR	FORM, TEXTURE	REMARKS
CHAMAECYPARIS lawsoniana PORT ORFORD CEDAR, LAWSON CYPRESS	To 60 ft. or higher.	To 30 ft. at base.	Blue-green, variable.	Pyramidal or columnar form with lacy, drooping flat foliage sprays and conical crown.	Can be planted as close as 3 ft. apart without becoming thin or straggly, and topped at 10 ft. or more for windbreak or sun screen.
C. l. 'Allumii' SCARAB CYPRESS, BLUE LAWSON CYPRESS	To 30 ft.	Narrow.	Blue-green, new foliage metallic blue.	Compact, narrow pyramidal form. Scalelike leaves are carried in regular vertical planes.	A widely adapted, slow-growing tree. Planted 2-3 ft. apart makes a narrow, formal hedge.
C. l. 'Azurea'	To 6 ft.	To 3 ft.	Silvery gray-blue.	Broad pyramidal form. Soft-textured, drooping branches.	Avoid crowding for shapely plants.
C. l. 'Compacta'	To 6 ft.	To 4 ft.	Gray-green.	Upright, rounded form. Light-textured, full-branched.	Background and large scale plantings.

Climate
Zone maps
pages 8-27

SPECIES OR VARIETY	HEIGHT	SPREAD	COLOR	FORM, TEXTURE	REMARKS
C. l. 'Ellwoodii' ELLWOOD CYPRESS	Slowly to 6 or 8 ft., higher with age.	To 2 or 3 ft.	Silvery blue.	Dense, compact columnar form. Light-textured with soft, prickly, needlelike leaves.	One of most widely planted and widely adapted trees.
C. l. 'Fletcheri' FLETCHER CYPRESS	6-8 ft., higher with age.	To 3 or 4 ft.	Blue-gray; purplish or brown in winter.	Dense, pyramidal form. Soft, prickly foliage.	Somewhat like "Ellwoodii" but taller, broader, and faster growing.
C. l. 'Forsteckensis' (C. l. 'Forsteckiana') FORSTECK CYPRESS	4 ft.	To 6 ft.	Dark green.	Dense, compact form. Moss-like texture; densely tufted branches.	A rock garden or container plant. Makes a dense, informal hedge.
C. l. 'Lutea' GOLDEN LAWSON CYPRESS	To 30 ft. or more.	To 10 or 12 ft.	New growth yellow, old growth blue-gray.	Soft fronds.	Probably best of the taller yellow false cypresses. Susceptible to sunburn.
C. l. 'Minima Glauca' LITTLE BLUE CYPRESS	To 3 ft.	To 2½ ft.	Blue-green.	Compact, nearly globular form. Dense foliage; soft texture.	A shrub well suited for pots, boxes, rock gardens, low uniform landscape plantings.
C. l. 'Stewartii' STEWART GOLDEN CYPRESS	To 30 ft.	10-12 ft. at 18-foot height.	New growth yellow, old growth dark green.	Upright, slender, pyramidal form. Soft texture; drooping branchlets.	Handsome and widely planted. Needs room for good growth. Used in parks, public playgrounds.
C. l. 'Wisselii' WISSEL CYPRESS	To 15 or 18 ft., higher in 15 to 20 years.	4-5 ft.	Dark blue-green.	Slender, upright form with twisted foliage; irregular branches, somewhat like those of Juniperus chinensis 'Torulosa'.	Subject to insects and diseases, especially in hot, dry climates. Keep sprayed for red spider mites.
C. nidifera (C. nestoides, C. lawsoniana nestoides, C. l. nidiformis) BIRD NEST CYPRESS	Variable from 3-12 ft. (see remarks).	6-8 ft.	Dark green.	Spreading, flat-topped form with dense center; outward spraying branches.	There are two forms of this plant: One sold as variety 'Nestoides' grows 3 to 4 ft. high. The other, sold as variety 'Nidiformis', grows 10-12 ft. high. Good for informal screening hedge.
C. nootkatensis NOOTKA CYPRESS, ALASKA YELLOW CEDAR	80 ft.	20-30 ft.	Bluish green.	Pyramidal form, with dense, fine-textured foliage. Often has pendulous branches. Coarser than Lawson cypress.	Slow growing, it will stand greater cold and poorer soil than Lawson cypress, though latter can probably stand more heat.
C. nootkatensis 'Compacta'	To 3 or 5 ft.	To 2 or 2½ ft.	Blue-green.	Narrow, pyramidal form.	Handsome in containers—a miniature tree rather than a shrub.
C. obtusa HINOKI FALSE CYPRESS	40-50 ft., higher with great age.	15-30 ft.	Dark glossy green.	Spreading, irregular, open form.	Very slow growing and suited principally to a large, Oriental garden. Splendid bonsai subject. Prune to shape.
C. o. 'Aurea' GOLDEN HINOKI CYPRESS	30-40 ft.	10-15 ft.	Dark green. Young growth is golden.	Foliage is bunched, flattened in horizontal plane.	Slow growing. For Oriental garden, woodland edge. Color hard to blend. Useful with dark greens. Subject to sunburn.
C. o. 'Crippsii' CRIPPS GOLDEN CYPRESS	To 30 ft. Can be kept smaller.	To 10 ft.	Yellow when young. Later dark green.	Somewhat open pyramidal habit.	Use for line and pattern in Oriental gardens or against fence, screen, wall. Can be pruned effectively by spacing branches at various levels.
C. o. 'Filicoides' FERNSPRAY CYPRESS	To 15 ft.	To 6 ft.	Medium green.	Dense foliage; branchlets short, crowded, frondlike.	Slow growing, with gracefully curved limbs. For Oriental gardens, entryways, large planting boxes.
C. o. 'Gracilis' (Often sold as C. obtusa). SLENDER HINOKI CYPRESS	Slow to 20 ft.	4-5 ft.	Very dark, glossy green.	Slender, somewhat weeping form. Soft and dense, with nodding tip and branch ends.	Choice plant that is slow to outgrow its place. Good entryway plant, or in containers.

(Continued on next page)

SPECIES OR VARIETY	HEIGHT	SPREAD	COLOR	FORM, TEXTURE	REMARKS
C. o. 'Lycopodioides' CLUB-MOSS CYPRESS	Slow to 3 ft.	3 ft.	Dark green.	Branchlets short, irregular. crowded or bunched.	Unusual plant for close-range viewing. Rock garden or container.
C. o. 'Nana' DWARF HINOKI CYPRESS	Very slow to 3 ft.	2 ft. or more.	Dark green.	Dense foliage in flat, stratified planes.	A 60-year-old plant may be 3 ft. tall, 2 ft. across. Rock gardens, mass plantings on slopes.
C. o. 'Nana Aurea' GOLDEN DWARF HINOKI CYPRESS	To 4 ft.	To 3 ft.	New foliage yellow. Old foliage dark green.	Dense foliage in flat-sided sprays.	Useful where a touch of yellow is needed; Oriental and rock gardens.
C. o. 'Nana Gracilis' (Usually sold as C. o. 'Nana') DWARF HINOKI CYPRESS	To 4 ft.	To 3 ft.	Dark green.	Dense foliage; flattened, cupped fronds.	Most commonly used dwarf hinoki cypress; Oriental and rock gardens.
C. o. 'Sanderi' (C. o. 'Ericoides')	4-6 ft.	4-6 ft.	Gray-green, purple-brown in winter.	Fluffy, needlelike rather than scalelike foliage.	Winter color interest; grows scraggly with age.
C. o. 'Torulosa' (C. o. 'Coralliformis')	To 3 ft.	3 ft.	Dark green. Red-tinted twigs.	Twisted, threadlike branches.	Slow growing; rock gardens, bonsai containers.
C. pisifera (Retinospora pisifera) SAWARA FALSE CYPRESS	20-30 ft. or more.	To 20 ft.	Dark green above, lighter beneath.	Spine-tipped, scalelike leaves; rather loose, open growth.	Good in large Oriental gardens. Prune heavily to force new growth, hide dead foliage on inner branches.
C. p. 'Cyano-Viridis'	Rather slow to 5-8 ft.	3-4 ft.	Light, silvery blue-green.	Good, dense form; soft, fine-textured, fluffy-looking foliage.	Good for color and texture contrast with other evergreens.
C. p. 'Filifera' THREAD CYPRESS, THREADBRANCH CYPRESS	To 8 ft. or higher.	To 6 ft.	Dark green.	Loose mound, attractive when young. Too open in old age. Weeping, threadlike twigs.	Oriental and rock gardens. Contrast with dense, solid shrubs. Prune to keep in bounds. C. p. 'Filifera Aurea', GOLDEN THREAD CYPRESS, has yellow foliage.
C. p. 'Plumosa' PLUME FALSE CYPRESS	20-30 ft.	10-12 ft.	Bright green.	Upright branches, compact, cone-shaped. Short, soft needles. Frondlike, feathery twig structure.	Carefully pruned, a big shrub. Unpruned, a tree. Slow growing at first.
C. p. 'Plumosa Aurea'	20-30 ft.	10-12 ft.	New growth golden yellow, old growth green.	As above.	Prune hard by pinching tips to restrain growth, promote density. Like variety 'Plumosa', tends to lose lower branches as it ages.
C. p. 'Squarrosa' MOSS CYPRESS	20-30 ft. or much higher.	10-30 ft.	Silvery gray-green.	Soft, feathery, with long, needlelike leaves.	Attractive while young. As it ages thin it out for greater character, picturesqueness. Big background plantings, massive yet soft-textured area cover.
C. p. 'Squarrosa Minima' (C. p. 'Pygmaea', C. p. 'Squarrosa Pygmaea')	Dwarf (see remarks).	(See remarks).	Gray-green to dark green depending on form.	Sharp-pointed leaves.	Several forms go under this name. One is a very compact, very slow-growing globe form to 6 by 6 inches in 5 years, with dark green, very short needles. Another is gray-green, lacy-foliaged, grows to 18 in. high and spreads much wider.
C. p. 'Squarrosa Veitchii'	To 20 or 30 ft.	10-30 ft.	Blue-green.	Lighter, airier than variety 'Squarrosa'.	An improvement in color and texture over variety 'Squarrosa'.

Climate
Zone maps
pages 8-27

for this use, climate restrictions are less severe.

In growing chamaecyparis, be sure to provide fast drainage. They are susceptible to root rot in heavy, slow-draining soils. Many forms develop dead foliage on the inner parts. Too much shade and red spider mites contribute to this condition. Spray in summer for spider mites. Stimulate new growth by pinching branch tips.

CHAMAEDOREA. Palm. House plant and outdoors Zones 16, 17, 22-24. Small shade-tolerant feather type. Generally slow growing, they are good in containers indoors or on a shaded patio. Some have single trunks, others clustered trunks. Leaves variable in shape.

C. cataractarum. Single-stemmed palm growing slowly to 4-5 ft.; trunk speckled. Older plants take some frost.

C. costaricana. Develops fairly fast into bamboolike clumps of 8-10-ft. trunks if well fed and liberally watered. Good pot palm; will eventually need good-sized container. Lacy, feathery leaves 3-4 ft. long.

C. elegans. (Widely sold as *Neanthe bella*.) Often called parlor palm, and the best indoor chamaedorea, tolerating crowded roots, poor light. Single-stemmed; grows very slowly to an eventual 3-4 ft. Douse

Chamaedorea elegans, easy indoors. Other chamaedoreas look less palmlike.

potted plants with water occasionally; feed regularly. Groom by removing old leaf stalks. Repot every 2-3 years, carefully washing off old soil and replacing with a good potting mix. Effective potted 3 or more to a container.

C. ernesti-augustii. Slow growing to 5 ft., with dark green, fishtail-shaped leaves. Needs shade and a protected location.

C. erumpens. Cluster-forming, bamboolike dwarf with drooping leaves. Slow grower to 4-5 ft. Needs shade or part shade, no frost.

C. geonomaeformis. Fine palm for pots. Grows slowly to 4 ft. Broad, oblong leaves are not cut featherwise, but are deeply split at the tips in fishtail effect.

C. glaucifolia. Slow to 8 ft. or more, with fine-textured feather leaves 4-6 ft. long with bluish green tint on both sides (most marked on underside).

C. klotzschiana. Single-trunk palm of slow growth to 4-5 ft. Handsome, dark green feathery leaves. Hardy to 28°.

C. radicalis. Slow, single-stemmed plant to 4 ft. tall. Strong-patterned dark green leaves. Interesting, colorful seed formation. Hardiest of chamaedoreas; will take temperatures down to 22-28°.

C. seifrizii. Cluster palm of dense, compact growth to 8-10 ft. Feathery leaves with narrow leaflets. Takes 28° and can be used outdoors in protected areas in part shade. Needs ample moisture.

C. tenella. Single trunk to 3-4 ft. Dark bluish green leaves are exceptionally strong, large, broad, undivided but deeply cleft at ends.

C. tepejilote. Single trunk, ringed with swollen joints like bamboo. Moderate growth to 10 ft.; leaves 4 ft. long, feathery. Grows well in frost-protected, shady areas inland.

CHAMAELAUCIUM uncinatum. (Sometimes sold as *C. ciliatum*.) GERALDTON WAX-FLOWER. Evergreen shrub. Zones 8, 9, 12-24. Native to Australia. The bright green needlelike leaves and showy sprays of winter-blooming, pale pink or rosy ½-in. flowers are cherished for flower arrangements of long-lasting beauty. Light and airy, loose and sprawling, fast growth to 6-8 ft., or, when staked, to 10-12 ft. with equal spread. Looks somewhat like a loose-growing heather. Very old plants have interesting twisted trunks and shaggy bark.

Plant on sunny dry bank or in cutting garden in fast-draining soil and water deeply but infrequently in summer. Or combine with plants that don't require regular summer watering such as *Cassia artemisioides*, rosemary. Prune freely for arrangements or cut back after flowering. Seedling plants vary. Select in bloom to get color you want.

CHAMAEROPS humilis. MEDITERRANEAN FAN PALM. Zones 5-24. Probably the hardiest palm; has survived 6°. Clumps develop slowly from offshoots, curve to a height of 20 ft., may be 20 ft. wide. Growth extremely slow in Portland, Seattle. Leaves green to bluish green. Versatile: use in containers, mass under trees, use for an impenetrable hedge. Drought and wind resistant. Feed and water in summer to speed growth.

CHAMOMILE. See Anthemis nobilis

CHAPARRAL BROOM. See Baccharis

CHARD. See Swiss chard

CHASTE TREE. See Vitex

CHAYOTE. Vine with edible fruits, young leaves, and tubers. Related to squashes. Perennial in Zones 14-16, 19-24, annual elsewhere. The fruit is the principal crop. It is green or yellow-green, irregularly oval, grooved, and contains a large seed surrounded by meaty, solid flesh. Both meat and seed, when boiled or baked have a flavor somewhat like squash. A well-grown plant should produce 200 or more fruits. Fruits measure 3-8 in. long.

Needs full sun; warm, rich soil; ample water; and a fence or trellis to climb. Buy fruits at store in fall, allow to sprout, plant the whole fruit edgewise, sprouted end at

lowest point, narrow end exposed. If shoot is long, cut it back to 1-2 in. Plant 2 or more fruits to assure pollination. Plant in February or March; in area where roots might freeze, plant in a 5-gallon can or tub and store the plant until after frost. Plants can produce 20-30 feet of vine the first year, 40-50 ft. the second. Tops die down in frost. Bloom starts when day-length shortens in fall, and fruits are ready a month later.

CHECKERBERRY. See Gaultheria procumbens

CHEIRANTHUS allionii. See Erysimum asperum

CHEIRANTHUS cheiri. WALLFLOWER. Perennial or biennial. Zones 4-6, 16, 17, 22, 23. Old timers esteemed for sweet fragrance and rich colors of flowers that bloom in spring and early summer. Erect bushy plants to 1-2½ feet; narrow, bright green leaves 3 in. long. Flowers ½ in. across, in velvety tones of yellow, orange, brown, red, pink, rose, burgundy, in dense clusters at tops of leafy stems. Excellent with tulips in yellow, orange, or lilac shades; or beneath lilacs, which bloom at same time.

Locate in full sun, or in light shade, where spring sun is bright. Plant in mounded or raised beds to provide best possible drainage. Sow seeds in spring for bloom following year; or set out nursery transplants in fall or early spring. Young plants need long period to develop vegetative growth.

CHENILLE PLANT. See Acalypha hispida

CHERIMOYA. See Annona

CHERRY. Here we consider the sweet cherries, sour cherries, and Duke cherries (hybrids between sweet and sour cherries).

SWEET CHERRIES

Most seen at markets and most widely known in the West. Trees 30-35 ft. tall, as broad in some varieties. They are at their best in deep well drained soils in Zones 2, 6, 7, 14, 15. They have a high chilling requirement (need many winter hours at below 45° temperature), and therefore are not adapted to the mild-winter areas of southern California or the low desert.

Fruiting spurs are long-lived, do not need to be renewed by pruning. Prune trees only to maintain good structure and shape.

Birds everywhere like sweet cherries. Protect with netting over tree or strings of pennants outside the tree, hanging from a revolving arm above tree, turned by electric motor.

Spray in winter with a copper spray, in spring before buds open with an insecticide-miticide, and when first blooms appear and weekly during bloom with a fungicide for control of brown rot and blossom blight.

Varieties:

'Bing'. Top quality. Large, dark red, meaty, fruit of fine flavor. Midseason.

'Black Tartarian'. Smaller than 'Bing', purplish black, firm, sweet fruit. Ripens early.

'Chinook'. Resembles 'Bing', ripens 4-10 days earlier.

'Corum'. Light-colored fruit with colorless juice, flesh whitish. Excellent flavor. Ripens 7 days before 'Royal Ann'.

C

Climate
Zone maps
pages 8-27

'Deacon'. Large tree. Large to medium-size black fruit, firm. Sweet pleasant flavor. Ripens 7 days earlier than 'Bing'.

'Lambert'. Large, vigorous tree, less spreading than 'Bing' and 'Royal Ann'. Very large, black, latest ripening fruit, very firm. Flavor more sprightly than 'Bing'.

'Rainier'. Has yellow skin with a pink blush; ripens a few days before 'Bing'.

'Republican' ('Black Oregon'). Large, spreading tree. Purplish black, small round fruit, dark juice, tender, crisp. Good flavor. Late season.

'Royal Ann' ('Napoleon'). Large, spreading tree, very productive. Light yellow fruit with pink blush, tender, crisp. Sprightly flavored. Midseason.

'Sam'. Vigorous, dense tree. Black fruit, large, firm. Excellent flavor.

'Van'. Heavy-bearing tree. Black shiny fruit, firmer and slightly smaller than 'Bing'. Good flavor. Ripens earlier than 'Bing' in Northwest, right with it in California.

Two trees are needed to produce fruit, and the second tree must be chosen with care. No combination of these will produce fruit: 'Bing', 'Lambert', 'Royal Ann'. These varieties will pollenize any other cherry: 'Black Tartarian', 'Corum', 'Deacon', 'Republican', 'Sam', and 'Van'. However, because 'Lambert' blooms late, it is pollenized best by 'Republican'.

SOUR CHERRIES

The sour cherry is a spreading, irregular growing, garden-sized tree to 20 ft. You can prune to increase the irregularity if you want an ornamental tree, or force a more regular, upright pattern by pruning out drooping side branches. The sour cherries are self-fruitful, and are reasonably good pollenizers for sweet cherries. 'Montmorency' and 'Early Richmond' are preferred varieties with small, bright red, soft, juicy, sweet-tart fruit. 'English Morello', darker, more tart fruits, and red juice. 'Meteor', fruit like 'Montmorency', but smaller tree.

DUKE CHERRIES

Trees are somewhat larger than sour cherries. Climate adaptation same as sweet cherries. The Duke cherries are self-fruitful. Their fruits have shape and color of sweet cherries, flavor, texture of sour cherries. Varieties: 'May Duke', medium-sized, early, dark red. 'Late Duke', large, light red fruit ripening in July.

CHERRY, BRUSH. See Syzygium

CHERRY, CATALINA. See Prunus lyonii

CHERRY, CORNELIAN. See Cornus mas

CHERRY, FLOWERING. See Prunus

CHERRY, GROUND. See Physalis pruinosa

CHERRY, JERUSALEM. See Solanum pseudocapsicum

CHERRY, SURINAM. See Eugenia uniflora

CHERVIL. See Anthriscus

CHESTNUT. See Castanea

CHESTNUT, CAPE. See Calodendrum

CHESTNUT, MORETON BAY. See Castanospermum

CHICORY. Botanically known as *Cichorium intybus*. Inner leaves and hearts used in salads. Dried ground roots can be roasted and used as a substitute for coffee. Grows as roadside weed in much of the West and recognized by its pretty sky blue flowers. 'Witloof' or French endive is the standard variety. For how to grow, see Endive.

CHILOPSIS linearis. DESERT WILLOW. Deciduous large shrub or small tree. Zones 11-13, 18-21. Native to desert washes and stream beds below 5,000 ft., southern California, east to Texas; Mexico.

Open and airy when trained as a small tree. Grows fast (to 3 ft. in a season) at first, then slows down, levels off at about 25 ft. In age, develops shaggy bark and twisting trunks somewhat like the Australian tea tree (*Leptospermum laevigatum*). As a native, drops leaves early and can look scraggly. But watering and pruning can make it most handsome.

Long, narrow, 2-5-in. leaves. Flowers look somewhat like catalpa's, trumpet-shaped with crimped lobes—pink, white, rose, or lavender, marked with purple. Flower color varies among seedlings. Nurseries select the most colorful. Flowers appear in spring and often through fall, borne first year from gallon cans. Easy to propagate from hardwood cuttings.

CHIMONANTHUS praecox (*C. fragrans, Meratia praecox*). WINTERSWEET. Deciduous shrub. Zones 4-7 (where it blooms February-March), 8, 9, 14-17 (where it blooms December-May). Native to China and Japan. Needs some winter cold. Its outstanding virtue: a spicy fragrance in the winter garden.

Tall, open, growing slowly to 10-15 ft. high and 6-8 ft. wide and many basal stems. Keep lower by pruning while in flower. Or prune as a small tree by removing excess stems. Leaves medium green, tapering, 3-6 in. long and half as wide. Flowers on leafless stems, 1 in. across, outer sepals pale yellow; the inner sepals chocolate colored, smaller. Plant where its winter fragrance can be enjoyed. In hot-summer areas it grows best if shaded from afternoon sun.

Variety 'Grandiflorus' has larger leaves and flowers; variety 'Luteus' has flowers of brighter yellow.

CHIMONOBAMBUSA. See Bamboo

CHINA-BERRY. See Melia azedarach

CHINCHERINCHEE. See Ornithogalum thyrsoides

CHINESE CABBAGE. Makes a tall head somewhat looser than cabbage, and sometimes called "celery cabbage". More delicate flavor than cabbage in salads or cooked. Favored varieties are 'Michihli' and 'Mandarin'. Definitely a cool-season crop; very prone to bolt to seed in hot weather, or in the long days of spring and early summer. Plant seeds directly in the open ground in July in Zones 1-6, 10, 11, in August or September in other areas. Sow seeds thinly in rows 24-30 in. apart and thin the plants to 18-24 in. apart in the rows. Heads should be ready in 70-80 days.

CHINESE EVERGREEN. See Aglaonema modestum

CHINESE GOOSEBERRY. See Actinidia chinensis

CHINESE HOUSES. See Collinsia

CHINESE PARSLEY. See Coriandrum

CHINQUAPIN. See Castanopsis

CHIONANTHUS. FRINGE TREE. Deciduous trees. Earn common name from the narrow, fringelike, white petals. These flowers are borne in impressive, ample, lacy clusters. Broad leaves turn deep yellow in fall.

C. retusus. CHINESE FRINGE TREE. Zones 2-9, 14-24. Generally smaller growing than *C. virginicus*—to 20 ft. Leaves 2-4 in. long. Flower clusters to 4 in. long; blooms in June and July. In bloom, it's a magnificent tree, something like a tremendous white lilac.

C. virginicus. FRINGE TREE. Zones 1-6, 15-17. Native Pennsylvania to Florida and Texas. Grows to 30 ft. where well adapted.

Fringe trees are named for the narrow, fringelike, 1-in., white flower petals.

Leaves and flower clusters twice the size of *C. retusus*, and it blooms earlier (May). Fragrant. In western Washington it is lucky to reach 12 ft. in 10 years, and is best used as a very slow-growing, airy shrub (it blooms profusely when only 2-3 ft. tall). Flowers are more greenish than white there, and it is one of the last deciduous plants to leaf out in spring.

CHIONODOXA. GLORY-OF-THE-SNOW. Bulb. Zones 1-7. Native to alpine meadows in Asia Minor. Charming small bulbous plants 4-6 in. high; among first to bloom in spring. Narrow basal leaves, 2 or 3 to each flower stalk. Blue or white, short, tubular, open flowers in loose spikes. Plant bulbs 3 in. deep in September or October in half shade. Under favorable conditions plants self-sow freely.

C. luciliae. Most generally available. About 10 brilliant blue, white-centered, star-like flowers on 6-in. stalks. Variety 'Alba', larger white flowers, 'Gigantea' has larger leaves, larger flowers of violet-blue with white throat.

C. sardensis. Deep true gentian blue flowers with very small white eye.

CHIRANTHODENDRON pentadactylon (*C. platanoides*). MONKEY HAND TREE. Evergreen tree. Zones 20-24. Fast growing to 40-50 ft. with a spread of 20-30 ft. Leaves 8-10 in. long, shaped like sycamore, medium green with a rusty underside. Odd flowers somewhat resemble waxy, deep red, smallish tulips, covered on outside with a soft fuzz. Projecting from the flower is a fantastic structure that resembles a tiny red hand, complete with fingernails. Blooms appear from March to October; borne toward ends of branches, leaves almost cover them.

Tree has survived temperatures in the upper twenties.

Continual leaf drop in summer and strong surface rooting rules it out as patio or street tree. Best in deep soil with infrequent but deep watering.

CHIVES. A small, clump-forming, perennial onion relative. Its leaves are grasslike in general appearance, but are round and hollow in cross-section. Clumps may reach 2 ft. in height but are usually less. The cloverlike spring flowers are in clusters atop thin stems and are rose-purple. The plant is pretty enough to use as an edging for a flower border or herb garden. Does best in moist, fairly rich soil. May be increased by divisions or grown from seed. Evergreen (or nearly so) in mild regions, goes dormant where winters are severe, but small divisions may be potted in rich soil and grown on a kitchen window sill. Chop or snip the leaves into salads, cream cheese, cottage cheese, egg dishes, gravies, and soups for delicate onionlike flavor and as a pretty garnish.

CHIVES, GARLIC. Sometimes known as Chinese garlic or Chinese chives. Plant resembles common chives in clumping habit, but leaves are flat and somewhat gray-powdery. Clustered summer flowers are white. Less vigorous than chives and more inclined to winter dormancy. Leaves have a mild garlic flavor. Culture is same as for chives.

CHLOROPHYTUM comosum (*C. capense*). SPIDER PLANT. Evergreen perennial. House plant; outdoor ground cover in Zones 15-17, 19-24. Native to tropics. Shade and moisture loving plant forming 1-3-ft.-high clumps of soft, curving leaves like long, broad grass blades. Form with white-margined leaves, often sold as *C. elatum vittatum*, most popular. Flowers white, ½-in. long, in loose leafy-tipped spikes standing above foliage. Greatest attraction: Miniature duplicates of the mother plant, complete with root, at end

Spider plant (Chlorophytum), familiar in hanging baskets, also good ground cover.

of curved stems (as with strawberry plant offsets); these offsets can be cut off, potted individually. Excellent, easily grown house plant for fully lighted window, greenhouse. Ground cover or hanging basket plant in partial shade.

CHOISYA ternata. MEXICAN ORANGE. Evergreen shrub. Borderline Zones 4-6, good in 7-9, 12-17, good but often suffers from pests and soil problems in Zones 18-24. Hardy to 15°. Rapid growing to 6-8 ft. high and as wide. Lustrous, yellow-green leaves held toward the end of the branches, are divided into fans of 3 leaflets (to 3 in. long); fans give shrub a dense, massive look but with highlights and shadows. Clusters of fragrant white flowers, somewhat like small orange blossoms, open in very early spring and bloom continuously into April, intermittently through summer.

Use as attractive informal hedge or screen. Mass to fill large spaces. Prune throughout growing season to shape and thin out branches, forcing replacement wood from inside the plant. Cut freely for decoration when in bloom.

Grows in full sun in cool-summer areas; elsewhere in light shade. Gets straggly and bears few flowers when in too much shade. It's touchy about soil conditions. Difficult in alkaline soils or where water is poor quality. Under such conditions, prepare special soil mix as for azaleas. Subject to root rot and crown rot if drainage is not fast. Water it infrequently but deeply. Subject to damage from thrips, aphids, mealybugs, scale, and red spider mites. Spray with all-purpose insecticide every 2 weeks through the growing season.

CHOKEBERRY, RED. See Aronia

CHOLLA. See Opuntia

CHORISIA speciosa. FLOSS SILK TREE. Evergreen to briefly deciduous tree. Zones 12-24. Native to Brazil. A gay springlike flower show comes in October, November, or December. All or part of the leaves drop as it blooms and when winter temperatures drop to 27° or lower. Blooms most profusely in warm foothills. Reducing water in late summer (on blooming-sized trees) encourages more flowers.

Grows 3-5 ft. a year in first years, then slowly to 30-60 ft. Young trees are lance-straight and narrow; the crown becomes broad (25-35 ft.) with age. Young trunk heavy and tapering, grass green, studded with thick-based spines; turns gray with age. Light green leaves are divided fanwise into 5-7 leaflets. Flowers somewhat resemble a narrow-petaled hibiscus in orchid pink, purplish rose, or burgundy. The petal bases are ivory or white, spotted or striped brown. Fast drainage and controlled watering are keys to success. Never plant in lawn. Water established trees once a month.

CHORIZEMA. FLAME PEA. Evergreen shrubs. Zones 15-17, 19-24. Native to Australia. Hardy to about 24°. All three species present a riotous, gaudy display of blended orange and red flowers resembling sweet peas in clusters, February-June. Fast growing with slender graceful branches.

Take sun but flower color is more intense in part shade. Left to go their own way, they are attractive spilling over a wall, on banks, in containers, hanging baskets. Pruned, pinched, and cut back severely after flowering, they make compact 2-ft. shrubs for ground cover, edging, or flower border. Source of late winter color.

C. cordatum. (Sometimes erroneously sold as *C. ilicifolium*.) HEART-LEAF FLAME PEA. Grows 3-5 ft. high, sometimes more under ideal conditions. Dark green leaves 1-2 in. long, with small prickly teeth along the edges.

C. ilicifolium. HOLLY FLAME PEA. A low spreading shrub 2-3 ft. high. Oval, ¾-1-in. leaves similar to *C. cordatum* but the edges are wavy and have deep prickly teeth; vaguely resemble holly leaves.

C. varium. BUSH FLAME PEA. More compact growth habit, to 3 ft., and the branches and leaves are hairy.

Chorizema species have many brilliant orange and red flowers in the spring.

CHRISTMAS BERRY. See Heteromeles arbutifolia

CHRISTMAS TREE, NEW ZEALAND. See Metrosideros excelsa

CHRYSALIDOCARPUS lutescens. (Often sold as *Areca lutescens.*) Zone 24. Clumping feather palm of slow growth to 10-15 ft. Graceful plant with smooth trunks and yellowish green leaves. Can grow in pots or in a shady, sheltered spot in frost-free areas. Takes sun near coast. Gets spider mites when grown indoors. Tricky to maintain, but a lovely palm.

CHRYSANTHEMUM. Annuals, perennials. All Zones. There are about 160 species of chrysanthemum, mostly native to China, Japan, and Europe. Included are some of the most popular and useful of garden plants—the top favorite being *C. morifolium*, whose modern descendants are known as florists' chrysanthemums. But there are many other worthwhile species in cultivation, capable of producing summer and fall color in borders, containers, or (widest use) as cut flowers.

C. arcticum. ARCTIC CHRYSANTHEMUM. Very hardy autumn-blooming perennial forming a clump with stems 6-12 in. high. Spoon-shaped leaves, usually 3-lobed, 1-3 in. long, leathery in texture. White or pinkish flower heads 1-2 in. across. From this species have been developed a group of hybrids known as Northland daisies with single flowers 3 in. or more across, in shades of pink, rose, rosy purple, and yellow. *C. arcticum* itself is primarily a rock garden plant. Taller growing varieties serve best in borders.

C

Climate Zone maps pages 8-27

C

Climate
Zone maps
pages 8-27

C. balsamita. COSTMARY. A weedy 2-4 ft. perennial with sweet-scented foliage that justifies its presence in the herb garden (use leaves in salads and in sachets). If the leggy stems are cut back, fragrant, gray-green basal leaves with tiny scalloped margins can make an herb garden edging. Divide clumps and reset divisions in late summer or fall.

C. carinatum. SUMMER CHRYSANTHE-MUM, TRICOLOR CHRYSANTHEMUM. Summer and fall-blooming annual, growing 1-3 ft. high, about 3 ft. wide. Deeply cut foliage; showy single, daisylike, 2-in.-wide flower heads in purple, orange, scarlet, salmon, rose, yellow and white, with contrasting bands around a dark center. Satisfactory, long-lasting cut flowers. Sow seeds in spring either in flats or in open ground. Full sun. Light or heavy soil; grows wild in sand dunes along sections of southern California coast.

C. coccineum *(Pyrethrum roseum)*. PAINTED DAISY, PYRETHRUM. Bushy perennial to 2-3 ft. with very finely divided, bright green leaves and single, daisylike, long-stemmed flowers in pink, red, and white. Also available in double and anemone-flowered forms. Starts blooming in April in mild-winter climates, in May or June in colder areas; if cut back, blooms again in late summer. Excellent for cutting, borders; combine with *Campanula persicifolia*, columbine, delphinium, dianthus. Best in full sun. Needs summer heat to perform well. Divide clumps or sow seeds in spring; double forms do not always come true from seed.

C. frutescens. MARGUERITE, PARIS DAISY. Rapid growing, much branched perennial, woody at base, tender in cold climates. Bright green, coarsely divided leaves; abundant daisylike flowers, 1½-2½ in. across, in white, yellow, or pink. 'Snow White', double anemone type, has pure white flowers, more restrained growth habit; 'White Lady' and 'Pink Lady' have buttonlike flower heads; 'Silver Leaf' has gray-green leaves and masses of white flowers that are much smaller than those of the regular marguerite. All kinds, but particularly the familiar white and yellow marguerites, are splendid for quick effects in borders, mass displays in new gardens, and containers.

Small plants set out in spring will grow 4 ft. across by summer. In buying plants, avoid large, vigorous looking ones with large leaves—they will bloom sparsely. Also avoid plants showing signs of fasciation (flattening or widening of stems) near the crown.

Plant in full sun, in light soil. Grows exceptionally well near coast; with sufficient water, good drainage, also succeeds inland, but may freeze in cold winters. For continued bloom, prune lightly at frequent intervals. Do not prune older plants severely —they seldom produce new growth from hardened wood. Replace every 2-3 years with new plants. Few pests, although subject to leaf miner.

C. maximum. SHASTA DAISY. Hardy, sturdy perennial, indispensable for summer and fall bloom in all climates. The original 2-4-ft.-tall Shasta daisy with its coarse leathery leaves and white, gold-centered flower heads 2-4 in. across has been largely superseded by varieties with larger, better

formed, longer-blooming flowers. They are available in single, double, quilled, and shaggy-flowered forms. All are white, but two show a touch of yellow. Some bloom from May to October. Shasta daisies are splendid in borders and cut arrangements. Cut blooms may be dyed by plunging freshly cut stems into water containing household dye or food coloring.

Following are some of the varieties available in nurseries:

'Esther Read', most popular double white, longest bloom; 'Marconi', a large frilly double; 'Aglaya', similar to 'Marconi', longest blooming season; 'Alaska', a big old-fashioned single; 'Horace Read', 4-in.-wide, dahlialike flower; 'Majestic', large yellow-centered flower; **'Thomas Killin'**, 6-in.-wide (largest) yellow-centered flower. 'Cobham's Gold' has distinctive flowers in a yellow-tinted, off-white shade. 'Canarybird', another yellow, is dwarf, with attractive dark green foliage.

Most popular varieties for cut flowers are 'Esther Read', 'Majestic', 'Aglaya', and **'Thomas Killin'**.

Set out divisions of Shasta daisies in fall or early spring, container-grown plants at any time. Thrive in fairly rich, moist, well-drained soil. Prefer sun, but do well in partial shade in hot-summer climates; double-flowered kinds hold up better in very light shade. In coldest regions mulch around plants, but do not smother foliage. Divide clumps every 2-3 years in early spring (or in fall in mild-winter areas). Shasta daisies generally easy to grow, but have a few problems. The disease called "gall" causes root crown to split into many weak, poorly rooted growing points that soon die. Dig and burn affected plants. Sterilize soil before planting in the same spot. Bait to control snails and slugs.

Shasta daisies in well drained soils can take plenty of water, especially before and during bloom; at this time apply liquid fertilizer to encourage large flowers. Also cut old flowers to prolong bloom.

C. morifolium. FLORISTS' CHRYSANTHE-MUM. The most useful of all autumn blooming perennials for borders, containers, and cutting, and the most versatile and varied of all chrysanthemum species, available in many flower forms, colors, and growth habits. Following are flower forms as designated by chrysanthemum hobbyists:

Button pompon. Smallest pompon, less than 1½ in. across.

Pompon. Globular, neat, compact flowers with flat, fluted, or quilled rays. Disbudded pompons may reach about 5 in. in diameter. Extremely large number of varieties in wide color range covering a long period of bloom.

Single or *daisy.* Come in all sizes and forms. Rays may be short and rigid or long and drooping, but are arranged regularly and form a fringe.

Spoon. Unusual tubular rays broaden at ends to form distinct spoons that are frequently of a different color from rest of rays, producing interesting contrasts.

Cushion. Flowers made up of unequal tiered rays; most varieties bloom prolifically from late September until frosts; some begin as early as June. Very dwarf, compact type. Useful in containers.

Anemone. One or more rows of rays with large raised center disk or cushion,

same color as rays or different. (Disbud for very large flowers.)

Spider. Some with rays only, others with varying number of disk flowers at center. True spiders have curling tubular rays ending in fish-hook tips. Disbud for large flowers.

Rayonnante. Most flowers with rays only; rays are long, closed tubes except for small openings near pointed tips.

Exhibition. Two types—*incurved* and *reflexed*. Rays of incurved type close in toward the center, forming a round ball-shaped flower. Rays of reflexed type turn back. Both types, when disbudded, produce the large flowers traditionally worn as corsages at football games.

Decorative. One of the so-called unclassified types. Slender rays variable: may be long, narrow or broad, and flat (overlapping like roof shingles), or may resemble cactus-flowered dahlias.

Feathery. Carnationlike with cupped or twisted and curled rays.

Japanese. Rays usually long and more or less curled, twisted and intertwined, giving entire flower a shaggy appearance.

It's easy to grow chrysanthemums, not so easy to grow prize-winning chrysanthemums. The latter need more water, feeding, pinching, pruning, grooming, and pest control than most perennials.

Plant in good, well drained garden soil improved by organic matter and a complete fertilizer dug in 2 or 3 weeks before planting. In most areas chrysanthemums do best in full sun; in hot climates provide shade from afternoon sun. Don't plant near large trees or hedges with invasive roots.

Set out young plants (rooted cuttings or vigorous, single-stem divisions) in early spring. When dividing clumps, take divisions from outside; discard woody centers. Water deeply at intervals determined by your soil structure—frequently in porous soils, less frequently in heavy soils. Too little water causes woody stems and loss of lower leaves; overwatering causes leaves to turn yellow, blacken, and drop. Stems attacked by borers in desert areas. Aphids are the only notable pest in all areas.

Feed plants in the ground 2 or 3 times during the growing season; make the last application with low-nitrogen fertilizer not less than 2 weeks before bloom.

Sturdy plants and big flowers are the result of frequent pinching, which should begin at planting time with removal of the tip of the new plant. Lateral shoots will form; select 1-4 of these for continued growth. Continue this pinching all summer, nipping the top pair of leaves on every shoot that reaches 5 in. in length. On some of the early-blooming cushion varieties, or in the coldest regions, pinching should be stopped earlier. Stake plants to keep them upright. To produce huge blooms, remove all flower buds except for 1 (or 2) in each cluster— this is called *disbudding*.

Pot Culture: Pot up rooted cuttings in February, March, or April, using a porous, fibrous, moisture-holding planting mix. Move plants on to larger pots as growth requires — don't let them become pot-bound. Pinch as directed above, and stake as required. Plants need water every day in warm weather; every other day when cool. Feed with liquid fertilizer every 7 to 10 days until buds show color.

C

Climate
Zone maps
pages 8-27

Cascade chrysanthemums: Grow in pots or boxes, shifting as the plants become larger; plants usually bloom in 10-12-in. pot or box of equivalent size. Pinch out tips of side shoots when 4-5 in. long starting when plants are 12 in. high. Pinch later side shoots as they form, leaving 2-3 leaves. When plant is 12 in. high, pinch out tip so that 3 to 5 side stems will ultimately form. Make frame like this: Bend 9 ft. of 12-gauge wire into a U. Run 14-gauge wire up center and use for crosspieces. Insert frame 1 in. from plant; bend at 45° angle 6 in. from base. Tie stem to frame. Point tip toward north. Protect from wind; top-heavy plants will blow over easily. As main stems grow, tie to frame at 5-in. intervals. Once a week, until September 15, pinch all side shoots (not tip of main stems) back to second or third leaf joint to encourage bushy growth. Gradually bend frame into a horizontal position. On September 15, reverse position of containers so that the wire points south. Continue to bend wire down to cascade position. This should be completed by October 15.

Steps in training a cascade chrysanthemum from 12-in. height (left) to full bloom.

Care after bloom: Cut back plants to within 8 in. of the ground. Check or renew labels. When soils are heavy and likely to remain wet in winter, dig clumps with soil intact, and set on top of ground in an inconspicuous place. Cover with sand or sawdust if you wish. Take cuttings from early to late spring (up until May for some varieties); or when shoots are 3-4 in. long. As new shoots develop, you can make additional cuttings. In cold-winter areas, store in a coldframe or mulch with a light, non-compacting material like excelsior.

Off-season, potted chrysanthemums: Florists and stores sell potted chrysanthemums in bloom every day of the year, even though by nature a chrysanthemum blooms in late summer or fall. The growers force these plants to bloom out of season by subjecting them to artificial day-lengths, using lights and dark cloths. You can plunge the potted flowering plants right into a garden bed or border as an immediate (but expensive) display of chrysanthemums. Or you can enjoy them in the house while the flowers remain fresh, and then plant them

out. Either way, they will not bloom again at the same off-season time the next year. Instead, they will revert to nature and commence once again to bloom in fall.

Cut off the flowers when they fade, leaving stems about 6-8 in. long. Remove the soil clump from the pot and break apart the several individual plants that were grown in the pot. Plant these individual plants. When new growth shows from the roots, cut off the remainder of the old flower stems.

C. parthenium. FEVERFEW. Compact, leafy, aggressive perennial, once favored in Victorian gardens. The old-fashioned single, white-flowered forms self-sow freely, grow as weeds in some areas. Leaves have strong odor, offensive to some. Named varieties vary in height from 1-3 ft. 'Golden Ball' has bright yellow flower heads and no rays; 'Silver Ball' is completely double with only the white rays showing. In 'Aureum', commonly sold in flats as 'Golden Feather', chartreuse colored foliage is the principal attraction. Sow seeds in spring for bloom by midsummer, or divide in fall or spring (in cold climates). Can also grow from cuttings. Full sun or light shade.

CHRYSOLARIX amabilis (*Pseudolarix amabilis, P. kaempferi*). GOLDEN LARCH. Deciduous conifer. Zones 2-7, 14-17. Slow growing to 40-70 ft. high, often nearly as broad at base. Wide-spreading branches, pendulous at tips, grow in whorls to form symmetrical, pyramidal tree. Needles 1½-2 in. long, about ⅛ in. wide, clustered in tufts except near branch ends where they are single. Foliage effect feathery, bluish green, turning golden yellow in fall. Cones and bare branches make interesting winter patterns. Give it a sunny, open spot sheltered from cold winds. Best in deep, rich, well drained, acid or neutral soil. Needs regular supply of moisture. Fine for spacious lawns.

CHUPAROSA. See Beloperone californica

CIBOTIUM. Tree ferns. One fairly common, one quite rare.

C. glaucum. (Usually sold as *C. chamissoi.*) HAWAIIAN TREE FERN. Zones 17, 24. Grows to 6 ft. high, 8 ft. wide, and has feathery, golden green fronds (apple green if shaded). Bare trunks imported from Hawaii by the thousands; these trunks can be potted up in loose fast-draining, rich in organic material. If temperatures and humidity are kept high, and the soil is not too wet, plants will root and grow. Leaf crowns can become very broad. Hardy to 32°.

C. schiedei. MEXICAN TREE FERN. Zones 16, 17, 21-24. Can reach 15 ft. tall, with wide-spreading, lacy, arching and drooping, chartreuse-green fronds. Hardy to 24° when mature. Rare.

CIGAR PLANT. See Cuphea ignea

CILANTRO. See Coriandrum

CIMICIFUGA. BUGBANE. Perennials. Zones 1-7, 17. Stately, upright, slim flower spikes of small white flowers grow from clumps of shiny, dark green leaves divided into many 1½-3 in.-long, deeply toothed leaflets. Flowers late summer to fall. Handsome among large ferns in woodland garden. Best in partial shade, rich, well drained, moist soil. Will

take considerable sun with ample water. Clumps can remain undisturbed for many years. Divide in fall or (in cold areas) in early spring before growth starts. Dried seed clusters useful in flower arrangements.

C. racemosa. BLACK SNAKEROOT. Native to eastern U.S. Flower spikes grow to 7 ft.

C. simplex. KAMCHATKA BUGBANE. Flowers spikes grow 3-5 ft. high.

CINERARIA. See Senecio cruentus

CINNAMOMUM. Evergreen trees. Slow to moderate growing, eventually reaching considerable size. Both species have aromatic leaves that smell like camphor when crushed. Good for large lawns and as street trees but competitive root system make it poor choice for garden beds. Thrives in hot summer areas where winter temperatures stay above 20°.

Not much bothered by pests, but subject to a root rot—verticillium wilt. Symptoms: wilting and dying of twigs, branches, entire center of the tree, or entire tree. Wood in twigs or branches shows brownish discoloration. No cure is known; cut out damaged branches. Fertilize trees with nitrogen fertilizer and water deeply. Trees often outgrow it. Most susceptible after wet winters or in poorly drained soils.

C. camphora. CAMPHOR TREE. Zones 8, 9, 12-24. Native to China, Japan. A delight to the eye in every season. In winter the foliage is a shiny yellow-green. Beautiful in rain when the trunks look black. In early spring new foliage may be pink, red, bronze depending on the tree. Unusually strong structure, heavy trunk, and heavy upright spreading limbs. Grows slowly to 50 ft. or more with a wider spread. Leaves 2½-5 in. long. Drops leaves quite heavily in March but fairly clean otherwise. Clusters of tiny, fragrant yellow flowers in profusion in May, followed by small blackish fruits.

C. glanduliferum. NEPAL CAMPHOR TREE. Zones 15-17, 19-24. Native to the Himalayas. Differs in having larger, richer green, more leathery leaves. Apparently faster growing than the common camphor tree, more upright in branching habit, and tenderer (shows some leaf burn at 25°).

CINQUEFOIL. See Potentilla

CISSUS. Evergreen vines distinguished for their foliage. All climb by tendrils. Related to Virginia creeper, Boston ivy, and grape. Easy to grow. Not fussy about soil, water, or fertilizer.

C. antarctica. KANGAROO TREEBINE. Zones 13, 16-24. Native to Australia. Vigorous once established. To 10 ft. A graceful vine. Medium green, shiny leaves, 2-3½ in. long and almost as wide, toothed edges. Good tub plant indoors or out, in sun or shade, for climbing up or tumbling down, for trellis or wall.

C. capensis. See Rhoicissus capensis

C. hypoglauca. Zones 13, 19-24. Native to Australia. Rapid growth to 15 ft. in one season. Eventually 30-50 ft. ta'l. Leaves highly polished, divided into 5 roundish, leathery leaflets 3 in. long; foliage strong in texture with bronzy color tones. New growth covered with rust-colored fuzz. Use in same way as *C. antarctica.* Makes a good bank cover.

Climate Zone maps pages 8-27

C. rhombifolia. GRAPE IVY. Zones 13, 15, 16, 21-24 (needs all-year warmth). Native to South America. To 20 ft. Beautiful dark green foliage. Leaves divided into diamond-shaped leaflets 1-4 in. long, with sharp-toothed edges; show bronze overtones because of reddish hairs on veins beneath. Widely used indoors. Outdoors it grows to good size and can be trained on trellis, pergola, or driftwood branches. Grows in sun or fairly deep shade, tolerating low light intensity indoors. The variety 'Mandaiana' is more upright and compact, with larger, more substantial leaflets.

C. striata. Zones 13, 16-24. Native to South America. In effect a miniature Virginia creeper, with small leaves divided into 3-5 leaflets, each 1-3 in. long, leathery. Stems reddish. To 10 ft. Use to make long traceries against plain surfaces, as ground or wall cover, or to spill over a wall. Sun or shade. Useful and beautiful.

C. voinieriana. See Tetrastigma

C. vomerensis. See Tetrastigma

CISTUS. ROCKROSE. Evergreen shrubs. Borderline in Zones 4-6; satisfactory in Zones 7-9, 12-15, 18-22; best in Zones 16, 17, 23, 24. Native to Mediterranean region. Hardy to 15°. Producers of showy flowers, the rockroses are also sun-loving, fast growing, drought-resistant, recommended for planting in fire hazard areas, tolerant of poor, dry soil. Will take cold ocean winds, salt spray, or desert heat. Rockroses should have well drained soil if they are to be watered frequently. To keep plants vigorous and neat, cut out a few old stems from time to time. Tip pinch young plants to thicken growth.

When planting in an area that will be neglected—no water once the plant is established—don't root prune plants. Cut circling roots and spread out the mass so the plant will have a chance to root down to lower soil levels.

Use as dry-bank cover, massed by themselves, or interplanted with ceanothus, wild buckwheat, or sunroses (*Helianthemum*). The taller kinds make good informal screens or low dividers. Useful in big rock gardens or in rough areas along drives and roads; for sunny wild areas.

C. corbariensis. See *C. hybridus*.

C. 'Doris Hibberson'. Compact, to 3 ft. tall and as wide. Gray-green foliage. Clear pink, 3-in.-wide flowers with crinkled, silky petals in June-July. Flower color is easier to work into combinations than that of the more commonly grown *C. purpureus*.

C. hybridus (*C. corbariensis*). WHITE ROCKROSE. Spreading growth to 2-5 ft. high and almost as wide. Leaves to 2 in. long, gray-green, crinkly, fragrant on warm days. Flowers 1½ in. across, white with yellow centers in late spring. Widely grown.

C. ladaniferus maculatus. CRIMSON-SPOT ROCKROSE. Compact, to 3-5 ft. high, with equal spread. Leaves to 4 in. long, dark green above, whitish beneath, fragrant. Large, 3-in.-wide, white flowers with dark crimson spot at the base of each petal, June-July.

C. laurifolius. LAUREL ROCKROSE. Open growth to 6-8 ft. high by 3-4 ft. wide; leggy if not pruned. Dark, grayish green, 2½-in.-long leaves. Large, white, 2-3-in.-wide flowers in July. Aromatic on hot days.

C. purpureus. ORCHID ROCKROSE. Compact grower to 4 ft. and equally wide, often lower and wider where constant ocean winds keep the plants low. Leaves 1-2 in. long, dark green above, gray hairy beneath. Reddish purple, 3-in.-wide flowers with a red spot at the base of each petal, June-July. Very fine where cool winds and salt spray limit choice of plants.

C. salvifolius. (Usually sold as *C. villosus* 'Prostratus'.) SAGELEAF ROCKROSE. Wide-spreading shrub to 2 ft. high and 6 ft. across. Leaves light gray-green, about 1 in. long, crinkle-veined, crisp looking. Flowers 1½ in. wide, white with yellow spots at base of petals, very profuse in late spring. Good bank or ground cover for rough situations.

C. villosus. Bushy plant 3-5 ft. tall and equally wide. Oval, 1-3-in.-long leaves densely covered with down. Flowers purplish pink, 2-2½ in. across in late spring and early summer. Used in fire-hazard areas.

CITRON. See Citrus

CITRUS. Evergreen trees and shrubs highly valued for fruit and as landscaping plants. Outdoors in Zones 8, 9, 12-24; indoor-outdoor container plants anywhere. As landscaping plants, they offer attractive form and foliage all year, fragrant flowers in season, and decorative fruit in season. As producers of quality fruit, varieties must be selected according to two considerations: total amount of heat available through fruit developing period (need varies according to type), and winter cold they will get. Choice and use is also determined by whether plants are standard trees or dwarfs.

CULTURE

Heat requirements. Lemons and limes need the least heat, and will produce usable fruit in cool-summer areas (where winter temperatures are not too low). 'Valencia' orange has a higher heat requirement and a greater frost tolerance. Navel oranges need even more heat. But their fruit development period is shorter than 'Valencia' and a tree will produce fruit between winter frosts if summer heat is high. Navel, therefore, is a good selection for northern Sacramento Valley and Arizona areas. Mandarin oranges (tangerine group) need high heat for top flavor. Grapefruit develops full flavor only in areas of prolonged high heat.

Hardiness. Citrus of one kind or another are grown in every Arizona and California climate where winter temperatures do not fall below 20°. From least hardy to hardiest they rank generally in this order: 'Mexican' lime (28°), limequat, grapefruit, regular lemon, tangelo and tangor, 'Bearss' lime, sweet orange, most mandarin oranges (tangerines), 'Rangpur' lime and 'Meyer' lemon, 'Owari' mandarin, sour orange, kumquat, calamondin (20°).

Standard or dwarf. Most standard citrus trees grow to 20-30 ft. high and almost as wide. Dwarfs (grown on dwarfing rootstock) become 4-10 ft. shrubs or small trees of equal beauty and greater landscaping utility. They can be located more easily than standards in garden warm spots and in containers they can be easily protected from frost and placed in wind-protected warm spots for extra heat. Some 30

varieties of citrus are available on dwarf rootstocks.

Drainage. The first requirement is fast drainage. If soil drains slowly, don't attempt to plant citrus in it regardless of how you condition planting soil. In poorly drained soil, plant above soil level in raised beds or by mounding up soil around the plant. Drainage in average soil and water retention in very light soils will be improved by digging in a 4-6 in. layer of peat moss, sawdust, or ground bark to a depth of 12 inches.

Watering. Citrus needs moist soil, but never free-standing water. It needs air in the soil. Danger from overwatering is greatest in clay soil where air spaces are minute. In soil with proper drainage, water newly planted trees almost as frequently as trees in containers—twice a week in normal summer weather, more frequently during a hot spell. Water established trees every other week. In clay soils, space watering intervals so top part of soil dries between irrigations. Don't let tree reach wilting point (as has been advised in the past).

If you build basins, make them wider than the spread of branches. Citrus roots extend out twice as far as the distance from the trunk to branch ends. Keep trunk dry by starting basin 6 in. or more from trunk. When you water, put on enough to wet entire root zone (that is, wet to a depth of 4 ft.).

Mulching. Since citrus roots grow near the surface as well as deep, a mulch over soil is beneficial. Use a 2-3-in.-deep layer of sawdust or the like, or large pebbles or gravel.

Fertilizing. Universities recommend from 1½ to 2 lbs. of actual nitrogen for mature trees each year (to get pounds of "actual nitrogen", take percentage of total nitrogen, as stated on label, times weight of the fertilizer). It's best to apply 1/3 in late winter, 1/3 in June, and 1/3 in August. Spread fertilizer beneath and well beyond branch spread of tree, and water in deeply. Use a high nitrogen formula; large quantities of phosphorus and potash are not needed.

Citrus may suffer from iron chlorosis or zinc deficiency. Iron chlorosis (yellowing leaves with dark green veins) may also be caused by excess water, so check your irrigation practice. Treat with chelated iron or iron sulfate. Zinc deficiency shows up as a yellowish blotch or mottle between leaf veins. Control with zinc foliar sprays. Commercial products are available as sprays containing both iron chelates and zinc.

Pests and diseases. Citrus can get aphids, mites, scale insects, and mealybugs. All of these pests can be controlled with the same insecticide: malathion. Use it whenever you see twisted leaves, a shiny film on leaves, or leaves stippled irregularly with yellow. If scale remains troublesome spray with light oil in early spring. Bait or spray for snails and slugs whenever necessary, especially during warm-night spells of winter and spring. Spray soil around the trees in March for ants and earwigs.

The few fungus ailments of citrus occur in poorly drained soil. Water molds, causing root rot, show up in yellowing and dropping foliage. Best control is to correct your watering schedule.

Brown rot gummosis usually occurs in older trees at base of trunk. Keep base of trunk dry; trim and clean the oozing wounds, removing decayed bark to a point where the discolored wood does not show. Paint areas with Bordeaux paste mixture.

Sunburn. Citrus bark sunburns in hot-sun areas. Trunks should be wrapped (commercial paper trunk band is available). When exposing trunks or limbs by heavy pruning, protect bark with whitewash or cold-water paint. Common cold-water wall paint in tan or brown, similar to bark color, is satisfactory.

Pruning. Commercial trees are allowed to carry branches right to the ground. Production is heaviest on the lower branches. Growers prune only to remove twiggy growth and weak branches, or, in a young plant, to nip back wild growth and balance the plant. You can prune garden trees to shape as desired. Lemons and sour oranges are often planted close and pruned as hedges. Many citrus are thorny. Pruners and pickers should wear gloves and long sleeves.

Gardening in old orange grove. Home owners moving into an orange grove should remember that the tree they inherit has had orchard care—deep watering, regular feeding, and periodic pest control. Roots spread far beyond tree branches. To keep the tree healthy, water deeply with slow irrigation and follow feeding and pest control schedule as outlined above. If lawn is planted near the tree, water near the tree deeply once a month in addition to regular lawn water.

Citrus in containers. Daily watering may be necessary in hot weather. For most dwarf citrus, containers should be at least 18 in. in diameter.

Citrus indoors. Gardeners in cold-winter, warm-summer areas can store plants indoors for winter protection. A cool greenhouse is best, but a basement area with good bright light is satisfactory. Use very little water.

GRAPEFRUITS

'Marsh' seedless. The West's main commercial type. Large, light yellow fruit. Ripens 18 months after bloom. Late November to June in desert areas. Needs highest, most prolonged summer heat for top quality. Even out of best climate it's a beautiful tree. Standard tree grows to 30 ft. or more; on dwarf rootstock, less than half size. Large glossy leaves.

'Ruby'. Pink grapefruit. Like 'Marsh' except for red blush of skin and pinkish flesh. Does not color well except in desert.

LEMONS

'Eureka'. The standard lemon of markets. Bears throughout year. Not as vigorous as 'Lisbon'. Somewhat open growth, branches with few thorns. As a dwarf, it's dense with large, dark leaves. New growth bronzy purple.

'Lisbon'. Vigorous growth, thorny, upright, denser than 'Eureka', to 20-25 ft. Can be trimmed up into highly decorative small tree. Fruit practically identical to 'Eureka'. Ripens mostly in fall, but some all year. More resistant to cold than 'Eureka', and better adapted to high heat. Best lemon for Arizona.

'Meyer'. Fruit is quite different from commercial lemon—rounder, thin-skinned, more orange colored. Tangy aroma, very juicy, but less acid than standard lemon. Bears fruit at early age. Tree is not a dwarf on its own roots. Will grow to 12 ft. with a 15-ft. spread. On dwarf rootstock it's half that size. This lemon carries a disease causing citrus "quick decline", and is banned in Arizona and the San Joaquin Valley, but widely sold elsewhere.

'Millsweet'. Known as sweet lime or sweet lemon. Fruits small, roundish, yellowish orange, with thin rind. Sweet flesh has mild lemon flavor and very little acid. Vigorous, medium-large tree.

'Ponderosa'. A novelty. Bears huge, rough lemons with thick coarse skin. Two-pound fruits not unusual. Mild lemon flavor. Bears at early age, frequently in gallon-can size. Main crop winter with some fruit through the year. Tree angular branched, open; large leaves widely spaced. To 8-10 ft.; dwarf size, 4-6 ft.

'Villa Franca'. Generally similar to 'Eureka' but tree is larger, more vigorous, and has denser foliage and thornier branches. Fruit is similar to 'Eureka'. Sold in Arizona to grow in protected spots; not common in California.

LIMES

'Bearss'. Best lime for California gardens. Succeeds where the orange is successful. Tree is quite angular and open when young but forms a dense round crown to 15-20 ft. when mature. Half that size on dwarf rootstock. It's thorny and inclined to drop many leaves in winter. Young fruit green, light yellow when ripe, almost size of a lemon. When fully ripe it is especially juicy. Seedless. Main crop winter to late spring, some fruit all year.

'Mexican'. The standard bartender's lime—small, green to yellow-green. Plant in mildest areas only. Grows to 12-15 ft. with upright twiggy branches.

LIMEQUAT

'Eustis'. Hybrid of 'Mexican' lime and kumquat. Fruit is jumbo olive in shape and size, light yellow when ripe. Rind edible. Flavor and aroma of lime. Ripens late fall and winter. Some fruit all year. Tree is shrublike, angular branching, twiggy, and rather open. Dwarf plant excellent in container.

MANDARIN ORANGES (Tangerines)

'Clementine'. Algerian tangerine. Fruit a little larger than 'Dancy', fewer seeds, ripens November to December. Fruit remains on tree, juicy and sweet, for months. Grows to 12 ft., semi-open with vertical, spreading, somewhat willowy branches. Seems to develop full flavor in areas too cool for a good 'Dancy'. 'Clementine' usually bears light crops unless planted with another variety for pollination.

'Dancy'. The standard tangerine in markets before Christmas. Fruits smaller and seedier than other mandarins. Best flavor in desert areas but good in warm coastal areas. Ripens December to January. Holds well on tree. Upright tree with erect branches. Dwarf tree handsome in container or as espalier.

'Honey.' Hybrid between 'King' and 'Willow' mandarin. Small, seedy fruit with rich and sweet flavor. Tends to bear heavily in alternate years. Vigorous tree.

'Kara'. Hybrid between 'King' and 'Owari'. Fruit large (2½ in.) for mandarin. Tart-sweet, aromatic flavor when ripened in warm interior climates. Ripens January and February in desert, March to May and June elsewhere. May be very seedy or nearly seedless some seasons. Tree form resembles 'Owari'. Spreading, often drooping branches with large leaves. To a rounded 15-20 ft. Half size as dwarf.

'Kinnow'. Hybrid between 'King' and 'Willow' mandarin. Medium-sized fruit has rich, aromatic flavor. Stores well on tree. Ripens January to May. Handsomely shaped tree—columnar, dense, very symmetrical to 20 ft. (dwarf will reach 10 ft.). Densely foliaged with slender leaves. Good in any citrus climate.

'Owari'. Owari Satsuma. Source of imported mandarins. Sweet, delicate flavor, nearly seedless, medium to large fruit. Loose skin. Earliest mandarin to ripen—October to Christmas. Gets overripe soon if left on tree, but keeps well in cool storage. Standard trees are spreading, to 10-15 ft. high. Dwarf trees can be used as 6-ft. shrubs. Open, angular growth in early age; then more compact. Not suited to desert.

'Wilking.' From same parents as 'Honey' and 'Kinnow.' Small to medium size fruit with relatively thin rind; very juicy with rich, distinctive flavor. Fruit stores well on tree. Tends to bear heavily in alternate years. Tree is rounded, medium height, and nearly thornless.

ORANGES

The commercial oranges of the West are typified by the 'Washington' navel and the 'Valencia'. Listed here are first 'Washington' and the other navel varieties, then 'Valencia' and its counterparts, and finally the other less-known oranges.

'Washington' navel. Widely adapted except desert regions; best in warm interiors. Standard tree is a 20-25-ft. globe. On dwarf stock it becomes an 8-ft. mound. Bears December to February.

'Robertson' navel. Variant of 'Washington' navel. Fruit identical but earlier by 2 to 3 weeks. Tends to carry fruit in clusters. Tree generally smaller in size than 'Washington'. Has same climate adaptation. Dwarf trees produce amazing amount of fruit.

At some seasons navel oranges are subject to split navels. This generally occurs when weather conditions favor fast fruit development and seems unrelated to culture. However, it's best to keep tree in even growth by avoiding excess fertilizer. Watch leaf color: yellowish leaves are signs of nitrogen need; dark green, lush leaves with burning tips or edges indicates too much nitrogen.

'Summernavel'. Fruit much like 'Washington'. Sometimes fails to color as well, but flavor is good. Later ripening—well into summer months. Tree is more openly branched with much larger leaves than 'Washington'. A dwarf tree will cover better than 8 feet square quite rapidly.

'Valencia'. The juice-orange of stores. Most widely planted orange in the world, widely adapted in California. Poor risk in Arizona; plant 'Dillar' or 'Hamlin' there instead. Fruit matures in summer and stores on tree for months, improving in sweetness. Tree vigorous and fuller growing than 'Washington' navel, both as standard and dwarf.

C

Climate Zone maps pages 8-27

C

Climate
Zone maps
pages 8-27

'Seedless Valencia'. Variant of 'Valencia'. Fruit size, quality, and season are same. May not bear as prolifically.

'Diller'. An Arizona variety, produces small to medium-sized oranges with few seeds, high quality juice. Ripen November-December (before heavy frost). Vigorous, large, dense tree with large leaves.

'Hamlin'. Similar to 'Diller', with medium-sized fruits, not as hardy.

'Shamouti'. Originated in Palestine and considered there to be the finest orange. Large, seedless, no navel. Not a commercial orange in California because not sufficiently superior to 'Washington' navel. Grown on dwarf rootstock for home gardeners because of beauty in form and foliage. It's wider than tall. Leaves larger than navel. Heavy crop of fruit in early spring.

'Tarocco'. Red or red suffused pulp, pink to red juice. Color varies. The less heat the more color. Good quality in cooler areas. Ripens late spring. Tree is very vigorous, open growing with long, willowy, vinelike branches. Dwarf tree makes ideal espalier.

'Trovita'. Originated from seedling of 'Washington' navel. About navel size with thin skin, but without navel. Ripens in early spring. Apparently requires less heat than other sweet oranges and develops good quality fruit near—not on—the coast. Dwarf tree has 'Washington' navel look with handsome dark green leaves.

NAGAMI KUMQUAT (*Fortunella margarita*)

Very hardy. May not flower or fruit in cold areas, but always worthwhile for form and foliage. Leaves bright green, 3 in. long, oval, pointed. White flowers have rich orange blossom perfume. Fruit is bright orange, oval, about 1 in. across. Edible rind is sweet, flesh tart. Fruit used in marmalade, jelly, candied, preserved whole. Expect regular fruit production only in warm-summer areas. Plant size variable when grown on its own roots—from 6 to 25 ft. On dwarf rootstock, a compact, dense, shrub-tree to 4 ft. Admirably suited, in pots or tubs, for patio or garden.

SOUR-ACID MANDARIN ORANGES

Calamondin. Fruit looks like a small (¾-1½-in.) orange. Hundreds hang from tall (8 to 10 ft. as dwarf), columnar plant. Most attractive in containers. Flesh is tender, juicy, sour, with a few small seeds. Not a fruit to eat fresh. Skin and flesh good in marmalades.

'Otaheite' orange. Natural dwarf only a few feet tall. Usually grown indoors as a decorative pot plant. Not a true orange. Will bear very young. Fruit is orange to reddish orange, small, round, rough-skinned, insipid in flavor. About as hardy as lemon.

'Rangpur' lime. Probably not a lime at all. Fruit looks and peels like a mandarin, does not have lime taste. Less acid than lemon but with other flavors that make it a rich interesting base for ades and mixed drinks. Good landscape tree, vigorous, sturdy, bushy. Fast growth to 15 ft. and as wide (as dwarf, to 8 ft.). Dense when pruned, open otherwise. Fruits colorful as ornaments hanging on the tree throughout the year. Has wide climate tolerance.

TANGELOS

'Minneola'. Hybrid of 'Dancy' tangerine and grapefruit. Fruit is bright orange-red, smooth, large. Flavor similar to tangerine. Few seeds. Ripens February to March. Stores well on tree for 2 months. Tree is not as large or dense as grapefruit. Leaves 3½-5 in. long and pointed. Thrives in all citrus districts.

'Orlando.' Fruit medium-large, like flattened orange. Rind is orange, adheres to orange colored flesh. Very juicy, mildly sweet, matures eariiy in season. Tree is similar to 'Minneola' but with distinctively cupped leaves. Less vigorous and more cold-resistant than 'Minneola.'

'Sampson'. Hybrid of tangerine and grapefruit, but fruit more like small grapefruit with orange-red pulp. Best for juice and marmalades. Ripens February to April. Standard tree is vigorous, fast, to 30 ft. Form similar to grapefruit. Most decorative as dwarf tree. Dark green, oval (2-3-in.) leaves, golden fruits in winter. Best in coastal valleys. Subject to sunburn in desert areas.

TANGORS

'Dweet'. Hybrid of orange and tangerine. Fruit is egg-shaped with neck and as large as 'Valencia' orange. Skin is tight. Seedy, but packed with rich juice. Ripens May to August. Dwarf tree to 8 ft. is moderately branched and rather open. Fruit at end of branches bends branches down. Susceptible to sunburn, defoliation, dieback. Unsatisfactory in desert areas. Best in warm, fairly frost-free areas away from coastal cooling.

'King'. Hybrid of hybrids, but has definite tangor characteristic. Fruit as large as 'Valencia' orange with rough, bumpy, deep orange skin. Ripens March to May. Fruits stay on tree for months, but become dry if not picked. Needs high summer heat for sweet fruit, but branches and fruit sunburn in desert areas. Upright, erect growth; large leaves.

'Temple'. Tangerine-orange hybrid (a tangor). High quality fruit in California's low deserts. Flat, deep bright orange; loose skin, easily peeled. Pulp more tender than sweet orange, juicy, of "different" good flavor. Ripens in early spring. Tree spreads wider than high, to 12 ft., bushy and thorny. To a wide 6 ft. on dwarf stock. Leaves are similar to the mandarin, smaller and narrower than the orange.

MISCELLANEOUS

Sour orange, Seville orange. (*Citrus aurantium.*) Many old trees doing good service from Sacramento Valley to Phoenix. Make large hedges, street trees, lawn trees. Fragrant flowers. Spectacular orange-red, 3-in. fruits in clusters. Fruit is bitter and makes excellent bitter marmalade. Tree grows to 20-30 ft. with 15-20-ft. spread, dense foliage. Plant 6-10 ft. apart for tall screen; 3-4 ft., and prune heavily for hedge.

'Bouquet'. Bouquet orange, 'Bouquet des Fleurs', often sold as Bergamot orange. Another very hardy sour orange for desert and hot interior areas. A big shrub or small tree to 8-10 ft. Graceful foliage, dark green. Used as a hedge or windbreak. Flowers unusually large and extremely fragrant. Fruit small, bitter, used only in marmalades.

'Chinotto' orange. Smaller in all ways than other sour oranges. Dense, bushy,

round-headed, with closely set, small almost myrtlelike leaves. Very slow growing to 7-10 ft. Formal appearance, often headed high on stem and clipped. Ideal tub plant. Fruit ornamental, small, round, bright orange; used in Europe for candying.

'Etrog' citron. Attractive foliage. Fruit is small, oblong, yellow, fragrant and usually lumpy on the surface. Peel used in candying.

CLADRASTIS lutea. YELLOW WOOD. Deciduous tree. Zones 1-9. Native to Kentucky, Tennessee, and North Carolina. Slow growing to 30-35 ft. with a broad rounded head half as wide as tree is high. Divided, 8-12-in.-wide leaves look somewhat like English walnut, bright green in summer, brilliant yellow in fall.

May not flower until 10 years old, and may skip bloom some years, but spectacular when it does. In May or early June it produces long (6-10-in.) clusters of white flowers (like wisteria's), very fragrant. Blooms followed by flat, 3-4-in.-long seed pods. Useful and attractive as a terrace, patio, or lawn tree even if it never bloomed. It's a tree you can garden under.

Prune when young to shorten side branches. Remove lower branches entirely when tree has height you want.

CLARKIA (includes *Godetia*). Annuals. Native to western South and North America, especially numerous in California. They grow in the cool season, bloom in spring and early summer. Attractive in mixed borders or in mass displays, alone or with love-in-a-mist (*Nigella*), cornflower, violas, sweet alyssum. Cut branches keep for several days; cut when top bud opens—others open successively.

Sow seeds in place in fall (in mild-winter areas) or spring. Seedlings difficult to transplant. Keep soil moist during and after germination, and until flowering. Best in sandy soil without added fertilizer.

C. amoena (*Godetia amoena, G. grandiflora*). FAREWELL TO SPRING. Native California to British Columbia. Two wild forms coarse-stemmed and sprawling, 4-5 in. high; slender-stemmed, 1½-2½ ft. high. On both forms, upright buds open into cup-shaped, slightly flaring, pink or lavender flowers, 2 in. across, usually blotched or penciled crimson. Among named varieties available are: 'Sybil Sherwood', single salmon pink edged with white; 'Kelvedon Glory', deep salmon orange; 'White Swan', pure white. All have single satiny flowers on branched plants growing about 18 in. high. Double flowered and lower-growing varieties have also been developed.

C. concinna. RED RIBBONS. Native to California. To 2-ft. Deep pink to lavender flowers with 3-lobed, fan-shaped petals. May be found in wildflower seed mixes.

C. pulchella. Native to Pacific Northwest. Slender, upright, reddish-stemmed, mostly unbranched, 1-1½ ft. high. Leaves narrow, 1-2 in. long, sparse. Flowers single, with 4 petals tapered to c'awlike base, 3-lobed at tip; semi-double and dwarf forms. Some garden clarkias probably hybrids between *C. pulchella* and *C. unguiculata.*

C. unguiculata (*C. elegans*). MOUNTAIN GARLAND. Erect, 1-4 ft. with reddish stems; leaves 1-1¾ in long; flowers 1 in. across, rose, purple, white; varieties with double

Climate Zone maps pages 8-27

white, orange, salmon, crimson, purple, rose, pink, and creamy yellow flowers. The double-flowered kinds are the ones usually sold in seed packets.

CLEMATIS. Most of the 200-odd species are deciduous vines; exceptions are the evergreen *C. armandii*, and a few interesting free-standing or sprawling perennials or subshrubs. All have attractive flowers and most are spectacular. The flowers are followed by clusters of seeds with tails, often quite effective in flower arrangements. Although the deciduous clematis are hardy in all Western climates and are enjoyed in most, they perform best in the Pacific Northwest (Zones 1-6) and in coastal northern California (Zones 15-17).

Clematis are not demanding, but their few specific requirements should be met. Plant the vine types next to a trellis or open framework for the stems to grow on. Plant so that roots are cool while tops are in full sun. Give them rich, loose, fast-draining soil; add generous quantities of peat moss, ground bark, and the like. Where soils are strongly acid, add lime. Where soils tend to be neutral or alkaline, add bone meal. Unlike most plants, clematis should be planted deep. Set root ball 2 in. below soil surface and cover with soil.

To provide cool root run, add mulch; or place a large flat rock over the soil; or plant a shallow-rooted ground cover over the root area; or plant in shade of a small shrub or an evergreen vine, and stake so the top can catch the sun. Put in support when planting, and tie up stems at once. Stems are easily broken. Protect with wire

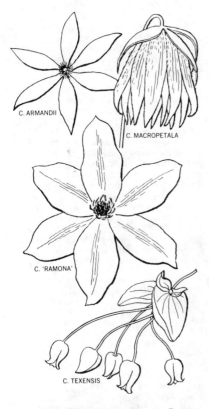

Four different kinds of clematis flowers. C. armandii, C. 'Ramona' most typical.

netting if child or dog traffic is heavy. Clematis need constant moisture and nutrients to make their great rush of growth. Fertilize every month in growing season.

In the list of species and hybrids that follows we have noted the type of pruning each should receive to give its best flower crop. Since there are many kinds not included in the list and more will be introduced by hybrid name only, here's how to let common sense guide your pruning: The time of flowering dictates the time and kind of pruning. Kinds that bloom in summer only are blooming on wood produced in spring. To get this new wood, cut back after flowering in late fall or early spring as buds swell. Cut to within 6-12 in. of the ground, or to 2-3 buds, for first 2 or 3 years. Cut older plants to 2 ft. or less. *C. jackmanii* is typical of this group. For convenience in pruning instructions, call this method "J".

Kinds that bloom in spring and again in summer are blooming on old wood in spring, new wood in summer. Make the fall or early spring pruning a light corrective one and prune the flowered portions immediately after bloom in spring. Call this pruning "L" (for *C. lanuginosa*).

Kinds that bloom in spring and spring only are blooming on wood of the previous year. Prune these severely after flowering in the spring.

To sum it up: If you don't know which type you have, watch it for a year to see when it blooms (in spring only, in summer only, or both) and prune accordingly.

Cut flowers choice for indoors (float in a bowl). Burn cut stems with a match to make flowers last longer.

C. armandii. EVERGREEN CLEMATIS. Hardy Zones 4-9, 12-24 but best adapted Zones 4-6, 15-17. Native to China. Leaves tip-burn badly where soil or water contain excess salts. Fast growing to 20 ft. Leaves divided into 3 glossy dark green leaflets, 3-5 in. long; they droop downward to create a strongly textured pattern. Glistening white 2½-in.-wide fragrant flowers in large, branched clusters in March-April.

Slow to start, races when established. Needs constant pruning after flowering to prevent tangling and build-up of dead thatch on inner parts of vine. Keep and tie up stems you want, and cut out all others. Frequent pinching will hold foliage to eye level.

Train along fence tops or rails, roof gables. Allow to climb tall trees. Trained on a substantial frame, makes a privacy screen if not allowed to become bare at the base.

There is a light pink flowered form, *C. a.* 'Hendersoni Rubra'.

C. chrysocoma. Deciduous vine. Native to western China. To 6-8 ft. or more in height and fairly open. Young branches, leaves, and flower stalks covered with yellow down. Flowers long-stalked, white, shaded pink, 2 in. wide, in clusters from old wood in spring, with later flowers following from new wood. Will take considerable shade. Pruning: "L".

C. 'Crimson King'. Large rosy red flowers early spring, again in summer. Best in partial shade. Pruning: "L".

C. davidiana. See *C. heracleifolia davidiana*

C. dioscoreifolia (*C. paniculata*). SWEET AUTUMN CLEMATIS. Native to Japan. Tall, vigorous, forming billowy masses of small (1-in.-wide) creamy white, fragrant flowers in late summer and fall. Leaves, dark green, glossy, divided into 3-5 oval, 1-2½-in.-long leaflets. After bloom or in early spring, prune year's growth to 1 or 2 buds. Good privacy screen, arbor cover.

C. 'Duchess of Edinburgh'. Fully double white flowers early spring, again in summer. Pruning: "L".

C. 'Ernest Markham'. One of best reds. Grows like *C. jackmanii*. Pruning: "J".

C. 'Gypsy Queen'. Flowers deep violet with wine crimson tints summer and fall. Pruning: "J".

C. 'Hagley Hybrid' ('Pink Chiffon'). Deep shell pink flowers. Pruning: "J".

C. heracleifolia davidiana (*C. davidiana*). Native to China. Half-woody perennial to 4 ft. high. Deep green leaves, divided into 3 broad oval, 3-6-in.-long leaflets. Dense clusters of 1-in.-long tubular, medium to deep blue, fragrant flowers July-August. Use in perennial or shrub border. Pruning: "J".

C. integrifolia. Native to Europe and Asia. Semi-shrubby perennial to 3 ft. with dark green, undivided, 2-4-in.-long leaves and nodding, urn-shaped, 1½-in.-long, blue flowers in June-July. Prune after bloom.

C. jackmanii. Series of hybrids between forms of *C. lanuginosa* and *C. viticella*. All are vigorous plants of rapid growth to 10 ft. or more in one season. The best known of the older large-flowered hybrids is known simply as *C. jackmanii*. It has a profusion of 4-5-in., rich purple flowers with 4 sepals. Blooms heavily June-July on. Later hybrids have larger flowers with more sepals, but none has as many flowers. *C. j.* 'Comtesse de Bouchaud' has silvery rose pink flowers, *C. j.* 'Mme. Edouard Andre' purplish red. All flower on new wood; all do best with severe pruning in early spring as buds begin to swell. Freezes to ground in cold winter areas. Pruning: "J".

C. lanuginosa. Native to China. A parent of many of the finest large-flowered hybrids. Grows only to about 6-9 ft. but produces a magnificent display of large (6-in.) lilac to white flowers in May-July. Best known for its variety *C. l.* 'Candida', with 8-in. white flowers and light yellow stamens. Blooms on new and old wood. In favorable climates will bloom in March-April. Prune only to remove dead or weak growth in early spring. Then after first flush of flowers, cut back the flowered portions promptly for another crop later in the summer. Pruning: "L".

C. 'Lasurstern'. Large, deep lavender-blue flowers with striking white stamens. Pruning: "L".

C. lawsoniana. Thought to be a hybrid of *C. lanuginosa* and *C. patens*. To 6-10 ft. Large (6-9-in.) flowers, rosy purple and dark veined. Its best known form is *C. l.* 'Henryi' with tremendous 8-in. flowers, white with dark stamens, June-August. Pruning: "L".

C. 'Lord Neville'. Flowers rich, deep blue, sepal edges crimped. Pruning: "L".

C. macropetala. DOWNY CLEMATIS. Native to China, Siberia. Variable in size, may be 6-30 ft. high. In early spring, produces

Climate
Zone maps
pages 8-27

4-in. lavender to powder blue flowers that have the appearance of doubleness; they look like ballet skirts. They are followed by showy, bronzy pink and silvery tailed seed clusters. *C. m.* 'Markhamii' has lavender-pink flowers. Prune lightly in February to remove weak shoots, and shorten vigorous growth to sound wood.

C. 'Mme. Baron-Veillard'. Vigorous plant of *C. jackmanii* type. Medium-sized 5-in. flowers of warm lilac rose. Pruning: "J".

C. montana. ANEMONE CLEMATIS. Native to the Himalayas, China. Vigorous to 20 ft. or more. Extremely hardy, easy to grow. Massive display in early spring of 2-2½-in. anemonelike flowers, opening white, turning pink. Flowers on old wood, so can be heavily thinned or pruned immediately after flowering to rejuvenate or reduce size.

C. m. 'Rubens'. To 15-25 ft. Foliage is bronzy green, the new growth crimson. Fragrant flowers, rose red changing to pink, are carried throughout the vine fabric.

C. m. 'Tetrarose'. Considered more vigorous than *C. m.* 'Rubens'.

C. 'Mrs. Cholmondeley' (pronounced "Chumley"). Vigorous vine of *C. jackmanii* type. Lavender-blue flowers with long, pointed sepals. Pruning: "J".

C. 'Nelly Moser'. Mauve sepals marked by a dark red stripe in the center of each. Pruning: "L".

C. paniculata. See *C. dioscoreifolia.*

C. 'Prins Hendrik'. Big flowers of near azure blue with ruffled sepals. Pruning: "L".

C. 'Ramona'. Lavender-blue; a classic for planting with yellow or coppery climbing roses. Pruning: "L".

C. 'Susan P. Emory'. Azure blue with red bars. Pruning: "L".

C. tangutica. GOLDEN CLEMATIS. Native to Mongolia, northern China. To 10-15 ft. high, with gray-green, finely divided foliage. Bright yellow, 2-4-in., nodding, lantern-shaped flowers in great profusion from July on. They are followed by handsome silvery-tailed seed clusters. Prune like *C. dioscoreifolia.* Uncommon.

C. texensis. SCARLET CLEMATIS. Native to Texas. Fast growing to 6-10 ft. Dense, bluish green foliage. Flowers bright scarlet, urn-shaped to 1 in. long, in July-August. Has not done well in Seattle, but flourishes in Reno. More tolerant of dry soils than most clematis. Pruning: "J".

C. 'The President'. Deep purple-blue with dark stamens. Pruning: "L".

C. viticella. Native to southern Europe, western Asia. To 12-15 ft. Purple or rose purple, 2-in. flowers, June-August. Very hardy. Pruning: "J". Better known is the variety 'Lady Betty Balfour', with much larger deep velvety purple flowers.

CLEOME spinosa. SPIDER FLOWER. Annual. Shrubby, branching plant topped in late summer and fall with many open, fluffy clusters of pink or white flowers with extremely long, protruding stamens. Slender seed capsules follow the blossoms. Short, strong spines on stems; lower leaves divided, upper ones not divided. The leaves and stems have a clammy feeling to the touch and a strong, but not unpleasant, odor. Plants grow 4-6 ft. tall, 4-5 ft. wide,

especially vigorous in warm dry inland areas. Grow in background, as summer hedge, against walls or fences, in large containers, or naturalize in fringe areas of garden. Flowers and dry capsules useful in arrangements.

Sow seed in place in full sun; they sprout rapidly in warm soil. Keep plants on dry side or they will become too rank. 'Pink Queen' has shrimp pink flowers; 'Helen Campbell' is pure white.

CLERODENDRUM. GLORYBOWER. Evergreen and deciduous; shrubs, trees, or vinelike. Some outdoor; some houseplants.

C. bungei (*C. foetidum*). CASHMERE BOUQUET. Evergreen shrub. Zones 5-9, 12-24. Native to China. Rapid growing, softwooded, to 6 ft. Prune severely in spring and pinch back through the growing season to make it a 2-3-ft. compact shrub. Spreads by suckers, eventually forming thicket if not restrained. Big leaves (to 12 in.), broadly oval with toothed edges, dark green above, with rusty fuzz beneath; ill-smelling when crushed. Delightfully fragrant flowers in summer: ¾ in. wide, rosy red, in large (to 8 in.) loose clusters. Plant in part shade where its appearance, except in the flowering season, is not important.

C. thomsoniae (*C. balfouri*). BLEEDING HEART GLORYBOWER. Evergreen shrubby vine. Zones: outdoors in most protected spots of 22-24; elsewhere indoor-outdoor pot plant. Native to west Africa. Leaves oval, 4-7 in. long, dark green, shiny, distinctly ribbed. Flowers, a study in color contrast, scarlet 1-in. tubes surrounded by a large (¾-in.-long) white calyx; carried in flattish 5-in.-wide clusters from August-October. Will flower in a 6-in. pot. Does well as indoor-outdoor tubbed vine. Give support for twining. Needs rich, loose soil mix, plenty of water with good drainage. Prune after flowering.

C. trichotomum. HARLEQUIN GLORYBOWER. Deciduous shrub-tree. May freeze to ground in Zones 5, 6 and come back from the roots, adapted Zones 15-17, 20-24. Native to Japan. Grows with many stems from the base to 10-15 ft. or more. Leaves oval, to 5 in. long, dark green, soft, hairy. Fragrant clusters of white tubular flowers almost twice as long as the prominent, fleshy, ½-in.-long scarlet calyces. Late summer bloom. The calyces hang on and contrast pleasingly with the turquoise or blue-green metallic-looking fruits. The variety *fargesii*, from China, is somewhat hardier, smaller, has smooth leaves, and green calyces that later turn pink. Grow in sun or partial shade. Routine care. Give room to spread at top and underplant to hide its legginess.

CLETHRA. Deciduous shrub and evergreen tree. Distinctive plants with definite climate and soil preferences.

C. alnifolia. SUMMERSWEET, SWEET PEPPERBUSH. Deciduous shrub. Zones 2-6. Native to eastern U.S. To 10 ft. high with thin strong branches forming a vertical pattern. Spreads slowly by suckers into broad clumps. Dark green leaves, 2-4 in. long, half as wide, toothed edges. Leafs out very late in mid-May. Blooms in late summer. Each branch tip carries several 4-6-in.-long spires of tiny, gleaming white flowers, spicily perfumed. Grows best in soils where

rhododendrons thrive. Full sun in cool gardens, some shade where summers are warm. *C. a.* 'Pinkspire' has deep pink flowers, *C. a.* 'Rosea', pale pink.

C. arborea. LILY-OF-THE-VALLEY TREE. Evergreen tree. Zones 15-17, 21-24. Native to Madeira. (For another lily-of-the-valley tree, see *Crinodendron.*) A beautiful small tree. Grows at moderate rate to 20 ft., rather stiffly upright, with a 10-ft. spread. Densely clothed with glossy, bronzy green, 4-in.-long leaves. White flowers in upright,

Clethra arborea—sprays of white, fragrant flowers at tips of leafy branches.

branched clusters resemble the lily-of-the-valley, even to their fragrance. They appear in late summer.

Tip burns with frost, but comes back from old wood or from roots when damaged.

Easy to grow in soils where azaleas or rhododendrons thrive. Where salts build up, condition soil with peat moss or ground bark and make sure drainage is fast. Abundant moisture necessary. Spray for red spider mites in summer.

CLEYERA japonica (*Eurya ochnacea*). Evergreen shrub. Zones 4-6, 8, 9, 14-24. Native to Japan and southeast Asia. A handsome foliage shrub related to camellia. Similar in character to ternstroemia. Grows slowly to 6-8 ft. and as wide with graceful, spreading, arching branches. Leaves of new growth are a beautiful deep brownish red. Mature leaves, 3-6 in. long, are a glossy dark green with a reddish midrib. Small clusters of fragrant, creamy white flowers in September-October are followed by small, dark red, puffy berries which last through the winter. Flowers and berries are attractive but not showy, don't form on young plants. Same soil and care as camellias.

CLIANTHUS puniceus. PARROT-BEAK. Evergreen shrublike vine. Zones 8, 9, 14-24. Native to New Zealand. Moderate growth to 12 ft. Foliage hangs gracefully in an open pattern made up of sprays of glistening, dark green, 3-6 in. leaves divided into many narrow leaflets. Flowers rose scarlet, sweet pea-shaped, with 3-in. parrot-beak keels, swung downward between the leaves. June blooming. Pods that follow are 3 in. long. Full sun on coast, in part shade inland. Train as espalier or on support to bring out full beauty of leaves and flowers. Routine garden care with ample water through blooming season. If soil is heavy,

Climate
Zone maps
pages 8-27

mix in organic soil amendment. Watch for snails and spider mites.

CLIFF-BRAKE. See Pellaea

CLIVIA miniata. KAFFIR LILY. Evergreen perennial with tuberous roots. Zones 15-17, 19-24. Native to South Africa. A striking member of the amaryllis family with brilliant clusters of orange, funnel-shaped flowers rising from dense clumps of dark green strap-shaped, 1½-ft.-long leaves. Blooming period is December to April; most bloom March-April. Ornamental red berries follow flowers. Belgian hybrids have deep red-orange blooms on thick, rigid stalks, and very wide, dark green leaves. Zimmerman hybrids have flowers in white, soft shades of yellow, orange, or red.

In frostless areas, or well protected parts of the garden clivias are handsome in shaded borders with ferns, azaleas, other shade plants. Superb in containers; grow indoors in cold climates. For best growth, clivia needs ample light, no direct sun, rich, moist soil. Plant with top of tuber just above soil line. Fertilize 2 or 3 times during growing season. Let clumps grow undisturbed for several years.

CLOCK VINE, ORANGE. See Thunbergia gibsonii

CLUSTERBERRY, RED. See Cotoneaster parneyi

CLYTOSTOMA callistegioides (*Bignonia violacea, B. speciosa*). VIOLET TRUMPET VINE. Evergreen. Permanent in Zones 9, 13-24; perennial elsewhere. Tops hardy to 20°; roots to 10°. Strong growing, will clamber over anything by tendrils. Needs support on walls. Extended terminal shoots hang down in curtain effect. Leaves divided into 2 glossy, dark green leaflets with wavy margins. Violet-lavender or pale purple trumpet flowers 3 in. long and nearly as wide at the top, in sprays at end of shoots, late spring to fall. Full sun or shade. Prune in late winter to discipline growth, prevent tangling. At other times of year, remove unwanted long runners and spent flower spikes.

COBAEA scandens. CUP-AND-SAUCER-VINE. Perennial. All Zones (treated as an annual). Native of Mexico. Extremely vigorous growth to 25 ft. Flowers bell-shaped, first greenish, then violet or rose-purple; also a white-flowered form. Called cup-and-saucer-vine because the 2-in.-long cup of petals sits in a large green saucerlike calyx. Leaves divided into 2 or 3 pairs of oval, 4-in. leaflets. At ends of leaves are curling tendrils that enable vine to climb rough surfaces without support.

The hard-coated seeds may rot if sown out of doors in cool weather. Start seeds indoors in 4-in. pots; notch seeds with a knife and press edgewise into moistened potting mix. Barely cover seed. Keep moist but not wet, and transplant to a warm, sunny location when weather warms up.

COCCULUS laurifolius. Evergreen shrub or small tree. Zones 8, 9, 12-24. Native to the Himalayas. Slow at first then moderately fast to 25 ft. or more. Can be kept lower by pruning or trained as an espalier. Usually a multi-stemmed shrub with arching spreading growth as wide as high. Staked

and trained as a tree, it takes on umbrella shape. Leaves shiny, leathery, oblong to 6 in., with 3 strongly marked veins running from base to tip. Will grow in sun or dense shade; tolerates many soil types.

COCKSCOMB. See Celosia

COCOS plumosa. See Arecastrum

CODIAEUM variegatum. CROTON. Greenhouse or house plant, outdoor annual in Zone 24. Grown principally for the coloring of the large, leathery, glossy leaves, which may be green, yellow, red, purple, bronze, pink, or almost any combination of these. Leaves may be oval, lance-shaped, or very narrow, straight-edged or lobed. Dozens of named forms combine these differing features. Can reach 6 ft. or more, but is usually seen as single-stemmed plant 6-24 in. tall. Best in warm, bright, humid greenhouse.

COELOGYNE. Epiphytic orchids. Native to the eastern hemisphere. Close to five dozen species varying widely in growth habit, but most are not sold. Grow like cattleyas: 55° to 60° night temperature, regular feeding during the growing season, partial shade. Osmunda, firmly packed, is one of the best potting media for these orchids. Keep water out of new growth where flower cluster forms to prevent rot.

C. cristata. Probably most popular species in collections. Light green 1-3-in. pseudobulbs topped by 6-9-in. leaves. Large, showy, 3-4-in. white flowers with yellow throat; 3 to 8 pendulous flowers to a stem. Bloom in winter to spring. Can be grown outdoors all winter in mildest climate areas. Keep plant on dry side once growth has matured—October or November—until after flowers have faded. Slight shriveling of the pseudobulbs will not be harmful.

COFFEA arabica. COFFEE. House or patio plant (outdoor shrub Zone 24). Native to east Africa. The coffee tree of commerce is sold as a handsome container plant for patio, lanai, and large, well-lit rooms. Must be protected from frosts. It's an upright shrub to 15 ft. with evenly-spaced tiers of branches, clothed with shining, dark green, oval leaves, to 6 in. long. Small, ¾-in., white, fragrant flowers are clustered near leaf bases. They are followed by shining red ½-in. fruits. Each contains 2 seeds—coffee beans. Grow in container, using same soil mixes and culture as with camellias. Needs shade outdoors.

COFFEEBERRY. See Rhamnus californica

COIX lacryma-jobi. JOB'S TEARS. Perennial grass grown as an annual in colder climates. A curiosity grown for its ornamental "beads". Loose-growing with smooth prominently jointed stems to 6 ft. Leaves to 2 ft. long, 1½ in. wide, sword-shaped. Outside covering of the female flower hardens as seed ripens; becomes a shining, pearly white, gray, or violet bead ¼-1½ in. across. String them in bracelets, rosaries, other articles. Cut stems for winter arrangements before seeds dry and shatter. Sun or shade; ordinary soil.

COLCHICUM autumnale. MEADOW SAFFRON. Corm. All Zones. A Mediterranean plant of the lily family sometimes called autumn crocus, but not a true crocus. The shining, brown-skinned, thick-scaled corms

send up clusters of long-tubed, flaring, lavender-pink, rose-purple, or white flowers to 4 in. across in late summer right from the corm itself, whether it is sitting in a dish on the window sill or planted in the soil. When planted out, broad, 6-12.-in.-long leaves show in spring and then die long before the flower cluster arises from the ground. Best planted in sun in average soil where they need not be disturbed oftener than every 3 years or so. Corms available during brief dormant period in July-August. Plant with tips 3-4 in. under soil surface. To plant in bowls, set upright on 1-2 in. of pebbles, or in special fiber sold for this purpose, and fill with water to base of corm.

COLEONEMA and DIOSMA. BREATH OF HEAVEN. Evergreen shrubs. Zones 7-9, 14-24. Native to South Africa. Filmy and delicate characters with slender branches and narrow heathlike leaves, fragrant when brushed or bruised. Flowers tiny, freely carried over a long season in winter and spring, with scattered bloom to be expected at any time. You will find them in the nurseries under either name, *Coleonema* or *Diosma*. Actually, your choice amounts to a white or a pink-flowering breath of heaven.

Plant in light soil and full sun. They can take some shade, but are likely to grow rather taller there than expected. Fast drainage is a must. To control size and promote compactness, shear lightly after main bloom is over. For an even more filmy look, thin out some interior stems.

Good on banks or hillsides, along paths where you can break off and bruise a twig to enjoy the foliage fragrance. Frequently used as a foundation plant, although a little wispy for such use.

C. album. (Almost universally sold as either *Diosma reevesii*, or *D. alba*.) WHITE BREATH OF HEAVEN. Grows to 5 ft. or more and as wide. White flowers.

C. pulchrum. PINK BREATH OF HEAVEN, PINK DIOSMA. (Often sold as *Diosma pulchra*.) Grows usually to 5 ft., occasionally to 10 ft. Flowers pink.

Diosma ericoides. BREATH OF HEAVEN. Introduced into California in 1890. However, most plants sold under this name now are *Coleonema album*. Has similar form and white flowers.

COLEUS blumei. COLEUS. Perennial, treated as an annual, winter-greenhouse or house plant. Native to tropics and subtropics. Grown for brilliantly colored leaves. Little-branched plants 2-3 ft. high with 3-6-in.-long, oval leaves with scalloped, toothed, or fringed margins, in shades of green, chartreuse, yellow, buff, salmon, peach, orange, red, magenta, purple, and brown, often with several colors to a leaf.

Useful for summer borders and as outdoor-indoor container plants. Plant from flats in spring. Best in strong, indirect light or thin shade—color less vivid in too much shade or too much sun. Needs warmth, rich, loose, well drained soil, ample water. Feed regularly with high-nitrogen fertilizer. Pinch stems to encourage branching and compact habit; remove flower buds to keep plant growing vigorously. Bait for slugs and snails. Control mealybug and aphids.

COLLARDS. See Kale

Climate Zone maps pages 8-27

COLLINSIA heterophylla (*C. bicolor*). CHINESE HOUSES. Annual. Native to California. Rather uncommon spring to early summer blooming plant with snapdragon-like flowers to 1 in. long, held in tiers at the top of 1-2-ft.-tall somewhat hairy stems; upper lip of flower white, lower one rose or violet. Leaves oblong, to 2 in. long. Gives light, dainty effect in front of borders, naturalized under deciduous trees, or as ground cover for bulbs. Sow seed in place in fall or spring in rich, moist soil. Self-sows under favorable conditions.

COLOCASIA esculenta (*Caladium esculentum*). TARO, ELEPHANT'S EAR. Perennial with tuberous roots. Evergreen only in Zones 23, 24 (tops freeze at 30°); grow as herbaceous perennial in Zones 13, 16-22 where tubers may be left in ground; in Zones 1-12, 14, 15 grow in containers, or lift and store tubers over winter. Native to tropical Asia and Polynesia. Fast growing to 6 ft. Mammoth, heart-shaped, gray-green leaves add lush effect to any tropical planting within one season. Effective with tree ferns, araliads, ginger, strelitzia. Handsome in large tub, raised beds.

Thrives in warm filtered shade with protection from wind which tears leaves. Plant tubers in spring in rich moist soil. Give lots of water, feed lightly once a month in growing season.

COLUMBINE. See Aquilegia

COLUMNEA. House plants. Some shrubby, but most arching or trailing with attractive foliage and showy flowers in shades of red, orange, and yellow. Related to African violets; they don't look it, but do require the same care although they prefer slightly cooler temperatures. Paired leaves are usually shiny; flowers are long tubes with flaring mouths.

There are many named varieties, all good-looking, and many species from Central and South America. These two are widely distributed:

C. crassifolia. Upright then arching, with narrow oval, pointed, thick, shiny leaves to 4 in. long and orange, 4-in.-long flowers.

C. 'Stavanger'. NORSE FIRE PLANT. Trailing stems can reach several feet if plant is grown in hanging basket. Neat pairs of rounded, shiny leaves ½ inch across, 3 to 4-in.-long red flowers.

COMAROSTAPHYLIS diversifolia. SUMMER HOLLY. Evergreen shrub or small tree. Zones 7-9, 14-24. Native to coastal southern California and Baja California. It's handsome, deserves to be used more. Related to manzanita. Rather formal growth to 6 ft. as a shrub, 18 ft. as a small tree. Gray bark. Leathery, 1-3-in.-long leaves, shiny dark green above, white hairy beneath, the margins inrolled. (Variety *planifolia* has flat leaves.) Small, white manzanitalike flowers in April-May; followed by clusters of red, warty berries similar to those of the madrone. Adaptable to many situations, but grows best in half shade with some moisture, good drainage.

CONEFLOWER, PURPLE. See Echinacea

CONVALLARIA majalis. LILY-OF-THE-VALLEY. Perennial grown from a pip (upright small rootstock). Zones 1-7; generally not successful as garden plant in mild-winter

areas. Small, fragrant, drooping, waxy, white, bell-shaped, spring-blooming flowers on 6-8-in. stems rising above 2 broad basal leaves. Ground cover in partial shade; carpet between camellias, rhododendrons, pieris, under deciduous trees, or high branching, not-too-dense evergreen trees.

Plant clumps or single pips in November, December in rich soil with ample humus. Set clumps 1-2 ft. apart, single pips 4-6 in. apart, 1½ in. deep. Topdress yearly with leaf mold, peat moss, or ground bark. Divide clumps when crowded—about every 5-6 years. Large, pre-chilled forcing pips, available in December, January (even in mild-climate areas) can be potted up for bloom indoors. After bloom, plunge pots in ground in cool, shaded area. When dormant, either remove plants from pots and plant in the garden, or wash soil off pips, place in plastic bags, and store in vegetable compartment of refrigerator until December or January; at this time, either pot up (as before, for bloom indoors), or plant out in permanent spot in the garden.

CONVOLVULUS. Evergreen shrub, evergreen perennial, and an annual. All have funnel-shaped flowers much like morning glories.

C. cneorum. BUSH MORNING GLORY. Evergreen shrub. Marginal Zones 5, 6; best Zones 7-9, 12-24. Native to southern Europe. Rapid growing to 2-4 ft. and as wide. Smooth-as-silk, silvery gray, roundish to oval leaves 2½ in. long. White or pink-tinted morning glories with yellow throats open from pink buds May-September. Compact and fully flowered if grown in full sun, looser habit with flowers more closed in light shade. Give it light soil and fast drainage. Avoid planting where it will get frequent sprinklings. Prune severely to renew plant; can get leggy if left alone. Spray for spider mites. Rabbits consider it a delicacy. Effective massed or in a border with *Teucrium fruticans, Achillea tomentosa.* Excellent on banks or in large rock gardens.

C. mauritanicus. GROUND MORNING GLORY. Evergreen perennial. Zones 4-9, 12-24. Native to Africa. Grows 1-2 ft. high with branches trailing to 3 ft. or more wide. Soft, hairy, gray-green, roundish leaves ½-1½ in. long. Flowers lavender-blue, 1-2 in. wide, June-November. Grows well in light, gravelly soil with good drainage, but will take clay soil if not over-watered. Full sun. Tends to become woody; prevent by trimming in late winter. Good for informal effects. Use on dry banks as a ground cover (plant 3 ft. apart), or group with helianthemum or cerastium. Trail over a low wall or raised planting bed, hanging baskets.

C. tricolor. DWARF MORNING GLORY. Annual. All Zones. Native to southern Europe. Bushy, branching, somewhat trailing plants to 1 ft. high and 2 ft. wide. Flowers, 1½ in. across, variable in color but usually blue with a yellow throat. Nick the tough seed coats with a knife and plant in place when soil has warmed up. Needs sun and warmth; blooms best when kept on the dry side. Use as edging, against a low trellis, or at the top of a wall. Excellent in pots or hanging baskets.

C. t. 'Crimson Monarch'. Dark red flowers.

C. t. 'Royal Ensign'. Flowers bright blue with a yellow throat, white markings.

COPPER LEAF. See Acalypha wilkesiana.

COPROSMA. Evergreen shrubs. Zones 8, 9, 14-17, 21-24. Native to New Zealand.

C. kirkii. Spreading shrub to 2-3 ft. high or nearly prostrate, with long, straight stems slanting outward from the base. Leaves, closely set on stems, are yellow-green, small, narrow (½-1 in. long). Tolerant of sun or partial shade, and grows in a wide range of soils. Drought tolerant once established. Prune regularly to keep plants dense. A tough, medium-height ground cover or bank cover. Tolerates sea wind, salt spray.

C. repens (*C. baueri*). MIRROR PLANT. Rapid growth to 10 ft. with 6-ft. spread. An open, straggly shrub if neglected but a beautiful plant when cared for. You can't imagine shinier, glossier leaves. They're dark to light green, 3 in. long, oval or oblong. Inconspicuous greenish or white flowers; often followed by small yellow or orange fruits. Variety 'Variegata' has leaves blotched with yellowish green. Variety 'Argentea' is blotched with white. There are dwarf forms available of both the species and the varieties.

Two prunings a year will keep it dense and at any height desired. Where shrub receives ocean wind, no pruning necessary. Except in foggy areas, give it part shade; water generously. Use as a hedge, screen, wall shrub, informal espalier.

CORAL BELLS. See Heuchera sanguinea

CORALBERRY. See Symphoricarpos orbiculatus

CORAL GUM. See Eucalyptus torquata

CORAL TREE. See Erythrina

CORAL VINE. See Antigonon

CORDYLINE. Evergreen palmlike shrubs or trees. (Often sold as *Dracaena;* for true *Dracaena,* see that entry.) Woody plants with swordlike leaves related to yuccas and agaves, but usually ranked with palms in nurseries and in the landscape.

C. australis (*Dracaena australis*). Zones 8-11, 14-24. In youth, a fountain of 3-ft.-long, narrow (2-5 in. wide), swordlike leaves. Upper leaves erect; lower leaves arch and droop. In maturity, a 20-30-ft. tree, branching high on the trunk, rather stiff like a Joshua tree. Fragrant tiny ¼-in. flowers in late spring are carried in long, branching clusters.

For a more graceful plant, head back when young to force multiple trunks. Or plant in clumps of 6 to 8. Cut back to the ground a few each year until all develop multiple trunks. Hardiest of the cordylines to 15° or lower. Takes almost any soil but grows fastest in soil deep enough for big carrottlike root. Used for tropical effects; with boulders and gravel for desert look; patio or terrace where there's room for a strong character.

C. a. 'Atropurpurea.' BRONZE DRACAENA. Like the above, but with bronzy red foliage. Slower in growth. Combine with gray or a warm yellowish green to bring out color.

C. indivisa. BLUE DRACAENA. Zones 16, 17, 20-24. Trunk to 25 ft., topped with crown of rather stiff, huge (6-ft.-long, 6-in.-wide) leaves. White flowers in 4-ft.-long clusters. Plant in groups of varying heights. Hardy to 26°.

C. stricta. Zones 16, 17, 20-24. Slender stems clustered at the base, or branching low with branches quite erect. Swordlike, 2-ft.-long leaves are dark green with hint of purple. Lavender flowers in large, branched clusters, very decorative in spring. Will grow to 15 ft., but can be kept lower by cutting tall canes to the ground. New canes

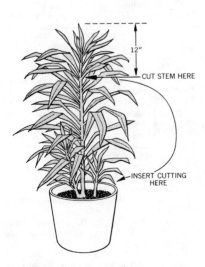

Foot-long cuttings of Cordyline stricta *root easily in pot or open ground bed.*

replace them. Stick long cuttings in the ground; root quickly. Hardy to 26°. Needs shade except near coast. Takes desert heat with ample water in shade. Fine container plant indoors or out; good for tall tropical-looking background in narrow,shaded areas. in lanais, or in narrow side gardens.

C. terminalis. Tɪ. Outdoors Zones 21-24, house plant elsewhere. Plants are usually started from "logs"—sections of stem imported from Hawaii. Lay short lengths in peat moss-sand mixture, burying them about ½ their diameter. Keep moist. When shoots grow out and root, cut them off and pot them. Takes ordinary indoor care. Tolerates low light intensity. Plant has many named forms with red, yellow, or variegated leaves. Outdoors, in Hawaii, it's a 10-ft. plant with 30-in.-long, 5-in.-wide leaves; usually much smaller when grown indoors. Outdoors in southern California, reaches 6-8 ft., in those special locations where soil and air drainage is good—the papaya climates.

COREOPSIS. Annual and perennial. Easily grown member of the sunflower family yielding a profusion of yellow, orange, maroon, or reddish flowers from late spring to fall. Remove old flowers from all types to prolong bloom. Both annual and perennial kinds are easy to propagate—the annuals from seed sown in place (full sun) or in flats, the perennials from seed or division of the root crown. Tend to self-sow.

C. auriculata 'Nana'. Perennial. Evergreen to semi-evergreen in Zones 17-24; deciduous elsewhere. Makes a 5-6-in.-high mat of 2-5-in.-long leaves. Under ideal conditions it will spread by stolons to form a

2-ft. broad clump in a year. Flower heads bright orange-yellow, 1-2½ in. wide, rise well above the foliage mat. Long and profuse blooming season from spring to fall if you remove flowers as they fade. Best used in foreground of taller plants, in a border, or as edging. Can be used in larger areas, but it's quite a chore keeping the unsightly faded flowers removed.

C. grandiflora. Perennial, 1-2 ft. high, spreading to 3 ft. with narrow, dark green, 3-5 lobed leaves. Large, bright yellow flowers, 2½-3 in. across, on long slender stems high above foliage, bloom all summer. Variety 'Sunburst' has large, semi-double flowers.

C. lanceolata. COREOPSIS. Perennial 1-2 ft. high. Leaves somewhat hairy, narrow, mostly in tuft near base. Flower heads 1½-2 in. across, yellow, on pale green stems. Some of lower stem leaves have a few lobes. when well established will persist year after year. Excellent cut flower.

C. maritima. Perennial. Native to coast of southern California. Sometimes called sea dahlia. Grows 1-3 ft. high from tuberous tap root. Stems hollow. Leaves somewhat succulent, divided into very narrow lobes. Clear yellow flower heads 2½-4 in. across on 9-12-in. long stems; bloom in spring. Borders, naturalizing, striking cut flowers.

C. tinctoria. ANNUAL COREOPSIS, CALLIOPSIS. Slender, upright, 1½-3-ft.-tall annual with wiry stems; much like cosmos in growth habit. Leaves and stems smooth. Flowers similar to perennial coreopsis, in yellow, orange, maroon, bronze, and reddish, banded with contrasting colors; purple-brown centers. Dwarf and double varieties. Sow seed in place in full sun and dryish soil.

CORIANDRUM sativum. CORIANDER. Annual herb. Grows 12-15 in. high. Delicate fernlike foliage; flat clusters of pinkish white flowers. Aromatic seeds crushed before use in seasoning sausage, beans, stews, cookies, wines. Young leaves used in salads, soups, poultry recipes, and a variety of Mexican and Chinese dishes. Grow in good, well drained soil, full sun. Start from seed (including coriander seed sold in grocery stores); grows quickly, self sows.

CORK TREE, AMUR. See Phellodendron

CORN, ORNAMENTAL *(Zea mays).* A variety of corn called 'Rainbow' or 'Squaw Corn' is sometimes grown for its brightly colored kernels of deep red, orange, yellow, blue, or black; two or more colors commonly appear marbled on each ear. Use for autumn decoration. Grow just like sweet corn, but permit ears to ripen to full hardness. Break down the mature green ears and let them hang down on the stalk; husks will turn yellowish and dry; after picking, peel the husks back to display some of the ear, or remove them completely.

CORN, POP. Logically enough, this name is applied to any corn that will pop under proper application of heat. Some kinds look like ordinary corn ('South American', 'Hybrid South American', 'Burpee's Peppy'); while others have narrow, deep kernels ('Japanese Hulless' and 'Strawberry'). 'Strawberry' is also a good ornamental corn; the ears (2 in. long, 1½ in. wide) have rich

dark red kernels. Grow like sweet corn, but permit ears to ripen fully before harvesting them; store in a dry place, shelled or on the cob. If your popcorn doesn't want to pop, it's too dry. Store in a moist atmosphere for two weeks and it will pick up moisture.

CORN, SWEET. The one cereal crop that home gardeners are likely to grow; it requires considerable space, but is still well worth growing. In picked corn the sugar changes to starch very quickly, and only by rushing the ears from garden direct to boiling water can you capture the full sweetness. Corn needs heat, but suitable early hybrid varieties will grow even in cool-summer areas of the Northwest. Most people prefer yellow corn of the 'Golden Bantam' type, but old-timers swear by white varieties like 'Stowell's Evergreen' and 'Country Gentleman' ('Shoe Peg'). Favorite yellow varieties are the early 'Early Sunglow', 'Golden Beauty', and 'Gold Crest'; and the mid-season 'Jubilee', 'F-M Cross', 'Golden Cross Bantam', 'Iochief', and 'Illinichief Super Sweet'. 'Stowell's Evergreen Hybrid' and 'Country Gentleman Hybrid' are improvements on their parent varieties. Corn is widely adapted but grows best in deep, rich soils; good drainage is important. Sow seed 2 weeks after average date of last frost. and make 3 or 4 more plantings at 2-week intervals; or plant early, midseason, and late varieties. Plant corn in blocks of short rows rather than stringing out single long rows; pollination is by wind, and unless a good supply of pollen falls on the silks the ears will be poorly filled. Plant either in rows 3 ft. apart and thin seedlings to stand 12 in. apart, or plant in "hills" (actually clumps) 3 ft. apart each way. Place 6 or 7 seeds in each hill and thin to the 3 strongest plants. Give plants ample water and one feeding when stalks are 7-8 in. tall. Make certain that you apply a good deep watering that thoroughly wets the entire root zone just as the tassel emerges from the stalk; repeat again at silking. Don't remove suckers that appear. Check carefully when ears are plump and silk has withered; pull back husks and try popping a grain with your thumb. Generally, corn is ready to eat 3 weeks after silks first appear. The kernels should squirt milky juice; watery juice means that the corn is immature. A doughy consistency indicates over-maturity. Over-age sweet corn is no better than market sweet corn.

Corn earworm is the principal insect pest. Control it by spraying sevin directly on the silk clusters when silks first become visible; or squirt silks with a mixture of 1 teaspoon malathion in ½ pint mineral oil, about ½ teaspoon of it onto each cluster of silks, using a medicine dropper or oil can. Make 3-4 applications at 3-4 day intervals.

Stunted ears or skips in kernels often indicate plant food shortage.

CORNFLOWER. See Centaurea cyanus

CORNUS. DOGWOOD. Deciduous (except where noted) shrub or tree (one's a ground cover perennial).

C. alba. TATARIAN DOGWOOD. Shrub. Zones 1-9, 14-24. In cold-winter areas its blood red, bare twigs are colorful against

C

Climate
Zone maps
pages 8-27

the snow. Upright to about 10 ft. high, and spreads wide, eventually producing a thicket of many stems. Branches densely clothed with 2½-5-in.-long leaves, to 2½ in. wide, deep rich green above, lighter beneath; red in fall. Fragrant, creamy white, small flowers in 1-2-in.-wide, flattish clusters in April, May. Bluish white to whitish small fruits.

C. a. 'Sibirica'. SIBERIAN DOGWOOD. Less rampant than species, it grows to about 7 ft. high with a 5-ft. spread. Gleaming coral red branches in winter.

With both plants, new wood is brightest, so cut back in spring to force new growth.

C. canadensis. BUNCHBERRY. Deciduous carpet plant. Zones 1-6. Native northern California to Alaska, and eastward. It's difficult to believe this 6-9-inch-high perennial is related to the dogwoods when you see it under trees by lakes and streams in the Northwest. Creeping rootstocks send up stems topped by a whorl of 4-6 oval or roundish, 1-2-in.-long leaves, deep rich green; they turn yellow in fall, die down in winter.

Flowers in May or June—a small compact cluster of tiny flowers surrounded by usually 4 oval, ½-¾-in.-long, pure white bracts. Clusters of small, shiny, bright red fruits in August and September.

For cool moist climates, in acid soil, with generous amounts of humus or rotten wood. Considered hard to establish, but transplanted with a piece of rotten log with bark attached, it establishes readily.

C. capitata. EVERGREEN DOGWOOD. Big shrub or small tree. Zones 8, 9, 14-20. From the Himalayas. Hardy to 15°. Not reliably evergreen in cold weather. Often in mild winters it loses half its leaves. Moderate growth to 20-30 ft. high and eventually an equal spread. Green to grayish green, 2-4-in.-long by ¾-1 ¾ in.-wide leaves; some turn red or purplish in the fall.

Although trees don't flower until about 8 or 10 years old, when they do they are delightful. Small flower cluster is surrounded by 4-6 creamy to pale yellow, 1½-2-in.-long bracts, in May and June. Large, fleshy, reddish purple fruits in October and November can be a litter problem. Birds may clean up some of the fruit.

C. controversa. GIANT DOGWOOD. Tree. Zones 3-9, 14, 18, 19. From the Orient. Hardy to 5°. Leaves, flowers, and fruits like the big shrubby dogwoods, but grows rapidly into a magnificent 40-60-ft. tree with picturesque horizontal branches; luxuriant 3-6-in.-long, oval leaves, 2-3 in. wide are dark green above, silvery green beneath, glowing red in fall. Creamy white flowers are not spectacular, but so abundant in May they give a good show. They form in fluffy, flattish clusters 3-7 in. wide. Shiny, bluish black, ½-in.-wide fruits ripen in August and September; enjoyed by birds.

Locate plants in full sun for most flowers and best autumn color. Keep soil moist.

C. florida. FLOWERING DOGWOOD, EASTERN DOGWOOD. Tree. Zones 1-9, 14-16. Native to eastern U.S. To 20 ft. high. Most commonly planted of the flowering dogwoods in the Northwest and intermountain areas where it's easy to grow and much a part of the spring flower display.

In form, it somewhat resembles our Western native, C. nuttallii, with its horizontal branching pattern. But the gray twigs

at branch ends tend to be upright. It usually has a shorter trunk. Small flower clusters are surrounded by 4 roundish, 2-4-in.-wide, white bracts with notched tips. Flowers almost cover tree in May before leaves expand. Oval, 2-6-in.-long by 2½-in.-wide leaves bright green above, lighter beneath; turn glowing red before they fall.

C. f. 'Cherokee Chief'. Deep rosy red flower bracts that are paler at base.

C. f. 'Cherokee Princess'. Gives unusually heavy display of white blooms.

C. f. 'Rubra'. A long-time favorite for its pink or rose flower bracts.

C. f. 'Welchii'. TRICOLOR DOGWOOD. Best known for its variegated, 4-in.-long leaves of creamy white, pink, deep rose, and green throughout spring and summer; turn deep rose to almost red in fall. Rather inconspicuous pinkish to white flower bracts are not as profuse.

C. kousa. KOUSA DOGWOOD. Big shrub or small tree. Zones 3-9, 14, 15, 18, 19. Native to Japan and Korea. Later blooming than other flowering dogwoods—in June and July. A big multi-stemmed shrub, or (with training) a small tree to 20 ft. Delicate limb structure, and spreading, dense horizontal growth habit. Lustrous, medium green leaves, 4 in. long, have rusty brown hairs at base of veins on under surface. Yellow and scarlet fall color.

Flowers, along tops of branches, show above leaves. Creamy white, slender-pointed, 2-3-in.-long, rather narrow bracts surround flower cluster; turn pink along edges. In October red fruits hang below branches like big strawberries.

C. k. chinensis. Native to China, has larger leaves and larger flower bracts.

C. mas. CORNELIAN CHERRY. Shrub or tree. Zones 1-6. Native to southern Europe and the Orient. One of the earliest dogwoods to bloom, it shows mass of clustered, small, yellow blossoms on bare twigs in February and March. It's usually an airy twiggy shrub but it can be trained as 15-20-ft. small tree. Oval leaves, 2-4 in. long, shiny green turning to yellow; some forms turn red in fall. Autumn color is enhanced by clusters of bright scarlet, ¾-in.-long fruits which hang on from September until birds get them. Fruit edible; used in making preserves. Withstands subzero temperatures. Tolerates alkaline soils.

C. nuttallii. PACIFIC DOGWOOD, WESTERN DOGWOOD. Tree. Zones 2-9, 14-20. Native to Pacific Northwest and northern California. One of our most spectacular natives when it wears its gleaming white flower bracts on bare branches in April or May. Often there's a second flowering with the leaves in September. Unfortunately, it's not as easy to grow in gardens as Eastern dogwood (C. florida). It reacts unfavorably to routine garden watering, fertilizing, pruning. Injury to its tender bark provides entrance for insects and diseases. But if you give plants exceptionally good drainage, infrequent summer watering, and plant under high branching trees, so bark will not sunburn, you have a chance of success.

Where adapted this tree will grow to 50 ft. or more high with a 20-ft. spread. It may grow one trunk or several. Gray-barked branches grow in a pleasing horizontal pattern, effective in winter. Oval, 3-5-in.-long leaves are a rich green above, grayish green

beneath; they turn to beautiful yellows and reds in fall. The 4-8 flower bracts are 2-3 in. long, roundish, rounded or pointed, white or tinged with pink. Decorative red to orange-red fruits in buttonlike clusters form in fall.

C. n. 'Goldspot'. Leaves splashed with creamy yellow. Flowers when only 2 ft. tall. Bracts are larger than species. Long, 2-month flowering season, often with some fall bloom.

C. sanguinea. BLOODTWIG DOGWOOD. Shrub. Zones 1-7. The big show comes in fall with dark blood red foliage, and in winter with purplish to dark red bare twigs and branches. Prune severely in spring to produce new branches and twigs for winter color. Grows as a big many-stemmed shrub to 12 ft. high, about 8 ft. wide. Dark green leaves 1½-3 in. long. June flowers are greenish white in 2-in.-wide clusters. Black fruits.

C. stolonifera. REDTWIG DOGWOOD, REDOSIER DOGWOOD. Shrub. Zones 1-9, 14-21. Native to moist places northern California to Alaska and eastward. Another dogwood with a brilliant show of red fall color and bright red winter twigs. Not only thrives in the coldest areas of the West, but throughout California, even the intermediate valleys of southern California if given frequent watering. Grows rapidly as a big multistemmed shrub to 15 ft. or more high. Spreads widely by creeping underground stems and rooting branches. To control, cut off with a spade roots that have gone too far. Cut off branches that touch the ground. Small creamy white flowers in 2-in.-wide clusters appear among the leaves (oval, 1½-2½ in. long, fresh deep green) throughout summer and into fall. Fruits are white or bluish.

C. s. 'Flaviramea'. YELLOWTWIG DOGWOOD. Has yellow twigs and branches.

COROKIA. Evergreen shrubs. Zones 4-24. Native to New Zealand. Tiny, starlike, ½-in. flowers in spring, followed by small bright fruits (on older plants). Notable for unusual branching patterns.

C. cheesemanii. Slender twiggy growth with spreading branches, to 8-12 ft. Leaves dark green above, felted white beneath; to 2 in. Small yellow flowers in clusters followed by ¼-in. red fruits. In many ways, a large version of C. cotoneaster. Espalier, pattern plant behind translucent panel. Good near ocean.

C. cotoneaster. Slow growing to 10 ft. Usually seen as 2-4-ft. container plant. Intricate branch pattern made up of many slim, contorted, interlaced, nearly black branches. Leaves ¾-in. long, dark green above, white underneath. Sun or part shade. Tolerates alkaline soils. Thrives in containers with fast-draining mix. Night lighting from beneath enhances bizarre quality of branch pattern.

C. macrocarpa. Upright, narrow, dense growth to 12-20 ft. Broad oval gray-green leaves are silvery on lower sides. Small yellow flowers followed by orange-red berries. Little-known shrub; excellent screen plant in ocean wind.

CORONILLA varia. CROWN VETCH. Perennial. All Zones. Relative of peas, beans, and clovers. Creeping roots and rhizomes make it a tenacious ground cover with straggling stems to 2 ft. Leaves made up of 11-25 oval leaflets ½-¾ in. long. Lavender-pink flowers in 1-in. clusters soon become bundles of brown, slender, fingerlike seedpods. Goes dormant and looks ratty during coldest weather. In spring, mow it, feed and water several times, and it will make a lush green summer cover. Too invasive and rank for flower beds. Use for covering cut banks and remote places. Once established, difficult to eliminate; selective weed killers can do the job.

CORREA. AUSTRALIAN FUCHSIA. Evergreen shrubs. Successful in Zones 5, 6 when winters aren't too cold (hardy to about 20°); generally successful Zones 14-24. Flower form may suggest the fuchsia, but in all other ways far from fuchsialike. Low to medium height, usually dense and spreading. Leaves small (to 1 in.), roundish, densely felted underneath and give a gray or gray-green effect that contrasts subtly with other grays and distinctly with dark greens. All (except summer-flowering *C. alba)* are valued for their long winter flowering season, normally from November-April. Flowers small, ½-¾ in., individually handsome but not showy, hang down along the branches like small bells.

Must have fast-draining soil. Do well in poor, even rocky soil. Easy to kill with kindness—over-watering and over-feeding.

Use as ground covers on banks or slopes. Attractive in large containers placed where flowers can be enjoyed close up. Generally thought to do best in full sun in coastal areas, partial shade inland, but many can be seen in full sun, all climates. Should not get reflected heat from wall or paving.

C. alba. To 4 ft. with arching branches. White flowers in summer.

C. backhousiana. (Often sold as *C. magnifica.)* More successful in southern California than *C. pulchella.* Growth habit upright and rather sprawling to 4-5 ft. and as wide. Flowers chartreuse.

C. harrisii. To 2½ ft. high and more compact than the other correas. Flowers a beautiful, clear red.

C. pulchella. Most widely grown correa in northern California. To 2-2½ ft. high and spread to as much at 8 ft. Leaves green above, gray-green below. Light pink flowers.

CORTADERIA selloana. PAMPAS GRASS. Evergreen giant ornamental grass. Zones 4-24. Root-hardy but deciduous in cold-winter areas. Native to Argentina. Very fast growing in rich soil in mild climates; from gallon can size to 8 ft. in one season. Established, may reach 20 ft. in height. A fountain of saw-toothed, grassy leaves above which, in late summer, arise long stalks bearing white to chamois or pink 1-3-ft. flower plumes.

Will grow in any soil from the driest to the wettest, acid to alkaline. Takes hot dry winds of deserts and fog winds of the coast. Its willingness to grow under rough conditions gives it value in large bank planting and as first line of defense in a wide windbreak. But the sheer bulk of the plant can become a problem in the small garden, and it's not easy to reduce in size. Roots and stems are tough and woody, and leaf edges are like sharp saws. Most efficient way to keep it under control is to burn it to the ground periodically.

CORYDALIS. Perennials. Zones 4-9, 14-24. Handsome clumps of dainty divided leaves similar to bleeding heart (to which it is closely related), or maidenhair fern. Clusters of small spurred flowers, usually yellow. Plant in partial shade, rich moist soil. Effective in rock crevices, in open woodland, near pool or streamside. Combine with ferns, columbine, bleeding heart, primroses. Divide clumps or sow seeds in spring or fall. Plants self-sow in garden.

C. cheilanthifolia. Hardy Chinese native, 8-10 in. high with fernlike green foliage. Clusters of yellow, ½-in.-long flowers in May and June.

C. lutea. Native to southern Europe. To 15 in. tall. Masses of gray-green foliage on many stems. Golden yellow, ¾-in.-long, short-spurred flowers throughout summer.

CORYLOPSIS. WINTER HAZEL. Deciduous shrubs. Zones 4-7, 15-17. Valued for show of soft yellow, fragrant flowers that come on bare branches in March or earlier. New leaves that follow bloom are often tinged pink, then bright green, roundish, somewhat resembling hazelnut (filbert) leaves. Slow growing to 5 ft. and as wide. Makes a rather open structure with attractive delicate branching pattern.

Plant in a sheltered location in sun or partial shade. Needs same type soil as rhododendrons. Use in shrub border, edge of woodland.

C. pauciflora. BUTTERCUP WINTER HAZEL. Flowers are primrose yellow, ¾ in., bell-shaped, in drooping clusters of 2 or 3. Leaves 1-3 in. long, with sharply toothed edges.

C. spicata. SPIKE WINTER HAZEL. Flowers are pale yellow, ½ in., bell-shaped in 1½-in.-long drooping clusters of 6-12. Leaves to 4 in. long with toothed edges.

CORYLUS. FILBERT, HAZELNUT. Deciduous shrubs or small trees. Zones 1-9, 14-20. Although mostly thought of as producing edible nuts (see Filbert) the following types are grown as ornamentals; one is a Western native.

C. avellana. EUROPEAN FILBERT. Not as widely grown as its two varieties described below. A shrub 10-15 ft. high and as wide. Leaves broad, roundish, 3-4 in. long; turn yellow in fall. Ornamental greenish yellow male flower catkins hang on all winter, turn yellow in earliest spring before leaves appear. Roundish nuts, enclosed by 2 irregularly lobed bracts, of good flavor.

C. a. 'Contorta'. HARRY LAUDER'S WALKING STICK. Fantastically gnarled and twisted branches and twigs. Takes well to container culture, and lends itself to display as a curiosity. Will grow to 8-10 ft. Leaves smaller than species.

C. a. 'Fusco-rubra' (*C. a.* 'Atropurpurea'). Identical to the species except for its handsome purple leaf color.

C. cornuta californica. WESTERN HAZELNUT. Native to damp slopes below 7,000 ft. elevation, north Coast Ranges and Sierra Nevada of California, north to B. C. Grows as an open, spreading multi-stemmed shrub 5-12 ft. high. Roundish, somewhat hairy leaves, 1½-3 in. long, with coarsely toothed edges; turn yellowish in fall. Like *C. avellana,* male flower catkins decorative. Nuts small, kernel flavorful; enveloped in leafy husk with long drawn-out beak.

C. maxima. See Filbert

C. m. 'Purpurea'. Makes a handsome, well-structured, small tree to 20 ft., or a suckering shrub to 12-15 ft. Roundish leaves 2-6 in. long, dark purple in spring and summer. Burns quite badly in southern California hot-summer areas.

C

Climate Zone maps pages 8-27

CORYNOCARPUS laevigatus. NEW ZEALAND LAUREL. Evergreen shrub or small tree. Good in Zones 16, 23; best in Zones 17, 24. Handsome, upright, growing 20 to 40 ft. high. Beautiful dark green, very glossy, leathery leaves, oblong to 7 in. by 2 in. wide. Flowers noticeable but of no importance—tiny, whitish, in 3-8-in.-long upright clusters. Fruit orange, oblong, 1 in. long, extremely poisonous.

Easy to grow in sun or part shade. Requires moist conditions. Good in containers. Slow growing; keeps attractive form for years. Use as screen or large hedge, background. Good in sheltered areas, entryways, under overhangs.

CORYPHANTHA vivipara. (Usually sold as *Mammillaria vivipara.)* Little cactus. All Zones. Native Alberta to north Texas. Has single or clustered globular, 2-in. bodies covered with little knobs which bear white spines. Flowers purple, showy, to 2 in. long. One of the hardiest forms of cactus, taking temperatures far below zero.

COSMOS. Annual. Native to tropical America, mostly Mexico. Showy summer and fall blooming plants, open and branching in habit, with bright green divided leaves and daisylike flowers in many colors and forms (single, double, crested, and frilled). Heights vary from 2½-8 ft. Give mass color in borders, background, or as filler among shrubs. Useful in arrangements if flowers are cut when freshly opened, and placed immediately in deep cool water. Sow seed in open ground from spring to summer, or set out transplants from flats. Plant in full sun in not-too-rich soil. Drought resistant. Self-sow freely.

C. bipinnatus. Flowers in white and shades of pink, rose, lavender, purple, or crimson, with tufted yellow centers. Heights up to 8 ft. Sensation strain grows 3-6 ft. high, comes in named white and pink varieties, blooms earlier than other kinds. 'Radiance' has deep rose flowers overlaid with crimson on tall robust plants.

C. sulphureus. YELLOW COSMOS. Grows to 7 feet, with yellow or golden yellow flowers with yellow centers. Tends to become weedy looking at end of season. Varieties include 'Mandarin', vermilion flowers, 'Orange Flare', and 'Yellow Flare'. Quite late blooming, especially 'Orange Flare'.

COSTMARY. See Chrysanthemum balsamita

COTINUS coggygria *(Rhus cotinus).* SMOKE TREE. Deciduous. All Zones, especially good in 1-3, 10, 11. (For another smoke tree, see *Dalea spinosa.)* An unusual shrub-tree creating a broad urn-shaped mass usually as wide as high — eventually to 25 ft. Roundish leaves 1½-3 in. long, bluish green in summer, turn yellow to orange-red in

C

Climate Zone maps pages 8-27

fall. Dramatic puffs of purple to lavender "smoke" come from large loose clusters of fading flowers. As the tiny greenish blossoms fade, stalks of sterile flowers elongate and become clothed with purple fuzzy hairs.

C. c. 'Purpureus' has purple leaves which gradually turn to green, and richer purple smoke puffs. *C. c.* 'Royal Purple' retains purple leaves through the summer.

At its best under stress in poor or rocky soil. When grown in highly cultivated gardens, must have fast drainage and infrequent watering to avoid root rot.

COTONEASTER. Evergreen, semi-deciduous, and deciduous shrubs. They range from ground covers to stiffly upright, small shrubs to tall growing (20 ft.) shrubs of fountain-like growth with graceful arching branches. All grow vigorously and thrive with little or no maintenance. In fact they look better and produce better crops of fall and winter berries if planted on dry slopes or in poor soil than in rich moist garden soil. Spring bloom.

While some of the medium and tall growers can be sheared, they look best when allowed to maintain natural fountain shapes. Prune only to enhance the graceful arch of the branches. Keep medium growers looking young by pruning out a portion of the oldest wood each year. Prune ground covers to remove dead or awkward branches. Give the flat growers room to spread. Don't plant near a walk or a drive where branch ends will need shearing. Stubbed branches unattractive.

Cranberry cotoneaster (C. apiculata) has big (¹/₂-in.) bright red berries.

COTONEASTER

SPECIES OR VARIETY	HARDINESS	SIZE, HABIT	LEAVES	FLOWERS, FRUIT	USES, COMMENTS
COTONEASTER adpressa CREEPING COTONEASTER	Deciduous. All Zones.	Slow growing (3-year-old 4 in. high and 2 ft. wide); eventually to 1 ft. with 6-ft. spread.	Dark green (to ¹/₂ in. long), nearly smooth.	Flowers pink-tinted. Good show of ¹/₄-in., bright red fruit.	Bank or ground cover. Will follow contours of ground, rocks, drape down a wall.
C. a. praecox (C. praecox)	Deciduous. All Zones.	More vigorous than species; to 1-1¹/₂ ft. high and spreading.	Oval (to 1 in. long), with wavy margins.	Fruits larger than species—to ¹/₂ in., bright red.	Same as C. adpressa.
C. apiculata CRANBERRY COTONEASTER	Deciduous. All Zones.	To 4 ft. high and spreading wider; growth similar to C. horizontalis	Roundish (less than ¹/₂ inch), shiny bright green above, slightly hairy beneath.	Flowers pinkish white. Large cranberry-size, bright red fruits in clusters.	Use as hedge, background planting. Berries color early and hold long. An improved variety 'Blackburn', more compact, larger fruits.
C. bullata macrophylla	Deciduous. Zones 4-24.	To 6-12 ft. tall, open, arching.	Dark green above, downy beneath, heavily veined with puckered appearance. 2¹/₂-5 in. long, half as wide.	Bright red fruits, ¹/₃-¹/₂ in. across, in 2-in. clusters.	Background, free-standing, large shrub borders. C. bullata is similar, but with smaller leaves.
C. congesta (C. microphylla glacialis)	Evergreen. Zones 2-24.	Slow growing to 3 ft. (spreading 8 in. a year) to a dense rounded form with branches curving downward.	Small (¹/₃ in.), rounded, dark green above, whitish beneath.	Flowers pink to white. Fruit small (¹/₄ in.) bright red.	Rock hugging, attractive in containers, foreground planting. Equally well grown in Zone 2 and the desert zones.
C. conspicua WINTERGREEN COTONEASTER	Evergreen. Zones 3-24.	Arching branches. Same growth habit as C. microphylla but taller, to 4-6 ft.	Small (¹/₄ in.) narrow, oval, dark green above, pale beneath.	Flowers white. Bright red fruit, ³/₈ in., in profusion.	This upright form is not much grown. Its variety (see below) is widely available.

C

Climate
Zone maps
pages 8-27

SPECIES OR VARIETY	HARDINESS	SIZE, HABIT	LEAVES	FLOWERS, FRUIT	USES, COMMENTS
C. c. 'Decora' NECKLACE COTONEASTER	Evergreen. Zones 3-24.	Almost prostrate. Grows with short rigid branches from main stems.	Same as *C. conspicua.*	Same as *C. conspicua.*	Ground cover, containers, rock gardens.
C. dammeri (*C. humifusa*) BEARBERRY COTONEASTER	Evergreen. All Zones.	Vigorous. Long, prostrate, rooting branches; to 3-6 in. high and spreading to 10 ft.	Oval, 1 in. long, bright green, glossy above, whitish beneath. *C. dammeri radicans* has blunt, often notched leaves.	Good show of white flowers (to $\frac{1}{2}$ in. wide). Fruit ($\frac{1}{2}$ in.) brilliant red, showy.	Use as ground-hugging carpet in sun or part shade. Will cascade down a wall, flow over and around rocks.
C. divaricata SPREADING COTONEASTER	Deciduous. All Zones.	To 6 ft. high, with many stiff branches spreading out from the center.	Oval, $\frac{3}{4}$ in. long, dark green above, pale green beneath, thickly set along branches. Turn orange to red in fall.	Flowers in profusion, pink, followed by great show of $\frac{1}{3}$-in.-long, egg-shaped, red fruits.	Use as boundary, informal hedge or screen, or large bank planting.
C. franchetii	Evergreen. Zones 4-13.	Fountainlike, arching growth to 10 ft. or more. In poor soil with little water, to 5-6 ft.	Thickish, oval (to $1\frac{1}{4}$ in. long), downy when young, dull green above when mature.	Flowers pink. Fruit ($\frac{1}{3}$ in.) orange-red in clusters.	Attractive as a tree-shrub or multi-stemmed small tree. Not a plant to shear or clip.
C. glaucophylla BRIGHT-BEAD COTONEASTER	Semi-evergreen or evergreen. Zones 4-24.	Erect arching growth habit to about 6 ft. and as wide, but can be pruned to any height.	Oval (to 2 in. long), gray-green, closely set on branches.	Flowers pinkish, followed by dull red fruits in clusters carried into winter.	Hedging, screening, border planting. Widely adapted. Good in desert Zones 11-13.
C. henryana	Semi-evergreen. Zones 4-24.	Arching, spreading growth to 8-12 ft.	Large (to 5 in. long), willowlike, deeply veined, green above, tawny hairy beneath.	Flowers white. Fruits red, in dense clusters.	Useful for Christmas greens as fruit is long-lasting. Beautiful as an individual shrub-tree.
C. horizontalis ROCK COTONEASTER	Deciduous, but out of leaf a very short time. All Zones.	Low growing (2-3 ft.), wide spreading (to 15 ft.) with stiffly angled branches with fanlike secondary branches.	Small ($\frac{1}{2}$ in. long or less), roundish, glossy bright green above, pale beneath, hold late, then color orange and red.	White flowers followed by shiny bright red fruits, in mass display.	Don't plant along walks or drive where branch ends must be pruned. Give it room to spread. Bank cover, filler, espalier. Low traffic barrier.
C. h. perpusilla	Same as *C. horizontalis.*	Lower growing, more compact than species.	Small roundish leaves to $\frac{1}{4}$ in., dark green above, pale green beneath.	Same as *C. horizontalis.*	More even and uniform as a ground cover than species.
C. h. 'Variegata'	Same as *C. horizontalis.*	Same as *C. horizontalis.*	Leaves edged with white.	Same as *C. horizontalis.*	Small plants effective in containers or grow atop low walls, so foliage detail can be seen.
C. lactea	Evergreen. Zones 4-24.	Arching growth to 6-8 ft. or more. Foliage growth to base of plant.	Leathery (to 2 in. long), heavily-veined, deep green above, white hairy beneath.	White flowers in $1\frac{1}{2}$-in.-wide clusters. Fruits, red, in 2-3-in. clusters, are long-lasting.	Use for screen or clip into formal hedge. Effective as espalier or in container. Cut sprays valued for arrangements.
C. 'Lowfast'	Evergreen. Zones 4-13.	Very vigorous, prostrate, rooting from trailing branches; to 12 in. high, and spreading to 10-15 ft.	Oval, $\frac{3}{4}$ in. long, dark green above, gray-green beneath; somewhat like *C. dammeri* but not as closely set along the branches.	Showy white flowers followed by red fruits.	Fast ground cover; spreads as much as 2 ft. a year. Other uses same as *C. dammeri.*
C. microphylla ROCKSPRAY COTONEASTER	Evergreen. Zones 2-9, 14-24.	Main branches usually trailing and rooting, secondary branches upright; to 2-3 ft. high, spreading 6 ft. and more.	Very small ($\frac{1}{3}$ in.) dark green above, gray-hairy beneath.	White flowers followed by rosy red, fairly large fruits usually borne singly.	Good bank cover if not overfed and over-watered. Occasional upright branches may be pruned or not, depending on desired effect. Useful in largest rock gardens, above walls.

(Continued on next page)

Climate Zone maps pages 8-27

SPECIES OR VARIETY	HARDINESS	SIZE, HABIT	LEAVES	FLOWERS, FRUIT	USES, COMMENTS
C. m. cochleata	Evergreen. Hardy to —5°. Not tested except Zones 4-6, 16-17.	More prostrate, more compact than C. microphylla.	Like C. microphylla but often with edges rolled back.	As in C. microphylla.	Moulds its growth to the contours of ground or rock. The best ground cover of the C. microphylla group.
C. m. thymifolia	Evergreen. Hardy to —5°. Zones 2-9, 14-24.	More compact than C. micro-phylla but with stiff upright branches.	Narrower than C. microphylla.	As in C. microphylla but fruits somewhat smaller, sometimes in small clusters.	Like other varieties, may become woody with foliage at ends of stems. Prune to thin and shorten.
C. pannosa SILVERLEAF COTONEASTER	Evergreen, half-ever-green in coldest winters. 0°. Zones 4-24.	Erect shrub with arching branches to 10 ft. high and spreading as wide.	Oval (1 in. long) gray-green above, white felted beneath.	Flowers white. Coral-red fruits in clusters.	Valuable as wind screen. Avoid excessive pruning.
C. p. 'Nana' DWARF SILVERLEAF COTONEASTER	Same as C. pannosa.	To 2-3 ft. high, spreading to 5 ft.	Leaves smaller than above, closely spaced, silvery.	Same as C. pannosa.	High ground cover or barrier or low screen plantings. Contrast with rich dark greens in mixed shrub planting.
C. parneyi PARNEY COTONEASTER, RED CLUSTERBERRY					Plants sold under this name are usually C. lactea. The two are very similar.
C. 'Pendula'	Evergreen or semi-deciduous. Zones 4-24.	To 6 ft., spreading wider. Vertical main branches, curving, weeping branches.	Deep green, to 2 in. long. Closely set on branches.	White flowers, fol-lowed early by red ¼-in. fruits.	Use as individual plant, espalier. Sometimes grafted high to make a small spreading, weeping patio tree.
C. rotundifolia	Evergreen or semi-deciduous. Zones 4-24.	Erect growth to 5-8 ft. high, branches spread-ing fan-fashion.	Roundish, dark glossy green.	Flowers white. Long-lasting fruits (to ½ in.) bright scarlet.	Use for massing, screening, informal hedge. Like a larger, more upright C. horizontalis.
C. salicifolia WILLOWLEAF COTONEASTER	Evergreen or semi-evergreen. Zones 4-24.	Vigorous, upright growth to 15 ft. high, arching branches spread-ing to 15-18 ft.	Narrow, willowlike (1-3½ in. long) wrinkled, dark green above, grayish-green beneath. The variety C. s. floccosa has leaves glossy green above.	Flowers white in 2-in. clusters. Bright red fruits.	Useful for big-scale screening, back-grounds. Or use as a single- or multi-stem tree.
C. salicifolia 'Herbstfeuer' ("Autumn Fire")	Same as C. salicifolia	Prostrate, to 6 in. high, spread-ing to 8 ft.	Same as C. salicifolia.	Same as C. salicifolia.	Plant 4-6 ft. apart for bank, ground cover.
C. simonsii	Deciduous to semi-evergreen. Zones 4-7. Not tested south.	Erect, stiffish growth to 9-12 ft.	Dark, glossy green, smooth, roundish to oval, ¾-1 in. long.	Scarlet, fairly large.	Vigorous plant for shrub border, group plantings.
C. wardii	Evergreen. Zones 4-24.	Erect growth to 8-9 ft. high, with arching branches spreading as wide.	Oval, (to 1¾ in. long), dark glossy green above, white felted beneath.	White or pinkish flowers. Fruit, ⅜ in., bright orange-red, clustered, profuse.	Can be sheared, but looks best alone or in informal groupings.
C. watereri 'Cornubia'	Evergreen. Zones 4-7, 14-17. Deciduous. Zones 2-3.	Vigorous, arching growth to 20 ft. high and as wide.	Dark green (4-5 in. long), red-veined, slightly downy beneath.	Unusually large dark red fruits in clusters, in profusion.	Striking as single- or multi-stem tree, or as really big screen. Not widely grown.
C. zabelii	Deciduous. Zones 2-24.	To 6 ft. spread-ing, with slender branches.	Dark green above, whitish beneath, to 1¼ in. long.	Bright red fruits in clusters.	Shrub border, wood-land edge, screen.

COTTONWOOD. See Populus

COTULA squalida. NEW ZEALAND BRASS BUTTONS. Evergreen perennial. Grows only a few in. high but branches creep to 1 ft. or more. Leaves are soft hairy, fernlike, bronzy green. Flowers are like yellow brass buttons about ¼-in. diameter. Calyxlike bracts below the heads fit tightly against the "buttons". Can be used as a ground cover in full sun to medium shade. Can be increased by planting divisions.

COTYLEDON. Succulents. Various sizes and appearances. Easily grown from cuttings and handsome in containers, raised beds, or open ground beds.

C. orbiculata. Zones 16, 17, 21-24. Shrubby, compact, to 3 ft. tall. The opposing pairs of fleshy leaves are 2-3 in. long, rounded, gray-green to nearly white, narrowly edged red. Green leafed forms are available. Flower stems rise above the plant and carry clusters of orange, bell-shaped, drooping flowers in summer. Good landscaping shrub in mild climates and well drained soils. Splendid container plant.

C. undulata. Zones 17, 23, 24. Striking 18-in. plant with broad, thick leaves thickly dusted with pure white powder. Leaf edges wavy. Flowers (spring and early summer) orange, drooping, clustered. Overhead watering washes off the powder.

COWANIA mexicana stansburiana. CLIFF ROSE. Evergreen shrub. Zones 1-3, 10-13. Native to California's Mojave Desert, Nevada, Arizona, Utah, Colorado, New Mexico, and Mexico. Much branched, straggly shrub to 6 ft. high and as wide. Tiny, ½ in. deeply toothed leaves. Flowers like ½-in.-wide, miniature, single roses, creamy or sulfur yellow, rarely white, in April-June. Its moment of glory comes following bloom when the many very tiny fruits with their long plumy tails soften the shrub to a feathery haze. Pruning and infrequent watering will make it acceptable subject in desert gardens.

COW-ITCH TREE. See Lagunaria

COYOTE BRUSH. See Baccharis

CRABAPPLE. Deciduous fruit tree. A crabapple is a small, usually tart apple. Many kinds are valued more for their springtime flowers than for their fruit. These are the flowering crabapples, described under *Malus.* Crabapple varieties grown mostly for fruit (used for jelly making and pickling) are infrequently sold at Western nurseries. Of the several that may be sold, the most popular is 'Transcendent', a yellow apple to 2 in. wide, with red cheeks. Ripens in late summer. Zones 1-9, 11-21. For culture, see Apple.

CRABAPPLE, FLOWERING. See Malus

CRANBERRY, MOUNTAIN. See Vaccinium vitis-idaea minus

CRANBERRY BUSH. See Viburnum trilobum

CRANBERRY BUSH, EUROPEAN. See Viburnum opulus

CRANE'S BILL. See Erodium, Geranium

CRAPE MYRTLE. See Lagerstroemia indica

CRAPE MYRTLE, QUEEN. See Lagerstroemia speciosa

CRASSULA. Succulents. Outdoors Zones 16, 17, 22-24; outdoors with overhead protection 8, 9, 12-15, 18-21; house plant anywhere. Mostly from South Africa. Most

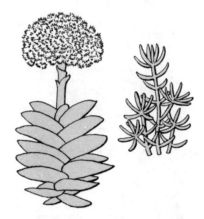

Crassula falcata *(left) has showy flowers; use C. tetragona as "tree" in dish gardens.*

soils, sun or shade. The flowers, as described for the various species below, can be counted on only when grown outdoors in some sunshine.

C. arborescens. Shrubby, heavy-branched plant very like the jade plant, but with gray-green, red-edged, red-dotted leaves. Flowers (usually seen only on old plants) white, fading pink, star-shaped. Good change of pace from jade plant; smaller and slower growing.

C. argentea. (Sometimes sold as *C. portulacea*.) JADE PLANT. Top-notch house plant, large container plant, landscaping shrub in mildest climates. Stout trunk, sturdy limbs even on small plants—and plants will stay small in small container. Can reach 9 ft. in time, but is usually less. Leaves are thick, oblong, fleshy pads 1-2 in. long, glossy bright green, sometimes with red-tinged edges. Clusters of pink, star-shaped flowers form in profusion from November-April.

C. corymbulosa. Low growing, slightly branched with rosettes of long, triangular fleshy leaves. These are dark red when plant is grown in full sun and in poor soil.

C. falcata. Full grown plants reach 4 ft., with equal spread. Leaves fleshy, sickle-shaped, gray-green, vertically arranged in opposite rows on the stems. Dense, branched clusters of scarlet flowers late summer.

C. lactea. Spreading, semi-shrubby plant 12-24 in. tall. Fleshy dark green leaves, white flowers in 4-6-in. clusters, October-December. Grows in shade—even dense shade. Fine rock garden plant.

C. lycopodioides. Leafy, branching, erect stems to a foot high, closely packed with tiny green leaves in 4 rows; effect is that of a braided watch chain or of some strange green coral. Easy and useful in miniature and dish gardens.

C. 'Morgan's Pink'. Fine miniature hybrid. Densely packed, fleshy leaves in a

tight cluster to 4 in. tall. Big brushlike clusters of pink flowers are nearly as big as the plant. Spring bloom.

C. multicava. Dark green, spreading ground cover or hanging plant. Light pink mosquitolike flowers in loose clusters late winter, spring. Rampant grower in sun or shade, in any soil.

C. pyramidalis. Interesting oddity to 3-4 in. high, the flat, triangular leaves closely packed in 4 rows, giving the plant a squarish cross section.

C. schmidtii. Mat-forming, spreading plant to 4 in. tall with long, slender, rich green leaves. Winter-spring flowers small, heavily borne, clustered, dark rose or purplish. Good pot or rock garden plant.

C. tetragona. Upright plants with treelike habit, 1-2 ft. high. Leaves narrow, an inch long. Flowers white. Widely used in dish gardens suggest miniature pine trees.

CRATAEGUS. HAWTHORN. Deciduous trees. Zones 1-11, 14-17. These trees, members of the rose family, are known for their pretty spring flowers and showy fruits in summer, fall. Need more pest control than most trees. Spray with an all-purpose insecticide as new leaves form and again 3 weeks later for aphids and other pests. Fireblight makes entire branches die back quickly. Cut out blighted branches well below dead part; wash pruning tools with disinfectant between each cut.

Hawthorns have thorny branches and need some pruning to thin out excess twiggy growth. Grow plants on the dry side to avoid rank, succulent growth.

C. 'Autumn Glory'. Hybrid origin. Vigorous growth to 25 ft. with 15-ft. spread. Twiggy, dense. Dark green leaves similar to *C. oxyacantha* but more leathery. Clusters of single white flowers in spring. Very large, bright red fruits autumn into winter. The type most susceptible to fireblight.

C. lavallei (*C. carrierei*). CARRIERE HAWTHORN. Hybrid origin. To 25 ft. with 10-ft. spread. More erect and open branching with less twiggy growth than other hawthorns. Very handsome. Leaves, dark green, leathery, 2-4 in. long, toothed; turn bronze red after first sharp frost and hang on well into winter. White flowers in spring followed by loose clusters of very large orange to red fruits that persist all winter.

C. monogyna. Native to Europe, North Africa, and western Asia. Classic hawthorn of English countryside for hedges and boundary plantings. Represented in Western nurseries by the variety 'Stricta'. Narrow growth habit to 30 ft. and 8 ft. wide. Plant 5 ft. apart for a dense narrow screen. Leaves 2 in. long, with 3-7, deep, smooth-edged lobes. Flowers white.

C. oxyacantha. ENGLISH HAWTHORN. Native to Europe and north Africa. Moderate growth to 18-25 ft. with 15-20-ft. spread. Leaves similar to *C. monogyna* but the lobes are toothed. Best known through its varieties: 'Paul's Scarlet', clusters of double rose to red flowers; 'Double White'; 'Double Pink'. Doubles set little fruit.

C. phaenopyrum (*C. cordata*). WASHINGTON THORN. Native to southeastern United States. Moderate growth to 25 ft. with 20-ft. spread. Light and open limb structure. Glossy leaves 2-3 in. long with

C

Climate Zone maps pages 8-27

Climate Zone maps pages 8-27

3-5 sharp pointed lobes (like some maples); foliage turns to a beautiful orange and red in fall. Small white flowers in broad clusters in late spring or early summer. Shiny Chinese red fruits in autumn hang on well into winter. More graceful and delicate than other hawthorns, and a preferred street or lawn tree. The least susceptible to fireblight.

C. pinnatifida major. Native to northeastern Asia. To 20 ft. high, 10-12 ft. wide. Leaves lobed like those of *C. oxycantha* but bigger and thicker. Tree habit is more open and upright than on *C. oxycantha.* Sets big fruits like those of *C. lavallei.*

C. 'Toba'. A Canadian hybrid of great cold tolerance. To 20 ft. White flowers age to pink. Sets few fruits.

CREAM BUSH. See Holodiscus

CREEPER, REDONDO. See Lampranthus under Ice Plant

CREEPER, VIRGINIA. See Parthenocissus quinquefolia

CREEPING JENNIE. See Lysimachia

CREOSOTE BUSH. See Larrea

CRESS, GARDEN. Sometimes called "pepper grass". Flavor resembles watercress. Easy to grow as long as weather is cool. Sow seed as early in spring as possible. Plant in rich, moist soil. Make rows 1 ft. apart, thin plants to 3 in. apart. Eat the thinnings. Make successive sowings every 2 weeks up to the middle of May. Cress matures fast. Where frosts are mild, sow through fall and winter.

CRINODENDRON patagua (*C. dependens, Tricuspidaria dependens*). LILY-OF-THE-VALLEY TREE. Evergreen tree. Zones 14-24. Native to Chile. (For another lily-of-the-valley tree, see *Clethra.*) Somewhat like an evergreen oak in general appearance; sometimes called flowering oak. Grows at moderate rate to 25 ft. and almost as wide, with upright, branching and rounded crown. Leaves 2½ in. long, ½-1 in. wide, dark green above, gray-green beneath with irregularly toothed edges.

In June and July, sometimes into October, it wears hundreds of ¾-in.-long, white, bell-shaped flowers. These are followed by numerous attractive cream and red seed capsules which drop and can be messy on paving. Tends to grow shrublike, or some branches turn down while others stick up. Early staking and pruning important. Prune out brushy growth toward the center; remove branches that tend to hang down.

Does well in wet spots, and thrives on lawn watering. In a lawn, water deeply once a month to discourage surface rooting.

CRINUM. Bulb. Zones 23, 24; or in sheltered garden situations Zones 16-22; other areas in containers. Distinguish from near-relative amaryllis by crinum's long, slender flower tube that is longer than flower segments. Long-stalked cluster of lily-shaped, 4-6-in.-long, fragrant flowers rises in spring or summer from the persistent clump of long, strap-shaped or sword-shaped leaves. Bulbs large, rather slender, tapering to stemlike

neck; thick fleshy roots. Bulbs generally available (from specialists) all year, but spring, fall planting preferred.

Provide soil with plenty of humus; set bulbs 6 in. under surface; give ample water, space to develop. Divide infrequently. In colder sections, mulch heavily in winter; or in containers, move into frostproof place.

C. asiaticum. Extremely large bulbs (1 ft. or so long, 4-5 in. thick). Leaves 3 ft. or more long, 3-5 in. wide, light bluish green. Typically has clusters of 20 or more very fragrant, pure white, narrow-petaled flowers with red stamens.

C. moorei. Large bulbs, 6-8 in. in diameter, with stemlike neck 12 in. or more long. Long, thin, wavy-edged, bright green leaves. Bell-shaped pinkish red flowers.

C. powellii. Resembles *C. moorei,* one of its parents, having dark rose-colored flowers. 'Alba' is a good pure white.

CROCOSMIA. Corm. Zones 5-24, but needs sheltered location and winter mulch in colder zones. Native to tropical and South Africa. Formerly called tritonia, and related to freesia, ixia, sparaxis. Sword-shaped leaves in basal clumps. Small orange, red, yellow flowers bloom in summer on branched stems. Useful for splashes of garden color and for cutting. Plant in full sun near coast and in coastal valleys, part shade inland.

C. crocosmaeflora (*Tritonia crocosmaeflora*). MONTBRETIA. A favorite for generations, montbretias can still be seen in older gardens where they have spread freely, as though native, producing orange-crimson flowers 1½-2 in. across on 3-4-ft. stems. Sword-shaped leaves to 3 ft., ½-1 in. broad. Many named forms once common; now little grown. Good for naturalizing on slopes or in fringe areas.

C. masonorum. From South Africa. Leaves 2½ ft. long, 2 in. wide. Flowers flaming orange to orange-scarlet, 1½ in. across, in dense, one-sided clusters on 2½-3-ft. stems which arch over at the top. Buds open slowly from base to tip of clusters, and old flowers drop clean. Flowers last 2 weeks when cut.

CROCUS. Corm. All Zones but most species best adapted to colder climates. The leaves are basal and grasslike — often with a silvery midrib — and appear before, with, or after the flowers, depending on the species. The flowers with long stemlike tubes and flaring or cup-shaped petals are 3-6 in. long; the short (true) stems are hidden underground.

Most crocus bloom in earliest spring or late winter, but some species bloom August-November, the flowers arising from the bare earth weeks or days after planting. All thrive in sun or light shade; mass them for best effect. Attractive in rock gardens, between stepping stones, in containers. Set corms 2-3 in. deep in a light, porous soil. Divide every 3-4 years.

C. angustifolius. (Formerly *C. susianus.*) CLOTH OF GOLD CROCUS. Orange-gold, starlike flowers with dark brown center stripe. January-February bloom, March in cold climates.

C. balansae. Deep orange, tinted brown on back of segments. Early spring.

C. biflorus. SCOTCH CROCUS. White, veined and feathered purple; yellowish, hairy throat. Spring.

C. chrysanthus. Orange yellow, sweet scented. Hybrids and selections from this range from white and cream through the yellow and blues, often marked with deeper color. Usually even more freely flowering than Dutch crocus, but with smaller flowers. Spring.

C. etruscus. Lilac and cream, yellow throat. Early spring.

Use crocus as flowering carpet under azalea, rhododendron, quince, or pieris.

C. flavus. (Formerly *C. aureus.*) Rich, deep golden yellow. Very early.

C. imperati. Bright lilac inside, buff veined purple outside, saucer-shaped. Early spring.

C. kotschyanus. (Formerly *C. zonatus.*) Pinkish lavender or lilac. September bloom.

C. medius. Light lilac-purple, showy. October-November.

C. sativus. SAFFRON CROCUS. Lilac. The orange-red stigma is the true saffron of commerce. Interesting rather than showy. Autumn.

C. sieberi. Delicate lavender-blue with golden throat. One of the earliest.

C. speciosus. Showy blue-violet flowers in October. Lavender and mauve varieties available. Fast increase by seed and division. Showiest autumn-flowering crocus.

Here, crocus blooms by stepping stones, with low ground cover of creeping thyme.

C

C. tomasinianus. Slender buds, star-shaped silvery lavender-blue flowers, sometimes with dark blotch at tips of segments. Very early—January or February in milder climates.

C. vernus. DUTCH CROCUS. The familiar crocus in shades of white, yellow, lavender, and purple, often penciled and streaked. February-April (depending on climate). Most vigorous crocus, and the only one much planted in mild-winter areas.

Colonies of crocus in low container with dwarf conifer, fine-leafed sedum, stone.

CROSSANDRA infundibuliformis. Evergreen greenhouse or house plant. Native to India. Grow it in a 4-5-in. pot as a 1-1½-ft. plant. Its glossy, very dark green, gardenia-like leaves are attractive all year, and the short, full spikes of scarlet-orange or coral orange flowers are showy for a long period in summer. Grow in warmest spot with good light, as with African violet. Feed with liquid fertilizer once a month. Buy plants from florist or nurseryman, or raise from seed. Blooms in 6-9 months from seed.

CROTALARIA agatiflora. CANARY BIRD BUSH. Evergreen shrub. Zones 13, 15-24. Native to east Africa. Recovers quickly after frost damage. Fast, rank growth to 12 ft. and as wide unless frequently pruned (which it should be). Common name is well-earned. The unique (1½-in.) flowers are strung along the flower spike (to 14 in. long) like so many chartreuse birds. Heaviest bloom in summer or fall but in frost-free areas blooms intermittently for 10 months. Foliage a pleasing gray-green, with leaves divided into 3-in.-long leaflets.

Yellow-green flowers harmonize with most colors. Try with red geraniums, zinnias, coral tree (*Erythrina*), or with other yellow-flowered shrubs for long succession of bloom. Will grow in almost any soil, in either sun or part shade. Prune 2 or 3 times a year to correct open, weak-stemmed growth, condense and improve the outline, and keep growth within bounds.

CROTON. See Codiaeum

CROWN IMPERIAL. See Fritillaria imperialis

CROWN OF GOLD TREE. See Cassia excelsa

CROWN OF THORNS. See Euphorbia milii

CROWN-PINK. See Lychnis coronaria

CRYOPHYTUM. See Mesembryanthemum crystallinum under Ice Plant

CRYPTANTHUS zonatus. Perennial used as house plant; outdoors Zones 17, 23, 24. Native to Brazil. A bromeliad (pineapple relative) grown for showy leaves — in spreading, low-growing clusters to 18 in. wide, usually less. Individual leaves wavy, dark brown-red, banded crosswise with green, brown, or white. Unimportant little white flowers grow among leaves. Pot in equal parts coarse sand, ground bark or peat moss, and shredded or chopped osmunda.

CRYPTOCARYA miersii. See Beilschmiedia

CRYPTOCARYA rubra. Evergreen tree. Zones 14-17, 20-24. Native to Chile. Slow to moderate growth to 30-40 ft. Dense, slightly spreading crown. Distinguished by its rich brown bark and beautiful coppery red new foliage. The 2-3-in.-long, roundish leaves, thick in texture, mature to a very glossy dark green above, bluish green beneath, spicily fragrant when crushed. Stake and prune unless a multiple trunk is desired. Occasional frost damage in Zones 14-16.

CRYPTOMERIA japonica. JAPANESE CRYPTOMERIA. Evergreen tree. Zones 4-9, 14-24. Graceful conifer, fast growing (3-4 ft. a year) in youth. Eventually a skyline tree with straight columnar trunk; thin red-brown bark peeling in strips. Foliage a soft bright green to bluish green. Branches, slightly pendulous, are clothed with short, ½-1-in.-long, needlelike leaves. Roundish, red-brown cones ¾-1 in. wide. Needs deep soil and ample water.

C. j. 'Elegans'. PLUME CEDAR, PLUME CRYPTOMERIA. Quite unlike the species. Feathery, grayish green, soft-textured foliage. Turns rich coppery red or purplish in winter. Grows slowly into a broad-based, dense pyramid, 20-25 ft. high. For Oriental effect, prune out some branches to give tiered effect. Give it space to show it off.

C. j. 'Lobbii Nana'. Upright, dwarf, very slow to about 4 ft. Foliage dark green.

C. j. 'Pygmaea' (*C. j. 'Nana'*). DWARF CRYPTOMERIA. Bushy dwarf 1½-2 ft. high, 2½ ft. wide. Dark green needlelike leaves, twisted branches.

C. j. 'Vilmoriniana'. Slow growing dwarf to about 1-2 ft. Fluffy gray-green summer foliage turns bronze during late fall and winter. Rock garden or container plant.

CTENANTHE. House plants; foliage plants for patio containers or gardens in Zones 23, 24. Leaves are the big feature. They may be short-stalked along the stem or long-stalked and rising from the base only. Insignificant white flowers form under bracts in spikes at ends of branches. Use with other tropical foliage plants such as philodendron, alocasia, tree ferns. Plant in partial shade in rich moist soil, feed with liquid fertilizer.

C. 'Burle Marx'. Grows to 15 in. Leaves gray-green above, feathered with dark green; maroon underneath. Leaf stalks maroon. Tender; best as a house plant, even in Zones 23, 24.

C. compressa. (Often sold as *Bamburanta arnoldiana*.) BAMBURANTA. Plants to 2-3 ft. high. Leathery leaves are oblong, unequal sided, to about 15 in. long, waxy green on top, gray-green beneath, held at an angle on top of wiry stems.

C. oppenheimiana. GIANT BAMBURANTA. Compact, branching, 3-5 ft. high. Narrow, leathery leaves, dark green banded with silver above, purple beneath, set at an angle on downy stalks. Very good tub plant for patio or porch in Zones 23, 24.

CTENITIS pentangularis. Fern. Zones 17, 21-24. Native to New Zealand. This low growing fern makes dense clumps of triangular, finely cut fronds. Will take moderately dry conditions and temperatures down to 26°.

CUCUMBER. Vines need at least 25 sq. ft. per hill, but you can grow the vines on fence or trellis to conserve space. Principal types are the long, smooth, green, slicing cucumbers; the small, heavy-bearing pickling cucumbers; and the roundish, yellow mild-flavored lemon cucumbers. Novelties include Japanese 'Sooyou', a mild, often curving variety; and Armenian cucumber, a very large, curved yellowish type.

Plant seeds 1 or 2 weeks after average date of last frost. To grow cucumbers on a trellis, plant seeds 1 in. deep and 2-3 in. apart and permit main stem to reach top of support. For pests see Melon.

CUNNINGHAMIA lanceolata. CHINA FIR. Evergreen tree. Zones 4-6, 14-21. Native to China. Picturesque conifer with heavy trunk, stout whorled branches, and drooping branchlets. Grows moderately to 30 ft. with 20-ft. spread. Stiff, needlelike leaves 1½-2½ in. long, sharp pointed, green above, whitish beneath. Brown cones (1-2 in.) interesting, but not profuse. Among the palest of needled evergreens in spring and summer; turns red bronze in cold winters. Needs protection from hot dry wind. Becomes less attractive as it ages. Dead branchlets need to be pruned out.

C. l. 'Glauca' is more widely grown and hardier than *C. lanceolata*. Its foliage is a striking gray-blue.

CUNONIA capensis. AFRICAN RED ALDER. Evergreen large shrub or small tree. Zones 9, 13-24. Native to South Africa. A small tree with single or multiple trunks, or a large shrub. Slow to moderate growth to 25-35 ft. as a tree. Good large tub plant. Foliage effective at close range. Twigs are wine red and new growth bronzy red, turning dark green. Leaves divided into 5-9 narrowish, toothed leaflets 3 in. long, 1 in. wide. Dense spiky clusters of small white flowers in late summer. Hardy to 20°. Severely damaged at 16°.

CUP-AND-SAUCER VINE. See Cobaea

CUPANIA. See Cupaniopsis

CUPANIOPSIS anacardioides (*Cupania anacardioides*, often incorrectly labeled *Blighia sapida*). CARROT WOOD, TUCKEROO. Evergreen tree. Zones 16, 17, 19-24. Slow to moderate growth to 30 ft. high, 20-ft. spread. Open branching in youth, becoming dense with age. Leaves made up of 6-10

Climate Zone maps pages 8-27

leathery, 4-in.-long leaflets. Somewhat resembles carob, but more delicate and airy. Gives heavy dense shade. Clean, handsome patio, lawn, or street tree. Prune to enhance structure, remove excess branches. Interesting as a multi-stemmed tree. Deep rooting. Tolerates poorly drained soil. Mature trees hardy to 22°; young trees more tender. Stands salt wind on coast or dry hot wind inland.

CUP FLOWER. See Nierembergia

CUPHEA. Shrubby perennials or dwarf shrubs. Outdoors all year in Zones 16, 17, 21-24; summer bedding or indoor-outdoor pot plant elsewhere. Native Mexico and Guatemala. Interesting for summer color in small beds, as formal edging for border, along paths. Take ordinary soil, sun or part shade (potted plants best in light shade); lots of moisture. Pinch tips for compact growth; cut back older plants severely in late fall or early spring. Easy from cuttings.

C. hyssopifolia. FALSE HEATHER. Compact shrublet 6 in. to 2 ft. with flexible, leafy branchlets. Leaves evergreen, ½-¾ in. long, very narrow. Tiny summer flowers in pink, purple, or white are scarcely half as long as leaves. White form most useful.

C. ignea. CIGAR PLANT. Leafy, compact, 1 ft. high and across. Leaves narrow, dark green, 1-1½ in. long. Flowers tubular, ¾ in. long, bright red with dark ring at end and white tip (hence the name cigar plant); blooms summer and fall.

CUPID'S DART. See Catananche

CUP-OF-GOLD VINE. See Solandra

CUPRESSOCYPARIS leylandii. Evergreen tree. All Zones. Hybrid between *Chamaecyparis nootkatensis* and *Cupressus macrocarpa*. Grows extremely fast (from cuttings to 15-20 ft. in 5 years). Most planted as a quick screening. However, some 10-year-old plantings have become open and floppy with age. Long, slender, upright branches of flattened, gray-green foliage sprays give youthful tree a narrow pyramidal form. Accepts a wide variety of soils and climate.

CUPRESSUS. CYPRESS. Evergreen trees. These coniferous trees have tiny scalelike leaves closely set on cordlike branches.

C. forbesii. TECATE CYPRESS. Zones 8-14, 18-20. Native to Santa Ana Mountains, Orange Co., and mountains of San Diego Co., California. Grows as a low-branching tree to 20 ft., with cherry red bark and green foliage. Very fast growing—in fact it may get too top heavy for size of root system. Needs to be kept on the dry side for wind resistance. Can be pruned as a hedge.

C. glabra. (Often sold as *C. arizonica*.) SMOOTH ARIZONA CYPRESS. Grown in Zones 8-24 but at its best in high desert and hot interiors, where it's valued as a fast-growing windbreak tree, tall screen. Native to central Arizona. Unusually drought resistant when established. Seedlings vary in form and foliage color. Usually to 40 ft., spreading to 20 ft. Smooth, cherry red bark, with green to blue-green to gray foliage. If you want uniformity in growth habit and color look for selected forms: *C. g.* 'Compacta', globe-shaped; *C. g.* 'Gareei', rich, silvery,

blue-green foliage; *C. g.* 'Pyramidalis', compact and symmetrical.

C. macrocarpa. MONTEREY CYPRESS. Zone 17. Native to California's Monterey Peninsula. Beautiful tree to 40 ft. or more, with rich bright green foliage. Narrow and pyramidal in youth, spreading and picturesque in age or in windy coastal conditions. Very subject to coryneum canker fungus for which there is no cure. Look for foliage that first turns yellow, then deep reddish brown, and falls off slowly. Destroy infected trees.

C. sempervirens. ITALIAN CYPRESS. Zones 4-24; best in 8-15, 18-20. Native to southern Europe, western Asia. The species itself, with horizontal branches and dark green foliage, is seldom sold. Instead, you usually have a choice of three varieties: *C. s. indica* (*C. roylei*) is stiff and upright in habit with bright green foliage; *C. s.* 'Stricta' (*C. s.* 'Fastigiata'), COLUMNAR ITALIAN CYPRESS, and *C. s.* 'Glauca', BLUE ITALIAN CYPRESS (really blue-green) are the classic Mediterranean cypresses. They grow eventually into dense, narrow, columnar trees to 60 ft. Often need shearing and tying to keep within limited areas. Spray with malathion for spider mites.

CURRANT. Deciduous shrub. Best in Zones 1-6, 17, but grown in all Zones except where irrigation water or soil is high in sodium. Grow in shade in hot-summer areas, full sun in coastal areas. A many-stemmed shrub to 3-5 ft. high and equally broad, depending on vigor and variety. Attractive foliage of lobed and toothed leaves to 3 in. wide.

Flowers, yellowish in drooping clusters, are followed by clusters of red or white fruits in early summer. Leaves drop rather early in the fall. Currants bear at the base of year-old wood and on spurs on 2- and 3-year wood. Prune so that you keep a balance of 1-, 2-, and 3-year canes; prune out older canes and weak growth. 'Red Lake', 'Perfection', 'Fay's Prolific', and 'Cherry' are preferred varieties.

In some areas of the West it is illegal to plant currants, which might be hosts to white pine blister rust. Ask your nurseryman or county agent.

For ornamental currants, see *Ribes*.

CURRANT, INDIAN. See Symphoricarpos orbiculatus

CUSHION BUSH. See Calocephalus

CUSHION PINK. See Silene acaulis

CUSSONIA spicata. SPIKED CABBAGE TREE. Evergreen tree. Zones 16, 17, 19-24. Native to South Africa. Known chiefly for its lobed, toothed, and cut leaves—something like giant dark green snowflakes. The leaves grow on 6-10-in. stalks, are 4-7 in. long, divided into 5-9 leaflets. This foliage display takes place on a 10-20 ft., smooth trunked tree, with branches in rounded crown. Under best conditions, tree blooms: small flowers, yellowish, in dense spikes 3-9 in. long, stand above leaves. Hardy to about 20°. Give it full sun, plenty of water in summer (with fast drainage).

CYATHEA medullaris. Tree fern. Zones 17, 22-24. Native to New Zealand. Biggest of

the hardier tree ferns; can reach 35 ft. Mature trunks black, covered with coarse, dark scales. Black-ribbed fronds 8-12 ft. long. Hardy to 25°.

CYCAD. A member of the Cycadales, an order of slow-growing evergreen plants with large, firm, palmlike or fernlike leaves and fruits borne in cones. Most people think of them as a kind of palm.

Most are native to tropical regions; some are subtropical, and some of these are hardy enough to grow out of doors in mild-winter climates. All are choice house plants—tough leaves, slow growth, and a smallish root system make them adapted to pot culture indoors.

The most common one is *Cycas revoluta* (see next entry). For others, see *Ceratozamia* and *Dioon*.

CYCAS revoluta. SAGO PALM. Cycad. Zones 8-24. In youth (2-3 feet high), they have airy, lacy appearance of ferns. With age (grow very slowly to as high as 10 ft.) they look more like palms than ferns. But they are neither—they are primitive, cone-bearing plants related to conifers. From central point at top of single trunk (sometimes several trunks), featherlike leaves grow out in rosettes. Leaves 2-3 ft. long (larger on very old plants), divided into many, narrow, leathery, dark glossy green segments. Makes offsets.

Choice container or bonsai plant; useful for tropical look. Tough, tolerant house or patio plant that looks best in partial shade. This is the hardiest (to 15°) and most widely grown cycad.

CYCLAMEN. Tuberous-rooted perennials. Grown for pretty white, pink, rose, or red flowers that resemble shooting stars. Attractive leaves in basal clumps. Zones and uses for the large-flowered florists' cyclamen (*C. persicum*) are given under that name.

All other types are small-flowered, hardy, best adapted Zones 1-9, 14-17. They bloom as described in listing below, and all lose leaves during part of the year. Leaves may appear before or with flowers. Use hardy types in rock gardens, in naturalized clumps under trees, as carpets under camellias, rhododendrons, and large, non-invasive ferns. Or grow them in pots out of direct sun.

All kinds of cyclamen grow best in fairly rich, porous soil with lots of humus. Plant tubers 6-10 in. apart, cover with ½-in. soil (except florists', in which upper half of tuber should protrude above soil level). Best planting time is dormant period, June-August. Keep soil moist; topdress annually with light application of potting soil with complete fertilizer added. Do not cultivate around roots.

Cyclamen grow readily from seed but require several years to flower.

C. atkinsii. Crimson flowers, deep green, silvery mottled leaves. Also pink, white varieties. January-March.

C. cilicium. Pale pink, purple-blotched, fragrant flowers, mottled leaves. September-January.

C. coum. Deep crimson-rose flowers, round, deep green leaves. White, pink varieties. Bloom January to March.

C. europaeum. Fragrant crimson flowers July-August, bright green leaves marbled silvery white, almost evergreen.

C. neapolitanum. Rose-pink flowers August-September, large light green leaves marbled silver and white. Also white variety. One of easiest and most vigorous, very reliable in colder climates.

C. persicum. FLORISTS' CYCLAMEN. Potted plant all areas; outdoors Zones 16-24. Blooms late fall to spring. Good choice for color in places occupied by tuberous begonias in summer. Must have shade in warm summer climates.

C. repandum. Bright crimson flowers, long narrow petals, rich green leaves, marbled silver, toothed on edges. Spring.

CYCLOPHORUS. See Pyrrosia

CYDONIA. See Chaenomeles

CYDONIA oblonga. See Quince, Fruiting

CYLINDROPHYLLUM. See Cephalophyllum under Ice Plant

CYMBALARIA muralis. (Formerly called *Linaria cymbalaria*.) KENILWORTH IVY. Perennial, mostly growing as an annual. A dainty creeper which may appear uninvited in shadier parts of the garden. Trailing stems root at the joints. Leaves small, smooth, rounded, almost kidney-shaped, with 3-7 toothlike lobes. Spring to fall, flowers like tiny snapdragons, lilac-blue marked with white and yellow, grow on stalks a little longer than the leaves.

Use as ground cover in moist shade where invasive habit not a disadvantage. Trails over rocks, front of walls, and raised beds, from hanging baskets; grown as house plant, in terrariums if controlled. Sow seeds in spring or make divisions. Self-seeds readily. Naturalized in favorable situations.

CYMBIDIUM. Terrestrial orchids. Native to high altitudes in southeast Asia, where rainfall is heavy and nights cool. Very popular because of their relatively easy culture.

Long, narrow, grasslike foliage forms a sheath around short, stout, oval pseudobulbs. Flowers grow on erect or arching spikes, usually from February to early May. There are a few new crosses that bloom in December, a few late blooming ones to prolong the flowering period.

Flower best if given as much light as possible without burning foliage. In general, plants do well with 50 per cent shade—under plastic cloth shading or under lath. Let leaf color be your guide: plants with yellow-green leaves generally flower best; dark green foliage denotes too much shade. (Shade plants during flowering period to prolong bloom life, keep from fading.)

Plants prefer 45° to 55° night temperature rising to as much as 80° to 90° during the day. They'll stand temperatures as low as 28° for short time only; therefore, where there's danger of harder frosts, protect plants with covering of polyethylene film in winter. Flower spikes are more tender than other plant tissues.

Keep potting medium moist during period when new growth is developing and maturing—usually March to September. In winter water just enough to keep bulbs from shriveling. On hot summer days syringe foliage early in day.

A good soil mix for cymbidiums: 2 parts redwood bark or sawdust, 2 parts peat moss, 1 part sand. Add a 4-in. pot of complete fertilizer to each wheelbarrow of mix. Ready-blended mixes are excellent. Whatever the medium, it should drain fast and still retain moisture.

Feed with a complete liquid fertilizer high in nitrogen every 10 days to 2 weeks January-July. Use low nitrogen fertilizer August-December.

Transplant potted plants when bulbs fill pots. When dividing plants keep a minimum of 3 healthy bulbs (with foliage) in each division. Dust cuts with sulfur or paint them with tree seal to discourage rot. Watch for slugs and snails at all times.

Except in frost-free areas, grow plants in containers in lathhouse, greenhouse, or under an overhang or high branching tree. For added enjoyment bring indoors when in flower. Excellent cut flower.

Most cymbidium growers list only hybrids in their catalogs—large-flowered varieties with white, pink, yellow, green, or bronze blooms. Most have yellow throat, dark red markings on lip. Large flowered forms produce a dozen or more 4½-5-in. flowers per stem. Miniature varieties, about a quarter the size of the large flowered forms, are popular for their size, free blooming qualities, flower color.

CYNOGLOSSUM. Biennial, usually treated as annual; perennial. Bedding, border, or wild garden plants with blue, white, or pink flowers like forget-me-nots.

C. amabile. CHINESE FORGET-ME-NOT. Biennial grown as annual, 1½-2 ft. tall. Leaves grayish green, soft hairy, lance-shaped. Loose sprays of rich blue, pink, or white flowers, larger than forget-me-nots, spring, into summer where weather is cool. 'Firmament', widely available, most popular variety, has rich blue flowers on compact, 18-in.-high plants. Combine with snapdragons, godetias, candytuft, clarkia, violas; especially effective with white, yellow, pink, salmon, or coral flowers.

Blooms first year from seed sown (preferably where plants are to grow) in fall or early spring. Hardy except in most severe winters. Sun, regular watering.

C. grande. WESTERN HOUNDS TONGUE. Perennial. Zones 4-9, 14-24. Native to Coast Ranges and Sierra Nevada slopes below 4,000 ft. Blooms March-June. Flowers blue, 1/3-½ in. across, white in center. Plants 1-2½ ft. tall, die back in summer to heavy underground root. Leaves hairy, mostly basal, spreading, 6-12 in. long.

CYPERUS. Perennials. Zones 8, 9, 12-24 as outdoor plant. Rush or grasslike plants, distinguished from true grasses by 3-angled, solid stems and very different flowering parts. Valued for striking form, interesting silhouette or shadow pattern.

Most cyperus are bog plants by nature; they grow in rich, moist soil or with roots submerged in water. Groom plants by removing dead or broken stems; divide and replant vigorous ones when clump becomes too large, saving smaller, outside divisions and discarding overgrown centers. In cold climates, pot up divisions, keep over winter as house plants.

C. alternifolius. UMBRELLA PLANT. Narrow, firm, spreading leaves arranged like ribs of an umbrella at tops of 2-4 ft. stems. Flowers in dry greenish-brown clusters. *C. a.* 'Nanus' (or 'Nanus Compactus') dwarf form. Grows in or out of water. Effective near pools, in pots, planters; or dry stream beds or small rock gardens. Self-sows.

C. diffusus. Much like umbrella plant but with broader leaves, more lush appearance. Usually lower growing (to 12-18 in.) but can grow taller. Vigorous, invasive, best used in contained space.

C. haspan. DWARF PAPYRUS. Flowers and long thin leaves combine to make filmy brown and green clusters on slender stems about 18 in. high. Sink in pots in water gardens where slender leafless stems will not lose delicately shaped design among larger and coarser plants. Oriental gardens.

C. papyrus. PAPYRUS. Tall, graceful, dark green stems 6-10 ft. high. Clusters of green threadlike parts to 18 in. long, longer than small leaves at base of cluster. Will grow in 2 in. of water in shallow pool or can be potted and placed on bricks or inverted pot in deeper water. Protect from strong wind. Also grows well in rich, moist soil out of water. Used by flower arrangers.

CYPHOMANDRA betacea. TREE TOMATO. Evergreen or partially evergreen shrub. Zones 16, 17, 22-24; with overhead protection in 14, 15, 18-21; elsewhere indoor-outdoor or greenhouse. Fast growth to 10-12 ft. Treelike habit. Leaves 4-10 in. long, pointed oval. Summer and fall flowers small, pinkish. Winter fruit red, 2-3 in. long, egg-shaped, edible, with acid, slightly tomatolike flavor. Grow from seed like tomato. Shelter from frost, and spray to control sucking insects.

CYPRESS. See Cupressus
True cypresses are all *Cupressus;* many plants erroneously called cypress will be found under *Chamaecyparis*.

CYPRESS, BALD. See Taxodium distichum

CYPRESS, FALSE. See Chamaecyparis

CYPRESS, MONTEZUMA. See Taxodium mucronatum

CYPRESS, SUMMER. See Kochia scoparia

CYPRESS VINE. See Quamoclit

CYPRIPEDIUM. LADY SLIPPER or MOCCASIN FLOWER. See also *Paphiopedilum*. Terrestrial orchids. Native to the northern hemisphere, two to the West. Short stem with pair of leaves near ground or long stem with many leaves up stem. Flowers, on straight stems well above foliage, have pouchlike lip. All like a moist but well drained, neutral to slightly acid soil rich in humus. Plant them in a cool spot which receives filtered sun. Use in a woodland setting with ferns and native wildflowers.

C. acaule. PINK LADY SLIPPER. Native to eastern U. S. Rose-pink flower, one to stem in May and June. Two oval, 6-9-in.-long leaves flat to ground. Needs cold winters, acid, leafy soil to thrive.

C. calceolus pubescens. YELLOW LADY SLIPPER. Native to eastern U. S. Yellow flowers, 1 to 3 to a stem, have twisted sepals, bloom in May and June. Oval, hairy leaves. Height: 1-2 ft. Needs cold winters to thrive.

C. californicum. Native to boggy areas of northern California, southern Oregon. Small, greenish yellow to brown sepals, yellow petals, pouch white to pinkish, spotted with brown. Often as many as a dozen flowers to a leafy stem in summer. Plant varies in height from 12 to 18 in. Oval leaves. Plant it and let it alone. Dislikes root disturbance.

C. montanum. Grows in clumps in forests below 5,000 feet in California north to British Columbia, east to Wyoming. In summer 1 to 3 fragrant flowers with purplish brown sepals and petals, and white pouch veined purple. Grows 1-2 ft. high. Hairy 4-6-in.-long leaves. Difficult to grow outside its native regions.

C. reginae. SHOWY LADY SLIPPER. Native to eastern U. S. In June, 1 to 3 flowers with white sepals and petals, rose pink pouch. Plant 2 ft. or more high. Oval leaves. Needs cold winters to thrive.

CYRTANTHUS mackenii. Bulb. Zones 23, 24, or sheltered situations in zones 16-22, elsewhere a container plant. South African native. Foot-long, narrow (⅓-in.-wide) leaves have somewhat wavy edges. Tubular, curved, 2-in.-long, white flowers nod in loose clusters at ends of stems. Blooms in spring. There are also cream and yellow-flowered forms. Plants are actively growing throughout year; produce numerous offsets. Grow them in well drained acid soil; keep soil moist. If grown in pots, you'll need to repot them annually.

CYRTOMIUM falcatum. HOLLY FERN. Zones 16, 17, 22-24. Coarse-textured but handsome fern 2-3 ft. tall, sometimes more. Leaflets large, dark green, glossy, leathery. Takes indoor conditions well, and thrives outside in milder areas. Hardy to 25°. Take care not to plant too deeply. Forms with fringed leaflets available.

CYTISUS, GENISTA, SPARTIUM. BROOMS. Evergreen or deciduous shrubs and shrublets. *Cytisus, Genista,* and *Spartium* carry the common name broom, and all are included together here. They range in size from large spreading shrubs to low spreading shrubs for ground covers to miniatures valued in rock gardens and collections. Leaves are not important elements in brooms except for *Cytisus battandieri, C. canariensis,* and *C. racemosus.* Other species may show a few leaves, but the green or gray-green stems perform most of the functions of leaves and create the impression of evergreen plants.

Brooms are valued chiefly for their displays of sweet pea-shaped flowers, which are often fragrant.

Brooms do best in full sun and in light soil that drains fast. Most are fairly drought resistant but look better with infrequent deep watering in summer. Prune tall growers immediately after flowering to induce bushiness and reduce formation of bean-like, unsightly seed pods. Seeds of some brooms are poisonous.

Climate and soil adaptability are not clearly defined. Generally the brooms are best in cool summer areas with at least neutral soil, but several do well in the alkaline soils and heat of desert areas. Generally all brooms benefit from the addition of iron sulfate to highly alkaline soils.

In southern California brooms are host to a caterpillar (genista worm) which defoliates the plant unless checked. Spray with an insecticide containing sevin, dibrom, or diazinon when first seen.

The vigor (or weediness) of the large-growing brooms is an advantage in impoverished soil on large dry banks, along country lanes. The medium growers, beautiful in bloom, serve best as backgrounds in the small garden. The dwarf shrublets, hardiest of the lot, are valuable in rock gardens and as small area ground covers.

Cytisus battandieri. ATLAS BROOM. Deciduous. Zones 5, 6. Fast growth to 12-15 ft. high and as wide. Can be trained as a small tree. Leaves divided into 3 roundish leaflets to 3½ in. long, to 1½ in. wide, covered with silvery, silky hairs. Fragrant, clear yellow flowers in spikelike (5-in.) clusters at branch ends June-September.

C. canariensis (*Genista canariensis*). CANARY ISLAND BROOM. Evergreen. Zones 8, 9, 12-24. Damaged at 15° but recovers quickly. Many-branched, upright shrub to 6-8 ft. high, 5-6 ft. wide. Bright green leaves divided into ½-in. leaflets. Bright yellow, fragrant flowers in short clusters at ends of branches, spring and summer. The genista of florists. Grows like a weed and spreads by seedlings.

C. decumbens. PROSTRATE BROOM. Shrublet. Zones 2-6, 16, 17; performance elsewhere not known. Prostrate, creeping to 8 in. high with a 4-ft. spread. Roundish, hairy, ½-¾-in.-long leaflets. Bright yellow flowers, 1 or 3 in cluster, in May and June.

C. kewensis. KEW BROOM. Dwarf shrublet. Best in Zones 4-6; less vigorous but satisfactory in 16, 17. Low, less than 1 ft. high, spreading with trailing branches to 4 ft. or more. Creamy white (½-in.) flowers in April-May. Branches will cascade in an open pattern over a wall or steep bank. One of the best prostrate forms.

C. lydia. See *Genista lydia.*

C. multiflorus. (Often mistakenly sold as *C. albus.*) WHITE SPANISH BROOM. Zones 4-6, 15-17. Fast growth to 10 ft. with erect grooved branchlets. May be held to 4-5 ft. Leaves single, or sometimes divided into 3 roundish, ½-in. leaflets. Sprays of small (½-in.) white flowers in profusion in May.

C. praecox. WARMINSTER BROOM, MOON-LIGHT BROOM. Zones 2-9, 12-22. Compact growth with many slender stems to 3-5 ft. high and 4-6 ft. wide. A mounding mass of pale yellow to creamy white flowers in March-April in the south, April-May, north. Effective as informal screen or hedge, along drives, paths, garden steps. There is a variety, 'Hollandia', with pink flowers.

C. purgans. PROVENCE BROOM. Zones 4-6. Dense mounding growth to 3 ft. high with equal spread. Silky hairy leaves roundish, ¼-½ in. long. Fragrant chrome yellow flowers. May-July.

C. purpureus. PURPLE BROOM. Zones 2-6, 16, 17. Performance elsewhere not known. Slender spreading branches arching to 1½ ft. high, spreading to 4 ft. Roundish leaflets, ½-1 in. long, dark green above. Orchid lavender flowers scattered along stems April-May.

C. racemosus (*Genista racemosa;* often mistakenly sold as *G. fragrans*). Evergreen. Zones 7-9, 11-24. Similar in growth habit to *C. canariensis,* but with larger leaflets and longer, looser spikes of yellow, fragrant flowers in late spring. Naturalizes where adapted.

C. scoparius. SCOTCH BROOM. Zones 4-9, 14-22. This one has given all brooms a bad name. Has spread like a weed over thousands of acres of open land in northern California and the Northwest. Upright growing mass of wandlike green stems (often leafless or nearly so) may reach 10 ft. Golden yellow (¾-in.) flowers, spring and early summer.

Much less aggressive are the lower growing (5-8 ft.) more colorful forms. Of the many, these particular varieties are the most popular: 'Andreanus', brownish red and yellow flowers; 'Burkwoodii', red flowers shaded rose and touched with yellow; 'Lord Lambourne', scarlet and cream; 'Pomona', orange and apricot; 'San Francisco' and 'Stanford', red; and 'St. Mary's', white.

Genista aethnensis. MT. AETNA BROOM. Zones 4-9, 12-22. Slender, nearly leafless green stems grow to 15 ft. high. Fragrant, yellow flowers (⅓ in. long) scattered near ends of the branches in July-August.

G. canariensis. See *Cytisus canariensis.*

G. fragrans. This white-flowered species is not in the nursery trade. Plants sold under this name are *Cytisus racemosus.*

G. germanica 'Prostrata'. Zones 2-9, 11-22. Very hardy. Low growing to 1½ ft. and spreading to 3 ft. Dark green leaves, ½-¾ in. long, clothe spiny branches well. Bright yellow flowers in 2-in.-long spikes on branch tips, May-June.

G. hirsutus decumbens. Plant sold under this name is a shrublet with green branches. Zones 2-9, 11-22. To 4 in. with an 18-in. spread. Bright yellow flowers in May. Useful as ground cover in small areas. Will drape over rocks.

G. hispanica. SPANISH BROOM. Zones 2-9, 11-22. Mass of spiny stems, with ½-in.-long leaves, to 1-2 ft. high and spreading wide. Golden yellow flowers in clusters at tips of stems in May-June.

G. horrida. Low shrub. Zones 4-9, 12-22. Spiny, to 15 in. high, 30 in. wide, slow growing. Tiny gray-green leaves. Golden yellow flowers profuse in June-August.

G. lydia. (Often sold, erroneously, as *Cytisus lydia.*) Shrublet. Zones 4-6; performance elsewhere not known. To 2 ft. high, spreading. Good ground cover. Bright yellow flowers in profusion at ends of shoots, June. Sets little seed.

G. monosperma. BRIDAL VEIL BROOM. Zones 16, 17, 22-24. Upright growth to 20 ft. high, 10 ft. wide, with slender, graceful, gray-green, almost leafless branches. White fragrant flowers in late winter and spring.

G. pilosa. Zones 2-9, 11-22. Fairly fast-growing prostrate shrub, ultimately to 4 in. with 7-ft. spread. Roots take hold as they spread. Intricately branched gray-green twigs. Roundish, ¼-½-in.-long leaves. Yellow flowers in May-June.

G. racemosa. See *Cytisus racemosus.*

G. sagittalis. Zones 2-9, 11-22. Plants spread along ground. Upright, winged, bright green branchlets appear jointed. Rather rapid grower to 12 in., spreading widely. Makes sheet of golden yellow bloom, late spring and early summer.

G. sylvestris pungens (*G. dalmatica*). Zones 2-9, 11-22. Slow growth to 1 ft. high, 2 ft. wide. Small (½-in.-long) leaves on many wiry branches, the flowering branches

Climate
Zone maps
pages 8-27

very spiny. Mass of ¼-in.-long, golden yellow flowers in June.

Spartium junceum. SPANISH BROOM. Evergreen. Zones 5-9, 11-24. Grows 6-10 ft. to make dense, bushy shrub of many, green, erect, almost leafless stems. Bright yellow, fragrant, 1-in.-long flowers in clusters at branch ends bloom continuously from July to frost in north, March to August south. Flowers followed by hairy pods like flattened, 4-in. string beans.

Gaunt-looking, woody shrub, but pruning will fatten it up. Does best with little water. Takes poor, rocky soil. Has naturalized at many places in the West. Good rough bank cover with native shrubs.

In southern California, especially Zone 24, extremely subject to caterpillars in summer. By fall, they often leave plants without flowers or stems—may resprout at base in winter.

DABOECIA. See Heaths and Heathers

DAFFODIL. See Narcissus

DAFFODIL, PERUVIAN. See Hymenocallis calathina

DAHLIA. Perennial grown from tuberous roots. All Zones. Native to Mexico, Guatemala. Except for tree dahlia (*D. imperialis*) described at end of this section, dahlias are represented today exclusively by hybrids and strains, hundreds of them. Through centuries of hybridizing and selection, these bush and bedding dahlias have become tremendously diversified with numerous flower types in all colors but true blue. Sketches illustrate type based on flower form as classified by the American Dahlia Society.

Bush and bedding plant dahlias grow from 15 in. to over 6 ft. high. Taller bush forms make summer hedges, screens, fillers among shrubs; lower kinds give mass color in borders and containers. Modern dahlias, with strong stems, long-lasting blooms that face outward or upward, and substantial attractive foliage, have become useful as cut flowers.

Planting. Most dahlias are started from tubers. Plant them after frost is past and soil is warm. Full sun; light afternoon shade in hottest areas. Several weeks before planting, dig soil 1 ft. deep, work in ground bark, composted redwood sawdust, or peat moss; also add coarse sand to heavy soils.

Make holes 1 ft. deep and 3 ft. apart for most varieties; space largest kinds 4-5 ft.; smaller ones 1-2 ft. If you use fertilizer at planting time, thoroughly incorporate ¼ cup of complete fertilizer in bottom of hole, then add 4 in. of plain soil. Drive 5-ft. stake into hole, place tuber horizontally with eye pointing toward stake and 2 in. from it. Cover tuber with 3 in. of soil. Water thoroughly if no rains expected. As shoots grow, gradually fill hole with soil.

Plant seeds of tall dahlias early indoors; transplant seedlings to garden position after frosts are over. Following fall and thereafter, dig and store tubers as described below. Sow seed of dwarf dahlias in place after soil is warm; or buy and plant started seedlings from nursery. Lift dwarf dahlia tubers in climates where ground freezes in winter; elsewhere they can remain permanently in place.

Thinning, pinching. On tall-growing types, thin to strongest shoot or 2 shoots (you can make cuttings of removed shoots). When remaining shoots have 3 sets of leaves, pinch off tips just above top set; 2 side shoots develop from each pair of leaves. For large

Tip-pinch dahlias to get bushy plants; disbud if you want larger flowers.

flowers, remove all but terminal buds on side shoots. Smaller flowering dahlias such as miniatures, pompons, singles, or dwarfs, need only the first pinching.

Watering. Start watering regularly after shoots are above ground. Throughout active growth, keep soil moist to depth of 1 ft. Dahlias planted in enriched soil don't need additional food. If soil lacks nutrients, side-dress plants with fertilizer high in phosphates and potash when first flower buds appear. Avoid high-nitrogen fertilizers: they result in soft growth, weak stems, tubers liable to rot in storage. Mulch to keep down weeds, eliminate cultivating which may injure feeder roots.

Cut flowers. Pick nearly mature flowers in early morning or evening. Place cut stems immediately in 2-3 in. of hot water, let stand in gradually cooling water for several hours or overnight.

Lifting, storing. After tops turn yellow or are frosted, cut stalks to 4 in. above ground. Dig around plant 1 ft. from center, carefully pry up clump with spading fork, shake off loose soil, let clump dry in sun for several hours. From that point, follow either of two methods:

(1) Divide clumps immediately (as described under method 2, below). This saves storage space. Freshly dug tubers are easy to cut; it is easy to recognize eyes or growth buds at this time. Dust cut surfaces with sulfur to prevent rot, bury the tubers in sand, sawdust, or vermiculite, and store through winter in a cool dry place.

(2) Leave clumps intact, cover them with dry sand, sawdust, peat moss, perlite, or vermiculite; store in a cool (40° to 45°) dry place. There is less danger of shrinking with this storage method. About 2-4 weeks before planting in spring, separate tubers by cutting from the stalk with sharp knife; leave 1 in. of stalk attached to each tuber, which must have an eye or bud in order to produce a new plant. Place tubers in moist sand to encourage development of sprouts.

D. imperialis. TREE DAHLIA. Zones 4-6, 8, 9, 14-24. A 10-20-ft. multi-stemmed tree grows each year from permanent roots, produces 4-8-in. lavender, daisy-type flowers with yellow centers, at branch ends in late fall. Leaves of many leaflets. Frosts kill tops completely. Cut back to ground after frost-kill. If it bloomed longer or remained evergreen, would be valued landscape plant, but annual live-and-die cycle relegates it to tall novelty class. Seldom sold in nurseries. Grow from cuttings taken near tops of branches in fall, root in containers of moist sand kept in protected place over winter. Or dig root clump and divide in fall. Full sun or half shade. *D. excelsa, D. maxonii* are similar.

DAHLIA, TREE. See Dahlia imperialis

Decorative and cactus dahlias reach impressive sizes; many reach or exceed 1 ft. in diameter. Other kinds shown are equally good for cutting, are easier to arrange.

Climate Zone maps pages 8-27

DAIS cotinifolia. POMPON TREE. Briefly deciduous. Zones 16-24. Native to South Africa. A worthwhile flowering shrub or small tree, somewhat like crape myrtle in size and shape. Slow to 12 ft. with 10-ft. spread. Flower clusters resemble 1½-in. balls of pink shredded coconut; carried at the ends of twigs in June and July. The flowers remain after fading and are then rather unsightly. Bluish green leaves to 2½ in. long drop in sharp frosts. By nature, a multiple-trunked shrub-tree, it looks best trained to single trunk. Unusually tolerant of heat. Will stand reflected light and heat of pavement and walls.

DAISY, AFRICAN. See Arctotis, Dimorphotheca

DAISY, AFRICAN TRAILING. See Osteospermum fruticosum

DAISY, ALPINE. See Aster alpinus

DAISY, DAHLBERG. See Thymophylla

DAISY, ENGLISH. See Bellis

DAISY, GLORIOSA. See Rudbeckia hirta

DAISY, LIVINGSTON. See Dorotheanthus under Ice Plant

DAISY, PAINTED. See Chrysanthemum coccineum

DAISY, PARIS. See Chrysanthemum frutescens

DAISY, SEASIDE. See Erigeron glaucus

DAISY, SHASTA. See Chrysanthemum maximum

DAISY, SWAN RIVER. See Brachycome

DAISY, TRANSVAAL. See Gerbera

DAISY, WOODLAND. See Arnica

DAISY BUSH. See Olearia

DAISY TREE. See Montanoa

DALEA spinosa. SMOKE TREE. Deciduous. Zones 11-13. Native to desert washes below 1,500 ft. in southern California, Arizona, Baja California. The few small leaves drop early. When out of leaf, its intricate network of gray spiny branches resembles a cloud of smoke. Good show of fragrant, violet-blue flowers, April-June (flower branches make choice dry arrangements).

Useful in natural desert gardens. Seems happy at edge of irrigation. Usually grows to 12 ft., but with water in summer grows in bursts to as much as 30 ft. Easily grown from seed sown in warm weather. Sow in place or in small container and plant out.

DANCING LADY. See Oncidium varicosum rogersii

DANDELION. It's a weed in lawns and flower beds but it can also be a cultivated edible-leaf crop. Seeds sold in packets. The cultivated forms have been selected for larger and thicker leaves than on common weed form. Tie leaves together to bleach interiors and eat it like endive. Or boil thick leaves as "greens".

DAPHNE. Evergreen and deciduous shrubs. Of the many kinds, three are widely grown in the West and most of the others are choice rock garden subjects with limited distribution in the nursery trade.

Although some daphnes are easier to grow than others, all require a fast draining soil and a careful hand with summer watering. They are far more temperamental in California than in the Northwest. In California, the widely planted *D. odora* is especially susceptible to root rot. Even commercial growers are never sure of bringing a crop through to salable size. However, when a plant finds a place in the garden that is favorable, it just grows and grows.

Daphne odora: *to cut flowers or to prune, always cut to a side branch or bud.*

So give them fast drainage (plant in a raised bed if drainage can't be corrected any other way). Let the soil partially dry out between waterings.

D. blagayana. Evergreen. Zones 4-6. Spreading, almost prostrate (to 6-in. high), rooting along trailing branches. Fragrant white flowers at ends of leafy twigs from March through April. Use in rock gardens or as small-area ground cover in part shade.

D. burkwoodii. Evergreen or semi-evergreen to deciduous. Zones 4-6, 15-17. Erect, compact growth to 3-4 ft. with closely set narrow leaves and numerous small clusters of fragrant white (fading pink) flowers around the branch ends in late spring and again in late summer. Sun or light shade. Use in shrub borders, woodland edge, foundation planting.

D. b. 'Somerset'. Similar to above but larger plants (4-5 ft.) and deeper pink flowers, May-June.

D. cneorum. GARLAND DAPHNE. Evergreen. Zones 2-9, 14-17. Matting and spreading, less than 1 ft. high and 3 ft. wide. Trailing branches covered with narrow, 1-in.-long, dark green leaves. Clusters of fragrant rosy pink flowers in April and May. Choice rock garden plant; give it partial shade in warm areas, full sun in cool-summer areas. After bloom, topdress with mix of peat moss and sand to keep roots cool and induce additional rooting of trailing stems.

D. c. 'Ruby Glow'. Has larger flower clusters and deeper color than above. Repeats bloom in late summer and early fall.

D. collina. Evergreen. Zones 5, 6 with protection; as rock garden plant in 16, 17. Neat dense mound to 2 ft. high and wide. Small (2-in. long) dark green leaves, paler beneath. Fragrant deep rose flowers in clusters at branch tips in April-May. Sometimes repeats bloom in fall.

D. c. 'Neapolitana'. The variety is smaller growing, more open and spreading, and perhaps easier to grow.

D. genkwa. LILAC DAPHNE. Deciduous. Best in Zones 4-6, 16, 17. Erect open growth to 3-4 ft. high and as wide. Before leaves expand, clusters of lilac-blue, scentless flowers wreathe the branches, making foot-long blossom wands. White fruits follow the flowers. Leaves are oval, 2 in. long. Use in rock garden, shrub border. Full sun or partial shade.

D. giraldii. Deciduous. Zones 2-7, 16, 17. Spreading bushy growth to 2½ ft. high, 4-5 ft. wide. Clusters of golden yellow, lightly fragrant flowers in late May.

D. laureola. SPURGE LAUREL. Evergreen. Zones 4-6. Best in woodland plantings. Erect growth to 4 ft. high, 3 ft. wide. Glossy, dark green leaves, 2-3 in. long. Stalkless clusters of yellow-green flowers nestled among leaves are faintly fragrant, December through April.

D. mantensiana. Evergreen. Zones 4-6, 15-17. Grows slowly to 1½ ft., spreading to 3 ft. Clusters of perfumed purple flowers tip the branches in May-June and often through the summer. Densely branched and well-foliaged, it can be used in the same way as low-growing azaleas.

D. mezereum. FEBRUARY DAPHNE. Zones 2-6, 15-17. Rather gawky, stiffly twigged, erect growth to 4 ft. with roundish 2-3-in.-long, thin leaves. Should be planted in groups. Fragrant, reddish purple flowers in short stalkless clusters are carried along the branches before the leaves come out in February and continue until April. Clusters of red fruits follow (poisonous if eaten).

D. m. 'Alba'. Same as above but with white flowers, yellow fruits, and not as rangy in growth.

D. odora. WINTER DAPHNE. Evergreen. Zones 4-9, 14-24. So much loved, so prized for its pervasive, pre-spring fragrance that it continues to be widely planted in spite of its unpredictable behavior. A very neat handsome plant usually to about 4 ft. high and spreading wider; occasionally grows 8-10 ft. high. Rather narrow, 3-in.-long leaves are thick and glossy. Flowers—pink to deep red on the outside with creamy pink throats—appear in nosegay clusters at ends of branches, February-March.

Other varieties of *D. odora* are: 'Alba', plain green leaves and pure white flowers; 'Alba Marginata', leaves edged with yellow and white flowers; 'Rose Queen', larger clusters of pink flowers.

Plant *D. odora* or any of its varieties in light shade or afternoon shade. Will grow in full sun, but don't expect it to take full sun plus reflected heat from walls or paving. In summer-cool areas give it a warm, sunny location sheltered from wind. Feed once a year just after bloom. Shape plants by cutting at bloom season; cut flowering twigs back to larger branches. Cut large

D

*Climate
Zone maps
pages 8-27*

sprays back to a good bud or small shoot. Cutting to outward facing buds gives spreading plants; cutting to inside facing buds will produce erect plants.

D. o. 'Marginata'. More widely grown than the species. Leaves are edged with a band of yellow.

D. retusa. Evergreen. Zones 5, 6, 15-17. Sturdy, compact growth to 1-2 ft. high and as broad. Lilac-scented flowers in 3-inch clusters, white tinged with pink or rose, in May-June, are followed by red fruits. Combines well with dwarf rhododendrons.

DARLINGTONIA californica. CALIFORNIA PITCHER PLANT, COBRA LILY. Novelty perennial. Native to bogs in mountains of northern California and Oregon. Grow in containers in sunny spot indoors or in greenhouse. Interesting for its unusual leaves and habit of digesting insects. Plant makes clumps of 1-2-ft., tubelike, yellow-green veiny leaves, hooded at top. Hood has translucent spots. At mouth opening are 2 flared lobes, often reddish in color. Insects are lured into this leafy trap by sticky glands. Once insects are inside, downward pointing hairs prevent escape. Insects fall to base of leaf, decay, and when they are in a soluble state they become plant's protein food absorbed by the cells.

The striking flowers, nodding at ends of 2½-4-ft. stems, appear April-June. Long, slender, pale green sepals, shorter dark purple petals. Blooms followed by mahogany brown seed capsules.

Pot in live sphagnum moss; keep moist at all times. Water overhead. Dry fertilizer, saline water are harmful. Collected plants are packaged and sold in a few nurseries and specialty shops, generally from October through June.

DATURA. Evergreen shrubs. Zones 16-24. All kinds sold have tubular flowers and are known as "angel's trumpet". Flowers and seeds poisonous if eaten. Some are used in producing drugs and many have been used by primitive peoples either as medicines, narcotics, or poisons. Identification of the white-flowered species sold has been thoroughly confused. However, as far as performance in the garden is concerned, it makes little difference by which name you acquire it.

All are large shrubs that can be trained as small trees. Garden care is the same for all: Plant in a wind-sheltered location. Expect frost damage and unattractive winter appearance. Prune in early spring after last frost. Cut back branchlets to 1 or 2 buds. (Tubbed plants can be wintered indoors with a little light and very little water.)

Large of leaf and flower, they are dominating shrubs and should be brought into the garden with that in mind. The white-flowered angel's trumpet is quite a plant in the moonlight.

D. arborea. Plants usually offered under this name are either one of the two white-flowered species described below. The true *D. arborea* has less impressive flowers.

D. candida. Native to Peru. Fast and rank growing with soft pulpy growth to 10-15 ft. (6 ft. or more in one season). Dull green large leaves in the 8-12-in. range. The heavy white trumpets, single or double, 8 in. or more long, are fragrant especially at night. They appear in summer and fall,

often as late as November or December in warm, sheltered gardens.

D. sanguinea. Native to Peru. Fast growing to 12-15 ft. Leaves bright green to 8 in. long. Trumpets orange-red with yellow veinings, about 10 in. long, hang straight down bell-fashion from new growth.

D. suaveolens. Native to Brazil. Similar to *D. candida,* except leaves and flowers are somewhat larger and flowers less fragrant. Some observers see it as bushier and wider spreading. As with *D. candida* the white flowers are veined with green.

DAUBENTONIA tripetii. SCARLET WISTERIA TREE. Deciduous shrub or small tree. Zones 8, 9, 12-16, 18-23. Native to Argentina. Neither a wisteria nor a tree, and the flower color is more burnt orange than scarlet. Fast growing to 8-10 ft. high and 6-8 ft. wide, with fernlike leaves. Showy, drooping clusters of yellow and orange-red, sweet pea-shaped flowers from May through summer. The pods that follow are 4-angled or winged. Remove pods as they form to prolong flowering.

Give full sun and the warmest spot in the garden. Prune severely in early spring to thin and shorten side branches to stubs.

Not a long-lived plant and appears a little out of place with glossy-leafed, refined plants, but valued for exciting color and quick effects. Most often seen trained into a flat-topped standard tree on a 6-ft. trunk. Can be grown in containers, blooming quite heavily in 12-in. pots.

DAVALLIA trichomanoides. SQUIRREL'S FOOT FERN. Outdoors in Zones 17, 23, 24; elsewhere an indoor or greenhouse plant. Very finely divided fronds to 12 in. long, 6 in. wide, rise from light reddish brown, furry rhizomes (like squirrel's feet) that creep over the soil surface. Can be used in mild-winter areas (hardy to 30°) as a small-scale ground cover in partly shaded areas. Best use in any climate is as a hanging basket plant. Use light, fast-draining soil mix. Feed occasionally. (For a similar fern, see *Humata.*)

DAVIDIA involucrata. DOVE TREE. Deciduous. Zones 4-9, 14-21. Native to China. Tree to 30 feet in Pacific Northwest (higher in California), with rounded crown and strong branching pattern. Has a clean look in and out of leaf. When it flowers in May

Dove tree draws attention when it blooms. White contrasts nicely with vivid green.

the general effect is that of white doves resting among green leaves—or as some say, like handkerchiefs drying on the branches.

Leaves are vivid green, 3-6 in. long, roundish to heart-shaped. The small, clustered, red-anthered flowers are carried between two large, unequal, white or creamy white bracts; one 6 in. long, the other about 4 in. Fruits brown, about the size of a golf ball, hang on tree well into winter.

In Zones 7-9, 14, 18-21, give it partial or afternoon shade. Plant it by itself; it should not compete with other flowering trees. Nice in front of dark conifers where vivid green and white stand out.

DAWN REDWOOD. See Metasequoia

DAYLILY. See Hemerocallis

DEER BRUSH. See Ceanothus integerrimus

DELOSPERMA. See Ice Plant

DELPHINIUM. Perennials, biennials, annuals. Most people associate delphiniums with blue flowers, but the color range also includes shades of red, pink, lavender, purple, white, and yellow. Leaves are lobed or fanlike, variously cut and divided. Taller hybrids offer rich colors in elegant spirelike form. Both perennial and annual kinds are effective in borders, and make good cut flowers. Lower-growing kinds serve well as container plants.

All kinds are easy to grow from seed. Sow annual (larkspur) seed in place in fall or spring; fall best except in heavy, slow draining soils. Sow fresh seed of perennial delphinium in flats of light soil mix in July-August in mild-winter areas; set out transplants in October for bloom in late spring and early summer. (In mild-winter climates, most perennial forms are short-lived, often treated as annuals.) In cold climates, refrigerate summer-harvested seed in airtight containers until time to sow. Sow seed in March-April, set out transplants in June-July for first bloom by September (and more bloom the following summer).

Delphiniums need full sun, rich porous soil, regular watering, and fertilizing. Improve poor or heavy soils by blending in soil conditioners. Add lime to strongly acid soils. Work a small handful of bonemeal or superphosphate into bottom of each hole before setting out plant. Be careful not to cover root crown.

When new shoots of perennial forms develop in spring, remove all but 2 or 3 strongest, and apply complete fertilizer alongside plants. Bait for slugs and snails. Stake flower stalks early. After bloom, cut back flower spikes, leaving foliage at bottom; after new shoots are several inches high, cut old stalks to ground; fertilize to encourage good second bloom in late summer, early fall.

D. ajacis. LARKSPUR, ANNUAL DELPHINIUM. Native to southern Europe. Upright, 1-5 ft. tall, with deeply cut leaves, spikes densely set with 1-1½-in.-wide flowers (most are double) in white and shades of blue, lilac, pink, rose, salmon, carmine, and blue-and-white bicolor. Best bloom in cooler spring and early summer months. Giant Imperial strain, many 4-5-ft. vertical stalks compactly placed. Regal strain, 4-5 ft., base-branching stems, large flowers similar to

Climate
Zone maps
pages 8-27

perennial delphiniums, in thick spikes. Super Imperial strain, base-branching; large flowers in 18-in., cone-shaped spikes. Steeplechase, base-branching, biggest double flowers, 4-5-ft. spikes; heat-resistant.

D. cardinale. SCARLET LARKSPUR. Perennial. Zones 14-24. Native to California coastal mountains, Monterey County south. Erect stems grow 3-6 ft. from deep, thick, woody roots. Leaves 3-9-in. wide, with deep narrow lobes. Flowers 1 in. across, with scarlet calyx and spur and yellow, scarlet-tipped petals; May-June bloom. Sow seed early for first-year bloom.

D. cheilanthum. Sturdy, bushy perennial. Zones 1-9, 14-24. To 3-4 ft.; deeply cut leaves; short-stemmed, airy flower clusters. Varieties: 'Belladonna', light blue, 'Bellamosum', dark blue, 'Cliveden Beauty', deep turquoise blue. All have flowers 1½-2-in. across, are longer lived than tall hybrids (see below).

Connecticut Yankee strain, extremely vigorous, base-branching, 2½-3 ft. tall; has larger flowers than 3 foregoing varieties in shades of blue, lilac, lavender, purple, rarely white.

D. elatum. CANDLE DELPHINIUM, CANDLE LARKSPUR. Perennial. Zones 1-9, 14-24. This 3-6-ft. Siberian species, with small dark or dull purple flowers, together with *D. cheilanthum* and others, is a parent of modern tall-growing delphinium strains such as the spectacular Pacific strain.

Pacific strain delphinium hybrids (also called Giant Pacific, Pacific Hybrids, and Pacific Coast hybrids) grow up to 8 ft., come in selected color series such as 'Summer Skies', light blue; 'Blue Bird', medium blue; 'Blue Jay', medium to dark blue; 'Galahad', clear white with white bee center; 'Percival', white and black bee.

Other series have flowers in shades of lilac pink to deep raspberry rose, clear lilac, lavender, royal purple, and darkest violet. The Wrexham strain, tall growing with large spikes, developed in England.

D. grandiflorum (*D. chinense*). CHINESE or BOUQUET DELPHINIUM. Short-lived perennial treated as biennial or annual. Bushy, branching, 1-1½ ft. Single, 1-in. flowers in loose, branching sprays. Varieties: 'Azure Fairy', light blue; 'Blue Butterfly', bright blue; 'Blue Mirror', deep gentian blue.

D. nudicaule. SCARLET LARKSPUR. Perennial. Zones 5-7, 14-24. Native of northern California, southwestern Oregon. Slender plant 1-3 ft. Leaves long-stalked, mostly basal, broadly divided. Flowers few, long-spurred, red. Sun or half shade; best in woodland situation.

DENDROBIUM. Epiphytic orchid. Native to east and southeast Asia. Distributed over a wide range of climates; the many species differ in cultural needs.

D. nobile hybrids are best for the novice. They vary from white through pink to rosy purple in color. Flowers grow in clusters all along well-ripened stems. Well-grown plants may have hundreds of 3-in. flowers. Grow under same conditions as cattleyas until new growths mature in the fall. Then move them into a cool, bright greenhouse with little water and no feeding. Resume normal cattleya treatment after flower buds form. Splendid orchids for the greenhouse,

they seldom get enough light to bloom well in living rooms or sun porches.

DENDROCALAMUS. See Bamboo

DENDROMECON. BUSH POPPY. Evergreen shrubs. Zones 5-8, 14-24. Has been grown as south-wall shrub in Zone 5. Both species give showy display of bright yellow, 2-in.-wide, poppylike flowers. Thrive in dry, well drained soil. Use on banks, roadsides, with other native shrubs.

D. harfordii. ISLAND BUSH POPPY. Native to Santa Cruz and Santa Rosa Islands off coast of southern California. Rounded or spreading large shrub or small tree to 20 ft. Leaves deep green, to 3 in. long, half as wide. Free flowering April-July and scattered bloom throughout year. Prune to thin or shape after bloom.

D. rigida. BUSH POPPY. Native to dry chaparral in lower elevations in California. Untidy in native state. Freely branched shrub 2-8 ft. with shreddy, yellowish gray or white bark. Thick, veiny, gray-green leaves 1-4 in. long. Flowers March-June. Prune back to 2 ft. after flowering.

DESERT CANDLE. See Eremurus

DESERT GUM. See Eucalyptus rudis

DEUTZIA. Deciduous flowering shrubs. Zones 1-11, 14-17. They are best used among evergreens where they can make a show when in flower, blend back with other greenery during the rest of the year. Their May-flowering coincides with that of late spring bulbs—tulips and Dutch iris.

Plant in sun or light shade. Prune after flowering. With low or medium-growing kinds, cut to the ground some of the oldest stems every other year. Prune tall-growing kinds severely by cutting back wood that has flowered. Cut to outward-facing side branches.

D. gracilis. SLENDER DEUTZIA. Native to Japan. To 3 ft. or less. Many slender stems arch gracefully to 3 ft. and spread to 5 ft. Bright green, 2½-in.-long leaves with sharply toothed edges. Clusters of snowy white flowers cover branches.

D. lemoinei. A hybrid. Neat, compact shrub to 6 ft. high. Leaves with finely toothed edges, 1-4 in. long. White flowers, tinged pinkish or purplish outside, in large broad clusters.

D. rosea. Hybrid. Low growing shrub (to 3-4 ft.), with finely-toothed, 1-3-in.-long leaves. Flowers pinkish outside, white inside, in short clusters.

D. scabra. Native to Japan, China. This and its varieties are tall robust shrubs 7-10 ft. Leaves oval, 3 in. long, dull green, roughish to touch, with scallop-toothed edges. May-June flowers white or pinkish in narrow, upright clusters. *D. s.* 'Candidissima' has pure white, double flowers. *D. s.* 'Pride of Rochester', best known, bears large clusters of small, double, frilled flowers, rosy purple outside.

DEVIL'S WALKING STICK. See Aralia spinosa

DEVIL TREE, INDIA. See Rauwolfia samarensis

DEVILWOOD. See Osmanthus

DEWDROP, GOLDEN. See Duranta erecta

DIANELLA tasmanica. Perennial. Zones 8, 9, 14-24. Fibrous-rooted plant with sturdy, swordlike leaves to 4-5 ft. Small, pale blue, summer-blooming flowers in loose clusters on straight, slender stalks, followed by glistening turquoise blue berries lasting 2 or more months. Grow in partial shade, or full sun along coast. Provide rich, porous soil, lots of water, routine feeding. Groom by removing shabby leaves.

DIANTHUS. PINK. Perennials, biennials, annuals. All Zones. Over 300 species, many with high garden value, and an extremely large number of hybrids. Most kinds form attractive evergreen mats or tufts of grass-like green, gray-green, blue-green, or blue-gray leaves. Single or double flowers in white and shades of pink, rose, red, yellow, and orange, bloom in spring or summer, sometimes until frost. Many have rich spicy fragrance.

Among dianthus are appealing border favorites such as cottage pink and sweet William, indispensable cut flowers such as carnation or clove pink, and rock garden miniatures.

All kinds of dianthus thrive in full sun (light afternoon shade in hot areas), and in light, fast draining soil. Carnations, sweet William, and cottage pinks need a fairly rich soil; rock garden or alpine types require a gritty growing medium, with added lime if soil is acid. Avoid overwatering. Shear off faded blooms. Sow seed of annual kinds in flats or directly in the garden. Propagate perennial kinds by cuttings made from tips of growing shoots, or by division, layers, or seed.

Carnations and sweet William subject to rust and fusarium wilt. Control rust by spraying foliage weekly with zineb. Remove and destroy plants infected with wilt. Replant only in clean or sterilized soil. Take cuttings of carnations only from disease-free plants.

D. 'Allwoodii'. Perennial. A group of hybrids developed in England between *D. plumarius* and *D. caryophyllus*. Plants 4-24 in. tall, with compact tufts of firm, broad, somewhat blue-gray leaves. Single or double flowers, some with fringed petals, in many colors. Allwood hybrids crossed with alpine species produced a dwarf plant, Allwoodii Alpinus, available in many colors.

D. barbatus. SWEET WILLIAM. Vigorous biennial often grown as an annual. Sturdy stems 10-30 in. high; leaves are flat, light to dark green, 1½-3 in. long. Dense clusters of white, pink, rose, red, purplish, or bi-colored flowers about ½ in. across, set among leafy bracts; not very fragrant. Sow seed in late spring for bloom next year. Available in dwarf forms (8-10 in. tall), also in taller named varieties such as 'Copper Red', 'Giant White', 'Newport Pink', and 'Red Monarch'.

D. 'Beatrix'. Perennial. A free-blooming plant to 8 in. high and 2 ft. wide. Clusters of double salmon pink flowers. Bright green, fairly wide leaves.

D. caryophyllus. CARNATION, CLOVE PINK. Perennial. There are two distinct categories of carnations: the florist and border types. Both have double flowers, bluish green leaves, and branching, leafy stems often becoming woody at the base.

Florist carnations. Grown commercially in greenhouses, outdoors in gardens in mild-winter areas. Greenhouse-grown plants reach 4 ft., have fragrant flowers 3 in. wide in many colors—white, pink and red shades, orange, purple, yellow, and variegated. For large flowers, leave only terminal bloom on each stem, pinch out all other buds down to fifth joint, below which new flowering stems will develop. Stake to prevent sprawling.

Florist's carnations come in a wide variety of colors and markings, need staking.

Start with strong cuttings taken from most vigorous plants of selected named varieties. Sturdy plants conceal supports, look quite tidy.

Miniature florist carnations, with smaller (1½-in.-wide) blooms, available in named varieties, including 'Elegance', pink with white edging; 'White Elegance'; 'Exquisite', purple with silver fringe. Remove only terminal bud on miniature carnations; encourage low branching by pinching stems when young.

Border carnations. Bushier, more compact than florist type, 12-14 in. high. Flowers 2-2½ in. wide, fragrant, borne in profusion. Enfant de Nice strain has blooms in red, rose, salmon, white. Dwarf Fragrance mixture comes in similar colors. Effective as shrub border edgings, in mixed flower borders, and in containers.

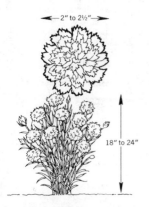

Border carnations are lower, bushier, less sprawling than the florist's type.

D. chinensis. CHINESE PINK, RAINBOW PINK. Biennial or short-lived perennial; most varieties grown as annuals. Erect, 6-30 in. high, stems branching only at top. Stem leaves narrow, 1-3 in. long, ½ in. wide, hairy on margins. Basal leaves usually gone by flowering time. Flowers about 1 in. across, rose-lilac with deeper colored eye, lack fragrance. 'Laciniatus', double flowers with petals cut and fringed; Gaiety, a strain derived from 'Laciniatus', has brightly colored blooms with fringed, twisted petals, is extremely vigorous, free-blooming, but not fragrant. Effective edging, for low massed bedding. 'Heddewigii', the fringed pink, has large, single or double flowers borne individually in loose clusters on 1-ft. stems.

You can buy seed of mixed annual pinks (some actually may be biennials or perennials). Peppermint Pinks and Fordhook Favorites are two such blends offered by seedhouses. The kinds in such blends mostly belong to *D. chinensis*. Sow directly on the ground in spring, full sun, for summer bloom. Plants grow 8-28 in. high, have single and semi-double flowers, 1-2 in. wide, in white, pink, red, lavender, purple, and two-color combinations. Petals on some are deeply fringed, on others are smooth-edged. Some flowers have intricately marked eyes. Pick off faded flowers with their bases to prolong bloom.

D. deltoides. MAIDEN PINK. Hardy perennial forming loose mats. Flowering stems 8-12 in. high with short leaves. Flowers about ¾ in. across, borne at end of forked stems; petals sharp-toothed, light or dark rose to purple or white, spotted with lighter colors. Blooms in summer, sometimes again in fall. In time makes a rough, light green ground cover.

D. graniticus. Hardy perennial with loose, spreading habit similar to preceding species, but doesn't grow as vigorously. Flowers reddish purple, about ½ in. across, 1 to a few at top of stem.

D. gratianopolitanus (*D. caesius*). CHEDDAR PINK. Perennial. Neat, compact mounds of blue-gray foliage on weak, branching stems up to 12 in. long. Flowering stems erect, 3-12 in. high. Very fragrant pink blooms with toothed petals. May-June.

D. 'Heddensis'. Hybrid between *D. chinensis* and its variety 'Heddewigii'. Single 2-in.-wide flowers on 16-in. stems. Treated as an annual.

D. 'Little Joe'. Perennial. An irresistible little plant forming clump of deep blue-gray foliage 4-6 in. high and about 6 in. across. Crimson-red single flowers bloom from May to November if dead blooms are removed. Especially effective with rock garden campanulas.

D. 'Mrs. Dina Weller'. Perennial. Compact, growing to 6 in., profusely covered in May and June with single lavender-pink flowers with deeper colored centers.

D. neglectus. ROCK PINK. Perennial. One of the smallest of the miniature dianthus. Sometimes considered merely a variety of *D. glacialis,* another rock pink, but is much stronger and more permanent in the garden. Narrow green leaves 1-2 in. long form a grassy tuft only a few inches in diameter. Single flowers on 6-in. stems, brilliant crimson-pink with lighter eye, buff-colored on back, to 1 in. across.

D. noeanus. Perennial. Mounding rock garden plant, 6-10 in. high, distinctive with its stiffish, needle-pointed leaves 1 in. or less long. Flowers white, fragrant, about ¾ in. across, with deeply fringed petals. Summer bloom.

D. plumarius. COTTAGE PINK. Perennial. Charming almost legendary plant, cultivated for hundreds of years, used in developing many hybrids. Typically has loosely matted, gray-green foliage. Flowering stems 10-18 in. tall; flowers spicily fragrant, single or double, with petals more or less fringed, rose, pink, or white with dark centers. Blooms from June to October. Indispensable edging for borders, or peony or rose beds. Perfect in small arrangements and old-fashioned bouquets.

D. 'Rose Bowl'. Perennial. Gray-green, very narrow leaves form a tight mat 2-3 in. high. Richly fragrant, cerise-rose flowers 1 in. across on 6-in. stems. Blooms almost continuously if spent blooms are removed regularly.

D. superbus. Grown as a biennial. Reseeds. Stems to 18 in., with few green leaves, 2½ in. or less long, ⅜ in. wide. Flowers in clusters of 2-12, showy, very fragrant, pink, rose, and white, to 2 in. across, with petals deeply cut. Dainty in summer bouquets.

D. 'Tiny Rubies'. Perennial. Tufts of gray foliage to 3 in. high, spreading to 4 in. Small, double, fragrant, ruby red flowers in early summer. This and other dwarf kinds of dianthus are among the longest lived and most attractive rock garden subjects and small-scale ground covers, with fresh-looking foliage at all seasons.

D. 'Wallace Red'. Perennial. Blue-gray foliage in a 10-in. mound topped with double, crimson-red flowers. Blooms from April to November in mild climates.

DIASCIA barberae. TWINSPUR. Annual. Native to South Africa. Oval leaves to 1½ in. long. Flowers ½ in. wide, 2 prominent spurs on back; rich salmon or coral-pink with yellow, green-dotted throat. Flowers in spikelike clusters at ends of slender 6-12-in. stems. Sow seed in place thickly in full sun, or partial shade where summers are hot. Later thin seedlings to 6-8 in. apart. Useful in rock gardens, low borders, containers; combine with ageratum, lobelia, sweet alyssum.

DICENTRA. BLEEDING HEART. Perennials. Zones 1-9, 14-24. Short-lived in mild-winter areas. Graceful, divided, fernlike foliage. Dainty flowers, usually heart-shaped, pink, rose, or white on leafless stems. Most kinds need shade, combine handsomely with ferns, begonias, primroses, fuchsias, bergenias, hellebores. In general, dicentras need rich, light, moist, porous soil. Never let water stand around roots. Since foliage dies down in winter, mark clumps to avoid digging into roots in dormant season.

D. chrysantha. GOLDEN EARDROPS. Native to inner Coast Ranges and Sierra Nevada foothills of California. Erect perennial with sparse, blue-gray, divided leaves on stout hollow stems 4-5 ft. high. Flowers golden yellow, short-spurred, held upright in large clusters. Requires warmth, good drainage, not-too-rich soil. Has a deep tap root, needs little water during flowering in spring and summer. Seed available from wildflower specialists.

Climate Zone maps pages 8-27

D. eximia. FRINGED BLEEDING HEART. Native of northeastern U. S. Forms tidy, non-spreading clumps 12-18 in. high. Leaves blue-gray, at base of plant, more finely divided than those of Western bleeding heart. Flowers deep rose-pink with short, rounded spurs, bloom May-August. Cut back in July or August for second growth and sometimes repeat bloom. Var. 'Alba' has white flowers.

Several hybrids with *D. eximia* as one parent: 'Bountiful', dark blue-green foliage, fuchsia red flowers; 'Clay's Variety', vivid pink flowers, blue-green foliage; 'Debutante', blush pink flowers, silver green foliage.

D. formosa. WESTERN BLEEDING HEART. Native to moist woods along Pacific Coast. Leafless flower stalks 8-18 in. high, with clusters of pendulous pale or deep rose flowers on reddish stems from April-June. Blue-green foliage. Var. 'Sweetheart', beautiful white flowers, light green leaves, blooms May-October. *D. f. oregana*, native of Siskiyou Mountains in southern Oregon and northern California, grows about 8 in. high, has translucent blue-green leaves, cream-colored flowers with rosy-tipped petals.

D. spectabilis. COMMON BLEEDING HEART. Native of Japan. An old garden favorite, showiest of the bleeding hearts. Leafy-stemmed plants 2-3 ft. high. Leaves soft green, largest of all dicentras. Rose-pink, pendulous 1-in. or more long, heart-shaped flowers, with white petals protruding, borne on one side of arching stems, bloom in late spring. Beautiful with maidenhair ferns and in arrangements with tulips and lilacs. In Southwest, can sometimes establish bleeding heart permanently in cool moist spot, in foothill canyons, but usual practice is to plant or pot up new roots each year, and discard plants in early summer after blooming.

DICHONDRA. See Lawn Chapter

DICKSONIA. Tree ferns. Hardy, slow growing, from southern hemisphere. See Ferns for culture.

D. antarctica. TASMANIAN TREE FERN. Zones 8, 9, 14-17, 19-24. Native to southeastern Australia, Tasmania. Hardiest of the tree ferns; well established plants tolerate 20°. Thick, red-brown, fuzzy trunks grow slowly to 15 ft. Out from top of trunk grow many arching 3-6-ft. fronds; mature fronds are darker green than either Hawaiian tree fern (*Cibotium*) or Australian tree fern (*Alsophila*). Not a plant for quick effects, but begins to make good display after 2-3 years.

D. squarrosa. Zones 17, 23, 24. Native to New Zealand. Slender, dark trunk to eventual 20 ft., but slow. Flat crown of 8 ft.-long, stiff, leathery fronds. Much less frequently grown than *D. antarctica*.

DICTAMNUS albus. GAS PLANT, FRAXINELLA. Perennial. Zones 1-9. Sturdy, long-lived, extremely permanent in colder climates. Once established, needs little care. Forms clump 2½-4 ft. high. Strong, lemony odor when rubbed or brushed against. Attractive, glossy, olive green leaves with 9-11 leaflets 1-3 in. long. Spikelike clusters of white flowers about 1 in. long (prominent greenish stamens). June-July. There are varieties with pink and rosy purple flowers and darker green leaves, growing taller and more robust than the species.

Effective in borders; combine white flowered kind with yellow daylily, Siberian iris, taller campanulas. Good cut flower. Plant in sun or part shade in good soil. Divide infrequently; divisions take 2-3 years before making a show. Propagate from seed sown in fall or spring. or from root cuttings in spring. The common name, gas plant, derives from this phenomenon: if a lighted match is held near the flowers on a warm, still evening, a volatile oil exuded from glands on that part of the plant will ignite and burn briefly.

DIDISCUS caeruleus. See Trachymene

DIEFFENBACHIA. DUMB CANE. Evergreen indoor foliage plant (you can move it into a sheltered patio or lanai in summer). Striking variegated leaves. Colors vary from dark green to yellow-green and chartreuse, with variegations in white or pale cream. Small plants generally have single stems; older plant may develop multiple stems. Common name reflects fact that the acrid sap will burn mouth and throat, and may paralyze vocal cords.

Give ample north light; turn occasionally, and water when soil surface feels dry. If a plant gets leggy, air-layer it or root cuttings in water. Repot when roots begin pushing plant up in pot. Once repotted, plant usually sends out new basal shoots. Potting soil should drain freely. Feed bimonthly in spring and summer with half-strength liquid fertilizer.

D. amoena. To 6 ft. or higher. Broad, dark green, 18-in.-long leaves marked with narrow, white, slanting stripes on either side of midrib.

D. 'Exotica'. More compact and smaller leaves than others. Leaves have dull green edges and much creamy white variegation. Midrib is creamy white.

D. picta. To 6 ft. or higher. Wide, oval green leaves, 10 in. or more in length, have greenish white dots and patches.

D. p. 'Rudolph Roehrs'. To 6 ft., with 10-in. leaves of pale chartreuse, blotched with ivory and edged with green.

D. p. 'Superba'. Foliage thicker and slightly more durable than species; more creamy white dots and patches.

DIERAMA. FAIRY WAND. Corm. Zones 4-24. Native to South Africa. Swordlike 2-ft. leaves; slender, tough, arching stems 4-7 ft. tall, topped with pendulous, bell-shaped, mauve, purple, or white flowers. Effective against a background of dark green shrubs or at edge of a pool where graceful form can be displayed. Plant in sun, moist soil. When dividing clumps, include several corms in each division.

D. pendula. Flowers white, lavender-pink, or mauve, 1 in. long, March or April.

D. pulcherrima. Leaves very stiff. Flowers bright purple to almost white, 1½ in. long, May, June.

DIGITALIS. FOXGLOVE. Biennials or perennials. All Zones. Erect plants 2-8 ft. high with tubular flowers shaped like fingers of a glove, in purple, yellow, white, pastels. Bloom May-September. Hairy, gray-green leaves grow in clumps at base of plant. Use foxgloves for a vertical display among shrubs, or with ferns, taller campanulas, meadow rue. Hummingbirds like foxglove blooms.

Plant in full or partial shade in rich, moist soil. Set out plants in fall for bloom following spring, summer. Sow seed in spring. Bait for snails, slugs. After first flowering cut main spike; side shoots develop, bloom until September. Plants self-sow freely.

D. ferruginea. RUSTY FOXGLOVE. Biennial or perennial with very leafy stems to 6 ft. Leaves deeply veined. Flowers ¾-1¼ in. long, yellowish, netted with rusty red, in long dense spikes.

D. grandiflora (*D. ambigua*). YELLOW FOXGLOVE. Biennial or perennial. Hairy leafed plant 2-3 ft. high. Toothed leaves wrap around stem. Large flowers, 2-3 in. long, yellowish marked with brown.

D. laevigata. Perennial. To 2-3 ft. Flowers ¾-1¼ in. long, yellow, marked with brown-purple, in long, loose spikes.

D. lutea. STRAW FOXGLOVE. Biennial or perennial, 2-3 ft. high. Flowers ¾ in. long, numerous, yellow to white.

D. purpurea. COMMON FOXGLOVE. Biennial, sometimes perennial. Naturalizes in shaded places. Variable, appears in many garden forms. Bold, erect, to 4 ft. or more high. Clumps of large, rough, woolly, light green leaves; stem leaves short-stalked, becoming smaller toward top of plant. Flowers 2-3 in. long, pendulous, purple, spotted

Tall spikes of common foxglove make their show in late spring, in shady places.

on lower, paler side, borne in one-sided, 1-2-ft.-long spike. Variety 'Gloxiniaeflora' more robust, with longer spikes, more wide-open, strongly spotted flowers. The following plants are closely related to *D. purpurea*: *D.* 'Isabellina', yellow flowers; and *D.* 'Lutzii', hybrid group with flowers in shades of pink, crimson.

DILL. See Anethum graveolens

DIMORPHOTHECA. CAPE MARIGOLD, AFRICAN DAISY. Annual. Gay, free-blooming, daisy-flowered plants, unsurpassed for winter and spring color in dry warm-winter areas. Not as well adapted in cool, moist coastal climate. Broadcast seed in late summer or early fall where plants are to grow. Best in light soil; moderate watering. Needs full sun; flowers close when shaded, during heavy overcast, and at night. Use in broad masses as ground cover, in borders, parking strips, along rural roadsides, as filler among low shrubs.

Climate
Zone maps
pages 8-27

D. barberiae. See Osteospermum

D. ecklonis. See Osteospermum

D. fruticosa. See Osteospermum

D. pluvialis (*D. annua*). Branched stems 4-16 in. high. Leaves to 3½ in. long, 1 in. wide, coarsely toothed. Flower heads 1-2 in. across; rays white above, violet or purple beneath; yellow center. Variety 'Ringens', 6-8 in. high, has large pure white flower heads with blue ring around center. Variety 'Glistening White', dwarf form, flower heads 4 in. across, is especially desirable.

D. sinuata. (Usually sold as *D.* 'Aurantiaca'.) Best known of the annual African daisies. Plants 4-12 in. high. Flower heads 1½ in. across, with orange-yellow rays, sometimes deep violet at base, yellow center. Hybrids between this species and *D. pluvialis* in white and shades of yellow, orange, apricot, salmon, often with contrasting dark centers.

DIOON. Cycads. In general, resemble *Cycas revoluta* and take same culture. Dioons are more tender and less frequently used.

D. edule. Zones 13, 17, 19-24. Very slow. Eventually forms cylindrical trunk 6-10 in. wide, 3 ft. high. Leaves spreading, slightly arching, 3-5 ft. long, made of many leaflets toothed at tip or smooth-edged. Leaves dusty blue-green, soft, feathery on young plants; darker green, more rigid, hard, shiny on mature plants.

D. spinulosum. Zones 21-24. Slow growth to 12 ft. Leaves to 5 ft. long, with up to 100 narrow, spine-toothed, dark green 6-8-in.-long leaflets. Protect from frosts.

DIOSMA. See Coleonema

DIOSPYROS. See Persimmon

DIPLACUS. SHRUBBY MONKEY FLOWER. Shrubby perennial or evergreen shrub or shrublet. All native to California. Zones 7-9, 14-24. Erect plants 1-4 ft. high, branching from base. When well grown, make excellent garden plants, blooming freely over a long period. Glossy leaves, usually dark green, often sticky. Tubular flowers, 1-3 in. long; upper lip has 2 lobes, lower lip has 3 spreading lobes. Wide color range, from cream through yellow and orange to red.

Use in sunny borders with ceanothus, lupine, native penstemon. Sun, well drained soil. Water hybrid types once a week in summer. Species can survive with very little summer water. Prune after first flowering; will bloom again in fall. Also prune in spring before new growth starts. Sow seed in fall for bloom following summer. Plants reseed. Make cuttings of desirable plants; not true from seed.

D. grandiflorus. PLUMAS MONKEY FLOWER. Large, buff-colored flowers; often called azalea-flowered diplacus.

D. longiflorus. MONKEY FLOWER. Erect, much branched; flowers vary from cream to orange-yellow. *D. l. rutilis* has velvety deep red flowers. McMinn Hybrids have flowers in cream, yellow, orange, buff, rose, pink, salmon, chamois, red, mahogany.

DIPLADENIA. See Mandevilla

DIPLOPAPPUS filifolius (*Aster fruticosus*). SHRUB ASTER. Evergreen shrub. Zones 8, 9, 14-24. Native of South Africa. Bushy, densely branched, 2-4 ft. high, 3 ft. wide.

Leaves narrow, dark green, ½-¾ in. long. Flowers lavender, 1 in. across, profuse from April to June. Good in sunny, dry locations. Prune after bloom.

DISTICTIS. Evergreen vines. Zones 16, 22-24. Climb by tendrils and have trumpet-shaped flowers. To 20-30 ft. tall. Hardy to 24°. Sun or part shade.

D. laxiflora (*D. lactiflora, D. cinerea*). VANILLA TRUMPET VINE. Native to Mexico. More restrained than most trumpet vines and requires less pruning. Leaves, with 2-3 deep green, oblong (2½-in.-long) leaflets, make attractive pattern all year. The 3½-in.-long, vanilla-scented trumpets, at first violet, fading to lavender and white, appear in generous clusters throughout the warmer months, sometimes giving 8 months of bloom.

D. 'Rivers'. (Sometimes labeled *D. riversii*.) ROYAL TRUMPET VINE. Plants sold under this name have larger leaves and flowers than the above. Much more vigorous with substantial glossy, deep green leaves giving it a better winter appearance. Purple trumpets (to 5 in.) marked orange inside.

DISTYLIUM racemosum. Evergreen shrub. Zones 15-24; not tested but seems worth trying in Zones 4-9, 11-14. Native to Japan where it's a tree to 80 ft. Introduced to Western gardens in 1940's, became commercially available in 1960's.

Admired for beauty of glossy leaves, 3-in.-long, leathery, dark green, resembling Japanese privet. Slow growing, it is usually seen here as a dense clipped screen or an espaliered wall plant. Tiny flowers consisting principally of dark, dull red anthers, appear in clusters March-April. A variegated form—*D. r.* 'Variegatum'—has leaves edged and splashed with white.

DITTANY, CRETE. See Amaracus

DIZYGOTHECA elegantissima. (Often sold as *Aralia elegantissima*.) THREADLEAF FALSE ARALIA. House plant (juvenile stage); evergreen garden shrub (mature form) for Zones 16, 17, 22-24. Leaves on juvenile plants are lacy—divided fanwise into very narrow (⅜-in.), 4-9-in.-long leaflets with notched edges—dark shiny green above, reddish beneath. As plants mature, leaves become bigger with coarsely notched leaflets to 12 in. long and 3 in. wide.

As house plant, give it ample light but no direct sunshine. Fast-draining, moisture-retentive soil mix (water-logged or dry soil will make leaves drop). Feed monthly. Subject to pests in dry atmosphere.

In mild climates, plant in sheltered areas. Can become 5-6-ft. shrub or even small tree with 10-12-ft. spread. As single plant, makes lacy pattern against a wall. Attractive seen through translucent glass or plastic panel.

DODECATHEON. SHOOTING STAR. Perennial. Hardiness varies with species. Mostly native to West. The spring flowers somewhat like a small cyclamen, few to many in a cluster on a leafless stem. Colors of the many species range from white to pink, lavender, or magenta. Pale green leaves in basal rosettes dry up in summer heat. Needs porous, rich, well drained soil, ample water while growing or blooming. Dry out after bloom.

Collector's items, rarely available in nurseries. Buy seed from native plant seed specialists or gather from wild plants (with owner's permission). Grow the species that are native to your area; not all are hardy everywhere.

DODONAEA viscosa. HOP BUSH, HOPSEED BUSH. Evergreen shrub. Zones 7-9, 12-24. Native to Arizona and elsewhere in warmer parts of the world. Plants grown from seed of Arizona natives appear more cold resistant than the introductions from Australia. Fast growing, with many upright stems to 12-15 ft. high, spreading almost as wide (can be trained to tree form by cutting out all but a single stem). Willowlike, green leaves to 4 in. long.

The most popular variety is 'Purpurea', PURPLE HOP BUSH, a selected form with rich bronzy green leaves that turn deeper in winter. Seedlings vary some in color. The variety 'Saratoga' (grown from cuttings) is uniformly rich purple in color. Plant the purple-leafed kinds in full sun to retain rich coloration; will turn green in shade.

Can be pruned as hedge or espalier, or planted 6-8 ft. apart and left unpruned to become a big, informal screen. Probably its biggest asset is its wide cultural tolerance. It takes any kind of soil, ocean winds, dry desert heat. It's quite drought resistant when established, but it will also take ample water (grows well in flower beds).

Clusters of flowers are insignificant. Creamy to pinkish winged fruits attractive in late summer.

DOGWOOD. See Cornus

DOLICHOS. Perennial twining vines which produce a dense cover of light green leaves divided fanwise into 3 leaflets.

D. lablab. HYACINTH BEAN. Perennial vine usually grown as an annual. Fast to 10 ft. Broad, oval leaflets to 3-6 in. long. Sweet-pea-like flowers in loose clusters on long stems standing out from foliage. 'Daylight' has white flowers, 'Darkness', purple ones. Flowers followed by velvety, beanlike pods to 2½ in. long. Grow the plants like string beans. Quick screening. Sun.

D. lignosus. AUSTRALIAN PEA VINE. Zones 16, 17, 21-24. Somewhat woody vine with small triangular 1½-in.-long leaflets and small white or rose-purple flowers clustered at ends of long stalks. Evergreen in mild winters. Grow from seed and train on trellis, or frame for summer screen. Sun.

DOMBEYA. Evergreen shrubs. Zones 21-24. Tender to frost, they make quick comebacks. They have big, tropical-looking, toothed leaves and large, dense, hydrangea-like flower clusters that droop from the branches. Dombeyas need only sun, warmth, reasonably good soil, and ample water. Faded flower clusters hang on and look untidy unless removed. Can be espaliered or trained over arbors to display flowers. Mix with trees for a jungle background.

D. cayeuxii. PINK BALL DOMBEYA. To 10 ft. Pink flowers in dense, heavy, drooping clusters. Winter bloom.

D. wallichii. To 30 ft., but usually seen as a big, rounded shrub 12-15 ft. high, with big leaves to 6-10 in. long and as wide. Big ball-shaped flower clusters in coral-pink to red. Blooms late August into winter.

DONKEY TAIL. See Sedum morganianum

Climate Zone maps pages 8-27

DORONICUM. LEOPARDS BANE. Perennial. Zones 1-6, 15-17. Showy, bright yellow, daisylike flowers on long stems arise from mounds of dense, dark green, usually heart-shaped leaves. Blooms in late spring. Grow in partial shade, good soil. Divide clumps every 2-3 years; young plants bloom best.

Use in groups under high branching deciduous trees; combine with white, purple, or lavender tulips, blue violas, forget-me-nots; use in front of purple lilacs; or with hellebores at edge of woodland or shade border. Good cut flower.

D. caucasicum. Stem 1-1½ ft. high. Flower heads 2 in. across, borne singly on 1-1½ ft.-stems. Increases by stolons. Variety 'Magnificum' more robust, with larger flowers.

Doronicum caucasicum: *brings summer sunshine in spring. Grow in part shade.*

D. clusii. To 2 ft. high, with creeping rhizomes. Flower heads 1½-2 in. across, 1 to a stem, brightest yellow of all.

D. pardalianches. Grows 1-4 ft. high. Flower heads 2 in. across, several to a stem. Starts blooming when *D. plantagineum* is through. Tuberous rooted. Will bloom again in autumn, if cut back as flowers die.

D. plantagineum. PLANTAIN LEOPARDS BANE. Early blooming, rather coarse, with tuberous rhizomes. Stout stems 2-5 ft. tall. Flowers 2-4 in. across, few to a stem. Best in wild garden.

DOROTHEANTHUS. See Ice Plant

DORYANTHES palmeri. SPEAR LILY. Enormous succulent. Zones 15-17, 19-24. Native to Australia. Gigantic cluster of 100 or so leaves which may reach 8 ft. in length by 6 in. wide. Flower stalk 6-9 ft. high; clustered flowers crimson, white within. Summer bloom. Striking in big gardens. Grow as you would century plant but requires more water to look well, and will tolerate more shade. *D. excelsa*, sometimes offered, has taller flower spikes (to 18 ft.), shorter leaves.

DOUGLAS FIR. See Pseudotsuga menziesii

DOVE TREE. See Davidia

DOVYALIS caffra (*Aberia caffra*). KEI APPLE. Zones 21-24. Evergreen shrub. Native to South Africa. Grows at moderate rate to 10 ft. high by as much as 25 ft. wide. Thick, stiff branches very thorny, densely clothed with 2-in.-long, roundish glossy, rather succulent, bright yellow-green leaves (reported to be fire-resistant). Flowers inconspicuous; fruits (only on female plants, and then only if pollinated by a male plant) 1 in. wide, edible, juicy, bright orange-yellow, acid. Fruit used in preserves.

A tough, long-lived plant that survives in the poorest soils, even alkaline ones. Needs little or no water once established. Tolerates winds. In full sun, makes a good, dense, impenetrable hedge that can be maintained at 1-8 ft. high, and 1 ft. or more thick.

DOXANTHA unguis-cati. (*Bignonia tweediana;* also sometimes sold as *Bignonia* or *Anemopaegma chamberlaynii*, a different plant. For differences between the two, see *Anemopaegma.*) CAT'S CLAW, YELLOW TRUMPET VINE. Zones 8-24. Partly deciduous vine that loses all its leaves when winters are cold. Climbs high and fast by the hooked, clawlike, forked tendrils. To 25-40 ft. Leaves divided into 2 oval, glossy green, 2-in. leaflets. Yellow trumpets to 2 in. long, 1¼ in. across, early spring.

Grows near the coast, but faster and stronger where summer heat is high—even on south walls in Phoenix, Tucson, the Imperial Valley. Will cling to any support—stone, wood, fence, tree trunk. Some even are seen clinging to the undersides of freeway overpasses. Tends to produce leaves and flowers at the ends of stems; cut back some stems nearly to the ground to stimulate new growth lower down, and prune the whole plant hard after bloom.

DRABA. Annuals, biennials, perennials. Zones 1-6. Many kinds exist but few are cultivated or available. All are best adapted to alpine, rock, or scree gardens. Small leaves, mostly in basal rosettes. Dainty, profuse, white, yellow, rose, or purplish flowers in clusters.

D. olympica. (Often confused with *D. bruniifolia.*) Forms a mossy green cushion 2-4 in. high, becoming 16 in. across in a few years. In spring, golden yellow flowers in compact clusters form just above the foliage. Combine with smaller kinds of dianthus or dwarf perennial phlox.

DRACAENA. (For other plants often called dracaena, see *Cordyline.*) Evergreen plants (small palmlike trees). Essentially foliage plants, grown in the house or on lanais—certain kinds can be grown outdoors as noted below. Some show graceful fountain forms with broad, curved, ribbon leaves, occasionally striped with chartreuse or white. Some have very stiff, swordlike leaves.

D. australis. See Cordyline australis

D. deremensis. Outdoors, out of wind, in Zone 24; otherwise, a house plant. Native to tropical Africa. The one usually sold is variety 'Warneckii'. Erect, slow growing, but eventually 15 ft. tall. Long, 2-ft. leaves, 2 in. wide, rich green, striped white and gray.

D. draco. DRAGON TREE. Outdoors in Zones 16, 17, 21-24. Native to Canary Islands. Stout trunk with upward-reaching or spreading branches topped by clusters of heavy, 2-ft.-long sword-shaped leaves. Grows slowly to 20 ft. high and as wide. Makes an odd but interesting silhouette.

Clusters of greenish white flowers form at branch ends. After blossoms drop, stemmy clusters remain. Trim them off to keep plants neat.

D. fragrans. Outdoors, out of wind, in Zones 21, 23, 24: other than that, a house plant. Native to west Africa. Upright, eventually to 20 ft. high, but slow growing. Heavy, ribbonlike, blue-green leaves to 3 ft. long, 4 in. wide. (Typical plant in 8-in. pot will bear leaves about 18 in. long.) Tolerates darker position in house than other dracaenas. The variety 'Massangeana' has a broad yellow stripe in center of leaf.

D. godseffiana. House plant. Native to west Africa. Slow grower, smaller than other dracaenas. Slender erect or spreading stems set with pairs or trios of 5-in.-long, 2-in.-wide, dark green leaves spotted with white.

D. sanderiana. Outdoors, out of wind, Zones 21, 23, 24; or a house plant anywhere. Native to west Africa. Neat and upright, somewhat resembling a young corn plant. Strap-shaped 9-in.-long leaves striped with white.

DRAGONHEAD, FALSE. See Physostegia

DRAGON TREE. See Dracaena draco

DRIMYS winteri. WINTER'S BARK. Small evergreen tree. Zones 8, 9, 14-24. Native to southern Chile and Argentina. Slender, to 25 ft. Distinguished chiefly for clean foliage and dignified presence. Stems and branches, which tend to droop gracefully, are mahogany red. Bright green, leathery, aromatic leaves are elliptical, 5-10 in. long. Jasmine-scented, creamy white flowers about 1 in. wide, in small clusters. Usually multi-stemmed, but easily trained to single trunk. May require pruning from time to time to maintain outline of pleasing symmetry. Give plenty of water with good drainage. Will take some sun near coast; shade inland.

DROSANTHEMUM. See Ice Plant

DRYAS. Perennials. Zones 1-6. Choice plants for rock gardens. Evergreen, or partially so, somewhat shrubby at base, forming a carpet of leafy creeping stems. Shiny, white or yellow, strawberrylike flowers May-July; ornamental seed capsules with silvery white tails. Sun; average soil.

D. drummondii. To 4 in. high. Leaves oblong. 1½ in. long, white-woolly beneath. Flowers nodding, bright yellow, ¾ in. across.

D. octopetala. Leaves 1 in. long. Flowers white, 1½ in. across, erect.

D. suendermannii. Hybrid between two species above. Leaves oblong, 1-1½ in. long, thick-textured, similar to oak leaves. Flowers yellowish in bud, white in full bloom, nodding.

DRYOPTERIS. WOOD FERN. Native to many parts of the world. Two natives of Western U. S. and one exotic species are sometimes sold.

D. arguta. COASTAL or CALIFORNIA WOOD FERN. Zones 4-9, 14-24. Native Washington to southern California. Dark green, finely cut, airy fronds to 2½ ft. tall. Not easy in gardens; best naturalized in woods. Avoid overwatering.

D. dilatata. SPREADING WOOD FERN. Zone 4-9, 14-24. Leaves even more finely cut than *D. arguta*. Named varieties sometimes seen in Northwestern nurseries. In southern California, best in pots.

D. erythrosora. All Zones. Native to China, Japan. One of few ferns with seasonal color value: young fronds reddish, deep green in late spring and summer. Spreading habit, 1½-2 ft. tall.

DUCHESNEA indica. INDIAN MOCK STRAWBERRY. Perennial. All Zones. Grows like strawberry, with trailing stems that root firmly along the ground. Bright green, long-stalked leaves with 3 leaflets. Yellow flowers ½ in. across, followed by ½-in., insipid-tasting fruits that stand above foliage rather than under leaves as in true strawberry. Grows readily in sun or shade without much care. Best used as a ground cover among open shrubs or small trees. Plant 12-18 in. apart. If neglected, can become a nuisance. Trim to keep under control.

DUDLEYA. Rosette-forming succulents. Zones 16, 17, 21-24. Native to California, Arizona, Baja California and other parts of Mexico. About 40 species are known and some of these are common on California's coastal cliffs or inland hills. Best known in cultivation is *D. brittonii* (from Baja California), with 18-in.-wide leaf rosettes on stems that gradually lengthen into trunks. Leaves fleshy, covered with a heavy coat of chalky powder which can be rubbed off. A striking plant when well grown.

DUMB CANE. See Dieffenbachia

DURANTA. Evergreen shrubs. Glossy green leaves arranged in pairs or whorls along the stem. Attractive blue flowers in clusters attract butterflies in summer, followed by bunches of yellow berrylike fruits. Many of the plants sold as *D. stenostachya* are actually *D. erecta*. Distinguishing characteristics described below.

Valued for summer flowers and fruits. Use as quick tall screen. Thrives in hot summer areas but requires constant level of moisture. Needs continual thinning and pruning to keep under control.

D. erecta (*D. repens, D. plumieri*). SKY FLOWER, GOLDEN DEWDROP, PIGEON BERRY. Zones 13, 16, 17, 21-24. Native to southern Florida, West Indies, Mexico to Brazil. Fast growing to 10-25 ft. Tends to form multi-stemmed clumps, branches often drooping and vinelike. Stems may or may not have sharp spines. Oval to roundish leaves 1-2 in. long, rounded or pointed at tip. Tubular violet-blue flowers flare to less than ½ in. wide. Fruit clusters 1-6 in. long.

D. stenostachya. BRAZILIAN SKY FLOWER. Not as hardy as *D. erecta*, seems to require more heat, and is not at its best in Zones 17, 24. Makes a neater more compact shrub than *D. erecta*, usually growing to about 4-6 ft. (under ideal conditions, 15 ft.). Stems are spineless. Leaves are larger (3-8 in. long) than *D. erecta* and taper to a long, slender point. The lavender-blue flowers are also somewhat larger, and the fruit clusters grow to 1 ft. long.

DUSTY MILLER. See Artemisia stelleriana, Centaurea cineraria, C. gymnocarpa, Senecio cineraria

DUTCHMAN'S PIPE. See Aristolochia

EASTER LILY VINE. See Beaumontia

ECHEVERIA. Succulents. All make rosettes of fleshy leaves of green or gray-green, often marked or overlaid with deeper colors. Flowers bell-shaped, nodding, usually pink, red, or yellow, on long, slender, sometimes branched clusters.

E. agavoides (*Urbinia agavoides*). Zones 8, 9, 13-24. Rosettes 6-8 in. across, with stiff, fleshy, smooth, bright green, sharp-pointed leaves which may be marked deep

Echeveria agavoides is far less prolific in offsets than other echeverias.

reddish brown at tips and edges. Flower stalk to 18 in. Flowers small, red and yellow.

E. crenulata. Zones 17, 21-24. Loose rosettes on short, thick stems. Leaves pale green or white-powdered, to 1 ft. long and 6 in. wide, with edges waved and crisped, purplish red. Flower clusters to 3 ft. high, with a few yellow and red flowers. Striking plant; shelter from hottest sun. Water frequently in summer.

E. derenbergii. Zones 17, 20-24. Small, tight rosettes spreading to form mats. Leaves grayish white with red edges and a sharp tip. Flowers reddish and yellow, in 1-sided clusters to 2½ in. long.

E. elegans. HEN AND CHICKS. Zones 8, 9, 12-24. Tight grayish white rosettes to 4 in. across, spreading freely by offsets. Flowers pink, lined yellow, in clusters to 8 in. long. Common, useful for pattern planting, edging, containers.

E. glauca. (*E. secunda glauca.*) HEN AND CHICKS. Zones 8, 9, 12-24. Rosettes purple-tinted gray-green, to 4 in. across. Makes offsets freely.

E. imbricata. HEN AND CHICKS. Zones 8, 9, 12-24. Rosettes 4-6 in. across, saucer-shaped, gray-green. Makes offsets very freely. Probably commonest hen and chicks in California gardens.

E. pulvinata. Zones 16, 17, 21-24. Small, loose rosettes of very thick leaves covered with silvery down which later turns red or brownish. Early spring flowers are bright red.

E. setosa. Zones 17, 23, 24. Dense rosettes to 4 in. across, dark green, densely covered with white stiff hairs. Flowers red tipped yellow. Good in rock gardens, shallow containers. Very tender.

E. 'Set-oliver'. Zones 16, 17, 21-24. Rosettes looser than in *E. setosa*. Flowers profuse, red and yellow, very showy in mass plantings.

E. hybrids. Generally have large, loose rosettes of big leaves on single or branched stems. Some have leaves crisped, waved, wattled, and heavily shaded with red, bronze, or purple. All are splendid pot plants; they do well in the open ground in mild coastal gardens.

Widely used for bedding, rock gardens, containers, edging: Echeveria imbricata.

ECHINACEA purpurea (*Rudbeckia purpurea*). PURPLE CONEFLOWER. Perennial. All Zones. Coarse, stiff plant forming large clumps of erect stems 4-5 ft. tall. Leaves oblong, 3-8 in. long. Showy flower heads with drooping purple rays and dark purple centers; blooms over a long period in late summer. Use on outskirts of garden or in wide borders with other robust perennials such as Shasta daisies, sunflowers, Michaelmas daisies. Plant in full sun; average soil, watering. Divide clumps in spring or fall.

Varieties are: 'The King', large coral crimson rays, brownish centers; 'Bright Star', similar to foregoing, but with brighter flowers; 'White Lustre', also called 'White King', dwarfer, to 3 ft., with white rays and greenish brown center, long blooming.

ECHINOCACTUS. BARREL CACTUS. Zones 12-24. Numerous kinds of large, cylindrical cactus with prominent ribs and stout thorns. Many native to the Southwest. Best known in gardens is *E. grusonii*, GOLDEN BARREL, a Mexican cactus of slow growth to 4 ft. high, 2½ ft. in diameter, with showy yellow, stiff 3-in. spines and yellow 1½-2-in. flowers at top of plant in April-May. It needs protection from hard frosts.

ECHINOPS exaltatus. GLOBE THISTLE. Perennial. All Zones. Rugged looking, erect, rigidly branched plants 3-4 ft. high. Coarse, prickly, deeply cut, gray-green leaves. Small, steel blue flowers in round heads 2 in. across, midsummer to late fall. 'Taplow Blue' is desirable selected form. Plants often mistakenly sold under names of *E. ritro* and *E. sphaerocephalus*.

Flowers long lasting when cut; hold color when dry. Plant in full sun, ordinary soil with good drainage. Grow from divisions in spring or fall; or sow seed in flats or in open ground in spring. Color and interesting form complement yellow and orange rudbeckias, heleniums; combine well with Michaelmas daisies and perennial phlox.

Climate Zone maps pages 8-27

ECHINOPSIS. EASTER LILY CACTUS, SEA URCHIN CACTUS. Outdoors Zones 16, 17, 21-24; grow inside sunny windows elsewhere. Small cylindrical or globular cactus from South America, generally grown in pots. Big, long-tubed, many-petaled flowers in shades of white, yellow, pink, and red can reach 6-8 in. in length. Free-blooming in summer if given good light, frequent feeding, fast-draining soil. Many kinds, all showy and easy.

ECHIUM. Biennials or shrubby perennials. Striking form and flower clusters. All take full sun, do well in dry, poor soil, but need good drainage. All are excellent for seacoast gardens.

E. candicans. Perennial. Zones 7-9, 14-24. Grows 2 to 6 ft. high, with branched stems. The flowers, in long, rather loose spikes, are blue with pink stamens.

E. fastuosum. PRIDE OF MADEIRA. Shrubby perennial. Zones 7-9, 14-24. Large picturesque plant with many coarse heavy branches 3-6 ft. high. Hairy, gray-green, narrow leaves form roundish irregular mounds at ends of stems. Great spikelike clusters of blue-purple, ½-in.-long flowers stand out dramatically, well above the foliage, in May-June. Branch tips and developing flower spikes may be killed by March

Big blue-purple flower spikes stand at eye level. Foliage is gray-green, hairy.

frosts in inland areas. Use for bold effects against walls, at back of a wide flower border, and on slopes. Very effective with *Limonium perezii.* Prune lightly to keep plant bushy. Cut off faded flower spikes.

E. pininana. PRIDE OF TENERIFFE. Biennial. Zones 7-9, 14-24. Looks similar to *E. fastuosum,* but it's taller growing (to 12 ft. or more), more openly branched, and the stems more slender. Blue flowers in long slender spikes. When flowers fade, plant dies but quantities of seed produced will give abundance of seedlings.

E. wildpretii. TOWER OF JEWELS. Biennial. Zones 16, 17, 21-24. Striking plant from 4-10 ft. Its first year is spent as a roundish mass of long, narrow leaves covered with silvery gray hairs. In its second year it starts to grow. By mid- or late spring it will form a thick column of rose to rose red flowers 6-10 ft. high and a foot or more thick. When all the countless little flowers have faded, the plant dies, leaving

behind a vast amount of seed. If resulting seedlings are not hoed out, these may be grown on to flower next year. An interesting oddity.

EDELWEISS. See Leontopodium

EGGPLANT. Few vegetable plants are handsomer than eggplant. Bushes resemble little trees 2-3 ft. high and equally wide. The big leaves (usually lobed) are purple tinged, and the drooping violet-purple flowers are 1½ in. across. And of course the big purple fruit is spectacular. Plants are effective in large containers or raised beds; a well-spaced row of them makes a distinguished border between vegetable and flower garden. Most people plant the large roundish or oval varieties such as 'Black Beauty' or 'Improved Large Purple'; the Japanese, who prefer their eggplant small and very tender, prefer a long, slender variety usually sold as 'Japanese'.

Can be grown from seed (sow indoors 8-10 weeks before date of last expected frost) but it's much easier to buy and plant nursery-grown plants. Set plants out in spring, when frosts are over and soil is warm. Space 3 feet apart in loose, fertile soil. Feed once every 6 weeks with commercial fertilizer, water when soil at roots is dry, and keep weeds out. Prevent too much fruit setting by pinching out some terminal growth and some blossoms. Three to 6 fruits per plant are enough. If you enjoy tiny whole eggplants, allow plants to produce freely. Harvest fruits after they develop some color, but never wait until they lose their glossy shine. Dust or spray to control aphids and whiteflies.

EGRET FLOWER. See Habenaria

EICHHORNIA crassipes. WATER HYACINTH. Aquatic plant. Zones 8, 9, 13-24. Where winters are cold, replace annually or winter indoors. Native to tropical America. Floating or submerged leaves and feathery roots. Leaves ½-5 in. broad, nearly circular in shape; leaf stems inflated. Blooms showy, lilac blue, about 2 in. long, upper petals with yellow spot in center, in many-flowered spikes. Attractive in pools, ponds, but can become a pest where unrestrained. Needs warmth to flower profusely.

ELAEAGNUS. Deciduous and evergreen large shrubs or small trees. All are splendid screen plants. Although one kind is a tree and the rest are big shrubs, and although some are deciduous and some are evergreen, all grow fast (as young plants), dense, full, firm, and tough, and do it with little upkeep. All tolerate heat and wind. Plant 10-12 ft. apart for screening.

Foliage is distinguished in evergreen forms by silvery (sometimes brown) dots that cover leaves. Reflecting sunlight, these dots give the plants a special sparkle. The deciduous kinds have silvery gray leaves. Small, insignificant, but usually fragrant flowers are followed by decorative fruits, usually red with silvery flecks. Evergreen kinds bloom in fall. The evergreen kinds are useful as natural espaliers, clipped hedges, or high bank covers, in addition to prime role as screen plants.

E. angustifolia. RUSSIAN OLIVE. Small deciduous tree. Zones 1-3, 7-14, 18, 19. To 20 ft. high, but can be clipped as a medium-height hedge. Angular trunk and branches

(sometimes thorny) are covered with shredding, dark brown bark that is picturesque in winter. Bark contrasts with willowlike, 2-in.-long, silvery gray leaves. Small, greenish yellow flowers in early summer are very fragrant, followed by berrylike fruits that resemble miniature olives. Can take almost any amount of punishment in interior. Does poorly and is out of character in mild-winter, cool-summer climates.

E. 'Coral Silver'. Large evergreen or deciduous shrub. All Zones. Has unusually bright gray foliage, coral red berries in fall. Evergreen in Zones 19-24, deciduous or partially deciduous elsewhere.

E. fruitlandii. FRUITLAND SILVERBERRY. Evergreen shrub. Zones 5-24. Grows 6-12 ft. high. Much like *E. pungens* (see below) but the total impression is of more silvery foliage; leaves larger than *E. pungens.*

E. macrophylla 'Ebbingi'. Evergreen shrub. Zones 5-24. More upright (to 10-12 ft.) than *E. pungens* (see below) and has thornless branches. Dark green leaves 2-4 in. long, silvery both sides when young, later dark green above, silvery beneath. Tiny fragrant silvery flowers. Fruits red.

E. philippensis. Evergreen shrub. Zones 15-17, 19-24. More open and erect (to 10 ft.) than other evergreen forms with somewhat spreading and drooping branches. The 3-in.-long, olive green leaves with silvery cast are quite silvery beneath.

E. pungens. SILVERBERRY. Large evergreen shrub. Zones 4-24. A rather rigid, sprawling, angular habit of growth to a height of 6-15 ft., but can be kept lower and denser by pruning. Grayish green, 1-3-in.-long leaves have wavy edges, brown tinting from rusty dots. Branches are spiny, and also are covered with rusty dots. Overall color of shrub is olive drab. Tough container plant in reflected heat, wind.

E. p. 'Maculata'. GOLDEN ELAEAGNUS. Leaves have gold blotch in center.

E. p. 'Marginata'. SILVER-EDGE ELAEAGNUS. Leaves have silvery white margins.

E. p. 'Variegata'. YELLOW-EDGE ELAEAGNUS. Leaves have yellowish white margins.

ELDERBERRY. See Sambucus

ELEPHANT'S EAR. See Alocasia, Colocasia

ELEPHANT'S FOOD. See Portulacaria

ELM. See Ulmus

EMPRESS TREE. See Paulownia

ENDIVE. Botanically known as *Cichorium endivia.* This species includes curly endive and broad-leafed endive (escarole). They take more heat than lettuce. Grow faster in cold weather. Sow in late summer for maturity during the rainy season (in cold-winter areas sow seed June to August). Endive matures in 90-95 days. Space plants 10-12 in. apart in rows 15-18 in. apart. When plants have reached full size, pull outer leaves over center and tie them up; center leaves will blanch to yellow or white. 'Green Curled' is the standard curly endive, 'Broad-leaved Batavian' best broad-leafed kind.

ENKIANTHUS. Deciduous shrubs. Zones 2-9, 14-21. Native to Japan. Upright stems with tiers of nearly horizontal branches,

Climate
Zone maps
pages 8-27

narrow in youth, broad in age, but always good-looking. Leaves whorled or crowded at branch ends, turn orange or red in autumn. Nodding, bell-shaped flowers in clusters. Grow in light shade, in well drained soil to which plenty of peat moss

Flowers of enkianthus are not dazzling, but markings, colors merit close viewing.

or ground bark has been added. Keep soil moist. Prune only to remove dead or broken branches. Plant with other acid-loving plants. Place where silhouette and fall color can be effective.

E. campanulatus. Slow-growing, handsome shrub to 20 ft. in 20 years (10 ft. by 4 ft. wide in 10 years). Bluish green leaves 1½-3 in. long, turn brilliant red in fall. In May, pendulous clusters of yellow-green, red-veined, ½-in.-long bells hang below the leaves. *E. c. palibinii* has deep red flowers; its variety 'Albiflorus' white ones.

E. cernuus. Seldom over 10 ft. tall, with 1-2-in.-long leaves. White flowers. Not as well known as its variety *rubens*, with translucent deep red flowers in May.

E. perulatus. Grows to 6-8 ft. high. Roundish, 1-2-in.-long leaves; exceptionally good scarlet fall color. Nodding clusters of small white flowers open before leaves.

ENSETE. Big, palmlike perennials. Evergreen in Zones 17, 19-24; die back each winter, regrow in spring in Zones 13, 15, 16, 18; outdoors in summer, indoors or in greenhouse over winter elsewhere.

E. ventricosum (*Musa ensete*). ABYSSINIAN BANANA. Lush, tropical looking, dark green leaves 10-20 ft. long, 2-4 ft. wide, with stout midrib, grow out in arching form from single vertical stem, 6-20 ft. high. Fast growing. Leaves easily shredded by winds, so plant in wind-sheltered place. Sun or part shade. Give normal garden watering, little or no fertilizing. Flowers typically form 2-5 years after planting; plant dies to roots after flowering. Possible then to grow new plants from shoots at crown, but easier to discard, replace with new nursery plants. Flowers (insignificant) form within cylinder of bronze red bracts at end of stem.

E. maurelii. (Usually sold as *Musa maurelii*.) ETHIOPIAN BANANA. Similar to *E. ventricosum* except leaves are tinged with red on upper surface, especially along edges, leaf stalks dark red, plant is slightly smaller (stems only 12-15 ft. high).

EPAULETTE TREE. See Pterostyrax

EPIDENDRUM. Epiphytic or terrestrial orchids. All are easy to grow. Most species

bear large clusters of blooms. On the whole they take same culture as cattleya. Those with hard, round pseudobulbs and thick leathery leaves are sun and drought tolerant and need a rest period. These grow in ground bark or other orchid media. Softer-textured plants with thin stemlike pseudobulbs do best with more shade and year around moisture.

Reed-stemmed types need abundance of sun to flower, but shaded roots to provide a cool root run. Mulch plants in ground beds. If sun is too hot, foliage turns bright red and burns. Grow outdoors in Zones 17, 23, 24. Tip growth will burn at 28°, plants are killed to ground at about 22°. In cold winter areas grow reed-stemmed plants in pots, move them indoors in winter.

Feed regularly with a mild liquid fertilizer during the growing season. In pure ground bark feed at every other watering

To keep reed-stem epidendrum plants neat, cut spent blooms as shown at right.

with a high nitrogen liquid feed. Feed plants grown in other media monthly. When blooms fade, cut flower stem back to within 1 or 2 joints of the ground.

E. cochleatum. Native to tropical America. Pear-shaped pseudobulbs 2-5 in. high with one or more leaves as long or longer. Erect flower stem bears 5-10 flowers, 2-3 in. across. Narrow, twisted yellow-green sepals and petals, purplish black lip shaped like cockleshell with lighter veins. Blooms at various times. Hardy to about 25°; grows outdoors in mildest winter climates.

E. ibaguense (*E. radicans*). Native to Colombia. Erect 2-4 ft. reedlike leafy stems. Dense, globular clusters of 1-1½-in. flowers at tips of slender stems well above foliage. Orange-yellow flower, fringed lip. Bloom season varies. Numerous hybrids in shades of yellow, orange, pink, red, lavender, and white, generally sold by color rather than by a name.

E. o'brienianum. Best known of reed-stem hybrids. Dense clusters of vivid red flowers, each the shape of a miniature cattleya orchid—on slender stems 1-2 ft. above foliage. Two outstanding hybrids have *E. o'brienianum* as one parent: *E. ibaguense* 'Braceyi' with scarlet flowers; and

E. burtonii with bright orange ones. Both are shorter and more compact in growth habit than *E. o'brienianum*.

EPIGAEA repens. TRAILING ARBUTUS. Evergreen low shrublet. Zones 1-7. Native to eastern North America. Difficult to grow except under ideal conditions: acid soil well fortified with leaf mold, pine needles, or peat moss; excellent drainage; shade from summer sun. Choice woodland ground cover. Do not fertilize. Mulch with leaf mold or peat moss when weather warms, keep plants moist all summer. Bait for slugs. Will take any amount of cold.

Each plant can cover a patch 12-24 in. wide, the stems rooting as they grow. Oval to roundish leaves 1-3 in. long. Waxy, pink or white, ½-in.-wide flowers (with a delightful fragrance) cluster at tips of branches, April or May.

Another species, *E. asiatica*, occasionally sold, is quite similar to the above but considered easier to grow.

EPIMEDIUM. Perennials. Zones 1-9, 14-17. Low growing evergreen, or nearly evergreen plant with creeping underground stems. Leathery, divided leaves on thin wiry stems. Heart-shaped leaflets, up to 3 in. long, unfold bronzy pink in spring, turn green in summer, bronzy in fall. Loose spikes of small, waxy-textured, pink, red, creamy yellow, or white flowers in spring. Use as ground cover under trees, among rhododendrons, azaleas, camellias; good in larger rock gardens. Foliage, flowers long-lasting in arrangements. Divide large clumps in spring or fall by cutting through tough roots with sharp spade. Cut off old leaves in early spring.

E. grandiflorum. BISHOP'S HAT, LONG-SPUR EPIMEDIUM. About 1 ft. high. Flowers 1-2 in. across, shaped like a bishop's hat; outer sepals red, inner sepals pale violet, petals white with long spurs. Varieties have white, pinkish, or violet flowers. 'Rose Queen', crimson carmine flowers with white-tipped spurs, is outstanding.

E. pinnatum. Grows 12-15 in. high, having yellow flowers ⅔ in. across, with red petals and protruding stamens. *E. p. colchicum* (often sold as *E. p. elegans*) is larger, with more and showier flowers.

You can enjoy epimedium's attractive foliage all year, the waxy flowers in spring.

Climate
Zone maps
pages 8-27

E. rubrum. To 1 ft. with showy clusters of flowers with bright crimson sepals, pale yellow or white, slipperlike petals, up-curved spurs. 'Pink Queen', rosy pink, and 'Snow Queen', white, are desirable varieties offered in specialty nurseries.

EPIPACTIS gigantea. STREAM ORCHIS. Hardy terrestrial orchid. Zones 1-9, 14-24. Native from Washington to southern California, east to southern Utah and west Texas. Oval or lance-shaped leaves with plaited veins. Creeping rootstocks. Stems 1-3 ft. tall. Flowers, 3-10 to the stalk, greenish, purple-veined, an inch wide, some-what resembling birds in flight. Blooms June-July. Grows near brooks and is probably the easiest native orchid to grow. Give it rich, moist soil in sun or partial shade.

EPIPHYLLUM. ORCHID CACTUS. House plants anywhere; lathhouse, shade and shelter plants in Zones 8, 9, 14-24. Growers use *Epiphyllum* to cover a wide range of plants including epiphyllum itself and a number of crosses with related plants—*Heliocereus, Nopalxochia, Selenicereus, Chiapasia, Aporocactus*. All are similar in being jungle (not desert) cactus, and most grow on tree branches as epiphytes, like some orchids. Here we grow them in pots. They need rich,

Orchid cactus (Epiphyllum) comes in a wide variety of flower colors, sizes, shapes.

quick-draining soil with plenty of leaf mold, peat moss, or ground bark, and sand. Over-watering and poor drainage cause bud drop.

During summer epiphyllums do best in broken shade under trees or lath. They need protection from frost. Most have arch-ing, trailing stems and look best in hanging pots, tubs, or baskets. Stems are long, flat, smooth, usually notched along edges, and are quite spineless. Flowers range from medium to very large—as much as 10 in. across—and the color range includes white, cream, yellow, pink, rose, lavender, scarlet, and orange. Many varieties have blends of 2 or more colors. Bloom season April-June. Feed with low-nitrogen fertilizer before and after bloom. Bait for snails and slugs. Spray to control aphids, scale, and mealybugs.

EPISCIA cupreata. FLAME VIOLET. House plant related to African violet. The plants are low and spread by runners much like strawberry. The oval 4-in. leaves are velvety-hairy and beautifully colored. Typically they

are deep coppery; the variety 'Metallica' has olive green leaves with pale stripes and red edges; 'Viridifolia' has light green leaves with creamy veins. Flowers resemble long-tubed, orange-red African violets. Grow like African violets. Use as hanging basket plants or as ground cover under greenhouse benches or in terrariums. Needs high hu-midity.

EQUISETUM hyemale. HORSETAIL. Perenni-al. All Zones. Rushlike survivor of the car-boniferous age. Slender, hollow, 4-ft. stems bright green with black and ash-colored ring at each joint. Spores borne in conelike spikes at end of stem. Several species, but *E. hyemale* most common. Called horsetail be-cause many of the species have a bushy look from many whorls of slender, jointed green stems that radiate out from joints of the main stem.

Although effective in garden situations, especially near water, use with caution; ex-tremely invasive, difficult to get rid of. Best confined to containers. Useful in marshy areas, pools, roadside ditches. In open ground, root prune rigorously, keep cutting back unwanted shoots.

ERANTHEMUM nervosum. (Sometimes sold as *E. pulchellum*.) Evergreen shrub. Out-doors Zones 23, 24; elsewhere in green-houses. Native to India. Grows rapidly to 2-4 ft. high. Handsome dark green, oval, long-stalked leaves 4 in. long in pairs, with prominent veins and somewhat scallop-toothed edge.

Deep blue (sometimes rose) tubular flowers protrude from prominent overlap-ping bracts in 3-in.-long solitary or branch-ing spikes at ends of branches and among leaves, January to April.

Best grown as a container plant, or in ground bed on shady wind-sheltered patio or terrace. Give plants loose, well-drained soil, rich in humus material. Keep plants moist at all times. Pinch back stem tips 2 or 3 times early in growing season to keep plants compact, and encourage more flower production. Cut to ground to stimulate fresh new growth and overcome legginess.

ERANTHIS hyemalis. WINTER ACONITE. Tuber. Zones 1-9, 15-17. Charming butter-cuplike plant 2-8 in. high, blooming in early spring. Each single, yellow flower, to 1½ in. across, with 5-9 petal-like sepals, sits on a single, deeply lobed, bright green leaf that looks like a ruff. Basal leaves round, divided into narrow lobes, appear immediately after flowers. Ideal companions for other small bulbs or bulb-like plants that bloom at same time, such as snow-drop (*Galanthus nivalis*) and Siberian squill (*Scilla sibirica*). Plant tubers in August, early September before they shrivel. If tub-ers are dry, plump up in wet sand before planting. When dividing, separate into small clumps rather than single tubers. Plant tubers 3 in. deep, 4 in. apart, in moist, porous soil in part shade.

EREMURUS. FOXTAIL LILY, DESERT CANDLE. Perennials. Zones 1-9. An imposing lily rela-tive with spirelike flowering stems 6-9 ft. tall. White, pink, or yellow, bell-shaped flowers, ½-1 in. in diameter, massed closely in graceful, pointed spikes. Blooming time: late spring, early summer. Strap-shaped basal leaves in rosettes appear in early spring, fade away after bloom in summer.

Magnificent in large borders against back-ground of dark green foliage, wall, or solid fence. Dramatic in arrangements; cut when lowest flowers on spike open. Plant in sun in rich, readily drained soil. Handle the thick, brittle roots carefully; tend to rot when bruised or broken. When leaves die down, mark the spot and avoid disturbing roots.

E. himalaicus. Leaves bright green, to 1½ ft. long. Flowers white, about 1 in. across in 2-ft. spikes on tall stems 3 ft. or more long.

E. robustus. Leaves 2 ft. or so long, in dense basal rosettes. Stems 8-9 ft. high, topped with 2-3-ft. spikes of clear pink flowers lightly veined with brown.

Shelford Hybrids. To 4-5 ft. tall; flowers in white and shades of buff, pink, yellow, and orange.

ERICA. See Heaths and Heathers

ERIGERON. FLEABANE. Perennials. Free-blooming plants with daisylike flowers similar to closely-related Michaelmas daisy (*Aster*), except that erigeron's flower heads have threadlike rays in 2 or more rows rather than broader rays in a single row. White, pink, lavender, or violet flowers usually with yellow centers, early summer into fall. Sun or light shade; sandy soil; moderate watering. Cut back after flower-ing to prolong bloom. Rock garden species need especially fast drainage.

E. compositus. All Zones. Western al-pine for rock garden. Forms cushion of soft green, hairy, finely-divided leaves. White or purplish flower heads, ¾ in. across, borne singly on stems 4-8 in. high in May-August.

E. glaucus. BEACH ASTER, SEASIDE DAISY. Zones 4-6, 15-17, 22-24. Native of Califor-nia, Oregon coast. Burns in hot sun inland. Basal leaves in clumps. Stout hairy stems 10-12 in. high, topped by lavender flower heads 1½-2 in. across in spring, summer. Use in rock garden, border, beside path. Sun or part shade.

E. karvinskianus. (Often called *Vitta-dinia*.) Zones 8, 9, 12-24. Native to Mexico. Graceful, trailing plant 10-20 in. high. Leaves 1 in. long, often toothed at tips. Dainty flower heads ¾ in. across with nu-merous white or pinkish rays. Use as ground cover, in rock gardens, dry walls, hanging baskets. Naturalizes easily; invasive unless controlled.

E. speciosus. Zones 4-9, 12-24. Native to coast, Pacific Northwest. Erect, leafy-stemmed, 2 ft. high. Flower heads 1-1½ in. across, dark violet or lavender rays; sum-mer bloom. Named varieties with larger flowers available.

ERIOBOTRYA. LOQUAT. Evergreen trees or big shrubs. Both kinds have large, promin-ently veined, sharply toothed leaves. One bears edible fruit.

E. deflexa. BRONZE LOQUAT. Zones 8, 9, 14-24. Shrubby, but easily trained into small tree form. New leaves have bright coppery color which they hold for a long time be-fore turning green. Leaves lie deeply veined, wrinkled, and not as leathery as *E. japonica*, more pointed, and shinier. No edible fruit. Good for espaliers (not on hot wall), patio planting, containers.

Climate
Zone maps
pages 8-27

E. japonica. LOQUAT. Zones 4-24. Grows 15-30 ft. tall, equally broad in sun, slenderer in shade. Big, leathery, crisp leaves, stoutly veined and netted, 6-12 in. long, 2-4 in. wide, sharply toothed. They are glossy deep green above, and show rust-colored wool beneath. New branches woolly; small, dull white flowers in woolly 3-6-in. clusters borne in fall. These are fragrant, but not showy. Fruits 1-2 in. long, orange to yellow, sweet, aromatic, and acid with seeds (usually big) in center. Hardy to 20°; has survived 12°, but fruit often injured by low temperatures.

Plant in well drained soil; will thrive in some drought when established, but grows best with abundant moisture. Prune to shape; if you like the fruit, thin branches somewhat to let light into tree's interior. If tree sets fruit heavily, remove some while it's small to increase size of remaining fruits and to prevent limb breakage. Insect-free, except for aphids and scale. Fireblight is a danger; if leaves and stems blacken from top downward, prune back 12 in. or more into healthy wood. Burn prunings and sterilize shears between cuts. Use as lawn or patio tree for sunny or shady spots; espalier on fence or trellis—but not in reflected heat. Can be held in a container for several years. Cut foliage good for indoor decorating.

Most trees sold are seedlings, good ornamental plants with unpredictable fruit quality; if you definitely want fruit, look for a grafted variety. 'Champagne' (March-May), best in warm areas, has a yellow-skinned, white-fleshed, juicy, tart fruit. 'Gold Nugget' (May-June), best near the coast, has sweeter fruit with orange skin and flesh.

ERIOGONUM. WILD BUCKWHEAT. Annuals, perennials, shrubs. Zones 14-24 (possibly 7-13). Native to most areas of the West (the few sold at nurseries mostly native to California coast). Grow best in full sun in well drained, loose, gravelly soil. Once established they take little water. Useful to cover dry banks, mass among rocks or use in rock gardens. Most of the available kinds withstand wind well.

Flower arrangers use the flower clusters in dried bouquets. The individual blossoms are tiny but they grow in long-stemmed or branched clusters—domed, flattish, or ball-like. They turn to shades of tan or rust as the seeds ripen. If you leave flower clusters on the plant, seeds will drop and volunteer seedlings will appear. Transplant them when they're small to extend planting or replace overgrown plants. Shrubby kinds get leggy after several years. You can do some pruning to shape if you start when plants are young, but if they've had no attention, it's better to replace them.

E. arborescens. SANTA CRUZ ISLAND BUCKWHEAT. Shrub. Native to Santa Cruz, Santa Rosa, and Anacapa islands, southern California, grows 3-4 (sometimes 8) ft. high, spreading 4-5 ft. or more. Trunk and branches with shreddy gray to reddish bark make attractive open pattern. Rather narrow, ½-1½-in.-long, gray-green leaves tend to cluster at the ends of the branches. Long-stalked, flat clusters of pale pink to rose flowers in profusion, May-September.

E. crocatum. SAFFRON BUCKWHEAT. Perennial. Native to Ventura County, California. Low compact, to 18 in. high with white woolly stems. Roundish 1-in.-long leaves

covered with white wool; attractive all year. Sulfur yellow flowers in broad flattish clusters April-August.

E. fasciculatum. CALIFORNIA BUCKWHEAT. Shrub. Native to foothills of California (Santa Clara to San Diego counties), and desert slopes of mountains of southern California. Forms clump of many semi-upright stems 1-3 ft. high, spreading to 4 ft. Leaves usually narrow, ½-¾ in. long, vary from dark green above, white woolly beneath (typical form) to gray hairy on both sides. White or pinkish flowers in headlike clusters, May-October. Good erosion control plant.

E. giganteum. ST. CATHERINE'S LACE. Shrub. Native to Santa Catalina and San Clemente islands. Differs from E. arborescens in its more freely branching habit, grayish white, broadly oval, 1-2½-in.-long leaves, and longer period of bloom.

E. latifolium rubescens (E. rubescens). RED BUCKWHEAT. Perennial. Native to San Miguel, Santa Rosa, and Santa Cruz islands, southern California. Woody-based; branches tend to lie on ground with upright tips about 10-12 in. high, spreading to 12-18 in. Gray-green oval leaves, 1-3½ in. long. Sturdy, upright branches, flower stalks topped by headlike clusters of rosy red flowers.

ERODIUM chamaedryoides. CRANE'S BILL. Perennial. Zones 7-9, 14-24. Native to Balearic Islands and Corsica. Dainty plant in the geranium family. Forms dense foliage tuft 3-6 in. high, 12 in. across. Long-stalked, roundish, dark green leaves ⅓ in. long, with scalloped edges. Profuse, cup-shaped, ½-in.-wide flowers with white, rosy-veined petals notched at tips, April to October.

Cushions of Erodium chamaedryoides are dotted with bloom over long season.

Good small-scale ground cover, rock plant. Plant in sun or part shade in porous soil; ample moisture. Rather slow growing. Not entirely hardy in cold winters.

ERYNGIUM amethystinum (E. coelestinum). SEA HOLLY, AMETHYST ERYNGIUM. Perennial. All Zones. Erect, stiff-branched thistlelike plant 2-3 ft. high, blooming July-September. Striking steel blue or amethyst, oval, ½-in.-long flower heads surrounded by spiny blue bracts; upper stems also blue (flowers last long when cut, fresh or dried). Leaves sparse, dark green, deeply cut, spiny toothed. Plant in borders or fringe areas, full sun, deep sandy soil. Tap-rooted; difficult to divide. Make root cuttings, or sow seed in place, thin to 1 ft. Often self-sows.

ERYSIMUM. BLISTER CRESS. Perennial or annual. Closely related to wallflower (Cheiranthus), with similar 4-petalled flowers, mostly yellow or orange.

E. asperum (Cheiranthus allionii). SIBERIAN WALLFLOWER. Perennial, usually grown as annual. All Zones. Branching plants 1-1½ ft. high smothered in spring with rich orange flowers. Leaves firm, narrow, 2-4 in. long. Combine with yellow, orange, or bronze tulips; blue forget-me-not (Myosotis) or Chinese forget-me-not (Cynoglossum). Sow seed in fall in mild climates; elsewhere in summer for well established plants by fall. Thin seedlings to 1 ft. apart.

E. kotschyanum. Perennial treated as annual in warm climates. Zones 1-11, 14-21. Forms attractive mats 6 in. high. Leaves pale green, finely toothed, crowded. Deep yellow flowers on 2-in. stems. Plant in sun. Use in rock gardens, rock crevices, between paving, or in small pattern plantings with mat-forming perennials such as aubrieta, dwarf candytuft (Iberis). If plants hump up, cut out raised portion; new growth will fill in the void.

ERYTHEA. Palms. These fan palms from Mexico are somewhat like the more familiar washingtonias in appearance, but with important differences.

E. armata. MEXICAN BLUE PALM. Zones 13-17, 19-24. Grows slowly to 40 ft., top spreading 6-8 ft. Leaves silvery blue, almost

Striking silvery blue fronds, hardiness characterize Mexican blue palm.

white. Conspicuous creamy flowers. Hardy to 18° and takes drought, heat, and wind.

E. brandegeei. SAN JOSE HESPER PALM. Zones 19, 21-24. Slow grower with slender flexible trunk. Eventually tall; reaches 125 ft. in its native Baja California. Trunk sheds leaves when old. When leaf stalks are trimmed, they often leave a spiral pattern. Three-foot leaves are light gray-green. Hardy to 26°.

E. edulis. GUADALUPE PALM. Zones 13-24. From Guadalupe Island off Baja California. Like E. armata but leaves are light green, flowers less conspicuous. Old leaves drop, leaving the naked, elephant-hide trunk ringed with scars. Slow grower to 30 ft., stout-trunked. Hardy to below 20° and takes beach and desert conditions.

E. elegans. FRANCESCHI PALM. Zones 13-17, 19-24. Slowest growing of erytheas; develops a trunk very slowly and reaches only 15 ft. Leaves gray-green. From northern Mexico; hardy to 22°.

Climate Zone maps pages 8-27

ERYTHRINA. CORAL TREE. Mostly deciduous (some nearly evergreen) trees or shrubs. Many kinds, known and used chiefly in southern California. Brilliant flowers from greenish white through yellow, light orange and light red to orange and red. Thorny plants have strong structural value, in or out of leaf. Leaves divided into 3 leaflets. Unless otherwise noted, plants do best in full sun, most soils (but best with good drainage), and with regular watering during dry season.

E. americana. (Sometimes sold as *E. corallodendrum.*) Briefly deciduous tree. Zones 12, 13, 19-24. Native to Mexico. Grows 15-25 ft. high. Short trunk, branches low. Bears coral red or crimson flowers in short clusters before leaves emerge in spring.

E. bidwillii. Large deciduous shrub. Zones 8, 9, 12-24. To 8 ft., sometimes tree-like to 20 ft. or more, wide spreading. Hybrid origin. Spectacular display—2-ft.-long clusters of pure red flowers on long, willowy stalks from spring until winter, main show in summer. Cut back flowering wood when flowers are spent. Very thorny so plant away from paths and prune with long-handled shears. Best in hot sun.

E. caffra (*E. constantiana, E. embryana*). KAFFIRBOOM CORAL TREE. Briefly deciduous tree. Zones 21-24. Native to South Africa. Grows 24-40 ft. high, spreads to 40-60 ft. wide. Drops leaves in January and then the angular bare branches produce big clusters of deep red-orange tubular flowers that drip honey. In March or earlier, flowers give way to fresh, light green, often dense foliage. Magnificent shade tree in summer. Wicked thorns disappear as wood matures.

E. coralloides (*E. poianthes*). NAKED CORAL TREE. Deciduous tree. Zones 12, 13, 19-24. Native to Mexico (some doubt about place of origin). To 30 ft. high and as wide or wider, but easily contained by pruning. Fiery red blossoms like fat candles or pine cones tip naked, twisted, black-thorned branches March to May. At end of flowering season, 8-10-in. leaves develop, give shade in summer, turn yellow in late fall before dropping. Bizarre form of branch structure when tree is out of leaf is almost as valuable as spring flower display.

Spikes of pink to wine red flowers at branch ends on Erythrina crista-galli.

E. crista-galli. COCKSPUR CORAL TREE. Deciduous shrub or tree. Native to rainy sections of Brazil. Zones 7-9, 12-17, 19-24. Unusual plant with habit all its own. In frost-free areas, becomes many-stemmed, rough-barked tree to 15-20 ft. high and wide. In colder climates, dies to ground in winter but comes back in spring like perennial (cut back dead growth). First flowers form after leaves come in spring—at each branch tip a big, loose, spikelike cluster of velvety birdlike blossoms, warm pink to wine red (plants vary). Depending on environment, there can be as many as three distinct flowering periods, spring through fall. Cut back old flower stems and deadened branch-ends after each wave of bloom. Leaves 6 in. long, leaflets 2-3 in. long.

E. falcata. Nearly evergreen tree. Zones 19-24. Native to Brazil and Peru. Grows to 30-40 ft. high, upright. Must be in ground several years before it flowers (may take 10-12 years). Rich, deep red, or occasionally orange-red, sickle-shaped flowers in down-hanging spikelike clusters at branch ends in late winter, early spring. Some leaves fall at flowering time.

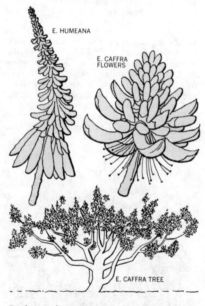

E. HUMEANA

E. CAFFRA FLOWERS

E. CAFFRA TREE

Erythrina humeana (upper left) blooms young; E. caffra has striking branches.

E. humeana. NATAL CORAL TREE. Normally deciduous shrub or tree (sometimes almost evergreen). Zones 12, 13, 20-24. Native to South Africa. May grow to 30 ft. but begins to wear its bright orange-red flowers when only 3 ft. high. Flowers in long-stalked clusters at branch ends well above foliage (unlike many other types). Bloom continuously from late summer to late November. Dark green leaves.

E. lysistemon. Deciduous tree. Zones 13, 21-24. Native to South Africa. Similar to *E. caffra* in size; slower growing. Light orange flowers, sometimes shrimp-colored, intermittently October to May, occasionally in summer. Time of bloom varies greatly. Many handsome black thorns. Altogether, a magnificent tree of great landscape value. Very sensitive to heavy wet soil.

E. ovalifolia. Nearly evergreen tree. Zones 12, 13, 19-24. Native to Malaysia. To 20-25 ft., upright and slightly spreading. Deep red flowers shaped like those of *E. coralloides,* but on long stems above leaves in March, April. Leaves become sparse in winter.

E. sandwicensis (*E. monosperma*). Deciduous tree or large shrub. Zones 21-24. Native to Hawaii. Grows to 15-30 ft. high. Flowers bright orange through yellow and yellow-green to nearly white, early spring.

E. umbrosa (*E. mitis*). Nearly evergreen tree. Zones 12, 13, 19-24. Native to Chile. To 20-25 ft., upright. Brick red flowers in clusters in spring, hang down from branches. Good shade tree.

ERYTHRONIUM. Corm. Zones 1-7, 15-17. Most native to West. Dainty, spring-blooming, nodding, lily-shaped flowers 1-1½ in. across, on stems usually 1 ft. or less high. All have 2 (rarely 3) broad, tongue-shaped, basal leaves, mottled in many species. Plant in shade or partial shade (except *E. dens-canis*) in groups under trees, in rock gardens, beside pools or streams. Plant corms in fall 2-3 in. deep, 4-5 in. apart, in rich, porous soil. Need moisture during summer.

Erythroniums are called by many common names—trout lily, fawn lily, adder's tongue, dog-tooth violet, avalanche lily, or alpine lily. What common names you hear depends to a great extent on what species they are or what they are commonly called in your part of the West.

E. californicum. FAWN LILY. Leaves mottled with brown. Flowers creamy white or yellow with deeper yellow band at base.

E. dens-canis. DOG-TOOTH VIOLET. European species with purple or rose flowers 1 in. long; stems 6 in. high. Leaves mottled with reddish brown. Needs more sun than others.

E. hendersonii. Flowers deeply curled back at tips, 1½ in. across, light to deep lavender, deep maroon at base surrounded by white band. Leaves mottled.

E. revolutum. Similar to *E. californicum,* with mottled leaves, large rose-pink or lavender flowers, banded yellow at base.

E. tuolumnense. All-green leaves. Flowers golden yellow, greenish yellow at base. Robust, with stems 12-15 in. tall.

ESCALLONIA. Evergreen shrubs. Zones 4-9, 14-17, 20-24. Native to South America, principally Chile. Wind-hardy, clean-looking, with glossy leaves. Clusters of flowers in summer and fall, nearly the year around in mild climates. May freeze badly at 10°-15°, but recover quickly. Will take direct coastal conditions and coastal winds. Grow in full sun near coast, part shade in hot interior valleys. Can take some drought once established, but look better with ample water. Tolerant of most soils but damaged by high alkalinity. Prune the taller ones by removing one-third of the old wood each year, cutting to the base, or shape into multiple trunk trees. Prune after flowers fade. Tip-pinch smaller kinds to keep them compact. Can be sheared as hedges, but this sacrifices some bloom. Good screen plants. Foliage of some exudes a resinous fragrance.

E. 'Alice'. Compact plant to 3-4 ft., with glossy, roundish 2-in. leaves and 2-in.-long clusters of bright red flowers.

E. 'Apple Blossom'. *E.* 'Glasneviensis'.

E. 'Balfouri'. Graceful plant to 10 ft., with drooping branchlets. Flowers white tinted pink in narrow clusters.

E. 'C. F. Ball'. Very similar to *E.* 'Alice'. With some pinching can be kept to 3 ft.

E. 'Fradesi'. Compact growth to 5-6 ft.; can be kept lower by tip-pinching. Glossy leaves smaller than those of *E. organensis,* which it resembles. Prolific show of clear pink to rose flowers nearly the year round.

E. franciscana. (Often sold as *E. rosea.*) Loose growth to 10 ft., with a tendency to throw long branches. Chocolate-colored bark and dark green leaves ½-1 in. long. Rosy pink flowers all summer. Informal espalier against wall or fence.

E. 'Glasneviensis' (*E.* 'Apple Blossom'). Twiggy shrub to 5 ft., sprawling unless pruned back. Flowers pinkish white from pink buds. Blooms all summer, with peaks in late spring, early fall.

E. 'Ingramii'. Densely leafy, 6-10 ft. tall, with red flowers in clusters in summer. Can be clipped as a hedge. Leaves glittering dark green.

E. 'Jubilee'. Compact 6-ft. shrub, densely leafy right to the ground. Clustered pinkish to rose flowers, at intervals throughout the year. Set 4 ft. apart for informal hedge or low screen.

E. langleyensis. Semi-evergreen in coldest winters. To 8-10 ft. with slender, arching branches. Foliage dense; leaves ½-1 in. long, glossy. Flowers rosy red in many short clusters June-July. Some repeat bloom.

E. 'Lou Allen'. Dwarf, bushy plant. At 3 years only 1 ft. tall, 1 ft. wide. Few pale pink flowers. Good edging or low foundation plant.

E. montevidensis. WHITE ESCALLONIA. Tall, broad shrub 8-10 ft. or a small tree to 25 ft. Leaves dark green, glossy, 3-4 in. long. White flowers in large, rounded clusters at branch ends late summer, fall. Big screening plant, or can be grown as a multiple trunk small tree. Many plants sold under this name are *E. illinita,* a smaller plant to 10 ft. tall with smaller flower clusters and a pronounced resinous odor.

E. organensis. PINK ESCALLONIA. Leafy, dense-growing shrub to 12-15 ft. Leaves bronzy green. Pink to red buds open into white to pink flowers in short, broad clusters. Early summer bloom. Use like *E. montevidensis.* Leaves burn in beach plantings.

E. pulverulenta. To 12 ft. Foliage markedly gummy and downy. White flowers in long, slender clusters. Summer bloom. Scarce.

E. rosea. Plants sold under this name are usually *E. franciscana,* but may belong to other pink-flowering kinds.

E. rubra. Upright, compact shrub 6-15 ft. tall. Leaves smooth, very glossy dark green. Red or crimson flowers in 1-3-in. clusters throughout warmer months. Much used as screen or hedge, especially near the coast.

E. 'William Watson'. To 4 ft. Growth rather spindly unless pruned. Ruddy cerise flowers.

ESCHSCHOLZIA californica. CALIFORNIA POPPY. Perennial usually grown as annual. Native to California, Oregon. State flower of California, where it is most familiar, covering fields, slopes, roadsides in spring

and early summer. Free-branching from base; stems 8-24 in. long. Leaves blue-green, finely divided. Single flowers vary from pale yellow to deep orange, about 2 in. wide, with satiny petals. Blooms close at night and on gray days.

Not the best choice for important, close-in garden beds because unless you trim off dead flowers regularly, plants go to seed and all parts turn straw color. But can't be surpassed for naturalizing on sunny hillsides, in dry fields, vacant lots, along drives, in parking strips, in country gardens. Broadcast seed in fall on cultivated, well drained soil; if rains are late, water to keep ground moist until seeds germinate. For large-scale sowing, use 3-4 pounds of seed per acre. Reseeds freely if not crowded out by weeds.

There are also garden forms available in pink, rose red, white, and cream-colored. Some of these have double flowers.

ESPOSTOA lanata. PERUVIAN OLD MAN CACTUS. Zones 12-24. Columnar cactus branching with age. Slow growing in pots, fairly fast to 8 ft. in open ground. Plant has light brown bristly thorns ½-2 in. long, usually concealed in the long, white hair that covers the plant and is especially long and dense near the summit. Pink 2-in.-long tubular flowers May-June. Protect from hard frosts.

EUCALYPTUS. Evergreen trees and shrubs. Zones 8-24. Native to Australia. The most widely planted non-native trees in California and Arizona. For several hundred miles in parts of California you never lose sight of a eucalypt. First ones were planted in California in 1856. From 1870 on, they were widely planted for windbreaks, firewood, shade, and beauty. From 1904 to 1912, thousands of acres were planted in an ill-advised hardwood timber scheme. Over the years, eucalyptus proved themselves well in these climates. They remain ever-

popular landscaping subjects. Reasons:

Great beauty. Some kinds are basically landscape structure trees or shrubs, with unimportant flowers. These kinds are grown for their attractive and functional form and texture. Others grow flowers as striking as roses or rhododendrons, or foliage so handsome that florists sell it. Some species serve basic landscaping functions and produce pretty flowers, too. The chart indicates the most noteworthy features of each species.

Climate tolerance. Much of Australia has either a desert, Mediterranean, or subtropical climate as do sections of California and Arizona. Dozens of eucalypts are naturally adapted to our coast, coastal hills, valleys, deserts—with or without irrigation. Drought tolerance is common to most.

No pests. In Australia, you seldom find a eucalyptus leaf unchewed by insects; here, by contrast, you almost never find one insect-chewed. Importing has been entirely by seed; no natural pests have been imported by way of living plants. There are no foliage-attacking diseases of eucalypts here.

Fast growth. Some of the tree types grow as fast as 10-15 ft. a year in early stages. Such growth rate is typically associated with short-lived trees, but not in this case; the fast-growing tree eucalypts can live for at least a century if planted right.

Eucalypts are influenced through their lives by their condition at planting time and the kind of planting they get. Select the most vigorous looking, not the biggest plants. Avoid ones with many leafless twigs or evidence of having been pruned hard. If possible, do not buy plants with canbound roots. If such plants are all that you can get, do this: Wash soil off roots, spread roots out as straight and fanlike as possible in a pre-moistened planting hole (with stem's old soil line ½-1 in. below grade level), fill in thoroughly around fanned-out

Climate Zone maps pages 8-27

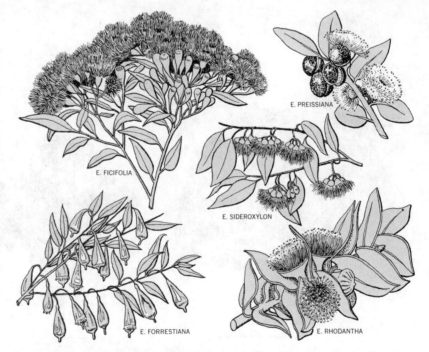

E. PREISSIANA

E. FICIFOLIA

E. SIDEROXYLON

E. FORRESTIANA

E. RHODANTHA

These five examples illustrate some of the variety that exists in eucalyptus flower size and formation. With E. forrestiana, *show comes from woody, red flower bases.*

Climate
Zone maps
pages 8-27

roots at once with moistened soil, and irrigate heavily. If plants are topheavy, cut back and stake (chart specifically prescribes staking for certain species).

Some descriptions in the chart recommend cutting plants back to make them bushier or stouter. Do this between March and August, preferably when a tree has been in the ground at least a year. If possible, cut back to just above a side branch or bud. If you can't find such a growth point, cut right into a smooth trunk; if the plant is established, new growth will break out beneath the cut. Later, come back and remove all excess new branches—keep only those that are mechanically well placed.

Best way to plant a eucalyptus is directly from seed flats. Seeding is as easy as with many annuals and perennials. Sow seed on flat of prepared soil in spring or summer. Keep flat shaded and moist. When seedlings are 2-3 in. high, lift gently, separate, and plant into another flat of prepared soil, spaced 3 in. apart. Or transplant into gallon cans or cleaned quart oil cans (puncture at bottom for drainage). Plant seedlings in 2-3 months when 6-12 in. high.

Take seeds from ripe seed capsules off trees. When ready, the fine seeds shake out of capsules like pepper from a shaker. Seed gathering is one reason the chart describes seed capsules in detail; the other reason is that seed capsules are distinctive identifying features. Seeds are sold by a few specialty seed houses in U. S. and Australia.

A eucalyptus tree in a suitable climate, properly planted and irrigated, is a vigorous, strong, and durable plant. Complete fertilizer is seldom needed, although iron often is required for eucalypts that chronically form yellow leaves.

Buds open to display flowers; fluffy parts disappear and leave seed capsules.

The chart gives approximate hardiness for each of the eucalyptus species sold in nurseries. But it is important to remember that these temperatures are not absolute. In addition to air temperature, you must take into consideration: age of the tree (generally, the older, the hardier); condition of the tree or shrub; date of the frost (24° in November is more damaging than 24° in January after weeks of frosts); dura-

tion of the frost. As a guide: If temperatures in your area are likely to fall within the frost-damage range for a certain species, plant it as a risk. If they regularly fall below the given range, don't plant it.

Most eucalypts have two conspicuous kinds of foliage: soft, variously shaped juvenile leaves found on seedlings, saplings, and new branches that grow from stumps; and the usually tougher adult or mature foliage. Where a species' juvenile foliage is significant, it is mentioned in the chart. Almost all eucalyptus leaves, juvenile and adult, have a distinguishing pungent fragrance. Sometimes you must crush leaves to smell it. There is a common denominator to the fragrance of all types, but various ones are additionally spiked with peppermint, lemon, medicinal, or other scents.

Several Australian words are used repeatedly in the common names for various eucalypts. Here are their meanings as applied to eucalyptus: *gum,* a name generally applied to any eucalypt, specifically to any of various smooth-barked (often peeling) species; *ironbark,* any with hard, rough bark; *mallee,* originally a native term for a eucalyptus thicket, here specifically for any shrubby species with round, swollen rootstock from which grow several slender stems; *marlock,* a dwarf species; *messmate,* an interesting name of no particular significance, applied to several stringybark species; *peppermint,* any with peppermint odor in crushed leaves, usually with finely fibrous bark; *yate,* a native word of Western Australia, applied to certain species.

Over 700 kinds of eucalyptus have been recorded in Australia. About 150 have been grown in California and Arizona (many as solitary representatives in arboretums).

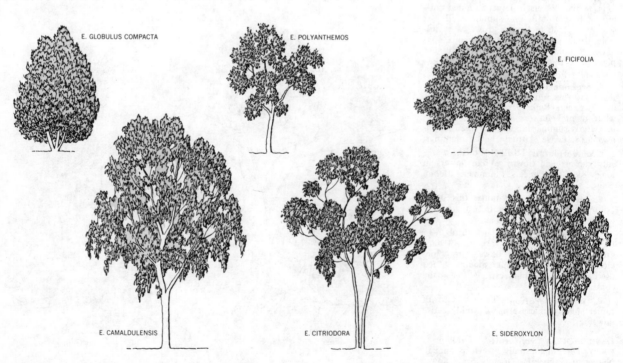

Six widely-planted tree-type eucalypts, showing relative sizes and differences in form. Of these, E. ficifolia and E. sideroxylon give most colorful flower display. E. globulus compacta is a screening tree. E. polyanthemos yields pretty cut foliage.

EUCALYPTUS

NAME	HARDINESS	FORM AND SIZE	LEAVES AND BARK	FLOWERS AND FRUIT	BEST FEATURES AND HOW TO ENCOURAGE THEM
EUCALYPTUS caesia (*caesia* means "bluish gray")	22°-25°	Graceful, weeping, open habit as mallee or small, weak-structured tree, 15-20 ft.	Gray-green small leaves, contrasting with red stems. Bark white and mottled when young, curling when older.	Outstanding dusty pink to deep rose flowers in loose clusters, blooming heavily late winter to early spring. Flowering scattered rest of the year. Seed capsules shaped like bells, lavender-gray, 3/4 in.	Not good in wind **or in** heavy soils. Use as thin screen in protected place. Or, with pruning and training use as espalier, shrub, or multi-trunked tree. Prune and stake to give it body.
E. calophylla (*calophylla* means "beautiful leaf")	25°-28°	Medium to large, roundheaded tree —90-150 ft. high in Australia, has reached 50 ft. in California.	Broad-oval leaves, 4-7 in. long. Rough, fissured bark.	Showy flowers in 1-ft. clusters—white, rose, or red, on and off all year. Bulbous seed capsules, 1 1/2 in. wide. Light pink-flowered form often sold as *E. c.* 'Rosea'; rose pink kind is *E. c.* 'Hawkeyi'.	Sturdy, drought-tolerant, easy to grow—and it produces showy flowers against nice leaves as part of the package. Similar to *E. ficifolia* in many ways (also hybridizes frequently with it).
E. camaldulensis (*E. rostrata*) RED GUM, RIVER RED GUM	12°-15°	Ultimately 80-120 ft. Form varies; typically has curved trunk, spreading crown, gracefully weeping branches.	Long, slender, lance-shaped, medium green leaves, pendulous in varying degrees. Tan, mottled trunk.	Unimportant white to pale yellow flowers in drooping clusters, summer. Followed by many, rounded, pea-sized seed capsules in long clusters. Not grown for flowers; a structural tree. One of the most widely planted eucalypts around the world.	A mighty eucalypt for highways, broad streets, parks, skylines. Grows in lawns. Widely planted in California and Arizona valleys and deserts. Takes more heat and cold than *E. globulus*. Good in alkaline soil. Has resprouted after 11° freeze.
E. cinerea (*cinerea* means "ash colored")	14°-17°	Medium-sized tree, 20-50 ft. high, almost as wide. Irregular outline. Can be scrawny.	Juvenile leaves gray-green, roundish, 1-2 in. long, in pairs. Mature leaves long. Furrowed bark.	Small white flowers near stems in winter and spring, followed by small conical seed capsules. The flowers are incidental—decorative juvenile foliage is main reason for growing it.	Inclined to grow snake-like. Corrective pruning yields and encourages juvenile gray-foliaged branches used for indoor decorating. Fast growing. Withstands wind. Best in dry site or with fast drainage.
E. citriodora LEMON-SCENTED GUM	24°-28°	One of the most graceful of trees, slender, tall (50-75 ft.). Trunk usually straight, sometimes curved.	Leaves long (3-7 in.), narrow, golden green, lemon-scented. Trunk and branches powder white to pinkish.	Once tree gets up in the air, you'd need a telescope to see flowers (lower 1/2 or 2/3 of tree is bare trunk). Blooms whitish, indistinctive, in clusters, mostly during winter. Seed capsules that follow are urn-shaped, 3/8 in. wide.	Designer's tree. Enhances any architecture. Can grow close to walls, walks. Perfect for groves. Very fast. Weak-trunked when young. Stake stoutly. Cut back and thin often to strengthen trunk. Tolerates much or little water. Tenderness to frosts is only real drawback.
E. cladocalyx (*E. corynocalyx*) SUGAR GUM	23°-28°	Large, upright, graceful, round-topped, very open, 75-100 ft. high. Straight trunk.	Oval or variably-shaped leaves, 3-5 in., shiny reddish. Tan bark peels to show cream patches.	Creamy white flowers of little significance, in dense 3-in. clusters, blooming June-August. Oval seed capsules (3/8 in. wide) in clusters. Not planted for flowers; used for its structure.	Dramatic skyline tree on southern California coast. Puffy clouds of leaves separated by open spaces —a Japanese print in its mature silhouette. Tough, drought-resistant. Variety 'Nana' to 20-25 ft.

(Continued on next page)

E

Climate Zone maps pages 8-27

NAME	HARDINESS	FORM AND SIZE	LEAVES AND BARK	FLOWERS AND FRUIT	BEST FEATURES AND HOW TO ENCOURAGE THEM
E. cloeziana YELLOW MESSMATE	25°-28°	Medium size (30-50 ft.). Straight central trunk. Usually narrow.	Light green 4-in.-long leaves, red and purple fall, winter. Brown bark.	Small clusters of white to yellowish flowers, spring, early summer. Round seed capsules like miniature ($1/4$-in.) half grapefruits in tight clusters.	Reddish new foliage is its best feature. Has made variable performance in California, including a tendency to become chlorotic (supply iron in soil).
E. cornuta (*cornuta* means "horn shaped") YATE	22°-25°	Large-headed, spreading tree, to 35-60 ft. high. Attractive dense crown gives shade.	Lance-shaped, shiny, leaves. 3-6 in. long (young leaves round, gray). Bark peels in strips.	Flower buds have interesting, fingerlike, buff caps, pushed off by opening flowers. Greenish yellow flowers make round fuzzy clusters, 3 in. wide, summer. Clusters of round seed capsules with short horns.	Appreciated for its flowers, form, and landscape uses. Grows under many kinds of soil and water and climate conditions. Does well even when neglected. Not subject to wind breakage. Good shade tree.
E. eremophila TALL SAND MALLEE	24°-27°	Multi-trunk, small, bushy tree, 25 ft.	Dark green, narrow, lance-shaped, shiny leaves. Scaly bark.	Round, yellow, fuzzy, 1-2 in. flowers in clusters, June. Opening flowers push off long, pointed caps. Capsules slightly cylindrical, $1/4$-in. wide.	Very drought-tolerant tree for banks, hillsides, beach areas. No good in lawns. Better liked in southern than in northern California.
E. erythrocorys RED-CAP GUM	23°-26°	Small tree, 10-30 ft., best with multiple trunk; a sprawling but attractive bush.	Thick, shiny, 4-7 in., lance-shaped leaves, greener than most eucalyptus leaves. White trunk.	Spectacular. Bright red caps tilt up and drop off to reveal yellow flowers, several in cluster that looks like shaving brush. Blooms any time, peak fall to early spring. Cone-shaped seed capsules.	Takes much water if drainage is good. Can be grown in lawn. To make a dense multi-trunk bush or tree, head back main shoots several times.
E. erythronema RED-FLOWERED MALLEE	22°-24°	Mallee or small, bushy, crooked or sinuous tree, 10-25 ft.	Narrow, dull green leaves $1\frac{1}{2}$-3 in. long. Smooth bark in patches of pink, white, tan, pale green.	Watermelon to deep red flowers, 1 in. wide, open from conical, pointed buds, 1 in. long, pinkish green to red. Flowers often hidden by leaves. Conical, square-sided seed capsules, $1/2$ in. wide.	The trunk and the flowers are its best features. You may have to thin some to make it a presentable tree. Resists wind and drought. Good near ocean.
E. ficifolia RED-FLOWERING GUM	25°-30°	Usually a single-trunk, round-headed tree to 40 ft. Compact crown. Can be multi-stemmed big bush.	Leaves 3-7 in. long, shape and texture of rubber plant leaves. Bark red stringy to gray fibrous.	Spectacular, 1-ft. clusters of flowers, cream, light pink, salmon, orange, or light red (most common); all year, peak July-August. Seed capsules 1 in. wide, like miniature dice cups with swollen bottoms.	Not like other eucalypts except *E. calophylla*. Prune off seed capsules from young trees so they won't pull branches down. Best on coast; seldom successful inland. Rarely good in lawns.
E. forrestiana FUCHSIA EUCALYPTUS	25°-30°	Shrub or short-trunked tree to 12 ft. (needs staking, pruning as tree).	Narrow leaves $1\frac{1}{2}$-$2\frac{1}{2}$ in. long. Gray-brown smooth trunk, reddish branches.	Flowers are unimportant; the woody, pendant, red flower bases, resemble fuchsias, give the decoration. Intermittent all year. Capsules 1 in. wide.	Fuchsialike flower bases last long when cut. Good performance coast or dry areas. Any soil. To strengthen, cut back when young.
E. globulus BLUE GUM	17°-22°	Tall, solemn trees of grandeur, to 200 ft. Straight trunks. Heavy masses of foliage.	Sickle-shaped leaves dark green, 6-10 in. long. Young leaves oval, silvery, soft. Bark sheds.	Flowers creamy white to yellow in winter and spring. Warty, ribbed, blue-gray seed capsules, 1 in. wide. Fruit drop added to leaf and bark litter makes tree very messy.	The most common eucalypt in California. Very aromatic. Magnificent windbreak but too messy, greedy, and brittle for garden or city street. Needs deep soil and plenty of room. Best on coastal slopes.

E

Climate Zone maps pages 8-27

NAME	HARDINESS	FORM AND SIZE	LEAVES AND BARK	FLOWERS AND FRUIT	BEST FEATURES AND HOW TO ENCOURAGE THEM
E. globulus 'Compacta' DWARF BLUE GUM	17°-22°	Many-branched, bushy, shrublike tree, as high as 60-70 ft.	Same as *E. globulus*. Foliage persists to ground for 10-15 years.	Flowers and seed capsules same as on *E. globulus*.	Lacks noble silhouette of *E. globulus*, just as greedy, almost as messy. Good low windbreak in coastal areas—can be sheared as low as 10 ft.
E. grossa COARSE-FLOWERED MALLEE	22°-26°	Multiple-trunked, spreading shrub, 9-15 ft., sometimes dense.	Thick, glistening, deep green, 3-in., broad-oval leaves. Red, green stems.	Noticeable yellow flowers in clusters open from bullet-shaped buds in spring and summer. Cylindrical seed capsules, ³/₈ in. wide.	Best feature is clean green foliage. Often erratic, can be made into dense hedge if pruned. Gets scraggly when old if watered heavily.
E. gunnii CIDER GUM	0°-10°	Medium to large, dense, vertical tree, 40-75 ft.	Mature leaves lance-shaped, 3-5 in. long. Bark smooth, green, tan.	• Small creamy white flowers April-June from shiny green, round buds. Seed capsules ¹/₄ in. wide, bell-shaped, in clusters.	Strong, vigorous, tall grower. Impressively healthy and vigorous looking. Good shade, windbreak, or privacy screening tree in cold areas (very hardy).
E. kruseana KRUSE'S MALLEE	25°-28°	Thin, open, angular shrub, almost a ground cover. Maximum: 5-8 ft.	Silver-blue, round, 1-in. leaves like tiny *E. pulverulenta*. Smooth bark.	Little (¹/₂-in.) yellow flowers along stems between round leaves. Flower bud caps cone-shaped. Seed capsules size and shape of small (¹/₄-in.) acorns.	Attractive foliage and flowers on slow-growing shrub small and dainty enough for Japanese garden. Conversation plant. Cut back often.
E. lehmannii BUSHY YATE	25°-28°	Small tree, 20-30 ft. Dense, flat-topped, wide-spreading.	Light green, long-oval, 2-in. leaves, some turn red in fall. Old ones rough. Brown bark.	Apple green flowers in huge (4-in.-wide), round clusters open from curved, horn-shaped buds in clusters. (Horns straight in form 'Max Watson'.) Large, fused seed capsules remain on branches.	Fast-growing, densely-leafed tree, very good for screening on coast, or street tree with lower branches pruned. Unpruned, branches persist to ground. Form 'Max Watson' grows low and compact.
E. leucoxylon WHITE IRONBARK	14°-18°	Somewhat variable, usually slender, upright, open, with pendulous branches, 20-80 ft.	Gray-green, sickle-shaped leaves, 3-6 in. long. Bark sheds leaving white to mottled trunk.	White flowers intermittently, winter, spring. Goblet-shaped seed capsules, ³/₈ in. wide. (*E. l.* 'Rosea' has pink flowers, larger seed capsule, may not come true from seed.)	Free-flowering, fast-growing, moderate-sized tree that tolerates many adverse conditions including heavy soil, light rocky soil, heat, wind.
E. l. macrocarpa 'Rosea' LARGE-FRUITED RED-FLOWERING GUM	14°-18°	Much branched, shrublike tree, 15-25 ft., variable.	Gray-green leaves. Gray to pinkish trunk.	Clear vivid crimson flowers borne profusely at early age. Seed capsules goblet-shaped, ³/₄ in. wide.	Very ornamental tree. Good on most soils, most sites, even near beach.
E. linearis (*E. pulchella, E. amygdalina angustifolia*) WHITE PEPPERMINT	18°-22°	Graceful tree to 20-50 ft. with weeping branches. Can be either asymmetrical or round-headed.	Long, very narrow, dark green, pendulous leaves. White to light tan bark peels in thin strips.	Clusters of tiny, creamy white flowers open from pinhead size buds, June-Oct. Goblet-shaped seed capsules, 3/16 in. wide, in tight clusters.	Fine landscaping and street tree. Beautiful form, willowy, well-mannered. Dark, dense foliage masses contrast with light trunk. Good in light soils with little water.
E. macrandra LONG-FLOWERED MARLOCK	8°-12°	Round-headed, open tree to 25-35 ft. Main branches often develop curves.	Light golden green, lance-shaped leaves, 2¹/₂-5 in. long. Slick bark peels in ribbons.	Cream to green flowers in clusters. Bud caps distinctive: light green fingers 1-1¹/₂ in. long, ¹/₈ in. wide. Seed capsules slightly elongated, too. Flowering is incidental.	Plant to hide a utility pole or soften a house corner. (Some nurseries mistakenly sell this as *E. angulosa*; real *E. angulosa* is a mallee with yellow-white flowers and prominently ribbed seed capsules.)

(Continued on next page)

E

Climate Zone maps pages 8-27

NAME	HARDINESS	FORM AND SIZE	LEAVES AND BARK	FLOWERS AND FRUIT	BEST FEATURES AND HOW TO ENCOURAGE THEM
E. macrocarpa (*macrocarpa* means "big-fruited")	8°-12°	Erratic, sprawling shrub 4-15 ft. Tries to be a vine but stems are too stiff. Similar to *E. rhodantha* (compare them).	Light gray-blue leaves, 2-5 in. long, round with definite point, set close to stem. Greenish white bark.	Golf-ball-size gray buds (point on top) open to show flat-topped, round, fluffy flowers 4-7 in. wide, usually pink, also white, red, or yellow-white (seedlings vary). No stems on flowers; grow right on branch. Flat-topped, bowl-shaped seed capsules, 3 in. wide.	Sprawling plant good for seasonal display in a dry, sunny place. Not for irrigated areas (over-watering causes blackening of leaves). New growth begins vertical, becomes horizontal when weighted down with buds and capsules. Stems tend to die back from pruning.
E. maculata (*maculata* means "spotted")	19°-23°	Erect single-trunked tree, branching to make wide head. Graceful, strong. To 50-75 ft.	Dark green leaves, 3-6 in. long. Pearl gray bark patched dark red to violet.	White flowers in branch-end clusters, 1-3 in. wide. Seed capsules urn-shaped, 1/2 in. wide, rough on outside. Not grown for flowers; a landscaping tree.	Good singly or in groves. Smooth, spotted trunks are usually quite handsome; they vary in degree of spottiness. Best in sandy, well drained soil.
E. maculosa RED-SPOTTED GUM	23°-25°	Tall, slender tree, 20-50 ft. Gracefully pendant branches sway prettily in wind.	Leaves 1/2 in. wide, 4-6 in. long, light green with gray cast. Bark brown, gray, off-white.	Unimportant light-colored flowers open from pointed oval buds in clusters of 3-7, and leave 1/2-in. goblet-shaped seed capsules.	A landscaping tree to feature in place of honor. When mature, brownish and grayish bark flakes off in summer, leaving powdery white surface. Australian aborigines paint their faces with the white dust.
E. megacornuta (*megacornuta* means "big-horned")	20°-23°	Big shrub or small tree, 20-30 ft. Multi-stemmed or single trunk. Spindly.	Shiny, bronzy green leaves. Smooth, gray to tan bark.	Clusters of St. Patrick's green flowers, 1 1/2 in. long, each shaped like a shaving brush, open from buds that look like warty fingers. Clawlike seed capsules.	Arrangers like the 2-in.-long, bronzy green buds, the flowers, and the seed capsules. Sometimes the form makes it acceptable for landscaping purposes.
E. melliodora (*melliodora* means "honey-scented")	18°-20°	Upright, graceful tree, 30-100 ft., with slightly weeping branches. Top fills in well.	Boat-shaped to sickle-shaped leaves, 2-6 in. long, grayish green. Old bark scaly-flaky, tan.	Late winter, early spring flowers are off-white, in clusters about 1 1/2 in. wide, not showy but sweet smelling (truly the smell of honey) and attractive to bees. Seed capsules goblet-shaped, 1/4 in. wide, in clusters.	Clean tree, well mannered, very little litter. Good for shade tree, street tree, windbreak (takes wind very well). The form 'Rosea' has pink flowers.
E. microtheca (*microtheca* means "tiny capsules")	5°-10°	Bushy tree, 35-40 ft., round head. May be single or many-trunked.	Blue-green, ribbon-like leaves, 8 in. long. Smooth bark.	Insignificant creamy white flowers. Seed capsules tiny (match head size) in clusters of 3-5. Seed capsules create no litter.	Strong-looking, strong-growing tree of character. Drought tolerant. No breakage from wind. One of Arizona's best eucalypts.
E. nicholii NICHOL'S WILLOW-LEAFED PEPPERMINT	12°-15°	Graceful, weeping tree, to 40 ft. Upright main trunk. Spreading crown.	Light green, often purple-tinged, very narrow leaves 3-5 in. Soft brown bark.	Small, inconspicuous whitish flowers mostly in summer. Very small, round seed capsules in roundish clusters.	A garden or street tree. The beauty is in the fine-textured foliage and the billowing, willowy form. Grows fast. Crushed leaves smell like peppermint.
E. niphophila SNOW GUM	5°-10°	Small, wide-spreading, open tree to 20 ft. Trunk usually crooked.	Silvery blue, lance-shaped, 1 1/2-4-in. leaves. Smooth, white, peeling bark.	Creamy white flowers in tight clusters 1 1/2 in. wide, summer. Seed capsules round, 3/8 in. wide, very gray, also in tight clusters, close to stem.	Acclaimed chiefly for its hardiness and silvery look of its leaves. Slow growing. Drought, wind tolerant. Good on slopes. Can be picturesque.

NAME	HARDINESS	FORM AND SIZE	LEAVES AND BARK	FLOWERS AND FRUIT	BEST FEATURES AND HOW TO ENCOURAGE THEM
E. orbifolia ROUND-LEAFED MALLEE	23°-25°	A large mallee of irregular, clambering habit. Not a tree.	Leaves nearly round (slightly pointed), 2 in. long. Thin red bark.	Little (½-in.-wide) yellow flowers in late spring. Round flower bud cap has a point like a Kaiser Wilhelm helmet. Seldom sets seed capsules.	Use as a ground cover in a difficult sunny place; native to rocky desert. Can be espaliered to show off round leaves and flowers. Slender vinelike stems.
E. orpetii ORPET HYBRID EUCALYPTUS (California hybrid)	24°-28°	A mallee or weak-stemmed small tree, 6-20 ft.—usually not over 10 ft.	Leaves vary in color, shape. Most are silvery green, tapered, 1½ in. long.	Many fluffy flowers, 2 in. wide, pink to red with yellow anthers, at branch ends in winter-spring. Buds and seed capsules interestingly ribbed.	Grow for the attractive flowers and leaves. Cut flowers keep a week or 10 days. Believed to be hybrid between *E. macrocarpa* and *E. caesia*.
E. pauciflora GHOST GUM	10°-15°	Tree. Branches spread to make crown as wide as height (40 by 40 ft.). Graceful, airy, open.	All-white trunk and branches, and narrow gray-green leaves 3-6 in. long—hence: "ghost gum."	Insignificant flowers and little or no seed-setting. Among other good points, ghost gum doesn't litter the ground beneath it.	White trunk and branches, and open, see-through foliage makes it valuable individual display tree. Takes most soils, including heavy and wet. Good in lawns. In youth, remove erratic branches.
E. perriniana ROUND-LEAFED SNOW GUM	10°-15°	Small straggly tree 15-30 ft. Best cut back as shrub.	Juvenile leaves silvery, form circle around stem, spin on stem when dry.	Many small white flowers in summer, clusters of 3. Seed capsules, also in 3's, cup-shaped, ¼ in. wide.	Silvery foliage nice for arrangements. If you cut enough, silvery juvenile growth remains (mature leaves are long). Use as gray-leafed plant in border.
E. platypus ROUND-LEAFED MOORT	23°-26°	Large bush or small tree, 20-30 ft. Many stems; may ultimately form one trunk.	Dark, dull green leaves, round-ended, 1-2 in. long, rough. Tan, smooth bark.	Many flowers, red or green (two forms), open at ends of flattened stems, make showy clusters 2 in. wide. Cluster of many ½-in. goblet-shaped seed capsules.	Dense, fast, pyramidal form, good for solid screening (space 12 ft. apart). Plants give general effect of stiff birches. Hummingbirds enjoy flowers.
E. polyanthemos SILVER DOLLAR GUM	14°-18°	Slender, erect tree, single or multi-stem, 20-60 ft. Fairly fast.	Juvenile leaves green-gray, oval or round, 2-3 in. Mature leaves lance-shaped. Mottled bark.	Creamy white flowers in 1-in. clusters, spring-summer. Seed capsules are cylindrical cups, ½ in. wide, in clusters. Flowers incidental—grow it for cut foliage or landscape uses.	Popular landscaping and street tree. Excellent cut foliage. Select young trees carefully; some have leaves less round and gray than others. Grows almost anywhere. Not good in wet places.
E. preissiana BELL-FRUITED MALLEE	24°-26°	Mallee—typically an open, many-stemmed shrub to 12 ft. Sometimes a tree to 15 ft.	Oval leaves, 2-3 in. long, thick, dull, bluish cast, red stems. Smooth gray bark.	Very showy. Round, flat, yellow flowers 2-3 in. wide open from brown globelike buds, 1 in. wide. Seed capsules cup-shaped, ¾ in. wide. Flower color contrasts nicely with leaf, stem, trunk.	A first-rate flower producer that also can hold its own as a garden shrub. Cut flowers keep well. Blooms heaviest January-March.
E. pulverulenta (*pulverulenta* means "powdered as with dust") SILVER MOUNTAIN GUM	15°-21°	Irregular, sprawling small tree or large shrub, 15-30 ft. Poor form unless pruned.	Silver-gray shish kebab juvenile foliage (stems appear to go through leaves). Ribbony bark.	Creamy white, ½-in., fuzzy flowers in 3's sandwiched between the round leaves along stems. Fall to spring. Flowers are simply an extra. They are followed by ½-in. wide cup-shaped seed capsules.	Use in garden as curiosity feature and source of branches for arrangements (use natural or gilded). Cut back often to get and encourage decorative juvenile leaf growth; mature leaves are usually long and pointed.

E

Climate Zone maps pages 8-27

(Continued on next page)

E

Climate Zone maps pages 8-27

NAME	HARDINESS	FORM AND SIZE	LEAVES AND BARK	FLOWERS AND FRUIT	BEST FEATURES AND HOW TO ENCOURAGE THEM
E. pyriformis (*pyriformis* means "pear-shaped")	25°-28°	Shrub or treelike shrub (mallee), 10-20 ft. Long, weak, rangy stems.	Broad, oval, light green leaves 2-4 in. long. Light brown bark.	Showy, large (2-3-in.-wide) flowers in clusters late winter to early summer. May be red, pink, orange, yellow, or cream. Pear-shaped 1-in. capsules.	Collector's item. Sometimes "an elegant slender tree," sometimes "weak, rangy shrub." Flowers are best feature. Good performance in dry or sandy soil.
E. rhodantha (*rhodantha* means "roselike")	8°-12°	Erratic sprawling shrub 4-8 ft. Branches tend to grow out horizontally.	Light gray-blue leaves sometimes with greenish cast, 2-4 in. long, nearly round, close to stem. Greenish white bark.	Buds same as *E. macrocarpa* but with shorter point on lid. Flowers, on 1-2-in.-long stems, same shape as *E. macrocarpa* but 3-5 in. wide and almost always carmine red. Capsules like *E. macrocarpa*. The two are similar but differ in some ways; compare them.	Sprawling plant good for almost continual flower display. For dry sunny place and little water, same as *E. macrocarpa*. Better for spilling down slope than *E. macrocarpa* (follows terrain better). Put supports under branches to keep mud off.
E. robusta SWAMP MAHOGANY	11°-15°	Tall, densely-foliaged, ultimately round-headed, 80-90 ft.	Leathery, shiny leaves 4-7 in. long. Rough dark red-brown stringy bark.	Attractive flowers for a large tree: masses of pink-tinted creamy white flowers any time, chiefly in winter. Cylindrical ³/₈-in. seed capsules in clusters.	Big strong tree performs well in moist or saline soil. Good for windy places at beach or inland. Windbreak. Attractive foliage.
E. rudis DESERT GUM, SWAMP GUM	12°-18°	Upright, spreading, often weeping, 30-60 ft. high. Robust.	Mature leaves gray-green to green, lance-shaped, 4-6 in. long. Rough trunk.	White flowers in clusters, spring and summer (not showy but good for a large tree). Seed capsules ¹/₄ in. wide.	A good, large shade tree, street tree. Tolerates: desert, valleys, beach, windy places, much or little water (but best with irrigation), any soil including saline.
E. saligna SYDNEY BLUE GUM	18°-20°	Tall, slender, shaft-like tree, dense when young, thins out later to open crown. To 60-80 ft.	Young leaves mahogany, mature medium green, 4-8 in. long, lance shape. Red to pinkish bark, sheds.	Flowers pinkish to cream in spring and summer, not showy. Smooth, seed capsules, ¹/₄ in. wide, in tight clusters 1 in. wide.	Probably the fastest-growing eucalypt ("Fastest gum in the West"); gallon can plant not rootbound can grow 10 ft. first year. Best near coast; not recommended inland. Can grow in lawns.
E. sideroxylon (Often sold as *E. sideroxylon* 'Rosea') RED IRONBARK, PINK IRONBARK	20°-25°	Varies: 20-80 ft. high, open or dense, slender or squatty, weeping or upright.	Slim blue-green leaves turn bronze in winter. Furrowed, non-shedding, nearly black trunk.	Fluffy flowers, light pink to pinkish crimson, in pendulous clusters, mostly from fall to late spring. Usually, the darker the foliage the darker the flowers. Seed capsules goblet-shaped, ³/₈ in.	Use singly, or as screen, or as street or highway tree. Wide variation in individuals—try to select according to characteristics you desire. Grows fast. Coast or inland. Gets chlorotic in wet adobe soils.
E. spathulata NARROW-LEAFED GIMLET	22°-25°	Small, erect, multi-trunked tree, 6-20 ft.	Ribbonlike leaves 2-3 in. long. Smooth red bark.	Many ¹/₂-in. cream and gold flowers open in summer from long, oval buds. Bell-shaped seed capsules.	Versatile. Tolerates poor soil drainage. Bushy wind screen. Branches move nicely in breezes.
E. stellulata BLACK SALLY	12°-18°	Medium size (20-50 ft.), spreading tree, pendulous branches.	Broad elliptical leaves. Smooth gray bark changes to olive green.	White to cream flowers, October-April. Not known for its flower display. Roundish seed capsules, size of small peas, in tight clusters along stem.	Unusual colored bark. Nice spreading form. Good small screening tree or shade tree.

NAME	HARDINESS	FORM AND SIZE	LEAVES AND BARK	FLOWERS AND FRUIT	BEST FEATURES AND HOW TO ENCOURAGE THEM
E. tetraptera SQUARE-FRUITED MALLEE	22°-26°	Shrub, 4-10 ft. (occasionally to 15 ft.). Straggly but interesting.	Thick, rubbery, dark leaves, 4-5 in. long. Green to gray bark.	Big (1½-in.), smooth, salmon buds open to show big round red flowers. Blooms almost continuously. Seed capsules, square with 4 flanges, are 1½ in. wide.	A novelty with striking flowers, fruits, unusual form. Not for basic landscaping. Grows in sand. Wind-resistant, salt-tolerant. Prune to make bushy.
E. torquata CORAL GUM	27°-29°	Slender, upright, narrow-headed, 15-20 ft. Branches often droop from weight of many flowers and seed capsules.	Light green to golden green leaves, long and narrow or blunt and round. Rough, flaky bark.	Flower buds are like little (¾-in.) Japanese lanterns. From them open beautiful coral red and yellow flowers, on and off all year. Seed capsules ½ in. long, grooved, squarish at bottom.	Grown for bloom (good cut flowers) and small size. Good as free-standing tree in narrow area. Stake and prune or head back to make it graceful and attractive. Select individuals by plant form.
E. viminalis (*viminalis* means "long, flexible shoot") MANNA GUM	12°-15°	Tall, spreading patriarch tree to 150 ft., drooping willowlike branches.	Light green, narrow, 4-6-in.-long leaves. Trunk whitish, bark sheds.	Little white flowers in long, thin, open clusters all year—usually too high to be seen. Small roundish seed capsules size of peas.	Can make significant silhouette. Grows best in good soil but can take poor soil. Needs room—for ranches, parks, highways, not small gardens. Debris.

E

Climate Zone maps pages 8-27

EUCOMIS comosa (*E. punctata*). PINEAPPLE FLOWER. Bulb. Zones 4-24. Native to South Africa. Unusual looking member of the lily family. Thick spikes 2-3 ft. tall closely-set with ½-in.-long, 6-petaled, scented, greenish white flowers sometimes tinged pink or purple; spike topped with a tuft of leaflike bracts. Bloom in July-August. Fruit violet-purple. Stems spotted with purple at base. Leaves to 2 ft. long, bright green, spotted with purple at base. Garden or container plant, handsome over long period; good cut flower. Sun or light shade. Plant in rich soil with plenty of humus. Water in summer. Can be grown from seed.

EUGENIA jambos. See Syzygium jambos

E. myrtifolia. See Syzygium paniculatum

E. paniculatum. See Syzygium paniculatum

E. smithii. See Acmena

EUGENIA uniflora. SURINAM CHERRY, PITANGA. Evergreen compact shrub or small tree. Zones 21-24. Very slow and open growth to 15-25 ft., usually to 6-8 ft., with equal spread. Leaves glossy, coppery green deepening to purplish or red in cold weather, oval, to 2 in. long. White, fragrant flowers like little brushes, ½ in. across. Fruits, size of a small tomato, change color from green to yellow to orange to deep red, at which stage they are edible. Grow in well drained soil, and water freely. Best in a moist atmosphere and a sheltered spot in sun or partial shade. Can be sheared into a hedge, but this will reduce flowering and fruiting. Prune to shape.

EUONYMUS. Evergreen or deciduous shrubs, evergreen vines. Evergreen kinds are highly valued for their foliage, texture, and form; they are almost always used as landscape structure plants, never for flower display. The deciduous species is a shapely shrub with unusually good fall color. Some types display colorful fruits—pink, red, or yellow capsules which open to show orange-red seeds in fall. Climate adaptation is quite significant because of varying degrees of hardiness and susceptibility to mildew.

E. alata. WINGED EUONYMUS. Deciduous shrub. Zones 1-9, 14-16. Slow to medium growth 7-10 ft. high, to 10-15 ft. wide. Dense, twiggy, with horizontal branching and a flat-topped appearance. Twigs have flat, corky wings which disappear on older growth. Dark green leaves turn rich rose-red in fall. Inconspicuous flowers followed by sparse crop of bright orange-red fruits. Use as background, screen, or single isolated plant. Best against dark evergreens.

Variety 'Compacta' grows 4-6 ft. tall and equally wide, has less prominent wings. Use as a screen or unclipped hedge.

E. fortunei. (Formerly *E. radicans acuta*.) Evergreen vine or shrub. Zones 1-17. One of the best broad-leafed evergreens where temperatures drop below 0°. An evergreen vine which trails or climbs by rootlets. Used as a shrub, its branches will trail and sometimes root; allowed to climb, it will be a spreading mass to 20 ft. or more. Leaves dark rich green, 1-2½ in. long with scalloped-toothed edges. Sun or full shade. Mature growth, like that of ivy, is shrubby and bears fruit; cuttings taken from this shrubby wood produces comparatively upright plants.

E. radicans (native to Korea, Japan), once thought to be the species, was later classed as variety of *E. fortunei*. Many nurserymen have not made the change in names, and still sell many varieties as forms of *E. radicans*; translate *radicans* to *fortunei* wherever you see it, except in *E. fortunei radicans*. Varieties of *E. fortunei*, listed below are better known than the species itself.

'Azusa'. Prostrate grower for ground cover use. Small dark green leaves with light colored veins. Undersides of leaves turn maroon in winter.

'Carrierei'. A shrubby spreading form. Plant where it can lean or sprawl against wall or fence; will not climb. Mature form; bears handsome orange fruits.

'Colorata'. PURPLE-LEAF WINTER CREEPER. Same sprawling growth habit as *E. f. radicans*. Leaves turn dark purple in fall and winter. Growth is more even as a ground cover than *E. f. radicans*.

'Gracilis'. (Often sold as *E. radicans argentea variegata*, *E. f. variegata*, *E. f.* 'Silver Edge'.) Trailing, less vigorous, more restrained than the species. Leaves variegated with white or cream; lighter portions turn pinkish in cold weather. Use in hanging baskets, as ground cover in small areas, to spill over a wall.

'Kewensis'. Delightful trailing or climbing form with very small (¼ in.) leaves. Use it to create delicate traceries against stone or wood, or as a dense, fine-textured ground cover.

'Minima'. Very similar to 'Kewensis' but with slightly longer leaves. There is a green and white variegated form.

E. f. radicans. COMMON WINTER CREEPER. Tough, hardy, trailing or vining shrub with dark green, thick-textured, 1-in.-long leaves. Given no support, it sprawls; given a masonry wall to cover, it does the job completely.

'Sarcoxie'. As hardy as *E. fortunei*, but with the upright habit of *E. japonica*. To 4 ft. high. Use for hedges, as sheared tubbed plant, or as an espalier.

'Silver Queen'. Seems identical to 'Carrierei' except for having white margins around the leaves. (There is also an *E. japonica* 'Silver Queen'.)

'Vegeta'. BIG-LEAF WINTER CREEPER. A shrub woody enough to support itself in

E

Climate
Zone maps
pages 8-27

a mound or (with support and training) a vine that will cover an area 15-20 ft. square. Irregular growth habit; sends out large branches, with side branches developing later. Attractive fruits—orange seeds in little "hat boxes"—in early fall. New spring growth an interesting chartreuse.

E. japonica. EVERGREEN EUONYMUS. Evergreen shrub. Zones 4-13, 18-20. Upright, 8-10 ft. with a 6-foot spread, usually held lower by pruning or shearing. Older shrubs attractive trained as trees with their curving trunks and umbrella-shaped tops. Leaves very glossy, leathery, deep green, 1-2½ in. long, broadly oval to roundish.

This and its varieties are "cast-iron" shrubs where heat tolerance is important and soil conditions unfavorable. Notorious for mildew except in Zones 4-6, where plants grow well even in coastal wind and salt spray. To lessen risk of mildew further south locate plants in full sun, where air drainage is good. Since plants are also attacked by scale insects, thrips, and red spider, it's a good idea to include them in your regular rose spray program for mildew and insects.

Variegated forms are most popular; they are among the few shrubs that maintain variegations in full sun in such hot summer climates as southern California's San Fernando Valley. They are labeled in many ways; there may be some overlapping in the names.

'Albo-marginata'. Green leaves edged white.

'Aureo-marginata'. Dark green leaves have golden yellow edge.

'Aureo-variegata'. Leaves have brilliant yellow blotches, green edges.

'Giltedge'. Green leaves yellow edged.

'Golden'. Green leaves edged yellow.

'Gold Center'. Green leaves, yellow center.

'Gold Spot'. Green edges, yellow blotches. Probably same as 'Aureo-variegata'.

'Grandifolia'. Plants sold under this name have shiny dark green leaves larger than the species. Compact, well branched, good for shearing as pyramids, globes.

'Microphylla' (E. j. pulchella). BOX-LEAF EUONYMUS. Compact, small leafed, 1-2 ft. tall and half as wide. Formal looking; usually trimmed as a low hedge.

'Microphylla Variegata'. Like 'Microphylla', but with leaves splashed white.

'President Gauthier'. Leaves deep green with cream-colored margins.

'Silver King'. Green leaves with silvery white edges.

'Silver Queen'. Green leaves, creamy white edges.

E. kiautschovica (E. patens). Evergreen shrub. Zones 4-13. Spreading shrub to 9 ft. tall; lower branches sometimes root in moist soil. Leaves partially evergreen or evergreen, damaged near 0°; light green, thinner textured than other species of evergreen euonymus. Fruits showy, pinkish with red seeds. Takes desert conditions if watered.

'Du Pont'. Compact, dense, fast growing, with dark green leaves. Hedge, screen, sheared formal plant.

'Manhattan'. Upright growth, dark green glossy leaves. Hedge, shearing, espalier.

EUPATORIUM coelestinum. MIST FLOWER. Perennial. All Zones. Upright, sparsely branched plant to 3 ft. high. Triangular,

coarsely toothed leaves to 3 in. long. Light blue to violet, somewhat fragrant flowers in fluffy clusters similar to ageratum. Blooms August-September. Useful for light quality in borders with chrysanthemums, rudbeckias, Michaelmas daisies. Plant in sun or light shade. Divide in spring or fall.

EUPHORBIA. SPURGE. Shrubs, subshrubs, perennials, biennials, annuals, succulents. Most have acrid, milky sap (poisonous in some species) which can irritate skin and cause pain in contact with open cuts or in the eyes. What is called the "flower" is really a group of colored bracts. True flowers, centered in the bracts, are inconspicuous.

E. biglandulosa. Evergreen perennial or subshrub. Zones 4-24. Stems angle outward, then rise up to 2 ft. Long, narrow, pointed, fleshy gray-green leaves, 1½ in. long, their bases tightly set against the stalks. Flower clusters in late winter—early spring are broad, domed, chartreuse-yellow in color, fading to pinkish. Valuable display plant in garden or container, especially with contrasting mulch of black pebbles or brown bark chips. Stems die back after seeds set and should be removed. New ones come up to take their places.

E. heterophylla. MEXICAN FIRE PLANT. Annual. To 3 ft. tall. Bright green leaves of varying shapes, larger ones resembling poinsettia. In summer, upper leaves are blotched bright red and white, giving appearance of second-rate poinsettias. Useful in hot, dry borders in poor soil. Sow seed in place after frost danger is over.

E. lathyrus. GOPHER PLANT, MOLE PLANT. Biennial. Legend claims that it repels gophers and moles. Stems have milky juice which is poisonous and caustic. It could bother a gopher or mole and make him go away. Grows as a tall single stem to 5 ft. by second summer, when it sets cluster of yellow flowers at top of stem. Flowers soon become seeds and plant dies. Leaves long, narrow, pointed, at right angles to stem and to each other. Grow from seed.

E. marginata. SNOW-ON-THE-MOUNTAIN. Annual. To 2 ft. Leaves light green, oval, the upper ones striped and margined white, the uppermost sometimes all white. Flowers unimportant. Used for contrast with bright colored bedding dahlias, scarlet sage, or zinnias, or dark-colored plume celosia. To use in arrangements, dip stems in boiling water or hold in flame for a few seconds. Sow seed in place in spring—sun or part shade. Thin to only a few inches apart, as plants are somewhat rangy.

E. milii (E. splendens). CROWN OF THORNS. Woody perennial or subshrub. Zones 21-24 (in gardens); elsewhere as greenhouse or indoor plant. Shrubby, climbing stems to 3-4 ft. armed with long, sharp thorns. Leaves roundish, thin, light green, 1½-2 in. long, usually found only near branch ends. Clustered pairs of bright red bracts borne nearly all year. Yellow, orange, pink varieties.

Train on small frame or trellis against sheltered wall or in container. Grow in porous soil, in full sun or light shade. Tolerates drought but does better with regular watering.

E. myrsinites. Perennial. All Zones. Growth similar to E. biglandulosa, but floppier and rising only to 8-12 in.; flattish

clusters of chartreuse to yellow flowers in winter, early spring. Leaves stiff, roundish, blue-gray, closely set around stems. Withstands cold, heat, but short-lived in warm-winter areas. Use in rock gardens, with succulents and gray-foliaged plants.

E. obesa. BASEBALL PLANT. Succulent. House plant or indoor-outdoor pot plant. Solid, fleshy gray-green sphere (or short cylinder) to 8 in., with brownish stripings, brown dots that resemble stitching on a baseball. Good drainage, bright light, warmth, no sudden temperature change. Moderate water; keep dryish in winter.

E. pulcherrima. POINSETTIA. Evergreen or deciduous shrub. Outdoors in Zones 16-24; greenhouse and indoor plant anywhere. Native to Mexico. Leggy, to 10 ft. tall and more. Showy part of plant consists of petal-like bracts; true flowers in center are yellowish, inconspicuous. Red single form most familiar; less well known are 'Henriette Ecke' (satisfactory only in the intense autumn light of southern California), 'Double Red', 'Flaming Sphere', all red doubles. Forms with smaller white, yellowish, or pink bracts last until Easter.

Useful garden plant when pruned to prevent legginess. Grow as informal hedge in frostless areas; where frosty (not severely cold) plant against sunny walls, in sheltered corners, under south-facing eaves.

Where adapted outdoors, needs no special care. Give slightly acid soil. Thin branches in summer to produce larger bracts; head back at 2-month intervals for bushy growth (but often smaller flowers). To improve red color, feed every 2 weeks with high-nitrogen fertilizer starting when color begins to show.

To care for Christmas gift plants: Keep plants in sunny window. Avoid sudden temperature changes. Keep soil moist; don't let water stand in pot saucer. When leaves fall in late winter or early spring, cut stems back to 2 buds, reduce watering to minimum. Store in a cool place until late spring. When frosts are past, set pots in sun outdoors. It's difficult to bring plants into bloom again indoors. They will probably grow too tall for indoor use next year, but may survive winter if well sheltered. Start new plants by making late summer cuttings of stems with 4 or 5 eyes (joints).

E. veneta (E. wulfenii). Shrubby evergreen perennial. Zones 4-24. Upright stems make a dome-shaped bush 4 ft. tall. Leaves crowded, slender, blue-green. Flowers striking chartreuse or lime green in big rounded clusters in late winter, spring. Effective against dark wood, evergreens, or in large borders. Full sun, well drained soil.

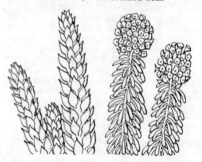

Euphorbia biglandulosa, *left: leaves gray-green.* E. veneta, *right: bloom lime green.*

F

Climate Zone maps pages 8-27

EURYA emarginata. Evergreen shrub. Zones 4-6, 15-17, 21-24. Native to Japan. Grown for refined foliage, form. Flowers insignificant, ill-scented (but only appearing on old plants). Slow growing to 6-8 ft., but easily kept to 3-4 ft. by pruning back to bud or side branches. Branches rise at a 45° angle from base of plant. Slightly teardrop-shaped, dark green, leathery leaves about ½ in. long, densely and symmetrically arranged along reddish brown branches. Part shade and same culture as rhododendrons, azaleas.

E. ochnacea. See Cleyera

EURYOPS. Shrubby evergreen perennials. Zones 15-17, 19-24. Native to South Africa. Leaves are finely divided, flower heads are daisylike. Long bloom season. They need little water once established but need excellent drainage. They thrive in buffeting ocean winds but are damaged by sharp frosts. Keep old blooms picked off, and prune in June.

E. athanasiae. Moderate growth to 5-6 ft. Leaves white-fuzzy, divided into needle-fine segments. Winter flowering; the 3-in. bright yellow daisies have foot-long stems.

E. pectinatus. Lower growing (to 3 ft.), with 1½-2-in. yellow daisies on 6-in. stems. Leaves green to grayish green. Flowers nearly the year around; heaviest bloom February-June.

EVODIA hupehensis. HUPEH EVODIA. Deciduous tree. Climate adaptation observed only in Zones 8, 9, 14-24. Reported hardy to −20°. Attractive, tropical-looking, round-headed, summer-flowering shade tree. Grows rapidly at first then moderately to 35 ft. Leaves, somewhat like a big-scale walnut leaf, are divided into 5-9 leaflets 3-5 in. long. Showy, large (5-in.-wide) clusters of small pink-stalked, white flowers in July-August followed by reddish brown, berry-like fruits with slender curved beaks. Brittle-wooded, not adapted in areas of high winds.

Some trees sold as *E. hupehensis* have turned out to be *E. daniellii*. The two are quite similar in growth, but flowers of *E. hupehensis* are in broad conical clusters; those of *E. daniellii* are in flattish clusters 4-6 in. wide.

EXOCHORDA. PEARL BUSH. Deciduous shrubs. Perform best in Zones 1-6, satisfactory in Zones 7, 9, 14-18. Loose, spike-like clusters of white 1½-2-in.-wide flowers

Exochorda: unopened buds resemble pearls. April flowers white, 1½-2 in. across.

open from a profusion of pearl-like buds. Flowers bloom about the same time as the roundish, 1½-2-in.-long leaves expand. Give plants a sunny spot, ordinary garden soil. Prune after bloom to control size and form.

E. macrantha. Hybrid. The only variety generally available is called 'The Bride'. Compact shrub to 4 ft. tall and as broad. Flowers in late April. Plant it beneath south or west facing windows.

E. racemosa (*E. grandiflora*). COMMON PEARL BUSH. Native to China. Loose, open, slender shrub to 10-15 ft. tall, and as wide. Blooms in April. In small gardens, trim it high to make upright, airy, multiple stemmed, small tree. In big shrub borders group three or more to give bulk, or plant against evergreens to show off the flowers.

FAGUS sylvatica. EUROPEAN BEECH. Deciduous tree. Zones 1-9, 14-24. Can reach 90 ft.; usually much less. Tree is a broad cone, with lower branches sweeping the ground unless pruned off. Needs space to look its best. Smooth gray bark contrasts well with dark, glossy green leaves, makes a handsome winter effect. Leaves turn red-brown in fall and hang on the tree well into winter. Little 3-sided nuts in spiny husks are edible, but inconsequential; they often fail to fill out, especially on solitary trees.

Grows in any good garden soil; salts in soil or water stunt growth, turn leaves brown. Many feeder roots grow near surface; don't disturb them with deep cultivation. These roots and heavy shade make lawn maintenance difficult under old or low-branched trees; good lawn trees in their early years. Spray for woolly beech aphids or whitefly. Seal pruning cuts to avoid wood rot.

Several varieties are available. Some of the best are:

'Atropunicea'. COPPER BEECH, PURPLE BEECH. Leaves deep reddish or purple. Good in containers. Often sold as 'Riversii' or 'Purpurea'. Seedlings of copper beech are usually bronzy purple, turning bronzy green in summer, widely sold but seldom as handsome as grafted plants.

'Laciniata'. CUTLEAF BEECH. Narrow green leaves, deeply cut and lobed. Densely foliaged. To 25-40 ft.

'Pendula'. WEEPING BEECH. Irregular, spreading form, long weeping branches reach to the ground. Green leaves. Without staking to establish a vertical trunk it will grow wider than high.

'Purpureo-pendula'. WEEPING COPPER BEECH. Purple-leafed weeping form. A splendid container plant. Can be held for many years in tubs or big pots.

'Rohanii'. Purple leaves with rounded lobes, like some oaks in outline.

'Tricolor'. TRICOLOR BEECH. Green leaves marked white and edged pink. Slow to 25-40 ft., usually much less. Foliage burns in hot sun or dry winds. Choice container plant, good contrasted with copper beech and evergreens.

'Zlatia'. GOLDEN BEECH. Young leaves yellow, aging to yellow-green. Subject to sunburn. Good container subject.

FAIRY DUSTER. See Calliandra eriophylla

FAIRY LANTERN. See Calochortus

FAIRY WAND. See Dierama

FALLUGIA paradoxa. APACHE PLUME. Partially evergreen shrub. Zones 8, 9, 11-23. Native to mountains of east San Bernardino County, California, Nevada, southern Utah, Arizona, Colorado to western Texas, northern Mexico. Grows 3-8 ft. high, with straw-colored branches and flaky bark. Small clustered, lobed leaves, deep green on top, rusty beneath. Flowers like single white roses (1½ in. wide) in April and May. Large clusters of feathery fruits follow—greenish at first turning pink or reddish tinged—create a soft-colored, changing haze through which you can see the rigid branch pattern. Important erosion control plant in arid regions of the Southwest.

FAREWELL-TO-SPRING. See Clarkia amoena

FARFUGIUM japonicum 'Aureo-maculatum' (*Ligularia tussilaginea, L. kaempferi*). LEOPARD PLANT. Perennial. Zones 4-10, 14-24. Leaves 6-10 in. broad, evergreen, thick and rather leathery, speckled and blotched with cream or yellow, all rising directly on 1-2 ft. stems from the rootstock. Nearly kidney-shaped but shallowly angled and toothed. Flower stalks 1-2 ft. tall bear a few flower heads, yellow-rayed, 1½-2 in. broad.

Choice foliage plant for shady beds or entryways. Good container plant. Tops hardy in 20° temperatures; plants die back to roots in zero cold, put on new growth again in spring. Bait for snails and slugs. *F. j.* 'Argenteum' has deep green leaves irregularly mottled, particularly on edges, with gray-green and ivory white. *F. j.* 'Crispatum' curled and crested leaf edges.

FATSHEDERA lizei. Evergreen vine, shrub, ground cover. Zones 4-9, 13-24. Hybrid between *Fatsia japonica* and *Hedera helix*, it shows characteristics of both parents. Highly polished, 6-8-in.-wide leaves with 3-5 pointed lobes look like those of a giant ivy. Shrubby like fatsia, yet sends out long trailing or climbing stems like ivy. Variety 'Variegata' has white-bordered leaves.

Leaves are injured at 15°, tender new growth at 20-25°; seems to suffer more from late frosts than from winter cold. Will take full sun only in mild, cool-summer coastal gardens. Give it partial shade and protection from hot, drying winds inland. Will take heavy shade, and can even thrive indoors. Give it plenty of water.

Fatshedera tends to go in a straight line, but it can be shaped, if you work at it. Pinch tip growth to force branching. Guide and tie stems before they become brittle. Do this 2-3 times a year. If the plant gets away from you, cut it back to the ground; it will regrow quickly. As a ground cover, cut back vertical growth every 2-3 weeks during growing season. Grown as a vine, the plants are heavy so give them strong supports. Even when well grown, vine will become leafless at base.

Protect leaves against aphids, scale insects, mealybugs, snails, and slugs.

FATSIA japonica (*Aralia sieboldii, A. japonica*). JAPANESE ARALIA. Evergreen shrub. Zones 4-9, 13-24. Tropical appearance with big, glossy, dark green, deeply lobed, fan-like leaves to 16 in. wide on long stalks. Moderate growth to 5-8 ft. (rarely more); sparingly branched. Many roundish clusters

Climate Zone maps pages 8-27

of small whitish flowers in fall-winter, followed by clusters of small, shiny black fruits (if you cut the flowers off as soon as they appear, the leaves will grow bigger and lustier).

Takes full shade; in cool-summer climates tolerates all but the hottest sun; foliage yellowish in full sun. Suffers in reflected heat from bright walls. Grows in nearly all soils; adapted to containers. Responds quickly to ample feeding, and watering. Foliage damaged in coldest Portland or Seattle winters. Wash occasionally with hose to clean leaves, lessen insect attack. Spray for aphids, scale insects, mealybugs. Bait for snails and slugs. Established plants sucker freely. Keep the suckers or remove them with a spade. Rejuvenate spindly plants by cutting back hard in early spring. Plants that set fruit often self-sow.

A natural landscaping choice where a bold pattern is wanted. Most effective when thinned to show some branch structure. Year-around good looks for shaded entryway or patio. Good house plant in a cool (not over 70°), bright room, north or east exposure good. Variety 'Moseri' grows compact and low. Variety 'Variegata' has leaves strikingly edged golden yellow to creamy white.

FAVA. See Bean, Broad

FEATHER BUSH. See Lysiloma thornberi

FEIJOA sellowiana. PINEAPPLE GUAVA. Evergreen shrub or small tree. Zones 7-9, 12-24. From South America. Hardiest of so-called subtropical fruits. Normally, a large plant of many stems, reaching 18-25 ft., with an equal spread—if not trained or killed back by frosts. Can take any amount of pruning or training to almost any shape: espalier, screen, hedge, small tree with some features of olive. Prune in late spring. Oval leaves 2-3 in. long, glossy green above, silvery white beneath. Unusual inch-wide flowers have 4 fleshy white petals tinged purplish on inside, and big tuft of red stamens. Petals edible and can be added to fruit salads. Blooms May or June.

Fruits ripen 4-5½ months after flowering in southern California, 5-7 months in cooler areas, can't be expected at all in deserts. They are 1-4 in. long, oval, grayish green, filled with soft, sweet-to-bland, somewhat pineapple-flavored pulp. Plants grow well in valley heat, but fruits seem better flavored in cooler coastal areas.

Varieties usually available are 'Choiceana', 'Coolidge', 'Pineapple Gem', and 'Superba'. If planting only one variety, choose either 'Coolidge' or 'Pineapple Gem', as the other two require cross-pollination. Combination of any two will do.

FELICIA amelloides (*F. aethiopica, Agathaea coelestis*). BLUE MARGUERITE. Shrubby perennial. Zones 8, 9, 13-24. Called a marguerite, but not the true marguerite (*Chrysanthemum frutescens*). About 1½ ft. tall, spreading to 4-5 ft. unless pinched or pruned back, with roughish, rather aromatic green foliage. Leaves oval, an inch long. Produces 1¼-in.-wide, sky blue, yellow-centered daisies almost continuously if dead flowers are picked off. Blooms even in mild winters.

Grow it in pots or containers, let it spill over a wall or raised bed, or plant in any sunny spot in the garden. Vigorous and likely to overgrow and look ragged; trim severely for cut flowers and prune back hard in late summer to encourage new blooming wood. One of most satisfactory perennials for warm regions.

Two improved varieties are grown: 'San Gabriel' has flowers of rich blue that do not fade even in hottest sun; 'Santa Anita' has larger (2½-3-in.) flowers of richer blue.

FENNEL, COMMON. See Foeniculum vulgare

FERN. Large group of perennial plants grown for their lovely and interesting foliage. Their leaves (fronds) are usually finely cut. They do not flower. They reproduce themselves by spores which form directly on the fronds. They vary in height from a few inches to 50 ft. or more, and are found in all parts of the world. Although most live in forests, some grow in deserts, in open fields, or near timberline in high mountains.

Most spectacular are the tree ferns, which display their finely cut fronds atop a treelike stem. These need moisture, rich, well drained soil, and shade (except in the coastal fog belt, where they can stand sun). Most tree ferns are rather tender to frost, and all suffer in hot, drying winds and under extremely low humidity. Frequent watering of tops, trunks, and root area will help pull them through unusually hot or windy weather. For the various kinds of tree fern, see *Alsophila, Blechnum, Cibotium, Cyathea, Dicksonia, Sadleria.*

Native ferns do not grow as high as tree ferns, but their fronds are handsome and they can perform a number of landscape jobs. Naturalize them in woodland or wild garden, or use them to fill shady beds, as ground cover, as interplantings between shrubs, or along a shady wall of the house. Many endure the long, dry summers in California but look lusher if given ample summer water. Some ferns native to eastern U. S. grow well in the Northwest and in northern California; these take extreme cold and are usually deciduous. For native ferns see *Adiantum, Asplenium, Athyrium, Blechnum, Dryopteris, Onoclea, Osmunda, Pellaea, Phyllitis, Pityrogramma, Polypodium, Polystichum, Pteridium, Woodwardia.*

Many ferns from other parts of the world grow well in the West; although some are house, greenhouse, or (in the mildest districts) lathhouse subjects, many are fairly hardy. Use them as you would native ferns, unless some peculiarity of habit makes it necessary to grow them in baskets or on slabs. Some exotic ferns will be found under *Adiantum, Asplenium, Ctenitis, Cyrtomium, Davallia, Humata, Lygodium, Microlepia, Nephrolepis, Pellaea, Pityrogramma, Platycerium, Polypodium, Polystichum, Pteris, Pyrrosia, Rumohra,* and *Woodwardia.*

All ferns look their best if groomed; remove dead or injured fronds by cutting them off near the ground or trunk—but don't cut back hardy outdoor ferns until new growth begins. The old fronds protect the growing tips. Feed frequently during the growing season, preferably with light applications of an organic-base fertilizer—blood meal or fish emulsion are both good. Mulch with peat moss occasionally, especially if the shallow fibrous roots are exposed by rain or irrigation.

FERN, BEAR'S FOOT. See Humata

FERN, BIRD'S NEST. See Asplenium nidus

FERN, BOSTON. See Nephrolepis exaltata 'Bostoniense'

FERN, CHAIN. See Woodwardia

FERN, CLIMBING. See Lygodium

FERN, COFFEE. See Pellaea andromedaefolia

FERN, DEER or DEER TONGUE. See Blechnum spicant

FERN, FIVE-FINGER. See Adiantum pedatum

FERN, GOLDBACK. See Pityrogramma

FERN, HARE'S FOOT. See Polypodium aureum

FERN, HART'S TONGUE. See Phyllitis

FERN, HOLLY. See Cyrtomium

FERN, JAPANESE FELT. See Pyrrosia

FERN, JAPANESE LACE. See Polystichum setosum

FERN, LADY. See Athyrium

FERN, LEATHERLEAF. See Rumohra

FERN, LICORICE. See Polypodium vulgare

FERN, MAIDENHAIR. See Adiantum

FERN, MOTHER. See Asplenium bulbiferum

FERN, ROUNDLEAF. See Pellaea rotundifolia

FERN, ROYAL. See Osmunda

FERN, SENSITIVE. See Onoclea

FERN, SILVER. See Pteris quadriaurita 'Argyraea'

FERN, SOUTHERN SWORD. See Nephrolepis cordifolia

FERN, SQUIRREL'S FOOT. See Davallia

FERN, STAGHORN. See Platycerium

FERN, SWORD. See Nephrolepis

FERN, TREE. See Alsophila, Blechnum, Cibotium, Cyathea, Dicksonia, Sadleria

Pineapple guava fruits are dull green, 1-4 in. long, filled with flavorsome pulp.

FERN, WESTERN SWORD. See Polystichum munitum

FERN, WOOD. See Dryopteris

FEROCACTUS. BARREL CACTUS. Zones 8-24. Medium to large cactus, globular when young, cylindrical with increasing age, ribbed, spiny.

F. acanthodes. COMPASS BARREL CACTUS. Native to southern California, Nevada, Baja California. Grows slowly to 8-9 ft. Flowers yellow to orange, bell-shaped, 3 in. across, bloom May-July. Grows faster on shady side of plant than on sunny side, producing a curve toward the south.

F. wislizenii. FISHHOOK BARREL CACTUS. Native to Arizona, Texas, and Mexico. Similar to above, with yellow or yellow-edged red flowers July-September. Hardy to near 0°.

FESCUE, BLUE. See Festuca ovina 'Glauca'

FESCUE LAWN GRASSES. See Lawn Chapter

FESTUCA ovina 'Glauca' (*F. glauca*). BLUE FESCUE. Ornamental grass. All Zones. Blue-gray, grows in distinct tufts 4-10 in. high. The fine color, the slender, bristly, hair-like leaves and the tufted habit make this a useful ground cover for sunny or partly shaded places, on slopes or level. Does not take traffic. Needs clipping after flowering and at any time when plants begin to look shabby. Used often in geometric pattern

When blue fescue looks shabby, cut back near ground. Fresh new growth follows.

planting. Does not make solid cover, so must be weeded regularly. Overgrown clumps should be dug, pulled apart, and small divisions replanted. Plant divisions or nursery plants 6-15 in. apart, depending on effect desired. Will not tolerate wet, poorly drained soil.

FEVERFEW. See Chrysanthemum parthenium

FICUS. Ornamental figs. Evergreen or deciduous trees, vines, shrubs, house plants. The average gardener would never expect to find the commercial edible fig, the small-leafed climbing fig, the banyan tree, and the potted rubber plant under one common heading. They are classed together because they all bear small or large figs.

F. benjamina. WEEPING CHINESE BANYAN. Evergreen tree. Outdoors in Zones 13, 23, 24; an indoor plant elsewhere. Native to India. To 30 ft. high and broadly spreading. Shining green, leathery, poplarlike leaves, 5 in. long densely clothe the drooping branches. Red figs. In frost-free, wind-

protected locations, grow it in sun or shade, out of prevailing wind. Probably best fig for heat tolerance in Zone 13 (damaged there by any frost but recovers quickly as the weather warms). Often used as small tree in entryway or patio. Good as an espalier. Excellent in containers as indoor plant.

F. carica. Edible fig. See Fig

F. diversifolia. MISTLETOE FIG. Evergreen shrubs. Outdoors in Zones 19-24; a house plant everywhere. Native to Malaya. Very slow growing to 8-10 ft. high. Interesting open, twisted branch pattern. Thick, dark green, roundish, 2-in. leaves are sparsely stippled with tan specks on upper surface and a few black glands below. Attractive, small, greenish to yellow fruits borne continuously. Most often grown in containers as a patio and house plant. Grow in part shade or strong diffused light.

F. elastica. RUBBER PLANT. Evergreen shrub or tree. Outdoors in Zones 16, 17, 19-24; house plant everywhere. Native to India and Malaya. This is the familiar rubber plant found in almost every florist shop. One of the most foolproof indoor pot subjects. Leaves are thick, glossy, leathery, dark green, 8-12 in. long by 4-6 in. wide. New leaves unfold from a rosy pink sheath which soon withers and drops. Can become 40-ft.-high tree in Zones 23, 24. As a small tree or shrub, useful in shaded "tunnel" garden entrances. Comes back in 3 months when cut to the ground by frost.

F. e. 'Decora' (*F. e.* 'Belgica'). Considered superior to the species on account of the broader, glossier leaves, bronzy when young.

F. e. 'Rubra'. New leaves are reddish and retain a red edge as rest of leaf turns green. Grown as shrub or small tree in Zones 22-24.

F. e. 'Variegata' (*F. doescheri*). Leaves are long, narrow, variegated yellow and

green. The variegation is interesting when viewed close up in a container, but as outdoor tree has an unhealthy look.

If a potted rubber plant becomes too tall and leggy, you can cut off top and select a side branch to form a new main shoot. Or you can get a new plant by air layering the top section. When roots have formed, cut the branch section with attached roots and plant it in a pot.

F. lyrata (*F. pandurata*). FIDDLELEAF FIG. Evergreen tree or large shrub. Outdoors in Zones 22-24. Native to tropical Africa. Dramatic structural form with huge, dark green, fiddle-shaped leaves to 15 in. long and 10 in. wide, prominently veined, with glossy surface. Highly effective as indoor pot plant. Stands reflected heat off building walls, but needs wind protection. In such locations can grow to 20 ft. with trunks 6 in. in diameter.

To increase branching, pinch back (house plants or garden plants) when young.

F. macrophylla. MORETON BAY FIG. Huge evergreen tree. Zones 17, 19-24. Native to north New South Wales and Queensland, Australia. Grows to enormous dimensions. A tree at Santa Barbara planted in 1877 has spread of 150 ft., with massive buttressed trunk and surface roots. Blunt, oval, leathery leaves, 10 in. long and 4 in. wide, glossy green above, brownish beneath. Rose-colored leaf sheaths appear like candles at the ends of the branches. Purple, white-spotted, 1-in. figs.

Although tender when young, acquires hardiness with size. Shows damage at 24°-26°.

F. microphylla. Plants sold under this name in California are *F. rubiginosa*.

F. mysorensis. MYSORE FIG. Evergreen tree. Zones 19-24. Native from India to

F

Climate Zone maps pages 8-27

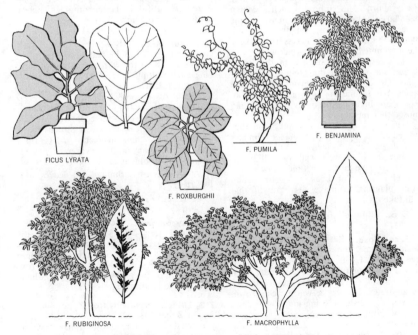

Ficus lyrata, F. roxburghii, F. benjamina *are good container plants;* F. pumila *a vine.* F. macrophylla, F. rubiginosa, *big evergreen trees, have substantial look.*

FICUS LYRATA · F. ROXBURGHII · F. PUMILA · F. BENJAMINA · F. RUBIGINOSA · F. MACROPHYLLA

*Climate
Zone maps
pages 8-27*

Burma. Grows quickly to 20 ft., and is as broad as tall. Rounded oval leaves 6-10 in. wide are borne in profusion to give the tree a most luxuriant look. In the juvenile stage leaves are fuzzy, bright green to almost yellow-green. As plant matures, leaves darken and develop a glossy upper surface. Orange-red 1-in. figs. Stands salt wind of the coast and heat of the foothills.

F. m. subrepanda. Upright in habit, with large orange-colored fruits.

F. m. pubescens. Spreading habit. Smaller fruits.

F. nekbudu (*F. utilis*). Evergreen tree. Zones 19-24. Native to tropical Africa. Similar in habit to *F. mysorensis* but leaves are much more leathery or rigid. Foliage pattern is more open, revealing the tree's structure and attractive pale gray bark of trunk and branches.

F. parcellii. CLOWN FIG. Large evergreen shrub. Zones 20-24. Native to the Pacific Islands. Has fanciful grass green, 4-8-in. leaves that are variously marbled with creamy white. Fruits are also variegated. Grows 12-18 ft. high, with many branches. Needs lots of water; dry air makes leaves drop. Needs wind protection. Good in containers.

F. pumila (*F. repens*). CREEPING FIG. Evergreen vine. Zones 8-24. Native to China, Japan, Australia. A most un-figlike habit. It is one of the few plants which attaches itself securely to wood, masonry, or even metal in barnacle fashion.

In young plants, gives very little indication of its potential vigor. The delicate tracery of tiny, heart-shaped leaves frequently seen patterned against a chimney or stucco wall is almost certain to be *F. pumila*, but in this growth phase gives no hint of its powerful character at maturity. There is almost no limit to the size of this vine and area it will cover. Neat little leaves of juvenile growth ultimately develop into large (2-4-in.-long), leathery, oblong leaves borne on stubby branches which bear large oblong fruits. The stems in time envelop a 3 or 4-story building so completely that it becomes necessary to keep them trimmed away from windows.

It is safe to use this fig on the house if the vine is cut to the ground every few years. Or, control by removing the fruiting stems from time to time as they form. Roots are invasive, probably more so than most other figs.

Because it is grown on walls, and thus protected, it is found in colder climates than any other evergreen fig. Will not climb on hot south or west wall, or will be an unattractive yellow. Sometimes slow to begin climbing. Cut back to ground soon after planting to make new growth that will take off fast.

F. p. 'Minima'. A slender, small-leafed variety.

F. religiosa. PEEPUL, BO-TREE. Briefly deciduous tree. Zones 13, 19, 21, 23, 24. Native to India. Large, upright with less spread than *F. macrophylla*. Foliage is quite open and delicate, revealing structure of the tree at all times. Bark is a warm rich brown. Leaves roundish, 4-7 in. long, with long tail-like point, pale green, rather crisp and thin-textured. They move easily even in the slightest breeze, giving the foliage a fluttering effect. Foliage drops completely in

April or May—a frightening experience to the gardener who has bought an "evergreen" fig.

F. retusa. INDIAN LAUREL FIG. Evergreen tree. Zones 9, 13-24. Native to India, Malaya. Both this and its variety *nitida* are widely used along streets throughout southern California and in the San Francisco Bay area. They differ definitely in growth habit and appearance.

F. retusa grows moderately to 25-30 ft. It has a beautiful weeping form with long drooping branches thickly clothed with 2-4-in. long leaves with blunt tips. New leaves, light rose to chartreuse, produced almost continuously, give the tree a pleasing two-tone effect. The slim light gray trunk supporting the massive crown may be concealed by the lower trailing branches if these are not trimmed off.

F. r. nitida. Has dense foliage on upright-growing branches, and is admirably suited to formal shearing. Leaves are a clear lustrous green, similar in size to *F. retusa*, but more pointed at base and apex. *F. r. nitida* may be pruned at almost any time of the year to size or shape desired.

Where pest-free, it would be difficult to find a more satisfactory tree or tub plant for warm climates.

Unfortunately, a thrips which attacks both the species and its variety has become established in California. This insect is difficult to control because it quickly curls the new leaves, stippling them and causing them to fall.

F. roxburghii. Briefly deciduous. Zones 20-24. Native to India. Usually takes the form of a large spreading shrub 6-10 ft. high and as wide. Leaves are unusually large—broadly oval to round, about 15 in. across. New growth is an interesting mahogany red, turning to a rich green. Leaves have a sandpapery texture. Large figs are borne in clusters on trunk and framework branches.

Can be shaped as small tree or espaliered. Beautiful in large container; needs ample space to show it off.

Grows in wind-protected locations.

F. rubiginosa. RUSTYLEAF FIG. Evergreen tree. Zones 18-24. Native to Australia. Grows to 20-50 ft., with broad crown and single or multiple trunks. Dense foliage of 5-in. oval leaves, deep green above, and generally rusty-woolly beneath.

Does well in sand on beach in Santa Monica and thrives in heat of interior valleys. A few trees in coastal gardens have developed the hanging aerial roots that characterize many of the evergreen figs in tropical environment.

F. r. australis. Similar but leaves are less rusty.

F. r. pubescens. Has leaves that are very rusty and hairy.

F. sycomorus. SYCOMORE FIG. Briefly deciduous tree. Zones 19-24. Native to Egypt, Syria. A large, round-headed tree with oval leaves, 4-10 in. long. Small figs grow in clusters. Sometimes goes bare for short period in mid-year, at time when new foliage is forming.

FIG, EDIBLE. Deciduous tree. Zones 4-9, 12-24. In Zones 1-3, 10, 11 as a tubbed plant, protected in winter. Grows fairly fast to 15-30 ft., generally low-branched and spreading; where hard freezes are common,

fig wood freezes back severely, and plant behaves as a big shrub.

Trunks heavy, smooth, gray-barked, gnarled in really old trees, picturesque in silhouette. Leaves rough, bright green, 3-5 lobed, 4-9 in. long and nearly as wide. Winter framework, tropical-looking foliage, strong trunk and branch pattern make fig a top-notch ornamental tree, especially near a patio where it can be illuminated from beneath. Fruit drop a problem immediately above deck or paving. Casts a dense shade. Can be held to 10 ft. in a big container, or trained as espalier along fence or wall.

Needs sun, good drainage; not particular about soil and drought resistant when established. In Northwest trees planted near or trained against south walls benefit from reflected heat. Cut back tops hard at planting. As tree grows, prune lightly each winter, cutting out dead wood, crossing branches, low-hanging branches that interfere with traffic. Pinch back runaway shoots any season. Avoid deep cultivation (may damage surface roots) and high nitrogen fertilizers (stimulate growth at the expense of fruit).

Home garden figs do not need pollenizing, and most varieties bear two crops a year: the first comes in June (July in the Northwest) on last year's wood; the second and more important comes in August-November from current summer's wood. Don't squeeze green or ripening figs; when ripe they come off easily. Keep picked as they ripen, and protect from birds (if you can). Pick off unripe figs and clean up fallen fruit in late fall.

Varieties differ in climate adaptability. Some are available only in the Northwest, others only in California and the Southwest.

'Adriatic'. Large green to yellowish green fig with red pulp of fine flavor. California, coast and interior.

'Blue Celeste' ('Celeste'). Hardy tree. Bronzy tinged violet, pulp rosy amber; fruit resistant to spoilage, dries well on tree in California.

'Brown Turkey'. ('San Piero'. Sold in Northwest as 'Black Spanish'.) Small tree; brownish purple fruit. Adaptable to most fig climates, Arizona to Northwest. Good garden tree. Cut back hard to scaffold limbs to lessen fruit formation and subsequent fruit-drop mess.

'Conadria'. Choice white fig blushed violet; thin-skinned, white to red flesh, fine flavor. Best in hot areas.

'Desert King'. Hardy, heavy bearing fig for Northwest. Fruit green, white-flecked, with violet-pink pulp. Ripens early August.

'Genoa' ('White Genoa'). Greenish yellow skin, amber to yellow flesh. Good quality, good home garden variety in California coastal and coastal valley gardens.

'Granata'. PERSIAN FIG. Somewhat more tender than other figs grown in Northwest, but survives and ripens fruit in Portland. Fruits large, blue-black with pink pulp. Large, silky leaves; easy to train as espalier.

'Kadota'. Fruit tough-skinned, greenish yellow in California's hot interior valleys where it bears best, green near coast. Commercial canning variety. Strong grower, needs little pruning. With severe pruning bears later, with fewer, larger fruits.

'Latterula'. WHITE ITALIAN HONEY FIG. Two-crop variety considered hardiest, best adapted to Northwest. Medium to large fruit, greenish yellow with honey-colored pulp.

'Mission' ('Black Mission'). Purple-black fig for desert and all California gardens except right on coast. Large tree.

'Negronne'. Jet black fruit in two crops. Figs small, with red pulp. Ornamental tree, with lacy, lobed leaves. Northwest.

'Neveralla'. LION FIG OF SYRIA. Many sweet, dark figs ripen September-November 15 in Northwest.

'Osborn Prolific'. Purplish brown fruit; good bearer in California coastal areas.

'Texas Everbearing'. Medium to large mahogany to purple fruit with strawberry-colored pulp. Bears young and gives good crop in short-season areas of Southwest.

FIG, HOTTENTOT. See Carpobrotus under Ice Plant

FIG, SEA. See Carpobrotus under Ice Plant

FILBERT. Deciduous nut tree. Zones 2-7. More treelike in form (15-25 ft.) than the other ornamental forms of *Corylus* (this is *C. maxima*). Makes a handsome, well-structured, small tree for garden or terrace. Spring to fall, the roundish, ruffled-edged leaves cast pleasant spot of shade. Showy male catkins hang long and full on bare branches in winter. Crop of roundish to oblong nuts (the ones sold in stores) comes as a bonus in fall. A 10-year-old tree may yield up to 10 lbs. of nuts a year. Nuts form inside frilled husks.

Set out plants in late winter or early spring, in well drained, deep soil. Tree tends to sucker; clear these out 3 or 4 times a year if you wish to maintain a clear trunk. Spray for aphids, bud mite, and filbert blight. Since cross-pollination is necessary, plant at least two varieties.

'Barcelona', slow or moderate growth to 18 ft., with greater spread. Roundish, large nuts.

'Du Chilly', slow to 15 ft. with equal spread. Shoots grow at right angles to limbs. Large, long nut of high quality, slow to drop and adhering in husks.

'Purpurea', ornamental variety with dark purple leaves.

'Royal', slow to 18 by 18 ft., with large nuts of excellent flavor.

'White Aveline' and 'Daviana', used as pollenizers. Light-crop varieties with medium-size, high-quality nuts.

FILBERT, EUROPEAN. See Corylus avellana

FINOCCHIO. See Foeniculum vulgare dulce

FIR. See Abies

FIR, CHINA. See Cunninghamia

FIREBUSH, MEXICAN. See Kochia scoparia 'Culta'

FIRECRACKER FLOWER. See Brodiaea idamaia

FIRE PLANT, MEXICAN. See Euphorbia heterophylla

FIRETHORN. See Pyracantha

FIREWHEEL TREE. See Stenocarpus

FIRMIANA platanifolia (*F. simplex*). CHINESE PARASOL TREE. Deciduous tree. Zones 5, 6, 8, 9, 12-24. Native to China, Japan. Small, usually slow-growing, 15-30 ft., with unique light gray-green bark. Trunk often has no side branches to 4 to 5 ft., at which point it divides into 3 or more slender, upright and slightly spreading stems which carry deeply lobed, tropical-looking, 12-in. leaves. Each stem looks as if it could be cut off and carried away as a parasol. Large, loose, upright clusters of greenish white flowers at ends of branches in July. Interesting fruits are like 2 opened, green, pea pods with seeds on the margins. Goes leafless for long period in winter (unusual for a tropical-looking tree).

Has been grown in mild-climate areas in all types of soil, but best in patios and courtyards, or other locations protected from wind.

FITTONIA verschaffeltii. FITTONIA. Evergreen house plant or greenhouse plant. Native to South America. Low and creeping with handsome foliage. Leaves dark green, oval, 4 in. long, conspicuously

Crisp, dark green, 4-in. leaves of fittonia are veined with red or with white.

veined with red. The variety 'Argyroneura' has leaves veined with white. Give north light. High humidity and an even warm temperature are among its requirements. Grow from cuttings.

FLAG, CRIMSON. See Schizostylis

FLAG, SPANISH. See Quamoclit lobata

FLAME BUSH, BRAZILIAN or TRINIDAD. See Calliandra tweedii

FLAME PEA. See Chorizema

FLAME TREE. See Brachychiton , Koelreuteria

FLAME VINE. See Pyrostegia

FLAME VINE, MEXICAN. See Senecio confusus

FLAME VIOLET. See Episcia cupreata

FLANNEL BUSH. See Fremontodendron

FLAX. See Linum

FLAX, NEW ZEALAND. See Phormium

FLAX, YELLOW. See Reinwardtia

FLEABANE. See Erigeron

FLEECEFLOWER, BOKHARA. See Polygonum baldschuanicum

FLOSS FLOWER. See Ageratum

FLOSS SILK TREE. See Chorisia

FOENICULUM vulgare. COMMON FENNEL. Perennial herb, usually grown as annual. To 3-5 ft. Similar to dill, but coarser. Yellow-green, finely cut leaves; flat clusters of yellow flowers. Grow in light, well drained soil, full sun. Start from seed where to be grown, thin seedlings to 1 ft. apart. Use seeds to season bread, pudding; use leaves as garnish for salads, fish. Young leaves and seeds have slight licorice taste.

F. v. dulce. FINOCCHIO. Lower growing, leaf bases larger and thicker. These are edible cooked or raw in salads.

FORGET-ME-NOT. See Myosotis

FORGET-ME-NOT, CAPE. See Anchusa capensis

FORGET-ME-NOT, CHINESE. See Cynoglossum amabile

FORSYTHIA. Deciduous shrubs. Zones 1-11, 14-16. Somewhat fountain-shaped shrubs, the bare branches covered with yellow flowers February-April. Rest of the year the medium green foliage blends well with other shrubs in border background. Branches can be forced for indoor bloom in winter.

Use as a screen, espalier, or bank cover. Or plant in shrub border. Tolerates most soils; likes sun, moderate water, and feeding. Prune established plants after bloom by cutting to the ground a third of the branches that have bloomed. Remove oldest branches, weak or dead wood.

F. 'Beatrix Farrand'. Upright grower to 7-10 ft. tall, 4-6 ft. wide. Branches thickly set with 2-2½-in.-wide deep yellow flowers marked orange.

F. intermedia. BORDER FORSYTHIA. Hybrid between *F. suspensa* and *F. viridissima*. To 10 ft. tall with long, arching branches. *F. i.* 'Karl Sax' resembles *F.* 'Beatrix Farrand' but is lower growing, neater, more graceful. *F. i.* 'Lynwood' ('Lynwood Gold') grows stiffly upright to 7 ft., with 4-6-ft. spread. Profuse tawny yellow blooms survive spring storms. *F. i.* 'Spectabilis' is a dense, upright, vigorous shrub to 9 ft. with deep yellow flowers. *F. i.* 'Spring Glory' has a heavy crop of pale yellow flowers.

F. suspensa. WEEPING FORSYTHIA. Dense, upright growth habit to 8-10 ft. with 6-8-ft. spread. Drooping, vinelike branches that root where they touch damp soil. Golden yellow flowers. Useful big-scale bank cover. Can be trained as a vine; support main branches and branchlets will cascade. *F. s.* 'Fortunei' is somewhat more upright, more available in nurseries.

F. viridissima. GREENSTEM FORSYTHIA. Stiff-looking shrub to 10 ft. with deep green foliage, olive green stems, greenish yellow flowers. 'Bronxensis' is a slow growing, dwarf form to 16 in. tall, for smaller shrub borders or ground cover.

FORSYTHIA, WHITE. See Abeliophyllum

F

Climate Zone maps pages 8-27

FORTUNELLA margarita. See Kumquat under Citrus

FOTHERGILLA. Deciduous shrubs. Zones 2-9, 14-17. Grown principally for fall color, but the small white flowers in 1-2-in. brushlike clusters are pretty. Plant in peaty soil, partial shade, especially where summers are long and hot.

F. gardenii. Low, rounded shrub to 3 ft. tall. Flower clusters at ends of bare branches in April. Roundish leaves 1-2½ in. long turn red in early autumn.

F. major. Erect shrub to 9 ft. with roundish, 4-in.-long leaves turning orange to purplish red in autumn. Flowers appear with the leaves. Fall color early and good in San Francisco Bay area even without chilly weather.

F. monticola. Spreading plant 3-4 ft. tall with broadly oval leaves. Flowers clusters somewhat larger than in *F. major*. Fall color scarlet to crimson.

FOUNTAIN GRASS. See Pennisetum

FOUQUIERIA splendens. OCOTILLO. Deciduous shrub ("character plant"). Zones 10-13, 18-20. Native to Mojave and Colorado deserts east to Texas, Mexico. Many stiff, whiplike gray stems 8-25 ft. high, heavily furrowed and covered with stout thorns. Fleshy, roundish, ½-1-in.-long leaves appear after rains, soon drop. Tubular ¾-1-in.-long red flowers in very attractive foot-long clusters after rains in summer. Can be used as screening, impenetrable hedge, or for silhouette against bare walls. Needs excellent drainage and full sun. Don't overwater. Cuttings stuck in ground will grow.

FOUR O'CLOCK. See Mirabilis

FOXGLOVE. See Digitalis

FRAGARIA chiloensis. WILD STRAWBERRY, SAND STRAWBERRY. Evergreen ground cover. Grow in part shade in Zones 4-24; in sun Zones 4-6, 15-17, 20-24. Native of Pacific beaches and bluffs, North and South America. Forms low, compact, lush mats 6-12 in. high. Dark green glossy leaves have 3 toothed leaflets. Leaves take on red tints in winter. Large (1-in.-wide) white flowers in spring. Bright red, ¾-in., seedy fruits in fall (seldom set in gardens). Plant rooted stolons in late spring or early summer. Flat-grown plants can be planted any time. Set plants 12-18 in. apart. Needs annual mowing or cutting back (early spring) to force new growth, prevent stem build-up. Feed annually in late spring. Needs regular watering. In late summer, if leaves show yellowing, apply iron sulfate.

F. c. ananassa. Fruiting strawberry. See Strawberry

'Number 25'. Hybrid of wild strawberry crossed with commercial fruiting variety. Bigger leaflets, grows higher (to 15 in.), and offers tasty fruit (birds like it, too) in addition to covering ground. Culture same as above.

FRANCOA ramosa. MAIDEN'S WREATH. Perennial. Hardy all Zones; evergreen in Zones 8, 9, 13-24. Native to Chile. Spreading plant with basal clumps of large, wavy-margined leaves which mass up 1-2 ft. In midsummer, the almost leafless, graceful

flowering stems stand 2-3 ft. high; the upper portions are spikes of many pure white (occasionally pinkish) tiny flowers. Ideal exposure is sun half the day or dappled sun all day. Needs just normal garden watering, very little fertilizer. Distribution seems mainly by neighborliness; more pass over back fences than through nursery channels. In just a few years, plants increase in size enough that you can divide and replant fresh new segments from outside edges of the clumps.

Good companion with foxgloves, primroses, azaleas camellias. Good cut flowers.

FRANGIPANI. See Plumeria rubra

FRANKLINIA alatamaha (*Gordonia alatamaha*). Deciduous tree. Zones 2-6, 14-17. Once native to Georgia, but apparently extinct in the wilds before 1800. Slender form, to 20-30 ft. high. Slow to moderate growth. Reddish brown bark with faint striping. Spoon-shaped bright green leaves 4-6 in. long, turn scarlet in autumn. Flowers 3 in. wide, white with a center cluster of yellow stamens, open from round white buds August-September, sometimes coinciding with fall foliage color. Give it well drained, rich, light acid soil, ample water, and partial shade in hot-summer areas (rhododendron conditions). During wet autumns in the Northwest it blooms shyly. Easy to grow from seed, blooming in 6-7 years. Use for contrast in rhododendron-azalea plantings. Unusual lawn or patio tree with right soil and exposure.

FRAXINELLA. See Dictamnus

FRAXINUS. ASH. Deciduous trees, one almost evergreen. Trees grow fairly fast, and most tolerate hot summers, cold winters, and many kinds of soil including alkaline. Chief uses as street trees, shade trees, lawn trees, patio shelter trees. Fairly pest-free (aphids sometimes infest).

In most cases, the leaves are divided into leaflets. Male and female flowers (generally inconspicuous, in clusters) grow on separate trees in some species, on same tree in others. In latter case flowers are often followed by clusters of 1-seeded, winged fruits, often in such abundance they can be litter problem. When flowers are on separate trees you'll only get fruit on female tree if it grows near male tree.

F. americana. WHITE ASH. Deciduous tree. Zones 1-11, 14-17. Native to eastern U. S. Grows to 80 ft. or more, with straight trunk, and oval-shaped crown. Leaves 8-15 in. long with 5-9 dark green, oval leaflets, paler beneath; turn purplish in fall. Edges show burning in hot windy areas. Male and female flowers on separate trees but plants sold are generally seedlings so you don't know what you get. If you have both, will get heavy crop of seed; both litter and seedlings can be problem. There is a male strain that doesn't produce seed. Trees are more pyramidal in shape; don't show leaf burn.

F. dipetala. FOOTHILL ASH. Deciduous tree or large shrub. Zones 7-24. Native to foothills of California; also in Baja California. Treelike shrub to 6 ft. high or small tree 18-20 ft. Leaves 2-5½ in. long with 3-9 leaflets (occasionally 1) about 1 in. long. White flowers in showy branched clusters, March-June, followed by many 1-in.-long fruits.

F. excelsior. EUROPEAN ASH. Deciduous tree. All Zones. Europe, Asia Minor. Round-headed tree 60-80 ft. high, or may grow to 140 ft. Dormant buds black. Leaves 10-12 in. long, divided into 7-11 oval, toothed leaflets, dark green above, paler beneath; do not change color but drop while green.

F. e. 'Kimberly'. (Sometimes sold as *F. quadrangulata* 'Kimberly'.) All Zones, but especially valued as a shade tree in Zones 1-3. A selected male variety, so doesn't produce seed.

F. e. 'Pendula'. WEEPING EUROPEAN ASH. All Zones. Spreading, rather asymmetrical, umbrella-shaped tree with weeping branches that reach the ground.

F. holotricha. Deciduous tree. Zones 4-24. Native to eastern Balkan Peninsula. Upright, rather narrow tree to 40 ft. Leaves of 9-13, dull green, 2-3-in.-long leaflets, with toothed edges. Casts light, filtered shade. Leaves turn yellow in fall, dry up, and sift down into lawn or ground cover, thus lessening litter problem.

F. h. 'Moraine'. Selected variety; more round headed than species, produces few seeds. A good lawn tree.

F. latifolia (*F. oregona*). OREGON ASH. Deciduous tree. Zones 4-24. Native to Sierra Nevada and along coast northern California to B.C. Grows to 40-80 ft. Leaves 6-12 in. long, divided into 5-7 oblong to oval, light green, hairy or smooth leaflets, the end leaflet to 4 in. long, larger than the side leaflets. Male and female flowers on separate trees. Will grow in standing water during the winter months.

F. ornus. FLOWERING ASH. Deciduous tree. Zones 1-9, 14-17. Native to southern Europe and Asia Minor. Grows rapidly to 40-50 ft. with broad rounded crown 20-30 ft. wide. Supplies luxuriant mass of foliage. Leaves 8-10 in. long, divided into 7-11, oval, medium green, 2-3-in.-long leaflets with toothed edges. Foliage turns to soft shades of lavender and yellow in fall. In May displays quantities of fluffy, branched, 3-5-in.-long clusters of fragrant white to greenish white blossoms followed by unsightly seed clusters that hang on until late winter unless removed.

F. pennsylvanica (*F. lanceolata*). GREEN ASH. Deciduous tree. Zones 1-6. Native to eastern U. S. Moderate grower to 30-40 ft., forming a compact oval crown. Gray-brown bark; dense twiggy structure. Leaves 10-12 in. long, divided into 5-9 bright green, rather narrow, 4-6-in.-long leaflets. Male and female flowers on separate trees. Takes wet soil, severe cold, but foliage burns in hot, dry winds.

F. p. 'Marshall'. MARSHALL SEEDLESS GREEN ASH. Selected male form with large, glossy, dark green leaflets.

F. quadrangulata. BLUE ASH. Deciduous tree. Zones 1-6. Native to central U. S. Grows rapidly to 60-80 ft. or more. Branches distinctly square, usually with flanges along the edges. Oval, dark green leaflets (7-11) 2-5 in. long, with toothed edges. Foliage turns purplish in fall. Fruit may become litter problem if you have female tree with male tree to pollinate it.

F. uhdei. EVERGREEN ASH, SHAMEL ASH. Evergreen to semi-evergreen tree. Zones 9, 12-24. Native to Mexico. In mildest areas leaves stay through winter; in colder sections, trees lose most or all foliage, but often only for a short time. Sharp frosts may kill back branch tips; serious damage at about 15° or lower. A top favorite in southern California and low-elevation deserts.

Grows fast to 25-30 ft. in 10 years; 40 ft. in 20 years; eventually 70-80 ft. or more. Makes upright narrow tree when young, eventually spreading. Leaves divided into 5-9 glossy, dark green leaflets about 4 in. long, the edges with small teeth. Foliage may burn if subjected to hot winds. Shallow rooted; encourage deeper rooting by watering deeply. Cut back any long branches to well placed, strong side branches when tree is young. Eliminate deep crotches by pruning out weaker branches. Fusarium wilt sometimes causes dieback; will kill young trees, but established trees usually survive.

F. u. 'Tomlinson'. TOMLINSON ASH. Grows more slowly (about 18 ft. in 10 years). More upright and dense when young. Leaflets deep green, more leathery with deep wavy-toothed margins.

F. u. 'Sexton'. SEXTON ASH. Forms very compact, rounded crown. Leaflets larger and deeper green than the species.

F. velutina. ARIZONA ASH. Deciduous tree. Native to Arizona. Zones 8, 9, 10-24. Tree withstands hot dry conditions and cold down to about minus 10°. Pyramidal when young, spreading, and more open when mature. Leaves divided into 3-5, narrow to oval, 3-in.-long leaflets. Male and female flowers on separate trees.

F. v. corlacea. MONTEBELLO ASH. Zones 8, 9,13-24. Native mostly to southern California. Has broader, more leathery leaves than the species.

F. v. 'Modesto'. MODESTO ASH. Selection from tree in Westside Park, Modesto, Calif. Zones 3-24. It is one of the most popular shade trees in northern California. Vigorous form of Arizona ash. Grows to about 50 ft. with a 30-ft. spread. Medium green leaflets glossier than the species; turn bright yellow in fall. Like evergreen ash, damaged by heavy winds due to weakness of many deep V-shaped crotches. Prune off weaker branch at each crotch to get a stronger framework that will withstand wind better.

In many areas following a wet spring, Modesto ash leaves get a scorched look. This is caused by a fungus disease called anthracnose. Control by spraying with captan. Verticillium wilt prevalent in agricultural areas; no control once it's started in young trees, but established trees often survive. Control aphids, psyllas, and spider mites with a contact spray.

F. v. 'Rio Grande'. FANTEX ASH. Zones 8-24. Thrives in hot dry climates and alkaline soils. Has very large, darker green, more succulent leaflets than Modesto ash; unfold in early spring, turn golden yellow in late fall. Foliage resistant to wind burn.

FRECKLE FACE. See Hypoestes

FREESIA. Corm. Outdoors in Zones 8, 9, 12-24; indoors in pots anywhere. Native to South Africa. Prized for rich fragrance of the flowers. Slender branched stems to 1-1½ ft., about same height as lowest leaves; stem leaves shorter. Flowers tubular, 2 in. long, in one-sided spikes. Older variety 'Alba' has fragrant white or creamy white blooms; newer larger flowered varieties with 12-18-in. stems are: 'Marie', pure white;

'Carmelita', pure yellow; and Tecolote Hybrids with white, pink, red, lavender, purple, blue, yellow, orange flowers.

In mild climates plant 2 in. deep (pointed end up) in fall in sunny, well drained soil. Plants dry up after bloom, start growing again in fall with rains or watering; increase supply. In cold climates plant 2 in. deep, 2 in. apart in pots, grow indoors in sunny window. Keep room temperature as cool as possible at night. Easily grown from seed sown in July-August; often bloom following spring.

FREMONTIA. See Fremontodendron

FREMONTODENDRON *(Fremontia).* FLANNEL BUSH. Evergreen shrubs or small trees. Zones 7-24. Fast growing to 6-20 ft. tall. Leathery leaves dark green above with feltlike covering beneath. Yellow saucerlike flowers. Conical seed capsules, covered with bristly, rusty hairs, hang on for a long time; some consider them unsightly. Needs excellent drainage; hillside planting best. Drought resistant; give plants little summer water especially in heavy soils. Roots shallow, so stake plants while young. Pinch and prune to shape. Plant with other native shrubs.

F. 'California Glory'. Hybrid between next two species. Plants to 20 ft. tall, possibly more. Flowers to 3 in. across, rich yellow inside, tinged red on outside. Very prolific bloom over a long period.

F. californicum. COMMON FLANNEL BUSH. Native to foothills Sierra Nevada and California Coast Ranges, and southern California mountains. Makes eye-catching show of lemon yellow, 1-1½-in.-wide flowers in May-June; flowers bloom all at once. Roundish 1-in.-long leaves, unlobed or 3-lobed.

F. c. napensis. Native to Napa, Lake, and Yolo counties in California. Somewhat shrubbier, with thinner leaves. Smaller yellow flowers sometimes tinged with rose.

F. mexicanum. SOUTHERN FLANNEL BUSH. Native to San Diego County and Baja California. Leaves have 3 to 5 distinct lobes, 1¼-3 in. long. Flowers larger (1½-2½ in. wide), yellow often tinged orange. Flowers over a longer period than *F. californicum*, but flowers form among the leaves so mass effect is not as showy.

FRINGE BELL. See Shortia soldanelloides

FRINGE TREE. See Chionanthus

FRITILLARIA. FRITILLARY. Bulb. Zones 1-7, 15-17. Native to Europe, Asia, North America; most numerous in West. Related to lilies. Give a variable performance in gardens, some kinds short-lived. Unbranched stems 6 in.-4 ft. high, topped by bell-like, nodding flowers often unusually colored and mottled. Use in woodland, rock garden, or as border plants in filtered shade. Plant bulbs in fall in porous soil with ample humus. Set smaller bulbs 3-4 in. deep; largest (crown imperial) 4-5 in. deep. Bulbs sometimes rest a year after planting or after blooming; use enough for yearly display.

F. imperialis. CROWN IMPERIAL. Stout stalk 3½-4 ft. tall clothed with broad, glossy leaves. Flowers large, drooping, bell-shaped, red, orange, or yellow in clusters at top of stem, with tuft of leaves above.

Use in borders, containers. Bulb and plant have somewhat unpleasant odor. Takes full sun near coast.

F. lanceolata. CHECKER LILY. Western native. Stems 2½ ft. high with several whorls of leaves. Flowers are bowl-shaped bells, brownish purple, mottled with yellow, greenish yellow, or purple.

F. meleagris. CHECKERED LILY, SNAKESHEAD. Nodding 2-in. bells on 12-18 in. stems. Showy flowers, checkered and veined with reddish brown and purple, bloom in late spring. There is a white form. Native to damp meadows in Europe and Asia, it tolerates occasional flooding. Long-lived in colder regions.

F. pudica. YELLOW FRITILLARY. Western native. To 6-12 in. tall with 1-3 nodding yellow or orange bells April-June. Flowers turn brick red with age.

Yellow or orange bells of yellow fritillary, ³/₄ in. long, turn brick red with age.

F. recurva. SCARLET FRITILLARY. Western native. Stem 2½ ft. high; flowers are scarlet bells marked yellow inside, tinged purple outside. Blooms March-July according to climate.

FUCHSIA. Evergreen to deciduous shrubs or shrublets. The popular, showy-flowered fuchsias that come in hundreds of named varieties are forms of *F. hybrida*, and are discussed under that heading. The other species are grown almost entirely by collectors, but some are good for basic landscaping purposes.

F. arborescens. Zones 16, 17, 22-24. Big shrub to 18 ft. tall, with 8-in. leaves and large clusters of small, erect, pinkish or purplish flowers in summer.

F. fulgens. Zones 16, 17, 22-24. To 4 ft., sometimes more if unpruned. Big oval leaves 2-7 in. long; clusters of scarlet, 3-in.-long, drooping flowers all summer.

F. hybrida. HYBRID FUCHSIA. Here belong nearly all the garden fuchsias. Zones 4-6, 15-17, 22-24 constitute the finest climate in North America for growing fuchsias, and the region in which most of the varieties were developed. The next strip —Zones 2, 3, 7-9, 14, 20, 21— finds fuchsias grown but with more difficulty. Outside of those two strips, fuchsias are

F

Climate
Zone maps
pages 8-27

little known, grown as summer annuals or in greenhouses.

Fuchsias bloom from early summer to first frost. At least 500 varieties grow in the West. Color combinations seem almost infinite. The sepals (the top parts that flare back) are always white, red, or pink. The corolla (inside part of the flower) may be almost any color possible within the range of white, blue-violet, purple, pink, red, and shades approaching orange. The flowers have no fragrance, but hummingbirds visit them.

There is considerable difference in flower sizes and shapes. Sizes range from the size of shelled peanuts to giants the size of a boy's fist. Within this range some are

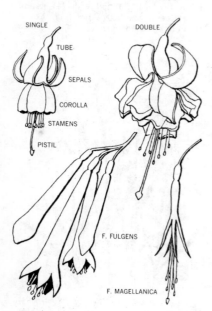

Upper left: hybrid fuchsia flowers showing parts; species have varied flower shapes.

single, meaning that there's just one layer of closely set petals in the corolla, and some are very double, with many sets of ruffled petals in the corolla. Quite frequently, the little-flowered types have little leaves, and the big-flowered types have big leaves.

Plant forms vary extremely: from erect growing shrubs, 3-12 ft. high to trailing

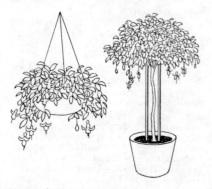

Use trailing fuchsias for hanging baskets. Upright kinds easier to train as "trees".

types (you grow them in hanging containers), and just about every possible form between the two extremes. Specifically, you can buy or train fuchsias in these forms: hanging basket, small shrub, medium shrub, large shrub, espalier, standard (miniature tree shape).

Best environment. Fuchsias grow best in cool summer temperatures, modified sunlight, and with much moisture in atmosphere and soil. If you live where fog rolls in on summer afternoons, any place in your garden will supply these conditions. Where summers are warm, windy, dry, or sunny, seek or create a favorable exposure protected from wind and in morning sun or all-day dappled shade—in short, a place where you, yourself, are comfortable on hot summer afternoons.

For containers or planting beds, soil mix should be porous and fast-draining but water-retentive.

Watering. Water as often as you can. It's almost impossible to give thriving fuchsias in well drained containers too much water. Hanging basket fuchsias need more watering than any other form. Fuchsias in the ground can go longer between watering if drainage is good. In hot-summer climates, heavy mulching (1½-3 in. deep) helps maintain soil moisture. Frequent overhead sprinkling is beneficial in several ways: keeps leaves clean, discourages pests, counteracts low humidity (especially important on windy days in inland climates).

Feeding. Apply a complete fertilizer frequently. Light doses every 10 days to 2 weeks, or label-recommended feedings every month, will keep plants growing and producing flowers. You can almost see the fertilizer take effect. Liquid and soluble fertilizers work well.

Grow from cuttings. You can take cuttings of a favorite variety and grow them into flowering plants in a few months, or—at the longest—in a year. Just cut 2-3-in. stem pieces (tips preferred) and put the lower halves in damp sand to root.

Summer pruning and pinching. If a plant is growing leggier than you'd like, pinch out tips of branches whenever you get the opportunity. Pinching forces growth into side branches, makes plant bushier. Pick off old flowers as they start to fade; never allow berries to form if you can help it—they reduce flower production.

Spraying. Worst pests in California are spider mites and whiteflies. If not controlled they cause leaves to yellow and drop. Frequent overhead watering will discourage mites; spray undersides of leaves with a miticide to control them. Spray undersides of leaves with malathion at two-week intervals to control whiteflies. In the Northwest, worst pest is aphids. Spray to control, using any of the good general-purpose insecticides.

Winters in cold climates. Where frosts are light, fuchsias lose their leaves, sometimes tender growth is killed. Where freezes are hard, most plants die back to hard wood, sometimes to roots. A few varieties, including 'Royal Purple', 'Checkerboard', and 'Marinka' stand outdoor exposures in winter in Zones 4-7. Generally, in the Northwest, best plan is to protect outdoor

fuchsias by mounding 5-6 in. of sawdust over roots (tops will be killed), and to store potted plants in greenhouse or indoors (40°-50° ideal) in bins of damp sawdust. Keep soil moist but not soggy all winter.

Early spring pruning. Fuchsias everywhere need some pruning in early spring. In frost-free areas, cut out approximately the volume of growth that formed the previous summer—leave about 2 healthy leaf buds on that growth. In mild frost areas, cut out frost-damaged wood, and enough more to remove most of last summer's growth. In cold-winter areas, prune lightly (remove leaves and twiggy growth) before storing. In spring prune out broken branches, and cut back into live wood.

F. magellanica. Zones 2-9, 14-24. Makes many arching, 3-ft.-long stems loaded with drooping, 1½-in.-long red and violet flowers, July to frost. Flowers frequented by hummingbirds. Where winters are mild, can reach 20 ft. trained against a wall. Treat as perennial in cold-climate areas. Roots hardy with mulching; tops die back with first hard frost.

F. procumbens. Zones 16, 17, 21-24. Prostrate, spreading fuchsia for containers, shady rock gardens. Leaves ½ in. long. Tiny flowers without petals in summer. Sepals pale orange with purple tips and marked green; anthers and pollen blue. Red berries, ¾ in. long, are showy.

FUCHSIA, AUSTRALIAN. See Correa

FUCHSIA, CALIFORNIA. See Zauschneria

FUCHSIA, CAPE. See Phygelius

FUNKIA. See Hosta

GAILLARDIA. Perennial and annual. All Zones. Native to central and western U.S. Low-growing, sun-loving plants with daisy-like flowers in warm colors—yellow, bronze, scarlet. They thrive in sun and heat, will take some drought, need good drainage. Easy from seed and fine for cutting and borders. Often reseed.

G. grandiflora. BLANKET FLOWER. Perennial. To 2-4 ft. high. Developed from the native species *G. aristata*. Flower heads 3-4 in. across with much variation in color. They are single or double, in warm shades of red and yellow with orange or maroon bands. Bloom June until frost. Flower the first year from seed. Foliage roughish, gray-green. Many strains and varieties obtainable, including dwarf and extra-large flowered kinds.

G. pulchella. Annual. Easy to grow. To 1½-2 ft. high. Flower heads 2-in. wide on long, whiplike stems in summer. Warm shades of red, yellow, gold. Leaves soft, hairy. Plant seeds in warm soil after frost danger past.

G. p. 'Lorenziana'. Has more nearly double heads. Double Gaiety strain yields many colors from near white to deep maroon, often bicolored.

GALANTHUS. SNOWDROP. Bulb. Zones 1-9, 14-17. Best adapted in cold climates. Closely related to, often confused with snowflake (*Leucojum*). White, nodding, bell-shaped flowers (1 to a stalk) with green tips on inner segments; larger outer

G

Climate
Zone maps
pages 8-27

segments pure white; 2-3 basal leaves. Sun or part shade. Use in rock garden, under flowering shrubs, naturalize in woodland, or grow in pots. Plant in fall, 3-4 in. deep, 2-3 in. apart, in moist soil with ample humus. Do not divide often; when needed, divide right after bloom; do not allow to dry out.

G. elwesii. GIANT SNOWDROP. Globular bells 1½ in. long on 12-in. stems; 2-3 leaves, 8 in. long, ¾ in. wide. January-February bloom in mild areas (where better adapted than *G. nivalis);* March-April in cold climates.

G. nivalis. COMMON SNOWDROP. Dainty, 1-in.-long bells on 6-9-in. stems in earliest spring.

GALAX aphylla. Perennial. Zones 1-6. Often used as a ground cover, although it spreads slowly. Must have medium to full shade, acid soil with much organic material, and preferably a mulch of leaf mold. Space plants 12 in. apart. Small white flowers on 2½-ft. stems in July. Leaves, in basal tufts, give the plant its real distinction. They are shiny, heart-shaped, 5-in. across, and they turn a beautiful bronze color in fall. Leaves are much used in indoor arrangements.

GALTONIA candicans. SUMMER HYACINTH. Bulb. Zones 8-24. Native to South Africa. Straplike leaves 2-3 ft. long; stout 2-4-ft. stems topped in summer with loose, spikelike clusters of drooping, funnel-shaped, 1-1½-in.-long, fragrant, white flowers with 3 outer segments often tipped green. Plant behind low bushy plants. Plant 6 in. deep in rich soil in fall. Don't disturb bulbs for many years. Where ground freezes, plant in spring; mulch deeply during winter or lift bulbs after foliage dies; store at 55°-60°. Bait for slugs and snails.

GAMOLEPIS chrysanthemoides. Evergreen shrub. Zones 8, 9, 13-24. From South Africa. A very fast-growing plant to 4-6 ft. high, spreading 4-8 ft. Produces bright yellow, daisylike flowers, to 1½ in. wide, almost continuously, but heaviest in spring, fall. Blooms even through frost. Quite resistant to heat and cold. Reseeds itself. Bright green leaves, 3 in. long, deeply toothed at edges. Tends to untidy ranginess if not pinched or pruned regularly. Has been used as clipped hedge. Best in full sun. Not fussy about soil conditions.

GARDENIA. Evergreen shrubs. White, highly fragrant flowers.

G. jasminoides. Zones 7-9, 12-16, 18-23. Native to China. Glossy, bright green leaves and double, white, highly fragrant flowers. Vigorous when conditions are right, plants need ample warmth, ample water, and steady feeding. Though hardy to 20° or even lower, plants fail to grow and bloom well without summer heat, are hard to grow in adobe soils. Takes full sun in coastal valleys; best with filtered shade in hot inland valleys; give north or east exposure in desert.

Soil should drain fast but retain water, too; use plenty of peat moss or ground bark in conditioning soil. Plant high (like azaleas and rhododendrons) and avoid crowding by other plants and competing roots. Mulch plants instead of cultivating. Syringe plants in early morning except when in bloom—unless water is high in salts; residue from this water may burn leaves. Keep soil moist; where water is poor, leach salts by monthly flooding. Feed every 3-4 weeks during growing season with acid plant food, fish emulsion, or blood meal. Treat chlorosis with iron sulfate or iron chelate. Prune to remove scraggly branches and faded flowers. Use all-purpose spray or dust to control aphids and other sucking insects.

All are useful in containers, raised beds, as hedges, low screens, or as single plants. Here are the named varieties:

'August Beauty'. Grows 4-6 ft. high and blooms heavily May-October or November. Large double flowers.

'Mystery'. Best known variety, has 4-5-in. double white flowers May-July. In warm Southwestern gardens may bloom through November. Can reach 6-8 ft.

'Radicans'. Grows 6-12 in. high and spreads to 2-3 ft. Small, dark green leaves often streaked with white. Summer flowers 1 in. wide, but with gardenia form and fragrance. A good small-scale ground cover, container plant.

'Veitchii'. Compact 3-4½-ft. plant with many 1-1½-in. blooms May-November, sometimes even during a warm winter. Prolific bloom, reliable grower.

'Veitchii Improved'. Taller (to 5 ft.) and produces a larger number of slightly larger blooms.

G. thunbergia. Zones 16, 17, 21-24. Native to South Africa. Angular-branched shrub to 10 ft. tall, 20 ft. wide. Leaves to 6 in. long, nearly black-green. Winter flowers long-tubed, single, 3-4 in. across. Very fragrant. Seems somewhat more tolerant of cool conditions and less-than-perfect soil than common gardenia, but tender to frost. Plants improve in vigor and floriferousness with age.

GARLAND FLOWER. See Hedychium coronarium

GARLIC. Seed stores and some mail order seed houses sell mother bulbs ("sets") for planting. In mild-winter areas plant October-December for early summer harvest. Where winters are cold, plant early in spring. Break the bulbs up into cloves and plant base downward, 1-2 in. deep, 2-3 in. apart, in rows 12 in. apart. Harvest when leafy tops fall over; air-dry bulbs, remove tops and roots, and store in a cool place.

GARLIC, GOLDEN. See Allium moly

GARRYA. SILKTASSEL. Evergreen shrubs. Pendulous male and female catkins on separate shrubs; the male catkins are exceptionally long, slender, and decorative. Both plants must be present to produce the grapelike clusters of purple fruit on the female plant.

G. elliptica. COAST SILKTASSEL. Zones 6-9, 14-21. Native to Coast Ranges southern Oregon to San Luis Obispo County, California. To 4-8 ft., or a small tree 20-30 ft. Elliptical leaves to 2½ in. long, dark green above, gray and woolly beneath, with wavy edges, densely clothe the branches. Flower tassels December-February in clusters. Yellowish to greenish yellow male catkins slender and graceful, 3-8 in. long. Pale green, rather stubby female catkins 2-3½ in. long. Female plants have clusters of purplish fruit which hangs on June-September or even longer if the robins don't eat it.

Excellent foliage plant for sun or part shade. Will take summer water and thrives near coast or inland as screen, informal hedge, or as a display shrub.

The variety 'James Roof' was selected for its unusually long catkins.

G. fremontii. FREMONT SILKTASSEL. Zones 4-9, 14-17. Native to Cascade Mountains, Sierra Nevada, California Coast Ranges. Differs from the above in its glossy, lively yellow-green leaves that are not gray and woolly beneath and have smooth edges. Catkins yellowish or purplish. Fruit purple or black. It does best in full sun. Tolerates drought, heat, and cold better than *G. elliptica.* Gets rangy in dense shade.

GAS PLANT. See Dictamnus

GAULTHERIA. Evergreen shrubs or shrublets. Zones 4-7, 14-17 except as noted. All have urn-shaped flowers and berrylike fruits. They need woodland soil and partial shade (except for the native *G. shallon).* Smaller kinds are favored for rock gardens and woodland plantings in the Northwest. Larger kinds are good companions for other acid-soil shrubs such as rhododendrons and azaleas.

G. cuneata. Compact shrub 1-1½ ft. tall. Leaves are ½-1 in. long, half as wide, glossy dark green, on reddish brown branches. Short clusters of white flowers in summer. White fruits ⅜ in. wide.

G. nummularioides. Slow-growing, dwarf shrublet 4-6 in. high, spreading by underground shoots. Roundish leaves ¼-⅝ in. long densely clothe slender, hairy stems. Tiny pinkish white flowers in summer, followed by bluish black fruits.

G. ovatifolia. Native to mountains northern California to British Columbia, east to northern Idaho. Spreading, trailing, with upright branches to about 8 in. high. Oval, leathery, dark green leaves ¾-1½ in. long, nearly as wide. Tiny white to pinkish flowers in summer. Bright red berries ¼ in. wide in fall and winter are edible, wintergreen-flavored, much liked by birds. Small-scale ground cover in woodland.

G. procumbens. WINTERGREEN, CHECKERBERRY. Zones 1-7, 14-17. Native to eastern U. S. Creeping stems, upright branches to 6 in. with 2-in. oval, glossy leaves clustered toward tips. Small, white, summer flowers followed by scarlet berries. Leaves and fruits have flavor of wintergreen. Used as ground cover; plant 12 in. apart.

G. shallon. SALAL. Native Santa Barbara County, California to British Columbia. In full sun and poor, dry soil a tufted plant 1-2 ft. tall. In shade and good soil can reach 4-10 ft. Nearly round, glossy bright green leaves 1¾-4 in. long. White or pinkish bell-like flowers on reddish stalks in loose, 6-in.-long clusters. Blooms March-June. Edible black fruits resemble large huckleberries, but are bland in flavor. Birds like them.

In sun a good low bank cover. In shade and acid soil, a good companion for rhododendrons, azaleas, ferns. Only neglected plantings need pruning; cut back in April, remove dead wood, and mulch with leaf mold or peat moss. Cut branches sold by florists as "lemon leaves".

G

Climate
Zone maps
pages 8-27

GAURA lindheimeri. GAURA. Perennial. All Zones. Native to the Southwest. Grows 3-4 ft. high. Leaves stalkless, growing directly on the stem, 1½-3½ in. long. Branching flower spikes with 1-in.-long white blossoms opening from many pink buds closely set on the stem. Long blooming period, with only a few blossoms opening at one time. Blossoms drop off cleanly when spent, but seed-bearing spikes should be cut to improve appearance and prevent too enthusiastic self-sowing. Plant in full sun. Can take neglect. One of the few long-lived perennials in Southwestern gardens.

GAYFEATHER. See Liatris

GAZANIA. Perennials. Zones 8-24. Native to South Africa. Daisy flowers give a dazzling color display during peak of bloom in late spring and early summer. In mild areas they continue to bloom intermittently throughout the year. Gazanias grow well in almost any soil. Once plants are established, water them about twice a month. Feed once in spring with a slow-acting fertilizer. Divide plants about every 3-4 years. In cold areas, carry gazanias through winter by taking cuttings in fall as you would pelargoniums.

There are two types—the clumping and the trailing.

The clumping kind (complex hybrids between a number of species) forms a mounding plant of evergreen leaves. The leaves are often lobed, dark green above, gray woolly beneath. The daisy flowers, on 6-10-in.-long stems are 3-4 in. wide. You can buy them in single colors, often marked with dark centers—yellow, orange, white, or rosy pink with reddish purple undersides. Or you can get a mixture of hybrids in the different colors—as plants or seeds.

Colorama strain (seeds) comes in white, yellow, gold, cream, yellow-orange, red-yellow, and pink. Fire Emerald strain (seeds) includes bronzy reds, lavender-pinks, pure pinks, rose, orange, yellow, and cream, all usually with a green center ring.

Two spectacular hybrids (sold in pots or flats) are 'Copper King', which has exceptionally large orange flowers with chestnut brown and violet markings, and 'Green Eye', coppery bronze with a green center.

Clumping gazanias serve well as temporary fillers between young growing shrubs

and as replaceable ground cover for relatively level areas that aren't subject to severe erosion. Try them in parking strips, or as edgings along sunny paths. They also do well in containers.

Trailing gazania (*G. uniflora*). (Sometimes sold as *G. leucolaena*.) Grows to about the same height as the clumping types but spreads rapidly by long, trailing stems. Foliage is a clean silvery gray. The yellow, orange, white, or bronze, 2½-in.-wide daisies grow in profusion, and contrast well with the gray foliage. Trailing gazania is useful on banks and on level ground. Or grow it at top of wall and allow it to trail over. It's especially attractive in hanging baskets.

GEIJERA parviflora. AUSTRALIAN WILLOW, WILGA. Evergreen tree. Zones 7-24. Graceful, fine-textured, to 25-30 ft. high, 20 ft. wide. Main branches sweep up and out, little branches hang down. Distant citrus relative, called Australian willow because its 3-6-in. long, narrow, medium green, drooping leaves give something of the effect of weeping willow. Old trees produce loose clusters of small, unimportant, creamy white flowers early spring, early fall. Well drained soil and full sun; plants stand light shade but tend to be thin in foliage. Established trees resist drought but respond to ample water with faster growth. Needs pruning only to correct form (much less pruning than willow). Quite pest-free.

Has much of the grace of willow, much of the toughness of eucalyptus, moderate growth rate, and deep, non-invasive roots. Casts light shade. Plant singly as patio or street tree, or in colonies for attractive grove effect.

GELSEMIUM sempervirens. CAROLINA JESSAMINE. Evergreen vine. Zones 8-24. Shrubby and twining moderate growth rate to about 20 ft. Clean pairs of shiny, light green 1-4-in.-long leaves on long streamerlike branches make neat but not dense foliage pattern. On a trellis, vine will cascade and swing in the wind; makes a delicate green curtain of branches when trained on house. Vine can get topheavy; if it does, cut it back severely. Fragrant, tubular, yellow flowers 1-1½ in. long in late winter, early spring. Can be used as ground cover; keep it trimmed to 3 ft. high. All parts of plant are poisonous.

GENISTA. See Cytisus

GENTIANA. GENTIAN. Zones 1-6, 14-17. Perennials. Low, spreading, or upright plants, generally with blue tubular flowers. Most are hard to grow, but prized by rock garden enthusiasts. Need full sun or light shade, perfect drainage, lime-free soil, ample moisture. If they thrive, they produce some of the richest blues in the garden.

G. acaulis. Leafy stems to 4 in. tall. Rich blue flowers 2 in. long in summer. Grows well; often fails to bloom.

G. asclepiadea. Upright or arching stems to 1½ ft. Leaves willowlike, 3 in. long. Flowers blue, 1½ in. long, in late summer, fall. Fairly easy in cool border, or rock garden.

G. septemfida. Arching or sprawling stems 9-18 in. long. Clusters of blue 2-in. flowers in late summer. Fairly easy.

G. sino-ornata. From rosettes of bright green leaves come trailing stems which end

in 2-in.-long flowers of brightest blue, early fall. Fairly easy in half shade.

GERANIUM. CRANESBILL. Perennials. Here we consider the true geraniums, hardy plants. Botanically the more common, in-door-outdoor plant most people know as a geranium is a pelargonium. Several of the true geraniums have handsome near-evergreen leaves, and bloom over a long period in summer and fall. Flowers attractive, but not as showy as pelargonium "geraniums". Borne singly or in clusters of 2 or 3, flowers have 5 overlapping petals, are usually rose to purple, some in blue shades; a few are pink or white. Leaves roundish or kidney-shaped, lobed, or deeply dissected. Plants upright or trailing in growth habit; alpine types form low tufts. Full sun.

G. argenteum. Zones 1-6. To 3-5 in. high. Densely covered with silky silvery hairs. Leaves basal, 5-7 lobed, 1 in. across. Flowers pink with darker veins, 1¼ in. across; notched petals, June-July.

G. cinereum. Zones 1-6. To 3-6 in. high. Deeply lobed, basal leaves, 1 in. wide, bluish green. Flowers violet with darker veins, 1-1½ in. across.

G. endressii. Zones 1-6. Bushy, 1-1½ ft. high. Leaves deeply 5-lobed, 2-3 in. across. Flowers rose pink, about 1 in. across; May-November.

G. grandiflorum. All Zones. Wiry, branching stems 12-15 in. high. Leaves roundish, 5-lobed, long-stalked, 1¾ in. across. Flowers in clusters, lilac with purple veins, red-purple eye, 1½-2 in. across. Blooms all summer.

G. pratense. All Zones. Common border perennial to 3 ft., branched above. Leaves deeply 7-lobed, 3-6 in. across. Flowers about 1 in. wide, typically blue, red-veined; often vary in color. Bloom June-August.

G. sanguineum. All Zones. Grows 1½ ft. high; trailing stems spread to 2 ft. Leaves roundish, 5-7 lobed, 1-2½ in. across, turn blood red in fall. Flowers deep purple to almost crimson, 1½ in across. Other forms of limited availability. A white variety, 'Album', is listed. Variety 'Prostratum' (*G. lancastriense*), neater, lower, more compact, has pure pink blooms. May-August bloom.

GERANIUM, CALIFORNIA. See Senecio petasitis

GERANIUM, COMMON. See Pelargonium

GERMANDER. See Teucrium

GERBERA jamesonii. TRANSVAAL DAISY. Perennial. Zones 8, 9, 12-24. Survives Zones 4-7 in coldframe with careful mulching, good drainage. House or greenhouse plant elsewhere. Native to South Africa. Most elegant and sophisticated of daisies. Lobed leaves to 10 in. long spring from root crowns which spread slowly to form big clumps. Slender-rayed, 4-in. daisies (one to a stem) rise directly from crowns on 18-in. erect or slightly curving stems. Colors range from cream through yellow to coral, orange, flame, and red. Flowers are first-rate for arrangements; cut as soon as fully open and slit an inch at the bottom of the stem before placing in water. Blooms May-December, with peaks in early summer, late fall.

Best in full sun, partial shade in hottest areas. Needs good soil with excellent drainage. Where drainage is poor, grow in

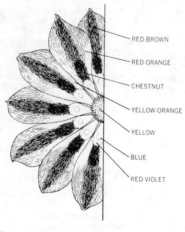

RED-BROWN

RED-ORANGE

CHESTNUT

YELLOW-ORANGE

YELLOW

BLUE

RED-VIOLET

Gazania 'Copper King' has large (3-4-in.-wide) flowers with these unusual markings.

raised beds. Plant 2 ft. apart with crowns at least ¼ in. above surface. Protect against snails and slugs. Water deeply and prevent soil from washing to cover crowns, then allow soil to become nearly dry before watering again. Feed frequently. Keep old leaves picked off. Let plants remain until crowded; divide February-April, leaving 2-3 buds on each division. As a house or greenhouse plant, grow in bright light with night temperature of 60°.

The wild Transvaal daisy was orange-red. Plants sold as hybrids are merely seedlings or divisions in mixed colors. Specialists have bred duplex and double strains. Duplex flowers have two rows of rays, and the daisies are often larger (to 5-6 in. across) on taller (2-2½ ft.) stems. In doubles, all flowers are rays and the flowers vary widely in form—some flat, some deep, some swirled, some bicolored. Buy in bloom to get desired colors and shapes.

Plant as seedlings from flats, as divisions, clumps, or from cans. To grow your own from seed, sow thinly in a sandy, peaty soil at 70°. Water carefully, and allow 4-6 weeks to sprout. Takes 12-18 months to flower. Seed must be fresh to germinate well; seed specialists can supply fresh seed of single, double, or duplex strains. Doubles come about 60 per cent true from seed.

GEUM. Perennials. All Zones. Double, semi-double, or single flowers in bright orange, yellow, and red over a long season (May-late summer) if dead blooms are removed. Foliage handsome; leaves divided into many leaflets. Plants evergreen except in coldest winters. Useful for mixed flower borders. Good cut flower.

Grows in sun, or part shade where summers are hot. Ordinary garden soil; needs good drainage. Grow from seed sown in early spring; or divide plants in autumn or early spring.

G. 'Borisii'. Plants sold under this name make 6-in.-high mounds of foliage, foothigh leafy stems with bright orange-red flowers. Use in rock garden, front of border. (The true G. borisii has yellow flowers.)

G. chiloense. (Often sold as G. coccineum.) Foliage mounds to 15 in. Leafy flowering stems to 2 ft. Flowers about 1½ in. wide. The following varieties are sold: 'Fire Opal' has semi-double orange-scarlet flowers; 'Lady Stratheden', double yellow; 'Mrs. Bradshaw', double scarlet; 'Princess Juliana', double coppery-orange.

GHOST GUM. See Eucalyptus pauciflora

GILIA. Annuals. Western natives related to phlox. Useful and colorful in wild garden or in borders. Sow seed in open ground early spring. Sun, well drained soil. Thin plants to avoid crowding.

G. achilleaefolia. YARROW GILIA. Plants to 3 ft. tall. Leaves very finely divided. Flowers (May-June) blue-violet, in dense clusters.

G. aggregata. See Ipomopsis

G. capitata. BLUE THIMBLE FLOWER. Slender plants 8-30 in. tall. Finely cut leaves. Flowers pale blue to violet-blue with blue pollen, in dense clusters like pincushions, ½-1½ in. across, June-October.

G. micrantha. See Linanthus

G. rubra. See Ipomopsis

G. tricolor. BIRD'S EYES. Branching plant 10-20 in. tall. Flowers ½ in. or more wide, single or in clusters of 2-5, pale to deep violet, with yellow throat spotted purple, blue pollen. June-September.

GILL-OVER-THE-GROUND. See Nepeta hederacea

GINGER, GINGER LILY. See Hedychium

GINGER, PORCELAIN. See Alpinia

GINGER, TRUE. See Zingiber

GINGER, WILD. See Asarum

GINKGO biloba. MAIDENHAIR TREE. Deciduous tree. Zones 1-9, 14-24. Graceful, hardy tree, attractive at any season, especially in fall when the leathery light green leaves of spring and summer suddenly turn to gold. Leaves hang on long, then drop quickly and cleanly to make golden carpet where they fall. Related to conifers but differs in having leaves broad and fanshaped (1-4 in. wide) rather than needlelike. Leaf shape and veining resembles leaflets of maidenhair fern, hence the name. Can grow to 70-80 ft., but most mature trees are 35-50 ft. May be gawky in youth, but becomes well proportioned with age—narrow to spreading or even umbrellashaped. Usually grow slowly, about 1 ft. a year, but under ideal conditions can grow up to 3 ft. a year.

Plant only male trees (ones grafted or grown from cuttings of male plants); female trees produce messy, fleshy, ill-smelling fruits in quantity. Named varieties listed below are reliably male. Use as street tree, lawn tree. Plant in deep, loose, well drained soil. Be sure plant is not root-bound in can. Stake young trees to keep stem straight; young growth may be brittle, but wood becomes strong with age. In general, ginkgos not bothered by insects or diseases.

G. b. 'Autumn Gold'. Upright, eventually rather broad.

G. b. 'Fairmount'. Fast growing, pyramidal form. Straighter main stem than 'Autumn Gold', requires less staking and tying.

GLADIOLUS. Corm. All Zones. All have sword-shaped leaves and tubular flowers, often flaring or ruffled, in simple or branching, usually one-sided spikes. Extremely wide color range. Bloom from spring to fall, depending on kind and time of planting. Superb cut flowers; also use in borders, beds behind mounding plants that cover lower parts of stems; or grow in large containers with low annuals at base. Plant in sun in rich sandy soil.

G. colvillei. BABY GLADIOLUS. Red and yellow hybrid, notable as the ancestor of the hybrid race called baby gladiolus. The latter have flaring 2½-3¼-in. flowers in short loose spikes on 18-in. stems. Flowers white, pink, red, or lilac, solid or blotched with contrasting color. Plant 4 in. deep in October-November for May-June bloom in mild-winter areas (June-July in the Northwest).

G. hybrids. GARDEN GLADIOLUS. The commonly grown garden gladiolus are a complex group of hybrids derived by variation and hybridization from several species.

Best-known gladiolus, with widest color range—white, cream, buff, yellow, orange, apricot, salmon, red shades, rose, lavender, purple, smoky shades, and more recently green shades. Individual blooms are occasionally as large as 8 in. across, stems 4-6 ft. tall.

Newer varieties of garden gladiolus, up to 5 ft. tall, with sturdier spikes bearing 12-14 open flowers at one time, are better garden plants than older varieties, stand upright without staking. Still another group of garden gladiolus, called miniature gladiolus, grow 3 ft. tall, have spikes of 15-20 flowers 2½-3 in. in diameter, are useful in gardens and for cutting. All varieties of garden gladiolus combine nicely in borders with delphiniums, Shasta daisies, gypsophila, perennial phlox.

High-crowned corms 1½-2 in. in diameter are more productive than older, larger corms (over 2 in. in diameter). Plant as early as possible to avoid damage by thrips. In frostless areas along the southern California coast, plant nearly all year. Along most of the coast, growers plant every 15 days from January-March for succession of bloom. In Zones 12, 13, plant November-February to avoid heat during bloom; plant April-June in Northwest; May-June where winters are severe. Corms bloom 65-100 days after planting.

If soil is poor, mix in complete fertilizer or superphosphate (4 pounds per 100 sq. ft.) before planting; do not place fertilizer in direct contact with corms. Treat with bulb dust (insecticide-fungicide) before planting. Set corms about 4 times their depth, somewhat less in heavy soils. Space big corms 6 in. apart, smaller ones 4 in. When plants have 5 leaves, apply complete fertilizer 6 in. from plants, water in thoroughly. Water regularly during growth. Control thrips and mites, as necessary.

Cut flower spikes when lowest buds begin to open; keep at least 4 leaves on plants to build up corms. Dig corms when foliage starts to yellow; cut tops off just above corms. (In rainy areas, growers dig corms while leaves are still green to avoid botrytis infection.) Burn tops; dry the corms in

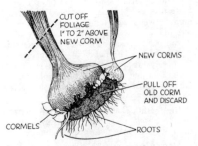

After digging gladiolus: discard old corms, save new corms to replant next season.

shaded ventilated area. In about 3 weeks pull off old corms and roots, dust new corms with diazinon dust, and store at 40°-50° in single layers in flats or ventilated trays.

G. murieliae. See Acidanthera bicolor

G. primulinus. Tropical African species to 3 ft. tall with hoodlike primrose yellow flowers on 3-ft. stems. Used extensively in hybridizing large flowered hybrids and miniature gladiolus. A strain called Butterfly gladiolus also belongs here. Flowers, medium-sized, frilled, with satiny sheen, vivid markings in throat. Strong, wiry, 2-ft. stems bear as many as 20 flowers, 6-8 open at one time. Colors include bright and pastel shades, and pure white.

G. tristis. Dainty gladiolus with 2½-3-in. flowers on slender, 18-in. stems. Bloom yellow, veined purple, fragrant at night. 'Concolor' has soft yellow to nearly white flowers. Bloom March and April; hardy except in severe winters. Plant corms in October-November.

GLAUCIUM. HORNED POPPY, SEA POPPY. Annual or perennial. Grows to about 2 ft. with gray-green lobed or finely cut leaves. Individual flowers short-lived, but bloom season continues June-August. Flowers followed by unusually long (to 1-ft.), slender seed capsules. Grow in full sun with other gray plants or with succulents.

G. corniculatum. Annual. Orange-red flowers with dark spot at base of petals.

G. flavum. YELLOW HORNED POPPY. Perennial or biennial. Zones 8-24. Grow as annual elsewhere. Orange to brilliant yellow flowers look as though they were varnished. Cutting back to new basal leaves once a year improves plants.

GLEDITSIA triacanthos. HONEY LOCUST. Deciduous tree. Zones 1-16, 18-20. Fast growing with upright trunk, spreading, arching branches. To 35-70 ft. Leaves divided into many oval, ¾-1½-in.-long leaflets. Late to leaf out: leaves turn yellow and drop early in fall. Inconspicuous flowers followed by broad, 12-18-in.-long pods filled with sweetish pulp and roundish, hard seeds.

Tolerant of acid or alkaline conditions, hardy to cold, heat, wind, some drought. Seems to do best in districts with sharply defined winters, hot summers. Good desert tree.

A good lawn tree. Leafs out late and goes dormant early, giving grass added sunlight in spring and fall. Small leaflets dry up and filter into the grass, decreasing raking chores. Stake until a good basic branch pattern is established. Not good in narrow area between curb and sidewalk; roots on old plants will heave paving. Don't plant if you need dense shade over a long season.

Trunks and branches of the species are formidably thorny, and pods make a mess; several garden varieties of a thornless form, *G. t. inermis*, are thornless and have a few or no pods.

'Imperial'. Tall, spreading, symmetrical tree to about 35 ft. More densely foliaged than other forms, gives heavier shade.

'Moraine'. MORAINE LOCUST. Best known; fast-growing, spreading tree with branches angled upward, then outward.

'Rubylace'. Deep red new growth.

'Shademaster'. More upright and faster growing than 'Moraine'—to 24 ft. tall, 16 ft. wide in 6 years.

'Skyline'. Pyramidal and symmetrical.

'Sunburst'. Golden yellow new foliage. Looks chlorotic unless combined with dark green or bronzy foliage. Showy in proper setting.

GLOBE AMARANTH. See Gomphrena

GLOBEFLOWER. See Trollius

GLOBE THISTLE. See Echinops

GLORIOSA rothschildiana. GLORY LILY, CLIMBING LILY. Tuber. Outdoors in Zone 24; anywhere as greenhouse or summer container plant. Native to tropical Africa. Climbs to 6 ft. by tendrils on leaf tips. Lily-like flowers 4 in. across with 6 wavy-edged, curved, brilliant red segments banded with yellow. Grow in light shade on terrace, patio, train on trellis or frame.

Set tuberous root horizontally about 4 in. deep in light, spongy soil. Start indoors or in greenhouse in February; set out after frosts. Keep moist; feed with liquid fertilizer every 3 weeks. Dry off gradually in fall; store in pot, or lift tubers and store over winter. May survive outdoors in frostless areas, but tubers rot in cold, wet soil.

GLORYBOWER. See Clerodendrum

GLORY-OF-THE-SNOW. See Chionodoxa

GLORY OF THE SUN. See Leucocoryne

GLOXINIA. See Sinningia

GNAPHALIUM. See Helichrysum petiolatum

GOATNUT. See Simmondsia

GODETIA. See Clarkia

GOLD FLOWER. See Hypericum moserianum

GOLDEN CUP. See Hunnemannia

GOLDEN DROPS. See Onosma

GOLDEN EARDROPS. See Dicentra chrysantha

GOLDEN FLEECE. See Thymophylla

GOLDEN FRAGRANCE. See Pittosporum napaulense

GOLDEN GLOW. See Rudbeckia laciniata 'Hortensia'

GOLDEN MEDALLION TREE. See Cassia leptophylla

GOLDEN SHOWER TREE. See Cassia fistula

GOLDEN TUFT. See Alyssum saxatile

GOLDENCHAIN TREE. See Laburnum

GOLDENRAIN TREE. See Koelreuteria paniculata

GOLDENROD. See Solidago

GOLDFISH PLANT. See Hypocyrta

GOMPHRENA globosa. GLOBE AMARANTH. Annual. All Zones. Stiffly branching plants 1-3 ft. high cover themselves in summer and fall with rounded, papery, cloverlike flower heads ¾-1 in. wide. These may be pink, purple, violet, or white. They can be dried quickly and easily, retaining color and shape for winter arrangements. Leaves are narrowly oval, 2-4 in. long,, somewhat hairy. Dwarf edging varieties are only 9 in. high. 'Buddy' is purple and 'Cissy' white. Plant in late spring.

GOOSEBERRY. Deciduous shrub. Zones 1-6, 17. Same culture as currant. Grown for pies and canning. The big European dessert

gooseberries do not do well in this country. 'Oregon Champion', a 3-5-ft. thornless bush is the preferred variety; green fruit. 'Pixwell', extremely hardy and with few thorns, has pink fruit. 'Poorman', a favorite in Zones 1-3, has red fruit sweet enough to eat off the bush. Gooseberry plants act as hosts to white pine blister rust organisms, so they cannot legally be planted in some areas of the West.

GOOSEBERRY VINE, CHINESE. See Actinidia chinensis

GOPHER PLANT. See Euphorbia lathyrus

GORDONIA. See Franklinia

GOURD. Annual vines. Many plants produce gourds; most commonly planted are the following three: *Cucurbita pepo ovifera*, YELLOW-FLOWERED GOURD. Produces the

Gourds come in a bewildering variety of sizes, colors, shapes, markings.

great majority of small ornamental gourds, in many shapes and sizes. These may be all one color or striped. *Luffa cylindrica*, DISH CLOTH GOURD, VEGETABLE SPONGE GOURD. Also has yellow flowers. Bears cylindrical gourds 1-2 ft. in length, the fibrous interior of which may be used in place of a sponge or cloth for scrubbing and bathing. *Lagenaria siceraria* (*L. vulgaris*), WHITE-FLOWERED GOURD. Bears gourds 3 in.-3 ft. long. May be round, bottle-shaped, dumbbell-shaped, crooknecked, coiled, or spoon-shaped.

All grow fast and will reach 10-15 ft. Sow seeds when ground is warm. Start indoors if growing season is short. Gourds need all the summer heat they can get to develop fruits by frost. If planting for ornamental gourd harvest, give vines wire or trellis support to hold ripening individual fruits off ground. Plant seedlings 2 ft. apart or thin seedlings to same spacing. Give deep, regular watering. Harvest when vines are dry. Cut some stem with each gourd so you can hang it up to dry slowly in a cool, airy spot. When thoroughly dry, preserve with coating of paste wax, lacquer, or shellac.

GRANADILLA, PURPLE. See Passiflora edulis

GRAPE. Deciduous vine. All Zones (but see limitations in chart). A single grapevine can produce enough new growth every year to arch a walk, roof an arbor, form a leafy wall, or put an umbrella of shade over a deck or terrace. The grape is one of the few ornamental vines with a dominant trunk and branch pattern for winter interest, bold-textured foliage, and colorful fruit.

To get quality fruit you must choose a variety that fits your climate, train it carefully, and prune it regularly.

The two basic classes are: European—tight skins, winelike flavor, generally high heat requirements, cold tolerance to about 5°; and American—slipskin, "foxy" Concord-type flavor, moderate summer heat requirements, cold tolerance well below 0°. Hybrids between classes are available; most are reasonably hardy, fall between either parent in flavor.

Choosing the right variety is important; varieties differ widely in hardiness and in heat requirements. The Northwest is primarily American grape country; the long warm-season areas of California and Arizona favor the European varieties. Everywhere the short-season, high-elevation areas must choose from American grapes.

The ideal climate for most table grapes in California is that of California's Central Valley—a long season of high heat; the ideal climate in the Northwest is the warmest parts of the Columbia Basin. If your climate is cooler, or the growing season is shorter than the ideal, look to the *early ripening* varieties: Or, create a warmer climate by giving the vine the added heat of a south-facing wall.

Nurseries in Oregon's Willamette Valley offer a number of European varieties to satisfy demand of experimenters. Only those varieties with lowest heat requirements will produce acceptable fruit.

Mildew is a serious pest of the European varieties (most American varieties are immune). To control, dust the vines with sulfur when shoots are 6 in. long, again when they are 12-15 in., then every 2 weeks until harvest. If vines are not in full sun, or are near lawns which are sprinkled repeatedly, it will be necessary to give them additional dustings.

To control grape leafhopper in California, add diazinon dust to sulfur at time of third sulfur dusting, just before blooming time. In the Northwest, dust with diazinon in June and again in August. Grape mealybugs may infest vines in Northwest. Control with dormant oil spray in late winter and with malathion in June.

Vines are deep rooted, grow best in deep soils. During growing season water to a depth of at least 3 ft. to develop a good root system. Nitrogen is the only fertilizing element they need.

See planting, training, and pruning in illustrations below and on next page.

GRAPE, CALIFORNIA HOLLY. See Mahonia pinnata

GRAPE, EVERGREEN. See Rhoicissus

GRAPE, OREGON. See Mahonia aquifolium

Climate Zone maps pages 8-27

GRAPE: PRUNING

1. *December-March: Dig deep hole, plant rooted cutting from nursery, leave only top bud exposed. Set stake for training. Mound soil over bud.*

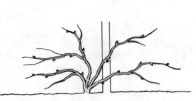

2. *First year: Let vine sprawl, develop as many leaves as possible to manufacture food for developing roots. This growth made by November. Leaves have fallen.*

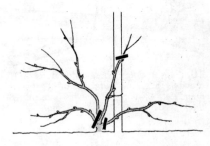

3. *First winter: Prune to one sturdy cane; shorten it to 3 lowest buds. If cane very vigorous, cut at 2-3 ft., or at good arbor branching point.*

4. *Second spring: When new shoots are 12 in. long, select one vigorous, upright shoot to form permanent trunk. Tie loosely to stake. Cut out other shoots.*

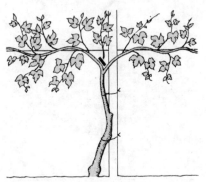

5. *Second summer: When shoot reaches branching point on arbor, trellis, or fence, pinch out tip. Allow 2 strongest subsequent shoots to develop. Pinch side shoots to 10 in.*

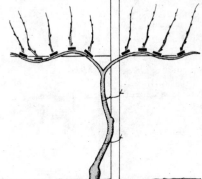

6. *Second winter: Cut spindly canes on arms back to old wood. Don't prune yet for fruit production; vines too immature. For fruit you'd leave 2 buds at base of canes.*

(Continued on next page)

GRAPE: PRUNING (CONT'D)

Climate
Zone maps
pages 8-27

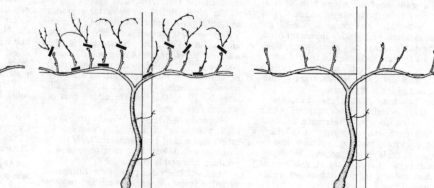

7. *Second winter's finished product. On arbor, arms would stretch along roof level of structure. Length of arms determines size, permanent framework of vine.*

8. *Third winter: These canes grew previous summer. To prune for fruit, cut out weak or crowding canes. Select sturdy canes 6-10 in. apart, cut them to 2 buds.*

9. *Third winter's finished product. Each bud will give 2 fruiting canes next summer. Following winter cut out one entirely, shorten other to 2 buds. See Nos. 10, 11.*

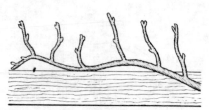

10. *Fourth winter: These canes bore fruit previous autumn. Cut one off at base. Branch at left already pruned. These short, thick branches are called fruit spurs.*

11. *Fourth winter: Shorten remaining cane to 2 buds. These will give next year's fruiting canes. Pruning in subsequent years the same. Cut out suckers on trunk, arms.*

12. *Well pruned arm in fourth year should look like this. Fruit spurs spaced approximately 6 in. apart, with 2 buds on each new cane at end of spurs.*

GRAPE: CANE PRUNING

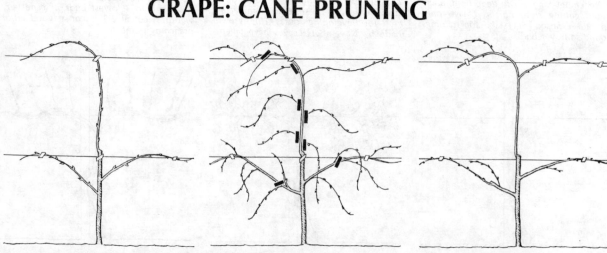

1. *Cane pruning in first two years is like spur pruning. Here, it's second winter after planting. Establish shape of vine on frame. American grapes usually grown with 4 arms.*

2. *Third Winter: Each cane has produced many canes. Prune to base of second cane from base of arm. (It will be pruned out next winter after fruiting.)*

3. *Third winter: Finished product. Second cane from base gives next summer's fruit. Cane nearest base (renewal cane) will give wood for next winter's pruning.*

GRAPE

*Climate
Zone maps
pages 8-27*

VARIETY	ZONES	SEASON	PRUNING	REMARKS
AMERICAN & AMERICAN HYBRID VARIETIES				
'Agawam'	2, 3, 7	Midseason to late	Cane	Pinkish red, aromatic, slightly foxy. Keeps well after picking. Some winter injury in coldest areas.
'Caco'	1-3, 7	Midseason to late	Cane	Light red berries. Aromatic and vinous in flavor. Thick skinned. Good for arbors. Hardy, thrifty.
'Campbell Early' ('Island Belle')	2-7, 17	Early	Cane	Dark purplish black with heavy bloom. High quality. Lacks foxy taste. Vine moderately vigorous. Excellent Concord type where too cool for 'Concord'.
'Catawba'	3, 14-16, 19-21	Late	Cane	Medium sized round, dull purplish red berries with a distinctive flavor all its own. Flavor both vinous and slightly foxy, aromatic.
'Concord'	1-3, 6-9, 14-16, 18-21	Midseason. Late in Northwest	Cane	Standard American slipskin. California's hot, dry summer areas are not to its liking. Fruit inferior to Northwest grown.
'Delaware' (American hybrid)	3, 5-7	Early midseason	Cane	Small, round, light red berries with lilac bloom. Aromatic, vinous in flavor.
'Diamond'	3, 5-7, 17	Early midseason	Cane	Round, medium-sized, yellowish green berries of high quality. Slightly aromatic. Pleasantly tart. Vine fairly vigorous, very productive.
'Fredonia'	1-7, 17	Early	Cane	Large black berries with thick, tough skin. Similar to 'Concord' but larger. Vigorous vine, clean foliage. Excellent for arbors.
'Golden Muscat' (American hybrid)	1-3, 6-9, 11-24	Early midseason	Cane	Golden green, with slipskin of American grapes but with Muscat flavor. Hybrid of the 'Muscat' and the green American grape, 'Diamond'. Vigorous.
'Interlaken Seedless' (American hybrid)	1-3, 5-7	Very early	Cane	Small, sweet, crisp, firm, greenish white berries. Tight skinned. Excellent flavor. Vine moderately vigorous, productive.
'Lucile'	1-3, 6-7	Midseason	Cane	Small, light red berries similar to 'Caco' but thin skinned. Vine strong growing, productive.
'Niabell'	7-9, 14-16, 18-22	Early	Spur or cane	Large black berries similar to 'Concord' at its best. Excellent arbor grape. Vigorous and productive in a wide range of climates. Succeeds in hot interiors where 'Concord' fails.
'Niagara'	3, 6-7	Midseason	Cane	Large, full clusters of medium to large green-gold berries. Sweet and juicy with strong foxy flavor. Attractive vigorous vine, excellent for arbors.
'Ontario'	1-3, 6-7	Early	Cane	Medium sized green berries of high quality. Vine moderately vigorous.
'Pierce'	7-9, 14-16, 18-21	Midseason	Cane	Called 'California Concord'. Berries larger, vine more vigorous than 'Concord'. Stands high heat better than 'Concord'.
'Portland'	5-7	Early	Cane	Large, round, green to amber berries. Skin very tender. Vine moderately vigorous.
'Romulus' (American hybrid)	3, 6-7	Late midseason	Cane	Yellow seedless berries similar to 'Interlaken' but 2 weeks later. Moderate vigor but productive.
'Schuyler' (American hybrid)	3, 5-7	Early	Spur or cane	Medium sized blue berries in large clusters. Very sweet and juicy. Vigorous and productive.
'Seneca'	1-7, 17	Very early	Cane	Sweet, aromatic, high quality, white berries. Skin thin and tender, adhering to pulp. Bunches sometimes loose; not a heavy yielder.

(Continued on next page)

G

VARIETY	ZONES	SEASON	PRUNING	REMARKS
AMERICAN & AMERICAN HYBRID VARIETIES (cont'd.)				
'Worden'	1-3, 6-7	Midseason	Cane	Large, round, purplish black to black berries of high Concord quality. Fairly productive; two weeks earlier than 'Concord.'
EUROPEAN VARIETIES				
'Almeria'	8, 9, 18, 19	Late	Cane	Large greenish white berries in large, high-shoulder bunches. Old standard white storage grape. Once imported from Spain in sawdust-filled kegs.
'Black Monukka'	3, 7-9, 11-16, 18-21	Early midseason	Cane or spur	Medium sized reddish black seedless berries in large, loose clusters. Popular home variety. One of the hardiest European grapes.
'Blackrose'	8, 9, 11-16, 18-20	Early midseason	Cane or spur	Beautiful black grapes, larger and more flavorful than 'Ribier'.
'Calmeria'	8, 9, 18, 19	Late	Cane or spur	Large, greenish yellow, tough-skinned, firm, crisp. Larger berries, not so tightly set in cluster as 'Almeria'.
'Cardinal'	8, 9, 11-16, 18-21	Early	Spur, short cane	Large, deep red, firm, crisp. Slight Muscat flavor when fully ripe. Heavy bearer. Thin some flower clusters off when shoots are 12-18 in. long.
'Csaba' ('Pearl of Csaba')	3, 6	Very early	Spur	Small to medium, yellowish white, moderately firm, some Muscat flavor. One of the hardiest European types. Grown in central Washington.
'Emperor'	8, 9, 18, 19	Late	Cane or spur	Large, reddish, very firm, crisp and crunchy. Neutral flavor.
'Italia' ('Italian Muscat')	8, 9, 11-14, 18-20	Midseason	Spur	Large, amber yellow berries. Crisp, with sweet Muscat flavor, tender skin.
'Lady Finger'	Two grapes with long slender berries are sold under this name. See 'Olivette Blanche', 'Rish Baba'.			
'Malaga, Red'	8, 9, 11-14, 18-19	Early midseason	Spur or cane	Pink to reddish purple, firm, crisp, neutral flavor. Large, irregular clusters. Good arbor grape.
'Malaga, White'	8, 9, 11-14, 18-19	Midseason	Spur or cane	Large, yellowish green; thick, tough skins. Flesh rather soft. Sweeter, more bland than 'Thompson Seedless'.
'Muscat' ('Muscat of Alexandria')	8, 9, 11-14, 18-19	Late midseason	Spur	Large, green to amber, round berries in loose clusters. Strongly aromatic. Renowned for its sweet, musky, aged-in-the-vat flavor.
'Olivette Blanche' ('Lady Finger')	8, 9, 11-14, 18-20	Late midseason	Cane	Berries long, slender, but broader, deeper green than those of 'Rish Baba'. Sometimes pink-blushed. Clusters large, tight, conical. More widely grown than 'Rish Baba'.
'Perlette'	3, 7-10, 11-16, 18-21	Early	Spur	Earlier, larger, less sweet than 'Thompson Seedless'. Needs far less heat than most European varieties.
'Queen'	8, 9, 11-14, 18, 19	Late midseason	Spur	Large, round, beautiful berries with a red glow. Very sweet and crisp. Heavy bearer; thin flower clusters to get top quality fruit.
'Ribier'	7-9, 11-16, 18-21	Early midseason	Spur	Huge, black, round berries in loose clusters. Sweet and juicy but insipid. Fruit lasts well on the vines. Not as flavorful as 'Blackrose'.
'Rish Baba' ('Lady Finger')	8, 9, 11-14, 18-20	Late midseason	Cane	Long, slender, greenish white berries sometimes slightly curved. Skins tender, brittle. Clusters slender, open.
'Thompson Seedless'	8, 9, 11-14, 18, 19	Early to midseason	Cane	Small, sweet, mild flavored, greenish amber in big bunches. Widely planted but top quality in warm interior areas only.
'Tokay'	8, 9, 14-16, 18-20	Late midseason	Spur	Brilliant red to dark red. Crackling crisp with distinctive winy flavor. Reaches perfection where summer heat is high but not excessive—Zone 14.

G

GRAPEFRUIT. See Citrus

GRAPTOPETALUM. Succulents. Zones 8-24. Native to Mexico. Leaves very thick, in loosely-packed, elongated rosettes. Good-looking in pots or in rock gardens in mildest regions. Leaves have a subtle, opalescent blending of colors. Flowers not showy. Detached leaves root easily.

G. amethystinum. Stems to 4 in. tall, eventually leaning or sprawling. Leaves bluish gray with pinkish purple overcast.

G. paraguayense. Leaves in a loose rosette or thickly borne on a stem to 7 in. tall, whitish gray with pinkish overcast.

GRASS NUT. See Brodiaea laxa

GRASSES, LAWN. See Lawn Chapter

GRASS TREE. See Xanthorrhea

GREVILLEA. Evergreen shrubs, trees. Native to Australia. Variable in size and appearance, generally with fine-textured foliage. Long, slender, curved flowers appear in (usually) dense clusters. Full sun. Once established they take poor, rocky, dry soil, but accept ordinary well drained garden soil. Rarely successful near lawns.

G. banksii. (Often sold as *G. banksii forsteri*.) Shrub or small tree. Zones 20-24. To 15-20 ft. Leaves 4-10 in. long, deeply cut into narrow lobes. Erect 3-6-in.-long clusters of dark red flowers sporadically throughout the year, heaviest in late spring. Showy used singly against a high wall, near entryway, or grouped with other big-scale shrubs. Freezes at 24°; takes wind, drought.

G. lanigera. WOOLLY GREVILLEA. Shrub. Zones 15-24. Spreading, mounding plant 3-6 ft. tall, 6-10 ft. across. Closely set, narrow, ½-in.-long leaves; general foliage effect gray-green. Clusters of narrow, curved, crimson and cream flowers profusely carried in summer; attractive to hummingbirds. Good bank cover in hot, sunny areas; good transition between garden and wild areas.

G. 'Noellii'. Shrub. Zones 8, 9, 12-24. Plant sold under this name reported to be a hybrid. Grows to 4 ft. tall, 4-5 ft. wide. Densely foliaged; narrow, 1-in.-long, medium green glossy leaves. Clusters of pink and white flowers 6-8 weeks in early and mid-spring. Takes more water than *G. lanigera;* far less drought-resistant.

G. robusta. SILK OAK. Tree. Zones 8, 9, 12-24. Fast growing to 50-60 (rarely 100) ft. Symmetrical, pyramidal when young. Old trees broad topped, picturesque against skyline, usually with a few heavy, horizontal limbs. Fernlike leaves are golden green to deep green above, silvery beneath. Heavy leaf fall in spring, sporadic leaf drop throughout year; frequent raking necessary. Large clusters of bright golden orange flowers in early spring; effective with jacaranda or with dark green background foliage.

Grows in poor, compact soils if not overwatered; takes fair amount of water in fast draining soils. Brittle, easily damaged in high wind. Stake securely. To make sturdier branches, lessen wind damage, cut leading shoot back hard at planting time, shorten branches to well balanced framework. Thrives in heat. Young trees damaged at 24°, older plants hardy to 16°.

Use for quick, tall screening or clip as a tall hedge. One of lushest greens for low desert. Fast shade producer, showy tree for unused space far from hose bib. Good temporary tree while you wait for a slower, tougher-wooded tree to grow up.

G. rosmarinifolia. ROSEMARY GREVILLEA. Zones 8, 9, 12-24. Compact shrub to 6 ft. tall, nearly as broad. Narrow, dark green 1½-in.-long leaves (silvery beneath) somewhat like rosemary. Red flower clusters (rarely pink or white) in fall and winter, with a scattering at other seasons. Use as clipped or unclipped hedge in dryish places.

G. thelemanniana. HUMMINGBIRD BUSH, SPIDER-NET GREVILLEA. Shrub. Zones 9, 14-17, 19-24. Graceful, rounded, 5-8 ft. tall, equally wide. Dark green leaves 1-2 in. long, divided into very narrow segments. Bright red flower clusters tipped yellow. Can bloom at any season. Water plants until established, then taper off. Somewhat temperamental. Plants airier, more open, less adapted to hedge and screen use than *G. rosmarinifolia.*

GREWIA caffra. LAVENDER STARFLOWER. Evergreen shrub. Zones 8, 9, 14-24. Native to South Africa. Fast growing, sprawling habit. Tends to branch freely in a flat pattern, making a natural espalier if given some support. Becomes dense with pinching and pruning. Grows 6-10 ft. tall (sometimes higher), with equal spread if unstaked. Deep green, oblong, finely-toothed leaves 3 in. long. Flowers an inch wide, starlike, lavender-pink with yellow centers. Blooms late spring with scattered bloom into autumn, especially if pruned after first heavy bloom.

Plant against a warm, sunny wall or fence. Can be planted 2 ft. apart and used as tall clipped hedge or screen. If upright growth is pruned out, it can be used as bank cover. Can be trained and staked to make a single-trunked tree or tied in place to cover an arbor or trellis. Takes wind well. Needs water, iron if chlorotic.

GRISELINIA. Evergreen shrubs. Zones 9, 14-17, 20-24. Native to New Zealand. Upright form and thick, leathery, lustrous leaves. Always look well groomed.

G. littoralis. A 50-ft. tree in New Zealand, it is usually seen in California as a 10-ft.-high shrub of equal spread. Leaves roundish, 4 in. long. In full sun with ample water it can reach 8 ft. in 3 years. A dense, compact screen or windbreak. Fine beach plant. Good espalier. Variety 'Variegata' has leaves marked with cream.

G. lucida. Slower growing, smaller, more open and slender than *G. littoralis,* with larger, 7-in.-long leaves. Excellent foliage plant for partial shade. Thrives in a container. Variety 'Variegata' has white markings on the leaves.

GROUND ORCHID, CHINESE. See Bletilla striata

GUAVA. See Psidium

GUAVA, CHILEAN. See Ugni

GUAVA, PINEAPPLE. See Feijoa

GUINEA GOLD VINE. See Hibbertia

GUM. See Eucalyptus

GUM, SOUR. See Nyssa

GUM, SWEET. See Liquidambar

GUNNERA. Perennial. Zones 4-6, 14-17, 20-24. Big, bold, awesome plants to 8 ft. high with giant leaves 4-8 ft. across. Leaves, on stiff-haired stalks 4-6 ft. long, conspicuously veined, with edges lobed and cut. Given the space (they need plenty) and necessary care, they can be the ultimate in summertime conversation pieces. New sets of leaves grow each spring. In mild-winter areas, old leaves remain green for more than one year. Elsewhere leaves die back completely in winter. Corncoblike 18-in. flower clusters down close to roots. Tiny fruits are red.

Part shade. Soil must be rich in nutrients and organic material, continually moist (but never soggy around root crown). Feed three times a year, beginning when new growth starts, to keep leaves maximum size. Give overhead sprinkling when humidity is low or drying winds occur. Use where can be focal point in summer, as beside a pool or dominating a bed of low, fine-textured ground cover. Makes confused scene when mixed with other plants of medium to large size leaves.

G. chilensis. Most common species. Lobed leaf margins are toothed and somewhat frilled. Leaves held in a bowl-like way, half upright and flaring.

G. manicata. Slightly smaller. Leaves carried fairly horizontal. Spinelike hairs on leaf stalks and ribs are red. Leaf lobes are flatter and lack the frills of *G. chilensis.*

GYMNOCLADUS dioica. KENTUCKY COFFEE TREE. Deciduous tree. Zones 1-3, 7-10, 12-16, 18-21. Native to eastern U. S. Saplings grow very fast, but slow down at 8-10 ft. Trees ultimately reach 50 ft. Narrowish habit in youth. Older trees broader, with fairly few heavy, contorted branches. These, together with the stout winter twigs, make bare tree picturesque. Leaves (1½-3 ft. long, divided into many leaflets 1-3 in. long) come out late in spring, are pinkish when expanding, deep green in summer, yellow in autumn. Inconspicuous flowers followed by 6-10-in.-long flat, reddish brown pods containing hard black seeds. Average garden soil and routine watering. Established trees will take some drought, much heat and cold, poor soil. Effective for structure and form in any cold-winter garden.

GYNURA aurantiaca. VELVET PLANT. House plant from the East Indies grown for its leaves and stems which have plush-like covering of violet hairs. Leaves lance-shaped, toothed, to 6 in. long, 2½ in. wide. Plant is somewhat shrubby, may reach 2-3 ft. or can spill out of a hanging basket. Yellow to orange ½-in. flowers have unpleasant odor; pinch out flower buds as they form. Needs strong indirect light for best color. Give plants wamth, and a rich, loose, well-drained soil.

GYPSOPHILA. Annual and perennials. Much branched, upright or spreading, slender-stemmed plants, 6 in. to 4 ft. tall, profusely covered in summer with small single or double white, pink, or rose flowers in clusters. Leaves blue-green, few when plant is in bloom. Use for airy grace in borders, bouquets; fine contrast with large-flowered, coarse-textured plants. Dwarf kinds ideal in rock gardens, trailing from wall pocket or over top of dry rock walls.

Full sun. Add lime to strongly acid soils. Thick, deep roots of some perennial kinds difficult to transplant; do not disturb often. Protect roots from gophers, tender top growth from snails, slugs. For repeat bloom on perennial kinds, cut back flowering stems before seed clusters form.

G. elegans. Annual. Upright, 1-1½ ft. Leaves lance-shaped, rather fleshy, to 3 in. long. Profuse single white flowers ½ in. or more across. Pink and rose forms available. Plants live only 5-6 weeks; for continuous bloom sow seed in open ground every 3-4 weeks from late spring into summer.

G. paniculata. BABY'S BREATH. Perennial. Zones 1-11, 14-16, 18-21. Much branched to 3 ft. or more. Leaves slender, sharp pointed, 2½-4 in. long. Single white flowers about 1/16 in. across, hundreds in a spray, July-October. Variety 'Bristol Fairy' improved form, more billowy, to 4 ft. high, covered with double blossoms ¼ in. wide. Propagate from root grafts or stem cuttings.

G. repens. Perennial. Zones 1-11, 14-16, 18-21. Alpine native 6-9 in. high, with trailing stems 18 in. long. Leaves narrow, less than 1 in. long. Clusters of small white or pink flowers in summer. Variety 'Rosea', usually less than 6 in. high, rosy pink flowers. Variety 'Bodgeri', to 1 ft. or more, stems prostrate at base, flowers white to pink, double, in loose clusters. Increase by cuttings in midsummer.

HABENARIA radiata. EGRET FLOWER. Terrestrial orchid. Outdoors in Zones 14-17, 19-24; greenhouse or indoor plant in winter elsewhere. Native of Japan. Flowers have green sepals, white petals—one of which flares to 1 in. wide with fringed edges like feathers on wing of bird in flight—and a large green trailing spur. From 3 to 5 blooms form on 12-15-in. stems which are leafy below.

Grow as potted plant in sun or part shade. For bloom most of year, store small tuberous roots in moist peat moss; plant a few each month. Set roots 1 in. deep, 6 to a 4-in. pot, in leaf mold or soil mix containing equal parts coarse sand, garden soil, peat moss. To get flowers, never let plants dry out. They will flower in about 6 months. Foliage dies back to ground in winter.

HABRANTHUS. Bulb. Outdoors in Zones 16, 17, 20-24; indoors or in greenhouses anywhere. Funnel-shaped blooms carried singly at an angle on 8-9-in. stems. Use in sunny border, rock garden, raised bed. Plant in fall or late summer in mild areas, spring in cold sections. Full sun or light shade. Set bulbs 1-2 in. deep, 3 in. apart. In cold climates dig and store in fall or mulch heavily. Usual bloom season summer and autumn, but may flower any time after rains or watering following dry spell.

H. robustus. Flowers 3 in. wide, 3 in. long, pale pink, veined deeper pink; green throat. Stems 6-9 in. tall. Narrow blue-green leaves follow flowers.

H. texanus. Flowers 1 in. long, coppery yellow, stained purple on outside. Stems 8 in. tall, leaves 4-6 in. long.

HACKBERRY. See Celtis

HAEMANTHUS katherinae. BLOOD LILY. Bulb. Tender South African plant closely related to amaryllis, grown in pots in greenhouse, as house plant; in mild climates move to terrace or patio for bloom in late spring. Large (4-in. diameter), white bulb stained red (hence common name). Leaves broad, wavy-edged, bright green, 12-15 in. long. Sturdy, succulent stem 2 ft. tall, topped by large, round clusters of salmon red flowers; protruding, showy, red stamens.

Pot 1 bulb to 10-in. pot in rich mix in winter or early spring. Set bulb with tip at soil surface; water sparingly, keep in 70° temperature. When leaves appear (8-10 weeks) move outdoors (in frostless sections) to sheltered, lightly shaded spot. Water thoroughly; feed monthly with complete fertilizer; bait for snails. After bloom, gradually reduce watering, dry out plant in cool, protected place. Do not repot next season; add new mix on top, or tip out root ball, scrape off some old soil, replace with fresh mix.

HAKEA. Evergreen shrubs or trees. Zones 9, 12-17, 19-24. Native to Australia. Tough, tolerant, relatively pest free, especially good for seacoast. Will take poor soil.

H. laurina. SEA URCHIN, PINCUSHION TREE. Small, dense, rounded tree or large shrub, to 30 ft. Narrow, gray-green, 6-in.-long leaves are often red-margined. Showy flower clusters look like round crimson pincushions stuck with golden pins. Blooms in winter, sometimes in late fall. Stake young trees securely. Good small patio tree.

H. suaveolens. SWEET HAKEA. Dense, broad, upright shrub to 10-20 ft. tall. Stiff, dark green, 4-in. leaves, branched into stiff, needlelike, stickery segments. Fragrant, small, white flowers, in dense, fluffy clusters, fall and winter. Useful barrier plant, background, or screen. Good with conifers. Can be pruned into tree form.

HALESIA. Deciduous trees. Zones 2-9, 14-24. Both kinds give best flower display in areas of winter cold, grow best in cool, deep, humus-rich soil with ample water.

H. carolina (*H. tetraptera*). SNOWDROP TREE, SILVER BELL. Moderate growth to 20-50 ft. with 15-30 ft. spread, depending on climate. Rates high as flowering tree in May when clusters of snowdrop white, ½-in. bell-shaped flowers hang from graceful branches just as leaves begin to appear. Leaves 4 in. long, oval, finely toothed, turn yellow in fall. Interesting brown fruits with 4 wings hang on most of winter. Prune to a single stem when it's young or it will grow as a large shrub. Flowers show off best when you can look up into tree. Attractive as overhead planting for azaleas and rhododendrons.

H. monticola. MOUNTAIN SILVER BELL. It's a larger tree, 40-60 ft., with larger (3-6 in.) leaves.

HALIMIOCISTUS sahucii. Evergreen shrub. Zones 4-24. Hybrid between *Halimium umbellatum* and *Cistus salvifolius*. Combines best characteristics of both parents. Densely foliaged with 1-in., narrow, gray-green leaves, it grows to 2 ft. high and spreads to 3 ft. or more. In summer, clusters of white, 1-2-in.-wide flowers with center tufts of yellow stamens, almost hide the foliage. Good choice for a sunny rock garden, a dry bank, cascading over a concrete retaining wall. Or, plant on sunny side of house under wide eaves where rains seldom reach. Will not live in wet soil, and can be watered with other plants only if drainage is better than average.

HALIMIUM. Evergreen shrublets. Zones 7-9, 12-24. Closely related to sunroses (*Helianthemum*) and sometimes sold under that name. Cultural requirements and uses are the same. Halimiums grow 2-3 ft. high, have gray-green foliage, yellow flowers in loose clusters in spring.

H. lasianthum (*Helianthemum formosum*). Spreading plant with leaves ½-1½ ft. long, ¼ in. wide. Flowers 1½ in. across, bright yellow with a brownish purple blotch near base of petals.

H. ocymoides (*Helianthemum ocymoides*). Erect plant with leaves slightly narrower than the above species. Flowers 1 in. wide, bright yellow, with a black and purple blotch at base of petals.

H. umbellatum (*Helianthemum umbellatum*). Grows to 18 in. Leaves very narrow, resembling rosemary. Flowers ¾ in. across, white with yellow stain at base of petals. Flower clusters 4-6 in. long.

HAMAMELIS. WITCH HAZEL. Deciduous trees or large shrubs. Yellow fall foliage. Fragrant, yellow flowers with very narrow crumpled looking petals in nodding few-flowered clusters. Plants grow in sun or light shade and need moderate moisture and some peat moss, ground bark, or leaf mold in the soil.

H. mollis. CHINESE WITCH HAZEL. Zones 4-7, 15-17. Moderately slow growing shrub to 8-10 ft. or eventually a small tree to 30 ft. Branches in a loose zigzag pattern. Roundish leaves, 3½-6 in. long, dark green and rough above, gray felted beneath, turn a good clear yellow in fall. Fragrant, rich golden yellow flowers, 1½ in. wide, with red-brown calyx, bloom on bare stems. December-March. Effective against red brick or gray stone. Flowering branches excellent for flower arrangements.

H. virginiana. COMMON WITCH HAZEL. Zones 1-9, 14-16, 18-21. Native to eastern U. S. Sometimes to 25 ft. but usually 10-15 ft. high, of open spreading, rather straggling habit. Moderately slow growing. Roundish leaves similar to *H. mollis* but not gray felted beneath; turn yellow to orange in fall. Golden yellow, ¾-in.-wide blooms appear in October and November and tend to be lost in the colored foliage.

HARDENBERGIA. Evergreen shrubby vines. Native to Australia. Moderate growing to 10 ft., climbing by twining stems. Pea-shaped flowers, several to many in clusters,

Lacy dark green foliage, 6-8-in.-long violet-blue flower clusters of lilac vine.

Climate
Zone maps
pages 8-27

late winter to early spring. Useful for light, delicate pattern on low walls, fences, screens, arches. Can be pegged down as a ground cover. Needs light, well drained soil in sun (partial shade in hot areas). Do not overwater. Provide support for climbing and cut back after bloom to prevent tangling. Fairly free of pests and diseases; subject to spider mites, nematodes.

H. comptoniana. LILAC VINE. Zones 15-24. Light, delicate foliage pattern; leaves divided into 3-5 dark green, narrow, 2-3-in.-long leaflets. Flowers violet-blue, ½ in. long, in long narrow clusters. Where temperatures drop below 24°, shelter blossoms, buds, tender tops by planting under overhang.

H. violacea (*H. monophylla*). Zones 9-24. Coarser texture; leaves usually with one 2-4-in.-long leaflet. Vining or shrubby. Flowers lilac, violet to rose or white. Denser, faster, hardier than *H. comptoniana*. Takes full sun, wind.

HARDTACK. See Cercocarpus betuloides

HAREBELL. See Campanula rotundifolia

HARLEQUIN FLOWER. See Sparaxis

HARPEPHYLLUM caffrum. KAFFIR PLUM. Evergreen tree. Zones 17, 19, 21-24. Fast growth to 30-35 ft. or higher with 20-25-ft. spread. Freezes back in cold weather but makes quick recovery, if frost not below 25°. (Usually has multiple trunks after such recovery.) Round-headed, but easily trained to structurally interesting small tree. Leathery, glossy leaves of 13-15 narrow, 2½-in.-long leaflets. These unfold as a rich red, but turn to dark green. Clusters of very small white or greenish flowers followed by tart but edible dark red fruits resembling large olives. The fruit drop is a problem near paving.

Tolerates considerable wind and heat. Prune to shape and to remove frost-damaged wood. Well-groomed appearance and quick growth make it a good shade or decorative tree for the small garden. Striking silhouette against a tall, light-colored wall.

HAT PLANT, CHINESE. See Holmskioldia

HAWORTHIA. Succulents of the lily family. Zones 8, 9, 12-24. Extremely variable in growth habit: the best-known ones resemble the smaller aloes (closely related), but others make small towers of neatly stacked fleshy leaves, and there are other forms, too. All make excellent pot plants, best in part shade.

H. attenuata. Dark green leaves heavily marked with raised white dots, grow in stemless or short-stemmed rosettes to 6 in. wide. Spreads to make clumps. Flowers dull pink in 2-ft. clusters.

H. fasciata. Stemless rosettes with many 3-in.-long, narrow, dark green leaves, marked strongly by crosswise bands of raised white dots. Flowers greenish white, in 6-in. clusters. Spreads freely by offsets.

H. setata. LACE HAWORTHIA. Small stemless rosettes of many leaves to 1¼ in. long, half as wide. Leaves dark green marked with white translucent areas and edged with long, bristly white teeth that give a lacy look.

HAWTHORN. See Crataegus

HAWTHORN, INDIA. See Raphiolepis indica

HAZEL NUT. See Corylus

HEART OF FLAME. Bromelia

HEATHS, HEATHERS. Evergreen shrubs. Three kinds of plants make up this group: *Calluna*, the true Scotch heather; *Daboecia*, which includes Irish heath, its color varieties, and a related plant from the Azores; and *Erica*, heath, the many species of which come from many lands.

Heaths and heathers resemble each other in having narrow, needlelike or scalelike leaves densely set on the branches, and in carrying a profusion of bell-shaped, urn-shaped, or tubular flowers. Only a few species are fragrant. They differ widely in size, habit, flower color, bloom season, and adaptability to Western soils and climates. Grow them in full sun (light shade in hot inland valleys) in soil that's slightly acid, peaty, and very well drained. A few tolerate neutral or alkaline soil and water; these will need treatment with iron or chelated iron to control chlorosis.

Do not fertilize heavily; light feeding with acid fertilizer will maintain good plant color in dry areas where watering must be frequent. They may need no feeding at all in the Northwest. Roots must never go dry; on the other hand they must never be soggy. Mulch to keep down weeds, minimize surface cultivation that damages surface roots.

Low-growing heaths and heathers may be sheared after bloom to remove dry blossoms, stimulate fresh growth. Shape taller kinds by cutting back wood that has bloomed. Save or shorten unbloomed branches, and make cut just above an unbloomed side branch. Never cut back into bare wood.

Use low-growing kinds for ground or bank cover, as bedding plants, in foregrounds, or in rock gardens. Excellent as edging or as colorful pot or planting box plants. They give convincing mountain meadow effects in woodland settings. Mass groups of one variety, or mix colors in natural-looking groups.

Taller heathers make good informal screens, featured plants in shrub borders, or contrasting elements with dark, heavy evergreens. They combine well with lower heathers and with heather relatives—rhododendron, azalea, huckleberry, pieris.

Good hobby plants where adapted; they give quick effects and come in a stimulating variety of sizes and shapes, most of which blend well with each other. By selecting species and varieties with care you can have some bloom the year around.

HEATHER, FALSE. See Cuphea hyssopifolia

HEATHS AND HEATHERS

NAME AND ZONES	GROWTH HABIT, SIZE	LEAVES	FLOWER COLOR, SEASON	COMMENTS
CALLUNA vulgaris SCOTCH HEATHER. Zones 2-6, 17. Europe, Asia Minor.	Upright shrub 15-30 in. tall.	Deep green.	Flowers in dense, slender clusters, rosy pink. June-Oct.	Its varieties are better known.
C. v. 'Alba Plena'	Loose mound to 12 in.	Medium green.	White, double. Aug-Sept.	One of the best whites.
C. v. 'Aurea'	Spreading, twiggy, to 8-12 in.	Gold in summer, russet in winter.	Purple. Aug.-Sept. Sparse bloom.	Gold foliage year around if in full sun.
C. v. 'Aureafolia'	Upright, to 18 in.	Chartreuse, golden tinge in summer.	White. Aug.-Sept.	Long irregular flower spikes.
C. v. 'County Wicklow'	Spreading mound, 9-18 in.	Medium green.	Pink, double. Aug.-Oct.	Excellent, white in bud.
C. v. 'Dainty Bess'	Tiny mat, to 2-4 in.	Gray.	Lavender. Aug-Sept.	Conforms to rocks.
C. v. 'David Eason'	Spreading mound, to 12-18 in.	Light green.	Reddish purple. Oct.-Nov.	Good late variety.
C. v. 'Else Frye'	Upright, to 24 in.	Medium green.	White, double. July-Aug.	Good clear white.

(Continued on next page)

H

Climate Zone maps pages 8-27

NAME AND ZONES	GROWTH HABIT, SIZE	LEAVES	FLOWER COLOR, SEASON	COMMENTS
C. v. 'Foxii Nana'	Small mound, to 6 in.	Dark green.	Purple. Aug.-Sept.	Dwarf pincushion.
C. v. 'Goldsworth Crimson'	Spreading mound, to 18 in.	Sage green.	Crimson. Oct.-Nov.	Good color in late fall.
C. v. 'H. E. Beale'	Loose mound, to 2 ft.	Dark green.	Soft pink, double. Aug.-Oct.	Long spikes, good for cutting.
C. v. 'J. H. Hamilton'	Prostrate, bushy, to 9 in.	Deep green.	Pink, double. Aug.-Sept.	Blooms generously.
C. v. 'Mair's Variety'	Upright, to 2-3 ft.	Medium green.	White. July-Sept.	Good background plant for lower heathers. Easy to grow.
C. v. 'Mrs. Pat'	Bushy mound, to 8 in.	Light green.	Light purple. July-Sept.	Good foreground plant. New spring growth is pink.
C. v. 'Mrs. Ronald Gray'	Creeping mound, to 3 in.	Dark green.	Reddish purple. Aug.-Sept.	Excellent ground cover.
C. v. 'Mullion'	Tight mound, to 9 in.	Medium green.	Rosy purple. Aug.-Sept.	Excellent ground cover.
C. v. 'Nana'	Low, spreading, to 4 in.	Dark green.	Purple. July-Sept.	Often called carpet heather.
C. v. 'Nana Compacta'	Compact mound, to 4 in.	Medium green.	Purple. July-Sept.	Rock garden. Often called pincushion heather.
C. v. 'Roma'	Compact, to 9 in.	Dark green.	Deep pink. Aug.-Oct.	Attractive form.
C. v. 'Searlei'	Bushy, 12-18 in.	Yellow-green.	White. Aug.-Oct.	Feathery foliage.
C. v. 'Tib'	Rounded bushy, to 12-18 in.	Medium green.	Rosy purple, double. Aug.-Sept.	Deepest in color of double callunas.
DABOECIA azorica Zones 8, 9, 14-24. Azores.	Low, dense growth, to 6 in.	Deep green.	Deep red, profuse in April-May. Some scattered blooms in Fall.	Rock garden plant.
D. cantabrica IRISH HEATH, IRISH BELL HEATH. Zones 3-9, 14-24. Ireland to northern Spain.	Erect, somewhat spreading stems, 1½-2 ft. tall.	Wider than those of other heaths, glossy dark green above, white hairy underneath.	Pinkish purple, ½ in. long, urn-shaped, in narrow clusters 3-5 in. long. June-Oct. In warmer areas bloom begins April.	Satisfactory in Zones 8, 9, 14, 18-24, if given good soil. Needs some shade except near coast. Cut back in fall to keep compact.
D. c. 'Alba'	As above.	Lighter green than above.	Pure white.	Masses well; plant 2 ft. apart.
D. c. 'Praegerae'	Grows to 12 in.	Deep green.	Pure pink.	Good rock garden plant.
ERICA arborea TREE HEATH Zones 15-17, 21-24. Southern Europe, north Africa.	Dense shrub or tree to 10-20 ft., single or many trunked, often with heavy burl at base.	Bright green, ¼ in. long. New growth lighter.	Fragrant white flowers. Mar.-May	Slow growing. Burls are the "briar" used for making pipes.
E. a. alpina	Dense, upright, fluffy looking shrub to 6 ft.	As above.	White. Mar.-May.	Slow to reach blooming age, but free blooming. Slightly hardier than above.
E. australis SOUTHERN HEATH. Zones 5-9, 14-24. Spain, Portugal.	Upright, spired, 6-10 ft. high.	Dark green.	Rosy or red. Mar.-June. Clustered at ends of shoots.	Needs protection in Northwest. There is a white form, 'Mr. Robert'.
E. blanda. See *E. verticillata*				
E. canaliculata (Usually sold as *E. melanthera*, and often called Scotch heather, which it is not.) Zones 15-17, 20-24.	Bushy, spreading, but with general spiry effect, to 6 ft.	Dark green above, white beneath.	Pink to rosy purple. Fall and winter.	The pink form is sold as 'Rosea', the reddish purple as 'Rubra'. Excellent winter bloom in California. Sometimes called Christmas heather. One of best for Zones 20-24.
E. c. 'Boscaweniana' (Sometimes sold as *E. melanthera*.)	Upright bush or small tree, to 18 ft.	As above.	Pale lilac-pink to nearly white. Winter, spring.	Like *E. canaliculata*, a good source of cut flowers.

Climate
Zone maps
pages 8-27

H

NAME AND ZONES	GROWTH HABIT, SIZE	LEAVES	FLOWER COLOR, SEASON	COMMENTS
E. carnea Zones 2-9, 14-24. European Alps.	Dwarf, 6-16 in. high. Upright branchlets rise from prostrate main branches.	Medium green.	Rosy red. Dec.-June.	Unsightly unless pruned every year. This and its varie- ties tolerate neutral or slight- ly alkaline soil. Takes part shade in hot-summer areas.
E. c. 'Ruby Glow'	To 8 in. high.	Dark green.	Deep ruby red. Jan.-June.	One of the richest in color.
E. c. 'Springwood' ('Springwood White')	Spreading, to 8 in.	Light green.	White, creamy buds. Jan.-April.	Toughest, fastest growing, one of the neatest heathers.
E. c. 'Springwood Pink'	Spreading mound, to 10 in.	Bright green.	Pure pink. Jan.-April.	Pinky rust new growth.
E. c. 'Vivellii'	Spreading mound, to 12 in.	Dark green, bronzy red in winter.	Carmine red. Feb.-Mar.	Interesting for seasonal change in foliage color as well as for bloom.
E. c. 'Winter Beauty' ('King George')	Bushy, spreading, compact, to 15 in.	Dark green.	Deep, rich pink. Dec.-April.	Often in bloom at Christmas.
E. ciliaris DORSET HEATH, Zones 4-6, 15-17. England, Ireland.	Trailing, 6-12 in.	Pale green.	Rosy red. July-Sept.	Good for massing.
E. c. 'Mrs. C. H. Gill'	Spreading, to 12 in.	Dark green.	Deep red. July-Oct.	Free blooming, showy.
E. c. 'Stoborough'	As above, but taller, to 18 in.	Medium green.	White. July-Oct.	Snowy, bell-like flowers.
E. cinerea TWISTED HEATH. Zones 4-6, 15-17. British Isles, northern Europe.	Spreading mound, to 12 in.	Dark green, dainty.	Purple. June-Sept.	Low, mat-making, good ground cover.
E. c. 'Atrosanguinea'	Low, spreading, bushy, to 9 in.	Dark green, dainty.	Scarlet. June-Oct.	Dwarf, slow growing.
E. c. 'C. D. Eason'	Compact, to 10 in.	Dark green.	Red. May-Aug.	Outstanding; good flower display.
E. c. 'G. Ford'	Compact, to 8 in.	Dark green.	Bright red. May-Aug.	Deeper color than 'C. D. Eason'.
E. c. 'P. S. Patrick'	Bushy, to 15 in.	Dark green.	Purple. June-Aug.	Sturdy, long spikes, large flowers.
E. darleyensis. See *E. purpurascens* 'Darleyensis'				
E. 'Dawn' Zones 4-9, 14-24.	Spreading mound, 12 in.	Green; new growth golden.	Deep pink. June-Oct.	Excellent ground cover. Easy to grow. Hybrid between *E. ciliaris, E. tetralix.*
E. 'Felix Faure' FRENCH HEATHER. Zones 15-17, 20-24.	Low, compact, to 1 ft.	Bright green.	Inch-long, tubular, lilac- pink tipped white, in winter.	Often used as a potted plant.
E. hyemalis (Often sold as *E. hieliana* or *E. hyalina*.) Zones 15-17, 20-24. South Africa.	Upright, spiky, to 2-3 ft.	Bright green.	Inch-long, tubular, lilac- pink tipped white, in winter.	There is a white form, 'Alba'. Sometimes sold as potted plant.
E. 'John McLaren'. See *E. mammosa*				
E. lusitanica (*E. codonodes*) SPANISH HEATH. Zones 5-9, 14-24. Spain, Portugal.	Upright, feathery shrub, to 6-12 ft.	Light green.	Pinkish white, slightly fragrant. Jan-Mar.	Remarkably profuse bloom. Needs sheltered spot in the Northwest. One of the best in Zones 20-24.

(Continued on next page)

H

Climate
Zone maps
pages 8-27

NAME AND ZONES	GROWTH HABIT, SIZE	LEAVES	FLOWER COLOR, SEASON	COMMENTS
E. mammosa Zones 15-17, 20-24. South Africa.	Stiff, erect, to 1-3 ft. tall.	Bright green.	Variable, but in shades of pink. Early spring, repeating through autumn.	Many varieties. 'Jubilee', a salmon pink, is the most generally available. Usually sold as 'John McLaren'.
E. mediterranea BISCAY HEATH. Zones 4-9, 14-24. Ireland, France, Spain.	Loose, upright, 4-7 ft.	Deep green.	Lilac-pink. Jan.-Apr.	Good background. Worth trial in Zones 12-13.
E. mediterranea hybrida. See E. purpurascens 'Darleyensis'				
E. melanthera. See E. canaliculata.				
E. persoluta Zones 15-17, 20-24. South Africa.	Stiff, upright shrub, to 2 ft. tall.	Bright green.	Tiny, rose or white. Late winter, early spring.	Offered as pot plants or sold as cut branches.
E. purpurascens 'Darleyensis' (E. mediterranea hybrida, E. darleyensis) Zones 4-9, 14-24.	Bushy grower, to 12 in. tall.	Medium green.	Light, rosy purple. Nov.-May.	Tough, hardy plant that takes both heat and cold surprisingly well. There is a white form.
E. p. 'George Rendall'	Bushy, compact, to 12 in.	Bluish green	Deeper purple than the above.	New growth gold tinted.
E. tetralix CROSS-LEAFED HEATH. Zones 4-6, 15-17. England, northern Europe.	Upright, to 12 in.	Dark green, silvery beneath.	Rosy pink. June-Oct.	Very hardy plant. New growth yellow, orange, or red.
E. t. 'Alba Mollis'	Upright, slightly spreading, to 12 in.	Silvery gray.	Clear white. June-Oct.	Foliage sheen pronounced in spring, summer.
E. t. 'Darleyensis'	Spreading, open growth, to 8 in.	Gray-green.	Salmon pink. June-Sept.	Good color. Do not confuse with winter-flowering E. purpurascens 'Darleyensis'.
E. t. 'Praegerae'	Spreading, to 6 in. high.	Medium green to gray-green.	Bright pink. June-Oct.	Not as gray as other E. tetralix varieties.
E. vagans CORNISH HEATH. Zones 3-6, 15-17, 20-24. Cornwall, Ireland.	Bushy, open, to 2-3 ft. tall.	Bright green.	Purplish pink. July-Sept.	Robust and hardy.
E. v. 'Lyonesse'	Bushy, rounded, to 18 in.	Bright, glossy green.	White. July-Oct.	Best white Cornish heath.
E. v. 'Mrs. D. F. Maxwell'	Bushy, rounded, to 18 in.	Dark green.	Cherry pink or red. July-Oct.	Outstanding for color and heavy bloom; widely grown.
E. v. 'St. Keverne'	Bushy, rounded, to 18 in.	Light green.	Rose pink. July-Oct.	Heavy bloom. Compact if pruned annually.
E. verticillata (Often sold as E. blanda, E. doliiformis.) Zones 15-17, 20-24.	Low growing, spiky plant, to 1 ft.	Rich green, needlelike.	Long, tubular, rosy red. June-Oct.	Blooms better if old blossoms picked off as they fade.

HEBE. Evergreen shrubs. Zones 14-24 except as noted. Native to New Zealand. Landscaping plants grown principally for form and foliage; some give good flower display. All do better in cool coastal gardens than in interior, where dry summer heat and winter frosts shorten their lives. The lower kinds are useful for edgings or ground cover; taller ones are good shrubs where sea winds and salt air are a problem. Most are fast growers.

Will take full sun on coast; give partial shade in warm valleys. Good drainage is essential, with plenty of moisture. Prune after bloom, shortening flowering branches considerably to keep plants compact and bushy.

Closely related to *Veronica* and still often sold under that name.

H. andersonii. Hybrid between *H. speciosa* and *H. salicifolia.* Compact, to 5-6 ft. Leaves fleshy, deep green. Summer flowers in 2-4-in. spikes, white at base, violet at tip.

H. 'Autumn Glory'. Zones 5, 6, 14-24. Mounding, compact, 2 ft. high, 2 ft. wide. Oval leaves 1½ in. long. Many 2-in.-long dark lavender-blue flower spikes in late summer and fall.

H. buxifolia. BOXLEAF HEBE. Rounded, symmetrical habit eventually 5 ft. tall, easily shaped into a 3-ft. hedge. Deep green leaves ⅓ in. long densely crowded on branches. Small white flowers in headlike clusters in summer.

H. 'Carnea'. Grows 3-5 ft. tall. Deep green, willowlike leaves 2½ in. long. Flowers rosy crimson in 2½-in.-long spikes, August-September.

H. chathamica. Ground cover shrub to 1½ ft. tall, the stems trailing to 3 ft. Leaves ½ in. long, deep green. Lavender flowers in summer.

H. 'Coed'. Compact plant to 3 ft. tall, equally broad. Reddish stems densely clothed with 1½-in.-long, dark green leaves. Spikelike clusters of small, pinkish purple flowers profusely carried May to August.

H. cupressoides. Slow grower to 4-5 ft. with slender branches clothed in bright green scalelike leaves that look like cypress. Small bluish flowers seldom produced. More widely sold is 'Nana', a compact, rounded, slow-growing plant to 2 ft. high. Often used in containers, rock gardens, or as a bonsai.

H. 'Desilor'. Dense, rounded shrub to 3 ft. tall, equally broad. Leaves somewhat smaller than in *H. elliptica.* Flowers deep purple-blue in 1½-in.-long clusters May-October.

H. elliptica (*H. decussata*). Much branched shrub 5-6 ft. high. Medium-green leaves 1¼ in. long. Fragrant bluish flowers in 1½-in.-long clusters bloom in summer.

H. glaucophylla. Broad, compact, rounded shrub about 2 ft. wide. Roundish, blue-green ½-in.-long leaves. Summer flowers white, in short, dense clusters. Use as a low foundation plant or divider between walk and lawn.

H. imperialis. Hybrid between *H. speciosa, H. salicifolia.* Resembles *H. speciosa,* but has reddish foliage, magenta flower clusters in summer. In nurseries *H. imperialis* and *H. speciosa* may be the same plant.

H. menziesii. Can reach 5 ft.; usually much lower. Narrow, closely spaced ¾-in.-long leaves are shiny bright green and slightly toothed. White flowers tinged lilac in short clusters; summer bloom. Spreading habit; good ground cover.

H. 'Patty's Purple'. To 3 ft. high, the stems wine red. Leaves ½ in. long, dark green. Purple flowers on slender spikes in summer. Use to back a flower border, or mass in groups.

H. pinguifolia. Zones 5, 6, 14-24. Erect or creeping shrub 1-3 ft. tall with roundish, blue-green leaves ¾ in. long, often with red edges. Fat, white, 1-in.-long flower spikes in summer. *H. p.* 'Pagei' has leaves ½-in. across, blue-gray edged rose. Grows 9 in. high, 5 ft. across. Rock garden plant.

H. 'Reevesii' (*H.* 'Evansii'). To 3 ft. high. The 2-in.-long leaves are a blend of dark green and reddish purple; flowers reddish purple, summer bloom.

H. salicifolia. Grows 10-12 ft. tall. Leaves 2-6 in. long, narrow, dark shiny green. Flowers in dense clusters in summer, white (usually) to mauve or purple. Clusters 2-5 in. long, slender.

H. speciosa. SHOWY HEBE. Spreading shrub 2-5 ft. high. Stout stems bear dark green, glossy leaves 2-4 in. long. Broad, dense, 3-4-in.-long spikes of reddish purple flowers, July-September.

H. traversii. Compact shrub 2-5 ft. tall. Leaves 1 in. long, 1/3 in. wide, dark green. Summer flowers white, in 2-in. clusters.

HEDERA. IVY. Evergreen woody vines. The most widely planted ground cover in California. Also, often a vine on walls, fences, trellises. Sometimes a planting does both—wall ivy spreads to become a surrounding ground cover, or vice versa. Ivy is dependable, uniform, and neat. Also, it is good for holding soil—discouraging soil erosion and slippage on slopes. Roots grow deep and fill soil densely. Branches root as they grow, further knitting the soil.

Ivy climbs almost any vertical surface by aerial rootlets—a factor to consider in planting against walls that need painting. A chain link fence planted to ivy soon becomes a wall of foliage. Ivy grows in sun or shade. Its only real shortcoming is monotony. All year long you get nothing from it but green or green and white.

Thick leathery leaves are usually lobed. Mature plants will eventually develop stiff branches toward top of the vine which bear round clusters of small greenish flowers followed by black berries. These branches have unlobed leaves; cuttings from such branches will have the same kind of leaves and will be shrubby, not vining. Such shrubs taken from variegated Algerian ivy are called "ghost ivy". *H. helix* 'Arborescens' is another variety of that type.

You can grow regular ivy from cuttings but many will die and growth will be very slow. Plants from flats grow much faster. Standard spacing: 18 in. Best planting time: early spring (March in California's ivy country).

Most critical needs in planting are for soil to be thoroughly pre-moistened, plant roots to be moist, and for plant tissues to be full of moisture (not wilted). Mix peat moss or ground bark into planting soil to a depth of 9-12 in., if possible. On a steep

slope, dig conditioner into each planting hole (6 in. deep, 6 in. wide). After spring planting, feed with high-nitrogen fertilizer. Feed again in August. For best possible growth, continue to feed in early spring and August of every year. In hot climates, the more water you give an ivy planting the better it will hold up through the summer.

Most ivy ground covers need trimming around the edges (hedge shears or sharp spade) 2-3 times a year. Fences and walls need shearing or trimming 2-3 times a year. When a ground cover builds up higher than you want, mow it with a rugged power rotary mower or cut it back with hedge shears. Do this in spring so ensuing growth will quickly cover the bald look.

Many trees and shrubs grow quite compatibly in ivy. But small, soft, or fragile plants will never exist for long with healthy ivy. The ivy simply smothers them out.

To kill Bermuda grass in ivy, spray with dalapon 2-3 times during Bermuda's active growing season. The chemical doesn't hurt ivy when used as directed for Bermuda. Add a wetting agent to make dalapon more effective.

A bacterial leaf spot causes light green, water-soaked spots on leaves. Spots turn brown or black, edged with red or brown; ultimately stems shrivel and blacken. A physiological trouble called edema brings on same symptoms. Prevent either malady by watering early in day, so foliage is dry by night. There is no chemical control for edema. To control the bacterial disease, spray infected beds with Morsodren or other locally recommended products.

If dodder, a yellow threadlike parasite, grows among ivy plants, use ammonium sulfate at 1 lb. per gal. of water. Treatment will kill ivy leaves but new leaves will grow out again.

Ivy can give haven to slugs and snails. If your garden has these pests put slug-snail poison in the ivy often.

H. canariensis. ALGERIAN IVY. Zones 8, 9, 12-24. Shiny, rich green leaves 5-8 in. wide with 3-5 shallow lobes, more widely spaced along stems then on English ivy. Requires more moisture than English ivy.

H. c. 'Variegata'. VARIEGATED ALGERIAN IVY. Leaves edged with yellowish white; the white sometimes suffused with reddish purple in cold weather.

H. helix. ENGLISH IVY. All Zones. Leaves dark, dull green with paler veins, 3-5 lobed, 2-4 in. wide at base and as long. Not as vigorous as Algerian ivy, easier to control, better for small spaces.

H. h. 'Baltica'. Hardiest, has leaves half the size of English ivy, whitish veins, turns purplish in winter.

Many small and miniature leafed forms are useful for small-area ground covers, hanging baskets, and training to intricate patterns on walls and in pots. Some of the small-leafed forms are: 'Hahn's Self Branching', light green leaves, dense branching, part shade best; 'Conglomerata', a slow-growing dwarf; 'Minima', leaves ½-1 in. across with 3-5 angular lobes. Names of some of the others give an idea of forms to be had: 'Dragon Tongue', 'Fan', 'Gold Dust', 'Maple Leaf', 'Needle Point', 'Pin Oak'.

HEDYCHIUM. GINGER LILY. Perennials. Outdoors in Zones 17, 22-24, greenhouse plants

Climate Zone maps pages 8-27

Climate
Zone maps
pages 8-27

anywhere. Foliage handsome under ideal conditions. Leaves on two sides of stems but in one plane. Richly fragrant flowers, in dense spikes, open from a cone of overlapping green bracts at ends of stalks. Flower in late summer or early fall. Remove old stems after flowers fade to encourage fresh new growth. Very useful in large containers, but will not grow as tall as in open ground. Container plants can be moved out of sight when unattractive. Grow in light shade, in soil high in organic matter. Frosts in mild areas can kill to ground, but new stalks appear in early spring.

H. coronarium. WHITE GINGER LILY, GARLAND FLOWER. Native to India and Indonesia. Grows 3-6 feet high. Leaves 8-24 in. long, 2-5 in. broad. Foliage usually unattractive in California because if it's given enough heat to bloom well, the foliage will burn. Flowers white in 6-12-in.-long clusters, wonderfully fragrant; make good cut flowers.

H. flavum. CREAM GINGER LILY. Native to India. About 5 ft. high. Foliage almost evergreen; the leaves to 14 in. long with long slender tips. Flowers yellow to buff, at best in late October, and reported to be more fragrant than the other two.

H. gardnerianum. KAHILI GINGER. Native to India. Grows to 8 ft. high, the 8 to 18-in.-long leaves 4-6 in. wide. Clear yellow flowers, with red stamens, in 18-in.-long spikes tip the branches from July to onset of cool weather.

HEDYSCEPE canterburyana. Palm. Outdoors in Zones 17, 23, 24; anywhere as house or greenhouse plant. Comes from Lord Howe Island in the South Pacific. Related to the better-known howeias (which see) but smaller, broader, lower growing, with broader leaf segments and more arching, lighter green feather-type leaves.

HELENIUM autumnale. COMMON SNEEZEWEED. Perennial. All Zones. Many branching, leafy stems to 1-6 ft. depending on variety. Daisylike flowers summer to early fall—the rays in shades of yellow, orange, red, and copper, surrounding brown pomponlike center. Needs full sun. Flowers best where summers hot. Trim off faded blossoms to encourage more blooms. Plants can take considerable neglect.

H. a. 'Chippersfield Orange'. To 4 ft.; copper and gold flowers, August to September or even later.

H. a. 'Moerheim Beauty'. To 2½-3 ft.; brownish red blossoms, June to September.

H. a. 'Peregrinum'. To 3 ft.; rays mahogany red tipped with yellow, July to August.

H. a. 'Pumilum'. To 1-2 ft.; flowers yellow, start to bloom in June.

H. a. 'Rubrum'. To 4 ft.; deep red flowers, summer.

HELIANTHEMUM nummularium. SUNROSE. Evergreen shrublets. All Zones. Commonly sold under this name are a number of forms as well as hybrids between this species and others. They grow to about 6-8 in. high, and spread to 3 ft. The ½-1-in.-long leaves may be glossy green above and fuzzy gray beneath, or gray on both sides depending on the kind. They give a delightful flower display in lovely, sunny colors—flame, red, apricot, orange, yellow, pink, rose, peach,

salmon, and white. Single and double-flowered forms. The 1-in.-wide flowers, in clusters, bloom April-June in California and Arizona, May-July in the Northwest. A blossom lasts only a day, but new buds continue to open. Shear plants back after flowering to encourage fall bloom.

Let sunroses tumble over rocks. Give them a niche in a dry rock wall. Set them in a planter inset in a sunny patio. Allow them to ramble over a gentle slope. If used as ground cover, plant 1-2 ft. apart. Plant in fall or early spring—from flats rather than from containers, if possible. Soil drainage must be good. Do not overwater. In cold-winter areas, lightly cover them with branches from evergreens to keep foliage from dehydrating in winter.

HELIANTHUS. SUNFLOWER. Annuals and perennials. All Zones. Coarse, sturdy plants with bold flowers. All are tough, tolerant plants for full sun, any garden soil. Perennial kinds spread rapidly, may become invasive. Not for tidy gardens. All bloom in late summer, fall.

H. annuus. COMMON SUNFLOWER. Annual. From this rough, hairy plant with 2-3-in.-wide flower heads have come many ornamental and useful garden varieties. Some of the ornamental varieties have double yellow flower heads 5-7 in. across ('Teddy Bear', 'Sungold', 'Chrysanthemum-Flowered'); others have large orange, red-brown, or mahogany heads. Best known form is the coarse, towering (to 10-ft.) plant with small rays outside and a cushiony center of disk flowers, 8-10 in. across. Usually sold as 'Mammoth Russian'. People eat the roasted seeds; birds like them raw, and visit the flower heads in fall and winter. For children, annual sunflowers are big, easy to grow, and bring a sense of great accomplishment. Sow seeds in spring where plants are to grow.

H. atrorubens (H. sparsifolius). Perennial. To 8 ft. tall, spreading by underground stems but not invasive. 'Gullick's Variety' has 4-5-in. dark-centered golden sunflowers. 'Monarch' has golden yellow which may reach 6 in. in diameter. Good for cutting, background planting in largest borders.

H. decapetalus multiflorus. Perennial. To 5 ft. with thin, toothed, 3-8-in.-long leaves and numerous 3-in.-wide flower heads with yellow central disks. 'Loddon Gold' and 'Soleil d'Or' are double-flowering varieties. Excellent for cutting.

H. tuberosus. JERUSALEM ARTICHOKE. Perennial. Grown to a certain extent as a commercial crop, the tubers being edible. Plants 6-7 ft. tall, with bright yellow flower heads. Spreads readily and can become a pest. Better harvest the tubers every year and just save out 2 or 3 for replanting.

HELICHRYSUM. Annual and shrubby perennial. Two quite different plants—one produces cut flowers for fresh and dried arrangements, the other is a landscaping plant.

H. bracteatum. STRAWFLOWER. Annual. Grows 2-3 ft. high with many flower heads. Known as an "everlasting" because the 2½-in. pomponlike flowers are papery and last indefinitely when dried. Also good in fresh arrangements. Flowers may be yellow, orange, red, pink, or white (seeds come in mixed colors). Plant seed in place, late

spring or early summer, same time as zinnias. Full sun. Dwarf forms available. Once plants well started, keep them on dry side. Inclined to have dry leaves at base. Best for hillside or dry areas.

H. petiolatum (Gnaphalium lanatum). Shrubby perennial. Zones 17, 22-24. Woody-based plants to 2 ft. with trailing stems that spread 4 ft. or more. Grown for 1-in.-long, oval, white-woolly leaves. If flower heads form, they are ⅛ in. wide in clusters 1-2 in. wide. Needs room. Trim to keep tidy. Good in sandy soils.

HELIOPSIS scabra. Perennial. Zones 1-16. Native to eastern U. S. Related to sunflower. Grows 3-4 ft. tall, has rough-textured foliage and yellow, 3-4-in. flowers on long wiry stems, July to fall. Flowers good for cutting. Plants die back in winter and make new growth each year. Plant in full sun. Among the several named varieties are: 'Gold Greenheart', with clear yellow double flowers; and 'Incomparabilis', a semi-double with gold-yellow flowers 3 in. across.

HELIOTROPIUM arborescens (H. peruvianum). COMMON HELIOTROPE. Perennial. All Zones as a house or summer bedding plant; outdoor plant Zones 8-24. Rather tender old-fashioned plants grown for the delicate, sweet fragrance of the flowers. In mild climates, grow shrubby and reach to 4 ft. high. Flowers dark violet to white, arranged in tightly grouped, curved, one-sided spikes which form rounded, massive clusters. The veined leaves have a darkish purple cast. If in pots, can be protected in winter and moved into patio or garden for spring and summer enjoyment. They take sun or partial shade (latter best in hot-summer climates). Avoid overwatering. Variety 'Black Beauty' is a form with deepest violet flowers.

HELIPTERUM roseum (Acroclinium roseum). Annual. Although grown for summer color in the garden, valued mostly for dried cut flowers. Plants to 2 ft. tall. Daisy flower heads 1-2 in. across, carried singly; pink or white rays, thicker, brownish or greenish colored near the base. Leaves narrow, numerous near top of stems. Easily grown in full sun in warm, dry soil. Sow seeds after frost where plants are to grow. Thin to 6-12 in. apart. To dry flowers, cut when fully open; cut after dew has dried from flowers. Tie in small bunches, hang upside down by stems in dry, cool, airy place until stems harden.

HELLEBORUS. HELLEBORE. Perennial. All Zones. Distinctive, long-lived, evergreen plants for shade or half shade, blooming for several months in winter and spring. Basal clumps of substantial, long-stalked leaves, usually divided fanwise into leaflets. Flowers large, in clusters or singly, centered with many stamens. Good cut flowers; sear ends of stems or dip in boiling water, then place in deep cold water.

Plant in good soil with lots of organic material added. Shade or partial shade; ample water. Feed once or twice a year. Do not move often; plants reestablish slowly. Mass under high-branching trees on north or east side of walls, in beds bordered with ajuga, wild ginger, primroses, violets. Use with azaleas, fatsia, pieris, rhododendrons, skimmia, ferns.

H. foetidus. Grows to 1½ ft. Attractive leaves—leathery, dark green, divided into 7-11 leaflets. Flowers 1 in. wide, light green with purplish margin; bloom February-April. Good with naturalized daffodils.

H. lividus corsicus. (Sometimes sold as *H. corsicus* or *H. lividus.*) CORSICAN HELLEBORE. Leafy stems to 3 ft. Leaves divided into 3 pale blue-green leaflets with sharply toothed edges. (The species *H. lividus* has leaflets with only a few fine teeth on the edges or none.) Clusters of large, firm-textured, light chartreuse flowers among upper leaves. In mild-winter climates blooms late fall to late spring; in Northwest blooms March-April. After shedding stamens, flowers stay attractive until summer. Best hellebore for southern California. Grows in neutral soil. Established plants take more sun, drought than other hellebores. Not reliably hardy in coldest areas.

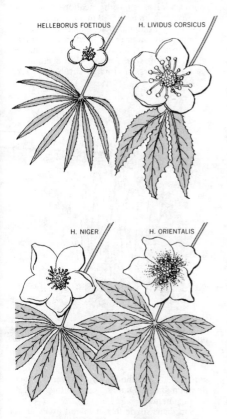

HELLEBORUS FOETIDUS   H. LIVIDUS CORSICUS

H. NIGER   H. ORIENTALIS

Leaves of hellebores, evergreen, substantial. Sober-colored flowers bloom early.

H. niger. CHRISTMAS ROSE. Elegant plant to 1½ ft. tall, blooming December-April. Not adapted to mild-winter climates. Lustrous, dark green leaves divided into 7-9 leaflets with a few large teeth. Flowers, about 2 in. wide, white or greenish white, becoming purplish with age.

H. orientalis. LENTEN ROSE. Much like *H. niger* in growth habit, but easier to transplant. Basal leaves with 5-11 sharply toothed leaflets. Blooms March-May. Flowering stems leafless, branched. Flowers greenish, purplish, or rose, often spotted or splashed with deep purple. Lenten rose often sold as Christmas rose: distinguished

by different flower color, by many small teeth on leaflets of Lenten rose, few large teeth on those of Christmas rose. Lenten rose does better in southern California than Christmas rose.

HELXINE. See Soleirolia

HEMEROCALLIS. DAYLILY. Perennial with tuberous, somewhat fleshy roots, deciduous and evergreen. All Zones. Large clumps of arching, sword-shaped leaves. Lily-like flowers in open or branched clusters at ends of generally leafless stems that stand well above foliage. Older yellow, orange, rust red daylilies mostly replaced by newer kinds (see below); both tall and dwarf varieties are available.

Use in borders with bearded iris, Michaelmas and Shasta daisies, poker plant (*Kniphofia*), dusty miller, agapanthus. Mass on banks under high-branching, deciduous trees, along driveways, and roadsides in country gardens. Group among evergreen shrubs, near pools, along streams. Plant dwarf daylilies in rock gardens, as edgings, low ground covers. Good cut flowers. Cut stems with well developed buds; buds open on successive days, although each flower slightly smaller than preceding one. Arrange individual blooms in low bowls. Snap off faded flowers daily.

Few plants tougher, more persistent, pest-free. Adapt to almost any kind of soil. Sun or part shade; in hottest areas flowers fade in full sun all day—give some afternoon shade. Red-flowered daylilies need warmth to develop best color. Water thoroughly while blooming; feed with complete fertilizer in spring and midsummer. Divide crowded plants in early spring or late fall.

H. aurantiaca. GOLDEN SUMMER DAYLILY. Evergreen, sturdy, early blooming. Leaves 2-3 ft. long, 1 in. or more broad. Flowers bright orange, fragrant, 3-4 in. long, not as wide open as in some species. Variety 'Major', larger, wide open flowers 6 in. across.

H. fulva. TAWNY DAYLILY, COMMON ORANGE DAYLILY. Deciduous. To 6 ft. Leaves 2 ft. or more long, 1 in. wide; flowers tawny orange-red, 3-5 in. long, bloom in summer. Old variety 'Kwanso', double flowers, superseded by newer, more handsome hybrids.

H. hybrids. Deciduous or evergreen. Modern hybrids grow 1-6 ft. tall, with flowers 3-8 in. across. Color range extends far beyond basic yellow, orange, rust, red; includes shell pink, vermilion, buff, apricot, creamy white, many bicolors. Early, mid-season, late varieties insure bloom from May to September or October (in mild climates). Some varieties bloom twice a year, some bloom in evening. Flowers single, semi-double, double; vary in shape from broad petaled to narrow and twisted. Few local nurseries carry many varieties; several specialists offer extensive lists in catalogs.

H. lilio-asphodelus (*H. flava*). LEMON DAYLILY. Deciduous. To 3 ft. Leaves 2 ft. long. Fragrant, clear yellow, 4-in. flowers in June. Old-timer, worthwhile for fragrance and moderate size.

H. middendorffii. BROAD DWARF DAYLILY. Deciduous. Leaves 12-18 in. long, ¾ in. wide, as tall or taller than flower stems. Flowers yellow, fragrant, bloom early, along with, or a little later than daffodils.

H. minor. DWARF YELLOW DAYLILY. Deciduous. Tuft of grasslike leaves 12-20 in. long, ¼ in. or less wide, usually lower than flower stems. Flowers yellow, fragrant, 4 in. or less long, bloom in spring.

HEMLOCK. See Tsuga

HEN AND CHICKENS. See Sempervivum tectorum

HEN AND CHICKS. See Echeveria

HEPATICA. LIVERLEAF. Perennials. Zones 1-11, 14-16. Attractive woodland plants for damp and shady places. Related to anemones. In really cold areas may bloom before the snow melts. Flower stems are 4-6 in. high and carry several white, brilliant blue-violet, or rose pink flowers about ¾ in. across. Flowers followed by silky fruits. Just the beautiful foliage is reason enough for planting—it's soft and furry when new, bronzed and thick when mature.

H. acutiloba. Leaves have three pointed lobes and flowering stems are usually taller.

H. americana. Leaves have three very blunt lobes.

HERALD'S TRUMPET. See Beaumontia

HERB-OF-GRACE. See Ruta

HERBS. This category includes all plants that at some time in history have been considered valuable for seasoning, medicine, fragrance, or general household use. As you look through lists of plants you can recognize certain herbs because they bear the species name *officinalis* (meaning: sold in shops, edible, medicinal, recognized in the pharmacopoeia).

Today the herb harvest is used almost entirely for the seasoning of foods. Herbs are versatile as garden plants. Some creep along the ground, making fragrant carpets. Others are shrublike and can be clipped to make formal hedges or grown informally in shrub or perennial borders. Many make attractive container plants. Those with gray foliage are a striking contrast to the green-leafed plants. However, many herbs do have a distinctly weedy look, especially when planted beside regular ornamental plants.

Many are hardy and adaptable. Although hot, dry, sunny conditions with a poor, but

Grow cooking herbs in boxes near kitchen for convenience in watering, gathering.

Climate Zone maps pages 8-27

well drained soil are usually considered best for most herbs, some thrive in shady, moist locations with light soil rich in humus.

Following are lists of herbs for specific landscape situations:

Kitchen garden. This can be a sunny raised bed near the kitchen door, a planter box near the barbecue, or a portion of the vegetable garden. Plant the basic cooking herbs: basil (*Ocimum*), chives, dill (*Anethum graveolens*), sweet marjoram (*Majorana hortensis*), mint (*Mentha*), oregano (*Origanum vulgare*), parsley, rosemary (*Rosmarinus*), sage (*Salvia officinalis*), savory (*Satureja*), tarragon (*Artemisia dracunculus*), thyme (*Thymus*). The connoisseur may wish to plant: angelica, anise (*Pimpinella anisum*), caraway (*Carum carvi*), chervil (*Anthriscus cerefolium*), coriander (*Coriandrum sativum*), common fennel (*Foeniculum vulgare*).

Ground cover for sun. Prostrate rosemary, mother-of-thyme (*Thymus serpyllum*), lemon thyme (*T. s. vulgaris*), woolly thyme (*T. lanuginosus*), caraway-scented thyme (*T. herba-barona*).

Ground covers for shade or part shade. Borage (*Borago officinalis*), chamomile (*Anthemis nobilis*).

Ground cover for shade. Sweet woodruff (*Asperula odorata*).

Perennial or shrub border. Common wormwood (*Artemisia absinthium*), Roman wormwood (*A. pontica*), small burnet (*Sanguisorba minor*), lavenders (*Lavandula*), monarda, rosemary, rue (*Ruta graveolens*), scented geraniums (*Pelargonium*), tansy (*Tanacetum vulgare*).

Hedges. Formal, clipped hedge—hyssop (*Hyssopus officinalis*), santolina, germander (*Teucrium*): informal hedge—lavenders, winter savory (*Satureja montana*).

Gray garden. Common wormwood, Roman wormwood, English lavender (*Lavandula spica*), germander, horehound (*Marrubium vulgare*), sage, woolly thyme.

Rock garden. French lavender (*Lavandula dentata*), sage, woolly thyme, mother-of-thyme, winter savory.

Herbs for moist areas. Angelica, mints, parsley, sweet woodruff.

Herbs for part shade. Chervil, costmary (*Chrysanthemum balsamita*), lemon balm (*Melissa officinalis*), parsley, sweet woodruff.

Herbs for containers. Crete dittany (*Amaracus dictamnus*), chives, costmary, lemon verbena (*Aloysia triphylla*), sage, pineapple sage (*Salvia longistyla*), summer savory (*Satureja hortensis*), sweet marjoram, mints, small burnet.

Potpourris and sachets. Costmary, English lavender flowers, lemon balm, sweet woodruff, lemon verbena, lemon-scented geranium (*Pelargonium crispum*), rose geranium (*P. graveolens*), monarda.

Drying herbs for cooking.

Leafy herbs. Cut leafy herbs for drying early in the day before sun gets too hot, but after dew has dried on foliage. Oil content highest then. Leafy herbs ready from when flower buds begin to form until flowers are half open. (Exceptions: parsley can be cut any time; sage and tarragon may take on a strong taste unless cut early in summer.) Don't cut perennial herbs back more than one third; annual herbs may be sheared back to about 4 inches from the ground. Generally you can cut 2 or 3 crops for drying during the summer. Don't cut

perennial herbs after September or new growth won't have a chance to mature before cold weather.

Before drying, sort weeds and grass from the herbs, remove dead or insect-damaged leaves. Wash off loose dirt in cool water; shake or blot off excess moisture. Tie woody-stemmed herbs such as sweet marjoram or thyme in small bundles and hang upside down from a line hung across the room. The room for drying herbs should be dark to preserve color, have good air circulation and warm temperature (about 70°) for rapid drying to retain aromatic oils. If drying area is fairly bright, surround herb bundles with loose cylinders of paper.

For large-leafed herbs such as basil, or short tips that don't bundle easily, dry in a tray made by knocking bottom from nursery flat and replacing it with screen. On top of screen place a double thickness of cheesecloth. Spread leaves out over surface. Stir leaves daily.

With good air circulation and low humidity, leafy herbs should be crumbly dry in a few days to a week. Strip leaves from stems and store whole in airtight containers —glass is best—until ready to use. Label each container with name of herb and date dried. Check jars first few days after filling to make sure moisture doesn't form inside. If it does, pour out contents and dry a few days longer.

Seed herbs. Gather seed clusters such as dill, anise, fennel, caraway when they turn brown. Seeds should begin to fall out of them when gently tapped. Leave a little of stem attached when you cut each cluster. Collect in a box. Flail seeds from clusters and spread them out in sun to dry for several days. Then separate chaff from seed and continue to dry in sun for another 1½ to 2 weeks. Store seed herbs the same way as leafy ones.

HERCULES' CLUB. See Aralia spinosa

HERNIARIA glabra. GREEN CARPET, RUPTURE WORT. Evergreen perennial. All Zones. Trailing plant under 2 or 3 inches with crowded, tiny, bright green leaves less than ¼ inch long. Bloom negligible.

Grows vigorously in full sun in hottest places, but does well in moist shade too. Foliage turns bronzy red in cold winters. Spreads well, but won't grow out of control; use it between stepping stones, on mounds, with rocks, or in parking strips.

HESPERALOE parviflora. Evergreen perennial. Zones 10-16, 18-21. Native to Texas, northern Mexico. Makes a dense, yuccalike clump of very narrow swordlike leaves 4 ft. long, about 1 in. wide. Pink to rose red, 1¼-in.-long, nodding flowers in slim 3-4-ft.-high clusters in early summer, with repeat bloom frequent in milder climates. Effective combined with other desert plants. Good large container plant with a loose, filmy, relaxed look.

Hardy to 0°. *H. p. engelmannii*, similar to the species but the 1-in.-long flowers are more bell-shaped.

HETEROMELES arbutifolia (*Photinia arbutifolia*). TOYON, CHRISTMAS BERRY, CALIFORNIA HOLLY. Evergreen shrub or small tree. Zones 5-24. Native to Sierra Nevada foothills, southern California to Baja California,

California Coast Ranges. Dense shrub 6-10 ft. tall or multiple-trunked small tree 15-25 ft. Thick, leathery, glossy dark green leaves 2-4 in. long with bristle-pointed teeth. Small white flowers in flattish clusters June-July. Bright red (rarely yellow) clustered berries November-January. Birds relish them. *H. a. macrocarpa*, from the Channel Islands, has larger berries.

Improves under cultivation. Drought-tolerant, but thrives with summer water in well drained soil. Needs summer water in desert. If trimmed to give an abundance of year-old wood, it produces even more berries than in the wild. Can be pruned to form a small single-trunked tree. Spray to control sucking insects which cause honeydew and subsequent sooty mold. Valuable as screen, bank planting, erosion control.

HEUCHERA. ALUM ROOT, CORAL BELLS. Perennials. Compact, evergreen clumps of roundish leaves with scalloped edges. Slender, wiry stems 15-30 in. high, bear open clusters of nodding, bell-shaped flowers ¼ in. or more across, in carmine, carmine pink, coral crimson, red, rose, greenish, or white. Bloom April-August. Use as edgings, mass in borders, in front of shrubs, in rock

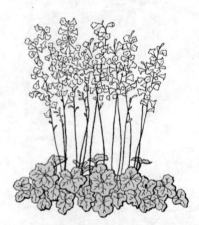

Red or pink coral bell flowers are held up in full view on 14-24-in., wiry stems.

gardens, as ground cover. Flowers attract hummingbirds. Dainty, long lasting in cut arrangements.

Sun, light shade in hot inland areas. Best with plenty of water. Divide clumps every 3 or 4 years in fall or spring (in colder sections). Use young, vigorous, rooted divisions; discard older woody rootstocks. Sow seed in spring.

H. maxima. ISLAND ALUM ROOT. Zones 15-24. Native to Channel islands, southern California. Foliage clumps 12-24 in. across. Leaves roundish heart-shaped, lobed, shining dark green. Flowers whitish or pinkish, hundreds in each narrow, 18-30-in.-long cluster. Blooms February-April. Partial shade; moisture. Good ground cover in untamed parts of garden.

H. micrantha. All Zones. Native to California, Washington, Oregon, Idaho. Adapts easily to garden conditions. Plant in protected spots in cold areas. Long-stalked,

H

Climate
Zone maps
pages 8-27

roundish leaves 1-3 in. long, hairy on both sides, toothed and lobed. Flowers whitish or greenish, about ⅛ in. long, in loose clusters on leafy stems 2-3 ft. high.

H. sanguinea. CORAL BELLS. All Zones. Native to Mexico and Arizona. A universal favorite. Makes neat foliage tufts of round 1-2-in.-long leaves with scalloped edges. Slender, wiry stems 14-24 in. tall bear open clusters of nodding, bell-shaped, bright red or coral pink flowers. White, pink, crimson varieties available. Good edging for beds of delphinium, iris, lilies, peonies, roses.

H. 'Santa Ana Cardinal'. Outstanding hybrid between garden forms of *H. sanguinea* and *H. maxima*. Unusually vigorous, free-flowering. Clumps 3-4 ft. wide. Vibrant rose red flowers, 50-100 in a spike, on 24-inch stems. Blooms 3-5 months, almost all year in mild areas.

HIBBERTIA scandens (*H. volubilis*). GUINEA GOLD VINE. Evergreen vine. Zones 16, 17, 21-24. Native to Australia. Fast-growing, shrubby, climbing by stems to 8-10 ft. Luxuriant foliage handsome all year in ideal climate. Waxy, dark green leaves, 3 in. long by 1 in. wide. Clear bright yellow flowers, like single roses, start to appear in May and will continue to bloom into October. Thrives in part shade, but will also grow in sun. Recovers quickly from burning by light frosts. Use it to cover stone or tile walls, or as ground cover. Good for small garden areas trained on trellis or against low fence. Can also use in containers.

HIBISCUS. Five species are grown in the West; one is a hardy perennial, two are deciduous shrubs, the others are evergreen shrubs. In Hawaii and the warmest areas of coastal southern California several more species are grown.

H. huegelii. BLUE HIBISCUS. Evergreen shrub. Zones 15-17, 20-24. Upright growth to 5-8 ft. Foliage dark green; leaves deeply cut, rough-textured. Flowers 4-5 in. across, lilac-blue, with glossy petals. Blooms off and on throughout year, and individual flowers last 2-3 days. Hardy to 27°. Pinch or prune occasionally to keep it compact. Best in dry, warm location.

H. moscheutos. PERENNIAL HIBISCUS, ROSE-MALLOW. Perennial. Zones 1-21. Hardy. To 6-8 ft. high. Stems rise each year and bloom starts in late June, continuing to frost. Plants die down in winter. Oval, toothed leaves deep green above, whitish beneath. Flowers the largest of all hibiscus; some reach 12 in. wide. Plants need regular, deep watering and protection from winds that may burn flowers. A 2-in.-deep mulch will help conserve moisture. Feed at 6-8-week intervals during growing season.

Varieties available are 'New Blood Red', 7-in., deep blood red flowers with reflexed petals; 'Raspberry Rose', 10-12-in., rich, deep rose flowers; 'Ruffled Cerise', 8-in. flowers; 'Strawberry Rose', 8-in. flowers; 'Super Clown', 9-in. flowers of ivory white suffused with pink, tips of petals shaded deep rose, deep red eye; 'Super Red', 7-in. flowers; and 'Super White', 8-12-in. white flowers with rose red centers.

H. mutabilis. CONFEDERATE ROSE. Deciduous shrub. Zones 4-24. Shrubby or tree-like in warmest climates, it behaves more like a perennial in colder areas, growing

flowering branches from a woody base or short trunk. Flowers 4-6 in. wide, opening white or pink and changing to deep red by evening. The variety 'Rubra' has red flowers.

H. rosa-sinensis. CHINESE HIBISCUS, TROPICAL HIBISCUS. Evergreen shrub. Zones 9, 12-16, 19-24. One of the showiest flowering shrubs. Reaches 30 ft. in the tropics, but seldom over 15 ft. tall in even the mildest parts of California. Glossy foliage varies somewhat in size and texture depending on variety. Growth habit may be dense and dwarfish or loose and open. Flowers 4-8 in. wide may be single or double. Colors range from white through pink to red, from yellow and apricot to orange.

Plants require good drainage; to check, dig a hole 18 in. across and as deep. Fill it with water; if water hasn't drained in an hour or so find another planting area, improve the drainage, or plant in raised bed or container. Plants also need sun, heat, and protection from frost and wind (especially ocean wind). In the warm inland areas they generally grow best if partially shaded from the very hot afternoon sun. In cool coastal climates such as San Francisco's they never get heat enough to thrive or bloom. Where winter temperatures frequently drop below 30°, even the hardier varieties will need overhead protection of roof overhang, or evergreen tree. Where temperatures drop much lower, grow plants in containers and shelter them indoors over winter. Or grow them as annuals, setting out fresh plants each spring.

Feed plants monthly (container plants twice monthly) from April to early September. Let growth harden after that. Water deeply and frequently. All varieties are quite susceptible to aphids.

Can be used as screen planting, in containers, as espaliers, or as free-standing shrubs or small trees. To keep mature plants growing vigorously, prune out about ⅓ of old wood in early spring. Pinching out the tips of stems in spring and summer increases flower production. Prune poorly shaped young plants when set out in spring to develop good branch structure. Here are a few of the many varieties sold in the West:

'Agnes Galt'. Big single pink flowers. Vigorous, hardy plant to 15 ft. Prune to prevent legginess.

'America Beauty'. Broad, deep rose flowers. Slow. Irregular form. To 8 ft. tall.

'Bride'. Very large, palest blush to white flowers. Slow or moderate growth to an open 6 ft.

'Brilliant' ('San Diego Red'). Bright red single flowers in profusion. Tall, vigorous, compact, to 15 ft. Hardy.

'Butterfly'. Small, single, bright yellow flowers. Slow, upright growth to 6 ft.

'California Gold'. Heavy yield of yellow, red-centered, single flowers. Slow or medium growth to a compact 7 ft.

'Crown of Bohemia'. Double gold flowers; petals shade to carmine orange toward base. Moderate or fast growth to 10 ft. Bushy, upright. Hardy.

'Delight'. Very large single yellow flowers. Upright growth to 6 ft. Large, dark green leaves.

'Flamingo Plume'. Double salmon pink flowers. Slow growth to 5 ft., spreading, irregular. Prolific bloom.

'Florida Sunset'. Coral orange to red, single. Low, compact plant. Slow growth to 4 ft. Rather tender.

'Fullmoon'. Double-pure yellow flowers. Moderately vigorous growth to a compact 8 ft.

'Kate Sessions'. Flowers large, single, broad-petaled, red tinged gold beneath. Moderate growth to 10 ft. Upright, open habit.

'Kona'. Double, ruffled pink flowers. Vigorous, upright, bushy, to 15-20 ft. Prune regularly.

'President'. Flowers single, 6-7 in. wide, intense red shading to deep pink in throat. Upright, compact, 8 ft. tall.

'Red Dragon' ('Celia'). Flowers small to medium, double, dark red. Upright, compact, 6-8 ft. tall.

'Rosea'. Heavy producer of double rose red flowers.

'Ross Estey'. Flowers very large, single, with broad, overlapping petals of pink shading coral orange toward tips. Flowers heavy-textured, lasting 2-3 days on bush. Vigorous grower to 8 ft. Leaves unusually large, ruffled, polished dark green.

'Sundown' ('Jigora'). Flowers double, salmon orange. Plant bushy, to 7 ft.

'White Wings'. Single, white, narrow-petaled flowers with small red eye. Profuse. Vigorous, open, upright growth to 20 ft.; prune to control legginess. A compact form with somewhat smaller flowers is available; it is generally sold under the name of 'White Wings Compacta'.

H. syriacus. ROSE OF SHARON, SHRUB ALTHAEA. Deciduous shrub. Zones 1-21. To 10-12 ft. tall, upright and compact when young, spreading and open with age. Easily trained to a single trunk with treelike top. Leaves medium-sized, often three-lobed, coarsely toothed. Summer flowers single or double, 2½-3 in. across. Single flowers slightly more effective, opening somewhat larger; but singles produce many unattractive capsule-type fruits.

Grows easily in sun or part shade. Water requirements moderate; established plants take some drought. Prune to shape; for bigger flowers, cut back (in winter) previous season's growth to 2 buds.

Varieties: 'Albus', single, pure white, 4-in. flowers; 'Anemonaeflorus', semi-double, red with deeper crimson eye; 'Ardens', double, purple; 'Boule de Feu', double, deep violet-pink; 'Coelestis', single, violet-blue with reddish purple throat; 'Collie Mullens', double, magenta rose with crimson eye; 'Hamabo', single pink with rose blotching eye, and veining; 'Jeanne d'Arc', double white flushed rose; 'Lucy', double, magenta rose with red eye; 'Pink Delight', semi-double to double, rose pink blotched and veined dark rose; 'Purpurea', semi-double, purple, red at base of petals; 'Woodbridge', single, magenta rose with red eye.

HILLS OF SNOW. See Hydrangea arborescens 'Grandiflora'

HIPPEASTRUM. AMARYLLIS. Bulb. Zones 19, 21-24; elsewhere as pot plant in greenhouse, indoors, or in frostproof outdoor area. Native to tropics and subtropics. Many species useful in hybridizing, but only hybrids generally available; usually sold as giant amaryllis or Royal Dutch amaryllis. Named varieties or color selections in reds, pinks, white, salmon, near orange, some variously marked and striped. From 2 to several flowers, often 8-9 in. across, form on stout,

2-ft. stems. Where grown outdoors, flowers bloom in spring. Where grown indoors, they bloom just a few weeks after planting. Leaves broad, strap-shaped, usually appearing after bloom, growing through summer, disappearing in fall.

Usually grown in pots. Pot in a rich, sandy mix with added bonemeal or superphosphate. Plant in November-February. Allow 2-in. space between bulb and edge of pot. Set upper half of bulb above soil surface. Firm soil, water well, keep barely moist until growth begins. Wet, airless soil causes root rot.

To force early bloom indoors, keep in warm, dark place until rooted. Growers maintain bottom heat and air temperatures of 75°-85° (or 70°-80°), until flower stalk 6 in. tall, then put in warm light shade. In homes, keep in warm, but not-too-dry atmosphere. Can grow in sunny indoor window boxes. Increase watering as leaves form. Feed lightly every 2 weeks through flowering period.

When flowers fade, cut off stem, keep up watering; feed to encourage leaf growth. When leaves yellow, withhold water, let plants dry out. Repot in late fall or early winter.

HIPPOCREPIS comosa. Perennial ground cover. Zones 8-24. Forms a mat 3 in. high; spreads to 3 ft. Leaves divided into 7-15 medium green, oval, ¼-½-in.-long leaflets. Flowers golden yellow, sweet pea-shaped, ½ in. long, in loose clusters of 5-12. Blooms in spring; some repeat bloom in summer.

Golden yellow flowers of hippocrepis are ½ in. long; clusters have 5-12 flowers.

Drought resistant and takes poor soils, but lusher-looking with good soil, adequate water. Roots bind soil on steep banks. Bank cover, rock garden, small-scale lawn substitute (mow once just after flowers fade). Set 1 ft. apart. Takes light foot traffic.

HOHERIA. Evergreen tree and deciduous tree or shrub. Native to New Zealand. Leaves are bright green, leathery, toothed, 3-5 in. long, 1½-2 in. wide. Flowers form in clusters among leaves, pure white, about 1 in. wide.

H. glabrata. MOUNTAIN RIBBONWOOD. Deciduous tree or large shrub. Zones 4-6. To 40 ft. high, usually much less. Attractive with azaleas or rhododendrons.

H. populnea. NEW ZEALAND LACEBARK. Evergreen tree. Zones 4-6, 15-17, 21-24. In growth habit as graceful as birch, but in addition it puts on a good show of flowers late summer into fall. Grows fast to eventual 50-60 ft., but enjoyable for many years as 20-30-ft., slender tree. Like birch, it's ideal for multiple planting and groves. Has deep, well behaved root system. Inner bark is interestingly perforated and used in New Zealand for ornamental purposes.

HOLLY. See Ilex

HOLLY, CALIFORNIA. See Heteromeles

HOLLY, COSTA RICAN. See Olmediella

HOLLY, GUATEMALAN. See Olmediella

HOLLY, SUMMER. See Comarostaphylis

HOLLY GRAPE, CALIFORNIA. See Mahonia pinnata

HOLLYHOCK. See Althaea rosea

HOLMSKIOLDIA sanguinea. CHINESE HAT PLANT. Evergreen shrub. Zones 13, 17, 22, 23. Rangy, fast growing, to 12-15 ft., with 4-in.-long, oval leaves. Clusters of small tubular, red flowers rise from nearly circular, flat, 1-in.-wide brick red bases. They bloom all summer; in especially favorable spots they may bloom all year. Hardy to about 22°. Near the coast give it full sun and reflected heat from a wall. Best with some midday shade inland. Good espalier or bank cover.

HOLODISCUS discolor. CREAM BUSH, OCEAN SPRAY. Deciduous shrub. Zones 1-7, 16, 17. Native to California Coast Ranges, Sierra Nevada; north to British Columbia east to Rocky Mountains. May grow to 20 ft. in moist rich soil and partial shade. In dry, sunny situations, such as east of the Cascades in Oregon and Washington, may get to only 3 ft. Triangular leaves, deep green above, white hairy beneath, to 3 in. long, the edges coarsely toothed. Nodding branched clusters (sometimes to 12 in. long) of small, creamy white flowers tip the branches May-July, make quite a show. Flowers fade to tannish gold and brown, remain attractive for long time. Prune back after flowering.

HOMALANTHUS populifolius. QUEENSLAND POPLAR. Evergreen or semi-evergreen small tree. Zones 14-24. Grows to 15 ft. high. Rather weedy but foliage interesting. Triangular leaves up to 6 in. long; older leaves turn bright red before falling; new leaves coppery. Leaves seem to drop most of year but cold weather causes all leaves to drop. Flowers insignificant, in 4-in.-long spikelike clusters, but produces quantities of seeds which by the next year pop up as seedlings. Fairly tolerant of drought and free of pests and diseases.

HOMALOCLADIUM platycladum. RIBBON BUSH, CENTIPEDE PLANT. Strange shrubby plant. Zones 8, 9, 12-24. Novelty or collector's plant, sometimes grown in raised beds or containers. Usually leafless, with long, narrow, flat, bright green, jointed stems reaching 2-4 ft. tall, usually less in pots. Small, narrow leaves sometimes show on stem edges. Flowers inconspicuous. Red, berrylike fruit.

HONESTY. See Lunaria

HONEY BELL. See Mahernia

HONEY BUSH. See Melianthus

HONEYSUCKLE. See Lonicera

HONEYSUCKLE, CAPE. See Tecomaria capensis

HONEYSUCKLE, DESERT. See Anisacanthus

HOP. See Humulus

HOP BUSH. See Dodonaea

HOREHOUND. See Marrubium

HORNBEAM. See Carpinus

HORSECHESTNUT. See Aesculus.

HORSERADISH. A large, coarse, weedy-looking plant grown for its large, coarse, white roots, which are peeled, shredded and mixed with vinegar or cream to make a condiment. Does best in rich, moist soils in cool regions. Grow it in some out-of-the-way corner. Start from roots planted 1 ft. apart in late winter or early spring. Dig the full grown roots in fall, winter, or spring. It's best to dig just a few outside roots at a time; then you'll have your horseradish fresh and hot.

HORSETAIL. See Equisetum

HOSTA (*Funkia*). PLANTAIN LILY. Perennials. Zones 1-10, 12-21. Their real glory is in their leaves — typically heart-shaped, shiny, distinctly veined. Flowers come as a dividend: thin spikes topped by several trumpet-shaped flowers grow up from foliage mounds in summer, last for several weeks. Sun, light shade, or heavy shade (north side of house). Feeding once a year will bring on extra leafy splendor. Blanket of peat moss around plants will prevent mud from splattering plants. Slugs and snails love the leaves; bait 3-4 times a year. All forms go dormant (collapse almost to nothing) in winter; new fresh leaves grow from roots in early spring. Good in containers. In ground, plants last for years, clumps expand in size, shade out weed growth.

H. decorata (*H. 'Thomas Hogg'*). Plants to 2 ft. high. Oval leaves, 6 in. long, bluntly pointed tips, green with silvery white margins. Lavender 2-in.-long flowers.

H. glauca (*H. sieboldiana*). Blue-green leaves 10-15 in. long, heavily veined. Many slender pale lilac flowers nestle close to leaves. Showpiece plant by shaded pool.

H. 'Honeybells'. Large grass green leaves. Fragrant lavender lilac flowers on 3-ft. stems.

H. lancifolia (*H. japonica*). NARROW LEAFED PLANTAIN LILY. Leaves dark green, 6 in. long, not heart-shaped, but tapering

Hostas valued chiefly for leaf masses; flowers a bonus. H. glauca (right), blue-green.

Climate Zone maps pages 8-27

into the long stalk. Lilac or pale lavender flowers 2 in. long on 2-ft. stems.

H. plantaginea (*H. grandiflora, H. subcordata*). FRAGRANT PLANTAIN LILY. Scented white flowers 4-5 in. long on 2-ft. stems. Leaves bright green, to 10 in. long.

H. undulata (*H. media picta, H. variegata*). WAVY-LEAFED PLANTAIN LILY. Leaves 6-8 in. long, have wavy margins, variegated white on green. Foliage used in arrangements. Pale lavender flowers on 3-ft. stalks.

H. ventricosa (*H. caerulea*). BLUE PLANTAIN LILY. Deep green broad leaves, prominently ribbed. Blue flowers on 3-ft. stems.

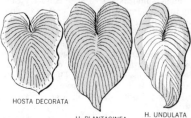

HOSTA DECORATA

H. PLANTAGINEA   H. UNDULATA

Hosta plantaginea: *big, bright green leaves.* H. decorata, H. undulata: *white markings.*

HOUND'S TONGUE, WESTERN. See Cynoglossum grande

HOUSELEEK. See Sempervivum

HOVENIA dulcis. JAPANESE RAISIN TREE. Deciduous tree. Zones 3-9, 13-24. Native to China, Japan, and the Himalayas. Moderate growth to 25-30 ft. (averages 2 ft. a year) with a 10-15-ft. spread. Glossy, heart-shaped leaves are 3-7 in. long and 3-6 in. wide, long pointed, with toothed edges. A good clean-foliage effect. The "raisins" come when the 2-3-in.-wide clusters of tiny greenish white flowers fade. Their red stalks swell, become very fleshy and contorted. Stalks are sweet, edible, and have chewy texture of raisins. Attractive as a shade tree for a small garden, and does well in lawns.

HOWEIA. Palm. Outdoors in Zones 17, 23, 24; anywhere as house or greenhouse plant. Native to Lord Howe Island. These feather palms are the kentia palms of the florists. Slow growing; with age, leaves drop to show a clean, green trunk ringed with leaf scars. Ideal pot plants.

Sentry (left) and paradise palms: clean green trunks ringed with leaf scars.

H. belmoreana. SENTRY PALM. Less common than the next, smaller and more compact, with over-arching leaves 6-7 ft. long. As a pot plant stands some watering neglect, drafts, dust.

H. forsteriana. PARADISE PALM. Larger than the above, with leaves to 9 ft. long and long, drooping leaflets.

HOYA. WAX FLOWER, WAX PLANT. Shrubby or climbing house plants, one used outdoors in mild climates. Thick, waxy evergreen leaves and tight clusters of small, waxy flowers. Commonly grown in sunny windows. Do best in rich, heavy, well drained soil. Bloom best when potbound; usually grown in containers even outdoors. Do not prune out flowering wood; new blossom clusters appear from stumps of old ones.

H. bella. House or greenhouse plant. Shrubby, to 3 ft., with slender upright branches which droop as they grow older, small leaves. Tight clusters of white, purple-centered ½-in. flowers in summer. Best in hanging basket.

H. carnosa. WAX FLOWER, WAX PLANT. Indoor plant or outdoors in Zones 15-24 with overhead protection—but even there it is quickly damaged by temperatures much below freezing. Vining to 10 ft. Has 2-4-in.-long, oval leaves; big, round, tight clusters of creamy white flowers ½ in. across, each flower with a perfect 5-pointed pink star in the center. Fragrant, summer-blooming. Red young leaves give an additional touch of color. Water deeply in summer, then allow soil to go partially dry before watering again. In cool climates let plant go dormant in winter, giving only enough water to keep it from shriveling. Outdoors, train on pillar or trellis in shade; indoors, train on wire in a sunny window.

'Variegata' has leaves edged with white suffused with pink. Color is variable and may change with age of plant, amount of available light. It is not as vigorous or hardy as the green form. 'Compacta' has crinkly leaves very closely spaced on short stems; it looks as if it had just undergone a severe attack of aphids.

HUCKLEBERRY, EVERGREEN. See Vaccinium ovatum

HUCKLEBERRY, RED. See Vaccinium parvifolium

HUMATA tyermannii. BEAR'S FOOT FERN. Outdoors in Zones 17, 23, 24; elsewhere an indoor or greenhouse plant. Native to China. This small fern has furry creeping rhizomes that look something like bear's feet. Fronds 8-10 in. long, very finely cut, rising at intervals from the rhizome. Like *Davallia* in appearance and uses, but slower growing.

HUMMINGBIRD BUSH. See Grevillea thelemanniana

HUMMINGBIRD FLOWER. See Zauschneria

HUMULUS. Hop. Annual and perennial vine. Extremely fast growth. Large, deeply lobed leaves. Useful for summer screening on trellises or arbors.

H. japonicus. JAPANESE HOP. Annual vine. To 20-30 ft. Flowers do not make true hops. Variety 'Variegatus' has foliage marked with white. Sow seeds in spring where plants are to grow.

H. lupulus. COMMON HOP. Perennial vine. All Zones. The plant that grows the hops used to flavor beer. Grow from roots (not easy to find in nurseries) planted in rich soil, early spring. Place thick end up, just below soil surface. Furnish supports for vertical climbing. Shoots come forth in May and grow quickly to 15-25 ft. by mid-summer. Give roots copious water once rapid growth starts. Leaves 3 to 5-lobed, toothed. Squarish, hairy stems twine vertically; to get horizontal growth, twine stem tips by hand. Light green hops (soft, flaky, 1-2-in. cones of bracts and flowers) form in August-September. They're attractive and have a fresh, piny fragrance. Cut back stems to ground after frost turns them brown. Regrowth comes the following spring.

HUNNEMANNIA fumariaefolia. MEXICAN TULIP POPPY, GOLDEN CUP. Perennial, usually treated as annual. Bushy, open plant, 2-3 ft. high, with very finely divided blue-green leaves. Its flowers are clear soft yellow, cup-shaped, 3 in. across, with crinkled petals; bloom July-October. Related to California poppy. Showy plant in masses; striking with scarlet *Zauschneria californica*, or with blues of ceratostigma, echium, or penstemon. Blooms last for a week in water if cut in bud and stem is burned or put in hot water. Plant from nursery flats or sow seed in place in warm, dry, sunny position and later thin seedlings to 12 in. apart. Reseeds. Dies out if overwatered.

HYACINTH. See Hyacinthus

HYACINTH, FEATHERED or PLUME. See Muscari comosum 'Monstrosum'

HYACINTH, FRINGE or TASSEL. See Muscari comosum

HYACINTH, GRAPE. See Muscari

HYACINTH, SUMMER. See Galtonia

HYACINTH, WATER. See Eichhornia

HYACINTH, WILD. See Brodiaea pulchella

HYACINTH, WOOD. See Scilla nonscripta

HYACINTH SHRUB. See Xanthoceras

HYACINTHUS. HYACINTH. Bulb. All Zones. As garden plant, best adapted in cold-winter climates. Bell-shaped, fragrant flowers in loose or tight spikes rise from a basal bundle of narrow, bright green leaves. All spring blooming. Plant in fall. Where winters are cold, plant in September-October. In mild areas plant October-December.

H. amethystinus. Little hyacinth for rock gardens or naturalizing. Stems 6-8 in. high with a loose spike of clear blue bells with paler colored streaks.

H. azureus (*Muscari azureum*). Nodding light and dark blue bells on 8-in. stem. March-April bloom. For naturalizing, rock gardens. Use with early yellow crocus.

H. orientalis. COMMON HYACINTH. Grows to 1 ft., with fragrant bell-shaped white, pale blue, or purple-blue flowers.

H. o. albulus. ROMAN OR FRENCH ROMAN HYACINTH. White, pink, or light blue flowers loosely carried on slender stems; usually several stems to a bulb. Bloom earlier than Dutch hyacinths; well adapted to mild winter areas where they

*Climate
Zone maps
pages 8-27*

naturalize in favorable situations. Where winters are cold, grow in pots for winter bloom.

DUTCH HYACINTH. Derived from *H. orientalis* through extensive cross breeding and selection. Most widely grown hyacinth, with large dense spikes of waxy, bell-like, fragrant flowers in white, shades of blue, purple, pink, red, cream, buff, and salmon. Size of spike directly related to bulb size. The biggest bulbs are desirable for exhibition or for potting; second size is most satisfactory for bedding outside. Small bulbs give smaller, looser clusters with flowers more widely spaced. Sometimes called miniature hyacinths. Set big bulbs 6 in. deep, smaller bulbs 4 in.

Hyacinths look best when massed or grouped; rows look stiff, formal. Mass bulbs of a single color beneath a flowering tree or in border. Leave bulbs in ground after bloom, continue to feed and water until foliage yellows. Flowers tend to be smaller in succeeding years, but maintain same color and fragrance.

Choice container plants. Pot in porous mix with tip of bulb near surface. After potting, cover containers with thick mulch of sawdust, wood shavings, or peat moss to keep bulbs cool, moist, shaded until roots well formed; remove mulch, place in full light when tops show. Also grow hyacinths in water in special hyacinth glass, the bottom filled with pebbles and water. Keep in dark, cool place until rooted, give light when top growth appears; place in sunny window when leaves are uniformly green.

HYBOPHRYNIUM brauneanum (*Bamburanta arnoldiana*). BAMBURANTA. Perennial. Zones 22-24; elsewhere an indoor plant. Grown for foliage only and not for flowers. The tall-growing canes suggest bamboo in habit; the spreading leaves all along the stems are oval and very short stalked. Best in containers. Needs light soil, good drainage, abundant water. Give light feedings frequently (every 2-4 weeks).

HYDRANGEA. Deciduous shrubs, vine. Big, bold foliage and large clusters of long-lasting flowers in white, pink, red, or (under some conditions) blue. Summer, fall bloom. Flower clusters may contain: sterile flowers (conspicuous, with large, petal-like sepals); fertile flowers (small, starry-petaled); or a cluster of small sterile flowers surrounded by a ring of big sterile ones. The last-named are called "lace cap" hydrangeas. Sterile flowers last long, often holding up for months, gradually fading in color. Effective when massed in partial shade or planted in tubs on a paved terrace.

Easy to grow in rich, porous soil; dependent on heavy watering. Protect against overhead sun inland; in cool coastal gardens they can take full sun. Prune to control size and form; cut out stems that have flowered, leaving those which have not. To get the biggest flower clusters, reduce the number of stems; for numerous middle-sized clusters nicely spaced, keep more stems.

H. anomala petiolaris (*H. petiolaris*). CLIMBING HYDRANGEA. Deciduous vine. Zones 1-21. Climbs high by clinging aerial rootlets. Shrubby and sprawling without support. Roundish, 2-4-in.-long green, heart-shaped leaves. Mature plants develop short, stiff flowering branches with flat white flower clusters 6-10 in. wide in lace-cap effect.

H. arborescens. SMOOTH HYDRANGEA. Deciduous shrubs. Zones 1-21. Upright, dense to 10 ft. with oval, grayish green 4-8-in. leaves. White flowers in 6-in. roundish clusters June to frost; a few large sterile flowers. Much better is the variety 'Grandiflora', HILLS OF SNOW, with very large clusters made up of large sterile flowers.

H. macrophylla (*H. hortensia, H. opuloides, H. otaksa*). BIGLEAF HYDRANGEA, GARDEN HYDRANGEA. Deciduous shrubs. Zones 2-24. Symmetrical, rounded habit, to 4-8, even 12 ft. with thick, shining, coarsely toothed leaves to 8 in. long.

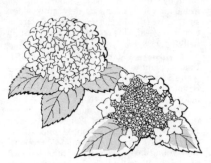

Large flowers in the cluster are sterile; smaller ones, as in "lace cap", fertile.

Flowers white, pink, red, or blue in big clusters.

Pink and red forms often turn blue or purple in acid soils. Florists grow the French hybrids as pot plants, controlling flower color by controlling soil mix. Blue-flowering plants from the florist may show pink flowers when planted out in neutral or alkaline soil. Plants can be made (or kept) blue by soil application of aluminum sulfate; plants can be kept red or made redder by liming or applying superphosphate in quantity to soil; treatment is not effective unless started well ahead of bloom.

A great performer in areas where winters are fairly mild, disappointing where plants freeze to the ground every year. May never bloom under these conditions. Protect in Zones 2, 3 by hilling soil or leaves over bases of plants.

There are hundreds of named varieties, and plants may be sold under many names. Florists' plants are usually French hybrids, dwarfer (1-3 ft. tall) and with larger flowers than old garden varieties. Two varieties are unmistakable: 'Domotoi' has clusters of pink or blue double sterile flowers; 'Tricolor' (usually sold as 'Variegata'), a lace cap, has dark green leaves strongly marked with cream and light green.

H. paniculata 'Grandiflora'. PEE GEE HYDRANGEA. Deciduous shrub. Zones 1-21. Upright, of coarse texture, can be trained as a 25-ft. tree. Best as a 10-15-ft. shrub. Leaves 5 in. long, turn bronzy in fall. White flowers in upright 10-15-in. long clusters slowly fade to pinky bronze.

H. quercifolia. OAKLEAF HYDRANGEA. Deciduous shrub. Zones 1-22. Broad, rounded shrub to 6 ft. with very handsome, deeply lobed, oaklike, 8-in.-long leaves that turn bronze or crimson in fall. Creamy white flowers in open clusters, June. Pruned to the ground each spring it makes a compact, 3-ft. shrub. Thinned out to well-spaced branches it makes a distinguished container plant. Takes considerable sun.

HYDRANGEA VINE, JAPANESE. See Schizophragma

HYMENOCALLIS. Bulb. Zones 5, 6, 8, 9, 14-24. Clumps of strap-shaped leaves like amaryllis. In June and July, 2-ft. stems bear several very fragrant flowers that resemble daffodils except that the center cup has six slender, spiderlike, free segments. Unusual summer-blooming plant for borders or containers. Plant in rich, well drained soil in late fall or early winter in frostless areas; after frosts in colder climates. Set bulbs with tips 1 in. below surface. Water well during growth and bloom, dry off when foliage begins to yellow. Dig and wash bulbs, dry in inverted position; do not cut off fleshy roots. Store in open trays at 60°-75°.

H. calathina (*Ismene calathina*). BASKET FLOWER, PERUVIAN DAFFODIL. Leaves 1½-2 ft. long, 1-2 in. wide. Two to 5 white, green-striped flowers in cluster. Variety 'Advance' has pure white flowers, faintly lined with green in throat.

H. festalis. Free-flowering, with 4 or more pure white flowers, the cup with very narrow curved segments.

H. 'Sulfur Queen'. Primrose yellow flowers with light yellow, green-striped throat.

HYMENOCYCLUS. See Malephora under Ice Plant

HYMENOSPORUM flavum. SWEETSHADE. Evergreen small tree or large shrub. Zones 8, 9, 14-16, 18-23. Native to Australia. Slow to moderate growth to 20-40 ft. with 15-20-ft. spread. Graceful, upright, slender, open habit in first 10 years. Leaves shiny, dark green, 2-6 in. long, 1-2 in. wide, with a tendency to cluster near ends of twigs and branches. Clusters of yellow flowers in early summer with pronounced orange blossom honey fragrance.

Best away from coastal winds. Should have fast soil drainage, routine feeding, and well-spaced deep watering rather than lawn watering. Watch for aphids and spray as needed. Early training necessary as branches spread out in almost equal threes, creating weak crotches that are likely to split. Strengthen branches by frequent pinching and shortening. As single tree, needs staking for several years. Attractive planted in small groves; in which case trees can grow without staking, training, or pruning.

HYPERICUM. ST. JOHNSWORT. Shrubs and perennials, evergreen or semi-evergreen. Zones 4-24, except as noted below. Best in mild, moist coastal areas. Open, cup-shaped, 5-petaled flowers range in color from creamy yellow to gold, and have prominent, sunburst of stamens in center. Leaves neat, vary in form and color. Plants useful for fresh green of foliage and summer flower color. Mass planting, ground cover, informal hedges, borders. Sun near coast, part shade in hot-summer areas. Any soil. Most kinds stand some drought, but are better with water.

H. calycinum. AARON'S BEARD, CREEPING ST. JOHNSWORT. Evergreen shrub; semideciduous where winters are cold. Zones 2-24. Grows to 1 ft. tall, spreads by vigorous underground stems. Leaves short-stalked, to 4 in. long, medium green in sun; yellow-green in shade. Flowers bright yellow, 3 in. across. Tough, dense ground cover for sun or shade; competes successfully with tree roots, takes poor soil, some drought. Can invade other plantings unless confined. Plant from flats or as rooted stems; set 18 in. apart. Clip or mow off tops every 2-3 years during dormant season.

H. coris. Evergreen subshrub. To 6-12 in. or more high. Leaves narrow, ½-1 in. long, in whorls of 4-6. Flowers yellow, ¾ in. across, in loose clusters. Bloom April-June. Good ground cover or rock garden plant.

H. moserianum. GOLD FLOWER. Evergreen shrub or perennial. To 3 ft. tall where winters are mild; grows as hardy perennial in cold-winter areas. Moundlike habit, with arching, reddish stems. Leaves 2 in. long, blue-green beneath. Flowers golden yellow, 2½ in. across, in clusters of 1-5; bloom June-August. Cut back in early spring.

H. patulum. Evergreen shrub. To 3 ft., spreading, with purplish, arching stems. Leaves about 2 in. long, blue-green beneath. Less grown than following two varieties: *H. p. henryi*, to 4 ft., with light green, oblong leaves on graceful, willowy branches. Flowers brilliant golden yellow, 2 in. across July-October. Shabby winter appearance in cold-winter areas. Good for low, untrimmed hedges, mass plantings. *H. p.* 'Hidcote', rounded shrub to 4 ft. In colder climates semi-evergreen, some winter damage to tops, stays at about 2 ft. tall. Flowers yellow, 3 in. across, bloom all summer.

H. 'Rowallane'. Evergreen shrub. Upright to 3-6 ft., rather straggly growth. Flowers bright yellow, 2½-3 in. across, profuse in late summer and fall. Remove older branches annually.

H. 'Sungold'. Twiggy, rounded shrub 1½-2 ft. tall, 2-3 ft. wide. Flowers golden yellow, 2-3 in. across, heavily produced in July-August.

HYPOCYRTA nummularia. GOLDFISH PLANT. Related to African violet, takes same culture. Foot-long arching branches set with neat pairs of shiny leaves and inch-long, fat, orange flowers with pinched mouths; blooms resemble goldfish.

HYPOESTES sanguinolenta. FRECKLE FACE, PINK POLKA-DOT PLANT. Indoor foliage plant. Can reach 1-2 ft. tall. Slender stems. Leaves 2-3 in. long, oval, spotted irregularly with pink. A selected form known as 'Splash' has larger spots. Blooms very seldom. Plant in loose, peaty mixture in pots or planters. Feed with liquid fertilizer. Pinch tips to make bushy.

HYSSOPUS officinalis. HYSSOP. Perennial herb. All Zones. Compact growth to 1½-2 ft. Narrow, dark green, pungent leaves; profusion of dark blue flower spikes from July to November. There are also white and pink-flowered forms. Full sun.

IBERIS. CANDYTUFT. Annuals, perennials. Free-blooming plants with clusters of white, lavender, lilac, pink, rose, purple, carmine, or crimson flowers, early spring to summer. Use annuals for borders, cutting; perennials for edging, rock gardens, small scale ground covers, containers.

Sow seed of annual kinds in place or in flats in fall (in mild areas) or in early spring. Set transplants 6-9 in. apart. Plant perennials in sun or partial shade in fall or spring; water deeply; shear lightly after bloom to stimulate new growth.

I. amara. HYACINTH-FLOWERED CANDYTUFT, ROCKET CANDYTUFT. Annual. Fragrant white flowers in tight round clusters that elongate into hyacinthlike spikes on 15-in. stems.

I. gibraltarica. GIBRALTAR CANDYTUFT. Perennial. Zones 4-24. Sprawling plant 12-16 in. high; growth habit less attractive than that of *I. sempervirens*. Flowers lilac-colored; variable from seed—colors range from white through pale lavender to an occasional lilac.

I. sempervirens. EVERGREEN CANDYTUFT. Perennial. All Zones. Grows 8-12 or even 18 in. high, spreading about as wide. Leaves dark green, good looking all year. Flower clusters pure white, on stems long enough to cut for bouquets; bloom early spring to June; first flowers as early as November in mild areas. Lower more compact varieties are 'Little Cushion', 3-6 in. or more, 1-ft. spread; 'Little Gem', 4-6 in. high; 'Snowflake', best variety, 4-12 in. high, spreads 1½-3 ft., with broader, more leathery leaves, larger flowers in larger clusters on shorter stems, most showy in spring—sporadic bloom all year in milder areas.

I. umbellata. GLOBE CANDYTUFT. Annual. Bushy plants 12-15 in. high. Flowers in pink, rose, carmine, crimson, salmon, lilac, and white. Dwarf hybrids, 6 in. tall, in same colors.

ICE PLANT. Succulent perennials, subshrubs, or annuals. Once conveniently lumped together as *Mesembryanthemum*, now classified under several different names. A brief summary of plants under new names:

Carpobrotus. Coarse, sturdy ice plants of beach and highway plantings.

Cephalophyllum. Slow-spreading, hardy, showy flowers.

Delosperma. Good ground cover, and bank cover.

Dorotheanthus. Annuals for summer bloom.

Drosanthemum. Profuse pink or purple flowers, useful on steep banks.

Lampranthus. Large-flowering, brilliantly colorful as ground cover, in rock gardens.

Malephora. Ground covers with good-looking foliage, long bloom season.

Mesembryanthemum. Botanists have reclassified plants formerly called *Mesembryanthemum*, so that ice plants you knew as *Mesembryanthemum* are now placed under other names.

Oscularia. Dainty form, fragrance.

All tolerate drought when established, but look best with some summer water; amount depends on heat, humidity. Plants require little summer water in coastal areas, more inland. Too much water can lead to dieback. Give just enough to keep plants looking lively. Feed lightly when fall rains begin, and again after bloom. All need full sun, take most soils; won't take walking on.

Carpobrotus. ICE PLANT, SEA FIG, HOTTENTOT FIG. Succulent perennials or subshrubs. Zones 12-24. Coarse-leafed, trailing plants useful for covering banks (but not steep ones), in binding loose sand at beach, for covering seldom-watered marginal areas. On steep slopes can become heavy and water-logged, cause slides. Fast growing, easy to increase by cuttings set 1½-2 ft. apart.

C. chilensis (*Mesembryanthemum aequilaterale*). Native along coast, Oregon to Baja California. The 3-sided fleshy leaves are straight, flowers lightly fragrant, rosy purple. Summer bloom.

C. edulis (*Mesembryanthemum edule*). From South Africa. Leaves curved. Flowers pale yellow to rose. Fruits edible, but not very good.

Cephalophyllum 'Red Spike'. (Often sold as *Cylindrophyllum speciosum*.) RED SPIKE ICE PLANT. Succulent perennial. Zones 8, 9, 11-24. Clumping plant 3-5 in. high, slowly spreading to 15-18 in. wide. Spiky, bronzy red leaves point straight up. Bright cerise red, 2-in.-wide flowers in winter, with scattering of bloom at other seasons. Plant 6-12 in. apart for ground cover.

Cryophytum crystallinum (*Mesembryanthemum crystallinum*). ICE PLANT. Annual. Native to South Africa, naturalized along California Coasts. Spreading stems carry broad, fleshy leaves to 4 in. long. Stems and leaves covered with clear, glistening blisters that look like ice crystals. Flowers 1 in. across, white to pink, not showy. This is the real ice plant; not handsome, but sometimes grown as an oddity.

Cylindrophyllum speciosum. See *Cephalophyllum*

Delosperma 'Alba'. WHITE TRAILING ICE PLANT. Succulent perennial. Zones 12-24. Dwarf, spreading, rooting freely from stems. Small, fleshy leaves of good green color. Small white flowers are not showy. Set 1 ft. apart for quick cover; does well as soil holder on fairly steep banks.

Dorotheanthus bellidiformis (*Mesembryanthemum criniflorum*). LIVINGSTON DAISY. Succulent. All Zones. Unlike most succulents, an annual. Not widely planted, but useful and pretty in poor, dry soil. A few inches high, spreading, with flattish, fleshy bright green leaves and daisylike, 2 in. wide flowers in white, pink, orange, red. Sow seed in warm weather; blooms quickly.

Drosanthemum. Succulent perennials. Zones 15-24. Dwarf, trailing, rooting stems. Small, dark green, fleshy leaves closely set on stems are covered with sparkling fleshy dots that give dew-sprinkled appearance. Grows to 6 in. tall, but trailing stems reach considerable length, will drape over rocks, walls. Grows well in poorest soils and is best for planting on steep slopes to prevent erosion. Plant 1-1½ ft. apart. Bees attracted by flowers.

D. floribundum. Profusion of ¾-in.-wide pink flowers late spring, early summer.

D. hispidum. ROSEA ICE PLANT. Great quantities of brilliant purple, inch-wide flowers late spring, early summer.

Hymenocyclus. See *Malephora*

Lampranthus. Succulent subshrubs. Most of the blindingly brilliant ice plants with large flowers belong here. Plants erect or

Climate
Zone maps
pages 8-27

trailing, woody at the base; leaves fleshy, either cylindrical or 3-sided. Select in bloom for color you like. Cut back lightly after bloom to eliminate fruit capsules, encourage new leafy growth.

L. aurantiacus. Zones 15-24. To 10-15 in. tall. Foliage gray-green; leaves an inch long, 3-sided. Flowers (February-May) 1½-2 in. across, bright orange. Variety 'Glaucus' has bright yellow flowers; 'Sunman' has golden yellow flowers. Plant 15-18 in. apart for bedding, borders, low bank cover.

L. filicaulis. REDONDO CREEPER. Zones 15-24. Thin, creeping stems, fine-textured foliage. Spreads slowly to form mats 3 in. deep. Flowers small, pink. Early spring bloom. Use for small-scale ground cover, mound or low bank cover.

L. productus. Zones 15-24. To 15 in. tall, spreading to 1½-2 ft. Gray-green fleshy leaves tipped bronze. Flowers an inch wide, purple. Blooms heavily January-April. Scattered bloom at other times. Plant 1-1½ ft. apart.

L. spectabilis. TRAILING ICE PLANT. Zones 15-24. Sprawling or trailing, to 12 in. tall, 1½-2 ft. wide. Gray-green foliage. Makes carpets of gleaming color March-May. Flowers 2-2½ in. across, very heavily borne. Available in pink, rose-pink, red, purple. Plant 1-1½ ft. apart.

Malephora (Hymenocyclus). Perennials. Dense, smooth, gray-green to blue-green foliage highly resistant to heat, wind, exhaust fumes. Widely used in streetside and freeway plantings. Flowers over a long season, but blooms are scattered rather than in sheets.

M. crocea. Zones 11-24. Trailing plant with smooth, gray-green foliage, sparse production of reddish yellow flowers nearly throughout the year, heaviest in spring. M. c. purpureo-crocea has salmon flowers, bluish green foliage. Both are good for erosion control on moderately steep slopes. Hardiest of trailing ice plants. Plant 1-1½ ft. apart.

M. luteola. Zones 15-24. To 1 ft. Light gray-green foliage, yellow flowers May-June and throughout the year. Bloom sparse. Not for erosion control.

Mesembryanthemum aequilaterale. See Carpobrotus chilensis

M. criniflorum. See Dorotheanthus

M. crystallinum. See Cryophytum

M. edule. See Carpobrotus edulis

Oscularia. Subshrubs. Zones 15- 24. Low plants with erect or trailing branches. To 1 ft. tall. Leaves very thick and fleshy, triangular, blue-green with pink flush. Flowers to ½ in. across, fragrant. Late spring, early summer. Best in pots, hanging baskets, rock gardens, borders. Can be used for small-scale ground cover.

O. deltoides. Purplish-rose flowers.

O. pedunculata. Paler, mauve pink flowers.

IDESIA polycarpa. Deciduous tree. Zones 9, 14-17, 19-24. Native to Japan, China. To 50 ft. tall, usually much less, with strongly horizontal branch structure and a broad crown. The leaves are thick, heart-shaped, 6-10 in. long, nearly as wide, on 5-7-in. stalks. Yellow-green flowers (June and July) in 10-in.-long, drooping clusters, fra-

grant but not showy; male and female flowers usually on separate trees. Fruit in clusters on female trees; individual berries the size of a pea, turning from green to brown to red, ornamental. Unusual lawn or shade tree. Large leaves and broad crown

Leaves of Idesia are 6-10 in. long. Red fruits on female plants are showy.

give idesia an exotic look; the berries are handsome in fall and early winter, but you must have both male and female plants for fruiting.

ILEX. HOLLY. Evergreen shrubs or trees (deciduous types not cultivated). English holly is most familiar, but other species are becoming popular, especially in warmer, drier parts of the West. They range from foothigh dwarfs to 50-ft. trees. Leaves may be tiny or large, toothed or smooth, green or variegated. Plants sold as Dutch holly are simply hollies without marginal spines. Berries may be red, orange, yellow, or black.

Most holly plants are either male or female, and both plants must be present for the female to bear fruits. There are exceptions: some female holly plants will set fruit without pollination, and hormone sprays may induce berry set on female flowers. Safest way to get berries is to have plants of both sexes, or to graft a male branch onto a female plant. Male plants will have no berries.

Holly prefers a rich, slightly acid, good garden soil; it tolerates sun or shade, is most compact and fruitful in sun. (See

descriptions for exceptions.) It needs ample water with good drainage. Add a thick mulch rather than cultivating around plant.

Scale and mealybug attack in all holly-growing areas. Holly bud moth and leaf miner need attention on English holly in the Northwest. Two sprays a year generally give good control. Use an oil late in March for scale and bud moth. Spray with systemics or malathion during May for leaf miner.

I. altaclarensis 'Camelliaefolia'. Vigorous, dense foliage pyramid. Large 3-5 in. long leaves without spines. Dark red berries in clusters.

I. a. 'Wilsonii' (I. wilsonii). WILSON HOLLY. Shrub or tree. Zones 3-24. Hybrid between English holly and a Canary Island species. One of the best hollies, especially in warmer regions. Takes sun, shade, wind, almost any soil. Usually a 6-8-ft. shrub, but easily grown as a 15-20-ft. single-stem tree. Leaves to 5 in. long, 3 in. wide, thick, leathery, rich green, evenly spine-toothed. Heavy producer of bright red berries. Use as standard tree, espalier, shrub, screen, clipped hedge.

I. aquifolium. ENGLISH HOLLY, CHRISTMAS HOLLY. Shrubs or trees. Zones 4-9, 14-24; at its best in Zones 4-6, 15-17. Native to southern and central Europe, British Isles. Slow growth to 40 ft., usually much less. Highly variable in leaf shape, color, and degree of spininess. Note that male plants will not have berries: females may or may not. Some varieties produce infertile berries without a pollinator but these berries are usually small, slow to develop, and quick to drop. English holly needs protection from sun in hot dry areas and soil conditioning where soils are alkaline. Best known varieties include:

I. a. angustifolia. Grows as a compact narrow pyramid. Very narrow (½-in.-wide, 1½-in.-long) spiny leaves. Small brilliant red berries.

'Bailey's Pride'. Identical to 'Rederly'. Berries redden in November. Tall, erect growing.

'Balkans'. Hardiest English holly. Seed collected in Yugoslavia. Upright, smooth, dark green leaves.

'Boulder Creek'. Typical English holly with large leaves.

'Chambers'. Typical Christmas holly.

'Ciliata Major'. Much like I. altaclarensis 'Camelliaefolia'. Vigorous open growth. Red berries very early. New growth is a rich brown.

'Fertilis'. Sets light crop of seedless berries without pollination.

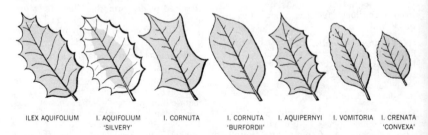

| ILEX AQUIFOLIUM | I. AQUIFOLIUM 'SILVERY' | I. CORNUTA | I. CORNUTA 'BURFORDII' | I. AQUIPERNYI | I. VOMITORIA | I. CRENATA 'CONVEXA' |

Ilex aquifolium *is the traditional Christmas holly; different, but still obviously hollies, are* I. cornuta, I. aquipernyi. *Others are hollies too, despite different appearances.*

Climate
Zone maps
pages 8-27

'Ferox'. HEDGEHOG, PORCUPINE HOLLY. Male with sterile pollen. Twisted, fiercely spined leaves give it its common names.

'J. G. Esson' ('Elderedge'). Leaves large and flat resembling *I. altaclarensis*. Turns purple in cold weather.

'Pendula'. Drooping branches. Heavy clusters of brilliant red berries.

'Rederly'. See 'Bailey's Pride'

'San Gabriel'. Bears seedless berries without pollination.

'Santa Ana'. Dense, bushy habit.

'Sparkler'. Strong upright grower. Heavy crop of glistening red berries at an early age.

'Teufel's Deluxe'. Exceptionally dark green leaves. Large, early ripening red berries.

'Teufel's Zero'. Upright with long slender branches, weeping. Unusually hardy.

'Van Tol'. Smooth, glossy green leaves. Early to mature.

Varieties with variegated leaves: Leaves edged with silver: 'Argentea Marginata', 'Silvery', 'Silver Queen', 'Silver King'. Leaves with silver centers: 'Argentea Medio-picta', 'Silver Star', 'Silver Milkmaid'. Leaves with golden margins: 'Aureo-marginata', 'Golden Queen', 'Lily Gold'. Leaves with golden centers: 'Golden Milkmaid', 'Pinto'.

I. aquipernyi. Shrub. Zones 4-9, 14-24. Hybrid between *I. aquifolium* and *I. pernyi*. The variety 'Brilliant' grows 8-10 ft. (possibly to 20 ft.), with cone-shaped habit and dense foliage. Leaves short-stalked, densely set on branches, twice as large as *I. pernyi*, with few but very pronounced teeth. Heavy crop of red berries without pollination.

I. cornuta. CHINESE HOLLY. Shrub or small tree. Zones 4-24; best in Zones 8, 9, 14-16, 18-21. Needs long warm season to set fruit. Give it an east or north exposure in desert climates. Dense or open growth to 10 ft. Typical leaves glossy, leathery, nearly rectangular, with spines at the 4 corners and at the tip. Berries exceptionally large, bright red, long lasting. Great variation among varieties in fruit set, leaf form, spininess. In the following list, all bear fruit without a pollinator except those noted:

'Azusa'. Medium to large shrub with deep green leaves. Needs pollinator.

'Burfordii'. BURFORD HOLLY. Widely planted throughout California. Leaves spineless.

'Burfordii Nana'. Same characteristics as above but smaller, more compact and slower growing.

'Dazzler'. Compact, upright growth. Leaves with high gloss. Loaded with berries.

'Femina'. Very spiny leaves. Good berry producer.

'Giant Beauty'. Upright, large growing. Lustrous, deep green, spiny leaves.

'Newport'. Unusually large leaves.

'Rotunda'. DWARF CHINESE HOLLY. Compact low grower. A 6-year-old may be 18 in. high and as wide. Does not produce berries.

'Tustin'. Unusually bushy.

I. crenata. JAPANESE HOLLY. Shrub. Zones 2-9, 14-24. Looks more like a boxwood than a holly. Dense, erect, usually to 3-4 ft., sometimes 20 ft. Narrow, finely toothed leaves, ½-¾ in. long. Berries are black. Extremely hardy and useful where winter cold limits choice of polished evergreens for hedges, edgings. All grow best in a slightly acid soil. Take sun or shade. Sold in following varieties:

'Compacta'. More densely branched, requires little pruning to hold its shape.

'Convexa'. (Often sold as *I. c. bullata*.) Compact, rounded shrub to 4-6 feet and broader than tall. Leaves, ½ in. long, roundish with edges cupped downward. Handsome clipped or unclipped.

'Green Island'. Low and spreading, to 24 in. high.

'Green Thumb'. Compact, upright to 20 in. Deep green leaves.

'Helleri'. Dwarf to 12 in. high, 2 ft. wide.

'Hetzi'. Similar to 'Convexa' with larger leaves, more vigorous growth.

'Latifolia'. Compact, upright, very bushy. Roundish leaves.

'Mariesii'. Smallest and slowest growing of Japanese hollies. Only 8 in. high in 10 years.

'Microphylla'. Stiff branching, compact. Very small leaves.

I. latifolia. Tree. Zones 4-7, 15-17, 20-24. Native to China and Japan. Largest leaves of the hollies, 6-8 in. long, dull dark green, thick and leathery, finely toothed. Slow growing tree with stout branches to 50-60 ft. Berries in large clusters, large, dull red.

I. 'Nellie Stevens'. Shrub. Zones 4-9, 14-24. Hybrid between *I. cornuta* and *I. aquifolium*. Leaves suggest both parents. Fast growing, large, can be trained as a tree.

I. opaca. AMERICAN HOLLY. Tree. Zones 2-9, 15, 16, 19-23. Native to eastern U. S. Slow growing, pyramidal or round-headed, to 50 ft. Leaves 2-4 in. long, dull or glossy green with spiny margins. Some of the many varieties are available in the West. They include 'Brilliantissima', 'East Palatka', 'Howard', 'Manig', 'Mrs. Sarver', 'Old Heavy Berry', 'Rosalind Sarver'.

I. pendunculosa. Shrub or small tree. Zones 3-7, 15-17, 20-24. Native to China, Japan. To 15 ft. high. Large oval, smooth-edged leaves. Bright red berries hang on long (1-1½-in.) stems like tiny cherries.

I. pernyi. Shrub or small tree. Zones 4-9, 14-24. Slow growth to 20-30 ft. Glossy, square-based leaves closely packed against branchlets, 1-2 in. long, with 1-3 spines on each side. Variety 'Veitchii' has larger leaves with 4-5 spines on each side. Both bear stemless red berries.

I. 'San Jose Hybrid'. Shrub or small tree. Zones 4-9, 14-24. Hybrid with *I. altaclarensis* 'Wilsonii' as one parent. To 15-20 ft. Resembles *I. altaclarensis* but with leaves somewhat longer and narrower. Growth upright, berry production heavy.

I. vomitoria. YAUPON. Shrub or small tree. Zones 3-9, 11-24. Native to southeastern U. S. Stands extreme alkaline soils better than other hollies. Large shrub or small tree to 15-20 ft. Often sheared into columnar form. Narrow, inch-long, dark green leaves. Tiny scarlet berries in profusion, without pollinator. The following varieties are available:

'Nana'. DWARF YAUPON. Low shrub. Compact to 18 in. high and twice as wide. Refined, attractive. Formal when sheared.

'Stokes'. Dark green leaves, close-set, compact. Smaller growing than 'Nana'.

IMMORTELLE, COMMON. See Xeranthemum

IMPATIENS. BALSAM, TOUCH-ME-NOT, SNAPWEED. Annuals, perennials. The annual kinds grow best in sun; the perennials thrive in all but coastal areas. Ripe seed capsules burst open when touched lightly and scatter seeds explosively.

I. balsamina. BALSAM. Annual. Erect, branching, 8-30 in. tall. Leaves 1½-6 in. long, sharply pointed, deeply toothed. Flowers large, spurred, borne among leaves along main stem and branches. Colors plain or variegated, in white, pink, rose, lilac, red. Double camellia-flowered forms most used, compact, bushy. Sow seeds in early spring, set out plants after frost in full sun (light shade in hot areas). Needs lots of water.

I. glandulifera (*I. roylei*). Annual. Coarse, much branched, to 12 in. Leaves 2-6 in. long, sharply toothed. Flowers large, pale lavender to purple, in clusters of 3 or more on long stalks. Grows easily, naturalizes.

I. holstii. See I. walleriana

I. oliveri. OLIVER'S SNAPWEED, POOR MAN'S RHODODENDRON. Perennial. Zones 15-17, 21-24; elsewhere as greenhouse or indoor-outdoor container plant. Shrubby to 4-8 feet tall, as much as 10 ft. wide. Bears many lilac, pale lavender, or pinkish, slender-spurred flowers 2¼ in. across. Glossy, dark green leaves to 8 in. long in whorls along stems. Blooms in partial or deep shade. Along coast grows in full sun, takes sea breezes, salt spray. Inland, frosts kill it to ground; regrows in spring.

I. sultanii. See I. walleriana

I. walleriana. BUSY LIZZIE. Perennial, usually grown as annual. Includes plants formerly known as *I. holstii* and *I. sultanii*. Rapid, vigorous growth to 2 ft. in tall varieties (usually called *I. holstii*), 4-8 in. dwarf, 8-12 in. in semi-dwarf varieties. Dark green, glossy, narrow 1-3 in.-long leaves on pale green, juicy stems. Flowers 1-2 in. across, scarlet, pink, rose, violet, orange, or white.

Useful for bright flowers in partial shade with begonias, fatsia, ferns, fuchsias, hydrangeas. Grow from seed, cuttings, or buy plants from flats. Rich, moist soil.

Popular dwarf and semi-dwarf strains are Baby, Imp, and Jewel. 'Blaze', with iridescent coral orange flowers, is an outstanding semi-dwarf.

INCARVILLEA delavayi. Perennial. All Zones. Fleshy roots. Basal leaves 1 ft. long, divided into toothed leaflets. Stems to 3 ft. topped with clusters of 2-12 trumpet-shaped flowers 3 in. long and wide, rosy purple outside, yellow and purple inside. Blooms May-July. Good in containers. Sun or light shade. Deep, porous soil. Roots rot in winter in water-logged soils. Sow seeds in spring for bloom following year. In extremely cold climates lift and store roots like dahlias. Cover with soil; do not let them dry out.

INDIAN BEAN. See Catalpa bignonioides

INDIAN FIG. See Opuntia ficus-indica

INDIAN MOCK STRAWBERRY. See Duchesnea

INDIGO, FALSE or WILD. See Baptisia

INSIDE-OUT FLOWER. See Vancouveria planipetala

IOCHROMA cyaneum (*I. lanceolatum, I. purpureum, I. tubulosum*). Evergreen shrub.

I

Climate Zone maps pages 8-27

Zones 16, 17, 19-24. To 8 ft. or more with oval to lance-shaped leaves, 5-6 in. long, of dark, dull green. Clusters of purplish blue, tubular, drooping, 2-in.-long flowers in summer. Seedlings sometimes vary to purplish rose or pink. Buy in bloom to get the color you want. Fast-growing, soft-wooded shrub that looks best espaliered or tied up against a wall. Prune it hard after bloom, and give it plenty of water, protection from hard frosts. Subject to infestation by measuring worms; spray with any broad-scope insecticide.

IPHEION uniflorum (*Brodiaea uniflora, Triteleia uniflora*). SPRING STAR FLOWER. Bulb. Zones 4-24. Native to Argentina. Flattish, bluish green leaves which smell like onions when bruised. Spring-blooming flowers 1½ in. across, broadly star-shaped, white tinged blue, on 6-8-in. stems. Edging, ground cover in semi-wild areas, under trees, large shrubs. Plant in fall in any soil; sun or part shade. Easy, persisting and multiplying for years.

IPOMOEA. MORNING GLORY. Annuals, perennials. The garden forms do not become pests; the pest is common bindweed, also called wild morning glory (*Convolvulus arvensis*). Leaves of garden morning glory are often lobed, heart-shaped. Flowers showy, funnel-shaped to bell-like, single or double, in solid colors of blue, lavender, pink, red, white, usually with throats in contrasting colors; some bicolored, striped. Most morning glories open only in morning, fade in afternoon; bloom until frost.

Use on fence, trellis, as ground cover; or in containers trained on stakes or wire cylinder, or allowed to cascade. For cut flowers, pick stems with buds in various stages of development, place in deep vase. Buds open on consecutive days.

Sow seeds in place in full sun after frost. To speed sprouting, notch seed coat with knife or file, or soak in warm water for 2 hours. Some growers sell scarified seed. For earlier start, sow seeds indoors in small pots or bands. Set out plants 6-8 in. apart. Ordinary soil; water moderately, do not feed. Exception: Imperial Japanese morning glory (below).

'Heavenly Blue' morning glory twines to 15 ft. Flowers 4-5 in. across, pure sky blue, yellow throat. 'Pearly Gates', large pure white flowers. 'Scarlet O'Hara', rosy red, veined scarlet, 3½ in. across. Other color forms available.

Imperial Japanese morning glory. Perennial usually treated as annual, grown in containers. Twining to 3-4 ft. Leaves large, hairy, 3-lobed. Flowers funnel-shaped, 5 in. or more across, in white, many rich shades, some with markings.

Start in small pots or bands, transplant into 7 or 8-in. pots in rich, porous soil. Pinch top when plant is 6 in. high, later pinch side shoots. Tie stems to bamboo stakes. Water around base, not on leaves. Feed regularly.

I. leari. BLUE DAWN FLOWER. Perennial. Zones 8, 9, 12-24. Vigorous, twines rapidly 15-30 ft. Leaves dark green; flowers bright blue, 3-5 in. across, in clusters. Use to cover large banks, walls. Blooms in 1 year from seed. Also grows from divisions, cuttings.

IPOMOPSIS. Biennials or short-lived perennials. Erect single stems, finely divided leaves, and tubular red, or yellow and red flowers. Startling in appearance, best massed; individual plants are very narrow. Sow seed spring or early summer for bloom following year. Sun, good drainage.

I. aggregata (*Gilia aggregata*). Biennial. Native California to British Columbia, Idaho. To 2½ ft. tall. Flowers in a long, narrow cluster, red marked yellow, sometimes yellow, an inch or so long. June-September.

I. rubra (*Gilia rubra*). Biennial or perennial. Native to southern U.S. To 6 ft. tall. Flowers red outside, yellow marked red inside. Summer bloom.

IRESINE herbstii. BLOOD-LEAF. Annual in all Zones, evergreen shrub in Zones 22-24. Desirable for leaf rather than flower color. The stalked leaves are 1-2 in. long, oval to round, most of them notched at the top, purplish red with lighter midrib and veins, or green or bronzed with yellowish veins. Leaf display best in summer and fall. Good in containers. Except in mildest coastal climates plants must be wintered indoors or treated as annuals. Easy to propagate from cuttings taken in fall and grown on for spring and summer display.

IRIS. Bulbs, rhizomes. All Zones, exceptions noted below. Large and remarkably diverse group of more than 150 species, varying in flower color and form, cultural needs, and blooming season, although the majority flower in spring or early summer. Leaves swordlike, or grasslike. Flowers showy, complex in structure. The 3 inner segments (petals or standards) usually erect, arching, or flaring; 3 outer ones (sepals or falls) hang or curve back. Following best known and most widely adapted species and varieties are listed in four main groups: bulbous iris, crested, beardless, and bearded. The last three have rhizomes.

BULBOUS IRIS

All have bulbs that become dormant in summer, can be lifted, stored until time to plant in fall. Flowers dainty, sometimes orchidlike.

I. reticulata. VIOLET-SCENTED IRIS. Bulbs have netted outer covering. Long-tubed, 2-in., delicately fragrant, violet-purple flowers edged gold. Stems 6-8 in. tall. Bloom March-April, or late January-early February in mild areas. Thin, 4-sided, blue-green leaves appear after bloom. Well adapted to pot culture. Cut flowers keep well.

I. xiphioides. ENGLISH IRIS. Zones 1-6, 15-17, 21-24. Plants to 18 in.; flowers larger than Dutch iris, have velvety texture of Japanese iris. Early summer blooms (after Dutch iris) are bluish purple, wine red, maroon, blue, mauve, white; no yellows. Need partial shade in warm-summer areas; moist, cool, acid soil; full sun where cool. In Zones 1-3, some gardeners find them easier than Dutch iris; no top growth in autumn that is liable to freeze. Set bulbs 3-4 in. deep, 4 in. apart in fall.

I. xiphium. SPANISH IRIS. Native to Spain, its surrounding areas, and north Africa. The native species grows 1½-2 ft. high, and has violet-purple flowers. However, from the original species have been developed many varieties and color strains. It's also one parent of the two following kinds. Spanish iris has smaller flowers and blooms about 2 weeks (or more) later than its descendants.

Dutch iris. Some growers lump Spanish and Dutch iris together. Others consider them separate. Dutch iris acquired their name because selecting and hybridizing of them was first carried out by Dutch growers. The result was a group of lovely iris with long straight stems, and flowers in many clear colors — white, blue, orange, purple, mauve, yellow, and bicolors. They flower in March-April in warm climates, May-June in colder areas. They make excellent cut flowers.

Plant in sun 4 in. deep, 3-4 in. apart in October-November. Bulbs hardy, but in coldest climates, mulch in winter. Ample water during growth; after bloom let foliage ripen before digging, store bulbs in a cool, dry place; do not let bulbs stay out of ground more than 2 months. Good in containers; plant 5 to a 5-6-in. pot.

Wedgwood iris. These are often sold as Dutch iris, but actually they are the result of a series of crosses between *I. xiphium* and the Moroccan native *I. tingitana*. The flowers are large, in shades of lavender-blue with yellow markings. The bulbs are larger than those of Dutch iris. They are also more tender and plants bloom several weeks earlier. Outstanding for cutting, containers, early color in borders (plant behind bushy annuals or perennials to hide the floppy leaves). 'Imperator', a darker blue, has more rigid leaves and is easier to use in the garden.

CRESTED IRIS

Dainty, closely related to bearded iris, generally shade-tolerant. Flowers distinguished by small narrow crest at base of falls.

I. cristata. Leaves 4-6 in. long, ½ in. wide, from slender, greenish, free-running rhizomes. Lavender or light blue flowers with golden crests in April-May. Hardy to -10°. Cool, damp soil, light shade, summer water. Divide crowded plantings right after bloom or in fall after leaves die down.

I. gracilipes. Graceful, delicate-looking, with several lilac to mauve pink flowers on branched stems 8-10 in. high, mid-spring.

I. japonica. Sometimes called orchid iris; considered most beautiful of crested iris. Widely branched, 2-ft. stems bear pale lavender, fringed flowers with orange crests, late spring. Outside only in milder climates; grow in containers in coldest areas.

I. tectorum. ROOF IRIS. Broad, ribbed leaves 1 ft. tall. Flowers purple-blue with white crests, or pure white, late spring. Rich, somewhat acid soil, half shade, ample water. Best in mild, moist areas; short-lived in very cold or dry climates. Planted on thatched roofs in Japan.

BEARDLESS IRIS

This group varies in size, appearance, and garden use. Distinguished by lack of beard (tufts of hairs on falls), short rhizomes with many fibrous roots, need for moisture—some need more than others.

I. dichotoma. VESPER IRIS. Native of Siberia, Manchuria, Mongolia. Hardy. Flowers white or pale lavender heavily marked purple, in branched, 3-ft. clusters in summer; each flower lasts but a short time; buds open over a long period. Plant short-lived, often dying after bloom, but easily raised from seed.

I. foetidissima. GLADWIN IRIS. Hardy iris with evergreen 1½-ft. leaves, ill-smelling if bruised. Stems 2-3 ft. tall; dull blue-gray flowers in spring. Real attraction is the large seed capsules which open in autumn to show numerous round, scarlet seeds, admired by flower arrangers. Plant will grow in sun or quite deep shade; needs little care.

I. kaempferi. JAPANESE IRIS. Graceful, upright sword-shaped leaves with distinct raised midrib. Stems to 4 ft. bear 1, 2, or more large (4-12-in.), flat, velvety, single or double flowers in late June-July. Colors are purple, violet, pink, rose, red, or white, often edged in contrasting shade.

Use in borders, at edge of pools or streams, grow in boxes or pots plunged halfway to rim in pond or pool during growing season. Plant in fall or spring. Set rhizomes 2 in. deep, 18 in. apart in rich, moist, acid soil. Provide sun in cool-summer areas, light shade in warm sections; shelter from wind; lots of water while growing and blooming. Not adapted to hot, dry climates. If soil or water is alkaline, apply aluminum sulfate or iron sulfate (1 oz. to 2 gallons water) several times during growing season. Divide crowded clumps in late summer or fall. Use rhizomes from outer edge of clump, cut back foliage halfway, replant quickly.

I. sibirica. SIBERIAN IRIS. Graceful iris for perennial borders, cut flowers. Leaves sword-shaped, narrow, erect, 1-2 ft. high. Flower stems 2-3 ft. Flowers shaped like Dutch iris appear as late bearded iris fade; range from pale to deep blue, purple, purple-red, or white; excellent named varieties. Full sun; neutral or slightly acid soil; plenty of water during growing season. When old clumps begin to get hollow in center, divide in September-October.

I. unguicularis (*I. stylosa*). WINTER IRIS. Zones 5-24. Dense clumps of narrow, dark green 1-2-ft. leaves. Lavender-blue flowers, with 6-9-in. tubes that look like stems, appear in November (where winters are mildest) to January-February. Use along paths, in borders. Good cut flowers; cut in bud, let flowers open indoors. Sun or shade; any soil; much or little water. To reveal flowers partly concealed by foliage, cut back the tallest leaves in September; also divide overgrown clumps at this time, or in March-April after flowering.

Louisiana Iris

A group consisting of 3 or more species, mostly native to Louisiana, have given rise to hybrids of great beauty and grace. The species are: *I. fulva*, with an unusual coppery red color; *I. giganticaerulea*, great size, height, good blue color; *I. foliosa*, hardiness and flower substance. Hybrids somewhat like Japanese iris, but more graceful in form, with colors including red, white, yellow, pink, purple, blue. Hardy except in Zone 1; mulch where ground freezes. Need rich, neutral or acid soil, ample water during growing season, partial shade in hot regions.

Pacific Coast Iris

Following 3 species native to Pacific Coast are used in Western gardens. Selections and hybrids of these iris also available from specialists.

I. douglasiana. Native to California coast from Santa Barbara north to Oregon. Large clump of evergreen 1-1½-ft. leaves.

Stems 1-2 ft. with 2 or 3 flowers in white, cream, yellow or lavender-blue to deep reddish purple. Naturalize on banks, in fringe areas of garden. Full sun or light shade; tolerates many soils. Once established, stands summer drought; also thrives with water.

I. innominata. From mountains of northern California, southwestern Oregon. Clumps of evergreen, 15-in. leaves. Flowers clear yellow to orange, lavender, purple. Best forms golden yellow striped brown. Woodland or rock garden plant.

I. tenax. From wooded areas of Washington and Oregon. Dense clumps of 6-in.-leaves. Dainty flowers dark purple blotched white, blue, lavender, pink, apricot, cream, and white on 6-12-in. stems. Rock garden. Porous soil, sun or light shade.

Spuria Iris

This is a group of similar species; they vary in height, but otherwise have similar growth habits, flower form, and culture. The name of the group comes from the species *I. spuria* which grows 1-2 ft. tall, and has flowers in shades of lilac, blue, purple. However, this species now also includes plants formerly known as *I. crocea* (*I. aurea*) — 3-4 ft. high, bright yellow flowers; *I. monnieri*—1-2 ft. tall, lemon yellow flowers; and *I. ochroleuca*—3-5 ft. tall, white to pale yellow flowers with deep yellow blotch on the falls. This group includes many hybrids which are replacing the species. They vary in height from 2-6 ft. They have somewhat larger flowers than the species and come in many shades—yellow, buff, bronze, lavender, blue, chartreuse.

All form clumps of stiff, erect, narrow, deep green leaves. Flowers, similar to Dutch iris, form on one side of tall rigid stems, bloom in spring, early summer. Stately plants in borders, for cutting. Full sun or light shade, rich soil, ample moisture while growing. Difficult to dig after firmly established. Avoid planting where necessary to lift and divide frequently. Plants often fail to bloom first year after dividing.

BEARDED IRIS

Probably most of the iris grown fall into this group. Many species, varieties, and many years of hybridizing by growers and iris fanciers have contributed to this great array of beautiful iris. All are characterized by having a beard (tuft of hairs) on the falls. The bearded iris can be separated into five groups which are described below. (Note that the Oncocyclus group need slightly different cultural requirements.)

Bearded iris need good drainage, full sun in cool climates, light shade in hottest areas. Adapt to most soils; not heavy feeders.

Plant July 1-September 15; earlier season best in cooler climates, later in warm areas. Set rhizomes 1-2 ft. apart, with top just below surface; spread roots well. Rhizomes grow from end with leaves; point that end in direction you want growth to take. For quick show, plant 3 rhizomes 8 in. apart, with growing ends pointed inward (clump will need thinning fairly soon). On slopes, set rhizomes with growing end facing upward. Water to settle soil, start growth; take care not to overwater later. Once in 2 weeks sufficient in most sections; established clumps need only occasional watering in cool areas. In warm climates, soak deeply 2 or 3 times during hot season.

Lift and divide overcrowded clumps right after bloom. Divide rhizomes with sharp knife; discard older, woody center, plant healthy sections with good fan of leaves. Trim leaves to 6 in. for convenient handling.

In late autumn remove old or dry leaves. Where winters are severe, mulch plantings to prevent alternate freezing and thawing.

Dwarf Bearded Iris

From 3-10 in. tall, flowers like miniature tall bearded iris. Many colors. Selected varieties bloom successively over 5-6 weeks; most varieties bloom earlier than tall bearded iris.

Intermediate Bearded Iris

From 15-28 in. tall, flowers 4-5 in. across. Bloom between dwarf and tall groups, some bloom again in September and October.

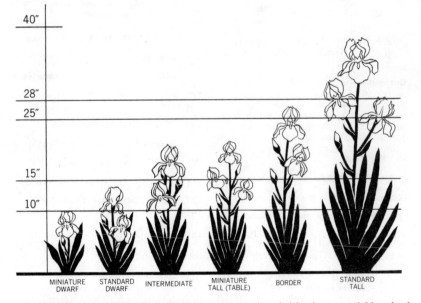

Tall bearded iris (right) most familiar. Lower-growing bearded kinds are available; check height against scale on left. Dwarf, median kinds have relatively large flowers.

I

Climate Zone maps pages 8-27

Tall Bearded Iris

Among very choicest perennials for borders, massing, cutting. Adapted in all climates, easy to grow. From 2-4 ft. high. All colors but pure red. Many named varieties available. Modern hybrids free branching, some with flowers ruffled, fringed, in two-tone colors. Many give a second bloom in fall.

Oncocyclus Iris

This is a group of bearded iris that have big, rounded flowers, generally veined in darker colors. Need perfect drainage, no summer water, and limy soil. Best in areas of fairly mild winters to protect the foliage which appears in autumn.

One of the most widely available species in this group is *I. susiana*, MOURNING IRIS, native to Asia Minor and Persia. It grows about 1 ft. high. Yellowish green leaves 6-9 in. or more long, ¾-1 in. wide. Large, round, silvery gray flowers, veined and stippled with purplish black; falls have large, round, dark brown, cushionlike beard.

More readily available are the Onco hybrids. These are Oncocyclus species crossed with tall bearded iris. They are as easy to grow as tall bearded kinds, but they retain the size and unusual flower form of the Oncocyclus species.

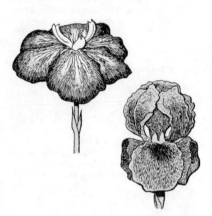

Japanese iris (left) has flowers to 1 ft. wide. I. susiana: flowers of gray, black.

Oncogelia Iris

Hybrids of Oncocyclus and closely related Regelia iris (including *I. hoogiana, I. korolkowii, I. stolonifera* — all with smaller, narrower flowers, smaller beards) are also beautiful and easy to grow. Flowers in rich, somber colors, with heavy veining, stippling.

IRIS, AFRICAN. See Moraea

IRIS pavonia. See Moraea glaucopis

IRIS, PEACOCK. See Moraea glaucopis

IRISH MOSS, SCOTCH MOSS. Perennial ground covers. All Zones. Two different plants of similar appearance, each sold in a green (Irish) and a golden green (Scotch) form. Both make dense, compact, mosslike masses of very slender leaves on slender stems. Both are grown primarily as ground covers for limited areas in full sun, semi-shade. Useful to fill in between paving

blocks. In cool Northwestern gardens they can seed themselves, become pests.

Although they look like moss, these plants won't grow well under conditions that suit true mosses. They need good soil, ample water, and an occasional feeding of slow-acting, non-burning fertilizer. In hot places, give partial shade; they don't do well in deep shade. They take some foot traffic and tend to hump up in time; control humping by occasionally cutting out narrow strips. Control snails, slugs, cutworms.

Cut squares from flats and set 6 in. apart for fast cover.

The two plants involved are: *Minuartia verna* (usually called *Arenaria verna caespitosa*), and *Sagina subulata*. The former has tiny white flowers in few-flowered clusters. The latter (far more common) bears flowers singly and differs in other technical details. In common usage, however, the green-colored forms of the two species are called Irish moss, and the golden green forms (*Minuartia verna* 'Aurea' and *Sagina subulata* 'Aurea') are called Scotch moss.

IRONBARK. See Eucalyptus

IRONWOOD, CATALINA. See Lyonothamnus floribundus

IRONWOOD, MOUNTAIN. See Cercocarpus betuloides

ISMENE. See Hymenocallis calathina

ITEA ilicifolia. HOLLYLEAF SWEETSPIRE. Zones 4-24. Evergreen shrub or small tree. Usually a graceful, open, arching shrub 6-10 ft., rarely to 18 ft. Leaves glossy, dark green, oval, 4 in. long, spiny-toothed. Small, greenish white, lightly fragrant flowers in nodding or drooping narrow clusters to 12 in. long. Fall bloom. Blooms sparsely where winters are very mild. Not a striking plant, but extremely graceful. Needs ample moisture and good soil; stands sun or partial shade near coast, should have part shade inland. Good near pools or waterfalls, as espalier against dark wood or stone backgrounds. Good informal screen.

ITHURIEL'S SPEAR. See Brodiaea laxa

IVY. See Hedera

IVY, ALGERIAN. See Hedera canariensis

IVY, BOSTON. See Parthenocissus tricuspidata

IVY, ENGLISH. See Hedera helix

IVY, GERMAN. See Senecio mikanioides

IVY, GRAPE. See Cissus rhombifolia

IVY, GROUND. See Nepeta hederacea

IVY, KENILWORTH. See Cymbalaria muralis

IXIA maculata. AFRICAN CORN LILY. Corm. Zones 5-24. Native to South Africa. Tender or half-hardy. Narrow, swordlike leaves, slender wiry stems 18-20 in. long, topped in May-June with spikelike clusters of 1-2-in. cup-shaped flowers in cream, yellow, red, orange, pink, all with dark centers. Long-lasting when cut. In mild areas, plant corms 3 in. deep in early fall; in Zones 5, 6 delay

planting until after November 1. Set corms 4 in. deep in sheltered spot, apply protective mulch. Can be left in ground several seasons; when crowded lift in summer, replant in fall. In mild climates, the plants reseed freely. In the coldest areas, grow in pots like freesias; plant 6-8 corms 1 in. deep in a 5-in. pot. Grow cool after bringing indoors—not over 55° night temperature.

IXIOLIRION montanum (*I. pallasii, I. tataricum*). Bulb. Zones 5-24. Native to central Asia. Narrow, greenish gray leaves; wiry stems 12-16 in. high bear loose clusters of violet-blue, trumpet-shaped, 1½-in. flowers in late May-June. Plant in sun in fall; set bulbs 3 in. deep, 6 in. apart. In cold areas, plant in warm sheltered location and mulch to protect leaves from severe frost in spring.

JACARANDA acutifolia (*J. mimosaefolia*). JACARANDA. Deciduous to semi-evergreen tree. Zones 9, 13-24. Native to Brazil. Grows 25-40 ft. high, 15-30 ft. wide. Open, irregular, oval head, sometimes multi-trunked or even shrubby. Finely cut, fernlike leaves, usually dropping in February-March. New leaves may grow quickly or branches may remain bare until flowering time. Many 8-in.-long clusters of lavender-blue, 2-in. tubular flowers, usually in June but can bloom any time April-September. Varieties with white and orchid pink flowers also exist. White form has more lush foliage, longer blooming period, and sparser flowers. All forms have roundish flat seed capsules, quite decorative in arrangements.

Fairly hardy after it attains some mature, hard wood; young plants are tender below 25° but often come back from freeze to make multi-stemmed, shrubby plants. Takes wide variety of soils but best in sandy soil.

Lavender-blue flowers of jacaranda. Individual blooms 2 in. long, 1½ in. wide.

Needs steady but not frequent irrigation. Too little water stunts it; too much encourages lush, loose, tender growth. Often fails to flower in path of ocean winds or where there isn't adequate heat.

Stake to produce single, sturdy trunk. Prune to shape. Usually branches profusely at 6-10 ft. In hillside gardens, a nice tree to look down on from above (as downslope from deck or terrace), or to view against sky (as planted on top of a knoll). But, it's also widely used in flat valley-floor gardens.

JACOBINIA. Evergreen shrubs Zones 6-9, 13-24; greenhouse plants anywhere. Erect, soft-wooded. Dense, showy clusters of red, pink, orange, or yellow, tubular, 2-lipped flowers. Partial shade. Need rich, porous, slightly acid soil, ample water. Unsightly if neglected. Cut back severely in early spring

Cluster of curving, tubular, 2-in. flowers give Brazilian plume flower its name.

as growth starts. Tops killed at about 29°, but come back strongly in spring.

J. carnea. BRAZILIAN PLUME FLOWER. Many upright stems to 4-5 ft. Leaves shiny dark green, purple-veined, 7 in. long. Dense clusters of crimson, rose to light pink flowers bloom July to early fall.

J. pauciflora. Shrub to 3 ft. or higher, and as wide. Leaves oblong, ¾ in. or less long. Red flowers, tipped in upper part with yellow, spring to early summer.

JACOB'S LADDER. See Polemonium

JADE PLANT. See Crassula argentea

JASMINE. See Jasminum

JASMINE, CHILEAN. See Mandevilla

JASMINE, MADAGASCAR. See Stephanotis

JASMINE, ROCK. See Androsace

JASMINE, STAR. See Trachelospermum

JASMINUM. JASMINE. Evergreen or deciduous shrubs or vines. This is one of the first plants that comes to mind when one thinks of fragrance. Yet not all jasmines are fragrant. Also, one of the best known and most fragrant plants commonly called jasmine—the star jasmine—is not a true jasmine at all but a *Trachelospermum.* All jasmines thrive in regular garden soil, sun or partial shade, and need frequent pinching and shaping to control growth.

J. floridum. Evergreen or partially evergreen, shrubby, sprawling, or half-climbing. Zones 4-9, 12-24. To 3-4 ft. Leaves divided into 3 (rarely 5) small leaflets ½-1½ in. long. Clusters of golden yellow, scentless, ½-¾-in. flowers over a long season in spring, summer, fall.

J. gracillimum. See J. multiflorum

J. grandiflorum (*J. officinale grandiflorum*). SPANISH JASMINE. Semi-evergreen to deciduous vine. Zones 9, 12-24. Rapid growth to 10-15 ft. Glossy green leaves with 5-7 leaflets 2 in. long. Flowers fragrant, white, 1½ in. across in loose clusters. Blooms all summer. Gives open, airy effect.

J. humile. ITALIAN JASMINE. Evergreen shrub or vine. Zones 8, 9, 12-24. Erect willowy shoots reach to 20 ft. and arch to make a 10-ft. mound. Can be trained as a shrub. Light green leaves with 3-7 leaflets 2 in. long. Fragrant clusters of bright yellow ½-in. flowers July-September. *J. h. revolutum* has larger, dull dark green leaves; flowers 1 in. across, up to 12 in a cluster. Side clusters make an even larger show.

J. magnificum. See J. nitidum

J. mesnyi (*J. primulinum*). PRIMROSE JASMINE. Evergreen shrub. Zones 4-24; protected spots in Zone 3. Long, arching branches 6-10 ft. tall—taller if trained against a wall. Leaves dark green, with 3 lance-shaped, 2-3-in. leaflets; square stems. Flowers bright lemon yellow, to 2 in. across, semi-double or double, unscented. They are scattered singly through plant November-April in mild-winter areas, February-April in colder climates. Needs space. Best tied up at the desired height and permitted to spill down in waterfall fashion. Use to cover pergola, banks, large walls. Sun or part shade.

J. multiflorum. (Often sold as *J. gracillimum.*) PINWHEEL JASMINE. Evergreen shrub or vine. Zones 8, 9, 14-24. Shrubby when free-standing. Reaches 20-30 ft. on support. Foliage light green. Leaves to 1½ in. long, uncut. Flowers white, fragrant, in dense hanging clusters spring-summer. Each flower looks like a 1-in.-wide pinwheel.

J. nitidum. (Often sold as *J. magnificum.*) ANGELWING JASMINE. Evergreen vine. Zone 13; semi-deciduous Zones 12, 16, 19-21. Needs long warm growing season to bloom satisfactorily. Not reliably hardy below 25°. Moderate growth to 10-20 ft. Leathery, uncut, medium glossy green leaves to 2 in. long. Flowers shaped like 1-in.-wide

Pinwheels of Jasminum nitidum *(upper). Clusters of* J. polyanthum *(below).*

pinwheels; very fragrant, white above, purplish beneath, purplish in bud, in 3-flowered clusters late spring and summer. Shrubby ground cover. Good container plant.

J. nudiflorum. WINTER JASMINE. Deciduous viny shrub. Zones 3-21; best adapted in cooler climates. To 10-15 ft. with slender, willowy branches. Glossy green leaves with 3 leaflets. Yellow 1-in. flowers in January-March before leaves unfold. Not fragrant. Train like *J. mesnyi* or use as trailer to cascade over wall or embankment.

J. officinale. COMMON WHITE JASMINE, POET'S JASMINE. Semi-evergreen to deciduous twining vine. Zones 12-24. Resembles *J. grandiflorum* but is taller (to 30 ft.), with smaller flowers (to 1 in. across). Somewhat tenderer than *J. grandiflorum.*

J. parkeri. DWARF JASMINE. Evergreen shrub. Zones 9, 12-24. Dwarf, twiggy, tufted habit. To 1 ft. tall, 1½-2 ft. across. Leaves bright green, ½-1 in. long, made up of 3-5 tiny leaflets. Small yellow flowers profusely borne in May, June. Not fragrant. Good rock garden shrub; containers.

J. polyanthum. Evergreen vine. Zones 9, 12-24. Fast-climbing, strong-growing to 20 ft. Finely divided leaflets. Flowers fragrant, white inside, rose-colored on outside, in dense clusters in February-July in Zones 22-24; April in colder areas. Needs sun to bloom well; regular summer watering; prune annually to keep it from tangling. Use as climber, ground cover, in containers.

J. sambac. ARABIAN JASMINE. Evergreen shrub. Zones 13, 21, 23. In Hawaii also called pikake, favorite flower for leis, used in making perfume; in Orient added to tea to make jasmine tea. Tender. To 5 ft. tall. Leaves undivided, glossy green, to 3 in. long. Flowers white, ¾-1 in. across, powerfully fragrant, in clusters. 'Grand Duke' (fully double) and 'Maid of Orleans' (semi-double) are good varieties. Grow as small compact shrub on trellis, or in container.

JERUSALEM THORN. See Parkinsonia

JESSAMINE, CAROLINA. See Gelsemium

JESSAMINE, GIANT ORANGE. See Murraya paniculata

JESSAMINE, NIGHT. See Cestrum nocturnum

JESSAMINE, WILLOW-LEAFED. See Cestrum parqui

JEWEL MINT OF CORSICA. See Mentha requienii

JOB'S TEARS. See Coix

JOHNNY-JUMP-UP. See Viola tricolor

JOJOBA. See Simmondsia

JOSEPH'S COAT. See Amaranthus tricolor

JOSHUA TREE. See Yucca brevifolia

JUBAEA chilensis (*J. spectabilis*). CHILEAN WINE PALM. Zones 15-24. Palm with fat trunk patterned with scars of leaf bases. Slow grower to 50-60 ft. Feather-type leaves 6-12 ft. long. Very hardy for a palm (20°).

JUDAS TREE. See Cercis siliquastrum

JUGLANS. See Walnut

JUJUBE. See Zizyphus

JUNIPER. See Juniperus

J

Climate
Zone maps
pages 8-27

JUNIPERUS. JUNIPER. Evergreen shrubs and trees. All Zones. Coniferous plants with fleshy berrylike cones. Foliage is needlelike, scalelike, or both. Junipers are the most widely used woody plants in the West. There's a form for almost every landscape use. Western nurserymen offer at least 120 junipers under 150 names. In the chart these offerings are grouped by common use and listed by botanical names with accompanying synonyms, nurserymen's names, and common names.

The ground cover group includes types ranging from a few inches to 2 or 3 ft. If you are planning large scale plantings, some of the taller junipers (such as the Pfitzer) could be included in this group. The prostrate and creeping junipers are almost in-

dispensable to rock gardens. As a ground cover, space plants 5-6 ft. apart; or for faster coverage, 2-3 ft., removing every other plant when they begin to crowd. In early years, a mulch will help keep soil cool and weeds down. Or interplant with annuals until junipers cover.

Shrub types range from low to quite tall, from spreading to stiffly upright and columnar. You can find a juniper in almost any height, width, shape, or foliage color. Use columnar forms with care; they become quite large with age. Many serve well as screens or windbreaks in cold areas.

The tree types are not widely used. They are interesting for picturesque habit of trunk and branch, tough, and drought-resistant.

Junipers succeed in every soil type the

West offers, acid or alkaline, heavy or light. However, you can expect root rot (yellowing and collapse) if soil is water-logged. In summer-cool climates they are best grown in full sun but will accept light shade. In hot areas they do well with partial shade.

Pests to watch for: spider mites (gray or yellow, dry-looking plants, fine webbing on twigs); aphids (sticky deposits, falling needles, sooty mildew); twig borers (browning and dying branch tips). Control the first two with malathion or other contact spray. Sevin or diazinon sprays in mid-June and early July (one month earlier in southern California) will control the latter. One important disease is juniper blight; twigs and branches die back. Control with copper sprays in July and August.

JUNIPERS

NAME	SYNONYMS OR NURSERYMEN'S NAMES	SIZE, HABIT	CHARACTERISTICS
GROUND COVERS			
J. chinensis 'San Jose'	J. procumbens 'San Jose' J. japonica 'San Jose' J. chinensis procumbens 'San Jose'	2 ft. by 6 ft. or more. Prostrate, dense.	Dark sage green with both needle and scale foliage. Heavy trunked, slow growing. One of the best.
J. c. sargentii SARGENT JUNIPER, SHIMPAKU	J. sargentii, J. sargentii viridis	To 1 ft. by 10 ft. Ground hugging.	Gray-green or green. Feathery. Classic bonsai plant.
J. c. sargentii 'Glauca'			A blue-green form of the above.
J. communis saxatilis	J. c. montana, J. sibirica	To 1 ft. by 6-8 ft. Prostrate, trailing.	Variable gray, gray-green. Upturned branchlets like tiny candles. Native alpine.
J. conferta SHORE JUNIPER	J. litoralis, J. conferta litoralis. Plants so named may be a grower's selected form.	To 1 ft. by 6-8 ft. Prostrate, trailing.	Bright green, soft needled. Excellent seashore and will stand interior valley heat if given moist, well drained soil.
J. davurica 'Parsonii'	J. squamata expansa 'Parsonii'	To 3 ft. by 6-8 ft.	Dense blue-green. Short heavy trunk and horizontal branches.
J. horizontalis PROSTRATA JUNIPER	J. prostrata, J. chinensis prostrata, J. communis prostrata, J. horizontalis prostrata.	To 18 in. by 8 ft. or more.	Selected form. Slow growing. Dense short twigs on flat, rather heavy branches.
J. h. 'Bar Harbor' BAR HARBOR JUNIPER		To 1 ft. by 10 ft. Hugs the ground.	Fast growing. Feathery, blue-gray foliage turns plum color in winter.
J. h. 'Douglasii' WAUKEGAN JUNIPER		To 1 ft. by 10 ft. Trailing.	Steel blue foliage turns purplish in fall. New growth rich green.
J. h. 'Plumosa' ANDORRA JUNIPER	J. depressa plumosa	To 18 in. by 10 ft. Wide spreading.	Gray-green in summer, plum color in winter. Flat branches, upright branchlets. Plumy.
J. h. 'Variegata' VARIEGATED PROSTRATA JUNIPER	J. prostrata variegata, J. communis prostrata variegated, J. horizontalis prostrata variegated.	To 18 in. by 4-5 ft.	See J. horizontalis. Patches of creamy yellow variegation. Not as rugged grower as green forms. Variegations burn in hot sun.
J. h. 'Venusta'		To 12 in. by 10 ft.	Similar to 'Bar Harbor'.
J. h. 'Webberi'		To 12 in. by 6-8 ft. Spreading, matlike.	Bluish green. Heavy texture.
J. h. 'Wiltonii' BLUE CARPET JUNIPER	J. horizontalis 'Blue Rug'	4 in. by 8-10 ft. Flattest juniper.	Intense silver blue. Dense, short branchlets on long trailing branches.

J

*Climate
Zone maps
pages 8-27*

NAME	SYNONYMS OR NURSERYMEN'S NAMES	SIZE, HABIT	CHARACTERISTICS
J. procumbens JAPANESE GARDEN JUNIPER	*J. chinensis procumbens*	To 3 ft. by 12-20 ft.	Feathery yet substantial blue-green foliage on strong, spreading branches.
J. p. 'Nana'		To 12 in. by 4-5 ft. Curved branches radiating in all directions.	Shorter needles than *J. procumbens.* More open in age than the following form.
J. p. 'Nana'	*J. procumbens compacta nana,* *J. procumbens 'Nana, Hill's Form'*	To 12 in. by 4-5 ft. Extremely dense.	Choice blue-gray. Slow growing. Mounds slightly. Never shows wood of branches.
J. p. 'Variegata'	*J. chinensis procumbens* 'Alba', *J. chinensis procumbens aureo-variegata.*	To 3 ft. by 8-10 ft.	*J. procumbens* with creamy white patches of foliage.
J. sabina 'Broadmoor'		To 14 in. by 10 ft. Dense, mounding.	Soft bright green foliage.
J. s. 'Buffalo'		To 12 in. by 8 ft. Lower than tamarix juniper.	Feathery, bright green. Wide-spreading.
J. s. 'Tamariscifolia' TAMARIX JUNIPER, TAM	*J. tamariscifolia*	To 18 in. by 10-20 ft. Dense. Symmetrically spreading.	Dense, blue-green. Widely used .
J. scopulorum 'Hughes'		To 18 in. by 10 ft. Wide spreading.	Bright silver blue foliage.
J. s. 'White's Silver King'		To 10 in. by 6-8 ft. Dense, spreading.	Pale silver blue foliage.
J. squamata 'Prostrata'		To 18 in. by 6-8 ft.	Slow growing. Grayish to bluish green foliage.
J. virginiana 'Silver Spreader'	*J. virginiana* 'Prostrata' and *J. virginiana prostrata* 'Lemon Hill' appear to be identical.	To 18 in. by 6-8 ft.	Silvery green, feathery, fine textured. Older branches become dark green.
SHRUBS			
J. chinensis 'Ames'		To 6 ft. Broad-based pyramid.	Blue-green. Slow growing. Massive.
J. c. 'Armstrongii' ARMSTRONG JUNIPER		4 by 4 ft. Upright.	Medium green. More compact than Pfitzer juniper.
J. c. 'Blaauwii' BLAAUW'S JUNIPER, BLUE SHIMPAKU		4 ft. by 3 ft. Vase-shaped.	Blue foliage. Dense, compact.
J. c. 'Blue Point'		To 8 ft. Dense pyramid.	Blue foliage. Needs no shearing.
J. c. 'Blue Vase' TEXAS STAR JUNIPER		3 ft. by 3 ft. Dense, blocky.	Blue prickly foliage. Good traffic stopper.
J. c. 'Corymbosa'	Probably a *J. chinensis* form.	To 10-15 ft. Irregular cone.	Much like Hollywood juniper but without twisted branches. Dark green.
J. c. 'Corymbosa Variegata' VARIEGATED HOLLYWOOD JUNIPER	*J. chinensis* 'Torulosa Variegata'	To 8-10 ft. Irregular cone.	Variegation of creamy yellow. Growth more regular than Hollywood juniper.
J. c. 'Fruitland'		3 ft. by 6 ft. Compact, dense.	Like a Pfitzer—but more compact.
J. c. 'Golden Armstrong'		4 ft. by 4 ft. Full, blocky.	Between golden Pfitzer and Armstrong juniper in appearance.
J. c. 'Hetzii' HETZ' BLUE JUNIPER	*J. chinensis hetzi glauca,* *J. glauca hetzi.*	To 15 ft. Fountainlike.	Blue-gray. Branches spread outward and upward at 45° angle.

(Continued on next page)

J

Climate Zone maps pages 8-27

NAME	SYNONYMS OR NURSERYMEN'S NAMES	SIZE, HABIT	CHARACTERISTICS
J. c. 'Maneyi'		To 15 ft. Semi-erect, massive.	Blue-gray. Steeply inclined, spreading branches.
J. c. 'Mint Julep'		2 ft. by 6 ft. Vase shape.	Mint green foliage, arching branches.
J. c. 'Mordigan'		To 7 ft. by 5 ft. Irregular, upright.	Dark green. Taller, narrower, more blocky than Pfitzer.
J. c. 'Pfitzeriana' PFITZER JUNIPER		5-6 ft. by 15-20 ft. Arching.	Feathery, gray-green. Sharp-needled foliage.
J. c. 'Pfitzeriana Aurea' GOLDEN PFITZER JUNIPER		Smaller than above.	Golden new foliage at tips.
J. c. 'Pfitzeriana Blue-Gold' GOLDEN PFITZER JUNIPER		3-4 ft. by 8-10 ft.	Blue-gray foliage with creamy yellow variegations.
J. c. 'Pfitzer Compacta' NICK'S COMPACT PFITZER JUNIPER	J. pfitzeriana nicksi, J. nicksi compacta	2 ft. by 4-6 ft. Densely branched.	Compact, gray-green foliage.
J. c. 'Pfitzeriana Glauca'		5-6 ft. by 10-15 ft. Arching branches.	Silvery blue foliage.
J. c. 'Pfitzeriana Mordigan Aurea'		3 ft. by 5 ft.	A denser, smaller golden Pfitzer.
J. c. 'Pfitzeriana Nana'		4 ft. by 2 ft.	Dense, nearly globular green juniper.
J. c. 'Pfitzeriana Nelson Blue'		2 ft. by 5 ft.	Blue form of compact Pfitzer.
J. c. 'Pfitzeriana Old Gold'	May be same as J. 'Golden Armstrong'		See J. c. 'Golden Armstrong'.
J. c. 'Pfitzeriana Plumosa'		2 ft. by 5 ft.	Horizontal-branching, table-topped Pfitzer.
J. c. 'Plumosa Aurea'	J. japonica aurea, J. bandai-sugi aurea, J. procumbens aurea.	3 ft. by 3 ft. Vase shaped.	Semi-upright, spreading, with bright gold new growth.
J. c. 'Richeson'	J. chinensis pfitzeriana compacta blue (in part).	2-3 ft. by 4-5 ft.	A dwarf gray-blue sport of Pfitzer.
J. c. 'Torulosa' HOLLYWOOD JUNIPER		To 15 ft. Irregular upright.	Rich green. Branches with irregular, twisted appearance. Give it enough room.
J. c. 'Weaver'		3 ft. by 2½ ft. Irregular upright.	Green, coarse-foliaged, compact.
J. c. 'Wilsonii'	Some growers sell J. c. 'Foemina' as J. 'Wilsonii'.	6-7 ft. by 4-5 ft. Dense, upright.	Dark green. Somewhat like a broader, more formal Hollywood.
J. communis 'Aureo-spica'	J. c. depressa aurea	1-2 ft. by 5-6 ft.	New foliage bright golden, older gray-green, brownish in winter. Best when young.
J. c. depressa PASTURE OR OLDFIELD JUNIPER		To 4 ft. and wide spreading.	Gray-green. Too large for average garden use.
J. c. d. 'Vase Shaped'		4 ft. by 3 ft. Dense.	Many nearly erect stems arise from ground. Gray-green.
J. c. 'Suecica Nana'		4 ft. by 4 ft. Dense.	Dark green. Resembles Armstrong juniper in size and shape.
J. sabina SAVIN, SAVIN JUNIPER		4 ft. by 10 ft.	Spreading with upturned branches. Dark green scale foliage. Foliage best on young plants.
J. s. 'Admirabilis'		1½ ft. by 4-5 ft.	Spreading, fine textured. Blue-green.
J. s. 'Arcadia'		1½ ft. by 4-5 ft.	Rich green, lacy. Like a very low, flat-topped Pfitzer.

J

Climate
Zone maps
pages 8-27

NAME	SYNONYMS OR NURSERYMEN'S NAMES	SIZE, HABIT	CHARACTERISTICS
J. s. 'Blue Danube'		3-4 ft. by 5 ft. Semi-erect.	Blue-green, upright habit with flat branching.
J. s. 'Scandia'		1 ft. by 4 ft.	More yellow-green than 'Arcadia'.
J. s. 'Variegated' HOARFROST JUNIPER		3-4 ft. by 6 ft.	Upright, spreading, lacy branch pattern. Every twig bears a small white tip.
J. s. 'Von Ehron'		3-4 ft. by 8 ft.	Deep green. Upright branching. Vigorous.
J. squamata meyeri MEYER or FISHBACK JUNIPER		6-8 ft. by 2-3 ft. Upright.	Oddly angled, stiff branches. Broad needled. Blend of green, gray, reddish foliage.
J. scopulorum 'Globosa'		4-6 ft. Globe	Silvery gray-green.
J. s. 'Lakewood Globe'		4-6 ft. Globe	Blue-green foliage.
J. s. 'Silver Star'		3 ft. by 6-8 ft.	Silvery gray. Wide spreading.
J. s. 'Table Top Blue'		6 ft. by 8 ft.	Gray, massive, flat-topped.
J. virginiana 'Kosteri'		2 ft. by 6 ft.	Blue-green. Slow, spreading.
J. v. 'Tripartita'	J. tripartita	4-5 ft. Upright, arching.	Green. Branches ascend from base, then spread out. Fast growing.

COLUMNAR TYPES

NAME	SYNONYMS OR NURSERYMEN'S NAMES	SIZE, HABIT	CHARACTERISTICS
J. chinensis 'Columnaris' CHINESE BLUE COLUMN JUNIPER		12-15 ft.	Blue-green narrow pyramid.
J. c. 'Foemina'	J. foemina, J. sylvestris, J. chinensis 'Reeves'.	12-15 ft.	Dark green, broad column with outward-spraying branchlets.
J. c. 'Hetz's Columnaris'		12-15 ft.	Rich green, dense column. Scale foliage predominant, branchlets threadlike.
J. c. 'Keteleeri' KETELEER JUNIPER		To 20 ft.	Bright green, broad pyramid with loose, ascending branches.
J. c. 'Mountbatten'		To 12 ft.	Gray-green, narrow column with needlelike juvenile foliage.
J. c. 'Obelisk'		To 20 ft.	Dense, stiff column. Steel blue foliage.
J. c. 'Pyramidalis'	Often sold as J. excelsa stricta.	15-30 ft.	Blue-gray, needlelike foliage. Narrow pyramid, broadening with age.
J. c. 'Robusta Green'		To 20 ft.	Brilliant green, dense, tufted column.
J. c. 'Spartan'	J. c. densaerecta 'Spartan'	To 20 ft.	Rich green, dense column.
J. c. 'Wintergreen'		To 20 ft.	Deep green, dense branching pyramid.
J. communis 'Stricta' IRISH JUNIPER	J. c. hibernica, J. c. fastigiata.	12-20 ft.	Dark green. Very narrow column with closely compact branch tips.
J. c. 'Suecica' SWEDISH JUNIPER		Possibly to 40 ft.	Blue-green, upright narrow pyramid with nodding branch tips. Heavy berry crop.
J. excelsa 'Stricta' SPINY GREEK JUNIPER	Plants sold under this name in colder areas are J. chinensis 'Pyramidalis'	20 ft. or more	Tall, narrow, spiny pyramid with gray-blue foliage. Tender.
J. e. 'Variegata' VARIEGATED SPINY GREEK	J. e. stricta variegata.	Probably to 20 ft.	Thick, full, blue-green pyramid with creamy white or yellowish branch tips.
J. sabina 'Fastigiata'		To 20 ft.	Dark green column.

(Continued on next page)

J

Climate Zone maps pages 8-27

NAME	SYNONYMS OR NURSERYMEN'S NAMES	SIZE, HABIT	CHARACTERISTICS
J. scopulorum ROCKY MOUNTAIN JUNIPER		To 50 ft.	All of these forms are tall growing. All are highly resistant to cold, heat, wind, drought, poor soil.
J. s. 'Blue Haven'	*J. s.* 'Blue Heaven'	To 20 ft.	Neat, compact, narrow gray-blue pyramid.
J. s. 'Emerald Green'			Compact, bright green pyramid.
J. s. 'Erecta Glauca'			Gray-blue upright pyramid. Very similar to 'Pathfinder'.
J. s. 'Gray Gleam'			Gray-blue symmetrical column. Slow grower.
J. s. 'Pathfinder'			Gray-blue, upright pyramid. Very similar to 'Erecta Glauca'.
J. s. 'Welchii'			Silvery green, very narrow spire.
J. virginiana 'Burkii' BURK RED CEDAR		15-20 ft. or more.	Steel blue, dense pyramid. Turns plum color in winter.
J. v. 'Cupressifolia' HILLSPIRE JUNIPER		15-20 ft.	Dark green, compact pyramid with same winter color.
J. v. 'Glauca' SILVER RED CEDAR		15-20 ft.	Silvery blue, dense, narrow column.
J. v. 'Manhattan Blue'	*J. scopulorum* 'Manhattan Blue'	10-15 ft.	Blue-green compact pyramid.
TREES			
J. californica CALIFORNIA JUNIPER		Shrubby or to 40 ft.	Yellowish to rich green. Useful in desert areas.
J. chinensis CHINESE JUNIPER	*J. reevesii, J. reevesiana.*	20-25 ft.	Never offered as a species. See preceding lists for garden forms.
J. deppeana pachyphlaea ALLIGATOR JUNIPER	*J. pachyphlaea.*	Shrubby or to 60 ft.	Blue-gray foliage, strikingly checked bark like alligator hide.
J. osteosperma 	*J. utahensis*	Shrubby or to 20-30 ft.	Yellowish green foliage. Adapted to high desert.
J. occidentalis 'Glauca' SIERRA JUNIPER		To 25 ft. or more.	Blue-gray foliage. Grows as column for years. Eventually a green, round-headed tree.
J. scopulorum 'Pendula' WEEPING ROCKY MOUNTAIN JUNIPER		Probably to 20 ft. if staked.	Silvery foliage, thin, weeping branchlets. Stake lead shoot to develop upright trunk.
J. virginiana RED CEDAR JUNIPER		40-50 ft. or more.	Conical dark green tree becoming reddish in cold weather.

JUPITER'S BEARD. See Centranthus

KADSURA japonica. SCARLET KADSURA. Twining evergreen vine. Zones 7-9, 14-22. Grow it for its foliage and berries. On support, grows fast to 15-20 ft. Leaves highly polished, leathery, dark green, oval, 2-4 in. long, toothed. Leaves turn reddish beneath with cold weather. Flowers yellowish white, ¾ in. across, inconspicuous. Bright scarlet fruit in roundish, headlike clusters, 1 in. wide, fall and winter. Train around a pillar or on a fence or pergola; takes full sun near coast, best in partial shade inland.

KAFFIR PLUM. See Harpephyllum

KALANCHOE. Succulents grown principally as house plants. Some hardy out of doors in the mildest coastal regions, but safest even there with protection of lath, eaves, or other overhead structure. Shapes and sizes varied. Flowers fairly large, bell-shaped, erect or drooping, brightly colored in a few species.

K. beharensis. (Often sold as *Kitchingia mandrakensis.*) FELT PLANT. Outdoors Zones 21-24, house plant anywhere. Stems usually unbranched, to 4-5 ft., possibly 10 ft. Leaves at tips of stems, usually 6-8 pairs, each leaf 4-8 in. or more long, half as wide, triangular to lance-shaped, thick, and thickly covered with dense white to brown felt-like hairs. Flowers not showy; foliage strikingly waved and crimped at edges. Hybrids between this and other species differ in leaf size, color, and degree of felting and scalloping. Striking in big rock garden, raised bed, in sun or considerable shade.

K. blossfeldiana. House plant; some hybrids hardy Zones 17, 21-24. Leaves fleshy, dark green edged red, shining, smooth-

Climate
Zone maps
pages 8-27

edged or slightly lobed, 2½ in. long, 1-1½ in. wide. Small, bright red flowers in big clusters held above the leaves. Hybrids and named varieties come in dwarf (6-in.) sizes, and in different colors, including yellow, orange, salmon. Blooms winter, early spring. Popular house plant at Christmas time.

K. daigremontiana. MATERNITY PLANT. House plant. Upright, single-stemmed plant 18-36 in. tall. Leaves fleshy, 6-8 in. long, 1¼ in. or more wide, gray-green spotted red. The leaf edges are notched, and young plants sprout in the notches; these root even on the plant. Flowers clustered, small, gray-ish purple.

K. flammea. House plant; some hybrids hardy Zones 17, 21-24. Lightly branched, 12-16 in. tall, with fleshy, gray-green, 2½-in. leaves and many-flowered clusters of orange-red or yellow flowers in winter and spring.

K. laciniata (*K. coccinea*). Zones 17, 21-24. To 4 ft. Leaves greenish bronze to red, to 5 in. long, fleshy, smooth-edged, scalloped, or cut. Clusters of ¼-in. yellow, orange, or red flowers late winter and spring.

K. longiflora coccinea. (Often sold as *K. petitiana*.) Zones 17, 21-24. Upright plant 1½ ft. tall. Blunt, thick, toothed leaves are greenish brown in part shade, orange-tinted to red in sun. Flowers orange-red or yellow.

K. pinnata (*Bryophyllum pinnatum*). AIR PLANT. Zones 17, 21-24. Fleshy stems eventually 2-3 ft. tall. Leaves fleshy; early ones undivided, scalloped, later ones divided into 3-5 leaflets, these also scalloped. Produces many plantlets in the notches of the scallops. Leaves can be removed and pinned to curtain, where they will produce plantlets until they dry up. Flowers greenish white to reddish. Sun or considerable shade. Likes moisture.

K. tomentosa. PANDA PLANT. House plant. Eventually 18 in. tall, branched. Leaves very fleshy, 2 in. long, coated with dense white felty hairs. Leaf tips and shallow notches in leaves strongly marked dark brown. A favorite with children.

Felt plant (left): densely furry leaves. Panda plant: brown markings on white.

KALE AND COLLARDS. The type of kale known as collards is a large smooth-leafed plant like a cabbage that does not form a head. Planted in early spring or late summer, collards will yield edible leaves in fall, winter, and spring. 'Georgia' is a typical variety. Collards not widely grown in the West.

Slightly more popular are the curly kales like 'Dwarf Blue Curled' and 'Blue Curled Scotch'; these are compact clusters of tightly curled leaves. They make decorative garden or container plants as well as supplying edible leaves. One kind, flowering kale, has brightly colored foliage, especially toward the centers of the rosettes. Grow just like late cabbage. Harvest leaves for cooking by removing from the outside of the cluster; or harvest the entire plant.

KALMIA. Evergreen shrubs. Zones 1-9, 14-17. Related to rhododendron. All have clusters of showy flowers and grow in part shade.

K. angustifolia. SHEEP LAUREL. Native to eastern North America. Grows 2-4 ft. tall, has shiny, bright green, 1-2½-in.-long leaves, paler beneath. Clusters of rosy red, ⅓-in.-wide flowers in May-June.

K. latifolia. MOUNTAIN LAUREL, CALICO BUSH. Native to eastern U.S. Slow growing to 6-8 ft. or more, with equal spread. Glossy, leathery, oval leaves, 3-5 in. long, dark green on top, yellowish green beneath. Clusters of pink buds open to pale pink flowers in apple blossom effect. May-June. Color rarely varies to white or near-red. Flowers 1 in. across, clusters to 5 in. across. Hardy well below 0°. Shares rhododendron's cultural needs—moist atmosphere, partial shade, acid soil rich in humus, regular watering.

K. polifolia. PALE LAUREL, BOG KALMIA. Native to damp ground from Cascades of Oregon and Washington to Alaska, east to Atlantic coast. Erect shrub to 2 ft. Leaves glossy dark green above, whitish beneath, to 1½ in. long. Pink to rose purple flowers, ½ in. across, in rounded clusters, June-August. Will grow in boggy acid soil. Needs good drainage if soil, water are alkaline.

K. p. microphylla. ALPINE BOG KALMIA. Native to high elevations, California to Alaska. Smaller plant to 8 in. tall with narrower, shorter leaves.

KALMIOPSIS leachiana. Evergreen shrub. Zones 4-6, 14-17. Native to mountains of southwest Oregon. Rhododendron relative, slow-growing to 1 ft. tall, with a 2-ft. spread. Many branches densely clothed with thick, dark green leaves. Flowers abundantly in early spring with flattish clusters of ½-in. rose-pink flowers. Best in light shade grown like rhododendron or azalea.

KANGAROO PAW. See Anigozanthus

KATSURA TREE. See Cercidiphyllum

KEI APPLE. See Dovyalis

KENTIA. See Howeia

KENTUCKY COFFEE TREE. See Gymnocladus

KERRIA japonica. Deciduous shrub. Zones 1-21. Green branches give welcome winter green in cold areas. Open, graceful, rounded shrub to 8 ft., with a 5-6-ft. spread. Leaves

bright green, heavily veined, somewhat triangular, 2-4 in. long with toothed edges, turning yellow in fall. Flowers (March-May) like small, single, yellow roses. Variety 'Pleniflora' has double yellow inch-wide flowers and is the more commonly planted form.

Give kerria part shade (will take sun in cooler areas) and room to arch and display its form. Remove suckers and prune heavily after bloom, cutting out branches that have flowered and all dead or weak wood.

KHAT. See Catha

KINNIKINNICK. See Arctostaphylos uva-ursi

KIWI. See Actinidia chinensis

KLEINIA. Succulents. Native to South Africa. Many species grown as pot plants; the two listed below are useful ground covers, especially when placed in contrast with dark green or bronze foliage. The daisylike whitish or yellowish flowers are unattractive; keep them cut off to preserve foliage quality. Roots somewhat invasive; sun or considerable shade, dry or moist soil.

K. mandraliscae (*Senecio mandraliscae*). Zones 16, 17, 21-24. Somewhat shrubby, with spreading branches to 12-18 in. tall, spreading wider. Leaves cylindrical, 3-3½ in. long, slightly curved, strikingly blue-gray.

K. repens (*Senecio serpens*). Zones 16, 17, 21-24. Like *K. mandraliscae*, but grows 1 ft. tall, has 1½-in.-long light gray or bluish leaves.

KNIPHOFIA uvaria (*Tritoma uvaria*). RED-HOT POKER, TORCH-LILY, POKER PLANT. Perennial. Zones 1-9, 14-24. Native to South Africa. Has been in cultivation long enough to give rise to garden varieties with some range in size and color. The typical plant

Glowing flowers of red-hot poker stand above grasslike leaves, can reach 6 ft.

is coarse with large, rather dense clumps of long grasslike leaves. Flower stalks (always taller than the leaves) are in dwarf kinds about 2 ft. and in the larger kinds 3-6 ft. tall. The many drooping orange-red or yellow tubular flowers of the typical one overlap, forming a pokerlike cluster 12 in. long. The named varieties, in both dwarf and taller forms, come in soft or saffron yellow, cream white, or coral. Flowers attract hummingbirds.

Flowering time varies — spring through summer. Cut out flower spikes after bloom. Cut old leaves at base in fall; new leaves will replace them by spring. Increase by root divisions. Poker plant is useful in large borders with other robust perennials such as hemerocallis, *Echinops exaltatus.*

KNOTWEED. See Polygonum

KOCHIA scoparia. SUMMER CYPRESS. Annual. Grow these foliage plants close together as a low, temporary hedge or individually for their gently rounded form—like fine-textured coniferous shrubs. To 3 ft. Branches densely clothed with very narrow, soft, light green leaves, making plants too dense to see through. Insignificant flowers. Sow in full sun. Tolerates high heat and will perform well in short-summer areas. Shear to shape if necessary.

K. s. 'Culta' (*K. s.* 'Trichophylla', *K.* 'Childsii'). MEXICAN FIRE BUSH, BURNING BUSH. Same as above, but foliage turns red with first frost. Reseeds profusely enough to become a pest.

KOELREUTERIA. Deciduous trees. Small yellow flowers in large, loose clusters in summer. Colorful fruits are fat, papery capsules, which seem to resemble clusters of little Japanese lanterns.

K. henryi. (Often sold as *K. formosana* or *K. bipinnata.*) CHINESE FLAME TREE. Zones 8-24. Slow to moderate growth to 20-40 ft. or taller, spreading, eventually flat-topped. Leaves 1-2 ft. long, divided into many oval leaflets, holding on the tree until December, then turning yellow briefly before dropping. Capsules 2 in. long, orange, red, or salmon colored, showy in late summer and fall, in large clusters. Fruit formation not always dependable. Takes to most well-drained soils and moderate watering. Stake and prune to develop high branching. Good patio shade tree, lawn, or street tree. Roots deep, not invasive. Good tree to plant under.

K. integrifoliola. Zones 8-24. Resembles *K. henryi.* The tree seems to have more flowers and fruits.

K. paniculata. GOLDENRAIN TREE. Zones 2-21. Slow to moderate growth to 20-35 ft. with 10-40-ft. spread. Open branching, giving slight shade. Leaves to 15 in. long, with 7-15 toothed or lobed leaflets, 1-3 in. long. Flower clusters in summer, 8-14 in. long. Fruits buff to brown in fall, hanging late. Takes cold, heat, drought, wind, alkaline soil; needs regular watering when young. Prune to shape; can be gawky without pruning. Valuable as street, lawn, or terrace tree in difficult soils and climates.

KOHLRABI. Cool-season vegetable related to cabbage. The edible portion is a bulblike enlarged portion of the stem, formed just above the soil surface. Varieties: 'Early White Vienna' and 'Early Purple Vienna'. Similar in size and flavor, they differ only in skin color. Sow seed ½ in. deep in rich soil about 2 weeks after average date of last frost. Follow first planting with successive plantings 2 weeks apart. In warm-winter areas plant again in late fall and early winter. Space rows 18 in. apart; thin seedlings 4 in. apart. To control aphids, dust or spray with rotenone. Harvest when round portions are 2-3 in. in diameter. Slice them up like cucumbers or cook them like turnips.

KOLKWITZIA amabilis. BEAUTY BUSH. Deciduous shrub. Zones 1-11, 14-20. Growth

upright, graceful to 10-12 ft., arching in part shade, denser and lower in full sun. Leaves gray-green. Clusters of small pink, yellow-throated flowers bloom heavily in May in California, June in Northwest and mountain states. Flowers followed by conspicuous pinkish brown, bristly fruits that prolong color. Thin out after bloom; to enjoy the fruits, thin lightly in early spring, removing wood which has bloomed the year before. Brown, flaky bark gradually peels from stems during winter.

KOREAN GRASS. See Zoysia tenuifolia

KOWHAI. See Sophora tetraptera

KUMQUAT. See Citrus

LA BELLA SOMBRA. See Phytolacca dioica

LABURNUM. GOLDENCHAIN TREE. Deciduous trees or large shrubs. Zones 1-10, 14-17. Upright growth; usually pruned into a single-stem tree; can be shrubby if permitted to keep basal suckers and branch low. Bark green, leaves bright green, divided into 3 leaflets (like clover). Flowers yellow, sweet pea-shaped, in hanging clusters like wisteria.

Protect from afternoon sun in hot regions. Well drained soil, adequate water. Subject to chlorosis in alkaline soils; use iron. Prune and trim regularly to keep plants tidy. Remove seed pods if possible. Not only are they poisonous, but too heavy a crop is a drain on the plant's strength. Handsome in bloom. Use as single tree in lawn or border or group in front of a neutral background, or space regularly in long borders of perennials, rhododendrons, or lilacs.

L. alpinum. SCOTCH LABURNUM. To 30-35 ft. Flowers clusters 10-15 in. long. Blooms late spring. The variety 'Pendulum' has weeping branches.

L. anagyroides. COMMON GOLDENCHAIN. To 20-30 ft. high, often wide spreading and bushy. Flower clusters 6-10 in. long in late spring. Like Scotch laburnum it has a weeping variety, 'Pendulum'.

L. watereri. A hybrid between the two preceding species, it has flower clusters 10-20 in. long. Most widely grown variety is 'Vossii', most graceful of the lot.

LACEBARK. See Brachychiton, Hoheria

LACHENALIA. CAPE COWSLIP. Bulb. Hardy outdoors only in Zones 17, 24; usually grown in pots indoors or in greenhouses. Native to South Africa. Strap-shaped, succulent leaves, often brown-spotted. Tubular, pendulous flowers in spikes on thick, fleshy stems; bloom in winter, early spring. Plant in August-September; put 6 bulbs in a 5-6-in. pot; set 1-1½ in. deep to prevent flowering stems from falling over. Water, keep cool and dark until roots form and leaves appear. When growth becomes active, water thoroughly, bring plants into light. Grow cool (50° night temperature). Feed when flower spikes show. When leaves start to yellow, gradually dry out plants. Keep dry until time to repot.

L. bulbifera (*L. pendula*). Basal leaves to 2 in. wide. Flowers 1½ in. long, coral red and yellow, purple-tipped, in spikes 12-15 in. tall. 'Superba', improved form, has orange-red flowers.

L. tricolor. Flowers yellow, inner segments tipped red, outer tipped green, on stems 1 ft. or less high. Leaves usually 2 to a plant, about 1 in. wide, about as tall or taller than flower stems. Variety 'Aurea' is bright orange-yellow; Variety 'Nelsonii' bright yellow tinged green.

LADY-OF-THE-NIGHT. See Brassavola nodosa

LADY SLIPPER. See Cypripedium, Paphiopedilum

LAELIA. Epiphytic orchids. Outdoors with protection Zones 16, 17, 21-24; greenhouse or indoors in winter elsewhere. All types listed below native to Mexico. Cattleya-type foliage and flowers. Blooms produced on long arching stems; flowers open in succession, stretching the bloom period to a month or more. Plants perform best in filtered shade. Grow on slab of tree bark or tree fern (hapuu) or in media used for cattleyas. Tack slabs on wall in patio, hang from tree trunk, or grow in pots on patio. During summer feed several times with fish emulsion or fertilizer packaged especially for orchids. Let potting medium dry out between waterings.

L. albida. Transparent white, 2-in. flowers with yellow rib in throat, lavender flush in lip. Bloom 2 to 8 on stem in winter and early spring. Fragrant. Oval 1-2-in.-high pseudobulbs topped by pair of narrow leaves.

L. anceps. Rose violet flowers to 4 in. across with yellow throat lined purple. Blooms 2 to 6 on stem in autumn and winter. Four-sided pseudobulb 3-5 in. high bearing one, sometimes two, 5-9-in.-long leaves. Repot plants as infrequently as possible.

L. autumnalis. Rose purple, 4-in. flowers with white at base of lip. Fragrant blooms 3 to 9 on erect stem in fall and winter. Pseudobulbs 2-4 in. high bear 2 to 3 leathery, 4-8-in.-long leaves.

LAGENARIA. See Gourd

LAGERSTROEMIA. Deciduous trees or shrubs. Noteworthy for spectacular show of flowers in summer and early fall.

L. indica. CRAPE MYRTLE. Shrub or tree. Root-hardy and sometimes treated as a perennial in Zones 1-3; hardy in Zones 4-6 but doesn't flower freely except in hottest summers; excellent in Zones 7-9, 12-14, 18-21; generally a shrub in Zones 10, 11; mildew is a serious problem in Zones 15-17, 22-24. Native to China. Dwarf shrubby forms and shrub-tree forms 6-30 ft. are available. Slow growing as shrub, spreads wide as high; trained as a tree, becomes vase-shaped with most attractive trunk and branch pattern. Smooth gray or light brown bark flakes off to reveal a smooth pinkish inner bark.

Spring foliage light green tinged bronzy-red; mature leaves 1-2 in. long, oval, deep glossy green. Fall foliage yellow, more rarely orange to red. Crinkled, crepelike, 1½-in. flowers in rounded, slightly conical clusters 6-12 in. long at ends of branches; smaller clusters form lower down on branches. Colors in shades of red, rose, pink, rosy orchid, purple, soft pink, white. Long flowering period, July-September.

L

Climate Zone maps pages 8-27

Plant in full sun; feed moderately; water infrequently but deeply. Where soil is alkaline or water high in salts, treat chlorosis or marginal leaf burn by occasional leaching and applications of iron. Check mildew with sprays just before plants bloom. Prune in dormant season to increase flowering wood the next summer. With dwarf shrub forms, remove spent flower clusters and prune out small twiggy growth. With large shrubs and trees cut back branches 12-18 in.

Many color selections are available in bush form and trained as trees. In the whites: 'White', 'Glendora White'; in the pinks: 'Shell Pink', 'Pink'; reds: 'Durant Red', 'Gray's Red', 'Rubra', 'Watermelon Red', 'Watermelon Red Improved'; other colors: 'Lavender', 'Purple', 'Select Purple', 'Majestic Orchid'. These are the dwarfer, shrubby forms (to 5-7 ft.): 'Petite Embers' (rose red), 'Petite Orchid', 'Petite Pinkie', 'Petite Snow', 'Snow White'.

L. speciosa (*L. reginae*). QUEEN CRAPE MYRTLE. Zones 22-24. A 60-ft. tree in the tropics; here, in warmest winter areas a large shrub or small tree 10-20 ft. Leaves leathery, dark green, 3-4 or more in. long. Large (to 3½-in.) light lavender flowers in big, heavy clusters, July-September.

LAGUNARIA patersonii. PRIMROSE TREE, COW ITCH TREE. Evergreen tree. Zones 13, 15-24. Native South Pacific and Australia. Rather fast growth to 20-40 ft. Young trees pyramidal, old trees sometimes spreading, flat topped. Densely foliaged. Leaves thick, oval, olive green, gray beneath, 2-4 in. long. Flowers, hibiscuslike, 2-in. wide, pink to rose, fading nearly white in summer. Brown seed capsules hang on for a long time; they are covered with short, stiff hairs which irritate the skin. Flower arrangers like them because the capsules split into 5 sections revealing bright brown seeds.

Foliage burns at 25° but recovers quickly. Tolerates wide variety of soils and growing conditions. Resists ocean wind, salt spray; tolerates soils and heat of low deserts. Best flowering under coastal conditions. Plant individually as garden tree or in groups as showy windbreak or screen.

LAMB'S EARS. See Stachys

LAMPRANTHUS. See Ice Plant

LANCE WOOD. See Pseudopanax crassifolium

LANTANA. Evergreen and deciduous vining shrubs. Seldom freeze in Zones 13, 17, 23, 24. May freeze but recover quickly in Zones 12, 15, 16, 18-22. In Zones 8, 9, 14 often persist, but may need replacement after a hard winter. Elsewhere, an annual. Valued for profuse show of color over a long season—every month in the year in frost-free areas.

Not particular as to soil. Plant in full sun. Subject to mildew in shade or continued overcast. Prune hard in spring to remove dead wood and prevent woodiness. Water deeply but infrequently, feed lightly. Much water and fertilizer cuts down on bloom. Watch for infestations of aphids, spider mites, whiteflies. Shrubby kinds used as substitutes for annuals in planting beds or containers, as low hedges, foundation shrubs. Spreading kinds excellent bank covers. Effective spilling from raised beds, planter boxes, hanging baskets. Crushed foliage has strong pungent odor that is objectionable to some people.

L. camara. One species used in development of kinds sold at nurseries. Coarse, upright to 6 ft. Rough, dark green leaves. Flowers in 1-2-in. clusters, yellow, orange, or red.

L. montevidensis (*L. sellowiana*). The other species used in cross breeding. This one is sold at nurseries. A little hardier than *L. camara*. It's a well-known ground cover whose branches may trail to as much as 3 or even 6 ft. Dark green leaves 1 in. long, with coarsely toothed edges; sometimes tinged red or purplish, especially in cold weather. Rosy lilac flowers in 1-1½-in.-wide clusters. A white-flowered variety is sold as 'Velutina White'.

The following list gives some of the named kinds of lantana that are available. Some are merely forms of *L. camara*, or hybrids between the forms. Others are hybrids between *L. camara* and *L. montevidensis*.

'Carnival'. 1½-2 ft. by 4 ft. Pink, yellow, crimson, lavender.
'Christine'. To 6 ft. tall, 5 ft. wide, cerise pink. Can be trained into a small patio tree.
'Confetti'. To 2-3 ft. by 6-8 ft. Yellow, pink and purple.
'Cream Carpet'. To 2-3 ft. by 6-8 ft. Cream with bright yellow throat.
'Dwarf Pink'. To 2-4 ft. by 3-4 ft. Light pink. Rather tender.
'Dwarf White'. To 2-4 ft. by 3-4 ft.
'Dwarf Yellow'. To 2-4 ft. and as wide as high.
'Gold Mound'. To 1½-2 ft. by 6 ft. Yellowish orange.
'Golden Glow'. To 2 ft. by 3 ft. Golden yellow.
'Irene'. To 3 ft. by 4 ft. Compact. Magenta with lemon yellow.
'Kathleen'. To 2 ft. by 5-6 ft. Blend of soft rose and gold.
'Moonglow'. To 2 ft. by 4 ft. Soft yellow.
'Orange'. To 4 ft. by 3 ft.
'Pink Frolic'. To 2-3 ft. by 6-8 ft. Pink and yellow.
'Radiation'. To 3-5 ft. by 3-5 ft. Rich orange-red. Try it as a staked small patio tree.
'Spreading Sunset'. To 2-3 ft. by 6-8 ft. Vivid orange-red.
'Spreading Sunshine'. To 2-3 ft. by 6-8 ft. Bright yellow.
'Sunburst'. To 2-3 ft. by 6-8 ft. Bright golden yellow.
'Tangerine'. To 2-3 ft. by 6-8 ft. Burnt orange.

LANTERN, CHINESE. See Abutilon

LANTERN PLANT, CHINESE. See Physalis alkekengi

LAPAGERIA rosea. CHILEAN BELLFLOWER. Evergreen vine. Zones 5, 6, 15-17, 23, 24. The national flower of Chile. Likes high humidity, moderate summer temperatures. Slender stems twine to 10-20 ft. Leaves glossy, leathery, oval, to 4 in. long. Blooms scattered through late spring, summer, and fall. Beautiful, 3-in.-long, rosy red, pendant, bell-shaped flowers (frequently spotted with white), have unusually heavy, waxy substance; hold up as long as 2 weeks after cutting. Give it partial shade, wind protection, loose soil with plenty of peat moss, ground bark, or sawdust, and ample water. Protect from snails and slugs.

LARCH. See Larix

LARCH, GOLDEN. See Chrysolarix

LARIX. LARCH. Deciduous conifers. Slender pyramids with horizontal branches and drooping branchlets. Needles (½-1½ in. long) soft to touch, in fluffy tufts. Woody, roundish cones, ½-1½ in. long, are scattered all along the branchlets. Notable for spring and fall color, and winter pattern. In spring, new needle tufts are pale green and new cones bright purple-red. In fall, needles turn brilliant yellow and orange before dropping. Winter interest is enhanced by many cones which create a delightful polka dot pattern against the sky. Not particular as to soils; accept lawn watering. Not for warm winter climates. Plant with dark evergreen conifers as background or near water for reflection.

L. decidua (*L. europaea*). EUROPEAN LARCH. Zones 1-9, 14-17. Moderate to fast growth to 30-60 ft. Summer color is a grass green, lighter than other species.

L. laricina. ALPINE LARCH. Zones 1-7. Native to British Columbia, both sides of Cascades in Washington. Does not take to lowland gardens. To 60 ft.

L. leptolepis. JAPANESE LARCH. Zones 1-9, 14-19. Fast growing to 60 ft. or more. Summer foliage color a soft bluish green. Most frequently planted larch in the West. Can be dwarfed in containers.

L. occidentalis. WESTERN LARCH. Zones 1-7. Native to British Columbia, Cascades of Washington to Columbia River, eastern Oregon, northern Rocky Mountains. Needles sharp and stiff. Grows to 150-200 ft. as a timber tree, 30-50 ft. in gardens.

LARKSPUR. See Delphinium ajacis

LARREA divaricata (*L. tridentata*). CREOSOTE BUSH. Evergreen shrub. Zones 10-13, 19. One of the commonest native shrubs in deserts of southeastern California, Arizona, southern Utah, Texas, northern Mexico. Grows with many upright branches 4-8 ft. high. Straggly and open in shallow dry soil. Attractive, dense, rounded but spreading where water accumulates. Leathery, yellow-green to dark green leaves divided into 2 tiny crescents ⅜ in. long. Gummy secretion makes leaves look varnished and yields a distinctive creosote odor, especially after a rain. Small yellow flowers off and on all year, followed by small roundish fruits covered with shiny white or rusty hairs. With water and fertilizer, grows taller, more dense, with larger shiny dark green leaves. Use as wind or privacy screens, or trim into more formal hedge.

LATHYRUS. Annual vines or bushlike, perennial vine. In this group is one of the best known garden flower producers—the delightfully fragrant and colorful sweet pea.

You will find through this book flower descriptions that say "sweet pea-shaped" or "sweet pealike". The flower of the sweet pea is typical of many members of the pea family (Leguminosae). This means that each flower has 1 large, upright, roundish petal (banner or standard), 2 narrow side petals (wings), and 2 lower petals that are somewhat united, forming a boat-shaped structure (keel).

L

Climate Zone maps pages 8-27

L. latifolius. PERENNIAL SWEET PEA. All Zones. Strong growing vine, up to 9 ft., with blue-green foliage. Flowers usually reddish purple, often white or rose. Straight colors —white and rose—sometimes sold. Long bloom season, June to September, if not allowed to go to seed. Plants grow with little care. May escape and become naturalized. Use as bank cover, trailing over rocks, on trellis, fence.

L. odoratus. SWEET PEA. Bears many spikelike clusters of crisp-looking flowers with a clean-sweet fragrance, in straight colors and mixtures. Color mixtures include deep rose, blue, purple, scarlet, white, cream, amethyst on white ground, salmon, salmon pink on cream. Sweet peas make magnificent cut flowers in quantity. Bush types offer cut flowers the same as vine types, and require no training.

To hasten germination, soak seeds for a few hours before planting. Treat seed with a fungicide. Sow seeds 1 in. deep and 1-2 in. apart. When seedlings are 4-5 in. high, thin to not less than 6 in. apart. Pinch out tops to encourage strong side branches. Where climate prevents early planting or soil is too wet to work, start 3-4 seeds in 2¼-3-in. peat pots, indoors or in a protected place, and set out when weather has settled. Plant 1 ft. apart, thinning to 1 strong plant. This method is ideal for bush types. Protect young seedlings from birds with a wire screen. Set out bait for slugs and snails. Never let vines lack for water. Soak heavily when you water. Cut flowers at least every other day and remove all seed pods.

For vining sweet peas, provide a trellis, strings, or wire before planting. Seedlings need support as soon as tendrils form. Free standing trellis running north and south is best. When planting against fence or wall keep supports away from wall to give air circulation.

Here is a special method of soil preparation—not essential but producing most perfect flowers on extra long stems: Dig a trench 12-18 in. deep. Mix 1 part peat moss, ground bark, or sawdust to 2 parts of soil. Add a complete commercial fertilizer according to label directions as you mix. Backfill the trench with the mix. This extra deep digging is not necessary in good garden soils. Regular monthly feeding with commercial fertilizer will keep vines vigorous and productive.

The many varieties of vine-type sweet peas are best understood if grouped by time of bloom.

Early flowering. (Early Flowering Multi-flora, Early Multiflora, formerly Early Spencers.) The name "Spencer" has been dropped by all seed growers. It described a type of frilled flowers (wavy petals) that is now characteristic of almost all varieties. The "Multiflora" indicates that the plants carry more flowers per stem than the old "Spencers". The value of the Early Flowering varieties is that they will bloom in midwinter when days are short. (Spring and summer-flowering types will not bloom until days have lengthened to 15 hours or more.) Where winter temperatures are mild (Zones 13, 17, 21-24), sow seeds in August or early September for late December or January bloom. Use these varieties for forcing in greenhouse. They are not heat-resistant. Generally sold in mixed colors.

Spring flowering. (Spring Flowering Heat-Resistant Cuthbertson Type, Cuthbertson's Floribunda. Floribunda—Zvolanek strain.) Seeds are packed in both mixtures and straight color named varieties. Wide color range: pink, lavender, purple, white, cream, rose, salmon, cerise, carmine, red, blue. Two advances in sweet peas are indicated in these names: "Cuthbertson" means heat-resistant; "Floribunda" means flowers on a stem have increased from 3-4 to 5-7.

In Zones 7-9, 12-24 plant between October and early January. Elsewhere, February to April, or just as soon as the soil can be worked.

Summer flowering. (Galaxy, Plenti-flora.) Available in named varieties and mixtures in wide color range. Heat-resistant, they bloom from early summer on. Large flowers, 5-7 on long stems. Heat-resistance is relative; not enough for Zones 7-15, 18-21.

Bush type. The so-called bush type sweet peas are strong vines with predetermined growth, heights. Unlike vining types that reach 5 ft. and more, these stop their upward growth at 12-30 in.

Bijou. To 12 in. Full color range in mixtures and straight varieties. Flowers 4-5 on 5-7-in. stems. Useful and spectacular in borders, beds, window boxes, containers. Not as heat-resistant or as long stemmed as Knee-Hi, performs better in containers.

Knee-Hi. To 30 in. Large, long-stemmed flowers 5-6 to the stem. Has all the virtues and color range of Cuthbertson Floribundas in self-supporting, bush-type vines. Provides cutting-type flowers in mass display in beds and borders. Growth will exceed 30 in. where planting bed joins fence or wall. Keep in open area for uniform height. Follow same planting dates as spring flowering sweet peas.

Sweet pea flowers. Broad petal above is banner. Below are wings, keel.

LAUREL, CALIFORNIA. See Umbellularia

LAUREL, ENGLISH. See Prunus laurocerasus

LAUREL, GRECIAN. See Laurus

LAUREL, MOUNTAIN. See Kalmia latifolia

LAUREL, NEW ZEALAND. See Corynocarpus

LAUREL, PALE. See Kalmia polifolia

LAUREL, PORTUGAL. See Prunus lusitanica

LAUREL, SHEEP. See Kalmia angustifolia

LAUREL, SIERRA. See Leucothoe davisiae

LAUREL, SPURGE. See Daphne laureola

LAUREL, TEXAS MOUNTAIN. See Sophora secundiflora

LAUREL CHERRY, CAROLINA. Prunus caroliniana

LAURUS nobilis. SWEET BAY, GRECIAN LAUREL. Evergreen tree or shrub. Zones 6-10, 12-24. Slow growth to 12-40 ft. Natural habit a compact, broad-based, often multi-stemmed, gradually tapering cone. Leaves leathery, aromatic, oval, 2-4 in. long, dark green; the traditional bay leaf of cookery. Clusters of small, yellow flowers, followed by ½-1-in. long black or dark purple berries.

Not fussy about soil, but needs good drainage; requires little water when established. In hot-summer climates, best in filtered shade or afternoon shade. Spray for black scale. Tends to sucker heavily. Dense habit makes it a good large background shrub or small tree. Takes well to clipping into formal shapes—globes, cones, topiary shapes, standards, or hedges. A classic formal container plant.

LAURUSTINUS. See Viburnum tinus

LAVANDULA. LAVENDER. Evergreen shrubs or subshrubs. Native to Mediterranean region. Prized for fragrant lavender or purple flowers used for perfume, sachets. Gray or gray-green aromatic foliage. Plant as hedge, edging, or in herb gardens; in borders with plants needing similar conditions—cistus, helianthemum, nepeta, rosemary, santolina, verbena.

All need full sun; loose, fast-draining soil. Little water or fertilizer. Prune immediately after bloom to keep plants compact, neat. For sachets, cut flower clusters or strip flowers from stems just as color shows; dry in a cool, shady place.

L. dentata. FRENCH LAVENDER. Zones 8, 9, 12-24. To 3 ft. tall. Bright green, narrow leaves, 1-1½ in. long, with square-toothed edges. Lavender-purple flowers in short spikelike clusters topped with a tuft of petal-like bracts. In mild-winter areas, blooms almost continually.

L. latifolia. SPIKE LAVENDER. Zones 4-24. Much like English lavender in appearance, but with broader leaves and flower stalks frequently branched.

L. spica (*L. officinalis, L. vera*). ENGLISH LAVENDER. All Zones. Most widely planted. Classic lavender used for perfume and sachets. To 3-4 ft. high and across. Leaves gray, smooth on margins, narrow, to 2 in. long. Flowers lavender, ½ in. long, on 18-24-in.-long spikes in July-August. Dwarf varieties: 'Compacta' ('Compacta Nana'), to 8 in. tall, 12-15 in. wide; 'Hidcote', slow growing to 1 ft. tall, deep purple flowers; 'Munstead', most popular dwarf, 18 in. tall, with deep lavender-blue flowers a month earlier than *L. spica;* 'Twickel Purple', 2-3 ft. high, with purple flowers in fanlike clusters on extra long spikes.

L. stoechas. SPANISH LAVENDER. Zones 4-24. Stocky plant 1½-3 ft. tall with narrow, gray leaves ½ in. long. Flowers dark purple, about ⅛ in. long, in dense, short spikes topped with a tuft of large purple petal-like bracts. Bloom in early summer.

LAVATERA. TREE MALLOW. Annuals, shrubs. Flowers resemble single hollyhocks.

L. arborea. Zones 14-24. Southern European plant naturalized along northern California coast. Evergreen shrub to 15 ft. tall. Maplelike leaves have 5-9 lobes and scalloped edges. Flowers purplish red with darker veins, 2 in. across, June-July. There is variety with white-variegated leaves.

L. assurgentiflora. Zones 14-24. Native to Channel Islands, but naturalized on California coastal mainland. Erect shrub to 12 ft., or treelike. Maplelike leaves 3-5 in. long, lobed and toothed. Rosy lavender flowers 2-3 in. wide, almost throughout the year, heaviest April-August. Resists drought, wind, salt spray. Use as fast-growing windbreak hedge. Will reach 5-10 ft. and bloom first year from seed. Shear to keep dense.

L. trimestris. ANNUAL MALLOW. Annual. To 3-6 ft. from spring-sown seed. Leaves roundish, angled on upper part of plant, toothed. Flowers satiny, to 4 in. across; named varieties in white, pink, rosy carmine. July-September bloom if spent flowers are removed to halt seed production. Thin seedlings to allow ample room to spread. Colorful summer hedge or background planting. Needs sun.

LAVENDER. See Lavandula

LAVENDER COTTON. See Santolina chamaecyparissus

LAVENDER MIST. See Thalictrum rochebrunianum

LAYIA platyglossa. TIDYTIPS. Annual. California native. Member of sunflower family. Often obtained in mixed wildflower packets, or from dealers in seeds of native plants. Rapid growth to 5-8 in. high. Flower heads about 2 in. across; the rays are light yellow with neatly marked white tips. Can grow in rather heavy soil. Plant in full sun.

LEEK. An onion relative that doesn't form a distinct bulb. The edible bottoms resemble long fat green onions and have a mild flavor. Leeks need a very rich soil. Best in cool weather. Sow in early spring (in cold-winter areas, sow indoors and set out plants in June or July). When plants have made considerable top growth, draw soil up around the fat, round stems to make the bottoms white and mild. Do not let soil into bases of the leaves. Begin to harvest in late autumn. Where winters are cold, dig plants with roots and plant them closely in boxes of soil in a cool but frost-free location. Where winters are mild, dig as needed from late fall until spring.

LEIOPHYLLUM buxifolium. BOX SAND MYRTLE. Evergreen shrub. Zones 4-7, 14-17. Native to eastern U.S. Neat, compact growth to 2 ft. Upright branches densely clothed with dark green, glossy, oval to roundish leaves about ½ in. long, half as wide. Foliage takes on a bronzy cast in the fall. Flowers (May-June) ¼ in. wide, white or pinkish from rosy pink buds, in inch-wide clusters. Long stamens have pinkish-brown anthers. Give it azalea culture, and combine with other acid-loving plants. *L. b. prostratum* is a more compact form.

LEMAIREOCEREUS thurberi. ORGANPIPE CACTUS. Zones 12-24. Native to Arizona, Mexico. Columnar, treelike cactus branching from base (also from top, if injured). Dark green or gray-green stems, with 12-17 ribs, grow slowly to 15 ft. Spines black, ½-1 in. long. Purplish, white-edged, 3-in. flowers May-June. Night-blooming. Fruit

1½ in. long, olive green, filled with sweet red pulp, edible.

LEMON. See Citrus

LEMONADE BERRY. See Rhus integrifolia

LEMON-SCENTED GUM. See Eucalyptus citriodora

LEONOTIS leonurus. LION'S TAIL. Perennial. Zones 8-24. Shrubby, branching, 3-6 ft. with hairy stems. Leaves 2-5 in. long, with coarsely toothed edges. Tubular, 2-in.-long flowers, in dense whorls, deep orange, covered with fine furlike hairs. Blooms in summer. Plant in full sun. Drought resistant. Striking if kept well groomed.

LEONTOPODIUM alpinum. ALPINE EDELWEISS. Perennial. Zones 1-9, 14-24. Short-lived, white-woolly plants 4-12 in. high, with small flower heads closely crowded on tips of stems and surrounded by a collar of slender white, woolly leaves radiating out from below the flower heads like the arms of a starfish. The tiny bracts of the flower heads, also white and woolly, are tipped with black. Blooms June-July. Sun, plenty of water, and excellent drainage. Seeds germinate easily.

LEOPARD PLANT. See Farfugium

LEOPARDS BANE. See Doronicum

LEPTOSPERMUM. TEA TREE. Evergreen shrubs or small trees. Zones 15-24. Native to Australia and New Zealand. Soft and casual looking (never rigid or formal)—partly because of branching habit. Substantial, useful landscape structure plants the year around. All make a springtime display of flowers along stems among small leaves. The flowers (white, pink, or red) are basically alike: about ½ in. wide with petals arranged around hard, central cone or cup. The single flowers look like tiny single roses. Petals fall to leave goblet-shaped seed capsules about ¼ in. wide.

Tolerate a fair amount of dryness, need good soil drainage and full sun. Subject to chlorosis in alkaline soils. Apparently pest-free above ground; sometimes succumb quickly to root troubles where drainage is poor. All take some surface shearing but in real pruning cut back only to side branches, never into bare wood. Called "tea tree" because Captain Cook brewed leaves of *L. scoparium* into tea to prevent scurvy among his crew.

Australian tea tree has graceful branches, rugged picturesque trunk (or trunks).

L. citratum (*L. citrinum*). Refined shrub or small tree with weeping see-through form (similar in form to *Callistemon viminalis* but smaller and fuller bodied). Attractive bark. Leaves pale green, oblong, ¾ in. wide, 1½ in. long. Strong lemon scent from crushed leaves. White single flowers.

L. flavescens 'Citriodora'. Shrub to 6-12 ft. high (occasionally to 20 ft.), upright and partially weeping. Leaves light green, oblong, to ½ in. wide and ¾ in. long. Flowers white. Lemon scent in crushed leaves but not as strong as in *L. citratum*.

L. laevigatum. AUSTRALIAN TEA TREE. Large shrub or small tree. To 30 ft. high, often as wide. Lives long and well with little care if soil conditions right (well drained, slightly acid). Oval or teardrop shaped leaves to ⅜ in. wide, 1 in. long, dull green to gray-green. The plant has two basic uses and the uses determine its appearance:

(1) Solitary plants allowed to grow full size develop picturesque character with muscular looking, twisted and gracefully curved, shaggy, gray-brown trunks, up to 24 in. diameter at the base. Equally handsome branches range out from the trunk and carry canopies of fine-textured foliage. Some pendulous branches weep down from foliage canopies. Single white flowers appear in great numbers along branches in spring.

(2) Planted close together (1½-6 ft.) to make a thick natural screen or clipped hedge, the plants do not develop any visible branching character but do make a solid bank of fine-textured green foliage, highlighted in spring by white flowers.

L. l. 'Compactum'. Similar to above but smaller—to 8 ft. high, 6 ft. wide—and slightly more open and loose. Does not flower as heavily as *L. laevigatum.*

L. l. 'Reevesii'. The leaves are rounder, slightly bigger and more densely set than on *L. laevigatum,* and plant grows only to 6-7 ft. high and wide. Heavier looking than either of the preceding two kinds.

L. lanigerum (*L. pubescens*). Erect growth to 8-15 ft. high. Noted for silky or downy surfaces on young shoots and on undersides of the dark, gray-green, tiny, narrow leaves (⅛ in. wide, ½ in. long). Flowers white, single, ¾ in. wide, appear singly on short leafy twigs in late spring.

L. rotundifolium. ROUND-LEAFED TEA TREE. Shrub 4-8 ft. high with dense growth. Dark green leaves are roundish ovals, ½ in. long, ⅜ in. wide. Heavy spring display of 1-in.-wide, apple-blossom pink, single flowers.

L. scoparium. NEW ZEALAND TEA TREE, MANUKA. Ground covers to large shrubs. The true species *L. scoparium* is of no interest in Western U.S. but its many varieties are valuable. These are not as bold of form or quite as serviceable in hedges and screens as the kinds listed above but they have showier flowers. Leaves are tiny (from almost needlelike and ¼ in. long to ⅛ in. wide and ½ in. long), pointed, densely set. Many flowers in spring or summer.

L. s. 'Boscawenii'. Dwarf shrub to 2 ft. high, 2 ft. wide, extremely compact. Purplish tinged leaves, tightly set (foliage seems stippled in green and purple). White flowers tinged with pink and red, spring.

L. s. 'Florepleno'. Double pale pink flowers on a compact bush. Blooms late winter to early spring, often with repeat bloom in late summer, fall.

Climate Zone maps pages 8-27

L. s. 'Horizontalis'. Ground cover shrub 1 ft. high, 3 ft. wide. Single pink flowers, spring.

L. s. 'Keatleyi'. Tallest (6-10 ft.) most open and rangy of the *L. scoparium* varieties—most inclined to develop picturesque habit. Single pink flowers, paler at edges, are extra large, sometimes as big as a quarter. Spring bloom, may repeat in summer.

L. s. 'Nanum'. Low, rounded shrub to 2 ft. high. Single flowers light pink, darker at center.

L. s. 'Pompon'. Compact to 6-8 ft. high. Many double pink flowers in late spring or summer. Dark green foliage.

L. s. 'Red Damask'. To 6-8 ft., dense in habit, double ruby red flowers, red-tinged leaves. Heavy bloom midwinter to spring.

L. s. 'Ruby Glow'. Compact, upright 6-8-ft. shrub with dark foliage, double, oxblood red flowers (¾ in. wide) in great profusion (entire shrub looks red) in winter, spring.

L. s. 'Scarlet Carnival'. Compact, to 6-8 ft., abundance of large, medium red, double flowers on long stems, late spring. Some red in leaves.

L. s. 'Snow Flurry'. Tall, spreading, 6-8 ft. high. Very double, white flowers with green eye, spring. Leaves tinged red.

L. s. 'Snow White'. Spreading compact plant 2-4 ft. high. Medium-sized double white flowers with green centers December-spring.

L. s. 'Waerengi'. Low, spreading ground cover shrub to 8-12 in. high, 18-24 in. wide. Many soft, pliant, arching twigs, reddish tinged. Soft, densely set leaves. Scattering of single, pale pink flowers in spring.

LETTUCE. Indispensable salad plant and easy to grow. A cool-season crop, but in all except the hottest summer areas it is possible to have some sort of lettuce throughout the frost-free period. There are four principle types.

Crisphead or heading lettuce is the most familiar kind in markets, the most exasperating for the home gardener to produce. Heads best when monthly average temperatures are around 55-60°. In cool coastal areas it does well over a long season; inland, timing becomes critical. Best varieties: various strains of 'Great Lakes', 'Imperial', and 'Iceberg'.

Butterhead or Boston types have loose heads with green, smooth outer leaves and yellow inner leaves. Good varieties: 'Bibb' ('Limestone'), 'Big Boston', and 'Buttercrunch'. 'Mignonette' stands heat without bolting quickly.

Loose-leaf lettuce makes rosettes rather than heads, stands heat better than the others, is summer mainstay in warm climates. Choice selections: 'Black-seeded Simpson', 'Oak Leaf', 'Slobolt', 'Prizehead' or 'Ruby' (red-tinged varieties), and 'Salad Bowl', with deeply-cut leaves.

Romaine lettuce has erect, cylindrical heads of smooth leaves, the outer green, the inner whitish. Stands heat moderately well. Try 'White Paris', 'Parris Island', 'Dark Green Cos', or 'Valmaine'.

Loose, well drained soil; (in hot-summer areas light shading in mid-day helps). Water regularly, feed lightly and frequently. Sow in open ground at 10-day intervals, starting after frost as soon as soil is workable. Plant seed ½ in. deep; space rows 18 in. apart. Thin head lettuce or romaine to 12 in. apart, moving seedlings with care to extend the plantings. Leaf lettuce can be grown 4 in. apart; harvest some whole plants as they begin to crowd.

In milder climates, make later sowings in late summer, fall. Where summers are very short, sow indoors, move seedlings outdoors after last frost. Control snails, slugs, earwigs with bait *on the ground*—not on the plants. Harvest when heads or leaves are of good size; lettuce doesn't stand long before going to seed, becoming quite bitter in the process.

LEUCADENDRON argenteum. SILVER TREE. Evergreen tree or large shrub. Zones 17, 20-24. Young trees (the most spectacular in effect) narrow and stiffly upright, mature trees spreading, with tortuous, gray-barked trunk, irregular silhouette. Can reach 40 ft. Silky, silvery white leaves 3-6 in. long densely cover the branches.

Needs fast draining soil; will not thrive in clay, alkaline soil, or soil with animal manure. Needs sunlight and humid air; takes ocean winds but not dry winds. Striking appearance and cultural problems make it hard to use. Small plants are picturesque container subjects for 3-4 years. Larger plants effective on slopes with boulders, suculents, pines in sheltered seaside gardens. Use singly or in groups.

LEUCOCORYNE ixioides. GLORY OF THE SUN. Bulb. Zones 13, 16, 19, 21-24. Native to Chile. Closely related to *Brodiaea*. Narrow, grasslike leaves to 1 ft. Slender, wiry stems 12-18 in. high, bear 4-6 lavender-blue, white-centered, beautifully scented flowers, 2 in. across; blooms in March-April. Variety 'Odorata' deep lilac and white blooms, very fragrant, is usually offered. In mild-winter climates use in rock gardens or naturalize in sections that get little summer watering. Use with ixia, sparaxis, freesia, tritonia, or grow in pots like freesias. Excellent, long lasting cut flowers.

Outdoors, plant bulbs in fall 6 in. deep, 3-4 in. apart in sun, in light, perfectly drained soil. Give ample water until after bloom, then let bulbs dry out. Bulbs tend to move downward in the soil; confine them by planting in containers or laying wire screen across bottom of planting area.

LEUCOJUM. SNOWFLAKE. Bulb. Strap-shaped leaves and nodding, bell-shaped

Snowflake (left), snowdrop (Galanthus) are similar. Note differences in flower shape.

white flowers with segments tipped green. Easy and permanent. Naturalize under deciduous trees, in shrub borders, orchards, or cool slopes. Plant 4 in. deep in fall. Do not disturb until really crowded; then dig, divide, and replant after foliage dies down.

L. aestivum. SUMMER SNOWFLAKE. All Zones. Most commonly grown. Leaves 12-18 in. long. Stems 18 in. long carry 3-5 flowers; variety 'Gravetye Giant' has as many as 9 flowers to a stem. In mild-winter areas blooms November through winter; flowers with narcissus in colder areas.

L. vernum. SPRING SNOWFLAKE. Zones 1-6; not successful in hot, dry climates. Leaves 9 in. long. Stems 1 ft. tall bear a single large, nodding, white flower. Very early spring (late winter in warmer areas). Needs a rich moist soil.

LEUCOPHYLLUM frutescens (*L. texanum*). TEXAS RANGER. Evergreen shrub. Zones 7-24. Native to Texas and Mexico. Compact, slow-growing, silvery-foliaged shrub to 5-12 ft. tall, 4-6 ft. wide. Does well in desert areas, taking any degree of heat and wind. Tolerates some alkali if drainage is good. Thrives with little water near the sea, but needs heat to produce its rose-purple, 1-in.-long, bell-shaped summer flowers. Useful either as a round-headed gray mass, as a clipped hedge, or in mixed dry plantings. Variety 'Compacta' is a smaller, denser selection.

LEUCOTHOE. Evergreen shrubs. Related to *Pieris*. All have leathery leaves and clusters of urn-shaped white flowers. Need acid, woodsy, deep soil and some shade, do best in woodland gardens or as facing for taller broad-leafed evergreens. Best used in masses; not especially attractive individually. Bronze-tinted winter foliage a bonus.

L. axillaris. Zones 4-7, 15-17. Native to eastern U. S. Very like *L. fontanesiana*, but with shorter-stalked, sharply-pointed leaves.

L. davisiae. SIERRA LAUREL. Zones 4-7, 15-17. Upright shrub to 3½ ft. Leaves oblong or egg-shaped, to 3 in. long, glossy rich green. Flowers white, in erect clusters 2-4 in. long. Blooms in summer. Grows in bogs and wet places in the Sierra Nevada, Trinity, and Siskiyou mountains.

L. fontanesiana (*L. catesbaei*). DROOPING LEUCOTHOE. Zones 4-7, 15-17. Borderline hardiness in Zones 1-3. Native to eastern U. S. Slow grower to 2-6 ft., the branches arching gracefully. Leathery, 3-6 in.-long leaves turn bronzy purple in fall (bronzy green, in deep shade). Spreads from underground stems. Drooping clusters of creamy white, lily-of-the-valleylike flowers in spring. Variety 'Rainbow', with leaves marked yellow, green, and pink, grows 3-4 ft. tall.

Can be controlled in height to make an 18-in. ground cover in shade; just cut older, taller stems to ground. Branches cut in bloom are decorative.

L. keiskei. Zones 3-6, 15-17. Native to Japan. Slow growth to 3 ft. Leaves to 3 in. long. Flower clusters short, with rather few (3-6), rather large (½-in.) flowers in spring.

LEVISTICUM officinale. LOVAGE. Perennial. All Zones. This herb is sometimes grown for its celery-flavored seeds, leaves, and stems. Reaches 2-3, even 6 ft., with cut and divided, glossy, deep green leaves. Flattish clusters of greenish yellow, small flowers. Ordinary garden care suits it. Grow from seeds or divisions.

LEWISIA. Perennials. Zones 1-7. Beautiful, often difficult plants for rock gardens, collections of alpine plants. Of many offered by specialists two are outstanding:

L. rediviva. BITTERROOT. Native to mountains of the West. State flower of Montana. Fleshy roots; short stems with short, succulent, strap-shaped leaves to 2 in. long that usually die back before flowers appear (seemingly from the bare earth) in spring. Flowers look like 2-in.-wide rose or white waterlilies. Not difficult if drainage is excellent.

L. tweedyi. Native to mountains, south central Washington. Stunning with big, satiny, salmon pink flowers 1-3 to a stem above the fleshy, evergreen, 4-in. leaves. Must have perfect drainage around root crown to prevent rot. Prune out side growths to keep root crown open to air.

LIATRIS. GAYFEATHER. Perennials. Zones 1-10, 14-24. Native to eastern and central United States. Showy plants. Basal tufts of narrow, grassy leaves grow from a thick, often tuberous rootstock. Tufts lengthen in summer to tall, narrow stems densely set

Flowering clusters of gayfeather (Liatris), 15 in. long, purplish rose, rarely white.

with narrow leaves and topped by a narrow plume of small rosy purple (sometimes white) fluffy flower heads.

They endure heat, cold, drought, and poor soil; are best used in mixed perennial borders. The rosy purple color calls for careful placing.

L. callilepis. Plants grown and sold under this name by Dutch bulb growers are *L. spicata*.

L. scariosa. Grows 1-3 ft. high. Each flower head in the cluster is ½-1 in. wide.

L. spicata. To 6 ft., usually only 2-3 ft., with 15-in.-long flower plumes; each individual flower head is ⅓ in. wide.

LIBOCEDRUS. See Calocedrus

LIGULARIA. See Farfugium

LIGUSTRUM. PRIVET. Deciduous or evergreen shrubs or small trees. Most widely used in hedges. Can also be clipped into formal shapes and featured in tubs or large

pots. One type makes a fine street tree. All have abundant, showy clusters of white to creamy white flowers in late spring or early summer. Fragrance is described as "pleasant" to "unpleasant" (never "wonderful" or "terrible"). Flowers draw bees. On clipped hedges, fewer flowers grow because most of the flower-bearing branches get trimmed off. Small blue-black berrylike fruits follow blossoms. Birds eat the fruits, thus distributing seeds which make privet plants come up like weeds.

Most grow easily in sun or in some shade, and in any soil. Give them lots of water. In some areas they are subject to lilac leaf miner which disfigures the leaves.

Confusion exists in identity of certain privets in nurseries. The one sold as *L. japonicum* usually turns out to be the small tree—*L. lucidum*. The true *L. japonicum* is usually sold as *L. texanum*. Actually two forms of *L. japonicum* are available and sold as *L. texanum*. The tall shrubby kind is the true species; the lower-growing, more densely-foliaged form probably should be called *L. japonicum* 'Texanum'.

L. japonicum. (Often sold as *L. texanum*.) JAPANESE PRIVET, WAXLEAF PRIVET. Evergreen shrub. Zones 4-24. Dense compact growth habit to 10-12 ft., but can be kept lower by trimming. Roundish oval leaves 2-4 in. long, dark to medium green and glossy above, distinctly paler to almost whitish beneath; have a thick slightly spongy feeling. Excellent plants for hedges, screens, or for shaping into globes, pyramids, other shapes, or small standard trees. In areas of caliche soil, or where Texas root rot prevails, grow it in containers.

L. j. 'Rotundifolium' (*L. j.* 'Coriaceum'). Grows to 4-5 ft. and has nearly round leaves to 2½ in. long. Part shade in inland valleys.

L. j. 'Texanum'. Very similar to the species but lower growing to 6-9 ft. and has somewhat denser, lusher foliage.

L. lucidum. GLOSSY PRIVET. Evergreen tree. Zones 5, 6, 8-24. Makes a round-headed tree that eventually reaches 35-40 ft. Can be kept lower as a big shrub, or may form multiple-trunked tree. Leaves 4-6 in. long, taper-pointed, glossy, dark to medium green on both sides; feel leathery but not slightly spongy like *L. japonicum*. Flowers in especially large feathery clusters followed by profusion of fruit. Fine street or lawn tree. Somewhat drought resistant but looks better with water. Can grow in narrow areas. Performs well in large containers. Or plant 10 ft. apart for tall privacy screen.

L. ovalifolium. CALIFORNIA PRIVET. Semideciduous shrub; evergreen only in mildest areas. Zones 4-24. Inexpensive hedge plant, once more widely used in California for hedges, especially variegated form. Grows rapidly to 15 ft., but can be kept sheared to any height. Dark green, oval, 2½-in.-long leaves. Set plants 9-12 in. apart for hedges. Clip early and frequently to encourage low dense branching. Greedy roots. Well-fed, well-watered plants hold leaves longest.

L. o. 'Aureum' (*L. o.* 'Variegatum'). GOLDEN PRIVET. Leaves have broad yellow edge.

L. 'Suwannee River'. Evergreen shrub. All Zones. Reported to be hybrid between

L. japonicum 'Rotundifolium' and *L. lucidum*. Slow growing to 18 in. in 3 years, eventually 3-4 ft.; compact habit. Dark green leaves leathery, somewhat twisted. No fruit produced. Low hedge, foundation planting, containers.

L. vicaryi. VICARY GOLDEN PRIVET. Deciduous shrub. All Zones. This one has yellow leaves—color strongest on plants in full sun. Best planted alone; color does not develop well under hedge shearing.

L. vulgare. COMMON PRIVET. Deciduous shrub. All Zones. To 15 ft., unsheared. Light green leaves less glossy than those of California privet. Clusters of black fruit conspicuous on unpruned or lightly pruned plants. Root system less greedy than California privet. Variety 'Lodense' ('Nanum') is a dense, dwarf form which reaches only 4 ft., with equal spread.

LILAC. See Syringa

LILAC, SUMMER. See Buddleia

LILAC VINE. See Hardenbergia comptoniana

LILAC, WILD. See Ceanothus

LILLY-PILLY TREE. See Acmena

LILIUM. LILY. Bulb. All Zones. Most stately and varied of bulbous plants. For many years only species—the same as plants growing wild in parts of Asia, Europe, and North America—were available; many of these were difficult and unpredictable.

Around 1925 lily growers entered upon a significant breeding program. Using species with desirable qualities, they bred new hybrids and also developed strains and varieties that were healthier, hardier, and easier to grow than the original species. They were able to produce new forms and new colors and, what is more important, they evolved the methods for growing healthy lilies in large quantities. Now, the new forms and new colors are the best garden lilies, but you can still get some desirable species lilies.

Lilies have three basic cultural requirements: (1) a deep, loose, well drained soil; (2) ample moisture the year around—they never stop growing completely; (3) coolness and shade at roots, and sun or filtered shade at tops where the flowers form.

Plant bulbs as soon as possible after you get them. If you must wait, keep them in a cool place until you plant. If bulbs are dry, place them in moist sand or peat moss until scales get plump and new roots begin to sprout.

In coastal fog belts, plant lilies in an open sunny position, but protect them from strong winds. In warmer, drier climates, high or filtered shade is desirable.

If soil is deep, well drained, and contains ample organic material, it will grow good lilies. If it is heavy clay, or very sandy and deficient in organic matter, add peat moss, ground bark, or sawdust. Spread a 3-4-in. layer of such material over the surface; on top of it, broadcast a complete fertilizer (follow label directions for pre-planting application), and thoroughly blend both into the soil as you dig to a depth of at least 12 in.

Before planting bulbs, remove any injured portions, and dust cuts with a disinfectant.

L

Climate Zone maps pages 8-27

For each bulb, dig a generous planting hole (6-12 in. deeper than depth of the bulb). Place enough soil at bottom of hole to bring it up to proper level for the bulb (see below). Set the bulb with its roots spread; fill in the hole with soil, firming it in around the bulb to eliminate air pockets.

Planting depths vary according to the size and rooting habit of the bulb. General rule is to cover smaller bulbs with 2-3 in. of soil; medium-sized bulbs with 3-4 in.; and larger bulbs with 4-6 in. Never cover Madonna lilies with more than 2 in. of soil. Planting depth can be quite flexible. It's better to err by planting shallowly than too deeply. Lily bulbs have contractile roots that draw them down to proper depth. Ideal spacing for lily bulbs is 12 in. apart; you can plant as close as 6 in. apart for a densely massed effect.

After planting, water well, and mulch the area with 2-3 in. of organic material to conserve moisture, keep soil cool, and reduce weed growth.

Lilies need constant moisture to about 6 in. deep. You can reduce watering somewhat after tops turn yellow in fall, but never allow roots to dry out completely. Flooding is preferable to overhead watering, which may help to spread disease spores. Pull weeds by hand if possible; hoeing may injure roots.

Virus or mosaic infection is a problem. No cure exists. To avoid it, buy healthy bulbs from reliable sources. Dig and destroy any lilies that show mottling in leaves or seriously stunted growth. Control aphids, which spread the infection. Control botrytis blight, a fungus disease, with phaltan or captan. Control gophers; they relish lily bulbs.

Remove faded flowers. Wait until stems and leaves turn yellow before you cut them back.

If clumps become too large and crowded, dig, divide, and transplant them in spring or fall. With care, lily clumps can be lifted at any time, even in bloom.

Following are the 16 lily species that are commonly grown in the West:

L. auratum. GOLD-BAND LILY. August or early September bloom on 4-6-ft. plants. Flowers fragrant, waxy white, spotted crimson, with a golden band on each segment. 'Platyphyllum' is the most robust selection. Flowers last better in light shade.

L. candidum. MADONNA LILY. Pure white, fragrant blooms on 3-4-ft. stems in June.

Unlike most lilies, dies down soon after bloom, makes new growth in fall. Plant while dormant in August. Does not have stem roots; set top of bulb only 1-2 in. deep in a sunny location. Subject to diseases that shorten its life. The lily of medieval romance, and a sentimental choice for many gardeners.

L. cernuum. Only 12-20 in. tall, with lilac flowers often dotted dark purple. Summer blooming; perfectly hardy. Sun.

L. concolor. To 2 ft., with 5-7 scarlet, unspotted, star-shaped flowers on wiry stems. Needs full sun and perfect drainage. 'Coridion' is a citron yellow variety.

L. formosanum. Long white Easter lily flowers appear very late. Plant bulbs 5-6 in. deep to allow for heavy stem roots. *L. f. wilsonii* 5-6 ft. tall, blooms October-November (December in mild climates). *L. f. pricei* blooms June-July on 18-in. plants.

L. hansonii. Sturdy lily to 4 ft. or more, with many thick-textured orange flowers spotted brown. June-July. Needs light shade. Highly resistant or immune to virus.

L. henryi. Slender stems to 8-9 ft. topped by 10-20 bright orange flowers with sharply recurved segments. Summer bloom. Best in light shade.

L. humboldtii. HUMBOLDT LILY. Native of open woodlands in Sierra Nevada. Grows 3-6 ft. tall. Nodding, recurved flowers of bright orange with large maroon dots. Early summer bloom.

L. japonicum. Deep pink to purple, fragrant, trumpet-shaped blooms on 2-3-ft. stems in July. 'Platyfolium' is the best variety.

L. lancifolium (*L. tigrinum*). TIGER LILY. To 4 ft. or more with pendulous orange flowers spotted black. Summer bloom. An old favorite.

L. longiflorum. EASTER LILY. Very fragrant, long, white, trumpet-shaped flowers on short stems. Usually purchased in bloom at Easter as forced plants. Set out in the garden after flowers fade. Sun or part shade, good drainage. Stem will ripen and die down. Plant may rebloom in fall; in 1-2 years may flower in midsummer, its normal bloom season. Varieties include 'Tetraploid', 1-1½ ft. tall; 'Croft', 1 ft. tall; 'Estate', to 3 ft. Not for severe winter climates. Don't plant forced Easter lilies near other lilies; may transmit virus.

L. martagon. TURK'S CAP LILY. Purplish pink, recurved, pendant flowers in June-July on 3-5-ft. stems. Slow to establish, but long-lived and makes big clumps. 'Album', pure white, is one of the most appealing lilies. There also is a deep wine purple variety that blooms July-August.

L. nepalense. Large, pendulous, trumpet-shaped flowers, soft green with purple centers in July-August. Stems 1½-4 ft. tall. Needs a long, warm growing season, humidity.

L. pardalinum. LEOPARD LILY. California native. Recurved flowers bright crimson at tips, lighter in the center, brown-spotted. Spring-summer bloom.

L. regale. REGAL LILY. Superseded in quality by modern hybrid trumpet lilies, but still popular and easy. To 6 ft., with white, fragrant flowers in July.

L. speciosum. Grows 2½-5 ft. tall. Large, wide, fragrant flowers with broad, deeply recurved segments in August-September; white, heavily suffused rose-pink, sprinkled with raised crimson dots. 'Rubrum', red; 'Album', pure white; also other named forms. Best in light and afternoon shade; needs rich soil with plenty of leaf mold.

L. tigrinum. See *L. lancifolium*

Following are the lily hybrids, listed approximately in order of bloom season:

Golden Chalice Hybrids. Stems 1½-3 ft. tall. Colors range from lemon yellow to apricot orange. 'Golden Wonder', 2½-4½ ft. tall, is a soft golden yellow variety. Blooms in May.

Coronado or Rainbow Hybrids. Tulip-shaped flowers golden yellow through orange to dark red, usually with dark spots; in upward facing clusters; bloom in June. Stems 2-3 ft. tall.

Martagon Hybrids. Mostly hybrids between *L. martagon* and *L. hansonii*. All bloom in June. 'Achievement' pale yellow, almost ivory white, 3 ft. tall. 'Gay Lights', 5 ft. tall, has pinkish bronze flowers, often as many as 30 on a stem. Paisley strain, 3½-5 ft. tall, many flowers to a stem. Segments recurved (curved sharply backward); colors range through yellow, orange, lilac, purple, tangerine, and mahogany.

Bellingham Hybrids. The result of crosses between a number of West Coast native lilies. Recurved flowers, 20 or more on 6-ft. stems in late June-July. Yellow

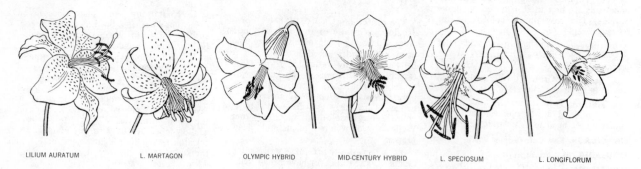

LILIUM AURATUM   L. MARTAGON   OLYMPIC HYBRID   MID-CENTURY HYBRID   L. SPECIOSUM   L. LONGIFLORUM

Flowers of lilies range from trumpet shape (L. longiflorum, Olympic hybrids) through flat (L. auratum, Mid-Century hybrids) to recurved (L. martagon, L. speciosum). Colors range from purest white to pink, red, purple, shades of yellow, orange.

Climate Zone maps pages 8-27

through orange to bright orange-red, spotted brown or reddish brown.

Fiesta Hybrids. Hardy, vigorous, sun-loving, bloom in July. Nodding flowers with strongly recurved segments in pale yellow through gold to deep maroon. Selections from Fiesta Hybrids are: Bronzino strain, sand, mahogany, and amber; Burgundy strain, cherry red, claret, and burgundy; Citronella strain, golden and lemon yellow flowers with small black dots; Golden Wedding strain, large golden yellow flowers.

Harlequin Hybrids. Largely derived from *L. cernuum.* June-July bloom. To 5 ft. tall. Flowers open with recurved segments; ivory white through pale lilac and old rose to violet and purple, with intermediate shades of salmon, terra cotta, and amber pink. Most are pink and tangerine.

Mid-Century Hybrids. Strong growing, hardy, tolerant of most soils. Plants from 2-4 ft. tall. July bloom. Colors range from yellow through orange to red; most dotted with black. Up-facing, wide open flowers spread like branches of candelabra. Many excellent named varieties; outstanding is 'Enchantment', nasturtium red, especially adapted to warm climates and pot culture.

Aurelian Hybrids. Offspring of *L. henryi* and various trumpet-shaped lilies. Contains 4 sections: Trumpet, which includes golden and lemon yellow, trumpet-shaped strains such as Golden Clarion and Golden Splendor; Bowl-shaped, including Heart's Desire strain, with flaring shallow flowers in white, yellow, cream, many with orange throats shading cream at segment tips; Pendant, with drooping flowers; and Sunburst, with flared flowers that have narrow segments. All grow 3-6 ft. high, bloom July-August.

Olympic Hybrids. Trumpet-shaped lilies bloom July-August on plants to 6 ft. high. Flowers range from pure white through cream, yellow, soft pink, or icy green, shaded on outside with greenish brown or wine. Many choice named varieties available, such as 'Black Dragon', 'Green Dragon', 'Quicksilver', 'Carrara'. Also available in strains such as Green Magic, Black Magic, and pure white Sentinel.

Oriental Hybrids. Hybrids derived from *L. auratum, L. japonicum, L. rubellum,* and *L. speciosum.* Most spectacular of all, with large flowers with broad segments in whites, pinks, or reds, often banded gold or red on white, and often spotted deep red; powerful fragrance. August-September. Best strains and named varieties expensive, but worth it. Among them are Imperial Crimson, Imperial Gold, Imperial Silver strains. Also Jamboree strain, a giant hybrid *L. speciosum* type.

LILY. See Lilium

LILY, ABYSSINIAN SWORD. See Acidanthera

LILY, AFRICAN CORN. See Ixia

LILY, AZTEC. See Sprekelia

LILY, BELLADONNA. See Amaryllis

LILY, BLACKBERRY. See Belamcanda

LILY, BLOOD. See Haemanthus

LILY, CHECKER. See Fritillaria lanceolata

LILY, CHECKERED. See Fritillaria meleagris

LILY, CHILEAN. See Alstroemeria

LILY, CLIMBING. See Gloriosa

LILY, COBRA. See Darlingtonia

LILY, FAIRY. See Zephyranthes

LILY, FAWN. See Erythronium californicum

LILY, FORTNIGHT. See Moraea

LILY, FOXTAIL. See Eremurus

LILY, GLORY. See Gloriosa

LILY, GUERNSEY. See Nerine sarniensis

LILY, JACOBEAN. See Sprekelia

LILY, KAFFIR. See Clivia, Schizostylis

LILY, MARIPOSA. See Calochortus

LILY, PERUVIAN. See Alstroemeria aurantiaca

LILY, PLANTAIN. See Hosta

LILY, RAIN. See Habranthus

LILY, SCARBOROUGH. See Vallota

LILY, SEGO. See Calochortus nuttallii

LILY, SNAKE. See Sauromatum guttatum 'Venosum'

LILY, SPEAR. See Doryanthes

LILY, SPIDER. See Hymenocallis, Lycoris

LILY, ST. JAMES. See Sprekelia

LILY, VOODOO. See Sauromatum

LILY, WATER. See Nymphaea

LILY, WHITE GLOBE. See Calochortus albus

LILY OF LIMA. See Alstroemeria pelegrina

LILY-OF-THE-NILE. See Agapanthus

LILY-OF-THE-VALLEY. See Convallaria

LILY-OF-THE-VALLEY SHRUB. See Pieris japonica

LILY-OF-THE-VALLEY TREE. See Clethra arborea, Crinodendron

LILY TURF. See Liriope and Ophiopogon

LIME. See Citrus

LIMEQUAT. See Citrus

LIME, 'Rangpur'. See Citrus

LIMONIUM (*Statice*). SEA LAVENDER. Annuals, perennials. Large, leathery, basal leaves contrast with airy clusters of small, delicate flowers on nearly leafless, many-branched stems. Tiny flowers consist of two parts: an outer, papery envelope which is the calyx; and an inner part called the corolla which is often of a different color. Flowers good for cutting, and keep color even when dried.

Tolerate heat, strong sun, some drought when established. Need good drainage; otherwise tolerant of many soils. Often self-sow.

Sow annual kinds indoors, move to garden when weather warms up for spring-summer bloom. Or sow outdoors in early spring for later bloom.

L. bonduellii. Annual or biennial. Grows 2 ft. tall, with 6-in. basal leaves lobed nearly to the midrib. The flower stems are distinctly winged; the calyx is yellow, the tiny corolla deeper yellow.

L. latifolium. Perennial. Zones 1-10, 14-24. To 2½ ft. tall. Leaves to 10 in. long with smooth edges. The calyx is white and the corolla bluish; white and pink kinds exist. Summer bloom. Well-grown plants may show a yard-wide haze of flowers.

L. perezii. Perennial. Zones 13, 16, 17, 20-24. Often freezes Zones 14, 15, 18, 19. Leaves up to 12 in. long, including stalks, rich green. Summer bloom over long season. In the flowers, the calyx is a rich purple and the tiny corolla white. Flower clusters may be 3 ft. tall, nearly as wide. First-rate beach plant. Damaged by 25° temperatures.

L. sinuatum. Annual. Growth habit like *L. bonduellii,* with lobed leaves and winged stems but calyx blue, lavender, or rose, the corolla white.

L. suworowii. Annual. To 1½ ft. Leaves 6-8 in. long and not lobed. Branched flower clusters rose-pink; branches upright and densely packed with flowers.

LINANTHUS. Annuals. California natives. Low-growing plants with finely divided leaves and dense clusters of small flowers atop single-stemmed or slightly branched plants. For culture and uses see *Gilia.*

L. androsaceus. Plants 3-5 in. tall. Flowers lavender, white, pink, or yellow depending on the form you get. Flowers in spring. Should be planted in fairly big patches.

L. grandiflorus. To 1 ft. tall or more; large, flat-topped, dense clusters of white or lilac flowers with ruffs or leaves beneath. Spring flowering.

LINARIA. TOADFLAX. Annuals or perennials. They have brightly colored flowers that resemble small, spurred snapdragons. Easy to grow. Best in masses; individual plants rather wispy.

L. cymbalaria. See Cymbalaria muralis

L. dalmatica. Perennial. All Zones. Grows 2-4 ft. high, with bluish green leaves and creeping roots which may spread too vigorously into other plantings. Flowers 1-2 in. long, on branching stalks from the upper stems. Yellow, with an orange blotch. May-September. Filmy, open effect. Plant in drier places in the garden where it will get little care; otherwise it can be a weed. Good in flower arrangements.

L. maroccana. BABY SNAPDRAGON, TOADFLAX. Annual. To 1½ ft. Flowers in red and gold, rose, pink, mauve, chamois, blue, violet, and purple, blotched with different shade on the lip. Spur longer than the flower. The Fairy Bouquet strain is only 9 in. tall and has larger flowers in pastel shades. Northern Lights strain has reds,

L

Climate Zone maps pages 8-27

oranges, and yellows as well as two-color forms. Flowers June-September. Sow in quantity for a show.

L. purpurea. Perennial. All Zones. Narrow, bushy, erect growth to 2½-3 ft. Blue-green foliage and violet-blue flowers. 'Canon Went' is a pink form. Summer blooming.

LINDEN. See Tilia

LINDEN, AFRICAN. See Sparmannia

LINDERA benzoin. SPICE BUSH. Deciduous shrub. Zones 1-7. To 6-15 ft. tall, equally wide, broad, dense, and twiggy. Leaves 3-5 in. long, bright green above, paler beneath, turning bright yellow in fall. Like all parts of the plant, leaves are spicily fragrant when bruised or brushed. Many tiny yellow or greenish yellow flowers early in spring before leaves appear. If plants of both sexes are present, female plants will show bright red, ⅓-in. fruits in fall. Needs moisture, prefers neutral to acid soil. Useful for screening, fall color.

LINGONBERRY. See Vaccinium vitis-idaea

LINNAEA borealis. TWINFLOWER. Shrubby perennial. Zones 1-7, 14-17. Native northern California to Alaska, Idaho, and much of northern hemisphere. Dainty, flat evergreen mats with 1-in.-long, glossy leaves. Spreads by runners. Pale pink, paired, trumpet-shaped flowers ⅓ in. long on 3-4-in. stems. Collector's item or small-scale ground cover for woodland garden. Keep area around plants mulched with leaf mold to induce spreading. In Northwest will grow in full sun if well watered.

LINOSPADIX monostachya *(Bacularia monostachya).* WALKING-STICK PALM. Zones 17, 22-24. Small feather palm to 6-8 ft. tall. Trunk very slender. Leaves 2-4 ft. long, with rather few, broad leaflets. Hardy to 28°. Very slow growing.

LINUM. FLAX. Annuals, perennials. All Zones. Flaxes are drought resistant, sun loving plants with erect, branching stems, narrow leaves, and abundant, shallow-cupped, 5-petaled flowers blooming from late spring into summer or fall. Each bloom lasts but a day, but others keep coming on. (The flax of commerce—*L. usitatissimum*—is grown for its fiber and seeds, which yield linseed oil.)

Use in borders; some naturalize freely in waste places. Full sun. Light, well drained soil. Most perennial kinds live only 3-4 years. Easy from seed; perennials also from cuttings; difficult to divide.

L. flavum. Perennial. (Often called yellow flax, a name correctly applied to closely related *Reinwardtia indica.*) Erect, compact, 12-15 in. tall, somewhat woody at base, grooved branches, green leaves. Flowers golden yellow, about 1 in. wide, in branched clusters April-June.

L. grandiflorum 'Rubrum'. SCARLET FLAX. Annual. Bright scarlet flowers, 1-1½ in. wide, on slender, leafy stems 1-1½ ft. tall. Narrow grayish green leaves. Also comes in rose-colored form. Sow seed thickly in place in fall (in mild areas) or early spring. Quick easy color in borders, over bulbs left in ground. Good with gray foliage or white-flowered plants. Reseeds, but doesn't become a pest.

L. narbonense. Perennial. Wiry stems to 2 ft. high. Leaves blue-green, narrow. Flowers large, 1¾ in. across, azure blue with white eye, in open clusters. Best variety, 'Six Hills', rich sky blue flowers.

L. perenne. PERENNIAL BLUE FLAX. Most vigorous blue-flowered flax with stems to 2 ft., usually leafless below. Branching clusters of light blue flowers, profuse from May-September. Flowers close in shade or late in the day. Self-sows freely.

LION'S TAIL. See Leonotis

LIPPIA citriodora. See Aloysia

LIPPIA. See Phyla

LIPSTICK PLANT. See Aeschynanthus

LIQUIDAMBAR. SWEET GUM. Deciduous trees. Valuable for form, foliage, and fall color, easy culture. Moderate growth rate; young and middle-aged trees generally upright, somewhat cone-shaped, spreading in age. Lobed, maplelike leaves. Flowers inconspicuous; fruits are spiny balls which ornament the trees in winter, need raking in spring.

Neutral or slightly acid, good garden soil; chlorosis in strongly alkaline soils hard to correct. Plant from containers or from ball and burlap; be sure roots are not canbound. Stake well. Prune only to shape. Trees branch from ground up, look most natural that way, but can be pruned up for easier foot traffic.

Good lawn or street trees. Effective in tall screens or groves, planted 6-10 ft. apart. Brilliant fall foliage. Leaves color best when trees are in full sun and in well drained soil; fall color less effective in mildest climates or in mild, late autumns.

L. formosana. CHINESE SWEET GUM. Zones 8, 9, 14-24. To 40-60 ft. tall, 25 ft. wide. Free-form outline; sometimes pyramidal, especially when young. Leaves 3 to 5-lobed, 3-4½ in. across, violet-red when expanding, then deep green. In southern California leaves turn yellow-beige in late December-January before falling. Further north leaves turn red. Variety 'Afterglow' has lavender-purple new growth, rose-red fall color.

L. orientalis. ORIENTAL SWEET GUM. Zones 5-9, 14-24. Native to Turkey. To 20-30 ft., spreading or round-headed. Leaves 2-3 in. wide, deeply 5-lobed, each lobe again lobed in lacy effect. Leafs out early after short dormant period. Fall color varies from deep gold and bright red in cooler areas to dull brown-purple in coastal southern California.

L. styraciflua. AMERICAN SWEET GUM. Zones 1-9, 14-24. Grows to 60 ft. (much taller in its native eastern U.S.). Narrow and erect in youth, with lower limbs eventually spreading to 20-25 ft. Good all-year tree: in winter, branching pattern, furrowed bark, corky wings on twigs, and hanging fruits give interest; in spring and summer, leaves 5-7 lobed, 3-7 in. wide, are deep green turning purple, yellow, or red in fall. Even seedling trees give good color (which may vary somewhat from year to year), but for uniformity match trees while they are in fall color or buy budded trees of a named variety, such as the following:

'Burgundy'. Leaves turn deep purple-red, hang late into winter or even early spring if storms are not heavy.

'Festival'. Narrow, columnar. Light green foliage turns to yellow, peach, pink, orange, and red.

'Palo Alto'. Turns orange-red to bright red in fall.

LIRIODENDRON tulipifera. TULIP TREE. Deciduous tree. Zones 1-10, 14-23. Native to eastern U. S. Fast growth to 60-80 ft., with an eventual spread of 40 ft. Straight columnar trunk, with spreading, rising branches that form a tall pyramidal crown. Bright yellow-green, lyre-shaped leaves 5-6 in. long and wide; these turn bright yellow (or yellow and brown) in fall. Tulip-shaped flowers in late spring are 2 in. wide, greenish yellow, orange at the base. Handsome at close range, they are not showy on the tree, being high up and well concealed by leaves. They are not usually produced until the tree is 10-12 years old.

Give this tree room; deep, rich, well drained neutral or slightly acid soil; and plenty of summer water. Best where constant wind from one direction won't strike it. Control scale insects and aphids.

Good large shade, lawn, or roadside tree. One of best deciduous trees for southern California; colors well there most autumns. Spreading root system makes it hard to garden under.

Two columnar varieties, 'Fastigiata' and 'Arnold', are useful in narrow planting areas. 'Arnold' will bloom 2-3 years after planting.

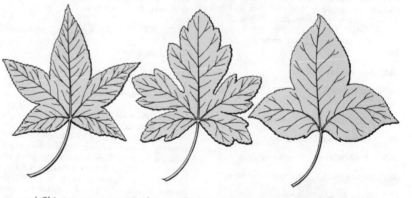

Leaves of Chinese sweet gum (right) usually have 3 lobes: leaves of Oriental sweet gum (center) are lacier, smaller. Leaves of American sweet gum may have 5 or 7 lobes.

LIRIOPE and OPHIOPOGON. LILY TURF. Evergreen grasslike perennials. Zones 5-9, 14-24 (*L. spicata* in All Zones). The two plants are similar in appearance and both belong to the lily family. They form clumps or tufts of grasslike leaves. White or lavender flowers grow in spikelike or branched clusters and in some kinds make quite a show. Last well in flower arrangements.

Use as casual ground cover in small areas. Also attractive as borders along paths, or between flower bed and lawn, among rock groupings, or in rock gardens. Grow well along streams and around garden pools. Try under bamboo or to cover bare soil at base of trees or shrubs in large containers. None satisfactory as mowed lawn. Tolerate indoor conditions in pots or planter beds.

Plant in partial shade in inland areas or foliage may turn yellow; along coast plant in sunny location. Well drained soil. Ample moisture needed but fleshy roots enable plants to withstand brief lapses in watering. Become ragged and brown with neglect. Cut back shaggy old foliage after new leaves appear. Plants don't need heavy feeding. Bait or spray for snails and slugs. Increase plants by dividing in early spring before new growth starts.

Plants look best from spring until cold weather of winter. Extended frosts may cause plants to turn yellow and it takes quite a while for them to recover. Can show tip burn on leaves if excess salts in soil, or if kept too wet where drainage is poor.

The chart compares the kinds you can buy, describes leaves and flowers, mentions uses and cultural needs.

L

Climate Zone maps pages 8-27

LIRIOPE AND OPHIOPOGON

NAME	GROWTH FORM	LEAVES	FLOWERS	COMMENTS
LIRIOPE exiliflora (*L. muscari exiliflora*)	Makes a rather loose clump that spreads by underground stems. Turf eventually 8-12 in. deep.	Dark green, 12-16 in. long, ³/₈ in. wide, rather upright to somewhat curved in age.	Small light violet buds and flowers in 3¹/₂-6¹/₂-in.-long, loose, spikelike clusters on foot-high stalks well above leaves, followed by numerous small, berrylike black fruits.	Flowers profusely but earlier than *L. muscari*. For ground cover, set plants 8 in. apart.
L. gigantea	To 3 ft. Use as high ground cover or singly. Spreads by underground stems.	Dark green.	Violet flowers.	Good for fountainlike effect. Tolerates sun or shade, best in light shade in hot climates.
L. muscari BIG BLUE LILY TURF (Often sold as 'Big Blue')	Forms large clumps but does not spread by underground stems. Rather loose growth habit 12-18 inches high.	Dark green but lighter than species above. To 2 ft. long, ¹/₂ in. wide.	Dark violet buds and flowers in rather dense 6-8-in.-long spikelike clusters on 5-12-in.-long stems (resemble grape hyacinths), followed by a few round shiny black fruits.	Profuse flowers July-August. Flowers held above leaves in young plants, partly hidden in older plants. Many garden varieties.
L. m. 'Majestic'	Resembles *L. muscari* but more open clumps and somewhat taller growing.	Similar to above.	Dark violet flowers and buds in clusters that look somewhat like cocks-combs on stems 8-10 in. long.	Heavy flowering. Clusters show up well above the leaves on young plants.
L. m. 'Monroe #1' (Sometimes sold as *L. m.* 'Monroe White')	Rather open clump 12-18 in. high.	Lighter green foliage, leaves curved.	White flowers in open spikes, the stems quite rigid, held well above the foliage clump.	One of the most distinct varieties of *L. muscari*. Foliage damaged in quite hot sun.
L. m. 'Monroe #2' (Sometimes sold as *L. m.* 'Christmas Tree')	Clumps distinctly open.	Leaves curved in almost half circle, usually 12-18 in. long.	Light violet in branched, conical cluster held well above leafy clump; look like miniature Christmas trees.	Flower buds profuse, do not open but are decorative and remain on stout stem until dry. Good in flower arrangements.
L. m. 'Silvery Sunproof'	Open growth, strongly vertical, partly arching, 15-18 in. high.	Leaves with gold stripes that turn white as they mature.	Lilac flowers in spikelike clusters rise well above foliage in early summer.	One of the best for open areas and flowers. Best in full sun along coast; inland partial or full shade.
L. m. 'Variegata' (May be sold as *Ophiopogon jaburan* 'Variegata')	Resembles *L. muscari*, but somewhat looser, softer.	New leaves green, 12-18 in. long, edged with yellow, becoming dark green second season.	Violet buds and flowers in spikelike clusters well above foliage. Flower stalk 12 in. high.	Does best in part shade.

(Continued on next page)

L

Climate Zone maps pages 8-27

NAME	GROWTH FORM	LEAVES	FLOWERS	COMMENTS
L. spicata CREEPING LILY TURF	Dense ground cover that spreads widely by underground stems. Grows 8-9 inches high.	Narrow (¼ in. wide) deep green grasslike leaves, soft and not as upright as *L. muscari*.	Pale lilac to white flowers in spikelike clusters barely taller than the leaves.	Hardy in All Zones. Inland, it looks rather shabby in winter. Should be mowed every year in spring prior to new growth development to get best effect. Good ground cover for cold areas where *Ophiopogon japonicus* won't grow.
OPHIOPOGON jaburan	Eventually forms large clump growing from fibrous roots.	Dark green, somewhat curved, firm leaves 18-36 in. long, about ½ in. wide.	Small, chalk white flowers in nodding clusters, somewhat hidden by the leaves, summer. Metallic, violet-blue fruits.	Does best in shade. Fruits very attractive feature; good for cutting.
O. japonicus MONDO GRASS	Forms dense clumps that spread by underground stems, many of which are tuberlike. Slow to establish as ground cover.	Dark green leaves ⅛ in. wide, 8-12 in. long.	Flowers light lilac in short spikes usually hidden by the leaves. Summer blooming. Fruit blue.	In hot dry areas grow in some shade. Can be cut back. Easy to divide. Set divisions 6-8 in. apart. Roots will kill at 10°. Looks best in partial shade but will take full sun along coast.
O. planiscapus 'Nigricans' (O. arabicum)	Makes a tuft 8 in. high and about 1 ft. wide.	Leaves to 10 in. long. New leaves green but soon turn black.	White sometimes flushed pink in loose spikelike clusters in summer.	Probably best grown in a container; valuable as a novelty, as black-leafed plants are rather rare.

LITCHI chinensis. LITCHI NUT. Evergreen tree. Zones 21-24. Slow growing, round-topped, spreading, 20-40 ft. tall. Leaves have 3-9, leathery, 3-6 in.-long leaflets that are coppery red when young, dark green later. Fruit, red and juicy when ripe, enclosed in brittle warty covering. Dried fruits have a raisinlike texture, sweet flavor.

Needs frost-free site, acid soil, ample water, moist air, feeding with nitrogen. Has fruited in a few warm areas near San Diego. Look for named varieties if you're interested in food production.

LITHOCARPUS densiflora. TANBARK OAK. Evergreen tree. Zones 4-7, 14-24. Native to Coast Ranges from southern Oregon to Santa Barbara County, California. Reaches 60-90 ft. under forest conditions; in the open, tree is lower, broader, the crown sometimes touching the ground. Leathery, 1½-4-in. sharply toothed leaves covered with whitish or yellowish wool on expanding, later smooth green above, gray-green beneath. Tiny whitish male flowers in large branched clusters have an odd odor which some find offensive. Acorns in bur-like cups.

Best in rich, moist soil; stands some drought when established. As street or lawn tree resembles holly oak, but has lusher foliage. One of the few broad-leafed evergreen trees for the Willamette Valley. Tends to be shrubby in Zones 4, 5.

LITHODORA diffusa (*Lithospermum diffusum, L. prostratum*). Perennial. Zones 5-7, 14-17. Prostrate, somewhat shrubby, slightly mounded, broad mass 6-12 in. tall. The evergreen leaves are narrow, ¾-1 in. long; foliage and stems are hairy. In May-June (and often later) plants become

sprinkled with tubular flowers ½ in. long and brilliantly blue. Full sun or light shade in hot exposures. Loose, well drained, lime-free soil. Rock gardens, walls.

'Heavenly Blue' and 'Grace Ward' are selected varieties of good form and color.

LITHOPS. STONEFACE. Succulents. Best grown indoors. Among the best known of "living rocks" or "pebble plants" of South Africa. Shaped like an inverted cone; top is shaped like a stone with a fissure across the middle. From this fissure emerge the

Plant of Lithops (³/₄ actual size); the roundish bodies are pairs of leaves.

large flower (it looks like an ice plant flower) and the new leaves. Many species, all interesting. Grow in pots of fast-draining soil. Water sparingly in summer; keep dry during cool winter weather. Fairly hardy in mild winters, but subject to rot outdoors in damp winter air.

LITHOSPERMUM. See Lithodora

LIVERLEAF. See Hepatica

LIVISTONA. Palms. Zones 13-17, 19-24. Native from China to Australia. These fan palms somewhat resemble washingtonias, but generally have shorter, darker, shinier leaves. All hardy to about 22°.

L. australis. In ground grows slowly to 40-50 ft. Has a clean, slender trunk with interesting-looking leaf scars. Dark green leaves 3-5 ft. wide. Good potted plant when young.

L. chinensis. CHINESE FOUNTAIN PALM. Slow growing; 40-year-old plants are only 15 ft. tall. Self-cleaning (no pruning of old leaves needed) with leaf-scarred trunk. Outer edges of 3-6-ft., roundish, bright green leaves droop strongly.

L. decipiens. To 30-40 ft. in 20 years. Stiff, open head of leaves 2-5 ft. across, green on top, bluish beneath, on long, spiny stems. Good in pots, gardens.

L. mariae. From hot, dry interior Australia. Grows slowly to 10-15 ft. Young or potted plants have attractive reddish leaves and leaf stems. Leaves 3-4 ft. wide.

LOBELIA. Perennials or annuals. Tubular, lipped flowers look like those of honeysuckle or salvia.

Climate Zone maps pages 8-27

L. cardinalis. CARDINAL FLOWER. Perennial. Zones 1-7, 14-17. Native to eastern U. S. Erect, single-stemmed, 2-4 ft. high with saw-edged leaves set directly on the stems. Spikes of flame red, inch-long flowers. Summer bloom. Needs constant moisture through growing season, rich soil (bog plant in nature). Sun or part shade.

L. erinus. Annual. Popular and dependable edging plant. Compact or trailing growth habit with leafy, branching stems. Flowers ¾ in. across, light blue to violet (sometimes pink, reddish purple, or white) with a white or yellowish throat. Bloom early summer to frost; lives over winter in mild areas.

Takes about 2 months for the seed in flats to grow to planting-out size. Moist, rich soil. Part shade in hot areas, full sun where summers are cool, foggy. Self-sows where adapted.

Trailing kinds are graceful as ground cover in large planters or in smaller pots, where the stems, loaded with flowers, spill over the edges. Also good for hanging baskets. Compact varieties make good edging, masses. Fine with begonias, ferns.

'Cambridge Blue' has clear, soft blue flowers, light green leaves on compact 4-6-in. plant. 'Crystal Palace' has rich, dark blue flowers on a compact plant with bronze green leaves. Takes morning or late afternoon sun inland. 'Emperor William', clear medium blue flowers, medium green leaves, on plant 4-6 in. high; combine with 'Cambridge Blue' for two-toned effect. Two trailing varieties for hanging baskets or wall planting are 'Hamburgia', light blue; and 'Sapphire', deep blue with white eyes.

LOBIVIA. Cactus. Grow outdoors in part shade in Zones 16, 17, 21-24; as house plant, or indoor-outdoor plant anywhere. Small globular or cylindrical shapes with big, showy flowers in shades of red, yellow, pink, orange, purplish, lilac. Flowers sometimes nearly as big as the plants, like flowers of *Echinopsis* but shorter, broader. Many species offered. Usually grown in pots by collectors. Need porous soil, ample water during summer bloom and growth, occasional feeding.

LOBIVOPSIS. Cactus. Hybrids between *Lobivia* and *Echinopsis*. Extremely free-flowering with big, long-tubed flowers on small plants. Culture, hardiness same as for *Echinopsis;* grow in fairly good-sized pots (5-in. pot for a 3-in. plant), feed monthly in summer and water freely during bloom season. The Paramount Hybrids come in red, pink, orange, rose, and white. Some may show a dozen or more 6-in.-long flowers on a 3-4-in. plant. Will take part shade, but do best in full sun.

LOBULARIA maritima. SWEET ALYSSUM. Annual. Low, branching, trailing plant to 1 ft. tall. Leaves narrow or lance-shaped, ½-2 in. long. Tiny four-petaled flowers crowded in clusters, white, honeylike fragrance. Spring and summer bloom in cold regions; where winters are mild, blooms the year around from self-sown seedlings. Has run wild in parts of the West.

Easy, quick, dependable. Blooms from seed in 6 weeks, grows in almost any soil. Best in sun, but takes light shade. Useful for carpeting, edging, bulb cover, temporary filler in rock garden or perennial border,

between flagstones, in window boxes or containers. If you shear plants halfway back 4 weeks after they come into bloom, new growth will make another crop of flowers, and plants won't become rangy.

Garden varieties better known than the species; these varieties self-sow too, but seedlings tend to revert to taller, looser growth, less intense color, smaller flowers. 'Carpet of Snow' (2-4 in. tall) and 'Little Gem' (4-6 in.) are good, compact whites. 'Tetra Snowdrift' (12 in.) has long stems, large white flowers. 'Rosie O'Day' (2-4 in.) and 'Pink Heather' (6 in.) are lavender-pinks. 'Royal Carpet' (2-4 in.), 'Violet King' (4 in.), and 'Violet Queen' (5 in.) are rich violet-purples.

LOCUST. See Robinia

LOCUST, HONEY. See Gleditsia

LOMARIA. See Blechnum

LONAS annua (*L. inodora*). Annual. Stems to 1 ft. tall, finely divided leaves, 2-in.-wide, flat-topped clusters of yellow flower heads that suggest yarrow. Takes coastal fog and wind. Sow where plants will bloom or grow in flats, transplant. Summer bloom in most areas, year-around bloom in Zone 17.

LONDON PRIDE. See Saxifraga umbrosa

LONICERA. HONEYSUCKLE. Evergreen or deciduous shrubs or vines. Most kinds valued for tubular, often fragrant flowers. Easily grown plants for sun, or light shade inland. Vining kinds need support when starting out.

L. ciliosa. Deciduous vine. All Zones. Native to mountains, British Columbia and Montana south to northern California and Arizona. To 15 ft. Leafs out early. Leaves oval, 1-3 in. long, green above, pale beneath. Flowers reddish orange, 1½ in. long in terminal whorl, May-July; followed by small red fruits. Becomes weedy if not controlled.

L. 'Clavey's Dwarf'. Deciduous shrub. All Zones. Dense, to 3 ft., rarely to 6 ft. tall, with equal spread. Flowers white, small, not showy. Useful foundation plant or low unclipped hedge in colder regions.

L. fragrantissima. WINTER HONEYSUCKLE. Deciduous shrub, partially evergreen in mild-winter areas. All Zones. Arching, rather stiff growth to 8 ft. Leaves oval, dull dark green above, blue-green beneath, 1-3 in. long. Creamy white flowers ⅝ in. long on previous year's wood, in early spring to fall depending on climate. Flowers not showy, but have rich fragrance, like *Daphne odora*. Red berrylike fruit. Can be used as clipped hedge or background.

L. heckrottii. GOLD FLAME HONEYSUCKLE, CORAL HONEYSUCKLE. Deciduous or semi-deciduous vine, or small shrub. Zones 2-24. Vigorous, to 12-15 ft. with oval, 2-in., blue-green leaves. Free blooming spring to frost, the clustered flowers 1½ in. long, bright coral pink outside, rich yellow within, opening from coral pink buds. Train as espalier, or on wire along eaves. Subject to aphids. Varieties sold as 'Gold Flame' and 'Pink Gold Flame' are similar, if not identical.

L. henryi. Zones 2-24. Evergreen or semi-evergreen twining vine. Has rather narrow, dark green, 3-in. leaves. Flowers ¾ in. long,

yellowish to purplish red, in summer, followed by black fruits. Less rampant than *L. japonica.* Good bank cover.

L. hildebrandiana. GIANT BURMESE HONEYSUCKLE. Evergreen vine. Zones 9, 14-17, 19-24. Big, fast growing, with 4-6-in., glossy, dark green, oval leaves on supple ropelike stems. Tubular, fragrant flowers to 6-7 in. long, open white, then fade yellow to dull orange; slow to drop. Summer bloom. Plants occasionally have dark green, inch-wide, berrylike fruits. Most widely planted kind in southern California. Any good soil, occasional feeding, plenty of water. Thin out older stems occasionally and remove some growth that has bloomed. Striking along eaves, on arbor or wall.

L. involucrata. TWINBERRY. Deciduous shrub. Zones 1-9, 14-17, 21-24. Native to moist areas, California to Alaska and eastward. Densely foliaged plants 5-10 ft. high. Dark green oval leaves 2-5 in. long. Small (½-in.-long), tubular, paired flowers, yellowish red, surrounded by 2 united bracts that enlarge as fruit forms, becoming bright red and finally black. The twin berries are black. Plants bloom March-July.

L. japonica. JAPANESE HONEYSUCKLE. Evergreen vine, partly or wholly deciduous in coldest regions. Zones 2-24. Rampant. Leaves deep green, oval. Flowers white, tinged purplish, with sweet fragrance. Late spring, summer bloom. Several varieties are grown, all better known than the species itself: *L. j.* 'Aureo-reticulata', GOLDNET HONEYSUCKLE, leaves veined yellow, especially in full sun. *L. j.* 'Halliana', HALL'S HONEYSUCKLE, most vigorous and most widely grown, climbs to 15 ft., covers 150 sq. ft., flowers pure white, changing to yellow. *L. j.* 'Purpurea', probably same as *L. j. chinensis*, leaves tinged purple underneath, flowers purplish red, white inside.

Of the above, Hall's honeysuckle most commonly used as bank and ground cover, for erosion control in large areas; unless curbed can become a weed, smothering less vigorous plants. Needs severe pruning once a year to prevent undergrowth from building up and becoming fire hazard. Cut back almost to framework with shears. Train as privacy or wind screen on chain link or wire fence. Fairly drought resistant when established; also tolerates poor drainage. For ground cover set 2-3 ft. apart.

L. korolkowii. Deciduous shrub. All Zones. Arching form to 12 ft. Leaves oval, 2 in. long, bluish green. A profusion of small, rose-colored flowers in May-June, followed by bright red fruits in early fall. Use in cold areas as big background shrub. Takes desert heat. *L. k.* 'Zabelii' has broader leaves, deeper rose flowers.

L. nitida. BOX HONEYSUCKLE. Evergreen shrub. Zones 4-9, 14-24. To 6 ft. with erect, densely leafy branches. Tiny dark green, oval, ½-in., shiny leaves. Flowers (in June) fragrant, creamy white, ½ in. long. Berries translucent, blue-purple. Rapid growth, tending toward untidiness, but easily pruned as hedge or single plant. Takes salt spray.

L. periclymenum. WOODBINE. Deciduous twining shrub or vine. Zones 3-24. To 20 ft. Leaves oval, 1½-3 in. long, dark green above, light beneath. Flowers very fragrant, yellowish white, deep purplish red outside, summer to fall, followed by red fruits. *L. p.* 'Belgica', DUTCH WOODBINE, flowers pale purple outside, most fragrant of all.

L. pileata. PRIVET HONEYSUCKLE. Semi-evergreen shrub. Zones 2-9, 14-24. Low, spreading, with stiff horizontal branches, to 3 ft. Dark green, 1½-in., privetlike leaves; small, white, fragrant flowers in May; translucent violet-purple berries. Sun, or light shade inland. Good bank cover with low-growing euonymus or barberries.

L. sempervirens. TRUMPET HONEYSUCKLE. Evergreen or semi-evergreen twining vine, shrubby if not given support. Zones 3-24. Showy, unscented orange-yellow to scarlet trumpet flowers 1½-2 in. long, in whorl at end of branches in summer. Fruit scarlet. Oval leaves, 1½-3 in. long, bluish green beneath.

L. tatarica. TATARIAN HONEYSUCKLE. Deciduous shrub. Zones 1-21. Forms big, upright, dense mass of twiggy branches, looser and more attractive in partial shade. Oval, 2-in.-long, dark green or bluish green leaves. Small pink flowers in late spring, early

Flowers of Tatarian honeysuckle may be white, pink or rose. Leaves 2 in. long.

summer. Bright red fruits. *L. t.* 'Alba' has white flowers; *L. t.* 'Rosea' rose outside, pink inside; *L. t.* 'Sibirica' has larger leaves, deep pink flowers margined white. All are neat-appearing plants for backgrounds, screens.

LOQUAT. See Eriobotrya

LOROPETALUM chinense. Evergreen shrub. Zones 6-9, 14-24. Borderline Zones 4, 5. Generally 3-5 ft. tall, possibly up to 12 ft. in great age. Neat, compact habit, with tiered, arching or drooping branches. Leaves roundish, light green, soft, 1-2 in. long. An occasional leaf turns yellow or red throughout the year for a nice touch of color. Flowers white to greenish white, in clusters of 4-8 at ends of branches. Each flower has 4 narrow, inch-long, twisted petals. Bloom heaviest March-April, but some bloom likely to appear any time.

Full sun in fog belt; sun or partial shade inland. Needs rich, well drained soil and lots of water. Subtle beauty, good in foregrounds, raised beds, hanging baskets,

woodland gardens, as ground cover. In Northwest needs protection against hard freezes.

LOTUS. Subshrubs or perennials, often with completely prostrate trailing stems. Leaves divided into leaflets. Flowers sweet pea-shaped, pink through shades of red to yellow.

L. berthelotii. Zones 9, 13-24. Trailing perennial with stems 2-3 ft. long, thickly covered with silvery gray foliage and very narrow 1-in.-long, scarlet blossoms. Blooms June-July. Dies back in cold weather, suffers root rot in poor drainage. Space 24 in. apart as ground cover, and cut back occasionally to induce bushiness. Also very effective in hanging baskets, as cascade over wall or rocks.

L. corniculatus. BIRDSFOOT TREFOIL. All Zones. Goes dormant where winters are cold. Use as ground cover or coarse lawn substitute. Makes a mat of dark green cloverlike leaves. Clusters of small yellow flowers in summer and fall. Seed pods at top of flower stem spread like a bird's foot, hence the common name. Sow seeds or set out plants. Takes much water in hot, dry months. Should be mowed occasionally.

L. mascaensis. Zones 16, 17, 20-24. Partially erect and bushy; will cascade in hanging containers, above walls. Narrow, silky, gray leaflets. Bright yellow flowers ½-¾ in. long in small clusters. Trim to induce flat growth. Short lived, freezes back at 30°.

LOTUS, AMERICAN. See Nelumbo pentapetala

LOTUS, INDIAN OR CHINESE. See Nelumbo nucifera

LOVAGE. See Levisticum

LOVE-IN-A-MIST. See Nigella

LOVE-LIES-BLEEDING. See Amaranthus caudatus

LUFFA. See Gourd

LUNARIA annua (*L. biennis*). MONEYPLANT, HONESTY. Biennial. Zones 1-10, 14-24. Old-fashioned garden plant grown for the translucent silvery circles (about 1¼ in. across) that stay on the flower stalks and are all that remain of the ripened seed pods after outer coverings drop with the seeds. Plants 1½-3 ft. high, with coarse, heart-shaped, toothed leaves. Plant in an out-of-the-way spot in poor soil, or in a mixed flower bed where the shining pods can be admired before they are picked for dry bouquets. Tough, persistent, can reseed and become weedy.

LUNGWORT. See Pulmonaria

LUPINUS. LUPINE. Annuals, perennials, shrubs. Leaves are divided like fingers into many leaflets. Flowers sweet pea-shaped, in dense spikes at ends of stems. Many species native to western U. S., ranging from beach sand to alpine rocks. Only best and easiest kinds covered here; native plant seed specialists can supply many others.

All need good drainage, are not otherwise fussy about soil. Start from seed sown winter-early spring; hard-coated seeds often slow to sprout, germinate quicker after

soaking in hot water or after having coats scratched or cut.

L. arboreus. Shrub. Zones 17, 24. Native to California coastal areas. Grows to 5-8 ft. tall. Flower clusters in March-June, 4-16 in. long, usually yellow but sometimes lilac or bluish. Striking beach plant.

L. hartwegii. Annual. Native to Mexico. Grows 1½-3 ft. tall and comes in shades of blue, white, and pink. Easy from seed sown April-May where plants are to bloom. Flowers in July-September.

L. nanus. SKY LUPINE. Annual. California 8-14 in. high, the flowers rich blue marked white. Sow seeds in fall or winter for spring bloom. Sow California poppies with it for contrast. April-May flowers.

L. polyphyllus. Perennial. All Zones. Native to moist places, northern California to British Columbia. Grows 1½-4 ft. tall, with dense flower clusters 6-24 in. long in summer. Flowers blue, purple, or reddish. One important ancestor of the Russell Hybrids. Spray for aphids.

L. Russell Hybrids. RUSSELL LUPINES. Perennials. Zones 1-7, 14-17. Large, spreading plants to 4-5 ft., with long spikes of flowers in May-June. Colors white, cream, yellow, pink, blue, red, orange, purple. Many bicolors. Grow from seed or buy started plants from flats, pots. Striking border plant where summers aren't too hot and dry. Give good air circulation to help avoid mildew. Often short lived.

LYCASTE. Epiphytic and terrestrial orchids. Greenhouse plants. Native to Central America. Plant has large oval pseudobulbs bearing 1 to 3 plaited leaves. Long lasting flowers produced in profusion are predominantly green; some are pink, white, yellow, or brown.

Thrive in cool (50° to 55° night, 10° higher day) location in bright light, good ventilation, and moist but very well drained soil. Plant in pots in a fibrous loam with just enough sphagnum and leaf mold to keep well drained. Reduce watering to minimum after plants have flowered. Increase watering when new growth appears, but keep water off leaves until mature to prevent rot.

L. skinneri. Native to Guatemala. Most popular species. Large numbers of 5-7-in. rose colored blooms with rose and crimson spotted lip. Produced singly on stem in winter. Plant 15-24 in. high.

LYCHNIS. Annual, perennial. Hardy, old-fashioned garden flowers, all very tolerant of adverse soils.

L. chalcedonica. MALTESE CROSS. Perennial. Zones 1-9, 11-24. Loose, open growing, 2-3 ft. high, with hairy leaves and stems. Flowers in dense terminal clusters, scarlet, the petals deeply cut. June-July bloom. Flower color harsh, plants best used in large borders with white flowers, gray foliage.

L. coeli-rosa. See Silene coeli-rosa

L. coronaria. CROWN-PINK, MULLEIN-PINK. Annual or biennial. All Zones. Plants 1½-2½ ft., with attractive silky white foliage and, in spring and early summer, magenta to crimson flowers a little less than an inch across. Effective massed, reseeds copiously, but any surplus is easily weeded out.

Climate
Zone maps
pages 8-27

L. viscaria 'Splendens'. Perennial. Zones 1-9, 11-24. Compact low evergreen clumps of grasslike leaves to 5 in. long. Flower stalks to 1 ft. with clusters of pink to rose ½-in. flowers in summer. A double flowered variety, 'Splendens Flore Pleno', is a good rock garden plant and lasts well when cut.

LYCORIS. SPIDER LILY. Bulb. Narrow, strap-shaped leaves appear in spring, ripen, and die down before bloom starts. Clusters of red, pink, or yellow flowers on bare stems up to 2 ft. in late summer, fall. Flowers spidery looking with narrow, wavy-edged segments curved backward, and long stamens. Grow in borders, depending on hardiness, or as pot plants. Some kinds are tender, some half-hardy. Bulbs available July-August. Set 3-4 in. deep (note exception below) in good soil; give ample water during growth, but let plants dry out during dormant period in late summer. Don't disturb plantings for several years. When potting, set with tops exposed; don't use too large pots; best growth with crowded roots.

L. aurea. GOLDEN SPIDER LILY. Outdoors in Zones 16, 17, 21-24; indoor-outdoor container plants elsewhere. Bright yellow 3-in. flowers in September-October.

L. radiata. Zones 4-9, 12-24. Best known and easiest. Coral red flowers with a gold sheen; stems 18 in. 'Alba' has white flowers. Nurseries sell a desirable form under the name 'Albiflora'; flowers are blend of cream, yellow, pink tints, fading to nearly white. Will take light shade. Give protection in cold-winter climates. August-September bloom.

L. sanguinea. Zones 4-9, 12-24. Orange-crimson flowers 2 in. long in loose clusters. August bloom. Holds color best in light shade.

L. squamigera (*Amaryllis hallii*). All Zones. Funnel-shaped, fragrant, pink or rosy lilac 3-in. flowers in clusters on 2-ft. stems. August bloom. Hardiest lycoris; winters in colder regions if bulbs are planted 6 in. deep in a protected location, as against a south wall.

LYGODIUM japonicum. CLIMBING FERN. Zones 17, 23, 24. Native to southeast Asia Delicate, lacy-textured, tightly twining climber to 8 ft., with light green leaflets. Fertile (spore-bearing) leaflets much narrower than the sterile ones. Grow on post or trellis, or in a hanging basket. Hardy to 30°.

LYONOTHAMNUS floribundus. CATALINA IRONWOOD. Evergreen tree. Zones 15-17, 19-24. Native to Channel Islands off coast of southern California. The species, with merely lobed or scallop-toothed leaves, is seldom seen in cultivation; *L. f. asplenifolius*, FERNLEAF CATALINA IRONWOOD, is well-known. Moderate growth to 30-60 ft. with a 20-40 ft. spread. Redwood-colored bark peels off in long, thin strips. Young twigs often reddish. The 4-6-in. leaves are divided into 3-7 deeply notched or lobed leaflets, deep glossy green above, gray hairy beneath. Small white blossoms in large, flat 8-18-in. clusters. These stand out well from the foliage, but should be cut off when they fade. Old clusters turn brown, are unattractive.

Needs excellent drainage and should be pruned in winter to shape and control

growth. Sometimes shows chlorosis in heavy soils. Easiest to grow near coast. Handsome in groves (like redwood), and effective with redwood, Torrey pines.

LYSILOMA thornberi. FEATHER BUSH. Shrub or small tree, evergreen in frostless areas, deciduous elsewhere. Zones 10, 12-24. Native to foothills of Rincon Mountains of Arizona. To 12 ft. Makes a broad canopy of finely cut bright green leaves somewhat like acacia. Sometimes killed by heavy frosts, but usually comes back. Flowers tiny, white, in ½-in. heads. May-June bloom. Seed pods flat, ridged, 4-8 in. long, 1 in. wide. Takes desert heat and drought when established. Good informal background shrub, patio tree, transitional planting between garden and desert.

LYSIMACHIA nummularia. MONEYWORT, CREEPING JENNIE. Perennial. Zones 1-9, 14-24. Evergreen creeping plant with long runners (to 2 ft.) that root at joints. Forms a pretty light green mat of roundish leaves. Flowers about 1 in. across, yellow, form singly in leaf joints. Summer blooming. Requires moisture and shade. Best use is in corners where it need not be restrained. Will spill from wall, hanging basket. Good ground cover (plant 12-18 in. apart) near streams or in low, damp places.

LYTHRUM salicaria. Perennial. All Zones. Showy magenta-flowered plants for pond margins or moist sunny areas. Grows in clumps 2 ft. wide with 2½-5-ft. stems; ¾-in. flowers densely set on the top 8-18 in. Varieties known as 'Roseum Superbum', 'Morden's Pink' or 'Morden's Dream' grown in the West. Valued for cut flowers in autumn and fall. In borders, tone down magenta by planting with white flowers.

MAACKIA amurensis. Deciduous tree. Zones 1-6. To 45 ft., with nearly equal spread; slow to moderate growth. Leaves 8-12 in. long, each composed of 7-11 dark green leaflets, 1½-3 in. long. Small, white, sweet pea-shaped flowers in tightly packed, upright, 4-8-in.-long clusters at branch ends. Each branch bears one or several of these clusters in summer, followed by flat, 2-in.-long pods that persist into winter. Very hardy to cold, heat, and wind. Plant in full sun; stake and prune to shape and develop a clear trunk. Unpruned trees often shrubby.

MACADAMIA. MACADAMIA NUT, QUEENSLAND NUT. Evergreen tree. Zones 9, 16, 17, 19-24. Clean, handsome ornamental tree where frosts are light. Where best adapted (Zones 23, 24) produces clusters of hard-shelled, delicious nuts; pick when they fall.

Best in deep, rich soil. Takes some drought when established but grows slowly if kept dry. Stake young trees. Prune to shape.

Most trees are sold under the name *M. ternifolia*. They are actually one of the species described below. Look for grafted, named varieties of proved nut-bearing ability.

Both species reach 25-30 ft. tall and more, 15-20 ft. wide. Long (5-12 in.), glossy, leathery leaves. Mature foliage is durable and attractive for cutting. Small flowers in winter and spring are white to pink in dense, hanging, 1 ft. clusters.

M. integrifolia. SMOOTH-SHELL MACADAMIA. Best near coast. Leaves are smooth edged. Nuts ripen in late fall to May.

M. tetraphylla. ROUGH-SHELL MACADAMIA. Best inland. Spiny leaves. Shell thinner, tree more open than *M. integrifolia*. Nuts appear fall through February.

MACLURA pomifera. OSAGE ORANGE. Deciduous tree. All Zones; little planted outside Zones 2, 3, 10-13. Fast growth to 60 ft. with spreading, open habit. Thorny branches. Leaves to 5 in. long, medium-green. If there's a male plant present, female plants may bear 4-in. inedible fruits which somewhat resemble bumpy, yellow-green oranges. Can stand heat, cold, wind, drought, poor soil, moderate alkalinity. Easily propagated by seed, cuttings, root cuttings; easily transplanted. Useful as big, tough, rough-looking hedge or background. Prune to any size from 6 ft. up. Pruned high, a desert shade tree, but needs some water until established. Can spread into a thicket.

MADAGASCAR PERIWINKLE. See Catharanthus

MADEIRA VINE. See Anredera

MADRONE, MADRONA. See Arbutus menziesii

MAGIC FLOWER. See Cantua

MAGNOLIA. Deciduous or evergreen trees and shrubs. A great number of magnificent flowering plants with a remarkable variety of colors, leaf shapes, and plant forms. The following classification by general appearance may help you find the magnolias that interest you (the chart lists all the kinds alphabetically).

EVERGREEN MAGNOLIAS

To gardeners in California and Arizona, magnolia usually means *M. grandiflora*, the big evergreen with glossy leaves and big, white, fragrant flowers. This one stands pretty much by itself. Generally considered a street or lawn tree, it can also be used as an espalier or grown in a large container for a few years. It has many named forms for different uses.

Other evergreen magnolias are *M. delavayi* and *M. virginiana* (sweet bay).

DECIDUOUS MAGNOLIAS WITH SAUCER FLOWERS

This group includes the saucer magnolia (*M. soulangiana*) and its many varieties, often miscalled "tulip trees" because of shape and bright colors of their flowers. Included here are the yulan magnolia (*M. denudata*) and the lily magnolia (*M. liliflora*). All are hardy to cold, thriving from southern California into the Northwest and the Columbia Basin; but early flowers of all forms are subject to frost damage, and all do poorly in hot, dry, windy areas. Related to these, but more tender to cold (and heat) are the big Oriental magnolias from western China and the Himalayas—*M. campbellii*, *M. dawsoniana*, *M. sargentiana robusta*, *M. sprengeri diva*. Most spectacular of all, these are borderline hardy in Zones 4 and 5, and subject to frost and storm damage to their very early flowers.

DECIDUOUS MAGNOLIAS WITH STAR FLOWERS

This garden group includes *M. kobus; M. k. stellata* and its varieties (the star magnolias); and *M. salicifolia*. All are hardy,

Climate Zone maps pages 8-27

slow-growing, early-blooming plants with wide climatic adaptablity.

LATE-FLOWERING MAGNOLIAS

These show fragrant, rather globular flowers during late spring and early summer and include *M. sieboldii, M. sinensis, M. watsonii,* and *M. wilsonii.* Blooming after the leaves appear, they make less splash than saucer magnolias, but they have quiet beauty, rich fragrance, and a fairly long bloom season.

OTHER MAGNOLIAS

Entirely different in effect are cucumber tree (*M. acuminata*), a big shade tree with little beauty of flower, and *M. macrophylla,* a huge-leafed, tropical-looking tree. Both are hardy.

Balled and burlapped plants are available in late winter and early spring, container plants any time. Do not set the plants lower than their original soil level. Stake single-trunk or very heavy plants against rocking by the wind, which will tear the thick, fleshy, sensitive roots. If you plant your magnolia in a lawn, try to provide a good-sized area free of grass for a watering basin. Water deeply and thoroughly, but do not drown the plants. A thick mulch will help hold moisture and reduce soil temperature. Surrounding grass cuts reflected heat.

Prevent soil compaction around root zone; this means reducing foot traffic to a minimum. Prune only when absolutely necessary. Best time is right after flowering, and the best way is to remove an entire twig or limb right to the base. Paint the wound with tree seal.

Pest and diseases are few. Watch for scale and aphids at any time, and for spider mites in hot weather. Snails and slugs eat the lower leaves of shrubby magnolias. Bait or spray will control them. Magnolias are not immune to oak root fungus (*Armillaria*), but they seem somewhat resistant.

Carefully pick the planting site for any magnolia. Except for *M. grandiflora* magnolias are hard to move once established, and many grow quite large. They never look their best when crowded, and may be severely damaged by digging around their roots, as might be necessary if you add other plants. They need moist, well drained, rich soil, neutral or slightly acid. Add plenty of organic matter at planting time—leaf

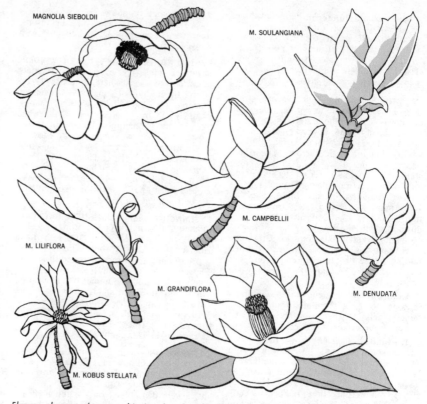

Flower shapes of seven kinds of magnolia. M. sieboldii *blooms after leaves appear.* M. grandiflora *blooms summer, fall. The others bloom early in year on bare branches.*

mold, peat moss, or ground bark. Full sun (light shade in desert regions).

More bothersome are deficiency problems: chlorosis from lack of iron in alkaline soils, and nitrogen starvation. Iron chelates will remedy the first condition, fertilizer will fix the second. Burning of leaf edges usually means salt damage from either overfertilizing, mineral salts in the soil, or salts in the irrigation water. This last is a problem in southern California, and is usually the factor limiting success of magnolias in the deserts. Regular, frequent, deep, heavy waterings will help leach out the salts and carry them to lower soil levels

—*if* drainage is good. In the Northwest late frosts sometimes burn leaf edges.

Uses are discussed in more detail in the chart. Generally speaking the larger deciduous magnolias are at their best standing alone against some background that will display their flowers and, in winter, their strongly patterned, usually gray limbs, and big, fuzzy flower buds. Smaller deciduous magnolias show up well in large flower or shrub borders, and make choice ornaments in the Oriental garden, where they are good companions for pine, bamboo, nandina, and azaleas. And all magnolias are excellent trees to grow in lawns.

MAGNOLIA

NAME	ZONES	DECIDUOUS OR EVERGREEN	HEIGHT IN FEET	SPREAD	BLOOMS AT AGE:	FLOWERS	USES	REMARKS
MAGNOLIA acuminata CUCUMBER TREE	1-9, 14-21	Dec.	60-80	25	12 yrs.	Small, greenish yellow, appearing after leaves expand. Late spring, summer. Not showy. Handsome reddish seed capsules, red seeds.	Shade or lawn tree.	Dense shade from handsome, glossy 5-9-in. leaves. Hardy to cold, but intolerant of hot, dry winds.

NAME	ZONES	DECIDUOUS OR EVERGREEN	HEIGHT IN FEET	SPREAD	BLOOMS AT AGE:	FLOWERS	USES	REMARKS
M. campbellii CAMPBELL MAGNOLIA	4-9, 14-21	Dec.	60-80	40	20 yrs. Grafts bloom younger.	Magnificent 6-10-in. bowls, deep rose outside, paler inside. Central petals cupped over rose stamens. Very early flowers. Varieties in white and pink.	Plant in lee of evergreens to protect blossoms from storm winds. Make it the focus of the garden and give it room.	Best in northern coastal California, Oregon. Borderline-hardy in Seattle. A plant for the patient gardener, or for posterity.
M. c. mollicomata	4-9, 14-21	Dec.	50-80	40	10 yrs. Grafts less— perhaps 5 yrs.	Rose pink, varying to white or pale pink. Early.	As above. As in *M. campbellii*, the broad leaves are handsome, being purplish when young and heavily parallel-veined, 8-12 in. long.	Much like *M. campbellii*; blooms younger.
M. dawsoniana DAWSON MAGNOLIA	5-9, 14-24	Dec.	40-50	25-30	12 yrs; less in grafted plants.	Large (8-10 in. wide), slightly pendulous, lightly scented. Petals strap-shaped.	Large growing magnolia for large gardens.	Very dark green leaves. Very heavy bloom on old, established plants.
M. delavayi	5-9, 14-24	Ev.	20-30	20	4-5 yrs.	Dull, creamy white, 7-8 in. across. Very fragrant, but short lived; flowers shatter the day they open. Summer bloom.	Use as a single tree in a lawn, or to fill a very large corner. Consider it a giant shrub, branching from ground.	Leaves are the feature: 8-14 in. long, 5-8 in. wide, stiff, leathery, gray-green.
M. denudata (*M. conspicua*) YULAN MAGNOLIA	2-9, 14-24	Dec.	35	30	6-7 yrs.	White, fragrant, sometimes tinged purple at base, held erect, somewhat tulip-shaped, 3-4 in. long, spreading to 6-7 in. across. Early; often shows a few summer flowers.	Place it where it can show off against a dark background or against the sky. Cut flowers striking in Oriental arrangements.	Tends toward irregular form— no handicap in an informal garden or at the woodland edge. Leaves 4-7 in. long.
M. grandiflora SOUTHERN MAGNOLIA, BULL BAY	4-12, 14-24.	Ev.	80	40	15 yrs., sometimes much less.	Pure white, aging buff, large (8-10 in. across), powerfully fragrant. Carried throughout summer and fall.	Street or lawn tree, big containers, wall or espalier plant. In cool-summer areas it appreciates a warm wall or pocket. Glossy leathery leaves 4-8 in. long.	Unpredictable in form and age of bloom. Grafted plants more predictable. Does well in desert heat if out of wind. Needs warm wall in Zones 4-5. Expect breakage, yearly pruning in Zones 6-7.
M. g. 'Exoniensis'	4-12, 14-24	Ev.	20-30 Slow	20	2-3 yrs. from grafts.	As above.	One of the hardiest forms of southern magnolia. Good in spots that require a narrowish evergreen.	Narrower, more upright than the species, with a narrower leaf.
M. g. 'Majestic Beauty'	4-12, 14-24	Ev.	Unknown. Probably large. Too new a variety to predict eventual size.		2 yrs. from grafts.	Very large, to 12 in. across, with 9 petals.	Vigorous, dense-branching street or shade tree of broadly pyramidal form.	Leaves exceptionally long, broad and heavy. The most luxuriant of the southern magnolias.

(Continued on next page)

M

Climate Zone maps pages 8-27

NAME	ZONES	DECIDUOUS OR EVERGREEN	HEIGHT IN FEET	SPREAD	BLOOMS AT AGE:	FLOWERS	USES	REMARKS
M. g. 'Samuel Sommer'	4-12, 14-24	Ev.	Unknown. Probably large. Too new a variety to predict eventual size.		2 yrs. from grafts.	Very large and full; to 10-14 in. across, with 12 petals.	See above. Like other grafted magnolias that bloom young, this will need pruning to become single-trunk tree. Can grow as a multiple-stem tree.	Leaves large, leathery, glossy, with a heavy rusty red felting on the underside. Very dark green above. Fairly fast growing. Comparable to *M. g.* 'Majestic Beauty' in quality.
M. g. 'St. Mary'	4-12, 14-24	Ev.	Usually 20 ft. by 20 ft. Slow.		2 yrs. grafts.	Heavy production of full-sized flowers on a small tree	Fine where a standard-size magnolia would be too tall. Good espalier and pot subject.	Left alone it will form a big, dense bush. Pruned and staked, it makes a small tree.
M. kobus KOBUS MAGNOLIA	1-9, 14-24	Dec.	30	20	15 yrs.	White, to 4 in. across; early.	Hardy, sturdy tree for planting singly on lawn or in informal shrub and tree groupings.	A superior selection named 'Wada's Memory' blooms younger, grows faster, has larger flowers.
M. k. stellata (Often sold as *M. stellata*.) STAR MAGNOLIA	1-9, 14-24	Dec.	10	20	3 yrs.	Very early white flowers with 19-21 narrow, strap-shaped petals. Profuse bloom in late winter, early spring.	Slow growing, shrubby, fine for borders, entryway gardens, edge of woods.	Quite hardy but flowers often nipped by frost. Fine texture to twig and leaf. Fair yellow and brown fall color.
M. k. s. 'Rosea' (Often sold as *M. s.* 'Rosea'.) PINK STAR MAGNOLIA	1-9, 14-24	Dec.	Same	Same	3 yrs.	Pink buds, flowers flushed pink, fading white.	As above. Place where you can see the flowers from living or family room; they often bloom so early that you won't want to walk out to see them.	In cold regions plant these early flowering sorts in a north exposure to delay bloom as long as possible, lessen frost damage.
M. k. s. 'Rubra' (Often sold as *M. s.* 'Rubra'.)	1-9, 14-24	Dec.	Same	Same	3 yrs.	Deeper pink, tinted purplish on backs of petals.	All the star magnolias have modest-sized (2-4-in.) leaves, finer foliage texture than other magnolias.	Same.
M. k. s. 'Waterlily' (Often sold as *M. s.* 'Waterlily')	1-9, 14-24	Dec.	Same	Same	3 yrs.	White, with broader petals than the type.	Same	Said to be faster growing, more vigorous than the type.
M. liliflora LILY MAGNOLIA	2-9, 14-24	Dec.	12	15	4 or 5 yrs.	White inside, purplish outside. Blooms in early spring and scatters bloom throughout summer. Long, slender buds.	Shrub border; for strong vertical effects in big flower border.	Good for cutting if taken before buds are fully open. Spreads slowly by suckering. Leaves 4-6 in. long.
M. l. 'Nigra' (*M. l.* 'Gracilis') Plants are sold under both names; probably identical.	2-9, 14-24	Dec.	12	15	As above.	Deep pink inside, deep purplish red outside. Slender, pansy black, curved buds.	As above	More slender in habit than species, with fewer suckers. Valuable for long blooming season—up to 2 months.

M

Climate Zone maps pages 8-27

NAME	ZONES	DECIDUOUS OR EVERGREEN	HEIGHT IN FEET	SPREAD	BLOOMS AT AGE:	FLOWERS	USES	REMARKS
M. macrophylla BIGLEAF MAGNOLIA	2-9, 14-21	Dec.	50 Slow	30	12-15 yrs.	White, fragrant, to 12 in. across, appearing after leaves are out. May-July.	Show-off tree with leaves 12-30 in. long, 9-12 in. wide. Needs to stand alone. Striking foliage, but hard to blend with other textures.	Plant where it is out of the wind; huge leaves easily tattered, branches brittle.
M. salicifolia ANISE MAGNOLIA	2-9, 14-21	Dec.	18-30 Slow	12	2-10 yrs.	White, narrow-petaled, to 4 in. across. Early.	Usually upright with slender branches, graceful appearance. In front of trees, shrub border. Leaves (3-6 in. long) bronze-red in fall.	An upright, large-flowered selection named 'Else Frye' is sold. Variety 'W. B. Clarke' blooms young, heavily.
M. sargentiana robusta	5-9, 14-24	Dec.	35	35	10-12 yrs. 8-10 yrs. for grafts.	Huge (8-12-in.) mauve pink bowls which open erect, then nod to horizontal. Early to midseason.	Must have ample room and protection from stormy winds which would tear the early blooms.	One of the most spectacular of flowering plants. Leaves 6-8 in. long. Not for hot, dry areas.
M. sieboldii (Sometimes sold as *M. parviflora.*) OYAMA MAGNOLIA	4-9, 14-24	Dec.	6-15	6-15	5 yrs.	White, cup-shaped, nodding, centered with crimson stamens, fragrant. Begins in May, and flowers open continuously over a long period.	Nice planted up-slope or at the top of a wall so that people can look into the flowers. Good for small gardens.	Popular in the Northwest for fragrance, long bloom, restrained growth. Buds like white Japanese lanterns. Leaves 3-6 in. long.
M. sinensis CHINESE MAGNOLIA	4-9, 14-24	Dec.	15-20	20-30	8-10 yrs. Less in grafts.	White, hanging, cup-shaped, fragrant, 3-5 in. wide. May and well into summer. Red stamens.	Usually a big shrub. Foliage glossy, thick, and leathery.	Long bloom, fragrance and crimson stamens make it a charming plant. Can be staked and pruned into a small tree.
M. soulangiana SAUCER MAGNOLIA often erroneously called TULIP TREE	1-10, 14-24	Dec.	To 25 ft.	To 25 ft. or more	3-5 yrs.	White to pink or purplish red, variable in size and form, blooming before leaves expand. Generally about 6 in. across.	Lawn ornament, shrub border, anchor plant in big corner plantings. Foliage good green rather coarse, leaves 4-6 in. (or more) long.	Seedlings highly variable; shop for named varieties. Hybrid of *M. denudata* and *M. liliflora.*
M. s. 'Alba' (*M. s.* 'Amabilis', *M. s.* 'Alba Superba')	1-10, 14-24	Dec.	Same	Same	Same	Flowers suffused purple, opening nearly pure white, large. Early.	As above. Rather more upright in growth than most.	
M. s. 'Alexandrina'	1-10, 14-24	Dec.	Same	Same	Same	Deep purplish pink, white inside, large. Mid-season.	As above. Large, rather heavy foliage.	Late bloom helps it escape frosts in colder sections.
M. s. 'Brozzonii'	1-10, 14-24	Dec.	Same	Same	Same	Huge, to 8 in. across. White, very slightly flushed at base. Early.	Large, vigorous plant.	One of handsomest whites.

(Continued on next page)

M

Climate Zone maps pages 8-27

NAME	ZONES	DECIDUOUS OR EVERGREEN	HEIGHT SPREAD IN FEET		BLOOMS AT AGE:	FLOWERS	USES	REMARKS
M. s. 'Burgundy'	1-10, 14-24	Dec.	Same	Same	Same	Large, well-rounded, deep purple halfway up to petal tips, then lightening to pink. Early.	San Francisco's Japanese Tea Garden has many of these artfully pruned and thinned to picturesque shapes.	
M. s. 'Grace McDade'	1-10, 14-24	Dec.	Same	Same	Same	Flowers very large, perhaps to 10 in. across, white, with pink tinting at base of petals. Early.	Striking with background of evergreens.	
M. s. 'Lennei'	1-10, 14-24	Dec.	Same	Same	Same	Very large, rather globe-shaped, deep purple on outside, white on inside. Late.	Plant spreading, vigorous.	Very late bloom helps it escape frosts in cold areas. 'Early Lennei' blooms 2 weeks earlier.
M. s. 'Lennei Alba'	1-10, 14-24	Dec.	Same	Same	Same	As above, except white in color, slightly smaller, earlier. Mid-season.	As above.	Two plants sold under this name. One form common in California is smaller in flower, creamy white, and earlier.
M. s. 'Lilliputian'	1-10, 14-24	Dec.	Smaller grower than others.		Same	Pink and white, somewhat smaller than other M. soulangiana varieties. Late flowering.	Good where a smaller magnolia is called for.	Late blooming.
M. s. 'Lombardy Rose'	1-10, 14-24	Dec.	Same as M. soulangiana		Same	To 8 in. wide, deep rose, white inside. Mid-season.	Readily trained into tree form.	Fast grower with treelike form.
M. s. 'Pink Superba'	1-10, 14-24	Dec.	Same	Same	Same	Large, deep pink, white inside. Early.	Best where late frosts are not a problem.	Identical to M. s. 'Alba' except for flower color.
M. s. 'Rubra' (M. s. 'Rustica Rubra')	1-10, 14-24	Dec.	To 25	To 25 ft. or more	Same	Large, cup-shaped, deep red-dish purple flowers. Midseason.	Tall, vigorous grower for large areas. More tree-like than many varieties.	Blooms somewhat past mid-season. Big 6-in. seed pods of dark rose.
M. s. 'San Jose'	1-10, 14-24	Dec.	Same	Same	Same	Large white flowers flushed pink to give general pale pink appearance. Very early.	Very early bloomer for sheltered spot.	Sometimes blooms late January in California.
M. sprengeri diva	5-9, 14-24	Dec.	To 40	To 30	7 yrs. from grafted plants.	To 8 in. wide, rose pink outside, white suffused pink with deeper lines inside. Scented; early to mid-season.	One of the brightest in color; young plants broad, twiggy.	Highly colored, erect, spectacular flowers. Buds seem more frost resistant than those of M. sargentiana robusta.
M. thompsoniana THOMPSON MAGNOLIA	4-9, 14-24	Dec.	10-20	10	4 yrs.	July flowering. Creamy white, fragrant, 4-5 in. across.	Big shrub for semi-shaded location, fragrant bloom at a dull season.	Long (4-10-in.) narrow leaves nearly white underneath. Hybrid of M. tripetala and and M. virginiana.

M

Climate Zone maps pages 8-27

NAME	ZONES	DECIDUOUS OR EVERGREEN	HEIGHT IN FEET	SPREAD	BLOOMS AT AGE:	FLOWERS	USES	REMARKS
M. veitchii VEITCH MAGNOLIA	4-9, 14-24	Dec.	30-40	30	4-5 yrs.	Blooms early, before leaves. Rose red at base, shading to white at tips, to 10 in. across.	Needs plenty of room and protection from wind. Fast-growing branches are brittle. Spectacular tree.	This hybrid between *M. campbellii* and *M. denudata* is exceptionally fast growing and vigorous. 'Rubra' has smaller purple-red flowers.
M. virginiana (*M. glauca*) SWEET BAY	4-9, 14-24	Dec. or semi-evergreen.	To 50 ft. Usually less.	To 20	8-10 yrs.	Nearly globular, 2-3 in. wide, creamy white, fragrant, June to September.	Prefers moist, acid soil. Grows in swamps in eastern U.S. Usually a massive, semi-evergreen shrub.	Variable in leaf drop. Some plants quite evergreen. Leaves grayish green, nearly white beneath, 2-5 in. long.
M. watsonii WATSON MAGNOLIA	4-9, 14-24	Dec.	20	20	12 yrs.	Creamy white, with crimson anthers, June-July after leaves expand. Often 5-6 in. across, fragrant.	Big shrub or stiff-looking small tree. At its best standing alone. Many think it a difficult plant to grow.	Hybrid between *M. sieboldii* and *M. obovata*, a big-leafed Japanese species. Leaves 4-8 in. long, dark green, nearly white underneath.
M. wilsonii WILSON MAGNOLIA	4-9, 14-24	Dec.	25	25	10 yrs.	White, with red stamens, pendulous, 3-4 in. across, fragrant. May and June.	Blooms at 4 ft., and tends to remain shrubby. Plant high on bank where flowers can be looked up to. Better in light shade.	Rich purple-brown twigs and narrow, tapered leaves, 3-6 in. long with silvery undersides.

MAHALA MAT. See Ceanothus prostratus

MAHERNIA verticillata. HONEY BELL. Evergreen perennial or subshrub. Zones 14-24. Straggly plant to 1 foot tall, 3 ft. wide. Leaves 1 in. long, finely divided. Yellow, bell-shaped, fragrant flowers in spring, then blooms sporadically all year. Needs good drainage. For longer plant life, keep dead flowers cut. Good in hanging basket or above a wall. Needs full sun.

MAHOBERBERIS miethkeana. Evergreen shrub. All Zones. Resembles *Mahonia aquifolium,* one of its parents; also has some traits of its barberry parent. Some leaves divided into leaflets. Leaves (or leaflets) oval, leathery, spiny-toothed or smooth, dark green showing bronzy purple in fall, winter. Dense, upright growth to 6-8 ft.; gets leggy, but can be pruned back. Clustered yellow flowers in early spring. Plant under some protection from wind and full sun.

MAHONIA. Evergreen shrubs. Related to barberry (*Berberis*) and described under that name by some botanists. Easily grown; good looking all year. Leaves divided into leaflets that usually have spiny teeth on the edges. Yellow flowers in dense rounded or spikelike clusters, followed by blue-black (sometimes red) berrylike fruit. Generally disease-resistant; sometimes foliage is disfigured by small looper caterpillar.

M. aquifolium. OREGON GRAPE. Zones 1-21. Native British Columbia to northern California. State flower of Oregon. To 6 ft. or more with tall, erect habit; spreads by underground stems. Leaves 4-10 in. long, with 5-9, very spiny-toothed, oval, 1-2½-in.-long leaflets that are glossy green in some forms, dull green in others. Young growth ruddy or bronzy; scattered mature red leaves through year (more pronounced in fall); purplish or bronzy leaves in winter, especially in cold-winter areas or where grown in full sun. Flowers in 2-3-in.-long clusters, March-May; fruits blue-black with gray bloom, edible (make good jelly).

Takes any exposure in most areas; north exposure best in Zones 12, 13. Control height and form by pruning; cut to ground any woody stems that extend too far above the mass; new growth quickly fills in. Lower growing varieties include 'Compacta', 'Mahani', 'Nana'.

Plant in masses as foundation planting, in woodland, in tubs, as low screen or garden divider. Resistant to oak root fungus (*Armillaria*) and especially valuable where gardens are heavily infested by this fungus.

M. bealei. LEATHERLEAF MAHONIA. All Zones. To 10-12 ft., with strong pattern of vertical stems, horizontal leaves over a foot long divided into 7-15 thick, leathery, broad leaflets as much as 5 in. long, yellowish green above, gray-green below, the edges spiny-toothed. Flowers in erect, 3-6-in.-

long, spikelike clusters at ends of branches in earliest spring. Berries powdery blue. Takes sun in fog belt, best in partial shade elsewhere. Plant in rich soil with ample organic material incorporated. Water generously. Truly distinguished plant against stone, brick, wood, glass.

M. fortunei. Zones 8-24. Stiffly upright with unbranched 5-6-ft. stems and 6-8-in. leaves divided into 7-13 rather narrow, 2-4-in.-long, dark dull green, toothed leaflets. Flowers (October-November) in short, narrow clusters. More tender than other mahonias, not so showy; pretty in a quiet way where vertical effect is desired.

M. fremontii. DESERT MAHONIA. Zones 8-24. Native to deserts of the Southwest. Erect habit, many stems, 3-12 ft. tall; the leaves with 3-5, thick, 1-in.-long leaflets, gray-green to yellowish green, the edges with very sharp, tough spines. Flowers in 1-1½-in.-long clusters, May-June; fruit dark blue to brown.

M. lomariifolia. Zones 6-9, 14-24. Showy plant with erect, little-branched stems to 6-10 ft. Young plants often have a single, vertical unbranched stem; with age plants produce more near-vertical branches from near base. Clustered near ends of these branches are the leaves, to 24 in. long, and held horizontally. Leaves have the outline of stiff, crinkly, barbed ferns. They are made of as many as 47 thick, spiny, glossy

M

Climate Zone maps pages 8-27

green leaflets arranged symmetrically along both sides of the central stem. Yellow flowers in winter or earliest spring grow in long erect clusters at branch tips, just above topmost cluster of leaves. They are followed by powdery blue berries which birds eat.

Needs shade at least in afternoon to keep its deep green. Prune stems at varying heights to induce branching. Dramatic in entryways, shaded patios, against shaded wall, in containers. Vertical habit, high leaf masses make it a dramatic plant for silhouette lighting effect. Good choice for narrow areas. Just don't place it so close to a walk that the sharp needles on its leaflets can scratch passers-by.

M. nervosa. LONGLEAF MAHONIA. Zones 2-9, 14-17. Native British Columbia to northern California. Low shrub 2 ft. (rarely 6 ft.) tall. Spreads by underground stems to make a good cover. Leaves clustered at stem tips, 10-18 in. long, with 7-21 glossy, bristle-toothed, green, 1-3¾-in.-long leaflets. Yellow flowers in upright clusters 3-6 in. long, April-June. Blue berries. Best in shade with ample moisture; will take sun in cooler areas, becoming very compact. Woodland ground cover, facing for taller mahonias, low barrier planting.

M. nevinii. NEVIN MAHONIA. Zones 8-24. Native to scattered localities, southern California. Many-branched shrub 3-10 ft. tall with gray foliage. Leaves with 3-5 leaflets, about 1 in. long, bristly or spiny. Flowers in loose, 1-2-in.-long clusters, March-May, followed by red berries. Sun or light shade, any soil, much or little water. Use individually or as screen, hedge.

M. pinnata. CALIFORNIA HOLLY GRAPE. Zones 8, 9, 14-24. Native southern Oregon to southern California. Similar to Oregon grape, but with more crinkly leaves. Stands heat and drought.

M. piperiana. Zones 6-9, 14-24. Coast ranges southern Oregon to Baja California. Compact and upright, usually 2-3 ft.

high in wilds, 4-5 ft. in gardens. Leaves of 5-9 oval leaflets, 1-2½ in. long, glossy dark green above, gray-green beneath, with spiny edges. Flowers in 2-in.-long clusters, March-April, followed by blue-black berries.

M. repens. CREEPING MAHONIA. Zones 1-21. Native northern California, eastward to Rocky Mountains. Creeps by underground stems. To 3 ft. tall, spreading habit. Dull bluish green leaves have 3-7 spine-toothed leaflets, turn bronzy in winter. Blooms April-June. Good ground cover in sun, partial shade.

MAIDENHAIR SPLEENWORT. See Asplenium trichomanes

MAIDENHAIR TREE. See Ginkgo

MAIDEN'S WREATH. See Francoa

MAJORANA hortensis. SWEET MARJORAM. Perennial herb, treated as annual in cold winter climates. To 1-2 ft. Tiny, oval, gray-green leaves; spikes of white flowers in loose clusters at top of plant. Grow in fairly moist soil, full sun. Keep blossoms cut off and plant trimmed to prevent woody growth. Propagate from seeds, cuttings, or root divisions. It's a favorite herb for seasoning meats, salads, vinegars, casserole dishes. Use leaves fresh or dried. Often grown in container indoors on windowsill in cold-winter areas.

MALCOLMIA maritima. VIRGINIAN STOCK. Annual. To 8-15 in., single-stemmed or branching from base, covered with nearly scentless 4-petaled flowers. Colors include white, yellow, pinks, and lilacs to magenta. Sow in place any time except in hot or very cold weather. As with sweet alyssum (*Lobularia maritima*), seed-sowing to bloom takes only 6 weeks. Does not readily reseed. Demands moderately rich soil and full sun for best performance. Good bulb cover.

MALEPHORA. See Ice Plant

MALLEE. See Eucalyptus

MALLOW, TREE. See Lavatera

MALTESE CROSS. See Lychnis chalcedonica

MALUS. CRABAPPLE. Deciduous trees, rarely shrubs. Zones 1-11, 14-21. Handsome pink, white, or red flowers and fruit which is edible, or showy, or sometimes both. For the crabapples we use in jellies see CRABAPPLE. Ornamental crabapples include at least two hundred named kinds, and new ones appear with each year's new catalogues. The chart describes two dozen of merit.

Longer lived than flowering peaches, hardier and more tolerant of wet soil than flowering cherries or other flowering stone fruits, flowering crabapples are among the most useful and least troublesome of flowering trees, even if spring color is less striking than that of flowering peach or cherry. Plant bare-root in winter or early spring; set out container plants any time. Good, well drained garden soil is best, but crabapples will take mildly acid or alkaline soil, or rocky soil. Prune only to build a good framework or to correct shape; annual pruning neither necessary nor desirable.

Diseases and pests are few; fireblight can be a problem, but usually is not. The same pests that affect apple also prey on crabapple; controls are simple. If you or your neighbors grow apples, or if you wish to use the crabapples from your tree, spray to control codling moth. Scale, aphids, spider mites, and tent caterpillars may require spraying. Scab, powdery mildew, and crabapple rust are serious problems in the Northwest. Fungicide sprays will control them. Some are rust resistant; see chart.

Fine lawn trees, or use in rows along driveways or walks. Planted near fences they will heighten the screening effect, provide blossoms and fruit, and still give planting room for primroses, spring bulbs, or shade-loving summer bedding plants.

MALUS

NAME	GROWTH RATE, HEIGHT & SPREAD IN FEET	STRUCTURE	FOLIAGE	FLOWERS	FRUIT
MALUS 'Almey'	Moderate to 15 by 15.	Upright growth.	Young leaves purplish, mature ones bronze green. Susceptible to rust in Northwest.	Single scarlet, white at base. April bloom.	Scarlet, hangs on well.
M. arnoldiana ARNOLD CRABAPPLE	Fairly rapid, 20 by 30.	Broad, spreading, with long, arching branches.	Medium texture, fairly large leaf.	Buds red. Flowers pink, fading white, fragrant, to 2 in. across.	Yellow and red, Sept. through Nov.
M. atrosanguinea CARMINE CRABAPPLE	Moderate growth to 18 by 18.	Upright branches, drooping tips. Open, irregular, rather sparse.	Purplish green, with more sheen than average crabapple.	Fragrant, crimson to rose pink; profuse; late April-May.	Yellow, aging brown and hanging through winter in withered state.
M. baccata mandschurica	Moderate to 40 by 20.	Vase shaped, bushy, dense.	Densely foliaged, dark green.	Fragrant white 1-in. flowers. First to bloom in April.	Bright yellow and scarlet, Aug.-Oct. Profuse.

M

Climate Zone maps pages 8-27

NAME	GROWTH RATE, HEIGHT & SPREAD IN FEET	STRUCTURE	FOLIAGE	FLOWERS	FRUIT
M. b. 'Columnaris'	Moderate to 30 by 5-8.	Narrow, upright, columnar, spreading somewhat in old plants.	Dense. Resistant to rust in Northwest.	White, fragrant, 1-in. flowers in April.	Yellow and scarlet.
M. coronaria 'Charlotte'	30 by 30.	Rounded, broad at base of crown.	Dense.	Pink, double, 2 in. across. Late May. Fragrant.	Large, green, sparsely produced.
M. 'Dolgo'	Moderate to 40 by 40.	Willowy, spreading; prune for good framework.	Reddish green, dense.	Early spring blooming. Flowers profuse, white, single.	Cherrylike clusters of red, 1¼-in. fruits, Aug.-Oct. Flavor good.
M. 'Dorothea'	Moderate to 25 by 25.	Dense, rounded.	Dense, fine textured.	May blooming, double, 2-in., pink flowers. Blooms young.	Marble-size, bright yellow, effective fall and early winter.
M. floribunda JAPANESE FLOWERING CRABAPPLE	Moderate to 20 by 30.	Rounded, densely branched. Irregular, angular branches.	Dense, fine textured. Resistant to rust in Northwest.	Red to pink in bud, opening white. Extremely profuse.	Small, yellow and red, Aug.-Oct.
M. halliana parkmanii PARKMAN CRABAPPLE	Slow to 15 by 12.	Arching branches, eventually rather globe-shaped crown.	Dark green, rather sparse.	Double, rose, 1¼ in. wide, in clusters on dark, wine red stems, May.	Small, dull red, of no value.
M. 'Hopa'	Fast to 25 by 20.	Upright branches spreading with weight of fruit.	Dense, dark green with brownish cast. Subject to rust in Northwest.	Fragrant, single, rose red, 1½ in. April flowering. One of best in southern California.	Orange-red, coloring early. Profuse. Good for jelly.
M. hupehensis (M. theifera) TEA CRABAPPLE	Moderate to 15 by 20.	Rigid branches grow in 45° angles from short trunk. Side branches short, spurlike. General effect Y-shaped.	Dense on side branches, but these are spaced well apart from each other.	Deep pink buds, pink flowers fading white, fragrant. Early May. Very profuse.	Not ornamental.
M. ioensis plena BECHTEL CRABAPPLE	Moderate to 25 by 20.	Coarse branches, rather angular, eventually vase-shaped.	Sparse, coarse, soft green.	Large, very double, pink, fragrant. Resemble rambler rose flowers.	Rarely borne, green, not ornamental.
M. 'Katherine'	Slow to 20 by 20.	Loose and open.	Dark green, not dense.	Double, light pink fading white, very large—to 2¼ in. Alternate bloom; heavy one year, light the next.	Dull red, not especially showy.
M. micromalus (M. kaido) MIDGET CRABAPPLE (Kaido is Japanese for crabapple)	Slow to 20 by 15.	Upright, dense.	Dark green.	Single, unfading pink, very profuse in April. Fragrant.	Red or greenish red, not showy.
M. 'Oekonomierat Echtermeyer' ('Pink Weeper') WEEPING CRABAPPLE	Moderate to 15 ft. Spread depends on pruning.	Weeping branches. Usually grafted high on a standard crabapple. Cut out branches that grow stiffly upright.	Opening purplish, later bronzy green.	Purplish red, 1½ in. in diameter, all along drooping branchlets.	Purple-red, 1 in., effective in fall.
M. pumila niedzwetzkyana REDVEIN CRABAPPLE	Fast to 25 by 18.	Upright, spreading, somewhat irregular.	Large, purplish green.	Purple-rose, 1½ in., April.	Wine red, 2 in., with purplish flesh.

(Continued on next page)

M

Climate Zone maps pages 8-27

NAME	GROWTH RATE, HEIGHT & SPREAD IN FEET	STRUCTURE	FOLIAGE	FLOWERS	FRUIT
M. purpurea 'Aldenhamensis' ALDENHAM CRABAPPLE	Fast to 20 by 20.	Somewhat irregular round head, dense.	Purplish leaves and purplish bark on twigs.	Semi-double, purplish red, large. May, sometimes reblooming in fall.	Purplish red, 1 in.
M. p. 'Eleyi' ELEY CRABAPPLE	Fast to 20 by 20.	Irregular, open, graceful.	Dark green, with reddish veins and stalks.	Wine red, 1¼ in., April.	Heavy bearer of ¾-in. purple-red fruits.
M. 'Red Jade'	Moderate to 15 by 15.	Long, slender, weeping branches. Charming, irregular habit.	Dark green.	Small, white, profuse in April-May.	Heavy crop of bright red fruits hold late into fall, are showy on weeping branches.
M. 'Red Silver'	Fast to 15 by 15.	Irregular, branches angular with tips drooping slightly.	Reddish or purplish bronze silvered with silky hairs.	Deep wine red, April.	Dark purplish red, ¾ in., good for jelly.
M. sargentii SARGENT CRABAPPLE	Slow to 10 by 20.	Dense, broad shrub with zig-zag branching.	Dark green, often lobed at base.	White, small but profuse, fragrant. Pink in *M. s.* 'Rosea'. Mid-May.	Red, tiny, profuse, lasting late.
M. scheideckeri SCHEIDECKER CRABAPPLE	Moderate to 20 by 15.	Dense, upright.	Dense, dark green.	Semi-double, rose pink. April to May.	Small, yellow, holding into November.
M. zumi calocarpa	Moderate to 25 by 15.	Pyramidal, dense, branching, branchlets weeping.	Densely foliaged, larger leaves lobed.	Opening soft pink, fading white, fragrant, late April-early May.	Small, ½ in., glossy, bright red, holding well into winter.

MAMMILLARIA. Cactus. Small, cylindrical or globe-shaped, either single-stemmed or clustered. Flowers generally small, arranged in a circle near the top of the plant, red, pink, yellow, or white. Easy to grow in sun; give ample water during summer. Chiefly grown in pots by collectors. Specialists offer as many as 100 species.

For the plant sold as *M. vivipara,* see *Coryphantha.*

MANDEVILLA. Evergreen or deciduous vines. Known for showy flowers. Includes plants formerly known as *Dipladenia.*

M. 'Alice du Pont' (*Mandevilla splendens, Dipladenia splendens, D. amoena*). House or greenhouse plant; outdoors Zones 21-24. Evergreen vine to 20-30 ft., much less as usually grown in pots or tubs. Twining stems produce dark green, glossy, oval leaves 3-8 in. long. Clusters of flowers appear among leaves from April-November. Flowers 2-4 in. across, pure pink, deeper when grown in shade. Even very small plants in 4-in. pots will bloom. Give plants frame, trellis, or stake for support. Pinch young plants to induce bushiness. Rich soil, ample water, full sun coastal areas, part shade inland. Spray for red spider mites.

M. laxa (*M. suaveolens*). CHILEAN JASMINE. Deciduous vine. Zones 4-9, 14-21. Twines to 15 ft. or more. Leaves long ovals, heart-shaped at base, 2-6 in. long. Summer flowers white, clustered, 2 in. across, trumpet-shaped, powerfully fragrant (like gardenia). Sun, rich soil, ample water. If plant becomes badly tangled, cut it to the ground in winter; it will bloom on new growth. Root-hardy to about 5°.

MANGIFERA indica. MANGO. Evergreen tree. Zones 23, 24. Grows to large size in tropics. In warmest parts of southern California often survives for years, but may remain shrubby and is likely to fruit only in most favored, frost-free locations. Leaves are large and handsome, often coppery red or purple at time of expanding, later dark green and 8-16 in. long. Needs steady moisture, but tolerates fairly poor, shallow soils.

MANGO. See Mangifera

MANNA GUM. See Eucalyptus viminalis

MANUKA. See Leptospermum scoparium

MANZANITA. See Arctostaphylos

MANZANOTE. See Olmediella

MAPLE. See Acer

MAPLE, FLOWERING. See Abutilon

MARANTA leuconeura. PRAYER PLANT, RABBIT TRACKS. Perennial. House or greenhouse plant with leafy stems, usually less than 1 ft. high. Leaves 7-8 in. long and half as wide, short stalked, becoming whitish along midrib and veins; brown spots toward margin account for name "rabbit tracks". Leaves fold upward at night; hence the

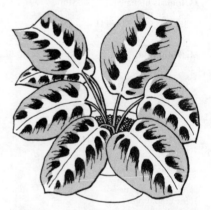

Paired brown spots give Maranta leuconeura the common name of rabbit tracks.

other common name, "prayer plant". In the variety 'Kerchoveana' undersurface of leaves is grayish and spotted with red.

Grow in north light. Must have warmth, occasional trimming, and regular feeding (fish emulsion is good) to be at its best. Excellent in dish gardens, terrariums, or shallow pots.

Climate Zone maps pages 8-27

MARGUERITE. See Chrysanthemum frutescens

MARGUERITE, BLUE. See Felicia

MARGUERITE, GOLDEN. See Anthemis tinctoria

MARIGOLD. See Tagetes

MARIGOLD, CAPE. See Dimorphotheca, Osteospermum

MARIGOLD, MARSH. See Caltha

MARIGOLD, POT. See Calendula

MARJORAM, SWEET. See Majorana

MARJORAM, WILD. See Origanum

MARMALADE BUSH. See Streptosolen

MARKHAMIA hildebrandtiana. Evergreen shrub or tree. Zones 23, 24. To 30 ft. Leaves bronzy when unfolding, later bronzy-green, 6-10 in. long, with leathery leaflets. Early summer flowers, clustered at ends of branches, 2 in. across, trumpet-shaped, soft yellow. Best near coast where air is moist, but out of sea winds.

MARLOCK. See Eucalyptus

MARRUBIUM vulgare. HOREHOUND. Perennial herb. All Zones. To 1-3 ft. Wrinkled, woolly, aromatic, gray-green leaves; white, mintlike flowers in whorls on foot-long, branching stems. Grows in poor, sandy, dry soil, full sun. Sow seeds in spring in flats, later transplant to 12 in. apart. As a garden plant, it's rather weedy-looking but can serve as edging in gray garden. Used for medicinal purposes and in candy. Foliage lasts well in bouquets.

MATERNITY PLANT. See Kalanchoe daigremontiana

MATTHIOLA. STOCK. Annuals (technically, biennials or perennials grown as annuals). All have gray-green, long, narrow leaves and flowers in erect clusters.

M. incana. STOCK. Valued for fragrance, cut flowers, garden decoration. Flowers single or double, an inch wide, in spikes. Colors include white, pink, red, purple, lavender, cream. Blues and reds are purple-toned, yellows tend toward cream. Spicy-sweet fragrance.

Stock needs light, fertile soil, good drainage, cool weather. Valuable winter flowers in Zones 8, 9, 12-24—there, set out plants in early fall for winter or early spring bloom. Plants take moderate frost, but will not set flower buds if nights are too chilly; late planting will mean late flowers. Where rainfall is heavy, plant in raised beds to insure good drainage, prevent root rot. In Zones 1-7, 10, 11, plant in earliest spring to get bloom before hot weather.

Many strains available. Column stock and Double Giant Flowering are unbranched, 2-3 ft. tall, and can be planted 6-8 in. apart in rows; ideal for cutting. Giant Imperial strain is branched, 2-2½ ft. tall, comes in straight colors or mixed. Trysomic or Ten Weeks stock are branched, 15-18 in. tall. Brompton stock in white or pink grows 18 in. tall. Trysomic Seven Weeks strain is 12-15 in. tall.

M. longipetala bicornis. EVENING SCENTED STOCK. Annual. Foot-tall plant with small purplish flowers that are closed and inconspicuous by day, wonderfully fragrant at night.

MATTRESS VINE. See Muehlenbeckia complexa

MAYPOP. See Passiflora incarnata

MAYTEN TREE. See Maytenus

MAYTENUS boaria. MAYTEN TREE. Evergreen tree. Zones 8, 9, 14-21. Slow to moderate growth to an eventual 30-50 ft.; 20 ft. by 15 ft. in spread at 12 years is typical. Long, pendulous branchlets hang down from branches, giving tree daintiness and grace. Habit and leaves (1-2 in. long) somewhat like small-scale weeping willow. A better tree for the patio than weeping willow —neater and not invasive rooted. Flowers and fruit inconspicuous.

Good drainage a necessity. Stake securely when planting. There will be much side growth; remove unwanted growth along trunk; or, if you wish, preserve some side branches for multiple trunk effect. Will take some drought when established, but is lusher and greener with adequate water. Sometimes may show partial defoliation after cold snaps or at blooming time; recovery is rapid.

Choice lawn tree. Locate to display its pattern effectively—against walls in entryway or patio, in featured raised planting beds, near outdoor living areas.

MAZUS reptans. Perennial. Zones 1-7 (freezes to ground in winter), 14-24 (evergreen). Slender stems creep and root along ground, send up leafy branches 1-2 in. tall. Leaves an inch long, narrowish, bright green, with a few teeth on edges. Flowers (spring, early summer) in clusters of 2-5, purplish blue with white and yellow markings, about ¾ in. across. In shape, the flowers resemble those of mimulus. Sun or very light shade; rich, moist soil. Rock gardens or small-scale ground cover. Takes very light foot traffic.

MEADOW RUE. See Thalictrum

MEADOW SWEET. See Astilbe

MECONOPSIS. Perennials. Rare plants related to poppy. Ardent collectors and shade garden enthusiasts sometimes attempt the many species offered by specialist seed firms. Most are difficult; two listed here are not too hard in the right climate.

M. betonicifolia (*M. baileyi*). HIMALAYAN POPPY. Zones 1-7, 17. Tall, leafy, short-lived perennial 2-4 ft. tall with hairy leaves and 3-4-in.-wide poppies of sky blue or rosy lavender, centered with yellow stamens. Needs shade, humid air, coolness, loose, acid soil. Try it with rhododendrons.

M. cambrica. WELSH POPPY. Zones 1-9, 14-17. Short-lived perennial with 3-in. yellow or orange flowers on 1-ft. stems. Fairly easy, self-sows. Gray-green divided leaves. Full sun or light shade near coast, part shade inland.

MEDICAGO. Group of plants related to clover. Most (including alfalfa) are grown for pasture or hay; two are ornamental:

M. arborea. TREE ALFALFA. Evergreen shrub. Zones 8-24. Native to southern Europe. To 6-8 ft. tall. Leaves cloverlike, 1-1½ in. long, the 3 leaflets ¼-¾ in. long, smooth green above, silvery beneath. Yellow, clustered, sweet pea-shaped flowers appear from early spring through fall, the year round in mildest climates. Seed pods spirally curled. Useful plant for long bloom, low maintenance.

M. lupulina. One of several plants grown as shamrock. See Shamrock.

MELALEUCA. Evergreen trees and shrubs. Narrow, sometimes needlelike leaves, and clustered flowers with prominent stamens. Each cluster resembles a bottlebrush, and some melaleucas are called bottlebrushes, although that name is more generally applied to Callistemon. Clusters of woody seed capsules hang on for several years, forming odd, decorative cylinders around twigs and branches.

Most melaleucas stand heat, wind, poor soil, drought, and salt air; exceptions, noted below, are important. Most are vigorous and fast growing; control by cutting back selected branches to a well-placed side branch. Shearing makes them dense and lumpish. The smaller melaleucas are good screening materials; some of the larger ones are useful as flowering or shade trees. Many have interestingly contorted branches and bark that peels in thick paperlike layers.

M. armillaris. DROOPING MELALEUCA. Shrub or small tree. Zones 9, 12-24. To 15-30 ft. Furrowed gray bark peels in strips near base of trunk. Drooping branches. Light green, needlelike leaves to 1 in. long. Fluffy white flowers in 1-3½-in.-long spikes spring to fall. Tough and adaptable, especially useful in sea winds. Clipped hedge or unclipped informal screen (prickly leaves a real deterrent), or, with training, a sprawling shrub or small tree. Becomes picturesque with age.

M. decussata. LILAC MELALEUCA. Large shrub or small tree. Zones 9, 12-24. Grows 8-20 ft. tall with equal spread. Brown, shreddy bark. Tiny (½-in.-long) leaves close-set on arching, pendulous branches. Lilac to purple flowers in 1-in. spikes late spring-summer. Will stand some neglect. Use it to supply big masses of fine-textured, bluish foliage. Thinning will improve its appearance by showing off trunk, branch character.

M. elliptica. Shrub or small tree. Zones 9, 12-24. To 8-15 ft. high. Brown, shreddy bark. Roundish, ½-in.-long leaves mostly at ends of fanlike branches. Large, showy, red to crimson bottlebrushes to 3½ in. long early spring to fall on side branches.

M. ericifolia. HEATH MELALEUCA. Shrub or small tree. Zones 9, 12-24. To 10-25 ft. Bark tan or gray, soft, fibrous. Dark green, needlelike, 1-in. leaves like those of heather. Yellowish white flowers in 1-in. spikes; blooms early spring. Fast growing and tolerant of alkaline soil and poor drainage; good near beach. Attractive multi-trunked tree.

M. hypericifolia. DOTTED MELALEUCA. Shrub. Zones 9, 12-24. Grows 6-10 ft. tall, with thin, peeling bark, drooping branches. Coppery green to dull green 1¼-in. leaves. bright orange-red flowers in dense 2-in clusters late spring through winter. Can be clipped into a hedge, but will bloom more profusely as an informal, unclipped screen. Not suited right at beach, but takes ocean wind, drought.

M. linariifolia. FLAXLEAF PAPERBARK. Tree. Zones 9, 13-23. To 30 ft., with umbrellalike crown. White bark sheds in papery flakes. Slender branchlets. Bright green or bluish green, 1¼-in.-long leaves are stiff, needlelike. Numerous fluffy spikes of small white flowers in summer give effect of snow on branches. Young plants willowy, need staking until trunk firms up; prune out lower branches to shape.

M. nesophila. PINK MELALEUCA. Tree or large shrub. Zones 9, 13, 16-24. Fast growth to 15-20, possibly 30 ft. Grows naturally as a small tree; unpruned, produces gnarled, heavy branches that sprawl or ascend in picturesque patterns. Thick, spongy bark. Gray-green, thick, roundish, 1-in. leaves. Mauve flower brushes fade to white, tipped yellow, roundish, to 1 in. wide, produced most of year. Takes beach winds and spray; poor, rocky soil; desert heat; much water or practically no water. Use as big informal screen, tree, or shear as hedge.

M. quinquenervia. (Usually sold as *M. leucadendra*). CAJEPUT TREE. Tree. Zones 9, 13, 16, 17, 20-24. Upright, open growth to 20-40 ft. Young branches pendulous. The trunk has thick, spongy, light brown to whitish bark that peels off in sheets. Leaves stiff, narrowly oval, pale green, shiny, 2-4 in. long. Young leaves have silky hairs. Foliage turns purple with light frost. Flowers yellowish white (sometimes pink or purple), 2-3-in. spikes, summer and fall. Can take much or little water. Good street tree.

M. styphelioides. Tree. Zones 9, 13-24. Grows 20-40 ft. Pendulous branchlets; lacy, open growth habit. Thick, pale, spongy, light tan bark becoming charcoal with age, peels off in papery layers. Leaves to ¾ in. long, ¼ in. wide, sometimes twisted, prickly to touch, light green. Creamy white flowers in 1-2-in. brushes, summer through fall. Thrives in any soil. Good lawn tree. Best trained with multiple trunks.

M. wilsonii. Shrub. Zones 9, 12-24. Wide spreading, 6-8 ft. high. Rough, scaly bark. Narrow ½-in.-long, medium green leaves closely set on slender branchlets. Spidery, pinkish magenta flowers in inch-wide clusters or cylindrical spikes, along stems in late spring.

MELIA azedarach. CHINA-BERRY. Deciduous tree. Zones 6, 8-24. Spreading tree to 30-50 ft. high. Leaves 1-3 ft. long, cut into many 1-2-in.-long, narrow or oval, toothed leaflets. Loose clusters of lilac flowers in early summer, followed by ½-in. yellow, hard, berrylike fruits. Fruits poisonous.

M. a. 'Umbraculifera'. TEXAS UMBRELLA TREE. Less picturesque but far more common. It has a dense, spreading, dome-shaped crown and drooping leaves. Grows to 30 ft. Gives rich green color, dense shade in hottest, driest climates, even in poor alkaline soil. Stands all except the strongest ocean winds. Sometimes suckers, and wood is brittle, but valuable where trees are hard to grow.

MELIANTHUS major. HONEY BUSH. Evergreen shrub. Zones 8, 9, 12-24. Soft-wooded plant of very fast growth to 12-14 ft., easily kept much lower. Stems upright or sprawling and spreading, slightly branched. Striking foliage. Leaves a foot long, grayish green, divided into 9-11 strongly toothed leaflets. Flowers reddish brown, 1 in. long, in foot-long spikes late winter, early spring.

Adaptable in most soils, most locations, but best in some shade in desert and valley gardens. To get tall plants, stake a few stems; for a sprawling, bulky effect, shorten some stems in early spring before new growth begins. Needs grooming. Spray to control whitefly. Use as silhouette in raised beds, sprawling over a wall, in containers, with succulents or foliage plants.

M. minor. Plants offered under this name usually turn out to be *M. major*. The true *M. minor* has much smaller (to 6 in. long) leaves on a 3-ft. plant.

MELISSA officinalis. LEMON BALM, SWEET BALM. Perennial herb. All Zones. To 2 ft. Light green, heavily veined leaves with lemon scent. White flowers unimportant. Shear occasionally to keep compact. Spreads rapidly. Grow in rich, moist soil in sun or part shade. Very hardy. Propagate from seed or root divisions. Leaves used in cold drinks; fragrant oil used in perfume. Cut branches keep well in arrangements.

MELON, MUSKMELON, CANTALOUPE. (The true cantaloupe, a hard-shelled melon, is not grown in this country.) To ripen to full sweetness, a melon needs 2½-4 months of heat. Foggy summer days or cool days don't help. Gardeners in cool-summer climates should plant their melons in the warmest south exposures. Both in cool-summer climates and interior short-summer climates, start plants indoors in peat pots a few weeks before the last frost date. Truly tropical plants, melons perish in even light frost.

Melons need considerable space (dimensions described below) in full sun. You can grow melons on sun-bathed trellises, but the heavy fruits have to be supported in individual cloth slings.

Principal types are the muskmelons ("cantaloupes") and the late melons. The former are ribbed and have a netted skin and (usually) salmon-colored flesh; these are most widely adapted to various Western climates. Good muskmelons (best for cooler climates) are 'Honey Rock', 'Gold Cup', 'Hale's Best', and the hybrids 'Samson' and 'Burpee Hybrid'. Late melons will ripen only where there is a long, hot, rather dry summer (Zones 8, 9, 12-14, 18, 19). 'Persian', 'Honey Dew', 'Honey Ball', 'Golden Beauty Casaba', and 'Crenshaw' are typical late melons.

Except as noted above, sow seeds 2 weeks after average date of last frost. Soil should be light and well drained. Best planted on gently rounded mounds 6 ft. wide and a few inches high at the center. On the south side of mounds make furrows 10 in. wide and 6 in. deep for irrigation. Water well until furrows are filled. Plant 6 or 7 seeds about 1 in. deep, spaced within an 8-10-in. circle 6 in. or so away from the furrow. Space these circles (hills) 3 ft. apart. This system permits watering the plants from below without wetting the foliage. When plants are well established, thin each circle to the best two, and begin to train them away from the furrow. Fill the furrow with water from time to time, but do not keep soil soaked. Feed (again in the furrow) every six weeks. Harvest muskmelon and 'Persian' melon when the stems begin to crack away from the melon end. 'Honey Dew' and 'Casaba' fruits are ready when the rinds turn yellow; 'Crenshaw' melons turn mostly yellow, but show some green even when ripe. Most reliable way to determine degree of ripeness of these melons is to smell the blossom end. Ripe ones have a pleasant, fruity perfume.

MENTHA. MINT. Perennial herbs and ground cover. Spread rapidly by underground stems. Grow almost anywhere but perform best in light, medium-rich, moist soil, partial shade. Contain in pot or box to keep in bounds. Propagate from runners. Keep flowers cut off. Replant every 3 years.

M. citrata. ORANGE MINT, BERGAMOT MINT. All Zones. Grows 2 ft. high. Broad, 2-in.-long, dark green, scented leaves; small lavender flowers. Use in potpourris, or like other mints in flavoring foods. Slight orange-like flavor when crushed.

M. gentilis. GOLDEN APPLE MINT. All Zones. To 2 ft. Smooth, deep green leaves, variegated yellow. Use in flavoring foods. Foliage excellent in mixed bouquets.

M. piperita. PEPPERMINT. All Zones. To 3 ft. Strong-scented, toothed, 3-in.-long leaves. Small purple flowers in 1-3-in. spikes. Leaves good for flavoring tea.

M. requienii. JEWEL MINT OF CORSICA. Creeping, mat-forming perennial. Zones 5-9, 12-24. Spreads at moderate to rapid rate, grows only ½ in. high. Tiny, round, bright green leaves give a mossy effect. Tiny light purple flowers in summer. Set divisions 6 in. apart for ground cover in sun or part shade. Needs moisture, and disappears during winter in colder areas. Delightful minty or sagelike fragrance when bruised or crushed under foot.

M. rotundifolia. APPLE MINT. All Zones. Stiff stems grow 20-30 in. high. Rounded leaves are slightly hairy and gray-green, about 1-4 in. long. Purplish white flowers are produced in 2-3 in. spikes.

M. spicata. SPEARMINT. All Zones. To 1½-2 ft. Dark green leaves, slightly smaller than peppermint; leafy spikes of purplish flowers. Use leaves fresh from the garden or dried for lamb, in cold drinks, as garnish, in apple jelly.

MENZIESIA purpurea. Deciduous shrub. Zones 4-7, 14-17. Low, spreading member of the heather family. Slow growth to 3-6 ft. Leaves oval, to 1½ in. long; some color red and orange in fall. Clustered, bell-shaped flowers in mid-spring, ½ in. long, bright red with slight grayish tint on the outside. Needs acid soil, ample water, partial shade in warmer areas.

MERATIA. See Chimonanthus

MERTENSIA virginica. VIRGINIA BLUEBELLS. Perennial. Zones 1-21. Native of eastern U. S. Comes up early in spring and blossoms early. The leafy flower stalks 1-2 ft. high bear several flowers in rather close, nodding clusters. Flowers trumpet-shaped, about 1

Climate Zone maps pages 8-27

in. long, blue with a purplish throat. The buds are bright pink. Leaves and stems die down after flowering season, and disappear by midsummer. Takes sun or shade; delightful in the woodland garden with trilliums, ferns.

Drooping, inch-long flowers of Virginia bluebells are soft blue, flower buds pink.

MESCAL BEAN. See Sophora secundiflora

MESEMBRYANTHEMUM. See Ice Plant

MESQUITE. See Prosopis glandulosa torreyana

MESQUITE, FALSE. See Calliandra eriophylla

MESSMATE. See Eucalyptus

METAKE. See Bamboo

METASEQUOIA glyptostroboides. DAWN REDWOOD. Deciduous conifer. Zones 3-24. To 80-90 ft. high. Looks somewhat like coast redwood *(Sequoia sempervirens)* but differs in several ways. Cones are much smaller than those of coast redwood. Leaves are soft to the touch and light, bright green; those of coast redwood are dark green and somewhat stiff. Dawn redwood's light brown branchlets turn upward; those of coast redwood usually stand out horizontally. Most important, foliage of dawn redwood turns light bronze in autumn and then it falls; coast redwood is evergreen.

Stands temperatures from −15° to 105°, but suffers winter wind damage in cold, dry areas. Salt winds cause foliage burn, as does hot sunlight in enclosed areas. Grows best in moist, well drained soil containing peat moss or leaf mold; takes lawn watering well. Rarely attacked by pests or diseases. Extremely sensitive to 2,4-D and similar hormone weed-killers.

Best use is in groves, where it brings something of the beauty of a redwood grove to cold-winter areas. However, also good for single planting—the swelling buds and bright, silky new needles are a real treat in spring. Structurally interesting even when bare. Grows very fast when young, sometimes 4-6 ft. a year in California, less in colder areas. A young tree will grow satisfactorily in a large tub or box.

METROSIDEROS. Evergreen trees or large shrubs. Native to New Zealand. Plants generally branch heavily from the ground up, require careful staking and pruning to bring into tree form. Leaves firm, leathery, densely spaced on branches. Flowers clustered at ends of branches, red (rarely yellow or white). Dense, clustered stamens make the show; along coast, trees rival *Eucalyptus ficifolia* in flower color.

Best near the coast; frost, dry air limit success inland. Most dependable first-line trees near the beach, tolerating wind and salt spray. Useful as street or lawn trees.

M. excelsa *(M. tomentosa)*. NEW ZEALAND CHRISTMAS TREE, POHUTUKAWA. Zones 17, 23, 24. Grows to 30 ft. or more; foliage on young plants smooth glossy green; older plants develop leaves which are dark green above, white-woolly underneath. Dark scarlet flowers in big clusters cover ends of branches in May-July (December in New Zealand, hence the common name "Christmas Tree"). "Pohutukawa" means "drenched with spray", and describes very well seashore locations where wild plants grow. There is a yellow-flowered variety, 'Aurea'.

M. robusta. NORTH ISLAND RATA. Zones 17, 23, 24. To 45 ft. or more. Leaves 1-1½ in. long, dark green, roundish. New shoots and foliage coppery red. Flowers (in midsummer) scarlet. Blooms young.

M. umbellata *(M. lucida)*. SOUTHERN RATA. Zones 16, 17, 20-24. Slow growth into a large bush, possibly eventually a tree 45-60 ft. tall. New leaves flushed red; mature leaves 1-3½ in. long, silky when young, finally glossy. Midsummer flowers scarlet. Slow growing, very slow to come into bloom (15-20 years), tolerant of frosts and constant wind. Needs plenty of water.

M. villosa *(M. kermadecensis)*. Zones 17, 20-24. Shrubby, fairly upright plant. Smaller than *M. excelsa*, with smaller grayish leaves, red flowers, sporadically through the year. Showier than *M. excelsa* when in bloom. Has withstood 22°. *M. v.* 'Variegata' has leaves with creamy markings.

MICHAELMAS DAISY. See Aster

MICHELIA. Evergreen trees or shrubs. Related to magnolias, but with flowers borne among the leaves rather than at ends of branches.

M. compressa. Evergreen tree. Zones 5-9, 14-24. Slow growth to 40 ft. Dense, rounded crown. Leaves polished dark green, 3 in. long, broad-oval. Flowers appear sporadically; they are pale yellow, 1½-2 in. across, very fragrant.

M. doltsopa. Big evergreen shrub or tree. Zones 14-24. Ultimate size in this country not known, but a tall tree in its native Himalayas. Has grown to 15 ft. in 12 years in San Francisco. Varies from bushy to narrow and upright; choose plants for desired form and prune to shape. Leaves thin, leathery, dark green, 3-8 in. long, 1-3 in. wide. Flowers open from brown furry buds that form in profusion among leaves near branch ends; blooms open January-March. Flowers creamy or white, slightly tinged green at base of petals, 5-7 in. wide, fragrant, with 12-16 1-in.-wide petals. They resemble somewhat the flowers of saucer magnolia *(M. soulangiana)*. Needs rich soil, ample water.

M. figo *(M. fuscata)*. BANANA SHRUB. Evergreen shrub. Zones 9, 14-24. Slow growth to 6-8 ft., possibly to 15 ft. Dense habit, with glossy, 3-in.-long, medium green leaves. Heavy bloom season March-May, but plants often show scattered bloom throughout summer. Flowers 1-1½ in. wide, creamy yellow shaded brownish purple, resembling small magnolias. Feature is the powerful, fruity fragrance; most people think it resembles the smell of ripe bananas. Rich, well drained soil in sun; partial shade best in hottest climates. Fragrance best in a warm, wind-free spot. Choice plant for entryway, patio, or near a bedroom window. Good espalier subject, container plant.

MICKEY MOUSE PLANT. See Ochna

MICROCOELUM weddellianum *(Syagrus weddelliana)*. Zones 23, 24. Small, decorative, thin-trunked feather palm to 7 ft. tall with a slightly wider spread. Grow in pots or outdoors in frost-free areas, but don't set out plants until they are 18-24 in. tall. Needs moisture and shade.

MICROLEPIA. Ferns. Sturdy, useful for landscaping shaded areas in mild climates.

M. firma. Zones 17, 23, 24. Native to India. Fronds dull green, delicately cut, triangular, to 3 ft. long. Surfaces densely hairy. Hardy to 28°.

M. platyphylla. Zones 15-17, 19-24. Large, coarse fern, to 10 ft. or higher. Leaflets broad, coarsely toothed, bluish green to yellow-green.

M. strigosa. Zones 17, 23, 24. Native to tropical Asia. Robust fern with delicate fronds. Grows 2-3 ft. tall. Hardy to 28°. Tolerates erratic watering, poor soil.

MICROMERIA chamissonis. See Satureja douglasii

MIGNONETTE. See Reseda

MILFOIL. See Achillea millefolium

MILLA biflora. MEXICAN STAR. Bulb. Zones 13, 16-24. Native to Arizona, New Mexico, northern Mexico. Grasslike basal leaves. Clusters of white, green-striped buds open to flat, starlike, fragrant flowers that are white inside, green outside. Spring bloom. Stems to 18 in. high. Hardy (with mulch) in fairly cold winters. Plant in October in sunny border, rock garden, or as edging. Or plant in pots for late winter, early spring bloom indoors.

MILTONIA. PANSY ORCHIDS. Epiphytic orchids. Greenhouse or indoors. Native to tropical or subtropical Americas. Many lovely large-flowered hybrids listed in catalogs. Flower colors: yellow, white, red, or blends of these colors. Blooms, single or in clusters on arching stems, are flat, resemble a pansy in appearance, and last a month or more on plant (not good cut flower). Plant has short pseudobulbs, long graceful, light green leaves that produce a clump of foliage a foot or more in diameter. Thrive in shade in a cool temperature. Keep moist and medium warm when flower spikes are forming, water less frequently in winter. Grow in finely cut but firmly packed osmunda fiber or in fine-sized ground bark or prepared, bark-based mix.

MIMOSA. Gardeners from the East and South often call silk tree (*Albizia julibrissin*) "mimosa".

MIMOSA, FLORIST'S. See Acacia baileyana

MIMOSA pudica. SENSITIVE PLANT. Tender perennial usually grown as an annual or under glass. Leaves finely cut into tiny leaflets. These leaves and the branchlets, when touched or otherwise disturbed, droop and fold up with astonishing speed. They quickly expand again. Grow from seed indoors or in a greenhouse; they will grow outdoors, but are not sufficiently attractive for garden. Transplant carefully to 4-in. pots. Avoid overwatering. Their only use is to demonstrate movement in plants; children find them fascinating.

MIMULUS. MONKEY FLOWER. Perennials, some treated as annuals. The three listed here need moist soil. Plant along edge of pool or in low, wet spot. Good in pots with lots of water, good drainage. (For the shrubby monkey flowers see *Diplacus*).

M. cardinalis. Perennial. Zones 4-24. Native to Oregon, California, Nevada, and Arizona. To 1-2 ft. with rather floppy stems. Leaves light green, 1-4½ in. long, sharply toothed, sticky. Flowers 1½-2 in. long, scarlet, 2-lipped, bloom July-October. Takes lots of heat if given partial shade and plenty of water.

M. lewisii. Perennial, often grown as annual. Native to streams and wet places in western mountains. Plants erect, to 2½ ft. high, slightly sticky. Leaves 1-3 in. long, irregularly toothed. Flowers rose red or pink, about 2 in. long, sometimes blotched or streaked maroon, with yellow lines in throat. Adapted to wet but well drained places in rock gardens.

M. tigrinus. Short-lived, usually grown as annual. Leaves smooth, succulent, toothed. Flowers 2-2½ in. across, yellow, splotched and spotted with brown and maroon; blooms spring and summer. Plant in shade with ferns, primroses, polemonium, tradescantia. Good in pots and hanging baskets. Sow seed in spring for summer bloom. Set out plants in rich moist soil. 'Queen's Prize' is a choice variety.

MINA lobata. See Quamoclit lobata

MINT. See Mentha

MINUARTIA verna. See Irish Moss, Scotch Moss

MIRABILIS jalapa. FOUR O'CLOCK. Perennial, grown as annual in cold-winter areas. Tuberous roots can be dug and stored like dahlia roots. Erect, many-branched stems form mounded clumps 3-4 ft. high and wide. Trumpet-shaped flowers open in midafternoon; red, yellow, or white with variations of shades between. Deep green, oval, 2-6-in.-long leaves of some forms are slightly sticky. Sow seed in sunny open location in early spring for blooms from midsummer through fall. Reseeds readily.

MIRROR PLANT. See Coprosma repens

MISTFLOWER. See Eupatorium

MISTLETOE. Partially-parasitic plants that grow on variety of hosts by pushing modified roots into host plant's stems. Leafy

mistletoes (*phoradendron*) are most common; they have range of leaf sizes usually in dull green. Dwarf mistletoes (*arceuthobium*) grow only on conifers, have scalelike leaves, yellowish to olive brown stems. Modest infestations do not harm host plants.

MOCCASIN FLOWER. See Cypripedium

MOLE PLANT. See Euphorbia lathyrus

MOLUCELLA laevis. BELLS-OF-IRELAND, SHELL FLOWER. Annual. Single-stemmed or branched, about 2 ft. high. Flowers are carried almost from the base, in whorls of 6. The showy part of the flower is the large shell-like or bell-like calyx—apple green, very veiny and crisp textured; the small white tube of united petals in the center is inconspicuous. As cut flowers the spikes of little bells are attractive fresh (long lasting) or dried (be sure to remove the unattractive leaves).

Needs a sunny location and loose, well drained soil. Sow seed in early spring or late fall; if weather is warm, refrigerate seed for a week before planting. For long spikes, water and fertilize regularly.

MONARDA didyma. BEE BALM, OSWEGO TEA. Perennial. All Zones. Bushy, leafy plant to 3 ft. with strong minty odor in foliage and flowers. Stems topped by clusters of scarlet flowers which rise from colored bracts. Bloom summer, early fall. The flowers attract hummingbirds. Useful in sun or shade. Mats of shallow roots spread rapidly. Needs cutting back to keep it compact and should be divided every 3-4 years. Named garden varieties are 'Cambridge Scarlet', a fiery red; 'Croftway Pink', a lavender-pink; and 'Granite Pink', a lovely clear pink.

MONDO GRASS. See Liriope and Ophiopogon

MONEY-PLANT. See Lunaria

MONEYWORT. See Lysimachia

MONKEY FLOWER. See Mimulus

MONKEY FLOWER, SHRUBBY. See Diplacus

MONKEY HAND TREE. See Chiranthodendron

MONKEY PUZZLE TREE. See Araucaria araucana

MONKSHOOD. See Aconitum

MONSTERA deliciosa. (Often sold as *Philodendron pertusum*.) SPLIT-LEAF PHILODENDRON. Evergreen vine. Zones 21-24; house plants anywhere. Eventually of great size if planted in open ground bed in greenhouse or (in mildest areas) outdoors. Long, hanging cordlike roots from stems root into soil, help support plant on trees or on moss "totem poles". Leaves on youngest plants uncut; mature leaves heavy, leathery, dark green, deeply cut and perforated with holes. Flowers may form on big plants; they are something like callas, with a thick, 10-in. spike surrounded by a white, boatlike bract. If heat, light, and humidity are high, the spike may ripen into an edible fruit.

Best in filtered shade with rich soil, ample water, stout support. A striking house

plant. For best results grow in a container with good drainage, feed occasionally, and keep leaves clean. In poor light or low humidity new leaves will be smaller. If tall plants get bare at the base, replant in a larger container and add a younger, lower plant to fill in; or cut the plant back and let new shoots start.

MONTANOA. DAISY TREE. Evergreen shrubs or small trees. Zones 16, 17, 20-24. Give them good soil, ample water, and groom by cutting off dead flower heads. Useful for winter flowers, tropical effects, background.

M. arborescens. To 12 ft. or more, usually seen as multiple trunk tree branching from the base. Covered with small, white, daisylike flower heads in winter. Needs little pruning.

M. bipinnatifida. To 7-8 ft. Bold-textured shrub with large, deeply lobed leaves. Flower heads to 3 in. across, mostly composed of white ray flowers to give a double effect; some yellow in center of heads. Blooms all fall, early winter. Prune hard after bloom; new stems grow quickly.

M. grandiflora. To 12 ft., with large, deeply cut leaves, 3-in. daisies in fall, winter. Prune like *M. bipinnatifida*.

MONTBRETIA. See Crocosmia crocosmaeflora, Tritonia

MOONFLOWER. See Calonyction

MORAEA. FORTNIGHT LILY, AFRICAN IRIS. Corms or rhizomes. Zones 8-24. Native to South Africa. Clumps of narrow, stiff, evergreen, irislike leaves. Flowers like miniature iris appear on branched stalks throughout spring, summer, fall, sometimes well into winter in mild areas. Each flower lasts a day, but is quickly replaced by another.

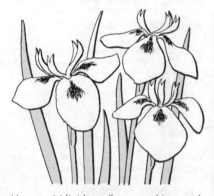

Moraea iridioides: *flowers white, with orange and brown blotch, purple markings.*

Bloom seems to come at 2-week intervals—hence the name fortnight lily. Grow in full sun, any fairly good soil. Ample water in summer.

M. bicolor (*Dietes bicolor*). Rhizome. To 2 ft. Flowers light yellow blotched maroon, about 2 in. wide. Cut flower stems back to ground after blossoms fade.

M. glaucopis (*Iris pavonia*). PEACOCK IRIS. Corm. Stems 1½-2 ft. tall. Flowers to 2 in. long, white or icy blue, outer segments with blue-black basal blotch.

M. iridioides (*Dietes iridioides*). Rhizome. To 4 ft. Flowers 3 in. across, waxy white with orange and brown blotch, purple

Climate Zone maps pages 8-27

stippling. 'Johnsonii' is robust variety with large leaves and flowers.

Tall flower stalks are perennial; don't cut them all the way to the ground for flower arrangements. Always leave at least one leaf joint at base.

MORNING GLORY. See Ipomoea

MORNING GLORY, BUSH.. See Convolvulus cneorum

MORNING GLORY, DWARF. See Convolvulus tricolor

MORNING GLORY, GROUND. See Convolvulus mauritanicus

MORUS. MULBERRY. Deciduous trees. Leaves of variable form, size, and shape—often on same tree. Fruits look like miniature blackberries and are favored by birds. Most important kinds to home gardeners, however, are the fruitless forms of *M. alba.*

M. alba. WHITE MULBERRY, SILKWORM MULBERRY. All Zones. Fruit bearing form grows to 20-60 ft., has inconspicuous flowers followed by rather insipid, sweet fruit which stains patios, clothing. 'Pendula' is a low-growing, strongly weeping variety.

Fruitless forms are better for home gardens. Excellent desert shade trees—bright green foliage, rapid growth in hot climates and alkaline soils. Resistant to Texas root rot. Take some drought once established, but grow faster with water and feeding. Beach plantings in southern California very successful. To 35 ft. tall, somewhat wider spread; often 20 ft. by 20 ft. in 3 years (slower in cool climates). 'Fruitless', 'Kingan', and 'Stribling' ('Mapleleaf') good varieties.

Stake new plants carefully; they develop large crowns rather fast, and these may snap from slender young trunks in high winds. For first few years branches may grow so long that they droop from own weight; shorten such branches to a well-placed upward-growing bud. Do not prune heavy branches to stubs; these are likely to rot.

M. nigra. BLACK OR PERSIAN MULBERRY. Zones 7-24. To 30 ft. with short trunk, dense, spreading head. Fruit large, juicy, dark red to black.

M. papyrifera. See Broussonetia

MOSES-IN-THE-BOAT, MOSES-IN-THE-CRADLE. See Rhoeo

MOSS CAMPION. See Silene acaulis

MOSS PINK. See Phlox subulata

MOSS, ROSE. See Portulaca

MOTHER-IN-LAW'S TONGUE. See Sansevieria

MOUNTAIN GARLAND. See Clarkia unguiculata

MOUNTAIN-MAHOGANY. See Cercocarpus

MOURNING BRIDE. See Scabiosa atropurpurea

MUEHLENBECKIA. WIRE VINE. Evergreen vines. Unusual plants with thin, wiry stems, tiny leaves, insignificant flowers. Sun to medium shade.

M. axillaris (*M. nana*). CREEPING WIRE VINE. Zones 4-9, 14-24. Small creeping plant to a few inches, or mounding up to 1 ft. high, dense, spreading by underground stems. Leaves ⅛ in. long, dark glossy green, closely spaced. Rock garden plant or small-scale ground cover.

M. complexa. MATTRESS VINE, WIRE VINE. Zones 8, 9, 14-24. Climbs to 20-30 ft. or more, or sprawls with no support. Dense tangle of thin black or brown stems. Leaves vary in shape, ⅛-¾ in. long. Tough vine for beach planting; good screen for an old stump or rock pile.

MUGWORT, WHITE. See Artemisia lactiflora

MULBERRY. See Morus

MULBERRY, PAPER. See Broussonetia

MULLEIN. See Verbascum

MULLEIN-PINK. See Lychnis coronaria

MURRAYA pániculata (*M. exotica*). GIANT ORANGE JESSAMINE. Evergreen shrub. Zones 21-24. To 6-15 ft. tall and wide, sometimes grown as a small multi- or single-stem tree. Open habit; graceful, pendulous branches with dark green, glossy leaves divided in 3-9 oval 1-2-in. leaflets. White, ¾-in., bell-shaped flowers have a jasmine fragrance. Blooms late summer and fall, sometimes spring as well. Mature plants have small red fruits.

Best in high shade or a half-day's sun without reflected heat. Need rich soil, ample water, frequent feeding. Recovers beauty slowly after cold wet winters. Good as hedge or filler; also for shaping.

M. p. 'Dwarf'. (Usually sold as *M. exotica*.) Slower growing, more upright and compact, to 6 ft. tall, 4 ft. wide. Leaves lighter green; leaflets smaller, stiffer. Bloom usually less profuse.

MUSA. BANANA. Perennials, some treelike in size. For the commonest bananas, see *Ensete.* The kinds described here include one tall, one medium-sized, and a number of dwarf (2-5-ft.) plants. All have soft, thickish stems and spread by suckers or underground roots to form clumps. Leaves are long, broad, spectacular, easily tattered by strong winds (a banana plant outdoors should be in a wind-sheltered spot). Most kinds are tender and should be grown in tubs, either beside a sunny window, in a greenhouse, or in such a location in winter and outdoors in warm season. *M. paradisiaca seminifera* can be grown outdoors all year in some mild climates. Give all types rich soil, plenty of water, heavy feeding.

M. cavendishii (*M. nana*). Tender. To 5-6, possibly 10 ft. Leaves 2-3 ft. long, 1 ft. wide, bluish green blotched red while young. Fruit yellow, seedless, edible, to 5 in. long.

M. coccinea. Tender. To 4 ft. tall. Leaves 3 ft. long, bright green. Upright bloom stalk has scarlet bracts with yellow tips.

M. ensete. See Ensete

M. mannii. Tender. To 2 ft. Slender stem tinged with black. Leaves 2-2½ ft. long, 7-8 in. wide. Erect bloom stalk has red bracts, yellow flowers.

M. maurelii. See Ensete maurelii

M. paradisiaca seminifera. Outdoors in Zones 16, 20-24. To 20 ft. or more.

Leaves 9 ft. long, 2 ft. wide. Drooping flower stalks occasionally form and are followed by small, inedible, seedy, greenish or yellow bananas. Plant for jungle effects.

M. sanguinea. Tender. To 4½ ft. tall; leaves 3 ft. long, 5-7 in. wide. Upright flower stalks with red bracts, yellow flowers.

M. velutina. Tender. To 4 ft. tall, with leaves 3 ft. long, 1 ft. wide. Upright flower stalks with red bracts, yellow flowers; red, velvety, inedible fruits follow. A plant sold as *M.* 'Velutina Hybrid' has burgundy red bracts and fruit, red markings on leaf edges.

MUSCARI. GRAPE HYACINTH. Bulb. All Zones. Clumps of narrow, grassy, fleshy leaves appear in autumn and live through cold and snow. Small, urn-shaped, blue or white flowers in tight spikes in early spring. Plant 2 in. deep in fall, setting bulbs in masses or drifts under flowering fruit trees or shrubs; in edgings, rock gardens; or in containers. Grows in sun or light shade. Very long-lived. Lift and divide when bulbs become crowded.

M. armeniacum. Bright blue flowers on 4-8-in. stems above a heavy cluster of floppy foliage. 'Cantab' has clear, light blue flowers, blooms later, is lower growing, has neater foliage.

M. azureum. See Hyacinthus azureus

M. botryoides. Medium blue flowers on 6-12-in. stems. 'Album' is white variety.

M. comosum. FRINGE OR TASSEL HYACINTH. Unusual, rather loose cluster of shredded-looking flowers — greenish brown fertile ones, bluish purple sterile ones. Stems 12-18 in. high. Leaves about same length and ⅜-1 in. wide.

M. c. 'Monstrosum (*M. c.* 'Plumosum'). FEATHERED OR PLUME HYACINTH. Sterile violet-blue to reddish purple flowers with finely divided and twisted segments.

M. tubergenianum. Stems to 8 in. tall; flowers at top of spike dark blue; lower flowers light blue. Leaves neater.

MUSTARD. Curly-leaf mustards somewhat resemble curly-leaf kales in appearance; they are cooked like spinach or cabbage, or young leaves are sometimes eaten raw in salads or used as garnishes. A fast and easy grower, ready for the table in 35-60 days. Sow in early spring and make succession sowings when young plants are established. Sow in late summer for fall use. In mild-winter areas, plant again in fall and winter. Thin seedlings to stand 6 in. apart in rows. Water well. Harvest leaves from the outside as needed. Mustard spinach or tendergreen mustard has smooth, dark green leaves. It ripens earlier than curly mustard and is more tolerant of hot, dry weather.

MYALL, WEEPING. See Acacia pendula

MYOPORUM. Evergreen shrubs or small trees. Bell-shaped flowers attractive at close range but not showy; fruits small but colorful. Features are dark green, shining leaves with translucent dots, fast growth, toughness.

M. debile. Shrub. Zones 15-17, 19-24. Low growing, with trailing branches. To 1 ft. tall, 2-4 ft. wide. Narrow, dark green leaves. Flowers in spring ½ in. across, pink; fruit ½ in. wide, rose-colored. Drought resistant. Rock garden, banks.

Climate Zone maps pages 8-27

M. insulare. Shrub or tree. Zones 8, 9, 14-17, 19-24. Generally shrubby near coast, taller and more treelike inland. Grows to 20-30 ft. Leaves and flowers much like those of *M. laetum,* somewhat smaller. Fruits bluish purple. Culture and uses same as *M. laetum*; plants more drought resistant.

M. laetum. Shrub or tree. Zones 8, 9, 14-17, 19-24. Exceptionally fast growth to 30 ft., 20-ft. spread. Dense foliage of rather narrow, 3-4-in.-long leaves. Natural habit a broad-based, billowing mass of dark green. An attractive multiple trunk tree if staked and pruned; thin to prevent top-heaviness and wind damage. Flowers in clusters of 2-6 in summer, about ½ in. wide, white with purple markings. Small reddish purple fruits.

Superb for seaside use—effectively blocks sound, wind, sun, blown sand (won't take drought, however). Can also make good ground cover; keep branches pegged down so they'll root and cover. Not for tailored garden areas or near pools; some leaf drop at all times, invasive roots.

M. l. 'Carsonii'. Cutting-grown selection; has darker, larger, broader leaves with fewer translucent dots; keeps its foliage right down to the base of the plant. Grows even faster than species.

M. parvifolium (*M. p. 'Prostratum'*). Ground cover. Zones 18-24. Bright green ½-1-in. leaves densely cover plant. Summer flowers are ½-in. wide, white, followed by purple berries. Grows to 3 in. high, 9 ft. wide. Plant 5 ft. apart. Plants will fill in within 6 months, branches rooting where stems touch moist ground. No traffic.

MYOSOTIS. FORGET-ME-NOT. Annual or biennial, perennial. Exquisite blue flowers, tiny but profuse. Best in partial shade; grows easily and thickly as a ground cover.

M. scorpioides. Perennial. All Zones. Similar in most respects to *M. sylvatica,* but grows lower, blooms even longer, and roots live over from year to year. Flowers, ¼ in. wide, are blue with yellow, pink, or white centers. Spreads by creeping roots.

M. sylvatica. Annual or biennial. To 6-12 in. Soft, hairy leaves ½-2 in. long, set closely along stem. Tiny, clear blue, white-eyed flowers, to ⅓ in. wide, loosely cover upper stems. Long bloom season, beginning in late winter or early spring. Flowers and seeds profusely for a long season. With the habit of reseeding will persist in a garden for years unless weeded out. Improved strains available, best of which is Blue Bird.

MYRICA. Evergreen and deciduous shrubs. The first one is from the Pacific Coast, the other from the Atlantic.

M. californica. PACIFIC WAX MYRTLE. Evergreen shrub or tree. Zones 4-6, 14-17, 20-24. Native to coast and coastal valleys southern California to Washington. At the beach a low, flattened mass; out of the wind a big shrub or tree to 30 ft., usually with many upright trunks. In the garden, one of the best-looking of native plants. Great virtue is clean looking foliage throughout the year. Branches densely clad with glossy, dark green leaves, 2-4½ in. long, about ½ in. wide, toothed on edges, paler beneath. Spring flowers inconspicuous; fall fruit purplish nutlets coated with wax. Useful screen or informal hedge 6-25 ft. tall. Can be used as a clipped hedge.

M. pensylvanica (*M. caroliniensis*). BAYBERRY. Deciduous or partly evergreen shrub. Zones 4-7. Native to eastern U. S. Dense, compact growth to 9 ft. Leaves to 4 in. long, narrowish, glossy green, dotted with resin glands, pungent in odor. Fruits tiny, roundish, covered with white wax—the bayberry wax used for candles. Will take poor, sandy soil, sun.

MYRRHIS odorata. SWEET CICELY. Perennial. All Zones. Thin, branching stems grow upright to 2-3 ft. Lacy, delicate green leaf consists of several finely cut pairs of leaflets so that mature plants resemble a fern. In early summer, small white flowers appear in terminal clusters about 2 in. wide. Seeds and leaves have slight anise flavor. Spicy green seeds flavor salads. Roots can be eaten raw or cooked. Shade or semi-shade. Moderately rich, moist, well drained soil. Seeds planted in fall make seedlings in spring. Increase stock by dividing roots.

(Another plant called sweet cicely, native to woods in Western states, is entirely different. It is *Osmorhiza*).

MYRSINE africana. AFRICAN BOXWOOD. Evergreen shrub. Zones 8, 9, 14-24. To 3-8 ft.; slightly floppy when young, but stiffens up into a dense, rounded bush easily kept at 3-4 ft. with moderate pinching, clipping. Stems vertical, dark red, closely set with very dark green, glossy, roundish, ½-in. leaves (excellent cut foliage).

Grows well in full sun or part shade with reasonable drainage. Smog resistant; relatively pest-free, although susceptible to red spider mites and, occasionally, brown scale. Good for low hedges, clipping into formal shapes, low green backgrounds, foundations, narrow beds, containers.

MYRTLE. See Myrtus, Vinca

MYRTLE, BOX SAND. See Leiophyllum

MYRTLE, JUNIPER. See Agonis juniperina

MYRTLE, OREGON. See Umbellularia

MYRTLE, PACIFIC WAX. See Myrica californica

MYRTUS. MYRTLE. Evergreen shrubs. Included here are several of the most useful, basic evergreen shrubs for California and Arizona gardens.

M. communis. TRUE MYRTLE. Zones 8-24. Rounded form to 5-6 ft. high and 4-5 ft. wide; old plants can reach treelike proportions—15 ft. tall, 20 ft. across. Glossy, bright green, pointed, 2-in. leaves, pleasantly aromatic when brushed or bruised. White, ¾-in.-wide flowers with many fuzzy stamens in summer, followed by bluish black, ½-in. berries. Grows well in part shade but also will take hot, bright sun. Any soil, but good drainage is important or tip chlorosis may occur. Good formal or informal hedge or screen. Can also be trained to reveal attractive branches.

M. c. 'Boetica'. Heavy, stiff, gnarled branches rise 4-6 ft. from base. Leaves large, leathery, very dark green, upward-pointing, very fragrant. Popular in desert.

M. c. 'Buxifolia'. BOXLEAF MYRTLE. Small, elliptical leaves.

M. c. 'Compacta'. DWARF MYRTLE. Slow growing, small, compact, with densely-set small leaves. Very popular for low edgings,

foundation plantings. Excellent low, compact, formal hedge.

M. c. 'Compacta Variegata'. VARIEGATED DWARF MYRTLE. Similar to 'Compacta', but leaves are edged in white.

M. c. 'Microphylla'. Dwarf myrtle with tiny, closely-set, overlapping leaves.

M. c. 'Variegata'. VARIEGATED MYRTLE. Leaves white-edged.

M. obcordata. Zones 16, 17, 20-24. Shrubby, dense, erect plant to 15 ft. Leaves leathery, glossy, roundish with notched tips, ½ in. long. Flowers ¼ in. across. Fruits dark red or purplish. Variety 'Purpurea' has purple leaves.

M. ugni. See Ugni molinae

NAKED LADY. See Amaryllis belladonna

NANDINA domestica. HEAVENLY BAMBOO, SACRED BAMBOO. Evergreen or semi-deciduous shrub. Zones 5-24. Loses leaves at 10°; killed to ground at 5°, but usually recovers fast. Not a bamboo but a member of the barberry family; reminiscent of bamboo in its lightly branched, canelike stems and delicate, fine-textured foliage.

Slow to moderate growth to 6-8 ft. (can be held at 3 ft. indefinitely by pruning oldest canes to ground). Leaves intricately divided into many 1-2-in., pointed, oval leaflets, creating a lacy pattern. New foliage pinkish and bronzy red on expanding, later soft, light green. Picks up purple and bronze tints in fall; often turns fiery crimson in winter, especially in some sun and with some frost. Flowers pinkish white or creamy white in loose, erect, 6-12-in. clusters at branch ends late spring or summer. Shiny red berries follow if plants are grouped; single plants seldom fruit heavily.

Sun or shade; colors better in sun, but needs some shade in desert and hot valley regions. Best in rich soil with ample water. Apply iron sulfate or chelates to correct chlorosis in alkaline soils. Most useful for light, airy vertical effects; narrow, restricted areas. Good screen, tub plant, bonsai. Dramatic with night lighting.

'Alba' has white berries and foliage that colors very little in fall; 'Chinese Princess' or 'Chinensis' is fairly low, very airy and open, sends up stems from underground runners to make broad clumps, colors well; 'Compacta' is lower-growing than the species (to 4-5 ft.); 'Nana' ('Nana Compacta', 'Lemon Hill') is only 12-18 in. tall, with broad leaflets of good color. This last does best in considerable shade.

NARCISSUS. DAFFODIL. Bulb. All Zones. Most valuable spring-flowering bulbous plants for most regions of the West: they are permanent, increasing from year to year; they are hardy to cold and heat; they are useful in many garden situations; they provide a fascinating variety in flower form and color; and gophers won't eat them.

Leaves straight and flat (strap-shaped) or narrow and rushlike. Flowers with a ring of segments ("petals") at right angles to the trumpet or crown (also called cup) in the center. Flowers may be single on a stem or clustered. Colors basically yellow and white, but with many variations—orange, red, apricot, pink, and cream.

Use under trees and flowering shrubs, among ground cover plantings, near water, in rock gardens and patios, or in borders. Naturalize in sweeping drifts where space

Climate
Zone maps
pages 8-27

is available. Good in containers, fine cut flowers.

Flowers usually face the sun; keep that in mind when selecting a planting place.

Plant bulbs as early in fall as obtainable. In southern California, wait until November so soil can cool. Look for solid, heavy bulbs. Number one double-nose bulbs are best; number one round, single-nose bulbs second choice. Plant with 5-6 in. of soil over top of bulbs, smaller bulbs covered

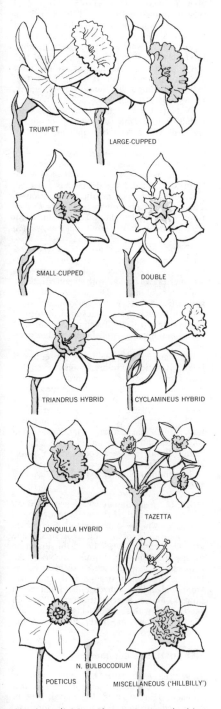

TRUMPET

LARGE-CUPPED

SMALL-CUPPED

DOUBLE

TRIANDRUS HYBRID

CYCLAMINEUS HYBRID

JONQUILLA HYBRID

TAZETTA

N. BULBOCODIUM

POETICUS

MISCELLANEOUS ('HILLBILLY')

Narcissus division. Flowers (except doubles) have 6 segments (perianth) and a cup.

by 4-5 in. Set bulbs 8 in. apart and you won't have to divide for at least 2-3 years. Full sun is best, but flowers of late-blooming kinds last better in light shade, as under high-branching, deciduous trees.

Water well after planting; if fall rains are on schedule, further watering usually unnecessary. Continued watering may be necessary where winters are dry. Apply a winter mulch in coldest areas. Water while growing and blooming. Control snails and slugs; they relish leaves and flowers of all kinds of narcissus and are particularly abundant during their flowering season.

Let foliage ripen naturally after bloom. Lift and divide clumps of daffodils where flowers get smaller and fewer in number. Wait until foliage has died down. Don't break away forcibly any bulbs that are tightly joined to mother bulb; remove only those that come away easily. Replant at once, or store for only a short time—preferably not over 3 weeks.

To grow in containers, set bulbs close together, with tips level with soil surface. Place pots in well drained trench or cold-frame and cover with 6-8 in. of moist peat moss, wood shavings, sawdust, or sand. Look for roots in 8-10 weeks (tip soil mass from pot carefully). Remove pots with well-started bulbs to greenhouse, cool room, or sheltered garden spot to bloom. Keep well watered until foliage yellows; then plant out in garden. Can sink pots or cans of bulbs in borders when flowers almost ready to bloom, lift containers when flowers fade.

Following are the 11 generally recognized divisions of daffodils, and representative varieties in each division:

Trumpet daffodils. The trumpet is as long as or longer than surrounding flower segments. Yellows are most popular: old variety 'King Alfred' best known, top seller, although newer 'Unsurpassable' and 'Diotima' superior. White varieties include 'Beersheba', 'Mount Hood'. Bicolors, with white segments, yellow cup are 'Spring Glory', 'President Lebrun'. Reverse bicolors like 'Nampa' and 'Spellbinder' have a white cup and yellow segments.

Large-cupped daffodils. Cups are more than 1⁄3, but less than equal to length of flower segments. Yellows are 'Carlton', 'Fortune'; whites 'Gertie Millar', 'Zero'; bicolors 'Mrs. R. O. Backhouse', 'Tunis'.

Small-cupped daffodils. Cups not more than 1⁄3 the length of segments. Yellow, with or without red in the cup; white with colored cups, 'Mrs. Nette O'Melveny'; all white, 'April Showers'.

Double daffodils. 'Yellow Cheerfulness', 'Mary Copeland', white and bright red; 'White Lion', creamy white and yellow; 'Twink', creamy yellow and orange.

Triandrus Hybrids. Cups not less than 2⁄3 the length of flower segments. Clusters of medium-sized, slender-cupped flowers. 'Thalia' is a favorite white with beautifully proportioned flowers.

Cyclamineus Hybrids. Early, medium-sized flowers with recurved segments. Gold, yellow, primrose, and white with yellow cup. 'February Gold' is the leading variety.

Jonquilla Hybrids. Clusters of 2-4 rather small, very fragrant flowers. Yellow, orange, ivory white. 'Trevithian' is well-known example.

Tazetta and *Tazetta Hybrids.* These are Polyanthus or bunch-flowered daffodils with

small-cupped white and yellow flowers in clusters. Also includes Poetaz narcissus, such as 'Geranium', paper white narcissus, and *N. tazetta* 'Orientalis' (Chinese sacred lilies). These last, along with 'Cragford' (yellow, scarlet cup) and 'Grand Soleil d'Or' (golden yellow) can be grown indoors in bowls of pebbles and water. Keep them dark and cool until growth is well along, then bring slowly into light.

Poeticus narcissus. POET'S NARCISSUS. White flowers with shallow, broad cups of yellow, edged red. 'Actaea' largest, white flower segments, yellow, red-rimmed cup.

Species, varieties, and *hybrids.* Many species and their varieties and hybrids delight the collector. Most are small, and some are true miniatures for rock gardens or very small containers. *N. bulbocodium,* HOOP PETTICOAT DAFFODIL. To 6 in. tall, has little up-facing flowers that are mostly trumpet, with very narrow pointed segments. Deep and pale yellow varieties. *N. cyclamineus,* 6 in. high, backward curved yellow segments and a narrow, tubular golden cup. *N. jonquilla,* JONQUIL. Round, rushlike leaves. Clusters of early, very fragrant, golden yellow flowers with short cups. *N.* 'Minimus' very early miniature trumpet flowers on 3-in. stems. *N. triandrus,* ANGEL'S TEARS. Clusters of small white flowers.

NASTURTIUM. See Tropaeolum

NATAL PLUM. See Carissa

NEANTHE bella. See Chamaedorea elegans

NECTARINE. See Peach and Nectarine

NECTARINE, FLOWERING. See Prunus

NELUMBO *(Nelumbium).* LOTUS. Perennials. All Zones. These are water plants. If you acquire started plants in containers, put them in pond with 8-12 in. of water over the soil surface. If you get roots, plant in spring, horizontally 4 in. deep, in a container (12-18 in. deep) of fairly rich soil, and place soil surface 8-12 in. under water. Huge round leaves attached at center to leaf stalks grow above water level. Large fragrant flowers form in summer, may grow above leaves or lower than leaves. Ornamental woody fruits perforated with holes in salt shaker effect. Good for dried arrangements. Roots should not freeze; where freezing is possible, cover pond with boards or fill it deeper with water.

N. nucifera *(Nelumbium nelumbo).* INDIAN OR CHINESE LOTUS. Round leaves 2 ft. or more wide carried 3-6 ft. above water surface. Pink flowers, one to each stem, 4-10 in. wide. White, rose, and double varieties available.

N. pentapetala *(Nelumbium luteum).* AMERICAN LOTUS. Similar to preceding but somewhat smaller in leaf and flower. Flowers are pale yellow.

NEMESIA strumosa. Annual. To 10-18 in., with irregularly shaped flowers. Every color of the spectrum (except green) appears in these 3⁄4-in. blossoms on their 3-4-in.-long spikes. Sometimes flowers are bicolored. The Sutton's strain is larger flowered. There is also a dwarf form, 'Nana Compacta'.

Sow outdoors in spring in cold climates, spring or fall where winters are mild, or

Climate Zone maps pages 8-27

buy in flats. Time plantings of this rapid grower to avoid frost but to bloom during cool weather. Does best in rich soil, moist but not wet. Pinch back to induce bushiness. Excellent bulb cover and container subject. A small bed of nemesia edged with blue lobelias or violas makes a dazzling patio planting.

NEMOPHILA. Annual. Often used as low cover for a bulb bed. Broadcast seed in place in early spring; will reseed if growth conditions are ideal. Both types listed here are native to western U. S.

N. menziesii (*N. insignis*). BABY BLUE EYES. To 6-10 in. tall, branching from base. Blooms as freely in gardens as it does in wilds. Cup-shaped flowers about 1 in. across, sky blue with whitish center. Leaves have rounded lobes. Spring blooming period short.

N. maculata. FIVE-SPOT NEMOPHILA. To 6 in. tall; growth habit, foliage, flower size same as *N. menziesii*. Flowers white, with fine purple lines; small dots and one large dot on each of the 5 lobes.

NEPETA. Perennials, ground covers. All Zones. Vigorous spreading plants of the mint family.

N. cataria. CATNIP. Perennial plant 2-3 ft. high with downy, gray-green leaves and clustered lavender or white flowers at branch tips in June. Easy grower in light soil in full sun; reseeds readily. Plant attractive to cats. Sprinkle its dried leaves over their food, or sew some into a toy cloth mouse. Some people use it for flavoring tea.

N. hederacea. GROUND IVY, GILL-OVER-THE-GROUND. Creeping perennial 3-6 in. high. Bright green, round leaves have coarsely scalloped edges. Light blue flowers among the leaves in spring and summer. Long creeping stems root at the joints. Can become a weed, especially in moist, shady places. Sometimes planted as a ground cover (plant 12 in. apart).

N. mussinii. CATMINT. Makes soft, gray-green undulating mounds to 2 ft. high. Leaves aromatic and (like catnip) attractive to cats, who enjoy rolling in plantings of it. Lavender-blue, ½-in. flowers in loose spikes make a display in early summer. If dead spikes prove unsightly, shear them back; this may bring on another bloom cycle. Set 12-18 in. apart for ground cover.

NEPHROLEPIS. SWORD FERN. (For the native Western sword fern, see *Polystichum munitum*.) Tough, easy-to-grow ferns for garden or house.

N. cordifolia. (Often sold as *N. exaltata*.) SOUTHERN SWORD FERN. Zones 16, 17, 19-24. Bright green, narrow, upright fronds in tufts to 2-3 ft. tall. Fronds have closely spaced, finely toothed leaflets. Roots often have small, roundish tubers. Plants spread by thin, fuzzy runners and can be invasive if not watched. Will not take hard frosts but otherwise adaptable — easily moved, tolerant of poor soil, light or heavy shade, erratic watering. Can be used in narrow, shaded beds.

N. exaltata. SWORD FERN. Outdoors in Zones 23, 24; house plant anywhere. Taller (to 5 ft.) than *N. cordifolia*, and with fronds to 6 in. wide. Not widely grown.

N. e. 'Bostoniense'. BOSTON FERN. House plant. Spreading and arching in habit, with graceful, eventually drooping fronds. The classic parlor fern of grandmother's day. Many more finely cut and feathery forms exist; 'Rooseveltii' and 'Whitmanii' are among the best known. North light in a cool room suits it. Plant in well drained, fibrous soil. Feed every month with dilute liquid fertilizer; water whenever soil surface dries out.

NEPHTHYTIS. See Syngonium

NERINE. Bulb. Zones 5, 8, 9, 13-24. Native to South Africa. Usually grown in pots, but can grow outdoors year around in mildest regions. Wide-leafed kinds need shade in warmer climates. Strap-shaped basal leaves appear during or after bloom. Flowers funnel-shaped with 6 spreading segments bent back at tips; in rounded clusters on 12-24-in. stems. Blooms August through January, depending on kind.

Plant August-December. Put 1 bulb in a 4-in. pot, 3 in a 5-6-in. pot. Cover only lower half of bulb. Wait for signs of flower stalk before watering. Water through winter and spring. In May move pots outdoors to a lightly shaded spot. Gradually dry off. Withhold water from July until growth resumes. Do not repot until quite crowded. To grow outdoors, plant in sun in perfectly drained soil; set bulb 3 in. deep. Do not disturb or divide for several years.

N. bowdenii. The hardiest; grows outdoors in milder parts of Northwest. Glossy green leaves 1 in. wide, 6-12 in. long. Flowers to 3 in. long, soft pink, marked deeper pink, in clusters of 8-12 on 2-ft.

Clustered flowers of Nerine bowdenii are pink, rose, or red on 2-ft. stems.

stems. Forms with taller stems, larger flower clusters, in deeper pink, crimson, and red. Blooms in fall; as late as December in southern California.

N. curvifolia. Best known is the variety 'Fothergillii Major', with clusters of 2-in.-wide, scarlet flowers overlaid with shimmering gold. Long stamens topped by greenish yellow anthers. Bloom stalks to 18 in.

N. filifolia. Leaves narrow, evergreen, 6-8 in. long. Flowers 1 in. long, rose-pink with slender, crinkled petals, in clusters of 8-12 on wiry 18-in. stems.

N. sarniensis. GUERNSEY LILY. Large clusters of iridescent crimson 1½-in.-long flowers on 2-ft. stalks. Pink, orange-scarlet, and pure white varieties.

NERIUM oleander. OLEANDER. Evergreen shrub. Zones 8-16, 18-23. One of the basic shrubs for desert and hot interior valleys. Moderate to fast growth; most varieties reach a maximum height of 8-12 ft. and as wide. Ordinarily broad and bulky, but easily trained into a handsome single or many-stemmed tree resembling (when out of bloom) an olive tree. Narrow leaves, dark green, leathery, and glossy, 4-12 in. long, attractive all seasons; a form with golden variegations in the leaf is sometimes available. Flowers 2-3 in. across, clustered at twig or branch ends May or June to October. A number of varieties have fragrant flowers. Varieties include double and single flower forms, with a color range from white to shades of yellow, pink, salmon, and red. 'Sister Agnes', a single white, is the most vigorous grower, often reaching 20 ft. tall; 'Mrs. Roeding', a double salmon pink, grows only 6 ft. tall.

Not at all particular about soil; it withstands considerable drought, poor drainage, soil with a relatively high salt content. Thrives in heat and strong light, even reflected light from paving. Weak or leggy growth, few flowers in shade or ocean fog.

Prune in early spring to control size and form. Cut out old wood that has flowered. Cut some branches nearly to the ground. To restrict height, pinch remaining tips or prune them back lightly. To prevent bushiness at base, pull (don't cut) unwanted suckers.

Chief insect pests are yellow oleander aphid (one spring spraying usually controls), and scale insects (spray in the midsummer crawler stage with cygon, diazinon, malathion, or sevin). One disease—bacterial gall which causes warty growths and splitting on branches and blackened, deformed flowers (control by pruning out infected parts, making cuts well below visible damage).

All parts of the plant are poisonous if eaten. Caution children against eating leaves or flowers; keep prunings, dead leaves away from hay or other animal feed; don't use wood for barbecue fires or skewers. Smoke can cause severe irritation.

Use as screens, borders for road or driveway, tubs, background plantings, small single or multiple trunked trees. Single white oleanders give a cool look to a hot-climate garden.

For another plant called yellow oleander, see *Thevetia*.

NERTERA granadensis (*N. depressa*). BEAD PLANT. Perennial. Extremely tender, generally grown as house plant. Sometimes used as rock garden subject or small-scale ground cover in Zones 17, 22-24. Prostrate habit. Tiny, smooth, rounded leaves make dense green mat an inch or so high; berry-like, ¼-in., bright orange fruit may last from midsummer into winter. Small green flowers are a lesser attraction. Plant in sandy loam with some leaf mold. Must have shade, constant moisture. Fine terrarium or dish-garden plant.

NET BUSH. See Calothamnus

NEW ZEALAND SPINACH. You cook and serve it like spinach but it's not a true spinach. Differs chiefly in that it can be harvested through the warm season; real spinach comes in cool season. You harvest the greens from the plants by plucking off the top 3 in. of tender stems and the attached leaves. A month later new shoots grow up for another harvest. Plants are spreading, 6-8 in. high, evergreen in mild-winter areas but going dormant in heavy frosts. Sow seed in early spring after frosts. Water deep and often. Feed 1-2 times a year with complete fertilizer. Expect self-sowing.

NICOTIANA. Tender perennial grown as an annual. May live over in mild-winter areas. Upright growing plants with slightly sticky leaves and stems. Flowers tubular, usually broadly flaring at ends into 5 pointed lobes; grow near top of branched stems in summer. Usually grown for the fragrance of the flowers which often open at night or on cloudy days; some kinds open during daytime. Plant in full sun or part shade. Some kinds reseed readily.

N. alata 'Grandiflora' *(N. affinis).* To 2-3 ft. high. Very fragrant, large, white flowers open towards evening. There are 3 good varieties: 'Dwarf White Bedder' ('White Bedder') grows only 1 ft. high. Flowers stay open during day. 'Lime Green' and 'Lime Sherbet' grow 2½ ft. high. Greenish yellow flowers not very fragrant but excellent in flower arrangements.

N. 'Daylight'. Grows 1½-2½ ft. Slightly fragrant, white flowers stay open all day.

N. sanderae. Flowers of most kinds stay open all day. Represented in gardens by 3 varieties: 'Crimson Bedder', to 1 ft. high; flowers rich deep crimson, slightly fragrant. 'Crimson King' grows to 2½ ft.; has dark velvety, crimson-red flowers, slightly fragrant. 'Knapton Scarlet' grows to 3 ft.; has brightest red flowers, delicately fragrant.

N. suaveolens. To 2 ft. high. White flowers rather small but most sweetly scented of all; some fragrance during day, more so at night. Suitable for planting under a window for fragrance in the house.

N. sylvestris. To 5 ft. Rather coarse foliage, but sweetly fragrant, large, white flowers in candelabralike clusters.

Sensation strain (Sensation Mixed, Daylight Sensation). Compact plants to 2½ ft. high. Flower colors — white, mauve, red, chocolate, chartreuse, lime green. Blooms open in daytime. Amount of fragrance varies according to environment.

NIDULARIUM innocentii. Perennial. Outdoors in Zones 23, 24; greenhouse plant anywhere. Stemless bromeliad, best adapted to pot culture and a shady, moist, warm atmosphere. Leaves straplike, 8 in. long or more, spiny-toothed along margin to pointed tip, reddish purple on underside. Smaller bractlike brilliant red leaves make flattened nestlike rosette at center of leaves, from which rises a dense bunch of white flowers with erect petals. Appropriately the name *Nidularium* means "bird's nest".

NIEREMBERGIA. CUP FLOWER. Perennials. Flowers tubular but flaring into a saucerlike or bell-like cup. Need sun, good soil.

N. frutescens. TALL CUP FLOWER. Zones 8-24. To 2-3 ft., shrubby, somewhat woody stems. Saucer-shaped flowers, 1 in. wide, white tinged with blue. Can be trimmed to low, rounded, shrublike shape.

N. hippomanica caerulea. DWARF CUP FLOWER. Zones 8-24. To 6-12 in. high. Much

branched mounded plant. Stiff, very narrow, ½-⅔-in.-long leaves. Covered all summer with blue to violet, widely spreading, bell-like flowers almost an inch across. Trimming back to induce new growth seems to lengthen life. Good edging plant for semi-shade in desert regions. *N. h. violacea* has deeper violet flowers. 'Purple Robe' readily available variety.

N. repens *(N. rivularis).* WHITE CUP. Zones 5-9, 14-17. Prostrate mat of bright green leaves covered in summer with white flowers as large or larger than the preceding and of same shape. For best performance, don't crowd it with more aggressive plants.

NIGELLA damascena. LOVE-IN-A-MIST. Annual. Branching, to 1-2½ ft. high. All leaves, even those that form a collar under each flower, finely cut into threadlike divisions. Blue, white, or rose flowers, 1-1½ in. across, are solitary on ends of branches. Curious papery-textured, horned seed capsules very decorative in dried bouquets; fresh material gives airiness in a bouquet or in a mixed border. Sow seeds among established plants. Plants come quickly into bloom in spring and dry up in summer. Will reseed. 'Miss Jekyll', semi-double corn flower blue blossoms, is superior variety.

NIGHTSHADE, COSTA RICAN. See Solanum wendlandii

NOTHOPANAX arboreum. Evergreen tree. Zones 16-24. Moderately fast to 15-25 ft. Outline dense, vase-shaped. Large, glossy deep green leaves divided fanwise into 3-7 leaflets 3-8 in. long, 1-3 in. wide. Flowers greenish brown, in large clusters, not showy. Rich soil, ample water. Takes part sun or considerable shade. Useful for rich, dark, dense foliage mass. Can be trained as a multiple stem small tree 6-8 ft. high; good tub subject for shady terrace or even indoors.

NUTMEG, CALIFORNIA. See Torreya

NYMPHAEA. WATER LILY. Water plants. All Zones. The leaves float and are rounded, with a deep notch at one side where leaf stalk is attached. Showy flowers either float on surface or stand above it on stiff stalks. Cultivated water lilies are largely hybrids that cannot be traced back to exact parentage. There are hardy and tropical types. Hardy kinds come in white, yellow, copper, pink, and red. Tropical types add blue and purple.

Hardy kinds are easiest for the beginner. Plant them from February through October in mild-winter areas, April through July where freezes prevail. Set 6-in.-long pieces of rhizome in a nearly horizontal position with bud end up, on soil at pool bottom, or plant in boxes of at least 8-in. depth. Top of soil should be 8-12 in. below water surface. Do not use redwood containers; they can discolor the water. Enrich soil with 1 lb. of complete fertilizer (3-5 per cent nitrogen) for each lily you plant.

Groom plants by removing spent leaves and blooms. They usually bloom throughout warm weather and go dormant in fall, re-appearing in spring. If you live in a very cold area, protect as you would *Nelumbo*.

The tropical kinds begin to grow and bloom later in summer, but they last longer in fall, too, often up to the first frost. Buy

started plants and set at same depth as hardy ones. The tropical types go dormant but do not survive really low winter temperatures. They usually live over where orange trees grow. Where winters are colder, store dormant tubers in damp sand over winter or buy new plants each year.

NYSSA sylvatica. SOUR GUM, TUPELO, PEPPERIDGE. Deciduous tree. Zones 1-10, 14-21. One of the best lawn trees for fall color; dependable color even in mild-winter areas. Slow to moderate growth to 30-50 ft., spreading to 15-25 ft. Pyramidal when young; spreading, irregular, and rugged in age. Crooked branches, twigs, and dark, red-tinged bark make a dramatic picture against a winter sky. Leaves dark green, glossy, 2-5 in. long, turning a hot, coppery red in fall before dropping; come out rather late in spring. Grows well in any soil, takes much or little water, withstands occasional drought, tolerates poor drainage.

OAK. See Quercus

OAK, TANBARK. See Lithocarpus

OCEAN SPRAY. See Holodiscus

OCHNA serrulata *(O. multiflora).* MICKEY MOUSE PLANT, BIRD'S-EYE BUSH. Evergreen shrub. Zones 14-24. Slow, spreading growth to 4-8 ft. high and as wide. Oblong leaves 2-5 in. long are leathery; finely toothed, bronzy in spring, deep green later. Early summer flowers are size of buttercups; when yellow petals fall, sepals turn vivid red. Next, 5 or more green, seedlike fruits protrude from red center. They later turn glossy jet black, in strong contrast with the red sepals; at this stage children see the configuration as the bright eyes and big ears of Mickey Mouse.

Partial shade, slightly acid soil, ample feeding and water. Good tub or box subject; sometimes grown indoors.

OCIMUM. BASIL. Annual herbs. One of the basic cooking herbs. Leaves in varying shades of green and purple. One type— 'Dark Opal'—is attractive enough to be sold for borders and mass plantings. Sow seed of any basil in early spring; plant outdoors after frost. Requires warm soil, full sun. Space plants 10-12 in. apart. Fertilize once during growing season with a complete fertilizer. Water regularly to keep growth succulent. An occasional overhead watering keeps foliage clean and bright.

Use leaves fresh or dried for seasoning many foods and dishes.

O. basilicum. SWEET BASIL. To 2 ft. Shiny green 1-2-in.-long leaves; spikes of white flowers. Forms with purple or variegated leaves, purple flowers. The most popular basil for cooking. Use fresh or dry; gives mild flavor of anise and spice to tomatoes, cheese, eggs, fish, shellfish, poultry stuffing, salads.

O. 'Dark Opal'. A large-leafed basil, known for its ornamental qualities. Dark purple bronze foliage; spikes of small lavender-pink flowers. Grows 12-18 in. tall with spread of about 1 ft. Attractive in mass planting with dusty miller or 'Carpet of Snow' sweet alyssum. As flavoring herb, has milder flavor than other purple basils.

OCONEE BELLS. See Shortia galacifolia

OCOTILLO. See Fouquieria

Climate Zone maps pages 8-27

OCTOPUS TREE. See Brassaia

ODONTOGLOSSUM. Epiphytic orchids. Outdoors in Zones 23, 24; greenhouse or indoors in winter everywhere. Few other orchids have as many natural crosses or as much variation between species. In general, pseudobulbs are flat and oval in shape with 2 or 3 pairs of leaves sheathing base and two more at top. In most cases flower stalks reach well above foliage.

Plant in medium or fine ground bark. Transplant after flowering in fall or in early spring, never in hot summer weather. Don't plant in oversize pot; the plants thrive under crowded conditions. Plants need abundant moisture year around, good ventilation but no drying winds, 45° to 55° temperature preferable, not above 65° in winter and as low as possible in summer. Thrive in well-lighted location, but burn in hot summer sun. Species listed here can be grown in garden beds, Zones 23, 24. Elsewhere, grow in pots or on slabs, suspended from trees, protected patio, or lathhouse in summer, indoors or in cool greenhouse in winter.

O. crispum. Large, 2-3-in. white flowers, often tinged with rose blotched with red, crowded on 15-30-in.-long stem. Usually blooms late spring, early summer, but may bloom any time. Oval 2-4-in.-high pseudobulbs; narrow, 9-15-in.-long leaves.

O. grande. TIGER ORCHID. Bright yellow flowers with mahogany brown stripes. Blooms 5-7 in. across, arranged 3 to 7 on a stalk to 12 in. long. Blooms in fall, lasting 3 to 4 weeks. Pseudobulbs 2-4 in. high with 2 dull green, broad, lance-shaped leaves 8-10 in. long. After bulbs mature, keep plant on dry side until growth shows again. Good cut flower.

O. pulchellum. LILY-OF-THE-VALLEY ORCHID. Six or more white, 1-in. flowers with touch of yellow in lip borne on 10-in. stems in spring. Flowers have fragrance of lily-of-the-valley. Pseudobulbs 2-3 in. high, stiff narrow 8-12-in.-long leaves. Keep on dry side from time growth matures until signs of new growth appears.

OENOTHERA. EVENING PRIMROSE. Biennials, perennials. All Zones. Valued for showy summertime flowers in tough, rough places.

O. biennis. Biennial. From very large fleshy roots grow much-branched plants 3-4 ft. high. Yellow flowers open in evening. Stems green to red.

O. erythrosepala (*O. lamarckiana*). Biennial or short-lived perennial. Escaped from gardens along coast, northern California to British Columbia. A tall unbranched plant to 2-6 ft. high. Bright yellow flowers an inch or more across are open from late afternoon until morning, turn orange-red as they fade. Reseeds readily; can become something of a pest but easily weeded out.

O. hookeri. Biennial. Western native. To 2-6 ft. high. Bright yellow, 3½-in. flowers open late afternoon to sunrise.

O. missouriensis. Perennial. Prostrate, sprawling stems to 10 in. long. Soft velvety 5-in. leaves. In summer, clear yellow flowers 3-5 in. across. One of the most beautiful of the evening primroses. Good rock garden subject.

O. speciosa childsii (*O. rosea mexicana*). MEXICAN EVENING PRIMROSE. Perennial.

During summer bloom period stems with their profusion of rose-pink, 1½-in. flowers are 10-12 in. high; stems then die back. Blooms in daytime. Once established, thrives with little or no care. Invasive if not controlled. Good for dry slopes, parking strips.

O. tetragona. SUNDROPS. Perennial. To 2 ft.; reddish stems, good green foliage. Daytime display of 1½-in.-wide, yellow blossoms throughout summer. Needs very little attention. Several varieties.

OKRA. A warm-season vegetable crop that grows well under the same conditions as sweet corn. Plant when ground begins to warm up. Soak seed 24 hours before planting to speed germination. Water regularly and fertilize at least once. Harvest pods every 2 or 3 days. Best size is 1-3 in. long; over-ripened pods are tough, and they shorten the plant's bearing life.

OLD MAN. See Artemisia abrotanum

OLD WOMAN. See Artemisia stelleriana

OLEA europaea. OLIVE. Evergreen tree. Zones 7-24. Along with palms, citrus, and eucalyptus, olives stand out like regional trademarks along avenues and in gardens of California and southern Arizona. The trees' beauty has been appreciated in those areas since the 18th century when Franciscan fathers brought them from Mediterranean lands to mission gardens for ornament and oil.

Willowlike foliage is a soft gray-green that combines well with most colors. Smooth, gray trunks and branches become gnarled and picturesque in maturity. The trees are slow growing, eventually getting to 25-30 ft. high and as wide; however, young trees put on height (if not substance) fairly fast. Begin training early. For a single trunk, prune out or shorten side branches below point where you want branching to begin, stake tree firmly, cut off basal suckers. For several trunks, stake lower branches or basal suckers to continue growth at desired angles.

Large old olive trees can (with reasonable care) be boxed and transplanted with near certainty of survival.

Olive trees need full sun. They're most lush when growing in deep, rich soil, but will also grow in shallow, alkaline, or stony soil and with little fertilizer. Thrive in areas of hot, dry summers, but also perform adequately in coastal areas. Take temperatures down to 15°. Withstand heavy pruning—thinning each year shows off branch pattern to best advantage, and removing flowering-fruiting branches reduces or eliminates the fruit crop, which is usually a nuisance.

Olives blacken and drop from the tree late in the year. Without leaching and processing, olives off the tree are inedible. The fruit can stain paving and harm a lawn if not removed. In addition to pruning, spray with fruit-control hormones when the tiny white flowers appear to reduce the crop. Or spread a tarpaulin at dropping time, knock off all fruit, and dispose of it. The so-called fruitless varieties are not always reliably barren.

Watch for scale insects and spray as needed. Olive knot occasionally forms galls on twigs and branches, eventually killing them; prune out infected wood, sterilizing instruments after each cut.

These varieties are sold:

'Ascolano'. Commercial variety. Large, tender-fleshed fruit, small pit.

'Barouni'. Large-fruited commercial variety, suited to hottest olive growing areas.

'Fruitless'. Landscaping variety. Advertised as non-fruiting, but some have borne fruit.

'Manzanillo'. Landscaping and commercial variety with lower, more spreading growth habit than most. Large fruit.

'Mission'. Landscaping and commercial variety. Taller, more compact, and hardier than 'Manzanillo'. Smaller fruit than most, but has fine flavor and high oil content.

'Sevillano'. Commercial variety. Very large fruit, low oil content.

OLEANDER. See Nerium

OLEANDER, YELLOW. See Thevetia peruviana

OLEARIA haastii. DAISY BUSH. Evergreen shrub. Zones 4-6, 14-17. Reaches 5-9 ft. tall, often broader than tall. Leaves roundish, leathery, to 1¼ in. long, shiny green above, white hairy beneath. Summer flowers in clusters; individual flowers like tiny yellow-centered white daisies. Plant and flowers pleasantly aromatic.

Needs sun; prefers sandy soil. Shear or tip to keep plants shapely; cut faded blooms or they will persist through winter. Good as bank cover or big borders where a touch of gray-green is needed. Stands wind and salt spray—excellent for beach gardens.

OLIVE. See Olea

OLIVE, RUSSIAN. See Elaeagnus angustifolia

OLIVE, SWEET. See Osmanthus fragrans

OLMEDIELLA betschleriana. GUATEMALAN HOLLY, COSTA RICAN HOLLY, MANZANOTE. Evergreen shrub or small tree. Zones 9, 14-24. Fairly fast to 20-25 ft., 10-15-ft. spread. Dense, dark green foliage, new growth bronzy. Leaves resemble English holly, but less prominent spines. Inconspicuous flowers. Female trees capable of producing few inedible fruits size of a small orange. Young plants tender (plant after spring frosts); established plants hardy to 19°. Sun or shade on coast; partial shade and ample water inland valleys. Train as single- or multi-trunked tree, or as big bush densely foliaged to base. Use as street or lawn tree, tall screen, trimmed hedge, container plant. Dry leaves very stickery; don't use near pool.

OMBU. See Phytolacca dioica

ONCIDIUM. Epiphytic orchids. Greenhouse or indoors. Native from Florida to Brazil, and from sea level to high, cool mountains. In general, growth habit similar to odontoglossums . Variable in size and form. Most species have yellow flowers spotted or striped with brown; a few have white or rose-colored blooms.

Water generously during growing season, sparingly during dormant period — just enough to keep pseudobulbs from shriveling. Give more light than odontoglossums. Give a definite rest period to Mexican and Central American species. Potting medium

O

Climate Zone maps pages 8-27

same as for odontoglossums. Most species grow well under conditions recommended for cattleyas. Excellent cut flower.

O. cheirophorum. Colombia. Miniature species with fragrant, bright yellow ½-in. flowers with green sepals. Dense, branched clusters in fall. Plant seldom over 6 in. high, with bright green, grasslike leaves.

O. crispum. Brazil. Shiny brown 1½-3-in. flowers with yellow and red at base of segments. Borne in profusion on 1-1½-ft., arching stems any time throughout year. Rough, flat, usually dark brown pseudobulbs 3-4 in. high, leathery 6-9-in. lance-shaped leaves. Never let plants dry out completely. Grows well in hanging containers.

O. papilio. BUTTERFLY ORCHID. West Indies. Flowers 4-5 in. long, 2½ in. across. Top sepals and petals stand erect, are brown with bands of yellow; lower sepals and petals curve downward and are yellow with bands of brown. Lip yellow, edged brown. Flowers open one at a time on 2-3-ft.-long stalk which continues to produce buds on old flower stems for several years. Blooms any time of year. Rounded, dark purple pseudobulbs. Olive green leaves, mottled with brownish purple.

O. splendidum. Guatemala and Mexico. Branched 2-3-ft. erect flower stems produce 3-in. flowers in profusion in winter. Sepals and petals yellow-green, barred and blotched with reddish brown, recurved at tips; large, flat, clear yellow lip. Two-inch pseudobulbs bear one stiff, leathery leaf 9-15 in. high.

O. varicosum rogersii. DANCING LADY. Brazil. Golden yellow, 2-in. flowers barred with reddish brown appear in great profusion in 3-ft.-long, branched, arching sprays in fall and winter. Oblong, 3-4-in.-high pseudobulbs bear pair of 6-9-in.-long leaves.

ONION. Grow onions either from seed or sets (small bulbs). Sets are easiest for beginners, but seed gives a larger crop for a smaller investment, and seed is the only way to start some of the varieties—the red onions, for instance. In mild climates, sets can go in 1-1½ in. deep and 1-2 in. apart all winter long and through April. Where winters are cold, plant sets in earliest spring. Start pulling green onions in 3 weeks or so; any not needed as green onions can grow on for later harvest as dry onions when the tops wither. Plant seed in early spring in rows 15-18 in. apart. Soil should be loose, rich, and well drained. When seedlings are pencil-size, thin to 3-4 in. apart, transplanting the thinnings to extend the plantings. Trim back tops of transplants about half way.

Never let onions go dry; they are shallow rooted and need moisture fairly near the surface. When tops have ripened, dig the bulbs and let them cure and dry on top of the ground for several days. Then pull off the tops, clean, and store in a dark, cool, airy place.

Of the more familiar varieties look for 'Crystal Wax Bermuda', 'Southport White Globe', and 'White Sweet Spanish' if you like white onions. Good yellow varieties are 'Early Yellow Globe', 'Yellow Globe Danvers', and 'Utah Sweet Spanish'. Fine red varieties are 'Early Red California' and 'Southport Red Globe'. An unusual onion is the long, red, very mild 'Italian Red' or 'Red Torpedo'.

ONOCLEA sensibilis. SENSITIVE FERN. All Zones. Native to eastern U. S. Coarse-textured fern with 2-4-ft. sterile fronds divided nearly to the midrib; fertile fronds smaller, with clusters of almost beadlike leaflets. Fronds come from an underground creeping rhizome which can be invasive in wet, rich soil. Dies down in winter. Takes sun if moisture is adequate. Fronds fascinate connoisseurs, but seem coarse to most gardeners.

ONOSMA stellulatum tauricum. GOLDEN DROPS. Perennial. Zones 1-9, 14-17. Low-growing, irregular clumps to 8 in. high, spreading to 18 in. wide, with rough, dull green, narrow, 1-2-in.-long leaves. One main vertical stem with smaller drooping side branches. Fragrant, long, tubular, yellow, 1½-in. flowers in fiddleneck clusters at tips of main stalk and side branches. Sun or part shade. Use in rock gardens, or include in a low planting scheme of grays and yellows.

OPHIOPOGON. See Liriope and Ophiopogon

OPUNTIA. Cactus. Many kinds of varied appearance. Most species fall into one of two sorts: those having flat, broad joints; or those having cylindrical joints. The first are often called prickly pears, the second chollas, but the terms are rather loose. Hardiness is variable. Flowers are generally large and showy. The fruit is a berry, often edible.

O. bigelovii. TEDDYBEAR CACTUS. Zones 11-24. Native to Arizona, Nevada, California, northern Mexico. Treelike plant of slow growth to 2-8 ft. Woody trunk covered with black spines. Branches cylindrical, easily detached, covered with vicious, silvery-yellow spines. Flowers pale green, yellow, or white marked with lavender, 1-1½ in. wide. April bloom. Grows freely in hottest, driest deserts.

O. ficus-indica. INDIAN FIG CACTUS. Zones 8, 9, 12-24. Big shrubby or treelike cactus to 15 ft., with woody trunks and smooth, flat green joints 15-20 in. long. Few or no spines, but has clusters of bristles. Yellow flowers 4 in. across, spring or early summer. Large fruit, red or yellow, edible, often sold in markets. Handle it carefully; bristles break off easily and are irritating.

O. microdasys. BUNNY EARS. Zones 13-24. Mexico. Fast growth to 2 ft. high, 4-5 ft. wide (much smaller in pots). Pads flat, thin, nearly round, to 6 in. across, velvety soft green with neatly spaced tufts of short golden bristles in polka dot effect. *O. m. albispina* has white bristles. Small round new pads atop larger old ones give the plant a silhouette of an animal's head. A favorite with children.

ORANGE. See Citrus

ORANGE, MANDARIN. See Citrus

ORANGE, MEXICAN. See Choisya

ORANGE, MOCK. See Philadelphus

ORANGE, OSAGE. See Maclura

ORCHID. Once considered "prestige flowers" for the very wealthy, primarily because plants were so expensive, many orchids are now no more expensive than choice garden shrubs or house plants. But they will always remain "prestige flowers".

Each of the kinds of orchids available to Westerners is described fully in this book under its name (i.e. *Cattleya, Cypripedium, Laelia,* etc.). Here we explain the orchid growers' terms that are used in those descriptions.

EPIPHYTIC

Some orchids are epiphytic, growing high in the branches of trees in tropical or subtropical jungles, clinging to the bark, but obtaining their nourishment from the air, rain, and whatever decaying vegetable matter they can trap in their root systems.

PSEUDOBULB

The epiphytic orchids have thickened stems called pseudobulbs which serve as storage for food and water, making it possible for the plants to survive seasons of drought. These may be short and fat like bulbs, or erect and slender. They vary from green to brown in color. Leaves may grow along the pseudobulbs or from their tips.

TERRESTRIAL

Other orchids are terrestrial, with their roots growing in a loose, moist soil rich in humus—often in wooded areas, but sometimes in open meadows as well. These orchids have no storage organs and require a constant source of moisture and food. Most of the native orchids fall in the latter classification.

SEPALS, PETALS, LIP, AND POUCH

The segments of an orchid flower include 3 sepals and 3 petals; one of the petals, usually the lowest one, is referred to in the descriptions as a lip. This lip is usually larger and more brightly colored than the other segments. Sometimes it is fantastically shaped, with various appendages and markings. It may be folded into a slipperlike "pouch".

RAFTS, BARK

Nearly all orchids, terrestrial or epiphytic, are grown in pots, A few are grown on "rafts" or slabs of bark or wood, or in baskets of wood slats; a few natives are grown in open ground.

OSMUNDA FIBER, HAPUU

Epiphytic orchids are grown in various kinds of organic material. Best known are osmunda fiber (the chopped roots of a kind of fern); hapuu (fibrous tree fern stem); and ground bark.

TEMPERATURE REQUIREMENTS

Below, we list orchids according to their temperature requirements.

Many of the cool-growing orchids are hardy enough to grow outdoors in mild-winter climate areas; some are native to our Western states.

The temperate-climate orchids can be grown in pots on a window sill along with other house plants, but will perform best if provided with additional humidity. An excellent method of supplying humidity is described under *Cattleya*. Most temperate-climate orchids can be moved outdoors in summer in the shade of high branching trees, on the patio, or in a lathhouse.

The warm-climate orchids need greenhouse conditions to provide the uniform

Climate Zone maps pages 8-27

warmer temperatures and high humidity they require.

Cool climate orchids: Bletilla, Calypso, Cymbidium, Cypripedium, Epidendrum, Epipactis, Habenaria, Laelia, Odontoglossum, Paphiopedilum (green leafed forms), Pleione. Some of these are hardy out of doors in the mildest parts of California. Some are thoroughly hardy.

Temperate climate orchids: Brassavola, Cattleya, Coelogyne, Dendrobium, Epidendrum, Laelia, Lycaste, Miltonia, Oncidium, Paphiopedilum (mottled leafed forms).

Warm climate orchids: Phalaenopsis, Vanda.

ORCHID, BUTTERFLY. See Oncidium papilio

    LILY-OF-THE-VALLEY. See Odontoglossum pulchellum

    MOTH. See Phalaenopsis

    PANSY. See Miltonia

    TIGER. See Odontoglossum grande

ORCHID, POOR MAN'S. See Schizanthus

ORCHID TREE. See Bauhinia

ORCHID VINE. See Stigmaphyllon

ORCHIS, STREAM. See Epipactis

OREGANO. See Origanum

OREOPANAX peltatus (*O. salvinii*). Evergreen shrub or small tree. Zones 17, 21-24. Slow growth to 10-15 ft. in partial shade or sun. Leaves large, on long stalks, deeply lobed, and with the divisions deeply lobed again, giving somewhat the effect of gigantic green snowflakes. This relative of fatsia is for bold tropical effects.

ORIGANUM vulgare. OREGANO, WILD MARJORAM. Perennial herb. All Zones. Upright growth to 2½ ft. Spreads by underground stems. Medium-sized, oval leaves; purplish pink blooms. Grow in sun, medium rich soil, good drainage, average watering. Keep trimmed to prevent flowering. Replant every 3 years. Leaves, fresh or dried, used in many dishes and sauces, especially Italian and Spanish ones.

ORNITHOGALUM. Bulb. Zones 5-24. Leaves vary from narrow to broad and tend to be floppy. Flowers mostly star-shaped, in rounded clusters. Most bloom in April-May. Use in borders or grow in pots.

    O. arabicum. Handsome clusters of 2-in., white, waxy flowers with beady black pistils in centers. Stems 2 ft. tall. Floppy leaves to 2 ft. long, 1 in. wide, bluish green. Bulbs hardy except in coldest winters; in cool-summer climates, bulbs may not bloom second year after planting because of lack of sufficient heat. Can be grown in pots. Excellent cut flower.

    O. caudatum. PREGNANT ONION, FALSE SEA ONION. House plant. Grown for bulb and foliage rather than for tall wands of small green and white flowers. Leaves are strap-shaped, down-hanging and up to 5 ft. long. Big, gray-green, smooth-skinned bulb (3-4 in. thick) grows on, not in, the ground. Bulblets form under the skin and grow quite large before they drop out and root. Hardy to 25°; will lose leaves in extended drought.

    O. miniatum (*O. aureum*). Stems 6-12 in. high; leaves 6-9 in. long. Round clusters of orange-yellow flowers, somewhat cup-shaped, with broad oval segments, bright yellow anthers.

    O. saundersiae. Vigorous plant with floppy, foot-long leaves and 4-6-ft. stalks bearing full clusters of white flowers with greenish black centers. Summer bloom. Group several bulbs in a border, or grow in large pots.

    O. thyrsoides. CHINCHERINCHEE. Tapering, compact clusters of white 2-in. flowers with brownish green centers. Leaves bright green, upright, 2 in. wide, 10-12 in. long. Flower stems 2 ft. high. Usually considered tender, but has survived cold winters in a sheltered south or southwest location and well mulched. Long lasting cut flower. Double-flowered form available.

    O. umbellatum. STAR OF BETHLEHEM. Probably the hardiest of the group. May naturalize widely once it's established. Clusters of 1-in.-wide flowers, striped green on outside, top 1-ft. stems. Grasslike leaves about as long as flower stems. Cut flowers last well but close at night.

OSCULARIA. See Ice Plant

OSMANTHUS. Evergreen shrubs or trees. All have clean, leathery, attractive foliage and inconspicuous but fragrant flowers.

    O. americanus. DEVILWOOD. Tree. Zones 8-10, 14-21. Native to southeastern U. S. Slow to moderate growth to 40 ft. Spreading, rather open round head. Leaves lance-shaped or oval 2-7 in. long, bright glossy green above, yellowish green beneath. Fragrant, tiny, white clustered flowers in early spring. Olivelike fruit in fall. Has done poorly as a street tree. Better performance in gardens where watered and fertilized generously. Susceptible to black scale.

    O. delavayi (*Siphonosmanthus delavayi*). DELAVAY OSMANTHUS. Shrub. Zones 4-9, 14-21. Slow growing, graceful, to 4-6 ft., with arching branches spreading wider. Leaves dark green, oval, to 1 in. long, with toothed edges. White, fragrant flowers in profusion (largest of any osmanthus) in clusters of 4-8, March-May. Partial shade in hot-summer areas. Attractive all year. Easily controlled by pruning. Good choice for foundations, massing. Handsome on top of retaining wall where arching branches hang down.

    O. fortunei. Shrub. Zones 7-10, 14-24. Hybrid between *O. heterophyllus* and *O. fragrans.* Slow, dense growth to 20 ft. Usually seen about 6 ft. high. Leaves, oval, hollylike to 4 in. long. Small, fragrant white flowers in spring, summer.

    O. f. 'San Jose'. Similar in appearance but has cream to orange flowers in October.

    O. fragrans. SWEET OLIVE. Shrub. Zones 8, 9, 12-24. Moderate growth to 10 ft. and more with age. Broad, dense, compact. Can be pruned to upright growth where space is limited. Can train as small tree, hedge, espalier, container plant. Pinch out growing tips of young plants to induce bushiness. Leaves glossy, medium green, oval, to 4 in. long, toothed or smooth-edged. Flowers tiny, white, inconspicuous except in their powerful, sweet, fruity fragrance. Bloom heaviest in spring and early summer, but is scattered throughout year in mild-winter areas. Young plants grow best in some shade, but tolerate sun as they mature. In Zones 12, 13, grow in east or north exposure.

    O. f. aurantiacus. Leaves less glossy than on *O. fragrans.* Concentrates its crop of wonderfully fragrant orange flowers in October.

    O. heterophyllus (*O. aquifolium, O. ilicifolius*). HOLLY-LEAF OSMANTHUS. Shrub. Zones 3-10, 14-24. A number of varieties are available:

    O. h. 'Gulftide'. Similar to 'Ilicifolius' but more compact.

    O. h. 'Ilicifolius'. Dense, symmetrical, upright growth to 6-8 ft., eventually to 20 ft. Leaves dark green, strongly toothed, hollylike, to 2½ in. long. Fragrant white flowers in fall, winter, early spring. Excellent for screening, background.

    O. h. 'Purpurascens'. Dark purple new growth, with purple tints through summer.

    O. h. 'Rotundifolius'. Slow growing to 5 ft., with roundish small leaves and few spines along the edges.

    O. h. 'Variegatus'. Slow growing to 4-5 ft., with densely set leaves edged creamy white. Useful to light up shady areas.

    O. yunnanensis (*O. forrestii*). Zones 4-10, 14-24. Similar to *O. armatus,* but eventually taller—to 20-25 ft. Flowers creamy yellow, appearing sporadically, but in greatest quantity in fall.

OSMAREA burkwoodii. Evergreen shrub. Zones 4-9, 14-17. Slow growing to 6 ft. and as wide. Bushy, compact, well-foliaged with dark green, glossy, toothed leaves 1-2 in. long. Small, fragrant white flowers in clusters, in April-May. Hybrid between *Osmanthus delavayi* and *Phillyrea vilmoriniana.* Similar to *Osmanthus delavayi* but does not flower as freely.

OSMUNDA regalis. ROYAL FERN. All Zones, best in Pacific Northwest. Big fern with twice-cut fronds, the leaflets large, texture coarser than that of most ferns, but extremely handsome. Fertile leaflets small, clustered at the tips of the fronds. Can reach 6 ft. in moist, shady places. Leaves die back in winter.

OSTEOSPERMUM. Evergreen subshrubs or perennials. Zones 8, 9, 14-24. South African plants closely related to *Dimorphotheca* (Cape marigold) and often sold as such. Except for the trailing perennial *O. fruticosum,* all are spreading, mounded shrubby plants with medium green foliage and a profusion of daisylike flowers over a long season. Leaves variable in size and shape, larger on young plants and vigorous young shoots, 2-4 in. long, narrowish oval, smooth edged or with a few large teeth. Flowers, on long stems, open only in sunlight.

Grow in full sun. Plants look best with moderate watering and good garden soil, but will stand drought and neglect when established. Tip-pinch young plants to induce bushiness; cutting back old, sprawling branches to young side branches will keep plants neat, often induce repeat bloom. Use in borders or mass plants along driveways, paths, on slopes, in front of screening shrubs. Grow from seeds or cuttings (named varieties from cuttings only).

    O. barberiae (*Dimorphotheca barberiae*). To 2-3 ft. tall, a little wider. Flower heads 2-3 in. across; rays pinkish lilac inside, with deep purplish blue stripes on reverse; dark purple blue centers. Blooms from fall through spring, frequently through summer.

O. 'Buttersweet'. Plant form resembles that of O. barberiae. Flower heads have primrose yellow rays fading to cream near center, lavender to brownish zone at base, lavender-blue to brownish center. Backs of rays yellow with pronounced brown stripe. Spring to frost.

O. ecklonis (Dimorphotheca ecklonis). Grows 2-4 ft. tall, equally broad. Long stems bear 3-in. flower heads with white rays (tinged lavender-blue on backs) dark blue center. Blooms early summer to frost.

O. fruticosum (Dimorphotheca fruticosa). TRAILING AFRICAN DAISY. Spreads rapidly by trailing, rooting branches. Rooted cuttings will cover a circle 2-4 ft. across in a year; plants 6-12 in. tall. Leaves shorter, thicker than in other species. Flowers intermittently during year, most heavily November-March. Heads to 2 in. across; rays lilac above, fading nearly white by second day, deeper lilac beneath and in bud; dark purple center. Excellent ground cover for sunny areas. Good bank cover. Will spill over a wall or grow in hanging basket (tip-pinch to induce bushiness). Used as annual (fall planting) in Zones 12, 13. A white form (sold as 'Hybrid White', 'White Cloud', 'Snow White') grows more upright, blooms in sheets in late winter and early spring.

O. 'Golden Charm'. Resembles O. 'Buttersweet', but rays, centers, bright yellow.

OSWEGO TEA. See Monarda

OUR LORD'S CANDLE. See Yucca whipplei

OXALIS. Perennials; some grow from bulbs or rhizomes. Leaves divided into leaflets (most commonly in the manner of clover leaves—3 leaflets). Flowers pink, white, shades of rose, or yellow. One yellow-flowered kind (O. corniculata and its purple-leafed form) is considered an aggressive weed everywhere in the West. Some of the cultivated kinds can spread aggressively, may become weeds. All except O. oregana can be grown as house plants anywhere—keep them in a sunny window.

O. acetosella. WOOD SORREL, SHAMROCK. One of several plants known as shamrock. See Shamrock.

O. adenophylla. Zones 4-9, 14-24. Low, dense, compact tuft of leaves, each leaf with 12-22 crinkly, gray-green leaflets. Flowers bell-shaped, lilac pink with deeper veins, bloom in late spring. Plant roots in fall. Needs good drainage, full sun. Good rock garden plant.

O. bowiei. Zones 4-9, 14-24. Cloverlike leaves of 3 leaflets. Pink or rose purple summer flowers 1½-2 in. across. Has survived 0° with only light mulching, but better known as house or basket plant.

O. crassipes. Zones 8, 9, 14-24. Compact, evergreen plant that seems to bloom at all seasons. Rose pink flowers small, but enough open at one time to be effective. There is a white-flowered form, O. c. 'Alba', and a blush pink one, O. c. 'Pinkie'.

O. hirta. Zones 8, 9, 14-24. Makes many upright, branching stems that gradually fall over with the weight of leaves and flowers. Leaves cloverlike, small, set directly against stems or on very short stalks. General effect feathery. Flowers (late fall or winter) bright rose pink, 1 in. wide. Plant bulbs in fall. Rock gardens, hanging baskets.

O. oregana. REDWOOD SORREL, OREGON OXALIS. Zones 4-9, 14-24. Native to coastal forests Washington to California. Creeping white roots send up velvety, medium green cloverlike leaves 1½-4 in. wide on stems 2-10 in. high. Flowers to 1 in. across, pink or white veined with lavender, borne in

Soft leaves of Oxalis oregana resemble clover. Flowers to 1 in. wide, striped.

spring, sometimes again in fall. Interesting ground cover for deep shade in mild-winter, cool-summer areas. Good with ferns. Looks most lush when watered frequently.

O. pes-caprae (O. cernua). BERMUDA BUTTERCUP. Zones 8, 9, 14-24. Clusters of bright green, cloverlike leaves (often spotted with dark brown) spring directly from soil in fall. Above them in winter and spring rise stems topped with clusters of inch-wide, bright yellow flowers. Handsome plant best grown in pots or baskets; it spreads rapidly by rhizomes and bulbs, and can become a troublesome pest in open garden.

O. purpurea (O. variabilis). Zones 8, 9, 14-24. Low growing (4-5 in. tall), with large cloverlike leaves and rose red flowers an inch across November-March. Spreads by bulbs and rhizomelike roots, but not aggressive or weedy. Plant bulbs in fall. Improved kinds with larger flowers sold under the name Grand Duchess; flowers are rose pink, white, or lavender.

OXERA pulchella. Zones 22-24. Evergreen vine or viny shrub. As a shrub, a mounding 6 ft. tall; with support, can be trained to 10 ft. Leaves leathery, glossy, very dark green, oblong, to 5 in. long. Clusters of white, waxy, 2-in. trumpets give winter or spring display of unusual quality. Refined appearance. Best in high shade or cool, sunny spot.

OXYDENDRUM arboreum. SOURWOOD, SORREL TREE. Deciduous tree. Zones 1-9, 14-17. Native to eastern U. S. Slow growth to 15-25 ft., eventually to 50 ft. Slender trunk, slightly spreading head. Leaves 5-8 in. long, narrow, somewhat resemble peach leaves; bronze tinted in early spring, rich green in summer, orange and scarlet in autumn. Creamy white, bell-shaped flowers in 10-in.-long, drooping clusters at branch tips in late July-August. In autumn, when foliage is brilliant scarlet, branching clusters of greenish seed capsules extend outward and downward like the fingers of a hand; the capsules turn light silver gray and hang on late into winter.

Best known in areas with cool summers, well defined winters. Requires acid soil, ample water. Not a competitive plant—doesn't do well in lawns or under trees. Avoid underplanting with anything needing cultivation. Good shade tree for patio or terrace. Distinguished branch and leaf pattern, spring leaf color, summer flowers, fall color.

Leaves of sourwood resemble peach leaves; flowers are creamy white in July-August.

PACHISTIMA. Evergreen shrubs. Zones 1-10, 14-21. Low growing with small, shiny, leathery leaves, insignificant flowers. Hardiness and compact habit make them useful as low hedges, edgings, ground cover. Full sun near coast; partial shade, ample water in hot interiors.

P. canbyi. RATSTRIPPER. Native to mountains, eastern U. S. Makes a mat 9-12 in. tall, with narrow leaves ¼-1 in. long, ¼ in. wide. Foliage dark green, turning bronze in fall and winter.

P. myrsinites. OREGON BOXWOOD. Native to mountains in the West. Dense growth to 2-4 ft. (usually much less), easily kept lower by pruning. More compact in sun. Leaves somewhat larger than the above.

PACHYSANDRA terminalis. JAPANESE SPURGE. Evergreen subshrub. Zones 1-10, 14-21. Excellent ground cover in shade. Spreads by underground runners. Stems reach 10 in. in deep shade, 6 in. in dappled shade. Leaves rich, dark green. 2-4 in. long, in clusters atop stems; yellowish in full sun. Small fluffy spikes of fragrant white flowers in summer; white fruits follow.

Set 6-12 in. apart in rich, preferably acid soil. Give plenty of water, especially while getting established. Feed during growing season for best color. Spreads moderately, but is not aggressive or weedy. Roots compete successfully with surface tree roots. Good transition between walks or lawns and shade-loving shrubs.

'Variegata' has leaves edged with white.

PÆONIA. PEONY. Practically all garden peonies are hybrids. These fall into two principal classes, herbaceous and tree peonies.

Herbaceous Peonies. Perennials. Zones 1-11, 14, 15. Well-grown clumps reach 2-4 ft. tall and spread wider from thickened,

P

Climate Zone maps pages 8-27

tuberous roots. Large, deep green, attractively divided leaves make effective background for the spectacular mid- to late spring flowers. These may be: single (uncommon but very effective); single filled with a mass of narrow, yellow, petal-like structures (Japanese type); semi-double; or fully double. Colors range from pure white through pale creams and pinks to red.

Semi-double (center), double (lower) peonies; Japanese type has yellow center.

Flowers may reach 10 in. across. Newer kinds have deeper reds and chocolate tones. There is even a pure yellow. Many have fragrance of old-fashioned roses.

Herbaceous peonies bloom really well only when they experience a pronounced winter chilling period. Winter cold and summer heat not a problem, but flowers do not last well where spring days are hot and dry—in such areas choose early-blooming varieties and give plants some afternoon shade and ample water. Where they grow best—in the Northwest and intermountain areas—they thrive in full sun.

Can grow in most soils, but because they live long prepare soil deep and well. Keep manure from direct contact with roots. Plant in early fall, being careful that eyes on tubers are no deeper than 2 in.; deeper planting may prevent blooming. Feed established clumps like other plants. Provide support for heavy flowers. Cut off stems carefully just below soil surface in fall after leaves turn brown. Fairly pest free; to control botrytis, which browns buds and spots leaves, spray with copper fungicide spray before buds open; cut out and burn all withered buds, stems, or brown-spotted leaves.

To divide in early fall, dig, cut off foliage, hose dirt from root cluster, and divide carefully into sections with at least 3 eyes (pink growth buds). But don't divide unless absolutely necessary.

Choice cut flowers. A mainstay of big perennial borders. Can be planted in bays of big shrub borders.

Tree Peonies. Deciduous shrubs. Zones 1-12, 14-21. Descendants of *P. suffruticosa*, a Chinese shrub to 6 ft. tall; yellow and salmon varieties are hybrids of this and *P. lutea*, a Tibetan plant with yellow flowers. Irregular, picturesque branching habit from

3-6 ft. tall, eventually as wide. Leaves large, divided, blue-green to bronzy green.

Flowers very large, up to 1 ft. across, single to fully double. Japanese types have single to double flowers held erect above the foliage; silky petals range from white through pink and red to lavender and purple. European types have very heavy double flowers that tend to droop and hide their heads; colors range chiefly through pinks and rosy shades. Hybrids with *P. lutea* have fully double to single flowers in yellow, salmon, or sunset shades; the singles and semi-doubles hold up their flowers best.

Very hardy to cold, and less dependent on winter chill than herbaceous peonies; can get botrytis in humid climates. Fragile blooms come in early to mid-spring and should be sheltered from strong winds. Give plants afternoon shade in hot summer climates. Plant in fall or earliest spring (from containers any time) in rich, deep, well-prepared soil away from competing tree roots. Plants are long lived, so take special pains to improve soil with peat moss or ground bark. Plant deep, setting plant several inches deeper than it grew in nursery can or growing field. To prune, remove spent flowers and cut back to live wood in spring when buds begin to swell.

Varieties available are many, and some nurseries sell unnamed seedlings; select the latter in bloom to get desired form and color.

PAGODA TREE, JAPANESE. See Sophora japonica

PAINTED-TONGUE. See Salpiglossis

PALM. It's difficult to generalize about any plant family as large and widespread as the palms. Generally speaking, they have single, unbranched trunks of considerable height; some grow in clusters, though, and some are dwarf or stemless. Again generally speaking, the leaves are divided into many leaflets, either like the ribs of a fan (fan palms) or like a feather, with many parallel leaflets growing outward from a long central stem. But some palms have undivided leaves.

Again, most palms are tropical or subtropical; a few are surprisingly hardy (to be seen in Edinburgh, London, and southern Russia, as well as Portland and Seattle).

Palms offer great opportunity for imaginative planting. In nature they grow not only in solid stands but also in company with other plants, notably broad-leafed evergreen trees and shrubs. Most young palms prefer shade and all tolerate it; this fact makes them good house or patio plants at a stage when they are small. As they grow, they can be moved into sun or part shade, depending on species.

Growth rates vary but keeping the plants in pots usually slows growth of faster-growing kinds. If temperatures are in the 60's or higher, fertilize potted palms often and wash them off frequently to provide some humidity, clean the foliage, and dislodge some of the insects which (indoors, at any rate) are protected from their natural enemies and can increase at an unnatural rate.

To pot up a palm, supply good potting soil, adequate drainage, and not too big a container. As with all potted plants, pot or

repot a palm in a container just slightly larger than the one it's in.

Some shade-tolerant palms such as *Rhapis*, *Chamaedorea*, and *Howeia* may spend decades in pots indoors. Others that later may reach great size—*Phoenix*, *Washingtonia*, *Chamaerops*—make charming temporary indoor plants but must eventually be moved.

To plant a palm of 5-gallon size in the ground, dig a hole 3 ft. wide and 8 in. deeper than the root ball. At bottom place 1 or 2 cubic ft. of manure, nitrolized sawdust, or other organic amendment, with a handful or two of blood meal added. Put a 6-in. layer of soil over this, set the palm, and fill around it with a mixture of half native soil, half nitrolized sawdust, ground bark, or peat moss. Water well, and continue watering throughout summer and fall. Give gallon-sized palms the same treatment scaled down.

Palms, even big ones, transplant easily in late spring or early summer. Since new roots form from the base of the trunk, root ball need not be large. A new root system will form and produce lush new growth. During the transplant of large palms, tie the leaves together over the center "bud" or heart, and stiffen or secure the latter by tying the leaf mass to a length of 2-by-4 tied to the trunk.

Palms need little maintenance; reasonably fertile soil and adequate water will produce thriving plants. All palms with a tropical background do their growing during the warm portions of the year. Winter rains wash them down and leach accumulated salts from the soil. Washing down with a hose is beneficial, especially for palms exposed to dust and beyond reach of rain or dew. Washing helps keep down sucking insects which find refuge in long leaf stems.

Feather palms and many fan palms look neater when old leaves are removed after they have turned brown. Make neat cuts close to the trunk, leaving the leaf bases. Some palms shed the old leaf bases on their own. Others, including arecastrums and chamaedoreas, may hold the old bases. You can remove them by slicing them off at the very bottom of the base (be careful not to cut into the trunk).

Many palm admirers say that the dead leaves of washingtonias should remain on the tree, the thatch being part of the palm's character. If you also feel this way, you can cut lower fronds in a uniform way close to the trunk, but leave the leaf bases which present a rather pleasant lattice surface.

Here are 10 roles that the right kinds of palms can fill (the palms named in each listing are described under their own names elsewhere in this book):

Sturdy palms for park and avenue plantings, and for vertical effects in large gardens: *Archontophoenix*, *Arecastrum*, *Erythea*, *Jubaea*, *Livistona*, *Phoenix canariensis*, *P. dactylifera*, *P. humilis*, *P. rupicola*, *Rhopalostylis*, *Sabal*, *Washingtonia*.

Small to medium-sized palms for sheltered areas in frost-free gardens: *Archontophoenix*, *Caryota*, *Chamaedorea*, *Chamaerops*, *Chrysalidocarpus*, *Hedyscepe*, *Howeia*, *Linospadix*.

Small to medium-sized palms for gardens in areas of occasional frosts: *Acoelorrhaphe*, *Acrocomia totai*, *Butia*, *Chamaedorea cataractarum*, *C. elegans*, *C. klotzschiana*,

Climate
Zone maps
pages 8-27

C. seifrizii, Chamaerops, Erythea, Linospadix, Livistona, Phoenix roebelenii, Rhapidophyllum, Trachycarpus, Trithrinax.

Hardy palms for cold areas: (The ones marked with an asterisk have withstood very cold winters in various parts of the world.) *Chamaerops, Erythea armata, E. edulis, *Jubaea, Livistona, *Phoenix canariensis, P. dactylifera, P. humilis, *Rhapidophyllum, Rhapis, Sabal mexicana, S. minor, S. palmetto, S. rosei, *Serenoa, *Trachycarpus, Trithrinax, Washingtonia filifera.*

Frost becomes more damaging to palms as it extends its stay and is repeated. Light frosts for half an hour may leave no damage, but the same degree during a period of four hours may damage some palms, kill others. Simplest damage is burned leaf edges, but frost may affect whole leaves, parts of trunks, or the crown. Damage in the crown is usually fatal (some have recovered). Hardiness is also a matter of size; larger plants may pass through severe frosts unharmed while smaller ones perish.

Garden palms for seaside planting: Palms in southern California beach plantings should be washed off occasionally to keep them free from salt accumulations. The following palms are listed in order of their salt tolerance, the most tolerant first: *Washingtonia robusta, Phoenix dactylifera, P. canariensis, P. reclinata, Chamaerops, Erythea edulis. Butia, Sabal domingensis, S. palmetto.*

Palms for inland and desert: *Butia, Chamaerops, Erythea armata, Livistona chinensis, L. mariae, Phoenix canariensis, P. dactylifera, P. humilis, P. sylvestris, Sabal mexicana, S. minor, S. rosei, S. texana, Washingtonia.*

Palms to grow under trees, lath, overhangs, or indoors: (Indoor palms should occasionally be brought outdoors into mild light.) *Acoelorrhaphe, Archontophoenix, Caryota mitis, C. ochlandra, C. urens, Chamaedorea, Hedyscepe, Howeia, Linospadix,* young *livistonas, Microcoelum, Phoenix reclinata* (when young), *P. roebelenii, Rhapis, Rhopalostylis, Trachycarpus* (when young), *Trithrinax.*

Palms near swimming pools: Palms have great value near swimming pools because they do not drop leaves. Mature plants of *Phoenix reclinata* or *Chamaerops humilis,* with their curved trunks arching near the pool give the feeling of a tropical island. But whether palm trunks are curved or upright, or topped with either fan or feather leaves, they create beautiful mirror effects in the water.

Palms as ground covers: Young palms, especially those that grow slowly such as *Livistona chinensis* or *Chamaerops humilis,* can be used effectively as ground covers. They'll stay low from 5 to 10 years, especially if they're in gardens that need little care. When they get too tall, move them to another location in the garden where you need height.

Palms to light at night: Because of their stateliness and their spectacular leaves, palms are good subjects for night lighting. You can back-light them, light them from below, or direct lights to silhouette palms against a light-colored building wall.

PALM, ALEXANDRA. See Archontophoenix alexandrae

CABBAGE. See Sabal palmetto

CALIFORNIA FAN. See Washingtonia filifera

CANARY ISLAND DATE. See Phoenix canariensis

CHILEAN WINE. See Jubaea

CHINESE FOUNTAIN. See Livistona chinensis

DATE. See Phoenix

FISHTAIL. See Caryota

FRANCESCHI. See Erythea elegans

GRUGRU. See Acrocomia

GUADALUPE. See Erythea edulis

KENTIA. See Howeia

LADY. See Rhapis

MEDITERRANEAN FAN. See Chamaerops

MEXICAN BLUE. See Erythea armata

MEXICAN FAN. See Washingtonia robusta

NEEDLE. See Rhapidophyllum

PARADISE. See Howeia forsteriana

PINDO. See Butia

QUEEN. See Arecastrum romanzoffianum

RATTAN. See Rhapis humilis

SAN JOSE HESPER. See Erythea brandegeei

SENTRY. See Howeia belmoreana

WALKING-STICK. See Linospadix

WINDMILL. See Trachycarpus fortunei

PALM, SAGO. See Cycas

PALMETTO. See Sabal

PALO VERDE. See Cercidium

PALO VERDE, MEXICAN. See Parkinsonia

PAMPAS GRASS. See Cortaderia

PANAMIGA, PANAMIGO. See Pilea involucrata

PANDA PLANT. See Kalanchoe tomentosa

PANDOREA. Evergreen vines. Zones 16-24. Leaves divided into glossy oval leaflets; flowers trumpet-shaped, clustered. Climb by twining.

P. jasminoides (*Bignonia jasminoides, Tecoma jasminoides*). BOWER VINE. Fast to 20-30 ft. Slender stems, distinguished glossy foliage, medium to dark green. Leaves have 5-9 egg-shaped leaflets 1-2 in. long. Flowers (June-October) 1½-2 in. long, white with pink throats, dropping cleanly after bloom. 'Alba' has pure white flowers; 'Rosea' has pink flowers with rose-pink throats. Plant in lee of prevailing wind. Ample moisture, sun near coast, part shade inland. Prolonged freezes will kill it.

P. pandorana (*Bignonia australis, Tecoma australis*). WONGA-WONGA VINE. Glossy foliage handsome all seasons. Flowers smaller (to ¾ in. long), yellow or pinkish white, throat usually spotted brown-purple. Prune ends of branches heavily after spring bloom.

PANSY. See Viola

PAPAVER. POPPY. Annuals, perennials. Provide gay color in spring and summer for borders and cutting. All kinds need full sun, ordinary soil, good drainage, not too much water, no fertilizer.

P. alpinum. ALPINE POPPY. Perennial. All Zones; best adapted in colder climates. Short-lived rock garden poppy with leaves in a basal rosette and flower stalk 5-8 in. high. Blue-green, nearly hairless divided leaves. Spring flowers 1-1½ in. across, white, orange, yellow, salmon.

P. nudicaule. ICELAND POPPY. Perennial, grown as annual in warm-winter areas. All Zones. Divided leaves with coarse hairs. Slender, hairy stems 1-2 ft. high. Flowers cup-shaped, to 3 in. across, slightly fragrant, yellow, orange, salmon, rose, pink, cream, or white. In mild climates blooms winter and early spring from plants set out in fall. Where winters are cold, sow seed in earliest spring for summer bloom. To prolong bloom, pick flowers frequently. Several good strains available. Cover young plants with screen to protect from birds.

P. orientale. ORIENTAL POPPY. Perennial. Zones 1-17. Short-lived in warm-winter climates. Strong, bold plants to 4 ft. Coarse, hairy, divided leaves. Flowers single or double, 3-6 in. across, in brilliant and pastel shades. Many named varieties. Plants die back in midsummer; new leafy growth appears in early fall, lasts over winter, develops rapidly in warm weather. Combine with bearded iris, lupine, nepeta, violas. Baby's breath (*Gypsophila*) makes a good summer filler when poppies go dormant. To use as cut flower, sear cut stems in flame before placing in water.

P. rhoeas. SHIRLEY POPPY. Annual. Slender, branching, hairy, 2-5 ft. high. Leaves short, irregularly divided. Flowers 2 in. or more across, single and double, in red, pink, white, orange, scarlet, salmon, bicolor. Broadcast seed mixed with fine sand. Sow successively for bloom from spring through summer (in cool areas). Take cut flowers when buds first show color. Remove seed capsules (old flower bases) weekly to prolong bloom season.

PAPAYA. See Carica

PAPERBARK, FLAXLEAF. See Melaleuca linariifolia

PAPHIOPEDILUM. LADY'S SLIPPER. Terrestrial orchids. Cool greenhouse or indoor plant. This name applies to the lady's slipper orchids (usually sold as *Cypripedium*) native to tropical regions of Asia. Under this name fall the large-flowered hybrids grown commercially for cut flowers. Blooms are perky, usually one, occasionally two or more to a stem. Many of them shine as if they'd been lacquered. Flowers may be white, yellow, green with white stripes, pure green, or a combination of background colors and markings in tan, mahogany brown, maroon, green, and white.

Graceful arching foliage (no pseudobulbs) either plain green or mottled. Usually the plain-leafed forms flower in winter, the mottled-leaf forms flower in summer. Most plants at orchid dealers' establishments are hybrids.

In general the mottled-leafed forms require about 60° to 65° night temperatures, 70° to 85° day temperature. The plain leafed forms require 55° to 65° night temperatures, and 65° to 75° day temperatures. They have no rest period, so should be kept moist at all times. A good potting

Climate Zone maps pages 8-27

medium: equal parts ground bark and sandy loam. Don't plant in oversize pot. The plants thrive when crowded. Hardiest kinds can be grown in pots indoors, treated as house plants. They thrive in less light than most orchids require.

P. insigne. Polished lady slipper-type flowers on stiff brown hairy stems any time October-March. Sepals and petals green and white spotted and striped brown; pouch reddish brown. Hardy to brief exposures of 28°.

PAPYRUS. See Cyperus papyrus

PARASOL TREE, CHINESE. See Firmiana

PARKINSONIA aculeata. JERUSALEM THORN. MEXICAN PALO VERDE. Deciduous tree. Zones 11-24; especially valuable in Zones 12 and 13. Rapid growth at first, slowing to eventual 15-30 ft. high and wide. Yellow-green bark, spiny twigs. Sparse foliage; leaves 6-9 in. long, with many tiny leaflets which quickly fall in drought or cold. Numerous yellow flowers in loose 3-7-in.-long clusters. Long bloom season in spring, intermittent bloom throughout year.

Tolerates alkaline soil. Resistant to pests, disease. Stake young trees, train for high or low branching. Requires minimum attention once established. Does not do well with lawn watering. As a shade tree, it filters sun rather than blocking it. Thorns, sparse foliage rule it out of tailored gardens. Flowering branches attractive in arrangements.

PARROT-BEAK. See Clianthus

PARROTIA persica. PERSIAN PARROTIA. Deciduous tree or large shrub. Zones 4-6, 15-17. Native to Persia. Choice and colorful; attractive at all seasons of the year. Most dramatic display comes in fall. Usually leaves turn from golden yellow to orange to rosy pink and finally scarlet. Slow growing to 30 ft. or more, but tends to be a shrub or a multiple trunked tree to 15 ft. Bark attractive in winter: smooth, gray, flakes off to leave white patches. Its dense foliage is made up of lustrous, dark green, oval, 3-4-in.-long leaves.

Its flowers with red stamens are in dense heads surrounded by woolly brown bracts. They appear in spring before leaves open to give the tree a hazy red effect.

To train as a tree, stake and shorten the lower side branches. Allow upper branches to take their wide-spreading habit. When tree reaches desired height, remove lower shortened side branches cleanly.

PARSLEY. The 6-12-in.-high plants with their tufted, finely-cut, dark green leaves, make an attractive edging for an herb, vegetable, or flower garden. You can use the leaves fresh or dried as seasoning, fresh as garnishes. Parsley is a biennial but is most satisfactorily grown from new sowing every year. Grow in sun. Buy plants at a nursery or sow seed in place (April in cold-winter climates; December-May in mild-winter climates; September-October in Zones 12, 13). Soak seed in warm water 24 hours before planting. Even then, it may not sprout for several weeks—an old story says that parsley seeds must go to the devil and come back before sprouting. Thin seedlings to 6-8 in. apart.

PARSNIP. Needs deep, well prepared, loose soil for the long roots; some varieties are 15 in. long. In cold-winter areas plant seeds in late spring, harvest in fall and leave surplus in ground to be dug as needed in winter. In mild-climate areas sow in fall and harvest in spring; in such areas parsnips can't stay in the ground even in winter, as they will become tough and woody. Remarkably free of pests and diseases.

PARTHENOCISSUS *(Ampelopsis)*. Deciduous vines. All Zones. Cling to walls by sucker discs at ends of tendrils. Superb and dependable fall leaf color, orange to scarlet. Ample water, moderate feeding. Think twice before planting them against wood or shingle siding; they can creep under, and their clinging tendrils are hard to remove at repainting time.

P. quinquefolia. VIRGINIA CREEPER. Big, vigorous vine that clings or runs over ground, fence, trellis. Looser growth than Boston ivy, and can be used to drape its trailing branches over a trellis. Leaves divided into 5 separate 6-in. leaflets with saw-toothed edges. Good ground cover on slopes. *P. q.* 'Engelmannii' has smaller leaves, denser growth.

P. tricuspidata. BOSTON IVY. Semi-evergreen in mild-winter areas. Glossy leaves variable in shape, usually 3-lobed, up to 8 in. wide. Clings tightly to make a fast, dense, even wall cover. This is the ivy of the "Ivy League"; covers brick or stone in areas where English ivy freezes. North or east walls only in hot desert regions. 'Lowii' has smaller (1½-in.), deeply lobed leaves. 'Veitchii' has small leaves, the younger ones purplish.

PASQUE FLOWER. See Anemone pulsatilla

PASSIFLORA. PASSION VINE. Evergreen, semi-evergreen, or deciduous vines. Climb by tendrils to 20-30 ft. Name comes from manner in which flower parts symbolize elements of the passion of the Lord; the lacy crown could be a halo or a crown of thorns; the five stamens the five wounds; the ten petal-like parts the ten faithful apostles.

Vigorous, likely to overgrow and tangle themselves; to keep plant open and prevent build-up of dead inner tangle, prune excess branches back to base or juncture with another branch. Do this annually after second year. Tolerant of many soils; average water and feeding. Subject to attack by caterpillars of the gulf fritillary butterfly. Control by sprays.

Use on trellises or walls for their vigor and bright, showy flowers, or use as soil-holding bank cover. In cold-winter climates use as greenhouse or house plants.

P. alato-caerulea *(P. pfordtii)*. Evergreen or semi-evergreen vine. Zones 12-24; root-hardy perennial in Zones 5-9. Hybrid between *P. alata, P. caerulea*. Best known, most widely planted, probably least subject to caterpillars. Leaves 3 in. long, 3-lobed. Fragrant 3½-4-in. flowers white shaded pink and lavender. Crown deep blue or purple. Blooms all summer. In colder areas give it a warm place out of wind; plant against wall or under overhang. Mulch roots in winter.

P. caerulea. BLUE CROWN PASSION FLOWER. Evergreen or semi-evergreen vine.

Zones 12-24; root-hardy perennial in Zones 5-9. Leaves smaller than *P. alato-caerulea*, 5-lobed. Flowers smaller, greenish white, crown white and purple. Fruits small, orange-colored, oval.

P. edulis. PASSION FRUIT, PURPLE GRANADILLA. Semi-evergreen vine. Zones 16, 17, 21-24. Leaves 3-lobed, deeply toothed, light yellow-green. Flowers white with white and purple crown, 2 in. across. Fruits deep purple, fragrant, 3 in. long, delicious in beverages, fruit salads, sherbets. Fruits in spring and fall. There is a yellow-fruited variety.

P. incarnata. MAYPOP. All Zones. Perennial vine. Only if you live in a really cold area and want a very hardy passion flower. Native to eastern U. S. Spreads prodigiously by root runners, dies back at first frost. Flowers 2 in. across, white with purple and white crown. Fruits 2 in. long, yellowish green, edible. Grow from seed.

P. jamesonii. Evergreen vine. Zones 14-24. Especially good in Zones 17, 24. Glossy leaves 3-lobed. Flowers long-tubed (to 4 in.), salmon to coral, profuse all summer. Fast growing bank, fence cover.

P. manicata. Evergreen vine. Zones 17, 23, 24. Leaves 3-lobed. Flowers to 4 in. across, scarlet with narrow blue crown.

P. mollissima. Evergreen vine. Zones 12-24. Soft green foliage; leaves 3-lobed, deeply toothed. Long-tubed pink to rose flowers 3 in. across. Yellow, 2-in. fruits. Rampant growth makes it a good bank cover, but a problem planted among trees and shrubs.

P. racemosa *(P. princeps)*. Evergreen vine. Zones 23, 24. Tall, slender. Leathery leaves fairly pest free. Showy deep rose maroon to coral flowers with purple and white crown hang from main stems in long, wiry clusters.

Passiflora alato-caerulea: crown (inner row of narrow segments) blue or purple.

PASSION FLOWER, BLUE CROWN. See Passiflora caerulea

PASSION FRUIT. See Passiflora edulis

PASSION VINE. See Passiflora

PAULOWNIA tomentosa *(P. imperialis)*. EMPRESS TREE. Deciduous tree. All Zones; young trees may need protection in Zones

Climate Zone maps pages 8-27

1-3. Somewhat similar to catalpa in growth habit, leaves. Fast to 40-50 ft. with nearly equal spread. Heavy trunk and heavy, nearly horizontal branches. Foliage gives tropical effect; leaves are light green, heart-shaped, 5-12 in. long, 4-7 in. wide. If tree is cut back annually or every other year, it will grow as a billowy foliage mass with giant-sized leaves up to 2 ft. However, this kind of pruning is done at the expense of flower production.

Flower buds form in autumn and persist over winter; they are brown and the size of a small olive. Buds open before leaves in early spring to form upright clusters (6-12 in. long) of trumpet-shaped 2-in.-long, fragrant flowers of lilac blue with darker spotting and yellow stripes inside. Flowers are followed by top-shaped seed capsules 1½-2 in. long. They hang on the tree so that both seed capsules and flower buds are present at the same time. Does not flower well where winters are very cold (buds freeze) or very mild (buds may drop off). In areas of strong winds, leaves will be damaged. Bark is apt to sunburn in Zones 7-14, 18-21. Give it a place where falling flowers and leaves are not objectionable. Not a tree to garden under because of dense shade and surface roots.

PAUROTIS wrightii. See Acoelorrhaphe wrightii

PEACH AND NECTARINE. Peach (*Prunus persica*) and nectarine (*Prunus persica nectarina*) trees look alike and have the same general cultural needs. Nectarine fruits differ from peaches only in having smooth skins and (in some varieties) a slightly different flavor. Climate adaptation of the nectarine is more limited.

In terms of landscaping and fruit growing, there are four kinds of peaches: flowering peaches, fruiting peaches, flowering-fruiting (dual-purpose) peaches, and dwarf fruiting peaches that form large bushes. Here we consider the three groups of fruiting peaches. For strictly flowering peaches, see *Prunus*.

The regular fruiting peach tree grows fast to 25 ft. high and spreads as wide; well pruned trees are usually less than 15 ft. tall and 15-18 ft. wide. The peach starts bearing large crops when 3-4 years old and reaches its peak at 8-12 years.

Peaches do best if they get some chilling in winter and clear hot weather during the growing season. Peaches generally set few flowers and pollinate poorly where spring is cool and rainy. Only specially selected varieties do well in extremely mild-winter areas. Lack of winter chilling results in delayed foliation, few fruits, and eventual death of the tree. The high desert satisfies chilling requirements but late frosts make early blooming varieties risky. Few are satisfactory in the mild-winter areas of the low desert.

To save space, you can graft different varieties on one tree or plant 3 or 4 varieties in one hole.

Peaches require a well drained soil and a regular fertilizing program. Prune these trees more heavily than any other fruit trees. When planting a bare-root tree, cut back to 2 ft. above ground. New branches will form below the cut. After the first year's growth, select three well placed branches for scaffold limbs. Remove all other branches. On mature trees, each dormant season cut off 2/3 of the previous year's growth by removing 2 of every 3 branches formed last year; or head back each branch to 1/3 its length. Or, head back some branches and cut out others.

Protect all kinds of peaches and nectarines from peach leaf curl and peach tree borer. Two dormant sprayings, one in November and again in January before the buds swell, will control leaf curl. Use Bordeaux mixture or lime sulfur. Sprays combining oil and lime sulfur or fixed copper will control both scale insects and peach leaf curl. Borers attack at or just below ground level. Pull away soil to expose 2-3 in. of roots. Spray with sevin or diazinon in early June and every 3 weeks until mid-August.

FLOWERING-FRUITING PEACHES

These dual purpose peaches were developed in southern California for southern California conditions, but are widely adapted. Zones 7-9, 12-22. Most likely to succeed in Zone 13 is 'Daily News Four Star'.

'Altair'. Large, double pink flowers. White fleshed freestone in mid-August.

'Daily News Two Star'. Deep pink flowers. Yellow fleshed, semi-freestone, early summer.

'Daily News Three Star'. Deep pink double flowers. Highly colored red freestone with white flesh, in midsummer.

'Daily News Four Star'. Salmon pink double flowers. Highly colored red fruit with white flesh. Freestone. Midseason.

'Double Delight'. Large pale pink double flowers. Yellow, blushed red, freestone, yellow flesh. Early midseason.

'Saturn'. Large, deep pink double flowers. High quality. Yellow fleshed freestone. Midseason.

NATURAL DWARF PEACHES AND NECTARINES

Most fruit trees are dwarfed by grafting standard varieties on dwarfing root stocks. In the case of peaches and nectarines, the best dwarfs are genetic (natural) dwarf varieties, not grafted. These are sold:

'Bonanza'. Peach. Blooms and bears fruit at 2 ft. high, 2 years old. Will eventually reach 6 ft. Semi-double rose-pink flowers. Blushed red, yellow fleshed freestone of good size and flavor. Early.

'Empress'. Peach. Semi-dwarf, reaching 4-5 ft. Pink to red skin, yellow fleshed cling of large size and fine flavor. Early August.

'Flory'. Peach. Grows slowly to 5 ft., with equal spread. White fleshed freestone. Bland flavor. Ripens July.

'Golden Gem'. Peach. To 5-6 ft. Double pink bloom. Large, yellow, red-blushed skin, yellow freestone. Midseason.

'Golden Glory'. Peach. To 6-7 ft. Large yellow fleshed freestone. Skin golden with red blush. Heavy bearer. Ripens mid- to late August.

'Golden Prolific'. Nectarine. Slow growing to 5-7 ft. Large yellow fleshed freestone. Skin yellow, mottled with orange-red. Ripens midseason.

'Golden Treasure'. Peach. To 5-6 ft. Golden, red-blushed, large yellow-fleshed freestone. Early August.

'Nectarina'. Nectarine. To 5-6 ft. Skin deep red and yellow. Orange-fleshed freestone ripening in late July.

'Silver Prolific'. Nectarine. Slow growing to 5-7 ft. Large yellow fleshed freestone. Skin light yellow, blushed red. Rich flavor. Midseason.

PEACH, FLOWERING. See Prunus

PEACH AND NECTARINE

NAME	ZONES	FRUIT	COMMENTS
PEACHES			
'Australian Saucer'	13, 18-24	White-fleshed, flattened end to end. Sweet, faint bitterish overtone. Very little acid. Freestone. Early.	Requires very little chilling and is nearly evergreen in mild regions.
'Babcock'	15-16, 19-24	White freestone, small to medium, sweet flavor with some tang. Early.	Needs little winter chilling. Old timer.
'Belle' ('Belle of Georgia')	10-12, 18-19	Large white freestone of fine flavor, attractive appearance. Early midseason.	Old favorite for table use.

(Continued on next page)

P

Climate Zone maps pages 8-27

NAME	ZONES	FRUIT	COMMENTS
PEACHES			
'Blazing Gold'	3, 6, 8, 9, 14-16	Yellow freestone, small to medium, firm-fleshed, good flavor. Early.	Not as high quality in Zones 3, 6 as in 8, 9, 14-16.
'Bonita'	15-24	Large yellow freestone with medium blush, firm flesh, fine flavor. Ripens in midseason.	Bred for mild-winter areas.
'Cardinal'	4-9, 14-16, 18	Medium to large clingstone. Bright red, yellow fleshed. One of the best early varieties.	Has ability to set fruit in cool, rainy spring weather.
'Dixie Gem'	2, 3, 6-9, 14	Medium to large, semi-cling, yellow fleshed. Early midseason.	Good canner.
'Dixie Red'	2, 3, 6-9, 14	Attractive red cling with yellow flesh. Very good flavor. Early.	Has tendency to split pits.
'Early Crawford'	1-3, 6-12, 14, 18	Medium-sized yellow freestone, blushed red. Firm flesh, excellent flavor. A week earlier than 'Elberta'.	Fruit irregular in shape and in ripening, but an old favorite.
'Early Elberta' ('Improved Elberta')	3-11, 14, 15	Superior in color and flavor to 'Elberta'. Freestone. Ripens a week earlier than 'Elberta'.	Needs somewhat less heat than 'Elberta' and less winter chill; less subject to fruit drop. Thin well for good-sized fruit.
'Elberta'	1-3, 6-11, 14	Medium to large yellow freestone, skin blushed red, high quality. Midseason (later in Zone 6.)	Needs good amount of winter chilling, high summer heat to ripen to full flavor.
'Fay Elberta' ('Gold Medal' in Northwest)	2, 3, 6-11, 14, 15, 18, 19	More colorful than 'Elberta', keeps a little better. Yellow-fleshed freestone. Ripens with 'Elberta'.	Has large, handsome single flowers. Thin it well.
'Giant Elberta'	1-3, 6	Large yellow-fleshed freestone of good quality. Early midseason.	Similar to 'July Elberta' in season, appearance, quality.
'Gold Dust'	6-9, 11, 14-16	Small to medium yellow freestone, high blush, good quality. Early.	Like 'Blazing Gold', but ripens a week later.
'Golden Blush'	18, 19	Medium large yellow-fleshed freestone of good flavor. Midseason.	Fast growing, vigorous tree.
'Golden Jubilee'	2, 3, 5, 6	Medium yellow freestone of fair flavor. Tender. Ripens 3 weeks before 'Elberta'.	Good early peach in Zones 2, 3.
'Halberta' ('Hal-Berta Giant')	1-3, 6-11, 14, 18	Very large yellow freestone, very smooth-skinned. Ripens with 'Elberta'.	Needs pollenizing; any other peach except 'J. H. Hale' or 'Indian Free' will do.
'Halehaven'	1-3, 6-11, 14-16	Medium to large, highly colored yellow freestone. Ripens two weeks ahead of 'Elberta'.	A fine large yellow freestone to use fresh or canned. Fruit and leaf buds very winter-hardy.
'Indian Blood Cling' ('Indian Cling')	1-3, 6-11, 14-16	Medium red-skinned clingstone. Flesh firm, yellow streaked red. Late.	Old variety with a small but devoted band of enthusiasts. Good for preserves.
'Indian Free'	7-11, 14-16	Large, round, yellow freestone, deep red at pit. Tart until fully ripe. Late midseason.	Needs pollenizing by any other peach.
'J. H. Hale'	1-3, 7-11, 14-16	Very large highly colored yellow freestone of high quality. Fine keeper. Ripens with 'Elberta'.	Needs pollenizing by any other peach except 'Halberta', 'Indian Blood'.
'July Elberta' ('Burbank Elberta' 'Kim Elberta')	2, 3, 6-12, 14-16, 18-19	Medium large, yellow-fleshed freestone of high quality. Ripens a month ahead of 'Elberta'.	Prolific bearer. May need extra thinning to get size.
'Meadowlark'	11, 12, 18, 20	Yellow-fleshed freestone much resembling 'Elberta'. Early.	Developed for these climate zones.
'Miller's Late'	7-11, 14, 18	Medium-sized yellow freestone peach of fair flavor. Very late ripening.	If you have to have peaches in mid-October. In cool-autumn areas, ripen off tree.

NAME	ZONES	FRUIT	COMMENTS
PEACHES			
'Nectar'	7-11, 14-16	Medium to large white freestone peach of excellent flavor. Early midseason.	White peach fanciers consider it the best.
'Orange Cling' ('Miller Cling')	1-3, 7-12, 14-16, 18	Large, late clingstone peach with firm, deep yellow flesh. Late.	A favorite for home canning.
'Pacific Gold' ('Rochester')	3-6	Small yellow freestone with medium blush, yellow flesh. Early midseason.	Long ripening season. One of best in Western Washington and Oregon for fresh use. Dependable producer.
'Ranger'	3, 5-9, 14-16, 18	Medium large, highly colored freestone, yellow fleshed, good flavor. Early midseason, a month before 'Elberta'.	Heavy fruit bud set. High yielder. Excellent early canner.
'Redglobe'	3, 6-11, 14-16	Highly colored, firm-fleshed yellow freestone of good flavor. Three weeks before 'Elberta'.	Good for canning or freezing. Sometimes sets a light crop in Zone 6.
'Redhaven'	3, 12, 14-16	Brightly blushed yellow freestone. Long ripening season permits numerous pickings. Ripens 3 to 4 weeks ahead of 'Elberta'.	Colors up early, so taste-test for ripeness. Thin early and well. One of the best for home planting.
'Redwing'	18-24	Small, highly colored white freestone. Soft-fleshed. Early.	Low winter chilling requirement.
'Richhaven'	3, 6-16	Brighter red than 'Redhaven'. Yellow freestone.	Not as good overall quality as 'Redhaven'.
'Rio Oso Gem'	3, 7-9, 14, 15	Medium large, yellow-fleshed freestone of excellent flavor. Ripens a week later than 'Elberta'.	Small tree. Not vigorous. One of the best.
'Robin'	18, 20	Small white clingstone. Bright color, soft flesh. Very early.	Mild flavor, low acid.
'Rochester' ('Pacific Gold')	3-6	Small yellow freestone with medium blush, yellow flesh. Early midseason.	Long ripening season. One of best for western Washington and Oregon for fresh use. Dependable producer.
'Rubidoux'	18, 20	Medium large yellow freestone, firm flesh, good keeper. Late midseason.	Developed specifically for these climate zones.
'Southland'	3, 6-9, 14-16	Attractive medium to large yellow fleshed freestone. Midseason.	Not consistently productive in Zone 6.
'Springtime'	18-23	Yellow freestone of high color, good flavor. Ripens late May-early June.	The earliest yellow-fleshed peach.
'Strawberry Cling'	7-9, 14-16, 18-20	Large, creamy white marbled red. Clingstone. Flesh white, juicy, richly flavored. Early midseason.	Favorite with home canners.
'Strawberry Free'	7-9, 14-16, 18-20	Medium size, white freestone. Medium blush, firm flesh, excellent flavor. Early midseason.	Old favorite of those who like white peaches.
'Tejon'	18-22	Small to medium semi-freestone, very juicy, yellow flesh. Very early.	Very low chilling requirement.
'Ventura'	18-24	Medium-sized attractive yellow freestone. Very smooth skin. Midseason.	Developed especially for these climate zones.
'Veteran'	4-6	Medium-sized yellow freestone of good flavor. Ripens 10 days earlier than 'Elberta'.	Resembles 'Elberta' but rounder, less fuzzy. Sets fruit under adverse conditions.
'White Heath Cling' ('Heath')	7-11, 14-16	Medium to large, firm-fleshed, white clingstone, excellent flavor. Late.	Distinctive flavor, and a favorite for home canning.

(Continued on next page)

P

NAME	ZONES	FRUIT	COMMENTS
NECTARINES			
'Boston' ('Boston Red')	2-3	Yellow with red cheek, yellow fleshed freestone. Late midseason.	Fine, sweet flavor. A favorite in eastern Washington.
'Flaming Gold'	7-9, 14-15	Large yellow freestone. Skin blushed red. Early midseason.	Showy fruit.
'Freedom'	7-9, 11	Large, highly colored, yellow-fleshed freestone of high quality. Early midseason.	Beautiful fruit.
'Fuzzless Berta'	2, 3, 6-9	Large, yellow freestone. Midseason.	One of few recommended for Willamette Valley.
'Garden State'	2, 3, 6-9	Large, yellow-fleshed freestone. Midseason.	Eastern variety doing well in the Northwest.
'Gold Mine'	7-9, 14-22	Red blush, white-fleshed freestone. Late midseason.	Low winter chilling requirement.
'Gower'	7-9, 11, 14-15	White freestone. Late midseason.	Good nectarine flavor.
'John Rivers'	7-9, 14, 15	White freestone or semi-freestone. Early.	Earliest good variety.
'Le Grand'	7-9, 14, 15	Very large, bright red and yellow nectarine. Firm yellow flesh. Clingstone. Ripens midseason.	Attractive and holds well. Many variants of this are entering trade—earlier and later forms, more colorful forms.
'Panamint'	7-9, 14-24	Bright red skin, yellow flesh, freestone. Midseason.	Very low chilling requirement.
'Philp'	7-9	Medium to large, yellow heavily blushed red. Yellow flesh tinged red at pit. Freestone. Early midseason.	Excellent flavor. Flowers large and showy.
'Pioneer'	7-9, 14-16, 18-23	Yellow overlaid with red. Flesh yellow touched with red. Freestone. Rich, distinctive flavor. Midseason.	Large pink flowers.
'Quetta'	7-9, 14, 15	Large white clingstone. Highly colored, very firm-fleshed. Midseason.	Attractive, rather tough fruit. Good for slicing.
'Redchief'	2-3	Red skinned, white-fleshed, free-stone. Small to medium. Midseason.	Keeps well in cold storage.
'Silver Lode'	7-9, 14-20	White flesh, freestone, scarlet and white skin. Early.	Low chilling requirement.
'Stanwick'	7-9, 14-15	Greenish white shaded purple-red. White fleshed, freestone. Late.	Excellent flavor. Good for freezing.

PEANUT. Best where summers are long and warm and soil is not acid. Plants resemble small sweet pea bushes 10-20 in. high. After bright yellow flower fades, a "peg" (shoot-like structure) develops at flower's base, grows down into soil and develops peanuts underground. Soil must be light-textured to admit penetration by the pegs. Sandy soil is ideal. Tender to frost but worth growing as novelty even in cool regions.

Buy seeds (unroasted peanuts) from mail order seed firms. Plant when soil warms up, setting nuts 2 in. deep in rows 3 ft. apart. Space shelled 'Jumbo Virginia' seeds 10 in. apart, 'Spanish' 4 in. apart (un-shelled seeds 20 in. apart). Fertilize at planting time. Water regularly, especially at blossom time, up to 2 weeks before harvest. In 110-120 days after planting, foliage begins to yellow and plants are ready to dig. Loosen soil around plants and pull them up. Cure peanuts on the vines in a warm, airy place out of sunlight for 2-3 weeks, then strip from plants.

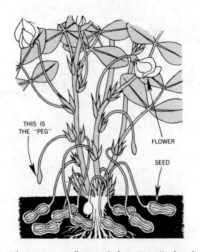

THIS IS THE "PEG"

FLOWER

SEED

When peanut flower fades, "peg" develops, thrusts seed into soil to ripen.

PEAR *(Pyrus communis).* Deciduous fruit tree. Zones 1-11, 14-16, 18. Pyramidal tree with strongly vertical branching; grows 30-40 ft. tall, sometimes more. Long-lived. Leaves leathery, glossy, bright green. Clustered white flowers handsome in early spring.

Takes damp, heavy soil better than most fruit trees. Good looking enough for garden use, and mature trees need little pruning, but trees need spraying for codling moth, aphids, and other pests. Fireblight can be a serious problem. It makes entire branches die back quickly. Cut out blighted branches well below dead part; wash pruning tools with disinfectant between each cut.

Train trees early to a good framework of main branches, then prune lightly to keep good form, eliminate crowding branches. Pears on dwarfing understock are good small garden trees, excellent espaliers.

See the accompanying chart for descriptions of pear varieties.

PEAR

NAME	CLIMATE ADAPTABILITY	FRUIT CHARACTERISTICS	COMMENTS
'Anjou', 'd'Anjou'	A favorite late variety in the Northwest, northern California mountains.	Medium to large, round or short necked, yellow to russeted yellow. Fine flavor, late ripening.	Tree upright and vigorous. Not always consistent in bearing. Moderately susceptible to fireblight.
'Bartlett'	Widely adaptable, but not at its best in mild winters. In southern California will succeed at high elevations or in cold canyon or valley floors.	Medium to large, with short but definite neck. Thin-skinned, yellow or slightly blushed, very sweet and tender. The standard summer pear of fruit markets.	Generally sets fruit without pollination, but may require pollinator in cool California coastal areas and Northwest. Any variety except 'Seckel' will do. Tree form not the best, and somewhat subject to fireblight. Nevertheless a good home variety.
'Bosc' ('Golden Russet')	Best in Northwest or at high altitudes further south.	Medium to large, quite long-necked, interesting and attractive in form. Heavy russeting on green or yellow ground color. Fine flavor. Midseason.	Large, upright, vigorous tree. Needs attention to pruning in youth. Highly susceptible to fireblight. Does not ripen well in cold storage; ripen it at room temperature.
'Clapp Favorite'	Very hardy to cold; good garden tree in Northwest, Intermountain areas.	Resembles 'Bartlett'. Early, soft, and sweet.	Tree productive and shapely. Good foliage; highly susceptible to fireblight.
'Comice' ('Royal Riviera')	At its best in Hood River and Medford regions of Oregon, Santa Clara County in California.	Large to very large, roundish to pear-shaped, thick skinned, russeted greenish yellow, sometimes blushed. Superb flavor and texture. Late.	Big, vigorous tree but slow to reach bearing age. Moderately susceptible to fireblight. Bears well only when soil, climate and exposure are right. Bears better in Northwest with pollinator.
'Douglas'	Has a short chilling requirement, but is also quite hardy.	Small to medium, oval in shape, greenish yellow. Flavor sweet to acid. Texture tender, with some grittiness.	Like other hybrids with sand pear, this one is highly resistant to fireblight.
'Flemish Beauty'	Grown in the Northwest.	Medium to large roundish pear, yellow, with pronounced red blush. Fine flavor. Early midseason.	Large, productive, very hardy tree. Fruit best ripened off tree.
'Forelle'	Offered principally in Northwest.	Medium size, variable in shape. Deep yellow, heavily blushed and spotted, decorative. White-fleshed, firm, fair quality. Midseason.	Tree vigorous and upright, highly susceptible to fireblight.
'Hardy'	Widely grown in northern California for canning. Grows in Northwest.	Medium to large, roundish pear-shaped. Dull greenish yellow, of good flavor. Flesh somewhat granular. Early midseason.	Well shaped, vigorous tree. Moderately susceptible to fireblight. Tends to alternate bearing. Needs pollination in Northwest.
'Kieffer'	Low winter chilling requirements, high tolerance to heat and cold. Grown in high desert.	Medium to large, oval, greenish-yellow blushed dark red. Gritty in texture, fair in flavor. Best picked from tree and ripened at 65°. Late.	A sand pear hybrid, and quite resistant to fireblight. Good pear for extreme climates.
'Le Conte'	Same as 'Kieffer'	Resembles 'Kieffer'. Roundish, gritty, late.	Most tolerant to summer heat; somewhat resistant to fireblight.
'Max-Red Bartlett'	See 'Bartlett'.	Like 'Bartlett' except bright red in skin color and somewhat sweeter.	The red color extends to twigs and tints leaves. Needs pollinator Northwest.
'Packham Triumph'	Widely grown in Northwest as pollinator for 'Bartlett'. Origin in New South Wales, Australia, should fit it for use in California.	Fine pear in its own right. Very high quality. Excellent keeper. Late.	Tree vigorous, spreading, somewhat susceptible to fireblight. Rapidly replacing some of the older varieties in commercial plantings.
'Seckel'	Widely adaptable.	Very small, very sweet and aromatic. Roundish to pear-shaped, yellow-brown. Flesh granular. Good for preserving and spicing. Early midseason.	Tree fairly resistant to fireblight, highly productive.
'Stewart Bartlett'	See 'Bartlett'. Developed in Northwest.	See 'Bartlett'.	Identical to 'Bartlett', but highly resistant to fireblight. Needs pollinator.
'Winter Bartlett'	See 'Bartlett'.	Smaller than 'Bartlett', firmer, later in ripening.	Tree spreading, loose, somewhat susceptible to fireblight.
'Winter Nelis'	Northwest. Mountains, cold valley floors in Southern California.	Small to medium, roundish, dull green or yellowish, rough. Very fine flavor. Late.	A very fine keeper, but not an attractive pear. Tree moderately susceptible to fireblight. Needs pollinator.

P

Climate
Zone maps
pages 8-27

PEAR, ORNAMENTAL. See Pyrus

PEARL BUSH. See Exochorda

PEAS. An easy crop to grow when conditions are right, and delicious when freshly picked. They need coolness and humidity and must be planted at just the right time. If you have the space and don't mind the bother, grow tall (vining) peas on trellises, strings, or screen; tall peas reach 4-5 ft. and bear heavily. Bush types are more commonly grown in home gardens; they require no support. A good tall variety is 'Alderman'. Fine bush varieties are 'Little Marvel', 'Morse's Progress No. 9', 'Freezonian', and 'Blue Bantam'. An unusually good vegetable (and one indispensable to Oriental cooking) is the edible-podded snow or sugar pea—'Mammoth Melting Sugar' is the tall-vining variety, 'Dwarf Gray Sugar' the bushy one.

Soil should be non-acid, water-retentive but fast draining. Peas are hardy and should be planted just as early in spring as the ground can be worked. Where winters are mild and spring days quickly become too warm for peas, plant from September through February, the later dates applying where winters are coldest. Sow 2 in. deep in light soil, shallower (½-1 in.) in heavy soil or in the winter. Moisten ground thoroughly before planting; do not water again until seedlings have broken through the surface. Leave 24 in. between rows, and thin seedlings to stand 2 in. apart. Successive plantings several days apart will lengthen the bearing season, but don't plant so late that summer heat will overtake the ripening peas; most are ready to bear in 60-70 days.

Plants need little fertilizer, but if the soil is very light give them one application of complete fertilizer. If weather becomes warm and atmosphere dry, supply water in furrows; overhead water encourages mildew. Provide support for climbing peas as soon as tendrils form. When peas begin to mature, pick *all* pods that are ready; if seeds ripen, the plant will stop producing. Vines are brittle; steady them with one hand while picking with the other. Above all—shell and cook (or freeze) the peas as soon after picking as you can.

PEASHRUB, SIBERIAN. See Caragana

PEA SHRUB, SWAN RIVER. See Brachysema

PEA VINE, AUSTRALIAN. See Dolichos lignosus

PECAN. See Carya

PELARGONIUM. GERANIUM. Shrubby perennials. Zones 17, 24 are the ideal climates; next best are Zones 15, 16, 22, 23; possible but less easy are Zones 8, 9, 12-14, 18-21; elsewhere a pelargonium or geranium is a house plant or summer bedding plant. The word geranium is used here as a common name only. The plant that botanists recognize as *Geranium* has somewhat similar flowers, but the plant is different in appearance and uses.

Most garden geraniums can be divided among 3 species of *Pelargonium*: Martha Washington geranium (*P. domesticum*); common geranium (*P. hortorum*) — this group also includes the variegated forms usually referred to as fancy-leafed or colored-leafed geraniums; and ivy geranium (*P. peltatum*). In addition, many other species have scented leaves.

All geraniums do well in pots. Common geraniums grow well in garden beds; Martha Washington geraniums are also planted in beds, but tend to get rangy. Some varieties of Martha Washington are used in hanging baskets. Ivy geraniums good in hanging containers, raised beds, as ground cover, bank cover. Use scented geraniums in close-up situations—in pots or in ground (in mild areas). For good bloom on a potted geranium indoors, place in a sunny window or in brightest light possible.

In the garden, plant geraniums in full sun in coastal areas, light shade in hot-summer climates; never in dense shade. Plant in any good, fast draining soil. If soil is alkaline, add peat moss, or nitrogen-fortified ground bark or sawdust to planting bed. Water common geraniums growing in the ground when soil dries to about 1 in. below surface—best slightly on dry side. In warm weather, water Martha Washington geraniums deeply once a week. Water ivy geraniums every 10 days-2 weeks. Geraniums of any kind in good garden soil need little feeding; if in light sandy soil feed 2-3 times during active growing season.

Remove faded geranium flowers regularly to encourage new bloom. Pinch growing tips in early growth stages to force side branches. Prune after last frost.

Geraniums in pots bloom best when somewhat pot bound. When needed repot only in next larger pot. In warm weather, water common geraniums in pots every other day; Martha Washington geraniums may need daily watering.

To control tobacco bud worm on common geraniums, use sevin before worms appear in summer, fall. Control aphids and whiteflies on Martha Washington geraniums with all-purpose spray. Use a miticide to control red spider mites on ivy geraniums.

P. crispum. LEMON-SCENTED GERANIUM. Small, crinkly, 1-in. leaves on narrow, upright plant 2-3 ft. tall. Lavender flowers. Float leaves in finger bowls, or dry in bunches for closets; use in potpourris. 'Variegated Prince Rupert' has green and white leaves.

P. domesticum. LADY WASHINGTON PELARGONIUM, MARTHA WASHINGTON GERANIUM, REGAL GERANIUM. Erect or somewhat spreading, to 3 ft. More rangy than common geranium. Leaves heart-shaped to kidney-shaped, dark green, 2-4 in. broad, with crinkled margins, unequal sharp teeth. Large showy flowers 2 in. or more across in loose rounded clusters, in white and many shades of pink, red, lavender, purple, with brilliant blotches and markings of darker colors.

P. fragrans. NUTMEG-SCENTED GERANIUM. Branching, rather bushy growth, 1-2 ft. high. Small roundish, gray-green leaves. Flowers white with pink veins.

P. graveolens. ROSE GERANIUM. To about 2 ft. Leaves deep green, slightly hairy, deeply lobed, with each of the lobes divided and toothed. Pungent, spicy, roselike fragrance. Small flowers, rose-colored or pink veined with purple, are not showy. Leaves used in potpourris, sachets, jellies, custards. 'Lady Plymouth', lower growing, small-leafed variety has smaller, variegated, rose-scented leaves.

P. hortorum. COMMON GERANIUM. GARDEN GERANIUM. Most popular, widely grown. Shrubby, succulent-stemmed, to 3 ft. or more; older plants grown in open (in mild areas) become woody. Leaves round or kidney-shaped, velvety and hairy, soft to the touch, edges indistinctly lobed and scallop-toothed; zones of color just inside margins. Flowers single or double,

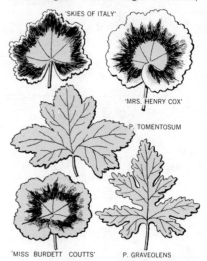

Plain-colored leaves belong to scented pelargoniums; others, forms of P. hortorum.

not as large as Lady Washington, flatter, usually in solid colors, many more flowers to a cluster. Many varieties in white, and shades of pink, rose, red, orange, and violet. Seed in mixed colors, also in red.

P. nervosum. LIME-SCENTED GERANIUM. Bushy plant with round, somewhat ruffled, light green leaves, toothed margins. Abundant, showy lavender flowers.

P. odoratissimum. APPLE-SCENTED GERANIUM. Trailing stems 1½ ft. long clothed with roundish, 1-2-in., ruffled leaves. White flowers in fluffy clusters.

P. peltatum. IVY GERANIUM. Trailing plants to 2-3 ft. or longer. Leaves rather succulent, glossy, bright green, 2-3 in. across, ivylike, with pointed lobes. Few to several 1-in., single or double flowers in rounded clusters are white, pink, rose, red, and lavender, 2 upper petals blotched or striped. Many named varieties. Flat-grown plants usually labeled only by color.

P. tomentosum. PEPPERMINT-SCENTED GERANIUM. Large, 3-to-5-in.-wide, lobed leaves, velvety to the touch. Spreads to about 2-4 ft. Small white flowers in fluffy clusters. Use as ground cover in partial shade in frost-free gardens. Leafy branches are striking draped over a wall or hanging from a basket.

PELLAEA. CLIFF-BRAKE. Ferns. Small plants, not striking in appearance, but with charmingly detailed foliage.

P. andromedaefolia. COFFEE FERN. Zones 6-9, 14-24. Native to California, southern Oregon. Finely cut fronds of gray-green to bluish green on thin, wiry stalks. To 18 in. high. Will take sun and drought, but under such conditions will be summer-dormant. With shade and ample water will remain green.

P. rotundifolia. ROUNDLEAF FERN. Zones 14-17, 19-24. Small fern with spreading fronds to 1 ft. long. The nearly round leaflets are evenly spaced, and about ¾ in. across. Pretty fern to contrast with finer-textured ferns or to show off in pots, baskets, or raised beds. Filtered shade. Hardy to 24°.

P. viridis (*P. adiantoides*). Zones 14-17, 19-24. Fronds to 2 ft. long, fresh green leaflets oval to lance-shaped. Ground cover, rock garden, containers. Filtered shade. Hardy to 24°.

PENNISETUM setaceum (*P. ruppelii*). FOUNTAIN GRASS. Perennial grass. All Zones. Dense rounded clump to 4 ft. Narrow arching leaves 2 ft. long. Hollow 3-4 ft. stems in summer tipped with fuzzy, showy, coppery pink or purplish flower spikes. Use in dry locations, as in gravel beds; as focal points in low ground covers. Any soil; full sun; drought resistant, pest-free. Goes dormant in winter. Cut stems for arrangements before flowers go to seed; a pest if not controlled. Variety 'Cupreum', reddish brown leaves, dark plumes, does not set seed; grow from division or cuttings.

PENSTEMON. BEARD TONGUE. Perennials, evergreen shrubs and shrublets. A few are widely grown; most of the others are sold only by specialists. All have tubular flowers in bright reds and blues (the commonest) but also soft pinks through salmon and peach to deep rose, lilac, deep purple, and white.

All penstemons best in full sun (light shade in hot-summer climates). Need fast drainage; many kinds best in loose, gravelly soil, with infrequent watering. Usually short-lived (3-4 years).

P. antirrhinoides. Evergreen shrub. Zones 8-24. Native to southern California and northern Baja California. Stiffly spreading, much-branched, to 6 ft. tall. The leaves are narrow, to ½ in. long. Flowers bright yellow, ½-¾ in. long, very broad, in leafy clusters; buds brownish red. Blooms April-June. Dormant in summer, loses lower leaves; use in fringe areas of garden. Water little in summer.

P. barbatus. Perennial. All Zones. Native to mountains from Utah to Mexico. Open, shrubby, somewhat sprawling habit, to 6 ft. Bright green leaves, 2-6 in. long. Long, loose spikes of red flowers about 1 in. long; early summer bloom. 'Rose Elf', a deep rose-flowered variety, 2½ ft. tall; short-lived in warm-winter areas.

P. barrettae. Perennial. Zones 1-7. Native to Columbia River gorge in Oregon and Washington. Shrubby, branching, to 1 ft. high. Leaves leathery, blue-green, to 3 in. long, toothed. Flowers abundant in short spikes, rose-purple, 1-1½ in. long. Blooms April-June.

P. cordifolius. Evergreen shrub. Zones 8, 9, 14-24. Native to coast of southern California. Loose-branching, half-climbing, with flexible, arching branches to 10 ft.; fuchsialike leaves ½-1½ in. long. Red, tubular flowers 1-1½ in. long, in dense clusters at tips of stems; April-June. Little water in summer if soil is heavy.

P. davidsonii (*P. menziesii davidsonii*). Perennial. Zones 1-7. Native to high mountains of Sierra Nevada and western Nevada north to Washington. Mat-forming alpine

to 3 in. high. Leaves oval, to ⅓ in. long, a little sticky. Flowers violet-blue, 1-1½ in. long; July-August. Ideal for a gravelly slope in rock garden.

P. gloxinioides. BORDER PENSTEMON, GARDEN PENSTEMON. Perennial treated as annual in cold-winter climates. All Zones. Compact, bushy, upright stems to 2-3 ft. Glossy bright green leaves 2-4 in. long. Tubular flowers in loose spikes at ends of stems, in almost all colors but blue and yellow. Mass in borders, or group with other summer-flowering plants.

Plant in full sun; partial shade in hot-summer areas. Subject to root rot in heavy, wet soil. In mild climates, set out flat-grown plants in fall for bloom in April. Older plants, if cut back after main bloom, flower again next year. Easy to grow from seed; several good mixed-color strains available. For plants in separate colors, make softwood cuttings from desirable plants. Some nurseries sell cutting-grown plants in separate colors.

P. heterophyllus purdyi. Perennial. Zones 6-24. Native to Sierra Nevada foothills and Coast Ranges of California. Stems upright or spreading, 12-24 in. high. Narrow pointed leaves 1-3 in. long. Spikelike clusters of flowers varying from rosy lavender to intense gentian blue. Blooms April-July. Most nurseries that stock this plant sell it under the name of 'Blue Bedder' penstemon.

P. newberryi. MOUNTAIN PRIDE. Perennial. Zones 1-9. Native to higher elevations of the Sierra Nevada. Matted plant to 20 in. high, woody at base. Leaves thick, roundish, toothed, ¼-½ in. long. Flowers rose-red, about 1 in. long; June-August.

P. rupicola. Evergreen subshrub. Zones 1-7. Native to Cascade Mountains. Trailing, much branched, to 4 in. high. Leaves roundish, blue-green, fine-toothed, ¼-½ in. long. Flowers bright rose crimson, ½-1½ in. long; June-August. Beautiful in dry wall near miniature campanulas. A lesser known, white-flowered form is available; it needs half shade, is somewhat more difficult than the species.

PEONY. See Paeonia

PEPEROMIA. Perennials. House or greenhouse plants grown for foliage. Evergreen, often succulent; usually prostrate or trailing. Tiny flowers in dense, small, slender spikes. Use in planters, dish gardens, or other containers. Can be used as ground cover in large indoor planting. Grow in north light,

or in diffused light protected from direct sun (as by wide overhang). Cool or warm temperature. Light, well drained soil; not too much water. Propagate by stem, crown, or leaf cuttings (insert lower ½ of leaf in 2-in. pot of ½ sand, ½ leaf mold).

P. caperata 'Emerald Ripple'. Plants 3-4 in. tall. Leaves rich green, heart-shaped, deeply veined, borne densely on very short, reddish stalks. Tiny, greenish white flowers in spikes. 'Little Fantasy', miniature variety with white flower spikes.

P. fosteri. Trailing; leaves fleshy, dark green, with lighter veins, pointed at both ends, 2 or 3 at each joint; reddish stems.

P. obtusifolia. Old favorite with thick, upright or trailing stems; dark green, fleshy, round, 4-in. leaves. 'Minima', miniature form, has dense stems; oval, stalked leaves 1½-2 in. long, dark green above, paler beneath.

P. rotundifolia (*P. nummularifolia, P. prostrata*). Tiny, dark green, round, ¼-in. leaves often reddish underneath, along slender, trailing stems.

P. sandersii. WATERMELON PEPEROMIA. Compact, nearly stemless, with a rosette of round, 3-5-in.-long, gray-striped leaves on long red stems.

PEPPER. The two kinds of peppers are the sweet and the hot. The first kind always remains mild, even when the flesh ripens to red; these are the big stuffing and salad peppers. Hot peppers range from pea-size to a long, narrow 6-7 in., but all are pungent, their flavor varying from the relatively mild heat of the Italian peperoncini to the almost incandescent chilipiquin and 'Chili Jalapeno'. 'California Wonder' and 'Yolo Wonder' are the best known sweet peppers; 'Pimiento' is a small, late-bearing, heart-shaped, thick-fleshed sweet pepper used for salads or for canning. 'Anaheim' is a long, slim pepper used for making canned green chiles; it is mild but spicy. 'Tabasco' and 'Long Red Cayenne' are both well-known very hot varieties for drying or sauce-making.

All grow on handsome, bushy plants. Use the plants as temporary low, informal hedge, or grow and display them in containers. Certain kinds have been bred for house plant use: 'Ball Christmas' and 'Red Boy' are typical ornamental forms with small, erect fruits that change from green through whitish and purple to bright red.

Buy started plants at a nursery, or sow seed indoors 8-10 weeks before average date

P

Climate Zone maps pages 8-27

Peperomias stay low and compact, are easy house plants where light is not too strong. Left to right: Peperomia obtusifolia, P. caperata 'Emerald Ripple', P. sandersii.

Climate Zone maps pages 8-27

of last frost. Set out when weather becomes warm, spacing plants 18-24 in. apart. Water thoroughly but not frequently as plants grow, and feed once or twice with commercial fertilizer after plants become established and before blossoms set. Pick peppers as soon as they have reached good size. Pick hot peppers when they are fully ripe. Control cutworms with baits. Aphids and whiteflies can be handled by an all-purpose vegetable garden dust or spray.

PEPPER, BRAZILIAN. See Schinus terebinthifolius

PEPPER, JAPAN. See Zanthoxylum

PEPPERBUSH, SWEET. See Clethra alnifolia

PEPPERMINT. See Mentha piperita

PEPPERMINT. For eucalypts known as peppermints, see Eucalyptus

PEPPERMINT TREE. See Agonis flexuosa

PEPPERIDGE. See Nyssa

PEPPER TREE. See Schinus

PEPPERWOOD. See Umbellularia

PERIWINKLE. See Vinca

PERNETTYA mucronata. Evergreen shrub. Zones 4-7, 14-17. Compact growth to 2-3 ft. tall, spreading by underground runners to make clumps. Glossy, dark green, oval or narrow, 1/3-3/4-in.-long leaves give fine-textured look. Some leaves turn red or bronzy in winter. Tiny, white to pink, bell-shaped flowers in late spring, followed by very colorful berries.

Berries are 1/2 in. across, fleshy, with a metallic sheen, purple, white, red, rose, pink, or near black. They hold until knocked off by a hard rain or frost, possibly until early spring. Plants set more fruit if you grow several together for better cross pollination.

Acid, peaty soil; ample water. Full sun in cold-winter regions, partial shade where summers are long and hot. Can be invasive; control by root-pruning with spade. Tops often need regular pruning to stay attractive. Use as informal low hedge or border. Tubs, window boxes. Berried branches good for table decoration.

PERSEA. Evergreen trees. Includes two ornamental species in addition to avocado.

P. americana. See Avocado

P. borbonia. Zones 5, 8, 9, 14-17, 18-24. To 40 ft., with long-oval, bluish green leaves to 6 in. long. Flowers inconspicuous; small (1/2-in.-long) blue-black fruits not edible.

P. indica. Zones 16, 17, 20-24. Resembles *P. borbonia* but tenderer to frost, smaller, denser in growth, with glossier foliage, reddish new growth, and has less littering fruit in maturity. Dense, round, slightly pointed crown of branches. A little stiff and uncompromising in shape. Use as street tree, tubbed tree.

PERSIMMON (*Diospyros*). Deciduous trees. Two species are grown in the West; one is a well-known fruit tree with outstanding ornamental qualities.

Oriental or Japanese Persimmon. (*Diospyros kaki*). Zones 7-9, 14-16, 18-23; borderline in Zones 4-6; grows in Zones 10-13, but rarely fruits. To 30 ft. or more with wide-spreading branches. New leaves soft, light green in spring, becoming dark green, leathery broad ovals to 6-7 in. long, 2-3½ in. wide. In late autumn leaves turn yellow, orange, or scarlet even in warm-winter climates. Then, after leaves drop, orange-scarlet fruits light the tree for weeks; when these drop, a handsome branch structure justifies a featured spot in the garden.

Easy to grow, with practically no pests or diseases. Prune only to remove dead wood, shape tree, or open up a too-dense interior. Only problem is fruit drop, common in young trees. To avoid it, be consistent in feeding and watering. Space deep irrigations so that root zone is neither too wet nor too dry. Feed plants in late winter or early spring; over-feeding with nitrogen causes excessive growth, excessive fruit drop. Mature plants usually bear consistently.

Persimmon fruits can be dried; pick when hard-ripe with some stem remaining. Peel and hang up by a string in the sun. Dried fruit has a flavor something like litchi or a very high quality prune.

One of the best fruit trees for ornamental use; good garden or small shade tree. Can be espaliered. Available varieties:

'Chocolate'. Brown-streaked, very sweet flesh.

'Fuyu'. Non-astringent, even when under-ripe, firm-fleshed (like an apple), reddish yellow, about the size of a baseball but flattened like a tomato.

'Hachiya'. Shapeliest tree for ornamental use. This variety yields the big (4-in.-long, 2½-3 in.-broad), slightly pointed persimmons usually found in produce stores. Pick before fully ripe to outwit birds, but allow to become soft-ripe before eating; astringent unless mushy.

'Tamopan'. Astringent until fully ripe; very large, turban-shaped.

American Persimmon (*Diospyros virginiana*). Zones 2-9, 14-16, 18-23; borderline Zone 1. Moderate-growing small tree to 20-30 ft. with broad oval crown, attractive gray-brown bark fissured into deep checkered pattern. Glossy, broadly oval leaves to 6 in. long. New foliage bronzy or reddish; leaves turn yellow, pink, and red in fall. Fruits round, yellow to orange (often blushed red), 1½-2 in. wide, very puckery until soft ripe, then very sweet.

PETUNIA hybrida. COMMON GARDEN PETUNIA. Tender perennial grown as an annual. Ranks with marigolds and zinnias as most popular spring-planted, summer-blooming bedding plant. (In mild-winter desert areas, planted in fall for color from spring to early summer.) Fragrant flowers single and funnel-shaped to very double, in many colors from soft pink to deepest red, light blue to deepest purple, cream (near yellow) and pure white. Leaves thick-ribbed and slightly sticky to touch.

Plant in full sun in good garden soil; single-flowered kinds will grow in poor soil if it's well drained; tolerate alkalinity. Plant 8-18 in. apart depending on size of variety. After plants established, pinch back about half for compact growth. Feed monthly with complete fertilizer. Near end

of summer, cut back rangy plants about half to force new growth. In some areas, smog causes spots on leaves of seedlings—plants outgrow damage in clear periods.

Most newer varieties of petunias belong to one of following strains: F_1 Hybrid Grandiflora and F_1 Hybrid Multiflora. (Also available but less commonly grown are F_2 Hybrid Grandiflora and F_2 Hybrid Multiflora.) F_1 hybrids, produced by crossing two different varieties, are more vigorous, more uniform in color, height, and growth habit than ordinary petunias. Most F_1 hybrid petunias are self-sterile, must be hand-pollinated in order to produce seed, thus are somewhat more expensive than petunias grown from open-pollinated seed.

F_1 Hybrid Grandiflora: Sturdy plants, 15-27 in. high, 24-36 in. across. Flowers usually single, ruffled or fringed, to 4½ in. across, in pink, rose, salmon, red, scarlet, blue, white, or striped. The Cascade series of petunias belongs here. Cascading growth habit makes them especially good for hanging containers. Large, single flowers, 4-5 in. across, in white, pink, red. Petunias of similar growth habit come in blue.

F_2 Hybrid Grandiflora: Excellent flowers, but irregular growth. Flowers variegated or in mixed colors; faded blooms tend to hang on plant.

F_1 Hybrid Multiflora: Plants about same size as F_1 Hybrid Grandiflora, but flowers generally smooth-edged and smaller (to 2 in. across), single or double. Neat, compact growth, ideal for bedding, massed planting. Many named varieties in pink, rose, salmon, yellow, white, blue. Multifloras resistant to botrytis disease which disfigures blossoms, and later foliage of other kinds in humid weather. Satin series of petunias belongs in F_1 Hybrid Multiflora strain. Flowers single, to 2½ in. wide, with satiny texture, in white, cream, pink, coral.

F_2 Hybrid Multiflora: Grown from F_1 seed, these are available only in mixed colors.

Bedding petunias, also called dwarf petunias: Plants 20-24 in. high, flowers smooth-edged, smaller than Grandifloras and Multifloras. Sprawling; good for large areas. Dwarf bedding petunias have same sized flowers as regular bedding kinds, but plants more compact, 12-16 in. high. Vigorous, floriferous; colors include red, ivory yellow, blue, white, pink, rose, purple.

Balcony petunias: Similar to bedding petunias, but stronger growing, with larger flowers; now largely replaced by superior Cascade series.

PHAEDRANTHUS buccinatorius (*Bignonia cherere*) BLOOD-RED TRUMPET VINE. Evergreen vine. Zones 8, 9, 14-24. Rampant growth. Climbs by tendrils to considerable height. Leaves have 2 oval or oblong leaflets, 2-4 in. long. Clusters of large 4-in.-long trumpet-shaped flowers stand well out from vine. Color is an orange-red which turns bluish red, yellow throat. Flowers appear in bursts throughout year whenever weather warms. Effective on a wall a high trellis or arbor, or a chain link fence. Prune yearly to keep under control. Needs sun. In interior valleys plant in a protected place. Feed and water young plants generously until well established.

PHALAENOPSIS. MOTH ORCHID. Epiphytic orchids. Greenhouse plants. Thick, broad,

Climate
Zone maps
pages 8-27

leathery leaves, no pseudobulbs. Long sprays of 3-6-in.-wide, white or light lavender-pink flowers in spring and fall.

Although very popular commercially, they require warmer growing conditions than most orchids (minimum 60-70° at night and about 70-85° during the day). More for advanced amateur than beginner. Require high humidity and moist potting medium at all times. Potting medium same as for cattleyas. When cutting flowers, leave part of the main stem so another set of flowers can develop from dormant buds. Many lovely, large-flowered hybrids. Some smaller-flowered new hybrids give promise of being easier to grow, taking somewhat lower night time temperatures.

PHASEOLUS caracalla. (Often sold as *P. gigantea.*) SNAIL VINE. Perennial vine. Zones 12-24. Looks much like a pole bean in foliage and general appearance. Climbs to 10-20 ft. Flowers (spring and summer) are fragrant, cream marked purple or pale purple. Common name comes from the twisted keel petals which are coiled like a snail shell. Odd and pretty. Cut to ground when frost kills tops. Summer screen or bank cover.

P. coccineus. See Bean, Scarlet Runner

PHELLODENDRON amurense. AMUR CORK TREE. Deciduous tree. Zones 1-17. Moderate growth to 30-45 ft. with equal or greater spread. Heavy trunk, heavy horizontal branches, and thick, deeply furrowed, corky bark create ruggedly handsome winter pattern. Leaves 10-15 in. long, with 5 to 13, 2½-4½-in.-long glossy green leaflets. Flowers inconspicuous; fruits black, pea-sized, with a turpentine odor. Plant in deep, rich soil. Tolerates drought when established. No special pests or diseases. Valuable in Idaho and Utah where it takes the high summer heat, deep winter cold. Gives filtered shade. Good lawn tree.

PHILADELPHUS. MOCK ORANGE. Deciduous shrubs. White, usually fragrant flowers in late spring (some species early summer). Most are large, vigorous plants of fountain form with medium green foliage. Full sun (part shade in hottest-summer areas), ordinary garden soil and watering. Prune every year just after bloom, cutting out oldest wood and surplus shoots at base. Taller ones are striking in lawns or as background and corner plantings. Smaller kinds can be planted near foundations or used as low screens or informal hedges.

P. coronarius. SWEET MOCK ORANGE. Zones 1-17. Strong growing, 8-10 ft. tall. Oval leaves 1-4 in. long. Clusters of very fragrant, 1½-in.-wide flowers in June. The old favorite.

P. gordonianus. See *P. lewisii gordonianus*

P. inodorus grandiflorus. Zones 1-7. Fast to 10 ft. Leaves 5 in. long, oval, larger than those of other mock oranges. Flowers scentless, 2 in. across, in small clusters.

P. lemoinei. Zones 1-17. This hybrid includes many garden varieties, most to 5-6 ft. tall and all with very fragrant flowers in clusters. 'Avalanche' and 'Innocence' have single flowers; 'Enchantment' and 'Mont Blanc' are good double-flowered varieties.

P. lewisii. WILD MOCK ORANGE. Zones 1-17. Native east of the Cascades in Pacific Northwest. Spreading habit, to 6 ft. tall. Satiny, fragrant blooms nearly 2 in. across. Blooms June-July. State flower of Idaho. *P. l. gordonianus (P. gordonianus)* from west of the Cascades, grows to 20 ft.

P. mexicanus. EVERGREEN MOCK ORANGE. Zones 8, 9, 14-24. Best used as a vine or bank cover; long, supple stems with 3-in. evergreen leaves will reach 15-20 ft. if given support. Fragrant flowers in small clusters spring and early summer, or intermittently.

P. polyanthus. Zones 1-17. One variety of this hybrid, 'Atlas', is a 4-5 ft. shrub with very large single flowers.

P. purpureo-maculatus. Zones 2-17. Group of hybrids including moderate-sized shrubs with flowers showing purple centers. 'Belle Etoile' has upright growth, to 5 ft. tall; fragrant, fringed, single flowers.

P. 'Silver Showers'. Zones 1-17. Compact growth to 3 ft. White, single, very fragrant flowers.

P. virginalis. Zones 1-17. Another hybrid which has produced several garden varieties, the flowers of which tend to be double: 'Bouquet Blanc', 'Minnesota Snowflake', and 'Virginal' all grow to 6-8 ft. tall; very fragrant flowers.

PHILLYREA. Evergreen shrubs or trees. Zones 4-9, 14-21. Neat, glossy evergreen foliage, low maintenance characterize these relatives of osmanthus. They have foliage quality of skimmia or camellia but grow well in ordinary garden soils and exposures, need little water when established. Flowers small, white or dull white, male and female on different plants. If both sexes are present, small red fruits follow bloom, turn purplish black in late fall.

P. latifolia. Shrub or small tree. Slow, dense growth to 10 ft. tall, equally wide; sometimes to 15-30 ft. Leaves oval or roundish oval, sharply toothed, to 2½ in. long, 1½ in. wide, shiny dark green above, lighter beneath. Flowers dull white, in short clusters in late spring.

P. l. media (*P. media*). Resembles *P. latifolia* but generally less likely to grow into a tree. Leaves ½-1½ in. long, slightly toothed or untoothed.

P. vilmoriniana (*P. decora*). Evergreen shrub. Slow growth to 6-8 ft. Glossy leaves 3-5 in. long, dark green above, yellowish green beneath. Small, pure white flowers April-May.

PHILODENDRON. Evergreen vines and shrubs. Philodendrons are tough, durable plants grown for their attractive, leathery, usually glossy leaves. They fall into two main classes; each species and variety in the list that follows is designated in one of these categories:

Arborescent and relatively hardy. These become big plants 6-8 ft. high (sometimes higher) and as wide. They develop large leaves and sturdy, self-supporting trunks. They will grow indoors, but need much more space than most house plants. They grow outdoors in certain milder climate zones—see descriptions below. As outdoor plants they do best in sun with shade at midday but can survive considerable shade. Use them for tropical jungle effects, or as

massive silhouettes against walls or glass. Excellent in large containers.

Vining or self-heading and tender. These forms can only be house plants. There are many kinds, with many different leaf shapes and sizes. Vining types do not really climb and must be tied to or leaned against a support until they eventually shape themselves to it. The support can be almost anything, but certain water-absorbent columns (sections of tree fern stems, wire and sphagnum "totem poles", slabs of redwood bark) serve especially well because they can be kept moist, and a moist column helps the plants grow better. Self-heading types form short, broad plants with sets of leaves radiating out from a central point.

Whether in containers or open ground, a philodendron should grow in rich, loose, well drained soil. House plant philodendrons grow best in good light but not the direct sun that comes through a window. All like ample water but will not take soggy soil. Feed lightly and frequently for good growth and color. Dust leaves of indoor plants once a month (commercial leaf polishes are available).

It's the nature of most philodendrons—especially when grown in containers—to drop lower leaves, leaving a bare stem. To fix a leggy philodendron you can air-layer the leafy top and, when it develops roots, sever it and replant it. Or cut the plant back to a short stub and let it start over again. Often the best answer is to throw out the overgrown, leggy plant and replace it with a new one. Aerial roots form on stems of some kinds; push them into the soil or cut them off—it won't hurt the plant.

Flowers may appear on old plants if heat, light, and humidity are high; they somewhat resemble callas, with a boat-shaped bract surrounding a club-shaped spikelike structure. Flower bracts are usually greenish, white, or reddish.

Here are the kinds. Note that the great favorite—the so-called "split-leaf philodendron"—is not a philodendron at all, but a *Monstera*.

P. barryi. Arborescent. Zones 15-24. Hybrid of *P. bipinnatifidum* and *P. selloum*. Big leaves, deeply lobed and cut, with red veins underneath.

P. bipinnatifidum. Arborescent. Zones 15-24. Similar to *P. selloum*, but carries more leaves at a time, and has more deeply and evenly cut leaves with reddish veins. Next to *P. selloum*, the hardiest for outdoor use.

P. eichleri. Arborescent. Zones 20-24. Giant elephant-ear leaves to 4 ft. or more in length, scalloped and shallowly lobed rather than deeply cut. Stunning, tropical-looking plant.

P. 'Emerald Queen'. Vining. Hybrid plant similar to *P. 'Hastatum'*, but with heavier-textured leaves that tend to remain uniform in size over the length of the plant. Compact and free of the leaf spot that affects *P. 'Hastatum'*.

P. erubescens. Vining. Leaves 9 in. long, arrow-shaped, reddish beneath, dark green edged with copper above, on reddish leaf stalks. Shows well against a wall.

P. 'Evansii'. Arborescent. Zones 20-24. Hybrid of *P. speciosum* and *P. selloum*. The elephant-ear lobes are scalloped and

P

*Climate
Zone maps
pages 8-27*

ruffled, but not deeply cut. Leaves on mature plants may reach 4-5 ft. long.

P. 'Fantasy'. Arborescent. Zones 20-24. Much like *P.* 'Evansii'.

P. 'Florida'. Vining. Hybrid of *P. laciniatum* and *P. squamiferum.* Leaves heavy-textured, split into 5 broad, sharp-pointed lobes, with pronounced veins and a reddish undersurface.

P. 'Florida Compacta'. Vining. Compact, slow to climb with deep green leaves similar to 'Florida' in shape. Leaf stalks red.

P. guttiferum. Vining. Slow, dense growth with narrow, pointed, very stiff, deep green leaves on short, broad, flattened leaf stalks. Close-held leaves give shingled effect to foliage.

P. 'Hastatum'. Vining. Fairly fast, open growth. Leaves 1 ft. long, arrow-shaped, rich green. Subject to leaf spot if kept too warm and moist. Plants sold as *P.* 'Hastatum Rubrum' may be *P. erubescens* or hybrids of it.

P. imbe. Vining. Foot-long, narrow, arrow-shaped leaves held well out from plant horizontally. Rich green above, reddish beneath.

P. 'Jungle Gardens'. Arborescent. Zones 20-24. Hybrid of *P. selloum* and *P.* 'Sao Paulo'. Leaves large, flat, much frilled and cut.

P. laciniatum. Vining. Dark green, 8-in. leaves slashed into unequal broad, sharp-pointed lobes. Holds lower leaves well.

P. 'Lynette'. Self-heading. Makes a close cluster of foot-long, broadish, bright green leaves with strong patterning formed by deeply sunken veins that run from midrib to edge. Good table top plant.

P. 'Mandaianum'. Vining. Leaves arrow-shaped, 12-15 in. long, dark green above, maroon underneath, on maroon stalks. Deeper in color than *P. erubescens.*

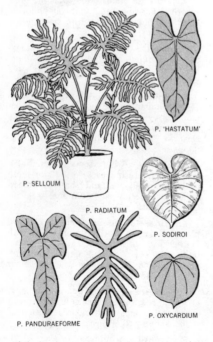

Philodendron selloum is arborescent; the others are vining kinds for indoors.

P. oxycardium. (Usually sold as *P. cordatum,* a different species.) Vining. The commonest philodendron. Leaves heart-shaped, deep green, usually 5 in. or less in length in juvenile plants, up to a foot long on mature plants in greenhouses. Easily grown (cut stems will live and grow for some time in vases of water). Thin stems will climb fast and high, or trail gracefully. Grow on moisture-retentive columns or train on strings or wires to frame a window or hang from a rafter.

P. panduraeforme. FIDDLE-LEAF PHILODENDRON. Vining. Fairly fast climber with rich green, 10-in. leaves oddly lobed to resemble a violin (or a horse's head; no two leaves are exactly alike). Excellent house plant, but sparse foliage on older plants suggests planting in multiples for dense effect.

P. pertusum. SPLIT-LEAF PHILODENDRON. See Monstera deliciosa

P. radiatum. (Often sold as *P. dubium.*) Vining. Slow to climb. The 9-in., deep green leaves are deeply cut into many narrow, spidery segments. More delicate in effect than *Monstera,* much slower-growing.

P. 'Ruby Queen'. Vining. Much resembles *P.* 'Emerald Queen', but with leaf stalks and undersides of leaves rich, deep red.

P. 'Sao Paulo'. Arborescent. Zones 20-24. Like *P. selloum,* but with leaf segments more frilled; leaves are flatter, less cupped.

P. selloum. Arborescent. Zones 8, 9, 12-24. Hardiest of the big-leafed philodendrons used outdoors. Leaves to 3 ft. long, deeply cut. The variety 'Lundii' is more compact.

P. sodiroi. Vining or self-heading. Leaves olive green, heart-shaped, mottled with silvery gray. If plant is staked upright in a 6-in. pot, leaves are 8 in. long; if kept small and unsupported in a 3-in. pot, leaves are 3 in. long.

P. squamiferum. Vining. Much like *P. laciniatum* in appearance, but with red-bristly leaf stalks and deeply sunken leaf veins.

P. verrucosum. Vining. Heart-shaped, 8-in. leaves, dark bronzy green with paler veins, deep green edges, purplish undersides. Leaf stalks red, with green bristles. Showy; not as tough and undemanding as most philodendrons.

P. wendlandii. Self-heading. Compact clusters of a dozen or more foot-long, broadly lance-shaped leaves of deep green on short, broad stalks. Useful where a tough, compact foliage plant is needed for table top or low, broad planting area.

PHILODENDRON, SPLIT-LEAF. See Monstera

PHLOMIS fruticosa. JERUSALEM SAGE. Shrubby perennial. All Zones. A deserving old time garden plant, rugged and woody. Coarse, woolly, gray-green wrinkled leaves. Yellow flowers 1 in. long in whorls around upper part of 4-ft. stems; bloom in early summer. Combine with echinops, eryngium, helenium, helianthus, kniphofia, rudbeckia. Full sun; adapted to poor soil, dry slopes. Stays evergreen in mild winters. Cut back ⅓ in fall to keep in shape.

PHLOX. Annuals, perennials. Most are natives of North America. Wide variation in growth form. All of them have showy flower clusters.

P. carolina (*P. suffruticosa*). THICK-LEAF PHLOX. Zones 1-14, 18-21. To 3-4 ft. tall, early-blooming, with flowers about ¾ in. wide, white with pale pink eye, to magenta, in clusters 15 in. long. Shiny foliage, free from mildew and red spider mites which often attacks summer phlox. 'Miss Lingard' is an excellent white-flowered variety to 3 ft. tall.

P. divaricata. SWEET WILLIAM PHLOX. Perennial. Zones 1-17. To 12 in., with slender, leafy stems and creeping underground shoots. Leaves oval, 1-2 in. long, ¾ in. wide. Flowers bluish or pinkish blue varying to white, ¾-1½ in. across, somewhat fragrant, in open clusters; bloom in spring. Use in rock gardens, as a bulb cover (see tulips). Light shade, good, deep soil.

P. drummondii. ANNUAL PHLOX. Grows 6-18 in. tall, with leafy, erect stems more or less covered with rather sticky hairs. Flowers numerous, showy, in close clusters at top of stems. Bright and pastel colors (no blue or orange); some with contrasting eye. Tetra strain has larger flowers on stronger stems. Art Shades strain has flowers of delicate, soft pastels. Starred and Fringed strain has fringed and pointed flower.

Dwarf forms 6 in. tall, in many colors, excellent for low bedding, edgings. Bloom from early summer until frost if faded flowers are removed. Plant in spring in colder climates—in fall in mild areas of southern California and desert. Give full sun and light, rich loam.

P. nivalis. TRAILING PHLOX. Perennial. Zones 4-7. Trailing plants form loose mats of narrow evergreen foliage. Big pink or white flowers in fairly large clusters in late spring or early summer. Excellent in rock garden.

P. paniculata. SUMMER PHLOX. Perennial. Zones 1-14, 18-21. Long-lived. Thrives in full sun, but in hottest areas colors may bleach. Flowers in summer, 1 in. wide, in large, dome-shaped clusters on 3-5-ft. stems. White, shades of lavender, pink, rose, or red; some with eyes of contrasting color. Many named varieties. Mulch around plant to keep roots cool. Plants subject to mildew at end of blooming season. Divide plants every few years, replanting young shoots from outside of clump. Plants do not come true from seed.

P. subulata. MOSS PINK. Perennial. Zones 1-17. Mat-forming, to 6 in. with ½-in., stiffish, needlelike, evergreen leaves on creeping stems. The ¾-in. flowers range in color from white through pinks to rose and lavender-blue. Late spring or early summer bloom, according to climate. Makes sheets of brilliant color in rock gardens. Ground cover. Grow in loose, not too rich soil. After flowering, cut back halfway.

P. suffruticosa. See *P. carolina*

PHOENIX. DATE PALM. Mostly large feather palms, but one a dwarf. Trunks patterned with bases of old leaf stalks. Phoenix palms hybridize freely; buy from a reliable nurseryman who knows his seed or plant source.

P. canariensis. CANARY ISLAND DATE PALM. Zones 9, 12-24. Big, heavy-trunked plant to 60 ft. tall, with a 50-ft. spread. Slow growing until it forms a trunk, then speeds up a little. Young plants do well in pots for many years, looking something like pineapples. Grow on slopes, in parks, big spaces, along wide streets; not for small city lots. Hardy to 20°.

P. dactylifera. DATE PALM. Zones 9, 12-24. The date palm of Indio, California, and of the Palm Springs golf courses. Native of the Middle East. Very tall palm with a slender trunk and gray-green waxy leaves, the leaflets stiff and sharp-pointed. Suckers from base. Too stiff and large for most home gardens, but adaptable and does well in both seaside and desert gardens. Leaves killed at 20°, but plants have survived 4° to 10°.

P. loureiri. (*P. humilis*) Zones 9, 12-24. Resembles a smaller, more slender and refined Canary Island date palm. Slow grower to 10-18 ft. tall. Leaves dark green, flexible, 10 ft. long. Good in containers or in the garden. Hardy to 20°.

P. reclinata. SENEGAL DATE PALM. Zones 23, 24. Native to tropical Africa. Makes picturesque clumps from offshoots, with several curving trunks 20-30 ft. high. Off-shoots can be removed to make single-trunk trees. Fertilize for fast growth. Below 28° expect trouble.

Clumping Phoenix reclinata grows to 20-30 ft. P. roebelenii is a 6 ft. dwarf.

P. roebelenii. PIGMY DATE PALM. Outdoors in Zones 23, 24; house plant anywhere. Native to Laos. Fine-leafed, small-scale palm. One stem grows slowly to 6 ft. or so. Curved leaves form a dense crown. Good pot plant. Requires moisture. Does best in shade or part shade, but not successful in dark indoor corners.

P. rupicola. CLIFF DATE PALM. Zones 17, 19-24. From India. Stately as Canary Island date palm, but much smaller, reaching only 25 ft. in height. Slender stem; lower leaves droop gracefully. Hardy to 26°.

P. sylvestris. SILVER DATE PALM. Zones 14-17, 19-24. Native to India. Hardy and beautiful date palm with single trunk to 30 ft. covered with old leaf bases. Trunk tapers from wide base to narrow top. Crown of gray-green leaves is thick and round. Hardy to 22°.

PHORMIUM. NEW ZEALAND FLAX. Evergreen perennials. Zones 7-24; may freeze to ground but regrow in Zones 5, 6. Big, dramatic plants composed of many sword-like, stiffly vertical leaves in a fan pattern. Flowers dull red or yellow, 1-2 in. long, in clusters on stems that reach high above the leaves. Use as point-of-interest display plant. Grow in containers. Use as windbreak along coast. Sturdy, grows in almost any soil or exposure—heat or cold, salt air or ocean spray; will take much or little water, even poor drainage to a point (in very poorly drained soil, crown rot can be a problem). Increase by dividing large clumps.

P. colensoi (*P. cookianum*). Leaves to 5 ft., 2½ in. wide; less rigid than *P. tenax*. Flowers yellow or amber yellow, on 7-ft. spikes. Not common, but useful for its moderate size.

P. tenax. NEW ZEALAND FLAX. Large, bold plant tending to spread. Leaves to 9 ft. long and as wide as 5 in. Reddish brown flower stalks bear many dark red to yellowish flowers. Variants in leaf color are available: 'Atropurpureum' is purple-red; 'Bronze' brownish red; 'Rubrum' has the deepest coloring, a dark purplish red; 'Variegatum' has green leaves striped with creamy white; dwarf forms (to 6 ft.) in most shades.

PHOTINIA. Evergreen or deciduous shrubs or small trees. Attractive foliage and fruit color. Related to hawthorn, pyracantha. Sun, good garden soil. In Northwest, withhold water in late summer to ripen growth, lessen frost damage. Prune to shape; never allow new growth to get away and make long, bare switches. Use as screens, background.

P. arbutifolia. See Heteromeles

P. fraseri. Evergreen shrub. Zones 4-24. Moderate growth to 10 ft. tall, spreading wider. Leaves glossy dark green above, lighter beneath, 2-5 in. long. New growth bright bronzy red, showy. Good espalier. Cut branches excellent in arrangements. Control aphids. Resists mildew where other kinds susceptible.

P. glabra. JAPANESE PHOTINIA. Evergreen shrub. Zones 4-24. Broad, dense growth to 6-10 ft or more. Leaves oval, broadest toward tip, to 3 in. long. New growth coppery; scattered leaves of bright red give touch of color through fall and winter. Summer pruning will restrict size of plant to a neat 5 ft. and give a continuing show of new foliage. White flowers with hawthorn fragrance in 4-in.-wide clusters. Berries red, turning black. May take setback with prolonged freeze, but usually recovers. Mildew a problem in many areas.

P. serrulata. CHINESE PHOTINIA. Evergreen shrub or small tree. Zones 4-16, 18-22. Broad, dense growth to 35 ft., but easily held to 10 by 10 ft. Leaves stiff, crisp, deep green, to 8 in. long, prickly along edges. New growth bright copper; scattered crimson leaves in fall, winter. Flowers white, in flat clusters 6 in. across April-May. Bright red berries often last until December. May freeze badly in continued 0° to 10° cold, but usually recovers. Mildew can be expected almost anywhere. Fairly drought-resistant when established. *P. s.* 'Aculeata' (often sold as *P. s.* 'Nova' or *P. s.* 'Nova Lineata') is more compact, has midrib and main leaf veins of ivory yellow.

P. villosa. Deciduous shrub or small tree. Zones 1-6. To 15 ft. tall, with spread of 10 ft. Leaves 1½-3 in. long, dark green. New foliage pale gold with rosy tints when expanding, bright red in fall. White flowers in 1-2-in.-wide clusters in mid-spring. Bright red fruits nearly ½ in. long decorate plant in fall, early winter.

PHYGELIUS capensis. CAPE FUCHSIA. Perennial in Northwest, tending to be shrubby in milder climates. Zones 4-9, 14-24. Perhaps it's called fuchsia because the flowers are pendant, but it is really related to penstemons and snapdragons. Stems 3-4 ft. high. Leaves 1-5 in. long, scalloped on margins, large at plant base, smaller toward top. Flowers red, tubular, slightly curved, 2 in. long, in loosely branched clusters July-September. Looks a bit weedy; use in outskirts of garden. Plant in sun in good garden soil. Spreads by underground roots. Prune for neat appearance. In colder areas, mulch to protect roots.

PHYLA nodiflora (*Lippia repens*). LIPPIA. Perennial. Zones 8-24. Creeps and spreads to form a flat, ground-hugging mat sturdy enough to serve as a lawn. Leaves to ¾ in. long, gray-green. Small lilac to rose flowers in tight round heads ½ in. across, spring-fall. Flowers attract bees; if objectionable, mow off tops. Full sun. Goes dormant, unattractive in winter. Feed regularly, especially in early spring to bring it out of dormancy fast. Water regularly. Particularly useful in desert areas, but subject to nematodes.

PHYLLITIS scolopendrium. HART'S TONGUE FERN. All Zones. Native to Europe, eastern United States. Odd fern with undivided, strap-shaped leaves 9-18 in. long. Fanciers collect various dwarf, crested, or forked varieties. In Pacific Northwest it is quite hardy and easy in full sun to full shade; seems fussy where summers are long and dry. Striking in woodland gardens, rock gardens, with rhododendrons and azaleas.

PHYLLOSTACHYS. See Bamboo

PHYSALIS. Perennials or annuals. The fruits are surrounded by a loose, papery husk (the enlarged calyx of the flower). One is ornamental, one edible.

P. alkekengi. CHINESE LANTERN PLANT. Perennial often grown as annual. All Zones. Plant angularly branched, 1-2 ft. high. Long, creeping, whitish, underground stems; may become invasive without control. Leaves long-stalked, light green, 2-3 in. long. Flowers white, rather inconspicuous, appearing in leaf joints. Ornamental part of plant is calyx which forms around ripened berry as a loose, papery, bright orange-red, 2-in.-long, inflated envelope shaped like a lantern. Dry leafless stalks hung with these gay lanterns make choice winter arrangements. Sow seed in spring in light soil. Sun or light shade. Increase by root division in fall or winter.

P. a. franchetii. Taller (1½-2½ ft.), more widely available. A dwarf variety, 'Pygmy', grows to 8 in., makes a good pot plant.

P. pruinosa. GROUND CHERRY, STRAWBERRY TOMATO. Tender perennial, grown as annual. Bushy, 1½ ft. high. Leaves 2-4 in. long. Flowers bell-shaped, ⅜ in. long, whitish yellow marked with 5 brown spots. Seedy yellow fruits are sweet, rather insipid, can be used for pies or preserves

Climate
Zone maps
pages 8-27

(after removing papery husks). Grow in the same way as tomatoes.

PHYSOSTEGIA virginiana. FALSE DRAGONHEAD. Perennial. All Zones. (Sometimes called obedience plant because flowers, if twisted on stem, remain in position.) Slender, upright, leafy stems to 4 ft. Leaves oblong, 3-5 in. long, toothed, pointed at tip. Flowers funnel-shaped, 1 in. long, glistening white, rose pink, or lavender rose, in dense, 10-in.-long spikes. Summer bloom. Spiky form useful in borders, cut arrangements. Combine with taller erigerons, *Scabiosa caucasica*, Michaelmas daisies. Sun or part shade. Any good garden soil. Stake taller stems to keep upright. Cut to ground after bloom. Vigorous; divide every 2 years to keep in bounds. 'Vivid', 2 ft., has rose pink flowers. 'Summer Snow', white, especially good, the least invasive.

PHYTOLACCA. A perennial and a semi-evergreen tree.

P. americana. POKE, POKEWEED, POKEBERRY, SCOKE. Perennial. All Zones. Native to eastern U. S. Vigorous, weedy plant to 4-10 ft. tall and as wide. Sprouts from a large, deep, fleshy, very poisonous root. Long-oval smooth leaves 4-12 in. long have (usually) red stalks, red veins. Summer flowers small, white, in narrow clusters 2-8 in. long. Juicy berries dark purple, ½ in. through, are eaten by birds but allegedly have poisoned children.

P. dioica. UMBU, OMBU, LA BELLA SOMBRA. Semi-evergreen tree. Zones 18-24. Native to Argentina. Large, very fast-growing tree to 50-60 ft., with equal or greater spread. Heavy trunk with huge surface buttress roots. Bark, wood very soft. Leaves (to 4 in. long) resemble avocado leaves. Flowers small, white, in narrow clusters. If you have a male and a female tree you'll get black-purple berries on the female tree. Tender to frost while young, less so as trees get older. Takes drought when established. Few pests or diseases.

PICEA. SPRUCE. Evergreen trees and shrubs. Zones 1-6, 15-17. The large cone-bearing trees take on a pyramidal or cone shape. Many kinds have dwarf varieties that are useful, where adapted, in foundation plantings, rock gardens, and in containers. Spruces have no special soil requirements. Dwarf forms need a reasonably cool location and ample water. Most kinds are attacked by small, dull green aphids in late winter. Their attack may not be noticed until the weather warms and the needles start dropping. Start spraying in February and repeat monthly until May. Pine needle scale (flat and white) may cause sooty mold. Spray when they are in the crawler stage in May.

Prune to shape only. If two main trunks develop, cut one out. If a branch grows too long, cut back to a well-placed side branch. To slow growth and make more dense, remove part of each year's growth to force side growth. When planting the larger spruces, don't place them too near buildings, fences, or walks. They need space to grow in. They can be grown in containers for years as living Christmas trees.

P. abies (*P. excelsa*). NORWAY SPRUCE. Native to northern Europe. Fast growth to 100-150 ft. Stiff, deep green, attractive pyramid in youth; in age branches tend to grow horizontally, with branches drooping strongly, and branches at base dying back. Extremely hardy and wind resistant, it is valued for windbreaks in cold areas. Norway spruce has produced a number of varieties. Some of the best are:

P. a. 'Clanbrasiliana'. Very dwarf, a tight, compressed ball, 2 ft. across in 20 years.

P. a. 'Maxwellii'. Picturesque, rounded dwarf with heavy short twigs, 2 ft. high and 3 ft. wide in 20 years.

P. a. 'Mucronata'. Dense dwarf, rounded in youth, growing into a broad pyramid with age. Reaches 3 ft. in 20 years and has the appearance of the larger spruces in miniature.

P. a. 'Nidiformis'. NEST SPRUCE, BIRD'S NEST SPRUCE. Very compact, dark green foliage; grows as a flattened globe, eventually to 3 ft. high and 4-6 ft. across.

P. a. 'Pendula'. Growing naturally it spreads over the ground with a height of about 1½ ft. and a spread of 10 ft. It will cascade downward from rocks or walls. When staked it becomes a dense irregular column with branches trailing downward to 8 ft. or more with outward sweeping recurved tips.

P. a. 'Procumbens'. Close-branched, irregular growth with upturned branch ends. Slow to 2 ft. high, 5 ft. across.

P. a. 'Pygmaea'. Broad rounded cone, very dense, 2 ft. high and 3 ft. across in 20 years.

P. a. 'Remontii'. An irregular, wide, cone-shaped dwarf, 3 ft. high, 4 ft. wide at base in 20 years, eventually to 20 ft.

P. a. 'Repens'. Low, irregular, rounded to 1½ ft. high and 3 ft. wide in 20 years. Fanlike branches held in layers.

P. a. 'Sherwood Gem'. Dense, heavily foliaged, regular, flattened globe to 2 ft. high, 4 ft. wide.

P. a. 'Sherwoodii'. Rugged, picturesque, compact but irregular in growth habit. Parent tree, 60 years old, is 5 ft. tall and 10 ft. across.

P. breweriana. BREWER'S WEEPING SPRUCE. To 100-120 ft. in its native Siskiyou Mountains in California and Oregon. The branchlets are pendulous, hanging vertically to 7-8 ft. or more. Rare in the wilds. Tenderer than most spruces, and requires much moisture.

P. engelmannii. ENGELMANN SPRUCE. Densely pyramidal tree to 150 ft., native from southwest Canada to Oregon and northern California, east to the Rockies. Resembles blue-green forms of Colorado spruce, but needles are softer and the tree is not so spreading at the base. Even 25-ft. specimens will be densely branched to the ground. A popular lawn tree in Rocky Mountain area.

P. glauca. WHITE SPRUCE. Native to Canada and northern U. S. Conical tree to 60-70 ft., dense when young, with pendulous twigs and silver-green foliage. Best in very cold-winter climates.

P. g. 'Conica'. (Often sold as *P. albertiana*.) DWARF WHITE SPRUCE, DWARF ALBERTA SPRUCE. Compact pyramidal tree of slow growth to 7 ft. in 35 years. Short, fine needles are soft to the touch, bright grass green when new, gray-green when mature. Handsome tub plant—a miniature Christmas tree for many years. Or, a fine small formal pyramid for the garden. Thoroughly hardy to cold, but needs shelter from hot or dry drying winds; and from strong reflected sunlight.

P. g. densata. BLACK HILLS SPRUCE. Slow-growing, dense pyramid, it can reach 20 ft. in height in 35 years. Use it in containers, or plant it out in groves for screening or for alpine meadow effects.

P. pungens. COLORADO SPRUCE. To 80-100 ft. Very stiff, regular, horizontal branches forming a broad pyramid. Foliage varies in seedlings from dark green through all shades of blue-green to a steely blue.

P. p. 'Glauca'. COLORADO BLUE SPRUCE. A positive gray-blue color.

P. p. 'Glauca Koster'. KOSTER BLUE SPRUCE. Even bluer than 'Glauca'.

P. p. 'Glauca Moerheimii'. Same blue as 'Glauca Koster' but tree has a more compact shape.

P. p. 'Pendens'. KOSTER WEEPING BLUE SPRUCE. Gray-blue with weeping branchlets.

P. sitchensis. SITKA SPRUCE. Native Alaska to California. Tall pyramidal tree to 100-150 ft. with wide-spreading, horizontal branches. Thin, quite narrow needles are prickly to the touch, bright green and silvery-white in color. Requires moisture in the soil and a moist atmosphere to look its best.

PIERIS. Evergreen shrubs. Leathery leaves and clusters of small white, urn-shaped

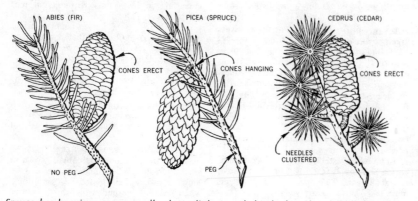

Spruce has hanging cones; needles leave little pegs behind when they fall; fir has erect cones, no pegs. Deodar, Atlas cedars, cedar of Lebanon have clustered needles.

flowers. Foliage and form excellent the year through; flower buds in early winter look like strings of tiny greenish pink beads. These begin to open February to April. At (or just after) bloom season, tinted new growth begins to appear. Related to rhododendron and azalea, they have the same cultural needs and make good companion plants. Fairly easy in coastal valleys of the Northwest, they become increasingly fussy south and inland. Require some shade, particularly in afternoon. Where water is high in salts, they need careful leaching. Protect from wind for maximum beauty. Prune by removing spent flowers. Splendid in containers, in Oriental and woodland gardens, in entryways where year-round quality is essential.

P. floribunda (*Andromeda floribunda*). MOUNTAIN PIERIS. Zones 2-9, 14-17; but needs protection in Zones 2, 3. Compact, rounded shrub 3-6 ft. tall with elliptic, dull green 1½-3-in. leaves. New growth pale green. Blossoms in upright clusters. Very hardy to cold, and takes hotter, dryer air than the others. Takes sun west of Cascades in Northwest.

P. formosa. HIMALAYAN PIERIS. Zones 5-9, 14-17. Rangy growth to 10 ft. Leaves dark green, to 6 in. long. New growth bronzy to scarlet. Pendulous flower clusters in April.

P. f. forrestii. CHINESE PIERIS. Zones 5-9, 14-17. Denser in growth, with spreading and drooping flower clusters, bright scarlet new growth. This color varies somewhat; select plants while they are making new growth. Needs more shade than other species.

P. japonica (*Andromeda japonica*). LILY-OF-THE-VALLEY SHRUB. Zones 1-9, 14-17; in Zones 1-3 requires protection from sun and wind. Upright, dense, tiered growth to 9-10 ft. Mature leaves glossy dark green, 3 in. long; new growth bronzy pink to red. Flowers in drooping clusters. Responds well to frequent feeding—a must in areas with heavy rainfall, or yellow foliage will result. Takes

Pieris japonica: *glossy, dark green leaves, drooping clusters of white flowers.*

full sun in cool climates, part shade elsewhere. 'Variegata', with smaller leaves edged creamy white, is a dense, compact variety. These also exist: pink-flowering varieties; a variety with rippled, wavy-leaf margins; dwarf forms.

PIGEON BERRY. See Duranta erecta

PIGGY-BACK PLANT. See Tolmiea

PILEA. Perennials. Grown in house or greenhouse. Juicy-stemmed foliage plants with inconspicuous flowers. Plant in porous soil mix (1 part sand, 1 part leaf mold, 1 part peat moss). Water thoroughly; don't water again until soil surface is dry. Feed monthly with house plant food. Grow at 65°-70° temperature. Light shade or bright light best; plant gets leggy in heavy shade.

Panamiga leaves, *up to 2 in. long, brownish green on top, seersucker texture.*

P. cadierei. ALUMINUM PLANT. Grows 1-1½ ft. tall. Erect, fast-growing with succulent stems. Leaves fleshy, toothed, 3-4 in. long; vivid green to bluish green with conspicuous silvery blotches. Flowers tiny.

P. involucrata. PANAMIGA, PANAMIGO. Freely branching plant 6-8 in. tall. Leaves roundish oval, to 2 in. long, brownish green above, purplish beneath, heavily veined in seersucker effect.

P. microphylla. ARTILLERY PLANT. Grows ½-1½ ft. tall, with many spreading branches and fine twigs. Leaves very tiny, thickly set, bright green. Total effect somewhat fernlike.

PIMELEA. Evergreen shrubs and shrublets. Native to Australia and New Zealand.

P. coarctata. Zones 4-7, 14-17. Gray, fine-leafed, compact mat 3-6 in. high and a foot across. Small white, fragrant flowers are followed by tiny white berries. Rock garden plant for cool, sandy, well drained soil in sun or very light shade.

P. ferruginea. ROSY RICE FLOWER. Zones 14-17. Rounded shrub to 3 ft. tall with crisp, pointed, shiny green ½-in. leaves. Long-lasting round clusters of rosy flowers intermittently through the year. Usually short lived (2-3 years). Needs good drainage. Partial shade except near coast.

PIMPERNEL. See Anagallis

PIMPINELLA anisum. ANISE. Annual herb. Bright green, toothed, basal leaves. Tiny, white flowers in umbrellalike clusters on 2-ft. stems in June. Start from seed in place when ground warms up in spring. Does not transplant easily. Grow in light soil, full sun. Use fresh leaves in salads. Seeds for flavoring cookies, confections.

PINCUSHION FLOWER. See Scabiosa

PINCUSHION TREE. See Hakea laurina

PINE. See Pinus

PINE, FERN. See Podocarpus gracilior

PINE, HOOP. See Araucaria cunninghamii

PINE, NORFOLK ISLAND. See Araucaria heterophylla

PINE, UMBRELLA. See Sciadopitys

PINEAPPLE. Bold, distinctive house plant that may bear fruit. Cut leafy top from a market pineapple. Root base of top in water or damp sand-peat moss. When roots have formed, move to a 7-in. pot of rich soil. Keep plants in greenhouse or in sunny room where temperatures stay above 68°. Water overhead when soil gets dry. Feed every 3-4 weeks with liquid fertilizer. Fruit forms, if you're lucky, in 2 years, on top of sturdy stalk at center of clump.

PINE, YEW. See Podocarpus macrophyllus

PINEAPPLE FLOWER. See Eucomis

PINK. See Dianthus

PINK IRONBARK. See Eucalyptus sideroxylon

PINK, CALIFORNIA INDIAN. See Silene californica

PINK, CROWN. See Lychnis coronaria

PINK, MULLEIN. See Lychnis coronaria

PINK POLKADOT PLANT. See Hypoestes

PINK POWDER PUFF. See Calliandra inaequilatera

PINON. See Pinus edulis

PINUS. PINE. Evergreen trees, rarely shrubs. See chart for climate adaptability. Pines are the great individualists of the garden, differing not only among species but also in the way they respond to sun, wind, and soil type. The number of long, slender needles in a bundle and the size and shape of the cones are two chief characteristics by which pines are classified.

Generally speaking, pines grow best in full sun; soil need not be rich, but it should be well drained (many pines naturally grow on rocky slopes or on sandy barrens where fertility is low but drainage excellent). They show the effects of bad drainage or overwatering by general poor appearance and an unusual number of yellowing needles, especially on older growth. Pines require little if any fertilizing; heavy feeding encourages too-rapid, rank growth. Never use a fertilizer high in nitrogen.

Pines are subject to a number of pests, but healthy, well-grown plants will stay that way with comparatively little attention. Most pines with 5 needles to a bundle are subject to a disease called white pine blister rust. Pines with 2 or 3 needles in a bundle are sometimes attacked by European pine shoot moth in the Northwest (symptoms are the distorted or dead new shoots). Aphids usually show their presence by sticky secretions, sooty mildew, yellowing needles. Beetle larvae sometimes bore into bark of Monterey, Canary Island, and Torrey pines in California; they often kill old trees weakened by drought.

All pines can be shaped, and usually improved, by some pruning. To slow a pine's growth or to fatten up a rangy one cut back the candles of new growth when

P

*Climate
Zone maps
pages 8-27*

new needles begin to emerge. Cut them back halfway or even more. Leave a few clusters of needles if you want growth to continue along the branch. To shape a pine in the Oriental manner is trickier, but not really difficult; it's just a matter of cutting out any branches that interfere with the effect, shortening other branches, and creating an upswept look by removing all twigs that grow downward. Cutting the vertical main trunk back to a well-placed side branch will induce side growth, and wiring or weighting branches will produce cascade effects.

It is unlikely that any one nursery will have *all* the pines described in the chart; in fact, any nursery which has even half of them is remarkably well stocked. Ask your nurseryman for help in locating any of the rarer ones you may wish to try.

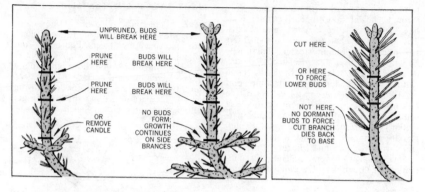

Two pine candles at left, center show spring pruning for greater denseness; shoot at right shows summer pruning. If shoots are young, tender, pinching as effective as pruning.

PINE

NAME	GROWTH RATE, SIZE	GROWTH HABIT	NEEDLES AND CONES	CLIMATE ADAPTABILITY	REMARKS
PINUS albicaulis WHITEBARK PINE Native to high mountains of Canada, Washington, Oregon, northern California, western Nevada, and east into Idaho, western Wyoming, central Montana.	Very slow to 20-40 ft.; usually much less.	Prostrate, spreading, or semi-upright. Often multi-trunked. In youth, slender and symmetrical.	Needles: in 5's, 1½-3 in., dark green, dense. Cones: 3 in., roundish, purple.	Hardy timberline tree. Does well in Northwest, east of Cascades.	Usually dug in mountains and sold by collectors as "alpine" conifer. Good for rock gardens, bonsai.
P. aristata BRISTLECONE PINE Native to high mountains of the West; very local and widely scattered.	Very slow to 45 ft., usually not above 20 ft.	Dense, bushy, heavy-trunked, with ground-sweeping branches. In youth a symmetrical, narrow-crowned tree with mature look.	Needles: in 5's, 1-1½ in., dark green, whitish below, flecked with white dots of resin. Cones: 3½ in., dark purplish brown.	Hardy. Does well at sea level in cool-summer areas of coastal California. Somewhat variable in Northwest. Best as pot plant in southern California.	So slow growing it is good for years as container plant. Needles persist many years, making crown extremely dense.
P. attenuata KNOBCONE PINE Native to northern and central Cascades in Oregon, Siskiyous, Sierra Nevada foothills in California, south to southern California, Baja California.	Rapid to 20-80 ft.	Open, irregular, and rough. In youth, rounded and regular.	Needles: in 3's, 3-5 in., yellow-green. Cones: 3-5 in., narrowly oval and asymmetrical, light brown.	Quite hardy, and adaptable to most areas from Puget Sound south to Baja California.	Very drought-tolerant when established. Grows well in poor soils. Holds its cones for many years.
P. banksiana JACK PINE Native from Nova Scotia, New York, Minnesota, west to Alberta.	Slow to moderate to 70 ft.; usually lower, shrubby.	Crooked, open, picturesque, with slender, spreading branches.	Needles: in 2's, an inch long, bright green, twisted. Cones: 2 in., conic-oblong, light brown.	Northernmost pine of North America. Very hardy. Well adapted to areas with long summer days.	A rare tree. Cones persist 12-15 years.
P. bungeana LACEBARK PINE Native to northern and central China.	Slow to 75 ft.	Often with several trunks, spreading. Sometimes shrubby. Picturesque.	Needles: in 3's, 3 in. long, bright green. Cones: 2-2½ in. long, roundish, light yellowish brown.	Hardy to sub-zero cold, tolerates heat of California's Central Valley.	Smooth, dull gray bark flakes off like sycamore bark to show smooth, creamy white branches and trunk.

P

Climate Zone maps pages 8-27

NAME	GROWTH RATE, SIZE	GROWTH HABIT	NEEDLES AND CONES	CLIMATE ADAPTABILITY	REMARKS
P. canariensis CANARY ISLAND PINE Native to Canary Islands.	Fast, to 60-80 ft., sometimes less.	In youth a slender, graceful pyramid. Later a tiered structure; finally a round-crowned tree.	Needles: in 3's, 9-12 in., blue-green in youth, dark green when older. Cones: 4-9 in., oval, glossy brown.	Tender in Northwest, but excellent in northern coastal and southern California, high desert.	Resistant to oak root fungus. Very young plants are gawky, but soon outgrow it. Drought tolerant, but needs water in southern California.
P. cembra SWISS STONE PINE Native to northern Asia and northern Europe.	Extremely slow to 70 ft. or higher.	Spreading, short branches form narrow, dense pyramid, becoming broad, open, and round-topped with age. In youth, handsome.	Needles: in 5's, 3-5 in., dark green. Cones: 3½ in., oval, light brown.	Very hardy (to —35°). Good in Northwest.	Resistant to white pine blister rust. A rare tree. Extremely slow growth and dense, regular foliage make a good plant for small gardens.
P. cembroides MEXICAN PINON PINE Native from Arizona to Baja California and northern Mexico.	Slow to 10-25 ft.	Stout, spreading branches form a round-topped head. In youth rather rangy.	Needles: in 3's, sometimes 2's, 1-2 in., slender, dark green. Cones: 1-2 in., roundish, yellowish or reddish brown.	Has succeeded in Northwest west of Cascades and in California coastal and valley gardens.	Most treelike of the pinons. Drought resistant, good in desert soils.
P. contorta SHORE PINE, BEACH PINE Native along coast from Mendocino County, California to Alaska.	Fairly fast to 20-35 ft.	Nursery-grown trees compact, pyramidal, somewhat irregular. Trees collected along coast dwarfed, contorted by winds.	Needles: in 2's, 1¼-2 in., dark green, dense. Cones: 1-2 in., light yellow-brown.	Hardy anywhere, but not at its best in hot, dry areas.	Good looking in youth. Dense foliage, takes training well. One of best small pines for small gardens. Does well in containers.
P. c. bolanderi DWARF SHORE PINE Native to Mendocino County, California.	Very slow to 2-5 ft.	Stiff, sparsely branched.	Needles: in 2's, short, dark green. Cones: very small.	Not very hardy. Performs well west of Cascades in Northwest but not east.	Poor soil in native habitat may contribute to dwarfism. Likely to grow taller and faster planted in good soil.
P. c. latifolia LODGEPOLE PINE Native to Blue Mountains of eastern Oregon; Cascade Mountains of Washington; throughout Rocky Mountains.	Rather slow to 80 ft., sometimes 150 ft., usually low, bushy tree in cultivation.	In cultivation rather irregular, open-branched, attractive. Planted close, they grow tall, slim-trunked. Solitary trees in mountains heavy-trunked, narrow, dense.	Needles: in 2's, 1½-3 in., yellow-green. Cones: 1½ in., shiny brown, persist many years.	Hardy. Widely adaptable except in areas of drought and low humidity.	All forms of *P. contorta* excellent in small garden, wild garden, or large rock garden.
P. c. murrayana LODGEPOLE PINE Native to Sierra Nevada and mountains of southern California, high north Coast Ranges of California, north in Cascades of Oregon to Columbia River.	Same as above.	Same as above.	Same as above.	Same as above.	Main difference between *P. c. latifolia* and *P. c. murrayana* is geographical distribution.
P. coulteri COULTER PINE Native to dry, rocky California mountain slopes: Mt. Diablo, Mt. Hamilton, Santa Lucia ranges and mountains of southern California, south to Baja California.	Moderate to fast, 30-80 ft.	Shapely open growth, lower branches spread widely, persist.	Needles: in 3's, 5-10, even 14 in., deep green, stiff. Cones: 10-13 in., buff colored, heavy, persist many years.	Hardy. Adaptable to area west of Cascades. Resistant to heat, drought, wind. Good in high desert.	Excellent in gardens where not crowded. Too spreading for small gardens.

(Continued on next page)

P

Climate Zone maps pages 8-27

NAME	GROWTH RATE, SIZE	GROWTH HABIT	NEEDLES AND CONES	CLIMATE ADAPTABILITY	REMARKS
P. densiflora JAPANESE RED PINE Native to Japan.	Rapid when young. May reach 100 ft., usually much less.	Broad, irregular head. Often develops two or more trunks at ground level.	Needles: in 2's 2½-5 in., bright blue-green or yellow-green, slender. Cones: 2 in., oval or oblong, tawny brown.	Hardy to —20°, but not a tree for desert areas. Will not tolerate cold winds.	Handsome pine for informal effects, especially multi-trunked trees. Makes moderate shade for woodland gardens.
P. d. 'Umbraculifera' TANYOSHO PINE Native to Japan.	Slow to moderate. 12-20 ft.	Broad, flat-topped, with numerous trunks from base. Spread greater than height.	Same as above.	Same as above.	Gallon and 5-gallon size trees frequently bear cones. Good for containers, rock and Oriental gardens.
P. edulis (*P. cembroides edulis*) PINON, NUT PINE Native to California's Little San Bernardino and New York Mountains, east to Arizona, New Mexico, and Texas, north to Wyoming.	Slow to 10-20 ft.	Horizontal branching tree; low, round or flat-crowned in age; bushy and symmetrical in youth.	Needles: usually in 2's, dark green, ¾-1½ in., dense, stiff. Cones: 2 in., roundish, light brown.	Hardy. Thrives in coastal California, Northwest, higher desert areas.	Beautiful small pine for containers, rock gardens. Collected plants bring look of age into new gardens. Cones contain edible seeds (pine nuts).
P. halepensis ALEPPO PINE Native to Mediterranean region.	Moderate to rapid growth to 30-60 ft.	Attractive as 2-year-old; rugged character at 5 years;.in age, an open irregular crown of many short, ascending branches. Often nearly columnar.	Needles: usually in 2's, 2½-4 in., light green. Cones: 3 in., oval to oblong, reddish to yellow-brown.	Semi-hardy. Thrives in desert heat, drought, and wind, good at seashore. Tender when young; established trees can take near-zero temperatures.	Most useful in poor soils and difficult, arid climates. Handsomer trees can be found for cooler, moister gardens. The standard desert pine.
P. jeffreyi JEFFREY PINE Native to mountains of California, southern Oregon, western Nevada, Baja California.	Moderate to 60-120 ft.	Symmetrical in youth; straight-trunked with short, spreading, often pendulous branches. Upper branches ascending, form open, pyramidal.	Needles: in 3's, 5-8 in., blue-green. Cones: 6-12 in., reddish brown, oval. Cone doesn't feel prickly when you hold it in hand (*P. ponderosa* cone does).	Hardy. A high altitude tree not at best in low areas. Drought resistant. Slow growing in Seattle.	Attractive in youth with silver-gray bark and bluish foliage. One of best natural bonsai trees. Furrows of bark have vanilla odor.
P. lambertiana SUGAR PINE Native to Sierra Nevada and California's higher Coast Ranges; high mountains of southern California; Baja California; north to Cascades of central Oregon.	Slow in youth, then faster, to 200 ft. or higher.	Young trees narrow, open pyramids with spreading, rather pendulous branches. Old trees usually flat-topped with wide-spreading, open head.	Needles: in 5's, 3-4 in., dark bluish green. Cones: 10-20 in., cylindric, light brown.	Hardy but temperamental. Grows well in Seattle.	World's tallest pine. Susceptible to white pine blister rust, but usually safe if no currants or gooseberry bushes (alternate hosts of blister rust) nearby.
P. monophylla SINGLELEAF PINON PINE Native to southeastern California south to Baja California, east to Utah, Arizona.	Very slow to 10-25 ft.	Young trees slender, symmetrical, narrow crowned. In maturity a small, roundheaded tree, with crooked trunk, open and broad topped in great age.	Needles: usually carried singly, ¾-1½ in., gray-green, stiff. Cones: 2 in., wide, roundish, brown.	Hardy and drought resistant. The only pinon common in southern California.	Good bonsai or rock garden plant—or a shrub of great character in dry, rocky places. Cones contain edible seeds (pine nuts).
P. montezumae MONTEZUMA PINE Native from Mexico to Guatemala.	Moderately fast to 70 ft. or more.	Broad, fairly dense, with horizontal, somewhat drooping branches.	Needles: usually in 5's, to 12 in. deep, often bluish, green. Cones: to 12 in., conical, yellow, reddish, or dark brown.	Unlikely to survive in low temperatures.	Rare, striking pine with unusually long needles. Does well in San Francisco Bay Area. Substitute *P. wallichiana* in colder areas.

NAME	GROWTH RATE, SIZE	GROWTH HABIT	NEEDLES AND CONES	CLIMATE ADAPTABILITY	REMARKS
P. monticola WESTERN WHITE PINE Native to northern California, north to British Columbia, east to Montana.	Fast first years, then slow to moderate to 60 ft.	Attractive, narrow, open crown in youth; spreading, somewhat drooping branches in age form pyramid.	Needles: in 5's, 1½-4 in., blue-green, white banded beneath, fine and soft. Cones: 5-11 in., light brown, slender.	Very hardy.	Susceptible to white pine blister rust throughout Northwest and northern California.
P. mugo *(P. montana)* SWISS MOUNTAIN PINE Native to mountains of Spain, central Europe to Balkans.	Slow to variable heights.	Variable. Prostrate shrub, low shrub, or pyramidal tree of moderate size.	Needles: in 2's, 2 in., dark green, stout, crowded. Cones: 1-2 in., ovoid, tawny to dark brown.	Hardy but suffers in desert heat.	In nurseries, generally a bushy, twisted, somewhat open pine. *P. m. pumilio* is eastern European form, shrubby and varying from prostrate to 5 or 10 ft. *P. m. rostrata* is western European form, may eventually reach 75 feet.
P. mugo mughus MUGHO PINE Native to eastern Alps and Balkan states.	Slow to 4 ft.	From infancy on a shrubby, symmetrical little pine. May become spreading in age.	Needles: darker green than *P. mugo.* Cones: a little shorter than those of *P. mugo.*	Very hardy; as above.	One of the most widely used pines because of low growth habit. Excellent container plant. Pick plants with dense, pleasing form.
P. muricata BISHOP PINE Native to northern coast of California, Santa Cruz Island, northwestern Baja California.	Rapid to 40-50 ft.	Open, pyramidal when young; dense, rounded in middle life; irregular in age.	Needles: in 2's, 4-6 in., dark green, crowded. Cones: 2-3 in., borne in whorls of 3, 4, or 5; broadly oval, brown.	Takes wind and salt air. Not reliably hardy in Northwest or interior.	Many people prefer *P. muricata* to Monterey pine because of its slower growth rate, greater denseness in youth.
P. nigra *(formerly P. austriaca)* AUSTRIAN BLACK PINE Native to Europe and western Asia.	Slow to moderate, usually not above 40 ft. in gardens.	Dense, stout pyramid with rather uniform crown. Branches in regular whorls; in age, broad and flat-topped.	Needles: in 2's, 3-6½ in., stiff, very dark green. Cones: 2-3½ in., ovate, brown.	Very hardy. Adaptable to winter cold and wind.	A tree of strong character which will serve either as landscape decoration or as windbreak in cold regions.

(Continued on next page)

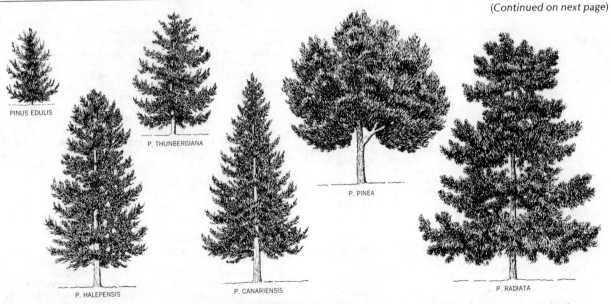

PINUS EDULIS

P. THUNBERGIANA

P. PINEA

P. HALEPENSIS

P. CANARIENSIS

P. RADIATA

Pines are variable in size and outline. At 20 years old, P. edulis is about 5 ft. tall, P. radiata 40 ft. or more. Structure varies from a symmetrical cone (P. canariensis) to informal cone (P. thunbergiana, P. halepensis) to umbrella (P. pinea).

P

Climate Zone maps pages 8-27

NAME	GROWTH RATE, SIZE	GROWTH HABIT	NEEDLES AND CONES	CLIMATE ADAPTABILITY	REMARKS
P. oocarpa (Identification not certain; plants sold under this name may be *P. pseudostrobus* or another Mexican long-needled pine.) Native to Central America, southern and western Mexico.	Rapid to about 70 ft.	Slender in youth, broadening with age. Stout branches and round, compact head.	Needles: usually in 5's, 10-12 in., bright green, soft. Cones: 2-3½ in., broad, ovate, yellowish brown.	Grown near coast in California.	Needles are strikingly long and pendulous. Cones persist for many years. A rare tree.
P. palustris LONGLEAF PINE Native to Virginia and Florida to Mississippi; along coast of southeastern United States.	Slow for 5-10 years, then fast to 55-80 ft.	Gaunt, sparse branches ascend to form open, oblong head.	Needles: in 3's, to 18 in. on young trees, to 9 in. on mature. Dark green. Cones: 6-10 in., dull brown.	Grows in northern and southern California. In native habitat it occasionally takes frosts down to 5° but is used to generally warm winters.	Gallon-size plants look like fountains of grass. Take several years to outgrow this stage. Larger young plants resemble green mops. Good tree for experimenters. Control chlorosis with iron chelates.
P. parviflora JAPANESE WHITE PINE Native to Japan and Formosa.	Slow to moderate to 20-50 ft. or higher.	In open ground a broad pyramid nearly as wide as high. Trees commonly grafted on *P. densiflora*; these grow slowly.	Needles: in 5's, 1½-2½ in., bluish gray to green. Cones: 2-3 in., oval, reddish brown.	Hardy. Grows well in Seattle and in northern California. Will survive —20°.	Widely used for bonsai or container plant.
P. patula JELECOTE PINE Native to Mexico.	Very fast to 40-80 ft.	Symmetrical pyramid with widely spaced tiers of branches.	Needles: In 3's, to 12 in., grass green, slender, hanging straight down. Cones: to 4½ in., conic-ovoid, lustrous pale brown.	Hardy to 15°; a borderline case in Seattle or inland, thriving in coastal California.	Graceful tree casts a light shade, provides handsome silhouette. One of the fastest growing pines in the world. Treat for chlorosis.
P. pinaster CLUSTER PINE, MARITIME PINE, FRENCH TURPENTINE PINE Native to Atlantic coast of France, western Mediterranean, northern Africa.	Very fast to 80-90 ft.	Spreading or sometimes pendulous branches form pyramidal head.	Needles: in 2's, 5-9 in., stiff, glossy green. Cones: 4-7 in., conic-oblong, clustered, glossy light brown.	Hardy to 0°. Best near coasts, in coastal valleys.	Well adapted to sandy soil, ocean exposure. Used in San Francisco's Golden Gate Park to help bind sand dunes. May be weak rooted when young; susceptible to woolly aphids.
P. pinea ITALIAN STONE PINE Native to southern Europe and Turkey.	Moderate to 40-80 ft.	In youth a stout, bushy globe; in middle life a thick trunk topped with umbrella form of many branches. In age broad and flat-topped.	Needles: in 2's, 5-8 in., bright to gray-green, stiff. Cones: 4-6 in., glossy, chestnut, brown, broadly oval.	Hardy. Takes heat and drought when established. Old trees hardy in Northwest, young ones tender. Good in California valleys and coast.	Excellent in beach gardens. Eventually too large for small gardens. Splendid roadside tree. Young trees are handsome, old trees striking.
P. ponderosa PONDEROSA PINE Native from British Columbia to Mexico, east to Nebraska, Texas, and northeast Oklahoma.	Moderate to rapid to 50-60 ft. in 50 years, eventually to 150 ft. or more.	In youth straight trunked and well branched. In age stately, with loosely arranged branches in spire-like crown.	Needles: in 3's, 4-11 in., glossy yellow-green to dark green, firm, in clusters at branch ends. Cones: 3-5 in., light to red-brown, prickly to touch.	Very hardy, but not good in desert heat and wind.	Bushy, attractive tree at all ages. Oddly enough, small ones make fine bonsai or large container plants.
P. pungens TABLE MOUNTAIN PINE Native from New Jersey to Georgia.	Fairly slow to 20-60 ft.	Stout, spreading branches form broad, open, often flat-topped or irregular picturesque crown.	Needles: in 2's or 3's, 2-3 in., stiff, prickly, dark green. Cones: 3½ in., bright brown, persist many years.	Hardy. Thriving in Seattle and in northern California.	Somewhat resembles Japanese red pine. Useful where an informal, rather open pine is desirable. Large, abundant, deep purple catkins are decorative.

P

Climate Zone maps pages 8-27

NAME	GROWTH RATE, SIZE	GROWTH HABIT	NEEDLES AND CONES	CLIMATE ADAPTABILITY	REMARKS
P. radiata MONTEREY PINE Native to California central coast.	Very fast to 80-100 ft.	Shapely broad cone in youth, then drops lower branches to develop rounded or flattish crown.	Needles: in 3's or 2's, 3-7 in., bright green. Cones: 3-6 in., lopsided, clustered, persist many years.	Most widely planted pine in California. Not reliably hardy when temperatures drop below 15°. Not for high or low desert areas.	Very fast growing, 6 ft. a year when young; 50 ft. in 12 years. Prune to maintain denseness (see introduction to Pines). In coastal California gets many pests, suffers smog damage.
P. resinosa RED PINE, NORWAY PINE Native to eastern United States.	Medium to 70 ft.	Dense crown of branches, slightly drooping branches.	Needles: in 2's, 4-6 in. long, dark shiny green. Cones: 2 in. long, shiny brown.	Very hardy to cold; popular in Northwest.	Bark reddish brown on older trees.
P. roxburghii *(P. longifolia)* CHIR PINE, INDIAN LONGLEAF PINE Native to Himalayan foothills.	Medium fast to 60-80 ft. or more.	Slender pyramid in youth with long, drooping foliage; later broad, spreading, with round-topped, symmetrical head.	Needles: in 3's, 8-13 in., slender, light green. Cones: 4-7 in., conic-ovate.	Adapted to California coastal areas, lower Oregon coast.	A rare pine. Similar in many ways to Canary Island pine.
P. sabiniana DIGGER PINE Native to California foothills.	Fast to 40-50 ft.	Wild trees in dry areas are sparse, open. Main trunk divides into secondary trunks.	Needles: in 3's, 8-12 in., gray-green, lacy. Cones: 6-10 in., oblong-ovate, contain edible seeds.	Though native to dry foothills, and very drought resistant, thrives in Seattle and is quite hardy there.	Unusual tree for large gardens. Bulky yet lacy, almost transparent crown. Little shade under digger pine. Very ornamental.
P. strobus WHITE PINE, EASTERN WHITE PINE Native to Newfoundland to Manitoba, south to Georgia, west to Illinois and Iowa.	Slow in seedling stage, then fast to 100 ft. or more.	Symmetrical cone with horizontal branches in regular whorls. In age, broad, open, irregular.	Needles: in 5's, 2-4 in., blue-green, soft. Cones: 3-8 in., slender, often curved.	Hardy in any cold but burns in windy areas. Needs regular water supply.	Fine-textured and handsome in form and color. Subject to blister rust.
P. s. 'Nana' DWARF WHITE PINE	Very slow to 3-7 ft.	Broad bush usually twice as wide as tall.	As above but needles shorter.	Hardy wherever *P. strobus* grows successfully.	Useful in containers or rock gardens.
P. sylvestris SCOTCH PINE Native to northern Europe, Asia.	Moderate to 70-100 ft.	Straight, well branched pyramid in youth; irregular and picturesque in age, with drooping branches.	Needles: in 2's, 1½-3 in., blue-green, stiff. Cones: 2 in., gray to reddish brown.	Very hardy. Not for desert areas; often turns red-brown in cold winters, but recovers.	Popular as a Christmas tree and in landscaping. Reddish bark, sparse foliage have own charm. Excellent in flower arrangements.
P. s. 'Fastigiata'	As above.	Dense, narrow column.	As above.	As above.	Handsome, very densely foliaged plant.
P. thunbergiana *(P. thunbergii)* JAPANESE BLACK PINE Native to Japan.	Fast to 100 ft. in Northwest. Slow or moderate to 20 ft. in southern California.	Spreading branches form a broad, conical tree, irregular and spreading in age.	Needles: in 2's, 3-4½ in., bright green, stiff. Cones: 3 in., brown, oval.	Hardy. Widely planted throughout California, in western Washington and Oregon, in intermediate and high desert.	Handsome tree in youth. Takes to pruning like cloth to scissors; shear it into Christmas tree form or make it into cascade. Excellent in planters or as bonsai.
P. torreyana TORREY PINE Native to California's San Diego coast and Santa Rosa Island.	Fast to 40-60 ft., sometimes higher.	Broad, open, irregular, picturesque habit when exposed to sea winds.	Needles: in 5's, 8-13 in., light gray-green to dark green. Cones: 4-6 in., chocolate brown.	Although native to the coast, it accepts inland, even high desert, conditions, with temperatures as low as 12°. Stands drought.	Less open growth when grown in heavy soil. Don't prune: cut branches die back to trunk.
P. wallichiana *(P. griffithii, P. excelsa)* HIMALAYAN WHITE PINE Native to Himalayas.	Slow to moderate to 40 ft., in gardens, 150 ft. in wilds.	Broad, conical.	Needles: in 5's, 6-8 in., blue-green, slender, drooping. Cones: 6-10 in., light brown.	Hardy to about —10°. Performance in dry, hot areas probably not good.	Resistant to blister rust. Eventually large, but good form and color make it a good choice for featured pine in big lawn or garden.

Climate
Zone maps
pages 8-27

PISTACHIO NUT. See Pistacia vera

PISTACIA. PISTACHE. Deciduous or semi-evergreen trees. Divided leaves on all species. Female trees bear fruit after several years if male trees nearby. Of the species described, only one bears edible fruits (nuts): *P. vera.* The others are ornamental trees.

P. atlantica. MT. ATLAS PISTACHE. Semi-evergreen or deciduous. Zones 8-24. Slow to moderate growth to 60 ft. More regular and pyramidal than other pistaches, especially as young tree. Leaflets 7-11, narrow, rounded at tip, glossy, medium green. Fruit dark blue or purple. Needs sun, good drainage. Takes desert heat and winds; tolerates drought when established. Holds its foliage very late—all winter in mild climates.

P. chinensis. CHINESE PISTACHE. Deciduous. Zones 8-16, 18-23. Moderate growth to 60 ft. tall, 50 feet. wide. Young trees often gawky and lopsided, but with reasonable care older trees become dense and shapely. Leaves with 10-16 paired leaflets 2-4 in. long by ¾ in. wide. Foliage colors beautifully in fall, scarlet, crimson, orange, sometimes yellow tones. Only tree to color scarlet in desert. Fruit on female trees bright red, turning dark blue. Not fussy as to soil or water; accepts moderately alkaline conditions, lawn watering, or no summer watering at all (this only in deep soils). Stake young trees and prune for first few years to develop a head high enough to walk under. A reliable tree for street or lawn, patio or garden corner planting.

P. vera. PISTACHIO, PISTACHIO NUT. Deciduous. Zones 7-12, 14, 15, 18-21. Broad, bushy tree to 30 ft. high, with one or several trunks. Leaves have 3-5 roundish, 2-4 in.-long leaflets. Fruits reddish, wrinkled, borne in heavy clusters. Inside the husks are hard-shelled pistachio nuts. Be sure to include a male tree in your planting. Pistachios are inclined to spread and droop; stake them and train branches to a good framework of 4 or 5 limbs beginning at 4 ft. or so above ground. Established trees will take considerable drought.

PITANGA. See Eugenia uniflora

PITCHER PLANT. See Sarracenia

PITCHER PLANT, CALIFORNIA. See Darlingtonia

PITTOSPORUM. Evergreen shrubs and trees. Some forms have attractive fragrant flowers and some have pretty fruits, but the pittosporums as a group are valued most by Californians for their foliage and form. All make basic, dependable shrubs or trees—the kind of plants that can be a garden's all-year backbone. Some make good clipped hedges; all have pleasing outlines when left unclipped.

Although they are fairly drought resistant, all respond with greener, lusher growth when watered regularly and when fed at least once each spring or summer with a nitrogenous or complete fertilizer. All are susceptible to aphids and scale insects. Black sooty covering on leaves (a mold growing on the insects' honeydew secretions) is a sure sign. All grow best in full sun to half shade.

P. crassifolium. Zones 9, 14-17, 19-24. Will grow to 25 ft. high in 8-10 years, but can easily be kept 6-10 ft. high and 6-8 ft. wide by yearly pruning. Gray-green leaves, 1-2 in. long with rounded ends, densely set on branches. Clusters of little (¼-in.-wide) maroon flowers in late spring. Conspicuous fruits. Good seashore plant.

P. eugenioides. Zones 9, 14-17, 19-22. Excellent hedge plant or free-standing shade tree. Leaves 2-4 in. long have distinctly wavy edges and a medium glossy finish. Depending on environment, leaf color may be yellow-green to a rather deep green. On unpruned plants, clusters of fragrant, yellow, ½-in. flowers form in spring. To grow as hedge, plant gallon-can plants 18 in. apart in row. Force bushiness by shearing off 2-6 in. of plant tops several times each year between February and October. Begin clipping sides when necessary. As free-standing tree (to 40 ft. high, 20 ft. wide), develops handsome curving, gray trunk and lush foliage canopy.

P. napaulense (*P. floribundum*). GOLDEN FRAGRANCE. Zones 17, 20-24. This shrub, to 12 ft. high, 8 ft. wide, is not like the others. Main differences: Leaves are thin-leathery texture, 4-8 in. long, 1-2 in. wide, shiny, pointed at tips; flowers are golden yellow, intensely fragrant, and in 3-in. clusters protruding beyond branch tips in spring. Use as display plant or fragrance maker, not as hedge or screen plant.

P. phillyraeoides. WILLOW PITTOSPORUM. Zones 9, 13-24. Also different from typical pittosporums. This one's a weeping plant, with trailing branches and deep, dusty green leaves, very narrow, 3 in. long. Grows slowly to 15-20 ft. high, 10-15 ft. wide. Always best standing alone; strong structure shouldn't be smothered by other foliage. Good by pool or patio. Small, yellow, bell-shaped, fragrant flowers borne along drooping branches in late winter, early spring, followed by deep yellow fruits. If drainage is poor, water very infrequently but deeply.

P. rhombifolium. QUEENSLAND PITTOSPORUM. Zones 12-24. Slow-growing shrub or tree, to 15-35 ft. Glossy, rich green leaves are nearly diamond-shaped, to 4 in. long. Small white flowers in late spring. Very showy, yellow to orange, ½-in., round fruits in clusters from fall through winter. Fruits contrast nicely with foliage. Growth is open enough that you can see the fruits. As a small tree, well suited for patio or lawn. Or use several as a not-too-dense screen that needs little pruning.

P. tenuifolium (*P. nigricans*). Zones 9, 14-17, 19-24. This is quite similar in most ways (size, growth habit, uses, culture) to *P. eugenioides.* The main difference is in the leaves and twigs, and therefore in the total texture effect. This one has shorter (1-1½ in.), more oval leaves than *P. eugenioides*, the leaf edges are less wavy, and the color is a deeper green. The small twigs and leaf stems are darker. Altogether, then, this one is finer textured, darker, and a little denser. If pruning allows flower formation, they will be dark purple, ½ in. wide in clusters. Plants more tolerant of beach conditions than *P. eugenioides.*

P. tobira. TOBIRA. Zones 8-24; borderline hardiness in Zones 4-7. Broad, dense shrub or small tree, 6-15 ft. tall, rarely to 30 ft. Can be held to 6 ft. by careful heading back and thinning (tobira does not respond as well to shearing as do some other pittosporums). Foliage clean-looking, dense; leaves leathery, shiny, dark green, 2-5 in. long, rounded at ends. Clusters of creamy white flowers at branch tips in early spring have fragrance of orange blossoms. Flowers become round, green fruits that turn brownish in fall and split to show orange seeds. Best for screens, massing, or individually as crooked-stemmed, free-standing small tree. Effective in containers. Variety 'Variegata' is smaller, usually growing to about 5 ft. high and as broad. Foliage gray-green edged white. Takes sun or shade.

P. undulatum. VICTORIAN BOX. Zones 16, 17, 21-24. Moderately fast growth to 15 ft., then slow to 30-40 high, equal width. Planted 5-8 ft. apart, can be kept to 10-15-ft. dense screen by pruning (not shearing). Makes a dense single or multi-trunked, dome-shaped tree of great beauty. Leaves medium to dark green, glossy, wavy-edged, 4-6 in. long. Fragrant creamy white flowers in early spring. Yellowish orange fruits open in fall to show sticky, golden orange seeds which are messy on lawn or paving. Lawn or street tree, screens, big containers. Strong roots become invasive with age.

P. viridiflorum. CAPE PITTOSPORUM. Zones 15-17, 20-24. Shrub or tree to 25 ft. Leaves to 3 in. long, sharp-pointed or blunt, often inrolled at the edges. Flowers fragrant, yellowish green, in dense clusters. Orange-yellow fruit. Resembles a large *P. tobira*; serves similar uses, also has great value as street or garden tree.

PITYROGRAMMA. GOLDBACK FERN. Finely cut fronds, dark green above, heavily coated beneath with bright golden or silvery white powder.

P. hybrida. Zones 23, 24. A large fern of hybrid origin. Brilliantly gold-backed fronds to 2-3 ft. long, broad, finely cut. Hardy to 32°.

P. triangularis. Zones 4-9, 14-24. Native California to Alaska. Small fern with fronds 7 in. long, 6 in. wide, often much less in dry woods. Reverse of fronds strikingly golden (silver in some varieties).

PLANE TREE. See Platanus

PLATANUS. PLANE TREE, SYCAMORE. Deciduous trees. All grow large, have lobed, maplelike leaves. Older bark sheds in patches to reveal pale, smooth, new bark beneath. Brown, ball-like seed clusters hang from branches on long stalks through winter; prized for winter arrangements. Subject to blight (anthracnose) which causes early, continued leaf fall; *P. racemosa* especially susceptible. Control with fungicide sprays.

P. acerifolia. (Often sold as *P. orientalis.*) LONDON PLANE TREE. All Zones. Fast to 40-80 ft., 30-40-ft. spread. Upper trunk and limbs cream-colored, smooth. Leaves 3-5 lobed, 4-10 in. wide. Tolerates most soils, stands up beautifully under city smog, soot, dust, reflected heat. Can be pollarded to create a dense, low canopy.

Fairly free of insects; watch for spider mites and scale. Good street, park, or lawn tree. Used in lines and blocks for formal plantings—avenues, screens, masses.

P. occidentalis. AMERICAN SYCAMORE, BUTTONWOOD. All Zones. Similar to London plane tree; new bark is whiter, tree is out of leaf longer. Very hardy. Occasionally grows with multiple or leaning trunks. Old trees near streams sometimes reach huge size and have heavy trunks.

P. racemosa. CALIFORNIA SYCAMORE. Zones 4-24. Native along streams in California foothills and Coast Ranges. Fast growth to a robust 50-100 ft. Main trunk often divides into spreading or leaning secondary trunk. Attractive patchy, buff-colored bark. Smooth branches often gracefully twisted and contorted. Deeply lobed, yellowish green leaves 4-9 in. long. Susceptible to leaf miner, red spider mites. Leaves naturally turn dusty brown too early in autumn to be considered as fall color. In mild coastal areas brown leaves hang on until new leaf growth starts. In winter the ball-like seed clusters hang 3-7 together along a single stalk. For native or wild gardens, or for big informal gardens generally. With care in pruning can be trained into a picturesque multi-trunked clump.

P. wrightii (*P. racemosa wrightii*). ARIZONA SYCAMORE. Zones 10-12. Native along streams and canyons in mountains of south and east Arizona. To 80 ft. Resembles *P. racemosa;* leaves more deeply lobed, seed clusters have individual stalks branching from the common stalk.

PLATYCERIUM. STAGHORN FERN. Odd epiphytic ferns from tropical regions. In nature, they grow on trees; gardeners grow them on slabs of bark or tree fern stem, occasionally in hanging baskets or on trees. Two kinds of fronds: sterile ones are flat, pale green aging tan and brown—they support the plant and accumulate organic matter to help feed it; fertile fronds are forked, resembling deer antlers. Striking decoration for lanai, shaded patio.

P. bifurcatum. Zones 15-17, 19-24. From Australia and New Guinea. Surprisingly hardy; survives 20°-22° with only lath structures for shelter. Fertile fronds clustered, gray-green, to 3 ft. long. Make numerous offsets which can be used in propagation.

P. grande. Zones 23, 24. From Australia. Fertile and sterile fronds both forked, the former broad but divided somewhat like moose antlers. Protect from frosts. Do not overwater.

PLATYCLADUS orientalis (*Thuja orientalis, Biota orientalis.*) ORIENTAL ARBORVITAE. Evergreen shrubs, trees. All Zones; damaged by severe winters in Zone 1. Shrubby forms common, but the tree from which they originate, a 25-50-ft. plant, is very rarely seen. Leaves scalelike, on twigs that are arranged in flat, vertical planes. Juvenile foliage needlelike; some varieties keep juvenile foliage throughout life. Cones small, fleshy, woody when ripe. Less hardy to cold than American arborvitae (*Thuja occidentalis*), but tolerates heat and low humidity better. Give good drainage, ample water, and protect from the reflected heat of light-colored walls or pavement. A blight of leaves and twigs in the Northwest is easily controlled by copper sprays in early fall and by pruning out and destroying diseased growth. Spray for spider mites.

Widely used around foundations, as pairs or groups by doorways or gates, singly in lawns or borders, or in formal rows. Most stay small, but some forms often end up bigger than the space they're meant for. Varieties are:

'Aurea' ('Aurea Nana', 'Berckmanii'). DWARF GOLDEN ARBORVITAE, BERCKMAN DWARF ARBORVITAE. Dwarf, compact, golden, globe-shaped, usually 3 ft. tall, 2 ft. wide. Can reach 5 ft.

'Bakeri'. Compact, cone-shaped, with bright green foliage.

'Beverleyensis'. BEVERLY HILLS ARBORVITAE, GOLDEN PYRAMID ARBORVITAE. Upright globe to cone-shaped, somewhat open habit. Branchlet tips golden yellow. Can grow to 10 ft. tall, 10 ft. wide in time. Give it room.

'Blue Cone'. Dense, upright, cone-shaped; good blue-green color.

'Blue Spire'. Similar to 'Blue Cone', but narrower.

'Bonita' ('Bonita Upright', 'Bonita Erecta'). Rounded, full, dense cone to 3 ft. tall. Dark green with slight golden tinting at branch tips.

'Chase's Golden'. Upright, cone-shaped, denser and more compact than 'Beverleyensis', with better golden color.

'Elegantissima'. Dense, broad column to 12-15 ft. New growth bright yellow, fading to yellowish green in summer.

'Fruitlandii'. FRUITLAND ARBORVITAE. Compact, upright, cone-shaped shrub with deep green foliage.

'Raffles'. Resembles 'Aurea' but denser in growth, smaller, brighter in color.

'Rosedalis'. To 4 ft. tall and as wide. Feathery foliage of needlelike juvenile leaves. Turns from blue-green to bronze in winter.

PLATYCODON grandiflorum. BALLOON FLOWER. Perennial. All Zones. Upright branched stems to 3½ ft. Leaves light olive green, 1-3 in. long. Balloonlike buds open into 2-in.-wide, star-shaped flowers in blue-violet, white, or soft pink. Bloom June-August if spent flowers (not entire stems) are removed.

Use in borders with astilbe, campanula, francoa, hosta, rehmannia. Plant in sun near coast; light shade in warmer areas. Protect roots from gophers. Good soil, moderate watering. Completely dormant in winter; mark position to avoid digging up fleshy roots. Takes 2-3 years to get well established. Easy to grow from seed. Variety 'Mariesii', dwarf form 12-18 in. high.

PLECTRANTHUS. Perennials. Outdoors in Zones 22-24; elsewhere lathhouse or greenhouse foliage plants. Leaves somewhat thickish, with scalloped edges and prominent veins. Small white flowers in spikes. Grow as ground cover in small shady areas, southern California coast. Especially good trailing over wall or edge of planter or raised bed. As indoor or lathhouse plant, grown in hanging or wall container.

P. australis. Shining, dark green leaves.

P. oertendahlii. Silvery-marked leaf veins and purplish scalloped margins on leaves.

PLEIONE. Terrestrial orchids. Outdoors in Zones 5-9, 14-24. Native to southeast Asia. Many species. All are deciduous. Flowers resemble a cattleya, appear before foliage in early spring. Grow them in pots with leaf mold or in peaty soil. Keep on the dry side in winter.

P. formosana. Two or three 2½-3-in. flowers on 3-5-in. stem in spring. Lavender-purple sepals and petals, paler lavender lip marked with brown and yellow.

PLEIOSPILOS. SPLIT ROCK. Succulents. Grow in pots; let them summer outside anywhere; bring indoors where winters are cold; leave outdoors in winter with overhead protection in Zones 16, 17, 21-24. Plants have 1-2 pairs of leaves that very much resemble gray or gray-green rounded pebbles. Flowers large, resembling those of ice plants, yellow or white. For culture see *Lithops.* Of many kinds offered *P. nelii* and *P. bolusii* are best known.

PLEROMA splendens. See Tibouchina

PLUM and PRUNE. The varieties of edible plums and prunes commonly grown in the West are described in the accompanying chart. Noted there beneath each variety is the group to which it belongs — Japanese (*Prunus salicina*), European (*P. domestica*).

As orchard trees both reach a height of 15-20 ft. with a spread somewhat wider than high. Differences in growth habit are discussed below under "pruning" and "thinning". The fruits of Japanese plums range in color from green through yellow and brilliant red to deep purple-black. With few exceptions the fruit is larger than that of European plum, juicier, with a pleasant blend of acid and sugar. Most of the Japanese plums are used for fresh fruit only. European plums range in color from green and yellow to almost black. Prunes are European plums that have a high sugar content which enables them to be sun-dried without fermenting at the pit.

European plums and prunes bloom late and are better adapted than the early blooming Japanese plums to areas with late frosts or cool, rainy, spring weather. Most European varieties have a moderately high chilling requirement that rules them out of extremely mild winter areas. Pollination requirements are listed in the chart; pollenizers recommended are not the only combinations possible, but those listed have worked.

You can grow plums in many soil types but, of course, they do best in well drained fertile soil. For larger fruit and vigorous growth, fertilize heavily.

Orchardists give Japanese plums 1-3 lbs. of actual nitrogen a year; European plums, 1-2 lbs. Japanese plums make tremendous shoot growth and rather severe pruning is necessary at all ages. Train young trees to the vase shape. After selecting framework branches, cut back to lateral branches. If tree tends to grow upright, cut to outside branches; if it is spreading, cut to inside branches.

European plums do not branch as freely and selection of framework branches is limited. Prune to avoid formation of V-crotches. Mature trees require little pruning —mainly thinning out annual shoot growth.

European plums and prunes do not require as heavy fruit thinning as the Japanese. Heavy bearing of Japanese varieties results in much small fruit and possibly damage to the tree. Thin drastically as soon as fruit is big enough to be seen. Space fruit 4-6 in. apart. Control insects and diseases like this: Dormant spray for scale, mite eggs, aphids. Spray when buds show

Climate Zone maps pages 8-27

white for twig borer and aphids; use insecticide containing sevin or diazinon. Brown rot and fruit and leaf spot may be severe in humid areas. To control, spray with wettable sulfur weekly as fruits mature. If borers attack, control as with peaches. To control mites and insects after leaves form, use an all-purpose fruit tree insecticide following carefully the instructions on spray label.

PLUM, FLOWERING. See Prunus

PLUM, JAPANESE FLOWERING. See Prunus mume

PLUM, NATAL. See Carissa grandiflora

PLUM AND PRUNE

NAME	ZONES	POLLINATION	FRUIT	REMARKS
'Beauty' JAPANESE *(P. salicina)*	7-10, 12, 14-20	Self-fertile; yield improved by pollination with 'Santa Rosa'.	Medium sized, bright, red skin, amber flesh streaked with scarlet, good flavor. Very early.	Fruit softens quickly.
'Becky Smith' JAPANESE	5-12, 14-20	Any other Japanese plum.	Large, showy yellow blushed light red. Light, mild-flavored yellow flesh. Midseason.	Cooking intensifies flavor.
'Burbank' JAPANESE	2-12, 14-20	'Beauty', 'Santa Rosa'.	Large, red. Amber yellow flesh of excellent flavor. Midseason.	Good choice in regions where hardiness to cold is important.
'Burmosa' JAPANESE	5-10	'Santa Rosa', 'Mariposa'.	Large, pinkish red. Light amber flesh. Early.	Handsome, delicious plum but softens quickly.
'Damson' EUROPEAN *(P. domestica insititia)*	2-21	Self-fertile.	Small, purple or blue-black, green fleshed, very tart.	Makes fine jam and jelly. Strains of this variety sold as 'French Damson', 'Shropshire'.
'Duarte' JAPANESE	2-12, 14-20	'Beauty', 'Santa Rosa', 'Satsuma', 'Howard Miracle'.	Medium to large, dull red, silvery markings. Deep red flesh. Midseason.	Firm and keeps well. Sweet flesh, fine flavor, tart skin.
'Eldorado' JAPANESE	7-10, 12, 14-20	'Santa Rosa', 'Wickson'.	Medium large, flattened, black-red. Firm, somewhat dry, amber flesh. Midseason.	Good keeper. Holds shape well for canning, slicing.
'Elephant Heart' JAPANESE	2, 3, 7-12, 14-22	'Santa Rosa'.	Very large dark red plum with rich red flesh. Freestone, highly flavored. Midseason to late.	Skin tart; some prefer it peeled. Long harvest season.
'Formosa' JAPANESE	7-9, 12-20	'Santa Rosa', 'Wickson', 'Duarte', 'Inca', 'Kelsey'.	Large yellow, blushed red. Cream-colored flesh of fine flavor. Early.	Softens quickly off tree.
'French Prune' ('Agen') EUROPEAN *(P. domestica)*	2, 3, 7-12, 14-22	Self-fertile.	Small, red to purplish black. Very sweet and mild. Late.	The standard drying prune of California. Suitable for drying or canning.
'Green Gage' *(P. d. italica)* EUROPEAN	2-12, 14-22	Self-fertile.	Small to medium, greenish yellow, amber fleshed. Good flavor. Midseason.	Very old variety; still a favorite for eating fresh, for cooking, canning, or jam. Selected strain sold as 'Jefferson'.
'Howard Miracle' JAPANESE	7-10, 14-20	Self-fertile.	Medium sized yellow with red blush. Yellow flesh with spicy, pineapple-like flavor. Midseason.	More acid than most Japanese plums, but truly distinctive in flavor.
'Imperial' ('Imperial Epineuse') EUROPEAN	7-12, 14-18	'French Prune' or other European plums.	Large, reddish purple to black purple, greenish yellow flesh, sweet, highly flavored, fine quality. Late midseason.	Excellent fresh. Makes a premium dried prune, canned product.
'Inca' JAPANESE	7-9, 12-24	'Beauty', 'Wickson', 'Kelsey', 'Santa Rosa', 'Satsuma'.	Medium sized yellow skinned, yellow-fleshed fruit. Firm fleshed. Late.	Good home variety. Fruit holds well. Discarded commercially. Very low chilling requirement.

"mitchelson"? — may be the name of the Tofino European plum.

NAME	ZONES	POLLINATION	FRUIT	REMARKS
'Italian Prune' ('Fellenburg') EUROPEAN	2-12, 14-18	Self-fertile.	Medium sized, purplish black, sweet prune. Late midseason.	Standard for prunes in the Northwest. Excellent fresh and for canning. Can be dried. 'Early Italian' ripens two weeks earlier.
'Kelsey' JAPANESE	7-12, 14-18	'Beauty', 'Formosa', 'Wickson', 'Inca'.	Large, green to greenish yellow splashed red. Yellow, firm, sweet flesh. Non-juicy. Late midseason.	Holds for several weeks off tree.
'Laroda' JAPANESE	7-12, 14-18	'Santa Rosa', 'Late Santa Rosa'.	Large, medium red. Light amber flesh. Thin, tender skin. Firm. Midseason.	Very sweet. Firm fleshed, but cooks apart easily.
'Late Santa Rosa' JAPANESE	7-12, 14-22	Self-fertile.	Medium to large, purplish crimson. Amber flesh red near skin, tart-sweet sprightly flavor. Late.	Follows 'Santa Rosa' by a month.
'Mariposa' ('Improved Satsuma') JAPANESE	7-12, 14-22	'Beauty', 'Santa Rosa', 'Wickson', 'Late Santa Rosa', 'Inca'.	Large, purple-red, deep red flesh. Nearly freestone. Sweet flavor. Midseason.	Good for cooking and eating.
'Nubiana' JAPANESE	2-12, 14-20	Self-fertile.	Large, deep black-purple, amber fleshed plum. Sweet and firm. Midseason.	Good for cooking and eating. Turns red when cooked. Good keeper.
'Peach Plum' JAPANESE	2-12, 14-20	Self-fertile.	Large, brownish red. Yellow fleshed, nearly freestone. Good flavor. Early midseason.	Matures rapidly.
'President' EUROPEAN	2-12, 14-20	'Imperial'	Large, purplish blue, amber fleshed, attractive. Flavor not outstanding. Late.	Used for cooking, eating fresh. Not for drying.
'Queen Ann' JAPANESE	7-12, 14-18	'Laroda'	Large, dark purple, heart-shaped fruit with amber flesh. Rich flavor when fully ripe. Late.	Holds shape well when cooked.
'Santa Rosa' JAPANESE	2, 3, 7-12, 14-22	Self-fertile.	Medium to large, purplish red with heavy blue bloom. Flesh yellow to dark red near the skin and of rich, pleasing, tart flavor. Early.	The most important commercial and home variety. Good canned if skin is removed.
'Satsuma' JAPANESE	2-12, 14-22	'Beauty', 'Santa Rosa', 'Wickson', 'Duarte'.	Small to medium, deep, dull red. Dark red, solid, meaty flesh, mild, sweet. Small pit. Early midseason.	Preferred for jams and jellies. Sometimes called blood plum because of its red juice.
'Shiro' bought 2005 JAPANESE	2-12, 14-22	'Beauty', 'Santa Rosa'.	Large golden yellow plum with yellow flesh of good quality. Early midseason.	Tree productive and hardy.
'Stanley' EUROPEAN	2-12, 14-22	Self-fertile.	Large, purplish black with yellow flesh. Sweet and juicy. Midseason.	Good canning variety; resembles a larger 'Italian Prune'.
'Sugar' EUROPEAN	2-12, 14-22	Self-fertile.	Medium, somewhat larger than 'French Prune'. Very sweet, highly flavored. Early midseason.	Good fresh, for home drying and canning. Trees tend to bear heavily in alternate years.
'Tragedy' EUROPEAN	2-12, 14-20	'President'	Small to medium, deep blue with heavy bloom. Green-amber flesh. Early.	Too tart for drying; good for eating fresh or cooking.
'Yellow Egg' EUROPEAN	2-12, 14-20	Self-fertile.	Large, oval, bright yellow, yellow fleshed, soft, sweet. Midseason.	Handsome, good-flavored plum for eating fresh, canning.
'Wickson' JAPANESE	2-12, 14-22	'Santa Rosa', 'Beauty'.	Large, showy yellow turning yellow-red when ripe. Firm yellow flesh of fine flavor. Early midseason.	Good keeper. Makes a fine-textured pink sauce.

P

Climate Zone maps pages 8-27

Casselman - Japanese - pale red, spotted

P

*Climate
Zone maps
pages 8-27*

PLUMBAGO auriculata *(P. capensis).* CAPE PLUMBAGO. Semi-evergreen shrub or vine. Zones 8, 9, 12-24. Unsupported, a sprawling, mounding bush to 6 ft. tall, 8-10 ft. wide; with support can reach 12 ft. or more. In Zone 12 usually a 2-ft. shrub. Leaves light to medium green, 1-2 in. long, fresh-looking. Flowers, an inch wide, in phloxlike clusters, varying (in seedling plants) from white to clear light blue. Select plants in bloom. Blooms March-December, throughout year in warm, frost-free areas. Hot desert sun bleaches flowers. Takes poor soil and (once established) very little water, but good drainage is important. Young growth blackens, leaves drop in heavy frosts, but recovery is good. Prune out damaged growth after frost danger is past. Propagate from cuttings. Slow to start, but tough. Good cover for bank, fence, hot wall; good background and filler plant. 'Alba' is a white-flowered variety.

For other plants called plumbago, see *Ceratostigma.*

PLUMBAGO, BURMESE. See Ceratostigma griffithii

PLUMBAGO, CAPE. See Plumbago

PLUMBAGO, CHINESE. See Ceratostigma willmottianum

PLUMBAGO, DWARF. See Ceratostigma plumbaginoides

PLUME, APACHE. See Fallugia

PLUME FLOWER, BRAZILIAN. See Jacobinia carnea

PLUMERIA. Evergreen and deciduous shrubs or small trees. Open, gaunt character, thick branches, leathery pointed leaves clustered near branch tips. Clustered flowers are large, showy, waxy, very fragrant. Tender to frost; won't take cold, wet soil. Sun near coast, part shade inland. Grow in containers, shelter from frosts. Keep dryish in winter. Feeding late in year will result in soft growth that will be nipped by lightest frosts. All are easy to grow from cuttings.

P. obtusa. SINGAPORE PLUMERIA. Evergreen shrub or small tree. Zone 24. Leaves dark green, 6 in. long, 2 in. wide, very glossy. White, fragrant flowers 2 in. across during warm weather. Very tender.

P. rubra. FRANGIPANI. Deciduous shrub or small tree. Zones 21-24. Thick, pointed, 8-16-in.-long leaves drop in winter or early spring. Flowers 2-2½ in. wide, red, or purplish, fragrant, blooming April-November. *P. r. acutifolia* has white or pink-tinted flowers with yellow centers. A dwarf variety has ¾-in.-wide white flowers.

PODOCARPUS. Evergreen trees, shrubs. Versatile plants with good-looking foliage, interesting form, adaptable to many climates, many garden uses. Foliage generally resembles that of the related yews (*Taxus*), but leaves of the better known species longer, broader, lighter in color.

Grow easily (if slowly) in ordinary garden soil, in sun or partial shade. Some shade best in hot valleys. Will grow many years in containers. Practically pest free; sometimes troubled by chlorosis, especially in cold, wet, heavy soils.

P. andinus. Shrub or shrubby tree. Zones 4-6, 8, 9, 14-24. Broad, dense, slow growing to 20 ft. Leaves ⅓-1 in. long, narrow, dark green, densely set on branches. Resembles yew, but brighter in color. Protect from reflected heat or drying winds. Good screen plant; can be clipped into hedge.

P. elongatus. See *P. gracilior*

P. falcatus. Tree. Zones 8, 9, 14-24. Native to South Africa. Slow growth. Differs from *P. gracilior* in technical details. For culture and uses, see *P. gracilior.*

P. gracilior. (Often sold as *P. elongatus.*) FERN PINE. Tree, often grown as an espaliered vine. Zones 8, 9, 13-24. Native to east Africa, where it grows to 70 ft. Old trees in California are 60 ft. tall.

Habit and foliage variable with age of plant and method of propagation. Leaves on mature wood closely spaced, soft grayish or bluish green, 1-2 in. long, narrow. Plants grown from cuttings or grafts taken from such wood will be limber-branched, slow to make vertical growth, and will have grayish or bluish short leaves. Such plants are usually sold as *P. elongatus.*

Leaves on seedlings, vigorous young plants, and unusually vigorous shoots of mature plants are twice as long, more sparsely set on the branches, and dark, glossy green. Seedlings are more upright in growth than plants grown from cuttings or grafts, and branches are less pendulous, more evenly spaced. Such plants are usually sold as *P. gracilior.* Stake these plants until a strong trunk develops. With age, foliage will become more dense, leaves shorter and bluish or grayish green in color.

Cutting-grown and grafted plants are slow to begin upright growth; branches are supple and limber, and a dominant, upright trunk is slow to form. Such plants are excellent for espaliering or for growing as vines along fences or eaves. With age they will become trees, either with single or multiple stems. Stake well to support heavy foliage masses.

Sun or light shade; needs shade in Zone 13. Among the cleanest and most pest free choices for street or lawn tree, patio or flower bed tree, espalier, hedge, big shrub, or container plant. Choice entryway plant or indoor-outdoor plant. Young plants sometimes used in dish gardens.

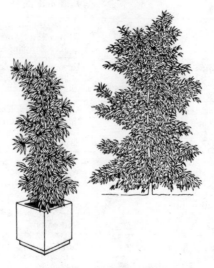

Podocarpus macrophyllus (left) is stiffer, has longer leaves than P. gracilior(right).

P. macrophyllus. YEW PINE. Shrub or tree. Zones 4-9, 12-24. Has been grown Zones 3, 11 with shelter from wind, hot sun, deep snow. Ultimately, to 50 ft. high. Bright green 4-in. leaves, broader than those of *P. gracilior.* Grows indoors or out, in tubs or open ground. Generally narrow and upright, but limber enough to espalier. Easily pruned to shape. Tub plant, large shrub, street or lawn tree (with staking and thinning), screen planting, topiary, clipped hedge.

P. m. maki. SHRUBBY YEW PINE. Smaller, slower growing than yew pine (to 6-8 ft. in 10 years). Dense, upright form. Leaves to 3 in. long, ¼ in. wide. One of the very best container plants for outdoor or indoor use, and a fine shrub generally.

P. nagi. Tree. Zones 8, 9, 14-24. Slow growth to 15-20 ft. (80-90 ft. in its native Japan). Branchlets drooping, sometimes to a considerable length. Leaves 1-3 in. long, ½-1½ in. wide, leathery, smooth, sharp-pointed. Takes considerable shade or sun, indoors or out. More treelike in youth than other podocarpus species. Makes a decorative foliage pattern against natural wood or masonry. Plant in groves for slender sapling effect.

P. totara. TOTARA. Tree. Zones 8, 9, 14-24. Reaches 100 ft. in New Zealand; likely to reach 25-30 ft. in gardens. Dense, rather narrow, with leathery, stiff, pointed, gray-green leaves to 1 in. long. General appearance like that of yew.

POHUTUKAWA. See Metrosideros excelsa

POINCIANA. Evergreen and deciduous shrubs, small tree. (The tropical royal poinciana is *Delonix regia.*) These members of the pea family grow quickly and easily in hot sun with light, well drained soil and infrequent, deep watering.

P. gilliesii *(Caesalpinia gilliesii).* BIRD OF PARADISE BUSH. Evergreen shrub or small tree. Zones 8-16, 18-23. It is occasionally seen Zones 6, 7. Tough, interesting, fast to 10 ft., with finely cut, filmy foliage on a rather open, angular branch structure. Drops leaves in cold winters. Blooms all summer, clusters of yellow flowers adorned with protruding, bright red, 4-5-in.-long stamens.

P. pulcherrima *(Caesalpinia pulcherrima).* DWARF POINCIANA, BARBADOS PRIDE. Deciduous shrub. Zones 12-16, 18-23. Fast, dense growth to 10 ft. tall, 10 ft. wide. Dark green leaves with many ¾-in.-long leaflets. Blooms throughout warm weather; flowers orange or red, clustered, with long red stamens. May be evergreen in mild winters. Useful for quick screening.

POINSETTIA. See Euphorbia pulcherrima

POISON OAK. See Rhus diversiloba

POKE, POKEBERRY, POKEWEED. See Phytolacca americana

POLEMONIUM. Perennials. Zones 1-11, 14-17. Plants for shaded or half shaded borders or under trees. Lush rosettes of finely divided, fernlike foliage; clusters of bell-shaped flowers in summer. Combine with bleeding heart, campanulas, ferns, hellebores, hosta, and lilies. Cool, moist conditions; good drainage. Grow from seed, or divide after flowering or in spring.

Climate Zone maps pages 8-27

P. caeruleum. JACOB'S LADDER. Clusters of lavender-blue pendulous flowers 1 in. long on leafy, 1½-2-ft.-high stems.

P. reptans. Best known is its variety 'Blue Pearl', a dwarf, spreading plant 9 in. tall. Profuse display of blue flowers in April and May. Good in shaded, dampish rock garden.

POLIANTHES tuberosa. TUBEROSE. Tuber. Garden plant in Zone 24; elsewhere planted in containers, moved outdoors after frosts. Native to Mexico. Noted for powerful, heady fragrance. Flowers white, tubular, loosely arranged in spikelike clusters, summer-fall. Basal leaves long, narrow, grass-like. Single forms are graceful, but double variety 'The Pearl' is best known and most widely available.

Long, slender bulblike tubers always show a point of green if alive and healthy. Start indoors like tuberous begonias or plant outside after soil is warm. Plant 2 in. deep, 4-6 in. apart. Needs steady heat, part shade. Water after leaves appear and heavily through growth season. Feed with acid-type fertilizer if soil or water are

Double-flowering tuberose 'The Pearl' has fragrant, white, 2-in.-wide flowers.

alkaline. Dry off when leaves yellow in fall, dig, and store in a warm place. Or plant 3 tubers in a 6-in. pot and treat as above. Tubers will bloom year after year; divide clumps every 4 years.

POLYANTHUS. See Primula polyantha

POLYGALA. Evergreen shrub, shrublets. Flowers irregular, with slight resemblance to sweet peas.

P. chamaebuxus. Shrublet. Zones 4-6. To 6-8 in. tall, spreading slowly by underground stems. Leaves dark green, 1-1½ in. long, shaped like those of boxwood. Flowers (April-May, and sporadically throughout year) creamy white or yellow and white, sometimes marked with red. Sun or filtered shade. Rock gardens.

P. dalmaisiana. SWEET-PEA SHRUB. Evergreen shrub. Zones 8, 9, 12-24. To 5 ft. tall, spreading habit, usually bare at base of plant. Leaves to 1 in. long. Useful for continuous production of purplish pink, oddly-shaped flowers. Sun or light shade. Color hard to handle; use it with whites or blues, preferably with low, bushy plants which conceal its legginess. Good temporary filler.

P. vayredae. Shrublet. Zones 4-6. Resembles *P. chamaebuxus* but only 2-4 in. tall, with yellow and red flowers.

POLYGONATUM multiflorum. SOLOMON'S SEAL. Perennial. Zones 1-7, 15-17. Arching leafy, 3-ft. stems. Greenish white, bell-like blossoms ½-⅔ in. long hang down beneath 2-6-in.-long leaves in spring. Leaves turn deep yellow in fall. Use in shaded woodland area with ferns, hosta, wild ginger, vancouveria. Spreads readily in loose, woodsy soil. (For Western native false Solomon's seal see *Smilacina*.)

POLYGONUM. KNOTWEED. Evergreen and deciduous perennials and vines. Sturdy sun-loving plants with jointed stems and small white or pink flowers in open sprays. Some kinds tend to get out of hand and need control.

P. affine. Evergreen perennial. All Zones. Tufted plant 1-1½ ft. tall. Leaves mostly basal, 2-4½ in. long, finely toothed, deep green, turn bronze in winter. Flowers bright rose red, in dense, erect spikes 2-3 in. long in August-October. Informal border.

P. aubertii. SILVER LACE VINE. Deciduous in Zones 1-7, 10-12; evergreen in Zones 8, 9, 13-24. Rapid growing; can cover 100 square feet in a season. Leaves heart-shaped, glossy, wavy edged, 1½-2½ in. long. Flowers creamy white, small, in frothy mass from late spring to fall. Use as fast-growing screen on fences, arbors. Water deeply once a month. Can prune severely (to ground) each year; bloom will be delayed until August.

P. baldschuanicum. BOKHARA FLEECE-FLOWER. Deciduous vine. All Zones. Much like *P. aubertii* in appearance, growth, vigor, and uses. The flowers are pink, fragrant, somewhat larger, and grow in large drooping clusters.

P. capitatum. Evergreen perennial. Zones 8, 9, 12-24. Rugged, tough, trailing ground cover to 6 in. high, spread to 20 in. Leaves 1½ in. long; new leaves dark green, old leaves tinged pink. Stems and flowers (in small round heads) also pink. Blooms most of year. Leaves discolor and die in temperatures below 28°. Good ground cover for waste places or in confined areas where invasive roots can be held in check. Seeds freely.

P. cuspidatum. JAPANESE KNOTWEED. Perennial. All Zones. Tough, vigorous, forming large clumps of wiry stems 4-8 ft. high. Greenish white blooms in late summer-fall. Extremely invasive; keep away from choice plants; useful in untamed parts of garden. Cut to ground in late fall or winter.

P. c. compactum (*P. reynoutria*). Fast-growing ground cover 10-24 in. high, with creeping roots, can become a nuisance near choice plants. Stiff, wiry red stems. Pale green leaves, 3-6 in. long, heart-shaped, red veined, turn red in fall. Plants die to ground in winter. Dense, showy clusters of small

flowers, red in bud and pale pink when open, late summer. Ground cover for sunny, dry banks, fringe areas of garden.

P. vaccinifolium. Evergreen perennial. Zones 4-7. Prostrate, with slender leafy, branching stems radiating 2-4 ft. Leaves ½ in. long, oval and shining, turning red in fall. Flowers rose pink in dense, upright, 2-3-in. spikes on 6-9-in. flower stalks, late summer. Excellent bank cover or drapery for a boulder in a large rock garden. Increase by cuttings.

POLYPODIUM. Ferns. A widespread and variable group, some native to the West.

P. aureum. HARE'S FOOT FERN. Zones 15-17, 19-24. From tropical America. Big fern for hanging basket culture. Heavy brown creeping rhizomes, coarse fronds 3-5 ft. long. Fronds drop after frost, but plants recover fast.

P. coronans (*Aglaomorpha coronans*). Zones 17, 23, 24. From tropical Asia. Leathery, dark green fronds 2-4 ft. long are uncut or scalloped near the base, coarsely cut above. It's epiphytic; grow it on slab or in a basket like staghorn fern (*Platycerium*). Hardy to 30°

P. vulgare. LICORICE FERN. All Zones. From Europe, Asia and North America. Forms mats from creeping rhizomes. Fronds once-cut, resembling those of smaller sword ferns. Several varieties and the closely related *P. scouleri* are native to California and the Northwest. Plant in leaf mold or other organic material. Plants in the wild often grow on rocks or dead logs. California natives tend to go summer dormant; European varieties are evergreen.

POLYSTICHUM. Ferns. Medium-sized, evergreen fronds on hardy, symmetrical plants. Among the most useful and widely planted ferns in the West; they blend well with other plants and are easy to grow.

P. dudleyi. Zones 4-9, 14-24. Native to Coast Ranges of northern California. Resembles *P. munitum* but has broader, shorter, more finely cut fronds. Not always easy to find, but choice.

P. munitum. SWORD FERN. All Zones. Native from California to Alaska and Montana. The most-seen fern of the redwood forests. Leathery, shiny, dark green fronds 2-4 ft. long, depending on soil and available moisture. Fronds once-cut, texture medium coarse, long-lasting when cut. Old plants may have 75-100 fronds. Good plant for shady beds, along house walls, big scale

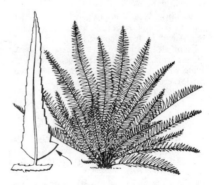

Dark green fronds of sword fern can reach 4 ft. in height in rich, moist soils.

P

*Climate
Zone maps
pages 8-27*

ground cover, in mixed woodland plantings. Grows best in rich soil with organic matter and ample water.

P. setiferum. Zones 4-9, 14-24. Low growing fern with spreading, finely cut fronds, giving the effect of dark green lace. Many cultivated varieties: 'Proliferum' makes plantlets on the midribs of older fronds; these make for a dense, lacy plant and can be used for propagation. Northwestern specialists offer many fancy varieties as "English ferns". All are splendid in shaded rock gardens or for bedding with tuberous begonias and other shade plants.

P. setosum. JAPANESE LACE FERN. Zones 4-9, 14-24. Handsome, dense, lacy. Resembles *P. setiferum* but is taller, darker green, somewhat coarser, fronds somewhat more upright (to 2 ft.).

POMEGRANATE. See Punica

POOR MAN'S RHODODENDRON. See Impatiens oliveri

POPLAR. See Populus

POPPY. See Papaver

POPPY, BUSH. See Dendromecon

POPPY, CALIFORNIA. See Eschscholzia

POPPY, HIMALAYAN. See Meconopsis betonicifolia

POPPY, HORNED. See Glaucium

POPPY, ICELAND. See Papaver nudicaule

POPPY, MATILIJA. See Romneya

POPPY, ORIENTAL. See Papaver orientale

POPPY, PRICKLY. See Argemone.

POPPY, SEA. See Glaucium

POPPY, SHIRLEY. See Papaver rhoeas

POPPY, WELSH. See Meconopsis cambrica

POPULUS. POPLAR, COTTONWOOD, ASPEN. Deciduous trees. All known for rapid growth. Eminently suitable for country places where fast growth, toughness, and low maintenance are considerations. Although most kinds can grow anywhere in the West, they are grown and appreciated far more in the cold-winter, hot-summer interior than near the coast. Roots extremely invasive—not for city streets, lawns, or small gardens.

P. alba. WHITE POPLAR. All Zones. Fast growth to 40-60 ft., broad and wide-spreading. The 5-in.-long leaves, usually with 3-5 lobes, are white-woolly underneath. A "lively" tree, even in light breezes, with flickering white and green highlights. Good tree for desert. Tolerates wide range of soils. Suckering a problem.

P. a. 'Pyramidalis'. (Usually sold as *P. bolleana.*) BOLLEANA POPLAR. Narrow columnar form. Good country windbreaks or sun screens. Suckers badly.

P. canadensis 'Eugenei'. CAROLINA POPLAR. All Zones. Fast growth to 40-150 ft., with narrow spread. Triangular leaves, 4 in. long, toothed at edges. Has a deservedly bad reputation for invading and breaking sewer lines.

P. candicans. BALM-OF-GILEAD. All Zones. Fast to 30-60 ft., broad-topped. Suckers profusely. Triangular leaves 4½-6 in. long, 3-4 in. wide. Thrives in Zones 12, 13.

P. fremontii. FREMONT COTTONWOOD. Zones 7-24. Fast to 40-60 ft. or more. Leaves are thick, glossy, yellow-green, 2-4 in. broad, triangular, coarsely toothed; turn bright lemon yellow in fall, remain on tree practically all winter in Zones 12, 13. Small, greenish yellow flowers in long, slender catkins appear before leaves. Female trees later bear masses of cottony seeds that blow about and become a nuisance; be sure to plant male trees (easily grown from cuttings). Requires little water. Valuable in desert areas as shade tree or windbreak.

P. nigra 'Italica'. LOMBARDY POPLAR. All Zones. Fast to 40-100 ft. Beautiful columnar trees with upward-reaching branches. Suckers profusely; invasive roots a problem. Indispensable to country driveways, valuable both as windbreak and skyline decoration. Bright green, triangular 4-in. long leaves turn beautiful golden yellow in fall. Subject to blight of branchlets in many areas.

P. tremuloides. QUAKING ASPEN. Zones 1-7. Native throughout the Western mountains. Fast growing to 20-60 ft. Trunk and limbs smooth, pale gray-green to whitish. Dainty, light green, round leaves that flutter and quake in slightest air movement. Brilliant golden yellow fall color. Generally performs poorly at low elevations, but grown successfully in Tilden Park, Berkeley, California. Collected plants are occasionally offered in nurseries. Good background tree for native shrubs and wildflowers. Apt to suffer from sudden dieback.

P. trichocarpa. BLACK COTTONWOOD. Zones 1-7. Native along mountain streams, California to Alaska. Tall, spreading tree to 40 ft. in 15 years, 150-180 ft. in age. Heavy-limbed, with dark gray, furrowed bark; wood very brittle. Leaves 3-5 in. across, triangular, deep green above and distinctly silver below; attractive when ruffled by breeze. Male trees shed quantities of catkins; female trees release myriad cottony seeds if male trees present.

PORTULACA grandiflora. PORTULACA, ROSE MOSS. Annual. Useful warm-weather plants for brilliant color, early summer until frost. Plants 6 in. high, 18 in. across. Leaves fleshy, succulent, cylindrical, pointed, 1 in. long. Trailing, branched reddish stems, also succulent. Flowers roselike, lustrous, in red, cerise, rose pink, orange, yellow, white, pastel shades; single and double strains sold. Flowers open fully only in sun, close in late afternoon.

Use on hot dry banks, in parking strips, rock gardens, gravel beds, patio insets, among succulents, as edgings. Plant in full sun. Any soil; best in sandy loam. Sow seed in place after weather is warm or plant flat-grown plants in late spring. Although drought-tolerant, better with occasional watering. Plants self-sow.

PORTULACARIA afra. ELEPHANT'S FOOD, PURSLANE TREE, SPEKBOOM. Succulent. Outdoors Zones 16, 17, 22-24; outdoors with overhead protection Zones 8, 9, 12-15, 18-21; house plant anywhere. Native to South Africa. Thick juicy-stemmed shrub to 12

ft. tall and nearly equal width, usually much smaller in pots. Looks a bit like jade plant (*Crassula argentea*) and is sometimes sold as jade plant. Elephant's food is faster growing, more loosely branched, has more limber, tapering branches, and smaller (½-in.-long) leaves. In South Africa, bears tiny pink flowers in clusters; seldom, if ever, blooms in western U. S.

Small plants are good, easy pot plants; where hardy can be used as a fast-growing informal screen, unclipped hedge, or cut back as high-growing ground cover. A form with leaves variegated yellow is *P. a.* 'Foliis Variegatis' (variegated forms usually dwarf and slow). Another form has larger, inch-long leaves. Same culture as jade plant.

POTATO. Few home gardeners bother to grow their own potatoes. The plants take too much garden space, are subject to several pests and diseases, and the potatoes need careful storage after harvesting. Potatoes need a sandy, fast-draining soil; tubers become deformed in heavy, poorly drained soils. For early crops, plant in spring as soon as the soil can be worked, or in midwinter where frosts are not severe; for fall and winter use, plant from mid-May to mid-June.

Buy certified (inspected, disease-free) seed potatoes from a seed or feed store. Cut potatoes into chunky pieces about 1½ in. square with at least 2 eyes. Place chunks 4 in. deep and 18 in. apart. Do not plant if soil is very wet. After top growth appears, give plants an occasional soaking.

Dig early (or new) potatoes when tops begin to flower; dig mature potatoes when tops die down. Dig potatoes carefully to avoid bruises and cuts. Well matured potatoes free of defects keep best in storage. Store in a cool dark place at a temperature of 40°.

POTATO, SWEET. See Sweet Potato

POTATO VINE. See Solanum jasminoides

POTENTILLA. CINQUEFOIL. Evergreen and deciduous perennials and shrubs. Hardy plants useful for ground covers and borders. Leaves bright green or gray-green, divided into small leaflets. Small, mostly single, roselike flowers cream to bright yellow, white or pink.

EVERGREEN PERENNIALS

P. cinerea. Zones 1-17. Matted stems 2-4 in. high. Leaves divided fanwise into 5 wedge-shaped, gray-hairy leaflets toothed at tip, white-woolly underneath. Flowers pale yellow, ½ in. wide. Ground cover or rock plants for sun, part shade.

P. nepalensis 'Willmottiae' (*P.n.* 'Miss Willmott'). All Zones. Good performance near coast. Grows to 10 in. high, spreads to 18 in. Leaves divided fanwise into 5 roundish, 2-3 in.-long, green leaflets. Branching clusters of salmon pink flowers ½-1 in. wide. Borders, cut flowers.

P. verna. SPRING CINQUEFOIL. All Zones. Dainty, bright green, tufted creeper 2-6 in. high. Leaves divided into 5 leaflets. Butter yellow flowers ¼ in. wide, 3-5 in clusters in spring and summer. Stands more moisture than other potentillas. May turn brown in cold winters. Ground cover, bulb cover.

Climate Zone maps pages 8-27

DECIDUOUS SHRUBBY POTENTILLAS

There's a group of shrubby potentillas (Zones 1-21) that are most often sold under the name of *P. fruticosa*. They all have their leaves divided into 3-7 leaflets; some are distinctly green on top, gray beneath; others look more gray-green. All bloom cheerfully from June-October in spite of poor soil, heat, and little water.

'Gold Drop' (variety 'Farreri') grows to 2 ft. high, 3 ft. wide. Deep yellow, ¾-in.-wide flowers.

'Katherine Dykes' can reach 5 feet but usually stays much lower. Pale yellow, inch-wide flowers.

'Snowflake' grows 2-4 ft. high. Semi-double, white blossoms.

'Sutter's Gold' grows 1 ft. high, spreading to 3 ft. Clear yellow flowers an inch wide.

POTERIUM sanguisorba. See Sanguisorba

POTHOS aureus. See Rhapidophora aurea

PRAYER PLANT. See Maranta

PREGNANT ONION. See Ornithogalum caudatum

PRICKLY PEAR. See Opuntia

PRIDE OF MADEIRA. See Echium fastuosum

PRIDE OF TENERIFFE. See Echium pininana

PRIMROSE. See Primula

PRIMROSE, BABY. See Primula malacoides

PRIMROSE, CAPE. See Streptocarpus

PRIMROSE, EVENING. See Oenothera

PRIMROSE, FAIRY. See Primula malacoides

PRIMROSE TREE. See Lagunaria

PRIMULA. PRIMROSE. Perennials; a few short-lived perennials treated as annuals. Fanciers reserve the name "primrose" for *Primula vulgaris*, but gardeners generally call both this plant and the polyanthus *(P. polyantha)*, "English primrose".

Out of some 600 species of primroses, only a few are widely adapted and distributed over the West. Long hot summers and low humidity are limiting factors. But almost any primrose can be grown to perfec-

tion in the cool, moist climates of western Oregon and Washington, and north coastal California. Most primroses are quite hardy; may thrive east of the Cascades and in the intermountain region.

Specialty nurseries in the Northwest offer seed and plants of many kinds of primroses. Fanciers exchange seeds and plants through local primrose societies, and through notices in the *Quarterly* of the American Primrose Society.

To systematize this large group of plants, specialists have set up sections—or groups of species that strongly resemble each other, often hybridize with each other, and usually respond to the same kind of care.

The primulas most commonly grown in the West fall into 11 of the 34 primula sections. Following are the basic characteristics and requirements of these sections. To learn how to grow a particular species, note which section it belongs to in the accompanying chart.

Section Auricula. Over 20 species native to European Alps. Rosettes of thick leaves, often with a mealy coating or white margin. Strong fleshy stems to 8 in. high bear clusters of yellow, cream, purple, rose, or brownish flowers; often fragrant. They grow in full sun in their native habitat but in most of Western U.S. do best in light

PRIMULA

NAME	SECTION	ZONES	LEAVES	FLOWERS	REMARKS
PRIMULA acaulis See *P. vulgaris*					
P. alpicola MOONLIGHT PRIMROSE	Sikkimensis	1-6, 17	Long-stalked, wrinkled, forming dense clumps in time.	Sulfur yellow, spreading, bell-shaped, in clusters on 20-in. stalk. Summer.	Powerfully fragrant. Flowers sometimes white or purple. Somewhat tender in coldest areas.
P. auricula AURICULA	Auricula	1-6, 17, 22-24 (in shade, preferably in pots)	Evergreen rosettes of broad, leathery leaves, toothed or plain-edged, gray-green, sometimes with mealy coating.	Clusters of yellow, cream, rose, purple, or brownish; fragrant; white or yellow eye. Early spring.	Three classes: Show Auriculas, usually grown in pots under glass to protect flowers against weather; garden Auriculas, sturdier; and alpine Auriculas. Flowers in shades of white, yellow, orange, pink, red, purple, blue, brownish. Double forms available.
P. beesiana	Candelabra	1-6, 17	Long leaves taper gradually into a leaf stalk. Leaves (including stalks) reach 14 in.	Reddish purple, in 5-7 dense whorls on a 2-ft. flower stem. Mid- or late spring.	Somewhat variable in color, but usually reddish purple with yellow eye. Very deep-rooted; needs deep watering.
P. bulleyana	Candelabra	1-6, 15-17	Like the above, but with reddish midribs.	Bright yellow, opening from orange buds. Whorls open in succession over long season in mid- and late spring.	Plants disappear in late fall; mark the spot. Older plants can be divided after bloom or in fall. Showy at woodland edge.
P. burmanica	Candelabra	1-6, 17	Like *P. beesiana*, but broader, longer-stalked.	Like *P. beesiana*, but with more densely-clustered flowers of deeper purple, with yellow eye.	One of the best and easiest of the Candelabra section.

(Continued on next page)

P

*Climate
Zone maps
pages 8-27*

NAME	SECTION	ZONES	LEAVES	FLOWERS	REMARKS
P. cockburniana	Candelabra	1-6, 17	Leaves 4-6 in. long, rather few in the clump.	Flowers orange-scarlet, in 3-5 whorls on 10-14 in. stalks.	Smaller and less vigorous than other Candelabra types. Striking color, most effective when massed.
P. denticulata (Often sold as *P. d. cachemiriana* or *P. cachemiriana*)	Denticulata	1-6	Leaves 6-12 in. long, only half-grown at flowering time.	Dense, ball-shaped clusters on foot-high, stout stems. Color ranges from blue-violet to purple. Very early spring bloom.	Pinkish, lavender, and white varieties are available. Not adapted to warm-winter areas.
P. florindae	Sikkimensis	1-6, 17	Leaves broad, heart-shaped, on long stems.	As many as 60 fragrant, yellow, bell-shaped, nodding flowers top 3 ft. stems in summer.	Will grow in a few inches of running water, or in a damp, low spot. Plants late to appear in spring. Hybrids have red, orange, or yellow flowers.
P. helodoxa	Candelabra	1-6, 17	Leaves smooth, large, nearly or quite evergreen in mild climates, unlike those of most Candelabra primroses.	Five to 7 whorls of large, golden yellow flowers in early to mid-spring. Stalks to 4 ft. tall.	Needs shade, much water. One of the most spectacular and stately for bog, damp woodland, waterside.
P. Inshriach hybrids	Candelabra	1-6, 17	Typical, lush Candelabra foliage.	Tiered clusters of flowers in bright and pastel shades of yellow, red, orange, peach, salmon, pink, purple. Mid-spring to early summer.	Easily grown from seed, blooming the second year.
P. japonica	Candelabra	1-6, 17	Leaves 6-9 in. long, to 3 in. wide.	Stout stems to 30 in. with up to 5 whorls of purple flowers with yellow eye. May-July.	White and pink varieties are obtainable. One of the toughest and hardiest of Candelabras. Needs semi-shade; lots of water.
P. juliae	Vernales	1-6, 17	Smooth, roundish leaves 1/2-1 in. long rise directly from a creeping rootstock.	Flowers 3/4-1 in. across, purplish red with yellow eye, borne singly on 1 in. stems. Bloom in early spring, appearing before or with new leaves.	Makes little flower-covered mats of great beauty.
P. juliae hybrids JULIANA PRIMROSE	Vernales	1-6, 17	Tuftlike rosettes of bright green leaves.	Flowers borne singly (cushion type) or in clusters. Very early.	Many named forms in white, blue, yellow, orange-red, pink, or purple. Excellent for edging, borders, woodland, rock garden.
P. kewensis	Verticillata	17. Greenhouse or house plant elsewhere.	Leaves 4-8 in. long, coarsely toothed, either deep green or powdered with white.	Borne in whorls on 18 in. stems, golden yellow, profuse. Long bloom season in winter, spring; scattered bloom possible any time.	Best as house plant, lathhouse Zones 15-16, 18-24. Long lived with reasonable care. Hybrid between *P. floribunda, P. verticillata*.
P. malacoides FAIRY PRIMROSE BABY PRIMROSE	Malacoides	14-24	Rosettes of soft, pale green, oval, long-stalked leaves 1 1/2-3 in. long. Edges lobed and cut.	Borne in loose, lacy whorls along numerous upright stems, 12-15 in. high. White, pink, rose, red, lavender, in February-May.	Splendid for winter-spring color in mild-winter areas of California. Set out plants in October-November. Use under high-branching trees, with spring bulbs, in containers. Grown as annual; stands light frost. Indoor or cool greenhouse pot plant in cold climates.
P. obconica	Obconica	15-24	Large, roundish, soft-hairy leaves on long, hairy stems; hairs cause skin irritation to some people.	Flowers 1 1/2-2 in. wide in large, broad clusters on stems to 1 ft. tall. Shades of white, pink, lavender, and reddish purple. Tends to be nearly everblooming in mild regions.	Perennial, best treated as annual. Use for bedding in light shade where winters are mild, as house plant in cold regions.

NAME	SECTION	ZONES	LEAVES	FLOWERS	REMARKS
P. Pagoda hybrids	Candelabra	1-6, 17	Typical, lush Candelabra foliage.	Tiered clusters of orange, red, yellow, pink, tangerine flowers on 2-3 ft. stems. Late spring through summer.	These are very fine Candelabra hybrids developed near Portland, Oregon.
P. polyantha POLYANTHUS PRIMROSES (Often called English primroses) A group of hybrids.	Vernales	1-9, 14-24	Fresh green leaves in tight clumps.	Flowers 1-2 in. across in large full clusters on stems to 12 in. high. Almost any color. Blooms from winter to early and mid-spring. Most adaptable and brilliant of primroses.	Fine, large-flowered strains are Clarke's, Barnhaven, and Pacific. Novelties include Gold Laced, mahogany petals edged with gold. Miniature Polyanthus have smaller flowers on shorter stalks. All excellent for massing in shade, for planting with bulbs, or as container plants.
P. polyneura	Cortusoides	1-6, 17	Leaves long-stalked, broad, lobed and toothed, green above, to 4 in. long.	Flower stems 9-18 in. high, with 1, 2, or more whorls of erect rose, purplish, or red flowers with orange-yellow eyes Spring bloom.	Handsome, spreading plant for shade; needs fast drainage, somewhat less water than Candelabra types.
P. pulverulenta	Candelabra	1-6, 17	Leaves a foot or more long, deep green, wrinkled.	Flowers red to red-purple, purple-eyed, in whorls on 3-ft. stems thickly dusted with white meal.	Bartley strain has flowers in pink and salmon range. Also a fine white with orange eye.
P. sieboldii	Cortusoides	1-6, 14-17	Leaves scalloped, toothed, on long, hairy stalks.	Flowers pink, rose, or white, clustered 1-1½ in. across. Stalk 4-8 in. high. Bloom in late spring.	Tolerates more heat and drought than most primroses. Spreads from creeping rootstocks. Often goes dormant in late summer. Easily propagated by cuttings of the rootstock.

(Continued on next page)

P

Climate Zone maps pages 8-27

shade—full sun in coastal areas. Tolerate more sun than Polyanthus primroses.

Section Candelabra. Native to and most abundant in meadows, bogs, or open woodland, principally in the Himalayan region. Vigorous growing; larger species have semi-erect leaves. Flowers in whorls, one above another on 2-3-ft. stems. Best in massed plantings. Need rich soil, partial shade, and much water; will take bog conditions.

Section Cortusoides. Called woodland primulas. Spread by underground creeping roots. After setting seed, plants become dormant and lose their leaves. Extremely hardy; can take somewhat drier conditions than other primroses, but thrive in rich moist soil with ample humus. Need shade.

Section Denticulata. Native to Himalayan meadows and moist slopes 6,000-14,000 ft. high. Winter over as large scale-covered buds from which emerge in spring a cluster of leaves and a stout stalk topped with a ball-like cluster of flowers. Grow best where winters are cold; mild days in fall and winter may force blossoms too early.

Section Malacoides. Semi-hardy primroses from western China, usually treated as annuals. Planted in mild-winter areas in early fall for bloom in winter and early spring. In cold climates grow in greenhouse.

Section Muscarioides. Short-lived, rather difficult, usually treated as biennial. Flowers

in this Chinese and Tibetan group are tightly crowded into long clusters resembling those of miniature red-hot pokers or grape hyacinths. For collectors.

Section Obconica. Semi-tropical, short-lived primroses from western China. Thick rhizomes; long-stalked, hairy leaves. Large, showy flower clusters over a long period in winter and spring. Good in pots. Hairy leaves irritate skin of some people.

Section Sikkimensis. Similar to Candelabra primroses, except that bell-shaped, drooping flowers on long stems are carried in a single large cluster, rarely with a second, lower whorl. Leaves have distinct stalks. Need abundant water, will take bog conditions.

Section Sinenses. Like the Obconica section includes semi-tropical, short-lived plants. Best grown indoors in pots, either in greenhouse or a cool, bright window.

Section Vernales. Includes the familiar species sometimes called English primroses —*P. vulgaris* and *P. polyantha*. Tuftlike rosettes of leaves, with flowers borne singly or in clusters on stiff stems. Grow best in rich soil with lots of humus. Partial shade inland, full sun in coastal fog belt.

Section Verticillata. Densely leafy tufts produce many stems bearing long-tubed yellow flowers. Long lived, with long bloom season. Rather tender plants grown in pots.

The accompanying chart does little more than introduce the great primrose group. Enthusiasts will be able to find and grow dozens of other species, some a real challenge to grow to flowering. But the primroses in the chart are not difficult if you live in the cool, moist primula belt and give the plants rich soil, ample water, and shade.

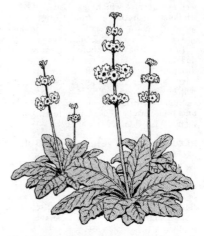

Candelabra primroses have tiered whorls of flowers on stiffly erect stems.

P

Climate Zone maps pages 8-27

NAME	SECTION	ZONES	LEAVES	FLOWERS	REMARKS
P. sikkimensis	Sikkimensis	1-6, 17	Leaves scanty, 3-5 in. long, with short stalks.	Up to 2 dozen yellow, bell-shaped, nodding flowers on a slender, 20-in.-high stalk. Summer bloom.	Largely supplanted by *P. florindae*, which is taller and somewhat easier to grow.
P. sinensis CHINESE PRIMROSE	Sinenses	Greenhouse or house plant.	Leaves on long stalks, roundish, lobed, toothed, soft-hairy, 2-4 in. long.	Flowers white, pink, lavender, reddish, coral, 1½ in. or more wide, many in a cluster on 4-8 in. stems. Stellata varieties have star-shaped flowers in whorls.	Tender, scarce. Favorite European pot plant; imported seed available from specialists.
P. veris COWSLIP	Vernales	1-6, 17	Leaves similar to those of Polyanthus primroses.	Bright yellow, fragrant flowers ½-1 in. wide in early spring. Stem 4-8 in. high.	Naturalize in a wild garden or rock garden. Charming, but not as sturdy as Polyanthus primroses.
P. vialii *(P. littoniana)*	Muscarioides	1-6, 17	Leaves to 8 in. long, 1½-2½ in. wide, hairy, irregularly toothed.	Flowers violet-blue, fragrant, ¼-½ in. across, opening from bright red calyces. Stems erect, 1-2 ft. high. Dense, narrow spikes 3-5 in. long.	Not long-lived, but quite easy from seed in cool-winter areas. For collectors. Use in rock gardens.
P. vulgaris *(P. acaulis)* PRIMROSE, ENGLISH PRIMROSE	Vernales	1-6, 17	Tufted; leaves much like those of Polyanthus primroses.	Flowers one to a stalk; vigorous garden strains often have 2 or 3 to a stalk. Early spring bloom. White, yellow, red, blue, and shades of bronze, brownish, and wine.	Generally found only in a cool, moist climate. Double varieties available. Blues and reds especially desirable. Use in woodland, rock garden, as edging.

PRINCE'S FEATHER. See Amaranthus hybridus hypochondriacus

PRINCESS FLOWER. See Tibouchina

PRIVET. See Ligustrum

PROSOPIS glandulosa torreyana *(P. juliflora torreyana).* (Often sold as *P. chilensis.*) MESQUITE. Deciduous tree or large shrub. Zones 10-13. Native to deserts in the Southwest. One of the wide spreading shade trees that help make outdoor living more comfortable in the desert. To 30 ft. high and over 40 ft. wide, with many tiny bright green leaflets all through the thicket-like tops. The leaflets and their stems make an airy kind of shade. Mesquite also serves well as screen or windbreak. Usually several trunks branch out at ground level. Small greenish yellow flowers in 1½-2½-in.-long spikes. Flat seed pods 2-6 in. long.

Best in deep soil where taproot will go down great distances for water. Tolerates drought, alkaline conditions, or irrigated lawn. Survives in shallow, rocky soil, but will be shrubby.

"Reese hybrid" is an evergreen tree of uncertain origin. Fast; may reach 30 ft. high, 60 ft. wide in 10 years.

PROSTANTHERA rotundifolia. ROUND-LEAFED MINT BUSH. Evergreen shrub. Zones 8, 9, 14-24. Dense, rounded growth to 4-10 ft. Tiny roundish leaves to ⅓ in. long, dark green above, paler beneath. Flowers (April-May) blue-purple, trumpet-shaped, to ½ in. long, profusely carried in short clusters. Takes sun or light shade, tolerates some drought.

PROTEA. Evergreen shrubs. Zones 16, 17, 21-24. Beautiful flowering plants from South Africa. Tubular flowers in large, tight clusters are surrounded by brightly colored bracts; effect is that of a large, very colorful artichoke or thistle. Superb cut flowers, they hold their color for weeks, and even after fading they retain their shape.

Difficult to grow; definitely not for beginners. They need perfect drainage (preferably on slopes), moderate summer water, protection from dry winds, good air circulation, full sun. Most need acid soil; some accept alkaline soil. Smaller species will grow in containers. Young plants tender to cold; older plants of most species hardy to 25°-27°. They bloom in 3-4 years from seed, but are not long-lived plants.

Some 150 species grow in South Africa. These few seem to do best here:

P. cynaroides. KING PROTEA. To 3-5 ft. tall with open, spreading habit. Leaves oval,

Flower head of Protea cynaroides (pink to red, with white center) may be 1 ft. wide.

leathery. Flower heads to 11-12 in. across. Bracts pale pink to crimson, flowers white (midsummer to winter, early spring). Needs regular watering throughout year. Can be grown in tubs.

P. neriifolia. To 10 ft., 6-8 ft. wide. Leaves narrow, shaped like oleander leaves. Flower heads (autumn, winter) 5 in. long, 3 in. wide. Bracts pink to salmon, with black, furry tips. Will take 17° and grow in alkaline soil.

P. susannae. To 6 ft. tall, fairly compact. Foliage heavy-scented. Flower heads to 4 in. long, pink shading to brown at the base. Has proven among the easiest to grow in California, withstanding alkaline soil and dry air.

PRUNE. See Plum and Prune

PRUNUS. Deciduous and evergreen trees and shrubs. The fruit trees that belong to *Prunus* are better known as the "stone fruits" and are described individually elsewhere in this encyclopedia under their common names. See Almond, Apricot, Cherry (sweet, sour, and Duke), Peach and Nectarine, Plum and Prune.

Take away the fruit trees and you have left the ornamentals, of which there are two classes: (1) the evergreens, used chiefly as structure plants (hedges, screens, shade trees, street trees); and (2) the deciduous flowering fruit trees (and shrubs) closely related to the fruit trees mentioned above and used chiefly for their springtime flower display. Following, in alphabetical order, are descriptions of the evergreen forms. After that comes an alphabetical listing of the flowering fruits, with certain kinds charted.

Climate
Zone maps
pages 8-27

EVERGREEN FORMS

P. caroliniana. CAROLINA LAUREL CHERRY. Evergreen shrub or tree. Zones 7-24. As an upright shrub, it can be well branched from the ground up and useful as a formal, clipped hedge or tall screen to 20 ft. Can be sheared into formal shapes. Trained as a tree, will become broad-topped and reach 35-40 ft. Attractive trained as multi-stemmed tree. Densely foliaged with glossy green, smooth-edged leaves 2-4 in. long. Small, creamy white flowers in 1-in. spikes, February-April. Fruit black, ½ in. or less in diameter. Varieties with greater denseness and less height are 'Bright 'n Tight' and 'Compacta'.

Litter from flowers and fruit is a problem when planted over paved areas. Appearance best in coastal areas. Often shows salt burn in alkaline soils but does withstand desert heat and wind. Give it average soil, full sun, pruning to shape. Once established it's quite drought tolerant.

P. ilicifolia. HOLLYLEAF CHERRY. Evergreen shrub or small tree. Zones 7-9, 12-24. Native to California Coast Ranges and Baja California. Grows at moderate rate to 20-30 ft. usually broader than high. Mature leaves deep, rich green, 1-2 in. long, resemble those of holly. New leaves, from March to May, are a light green, contrasting pleasantly with the dark older foliage. Often, variations in leaf color and size occur from plant to plant. Creamy white flowers, ½ in. across, in spikes 3-6 in. long, appear with the new leaves in March. Round fruits, ½-¾ in. wide, turn from green to red, then a reddish purple (never as dark or black as those of the Catalina cherry). Hybrids between hollyleaf and Catalina cherry appear frequently when plants are grown from seeds collected where both grow.

Hollyleaf cherry can be grown in almost any soil but thrives best in coarse, well drained types. May be attacked by whiteflies. For control, see *Prunus lyonii*. Does best in sun but will take light shade. Once established it will require no irrigation in normal rainfall years. However, growth rate and appearance are improved by deep but infrequent watering. When buying plants avoid rootbound, large plants. A gallon can size, properly grown (no coiled roots) will generally outgrow the larger plant in a 5 gallon can. Use as a small tree, tall screen, or formal clipped hedge of any height from 3-10 ft. (space plants 1 or 1½ ft. apart, train as described under *Pittosporum eugenioides*). It has unusually high resistance to oak root fungus *(Armillaria)*, (like *P. lyonii*). Very large, old trees resemble California live oak *(Quercus agrifolia)*.

P. laurocerasus. ENGLISH LAUREL. Evergreen large shrub or small tree. Zones 4-9, 14-24; best performance in Zones 4-6, 15-17. Native from southeastern Europe to Iran. Generally seen as clipped hedge. As a tree, fast growing to 30 ft. tall and as wide. Leaves leathery, glossy, dark green, 3-7 in. long, 1½-2 in. wide. Flowers creamy white in 3-5-in.-long spikes in summer, often hidden by leaves. Small black fruits in late summer and fall. No special soil requirements. Where adapted, it's a fast-growing, greedy plant that's difficult to garden under or around. Generous watering and fertilizing will speed growth and keep treetop dense. Grows best in part shade in hot summer areas. Full sun elsewhere. Few pests. A fungus may cause reddish brown spots on leaves. Use combination fungicide-insecticide-miticide to prevent further damage.

Stands heavy shearing, but at expense of considerable mutilation of leaves; best pruned not by shearing but one cut at a time, cutting overlong twigs just above a leaf. Maintenance of hedge a problem because of fast growth. Best used as tree or tall unclipped screen. A dwarf form of *P. laurocerasus* is sold. It is more compact, grows to 4-6 ft. Leaves are smaller. Can be sheared as hedge.

P. l. 'Schipkaensis'. SCHIPKA LAUREL. Zones 2-9, 14-17. Smaller plant than species, with narrow leaves 2-4½ in. long.

P. l. 'Zabeliana'. ZABEL LAUREL. Zones 3-9, 14-21. This narrow-leafed variety has branches which angle upward and outward from base. To 4 ft. high with equal or greater spread. More tolerant of full sun than English laurel. Use as a low screen, divider, or big foundation plant. With branches pegged down it makes an effective bank cover. Can be espaliered. Planted in a narrow strip between house and walk, half the branches will lie on the ground and the rest will fan up the wall.

P. lusitanica. PORTUGAL LAUREL. Evergreen shrub or tree. Zones 4-9, 14-24. Native to Portugal and Spain. Slower growing than English laurel. Becomes densely branched large shrub 10-20 ft. high or many-trunked spreading tree to 30 ft. or more; trained to a single trunk, it is used as a formal street tree. Dense branching habit and attractive dark green foliage make it a useful background plant. Leaves glossy dark green, to 5 in. long. Small creamy white flowers in 5-10-in. spikes extend beyond the leaves in spring and early summer, followed by long clusters of bright red to dark purple, ⅓-in. fruits. Takes heat, sun, and wind better than English laurel.

P. l. azorica. Native to the Azores and the Canary Islands where it grows 60-70 ft. high. Here, it grows into a gigantic columnar bush 20 ft. high and half as wide. Exceptionally dark green and glossy foliage.

P. lyonii *(P. integrifolia, P. ilicifolia integrifolia)*. CATALINA CHERRY. Evergreen shrub or tree. Zones 7-9, 12-24. Native to Channel Islands off southern California. Seen as broad, dense shrub in hedges and screens, clipped and informal. Trained as a tree it will reach 45 ft. in height with a spread of over 30 ft. and a trunk 6-8 in. in diameter. Leaves 3-5 in. long, dark green, smooth-margined or faintly toothed. (Leaves of young plants are more definitely toothed and usually are similar to the hollyleaf cherry.) Creamy white flowers in spikes 4-6 in. long are borne in profusion in April and May. Fruits, ¾-1-in. black cherries, ripen August-September. Fruit sweet but insipid, large stoned.

When used as a patio tree or street tree over sidewalks, the fruit litter is objectionable. As a garden tree it is easy to live with—not particular as to soil, water, or exposure and seldom troubled with diseases or pests. May be attacked by whitefly. Spray with all-purpose insecticide three times at weekly intervals, or use systemic insecticide. Valuable as a tall screen or hedge. Can be held to any height desired by pruning. Rates high in resistance to oak root fungus *(Armillaria)*.

FLOWERING FRUITS

Flowering Cherry. The several species and many varieties commonly called flowering cherries are described in the accompanying chart. They perform best in Zones 4-6, 15-17. Their cultural requirements are identical. They require a fast-draining well-aerated soil. If your soil is heavy clay, plant in raised beds. Do as little pruning as possible. Cut while the tree is in bloom and use the branches in arrangements. Remove awkward or crossing branches. Pinch back an occasional overly-ambitious shoot to force branching.

Pests and diseases are not usually a problem. Infestations of the tadpole-shaped slug and a yellowish to greenish caterpillar may skeletonize the leaves unless sprayed with an insecticide. If a branch or two dies back, treat the tree for cherry dead-bud like this: Prune out the affected areas, spray with a fungicide containing mercury or copper in November or December and again in February and several times during the spring and growing season.

Use the flowering cherries as their growth habit indicates. All are good trees to garden under. The large spreading kinds make good shade trees. The smaller cherries are almost a necessity in Oriental gardens.

Flowering Nectarine. There is but one flowering nectarine: 'Alma Stultz'. Fast growing to 20 ft. and as wide as high. In early spring it covers itself with large, 2-2½-in.-wide, waxy-petaled flowers that look somewhat like azalea blossoms. They are rosy white shaded pink, and the color deepens with age. Deliciously fragrant. The white-fleshed fruit is sparsely produced. Treat it as you would a flowering peach.

Flowering Peach. The flowering peach is identical to the fruiting peach in growth habit and height. But it's more widely adapted than fruiting peaches—the flowering peaches can be grown in Zones 2-24. However, they may be caught by late frosts in Zones 2, 10, 11, and suffer from delayed foliation in 13, 23, 24. Heavy pruning necessary for good show of flowers. Cut branches back to 6-in. stubs at flowering time. Many-branched new growth will be luxuriant by summer's end and it will flower profusely the following spring. Cultural requirements, insect and disease control are the same as for fruiting peaches. Use flowering peaches as giant seasonal bouquets. Place them where they will give maximum effect when in bloom and where they will be fairly unobtrusive out of bloom—behind evergreen shrubs, fence or wall.

Some peach varieties produce showy blossoms and good fruit. These are described in this encyclopedia under Peaches and Nectarines. The following varieties are strictly "flowering" in the sense that their blooms are showy and their fruit is either absent or worthless.

'Burbank'. Double pink. Late.
'Camelliaeflora'. Double red. Late.
'Double White'. Midseason.
'Early Double Pink'. Very early.
'Early Double Red'. Deep purplish red or rose red. Very early and brilliant, but color likely to clash with other pinks or red.
'Helen Borchers'. Clear pink, 2½-in.-wide flowers. Early.
'Icicle'. Double white flowers. Late.

P

*Climate
Zone maps
pages 8-27*

FLOWERING CHERRY

NAME	ZONES	FORM	HEIGHT & SPREAD	FLOWERS & SEASON
P. avium 'Plena' DOUBLE-FLOWERED MAZZARD CHERRY	1-11, 14-17	A double flowering form of sweet cherry, and identical in form, foliage.	To 30 ft.; nearly 25 ft. wide.	Double, pure white, roselike, in clusters. Midseason.
P. campanulata TAIWAN FLOWERING CHERRY	7-9, 14-23	Graceful, densely branched, bushy, upright, slender small tree. Performs well in California climates where other flowering cherries fail.	To 20-25 ft.; not as wide as high.	Single, bell-shaped, drooping, in clusters of 2-5. Strong positive color —an electric rose, almost a neon purple-pink. Blooms early, along with flowering peach.
P. jacquemontii	7-9, 14-23	A very fast-growing, bushy, rounded shrub in California. Straggly in colder climates.	To 10 ft. or more and almost as wide.	Single, rose pink, usually in pairs. Blooms in Feb.-Mar. Small 1/2-in. red fruit in May-June.
P. sargentii SARGENT CHERRY	1-7, 14-17	Upright spreading branches form rounded crown. Orange-red fall foliage.	To 40-50 ft. and more, not as wide as high.	Single blush pink flowers in clusters of 2-4. Midseason.
P. serrula BIRCH BARK CHERRY	1-7, 14-16	Valued for beauty of its bark—a glossy mahogany red color.	To 30 ft. and as wide.	Small white flowers are almost hidden by new leaves. Midseason.
P. serrulata JAPANESE FLOWERING CHERRY	2-7, 14-20	The species is known through its many cultivated varieties. The best of these are:		
'Amanogawa'		Columnar tree. Use as a small Lombardy poplar.	To 20-25 ft. tall, 8 ft. wide.	Semi-double, light pink with deep pink margins. Early midseason.
'Beni Hoshi' ('Pink Star')		Fast grower with arching, spreading branches; umbrella-shaped in outline.	To 20-25 ft. high and as wide.	Vivid pink single flower with long, slightly twisted petals hang below the branches. Midseason.
'Fugenzo' ('Kofugen', 'James H. Veitch')		Broad spreading, flat-topped.	To 20-25 ft. and as wide.	Large double pink, appear with the new coppery pink leaves. Late.
'Kwanzan' See 'Sekiyama'				
'Ojochin'		Up-sweeping, rather stiff branches, compact growth.	To 25-30 ft. and as wide.	Single, pink buds open white or white flushed pink. Midseason.
'Sekiyama' ('Kwanzan')		Branches stiffly upright, form an inverted cone.	To 30 ft. high, 20 ft. wide.	Large, double, deep rosy pink in pendant clusters displayed with red young leaves. Midseason.
'Shirofugen'		Wide horizontal branching	To 25 ft., and as wide.	Double, long-stalked, pink, fading to white. Latest to bloom.
'Shirotae' ('Mt. Fuji')		Strong horizontal branching	To 20 ft., wider than high.	Double and semi-double, pink in bud, white when fully open, purplish pink as flower ages. Early.
'Shogetsu'		Spreading growth, arching branches.	To 15 ft., wider than high.	Semi-double and very double, pale pink, often with white centers. Late.
'Sieboldii' ('Takasago')		Low, rounded head. Slow growth.	To 12-15 ft.	Large, semi-double, pale pink. Midseason.
'Tai-Haku'		Vigorous, upright, spreading. Leaves are large, to 7 in. long.	To 25 ft., and as wide.	Single white flowers in clusters of 2-3 show in striking contrast with copper red young foliage. Midseason.
'Tanko Shinju' (Sometimes sold as 'Pink Pearl')		Upright-spreading and branching from near the base of the trunk.	To 25 ft., and as wide.	Double soft pink in center shading deep pink toward edges. Early.
'Ukon'		Open sparse growth. Pinch branch tips in young plants to induce denser branching. Orange-red autumn color.	To 30 ft., and as wide.	Large semi-double greenish-yellow. Midseason.

NAME	ZONES	FORM	HEIGHT & SPREAD	FLOWERS & SEASON
P. subhirtella autumnalis	2-7, 14-20	Loose branching, bushy with round flattened crown.	To 25-30 ft., and as wide.	Double, white or pinkish white in autumn as well as early spring. Often in warm spells in January and February.
P. s. 'Hally Jolivette'		Small bushy, upright.	To 8 ft., 6 ft. wide.	Double white flowers; pink buds. Early.
P. s. pendula SINGLE WEEPING CHERRY		Usually sold grafted at 5-6 ft. high on an upright-growing understock. Graceful branches hang down, often to the ground.	Slow to 10-12 ft., and as wide.	Single small pale pink in profusion. Midseason.
P. s. 'Rosea' ('Beni Higan')		Bushy, wide spreading.	To 20-25 ft., and as wide.	Single pale pink, in great profusion. Early.
P. s. 'Whitcombi'	2-6	Wide spreading, horizontal branching.	To 20 ft., spreading 30 ft.	Buds, almost red, open to rosy pink, single flowers. Very early.
P. s. 'Yae-shidare-higan' DOUBLE WEEPING CHERRY		Same as *P. s. pendula*.	Same as *P. s. pendula*.	Double rose pink. Midseason.
P. yedoensis YOSHINO FLOWERING CHERRY	2-7, 14-20	Curving branches, graceful, open pattern.	Fast to 40 ft., with 30 ft. width.	Single, light pink to nearly white, fragrant. Early.
'Akebono' (Sometimes called 'Daybreak')		Variety is smaller than species.	To 25 ft., and as wide.	Flowers pinker than *P. yedoensis*.

P

Climate Zone maps pages 8-27

FLOWERING PLUM

NAME	ZONE	GROWTH HABIT	LEAF, FLOWER, FRUIT
P. blireiana Hybrid between P. cerasifera 'Atropurpurea' and P. mume	2-12, 14-20	Graceful, branches long and slender, to 25 ft, high, 20 ft. wide.	Leaves reddish purple, turning greenish bronze in summer. Flowers semi-double, fragrant, pink to rose. February-April. Fruit none or very few.
P. cerasifera CHERRY PLUM, MYROBALAN	2-20	Used as rootstock for various stone fruits. Will grow to 30 ft. and as wide.	Leaves dark green. Flowers pure white. $3/4$-1 in. wide. Small red plums 1-1$1/4$ in. thick. Seeds itself freely.
P. c. 'Atropurpurea' (P. 'Pissardii') PURPLE-LEAF PLUM	2-20	Fast growing to 25-30 ft. high, rounded in form.	New leaves copper red, deepening to dark purple, gradually becoming greenish bronze in late summer. White flowers. Sets heavy crop of small red plums.
'Hollywood' Hybrid between P. c. 'Atropurpurea' and Japanese plum 'Duarte'	7-20	Upright grower to 30-40 ft., 25 ft. wide.	Leaves dark green above, red beneath. Flowers, light pink to white. February-March. Good quality red plums 2-2$1/2$ in. in diameter.
'Krauter Vesuvius'	2-20	Smaller growing than *P. c.* 'Atropurpurea', to 18 ft. high, 12 ft. wide.	Darkest of the flowering plums. Leaves purple-black. Flowers light pink. February-March. Fruits none or few.
'Newport'	2-20	To 25 ft. high, 20 ft. wide.	Purplish red leaves. Single pink flowers. Will bear a few fruits.
'Thundercloud'	2-20	More rounded form than *P.c.*'Atropurpurea' to 20 ft. high, 20 ft. wide.	Dark coppery leaves. Flowers light pink to white. Sometimes sets good crop of red fruits.
P. cistena DWARF RED-LEAF PLUM	2-12, 14-20	Dainty, many-branched shrub to 6-10 ft. Can be trained as single stemmed tree.	Purple-leafed, white to pinkish flowers in early spring. Fruit blackish purple in July.

P

Climate Zone maps pages 8-27

'Late Double Red'. Later by 3-4 weeks than 'Early Double Red'.

'Peppermint Stick'. Flowers striped red and white; may also bear all-white and all-red flowers on same branch. Midseason.

'Royal Red Leaf'. Foliage red, deepening to maroon. Deep pink flowers. This might be classed as flowering-fruiting as it bears red, white-fleshed, edible fruit. Late.

'Weeping Double Pink'. Smaller than other flowering peaches, with weeping branches. Requires careful staking and tying to develop a main stem of suitable height. Midseason.

'Weeping Double Red'. Similar to above, but with deep rose red flowers. Midseason.

Flowering Plum. The many species and varieties of flowering plums are grouped in chart form.

Flowering plums will grow in almost any soil. If soil is wet for long periods, plant 6-12 in. above grade level in raised bed. Expect attacks from aphids, slugs, caterpillars, spider mites. Spray with an all-purpose fruit tree spray. Check trunk at and just below ground level for peach tree borers. Spray with sevin or diazinon (see Peach).

One of the most adaptable and choicest medium-sized flowering trees for lawn, patio, terrace, or small street tree is *P. blireiana*. It also does well in planters and large tubs. In choosing a plum to be planted in a paved area check its fruiting habits. When a flowering plum is planted in a patio, prune to establish a head at a height to walk under. As the tree develops, prune out crossing and inward-growing branches.

P. glandulosa. DWARF FLOWERING ALMOND. Deciduous shrub. Zones 1-10, 14-19. Native to Japan, China. Much-branched, upright, spreading growth to 6 ft. tall. Flowers, set close to the slender branches, appear early, before the leaves, and turn the branches into long wands of blossoms. In the species, seldom seen in gardens, flowers are single, pink, or white, and only ½ in. wide. Flowers of the commonly available varieties are double, 1-1¼ in. across, resembling light fluffy pompon chrysanthemums. Variety 'Albiplena' has double white flowers; 'Sinensis' has double pink flowers. Prune back hard, either just after blooming, or when in bloom, using the cut wands for arrangements.

P. mume. JAPANESE FLOWERING APRICOT, JAPANESE FLOWERING PLUM. Deciduous tree. Zones 2-9, 12-22. (Blooms may be frosted in Zones 2, 3.) Neither a true apricot nor plum. Considered the longest lived of flowering fruit trees, it eventually develops into a gnarled, picturesque 20-ft. tree. Flowers are small, profuse, with a clean, spicy fragrance. January-February in mild areas, February-March in cold-winter areas. Fruit is small, inedible. Prune heavily. Let tree grow for a year, then prune back all shoots to 6-in. stubs. Next year cut back half the young growth to 6-in. stubs; cut back the other half the following year, and continue the routine in succeeding years.

The varieties are:

'Bonita'. Double crimson flowers. Earliest to bloom.

'Dawn'. Large ruffled double pink.

'Peggy Clarke'. Double deep rose flowers with extremely long stamens and a red calyx.

'Rosemary Clarke'. Double white flowers with red calyx. Very early.

P. triloba. FLOWERING ALMOND. A small tree or treelike large shrub. Zones 1-11, 14-17. One of several plants known as "flowering almond". Slow growth to 15 ft., usually 8-10 ft. with equal spread. Rather broad 1-2½-in.-long leaves and double pink flowers about 1 in. wide in very early spring. Useful where a quite hardy small flowering plant of definite tree form is needed.

PSEUDOLARIX. See Chrysolarix

PSEUDOPANAX. Evergreen shrubs or trees. Slow growing. Leaves of *P. crassifolium*, *P. ferox* highly variable; young plants have long, narrow, spiny-toothed leaves; mature plants have divided or undivided leaves of no very remarkable shape. Young plants odd and decorative.

P. crassifolium. LANCE WOOD. Zones 16, 17, 21-24. In time, a 50-ft. tree. Usually seen as a single-stem plant 3-5 ft. tall with rigid, drooping leaves to 3 ft. long, less than 1 in. wide, strongly toothed, reddish bronzy in color. Upright growth habit—good choice for narrow areas.

P. ferox. Zones 16, 17, 21-24. Eventually a 20-ft. tree. Young plants with leaves 12-18 in. long, 1 in. wide, strongly toothed.

P. lessonii. Zones 17, 20-24. Moderate growth to 12-20 ft. tall. In open ground an effective multiple stemmed tree. Leaves dark green, leathery, divided into 3-5 leaflets 1-3 in. long. July-August flowers inconspicuous. Sun or deep shade; withstands wind. Excellent container plants; confining roots keeps plants shrubby.

PSEUDOSASA. See Bamboo

PSEUDOTSUGA. Conifers. The two species are quite similar but there's a great difference in status—the first is little known and the second is the most prominent tree in the Pacific Northwest.

P. macrocarpa. BIGCONE SPRUCE. Zones 1 (southerly parts), 10, 11, 18, 19. Native to southern California. Grows to about 60 ft. tall. Needles similar to *P. menziesii*. Has much larger cones—4-7½ in. long, 2-3 in. wide; the 3-pronged bracts on cones barely protrude from each scale.

P. menziesii (*P. taxifolia*). DOUGLAS FIR. Zones 1-10, 14-17. Since the pioneer days, Northwesterners have been gardening under and near this magnificent native tree. Its entire range includes not only western Oregon and Washington but also extends east to the Rocky Mountains, north to Alaska, and south into many forested parts of northern California.

Sharply pyramidal form when young; widely grown and cherished as a Christmas tree. Grows 70-250 ft. in forests. Densely-set, soft needles, dark green or blue-green, 1-1½ in. long, radiate out in all directions from branches and twigs. Sweet fragrance when crushed. Ends of branches swing up. Pointed wine red buds form at branch tips in winter. These open in spring to apple green tassels of new growth that add considerably to the tree's beauty. Reddish brown cones are oval, about 3 in. long, and have obvious 3-pronged bracts. Unlike the upright cone of the true firs (*Abies*), these hang down.

Best suited to its native areas or to areas with similar summer-winter climates. Will grow in any except undrained, swampy soils. Does well in sun or considerable

shade, and can take wind. Environment influences its appearance: where summers are dry, it is dense with shorter spaces between branches; where there is much moisture or too much shade, it tends to look awkward, thin, and gawky, especially as a young tree. As a garden tree, its height is difficult to control; you can't keep it down without butchering it. Yet it serves well as a 10-12 ft. clipped hedge—plant young trees 2 ft. apart and keep them topped and trimmed.

P. m. glauca. The common form in the Rocky Mountains. Usually has more bluish green needles.

PSIDIUM. GUAVA. Evergreen shrubs or small trees. White flowers (composed principally of a brush of stamens). Berrylike fruit, good in jellies, pastes. Best in rich soils, but adaptable, taking some drought when established.

P. cattleianum. STRAWBERRY GUAVA. Zones 9, 14-24. Moderate, open growth to 8-10 ft. as shrub; can be trained as a multiple trunk. 15-ft. tree. Especially beautiful bark and trunk—greenish gray to golden brown. Leaves glossy, golden green, to 3 in. long; new growth bronze. Dark red fruit in fall and winter, to 1½ in. long (if thinned). White flesh is sweet-tart, rather

Dark red fruits of strawberry guava are 1½ in. across. Glossy golden green leaves.

resinous in taste. Variety 'Lucidum' has yellow fruits, denser growth. Good informal hedge or screen. Excellent in containers; fine bonsai subject.

P. guajava. GUAVA. Zones 23, 24. Taller than strawberry guava, with strongly-veined leaves to 6 in. long. Semi-deciduous briefly in spring; new leaves an attractive salmon color. Fruits 1-3 in. across; white, pink, or yellow flesh, musky and mildly acid.

PTERIDIUM aquilinum. BRACKEN. Fern. All Zones. Worldwide native. The variety *pubescens* is native to the West. Fronds coarse, much divided, rising directly from deep, running rootstocks. Occurs wild in many places and can be tolerated in untamed gardens, but beware of planting it: the deep rootstocks can make it a tough, invasive weed.

PTERIS. BRAKE. Ferns. Mostly small ferns of subtropical or tropical origin, and mostly used in dish gardens or small pots; some are big enough for landscape use.

P. cretica. Zones 17, 23, 24. To 1½ ft. tall with comparatively few, long, narrow leaflets. Numerous varieties exist: some have forked or crested fronds, some are variegated. Variety 'Wimsetti' a light green form with forked tips on mature plants is so dense and frilly that it doesn't look like a fern.

P. 'Ouvrardii'. Zones 17, 22-24. Dark green 12-30-in.-tall fronds have extremely long, narrow, ribbonlike divisions. Splendid massed or grouped with azaleas, camellias.

P. quadriaurita 'Argyraea'. SILVER FERN. Zone 24. From India. Fronds 2-4 ft. tall, rather coarsely divided, heavily marked white. Showy, but the white markings seem out of place on ferns. Protect from frost and snails.

P. tremula. AUSTRALIAN BRAKE. Zones 16, 17, 22-24. Extremely graceful 2-4-ft. fronds on slender, upright stalks. Good landscape fern, with excellent silhouette. Fast growing, but tends to be short-lived.

PTEROCARYA stenoptera. CHINESE WING-NUT. Deciduous tree. Zones 5-24. Fast to 40-90 ft., with heavy, wide-spreading limbs. Shows its kinship to walnuts clearly in its leaves, 8-16 in. long and divided into 11-23 finely toothed, oval leaflets. Foot-long clusters of small, one-seeded, winged nuts hang from branches. A good looking tree, but with only one real virtue: It succeeds well in compacted, poorly aerated soil in play yards and other high-traffic areas. Aggressive roots make it unsuitable in lawn and garden.

PTEROSTYRAX hispida. EPAULETTE TREE. Deciduous tree. Zones 5-10, 14-21. Possibly to 40 ft., but more usually held to 15-20 ft. with 10 ft. spread. Trunk single or branched, branches open, spreading at the top. Light green leaves, gray-green beneath, 3-8 in. long, rather coarse. Creamy white, fringy, lightly fragrant flowers in drooping clusters 4-9 in. long, 2-3 in. wide. Blooms in early summer. Gray, furry, small fruits in pendant clusters hang on well into winter, are attractive on bare branches.

Sunny location in well drained soil. Prune to control shape, density. Best planted where you can look up into it—on bank beside path, above a bench, or in raised planting bed. Choice at edge of a woodland or as a focal point in a large shrub border.

PTYCHOSPERMA macarthuri (*Actinophloeus macarthuri*). Zones 23, 24. Native to New Guinea. Feather palm with several clustered, smooth green stems 10-15 ft.

The slender, clustered smooth green stems of Ptychosperma grow to 10-15 ft.

high. Soft green leaflets with jagged ends. Requires part shade in frost-free coastal locations.

PULMONARIA. LUNGWORT. Perennials. Zones 1-9, 14-17. Long-stalked leaves mostly in basal clumps, with few on the flower-bearing stalks. Flowers funnel-shaped, blue or purplish, in drooping clusters from April-June. Will grow in shade that discourages most flowering plants. Use with ferns, azaleas, rhododendrons; good under early spring-flowering trees, with blue scillas, pink tulips. Creeping roots. Needs moist, porous soil.

P. angustifolia. COWSLIP LUNGWORT. Tufts of narrowish, dark green leaves. Flowers dark blue, in clusters on 6-12-in. stems. Blooms in spring at same time as primroses. Divide in fall after leaves die down.

P. saccharata. BETHLEHEM SAGE. Grows to 1½ ft., spreads to 2 ft. White-spotted, roundish, evergreen leaves. Flowers reddish violet or white. Variety 'Maculata' is offered; it has pink buds, blue flowers.

PUMPKIN. Here's how to grow jumbo-sized pumpkins for Halloween. Varieties that grow to 30-40 in. across are 'Big Tom' (or 'Connecticut Field'), 'Jack O'Lantern', and 'Big Max'. Plant seeds in mid-May or early June. Choose a sunny location. Allow vine area of 8-12 sq. ft. in diameter. After soil is cultivated, scoop a hole 4 in. deep right under where you will plant the seeds. Put a shovelful of manure in the hole and cover it with enough soil to make ground level again.

Plant 6-8 seeds, 1 in. deep, within a circle 6 in. in diameter. If you want more than one set of vines, plant such circles 8 ft. apart. Water seeds after planting. When plants are 4-6 in. high, cut off tops of all but the two best plants in the circle. Water when you see signs of slightest wilting. Try not to wet foliage. When small pumpkins are tennis-ball size, remove all but 3 or 4 on each vine (for extra large pumpkins, remove all but one). Remove fruits towards ends of vines; save those near the main stem. Continue removing later flowers. In late summer, slide a wooden shingle under pumpkins to protect from wet soil (not necessary if soil is sandy).

PUNICA granatum. POMEGRANATE. Deciduous tree or shrub. Zones 7-24; also Zones 5 and 6 if used against a south or west wall. Showy flowers. Some varieties yield pomegranates. Narrow, glossy, bright green to golden green leaves, bronzy new growth, brilliant yellow fall color except in Zone 24. All varieties tolerate great heat and will live and grow well in alkaline soil that would kill most plants. Need sun for best bloom and fruit. When established, non-fruiting varieties need little water, but will take a lot if drainage is good.

'Albo-plena'. Shrubby, 6-10 ft. tall. Flowers double, creamy white or yellowish from a yellow, waxy calyx, June-August. New growth bright green. No fruit.

'Chico'. DWARF CARNATION-FLOWERED POMEGRANATE. Compact bush can be kept to 18 in. tall if pruned occasionally. Double orange-red flowers over a long season. No fruit. Excellent under low windows, in containers, as edging.

'Double Red'. Arching shrub to 12 ft. high with double orange-red flowers, no fruit.

'Legrelle' ('Mme. Legrelle'). Dense 6-8 ft. shrub with double creamy flowers heavily striped coral red. No fruit.

'Nana'. DWARF POMEGRANATE. Dense shrub to 3 ft., nearly evergreen in mild winters. Blooms when a foot tall or less. Orange-red single flowers followed by small, dry, red fruits. Excellent garden or container plant; effective bonsai.

'Sweet'. A fruiting pomegranate with very sweet fruit, much less acid than 'Wonderful'.

'Wonderful'. Best known fruiting pomegranate. Grow it as a 10-ft. fountain-shaped shrub, a tree, or an espalier. Burnished red fruits in autumn follow orange-red, single flowers up to 4 in. across. Will not fruit in cool coastal areas. Drought followed by flooding will cause fruit to split. Water deeply and regularly if fruit is important.

PURPLE HEART. See Setcreasea

PURSLANE TREE. See Portulacaria afra

PUSCHKINIA scilloides. Bulb. All Zones. Closely related to *Scilla* and *Chionodoxa*. Flowers bell-like, pale blue or whitish with darker, greenish blue stripe on each segment, in spikelike clusters on 3-6-in. stems. Leaves broad, strap-shaped, upright, bright green, a little shorter than flower stems. Plant bulbs 3 in. deep, 3 in. apart in fall. Will grow for years without disturbance. Best in cold climates. *P. s. libanotica*, a more vigorous plant, is the variety usually sold. *P. s. 'Alba'* has white flowers.

PUYA alpestris. Evergreen perennial. Zones 9, 13-17, 19-24. Native to Chile. A big, spectacular flowering plant. Massive flower clusters, resembling giant asparagus stalks as they develop, grow from a crowded clump of 2-ft.-long, 1-in.-wide swordlike leaves, gray-green, with sharp spines on edges and sharp tips. Flower cluster, including stalk, gets 4-6 ft. high. Bloom late April to early June. Cluster contains 2-in. bell-shaped flowers, metallic blue-green and steely turquoise, accented with vivid orange anthers. Stiff, spiky branchlet ends protrude from cluster.

Use in rock gardens, on banks, or in large containers. Good with cactus, succulents, aloes. Full sun. Soil can be poor. Water requirement same as for cactus, yuccas.

PYRACANTHA. FIRETHORN. Evergreen shrubs. Grown widely for bright fruits, evergreen foliage, variety of landscape uses, and easy culture. All grow fast and vigorously with habit from upright to sprawling; nearly all have thorns. All have glossy green leaves, generally oval or rounded at the ends, ½-1 in. wide and 1-4 in. long. All bear flowers and fruit on spurs along wood of the last year's growth. The clustered flowers are small, fragrant, dull creamy white, effective because numerous.

Fruits vary in color, size, season, and duration. Some color in late summer; others color late and hang on until birds, storms, or decay clear them out in late winter. Plants need full sun and do best where soil is not constantly wet; keep them away from lawn sprinklers. Control size and form by

P

Climate Zone maps pages 8-27

Climate
Zone maps
pages 8-27

pinching young growth or by shortening long branches just before growth starts. Cut out branches that have berried back to a well-placed side shoot. Subject to fireblight, aphids, woolly aphids, scale, and red spider mites.

Use as espaliers on wall or fence, as barrier plantings, screens, rough hedgerows or barriers along roads. Can be trained as standards; often clipped into hedges or topiary shapes (which spoils their rugged informality and often their fruit crop). Low growing kinds are good ground covers.

P. coccinea. All Zones except coldest parts of Zone 1. Rounded bush to 8-10 ft. (20 ft. trained against a wall). Flowers March-April; red-orange berries in October, November. Best known for its varieties 'Government Red' (red berries), 'Kasan' (red-orange, long-lasting berries), 'Lalandei' and 'Lalandei Monrovia' (orange berries), 'Pauciflora' (low and compact, with looser fruit clusters), and 'Wyatii' (orange-red berries coloring early). Best species for cold-winter areas. 'Lalandei' is hardiest of all.

P. 'Duvalii'. Zones 4-24. Large, bright red berries in very dense clusters. Good espalier. Tightly clustered fruits sometimes mold in wet autumns.

P. fortuneana (*P. crenato-serrata, P. yunnanensis*). Zones 4-24. Spreading growth to 15 ft. tall, 10 ft. wide. Limber branches make it a good espalier plant. Berries orange to coral, lasting through winter. Variety 'Graberi' has huge clusters of dark red fruits that color in mid-fall, last through winter; growth more upright than species.

P. koidzumii (*P. formosana*). Zones 4-24. Big, upright shrub to 10 ft. tall, 8 ft. wide. Large scarlet fruits in big clusters. Many pyracanthas of mixed parentage are sold as *P. koidzumii* varieties.

P. 'Lodense'. Zones 4-24. Low, dense, compact pyracantha with small, closely set leaves, sparse crops of orange-red fruit hidden by leaves. Edgings, low barriers.

P. 'Rosedale'. Zones 4-24. Upright growth with supple branches well adapted to espalier work. Bright red fruit is earliest to color, hangs late, is well distributed along branches.

P. 'Santa Cruz' (*P.* 'Santa Cruz Prostrata'). Zones 4-24. Low growing, branching from base, spreading. Easily kept below 3 ft. by pinching out an occasional upright branch. Red fruit. Plant 4-5 ft. apart for ground, bank cover.

P. 'Stribling'. Zones 4-24. Tall, upright to 15 ft., with pendulous branches. Red berries.

P. 'Tiny Tim'. Zones 4-24. Compact plant to 3 ft. tall. Small leaves, few or no thorns. Berries red. Prune once a year when fruit begins to color, shortening any runaway vertical shoots. Informal low hedge, barrier, tub plant.

P. 'Victory'. Zones 4-24. To 10 ft. tall, 8 ft. wide. Dark red fruits color late and hold on well.

P. 'Walderi' (*P.* 'Walderi Prostrata'). Zones 4-24. Low-growing, wide-spreading ground cover plant with red berries. Plant 4-5 ft. apart for fast cover.

PYRETHRUM. See Chrysanthemum coccineum

PYROSTEGIA venusta (*P. ignea, Bignonia venusta*). FLAME VINE. Evergreen vine. Zones 13, 16, 21-24. Fast to 20 ft. or more, climbing by tendrils. Leaves with oval, 2-3-in. leaflets. Orange, tubular flowers 3 in. long in clusters of 15-20 are an impressive sight during fall, early winter. Any soil. Will take some shade, but best in full sun. Thrives in low desert and other hot climates; outstanding against a west wall.

PYRROSIA lingua. (Usually sold as *Cyclophorus lingua.*) JAPANESE FELT FERN. Zones 16, 17, 19-24. Dark green, broad, undivided, lance-shaped fronds with feltlike texture from creeping rootstocks. Fronds to 15 in.

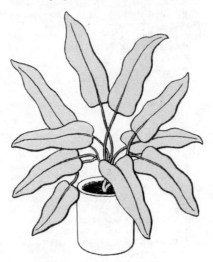

Unconventional fronds of Japanese felt fern have feltlike texture, are 15 in. long.

tall, densely clustered. Most often used in baskets, but makes a choice ground cover for small areas. Slow grower.

PYRUS. ORNAMENTAL PEAR. Deciduous or evergreen trees. The commercial fruiting pear is described under Pear. Following are the ornamental species. Most of these are subject to fireblight (see under Pear).

P. calleryana. Deciduous tree. Zones 2-9, 14-21. Grows to 15-25 ft. Strong horizontal branching pattern. Leaves 1½-3 in. long, broadly oval, scalloped, dark green, very glossy and leathery. Flowers clustered, pure white, ¾-1 in. broad; very early bloom. Fruit very small, round, inedible. Fairly resistant to fireblight.

Useful small shade tree with wine red to scarlet fall foliage. Variety 'Bradford', BRADFORD PEAR, grows to 50 ft., with a spread of 30 ft., has upsweeping branches, more erect form than species. Resists wind damage and grows well in most soils.

P. communis. See Pear

P. kawakamii. EVERGREEN PEAR. Evergreen shrub or tree. Zones 8, 9, 12-24. Partially deciduous in coldest winters in coldest zones. Branchlets drooping; leaves glossy, oval, pointed. Clustered white flowers appear in sheets and masses in winter-early spring. Fruit seldom seen, small, inedible.

Without support evergreen pear becomes a broad, sprawling shrub or in time a multi-trunked small tree. With willowy young branches fastened to fence or frame, it makes a good-looking espalier. To make a

tree of it, stake one or several branches, shorten side growth, and keep staked until trunk is self-supporting. Beef up framework branches by shortening (when young) to upward-facing buds or branchlets. Established, well-shaped plants need little pruning or shaping. Heavily pruned evergreen pears, such as those espaliered on small frames, seldom flower.

Tolerant of many soils, easy to grow wherever it doesn't freeze. Spray for aphids and watch for fireblight, which can disfigure or destroy plants.

P. pyrifolia. SAND PEAR, JAPANESE SAND PEAR. Deciduous tree. Zones 1-9, 14-21. Like common pear in appearance, but has glossier, more leathery leaves which turn brilliant reddish purple in fall. Fruit small, woody, gritty. Improved forms of this tree, *P. p. culta*, are grown for their fruit by the Japanese. The fruit is roundish, firm-fleshed, sweet, and gritty. One variety called 'Nihon Nashi' has been sold in California. Sand pears are resistant to fireblight and have been used in breeding this quality into common pear. 'Kieffer', 'Douglas', and 'Le Conte' have sand pear blood.

QUAIL BUSH. See Atriplex lentiformis

QUAKING GRASS. See Briza

QUAMOCLIT. Annual or perennial vines. Related to morning glories and like them, fast-twining vines. The clustered flowers in summer are bright red, orange, or white. Grow them on supports or trellises for filtered shade. Sow in spring after notching hard seed coat with a knife or soaking seeds in warm water until they swell.

Q. lobata (*Mina lobata*). SPANISH FLAG. Perennial. Zones 20-24. Can be grown as annual in colder areas. To 20 ft. tall. Leaves 3 in. across, heart-shaped at base, 3-lobed. Flowers orange-red, fading to yellow and white.

Q. pennata. CYPRESS VINE, CARDINAL CLIMBER. Annual vine twining to 20 ft. Leaves (2½-4 in. long) finely divided into slender threads. Flowers are 1½-in. tubes flaring at the mouth to a 5-lobed star. Usually scarlet, but white forms appear.

QUEENSLAND KAURI. See Agathis

QUEENSLAND NUT. See Macadamia

QUEENSLAND POPLAR. See Homalanthus

QUEENSLAND UMBRELLA TREE. See Brassaia

QUEEN'S TEARS. See Billbergia

QUEEN'S WREATH. See Antigonon

QUERCUS. OAK. Deciduous or evergreen trees. Western home owners acquire oak trees in either of two ways: For one, they (or a previous owner) either set out a nursery plant or plant an acorn (or a jay or squirrel plants an acorn for them). Or, they move into a place where a native oak tree remains from the days when the land was wild.

The method of acquisition is quite significant. An oak tree planted in a garden will grow vigorously and fast (1½-4 ft. a year). It will very likely not experience any unusual pest attacks or poor health—whether it's a Western native or not. The old wild trees, on the other hand, quite frequently cannot handle the surfeit of water and nutrients that they get in a garden and must be given special treatment.

Special treatment for existing native oaks. If possible, do not raise or lower grade level between the trunk and the drip line. If you must alter the grade, put a well around the base of the trunk so that grade level there is not changed. Never water within 4 ft. of the trunk or allow water to stand within that area. Any of a number of sucking and chewing insects, mites, and diseases can strike an existing native oak. It is definitely wise to contract with a commercial arborist or pest control firm to diagnose and spray or treat as necessary because of size of the tree (amateur equipment can seldom reach it), the complex chemicals that do the job best (seldom sold to consumers), and because high-pressure spraying is necessary for the material to act on many of the pests.

Oak root fungus *(Armillaria)* is a way of life in many California neighborhoods that once were oak forests. Get advice of an arborist on how to sustain infected trees. All old oaks, infected with the disease or not, can benefit from feeding and deep watering—fertilize and irrigate only out near drip line.

Old, existing, native oaks also benefit from periodic grooming to remove dead wood. Arborists should not cut thick branches unless they have good reasons for doing so. Excessive pruning may stimulate succulent new growth that will be subject to mildew.

How to plant an acorn. Select shiny, plump fallen acorns, free of worm holes. Remove the caps. Plant acorns on or just beneath soil surface and put up screen to protect from jays and squirrels. A surer way is to gather newly sprouted acorns or to sprout fresh ones between layers of damp peat moss (takes 2 weeks). Plant those with strong root sprouts. Make a crater deep enough so acorn can be just covered with soil. At bottom of crater poke a vertical hole to take sprouted tap root. Insert root and press soil around it. Water. Expect first leaves in 6-8 weeks. If you plant several acorns in one area you can thin later to the best seedling. After planting, water weekly (when there is no rain) the first 2 months, then monthly. Fertilize lightly once a month after leaves appear.

How to transplant an oak. It seems not to hurt an oak seedling of any size up to 5-8 ft. to have its vertical root cut in transplanting if the root ball is otherwise big and firm enough. The tree may wilt or lose leaves after a root-cutting transplant but if watered in well it should show new growth in 4-6 weeks. Oak seedlings from nursery containers never show spiralling of tap roots at bottom of containers. They form fibrous roots from the outset. Plant them just as any other tree from the nursery.

How to train a young oak. By nature, many young oaks grow twiggy. The growth is divided among so many twigs that none elongate fast. To promote fast vertical growth, pinch off the tips of unwanted small branches, meanwhile retaining all the leaf surface possible in order to sustain maximum growth.

Q. agrifolia. COAST LIVE OAK. Evergreen tree. Zones 7-9, 14-24. Native to California Coast Ranges. Round-headed, wide-spreading tree to 20-70 feet high, often with greater spread. Smooth, dark gray bark.

Dense foliage of rounded, hollylike, 1-3-in.-long leaves, slightly glossy on upper surface. As a planted tree from nursery or an acorn it can grow as high as 25 ft. in 10 years, 50 ft. in 25 years. Attractive green all year unless hit by oak moth larvae or other pests. Has greedy roots and drops almost all of its old leaves in early spring just when gardening time is most valuable. Regardless of these faults, it's a handsome and quite worthwhile shade tree or street tree.

Q. alba. WHITE OAK. Deciduous. All Zones. Native to eastern U.S. Grows to 70-90 ft. with broad open crown. Bright green 4-9-in., deeply lobed leaves turn reddish purple in fall. Interesting in winter with its gray bark and rugged framework.

Q. chrysolepis. CANYON LIVE OAK. Evergreen. Zones 5-9, 14-24. Native to mountain slopes and canyons of California, southern Oregon. Handsome round-headed or somewhat spreading tree to 20-60 ft., with smooth whitish bark. Oval, 1-2-in.-long leaves are shiny medium green above, grayish or whitish beneath. Leaf edges are smooth or toothed. Acorn cups covered with golden fuzz, look like turbans.

Q. coccinea. SCARLET OAK. Deciduous. All Zones. Native to eastern U.S. Moderate to rapid growth in deep, rich soil. Can reach 60-80 ft. High, light, open branching habit. Leaves bright green, to 6 in. long, with deeply cut, pointed lobes. Leaves turn bright scarlet in sharp autumn nights (Zones 1-11, 14, 15, 18-20); color less well where autumn is warm. Roots grow deep. Good street or lawn tree. Fine to garden under.

Q. douglasii. BLUE OAK. Deciduous. All Zones. Native to foothills around California's Central Valley. Low-branching, wide-spreading, to 50 ft. high. Finely textured light gray bark and decidedly bluish green leaves, shallowly lobed, oval, almost squarish. Good in dry, hot situations.

Q. engelmannii. MESA OAK. Evergreen. Zones 18-24. Native to southern California. Wide-spreading tree of character, to 60 ft. high. Leaves oval or oblong, 2 in. long, usually smooth-edged. In its area, has same cherished native status as coast live oak.

Q. garryana. OREGON WHITE OAK, GARRY OAK. Deciduous. Zones 4-6, 15-17. Native British Columbia south to Santa Cruz Mountains of California. Slow to moderate growth to 40-90 ft., with wide rounded crown, the branches often twisted. Bark grayish, scaly-checked. Leaves 3-6 in. long, with rounded lobes, leathery, dark glossy green above, rusty or downy on the lower surface. Casts moderate shade and has deep non-aggressive root system—good shelter for rhododendrons (but don't plant them within 4 ft. of tree's trunk).

Q. ilex. HOLLY OAK, HOLM OAK. Evergreen. Zones 4-24. Native to Mediterranean region. Moderate growth rate reaching 40-70 ft. high, equal spread. Leaves variable in shape and size, usually 1½-3 in. long, ½-1 in. wide, either toothed or smooth-edged, dark, rich green on upper surface, yellowish or silvery below.

Tolerates wind and salt air; will grow in constant sea wind, but tends to be shrubby there. Inland, growth rate can be moderately fast but this varies with soil and water conditions. Good evergreen street or lawn tree where pests and diseases make coast live oak difficult to maintain but it lacks open grace of coast live oak. Can take hard clipping into formal shapes or hedges.

Q. kelloggii. CALIFORNIA BLACK OAK. Deciduous. Zones 5 (inland portions), 6, 7, 15, 16. Native to mountains from southwestern Oregon to southern California. Moderate growth rate to 30-80 ft. Dark, furrowed, and checked bark. Handsome foliage; unfolding leaves are soft pink or dusty rose, becoming bright glossy green and turning yellow or yellow-orange in the fall. Leaves 4-10 in. long and 2½-6 in. wide, deeply lobed, the lobes ending in bristly points. Good moderate-sized tree for spring and fall color, winter trunk and branch pattern.

Q. lobata. VALLEY OAK, CALIFORNIA WHITE OAK. Deciduous. Zones 1-3, 6-16, 18-21. Native to interior valleys, Sierra foothills, and Coast Ranges away from direct coastal influence. California's mightiest oak, often reaching 70 ft. or more with equal or greater spread. Trunk and limbs massive, with thick, ashy-gray, distinctly checkered bark. Limbs often picturesquely twisted; outer branches long and drooping, sometimes sweeping the ground. Deeply-lobed leaves, the lobes rounded; 3-4 in. long, deep green above, paler beneath.

Tolerates high heat and moderate alkalinity in its native range. Best in deep soils where it can tap ground water—and in such situations it can grow fast (2½-3 ft. a year). A magnificent tree for shading a really big outdoor living area (debris makes its difficult for heavily-used paved areas). This is the tree that gives much of California's Central Valley its parklike look.

"Oak balls" which are lightweight, corky spheres about size of tennis balls, black and tan when they fall, result from insect activity, do not harm the tree.

Q. macrocarpa. BUR OAK, MOSSY CUP OAK. Deciduous. Zones 1-11, 14-24. Native to eastern U.S. Rugged looking, to 60-75 ft. high, 30 ft. wide. Leaves, glossy green above and whitish beneath, 8-10 in. long, broad at tip, tapered at base, deeply lobed. Large acorns form in a mossy cup. Similar

Oak leaves come in many sizes and forms. Most people consider lobed leaves typical.

Q

Climate
Zone maps
pages 8-27

to *Q. alba* but faster growing, more tolerant of adverse conditions.

Q. palustris. PIN OAK. Deciduous. All Zones. Native to eastern U.S. Moderate to fairly rapid growth to 50-80 ft. Slender and pyramidal form when young, open and round-headed at maturity. Brownish gray bark. Lower branches tend to droop almost to the ground; if the lowest whorl is cut away, the branches above will adopt the same habit. Only when fairly tall will it have good clearance beneath its lowest branches. Glossy, dark green leaves, deeply cut into bristle-pointed lobes; in brisk fall weather the leaves turn yellow, red, and finally russet brown. Many will hang on through winter.

Intolerant of drought. Develops chlorosis in alkaline soils; treat with iron chelate. Needs ample water and good drainage. Stake young trees and give only corrective pruning. Plant where its spread will not interfere with walks, drives, or street traffic, or trim it often. A fine tree for lawns.

Q. phellos. WILLOW OAK. Deciduous. Zones 1-4, 6-16, 18-21. Native to eastern U.S. To 50-90 ft., somewhat like pin oak in growth habit and spreading nature. Bark smooth, gray. Leaves unlike those of other common oaks, somewhat resemble willow leaves; 2½-5 in. long, ⅓-1 in. wide, smooth-edged, turning yellowish before falling. Of all oaks the most delicate in foliage pattern. Grown and used in the same way as pin oak.

Q. robur. ENGLISH OAK. Deciduous. Zones 2-21. To 90 ft. with rather short trunk and very wide, open head in maturity. Fairly fast growth. Leaves 3-4½ in. long, with 3 to 7 pairs of rounded lobes. Leaves hold until late in the fall and drop without much color change. The variety 'Fastigiata', UP-RIGHT ENGLISH OAK, is narrow and upright, like a Lombardy poplar when young; branches out to a broad, pyramidal shape when mature.

Q. rubra. (*Q. borealis*). RED OAK, NORTH-ERN RED OAK. Deciduous. All Zones. Fast growth to 90 ft. Broad, spreading branches and a round-topped crown. Leaves 5-8 in. long by 3-5 in. wide, with 3-7 pairs of sharp-pointed lobes. New leaves and leaf stalks are red in spring and turn to dark red, ruddy brown, or orange in the fall. Needs fertile soil and plenty of water. Stake young plants. High branching habit and reasonably open shade make it a good tree for big lawns, parks, broad avenues. Its deep roots make it a good tree to garden under.

Q. suber. CORK OAK. Evergreen. Zones 8-16, 18-23. Native to Mediterranean region. Moderate growth rate to 70-100 ft. high with equal spread. Trunk and principal limbs covered with thick, corky bark (the cork of commerce). The 3-in., toothed leaves are shining dark green above, gray beneath. The general effect is fine-textured. Needs good drainage; fairly tolerant of different soil types, but likely to yellow in alkaline soils. Established trees can take considerable drought.

A good garden shade tree with an interesting contrast between fairly light-textured foliage and massive, fissured trunk. Value as a street or park tree diminishes when small boys find out how easy it is to carve the bark.

Q. virginiana. SOUTHERN LIVE OAK. Evergreen, partly or wholly deciduous in cold-winter regions. Zones 4-24. Native to eastern U.S. Moderate to fast growth to an eventual 60 ft., with a broad, spreading, heavy-limbed crown twice as wide. Leaves 1½-5 in. long, smooth-edged, shining dark green above and whitish beneath. Thrives on ample water and does its best in deep, rich soil. In hot, interior climates, the most attractive of all evergreen oaks.

Q. wislizenii. INTERIOR LIVE OAK. Evergreen. Zones 7-9, 14-16, 18-21. Native to Sierra foothills and east side of California's Central Valley. To 30-75 ft. high, often broader than high. Wide-spreading branches form dense crown. Oblong leaves to 4 in. long, glossy green, smooth or spiny edges. Handsome tree for parks and big lawns.

QUILLAJA saponaria. SOAPBARK TREE. Evergreen tree. Zones 8, 9, 14-24. Usually to 25-30 ft.; occasionally to 60 ft. Young plants are dense columns foliaged right down to the ground; old trees develop a broad, flattened crown. Branchlets are pendulous, especially on younger plants, and the general effect of a young tree is that of a narrow, bushy, weeping live oak. Leaves 2 in. long, oval to nearly round, rather leathery, shiny green. White flowers, ½ in. across; handsome brown 1-in. fruits open into star form. Tends toward multiple trunks and excessive bushiness but responds quickly to pruning. Younger trees may blow down in strong winds without firm staking and occasional thinning. Fairly tolerant of different soils, and even of drought, once well-rooted. Good narrow screening tree. Can be pruned as a tall hedge.

QUINCE, FLOWERING. See Chaenomeles

QUINCE, FRUITING. Deciduous shrub or small tree. All Zones. Slow to 10-25 ft. Unlike flowering quince (*Chaenomeles*) its branches are thornless.

Generally overlooked by planters of flowering fruit trees and home orchard trees, yet the following virtues make common quince worth considering as an ornamental. In spring it wears white or pale pink, 2-in.-wide flowers at tips of leafed-out branches. Attractive, oval, 2-4-in. leaves, dark green above, whitish beneath, turn yellow in fall. Fruits are yellow, fragrant. Its winter form can be dramatic in pattern of gnarled and twisted branches.

Best in heavy, well drained soil but tolerates wet soil. Avoid deep cultivation, which damages shallow roots and causes suckers. Prune only to form a trunk and shape the frame; thin out and cut back only enough to stimulate new growth. Do not use high-nitrogen fertilizer, as this results in succulent growth which is susceptible to fireblight.

The large, fragrant fruits are inedible when raw but useful in making jams and jellies. Here are some popular varieties (the fruits ripen from late September to October):

'Apple' ('Orange'). An old favorite. Round, golden-skinned fruit. Tender, orange-yellow flesh.

'Champion'. Very large, pear-shaped, greenish yellow fruit; yellow flesh. Larger, taller tree than 'Apple'. Later ripening.

'Pineapple'. Roundish, light golden fruit. Tender, white flesh; pineapplelike flavor.

'Smyrna'. Round to oblong fruit, lemon yellow skin. Strong quince fragrance.

RABBIT TRACKS. See Maranta

RADISH. You can pull radishes for the table 3 weeks after you sow the seed (the slowest kinds take 2 months). They need continual moisture and some added nutrients to grow well. Supply the nutrients by blending rotted manure into the soil before planting, or—about 10 days after planting—feed the row as for carrots, or feed with liquid fertilizer. Sow seeds as early in spring as soon as ground can be worked, and at weekly intervals until warm weather approaches. In mild areas, radishes also make a fall and winter crop.

Sow seeds ½ in. deep and thin to 1 in. apart when tops are up. Space rows 12 in. apart. Most familiar kinds are the short, round, red or red and white ones like 'Cherry Belle', 'Crimson Giant', and 'Scarlet White-Tipped'. These should be used just as they reach full size. Slightly slower to reach edible size are the long white radishes, of which 'Icicle' is the best known. Late radishes 'Long Black Spanish' and 'White Chinese' grow 6-10 in. long and can be stored in moist sand in a frost-free place for winter use.

RAINTREE, BRAZIL. See Brunfelsia caly-cina

RAISIN TREE, JAPANESE. See Hovenia

RAMONDA myconi (*R. pyrenaica*). Perennial. Zones 1-6, 17. Relative of African violets; similar growth habit but hardy to sub-zero cold. Leaves in a conspicuous flat rosette that gets larger as the plant grows. Rusty hairs and veins strongly impressed on upper surface of leaves; edges deeply toothed. Flowers few, on 3-6-in. stalks, 5-parted and flat-faced, purple with orange eye. Needs shade, and moisture, but center of rosette will rot with excess moisture. Often planted in chinks in a wall or rockery so foliage will shed rain.

RANUNCULUS. Tubers, perennials. A very large group (up to 250 species); the two listed are only ones grown to any extent in Western gardens.

R. asiaticus. PERSIAN RANUNCULUS, TUR-BAN RANUNCULUS. Tuber. Most ranunculus sold in West are newer strains developed in southern California, Mexico, Australia, South Africa. Flowers are semi-double to fully double, 3-5 in. in diameter, 1-4 on stalks up to 18 in. or more tall. Blooms in many shades of yellow, orange, red, pink, cream, and white. Large tubers produce many stalks, 50-75 blooms. Popular strains, in straight or mixed colors, are: Claremont, El Rancho, Hadeco, Tecolote. Use in borders with Iceland poppies, snapdragons, nemesias. Plant for follow-up color in daffodil beds. Superb cut flowers. Leaves bright fresh green, divided into many leaflets—look almost fernlike.

In mild-winter areas, plant tubers in November. In western Washington, Oregon, plant November or mid-February. Need perfect drainage, full sun. Set tubers (prongs downward) 2 in. deep, 6-8 in. apart. Tubers come dry and hard; plump up after absorbing moisture. Water thoroughly after planting; unless weather is very hot and dry, do not water again until sprouts show above ground (10 days-2 weeks). Tubers rot if overwatered before roots form. In warm, dry regions, some

Climate Zone maps pages 8-27

soak tubers 3-4 hours before planting. Can start tubers in flats of moist sand, plant when sprouted and rooted. To protect young sprouts from birds, cover with netting. After blooms fade, let plants dry out, lift, cut off tops, and store tubers in dry, cool place.

Tubers, flower of Persian ranunculus; set tubers with prongs pointed downward.

Flat-grown seedlings sold in some areas in fall. In coldest climates grow ranunculus in greenhouse, plant after frosts. Early hot spell may shorten bloom period in such areas.

R. repens 'Pleniflorus'. CREEPING BUTTERCUP. All Zones. Vigorous plant with thick fibrous roots and runners growing several feet in a season, rooting at joints. Leaves glossy, roundish, deeply cut, toothed. Flowers fully double, button-shaped, bright yellow, about 1 in. across, on stems 1-2 ft. high. Spring bloom. Ground cover in moist soil, filtered or deep shade. Can be invasive in flower beds and lawns.

RAOULIA australis. Perennial. Zones 7-9, 13-24. Carpeting plant. Stems up to 6 in. long form very close mats. Stems are hidden by small gray leaves that overlap them completely. Inconspicuous pale yellow flowers in spring. Useful in dry rockery with ice plants and their relatives, or in a cactus bed. Needs sandy soil, full sun, moderate water, perfect drainage.

RAPHIOLEPIS. Evergreen shrubs. Zones 8-10, 14-24; grown as a worthwhile risk in Zones 4-7. These shrubs, with their glossy, leathery leaves, make attractive dense background plantings, large-scale ground covers, low dividers, or informal hedges. And they offer more than the constant greenery of most basic landscaping shrubs. From late fall or midwinter to late spring they carry a profusion of flowers ranging from white to near red. Dark blue berrylike fruits follow the flowers. New leaves often add to the color range with tones of bronze and red.

They stay low. Even the taller kinds rarely get higher than 5-6 ft.; with pruning they can be kept at 3 ft. almost indefinitely. Prune from beginning if you want sturdy, bushy, compact plants; pinch back tips of branches at least once each year, after flowering. For more open structure, let it grow naturally and occasionally thin out branches. Encourage spreading by shortening vertical branches. Pinch side branches to encourage upright growth.

Most kinds are easy to grow in full sun; in light shade they are less compact, bloom less. Raphiolepis stand fairly dry conditions but also tolerate the frequent waterings they get when planted near a lawn or flower bed. Aphids occasionally attack. A fungus sometimes causes leaf spotting, especially during cold, wet weather—to control, destroy infected leaves, spray with a fungicide, avoid overhead watering.

R. delacouri. A pink-flowered hybrid of *R. indica* and *R. umbellata.* To 6 ft. tall. Small pink flowers in upright clusters. October-May. Leaves smaller than most. The name is often used incorrectly for many different plants.

R. indica. INDIA HAWTHORN. White flowers, tinged with pink, about ½ in. across. Leaves pointed, 1½-3 in. long. Plants grow 4-5 ft. high. Grown infrequently but its varieties (below) are widely grown and sold. The varieties differ mainly in color of bloom and size and form of plant. Even plants of same variety may vary. Flower color is especially inconsistent. Flowers in warmer climates and exposures are usually lighter. Bloom is paler in fall than in spring.

R. i. 'Apple Blossom'. White and pink flowers.

R. i. 'Ballerina'. Deep rosy pink flowers. Stays low (not much taller than 2 ft.) and compact (no wider than 4 ft.). Leaves take on a reddish tinge in winter.

R. i. 'Bill Evans'. Light pink flowers, larger than most. Plants grow fast and vigorously. Usually to 5-7 ft. high. Upright, open, irregular. Thick, glossy, roundish leaves resemble those of *R. umbellata* more than *R. indica.*

R. i. 'Clara'. White flowers on compact plants 3-5 ft. high, about as wide. Red new growth.

R. i. 'Coates Crimson'. Crimson pink flowers. Compact, spreading plants grow slowly, stay small—2-4 ft. high and as wide. Best in part shade and with regular watering.

R. i. 'Enchantress'. Pink flowers. Faster, more vigorous, and taller than 'Coates Crimson', color not as deep.

R. i. 'Fascination'. Deep rosy pink flowers with white centers. Taller than 'Ballerina' but lower and more compact than most raphiolepis.

R. i. 'Flamingo'. Light pink flowers. Fast growing to at least 4 ft. high.

R. i. 'Jack Evans'. Bright pink flowers. To about 4 ft. with wider spread. Compact and spreading. Leaves sometimes have purplish tinge.

R. i. 'Pink Cloud'. Pink flowers. Compact growth to 3 ft. high, 3-4 ft. wide.

R. i. 'Rosea'. PINK INDIA HAWTHORN. This was the first of the selected, named seedlings. Very light to medium pink flowers. Slow growth to 3-5 ft. high, 5-6 ft. wide. Growth looser and more graceful than that of most of the stiffer, more compact newer varieties. New growth bronzy.

R. i. 'Rosea Dwarf'. Denser, more compact grower than 'Rosea'; flowers pale pink. Foliage purplish in winter.

R. i. 'Snow White'. White flowers. Growth habit about like 'Jack Evans'. Leaves paler than on most varieties.

R. i. 'Springtime'. Deep pink flowers. Vigorous, upright to 4-6 ft. high.

R. umbellata (*R. u. ovata, R. ovata*). Easily distinguished from *R. indica* by its roundish, leathery, dark green leaves, 1-3 in. long. White flowers about ¾ in. wide. Vigorous plants 4-6 ft. tall, sometimes to 10 ft. In full sun, thick and bushy.

RASPBERRY. These need a slowly warming, lingering springtime to reach perfection. Best in Zones 4-6, 15-17, but can be grown (perhaps with some setbacks or difficulties) anywhere else in the West.

Most popular and heaviest bearers are red raspberries. These can be grown as free-standing shrubs and staked, but in the Northwest (where they grow tall) they are easiest handled tied to wires as illustrated.

Set plants 2½-3 ft. apart in rows 7-9 ft. apart. Well drained soil is essential. Set plants about an inch deeper than they grew originally, and cut back the cane that rises from the roots, leaving only enough to serve as a marker. The plant should produce 3-5 sturdy canes the first year; these will bear the next year and should be cut out at ground level after fruiting.

The second year canes will come up all around the parent plant and even between hills and rows. Remove all except 8-12 closely spaced, vigorous canes that come up near the crown—be sure to pull up all suckers away from the crown. Tie the selected canes to the top wire. In spring before growth begins cut them back to 4½-5½ ft. and retie if necessary. Fruit-bearing laterals will appear from these canes.

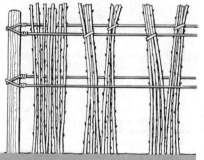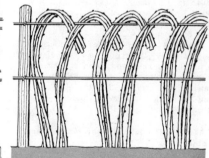

Red raspberries can be tied in bunches of 4 or 5, or interwoven on two wires. Top wires 4-5 ft. above ground, lower wires 2-2½ ft. Low trellis of poles can substitute.

Climate
Zone maps
pages 8-27

Fall-bearing raspberries differ slightly in pruning needs; these ripen canes earlier in summer and fruit laterals form and bear fruit near the top of the cane. Cut off the upper portion that has borne fruit; the lower parts of the cane will fruit next spring; cut out the cane after it has fruited along its whole length.

Plants need plenty of water, especially during blossoming and fruiting. Feed at blossoming time.

'Canby'. Large, bright red berries. Thornless, hardy.

'Cuthbert'. Medium berries of good quality.

'Fairview'. Variety for coastal Northwest. Bears young, and heavily. Early variety of good quality.

'Indian Summer'. Small crops of large, red, tasty berries in late spring and again in fall; fall crop often larger.

'Latham'. Older, very hardy variety for intermountain areas. Late. Berries tend to be crumbly. Mildews in summer-humid regions.

'Newburgh'. Hardy, late ripening variety. Large, light red berries. Takes heavy soil fairly well.

'Puyallup'. For west of the Cascades. Large, soft berries with very good flavor. Midseason.

'Ranere' ('St. Regis'). Everbearing. Long bearing season, from mid-spring to frost in California. Berries small, bright red. Needs steady irrigation for long bearing.

'Sumner'. Hardy, with some resistance to root rot in heavy soils. Fine fruit. Early.

'New Washington'. Smallish fruit of high quality. Hardy, but needs well drained soil.

'Willamette'. Large, firm, dark red berries which hold color and shape well.

A tasty novelty is 'Golden West', with yellow berries of excellent quality.

RASPBERRY, BLACK or BLACKCAP. Resembles the regular red raspberry in many ways, but the blue-black fruit is firmer, seedier, and has a more distinct flavor. Plants differ from red raspberries in not suckering from the roots; new plants form when the arching cane tips root in the soil.

Does well in all but the coldest intermountain areas of the Northwest where freezing destroys following year's crop. Not well adapted to California. You need no trellis. Head back new canes at 18-24 in. to force laterals. At end of growing season, cut out all weak canes (under ½-in.; if all are small leave best two), and remove canes that fruited during current season. In late winter or early spring, cut back laterals to 10-15 in. on strong canes, 3-4 in. on weak ones. Fruit is produced on sideshoots from these laterals. If you prefer trellising, head new canes at 2-3 ft.

Varieties usually sold as 'Cumberland'. an old variety;'Morrison', a large berry on a productive vine; and 'Munger', the most popular commercial variety. 'Sodus', the purple raspberry, is a hybrid between a red and black raspberry. A vigorous variety; head new canes at 30-36 in.

RATA, NORTH ISLAND. See Metrosideros robusta

RATA, SOUTHERN. See Metrosideros umbellata

RATTLESNAKE GRASS. See Briza

RATSTRIPPER. See Pachistima canbyi

RAUWOLFIA samarensis. (Often sold as *Alstonia scholaris.*) INDIA DEVIL TREE. Semi-deciduous tree. Zones 22-24. Fast to 30 ft. tall, 20 ft. wide. Beautiful structure, with tiers of foliage nicely separated by open spaces. Large, shiny dark green leaves 2-8 in. long, 1-2 in. wide, in whorls of 3-6 at ends of branches. Clusters of small white flowers; black seeds sometimes messy on paved areas. Subject to red spider mites. Needs rich soil and plenty of water. Remarkably wind resistant. Marvelous for tropical effect; handsome feature for front garden or near outdoor living. Don't dim its clear-cut outline by setting large shrubs too near it.

REDBERRY. See Rhamnus crocea

REDBUD. See Cercis

RED-HOT POKER. See Kniphofia

RED IRONBARK. See Eucalyptus sideroxylon

RED RIBBONS. See Clarkia concinna

REDWOOD. See Sequoia

REDWOOD SORREL. See Oxalis oregana

REED, GIANT. See Arundo

REHMANNIA angulata. Perennial. Zones 7-10, 12-24. The impressive thing about this plant is that it blooms in sun or shade from mid-April to November. Flower stalks rise to 2-3 ft., loosely set with 3-in.-long, tubular flowers that look something like big, gaping foxgloves. Common form is rose purple with yellow, red-dotted throat; there is a fine white and cream form that must be grown from cuttings or division. Coarse, deeply toothed leaves. Spreads by underground roots and forms big, evergreen clumps where winters are mild. Deciduous where winters are colder. Easy to grow; main requirements are rich soil, ample water, and shade. Handsome, long-lasting cut flowers.

REINWARDTIA indica (*R. trigyna*). YELLOW FLAX. Perennial. Zones 8-10, 12-24. Grows shrublike to 3-4 ft. Brilliant yellow, 2-in. flowers form in great profusion at an unusual season: in late fall and early winter. Blooms do not last long, but for weeks new ones open daily. Sun or part shade. Pinch to make more compact. Spreads by underground roots. Increase by rooted stems; divide in spring. Good choice for winter color in flower garden or with shrubs.

RESEDA odorata. MIGNONETTE. Annual. To 12-18 in. tall; rather sprawling habit. Not a particularly beautiful plant, but well worth growing because of remarkable flower fragrance. Dense spikes of bloom become loose and open as blossoms mature. Small, greenish flowers tinged with copper or yellow. Flowers dry up quickly in hot weather.

Sow seed in early spring—or late fall or winter in Zones 15-24. Successive sowings give a long bloom period. Best in rich soil. Sun in cool sections, part shade inland. Plant in masses to get the full effect of fragrance, or spot a few in a flower bed. Suitable for pots. There are other forms

with longer flower spikes and brighter colors, but they are less fragrant.

RETINOSPORA pisifera. See Chamaecyparis pisifera

RHAMNUS. Evergreen or deciduous shrubs or trees. Small flowers in clusters, rather inconspicuous; plants grown for form and foliage, occasionally for show of berrylike fruits.

R. alaternus. ITALIAN BUCKTHORN. Evergreen shrub. Zones 4-24. Fast, dense growth to 12-20 ft. or more, spreading as wide. Close planting or pruning will keep it narrow. Easily trained as a multi-stem or single stem small tree. Leaves oval to oblong, bright shiny green, ¾-2 in. long. April flowers tiny, greenish yellow. Fruit black, ¼ in. long.

Easily sheared or shaped. Takes drought, heat, wind, as well as regular watering. Grows in full sun or part shade. Valuable as fast screen or tall clipped hedge. Trained to a single stem, makes a good plant for tall screen above a 6-ft. fence. *R. a.* 'John Edwards' is cutting-grown and thus uniform in size, shape. *R. a.* 'Variegata' (*R. a.* 'Argenteo-variegata') has leaves edged with creamy white; striking against a dark background. Cut out plain green branches that occasionally appear.

R. californica. COFFEEBERRY. Evergreen shrub. Zones 4-24. Native to southwest Oregon, California, Arizona, New Mexico. Low and spreading or upright, 3-15 ft. tall. Leaves 1-3 in. long, shining dark green to dull green above (depending on variety), paler beneath (in some forms gray-hairy beneath). Large berries green, then red, then black when ripe. Near the ocean plants tend to be broad, spreading; taller in woodland or in hills. A selected coastal form, *R. c.* 'Seaview', can be kept to 18 in. high, 6-8 ft. wide if upright growth is pinched out.

R. crocea. REDBERRY. Evergreen shrub. Zones 14-21. Native to Coast Ranges, Lake County to San Diego County, California. To 2-3 ft. high and spreading, with many stiff or spiny branches. Leaves roundish, ½-in. long, glossy dark to pale green above, golden or brownish beneath, often finely toothed. Small bright red fruit August-October.

R. c. ilicifolia. HOLLY-LEAF REDBERRY. Evergreen shrub. Zones 7-16, 18-21. Native to Coast Ranges and Sierra Nevada foothills, mountains of southern California, Arizona, Baja California. Multi-stemmed, or often treelike, 3-15 ft. Leaves roundish, ½-1¼ in. long, spiny-toothed. A good ornamental plant for dry banks or informal screen in hot-sun areas. Drought resistant.

R. frangula. ALDER BUCKTHORN. Deciduous shrub or small tree. Zones 1-7, 10-13. To 15-18 ft. tall. Leaves roundish, glossy dark green, 1-3 in. long, half as wide. Fruit turns from red to black on ripening. *R. f.* 'Columnaris', TALLHEDGE BUCKTHORN, grows 12-15 ft. tall, 4 ft. wide. Set 2½ ft. apart for a tight, narrow hedge that needs a minimum of trimming and can be kept as low as 4 ft.

R. purshiana. CASCARA SAGRADA. Deciduous shrub or small tree. Zones 1-9, 14-17. Native northern California to British Columbia and Montana. To 20-40 ft., with smooth gray or brownish bark. Leaves el-

Climate
Zone maps
pages 8-27

liptical, prominently veined, dark green, 1½-8 in. long, to 2 in. wide, usually somewhat tufted at the ends of the branches. Foliage turns a good yellow in fall. Round black fruits attract birds. Will grow in dense shade or full sun with ample water. Picturesque branching pattern. Bark has medicinal value.

RHAPHIDOPHORA aurea (*Scindapsus aureus, Pothos aureus*). Evergreen perennial. Grown as house plant. Climbing plants related to philodendron and similar in appearance. Takes same treatment as climbing philodendrons. Oval, leathery leaves 2-4 in.

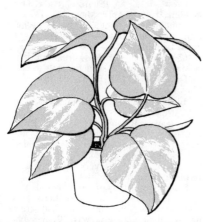

Leaves of Rhaphidophora are bright green splashed yellow, 2-4 in. long.

long, bright green splashed yellow. (Grown in a greenhouse, leaves can reach 1½ ft. in length and show deeply cut edges.) Best as a trailer in dish gardens, planting boxes, window boxes.

RHAPIDOPHYLLUM hystrix. NEEDLE PALM. Zones 7-9, 12-24. Hardy, slow-growing fan palm from southeastern U. S. Upright or creeping stems 5 ft. high. Rounded leaves, 3-4 ft. across, dark green above, silvery beneath. Well provided with strong black spines. Makes an impenetrable hedge. Hardy to 10°.

RHAPIS. LADY PALM. Fan palms which form bamboolike clumps with deep green foliage. Trunks covered with a net of dark, fibrous leaf sheaths. Slow growing, choice.

Rhapis excelsa is one of the finest palms for containers, indoors or outside.

R. excelsa. LADY PALM. Zones 15-17, 19-24. Small, slow, 5-12 ft. tall, often much lower. Best in shade, but will take considerable sun near the beach. One of the finest container palms; resists poor light, dust, and drought, but responds quickly to better light and fertilizer. Hardy to 20°.

R. humilis. RATTAN PALM, SLENDER LADY PALM. Zones 16, 17, 20-24. Tall, bamboolike stems (to 18 ft.) give a charming, graceful, tropical air. Larger, longer-leafed than *R. excelsa*, less tolerant of sun and wind. Hardy to 22°.

RHIPSALIDOPSIS gaertneri (*Schlumbergera gaertneri*). EASTER CACTUS. House plant; lathhouse or covered terrace plant in Zones 16, 17, 21-24. For culture and general description, see *Schlumbergera*. Much like *S. bridgesii* but plant more upright (has same drooping branches). Flowers to 3 in. long, bright red, upright or horizontal rather than drooping. Blooms April, May, often again in September. There are many varieties in shades of pink and red.

RHODODENDRON (including azalea). Evergreen or deciduous shrubs, rarely trees. A very large group: The number of species is near 1,000, and more are being discovered. There are some 10,000 named varieties in the International Register, of which about 2,000 are currently available. Botanists have arranged the species into series and subseries: One of these series includes the plants called azaleas.

The climate adaptation pattern of azaleas is very different from that of rhododendrons. For example, evergreen azaleas are planted by the hundreds of thousands in southern California where rhododendrons are relatively rare.

The widest choice in kinds of rhododendrons that can be grown is in Zones 4-6, 15-17. However, gardeners in every climate of the West—except the deserts and areas of coldest winters—can find ways to grow certain varieties.

The basic soil and water requirements of rhododendrons and azaleas are much the same. They require an acid soil. They need more air in the root zone than any other garden plants. At the same time, they need a constant moisture supply. In other words, they need a soil that drains rapidly and at the same time retains moisture. Soils rich in organic matter have those qualities.

If your soil lacks those qualities, add organic matter such as peat moss, ground bark, sawdust, or leaf mold. If your soil is alkaline, replace it with an acid mixture. Some growers use straight, pre-moistened peat moss; others use 75 per cent peat moss and 25 per cent perlite or fine sand; or 50 per cent peat and 50 per cent redwood sawdust; or ground bark—straight or with fine sand. Some swear by decayed pine needles.

Don't plant in a hole that doesn't drain. Instead, plant above soil level in raised beds.

Plant azaleas and rhododendrons at or slightly above soil level. Never allow soil to wash in and bury stems. Plants are surface rooters and benefit from a mulch. Never cultivate soil around these plants.

Sun tolerance of azaleas and rhododendrons differs by species and varieties. Most can take full sun in cool-summer areas. Ideal location is in the filtered shade of tall trees. East and north side of house and fence are next best. Too dense shade makes lanky, sparse-blooming plants.

Fertilize when growth starts in the spring, at bloom time or immediately afterward, and repeat monthly until August. Use a commercial acid fertilizer and follow directions carefully; to be extra safe, cut portions in half and feed twice as often.

Both azaleas and rhododendrons need special attention where soil or water is high in dissolved salts—as in many areas in California. To avoid damage, use one of the soil mixes listed above in containers or raised beds and periodically leach the mix by heavy watering—enough to drain through the mix 2 or 3 times. If leaves turn yellow while the veins remain green (chlorosis), apply iron chelate to the soil or spray with iron solution.

Control of insects and diseases is not difficult. Root weevil larvae feed on the roots. The adult weevils notch the leaves but damage is minor. You can prevent larvae from developing in the soil by applying diazinon dust to the soil and working it in to a depth of 6 in. at planting time. Or you can kill adults as they emerge from the soil about late May. Use poison bait or spray plant and soil with diazinon and repeat every 2 weeks until there is no sign of leaf feeding. In western Oregon the obscure root weevil (gray in color) is part of the root weevil group; control with malathion.

Poor drainage can result in root rot, which shows in yellowing, wilting, and collapse of plants. Too much sun causes bleaching or burning in leaf centers. Wind and soil salts burn leaf edges; windburn shows up most often on new foliage, saltburn on the older leaves. Late frosts often cause deformed leaves.

Prune evergreen azaleas by frequent pinching of tip growth from after flowering to August if you wish a compact plant with maximum flower production.

Prune large-flowered rhododendrons early in spring or at bloom time if needed. Tippinch young plants to make them bushy; prune older, leggy plants to restore shape by cutting back to a side branch, leaf whorl, or to a cluster of dormant buds. (Some varieties will not push new growth from dormant buds.) Prune off faded flower heads or break off spent flower trusses; take care not to injure new growth buds just beneath the truss.

KINDS OF RHODODENDRONS

Most people know rhododendrons as big, leathery-leafed shrubs with stunning, rounded clusters of white, pink, red, or purple blossoms. But there are other rhododendrons—dwarfs a few inches high; giants to 40, even 80 ft. in their native China; and a host of species and hybrids in every size between, in a color range that includes scarlet, yellow, near-blue, and a constellation of blends in the orange-apricot-salmon range.

Listed here are a number of the most generally available kinds.

Heights given are for plants 10 years old; older plants may be taller, and crowded or heavily shaded plants may reach up faster. Bloom seasons are approximate and vary with weather and location.

Climate Zone maps pages 8-27

The ratings for plant quality should be regarded as judgments that may change with every new issue of the Rhododendron Year Book. Furthermore, one rating cannot blanket the performance of a plant in a dozen different climates.

The list includes only 75 of the best species and hybrids grown in the West.

To give some idea of the great variety of experiences to be had with rhododendrons, we have brought together a few classifications from the alphabetical list of species and hybrids that follows.

There are a number of "ironclad" hardy hybrids that surprisingly do well in southern California: 'Cunningham's White', 'Fastuosum Flore Pleno', 'Gomer Waterer', 'Madame Mason', 'Mars'.

California specials. Rhododendrons too tender for Northwest gardens. Many of them fragrant: R. burmanicum, 'Countess of Haddington', 'Countess of Sefton', 'Forsterianum', 'Fragrantissimum', 'Saffron Queen'.

Good performers in California, rated low in Northwest: 'Anah Kruschke', 'Antoon Van Welie', 'Rainbow', 'Sappho', 'Unknown Warrior', 'Van Nes Sensation'.

Dwarfs and low growers with distinctive foliage and bell-shaped or funnel-shaped flowers, not in typical trusses: 'Bow Bells', 'Bric-a-Brac', 'Cilpinense', 'Racil', 'Snow Lady'.

If you call them azaleas you would love them. Low growing species rhododendrons of great charm: R. chryseum, R. impeditum, R. intricatum, R. keiskei, R. moupinense, R. pemakoense.

Highly regarded, dependable, popular, easy to grow, widely adapted: 'Anna Rose Whitney', 'Betty Wormald', 'Britannia', 'Countess of Derby' ('Eureka Maid'), 'Crest', 'David', 'Jan Dekens', 'Loder's White', 'Mrs. E. C. Stirling', 'Mrs. G. W. Leak' ('Cottage Gardens Pride'), 'Pink Pearl', 'Purple Splendour', 'The Hon. Jean Marie de Montague'.

RATINGS & HARDINESS

We have followed the American Rhododendron Society's system for rating plants for quality and hardiness.

Quality is expressed this way: 3/3. Flower quality is listed first, shrub quality second; 5 is superior, 4 above average, 3 average, 2 below average, 1 poor. A 5/5 rating is near perfection.

Hardiness rating indicates minimum temperatures a well matured plant can take without serious injury.

'A. Bedford'. 4/3. −5°. Lavender-blue, darker flare, large trusses. To 6 ft. Late May.

'Alice'. 3/4. −5°. Deep pink, fading to pale rose. Reliable, easy to grow. Flowers good for cutting. To about 6 ft. April and May.

'Anah Kruschke'. 2/3. −10°. Lavender. Color not the best, but plant has good foliage, tolerates heat, not fussy about soil. To 5 ft. May.

'Anna Rose Whitney'. 4/3. +5°. Big, rich, deep pink trusses on a compact, 5-ft. plant with excellent foliage. May.

'Antoon Van Welie'. 3/3. −5°. Carmine pink. Big trusses of 'Pink Pearl' type on a 6-ft. plant. Late May.

R. augustinii. 4/3. +5°. Open, moderate growth to 6 ft. Leaves to 3 in. long. Flowers 2-2½ in. wide in clusters of 3-4, blue or purple in best named forms. May.

'Betty Wormald'. 4/3. −5°. Carmine pink, darker markings on upper petals. Tall trusses. Informal growth to 6 ft. April, May.

'Blue Diamond'. 5/4. 0°. Compact, erect growth to 3 ft. Small leaves; lavender-blue flowers cover plant in April. Takes considerable sun in Northwest.

'Blue Peter'. 4/3. −10°. Broad, sprawling growth to 4 ft.; needs pruning. Large trusses of lavender-blue flowers blotched purple. May.

'Blue Tit'. 4/4. 0°. To 2-3 ft. Small leaves on a dense twiggy plant. Flowers lighter than 'Blue Diamond', near true blue.

'Bow Bells'. 3/4. 0°. Compact, rounded growth to 4 ft. Leaves rounded. Flowers bright pink, bell-shaped, in loose clusters. May. New growth bronzy.

'Bric-a-Brac'. 4/4. +5°. Low, compact grower to 3 ft. with greater spread. New growth dark red; leaves small. Flowers in pairs, pure white with chocolate anthers. Splendid for massing, containers. Protect March flowers from late frost.

'Britannia'. 4/4. −5°. Bright red, ruffled flowers in large, rounded truss. May. Slow growing, rounded shrub to 4 ft. Beautiful foliage yellows in too much sun.

'Broughtonii Aureum'. 3/2. 0°. Azalea-rhododendron hybrid of loose, willowy growth to 4 ft. Foliage dull green. Soft yellow flowers blotched orange in rounded trusses. Has shown good heat, sun resistance in California. Late May.

R. burmanicum. Greenish yellow bells in clusters of 4-6. April-May.

R. calophytum. 4/4. −5°. Small, stocky tree, to 4 ft. Noted for big leaves—4 in. wide, 10-14 in. long. Trusses of white or pink flowers with a deep blotch. Protect from wind. March and April.

'Carita'. 4/4. +5°. Large, pale primrose yellow, 12-13 flowers in truss. Late April. Outstanding flowers and foliage, but latter yellows badly in sun.

'Christmas Cheer'. 2/4. −5°. Pink to white in tight truss. Can take full sun. To 3 ft. Early bloom (February-March) compensates for any lack in flower quality.

R. chryseum. 2/2. −15°. Dwarf (1-ft.) densely branched plant with 1-in. leaves. Flowers are small, bright yellow bells, 4-5 in a cluster. April to May.

'Cilpinense'. 4/4. +5°. Funnel-shaped flowers of apple blossom pink fading white; loose clusters nearly cover plants in March. Low, spreading growth to 2½ ft.; small leaves. Easy to grow. Effective massed. Protect blossoms from late frosts.

'CIS'. 4/2. +10°. Flowers (in large trusses) are red in throat to cream yellow at edges of flower. To 3 ft. May.

'Conemaugh'. 4/3. −15°. Dainty, lavender-pink flowers in miniature trusses. Light, airy, open. To 3 ft. March.

'Cornubia'. 4/3. +15°. Strong, upright growth to 7 ft. Blood red flowers in large clusters February-March. Tender in Northwest.

'Countess of Derby' ('Eureka Maid'). 4/3. −5°. Rose pink, with deeper blotch. Easy, vigorous grower to 5 ft. Resembles 'Pink Pearl'. May.

'Countess of Haddington'. 4/4. +20°. Light pink to white, waxy, tubular, fragrant flowers in compact trusses. To 5 ft. May.

'Countess of Sefton'. 3/3. +20°. Large, tubular, fragrant, white flowers in loose truss. Not as rangy as 'Fragrantissimum'. To 4 ft. Late April.

'Crest'. 5/3. −5°. Primrose yellow. Outstanding. To 5 ft. April, May.

'Cunningham's White'. 2/3. −15°. White with greenish yellow blotch. Hardy old-timer. Late May.

'Cynthia'. 3/3. −10°. Rosy crimson trusses in May. Dependable, strong grower to 6 ft.

'David'. 4/3. +5°. Blood red trusses in May. Compact growth to 5 ft.

'Elizabeth'. 4/4. 0°. Several forms available. Broad grower to 3 ft. tall with middle-sized leaves. Blooms very young. Bright red, waxy, trumpet-shaped flowers in clusters of 3-6 at branch ends and in upper leaf joints. Main show in April; often reflowers in October. Very susceptible to fertilizer burn, salts in water.

Fabia. 3/3. +10°. Group of hybrids with 6-8 nodding flowers to a truss. Early May. Low, spreading growth; 4 ft. 'Tangerine' has vermilion-orange flowers; 'Roman Pottery' terra cotta; 'Exbury' pale apricot tinted pink.

R. falconeri. 3/3. +5°. One of the unusual tree rhododendrons (others not listed here). To 25 ft. high and wide. Leathery leaves 6-12 in. long, reddish felted beneath. Creamy white to pale yellow flowers, 2 in. wide, in clusters, shown on page 398. Won't bloom until 15-20 years old.

'Fastuosum Flore Pleno'. 3/3. −10°. Double mauve flowers in May. Dependable, hardy old-timer. To 5 ft.

R. forrestii repens. 3/3. +5°. Low, spreading dwarf. To 6 in. Tubular, bright red flowers in small clusters. April-May. Not easy to grow. Needs perfect drainage.

'Forsterianum'. 5/4. +20°. Tubular, frilled, fragrant white flowers tinted pink. March bloom; buds often damaged by frost in colder areas without overhead protection. Open, rangy growth to 5 ft. Attractive glossy, red-brown, peeling bark and medium-scale, glossy foliage.

'Fragrantissimum'. 4/3. +20°. Large, funnel-shaped white flowers touched with pink, April-May. Powerfully fragrant. Loose, open, rangy growth with medium-sized, bright green, bristly leaves. With hard pinching in youth a 5-ft. shrub. Easily trained as an espalier or vine, reaching to 10 ft. or more. Can spill over a wall.

'Gomer Waterer'. 3/4. −15°. White flushed lilac. Hardy old-timer. To 5 ft. Late May.

R. impeditum. 2/3. −10°. Twiggy, dwarf, dense shrub to 1 ft. with closely packed, tiny, gray-green leaves. Small flowers mauve to dark blue, April or May. Takes full sun in cooler areas.

R. intricatum. 2/3. −15°. Compact, upright to 3 ft. Mauve to lilac blue. April, May.

'Jan Dekens'. 2/3. 0°. Big, high trusses of rich pink, frilled flowers in May. Excellent habit and foliage. To 6 ft.

R

Climate
Zone maps
pages 8-27

R. keiskei. 2/1. −5°. At least two forms are available. The very dwarf, very compact form makes a 6-in.-high shrublet. The taller form will reach 3 ft., and is more open in growth. Both forms produce lovely lemon yellow bells in great profusion, 3-5 in a cluster. March-May.

'Letty Edwards'. 3/3. 0°. Pale yellow with greenish tinge. One of the older yellows. Several forms—one with pinkish tinge, another sulfur yellow. Sets buds as a youngster. Foliage does not yellow in sun. To 5 ft. Mid-May.

Loderi. 5/4. 0°. Spectacular group of hybrids with tall trusses of 6-7-in.-wide flowers in shades of pink or white. Fragrant; early May bloom. Informal, open growth to 8 ft. Too large for the small garden. Slow to reach blooming age and not easy to grow. Difficult to maintain good foliage color. Best known are 'King George', with white flowers opening from blush buds; 'Pink Diamond', with blush flowers; and 'Venus', with shell pink flowers.

'Loder's White'. 5/5. 0°. Big trusses of flowers open white tinged pink and mature pure white. May. Shapely growth to 5 ft. Blooms freely even when young. Best white for most regions.

R. macrophyllum (*R. californicum*). COAST RHODODENDRON, WESTERN RHODODENDRON. Unrated. +5°. Native near coast northern California to British Columbia. Rangy growth 4-10 ft. Leaves dark green, leathery, 2½-6 in. long; flower trusses rosy, rose-purple, rarely white. May-June. Rarely sold; should not be collected in wild.

'Madame Mason' ('Madame Masson'). 3/3. −5°. White with light yellow flare on upper petal. Needs pruning to keep it compact. To 5 ft. Late May.

'Mars'. 4/3.−10°. Dark red. Outstanding in form, foliage, flowers. To 4 ft. Late May.

'Moonstone'. 4/4. −5°. Flaring bells age from pale pink to creamy yellow in April. Attractive dense, dwarf growth to 2 ft. Leaves neat, small, rounded. Fine facing taller rhododendrons, as low foundation planting with 'Bow Bells'.

R. moupinense. 4/2. 0°. Open, spreading. To 1½ ft. Small (1½-in.-long), oval leaves. White or pink flowers, spotted red. New spring foliage deep red. February to March.

'Mrs. Betty Robertson'. 3/3. +5°. Pale yellow, large truss. May. Low, compact grower to 3 ft. Good foliage does not burn in sun.

'Mrs. Charles E. Pearson'. 4/4. −5°. Bluish mauve blotched orange-brown; fades to light pink. Big trusses. May.

'Mrs. E. C. Stirling'. 4/4. −5°. Opens blush pink, becomes light pink. May. Easy to grow. Vigorous growth to 5 ft.

'Mrs. Furnival'. 5/5. −10°. Clear pink flowers with light brown blotch in upper petals, in tight, round trusses. Late May. Compact growth to 4 ft.

'Mrs. G. W. Leak' ('Cottage Gardens Pride'). 4/4. +5° Deep pink, deep brown flare on upper petals. Strong growth to 5 ft. May.

R. mucronulatum. 4/3.−25°. Deciduous rhododendron with open growth to 5 ft. Makes up for bare branches by flowering in January-February. Flowers generally bright purple; there is a pink form, 'Cornell Pink'.

Naomi. 4/4. −10°. Group of top-notch hybrids with trusses of fragrant 4-5-in. flowers in May. Bloom younger than Loderi hybrids; lower, more compact, hardier. To 4-5 ft., and leggy unless carefully pruned while young. 'Exbury' (rosy pink blended with yellow); 'Nautilus' (pale pink, frilled, centered with creamy yellow and veined rose); and 'Stella Maris' (pink and yellow) are the three best known in this outstanding group. Take it easy with fertilizers.

R. pemakoense. 2/3. 0°. Compact, spreading. To 1½ ft. Tiny (1½-in.-long) leaves. Flowers pinkish purple, very free blooming. Useful in rock gardens. March-April.

'Pink Pearl'. 3/3. −5°. Rose pink, tall trusses in May. To 6 ft. and more. Open, rangy growth without pruning. Dependable grower and bloomer in all except coldest climates.

'Purple Splendour'. 4/3. −10°. Ruffled, rich deep purple blotched black-purple. Informal growth to 4 ft. Hardy and easy to grow. May.

R. racemosum. 3/3.−10°. Several forms include a 6-in. dwarf, a 2½-ft. compact upright shrub, and a tall 7-footer. Pink inch-wide flowers in clusters of 3-6 all along the stems in March-April. Easy; sun-tolerant in cooler areas.

'Racil'. 3/2. −5°. Shell pink, funnel-shaped flowers in open clusters. Most useful. To 2 ft. April.

'Rainbow'. 1/2. 0°. Light pink center, carmine edges. Very showy. Heavy foliage. Strong growth to 5 ft. April.

'Saffron Queen'. 4/3.+20°. Sulfur yellow,

darker spots on upper petals. April bloom. Flowers, trusses, foliage smaller than 'Pink Pearl' type. To 3 ft.

'Sapphire'. 4/4. 0°. Bright blue, small, azalealike flowers in March, April. Twiggy, rounded, dense shrublet to 1½ ft. Foliage gray-green, leaves tiny.

'Sappho'. 3/2. −5°. White, dark purple spot in throat. May. Easy to grow, gangly without pruning. Use it back of border.

'Snow Lady'. 4/4. 0°. White, black stamens. Wide, flat flowers in clusters. To 3 ft. April.

'Susan'. 3/4. −5°. Silvery lavender flowers in large trusses. May. Handsome foliage. To 4 ft.

'The Hon. Jean Marie de Montague'. 3/4. 0°. Brightest scarlet red in May. Good foliage. To 5 ft.

'Unique'. 3/5. +5°. Apricot buds open to deep cream, fade to light yellow; trusses tight, rounded. April, early May. Outstanding neat, rounded, compact habit. To 4 ft.

'Unknown Warrior'. 3/2. +5°. Light soft red, fades quickly when exposed to bright sun. Easy to grow. To 4 ft. April.

'Van Nes Sensation'. 3/4. 0°. Pale lilac flowers in large trusses. Strong grower. To 5 ft. May.

'Vulcan'. 3/4. −5°. Bright brick red flowers in late May, early June. New leaves often grow past flower buds, partially hiding flowers. To 4 ft.

R. yakusimanum. 4/4. −20°. Clear pink bells changing to white, about 12 in a truss. Late May. Dense, spreading growth to 3 ft. New foliage gray-felted; older leaves with heavy tan or white felt beneath.

KINDS OF EVERGREEN AZALEAS

The evergreen azaleas sold in the West fall into 11 groups. In many cases the group to which a variety belongs indicates the kind of growth and flowering that you can expect, hardiness, and the amount of sun the plants can take. But group characteristics are rather elastic. Here are the groups, the symbols used to designate them in the variety list, the zones in which they perform best, and descriptions of the groups' characteristics.

Belgian Indica (BI). Zones 15-24. This is a group of hybrids originally developed for greenhouse forcing. Where lowest temperatures are 20°-30°, many of them serve very well as landscape plants. Their foliage is lush and full. The large flowers open in profusion during their flowering season.

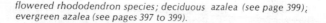

Left to right: 'Pink Pearl', typical of the dependable, large-trussed rhododendron hybrids; R. racemosum, one of the many small-flowered rhododendron species; deciduous azalea (see page 399); evergreen azalea (see pages 397 to 399).

R

Climate Zone maps pages 8-27

Brooks hybrids (Br). Zones 8, 9, 14-24. Bred in Modesto, California, for heat resistance, compactness, and large flowers.

Gable hybrids (G). Zones 4-9, 14-24. Developed to produce azaleas of the Kurume type that would take 0° temperatures. In Zones 4-6, they may lose some leaves but they bloom heavily from late April through May.

Glenn Dale hybrids (Gl). Zones 4-9, 14-24. Developed primarily for hardiness. But they do drop some leaves in cold winters. Some grow tall and rangy, others low and compact. They vary from rapid to slow growing. Some have small leaves like the Kurumes; others have large leaves.

Gold Cup hybrids (GC). Zones 15-24. Originally called Mossholder-Bristow hybrids. Plants combine large flowers of the Belgian Indicas with the vigor of the Rutherfordianas. Good landscape plants where temperatures don't go below 20°.

Kaempferi hybrids (Ka). Zones 1-7. Based on *R. kaempferi*, the torch azalea, a hardy group with orange-red flowers. Somewhat hardier than Kurumes, taller and more open in growth. Nearly leafless in coldest winters. Hardy to −15°. Flowers cover plants in early spring. Similar in every way to Vuykiana or Malvatica hybrids.

Kurume (K). Zones 4-9, 14-24. Compact, twiggy plants, densely foliaged with small leaves. Small flowers borne in incredible profusion. Plants mounded or tiered, handsome even out of bloom. Hardy to 5°-10°. Grow well outdoors in half sun.

Macrantha (Mac). Zones 4-9, 14-24. Includes azaleas sometimes referred to as Gumpo, Chugai, and Satsuki hybrids. Hardy to 5°. Plants low growing; some true dwarfs. Large flowers late, often in June.

Pericat (P). Zones 4-9, 14-24. Hybrids originally developed for greenhouse forcing, but as hardy as Kurumes. Similar to Kurumes but flowers tend to be somewhat larger.

Rutherfordiana (R). Zones 15-24. Greenhouse plants, good in garden where temperatures don't go below 20°. Bushy, 2-4-ft. plants with handsome foliage. Flowers intermediate between Kurume and Belgian Indica.

Southern Indica (SI). Zones 8, 9, 14-24. Varieties selected from Belgian Indicas for sun tolerance and vigor. Most take temperatures of 10°-20°, but some are damaged at 20°. Generally speaking, they grow faster, more vigorously, and taller than the other kinds.

In the descriptions that follow (the 70 most-sold kinds), flowers are described as single, semi-double, double, or hose-in-hose. The first three are familiar garden terms (defined in the chapter on gardeners' language that begins on page 161). The last term means that each flower appears as a tube within a tube.

'Alaska' ('Snowbank') (R). White; semi-double flowers, fall to April. Half sun.

'Albert and Elizabeth' (BI). White, pink edge; double, October to May, peak April. Rangy. Half sun.

'Anchorite' (Gl). Orange. Erect to broad, spreading to 4 ft. March-April. Three-quarters sun.

'Aphrodite' (Gl). Pale rose pink. Flowers partly cover in March-April. Bushy. Three-quarters sun.

'Avenir' (BI). Copper pink; double flowers in medium coverage fall to spring. Large, round leaves. Quarter sun.

'Bridesmaid' (K). Salmon pink; single flowers cover plant February, March. Glossy leaves. Half to full sun.

'Brilliant' (SI). Carmine red; single flowers cover plant March to May. Full sun if soil kept moist.

'Buccaneer' (Gl). Bright orange-red; flowers cover plant April, May. Upright to 5 ft. Like all orange reds it fades in the sun.

'Bunkwa' (Mac). Blush pink; single flowers, in May and June. Low, spreading. Small glossy leaves. Half sun.

'California Sunset' (BI). White, deep pink; fall through spring. Half sun.

'Caroline Gable' (G). Shocking pink; hose-in-hose flowers cover plant March, April. Half sun.

'Coral Bells' (K). Shell pink; single, small flowers cover plant all spring. Small leaves. Half sun. Often blooms in fall or winter in California.

'Dorothy Gish' (R). Brick red; hose-in-hose flowers partly cover plant February to April. Compact. Dark, glossy leaves. Quarter sun.

'Dr. Bergman' (BI). Orange-red; semi-double flowers partly cover plant February, March. Slow. Quarter sun.

'Duc de Rohan' (SI). Salmon pink; single flowers come in cycles. Adapts to low pruning. Half sun.

'Easter Bonnet' (GC). Lavender, white; semi-double, February to April. Half sun.

'Easter Parade' (GC). Pink and white; hose-in-hose, March to May. Half sun.

'Elegans Superba' ('Pride of Mobile') (SI). Watermelon pink; single flowers cover plant April, May. Loose grower. Full sun.

'Everest' (Gl). White blotched chartreuse; single, 2-in. flowers, early to mid-May. Broad, spreading, to 5 ft. tall. Good foliage; useful where *R. mucronatum* is tender.

'Fedora' (Ka). Bright salmon rose. Rangy if not pruned. Angular. May.

'Fielder's White' (SI). White; single flowers, February to May. Half to full sun.

'Flame Creeper' (Mac). Orange-red; single flowers partly cover in April, May. Low, spreading. Half sun.

'Flamingo' (Br). Red; small, single flowers partly cover, March. Dense, bushy. Half sun.

'Formosa' ('Phoenicia', 'Coccinea', or 'Vanessa') (SI). Brilliant red-purple; big, single flowers almost hide leaves in March, April. Vigorous, rangy; popular. Large leaves. 'Formosa' may be more dwarf than 'Phoenicia'; otherwise all are same. Half to full sun.

'Fred Sanders' ('Mrs. Fred Sanders') (BI). Salmon pink; double flowers cover plant autumn to June; peak in March. Half sun.

'Geisha' (Gl). White, striped red; bloom February, March. Upright. Half sun.

'George Lindley Taber' (SI). Light pink; large, single flowers, March, May. Full sun (if kept moist).

'Glacier' (Gl). Shiny white; large single flowers cover the plant in March, April. Glossy leaves. Half sun.

'Glory of Sunninghill' (SI). Vivid orange-red; single flowers in April, May. Half to full sun.

'Gumpo' (Mac). White; large, single flowers cover plant in May, June. Dense and flat habit. Quarter sun.

'Gumpo Pink' (Mac). Rose pink flowers with deeper flecks; 'Gumpo Variegated' ruffled pink flowers with white edge. May-June.

'Herbert' (G). Flowers frilled, 1¾ in., crimson purple; lighter than 'Purple Splendor'. Spreading and compact. April.

'Hexe' (K). Crimson red; single, hose-in-hose flowers, March to May. Half sun.

'Hino-crimson' (K). Brilliant red; single flowers cover flat, tiered branches February to April. Half to full sun.

'Hinodegiri' (K). Cerise; single flowers cover flat, tiered branches February to April. Dark glossy leaves are red in winter. Half to full sun.

'Iveryana' (SI). White; orchid streaks; single, April to May. Half to full sun.

'John Cairns' (Ka). Orange-red; April-May. Tallish, very hardy. Fades in full sun.

'L. J. Bobbink' (R). Orchid pink; hose-in-hose, frilled flowers partly cover plant March, April. Half sun. Sometimes sold as a Southern Indica.

'Louise Gable' (G). Pink with darker blotch; semi-double flowers, April, May. Low. Half to full sun.

'Mme. Mestdagh' (BI). Variegated pink, red, white; double to semi-double, fall to April. Tender. Half sun.

'Mme. Pericat' ('Pink Charm') (P). Light pink with some red markings; hose-in-hose flowers cover February to April. Quarter sun.

'Mme. Petrick' (BI). Cherry red; semi-double flowers cover February to April. Low, compact. Half sun.

'Mme. Petrick Alba' (BI). White; semi-double flowers cover September to April.

Above: Rhododendron falconeri *(see page 396). Below:* R. *'Moonstone' (page 397).*

Climate
Zone maps
pages 8-27

Slow, compact. Half sun.

'Madonna' (Br). White; double flowers partly cover February to April. Rapid, bushy. Lush leaves. Half sun.

R. mucronatum ('Indica Alba', 'Ledifolia Alba'). Zones 4-9, 14-24. Spreading growth to 6 ft. (but usually 3 ft.); large, hairy leaves. White or greenish flowers 2½-3 in. across March-April. Variety 'Sekidera' ('Indica Rosea', 'Ledifolia Rosea') has white flowers flushed and blotched rose, February, March.

'Orchidiflora' (BI). Orchid pink; large, double to semi-double flowers, January, April. Half sun or less.

'Palestrina' (Ka). White with chartreuse blotch. Can be used where *R. mucronatum* ('Ledifolia Alba') is not hardy. Flowers not as large as those of *R. mucronatum* but packed more closely on the plant. May.

'Paul Schame' (BI). Salmon pink; large, double, October to April. Half sun.

'Pride of Dorking' (SI). Brilliant carmine red; March, April. Upright, compact. Full sun (if kept moist).

'Prince of Wales' (SI). Rose red; single or semi-double flowers, February to April. Upright. Full sun.

'Purple Splendor' (G). Flowers, 2 in., crimson purple. April. Fast, open growing.

'Red Poppy' (BI). Dark red; single, huge flowers, October to May. Half sun.

'Redwing' (Br). Red; semi-double, hose-in-hose flowers February to April. Loose, needs pruning. Half sun.

'Rosaeflora' ('Balsaminaeflorum') (Mac). Rose pink; double flowers (buds like roses) partly cover April, May. Very low growing. Used for border edging, ground cover. Sun or little sun.

'Rosebud' (G). Rose pink; small, double flowers March, April. Compact. Difficult in climate extremes, but worth petting. Half sun.

'Rose Greeley' (G). White, chartreuse blotch; hose-in-hose, sweet scented flowers, February to May. Half sun.

'Rose Parade' (GC). Deep pink; very ruffled, double, large flowers, March to April. Glossy leaves. Half sun.

'Sherwood Orchid' (K). Reddish violet with darker blotch; single, large flowers, March, April. Half sun.

'Sherwood Red' (K). Brilliant orange-red; single flowers, February to April. Deciduous if very cold. Half sun.

'Shinnyo-No-Tsuki' (Mac). Violet-red with white center; single, large flowers, May, June. Half sun.

'Snow' (K). White; hose-in-hose flowers, March, April. Upright growth. Dead flowers hang on. Half sun.

'Southern Charm' ('Judge Solomon') (SI). Watermelon pink; large, single flowers partly cover plant February to April. Open, sprawling growth. Very large leaves. Half sun.

'Sun Valley' (GC). Shiny white with green throat; large, hose-in-hose flowers March to May. Half sun.

'Sweetheart Supreme' (P). Blush pink; semi-double, hose-in-hose flowers, February, March. Half sun.

'Twenty Grand' (P). Rose pink; semi-double, hose-in-hose flowers February to April. Half to full sun.

'Vivid' (K). Scarlet; single or semi-double flowers partly cover February, March. Small leaves. Half to full sun.

'Ward's Ruby' (K). Brilliant dark red; single, February to April. Half to full sun.

'White April' (SI). White; single, large, February, March. Upright. Half to full sun.

'White Orchid' (GC). White, red throat; semi-double. Ruffled, cover plants January to May. Half sun.

'William Van Orange' (BI). Orange-red; ruffled, large, double flowers partly cover fall to April. Little sun.

KINDS OF DECIDUOUS AZALEAS

Very few deciduous shrubs can equal the deciduous azaleas—in show and range of color. Their evergreen relatives can't match them in the yellow, orange, and flame red range. They are at their best in Zones 2-7, 15-17.

R. calendulaceum. FLAME AZALEA. Native to mountains of eastern U. S. Variable growth 4-10 ft. tall. Tubular, flaring flowers in clusters of 5-25. Colors range from gold and orange to scarlet. May-June bloom.

R. japonicum. JAPANESE AZALEA. Upright, fast growth to 6 ft. Flowers, 2-3 in., in clusters of 6-12, in salmon red, orange, and orange-red. The variety *aureum* has rich yellow flowers. Blooms in May.

R. luteum (*R. flavum*). PONTIC AZALEA. Tall growing to 8 ft. Flowers are single yellow with a darker blotch; fragrant. Blooms in May.

R. molle. CHINESE AZALEA. Erect grower to 6 ft. April flowers 2½ in. wide in clusters of 6-10, yellow to golden orange. Foliage turns yellow to orange in late fall.

R. occidentale. WESTERN AZALEA. Zones 4-24. Native to mountains and foothills of California and Oregon. Erect growth to 6-10 ft. Funnel-shaped flowers in clusters May-June. Color varies from white to pinkish white with yellow blotch; some are heavily marked carmine-rose. Fragrant.

R. quinquefolium. Shrub or small tree up to 25 ft., usually smaller. Flowers, in trusses of 1-3, up to 2 in. in diameter, pure white with green spots. Blooms April-May. Very attractive foliage, especially in fall color.

R. roseum. Up to 12 ft. Clove-scented flowers are clear deep pink to violet-red, sometimes paler, usually blotched with darker brown-red; tubular, funnel-shaped, in trusses of 5-9, about 1¾ in. across. Blooms in May.

R. schlippenbachii. ROYAL AZALEA. Native to Korea. Densely branched shrub to 6-8 ft. Leaves in whorls of 5 at tips of branches. Large (2-4-in.), pure light pink flowers in clusters of 3-6. April-May. There's no pink to compare with it. Good fall color—yellow, orange, scarlet, crimson. Protect from full sun to avoid leaf burn.

R. vaseyi. PINKSHELL AZALEA. Upright, irregular, spreading to 15 ft. Pink, almost white flowers in clusters of 5-8 in May.

R. viscosum. Up to 15 ft. Fragrant, sticky, white flowers, occasionally with some pink in them; in clusters of 4-12, about 1½ in. across. June-July.

Ghent hybrids. Extremely hardy. Many will take —25° temperatures. Upright growth variable in height. Flowers generally smaller than those of the Mollis hybrids. Color ranges in shades of yellow, orange, umber, pink, and red. May flowering. Some varieties:

'Altaclarense'. Vigorous growth to 10-12 ft. Flowers yellow-orange with orange-bronze markings. Handsome.

'Coccinea Speciosa'. Orange with yellow-orange blotch.

'Fanny'. Pink with copper shadings.

'Nancy Waterer'. Golden yellow.

Knap Hill-Exbury hybrids. Plants vary from spreading to upright, from 4-6 ft. tall. Flowers are large (3-5 in. across), in clusters of 7-18, sometimes ruffled or fragrant, white through pink and yellow to orange and red, often with contrasting blotches. Wide petals give a squarish look to the flowers.

Both Knap Hill and Exbury azaleas come from the same original crosses; the first crosses were made at Knap Hill, and subsequent improvements were made both at Exbury and Knap Hill. The "Rothschild" azaleas occasionally sold are Exbury plants. Ilam hybrids are from the same original stock, further improved in New Zealand.

A hundred or more named varieties are available in the Northwest and northern California. If you want to be sure of the color and size of flower of the plant you buy, choose from the named varieties. But don't consider all seedlings as inferior plants. Generally it's best to select seedlings in bloom. Here are a few representative named varieties:

'Berryrose'. Fragrant pale pink flowers with orange centers. June.

'Cecile'. Deep pink buds opening salmon pink with a yellow flare. Up to 12 flowers, 3½-4 in. across, in a truss. May-June.

'George Reynolds'. Large flowers of butter yellow with deep gold blotches, green throat. May-June.

'Oxydol'. Very large white flowers with yellow blotch in throat. Free-flowering. Bronze green leaves. May-June.

'Strawberry Ice'. Pink buds, coral pink flowers, yellow flare; 11-13 to a truss. May-June.

'Toucan'. Creamy white flowers with big yellow flare; flowers 3½ in. wide. Fragrant. ('Lila', with 4½-in. flowers, is an improved form of this one.) May-June.

Mollis hybrids. Hybrids of *R. molle* and *R. japonicum*. Upright growth 4-5 ft. Similar to *R. molle* but with larger (2½-4-in.) flowers in clusters of 7-13. Colors range from chrome yellow through poppy red. Good fall foliage color. Bloom in May. Some representative varieties:

'Adriaan Koster'. Deep pure yellow, large (4-in.) flowers.

'Christopher Wren'. Chrome yellow, tangerine blotch.

'Dr. Jacobi'. Deep red, 4½-in. flowers.

'Koster's Brilliant'. Red vermilion; reddest of all azaleas.

Occidentale hybrids. Hybrids between *R. occidentale* and Mollis hybrids. Flowers same size as Mollis hybrids; plants taller, to 8 ft. Colors range from white flushed rose and blotched yellow to red with orange blotch. Some of the varieties:

'Delicatissima'. Creamy white flushed rose, with yellow blotch.

'Exquisita'. Pink, white, with orange-yellow throat.

'Graciosa'. Orange-yellow, suffused red, tangerine blotch.

R

Climate
Zone maps
pages 8-27

RHOEO spathacea (*R. discolor*). MOSES-IN-THE-CRADLE, MOSES-IN-THE-BOAT. Perennial. Outdoor plant in Zones 16, 17, 20-24; sheltered spots in Zones 12-15, 18, 19. House plant everywhere. Stems to 8 in. high. Leaf tufts to 6-12 in. wide, with a dozen or so broad, sword-shaped, and rather erect leaves which are dark green above and deep purple underneath. Flowers interesting rather than beautiful. Small, white, 3-petaled, they are crowded into boat-shaped bracts borne down among the leaves. Best used as a pot plant or in hanging basket. A tough plant which will take high or low light intensity and casual watering. Variety 'Vittata' has leaves striped red and yellowish green.

RHOICISSUS capensis (*Cissus capensis*). EVERGREEN GRAPE. Evergreen vine. Outdoors in Zones 16, 17, 21-24; house plant anywhere. Leaves roundish to kidney-shaped, scallop-toothed, something like true grape in size and appearance. New growth (stem and leaf) rosy rusty with red hairs, mature leaves strong light green tinged coppery, rusty hairy beneath. Takes full sun outdoors but roots need shade, moisture. Will take heavy shade as a house plant. Good overhead screen or ground cover in milder regions.

RHOPALOSTYLIS. Zones 17, 23, 24. Feather palms with clean, long trunks. Moderate growth rate. Need shade and do best in frost-free gardens.

R. baueri. From Norfolk Island. Grows to 50 ft.; beautiful curving, arching leaves 6-9 ft. long.

R. sapida. NIKAU PALM. From New Zealand. Grows to 30 ft. A good pot plant where small space dictates an upright palm.

Rhopalostylis sapida: *flaring crown and bulge below it suggest a shaving brush.*

On outdoor plants, feathers 4-8 ft. long stand upright from a prominent bulge at top of clean, long trunk. (Often called shaving brush palm.)

RHUBARB. Grows best in Zones 1-11. An unconventional vegetable. It is used, as fruit is, in sauces and pies. And, its delicious leaf stalks bear poisonous leaves; always discard the leaf when preparing rhubarb. A perennial, it grows from large, fleshy rhizomes. Big leaves and red tinted leaf stalks are showy enough to qualify for a display spot in the garden. Preferred varieties are 'Victoria' (greenish stalks), 'MacDonald', and 'Cherry' (red stalks).

Plant in late winter or early spring. Divisions should contain at least one bud. Soil should be deep, rich, and well-drained. Place tops of the divisions at the soil line. Space divisions 3-4 ft. apart. Give plants some shade in hot inland gardens. Irrigate freely when active top growth indicates that roots are growing. Permit plants to grow two full seasons before harvesting. During the next spring you can pull off leaf stalks (to cook) for 4 or 5 weeks; older, huskier plants will take up to 8 weeks of pulling. Harvest stalks by grasping near base and pulling sideways and outward; cutting with a knife will leave a stub that will decay. Never remove all leaves from a single plant. Stop harvesting when slender leaf stalks appear. After harvest, feed and water freely. Cut out any blossom stalks that appear.

RHUS. SUMAC. Evergreen or deciduous shrubs or trees. Of the ornamental sumacs, the deciduous kinds are hardy anywhere and thrive in poor soils. They tend to produce suckers, especially if their roots are disturbed by soil cultivation. They need some water. The evergreen sumacs will grow in almost any soil, but they need good drainage; soggy soils may kill them. They are not as hardy as the deciduous kinds.

Rhus includes poison oak and poison ivy, both of which may cause severe dermatitis on contact; even breathing the smoke from burning plants is harmful. If you have either on your property, it's best to destroy the plants with a chemical brush killer.

Poison oak (*R. diversiloba*) is most common in California, western Oregon, and western Washington. In the open or in filtered sun, it grows as a dense leafy shrub. Where shaded, as in coast redwood country, it becomes a tall-climbing vine. Its leaves are divided into 3 leaflets the edges of which are scalloped, toothed, or lobed. Very similar is poison ivy (*R. toxicodendron*) which grows in eastern Oregon, eastern Washington (and eastward), but it's more sprawling in growth habit and rarely climbs. The foliage of both turns bright orange or scarlet in the fall—beautiful but to be avoided. It's hardest to identify the bare branches in winter and early spring; even brushing against these can cause the typical rash.

R. cotinus. See Cotinus coggygria

R. glabra. SMOOTH SUMAC. Deciduous large shrub, or small tree. Zones 1-9, 14-17. Native to eastern Oregon, eastern Washington, British Columbia, and eastward in North America. Upright to 10 ft., or sometimes treelike to 20 ft. In the wild spreads by underground roots to form large patches. Very similar in appearance to staghorn sumac (*R. typhina*), but it usually grows lower and its branches are not velvety.

Leaves divided into 11-23, rather narrow, 2-5-in.-long, toothed leaflets, deep green above, whitish beneath; turn brilliant scarlet in fall. Inconspicuous greenish flowers followed by showy autumn display of scarlet fruits in conical clusters which last on bare branches well into winter. *R. g.* 'Laciniata' has deeply cut and slashed leaflets giving a fernlike appearance. Garden use the same as staghorn sumac.

R. integrifolia. LEMONADE BERRY. Evergreen shrub. Zones 15-17, 20-24. Native to coastal southern California and Baja California. Generally 3-10 ft. high and as wide, rarely treelike to 30 ft. Oval to nearly round, leathery, dark green leaves, 1-2½ in. long, with smooth or shallowly-toothed edges. White or pinkish flowers in dense clusters Feb.-March, sometimes Jan.-July. Small, flat, clustered fruits, reddish, gummy, with an acid pulp which can be used to flavor drinks—hence the common name.

Set plants out in fall or winter. Although drought resistant, they thrive best if watered once per month, deeply during summer months. Will also take normal garden watering if drainage is good. Grows best near coast. Makes wonderful ground cover on rocky slopes exposed to salt-laden winds; one plant eventually sprawls over wide area, even down cliffs. In less windy places, use it as a tall screen or background. Makes an excellent espalier against fences and walls. Can be trimmed to dense formal hedge and kept only 10 in. wide.

R. lancea. AFRICAN SUMAC. Evergreen tree. Zones 8, 9, 12-24. Slow growing to 25 ft. with open, spreading habit, graceful weeping outer branchlets. Leaves divided into 3 willowlike, dark green leaflets 4-5 in. long. Pea-sized, yellow or red berrylike fruit in clusters on female tree.

Popular tree in desert areas because it can take high summer heat. Established plants drought resistant, but will also thrive in lawns. Hardy to 12°. Stake and prune to establish form you want. Makes an attractive, airy tree with interesting branch pattern and effective dark red, rough bark. You can train it to single trunk or let it grow as multi-trunked tree. Also useful for screens or clipped hedges. Old plants easy to transplant if grown under dry conditions.

R. laurina. LAUREL SUMAC. Evergreen shrub. Zones 20-24. Native mostly to coastal foothills of southern California. Grows rapidly to 6-15 ft.; sometimes almost treelike, with rounded crown. Gets rangy unless pruned and trimmed. Attractive reddish branchlets. Laurel-like leaves, 2-4 in. long, light green, often with pink margins and pink leaf stalks; foliage pleasantly aromatic. Small whitish flowers in dense, branched clusters 2-6 in. long; bloom May-July, sometimes to December. White berrylike fruit attracts birds. More tender to frost than the native sugar bush or lemonade berry. Sometimes freezes in its native range but comes back quickly from the stump. Useful as an espalier plant or as clipped hedge. Good bank cover where frost is rare.

R. ovata. SUGAR BUSH. Evergreen shrub. Zones 7-9, 11-24. Native to dry slopes away from coast in southern California, Baja California, Arizona. Upright or spreading shrub 2½-10 ft. high. Glossy, leathery leaves 1½-3 in. long; differ from *R. integrifolia* in being somewhat trough-shaped and with pointed tip instead of rounded. White or pinkish flowers in dense clusters, March-May; followed by small, reddish, hairy fruits coated with a sugary secretion. Culture and use the same as lemonade berry and can substitute for same in inland areas. Can be used along coast but not where exposed to salt spray and sea winds.

R. typhina. STAGHORN SUMAC. Deciduous shrub or small tree. Zones 1-9, 14-17. Upright growing from 15 to sometimes 30 ft., spreading wider. Very similar to *R. glabra*, except the branches are covered with velvety short brown hairs, like a deer's antler "in velvet". Leaves divided into 11-31, 5-in.-long, toothed leaflets deep green above, grayish beneath; they turn rich red in fall. Tiny greenish flowers in 4-8-in.-long clusters in June-July are followed by clusters of fuzzy crimson fruits which last all winter, gradually turn brown. *R. t.* 'Laciniata' is a variety with deeply cut leaflets. It doesn't grow quite as big as the species, and is said to have richer color in the fall.

Both staghorn sumac and smooth sumac take extreme heat and cold and will grow in any except the most alkaline soils. Big divided leaves give a tropical effect; when they turn color the show is brilliant. Bare branches make a fine winter silhouette, fruits are decorative. Good among evergreens that show off the bright fall foliage color. You can also grow them in large containers.

RHYNCHOSPERMUM. See Trachelospermum

RIBBON BUSH. See Homalocladium

RIBBONWOOD, MOUNTAIN. See Hoheria glabrata

RIBES. CURRANT, GOOSEBERRY. (See these entries for fruiting currants and gooseberries.) Deciduous and evergreen shrubs. Those without spines are called currants; those with, gooseberries. A number of native species are ornamental; four are sold in nurseries.

R. aureum. GOLDEN CURRANT. Deciduous shrub. All Zones. Native to inland regions of the West. Erect growth, 3-6 ft. tall with light green, lobed, toothed leaves. Clusters of small, bright yellow, spicily fragrant (usually) flowers are 1-2½ in. long. Spring bloom. Summer berries are yellow to red to black.

R. sanguineum. PINK WINTER CURRANT, RED FLOWERING CURRANT. Deciduous shrub. Zones 4-9, 14-24. Native California to British Columbia in Coast Ranges. To 4-12 ft. tall. Leaves 2½ in. wide, maplelike. Flowers March-June, deep pink to red, small, 10-30 in 2-4-in. drooping clusters. Berries blue-black, with whitish bloom. The variety *glutinosum* (more southerly in origin) is commonest in nurseries; it has 15-40 flowers to a cluster, generally deep or pale pink. 'Elk River Red', occasionally sold in the Northwest, has rich red flowers.

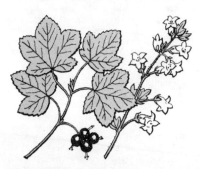

Ribes sanguineum *pink to red flowers in drooping clusters; fruits shown at left.*

R. speciosum. FUCHSIA-FLOWERING GOOSEBERRY. Nearly evergreen shrub. Zones 8, 9, 14-24. Native near coast from Santa Clara County south to Baja California. Erect, 3-6 ft. tall with spiny, often bristly stems. Thick, green, 1-in. leaves resemble those of fruiting gooseberry. Deep crimson drooping flowers are fuchsialike, with long, protruding stamens. January-May bloom. Berries gummy, bristly. An excellent barrier planting.

R. viburnifolium. CATALINA PERFUME, EVERGREEN CURRANT. Spreading evergreen shrub. Zones 8, 9, 14-24. Native to Catalina Island, Baja California. Low-growing plant. To 3 ft. tall and much wider (to 12 ft.). Low-arching or half-trailing wine-red stems may root in moist soil. Leaves leathery, roundish, dark green, an inch across, fragrant (some say like pine, others, like apples) after a rain or when crushed. Flowers light pink to purplish, February-April. Berries red. Ground or bank cover for sun or half shade on coast, part shade inland. Foliage yellows in hot sun. Drought tolerant when established. Excellent ground cover under native oaks where heavy watering is undesirable. Cut out upright-growing stems to keep low.

RICE FLOWER, ROSY. See Pimelea ferruginea

RICE PAPER PLANT. See Tetrapanax

RICINUS communis. CASTOR BEAN. Annual. A bold and striking shrublike plant. Can provide a tall screen or leafy background in a hurry; grows to 6-15 ft. in a season with full sun, plenty of heat and moisture.

Prickly husks of castor bean (left) contain poisonous seeds; leaves to 3 ft. wide.

Where winters are mild, will live over and become quite woody and treelike.

Should not be planted in an area where small children play—the large, mottled, attractive, shiny seeds are poisonous. Also, foliage or seeds occasionally cause severe contact allergies.

Large, lobed leaves 1-3 ft. across on vigorous young plants, smaller on older plants. Small, white, unimpressive flowers borne in clusters on foot-high stalks, followed by attractive prickly husks which contain seeds. Grown commercially for castor oil extracted from seeds. Many horticultural varieties: 'Zanzibarensis' has very large green leaves; 'Cambodgenis' has purplish red foliage and stems.

RIVER RED GUM. See Eucalyptus camaldulensis

ROBINIA. LOCUST. Deciduous trees or shrubs. All Zones. Leaves divided into feathers into many roundish leaflets; clusters of white or pink sweet pea-shaped flowers mid-spring to early summer. They are hardy everywhere, fairly fast growing, and well adapted to dry, hot regions. Will take poor soil, much drought when established. Drawbacks: wood is brittle, roots aggressive, plants often spread by suckers.

R. hispida. ROSE ACACIA. Deciduous shrub. Spreading, suckering habit, usually 6-8 ft. high. Branches and leaf stalks with bright red bristles. Leaves 6-10 in. long, with 7-13, oval to round, dark green leaflets 1½-2½ in. long and half as wide. Flowers deep rose, 1¼ in. long, in clusters 2-3 in. long and as wide with 5-10 flowers. Pods very rarely produced.

R. h. 'Macrophylla'. Better known than the species. Nearly free of bristles; larger, more brightly colored flowers; rounder leaflets. Often grafted on 6 or 8-ft. black locust trunks to produce small round-headed standard tree 12-15 ft. tall, equally broad. Such trees need stout stakes until well established.

R. h. 'Monument'. MONUMENT LOCUST. Tree to 10-12 ft. tall, 5-6 ft. wide. Lavender-pink flowers in 4-in. clusters. Useful small street tree in minimum-maintenance conditions.

R. 'Idaho'. (Often sold as *R.* 'Idaho Pink' or *R. idahoensis*.) Deciduous tree. Moderately fast growth to 40 ft. Shapely. Flowers bright magenta-rose, large, in large clusters (to 8 in. long). Showiest of locusts in bloom.

R. pseudoacacia. BLACK LOCUST. Deciduous tree. Fast growth to 75 ft., with rather open, sparse-branching habit. Deeply furrowed brown bark. Thorny branchlets. Leaves divided into 7-19 leaflets 1-2 in. long. Flowers white, fragrant, ½-¾ in. long, in dense hanging clusters 4-8 in. long. Bean-like, 4-in.-long pods turn brown and hang on tree all winter.

The emigrants brought seeds with them from eastern U. S. and black locust is now common everywhere in the West. In California's Gold Country it has gone native. With pruning and training in its early years, a truly handsome flowering tree, but so common, and so commonly neglected, that it's often overlooked. Has been used as a street tree, but not good in narrow parking strips or under power lines.

R. p. 'Decaisneana'. To 40-50 ft. tall, 20 ft. wide; flowers pale pink, fragrant.

R. p. 'Fastigiata'. Very narrow, columnar tree.

R. p. 'Frisia'. Leaves yellow; new growth nearly orange. Thorns, new wood red.

R. p. 'Tortuosa'. Slow growing, with twisted branches. Clusters few-flowered.

R. p. 'Umbraculifera'. Dense, round-headed. Usually grafted 6-8 ft. high on another locust. Very few flowers.

ROCHEA coccinea (*Crassula coccinea*). Succulent. Outdoors in Zones 17, 23, 24; greenhouse plant anywhere. From South Africa. Shrubby, well-branched plant 1-2 ft. Leaves closely set on stems, 1-1½ in. long by half as wide. Flowers once a year in late spring or summer—bright scarlet blooms 2 in. long, fragrant, in flat clusters at tops of stems.

In greenhouse, give plants rich, porous soil; grow cool bright, on the dryish side until January; then increase warmth, water. In mild-winter area gardens, root cuttings in late spring or very early summer, grow the rooted plants in porous, peaty soil with feeding. The plants will flower the following summer.

ROCKCRESS. See Arabis

ROCKROSE. See Cistus

ROHDEA japonica. Perennial. Zones 4-9, 14-24. Grown for its dense clumps of evergreen foliage. Leaves broadly strap-shaped, usually arched and recurving, dark green, to 2 ft. long and 3 in. wide. Cream-colored flowers in a thick, short spike among the

Dark green leaves of Rohdea are 2 ft. long, 3 in. wide. Good pot or outdoor shade plant.

leaves followed by short, dense cluster of red berries. Spreads slowly by thick rhizomes; old plants have many foliage clumps.

Grow it in shade outdoors; or pot it up as a house plant. Tough and sturdy. The many varieties with crested and variegated leaves are collector's items in Japan. Some are available from specialists here.

ROMNEYA coulteri. MATILIJA POPPY. Perennial. Zones 5-10, 12-24. Native to southern California and Mexico. Spectacular plant growing to 8 ft. or more. Stems and deeply cut, 3-4-in. leaves are gray-green. Flowers up to 9 in. wide, with 5 or 6 white, crinkled petals surrounding a round cluster of golden stamens. Fragrant. Bloom June-July. Flowers handsome in arrangements; if cut in bud, will open in water, last for a few days.

Use on hillsides as a soil binder, along roadsides and in marginal areas, in wide borders. Invasive, spreading by underground roots; don't place near less vigorous plants. Needs full sun, loose gravelly soil, not too much water. Withhold summer irrigation to keep growth in check. Cut nearly to ground in early fall. New shoots emerge after the first rains.

RONDELETIA. Evergreen shrubs. Borderline in Zones 8, 9, 18; reasonably safe in Zones 14-17, 19-24. Tubular flowers in clusters, brightly colored, sometimes fragrant. Best in slightly acid soil in part shade (sun along coast). Feed and water generously. Prune when young to make compact. Remove old spent flowers. Shelter from hard frosts.

R. amoena. Medium to fast growth to 6-8 (possibly 15) ft. Glossy golden green

to dark red-green, 5-in., oval leaves. New growth bronzy. Clustered flowers light salmon pink, yellow in throat. Late winter, spring, and intermittently later on.

R. cordata. Similar to *R. amoena*, but with shining green smooth leaves. Flowers near red in bud, open to become salmon pink in February-March, often into June.

R. odorata (*R. speciosa*). To 6 ft. Leaves smaller, to 2 in. long. Flowers orange-red with yellow throat.

ROSA. ROSE. Deciduous, bushy or climbing shrubs (a few evergreen in warm climates). Undoubtedly the best loved and most widely planted of shrubs in the West, and in all other temperate parts of the world. Even though the best known kinds are not completely hardy they will survive cold winters with some protection.

GROWING ROSES SUCCESSFULLY

To grow roses successfully, you must:
1. Buy healthy, No. 1 plants in varieties suited to your climate.
2. Locate and plant them properly.
3. Supply their four basic needs: water, nutrients, pruning, and pest and disease control.

Climate

Roses will grow in nearly any Western climate, but few varieties bloom equally well in all these climates, and each area requires a little different culture if plants are to give top performance.

In cool-summer areas, you should make certain allowances to get best rose performance: If possible, avoid varieties with an unusually great number of petals; they tend to "ball" (open poorly or not at all). Varieties with deep color tones tend to get "muddy" in cool summers; pastel colors are best. Choose varieties with high resistance to disease. Plant in open areas to assure good air circulation. Spray regularly for either mildew, rust, or black spot, depending on which cool-summer area you live in (see pests and diseases section below). Also, water conservatively but deeply to encourage deep root growth.

In hot-summer areas, rose plants grow fast and strong, but in hot sun and wind flowers often open prematurely, burn, or fade. Provide midday or afternoon shade for best summer flowers. Avoid reflected heat from light-colored walls and avoid south or west exposures. Mulch heavily to keep roots cool and to conserve moisture.

In cold-winter areas, select hardy plants. Plant them with bud union just below the soil surface. After planting, mound soil over canes for protection against freezing. Begin removing soil gradually when hard freezes are over. Cut out dead branch tips in spring.

To determine which varieties will flower best for you, visit municipal or private rose gardens, ask successful local rose gardeners, check with local nurserymen and rose growers, or read the *American Rose Annual's* "Proof of the Pudding" section, which lists performances of hundreds of rose varieties by region.

Get Healthy Plants

Reputable nurserymen and rose growers who sell by mail have top-grade plants and usually replace plants that fail to grow. They store their bare-root or packaged roses

properly and plant them in containers before root and top development are too advanced for proper growth. Bargain roses at supermarkets and department stores may be a good buy when they first arrive, but high storage temperatures dry out roots and stems and sometimes induce premature, spindly top growth which burns in sun and wind. The plants may be dead at the time of sale. Inspect them carefully. Healthy plants should have heavy, plump, fresh-looking canes. Mail order plants that have dried out slightly in shipping can be revived by burying them, tops and all, in moist soil, sand, or sawdust, for a few days. Immerse roots and tops of *all* roses in a bucket of water and let stand for several hours before planting.

Insist on No. 1 or No. 1½ plants. No. 2 grade will often prove disappointing. Presence or absence of a patent tag is less important. Many patent roses are excellent varieties (virtually all the newer roses are patented), but some may be unsatisfactory in your area. And many fine older varieties were never patented, or have patents which have expired. The All-American symbol (AARS), on the other hand, means that the rose has been observed for two seasons in test gardens around the country and has been found both reliable and beautiful.

Bare-root plants are always the best buy, but their planting is limited to the winter months. If you wish to plant roses at other times of the year you can pay more for plants in containers. These roses may be planted any time after rooting is sufficiently advanced to hold soil ball together—usually 3 months after planting in containers.

Plant in Right Location

Plant roses where they receive full sun all day or at least half the day, preferably morning. Avoid planting where roots of trees will steal food and water. Select a spot where air circulates freely.

Soil should drain reasonably well; if it does not, plant roses in raised beds. Allow adequate spacing between plants to promote free air circulation, lessen mildew and other diseases. Spacing of plants will vary with varieties. Many have plenty of room when 3 ft. is allowed between plants; some vigorous growers need as much as 5 ft.

Plant Properly

Aerate heavy clay soils by cultivating deeply and incorporating organic matter such as ground bark or peat moss; enrich sandy soils by adding a complete fertilizer before planting. Dig bonemeal and superphosphate into all planting holes to get nutrients down to where roots can use them.

Keep roots moist while preparing planting beds, either by covering roots with moist, loose soil, or by keeping roots in a bucket of water. Cut back broken canes and broken or badly bruised roots. Dig planting holes large enough to permit roots to be spread out.

In mild climates, set the plant in the hole so that the bud union is just above soil level; where temperatures drop consistently below 10° in winter, set union just below soil level.

Work fine soil around the roots; push it in so that no air pockets remain. Then fill hole to top. Water thoroughly to settle soil around roots. Check to make sure wires on labels aren't tightly wrapped around the canes. If you plant bare-root roses late in

Climate Zone maps pages 8-27

the season, or if the weather is unusually warm, dry, and windy, mound moist soil or peat moss around the canes, and remove carefully when leaves begin to expand.

As soon as plants leaf out in spring, feed them with a complete commercial fertilizer according to label directions for roses. Water in thoroughly.

Water Wisely

Roses need plenty of water to perform well; water deeply, but only as often as necessary. Inadequate water slows or halts growth, diminishes flower production; overwatering which results in constantly soggy soil will lead to root diseases. It's better to let the soil dry out slightly than to water too often, but plants should not wilt. Big, well-established plants in full growth and bloom will need more water than newly set plants. Hot, windy weather necessitates frequent watering.

Basin flooding is a simple way to water a modest-sized rose garden. Overhead sprinkling is popular in hot, dry areas. It removes dust, freshens foliage, and is a partial control for mildew, aphids, and spider mites, but it also washes off spray residues, leaves a calcium deposit on foliage if water is hard, and (by keeping foliage and atmosphere damp) may encourage black spot and rust. If you sprinkle overhead, do it early in the day, and give foliage a chance to dry off by nightfall. Even if you irrigate in basins give plants an occasional sprinkling to clean dust off foliage.

Mulch

A 2-3-in.-deep mulch will help save water, keep soil surface from baking hard, keep the soil cool in summer, warm in winter, keep weed growth down, and build a healthy soil structure. An excellent mulching material for rose gardens is ground bark. Many similar materials have been used successfully.

Feed Regularly

In mild-winter climates begin feeding established plants with a complete commercial fertilizer in February. Elsewhere, give the first feeding just as growth begins. Fertilizer application should be timed in relation to bloom period. The ideal time to make subsequent feedings is when a blooming period has come to an end and new growth is just beginning for the next blooming period.

Prune Properly

Pruning is based on the following facts about growth of roses:

1. Blooms are produced on new wood on Hybrid Teas, Polyanthas, and other bush roses, on year-old wood on climbers. Unless annual pruning produces strong new wood, blooms will grow on tiny outer twigs and be useless for cutting.
2. The more healthy wood you retain, the bigger the plant will be. The bigger the plant, the more flowers you get. So prune conservatively.
3. Best time for major pruning of bush roses is at end of the dormant season, when growth buds begin to swell. Date will vary with locality. Prune climbers after bloom in spring.

General pruning rules. Following pruning practices apply to all roses (except for certain shrub or species roses, where special cautions are indicated in descriptions):

1. Using sharp pruning shears, remove all obviously dead wood.
2. Remove wood that is heavily scaled, sun-scalded, or covered with lesions.
3. Remove branches that cross through center of plant or that rub against other canes.
4. Completely remove all suckers when they appear; dig down to where they leave the understock and remove the bud completely. Let wound air-dry, then paint it with asphalt emulsion.
5. Remove branches that make the bush seem lopsided.
6. If new, large basal canes have formed during the preceding growing season, remove any old canes that interfere with their proper development. Keep bud union well trimmed of dead snags.
7. Cut back wood of previous year, preferably to an outside bud. As a general rule, cut back a half to one third. Try to leave canes at least 18 in. long; in cold climates you will have to cut shorter.
8. Make all cuts as close to the bud as possible without damaging it.
9. If plants were badly infected with rust, mildew, or black spot the previous season, pull off all old leaves after pruning. Rake them up and dispose of them. With a strong stream of water, wash crowns clean of old leaves, dirt, and mulch. Follow up with a dormant spray of oil spray and lime sulfur.
10. Consider cutting for flowers as a form of pruning. Cut off enough stem to support the flower in a vase, but don't deprive the plant of too much foliage. Leave at least two sets of 5-leaflet leaves below a healthy bud.

Pruning Hybrid Teas. Follow the general rules above. In addition, these steps are important:

1. Remove interfering small branches and twiggy growth, but be sure to leave enough growth to keep all bark shaded after leaves form again.
2. Evaluate main canes: If the plant is getting larger than you desire, remove one or more of the oldest canes being careful to retain a good shape.
3. Cut back strong upper side branches to 3rd or 4th bud.

Pruning Floribunda roses. The object here is to get a shapely plant and a quantity of flowers.

1. Prune for balanced form, for uniform height (if plants are massed or planted as hedge or border).
2. Keep all good, healthy canes. Cut off spent clusters of bloom.
3. Cut back last year's growth only by one-fourth. Shape as you prune.
4. If strong, ambitious canes shoot above the bush, cut back to desired height after bloom. Or let them stay and bloom at will if you like the effect.

Pruning Grandifloras. Handle like Hybrid Teas.

Pruning tree roses. Be sure to keep tops balanced and not too large or wind will snap them off, even though they are well staked.

1. Cut back main branches same as for bush rose.

2. Cut back side branches to 2-3 buds.
3. Most important of all, check stake, ties, and labels. Half-inch steel pipe makes a good permanent stake, which can be unobtrusive if painted green. Use cross "X" ties between stake and plant to hold secure. Remove label wires that are apt to cut into bark.

Pruning large-flowered climbers. These "natural" climbers vary in bloom pattern. Prune conservatively until you're sure how your plants should be managed. Each year remove about a third of the oldest canes so that the plant is gradually renewed each year. Cut side branches to 2-3 buds.

Pruning Climbing Hybrid Teas and Climbing Floribundas.

1. Leave plants unpruned for 2 or 3 years; remove only dead and useless twiggy wood. Spread long canes, bring down toward horizontal line, and tie firmly down to support.
2. Wait to prune spring-blooming climbers until after bloom. Watch for and save vigorous new canes; remove at the base from $\frac{1}{3}$ to 1/5 of the oldest canes each year.
3. Flowers appear on lateral branches from long canes; best blooms appear on 2-3-year-old canes.
4. Remove spent flowers; cut back laterals on which they appear to 2-3 buds.
5. Climbing Floribundas can support many main canes.

Pruning Pillar roses. Remove dead and useless wood, cut back side branches to 2-3 buds, and look for renewal canes. In general, handle like very tall Hybrid Teas (which they are).

Control Pests and Diseases

Principal pests are aphids, spider mites, and — in some areas — thrips. To control aphids, spray with contact insecticides as soon as the aphids first appear, and repeat as needed; spraying may be necessary every week or even every few days, especially in late spring. Spider mites can cause serious harm during hot spells, particularly if plants are not watered enough or are otherwise weakened. They stipple leaves, give them a silvery cast, and make them fall off. Spider mites can sap growth to the point that flower formation stops. Control by spraying according to label directions with dibrom or diazinon until infestation is wiped out, or use a systemic insecticide.

Thrips do their damage inside rose buds, making brown streaks on petals, browning petals completely, or turning entire buds brown or so misshapen that flowers may not open. Control is difficult because the tiny thrips hide themselves so well.

Systemic insecticides are especially valuable in controlling the well-hidden thrips. Used every 30 days these products will also control other sucking insects and mites but will do nothing to chewing insects or diseases.

Any multi-purpose insecticide can take care of the leaf-eating insects.

Mites and the three main rose diseases have one thing in common—all four can be checked to a fair degree by a winter clean-up (pick off all leaves on the plants, rake up and dispose of all fallen leaves beneath the plants), followed by a thorough dormant spraying with a mixture of oil

ROSE VARIETIES

NAME	COLOR	FRAGRANCE	DISEASE RESISTANCE	HEIGHT	HABIT OF GROWTH	CLIMATE ADAPTABILITY	COMMENTS
HYBRID TEAS—RED							
'Charlotte Armstrong' (AARS)	Red to deep pink	Lightly fragrant	Good resistance	4-5 ft.	Upright, spreading, strong	General; best color in warmer areas	Reliable; heavy producer. Well-shaped buds open to well-shaped flowers.
'Chrysler Imperial' (AARS)	True red	Fragrant	Resistant; some mildew	3-4 ft.	Upright, compact	Not its best in cool fog	Well foliaged. Extreme weather changes hinder opening of blooms.
'Etoile de Hollande'	Velvety dark red	Very fragrant	Moderate resistance	3-4 ft.	Upright, spreading	General	One of best older roses. Good for cutting. Climbing form, too.
'Mister Lincoln' (AARS)	Dark red	Strong damask	Good resistance	3-4 ft.	Upright	General	Big (6-in.) flowers open flat. Buds shapely.
'Oklahoma'	Black-red	Very fragrant	Good resistance	3-4 ft.	Upright	General, not best in cool areas	Large, urn-shaped buds.
HYBRID TEAS—ORANGE TONES							
'Mojave' (AARS)	Orange-yellow, veined red	Slight fragrance	Resistant	3-4 ft.	Upright	General	Long-stemmed roses for cutting. Long buds.
'Tropicana' (AARS)	Reddish orange	Very fragrant	Generally resistant, some mildew	3-6 ft.	Upright, spreading	General	Heavy producer of medium-sized flowers good for cutting.
'Invitation'	Salmon pink	Very fragrant	Highly resistant	5 ft.	Upright	General	Heavy bloom over extended period.

spray and lime sulfur. This spraying kills mite eggs and overwintering spores of mildew, black spot, and rust.

But a dormant spray won't protect plants all year. In growing season, use materials and methods listed below to control or prevent the main rose diseases.

For mildew, starting in early spring when new growth first appears, spray or dust as often as every 7 days with one of these: dusts—sulfur, sulfur plus ferbam, phaltan; sprays—wettable sulfur, karathane, phaltan, or actidione. Mildew on roses is worst in regions of no rain during growing season. High humidity coupled with poor air circulation encourages it. Choose mildew-resistant rose varieties when possible. Red roses in general are susceptible, some more so than others. Watering foliage early in the day kills spores and aids in controlling mildew.

Black spot occurs in the Northwest, is rare in California and the Southwest. Black spots appear on leaves, which then turn yellow and fall. Control with sulfur dust, wettable sulfur spray, ferbam, or phaltan.

Rose rust first shows (usually in late spring) as small, bright orange spots beneath the leaves. The wintertime clean-up and spray is very important for arresting a rust infestation. If an infestation starts during the growing season, clean up fallen leaves and spray or dust at regular 14-day intervals with ferbam, zineb, lime sulfur, or dusting sulfur.

Chlorosis—yellowing of leaves—may result from a disease, a nutrient deficiency, or as physiological disorder. If the cause is a lack of available iron in soil (most frequent), leaves will turn yellow, with lines of green along veins. Iron chelate gives the fastest relief; iron sulfate can also be used, but acts more slowly. Apply as directed and water in well.

HOW TO USE ROSES

A rose bed can be a thing of great beauty if plants are combined for color harmony and if plants are thoughtfully displayed, with tree roses or tall Grandifloras at the rear or center of the bed, Hybrid Teas at center stage, and an edging of low Floribundas at the front. Resist the temptation to plant one of each variety; group planting of at least 3 of a variety is far more effective.

Raised beds bring blooms nearer eye level, simplify maintenance. Planting in containers supplies portable garden color. Given reasonable space and freedom from too-tough root competition, roses give useful color to shrubbery borders and flower beds.

Climbing roses need not be limited to wall, trellis, or fence. If their branches are pegged down, they make colorful ground covers.

MODERN ROSES

Hybrid Teas

Far and away the most popular class of rose is the Hybrid Tea; it outsells all other classes combined. Thousands of varieties are known and many new ones come out each year. No other flowering shrub is so widely grown or so thoroughly studied and tested. These are the roses of the formal garden, the cutting bed, and the greenhouse. Many varieties are obtainable as climbers, and many are trained to branch at 3 ft. to make trees. Hardy anywhere in the West, although they may need special winter care in Zones 1-3. See chart for some of the finest varieties.

Polyanthas

These produce small flowers (less than 2 in. in diameter) in large clusters. Color range is limited. Flowers have no fragrance or just a light scent. Plants hardy everywhere. Heavy and long-continued bloom makes them good bedding or hedge plants and excellent container plants. 'Cecile Brunner', sometimes called the baby rose, has

NAME	COLOR	FRAGRANCE	DISEASE RESISTANCE	HEIGHT	HABIT OF GROWTH	CLIMATE ADAPTABILITY	COMMENTS
HYBRID TEAS—PINK							
'Duet' (AARS)	Two-tone pink	Slight fragrance	Resistant	3½ ft.	Upright, spreading	General	Easy to grow; persistent bloom. Good cut flowers. Glossy leaves.
'Tiffany' (AARS)	Silvery pink, flushed gold	Very fragrant	Relatively resistant	3-4 ft.	Upright	General: best in warm areas	Good buds, long stems.
HYBRID TEAS—YELLOW							
'Eclipse'	Yellow	Some perfume	Resistant	3-4 ft.	Upright	Not for hot summer areas	Streamlined buds on long stems; fine for cutting.
'King's Ransom' (AARS)	Yellow	Fragrant	Resistant	4-6 ft.	Upright	Not for cool, foggy areas	Tall, vigorous plant. Good color in warm areas.
'Lowell Thomas' (AARS)	Yellow	Good fragrance	Resistant	3-3½ ft.	Upright	Poor color in hot areas	Reliable grower with dark green foliage.
'Summer Sunshine'	Golden yellow	Light fragrance	Resistant	3-5 ft.	Semi-upright, spreading	General	Good cut flower, non-fading in heat. Strong, vigorous grower.
HYBRID TEAS—WHITE							
'Matterhorn' (AARS)	Ivory white	No fragrance	Very resistant	4-5 ft.	Upright	General	Free blooming. Good cut flowers. Shiny foliage.
'Virgo'	White	Slight fragrance	Fair resistance	3-3½ ft.	Upright	Flowers poor in foggy areas	Very shapely long buds, medium-sized flowers.
'White Knight' (AARS)	Pure white	Mild fragrance	Low resistance	3-4 ft.	Upright	General; best in warmer areas	Plants sometimes slow to get started.

Climate Zone maps pages 8-27

(Continued on next page)

flowers which blend pink, gold, and cream. Buds are well shaped, and plants low and bushy. There is a climbing form. 'Margo Koster' has coral orange, very double, ranunculus-type flowers. A climbing form is available. 'The Fairy' has huge clusters of small light pink flowers. Normally 2-3 ft. tall and spreading much wider; it can be kept lower.

Floribundas

They tend to have clustered flowers somewhat smaller than Hybrid Teas. Hardy, disease resistant, and heavy flower producers. The best roses for landscape use: informal hedges, massing, borders, containers. Some varieties have climbing forms.

Grandifloras

Vigorous plants sometimes 8-10 ft. high with Hybrid Tea-type flowers borne singly or in long-stemmed clusters. This class is very close to Hybrid Teas, and some varieties have been switched from one class to the other. Valuable for its large number of cuttable flowers per plant and its mass color effect in the garden.

Miniature roses

True roses 6-12 in. tall or a little taller, with miniature canes, foliage, and flowers. They are derived from *R. chinensis minima* (*R. roulettii*) and come in white, pink, red, or yellow. Everblooming. Can be grown indoors in a cool, bright window; use 6-in. pots and rich garden soil. Use outdoors in rock gardens, window boxes, or containers. Plants are hardier than Hybrid Teas, but shallow roots demand constant water, careful feeding, and mulching.

Large-flowered climbers

Here belong the "natural" climbers, as opposed to the climbing sports of Hybrid Teas and Floribundas. They are quite hardy. 'Paul's Scarlet' and 'New Dawn' are typical.

OLD ROSES

Some of the wild or species roses and their immediate hybrid offspring are still grown by fanciers, and sold by specialists. Many are valuable landscape or flowering shrubs. All are as hardy as modern Hybrid Teas, except where noted.

R. banksiae. LADY BANKS' ROSE. Evergreen climber (deciduous in cold winters). Zones 4-9, 12-24. Vigorous grower to 20 ft. Aphid-resistant, almost immune to disease. Stems have no prickles; leaves with 3-5 leaflets to 2½ in. long, glossy and leathery. Flowers small, yellow or white, in large clusters late spring to midsummer depending on zone and season. Good for covering banks, ground, fence, or arbor in mild climates. The two varieties sold are 'Albaplena', whose white, double flowers smell like violets; and 'Lutea', which has scentless double yellow flowers.

R. bracteata 'Mermaid'. MERMAID ROSE. Evergreen climber. Zones 4-24. Vigorous (to 30-ft.), thorny, evergreen or semi-evergreen rose with glossy, leathery dark green leaves and many single, creamy yellow, lightly fragrant flowers, 5 in. across, in summer, fall, and intermittently through winter in mildest zones. Tough, disease-resistant, thrives in sun or part shade, at beach or inland. Plant 8 ft. apart for quick ground cover, or use to climb a wall (will need tying), run along a fence, or climb a tree.

R. centifolia. CABBAGE ROSE. Deciduous shrub. To 6 ft. tall, with prickly stems. Flowers pink, double, nodding, very fragrant, blooming in late spring, early summer. Selections range from pale pink to purplish. *R. c. muscosa*, MOSS ROSE, is grown in many named kinds. Moss roses have flower stalks and bases covered with hairy, green "moss". Flowers are mostly double, pink, white, or red, intensely fragrant with old-rose fragrance; some varieties bloom only one season each year, others bloom repeatedly.

R

Climate Zone maps pages 8-27

NAME	COLOR	FRAGRANCE	DISEASE RESISTANCE	HEIGHT	HABIT OF GROWTH	CLIMATE ADAPTABILITY	COMMENTS
HYBRID TEAS—BICOLOR AND BLEND							
'Chicago Peace'	Pink, copper blend	Slight	Resistant	5 ft.	Upright, spreading	General	Sport of 'Peace', with same good qualities, deeper color.
'Garden Party' (AARS)	White, pink shadings	Fragrant	Some mildew	4-5 ft.	Upright, spreading	Flowers poor where climate extreme	Vigorous growth.
'Helen Traubel' (AARS)	Peach pink	Mild fragrance	Relatively resistant	4-5 ft.	Upright, spreading	General	Large, vigorous plant. Large buds on long stems.
'Peace' (AARS)	Pale to deep yellow, shaded cerise	Delicate fragrance	Resistant	3-5 ft.	Upright, spreading	General; liked everywhere	Huge blooms, no two alike. Excellent foliage. Climbing form grows 15-20 ft. year.
'Sutter's Gold' (AARS)	Yellow, shaded orange	Very fragrant	Resistant	4-5 ft.	Upright, spreading	General	Long, pointed buds. Heavy continuous bloom.
HYBRID TEAS—OTHER COLORS							
'Sterling Silver'	Silvery lavender	Very fragrant	Subject to mildew	3 ft.	Upright	General	Vigorous once established. Fades slightly in heat.

R. chinensis. CHINA ROSE. Deciduous shrub with prickly or smooth stems, glossy foliage, and single, usually clustered flowers over a long period. An important source of everblooming quality in modern roses.

R. c. 'Gloire de Rosomanes'. (Better known as 'Ragged Robin'; has been sold as 'Red Robin'.) An old rose still widely planted as a hedge. Vigorous growth to 6-10 ft.; can be held lower. Semi-double, red, fragrant flowers over a long season. Plant 18 in. apart for hedging. Very susceptible to mites.

R. c. 'Minima' (R. roulettii). FAIRY or BABY ROSE. An important parent of the modern miniature roses. In its own right it is a good pot or rock garden plant to 9-10 in. (with age, to 30 in.) high, with tiny, red, single or double flowers in spring, scattered repeat bloom. Few flowers first year after planting.

R. damascena. DAMASK ROSE. Deciduous shrubs to 6 ft., with pale green foliage, and double, very fragrant blooms in large clusters. Color ranges from pure white to red. The different varieties bloom either in spring or repeatedly.

R. eglanteria (R. rubiginosa). SWEET BRIAR, EGLANTINE. Deciduous shrub or climber. All Zones. Vigorous growth to 8-12 ft. Stems prickly; leaves dark green, fragrant (like apples), especially after a rain. Flowers single, pink, 1½ in. across, appearing singly or in clusters in late spring. Fruit red-orange. Can be used as a hedge; plant 3-4 ft. apart and prune once a year in early spring. Can be held to 3-4 ft. Naturalized in some parts of the West. Good hybrid forms: 'Lady Penzance', 'Lord Penzance'.

R. foetida (R. lutea). AUSTRIAN BRIER. Deciduous shrub. All Zones. Slender, prickly stems 5-10 ft. long, erect or arching. Leaves dark green, smooth, or slightly hairy. May drop early in fall. Flowers (May-June) single, bright yellow, 2-3 in. across, with odd scent. Best known by its variety *bicolor*, AUSTRIAN COPPER ROSE, a 4-5-ft.-tall shrub with brilliant coppery red flowers, petals of which are yellow on the backs.

Austrian brier does best in warm, fairly dry, well drained soils and in full sun. Needs reflected heat in Zones 4-6. Prune only to remove dead or worn-out wood.

R. gallica. FRENCH ROSE. Deciduous shrub. Prickly stems to 3-4 ft. tall from creeping rootstocks. Leaves smooth, dark green. Flowers red, fragrant, 2-2½ in. across. All have old-rose fragrance, and some are strikingly striped red on white. Flowers pink through slate blues and purple, often mottled with these colors.

R. harisonii. HARISON'S YELLOW ROSE. Deciduous shrub. All Zones. Thickets of thorny stems to 6-8 ft.; fine-scale foliage; flowers (in late spring) profuse, semi-double, bright yellow, fragrant. Occasionally reblooms in fall in warmer climates. Showy fruits. Hybrid between Austrian brier and Scotch rose. Very old rose that came West with the pioneers and still persists in the gold country and around old farm houses. Vigorous growth, disease-free, hardy to cold and (once established) resistant to drought. A useful deciduous landscaping shrub.

R. hugonis. FATHER HUGO'S ROSE, GOLDEN ROSE OF CHINA. Deciduous shrub. All Zones. Dense growth to 8 ft. Stems arching or straight, with bristles near base. Handsome foliage; leaves deep green, 1-4 in. long with 5-11 tiny leaflets. Flowers profusely in May-June; branches become garlands of 2-in.-wide, bright yellow, faintly-scented flowers. Useful in borders, as screen plantings,

against a fence, trained as fan on trellis. Will take high filtered afternoon shade. Prune out oldest wood to ground each year to shape plant, get maximum bloom.

R. multiflora. Deciduous shrub. All Zones. Arching growth on a dense, vigorous plant 8-10 ft. tall and as wide. Very susceptible to mildew, spider mites. Many clustered, small, white flowers in June; profusion of ¼-in. red fruits in fall. Promoted as a hedge but truly useful for this purpose only on largest acreage—far too large and vigorous for most gardens. Spiny and smooth forms available; spiny form best for barrier hedge. Set plants a foot apart for fast fill-in. Birds love the fruits.

R. pimpinellifolia (R. spinosissima). SCOTCH ROSE, BURNET ROSE. Deciduous shrub. All Zones. Suckering, spreading shrub 3-4 ft. tall. Stems upright, spiny and bristly, closely set with small, ferny leaves. Handsome bank cover on good soils. Spring flowers white to pink, 1½-2 in. across. Fruits dark brown or blackish. Many varieties range to deep rose or yellow. Best known variety is R. p. altaica, sometimes 6 ft. tall, with larger leaves and 3-in. white flowers garlanding the branches. Best garden hybrid is 'Stanwell Perpetual', 4-6 ft., with blush to white double blooms.

R. roxburghii. CHESTNUT ROSE. Deciduous. Zones 2-24. Spreading plant with prickly stems 8-10 ft. long. Bark gray, peeling. Light green, very fine-textured, ferny foliage; immune to mildew; new growth bronze and gold tipped. Buds and fruits spiny like chestnut burs. Flowers generally double, soft rose-pink, very fragrant, appear in June. If stems are pegged down makes a good bank cover; normally a big shrub for screen or border.

R. rugosa. RAMANAS ROSE, SEA TOMATO. Deciduous shrub. All Zones. Vigorous, very

NAME	COLOR	FRAGRANCE	DISEASE RESISTANCE	HEIGHT	HABIT OF GROWTH	CLIMATE ADAPTABILITY	COMMENTS
FLORIBUNDAS—RED							
'Sarabande' (AARS)	Oriental red	Slight fragrance	Mildews slightly	2½-3 ft.	Low, spreading	General	Color difficult to use with others. Profusion of bloom.
FLORIBUNDAS—PINK							
'Rosenelfe'	Pink	Slightly fragrant	Resistant	2½-3 ft.	Upright	General	Excellent for cutting. Buds and flowers have fine form.
FLORIBUNDAS—WHITE							
'Iceberg'	White	Fragrant	Immune	2-8 ft.	Shrubby	General	Best white in trade.
'Ivory Fashion' (AARS)	Ivory white	Sweet fragrance	Relatively resistant	2-3 ft.	Upright, spreading	General, poor in Spokane	Long, slender buds, high centered flowers.
'Saratoga' (AARS)	White	Old-rose fragrance	Good resistance	2-3 ft.	Upright	General	Glossy foliage, sturdy plant.
FLORIBUNDAS—OTHER COLORS							
'Circus' (AARS)	Orange, buff, pink	None	Resistant	2-3 ft.	Upright, spreading	General	Large, glossy leaves.
'Little Darling'	Yellow-pink, orange	Fragrant	Resistant	4-5 ft.	Spreading, half-climber	General	Useful as small climber, ground cover.
GRANDIFLORAS							
'Buccaneer'	Non-fading, golden yellow	Slight fragrance	Resistant	5-7 ft.	Upright	General	Rich green foliage clothes entire plant.
'Camelot' (AARS)	Salmon coral	Fragrant	Resistant	5-7 ft.	Upright, vigorous	General	Deep green foliage. Flowers singly and in clusters.
'Mt. Shasta'	White, tinged green	Slight fragrance	Good resistance	6-7 ft.	Upright	General	Profusion of top quality bloom. Blue-green leaves.
'Olé'	Orange-red	Slight fragrance	Resistant	4-7 ft.	Upright	General	Good color even in heat. Profuse bloom, good cut flowers.
'Queen Elizabeth' (AARS)	Delicate clear pink	Mild fragrance	Resistant	5-6 ft. or higher	Upright	General	Good foliage. High-centered blooms borne singly.
CLIMBER AND PILLARS							
'Blaze'	Scarlet	Slight	Some mildew, rust	10-15 ft.		General	A favorite year after year.
'Clg. Cecile Brunner'	Light pink	Fragrant	Some mildew	20-30 ft.		General	The "sweetheart rose". Blooms profusely in clusters. Drought tolerant.
'Don Juan'	Deep red	Slight fragrance	Resistant	8-10 ft.		General	Can prune as bush. Non-burning in heat. Excellent foliage.
'Clg. Mrs. Sam McGredy'	Coppery red to salmon	Fragrant	Some mildew	15-20 ft.		General	Excellent rose for long bloom, varied color, coppery new foliage.
'Clg. Talisman'	Yellow shaded cerise	Slight fragrance	Some mildew	15-20 ft.		General	Rank grower; heavy bloom when established.

R

Climate Zone maps pages 8-27

R

Climate Zone maps pages 8-27

hardy shrub with prickly stems, 3-8 ft. tall. Leaves bright glossy green, distinctive in heavy veining which gives them a crinkled appearance. Flowers are 3-4 in. across and, in the many varieties, range from single to double and from pure white and creamy yellow through pink to deep purplish red. Bright red fruits, an inch or more across, are shaped like tomatoes, edible but seedy; sometimes used for preserves.

All rugosas are extremely tough and hardy. They take hard freezes, wind, drought, salt spray at ocean. Foliage remains quite free of diseases and insects except possibly for aphids.

R. soulieana. Deciduous shrub with vigorous climbing habit. Zones 2-24. Big clump with thick, 10-15-ft.-long canes. Dense foliage; leaves gray-green. Sprays of small, single, fragrant, white flowers intermittently all summer. Fruits orange-red, ½ in. long. Can be pegged down as a ground cover. Will do well in partial shade.

R. wichuraiana. MEMORIAL ROSE. Vine. All Zones; evergreen or partially evergreen Zones 4-24. Trailing plant, making stems 10-12 ft. long in one season. Stems root in contact with moist soil. Leaves 2-4 in. long, with 5-9 smooth, shining leaflets ¼-1 in. long. Flowers white, to 2 in. across, in clusters of 6-10. Blooms midsummer. Good ground cover in relatively poor soil.

Hybrid Musks

Large 6-8-ft. shrubs -or semi-climbers. Flowers, almost everblooming, bright red, heavily fragrant. Unlike most roses, Musks grow and bloom in afternoon shade or broken shade. 'Belinda', 4-6 ft. tall, has clusters of bright pink, fragrant, semi-double flowers throughout spring and summer. Outstanding for its long bloom period, striking floral display in Zones 8, 9. These clusters may be a foot tall, 10 in. through. 'Will Scarlet', to 8 ft. tall, has clusters of 2-in., semi-double, scarlet flowers over a long season. These are followed by clusters of orange fruits in fall.

Hybrid Perpetuals

Before Hybrid Teas became popular, these were *the* garden roses. Plants are big, vigorous, and hardy to –30° if cut back to 18 in. when ground freezes and mounded with soil until new growth pushes out in spring. Often very susceptible to rust. They need more frequent feeding and watering than Hybrid Teas to produce repeated bursts of bloom. Prune high and thin out oldest canes. Flowers are big (to 7 in. wide), opulent, full-petaled, and have strong old-rose fragrance. Buds are short and plump. Colors range from white through many shades of pink to deep red.

ROSA DE MONTANA. See Antigonon

ROSARY VINE. See Ceropegia

ROSE. See Rosa

ROSE ACACIA. See Robinia hispida

ROSE APPLE. See Syzygium jambos

ROSE, CHRISTMAS. See Helleborus niger

ROSE, CLIFF. See Cowania

ROSE, CONFEDERATE. See Hibiscus mutabilis

ROSE, LENTEN. See Helleborus orientalis

ROSE-MALLOW. See Hibiscus moscheutos

ROSE MOSS. See Portulaca

ROSE OF HEAVEN. See Silene coeli-rosa

ROSE OF SHARON. See Hibiscus syriacus

ROSECRESS. See Arabis blepharophylla

ROSEMARY. See Rosmarinus officinalis

ROSEMARY, BOG. See Andromeda polifolia

ROSMARINUS officinalis. ROSEMARY. Evergreen shrub, herb. Zones 4-24. Rugged, picturesque, to 2-6 ft. high. Narrow, aromatic leaves glossy dark green above, grayish-

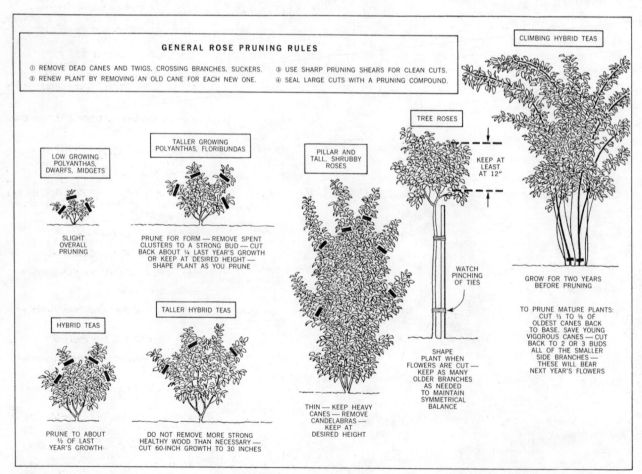

Different classes of roses have their own pruning requirements. Prune at end of dormant season when leaf buds are beginning to swell. Time varies with locality. Annual pruning, shown here, is made simpler if you've kept roses picked and trimmed all year.

Rosemary var. "ARP"
recommended by Brian minter
as most hardy

white beneath. Small clusters of light lavender-blue, ½-in. flowers in winter, spring; occasionally repeat in fall. Flowers attract bees. Leaves widely used as a seasoning.

Endures hot sun and poor soil, but good drainage is a must. Once established needs some watering in desert, little or no watering elsewhere. Feeding and excess water result in rank growth, subsequent woodiness. Control growth by frequent tip-pinching when plants are small. Prune older plants lightly; make cuts to side branch.

Some taller varieties are useful as clipped hedges or in dry borders with native and gray-leafed plants. Greatest use for lower growing varieties is as ground or bank covers. Set container-grown plants or rooted cuttings 2 ft. apart for moderately quick cover. Feed lightly, thin occasionally, and head back gently to encourage new growth.

R. o. 'Collingwood Ingram' (*R. ingramii*). To 2-2½ ft. tall, spreads 4 ft. or more. Branches curve gracefully. Flowers rich, bright blue-violet. Tallish bank or ground cover with high color value.

R. o. 'Lockwood de Forest' (*R. lockwoodii, R. forrestii*). Resembles *R. o.* 'Prostratus', but has lighter, bright foliage, bluer flowers.

R. o. 'Prostratus'. DWARF ROSEMARY. To 2 ft. tall, 4-8-ft. spread. Will trail over wall or edge of raised bed to make curtain of green.

R. o. 'Tuscan Blue'. Rigid, upright branches to 3 ft. tall grow directly from base of plant. Leaves rich green; flowers bright blue-violet.

ROSY RICE FLOWER. See Pimelea ferruginea

RUBBER PLANT. See Ficus elastica

RUDBECKIA. Annuals, biennials, perennials. All Zones. Garden rudbeckias are descendants of wild plants from eastern United States. All are tough, easy plants which thrive in any except soggy soils; full sun. The showy flowers are good for cutting and brighten summer and autumn borders.

R. hirta. GLORIOSA DAISY, BLACK-EYED SUSAN. Biennial or short-lived perennial; can be grown as an annual, blooming first summer from seed sown in early spring. To 3-4 ft., with upright, branching habit, rough,

Flowers of Gloriosa daisy are 5-7 in. wide. Flower at right shows typical dark zone.

hairy stems and leaves. The wild black-eyed Susan has single daisylike flowers 2-4 in. across, with orange-yellow rays and a black-purple center.

Gloriosa Daisy strain has single daisies 5-7 in. wide in shades of yellow, orange, russet, or mahogany, often zoned or banded. 'Irish Eyes' has golden yellow flowers with light green centers that turn brown as they mature. 'Pinwheel' has mahogany and gold flowers. Gloriosa Double Daisy strain has somewhat smaller (to 4-1/2 in.) double flower heads, nearly all in lighter yellow and orange shades.

R. laciniata 'Hortensia'. GOLDEN GLOW. Perennial to 6-7 ft. tall, spreading by underground stems, sometimes aggressively. Leaves deeply lobed, light green. Flowers (summer and fall) double, bright yellow. Tolerates heat remarkably well. Good summer screen or tall border plant. Does not seed, but spreads rapidly, is easily divided. Spray to control aphids. The variety 'Goldquelle' grows to 2½ ft., is less aggressive.

R. purpurea. See Echinacea.

RUE. See Ruta

RUMOHRA adiantiformis. (Usually sold as *Aspidium capense*.) LEATHERLEAF FERN. Zones 14-17, 19-24. Fronds deep glossy green, triangular, finely cut, to 3 ft. tall. They are firm-textured and last well when cut for arrangements. Although it does best in partial shade, this fern will grow in full sun. Hardy to 24°.

RUSCUS. BUTCHER'S BROOM. Evergreen shrublets. Zones 4-24. Unusual plants with some value as small-scale ground cover,

Ruscus hypoglossum: leaflike flattened stems. Lower 2 show flower bracts.

curiosity, or source of dry arrangement material and Christmas greens. Flattened leaflike branches do work of leaves. They bear tiny greenish white flowers in centers of upper surfaces. If male and female plants are present, or if you have a plant with male and female flowers, bright red (sometimes yellow) marble-sized fruits follow the flowers. Spread by underground stems. Best in shade but will take sun, except in hot desert areas. Will grow indoors.

R. aculeatus. To 1-4 ft. tall, with branched stems, "leaves" 1-3 in. long, a third as wide, spine-tipped, leathery, dull dark green. Fruits ½ in. across, red or yellow.

R. hypoglossum. To 1½ ft., unbranched stems, "leaves" to 4 in. long, 1½ in. wide, glossy green, not spine-tipped. Fruits ¼-½ in. across. Faster spreading than *R. aculeatus*. Superior as small-scale ground cover.

RUSSELL LUPINES. See Lupinus

RUTA graveolens. RUE, HERB-OF-GRACE. Perennial herb. All Zones. To 2-3 ft. Aromatic fernlike, blue-green leaves; small, greenish yellow flowers; decorative brown seed capsules. Sow seeds in flats, transplant to 12 in. apart. Good garden soil with additions of lime to strongly acid soil. Full sun. Plant at back of border. Dry seed clusters for use in wreaths or swags.

RYE GRASS. See Lawn Chapter

SABAL. PALMETTO. Zones 13-17, 19-24. Native from North Carolina to South America. Large, slow-growing fan palms, some with trunks, some without. Hardy, all withstanding 20°-22°, some even lower temperatures.

S. domingensis. (Often sold as *S. blackburniana* or *S. umbraculifera*.) HISPANIOLAN PALMETTO. Largest palmetto, ultimately 80 ft. or more, with immense green fans 9 ft. across.

S. mexicana. OAXACA PALMETTO. Leaf stems hang on trunk in early life, then fall to show attractive, slender trunk. Grows 30-50 ft. high.

S. minor. Leafy green palm, usually trunkless, but sometimes with a trunk to 6 ft. Old leaves fold at base, hang down like inverted umbrella.

S. palmetto. CABBAGE PALM. Trunk grows slowly to 20 ft. Big, green 5-8-ft. leaves grow in a dense globular head.

S. rosei. Grows slowly to a slender-trunked 20 ft. Many pale green leaves, pale green flowers.

S. texana. Tall Texan, 60-70 ft. tall there; not likely to reach that size in the West for many years. Light green leaves 3-5 ft. wide. Dense, round head; sheds dead leaves.

SACRED FLOWER OF THE INCAS. See Cantua

SADLERIA cyatheoides. DWARF HAWAIIAN TREE FERN. Zone 24. To 6 ft. tall, the trunk covered with dark, chaffy scales. Fronds clear light green, 3 ft. long, somewhat more erect and less finely divided than the big Hawaiian tree fern (*Cibotium glaucum*). Hardy to 32°.

SAFFLOWER. See Carthamus

SAFFRON, FALSE. See Carthamus

SAFFRON, MEADOW. See Colchicum

SAGE. See Salvia

SAGE, BETHLEHEM. See Pulmonaria saccharata

SAGE, JERUSALEM. See Phlomis

SAGE, SANDHILL. See Artemisia pycnocephala

SAGEBRUSH, BIG. See Artemisia tridentata

SAGINA subulata. See IRISH MOSS, SCOTCH MOSS

SAGUARO. See Carnegiea

SAINTPAULIA ionantha. AFRICAN VIOLET. Evergreen perennial. Probably the most popular house plant in the United States.

S

Climate Zone maps pages 8-27

S

Climate Zone maps pages 8-27

Fuzzy heart-shaped leaves, with smooth edges, grow in rosettes. Pale lavender flowers in clusters of 3 or more. On hybrids and named varieties leaves are plain or scalloped, green or variegated; flowers purple, violet, pink, white, or variegated. Best in east window with roof overhang or suffused morning sun. Keep where temperatures average 60°-70°. Preferably humidity should be high; if house air is quite dry, increase humidity around plants by setting each plant on a saucer filled with wet gravel.

African violets won't take just any potting mix. They need: acid conditions (use plenty of leaf mold); a suitable soil conditioner such as builder's sand or vermiculite; good loam (preferably sterilized if you use garden soil); and a small amount of slow-acting fertilizer such as bonemeal or manure. One good mix is 3 parts leaf mold, 1 part loam, ½ part builder's sand, and a small amount of bonemeal. (For a number of other good mixes, see the *Sunset* book *How to Grow African Violets*, by Carolyn K. Rector.) Don't use too large a pot—African violets bloom best when roots are crowded.

Water plants from top or below, but avoid watering crown or leaves. Use water at room temperature or slightly warmer, wet soil thoroughly, let potting mixture become dry to the touch before watering again. Don't let water stand in pot saucers for more than 2 hours after watering the plants. If plant is well established, feed—only when soil is moist—with a slightly acid fertilizer once every 2-4 weeks. Propagate from seeds, leaf cuttings, or divisions. Most common pests are aphids, cyclamen mites, thrips, and mealybugs.

SALAL. See Gaultheria shallon

SALIX. WILLOW. Deciduous trees or shrubs. Most kinds best where there are pronounced winters. Very fast growing. Will take any soil, and most kinds will even tolerate poor drainage. The one important need is plenty of water. All have invasive roots, are hard to garden under. Most are subject to tent caterpillars, aphids, borers, spider mites.

Weeping willows find their best use as single trees near a stream or lake. With training they can become satisfactory shade trees for patio or terrace. All leaf out very early in spring, hold leaves late (until Christmas in milder climates).

The shrubby willows are grown principally for their catkins ("pussy willows"), their colored twigs, as screen plants, or for erosion control on stream or river banks.

S. alba 'Tristis' (*S. babylonica aurea, S. 'Niobe'*) GOLDEN WEEPING WILLOW. Tree. All Zones; short-lived in desert areas. To 80 ft. or more, with greater spread. One-year-old twigs are bright yellow, quite pendulous. Leaves bright green or yellow-green, paler beneath.

Left to its own way, this (and other weeping willows) will head too low to furnish usable shade. Stake up a main stem and keep it staked—right up to 15-18 ft. Shorten side branches and remove them as they lose their vigor; keep early growth directed into a tall main stem and high-branching scaffold limbs. This treatment will give you a tree you can walk under. Subject to a twig blight in Northwest; use copper spray on new foliage.

S. babylonica. WEEPING WILLOW. Tree. All Zones. To 30-50 ft. with equal or greater spread. Smaller than golden weeping willow, with longer (3-6-in.) leaves, an even more pronounced weeping habit. Greenish or brown branchlets. Train to be a full-fledged weeper as described under *S. alba* 'Tristis'.

Variety 'Crispa' ('Annularis'), RINGLEAF or CORKSCREW WILLOW, an interesting oddity, has leaves twisted and curled into rings or circles and is somewhat narrower in spread.

S. blanda. WISCONSIN WEEPING WILLOW. Tree. All Zones. To 40-50 ft. or more, spreading wider. Less strongly weeping habit than *S. babylonica*, leaves broader, more bluish green.

S. caprea. FRENCH PUSSY WILLOW, PINK PUSSY WILLOW. Shrub or small tree. All Zones. To 25 ft. Broad leaves 3-6 in. long, dark green above, gray-hairy beneath. Fat, inch-long pinkish gray, woolly catkins before leaves in very early spring. Forces easily indoors, and can be cut for winter arrangements. For large gardens that can spare room for unusual shrubs, or for naturalizing. Can be kept to shrub size by cutting to ground every few years.

S. discolor. PUSSY WILLOW. Shrub or small tree. All Zones. To 20 ft., with slender, red-brown stems and bright green 2-4-in.-long, oval leaves bluish beneath. Catkins of male plants (usually the only kind sold) are feature attraction—soft, silky, pearl gray, and up to 1½ in. long. Branches can be cut in winter for early bouquets.

S. gracilistyla. ROSE-GOLD PUSSY WILLOW. Shrub. All Zones. Upright, spreading to 6-10 ft. tall, with 2-4-in.-long, ½-1¼-in.-wide leaves, gray-green above, bluish green beneath. Plump, 1½-in.-long, furry, gray catkins show numerous stamens with rose and gold anthers. Good-looking in the garden or in arrangements. Cutting branches for indoor use will help curb its size; every 3 or 4 years cut back the whole plant to short stubs. You'll be rewarded by especially vigorous shoots with large catkins.

S. humboldtiana (*S. chilensis*). Tree. Zones 9, 14-24. Native to Mexico, Central and South America. Upright, narrow growth 20-60 ft. tall. Habit like that of Lombardy poplar. Leaves 2-5 in. long, only ¼ in. wide, drooping, dull dark green both surfaces. Nearly evergreen in milder winters.

S. magnifica. Shrub or small tree. Zones 4-6, 14-17. Upright growth to 6-20 ft. Shoots turn green to red in winter, hold color for several years. Leaves very large, 4-10 in. long, 3-5 in. wide, gray-green, turning yellow in fall. Catkins very long (4-11 in.). Unwillowlike in appearance; some people think it looks like madrone or magnolia. Unlike other willows, not easy to grow from cuttings.

S. matsudana. HANKOW WILLOW. Tree. All Zones. Upright, pyramidal growth to 40-50 ft. Leaves narrow, bright green, 2-4 in. long, ½ in. wide. Can thrive on less water than most willows.

S. m. 'Navajo'. GLOBE NAVAJO WILLOW. Large, very tough and hardy, spreading, round-topped tree to 70 ft. tall, equally wide.

S. m. 'Tortuosa'. TWISTED HANKOW WILLOW, CORKSCREW WILLOW. To 30 ft. high, with 20-ft. spread. Branches and branchlets

fantastically twisted into upright, spiralling patterns. Use for silhouette value; cut branches good in arrangements.

Tree and branchlets of corkscrew willow (Salix matsudana 'Tortuosa').

S. m. 'Umbraculifera'. GLOBE WILLOW. To 35 ft. with equal spread. Round, umbrella-shaped head with upright branches, drooping branchlets.

S. purpurea. PURPLE OSIER, ALASKA BLUE WILLOW. Shrub. All Zones. To 10-18 ft. high with purple branches, 1-3-in.-long dark green leaves markedly bluish underneath. Variety 'Gracilis' ('Nana'), DWARF PURPLE OSIER, often seen in cold-winter regions, has slimmer branches and narrower leaves; it is usually grown as a clipped hedge and kept 1-3 ft. high and equally wide. General effect is fine-textured, color effect blue-gray. Grows easily from cuttings.

S. sachalinensis 'Sekka' (*S. s.* 'Setsuka'). Shrub or small tree. All Zones. Leaves 2-4 in. long, ½ in. wide, green above, silvery beneath. Catkins silvery, up to 2 in. long. Big feature: flattened branches often 1-2 in. wide, twisted and curled, picturesque in arrangements.

SALPIGLOSSIS sinuata. PAINTED-TONGUE. Annual. Upright, open habit, to 2-3 ft. tall. Sticky leaves and stems. Flowers much like petunias in shape and size (2-2½ in. wide), but more unusual in coloring—shades of mahogany red, reddish orange, yellow, purple and pink tones, marbled and penciled with contrasting color.

Seeds are rather difficult to start, especially when sown directly in garden bed. A good method: In late winter or early spring, plant in potting mixture in peat pots, several seeds to a pot. Keep in a warm, protected location; seeds should sprout in 7 to 10 days. Thin to one seedling in each pot. Later, when young plants are well established and all danger of frost is past, plant in sunny location. Best in rich soil; don't overwater. Pinch out tips of growing plants to induce branching. Best bloom in late spring and early summer, but plants will endure until frost. Good background plant for annual border; handsome cut flowers.

SALSIFY, OYSTER PLANT. Root looks something like a parsnip and has a creamy white flesh that tastes a little like oysters. Plant in a rich, deep, sandy soil spaded deep. Culture is same as for parsnips. It takes 150 days to grow to maturity. Cooked, mashed salsify, mixed with butter and

Climate
Zone maps
pages 8-27

beaten egg, can be made into patties and sauteed until brown to make mock oysters. If plant is allowed to overwinter it will produce a flower stalk topped by a large head of white, cottony, dandelionlike seeds that is quite ornamental.

SALTBUSH. See Atriplex

SALVIA. SAGE. Annuals, perennials, shrubs. Flowers in whorls, sometimes distinctly spaced, sometimes pushed close together so they appear as one dense spike. Tubular, flowers vary in color from deep blue through purple to bright red.

S. azurea grandiflora (*S. pitcheri*). Perennial. Zones 1-11, 14-24. To 5 ft. tall with hairy, 2-4-in.-long leaves. Gentian blue flowers, ½ in. long, provide a mass of color from early July to frost. Full sun.

S. clevelandii. Shrub. Zones 10-24. Native to chaparral slopes of San Diego County. Rounded form, to 4 ft. tall. Foliage and flowers have delightful fragrance. Smooth, gray-green leaves about an inch long. Blue, ¾-inch flowers May-August. Sun, well drained soil, practically no water in summer. For best appearance, prune after frosts have passed. Use with plants that have similar cultural requirements.

S. farinacea. MEALY-CUP SAGE. Perennial; annual where winters are cold. All Zones. Fast growth to 3-ft. mound. Gray-green, 4-in.-long leaves. Spikes of violet-blue, ½-in.-long flowers rise well above mound. Use with other annuals and perennials or by itself as foundation plant. A favorite of flower arrangers. 'Blue Bedder' and 'Royal Blue' good varieties.

S. gracilistyla. (Often sold as *S. rutilans*.) PINEAPPLE SAGE. Perennial herb. Zones 8-24. To 2-3 ft. Use woolly light green leaves fresh or dried as seasoning; milder, more fruity scent and taste than garden sage. Scarlet flowers in fall. Tender to frost, otherwise same care as garden sage.

S. greggii. Evergreen shrub. Zones 8-24. Upright branching, bushy plant to 3-4 ft. tall. Leaves ½-1 in. long, medium green. Flowers an inch long, rosy red, in loose spikelike clusters late spring and summer. Ordinary garden soil and watering, full sun or light shade.

S. leucantha. MEXICAN BUSH SAGE. Shrub. Zones 10-24. To 3-4 ft. tall and as wide; graceful habit. Long, slender, velvety purple or deep rose spikes with small white flowers; blooms summer and fall. Tolerates drought. Cut old stems to the ground; new ones bloom continuously. Grow from clump or pieces of old clumps with roots attached.

S. leucophylla. PURPLE SAGE. Shrub. Zones 10-24. Native to southern Coast Ranges and mountains of southern California. To 2-6 ft. tall with white stems and gray, crinkly, 1-3-in. leaves which drop in dry seasons. Flowers light purple, ½ in. long, in 3-5 whorled clusters May-June.

S. officinalis. GARDEN SAGE. Perennial herb. All Zones. To 18-24 in. high. Narrow, gray-green, 1-2-in.-long leaves. Tall spikes of violet-blue (rarely red or white) flowers attractive to bees in early summer. Variety 'Tricolor' has leaves variegated with white and purple-red. Poor but well drained soil, full sun. Fairly drought resistant. Cut back after bloom; fertilize if you cut continually. Divide every 3 to 4 years. Propagate from

cuttings, layers, or seeds. Excellent for rock gardens and containers. Fragrant, colorful cut flower. Use leaves (fresh or dried) for seasoning meat, sausage, cheese, poultry.

S. patens. GENTIAN SAGE. Perennial, evergreen in mild climates; use as annual where winters are cold. All Zones. To 2½ ft. stems with arrow-shaped, hairy, 2-5-in.-long, green leaves. Deep, dark blue flowers 2 in. long. Sun or part shade.

S. sclarea. CLARY SAGE. Biennial. Coarse-foliaged plant to 3-4 ft. Summer flower fountains of bluish white and rose. Easy from seed. Said to have medicinal value as eyewash.

S. splendens. SCARLET SAGE. Annual. Sturdy plant 1-3 ft. high (depends on variety) with dark green leaves topped by tall, dense clusters of magnificent scarlet flowers. Also rose, lavender varieties. Blooms early summer to frost. 'Scarlet Midget' and 'Blaze of Fire' are extremely dwarf varieties. Start from seed (slow) or buy young plants from nursery. Thrives in full sun, but will also flower in part shade. Any soil; water generously. Cut flowers don't last. Strong color is best with gray foliage or white flowers.

SAMBUCUS. ELDERBERRY. Deciduous shrubs or trees. In their natural state, these Western natives are rampant, fast-growing, wild looking. But they can be tamed to a degree. Use them in same way as spiraea or other large deciduous shrubs. In large gardens, they can be effective as a screen or windbreak. To keep them dense and shrubby, prune hard every dormant season. New growth sprouts readily from stumps.

S. caerulea (*S. glauca*). BLUE ELDERBERRY. Zones 1-17. Native California north to British Columbia, east to Rockies. Shrub 4-10 ft. tall, or spreading tree to 50 ft. Leaves 5-8 in. long, divided into 5-9 rather firm, toothed, 1-6-in.-long leaflets. Small white or creamy white flowers in flat-topped clusters 2-8 in. wide, April-August. Clusters of blue to nearly black ¼-in. berries usually covered with whitish powder. Berries edible, often used in jams, jellies, pies, and wine—if birds don't get them first.

S. callicarpa (*S. racemosa callicarpa*). COAST RED ELDERBERRY, RED ELDERBERRY. Zones 4-7, 14-17. Native to coastal regions, northern California to British Columbia. Shrub to 8 ft. or small tree to 20 ft. Leaves 3-6 in. long, divided into 5-7 smooth, sharply toothed leaflets. Flowers creamy-white, in dome-shaped clusters 2-5 in. across. Small berries are bright red, reputed to be poisonous. Requires ample water.

S. mexicana (*S. caerulea mexicana*). Zones 8-13. Like blue elderberry but with fewer, smaller leaflets, smaller flower clusters, smaller, drier berries of blue or white.

S. racemosa. RED ELDERBERRY. Zones 1-3. Native to high elevations, Sierra Nevada north to British Columbia, east across U. S. Bushy shrub 2-6 ft.; leaves 3-6 in. long, divided into 5 or 7 smooth, sharply toothed leaflets. Small creamy white flowers in dome-shaped clusters to 2½ in. wide, May-July, followed by bright red berries.

SANGUINARIA canadensis. BLOODROOT. Perennial. Zones 1-6. This member of the poppy family gets its common name because of the orange-red juice that seeps from cut roots and stems. Big, deeply lobed grayish

leaves. In early spring, 1½-in. white or pink tinged flowers are borne singly on 8-in. stalks. For the damp, shaded rock garden where it can spread, or for leafy soil beneath trees or open shrubs. 'Multiplex' has double flowers.

SANGUISORBA minor (*Poterium sanguisorba*). SMALL BURNET, SALAD BURNET. Perennial herb. All Zones. To 8-12 in. high. Leaves with deeply toothed leaflets grow in rosette close to ground. Unusual, thimble-shaped pinkish white flowers borne on long stems. Grow in sun, poor soil, adequate moisture, good drainage. Keep blossoms cut. Don't cut plant back more than half. Self seeds almost too freely if flowers not cut. Also propagated from division of roots (divide each year). Bushy ornamental. Good in containers. Leaves give cucumber aroma to salads, vinegar, cream cheese.

SANSEVIERIA. BOWSTRING HEMP, SNAKE PLANT, MOTHER-IN-LAW'S TONGUE. Evergreen perennials. Outdoors Zones 13-24, protected locations Zone 12. House plants everywhere. Appreciated for thick, patterned leaves that grow in a cluster and radiate up and out from base—leaves range in

Among most durable house plants: Sansevieria 'Hahnii' (left), S. trifasciata.

shape from short, blunt triangles to long swords. First common name comes from use of tough fibers in leaves as bowstrings; second comes from banding or mottling on leaves, which resembles some snakeskins; third probably comes from toughness of leaves and plants' persistence under neglect. Erect, narrow clusters of greenish white, fragrant flowers seldom appear.

No special soil requirements; water seldom but thoroughly. If grown outdoors, shelter from midday sun, which makes leaves pale and unsightly. Indoors they will grow in much or little light, seldom need repotting, and withstand considerable neglect—dry air, uneven temperatures, and light, capricious watering.

S. 'Hahnii'. Broad, fleshy, 6-in.-long, dark green leaves cross-banded with irregular silvery markings. Leaves pile up slowly to make the plant 1 ft. tall, 1 ft. wide. Good in small pots, or to give substantial mass to mixed dish gardens.

S. trifasciata. (Often sold as *S. zeylanica*.) Leaves 1-4 ft. long, 2 in. or more wide, fleshy, dark green, broadly banded with silvery gray, rise stiffly erect. Variety 'Laurentii', best known of all, is identical, but leaves have broad creamy yellow stripes on edges.

SANTOLINA. Herbs, evergreen subshrubs. All Zones. These have attractive foliage, a profusion of little round flower heads, and stout constitutions. Good as ground covers, bank covers, or low, clipped hedges. Grow in any soil in full sun. Both species are aromatic if bruised, and both look their best if kept low by pruning. Clip off spent flowers. Cut back in early spring. May kill to ground in coldest areas, but roots will live and resume growth.

S. chamaecyparissus. LAVENDER COTTON. Can reach 2 ft., but looks best clipped to 1 ft. or less. Brittle, woody stems densely clothed with rough, finely divided, whitish gray leaves. Bright yellow buttonlike heads in summer on unclipped plants. Plant 3 ft. apart as ground cover, closer as edging for walks, borders, foreground plantings. Replace after a few years if woodiness takes over.

S. virens. Similar to lavender cotton, but narrower, deep green leaves of striking texture. Creamy chartreuse flowers. Faster than *S. chamaecyparissus*, tolerates more water. Fire-retardant.

SAPIUM sebiferum. CHINESE TALLOW TREE. Deciduous tree. Zones 8, 9, 14-16, 18-21. To 35 ft., with dense round or conical crown of equal width. Outstanding fall color. Tends toward shrubbiness, multiple trunks, suckering, but easily trained to single trunk. In colder areas unripened branch tips freeze back each winter, but new growth quickly covers damage. Leaves poplarlike, roundish, tapering to a slender point, light green. Foliage dense, but general effect is airy; the leaves flutter in the lightest breeze. If the tree is in full sun and has moderate autumn chill its foliage turns a brilliant translucent neon red. Some trees color plum purple, yellow, orange, or a mixture of colors. If possible, select your tree while it is in fall color; a few specimens have shown a nondescript yellow instead of flaming red. Tiny yellowish flowers in spikes at branch tips; fruits small, clustered, grayish white with a waxy coating.

Hardy to 10° to 15°. Grows in most soils, but does somewhat better in mildly acid conditions. Give it ample water for fast growth and prune only to correct the shape. Stake young plants securely. Good lawn or street tree, patio or terrace shade. Good screening against low summer sun or an objectionable view. Gives light to moderate shade.

SAPONARIA ocymoides. Perennial. All Zones. Trailing habit, to 1 ft. high and 3 ft. across. Leaves oval, dark green; in spring plants are covered with small pink flowers in loose bunches shaped much like phlox. Any soil; easy to grow. Useful for covering walls and as ground cover in little-used areas.

SAPOTE, WHITE. See Casimiroa

SAPPHIRE BERRY. See Symplocos

SARCOCOCCA. Evergreen shrubs. Zones 4-9, 14-24 (see *S. saligna* for exception). Native to Himalayas, China. Of great value in landscaping shaded areas — under overhangs, in entryways, beneath low-branching, evergreen trees. They maintain a slow,

orderly growth and polished appearance in the deepest shade. Will take sun in cool-summer areas. Grow best in soil rich in organic matter. Add peat moss, ground bark, or the like to planting bed. Scale insects are only notable pests.

S. confusa. Very similar to, and generally sold as *S. ruscifolia*. However, the latter has red fruits in contrast to the jet black fruits of *S. confusa*.

S. humilis (*S. hookeriana humilis*). Low growing, seldom more than 1½ ft. high, spreading by underground runners to 8 ft. and more. Dark green, glossy, narrow oval, pointed leaves (1-3 in. long, ½-¾ in. wide) closely set on the branches. Fragrant tiny white flowers hidden in the foliage in early spring are followed by glossy blue-black fruits. Good ground cover in the shade.

S. ruscifolia. Slow growth (6 in. a year) to 4-6 ft., with a 3-7-ft. spread. Glossy, waxy, deep green, wavy edged leaves, 2 in. long, densely set on the branches. Flowers (in early spring) small, white, nearly hidden in the foliage, but fragrant enough to be noticed many feet away, are followed by red fruits. Will form a natural espalier against a wall, the branches fanning out to form dark patterns.

S. saligna. Least hardy of the species. Killed to ground in Zones 4-6 at lows of 8°. Grows to 3-4 ft. high with weeping branches. Dark green, willowlike leaves, 3-5 in. long, 1-1½ in. wide. Fragrant light yellow flowers. Purple fruits.

SARRACENIA. PITCHER PLANT. Perennial. Zones 4-7. Leaves rise from a creeping rhizome, look like hollow tubes or "pitchers". These leaves trap and digest insects in the same manner as our Western native pitcher plant—see Darlingtonia. Not easy to grow, requiring boggy, acid soil and high humidity. Will not tolerate hot dry air, strong fertilizers, or extended irrigation with hard water. Grow in bogs, in pots of wet sand-sphagnum mix, or try them in terrariums or enclosed, humid, glass frames.

S. flava. Leaves 1-2 ft. tall, erect, yellowish green veined red. Flowers solitary on 1-2-ft.-stalks, yellow, 4-5 in. across.

S. purpurea. Green to purple-red leaves 6-10 in. tall, rather plump. Flowers purple-red or greenish, to 2 in. across.

SASA. See Bamboo

SASSAFRAS albidum. SASSAFRAS. Deciduous tree. Zones 4-6, 14-17. Fast to 20-25 ft., then slower to eventual 50-60 ft. Dense and pyramidal, with heavy trunk and rather short branches. A pleasantly aromatic tree; bark of roots makes a pleasant, fragrant pink tea. Leaves 3-7 in. long, 2-4 in. wide; shape may be oval, lobed on one side (mitten-shaped), or lobed on both sides. They turn to orange and scarlet in fall, better some years than others. Flowers inconspicuous. Best in sandy, well drained soil; won't take long summer drought or alkaline soil. Hard to transplant. Suckers badly if roots cut in cultivating.

SATUREJA. Annual and perennial herbs, sometimes shrublike. Aromatic foliage.

S. douglasii (*Micromeria chamissonis*). YERBA BUENA. Creeping perennial. Zones 4-9, 14-24. Native from Los Angeles County to British Columbia (plant for which San

Francisco was given its original name of Yerba Buena). Slender stems root as they grow, spreading to 3 ft. Roundish, 1-in.-long leaves with scalloped edges have strong minty scent. Small, white or lavender-tinted flowers April-September. Needs rich, moist soil. Sun along coast, part shade inland. Dried leaves make pleasant tea.

S. hortensis. SUMMER SAVORY. Annual. Upright to 18 in. with loose open habit. Rather narrow, ½-1½-in.-long, aromatic leaves. Delicate ⅛-in.-long, pinkish white to rose flowers in whorls. Grow in light soil, rich in humus. Full sun. Excellent container plant. Sow seed where plants are to be grown, thin to 18 in. apart. Use fresh or dried leaves as mild seasoning for meats, fish, eggs, soups, vegetables.

S. montana. WINTER SAVORY. Perennial or subshrub. All Zones. Low, spreading, 6-15 in. high. Stiff, narrow to roundish ½-1-in.-long leaves. Profusion of white to lilac, ⅜-in.-long blooms in whorls, attractive to bees. Grow in sandy, well drained soil, average moisture. Keep clipped. Clip at start of flowering season for drying. Propagate from seed (germinates slowly), cuttings, divisions. Space plants 18 in. apart in rows. Use as edging in herb border, or in rock garden. Use leaves fresh or dried. Not as delicate a flavor as summer savory.

SAUROMATUM guttatum (*Arum cornutum*). VOODOO LILY. Tuber. Zones 5, 6, 8, 9, 14-24; also grown as house plant. Flower a 12-in.-long, greenish yellow flower bract marked deep purple, surrounding long blackish purple central spike. Bloom has extremely strong, unpleasant odor. Large, deeply lobed, fanlike, tropical-looking leaves on 3-ft. stalks appear after flowers. Big tuber will bloom without planting if large

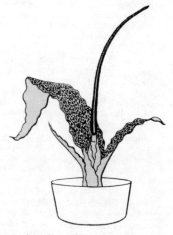

Greenish yellow bract of Sauromatum is spotted purple; spike blackish purple.

enough; just place it on window sill or table. After bloom, plant in a big pot or in garden. Loose, slightly acid soil.

S. g. 'Venosum', commonly called snake lily, has leaves 10-12 in. long, spotted stalk.

SAVORY, SUMMER. See Satureja hortensis

SAVORY, WINTER. See Satureja montana

SAXIFRAGA. SAXIFRAGE. Perennials. Some native to Western mountains and foothills, most from Europe. They thrive best in the rock gardens of the Northwest. Most saxifrages grow in full sun or light shade in cooler regions. They require good drainage. Bergenias were once classified as saxifrages, and are still often sold as such.

S. burseriana. Zones 1-7, 14-17. Mat-forming rock garden plant. Makes masses of tiny rosettes, each packed with narrow, sharp-pointed, blue-gray leaves. In early spring white flowers rise above the mats on 1-2-in. stems. Variety 'Crenata' has scalloped petal edges. Variety 'Sulphurea' has soft yellow flowers.

S. callosa (*S. lingulata*). Zones 1-7, 14-17. Basal leaves narrow, rounded at tip, edges encrusted with lime. Flower stalk 6-14 in., with many white, often red-spotted blossoms on upper half of stalk. Early summer bloom.

S. marginata. Zones 1-7, 14-17. A very small edition of the above with flower stalks to 4 in. in height. Flowers white, ½-¾ in. across. Spring-flowering.

S. paniculata (*S. aizoon*). Zones 1-7. Leaves with toothed edges, narrow, growing in dense rosettes. Flower stalks 6-10 in. tall, with many clustered white flowers spotted with red. Varieties and hybrids between this and other saxifrages have pink or yellow flowers. Early summer.

S. rosacea (*S. decipiens*). Zones 1-7, 14-17. Cushion-forming, spreading plant—a typical "mossy saxifrage". Spreads fairly rapidly; the narrow, fleshy leaves are divided into 3-5 narrow lobes. In Northwest, foliage turns crimson in late fall. Flower stalks rise in spring to 8-9 in. tall and display wide-open flowers of white. Afternoon shade best in cool-summer areas; shade essential where summers are hot. Many named varieties and hybrids exist, with flowers of apple-blossom pink, rose, and red.

S. sternbergii. Zones 1-7, 14-17. Fast-spreading mats of finely-divided, fleshy leaves, above which (in May) the white flowers rise on slender 6-in. stems. Sturdy and quick enough to serve as small-scale ground cover. Cut back by a third after bloom to keep plants compact.

S. stolonifera (*S. sarmentosa*). STRAWBERRY GERANIUM. Zones 4-9, 14-24; house plant everywhere. Creeping plant that makes runners like a strawberry. Nearly round, white-veined leaves to 4 in. across, pink underneath, blend well with pink azaleas. Flowers white, to 1 in. across, in loose, open clusters to 2 ft. tall. Used as a house plant in hanging baskets or pots. A ground cover where hard freezes are infrequent. Shade or part shade, considerable moisture.

S. umbrosa. LONDON PRIDE. Zones 1-7, 14-17. Rosettes of thick, strap-shaped, 2½-in.-long shiny green leaves. Open cluster of pink flowers on a wine red flower stalk, blooms in May. Does best in shade. Good ground cover for small areas; effective near rocks, stream beds.

SCABIOSA. PINCUSHION FLOWER. Annual, perennials. Stamens protrude beyond curved surface of flower cluster, giving illusion of pins stuck into a cushion. Easy to grow; needs sun. Bloom begins in midsummer, continues until winter if flowers are cut. Good in mixed or mass plantings. Excellent for arrangements.

S. atropurpurea. PINCUSHION FLOWER, MOURNING BRIDE. Annual; may persist as a perennial where winters are mild. Grows to 2½-3 ft. tall. Many long, wiry-stemmed

Flower heads of pincushion flower 2 in. or more wide, deep purple to pink, white.

flower clusters 2 in. or more across, in colors from blackish purple to salmon pink, rose, white.

S. caucasica. PERENNIAL PINCUSHION FLOWER. Perennial. All Zones. To 2½ ft. high. Leaves vary from finely cut to uncut. Flowers blue to bluish lavender or white depending on variety. Flower clusters 2½-3 in. across appear from June to frost.

S. columbaria. Perennial. Zones 4-24. To 2½ ft. tall. Leaves gray-green, finely cut. Flowers to 3 in. across; lavender-blue, pink, white varieties. Does particularly well in Zones 22-24.

SCHEFFLERA. Evergreen large shrubs, small trees. Zones 23, 24. For the plant widely sold as *Schefflera actinophylla*, see *Brassaia*. Fast growing, tropical-looking plants; long-stalked leaves divided into leaflets which spread like the fingers of a hand. Good use as wall plant—fasten main stem to wall. But can also stand alone. Rich soil, ample water, sun or shade.

S. actinophylla. See Brassaia

S. delavayi. Native to south China. Grows to 15-20 ft. Leaflets dark green, whitish beneath, lobed or with a few teeth, 5-10 in. long, 2-5 in. wide, 4-7 to a leaf. Tiny greenish flowers in branched clusters 1-1½ ft. long.

S. digitata. NEW ZEALAND SCHEFFLERA. Grows 10-20 ft. tall, generally with grouped leaning stems. Leaves with 5-10 leaflets, each 3-7 in. long, sometimes deeply lobed, dark, dull green; new leaves light green with brown tinge. Clusters of greenish flowers followed by clustered purplish black fruit.

SCHINUS. PEPPER TREE. Evergreen and semi-deciduous trees. Commonly planted in lowland parts of California and Arizona. Pepper trees are praised by some gardeners, heartily disliked by others. Actually, the three species discussed here are quite different from one another, and each should be judged on its own merits.

S. molle. CALIFORNIA PEPPER TREE. Evergreen tree. Zones 8, 9, 12-24. Fast to 25-40-ft. height and spread. Trunks of old trees heavy and fantastically gnarled, with knots and burls that frequently sprout leaves or small branches. Bark light brown, rough. Limbs heavy, branchlets light and gracefully drooping. Bright green leaves divided into many narrow 1½-to-2-in.-long leaflets. Numerous, tiny, yellowish white, summer flowers in drooping 4-6-in. clusters give way to pendant clusters of rose-colored berries in fall, winter. (Some trees have nearly all male flowers; these will not fruit.) Grows in any soil, tolerates drought when established, and will even get along with poor drainage. Stake young plants; prune for high branching if you wish to walk or grow lawn under them. To avoid heart rot, keep large pruning cuts sealed until well healed over. Spray for scale and aphids. Subject to root rot diseases in infected soils.

There's room for argument when it comes to usefulness. Some gardeners object to their messy litter, scale infestation, and greedy surface roots; and yet many newcomers to California consider them to be one of our most strikingly handsome trees. Properly used they are splendid. Don't plant them between sidewalk and curb, near house foundations, patio paving or entrances, in lawns, or near sewers or drains. Do plant them along roads or rustic streets without curbs—if you can give them room to spread. They are fine trees for shading a play area or rustic, gravel-surfaced, informal lounging area. One different use: plant young pepper trees 2 ft. apart and prune into a graceful, billowy hedge.

S. polygamus (*S. dependens*). PERUVIAN PEPPER TREE. Evergreen or semi-deciduous tree. Zones 8-24. Very fast to 15-25 ft. high and about as wide. Single or multiple trunked. Branches spiny. Leaves oblong, ⅓-1 in. long, dark green. Deep purple small fruits that follow the tiny yellowish flowers are in dense clusters, almost hide foliage in July. Any soil. No serious pests or diseases. Thin out excess twiggy growth to show off branch pattern. Street, lawn, or garden tree; also hedge. Especially useful in low desert.

S. terebinthifolius. BRAZILIAN PEPPER. Evergreen tree. Zones 15-17, 19-24. Moderate growth rate to 30 ft., with equal spread. Differs from California pepper in its non-pendulous growth; in its darker green, coarser, glossy leaves with only 7 leaflets instead of many; and in its bright red berries that are very showy in winter. With very little training it makes a broad, umbrella-shaped crown. Stake young trees well and prune to make a fairly high crown. Also popular as a multi-trunk tree. Variations in foliage and growth habit are often pronounced. When selecting a tree, try to choose one that has rich foliage and that has already set berries.

Feed and water infrequently and deeply to discourage surface roots. To reduce possibility of storm breakage, shorten overlong limbs and do some late summer thinning so wind can pass through. Subject to verticillium wilt. Good shade tree for patio or small garden; fine lawn tree.

SCHIZANTHUS pinnatus. POOR MAN'S ORCHID, BUTTERFLY FLOWER. Annual. To 1½ ft. high. Great quantities of small, orchid-like flowers in late winter and spring.

S

Climate Zone maps pages 8-27

Flowers have varicolored markings on pink, rose, lilac, purple, or white background and are quite showy against their ferny foliage. Sensitive to frost and to heat; best in cool coastal regions. Buy plants in flats, or start seeds indoors about 4 months ahead of planting time (germination is slow). Plant in filtered shade. Combines well with *Primula malacoides* and cineraria, and shares same cultural requirements. Good pot subject. Often grown in greenhouses and conservatories.

SCHIZOCENTRON elegans. SPANISH SHAWL. Perennial. Zones 17, 21-24; with protection from frost, lives over in Zones 15, 16, 18-20. Creeping, vinelike habit. Oval leaves ½-in. or less wide with 3 well-marked veins. Leaves and stems often acquire a red color as the season advances. In summer, 1-in.-wide magenta flowers appear among the leaves; calyx remains after blossom has withered. Grow in shade. When used as ground cover, plants in bloom give appearance of a carpet covered with bougainvillea-like blossoms. Good subject for hanging baskets.

SCHIZOPHRAGMA hydrangeoides. JAPANESE HYDRANGEA VINE. Deciduous vine. Zones 4-10, 14-22. Similar to *Hydrangea anomala petiolaris* in appearance and uses. Differs in that the hydrangea has sterile flowers with four petal-like lobes, *Schizophragma* has sterile flowers with a single large leaflike lobe.

SCHIZOSTYLIS coccinea. CRIMSON FLAG, KAFFIR LILY. Rhizome. Zones 5-9, 14-24; best in mild-winter climates. Narrow, evergreen leaves, 18 in. tall, resembling those of gladiolus. Spikes of showy, crimson, starlike, 2½-in. flowers on slender 18-24-in. stems in October-November. Variety 'Mrs. Hegarty' has rose-pink flowers. Excellent cut flower; each bloom lasts 4 days, other blooms follow. Plant in sun. Provide light shade in hot areas. Add peat moss or leaf mold to soil; water freely during growth. Divide overgrown clumps, leaving 5 shoots on each division.

SCHLUMBERGERA. CACTUS. House plants; lathhouse or covered terrace plants in Zones 16, 17, 21-24. Cactus that in nature live on trees like certain orchids. Plants often confused in nursery trade; many hybrids, selections differ principally in color. Remember, they come from the jungle—give them rich, porous soil with plenty of leaf mold and sand. Water frequently and feed often with liquid fertilizer. Feed as often as every 7-10 days. If grown outdoors in summer, give half shade.

S. bridgesii. (Often sold as *Zygocactus truncatus.*) CHRISTMAS CACTUS. Old favorite. Grown right, plants may be 3 ft. across, with arching, drooping branches made up of flattened, scalloped, smooth, bright green, spineless, 1½-in. joints; and may have hundreds of many-petaled, long-tubular, 3-in.-long, rosy purplish red flowers at Christmas time.

S. gaertneri. See Rhipsalidopsis gaertneri

S. truncata (*Zygocactus truncatus*). CRAB CACTUS. Joints 1-2 in. long, sharply toothed, with 2 large teeth at end of last joint. Flowers short-tubed, with spreading, pointed petals, scarlet. November-March.

Many varieties in white, pink, salmon, orange.

SCHOLAR TREE, CHINESE. See Sophora japonica

SCIADOPITYS verticillata. UMBRELLA PINE. Evergreen tree. Zones 4-9, 14-24; borderline Zones 1-3. To 100-120 ft. in its native Japan, but not likely to exceed 25-40 ft. in Western gardens. Very slow grower. Young plants symmetrical, dense, rather narrow; older plants open up and branches tend to droop. Small, scalelike leaves scattered along branches, bunched at branch ends. At branch and twig ends grow whorls of 20-30 long (3-6-in.), narrow, flattened, firm,

Glossy green needles of umbrella pine are 3-6 in. long. Young plants symmetrical.

fleshy needles of glossy dark green (they radiate out like the spokes in an umbrella). In time, 3-5-in.-long woody cones may appear.

Plant in rich, well drained, neutral or slightly acid soil. Full sun in cool-summer areas or near coast; afternoon shade in interior valleys. Give ample water. Can be left unpruned or can be thinned to create an Oriental effect. Choice decorative tree for open ground or container use. Good bonsai subject. Boughs are beautiful and long lasting in arrangements.

SCILLA. SQUILL, BLUEBELL. Bulb. All Zones; exceptions noted below. All have basal, strap-shaped leaves and bell-shaped or starlike flowers in clusters on leafless stalks. Best planted in informal drifts among shrubs, under deciduous trees, among low-growing spring perennials. Good in pots, for cutting.

S. bifolia. First to bloom. Carries up to 8 turquoise blue, inch-wide, starlike flowers on 8-in. stems. White, pale purplish pink, or violet-blue varieties. Plant 2 in. deep, 3-5 in. apart.

S. hispanica (*S. campanulata*). SPANISH BLUEBELL. Most widely planted. Prolific, vigorous, with sturdy 20-in. stems bearing 12 or more nodding bells about ¾ in. long. Blue most popular color; 'Excelsior', deep blue, best variety. Also white, pink, or rose forms. Plant 3 in. deep in fall.

S. nonscripta. ENGLISH BLUEBELL, WOOD HYACINTH. Flowers narrower and smaller than Spanish bluebell, on 1-ft. spikes. Culture and uses same as for Spanish bluebell.

S. peruviana. PERUVIAN SCILLA. Outdoors all year in Zones 14-17, 19-24; in

colder climates grow in pots (1 to a 6-in. pot, 3 in a 9-10-in. pot). Actually native to Mediterranean. Bluish purple, starlike flowers—50 or more in a large dome-shaped cluster, on 10-12-in. stalks. Long floppy, strap-shaped leaves die down after flowers bloom in May-June. Plant 4-6 in. deep. Bulbs dormant only a short time after leaves wither; replant, if necessary, then.

S. sibirica. SIBERIAN SQUILL. Satisfactory only in cold-winter areas. Very early blooming, with loose spikes of intense blue flowers on 3-6-in. stems. 'Spring Beauty', with darker blue stripes is choice. Also white, purplish pink, and violet-blue varieties.

S. tubergeniana. Blooms in January, at same time as snowdrops (*Galanthus*). Pale blue flowers, 4 or more on 4-in. stalks; 3 or more stalks to each bulb. Plant 2-3 in. deep.

SCIMITAR SHRUB. See Brachysema

SCINDAPSUS. See Rhaphidophora

SCIRPUS cernuus. LOW BULRUSH. Grasslike perennial. Zones 7-24. To 6-10 in. high, usually less. Drooping green, threadlike stems topped by small brown flower spikelet. Ample moisture is all it needs to grow; occasional division and resetting will keep it small. Ideal for edge of a shallow pond; highly attractive for streamside effect in Japanese gardens. Good pot subject.

SCOKE. See Phytolacca americana

SCOTCH MOSS. See Irish Moss, Scotch Moss

SEAFORTHIA elegans. See Archontophoenix cunninghamiana

SEA HOLLY. See Eryngium

SEA LAVENDER. See Limonium

SEA PINK. See Armeria

SEA TOMATO. See Rosa rugosa

SEA URCHIN. See Hakea laurina

SEDUM. STONECROP. Succulent perennials or subshrubs. They come from many parts of the world and vary in hardiness, cultural needs; some are among the hardiest succulent plants. Some tiny and trailing, others upright. Leaves fleshy, highly variable in size, shape, and color; evergreen unless otherwise noted. Flowers usually small, starlike, in fairly large clusters, sometimes brightly colored.

The smaller sedums are useful in rock gardens, as ground or bank cover, in small areas where unusual texture, color are needed. Larger kinds good in borders or containers, as shrubs. Most of the kinds propagate very easily by stem cuttings—even detached leaves will root and form new plants. Soft and easily crushed, they will not take foot traffic; otherwise they are tough, low-maintenance plants. Set ground cover kinds 10-12 in. apart.

S. acre. GOLDMOSS SEDUM. All Zones. Evergreen plant 2-5 in. tall, with upright branchlets from trailing, rooting stems. Tiny light green leaves; clustered yellow flowers in mid- or late spring. Extremely hardy but can get out of bounds, become a weed. Good as ground cover, between stepping stones, on dry walls.

S. album. (Often sold as *S. brevifo-lium.*) All Zones. Creeping evergreen plant 2-6 in. tall. Fleshy leaves ¼-½ in. long, light to medium green, sometimes red-tinted. Flowers white or pinkish white. Ground cover.

S. altissimum. See *S. sediforme, S. reflexum.*

S. amecamecanum. MEXICAN SEDUM. Zones 8, 9, 14-24. Spreading, branching plant 6-8 in. tall. Leaves fleshy, bright yellow-green, ¾ in. long. Flowers yellow, clustered; spring and summer bloom. Good ground cover, but sometimes afflicted by a

Leaves of Mexican sedum about ³/₄ in. long, bright yellow-green. Dense branching.

dieback, especially in hot weather and in wet soils. Best appearance in cool weather. Much like *S. confusum;* the two plants often sold interchangeably.

S. anglicum. All Zones. Low, spreading plants 2-4 in. tall. Dark green fleshy leaves to ⅛ in. long. Flowers (spring) pinkish white. Ground cover.

S. brevifolium. Zones 8, 9, 14-24. Europe, north Africa. Tiny, slowly spreading plants, 2-3 in. high with tightly-packed fleshy leaves less than ⅛ in. long. Leaves gray-white, flushed with red. Flowers pinkish or white. Sunburns in hot, dry places. Needs good drainage. Best in rock garden, with larger succulents in pots, containers, miniature gardens.

S. confusum. Zones 8, 9, 14-24. Native to Mexico. Plants much-branched, to 1 ft. tall. Leaves to 1½ in. long, ½-¾ in. wide. Dense clusters of yellow flowers in late spring. Borders, pots, or bank plantings, ground cover. Much like *S. amecamecanum.*

S. dasyphyllum. Zones 8, 9, 14-24. Mediterranean, north Africa. To 2 in. tall; tiny leaves closely packed on stems, soft bluegreen. Spring flowers small, white. Good color for small areas. Ground cover.

S. dendroideum. Zones 8, 9, 14-24. Native to Mexico. To 2 ft..Branching, spreading plant with rounded, fleshy leaves 2 in. long, yellow-green, often bronze tinted. Flowers deep yellow, in spring and early summer.

S. d. praealtum (*S. praealtum*). Like the one above but taller (to 3-5 ft.), with lighter yellow flowers and less bronze tinting on leaves. Both plants good for low-maintenance informal hedge or space divider; especially useful along semi-rural streets, lanes where watering is difficult.

S. guatemalense. See *S. rubrotinctum.*

S. lineare. (Often sold as *S. sarmentosum.*) All Zones. Spreading, trailing, rooting stems to 1 ft. long, closely set with very narrow, fleshy, light green leaves 1 in. long.

Flowers yellow, star-shaped, profuse in late spring, early summer. Ground cover. Vigorous spreader.

S. moranense. Zones 8-24. Native to Mexico. Small, spreading, much-branched plants to 3 in. tall. Leaves small, fleshy, cylindrical, bright green turning reddish in sun or in cool weather. Flowers sparse, small, white. Rock garden, or ground cover for small areas.

S. morganianum. DONKEY TAIL, BURRO TAIL. Safely outdoors in Zones 17, 22-24; house plant everywhere; much used under protection of lath or eaves in Zones 13-16, 18-21. Makes long, trailing stems that grow to 3-4 ft. in 6-8 years. Thick, fleshy, light gray-green leaves overlap each other along the stems to give a braided or ropelike effect. Flowers (rarely seen) pink to deep red. Choice plant if well grown. Because it grows such long, pendulous stems, the most practical place to grow it is in a hanging pot or wall pot. In mildest areas near coast try it at top of walls or high up in rock garden.

Trailing stems of donkey tail grow to 3-4 ft., are set with gray-green leaves.

Rich, fast draining soil. Protect from wind and give half shade; water freely and feed 2-3 times during summer with liquid fertilizer.

S. oaxacanum. Zones 8-24. Spreading, rooting stems a few inches tall. Leaves tiny, thick, gray-green. Yellow spring flowers. Takes poor soil. Ground cover.

S. oxypetalum. Zones 16, 17, 21-24. Native of Mexico. Grows to 3 ft. high, usually much less. Even tiny plants have look of a gnarled tree. Leaves 1-1½ in. long; flowers dull red, fragrant. Evergreen or semi-evergreen in mildest areas, deciduous elsewhere. Handsome pot plant.

S. reflexum. (Often sold as *S. altissimum.*) Zones 8-24. Much like *S. sediforme*, but with shorter leaves, yellow flowers. Ground cover.

S. rubrotinctum (*S. guatemalense*). PORK AND BEANS. Zones 8, 9, 14-24. Sprawling, leaning stems 6-8 in. tall. Leaves like jelly beans, ¾ in. long, green with reddish brown tips, often entirely bronze-red in sun. Flowers reddish yellow. The easily-detached leaves root readily. Rock gardens, pots, small-scale ground cover.

S. sediforme (*S. altissimum*). Zones 8-24. Native to Mediterranean region. Spreading, creeping plants to 16 in. tall. Leaves light blue-gray, fleshy, to 1½ in long, narrow, closely set on stems. Flowers small, greenish white. Rock garden, for blue-green

effects in carpet or pattern planting, small-scale ground cover.

S. sieboldii. All Zones. Native to Japan. Spreading, trailing, unbranched stems to 8-9 in. long. Fleshy leaves in 3's, nearly round, stalkless, toothed in the upper half, blue-gray edged red. Plant turns coppery red in fall, dies to ground in winter. Each stem shows a broad, dense, flat cluster of

Sedum sieboldii: blue-gray leaves edged red. Dusty pink flowers in fall.

dusty pink flowers in autumn. *S. s.* 'Variegatis' has leaves marked yellowish white. Beautiful rock garden or hanging basket plant.

S. spathulifolium. All Zones. Native from California's Coast Ranges and Sierra Nevada north to British Columbia. Leaves blue-green tinged reddish purple, spoon-shaped, fleshy, packed into rosettes on short, trailing stems. Flowers light yellow, spring-summer. Ground cover. 'Cape Blanco' is a selected form with good leaf color. 'Purpureum' has deep purple leaves.

S. spectabile. All Zones. China, Japan. Upright or slightly spreading stems to 18 in. tall, well set with blue-green, roundish, fleshy, 3-in. leaves. Flowers pink, in broad

Sedum spectabile: flower clusters 3-4 in. across, pink, rose, or carmine red.

dense clusters atop the stems in late summer, autumn. Dies down in winter. 'Brilliant' has deep rose-red flowers, 'Carmen' is soft rose, and 'Meteor', the brightest, has carmine red flowers.

S. spurium. All Zones. Evergreen perennial plant with trailing stems. Leaves thick, an inch or so long, nearly as wide, dark green or bronzy-tinted. Flowers pink, in dense clusters at ends of 4-5-in. stems in summer. A garden variety called 'Dragon's

Climate
Zone maps
pages 8-27

Blood' has bronzy leaves and rosy red flowers. Rock garden, ground cover, pattern planting.

S. stahlii. Zones 8, 9, 14-24. Native to Mexico. Twiggy, trailing, 4-8 in. tall. Leaves like tiny (¼-½-in.) beans closely packed toward ends of stems. Leaves dark green, usually brown-tinted or quite brown. Yellow flowers summer or autumn. Rock garden, miniature garden, pots, limited area ground cover.

SEMELE androgyna. CLIMBING BUTCHER'S BROOM. Evergreen vine. Zones 17, 19-24. Clean-cut, graceful, emphatic foliage pattern. Slow to start, then fast to 12-16 ft. or more. The leaflike, flat branchlets (cladodes) dark green, glossy, leathery, to 4 in. long, symmetrically arranged along branches. In June, inconspicuous yellowish flowers along edge of "leaf" followed by small red berries.

Best given protection of a wide overhang. Any soil, shade (full shade in warm climates), moderate water, and feeding. Needs fastening to its support. Prune occasionally to thin, shape, remove dead wood.

SEMPERVIVUM. HOUSELEEK. Succulents. All Zones. Evergreen perennial plants with tightly-packed rosettes of leaves. Little offsets cluster around the parent rosette. Flowers star-shaped, in tight or loose clusters, white, yellowish, pink, red, or greenish, pretty in detail but not showy. Summer bloom. Blooming rosettes die after setting seed, but the offsets carry on. Good in rock gardens, containers, even in pockets on boulders or pieces of porous rock. All need sun, good drainage, and generous summer watering. Many species, all good; these are fairly common:

S. arachnoideum. COBWEB HOUSELEEK. Europe. Tiny gray-green rosettes ¾ in. across, the many leaves joined by fine hairs which give a cobweb-covered look to the plant. Spreads slowly to make dense mats. Flowers bright red on 4-in. stems; seldom blooms.

S. tectorum. HEN AND CHICKENS. Rosettes gray-green, 4-6 in. across, spreading quickly by offsets. Leaves tipped red-brown, bristle-pointed. Flowers red or reddish in clusters on stems to 2 ft. tall. Easy in rock gardens, borders, pattern planting.

SENECIO. Perennials, shrubs, vines. Daisy relatives which range from the garden cineraria and dusty miller to vines, shrubs, perennials, succulents, even a few weeds.

S. cineraria. DUSTY MILLER. Shrubby perennial. All Zones (needs protection Zones 1-3). Spreading plant to 2-2½ ft.; woolly-white leaves cut into many blunt-tipped lobes. Clustered heads of yellow or creamy yellow flowers at almost any season. Plant gets leggy unless sheared occasionally. Easy to grow, needs only light watering. Use in combination with bright-flowered, sun-loving annuals and perennials. Striking in night garden.

S. confusus. MEXICAN FLAME VINE. Evergreen or deciduous vine. Zones 16-24. Sometimes grown as annual or perennial in colder climates. Twines to 8-10 ft. in frost-free areas; dies back to ground in mild frost, comes back fast from roots. Leaves light green, rather fleshy, 1-4 in. long, ½-1 in. wide, coarsely toothed. Daisylike flowers

in large clusters at ends of branches, ¾-1 in. wide, startling orange-red with golden centers. Blooms all year where winters are mild. Sun or light shade; moist, light soil. Use on trellis, column, to cascade over a bank or wall, or in a hanging basket.

S. cruentus. CINERARIA. Perennial usually grown as an annual. Valuable for bright colors in cool shady places; not for hot, dry climates. Most commonly grown are the large-flowered, dwarf kinds generally sold as Multiflora Nana or Hybrida Grandiflora. These are compact 12-15-in.-tall plants with lush, broad, green leaves and broad clusters of 3-5-in.-wide daisies that cover the top of the plant. Will self-sow when adapted. Colors range from white through pink and purplish red to sensational blues and purples, often with contrasting eyes or bands. Bloom late winter and early spring in mild regions, spring and early summer elsewhere. Plants sold as *Cineraria stellata* are taller (to 2½-3 ft.) with looser clusters of smaller, starlike daisies.

Frost is a hazard to fall-planted cinerarias; plant in spring, or protect by planting under shrubs, trees, overhang, or lath. Plant in shade in cool, moist, loose, rich soil. Water generously and often, but avoid soggy soil, which brings on stem rot. Principal pests are leaf miners, spider mites, slugs, snails.

To grow in large pots for patio display, begin by setting transplants in 3- or 4-in. pots in mixture of rich soil, leaf mold, sand. After several weeks (or before they become pot-bound) shift into 5-6-in. pots. Feed every 2 weeks with liquid fertilizer. Never let plants dry out.

Effective in mass plantings or combined with ferns, tuberous or other begonias, foliage plants. Use to decorate lanais, shaded terraces, sitting areas.

S. greyii. Evergreen shrub. Zones 5-9, 14-24. Spreading plant that grows 4-5 ft. high. Stiff, slightly curving stems bear 3½-in.-long, leathery leaves of gray-green outlined by silvery white. A profusion of 1-in.-wide, yellow daisies in 5-in.-wide, flattish clusters comes in summer—effective contrast with gray foliage.

Full sun, not-too-rich soil, good drainage, little or moderate water. Prune yearly to remove oldest or damaged growth, stimulate new wood. Attractive with geraniums, zauschneria, cistus, rosemary, purple or red leafed shrubs. Cut branches effective in arrangements, especially with scarlet and orange flowers; long lasting.

S. leucostachys. (Often sold as *S. cineraria* 'Candidissimus.') All Zones. To 4 ft. tall; broad, sprawling habit. Leaves like *S. cineraria* but more finely cut into much narrower, pointed segments, whiter. Flowers (summer) not showy, creamy white. In full sun brilliantly white, densely leafy; in part shade looser, more sparsely foliaged with larger, greener leaves. Tip-pinch young plants to keep them compact.

S. mandraliscae. See Kleinia mandraliscae

S. mikanioides. GERMAN IVY. Perennial vine. Zones 14-24. Evergreen in mildest areas, deciduous elsewhere. Twines to 18-20 ft. Leaves roundish, with 5-7 sharply pointed lobes, ivylike, ½-3 in. long. Winter flowers small, yellow, the daisies without rays. Trailer in window boxes, or screening vine.

S. petasitis. VELVET GROUNDSEL, CALIFORNIA GERANIUM. Perennial or shrubby perennial. Zones 15-17, 21-24, greenhouse plant anywhere. Bulky plant 6-8 (or more) ft. tall, equally wide. Leaves evergreen, tropical-looking, large, lobed, fanlike, velvety to the touch, to 8 in. across. Blooms in midwinter, with large clusters of small, bright yellow, daisylike flowers standing well above mass of plant. Best in sheltered locations in full sun. Needs ample water, some feeding. Prune hard after bloom to limit height and sprawl. Can be kept 2-4 ft. tall in big pots or tubs. Good filler in tropical garden.

S. rowleyanus. STRING OF BEADS. Succulent. Trailing or hanging stems to 6-8 ft. set with ½ in. spherical green leaves. Small white carnation-scented flowers. Hanging basket. Hardy to 25°.

S. serpens. See Kleinia repens

SENNA. See Cassia

SENSITIVE PLANT. See Mimosa pudica

SEQUOIA sempervirens. COAST REDWOOD. Evergreen tree. Zones 4-9, 14-24. Native to parts of Coast Ranges from Curry County, Oregon, to Monterey County, California. Tallest of the world's trees, and one of the West's most famous native trees (equally famous is its close relative *Sequoiadendron*, the giant sequoia or big tree). A fine landscaping tree—fast growing (3-5 ft. a year), substantial, practically pest free, and almost always fresh-looking and woodsy smelling.

Its red-brown, fibrous-barked trunk goes straight up (unless injured). Nearly parallel sides on a redwood's trunk indicate that the tree has fared well (if redwoods struggle they develop trunks with a noticeable taper). Branches grow straight out from the trunk and cup up a little at outer end. Branchlets hang down slightly from the branches. The flat, pointed, narrow leaves (½-1 in. long) grow in one plane on both sides of the stem like a feather. Leaves are medium green on top, grayish underneath. Small round cones are 1 in. long.

Plant in full sun to half shade. One of the best growing places is in or directly next to a lawn. The redwood thrives on the luxury supply of water (in 10-20 years, however, the tree may defeat the lawn). Away from lawns it needs occasional feeding and regular summer watering (at least for first 5 years).

Coast redwood (left) is darker green, softer in outline, less dense than giant sequoias.

Troubles the tree encounters are mostly physiological: (1) Not enough water makes it sulk and grow slowly; (2) Too much competition from bigger trees and structures makes it grow lanky, thin, and open; (3) Lack of iron makes needles turn yellow every summer, especially on new growth —apply iron sulfate or chelated iron; (4) It's normal for oldest leaves to turn yellow, then brown, and then drop in late summer and early fall.

Count on a branch spread at base (tip to tip) of 14-30 ft. Although mature, centuries-old natives surpass 350 ft. in height, 70-90 ft. seems to be the most to expect in a garden in one owner's lifetime. Use a redwood singly as a shade tree, a tree to look up into or to hang a swing from, a tree to be seen from 2 blocks away. Or, plant several in a grove. Or, plant several in a 40-ft.-diameter circle—inside it's cool, fragrant, and a fine spot for fuchsias, begonias, and people on hot summer days. For grove or circle planting, space trees 7 ft. apart. Trees can be planted 3-4 ft. apart and topped at least once a year to make a beautiful hedge.

SEQUOIADENDRON giganteum *(Sequoia gigantea).* BIG TREE, GIANT SEQUOIA. Evergreen tree. All Zones. Native to west slope of the Sierra Nevada from Placer County to Tulare County. The most massive-trunked and one of the tallest trees in the world, reaching 325 ft. in height with a 30-ft. trunk diameter. It has always shared fame and comparisons with its close relative, the coast redwood *(Sequoia).* But, horticulturally, the similarities are rather slim.

The dense foliage of giant sequoia (more bushy than coast redwood) is gray-green; the branchlets clothed with short, overlapping, scalelike leaves with sharp points. It's a somewhat prickly tree to reach into. Dark reddish brown cones 2-3½ in. long. The bark is reddish brown and generally similar to that of coast redwood.

Giant sequoia is hardier than coast redwood. It grows a little slower—2-3 ft. a year. It also needs less water. Plant in deep soil, full sun preferable, and water deeply but infrequently once trees are established.

Primary use is as a featured tree in a large lawn (roots may surface there in due time) or other open space. Trees hold lower branches throughout their long youth, and are likely to get too broad for the small garden. In essence, then, the giant sequoia is easier to grow than the coast redwood and more widely adaptable to climates but it doesn't have as many landscape uses.

SERENOA repens. SAW PALMETTO. Zones 7-9, 12-24. Native to southeastern U. S. Stems creeping, sometimes branching, forming low, wide-based clump. Fan-shaped leaves 2-4 ft. across, green or gray-green, on 2-4-ft. spiny-edged stalks. Hardy well below 20°. Makes an impenetrable hedge.

SERVICE BERRY. See Amelanchier

SETCREASEA purpurea. PURPLE HEART. Perennial. Zones 14-24; house plant anywhere. Stems a foot or more high, inclined to lop over. Leaves rather narrowly oval and pointed, very strongly shaded with purple, particularly underneath. Use discretion in planting, or the vivid foliage may create a

harsh effect, (pale or deep purple flowers are not important). Plants are generally unattractive in winter. Will take light shade; color best in sun. Frosts may kill tops, but growth resumes in warm weather and recovery is fast.

SHADBLOW, SHADBUSH. See Amelanchier

SHALLOT. A small onionlike plant that produces a cluster of edible bulbs from a single bulb. Prized in cooking for its distinctive flavor. Plant either sets (small dry bulbs) or nursery plants in fall in mild climates, early spring in cold-winter areas. Leaves 12-18 in. high develop from each bulb. Ultimately 2-8 bulbs will grow from each original set. At maturity (early summer if fall-planted, late summer if spring-planted), bulbs are formed and tops yellow and die. Harvest by pulling clumps and dividing bulbs. Let outer skin dry for about a month so that shallots can be stored for 4-6 months. Some seed firms sell sets; nurseries with large stocks of herbs may sell growing plants. If you plant sets, place in ground so that tips are just covered.

SHAMROCK. Around St. Patrick's Day nurseries and florists sell "shamrocks." These are small potted plants of *Medicago lupulina* (hop clover, yellow trefoil, black medick), an annual plant; *Oxalis acetosella* (wood sorrel), or *Trifolium repens* (white clover). The last is most common.

All have in common leaves divided into 3 leaflets (symbolic of the Trinity). They can be kept on a sunny window sill or planted out, but have little ornamental value and are likely to become weeds.

SHEEP BUR. See Acaena

SHELL FLOWER. See Alpinia, Molucella laevis

SHELL FLOWER, MEXICAN. See Tigridia

SHE-OAK. See Casuarina

SHOOTING STARS. See Dodecatheon

SHORTIA. Perennials. Zones 1-7. Beautiful small evergreen plants. Spread slowly by underground stems. Need shade, moisture. Acid, leafy or peaty soil. Grow with azaleas or rhododendrons.

S. galacifolia. OCONEE BELLS. Forms clump of round or oval, glossy green leaves 1-3 in. long, with scalloped-toothed edges. A single, nodding, white bell, 1 in. wide, with toothed edges, tops each of the many 4-6 in.-high stems in March, April.

S. soldanelloides. FRINGE BELLS. Coarsely toothed, round leaves form clumps similar to above. Flowers differ in being pink to rose in color, with deeply fringed edges.

S. uniflora 'Grandiflora'. Like *S. galacifolia* but with indented and wavy-edged leaves and flowers that are large fringed bells of clear soft pink.

SHRIMP PLANT. See Beloperone guttata

SILENE. Annuals, perennials. Many species, some with erect growth habit, others cushionlike. Sun, part shade.

S. acaulis. CUSHION PINK, MOSS CAMPION. Perennial. Zones 1-11, 14-16, 18-21. Mosslike mat of bright green, narrow leaves about ⅜ in. long. Reddish purple flowers,

½ in. across, borne singly March-April. For a gravelly, damp but well drained spot in the rock garden.

S. californica. CALIFORNIA INDIAN PINK. Perennial. Zones 7-11, 14-24. Native in California-southern Oregon foothills. Loosely branching to 6-16 in. tall. Foliage somewhat sticky. Flaming red, 1¼-in.-wide flowers, with petals cleft and fringed. Spring blooming. Occasionally sold in seed packets.

S. coeli-rosa *(Lychnis coeli-rosa, Viscaria oculata).* ROSE OF HEAVEN. Annual. Single, 1-in., saucer-shaped, summer flowers in tones of blue, lavender, and white and marked with a dark contrasting eye. Also dwarf (6-8-in.) or tall (18-in.) strains in blue, white, or pink. Much branched growth habit. Good cut flowers. Sow seed March-April in moist well fertilized soils.

S. schafta. MOSS CAMPION. Perennial. Zones 1-9, 14-16, 18-21. A tuft of upright, rather wiry stems to 6-12 in. high. Leaves small, tongue-shaped. Stalks with 1-2 rose-purple flowers in late summer, autumn.

SILK OAK. See Grevillea robusta

SILKTASSEL. See Garrya

SILK TREE. See Albizia julibrissin

SILVER BELL. See Halesia

SILVERBERRY. See Elaeagnus pungens

SILVER DOLLAR GUM. See Eucalyptus polyanthemos

SILVER LACE VINE. See Polygonum aubertii

SILVER MOUNTAIN GUM. See Eucalyptus pulverulenta

SILVER TREE. See Leucadendron

SIMMONDSIA chinensis. JOJOBA, GOATNUT. Evergreen shrub. Zones 10-13, 19-24. Native to deserts of southern California, Arizona, Mexico. Dense, rigid-branching, spreading shrub 3-6 (rarely 16) ft. tall. Foliage dull gray-green; leaves leathery, 1-2 in. long, to ½ in. wide. Flowers inconspicuous, male and female on different plants. If both are present, female plants bear edible, nutlike fruits about ¾ in. long. Flavor like filbert, slightly bitter until cured. High oil content of fruit gives plant possible commercial value.

Young plants rather tender; when established will take 15°. Needs little water. Of particular value as clipped hedge, foundation planting in desert garden.

SINNINGIA speciosa *(Gloxinia speciosa).* GLOXINIA. Tuber. House plant, or pot plant for shaded terrace or patio. Leaves oblong, dark green, toothed, fuzzy, 6 in. or more long. Flowers large, velvety, bell-shaped, ruffled on edges. Come in blue, purple, violet, pink, red, or white. Variable; some flowers have dark dots or blotches; leaves occasionally white-veined. Tubers usually available December-March. Plant 1 in. deep in rich, loose mix. Water sparingly until first leaves appear; increase watering after roots form. Apply water around base of plant, or from below; don't water on top of leaves. When roots fill pot, shift to larger pot. Feed regularly during growth. After bloom has finished, gradually dry off plants and store tubers in a cool, dark place with

S

just enough moisture to keep them from shriveling. Repot in January-February.

SINOCALAMUS. See Bamboo

SIPHONOSMANTHUS delavayi. See Osmanthus delavayi

SISYRINCHIUM. Perennials. Zones 4-24. Related to iris. Narrow, rather grasslike leaves. Small flowers made up of 6 segments; they open in sunshine. Pretty but not showy, best suited for informal gardens or naturalizing.

S. bellum. BLUE-EYED GRASS. Native to coastal California. To 4-16 in. tall. Narrow green or bluish green leaves. Flowers purple to bluish purple, ½ in. across, early to mid-spring.

S. californicum. YELLOW-EYED GRASS. Native to coast of California and Oregon. Dull green leaves, broader than those of blue-eyed grass. Yellow flowers open May-June. Can grow in wet, low, or poorly drained places.

SKIMMIA. Evergreen shrubs. Zones 4-9, 14-22 (grows best in Zones 4-6, 17; needs special handling elsewhere). Slow growing, compact with glossy, rich green leaves neatly arranged. Clusters of tiny white flowers open from clusters of pinkish buds held well above foliage. Blooms April-May. Red hollylike fruits in fall and through December if pollination requirements are met.

When massed, forms a level surface of leaves; individual plants are dense mounds. Light to moderate shade preferable; full sun yellows leaves, heavy shade makes plants lanky, inhibits bloom.

No special soil requirement in the Northwest. In California's alkaline soils add at least 50 per cent peat moss or the like to planting soil. Also expect attacks by thrips and red spider mites. In the Northwest, skimmia is attacked by a special skimmia mite that gives the leaves a sunburned look.

Good shrub under low windows. Use to flank entryways. Plant beside shaded walks. Blends well with all shade plants. Good in containers.

S. foremannii. Hybrid between following two species. Resembles *S. japonica* but more compact, with broader, heavier, darker green leaves. Seems to take northern California conditions better than either parent. Plants may be male, female, or self-fertile.

S. japonica. Variable in size. Slow growth to 2-5 ft. tall, 3-6 ft. wide. Leaves 3-4 in. long, an inch wide, oval, short-pointed, mostly clustered near twig ends. Flowers fragrant, in 2-3-in. clusters. Bright red berries on female plants if male plant present, and worth effort of planting both. A form with ivory white berries is available. *S. j.* 'Macrophylla' is a male form with large leaves and flowers. Makes a rounded, spreading shrub to 5-6 ft. high.

S. reevesiana (*S. fortunei*). Dwarf, dense-growing shrub 2 ft. tall. Self-fertile, with dull crimson fruits. Fragrant flowers.

SKY FLOWER. See Duranta, Thunbergia grandiflora

SMILACINA racemosa. FALSE SOLOMON'S SEAL. Perennial. Zones 1-7, 15-17. Grows 1-3 ft. tall. Each single arching stalk has several 3-10-in.-long leaves, hairy beneath. Stalk topped by fluffy, conical cluster of small creamy white flowers in March-May,

followed by red, purple-spotted berries. The most common form in the West is the variety *amplexicaulis* whose leaves sheath the stem at the base. You see it commonly in shaded woods—California to British Columbia, east to Rockies.

SMILAX ASPARAGUS. See Asparagus asparagoides

SMOKE TREE. See Cotinus, Dalea

SNAIL VINE. See Phaseolus caracalla

SNAKE PLANT. See Sansevieria

SNAKEROOT, BLACK. See Cimicifuga racemosa

SNAKESHEAD. See Fritillaria meleagris

SNAPDRAGON. See Antirrhinum

SNAPDRAGON, BABY. See Linaria maroccana

SNAPWEED. See Impatiens

SNEEZEWEED, COMMON. See Helenium autumnale

SNOW BUSH. See Ceanothus cordulatus

SNOWBALL, CHINESE. See Viburnum macrocephalum 'Sterile'

SNOWBALL, COMMON. See Viburnum opulus 'Roseum'

SNOWBALL, FRAGRANT. See Viburnum carlcephalum

SNOWBALL, JAPANESE. See Viburnum plicatum

SNOWBELL. See Styrax

SNOWBERRY, COMMON. See Symphoricarpos albus

SNOWBERRY, CREEPING. See Symphoricarpos mollis

SNOWBERRY, SPREADING. See Symphoricarpos mollis

SNOWDROP. See Galanthus

SNOWDROP TREE. See Halesia carolina

SNOWDROP TREE, JAPANESE. See Styrax japonica

SNOWFLAKE. See Leucojum

SNOWFLAKE TREE. See Trevesia

SNOW-IN-SUMMER. See Cerastium

SNOW-ON-THE-MOUNTAIN. See Euphorbia marginata

SOAPBARK TREE. See Quillaja

SOAPWEED, SMALL. See Yucca glauca

SOCIETY GARLIC. See Tulbaghia violacea

SOLANDRA hartwegii. (Usually sold as *S. guttata*). CUP-OF-GOLD-VINE. Evergreen vine. Zones 17, 21-24; with overhead protection in Zones 15, 16, 18-20. Fast, sprawling, rampant growth to 40 ft. Fasten to support. Large, broad, glossy leaves 4-6 in. long. Blooms February-April and intermittently at other times. Flowers fragrant,

golden yellow striped brownish purple, bowl-shaped, 6-8 in. across.

Full sun near coast; needs cool shaded root run in hot inland valleys. Prune to induce laterals and more flowers. Can be cut back to make a rough hedge. Takes salt spray directly above tide line; stands wind, fog. Use on big walls, pergolas, along eaves, or as bank cover.

SOLANUM. Evergreen and deciduous shrubs and vines. Includes, in addition to potato and eggplant (described under their own names), a number of ornamental plants. Ordinary garden care suits most of them.

S. jasminoides. POTATO VINE. Evergreen or deciduous vine. Zones 8, 9, 14-24. Fast growth to 30 ft., twining habit. Leaves 1½-3 in. long, evergreen in milder winters, medium to purplish green. Flowers pure white, or white tinged blue, an inch across, in clusters of 8-12. Nearly perpetual bloom; heaviest in spring. Sun or part shade. Grown for flowers or for light overhead shade. Cut back severely at any time to prevent tangling, promote vigorous new growth; control rampant runners that grow along the ground.

S. macrantherum. Evergreen or deciduous vine. Zones 21-24. Similar to *S. rantonnetii* but tends to be more a vine, less a shrub. Emerald foliage on yellow stems. Flowers violet with yellow eye, to 1½ in. across, in large, many-flowered clusters.

S. pseudo-capsicum. JERUSALEM CHERRY. Evergreen shrub. Zones 23, 24; anywhere pot or container plant for indoor use, outdoor summer decoration. Grows 3-4 ft. high. Foliage deep green; leaves 4 in. long, smooth, shiny. Flowers ½ in. wide, white. Fine show of scarlet (rarely yellow) ½-in. fruits like miniature tomatoes, October-December. Fruits may be poisonous; caution children against eating them. Usually grown as an annual. In Zones 23, 24, blooms, fruits, and seeds itself through the year. The many dwarf strains (to 12 in. high) are more popular than the taller kinds, have larger (to 1-in.) fruits.

S. rantonnetii. Evergreen or deciduous shrub or vine. Zones 15-24. As a free-standing plant makes a 6-8-ft. shrub. Can be staked into tree form. With support a vine 12-15 ft. or more. Informal, fast-growing, not easy to use in tailored landscape. Evergreen in mild winters; leaves drop in severe cold, branch tips may die back. Oval leaves to 4 in. long, bright green. Flowers violet-blue, yellow-centered, 1 in. wide, blooming

Violet-blue flowers of Solanum rantonnetii have yellow centers, are 1 in. wide.

throughout warm weather, often nearly throughout the year. Apparently all plants in cultivation are the variety 'Grandiflorum'. The wild species has flowers only half as large.

Prune severely to keep it a neat shrub. Give it support when used as a vine; or let it sprawl as a ground cover.

S. wendlandii. COSTA RICAN NIGHT-SHADE. Deciduous vine. Zones 16, 21-24. Tall, twining vine with prickly stems. Leaves larger than those of other species, lower ones divided into leaflets. Leaves drop in low temperatures even without frost. Slow to leaf out in spring. Big clusters of 2½-in. lilac blue flowers. Use to clamber into tall trees, to cover a pergola, to decorate eaves of large house.

SOLDANELLA montana. Perennial. Zones 1-6. Alpine plants, related to primula. Clumps of small, round, leathery leaves and fringed violet-blue bell-shaped flowers in earliest spring. Flower stems 6-14 in. high. Needs cool, partly shaded situation and ample moisture; best in rich soil.

SOLEIROLIA soleirolii (*Helxine soleirolii*). BABY'S TEARS, ANGEL'S TEARS. Perennial. Zones 8-24. Creeping plants with tiny round leaves make lush medium green mats 1-4 in. high. Flowers inconspicuous. Tender, juicy leaves and stems easily injured, but aggressive growth habit quickly repairs damage. Roots easily from pieces of stem and can become an invasive pest.

Grows best in shade, but takes full sun near coast if water supply ample. Freezes to black mush in hard frosts, but comes back fast. Cool-looking, neat cover for ferns or other shade-loving plants. Can be used to carpet terrariums or space under green-house benches.

SOLIDAGO. GOLDENROD. Perennial. All Zones. Not as widely known and grown in the West as east of the Rockies. A few can be grown here. Varieties of garden origin are sometimes sold. They grow 1-3 ft. high (sometimes to 5 ft.), with the characteristic goldenrod plume of yellow flowers topping the leafy stems. Varieties differ chiefly in size and in depth of yellow shading. Good meadow planting with black-eyed Susan and Michaelmas daisies, or can be used in a border for summer-fall color.

SOLLYA fusiformis (*S. heterophylla*). AUSTRALIAN BLUEBELL CREEPER. Evergreen shrub or vine. Zones 8, 9, 14-24. Grows 2-3 ft. tall as a loose, spreading shrub; given support and training, climbs to 6-8 ft. Foliage light and delicate; leaves narrow, glossy green, 1-2 in. long. Clusters of ½-in.-long, brilliant blue, bell-shaped flowers appear through most of summer.

Full or part sun in coastal areas, part shade inland. Drought tolerant when established, but looks better with regular watering. Dies if drainage is poor. Spray to control scale insects. Will grow under eucalyptus trees. Use as ground cover, border planting, along steps, on half-shaded banks. Plant over a low wall, where its branches can spill downward. Good container plant.

SOLOMON'S SEAL. See Polygonatum

SOLOMON'S SEAL, FALSE. See Smilacina

SOPHORA. Deciduous or evergreen trees or shrubs. Leaves divided into numerous leaflets. Drooping clusters of sweet pea-shaped flowers followed by pods bearing seeds.

S. japonica. JAPANESE PAGODA TREE, CHINESE SCHOLAR TREE. Deciduous tree. All Zones. Moderate growth to 20 ft.; from this point it grows slowly to 40 ft., with equal or greater spread. Young wood smooth, dark gray-green. Old branches and trunk gradually take on the rugged look of an oak. Dark green, 6-10-in. leaves divided into 7-17, oval, 1-2-in.-long leaflets. Long, open, 8-12-in. clusters of yellowish white ½-in.-long flowers July-September. Pods are 2-3½ in. long, narrowed between the big seeds in bead necklace effect. Unreliable bloom where summers are cold and damp. Not fussy as to soil, water; no special pests or diseases. One of the best spreading trees for giving shade to a lawn. Seed or pods may stain a patio.

S. secundiflora. MESCAL BEAN, TEXAS MOUNTAIN LAUREL. Evergreen shrub or tree. Zones 8-16, 18-24. Can be trained into a 25-ft. tree with a short, slender trunk, narrow crown, and upright branches. Very slow growth, especially in cool-summer regions. Leaves 4-6 in. long, divided into 7-9 glossy, dark green, oval leaflets, 1-2 in. long. Blooms February-April; the inch-wide, violet-blue, wisterialike flowers are carried in drooping 4-8-in. clusters. Rarely a white-flowered form appears. Flowers have sweet fragrance. Silvery gray, woody, 1-8-in.-long seed pods open in ripening to show bright red ½-in. seeds which are decorative but poisonous—remove pods before they mature. Thrives in hot sun and alkaline soil, but needs good drainage and some water. Choice small tree for street, lawn, or patio. Untrained, it is a good large screen, bank cover, or espalier.

S. tetraptera. KOWHAI, YELLOW KOWHAI. Evergreen or deciduous shrub or small tree. Zones 15-17. Slow growing to 40 ft. Young plants evergreen and shrubby, with wiry, tangled branches; as plant reaches blooming age it becomes a slender, open, rather narrow tree which drops its leaves in spring just before blooming. Leaves 1½-4 in. long, divided into tiny leaflets, their number ranging from 7 to as high as 80. Flowers bright golden yellow, 1-2 in. long, in hanging clusters of 4-8. Seed pods with 4 wings, narrowed between seeds, 2-8 in. long. Rather tender; doesn't take drought and low humidity. Well drained soil, ample water, full sun or partial shade.

SORBUS aucuparia. EUROPEAN MOUNTAIN ASH. Deciduous tree. Zones 1-6, 15-17. Moderate to rapid growth to 20-30 ft. with a 15-20-ft. spread; may reach eventual 50-ft. height. Sharply-rising branches make a dense, oval to round crown. Leaves divided into 9-15, 1-2-in.-long leaflets, dull green above, gray-green beneath; turn yellow or rusty yellow in fall (some strains red to orange). Broad, flat 3-5-in. clusters of white flowers in late spring, followed by clusters of bright orange-red, ¼-in. berrylike fruit which color in midsummer and hang on until midspring unless birds get them.

Sun best, but will take part shade. Plant in well drained good garden soil. Needs some summer water. Blight, borers, and scale sometimes a problem. Good street or lawn tree, although somewhat messy with leaf and fruit drop. Fruits effective with background of dark evergreens.

SORREL TREE. See Oxydendrum

SOURWOOD. See Oxydendrum

SPANISH BAYONET. See Yucca aloifolia

SPANISH DAGGER. See Yucca gloriosa

SPANISH FLAG. See Quamoclit lobata

SPANISH SHAWL. See Schizocentron

SPARAXIS tricolor. HARLEQUIN FLOWER. Corm. Zones 9, 13-24. Native to South Africa. Closely related to and similar to ixia in uses and culture. Small, funnel-shaped flowers in spikelike clusters on 12-in. stems. Flowers come in yellows, blues, purples, reds, and white. Usually blotched and splashed with contrasting colors. Blooms over long period in late spring. Use in borders, rock gardens, containers, for cutting. Naturalize like freesias in mild climates. Plant in full sun in fall; set corms 2 in. deep, 2-3 in. apart.

SPARMANNIA africana. AFRICAN LINDEN. Evergreen shrub, tree. Zones 17, 21-24; with special protection 16, 18-20; house plant anywhere. Fast to 10-20 ft., usually as a thicket, many trunks from base, especially if frosted back or pruned to control size. Dense, coarse foliage. Leaves broad, angled, to 9 in. across, light green, heavily veined, velvety with coarse hairs. Flowers white with a brush of yellow stamens, 1-1½ in. across, clustered, borne in midwinter.

Ample water and feeding, sun or shade. Susceptible to spider mites. Prune heavily every few years to give desired height and control legginess. Best used for furnishing bulk and mass near entryways, screening, combining with tropical foliage plants.

SPARTIUM. See Cytisus

SPATHIPHYLLUM. Evergreen perennial. House plant. Dark green leaves are large, oval or elliptical and narrowed to a point, erect on slender leaf stalks that rise directly from the soil. Flowers resemble calla lilies or anthuriums—a central column of closely set tiny flowers surrounded by a leaflike white flower bract.

Loose, fibrous potting mixture; weekly feedings of liquid fertilizer. Grow in good light, but avoid hot, sunny windows. One of the few flowering plants that grows and blooms readily indoors. Most commonly available: *S. wallisii*, *S.* 'Mauna Loa', *S.* 'Clevelandii', all quite similar in appearance. *S. wallisii* reaches 20 in. in height; 'Clevelandii' is larger, and 'Mauna Loa' larger still, well grown plants reaching 3 ft. in height and spread.

SPEARMINT. See Mentha spicata

SPEEDWELL. See Veronica

SPEKBOOM. See Portulacaria afra

SPICE BUSH. See Calycanthus occidentalis

SPIDER FLOWER. See Cleome

SPIDER PLANT. See Chlorophytum

SPIDERWORT. See Tradescantia virginiana

SPINACH. Sow in July to September so it can grow to maturity during fall, winter, and spring. Long daylight of late spring and heat of summer make it go to seed too fast. It requires a rich soil that drains well. Make small sowings at weekly intervals to get a succession. Grow in sun. Space rows 18 in. apart. After seedlings start growing, thin plants to 6 in. apart. Give plants plenty of water; one feeding will encourage lush foliage. When plants have reached full size,

harvest by cutting off entire clump at ground level.

SPIRAEA. Deciduous shrubs. Zones 1-11, 14-17. Easy to grow in all kinds of soils, in sun or light shade. Varying in form, height, and flowering season. They provide generous quantities of white, pink, or red flowers. Prune according to form and time of bloom. Those with the loose graceful look need annual renewal of new growth.

Remove old wood that has produced flowers —cutting back to the ground. Most shrubby types require less severe pruning. Prune spring-flowering kinds when they finish blooming. Prune summer-flowering species in late winter or very early spring. See chart for descriptions of kinds available.

SPIRAEA, BLUE. See Caryopteris incana

SPIRAEA, FALSE. See Astilbe

SPIRAEA

NAME	GROWTH HABIT	FLOWERS	SEASON
S. billiardii Hybrid—*S. douglasii* and *S. salicifolia*	To 4-6 ft. high with arching branches. Foliage green above, gray-green beneath.	Tiny, pale pink flowers in fluffy, 8-in.-long clusters at ends of the branches.	July-August
S. bullata Native to Japan	To 1-1½ ft., dense-growing, with roundish, puckered leaves that hang on all winter in mild climates.	Pink flowers in small dense clusters. Used in edgings, rock gardens.	July-August
S. bumalda Hybrid between *S. japonica* and *S. albiflora*.	Rounded, dense, to 2-3 ft. tall. Narrow oval leaves 1-4 in. long.	Flowers deep pink to nearly white in flat-topped clusters.	June to fall
S. b. 'Anthony Waterer' DWARF RED SPIRAEA Most commonly available form of *S. bumalda*	Same as above.	Flowers bright carmine in flat-topped clusters.	June to fall
S. b. 'Froebel'	Same growth habit but taller, to 3-4 ft. Good fall coloring.	Flowers rosy red, in flat-topped clusters 3 in. across.	June to fall
S. cantoniensis (*S. reevesiana, S. reevesii*) REEVES SPIRAEA	Upright with arching branches to 5-6 ft. Small dark green leaves turn red in fall.	White flowers in dense clusters along branches.	June-July
S. densiflora Native to California to British Columbia, east to Wyoming.	Mounding to 2 ft. Leaves oval or elliptic, to 1½ in. long, green above, paler beneath.	Flowers rose colored, in dense clusters to 1½ in. across.	June
S. douglasii WESTERN SPIRAEA Native California to British Columbia, east to Rocky Mountains.	Suckering shrub to 4-8 ft. tall, with 1½-3-in. leaves of dark green, velvety white beneath.	Flowers pale pink to deep rose in dense, steepled 8-in.-long clusters at ends of branches.	July-August
S. japonica Native to Japan	Upright to 6 ft. Leaves 1-3 in. long, pale underneath.	Flowers pale to deep pink, occasionally white, in large clusters at ends of branches.	June-July
S. nipponica tosaensis 'Snowmound' Native to Japan	Compact spreading growth to 2-3 ft. Dense foliage of small, blue-green leaves.	White flowers in round clusters all along the stems make wands of white.	June
S. prunifolia 'Plena' BRIDAL WREATH SPIRAEA, SHOE BUTTON SPIRAEA Native to Korea, China, Formosa	Graceful to 6 ft. high with equal spread. Small, dark green leaves turn rich red in fall.	Small double white flowers like little rosettes all along the branches.	April-May
S. thunbergii Native to Japan, China	Showy, billowy to 5 ft., with many arching branches. Turns soft reddish brown in fall.	Round clusters of small white flowers all along branches.	April
S. vanhouttei Hybrid between *S. cantoniensis* and *S. trilobata*. Probably most commonly planted.	Fountain-shaped growth to 6 ft. Blue-green leaves on arching branches.	Showy, snow white flowers in rounded clusters wreathe the branches.	June-July

SPLIT ROCK. See Pleiospilos

SPREKELIA formosissima. (Often sold as *Amaryllis formosissima*.) JACOBEAN LILY, ST. JAMES LILY, AZTEC LILY. Bulb. Zones 9, 13-24 as all-year garden plants; everywhere in pots or as spring-fall garden plants. Native to Mexico. Foliage resembles daffodils. Dark crimson blooms with 3 erect segments, 3 lower ones rolled together into a tube at the base, then separating again into drooping segments. Stems 12 in. tall. Plant in fall, setting bulbs 3-4 in. deep and 8 in. apart in full sun. Blooms 6-8 weeks after planting. Most effective in groups. In mild climates may flower several times a year, with alternating moisture and drying out.

Spidery, dark crimson blooms of Sprekelia are 4 in. wide, grow on 1 ft. stems.

Where winters are cold, plant outdoors in spring, lift plants in fall when foliage yellows and store over winter (leave dry tops on). Or grow in pots like amaryllis (*Hippeastrum*), only slightly cooler. Repot every 3-4 years.

SPRUCE. See Picea

SPRUCE, BIG CONE. See Pseudotsuga macrocarpa

SPURGE. See Euphorbia

SPURGE, JAPANESE. See Pachysandra terminalis

SQUASH. There are two kinds. Those that are harvested and cooked in the immature state are called summer squash; this group includes scalloped white squash, yellow crookneck varieties, and the cylindrical, green or gray zucchini or Italian squash. Winter squash varieties have hard rinds and firm, close-grained, fine-flavored flesh. They store well and are used for baking and for pies. They come in a variety of shapes—turban, warted, and banana are a few—and a variety of sizes and colors.

Many of the summer squashes grow on broad, squat bushes rather than on vines; these help economize on space. 'Early Summer Crookneck' and 'Early Prolific Straightneck' are good yellow summer squash. 'Early White Bush', is a scalloped variety. 'Caserta', 'Zucco', 'Greyzini', and 'Chefini

Hybrid' are excellent Italian or zucchini types. Fall and winter squash for storing are the small 'Bush Table Queen', 'Danish', 'Acorn', 'Butternut', and 'Buttercup'; and the large 'Hubbard', 'Blue Hubbard', and 'Pink Banana.' Spaghetti squash looks like any other winter squash but when you cook it (bake or boil) and open it, you find the flesh is made up of long, spaghetti-sized strands. It has a nutty flavor.

Bush varieties of summer squash can be planted 2 ft. apart in rows; planted in circles ("hills") they need more room, so space "hills" 4 by 4 feet. Runner-type winter squash needs 5 ft. spacing in rows, 8 by 8 ft. in "hills". Roots will need ample water, but keep the leaves and stems as dry as possible; irrigate in basins or furrows. Harvest summer squash when they are still small and tender; seeds should still be soft and you should be able to pierce the rind easily with your thumbnail. Late squash should stay on the vines until thoroughly hardened; harvest these with an inch of stem and store in a cool (55°), frost-free place.

SQUILL. See Scilla

STACHYS olympica *(S. lanata)*. LAMB'S EARS. Perennial. Zones 1-9, 12-24. Soft, thick, white-woolly, rather tongue-shaped leaves grow densely on spreading 12-18-in. stems. Flower stalks, with many whorls of small purplish flowers, form in June-July but the plant is most useful for foliage effect. Rain smashes it down, makes it mushy. Frost damages leaves. Cut back in spring. Use to contrast with dark green and differently shaped leaves such as strawberry or some of the sedums. Good edging plant for paths, flower border; highly effective edging for bearded iris. Excellent ground cover under high-branching oaks.

STACHYURUS praecox. Deciduous shrub. Zones 4-6 best; also 14-17. Slow to 10 ft., with spreading, slender polished chestnut brown branches. Pendulous flower stalks 3-4 in. long, each with 12-20 unopened buds, hang from branches in fall-winter. These open (February-March) into pale yellow or greenish yellow bell-shaped flowers $\frac{1}{3}$ in. wide. Berrylike fruits in August-September. Bright green leaves 3-7 in. long are toothed, taper to a sharp tip. Leaves often somewhat sparse. Fall color pleasant (but not bright) rosy red and yellowish.

Grow under deciduous trees to shelter winter buds from heavy freezes. With ample water will take full sunshine, give brighter fall color. Appropriate in woodland garden.

STAPELIA. STARFISH FLOWER, CARRION FLOWER. Succulents. House plants; outdoors under lath or other shelter Zones 16-24. Plants resemble cactus, with clumps of 4-sided, spineless stems. Flowers (summer) are large, fleshy, shaped like 5-pointed stars; they usually have an elaborate circular fleshy disk in the center. Most smell like carrion; the odor is not usually offensive on plants blooming outside in summer. They need cool, dry rest period in the winter, sun and moderate water in summer. Best managed in pots.

S. gigantea. Remarkable novelty, with 9-in.-tall stems and flowers 10-16 in. across, brown-purple marked yellow, with fringed edges.

S. variegata. The commonest. Stems to 6 in. Flowers to 3 in. across, yellow heavily spotted and barred dark purple-brown. There are many hybrids and color variants. Unscented flowers.

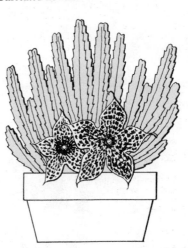

Star-shaped, fleshy flowers give starfish flower its name. Stapelia variegata.

STAR BUSH. See Turraea

STARFISH FLOWER. See Stapelia

STARFLOWER, LAVENDER. See Grewia

STAR, MEXICIAN. See Milla

STAR OF BETHLEHEM. See Campanula isophylla, Ornithogalum umbellatum

STAR OF PERSIA. See Allium albopilosum

STATICE. See Limonium

STAUNTONIA hexaphylla. Evergreen vine. Zones 4-7, 14-23. Twining growth to 40 ft. Old leaves dark, dullish green; new leaves light yellow green. Leaves have 3-7 leaflets, 2-4 in. long, on long stalks; whole leaf has long stalk, too. Early spring flowers clustered, bell-shaped, $\frac{3}{4}$ in. long, white tinged purplish or brownish. Plants either male or female; if both are present, latter bear edible purple fruit the size of a plum. Rich soil, ample water, part shade in hotter climates. Can become a tangled mess if not pruned occasionally. Train on trellis for privacy screen, or grow on pillar for foliage, flowers.

ST. CATHERINE'S LACE. See Eriogonum giganteum

STENOCARPUS sinuatus. FIREWHEEL TREE. Evergreen tree. Zones 16, 17, 20-24. Slow to 30 ft., with a spread of 15 ft. Foliage dense, shiny. Leaves on young plants to 12 in. long, lobed like oak leaves; on older plants leaves are smaller and usually unlobed. Tubular, 2-3-in. scarlet and yellow flowers arranged in clusters like spokes of a wheel. Plants will not bloom until established for several years. Bloom season varies; plants may flower at any time, but early fall is usually peak season. Blooms will sometimes come out of the trunk's bark, making a most unusual effect.

Rather tender, especially when young. Best in deep, rich, well drained, acid soil.

Climate Zone maps pages 8-27

S

Climate Zone maps pages 8-27

Needs occasional deep watering even when well established. Prune to shape in early years. Where climate, soil, and water is right, it can be a showy flowering tree for use near patio or terrace. Good lawn tree. Popular as indoor pot plant with beautiful juvenile leaves.

Each "spoke" in flower clusters of firewheel tree is a scarlet and yellow flower.

STENOLOBIUM stans (*Tecoma stans*). YELLOW BELLS, YELLOW TRUMPET FLOWER, YELLOW-ELDER. Evergreen shrub or small tree. Zones 12, 13, 21-24. In mildest-winter areas can be trained as a tree. Usually a large shrub where frosts are common, much of the wood dying back; quick recovery in warm weather, and very rapid, bushy growth to 20 ft. Leaves divided into 5-13, toothed 1½-4-in.-long leaflets. Flowers bright yellow, bell-shaped, 2 in. across in large clusters. Blooms June to January. Needs heat, water, deep soil, fairly heavy feeding. Cut faded flowers to prolong bloom, prune to remove dead and brushy growth. Very showy mass in the large garden. Boundary plantings, big shrub borders, screening.

STEPHANOTIS floribunda. MADAGASCAR JASMINE. Evergreen vine. Zones 23, 24; house or indoor-outdoor plant everywhere. Moderate growth to 10-15 ft. (more if grown in open ground). Can be kept small in pots. Leaves glossy green, waxy, to 4 in. long. Flowers funnel-shaped, white, waxy, very fragrant, 1-2 in. long in open clusters. Blooms June through summer as outdoor plant; grown indoors and properly rested by some drying out, will bloom 6 weeks after resuming growth. Favorite flower in bridal bouquets.

Grown outdoors, does best with roots in shade, tops in filtered sun. Needs warmth, support of frame or trellis. As indoor-outdoor plant, feed and water liberally, but dry out somewhat before bringing indoors. Grow in bright light out of direct sun. Spray for scale, mealybug.

STERCULIA. See Brachychiton

STERNBERGIA lutea. Bulb. All Zones. Narrow 6-12-in. leaves appear in fall at same time as flowers, and remain green for several months after blooms have gone. Flowers 1½ in. long, resemble large golden crocuses on 6-9-in. stems. Flowers give a pleasant autumn surprise in borders, rock gardens, and near pools. Good cut flowers. Plant bulbs as soon as available—August or September. Set 4 in. deep, 6 in. apart, in

sun. In coldest climates give sheltered location. Lift, divide, replant in August, but only when bulbs become crowded.

STEWARTIA. Deciduous shrubs or trees. Zones 4-6, 14-17, 20, 21. These are all-season performers; bare and exhibiting distinctive branch pattern in winter; leafing out in spring; displaying white flowers like single camellias in summer; and in autumn offering colored foliage. Slow growing. Best in moist, acid soil with a high content of organic matter. Needs ample moisture when young, otherwise leaves burn. Takes sun, but prefers partial shade in warm climates.

S. koreana. KOREAN STEWARTIA. Tree. To 20-25 ft.; may reach eventual 50 ft. Rather narrow, pyramidal habit. Leaves dark green, to 4 in. long, somewhat silky underneath, turning orange or orange-red in fall. Flowers in June-July, white with yellow-orange stamens, to 3 in. across, on short stalks among the leaves.

S. monadelpha. TALL STEWARTIA. Tree. To 25 ft., with upward-angled slender branches, 1½-2½-in.-long leaves. Summer flowers 1½ in. across, the stamens with violet anthers. Outstanding red fall leaf color.

S. ovata. MOUNTAIN STEWARTIA. Shrub or small tree. To 15 ft. Slender habit. The 2½-5-in. grayish green leaves turn brilliant orange in fall. Three-inch flowers with frilled petals in summer.

S. pseudo-camellia. JAPANESE STEWARTIA. Tree. To 60 ft. Leaves 1-3 in. long, turning bronze to dark purple in fall. July-August flowers to 2½ in. across with orange anthers.

Summer flowers of stewartias resemble single white camellias. Leaves color in fall.

STIGMAPHYLLON ciliatum. ORCHID VINE. Evergreen vine. Zones 19-24. Twines at moderate to fast rate to 25-30 ft.; easily kept smaller. Foliage open and delicate; leaves smooth, heart-shaped, bright green above, gray-green beneath, 1-3 in. long; new growth coppery color. Clusters of 3-7 flowers, 1½ in. across, bright yellow, shaped somewhat like pansy orchids (*Miltonia*). Heaviest bloom July-September; some bloom through year.

Sun, light shade in warm areas. Moist soil, ample water, some shade at roots. Support with trellis, prune out dead and weak wood.

ST. JOHN'S BREAD. See Ceratonia

ST. JOHNSWORT, CREEPING. See Hypericum calycinum

STOCK. See Matthiola

STOCK, VIRGINIAN. See Malcolmia

STOKESIA laevis. STOKES'ASTER. Perennial. Zones 1-9, 12-24. A rugged and most adaptable plant. Much branched, with stiff, erect stems 1½-2 ft. high. Smooth, firm-textured, medium green leaves 2-8 in. long, spiny toothed at the bottom. Flower heads aster-like, blue, purplish blue, or white, 3-4 in. across, with a button of small flowers in center, outer ring of larger flowers. Blooms summer, early autumn. Leafy, curved, finely toothed bracts surround tight, unopened flower buds. Use in borders with lythrum, penstemon; edge with *Nepeta mussinii* or verbena. Good in pots. Long-lasting cut flower.

STONECRESS. See Aethionema

STONECROP. See Sedum

STONEFACE. See Lithops

STRANVAESIA davidiana. Evergreen shrub or small tree. Zones 4-11, 14-17. Informal, wide-spreading, 6-20 ft. high; moderate growth rate. Leaves oblong, smooth-edged, to 4 in. long; new foliage reddish. Some leaves turn bronze or purple in late fall and winter—good foil for clusters of showy red berries that form at same time. White flowers in 4-in. clusters, June.

Best if given plenty of room, sun, not-too-rich soil. In hot interior gardens, protect from hot winds and supply adequate water. Subject to fireblight. Looks good with strong-growing native plants, or as screen or background. Berried branches handsome as holiday cut foliage.

S. d. undulata (*S. undulata*). Lower growing, to an irregularly-shaped 5 ft. New foliage and branch tips colorful bronzy red. Leaves are wavy along the edges.

STRAWBERRY. Plant strawberries in a sunny location and in soil that is well drained, fairly rich. To harvest just a few berries, you can simply plant a dozen or so plants, spaced 14-18 in. apart in a sunny patch within a flower or vegetable garden, or even in boxes or tubs on a patio.

To bring in a big crop of berries, plant in rows. If soil is heavy or poorly drained, set plants in rows along raised mounds 5-6 in. high and 28 in. from center to center. Use the furrows between mounds for irrigation and feeding. Set plants 14-16 in. apart.

If your soil drains well or if furrow irrigation would be difficult, plant on flat ground 14-18 in. apart in rows 18 in. apart, and irrigate by overhead sprinkler. It's best to use a flat bed wherever salinity is a problem. Strawberries are difficult to grow in the desert or other regions where soil and water salinity is a problem.

In the Northwest most gardeners set plants 2-3 ft. apart in rows 4-5 ft. apart, let runners fill in until plants are 7-10 in. apart, then keep additional runners pinched off. Keep rows 20-30 in. wide.

Planting season is usually determined by when your nursery can offer the plants. In mild-winter areas plants set out in late summer or fall produce a crop the following spring. Other than that, the rule is to plant in early spring. Everbearers will give a summer and fall crop from spring plantings; pinch off earliest blossoms to increase plant strength.

Set plants carefully; crown should be above soil level, topmost roots ¼ in. beneath soil level (buried crowns rot; exposed roots dry out). Mulch to keep down weeds, conserve moisture, keep berries clean.

Strawberries need frequent deep soaking, especially in the bearing season. In summer-arid areas they may need water every 2-3 days if soil is sandy, every week to 10 days if soil is heavy. In the humid Northwest early berries may ripen without irrigation, but everbearers will need summer water.

Feed plants twice a year—once when growth begins, again after the first crop. In California and the Southwest nitrogen is especially necessary. Northwest growers usually apply superphosphate at planting time and use complete fertilizers high in phosphorus.

Most varieties are reproduced by offset plants at the ends of runners. You can (a) pinch off all runners, which will give large plants and small yields of big berries; or (b) permit offset plants to grow either 7-10 in. apart (or even closer), which will give heavy yields of somewhat smaller berries. When your plants have made enough off-sets, pinch off further runners. (Some varieties make few or no offsets.)

Strawberries are subject to red stele (root rot), yellows (virus) and verticillium wilt (soil-borne fungus). Spray or dust to control aphids and spider mites; do not use chemicals if fruit has set. Replace plants every 3 years (everbearers every other year). Use your own runner-grown plants only if disease-free.

See variety chart for choices in regular strawberries.

Novelty Strawberries. 'Sonjana', the so-called climbing strawberry, makes runner on runner, and these bear even if not rooted. Plants can be tied to a trellis or permitted to hang over a wall. Fruit small, of

S

Climate Zone maps pages 8-27

STRAWBERRY

NAME	DESCRIPTION	ADAPTABILITY	RESISTANCE
'Chief Bemidji'	Everbearer. Bright red fruit of fine flavor.	Hardy to —40°. Not thoroughly tested in milder areas.	
'Gem'	Everbearer. Fruit highly flavored, tart. Few runners.	Good in cold winter climates and near coast.	Resistant to yellows, wilt.
'Honey Lump'	Everbearer. Very sweet fruit.	Very hardy to cold. Tolerance to warm winters not thoroughly tested.	
'Lassen'	Medium large berry with spring and fall crops. Use fresh or for freezing.	Good in southern California, inland valleys. Takes warm winters.	Moderate resistance to alkalinity. Highly subject to yellows.
'Marshall' ('Banner', 'Oregon Plum', 'Oregon', 'Pacific', 'Dewey')	Large, deep crimson fruit in late June. Excellent flavor.	Good in Northwest where yellows not prevalent.	Susceptible to yellows and red stele.
'Northwest'	Big, good-looking berry for use fresh, frozen, in preserves. June-July in Northwest.	Very popular in Washington, Oregon.	Resistant to yellows. Susceptible to red stele; give good drainage.
'Ogallala'	Everbearer. Hybrid with a wild Rocky Mountain berry.	Very cold tolerant. Blossoms fairly frost resistant.	
'Puget Beauty'	Sweet, glossy red. Good fresh, frozen, and for jam. Main crop June; light crop in August.	Good variety for heavy soils in Northwest.	Some resistance to red stele and mildew.
'Red Rich'	Medium large everbearer. Red clear through. June-October.	Good in all strawberry climates.	Moderate resistance to salinity. Susceptible to yellows, wilt.
'Rockhill'	Medium large, medium red everbearer. Heavy crop.	Does well in all strawberry climates. Best in sandy soil. Few runners; grow in hills.	Resistant to verticillium wilt, moderate salinity.
'Sequoia'	Medium to large, red fruit. Tastiest of modern strawberries. Prolific. Bears for many months.	Developed in and for coastal California. Does well in California's interior valleys, too.	Resistant to alkalinity, yellows, and most leaf diseases.
'Siletz'	Vigorous plant with good fruit.	Northwest.	Highly resistant to red stele.
'Solana'	Better quality than 'Lassen'.	Southern California.	
'Streamliner'	Everbearer of good size, excellent flavor. Bears quickly after planting.	Very cold tolerant. Good in coastal California. Poor flavor in southern California interior valleys.	Fair disease resistance.
'Tioga'	Yield, size, and appearance better than 'Lassen'.	Grows well in all strawberry areas of California.	
'20th Century' (Utah Centennial')	Medium to large fruit of high quality. Spring and fall crop.	Good in cold winter areas, northern California inland valleys.	Resistant to yellows. Susceptible to wilt.
'Wiltguard'	High quality for fresh fruit, freezing. Heavy yields after an early start.	Not widely tested outside southern California.	Fairly good wilt resistance.

S

Climate Zone maps pages 8-27

spicy flavor. 'Harzland' and 'Baron Sole-macher' are 18-in.-tall plants with no runners. Small, sweet berries throughout spring and summer. Grow from seed sown in fall or early spring, or divide plants.

STRAWBERRY GERANIUM. See Saxifraga stolonifera

STRAWBERRY, SAND. See Fragaria chiloensis

STRAWBERRY TREE. See Arbutus unedo

STRAWBERRY, WILD. See Fragaria chiloensis

STRAWFLOWER. See Helichrysum bracteatum

STRELITZIA. BIRD OF PARADISE. Evergreen perennials. Tropical plants of extremely individual character. Need full sun in coastal areas, light shade inland. Both kinds are good to use by pools—make no litter and seem to withstand some splashing.

S. nicolai. GIANT BIRD OF PARADISE. Zones 22-24. This one is grown for its dramatic display of bananalike leaves; flowers are incidental. Treelike, clumping, many stalks to 30 ft. Gray-green, leathery, 5-10-ft. leaves are arranged fanlike on erect or curving trunks. Floral envelope is purplish gray, flower is white with a dark blue tongue.

Feed young plants frequently to push to full dramatic size, then give little or no feeding. The goal is to acquire and maintain size without lush growth and need for dividing. Keep dead leaves cut off and thin out surplus growths. Endures temperatures only to 28°.

S. reginae. BIRD OF PARADISE. Outdoors in Zones 22-24; under overhangs where heat can be trapped, Zones 9, 12-21. This one is grown for its spectacular flowers, startlingly like tropical birds. The orange, blue, and white flowers on long stiff stems bloom intermittently throughout the year, but best in cool season, last extremely long. Trunkless plants grow 5 ft. high with leathery, long-stalked, blue-green, 1½-ft.-long leaves, 4-6 in. wide. Benefits greatly from frequent and heavy feedings. Divide infrequently since large crowded clumps bloom best. Good in containers.

STREPTANTHERA cuprea. Corm. Zones 9, 13-24. Related to and similar to ixia and sparaxis, but with flatter, rounder blooms 1½ in. wide, coppery orange with dark purple center spot and a yellow eye. Leaves 5-7 in. long, in fan-shaped basal tufts. Plant corms 2-3 in. deep, 3-4 in. apart in light soil. Full sun. Easy from seed; if sown early, may bloom first year. In colder areas grow in pots or mulch deeply over winter.

STREPTOCARPUS. CAPE PRIMROSE. Evergreen perennials. Outdoors in Zones 17, 22-24; house plants everywhere. Related to African violets and gloxinias (Sinningia), and something between them in appearance. Leaves are large, fleshy, sometimes velvety. Flowers trumpet-shaped, with long (2-3-in.) tube and spreading mouth 1½-2 in. wide. Autumn-winter bloom. Buy plants or grow from tiny seeds. Usually bloom one year from seed. Indoors, handle like African violet. Outdoors, give shady, cool, moist situation.

Many species interest collectors and hybridizers. Hybrids most common in nurseries and seed catalogs:

Giant Hybrids. Flowers range from white to blue, pink, rose, and red, often with contrasting blotches. Stems 1 ft. tall.

Wiesmoor Hybrids. Flowers fringed and crested, 4-5 in. across on tall (to 2-ft.) stems. Many colors. 'Wiesmoor Tetred' has bright rose flowers marked deep crimson.

STREPTOSOLEN jamesonii. MARMALADE BUSH. Evergreen viny shrub. Outdoors in Zones 17, 23, 24; indoor-outdoor plant or with careful protection Zones 13, 15, 16, 18-24. To 4-6 ft. tall and as wide (to 10-15 ft. trained against wall, bank, trellis). Leaves ribbed, oval, 1½ in. long. Flowers 1 in. across in large, loose clusters at branch ends. Color ranges from yellow to brilliant orange, mostly the latter.

Big bloom season April-October (in most frost-free parts of Zones 23, 24 occasionally everblooming, with good display in midwinter). Grow it in a warm spot with ample water, fast drainage.

In colder areas protect plants from frost; cut back dead wood after last frost, thin and prune to shape. Good hanging basket plant (needs some protection from hottest sun).

STRING OF BEADS. See Senecio rowleyanus

STYRAX. Deciduous trees. Zones 1-10, 12-21. Pretty white bell-like flowers in hanging clusters.

S. japonica. JAPANESE SNOWDROP TREE, JAPANESE SNOWBELL. Deciduous tree. Slow to moderate growth to 30 ft. Trunk slender, graceful; branches often strongly horizontal, giving the tree a broad, flat top. Leaves oval, dark green, to 3 in. long with scalloped edges, turning red or yellow in fall. Flowers white, faintly fragrant, hanging, ¾ in. long, on short side branches in June. Leaves angle upward from branches while flowers hang down, giving parallel tiers of green and white.

Drooping white flowers of Styrax japonica make it good tree to look up into.

Needs reasonably good well drained garden soil. Full sun or part shade. Plenty of water. Prune to control shape; tends to be shrubby unless lower side branches suppressed. A splendid tree to look up into; plant it in raised beds near outdoor entertaining areas, or on a high bank above a path. A good tree to garden under; roots are not aggressive.

S. obassia. FRAGRANT SNOWBELL. Deciduous tree. To 20-30 ft. tall, rather narrow in spread. Roundish leaves 3-8 in. long, deep green. June flowers fragrant, ¾-1 in. long, carried in 6-8-in. drooping clusters at the ends of branches. Culture same as S. japonica. Good against a background of evergreens, or for height and contrast above a border of rhododendrons and azaleas.

SUCCULENT. Strictly speaking, a succulent is any plant that stores water in juicy leaves, stems, or roots to withstand periodic drought. Practically speaking, fanciers of succulents exclude such fleshy plants as epiphytic orchids and include in their collections many desert plants (yuccas, puyas) which are not fleshy. Although cactus are succulents, common consent sets them up as a separate category (see Cactus).

Most succulents come from desert or semi-desert areas in the warmer parts of the world. Mexico and South Africa are two very important sources. Some (notably sedums and sempervivums) come from colder climates, where they grow on dry, sunny, rocky slopes and ledges.

Succulents are grown everywhere as house plants; in milder Western climates many are useful and decorative as landscaping plants, either in the open ground or in containers. When well grown and well groomed, they look good throughout the year, in bloom or out. Although considered low-maintenance plants, they look shabby if neglected. They may live through extended drought but will drop leaves, shrivel, or lose color. Amount of irrigation needed depends on summer heat, humidity of atmosphere. Plants in interior valleys may need water every week or two; near the coast water less. Give plants just enough water to keep them healthy, plump of leaf, and attractive.

One light feeding at the start of the growing season should be enough for plants in the open ground. Control aphids with sprays or dusts. Read insecticide labels and directions carefully; some succulents are sensitive to certain spray materials.

Some succulents make good ground covers. Some are sturdy and quick-growing enough for erosion control on large banks. Other, smaller kinds are useful among stepping stones or for creating patterns in small gardens. Most of these come easily from stem or leaf cuttings, and a stock can quickly be grown from a few plants. See: *Echeveria*, Ice plant, *Kleinia*, *Portulacaria*, *Sedum*.

Large-growing succulents have a decorative value in themselves. See: *Aeonium*, *Agave*, *Aloe*, *Cotyledon*, *Crassula*, *Doryanthes*, *Dudleya*, *Echeveria*, *Kalanchoe*, *Portulacaria*, *Yucca*.

Many succulents have showy flowers. For some of the best see *Aloe*, some species of *Crassula*, *Euphorbia*, *Hoya*, Ice plant, *Kalanchoe*, *Rochea*.

Some smaller succulents are primarily collectors' items, grown for odd form or flowers. See smaller species of *Aloe*, *Ceropegia*, *Crassula*, *Echeveria*, *Euphorbia*, *Graptopetalum*, *Haworthia*, *Lithops*, *Pleiospilos*, *Stapelia*.

A few words of caution to growers of succulents:

1. Not all succulents like hot sun; read species descriptions carefully.

2. The variety of forms, colors, textures, offers many possibilities for handsome combinations, but the line between a successful

grouping and a jumbled medley is thin. Beware of using too many kinds in one planting. Mass a few species instead of putting in one of each.

3. You can combine succulents with other types of plants, but plan combinations carefully. Not all plants look right with succulents.

SUGARBERRY. See Celtis laevigata

SUGAR BUSH. See Rhus ovata

SUGAR GUM. See Eucalyptus cladocalyx

SUMAC. See Rhus

SUMMERSWEET. See Clethra alnifolia

SUNDROPS. See Oenothera tetragona

SUNFLOWER. See Helianthus

SUNFLOWER, MEXICAN. See Tithonia

SUNROSE. See Helianthemum

SWEET BRUSH. See Cercocarpus betuloides

SWEET CICELY. See Myrrhis odorata

SWEETLEAF. See Symplocos

SWEET PEA. See Lathyrus

SWEET-PEA SHRUB. See Polygala dalmaisiana

SWEET POTATO. This vegetable is the thickened root of a tropical plant closely related to morning glory. Requires a long frost-free season; much space; warm, well drained, preferably sandy loam soils; and considerable work in getting started. They are, moreover, tricky to store. All in all, they are not recommended to the home gardener.

To grow a sweet potato vine as a house plant, push 3 toothpicks firmly into a sweet potato at equal distances around the tuber; these will support the potato within the rim of a glass or jar of water. Adjust water level so it just touches the tip end of the tuber; it doesn't matter which end. Keep water touching the base. Sprouts will grow from the tuber and in 6 weeks you'll have a lush vine with very attractive foliage. The vine will continue to grow until the tuber shrivels. If nothing happens for several weeks, your sweet potato probably has been kiln-dried or treated to prevent sprouting.

SWEET SHRUB. See Calycanthus

SWEETSPIRE, HOLLYLEAF. See Itea ilicifolia

SWEET WILLIAM. See Dianthus barbatus

SWEET WOODRUFF. See Asperula

SWISS CHARD. One of the easiest and most practical of vegetables for home gardens. Sow the big, crinkly, tan seeds ½-¾ in. deep on spaded soil, in a sunny position, any time from early spring to early summer. Thin seedlings to 12 in. apart. Water enough to keep them growing. About 2 months after sowing you can begin to cut outside leaves from plants as needed for meals. New leaves grow up in center of plants. Yield all summer and seldom bolt to seed (if one does, pull it up and throw it away).

Regular green and white chard looks presentable in a flower garden. Rhubarb chard has red stems, reddish green leaves, and makes quite attractive plant in garden beds or containers. Its leaves are valuable in floral arranging and they are tasty when cooked, too—sweeter and stronger flavored than green chard.

SYAGRUS. See Microcoelum

SYCAMORE. See Platanus

SYDNEY BLUE GUM. See Eucalyptus saligna

SYMPHORICARPOS. Deciduous shrubs. North American natives. Low-growing, often spreading by root suckers. Flowers small, pink-tinged or white, in clusters or spikes. Attractive round berrylike fruits remain on stems after leaves fall, nice in winter arrangements. Best used as wild thicket in sun or shade, erosion control on steep banks.

S. albus (*S. racemosus*). COMMON SNOWBERRY. All Zones. Upright or spreading shrub 2-6 ft. tall. Leaves roundish, dull green, ¾-2 in. long (to 4 in. and often lobed on sucker shoots). Pink flowers in May-June, white fruits ½ in. wide from late summer to winter.

S. chenaultii. All Zones. Hybrid of garden origin. Resembles *S. orbiculatus*, but red fruit is lightly spotted white and leaves are larger.

S. mollis. CREEPING SNOWBERRY, SPREADING SNOWBERRY. Zones 4-24. Like common snowberry, but usually less than 18 in. high, earlier flowering, fewer flowers, smaller fruits. Spreads like ground cover.

S. orbiculatus. CORAL BERRY, INDIAN CURRANT. All Zones. Resembles common snowberry, but with profusion of small, purplish red fruits in clusters.

SYMPLOCOS paniculata. SWEETLEAF, SAPPHIRE BERRY. Deciduous shrub, small tree. Zones 4-6. Usually 10-15 (sometimes 20) ft. tall in gardens; can grow larger. Leaves oval, 1½-3½ in. long, half as wide, bright green. Tiny, white, fragrant flowers in 1½-in. clusters appear in late spring. Clusters of showy, sapphire blue, ¼-in. fruits appear in fall.

Ordinary garden soil, moderate water, sun or light shade. Thin to prevent brushy look. Flowers, handsome fruits not long lasting, but foliage and form good-looking enough to give it a place as tall background shrub or in mixed shrubbery. Will thrive in a lawn.

SYNGONIUM podophyllum. Evergreen climbing vine. Grown as house plant. Dwarf, fast growing. Related to philodendron. Long-stalked, arrow-shaped, dull green leaves, sometimes lobed. Easy to grow in pots of rich house plant mix. Useful in terrarium, dish garden, as a trailer, or trained against a support in the manner of vining philodendron. Many varieties include 'Ruth Fraser', silvery leaves bordered green; 'Trileaf Wonder', green leaves covered with whitish powder; 'California Silver Wonder', narrow silvery leaves.

SYRINGA. LILAC. Deciduous shrubs. Best known is the common lilac (*S. vulgaris*) and its many named varieties, but there are other species of great usefulness. All are best where winter brings a pronounced chill, but some bloom well with light chilling.

Sun; light shade in hottest areas. All like an alkaline soil; in areas where soils are strongly acid, add lime and cultivate into soil beneath the drip line of the plants. Control growth during early years by pinching and shaping. Flower buds for next year form in pairs where leaves join stems. After bloom, remove spent flower clusters just above points where buds are forming. Heavy pruning results in loss of much of next year's bloom. Thin out dead and weak wood at same time. Renovate old, overgrown plants by cutting a few of oldest stems to the ground each year. Leaf miner and scale are only important pests; bacterial blight is occasional problem.

S. chinensis (*S. rothomagensis*). CHINESE LILAC. Zones 1-11, 14-16, 18-21. Hybrid between common and Persian lilacs. Moderate growth rate to 15 ft., usually much less. More graceful than common lilac, and with finer-textured foliage. Airy, open clusters of fragrant rose-purple flowers in May. Profuse bloom. Does well in mild-winter, hot-summer climates. Variety 'Alba' has white flowers.

S. josikaea. HUNGARIAN LILAC. Zones 1-11, 14-16, 18-21. Dense, upright growth to 12 ft. Dark green foliage. Flowers lilac purple, slightly fragrant, in narrow clusters 4-7 in. long. Blooms in May. Variety 'Sylvia' has pink flowers.

S. laciniata (*S. persica laciniata*). Zones 1-12, 14-16, 18-21. Moderate growth to 4 ft. tall, open habit, good rich green foliage color. Leaves to 2½ in. long, divided nearly to midrib into 3-9 segments. Many clusters of pale lilac, fragrant flowers in May.

S. persica. PERSIAN LILAC. Zones 1-12, 14-16, 18-21. Graceful, loose form to 6 ft., with arching branches and 2½-in.-long leaves. Many clusters of pale violet, fragrant flowers appear all along branches in May.

S. swegiflexa. Zones 1-9, 14-16. To 12 ft. Single pink flowers open from deep reddish buds. Clusters to 8 in. long. Blooms 3 weeks after common lilac. Sometimes sold as pink pearl lilac. Hybrid between two hardy Chinese species, *S. reflexa* and *S. sweginzowii*.

S. velutina. (Usually sold as *S. palibiniana*.) KOREAN LILAC. Zones 1-9, 14-16. Dense, twiggy growth to an eventual 8-9 ft., but stays at 3 ft. many years. Flowers pink to lavender, in clusters to 5 in. long. Blooms in May. Sometimes grafted high on common lilac to make a 3 ft. standard tree.

S. vulgaris. COMMON LILAC. Zones 1-11. In Zones 14-16, 18-22, force plants into dormancy by drying them off gradually but completely starting in August. Failure of plants to go dormant will result in third-rate off-season bloom, eventual failure of plant to bloom at all, gradual decline. Exception: 'Lavender Lady' takes very well to Zones 18-22 without special attention.

These bulky shrubs can eventually reach 20 ft. tall, with nearly equal spread. Leaves roundish oval, pointed, dark green, to 5 in. long. Flowers pinkish or bluish lavender ('Alba' has pure white flowers) in clusters to 10 in. long or more. Flowers in May, and the fragrance is legendary. Excellent cut flowers. Lilac fanciers swear these are more fragrant than the newer varieties.

The varieties, often called French hybrids, number in the hundreds. They generally flower a little later than the species

Climate
Zone maps
pages 8-27

and have larger clusters of single or double flowers in a wide range of colors. Singles are often as showy as doubles, sometimes even more so. All lilacs require 2-3 years to settle down and produce flowers of full size and true color. Here are just a few of the many choice varieties:

'Clarke's Giant'. Single, soft blue. Very large leaves, individual flowers, and clusters.

'Ellen Willmott'. Double, white. Heavy, compact clusters.

'Esther Staley'. Single, rose pink flowers opening from red buds.

'Firmament'. Single, sky blue.

'Maximowicz'. Double, deep purple.

'Monument'. Single, snowy white.

'President Lincoln'. Single, large Wedgwood blue flowers.

'Primrose'. Single, palest primrose yellow to cream. Unusual contrast to darker lilacs.

'Purple Heart'. Single, deep purple.

'Souvenir de Louis Chasset'. Single, ruby red, big flowers.

SYZYGIUM. Evergreen shrubs or trees. Closely related to *Eugenia,* and usually sold as such in nurseries. Foliage rich green, often tinted coppery; new foliage brightly tinted. Flowers conspicuous for tufts of stamens that look like little brushes. Fruit soft, edible, handsomely colored.

S. jambos (*Eugenia jambos*). ROSE APPLE. Zones 18-24. Slow growth to 25-30 ft., usually much smaller and shrubby. Leaves 5-8 in. long, narrow, thick, shiny, coppery green; new growth pinkish. Greenish white flower brushes 2-3 in. across in clusters at branch ends. Spring bloom. Fruit greenish or yellow sometimes blushed pink, 1-2 in. in diameter, sweetish, with mild flavor, fragrance of rosewater. Slow growth means little or no pruning.

S. paniculatum (*Eugenia myrtifolia, E. paniculata*). BRUSH CHERRY, AUSTRALIAN BRUSH CHERRY. Zones 16, 17, 19-24. Unclipped, a handsome, narrowish tree with single or multiple trunk, dense foliage crown, 30-60 ft. tall. Usually clipped into formal shapes and hedges, and a most popular hedging and screening plant in mild, nearly frost-free areas. Young foliage reddish bronze; mature leaves oblong, 1½-3 in. long, rich glossy green, often bronze-tinged. Flowers white or creamy, ½ in. wide, with feathery tufts of stamens. Fruit rose-purple, showy, ¾ in. long, edible but insipid.

Will not stand heavy frost; foliage burns at 25°-26° and even old plants may die if temperature drops much lower. Thrives in well drained garden soil. Hedges need frequent clipping to stay neat, and heavy root systems makes it hard to grow other plants nearby; new red foliage, showy fruit make it worth the effort. Don't plant where dropping fruit will squish on pavement. Spray for aphids; keep ants away; watch for scale insects, mealybugs.

The variety 'Compacta' is smaller, denser in growth. Very popular hedging plant.

TABEBUIA. Briefly deciduous, sometimes evergreen trees. Zones 15, 16, 20-24. Fast growth to 25-30 ft. Very showy trumpet-shaped flowers 2-4 in. long in rounded clusters which become larger, more profuse as trees mature, may contain as many as 23 flowers. Leaves dark olive green, usually divided into 3-7 leaflets arranged like the fingers of a hand.

Useful as patio trees, free-standing flowering trees for display, in lawns. Tolerate many soils and degrees of maintenance, but respond well to feeding and frequent watering. Stake while young and keep plants to a single leading shoot until 6-8 ft. tall, then allow to develop freely. Hardy to about 24°.

The two species below were the first to be introduced to the California nursery trade. Others will surely follow because there are many more species grown where the first ones came from (West Indies, Central and South America), and all are showy.

T. chrysotricha. (Sometimes sold as *T. pulcherrima.*) GOLDEN TRUMPET TREE. Rounded, spreading growth to 25 ft. Leaves with 5 leaflets (2-4 in. long, 1-2 in. wide); young twigs, undersides of leaves with tawny fuzz. Flowers 3-4 in. long, golden yellow, often with maroon stripes in throat. Bloom heaviest April-May, at which time trees lose leaves for a brief period. May give lighter bloom at other times with leaves present. Blooms young.

T. ipe. More erect, larger growing than *T. chrysotricha.* Leaves dark green, smooth. Tree usually evergreen. Flowers 2-3 in. long, lavender with white throat banded yellow. Blooms late winter, sometimes again late summer to fall. Does not bloom as young tree.

TAGETES. MARIGOLD. Annuals. Robust, free-branching, nearly trouble-free plants ranging from 6 in. to 4 ft. tall and with flowers from pale yellow through gold to orange and brown-maroon. Leaves finely divided, ferny, usually strongly scented. Bloom period early summer to frost if old flowers are picked off. Handsome, long-lasting cut flowers; strong scent permeates a room, but some odorless varieties are available. Easy from seed, which sprouts in a few days in warm spot; to get earlier bloom, start seeds in flats or buy flat-grown plants. Full sun, ample water. Smog will damage tender young plants, but they toughen up.

Pale yellow marigolds are good in the mixed border with most other colors. Those with stronger colors should be used where orange and maroon-red predominate.

T. erecta. AMERICAN MARIGOLD, AFRICAN MARIGOLD. (Often sold simply as tall marigold.) Original strains were plants 3-4 ft. tall with single flowers. Modern strains are more varied, and most have fully double flowers. The F₁ hybrid strains Gold Coin, X-15, and Climax have 5-in. double flowers in shades of yellow and orange. The Carnation-flowered strain has double flowers 3½-4 in. across on plants 2-2½ ft. tall. Two varieties have odorless foliage: 'Hawaii' (double, 2 ft. tall, 4-in. flowers) and 'Crown of Gold' (2 ft. tall, 2-in. flowers). Chrysanthemum-flowered strain has fully double flowers with narrow rays curved inward toward center. Many varieties available in yellow and orange. 'Cupid Orange' and 'Cupid Yellow' are interesting dwarfs with 2½-3 in. flowers on odorless, 8-10-in. bushy plants.

Avoid overhead watering on taller kinds, or stems will sag and perhaps break. To make tall-variety plants stand as stout as possible (and perhaps not need staking), dig planting holes extra deep, strip any leaves off lower 1-3 in. of stem, and plant extra deep with soil around lower 1-3 in. of stem.

T. patula. FRENCH MARIGOLD. Varieties from 6 in. to 18 in. tall, in flower colors from yellow to rich maroon-brown; flowers may be fully double or single, and many are strongly bi-colored. Among the best for edging are the Extra Dwarf Doubles, 6 in. tall, 10 in. wide, very floriferous: 'Petite Gold' (golden yellow), 'Petite Harmony' (mahogany and gold), 'Petite Orange', 'Petite Yellow', and 'Brownie Scout' (golden splashed red). Taller varieties for use as bedding plants are 9-18 in. tall: 'Naughty Marietta' (single, gold and maroon) and 'Spry' (double, yellow and mahogany), 9-12 in.; 'Tangerine' (double, bright orange), 15 in.

T. tenuifolia (*T. signata*). SIGNET MARIGOLD. Relatively little-planted species. Fewer ray flowers on smaller flower heads, but incredibly profuse in bloom. 'Ursula' and 'Gnome' grow to 2 ft. 'Golden Ring', a 10 in. dwarf, has golden orange, star-shaped blooms.

TALLOW TREE, CHINESE. See Sapium

TAMARIX. TAMARISK. Deciduous and evergreen-appearing shrubs and trees. In deserts of California and Arizona they have no equal in resistance to wind, drought, and they will grow in saline soils that are toxic to other plants. Nurseries can't keep them in containers long because they form deep tap roots. But they are easy to grow from ½-1-inch-thick cuttings set in place and kept watered.

There is much confusion in labeling of tamarisks in the nurseries. But as far as the gardener is concerned there are three kinds of tamarisk—an evergreen-appearing tree, spring-flowering, and summer-flowering. And it is in this way that you will find them below.

Evergreen-appearing tree

T. aphylla (*T. articulata*). ATHEL TREE. Widely used in Zones 10-13; useful in some difficult situations in Zones 7-9, 14-24. Heavily damaged at 0° temperature but comes back rapidly. An excellent windbreak tree. Fast growth from planted cuttings to 10 ft. or more in 3 years; eventually 30-50 ft. and more in 15 years with deep soil and water.

Greenish jointed branchlets give tree its evergreen appearance. Takes on grayish look in late summer where soils are saline due to secretions of salt. True leaves are minute. White to pinkish, very small flowers in clusters at ends of branches in late summer, but flowering not as spectacular as other tamarisks. Not a good selection for highly cultivated garden because its roots are too competitive.

Spring-flowering tamarisks

These are hardy and adapted in All Zones. Fast growth to 6-15 ft., depending on culture. Graceful, airy, arching branches with reddish bark. Pink flowers in clusters on branches of previous year. Prune after bloom in spring to maintain graceful effect, limit height, and produce new flowering wood.

T. africana. Grown in Arizona. Bears its flowers in 2-3-in.-long, upright clusters. For

Climate Zone maps pages 8-27

plants sold and widely used under this name in California, see *T. tetrandra.*

T. juniperina. (Sometimes sold as *T. japonica,* or *T. plumosa.)* Occasionally cultivated in California and Arizona. Flowers in drooping clusters 2-4 in. long.

T. parviflora. Plants sold under this name can scarcely be distinguished from the following.

T. tetrandra. Most frequently cultivated of the spring-flowering species. Flower clusters upright, 1-2 in. long.

Summer-flowering tamarisks

T. pentandra. SALT CEDAR. All Zones. This species is typical of the summer-flowering kinds. (Others you may find in the nurseries that closely resemble this species are *T. chinensis, T. gallica, T. hispida*—hairy branches and branched flower clusters, and *T. h.* 'Coolidgei'.)

Spreading feathery shrub that grows to 6-12 ft. if pruned to the ground in early spring. Otherwise it can become 20-30-ft. rank-growing shrub with highly competitive root system. Since the tiny pale pink flowers, in dense clusters, are borne on wood of the current season, this type of pruning will not only keep the plants down but also give a mass of flower plumes from July to fall. Small leaves are pale blue-green.

TANACETUM vulgare. COMMON TANSY. Perennial herb. All Zones. A coarse garden plant with history of medicinal use. To 3 ft. Finely cut, bright green, aromatic leaves; small, buttonlike flowers. Any soil, full sun. Start from seed or division of roots. Thin clumps yearly to keep in bounds. Foliage and flowers keep well in bouquets.

T. v. 'Crispum'. FRINGED OR FERN-LEAF TANSY. To 2½ ft.; more decorative.

TANBARK OAK. See Lithocarpus

TANGELO. See Citrus

TANGERINE. See Citrus

TANGOR. See Citrus

TANSY, COMMON. See Tanacetum

TARO. See Colocasia

TARRAGON. See Artemisia dracunculus

TASSEL FLOWER. See Amaranthus caudatus

TAXODIUM. Deciduous or evergreen trees. Conifers of considerable size bearing short, narrow, flat, needlelike leaves in graceful sprays.

T. distichum. BALD CYPRESS. Deciduous tree. Zones 1-9, 14-24. In nature can grow into a 100-ft. tall, broad-topped tree, but young and middle-aged garden trees are pyramidal. Foliage sprays very delicate and feathery; leaves about ½ in. long, very narrow, and of a delicate, pale, yellow-toned green. Foliage turns bright orange-brown in fall before dropping. Any soil except alkaline. Takes extremely wet conditions (even thrives in swamps), but also will tolerate rather dry soil. Hardy in all except coldest mountain areas. No particular pests or diseases. Requires only corrective pruning—removal of dead wood and unwanted branches. Outstanding tree to plant on the banks of a stream, lake, or pond. Also,

tolerates wet lawn conditions, unlike many conifers.

T. mucronatum. MONTEZUMA CYPRESS. Evergreen tree in mild climates; partially or wholly deciduous in cold regions. Zones 5, 6, 8, 9, 14-24. Has strongly weeping branches. A fast-grower in its youth; with ample water will reach 40 ft. in 14 years; it's likely to reach an eventual 75 ft. in gardens. Established plants are fairly drought tolerant, but growth is slow under drought conditions. Extremely graceful, fine-textured evergreen for large lawns or for background planting.

TAXUS. YEW. Evergreen shrubs or trees. Zones 1-9, 14-24. Conifers, but instead of cones they bear fleshy, scarlet (rarely yellow), cup-shaped, single-seeded fruits. In general, yews are more formal, darker green, and more shade and moisture-tolerant than most cultivated conifers. Slow growing, long-lived, tolerant of much shearing and pruning. Excellent basic landscape plants for hedges, screens, upright plants placed singly or in balanced groups, or for containers.

Easily moved even when large, but slow growth makes big plants a luxury item. Tolerate many soil conditions, but will not thrive in strongly alkaline or strongly acid soils. Once established, fairly drought tolerant. Grow well in shade or sun, but reflected light and heat from a hot south or west wall will burn foliage. Even cold-tolerant kinds show needle damage when exposed to bright winter sun, dry winds, and very low temperatures.

Only female plants produce berries, but many do so without male plants nearby. Considered disease-free; the few pests include vine weevils, scale, and spider mites. All yews benefit from being washed off with water from hose every 2 weeks during hot, dry weather.

T. baccata. ENGLISH YEW. Slow growth to 25-40 ft., with wide-spreading branches forming a broad, low crown. Needles ½-1½ in. long, dark green and glossy above, paler underneath. Red fruits have poisonous seeds. Garden varieties are far more common than the species.

T. b. 'Adpressa'. (Usually sold as *T. brevifolia,* which is really the native Western yew.) Wide-spreading, dense shrub, 4-5 ft. high with leaves about ½ in. long.

T. b. 'Aurea'. More compact than species, with new foliage golden yellow spring to autumn, then turning green.

T. b. 'Erecta'. Erect and formal. Less compact than Irish yew, and with smaller leaves.

T. b. 'Fastigiata Aurea'. Resembles Irish yew, but has golden yellow new foliage.

T. b. 'Repandens'. SPREADING ENGLISH YEW. Long, horizontal, spreading branches make a 2-ft. high ground cover. Useful low foundation plant. Will arch over a wall.

T. b. 'Repandens Aurea'. Golden new growth; otherwise like spreading English yew.

T. b. 'Stricta.' IRISH YEW. Makes a column of very dark green. Slow growing to 20 ft. or higher. Leaves larger than on English yew. Many crowded upright branches tend to spread near the top, especially in snowy regions or where water

is ample, growth lush. Branches can be tied together with wire. Striking against a big wall, in corner plantings, or as a background planting. Very drought tolerant once established.

T. b. 'Stricta Variegata'. Like Irish yew, except that the leaves show yellowish white variegations.

T. brevifolia. WESTERN, PACIFIC, OR OREGON YEW. Zones 1-17. Native of moist places California north to Alaska, inland to Montana. Tree of loose, open growth to 50-60 ft. with needles of dark yellowish green 1 in. or less in length. Very difficult to grow. Most plants sold under this name are *T. baccata* 'Adpressa' or *T. cuspidata* 'Nana'.

T. cuspidata. JAPANESE YEW. A tree to 50 ft. in Japan. Most useful yew in cold-winter areas east of the mountains. Usually grown as a compact, spreading shrub. Leaves ½-1 in. long, usually in two rows along twigs, making a flat or V-shaped spray. Foliage dark green above, tinged yellowish underneath.

T. c. 'Capitata'. Plants sold under this name are probably ordinary *T. cuspidata* in its upright, pyramidal form. Dense, slow growth to 10-25 ft. Can be held lower by pinching new growth. Fruits heavily.

T. c. 'Densiformis'. Much branched, very low, dense, spreading plant with dark green foliage.

T. c. 'Nana'. (Often sold as *T. brevifolia.)* Grows slowly (1-4 in. a year) to 3 ft. tall and spreads to 6 ft. (in 20 years). Good low barrier or foundation plant.

T. media. A group of hybrids between Japanese and English yew. Intermediate between the two in color of green and texture.

T. m. 'Andersonii'. Broad, spreading yew with branches angled up and out.

T. m. 'Brownii'. Slow-growing, compact, rounded yew eventually 4-8 ft. tall. Good for low, dense hedge.

T. m. 'Hatfieldii'. Broad columnar or pyramidal yew of good dark green color.

T. m. 'Hicksii'. Narrow, upright yew, slightly broader at the center than at top and bottom.

T. m. 'Hill's'. (Also sold as *T. m.* 'Pyramidalis Hillii'.) Upright, narrowly pyramidal, with dark green foliage. A heavy fruiting variety.

TEA. See Camellia sinensis

TEA TREE. See Leptospermum

TECOMA australis. See Pandorea pandorana

T. capensis. See Tecomaria

T. jasminoides. See Pandorea jasminoides

T. stans. See Stenolobium

TECOMARIA capensis *(Tecoma capensis).* CAPE HONEYSUCKLE. Evergreen vine or shrub. Zones 12, 13, 16, 18-24. Native to South Africa. Can scramble to 15-25 ft. if tied to a support. With hard pruning a 6-8-ft. upright shrub. Leaves divided into many dark, glistening green leaflets. Total foliage effect is of informality and fine texture. Brilliant orange-red, tubular, 2-in. blossoms in compact clusters, October through the winter.

Needs good soil drainage. Takes sun, heat, wind, salt air, some drought when established. Use as espalier, bank cover (especially good on hot, steep slopes), coarse barrier hedge.

The variety 'Aurea' has yellow flowers and lighter green foliage; it's smaller-growing and less showy. Requires more heat to perform well.

TERNSTROEMIA gymnanthera (*T. japonica*). Evergreen shrub. Zones 4-9, 12-24. It takes a long time to reach 6-8 ft., and is usually seen as a rounded plant 3-4 ft. tall and 4-6 ft. wide. Glossy, leathery foliage is the feature; rounded oval to narrow oval leaves are 1½-3 in. long, with red stalks. New growth bronzy red; mature foliage deep green to bronzy green to purplish red, depending on season, exposure, and the plant itself. Plants in deep shade tend to be dark green; with some sun, leaves may be bronzy green to nearly purple-red. Red tints are deeper in cold weather.

Summer flowers not showy but fragrant, ½ in. wide, creamy yellow. Fruits (uncommon on small plants) resemble little holly berries or cherries, yellow to red-orange; they split open to reveal shiny black seeds.

Full sun to partial shade (full shade in desert). Ample moisture—and the more sun the plants get, the greater the water need. Leaves turn yellow if soil isn't acid enough—feed with acid plant food. Pinch out tip growth to encourage compact growth. Use as basic landscaping shrub, informal hedge, tub plant. Grows well and blends well with camellias (to which it is related), azaleas, nandina, pieris, ferns.

TETRAPANAX papyriferus (*Aralia papyrifera*). RICE PAPER PLANT. Evergreen shrub. Zones 15-24. This is an often multi-stemmed plant of fast growth (to 10-15 ft.). Big, bold leaves 1-2 ft. wide, deeply lobed, on long stalks, in clusters at ends of stems, gray-green above, white-felted beneath. Tan trunks often curve or lean. Big branched clusters of creamy white flowers on tan furry stems show in December.

Sun or shade (midday shade in hottest summer areas). Young plants sunburn easily, older ones adapt. Nearly any soil. Few pests; seems to suffer only from high winds (which break or tatter leaves) or frost (foliage severely damaged at 22°). Plants recover fast from freezes, often put up suckers to form thickets. Can prove hard to

Gray-green leaves of rice paper plant, to 2 ft. across, create strong pattern.

eliminate because of deep root system that sometimes sprouts long after tops have been cut off. Digging around roots stimulates suckering.

Use as silhouette against walls, in patios; combine with other sturdy, bold-leafed plants.

TETRASTIGMA. Evergreen vines. Zones 13, 17, 20-24. Climb by tendrils or cover ground rapidly. Stems thick, fleshy. Leaves glossy, dark green, up to 1 ft. across, divided fanwise into 3-5 oval, leathery leaflets with toothed edges. Flowers, fruits rarely seen. Needs ample water; feed until well established. Plant so roots are shaded while top can run out or up to sun. Good eave-line decoration, large-scale bank or ground cover.

T. voinierianum (*Cissus voinieriana*). Fast growth to 50-60 ft. New growth covered with silvery fuzz.

T. vomerensis (*Cissus vomerensis*). Slightly less rampant than *T. voinierianum*. New growth covered with orange-brown fuzz which lingers on undersides of leaves, contrasts well with rich green of developed leaves.

TEUCRIUM. GERMANDER. Evergreen shrubs or subshrubs. Tough plants for sun and heat, enduring poor, rocky soils. They can't stand wet or poorly drained soils, but take ordinary garden watering where drainage is good.

T. chamaedrys. All Zones. Low growing (to 1 ft. tall), spreading to 2 ft., with many upright stems woody at the base. Toothed dark green leaves, ¾ in. long, densely set on stems. In summer red-purple or white ¾-in. flowers form in loose spikes. White flowered form is looser. Use as edging, foreground, low clipped hedge, or small-scale ground cover. To keep neat, shear back once or twice a year to force side branching. As ground cover, set 2 ft. apart.

T. c. 'Prostratum'. Foliage and flowers similar to *T. chamaedrys*, but growth habit is very prostrate (4-6 in. high and spreading to 3 ft. or more).

T. fruticans. BUSH GERMANDER. Zones 4-24. Loose, silvery-stemmed shrub to 4-8 ft. tall and as wide or wider. Leaves 1¼ in. long, gray-green above, silvery white beneath, giving overall silvery gray effect. Lavender-blue, ¾-in.-long flowers in spikes at branch ends through most of the year. Thin and cut back in late winter, early spring. Use as informal hedge, against a fence or screen, in mass at end of lawn area, but far enough from sprinklers to avoid overwatering. Attractive with reddish or purplish-leafed plants.

TEXAS RANGER. See Leucophyllum

THALICTRUM. MEADOW RUE. Perennial. All Zones; most species short-lived in Zones 18-24. Leaves resemble those of columbines; openly leafy stems on most species are 3-6 ft. in height, topped by airy clusters of small flowers. Summer bloom. Give wind-protected location with plenty of moisture and light shade. Superb for airy effect; delicate tracery of leaves and flowers is particularly effective against a dark green background. Pleasing contrast to sturdier perennials.

T. aquilegifolium. COLUMBINE MEADOW RUE. To 2-4 ft. Flowers purple, pink, or white, late spring to midsummer.

T. dipterocarpum. CHINESE MEADOW RUE. Plants 3-6 ft. Lavender to violet flowers with yellow stamens. Long-lived, even in Zones 18-24.

T. minus (*T. adiantifolium*). To 1-1½ ft. high. Unshowy greenish yellow flowers but especially fine foliage.

T. rochebrunianum. LAVENDER MIST. Clumps 4-6 ft. high, the lavender-violet flowers with pale yellow stamens. Quite hardy.

T. rugosum (*T. glaucum*). DUSTY MEADOW RUE. To 3-6 ft. Foliage blue-gray. Flowers slightly fragrant, soft yellow. Effective with blue delphiniums.

Feathery flower clusters of Thalictrum *come in lavender, purple, pink, white, yellow.*

THEA. See Camellia sinensis

THERMOPSIS caroliniana. Perennial. All Zones. To 3-4 ft. tall. Leaves gray-green, divided into three 2-3-in.-long leaflets. Canary yellow flowers in 10-in.-long clusters resemble lupine. Blooms June, July. Light, well drained soil; will take poor soil. Full sun, moderate water. Needs staking. Cut to ground after bloom. Use at back of mixed flower borders, or grow just for cut flowers. Hard to transplant; grow from seed sown in spring or fall.

THEVETIA. Evergreen shrubs, small trees. Fast-growing plants with narrow leaves; showy funnel-shaped, yellow or apricot flowers in clusters. They thrive in heat, take very little frost. Like their relatives the oleanders, they are poisonous.

T. peruviana (*T. nereifolia*). YELLOW OLEANDER. Zones 12 (with careful protection), 13, 21-24. Fast growth typically to 6-8 ft. or more. Can be trained into a 20-ft. small tree. Leaves 3-6 in. long, very narrow, with edges rolled under. Leaves have deep veins on upper surfaces, look wrinkled. Flowers any time (mostly June-November), fragrant, yellow to apricot, 2-3 in. long, in clusters at branch ends.

Takes any amount of heat and sun. Best with ample water, good drainage. Shallow rooted. Protect from wind or prune to lessen wind resistance. Can be grown as a tree or pruned into a 6-8-ft. hedge or screen. In cold-winter areas, mound dry sand 6-12 in. deep around base of stem. If top is frozen, new growth will come from uninjured basal wood, bloom same year.

Climate Zone maps pages 8-27

T. thevetioides. GIANT THEVETIA. Zones 22-24. Fast open growth to 12 ft. tall, 12 ft. wide. Leaves darker green than *T. peruviana*, resemble those of oleander but corrugated, white-downy beneath. Flowers brilliant yellow, to 4 in. across, in large clusters, June-July and into winter.

THIMBLE FLOWER, BLUE. See Gilia capitata

THORN, KANGAROO. See Acacia armata

THRIFT. See Armeria

THROATWORT, COMMON. See Trachelium

THUJA. (Sometimes spelled Thuya, and always so pronounced.) ARBORVITAE. Evergreen shrubs or trees. Neat, symmetrical, even, geometrical plants which run to globes, cones, or cylinders. Scalelike leaves in flat sprays; juvenile foliage feathery, with small needlelike leaves. Small cones with few scales. Foliage in better-known varieties is often yellow-green, or bright golden yellow.

T. occidentalis. AMERICAN ARBORVITAE. Tree. Zones 1-9, 15-17, 21-24. Native to eastern U. S. Upright, open growth to 40-60 ft. with branches that tend to turn up at the ends. Leaf sprays bright green to yellowish green. Foliage turns brown in severe cold. Needs moist soil, moist air to look its best. Spray for red spider mites.

The typical plant is seldom seen but certain garden varieties are fairly common. Among them, the taller kinds make good unclipped or clipped screens. Lower-growing kinds often planted around foundations, along walks or walls, as hedges. Some good varieties are:

'Douglas Pyramidal'. Tall, vigorous green pyramid of fairly fast growth.

'Fastigiata' ('Pyramidalis', 'Columnaris'). A narrow, tall, dense, columnar plant which can grow to 25 ft. high, 5 ft. wide. Can be kept lower by pruning. Good plant for tall (6-ft. or more) hedges and screens, especially in cold regions and damp soils. Set 4 ft. apart for neat, low-maintenance screen.

'Globosa' ('Nana' and 'Pumila' are very similar, if not identical.) GLOBE ARBORVITAE, TOM THUMB ARBORVITAE. Small, dense, rounded, with bright green foliage. Usually 2-3 ft. tall, with equal spread, but eventually larger.

'Little Gem' ('Pumila'). Dense, dark green; slow growth to 2 ft. tall, 4 ft. across. Larger in great old age.

'Nana'. Small, round, dense, to 1½-2 ft. in height.

'Rheingold' ('Improved Ellwangeriana Aurea'). Cone-shaped, slow-growing, bright golden plant which has a mixture of scalelike and needlelike leaves. Even very old plants seldom exceed 6 ft.

'Umbraculifera'. Globe-shaped in youth, gradually becoming flat-topped. At 10 years it should be 4 by 4 ft.

'Woodwardii'. Widely grown dense globular shrub of rich green color. May attain considerable size with age, but is a small plant over a reasonably long period. If you can wait 72 years, it may be 8 ft. high by 18 ft. wide.

T. orientalis. See Platycladus

T. plicata. WESTERN RED CEDAR. Tree. Zones 1-9, 14-24. Grows from coastal northern California north to Alaska and inland to Montana. Plants from inland seed are hardy anywhere in the West; those from coastal seed less hardy to cold. Can reach over 200 ft. in the coastal belt of Washington, but usually much less in gardens. Slender, drooping branchlets set closely with dark green scalelike leaves, forming flat, graceful, lacy sprays. Cones ½ in. across, cinnamon brown.

Single trees are magnificent on large lawns, but the lower branches spread quite broadly and trees lose their characteristic beauty when these are cut off.

Here are a few of its varieties:

'Aurea'. Younger branch tips golden-green.

'Aurea Variegata'. Patches of golden twigs scattered among the green.

'Fastigiata'. HOGAN CEDAR. Very dense, narrow, erect; fine for tall screen.

'Striblingii'. Dense, thick column 10-12 ft. tall, 2-3 ft. wide. For moderate-height screen planting or can be used as an upright sentinel.

THUJOPSIS dolabrata. FALSE ARBORVITAE, DEERHORN CEDAR, HIBA CEDAR. Evergreen tree. Zones 1-7, 14-17. Pyramidal, coniferous, of very slow growth to 50 ft. high; often shrubby. Foliage resembles *Thuja*, but twigs are coarser, branching in deerhorn effect. Will grow in part shade. Plant as a single tree where its foliage details can be appreciated. Slow growth makes it a good container plant.

THUNBERGIA. Perennial vines. Noted for showy flowers. Tropical in origin, but some are hardy in milder parts of California, and others grow fast enough to bloom the first season and, hence, be treated as annuals.

T. alata. BLACK-EYED SUSAN VINE. Perennial, grown as an annual. Trailing or twining plant with trianglular, 3-in. leaves. Flowers are flaring tubes to 1 in. wide, orange, yellow, or white, all with purple-black throat. Start seed indoors, set plants out in sunny spot as soon as weather warms.

Thunbergia alata: inch-wide flowers of white, yellow, orange, purple-black throat.

Use in hanging baskets, window boxes, as ground cover in small, sunny spots. Or train on strings or low trellis.

T. gibsonii. ORANGE CLOCK VINE. Perennial; may be grown as an annual. Resembles *T. gregorii* but semi-deciduous or herbaceous. Flowers slightly smaller, not as bright an orange.

T. grandiflora. SKY FLOWER. Zones 16, 21-24. Vigorous twiner to 20 ft. or more, with lush, green, 8-in., heart-shaped leaves. Slightly drooping clusters of tubular, flaring, 2½-3-in., delicate, pure blue flowers. Blooms fall, winter, spring. Takes a year to get started, then grows rapidly. Will come back to bloom in a year if frozen back. Full sun near coast, part shade inland. Use to cover arbor, lathhouse, or fence; makes dense shade. There is a white variety.

T. gregorii. Zones 21-24; warm lathhouse or greenhouse in Zones 16, 17; or grow as an annual. Twines to 6 ft. tall, or sprawls over ground to cover 6-ft. circle. Leaves 3 in. long, toothed, evergreen. Flowers tubular, flaring, bright orange, borne singly on 4-in. stems. Blooms nearly all year in mildest areas, in summer where winters are cool. Plant 3-4 ft. apart to cover a wire fence, 6 ft. apart as ground cover. Plant above a wall, over which vine will cascade, or grow in hanging basket. Easy and showy; watch color conflicts with pink and red flowers.

THYMOPHYLLA tenuiloba. DAHLBERG DAISY, GOLDEN FLEECE. Annual; may live over as a perennial where winters are mild. Southwest native. To 1 ft. high. Divided threadlike leaves make dark green background to yellow flower heads, which look much like miniature golden marguerites. Use for massed display or pockets of color. Start in flats or plant in place, in full sun and preferably in sandy soil. Blooms early summer to fall, or to early winter in warm climates. Pull out plants that get ragged with age.

THYMUS. THYME. Ground covers, erect shrubby perennial herb. All Zones. Foliage usually heavily scented. Grow in warm, light, well drained soil that is fairly dry. Full sun. Stands neglect. Restrain plants as needed by clipping back growing tips. Propagate from cuttings taken early in summer, or seed. Plant ground cover kinds 6-12 in. apart in fall or spring.

T. herba-barona. CARAWAY-SCENTED THYME. Ground cover. Fast growing, forms a thick flat mat of dark green, ¼-in.-long leaves with a caraway fragrance. Rose pink flowers in headlike clusters. Can use leaves to flavor vegetable dishes.

T. lanuginosus. WOOLLY THYME. Ground cover. Forms flat to undulating mat 2-3 in. high. Stems densely clothed with small gray-woolly leaves. Seldom shows its pinkish flowers. Plants become slightly rangy in winter. Use in rock crevices, between stepping stones, to spill over bank or raised bed, to cover small patches of ground.

T. serpyllum. MOTHER-OF-THYME, CREEPING THYME. Ground cover. Forms flat mat, the upright branches 2-6 in. high. Roundish, ¼-in.-long, dark green, aromatic leaves. Small purplish white flowers (white in one form) in headlike clusters June-September. For small areas or filler between stepping stones where foot traffic is light. Soft and fragrant under foot. Leaves can be used in seasoning and in potpourris.

T. s. 'Argenteus'. SILVER THYME. Leaves variegated with silver.

T. s. vulgaris. LEMON THYME. Lemon-scented green foliage.

T. vulgaris. COMMON THYME. Shrubby perennial herb. To 6-12 in. high. Narrow

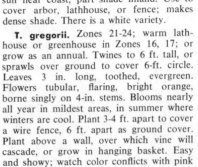

*Climate
Zone maps
pages 8-27*

to oval, ¼-in.-long, fragrant, gray-green leaves. Tiny lilac flowers in dense whorls, June and July. Low edging for flower, vegetable, or herb garden. Good container plant. Use leaves fresh or dried for seasoning vegetable juices, fish, shellfish, poultry stuffing, soups, vegetables.

TI. See Cordyline terminalis

TIBOUCHINA semidecandra (*Pleroma splendens*). PRINCESS FLOWER. Evergreen shrub or small tree. Zones 16, 17, 21-24; excellent greenhouse plant anywhere. Native to Brazil. Fast, rather open growth to 5-18 ft. Large, oval, velvety, 3-6-in.-long leaves are strongly ribbed, velvety green, often edged red. Branch tips, buds, new growth shaded with orange and bronze red velvety hairs. Older leaves add spots of red, orange, or yellow, especially in winter. Brilliant, royal purple, 3-in.-wide flowers in clusters at ends of branches appear intermittently May-January.

Best in somewhat acid, well drained soil, with roots in shade, top in sun. Protect from strong wind. Minimize legginess by light pruning after each bloom cycle, heavier pruning in early spring. Pinch tips of young plants to encourage bushiness. Feed after spring pruning and lightly after each bloom cycle. If buds fail to open, look for tobacco budworm. Hand pick and destroy worms in buds; spray plants with all-purpose insecticide.

TIDYTIPS. See Layia

TIGER FLOWER. See Tigridia

TIGRIDIA pavonia. TIGER FLOWER, MEXICAN SHELL FLOWER. Bulb. All Zones if treated like gladiolus; leave bulbs in ground only in mild-winter areas. Leaves narrow, ribbed, swordlike, 12-18 in. long; shorter leaves on 18-30-in. flower stalks. Showy bright flowers, 6 in. across, with 3 large segments forming a triangle, joined with 3 smaller segments to form a center cup. Larger segments usually vivid solid color—orange, pink, red, yellow; or white. Smaller segments usually spotted or blotched with darker colors. Immaculata strain in solid colors, unspotted. Bloom July-August; each flower lasts one day, but others follow for several weeks.

Plant after weather warms in rich, porous soil in groups of 10-12. Set bulbs 2-4 in.

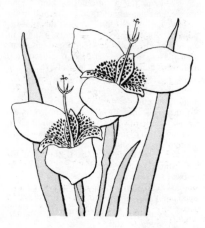

Flowers of Tigridia: outer segments show bright solid colors; inner ones blotched.

deep, 4-8 in. apart. Full sun near coast, afternoon shade in warmer areas. Or, plant 6-8 bulbs in a 9-in. pot. During active growth water regularly, and feed every 2 weeks with a mild solution of liquid fertilizer. In colder areas dig and store after foliage ripens. Do not break bulbs apart until just before planting in spring. Plants in open ground require division every 3-4 years. Easily grown from seed; may bloom first year. Control red spider mites, starting when leaves are few inches tall. Protect from gophers.

TILIA. LINDEN. Deciduous trees. Dense, compact crowns. Much used for street and park planting in Europe. All have small, quite fragrant, yellowish white flowers in drooping clusters. All respond well to deep, rich soil and plenty of water. All grow at slow to moderate rate (not fast trees). Young trees need staking and shaping. Older trees need only corrective pruning. Under certain circumstances, aphids cause a disagreeable drip of honeydew and an accompanying sooty mildew.

T. americana. AMERICAN LINDEN, BASSWOOD. Zones 1-17. To 40-60 ft. with a 20-25-ft. spread. Straight trunk; dense, compact, narrow crown. Dull, dark green leaves 4-6 in. long, 3-4 in. wide, sometimes larger, heart-shaped. Loose clusters of fragrant, yellowish white flowers in June-July. 'Fastigiata' and 'Pyramidal' are upright-branching, narrow forms.

T. cordata. LITTLE-LEAF LINDEN. Zones 1-17. To 30-50 ft. with 15-30-ft. spread. Form densely pyramidal. Leaves 1½-3 in. long, equally broad or broader, dark green above, silvery beneath. Flowers in July. Excellent medium-sized lawn or street tree. Given space to develop its symmetrical crown, it can be a fine patio shade tree (but expect bees in flowering season). It is the hardiest linden. 'Greenspire' and 'Rancho' are forms with especially upright or conical shapes.

T. euchlora. CRIMEAN LINDEN. Zones 1-17. To 25-35 ft., perhaps eventually to 50 ft., almost as wide. Branches slightly pendulous. Leaves oval or roundish, 2-4 in. long, rich glossy green above, paler beneath. Yellowish white flowers in July. Use in same way as little-leaf linden—the form is broader, the shade and foliage less dense. 'Redmond' is pyramidal in habit.

T. europea. EUROPEAN LINDEN. Zones 1-17. Symmetrical, to 40-60 ft. Dark green leaves. More inclined than other lindens to sucker, get aphids, and drop leaves early.

T. tomentosa. SILVER LINDEN. Zones 1-21. To 40-50 ft. high, 20-30 ft. wide. Light green, 3-5-in.-long leaves, silvery beneath, turn in slight breeze. Drought resistant once established.

TILLANDSIA lindeniana (*Vriesia lindenii*). Perennial. Outdoors in most frost-free locations of Zones 22-24; house plant anywhere. A bromeliad (pineapple relative) with rosettes of 1-ft., spreading leaves. Large flower spike, carried well above the leaves, has crimson bracts overlapping in a dense, flattened plume, with the small bluish purple flowers (which blossom few at a time) peeping out from between them. Good for pot culture, or can grow in its natural manner fastened to a tree branch in a pocket of sphagnum moss. There is a miniature form with leaves only 2-3 in. high.

TIPUANA tipu. TIPU TREE. Deciduous or semi-evergreen tree. Zones 14-16, 18-24. Fast to 25 ft.; can reach eventual 35-50 ft. Broad silhouette with flattened crown usually wider than high; can be pruned to umbrella shape to make a narrower, denser crown. Leaves divided into 11-21, 1½-in.-long, oblong, light green leaflets. Blooms June-July with clusters of sweet pea-shaped flowers, apricot to yellow. Blooms followed by 2½-in. pods. Hardy to 25°, well ripened wood will take 18° with minor damage. Any soil except strongly alkaline. Established trees need occasional deep soaking, young plants more frequent irrigation. Flowers best in warm-summer areas out of immediate ocean influence. Good street or lawn tree. Useful shade canopy for patio or terrace, although flower litter can be a slight problem.

TIPU TREE. See Tipuana

TITHONIA rotundifolia (*T. speciosa*). MEXICAN SUNFLOWER. Perennial grown as an annual. Husky, rather coarse and gaudy plant; rapid growth to 6 ft. tall. Spectacular flower heads 3-4 in. across with orange-scarlet rays and tufted yellow centers. Blooms July to frost. Inflated hollow stems; cut with care for bouquets so as not to bend stalks. Leaves velvety green. Sow seed in place in spring, in not-too-rich soil. Full sun. Drought resistant and heat resistant, good choice for desert gardens. Belongs in background where flowers can be seen above other plants. 'Torch', a lower growing variety to 4 ft., makes a bushy summer hedge, is a useful filler in new shrub borders.

TOADFLAX. See Linaria

TOBACCO BRUSH. See Ceanothus velutinus

TOBIRA. See Pittosporum tobira

TOLMIEA menziesii. PIGGY-BACK PLANT. Zones 5-9, 12-24; house plant everywhere. Native to the coastal ranges from northern California northward to Alaska. Chief asset is abundant production of attractive basal, 5-in.-wide leaves—shallowly lobed and toothed, rather hairy. Leaves can produce new plantlets at the junction of leaf stalk and blade. Tiny reddish brown flowers top 1-2-ft.-high stems, are rather inconspicuous. Tolerates wet soil. Good ground cover for shade.

TOMATO. The vines are easy to grow and they yield delicious fruit abundantly—that must be why tomatoes are just about the most widely grown of all garden plants, edible or otherwise. There is a sea of opinion among amateur and commercial growers about how the plants can best be grown. If you have developed your own particular scheme for growing them, continue to follow it. But, if you're a novice or dissatisfied with your previous attempts you may find useful the following spring-to-fall calendar for growing tomatoes (in the calendar, the word "vine" is used to denote the tomato plant—it's really a sprawling plant incapable of climbing, but by common usage it's a "vine"):

First, choose a variety suited to your climate, that will yield the kind of tomatoes you like that on the kind of vines that you can handle. Such varieties are described at the end of this section.

Climate
Zone maps
pages 8-27

To grow your own tomato plants from seed, sow in early March in a pot of light soil mix or in a ready-made seed starter, sold at stores. In pots, cover seed with ½ in. of fine soil. Firm soil over the seeds. Keep soil surface damp. Place seed container in coldframe or sunny window (sun and 65° to 70° temperature). Transplant seedlings when 2 in. high into 3 or 4-in. pots. Keep these pots in a sunny area, and grow them to transplant size.

The time to plant tomato seedlings— ones that you grew from seed (above) or ones that you buy from a nursery or garden store—depends on where you live: February or early March in Zones 12, 13; April, May, or early June in Zones 7-9, 14-24; May or early June in Zones 1-6, 10, 11. Typically, 6 plants can supply a family.

Plant in a sunny position in well drained soil. Space plants 18 in. to 3 ft. apart (staked or trained) to 3-4 ft. apart (untrained). Make planting hole extra deep. Set seedlings in the hole so first leaves are just above soil level. Additional roots will form on buried stem and provide a stronger root system.

Tomato management and harvest will be most satisfying if you train the vines to keep them mostly off the ground (left alone, they will sprawl across many square feet and some fruits will lie on the soil, often causing rot, pest damage, and discoloration). The commonest training method is to drive a 6-ft.-long stake (at least 1-by-1-in. size) into the ground a foot from each seedling. Tie plants to this stake as they grow.

Slightly easier in the long run, but more work at planting time, is to grow each plant in a wire cylinder made of concrete reinforcing screen (6-in. mesh). Form the cylinder with a 1½-ft. diameter. The screen is manufactured 84 in. wide, which is just

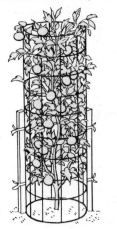

Wire cylinder supports tomato vine, eliminates tying up, keeps fruit clean.

right for the cylinder height. Most vines can grow to the top of such a cylinder. Put stakes at opposite sides of the cylinder and tie it firmly to them. As the vine grows, poke protruding branches back inside the cylinder every week or so. Reach through the screen to pick the fruit.

Or for a novelty, plant in a large suspended container and let the vine cascade down (quite useful and practical with small-fruited tomatoes).

Irrigate tomato plants frequently during the early part of the season, less frequently

after fruit begins to ripen. The tomato plant sends its roots deep, so water heavily when you do water.

If soil is fairly rich, you won't need to fertilize at all. But, in ordinary soils, give a light application of fertilizer every 2 weeks or at every alternate watering from the time the first blossoms set until the end of harvest.

If diseases or insects trouble or threaten plants, protect them with an all-purpose vegetable dust or spray—a mixture that contains both an insecticide and fungicide.

If your plants grow, set fruit, and then shrivel, wilt, and die, they probably are suffering from verticillium or fusarium wilt or both. Pull and dispose of such plants. The diseases live over in soil so the next year plant in a different location and try one of the wilt-resistant varieties suited to your climate.

If you have done everything right and your tomatoes have failed to set fruit in the spring, use a hormone to spray on the blossoms. Tomatoes often fail to set fruit when night temperatures drop below 55°. The fruit-setting hormone often speeds up bearing, in the earlier part of the season. Tomatoes can also fail to set fruit when temperatures rise above 100°, but hormones are not effective under those conditions.

Harvest fruits when they have turned full-red and juicy; keep ripe fruits picked to extend the season. When frost is predicted, harvest all fruit, green and partly ripe. Store these at 58° and bring into 70° to ripen as needed.

TOMATO VARIETIES

Following are the kinds of tomatoes you can buy as seeds or started plants—the listings are arranged according to fruit and vine types.

Large-fruited tomatoes. These are home gardener's specials. They are poor shippers. Unless they are grown locally, you won't find them at your produce market. Among the best are 'Ponderosa', 'Beefsteak' ('Crimson Cushion'), and 'Golden Yellow Ponderosa'. Fruits are very large, broad, rather shallow, very meaty, and mild in flavor. All varieties need moderate heat and are not recommended where nights are cool or in coastal areas. Vines are large.

Small-fruited tomatoes. Ripe fruits are the size of large marbles or small plums, but there's nothing small about the vines of the small-fruited tomatoes. Trained against a wall they will reach 8 ft. and spread almost as wide. These varieties set fruit well under greater climate extremes than do the larger-fruited varieties. Many shapes and colors are available as indicated by their names: 'Red Cherry', 'Red Plum', 'Red Pear', 'Yellow Cherry', 'Yellow Pear', 'Yellow Peach'. Two dwarf varieties that will grow in small pots or containers are 'Tiny Tim' and 'Atom'.

Early tomatoes. "Early" means more than early harvest. Early varieties set fruit at lower night temperatures than midseason or late varieties; most will ripen fruit in cool summer climates. The name 'Earliana' covers several varieties such as 'Early Market', 'First Early', 'Morse's 498', and 'Pennheart'. Early types grown in Oregon and Washington include 'Bonny Best', 'John Baer', 'Moreton Hybrid', and 'Valiant', all large-vine types; and 'Early Chatham', 'Willamette', and 'Medford', small-vine types.

Yellow-orange tomatoes. 'Jubilee' and 'Sunray' are strikingly handsome golden orange tomatoes. They taste just like good red tomatoes and look good too, especially sliced and mixed with sliced red tomatoes. There are even white tomatoes: 'New Snowball' and 'White Beauty' are interesting novelties with very low acid content.

Hybrid tomatoes. Hybrid vigor makes these tomatoes grow more vigorously, produce larger and more uniform fruit than other varieties. And they produce fruit in climate extremes. Of many hybrids 'Burpee Hybrid', a medium to large main crop variety; and 'Big Boy', a very large, deep, round red tomato, are best known.

Main crop of standard tomatoes. 'Ace' is a large tomato of very fine flavor that bears well in California's interior and inner coastal valleys. 'Pearson' will set fruit under a wide range of temperatures and produces well in California's coastal and interior valleys. 'Stone' is a late-maturing variety with scarlet red, globular fruit on large vines; it is a southern California favorite. 'Manalucie' and 'Homestead Elite' are other good main crop varieties for warm areas. 'Pritchard' produces a fairly early main crop and is useful in Northwestern gardens.

Cool-summer tomatoes. Where summers are unusually cool, nurseries offer locally adapted varieties: in Seattle you'll find 'Seattle Best of All'; in San Francisco look for 'Frisco Fogger'.

Wilt-resistant tomatoes. Several varieties are valued especially for their resistance to verticillium or fusarium wilt. They include: 'Pritchard', 'Manalucie', 'Homestead Elite', and 'Summerdawn'.

TOMATO, STRAWBERRY. See Physalis pruinosa

TOMATO, TREE. See Cyphomandra

TORCH-LILY. See Kniphofia

TORENIA fournieri. WISHBONE FLOWER. Annual. Compact, bushy, to 1 ft. high. Flowers look like miniature gloxinias, light blue marked deeper blue, bright yellow throat; white also available. Blooms summer and fall. Stamens arranged in shape of a wishbone. Full sun where summers are

Torenia: 1-in.-wide flowers show strong markings in light and deep blue, yellow.

cool and short, part shade elsewhere. Sow seed in flats, transplant to garden when frosts are over. Good for borders, pots, window boxes.

TORREYA californica. CALIFORNIA NUTMEG. Evergreen tree. Zones 7-9, 14-24.

T

Climate
Zone maps
pages 8-27

Conifer native to cool shaded canyons in scattered California mountain regions below 4,500 ft. elevation. Wide, open pyramidal crown, becoming domelike with age; slow growing to 15-50 ft. high with a trunk 1-3 ft. in diameter. Branches horizontal, slender, somewhat drooping at tips. Leaves dark green with two whitish bands underneath, flat, rigid, sharp-pointed, 1¼-2½ in. long, ⅛ in. wide, in flat sprays. Fruit plumlike, pale green with purplish markings. Easy to grow; needs occasional watering in summer months.

TOTARA. See Podocarpus totara

TOUCH-ME-NOT. See Impatiens

TOWER OF JEWELS. See Echium wildpretii

TOYON. See Heteromeles arbutifolia

TRACHELIUM caeruleum. COMMON THROATWORT. Perennial. Zones 8, 9, 12-24. A profusion of deep lavender-blue flowers in 3-5-in.-wide clusters cover plant in summer and fall. Plant grows 3-4 ft. high with many branches. Oval leaves 3 in. long, with toothed edges. Easy to grow from seed, persists with little care. Hardy to about 20°. Sun or part shade. Flower clusters good for cutting.

TRACHELOSPERMUM (*Rhynchospermum*). STAR JASMINE. Evergreen vines or sprawling shrubs. Used as ground covers, spillers, or climbers.

T. asiaticum. Zones 6-24. Twines to 15 ft. or sprawls on the ground with branchlets rising erect. Leaves smaller, darker, duller green than *T. jasminoides*. Flowers smaller, creamy yellow or yellowish white, fragrant, blooming April-June.

T. jasminoides. STAR JASMINE. Zones 8-24. One of the most widely used plants in California and Arizona. Given support, a twining vine to 20 ft., slow to start but eventually moderately fast growing. Without support and with some tip-pinching, a spreading shrub or ground cover 1½-2 ft. tall, 4-5 ft. wide. New foliage glossy light green; mature leaves lustrous dark green, to 3 in. long. Flowers white, to 1 in. across, profuse in small clusters on short side branches, sweetly fragrant. Blooms June-July.

To grow as a vine, start with a plant that has been staked, or that at least has not been tip-pinched to make it shrubby. Provide support immediately. Use heavy cord to lead vine in the direction you wish to take. Train on posts, baffles, walls, fences, trellises wherever its fragrance can be enjoyed, or where night lighting can pick out the white blossoms. Give some shade in hottest areas. Cut back older plants about ⅓ each year to prevent inner growth becoming too woody and bare.

To grow as a ground cover, set plants 1½-3 ft. apart (depending on how fast you want cover). Cut back upright shoots. Feed in spring, late summer. Spray for scale, mealybug, red spider mites. Keep well watered and weeded. In 3-4 years growth should be thick enough to discourage weeds.

Use in raised beds, entry gardens, for edging along walks or drives, to extend a lawn, or to cover ground under trees and shrubs that need summer water.

TRACHYCARPUS. Palms. Fan-leafed. Plants of moderate size and great hardiness. Characteristic blackish fiber grows at least at the tops of all but the oldest trunks.

T. fortunei. (Sometimes sold as *Chamaerops excelsa*.) WINDMILL PALM. Indoor potted palm anywhere; outdoors Zones 4-24. Native to China. Fast growing to 30 ft. in warm-winter areas. Trunk is dark, usually thicker at the top than at the bottom, covered with dense, hairy-looking fiber. Leaves 3 ft. across on 1½-ft. toothed stalks. Responds to water and feeding, but isn't demanding. Sometimes becomes untidy and ruffled in high winds. Very hardy—to 10° or lower.

T. martianus. Zones 15-17, 19-24. Native to Himalayas. Slower, taller, more slender than *T. fortunei*. Trunk without fiber except at the top, ringed with leaf scars. Hardy to 22°.

Windmill palm has dark trunk covered with coarse, dense, hairy-looking fiber.

T. takil. Zones 15-17, 19-24. Native to western Himalayas. Very slow grower with heavy, inclined trunk. Can reach 20 ft., but a dwarf for many years.

TRACHYMENE caerulea (*Didiscus caeruleus*). BLUE LACE FLOWER. Annual. To 2 ft. tall. Flowers small, lavender-blue, numerous, in flat-topped clusters 2-3 in. across and quite lacy in appearance, as are the divided leaves. Sow seeds in place in spring for summer bloom. Needs sunny location, but won't take too much heat.

TRADESCANTIA. Perennials. Flowers last only a day but they come along in rapid succession. Can be invasive.

T. fluminensis. WANDERING JEW. Zones 12-24; house plant everywhere. Prostrate or trailing habit. Fast growing. Succulent stems with swollen joints where 2½-in.-long, dark green, oval or oblong leaves are attached ('Variegata' has leaves striped yellow or white). Tiny white flowers, not showy. Very easy to grow. In warmer areas can be grown in shade as a ground cover. Excellent for window boxes and dish gardens, or for under a greenhouse bench. A few stems placed in a glass of water will live a long time, and will even make some growth.

T. virginiana. COMMON SPIDERWORT. All Zones. To 1½-3 ft. tall. Dense clusters of violet-blue flowers carried on stem above upright or arching, grasslike foliage. Only one flower in a cluster opens at a time, and it lasts only a day, but plants are seldom

out of bloom during summer. Named garden varieties come in shades of blue, white, pink, and rose-red. Propagate by divisions. Any soil. Sun or shade. Needs plenty of water. Best in informal borders.

TREE ALFALFA. See Medicago arborea

TREEBINE, KANGAROO. See Cissus antarctica

TREE-OF-HEAVEN. See Ailanthus

TREVESIA. SNOWFLAKE TREE. Evergreen shrubs or small trees. Zones 21-24; house plant everywhere. Resemble *Fatsia japonica* in growth habit, but taller (10-20 ft.), more treelike. Leaves on long stalks, 1-2 ft. across, deeply lobed like fatsia, but each lobe is deeply cut. Leaves have lacy look, like a caterpillar-chewed fatsia. Three species have been sold, all pretty much alike: *T. micholitzii, T. palmata,* and *T. sanderi.*

Filtered sun or afternoon shade; loose, leafy, fast-draining soil with liberal water and feeding. Watch for mealybug, spider

Deeply cut and lobed leaf of Trevesia shows outline of an enormous snowflake.

mites. Indoors, give good light but not hot sun from a west or south window. Young plants are good tub subjects, indoors or outdoors.

TRICHOSPORUM. See Aeschynanthus

TRICHOSTEMA lanatum. WOOLLY BLUE CURLS. Evergreen shrub. Zones 14-24. Native to dry slopes of Coast Ranges, California. Much branched, neat plant, 3-5 ft. high. Leaves pungently aromatic when bruised, narrow, 1¼-2 in. long, upper surface shining dark green, under surface white woolly; leaf edges rolled under. Flowers in separated clusters along the long stalk, blue with conspicuous arching stamens. Stalks and parts of flowers covered with blue, pink, or whitish wool. Blooms April and May. Do not water in summer. A good choice for hillsides.

TRICUSPIDARIA dependens. See Crinodendron

TRILLIUM. WAKE ROBIN. Perennials. Early spring blooming plants of the lily family. A whorl of three leaves tops each stem, and from the center of these springs a single flower with three maroon or white petals. Plant the thick, deep-growing, fleshy rhizomes in a shady, woodsy location. Let them alone; they will gradually increase.

T. chloropetalum. Zones 4-9, 14-17. Western native. To 1-1½ ft. high. Flower, with greenish white to yellowish petals about 2½ in. long, sits without a stalk on the three large (6-in.-long) mottled leaves. *T. c. giganteum* has deep maroon petals.

T. grandiflorum. Zones 1-6. Stout stems 8-18 in. Leaves 2½-6 in. long. Flower stalked, nodding, white aging to rose.

T. ovatum. Zones 1-6, 14-17. Western native similar to *T. grandiflorum* but with narrower petals and the flowers are usually

Western trillium (Trillium ovatum). White flowers (2 in. wide) fading to rose.

upright on their stalks. Very effective in a shady part of a wildflower garden or among ferns, azaleas, or Polyanthus primroses.

TRISTANIA. Evergreen trees. Zones 19-24; also grown in Zones 15-18, but hardiness is questionable where temperatures drop below 26°. Related to eucalyptus. The two species grown in California are of manageable size, and both have brightly colored shedding bark in addition to handsome evergreen foliage.

T. conferta. BRISBANE BOX. Moderate to fast growth rate to 30-60 ft. Trunk and limbs resemble those of madrone, reddish brown bark peeling away to show smooth, light-colored new bark underneath. Growth habit rather upright, crown eventually broad and rounded. Leaves 4-6 in. long, oval, leathery, bright green; they tend to cluster toward tips of branchlets. Flowers in clusters of 3-7 in summer, ¾ in. across, white to creamy. Fruit is a woody capsule something like that of eucalyptus.

Takes almost any soil, but young plants get a better start with good soil and liberal watering; established plants are quite drought resistant. Pinch and prune to get more twiggy growth. Not bothered by insects or diseases, but chlorosis sometimes a problem in Los Angeles area. A good street or lawn tree.

T. laurina. Small, slow-growing, rather formal-looking small tree or shrub. Trees 8 years old are 10 ft. tall and 5 ft. across, with a remarkably dense and rounded crown. Trunk covered with mahogany colored bark which peels to show satiny white new bark. Leaves to 4 in. long, usually narrow, but varying to somewhat broader,

heavy-textured, glossy medium green. Flowers small, yellow, clustered, borne with sufficient profusion to put on a good show in late spring or early summer. Young plants densely shrubby, and can be kept that way with a little pinching. To make a tree, stake the plant and shorten side branches. Remove shortened side branches when treelike growth pattern is established; then only light shaping will be necessary. Good tub subject.

TRITELEIA. See Ipheion

TRITHRINAX acanthocoma. Palm. Zones 15-17, 19-24. From Brazil. Slender, hairy, spiny trunk grows to 12-18 ft. Glossy, dark green fan-shaped leaves resemble those of *Trachycarpus.* Hardy to 22°.

TRITOMA. See Kniphofia

TRITONIA (*Montbretia*). Corm. Zones 9, 13-24. Native of South Africa. Related to freesia, ixia, and sparaxis. Leaves narrow, sword-shaped. Branched flower stems carry short, spikelike clusters of brilliant flowers. Rock gardens, borders, pots. Long lasting cut flowers.

T. crocata. Often called flame freesia. Flower stems to 12-18 in. Flowers orange-red, funnel-shaped, 2 in. long. Variety 'Miniata' has bright red blooms. 'Princess Beatrix' has deep orange flowers. Others in white and shades of pink, salmon, yellow, and apricot.

T. hyalina. Flowers bright orange; narrower segments than *T. crocata,* with transparent area near the base. Dwarfer than *T. crocata.*

TROCHODENDRON aralioides. Evergreen shrub or small tree. Zones 4-7, 14-17. Good looking foliage plant that takes on bronzy tones in winter when grown in sun. Slow growth to 15-20 ft. usually with multiple stems. Leaves long-stalked, lance-shaped or blunt-ended oval, 6 in. long, bright green, glossy, leathery. Flowers (in May) bright green, ½ in. wide, in clusters 4-6 in. tall. Will take shade but leaves remain green there. Needs good, rich soil, ample water.

TROLLIUS. GLOBEFLOWER. Perennials. All Zones. Shiny, finely cut, dark green leaves. Yellow to orange flowers resemble those of ranunculus. Bloom season late spring to late summer. Need shade or part shade, rich soil,

Finely cut foliage of Trollius ledebouri a good contrast for big orange flowers.

plenty of moisture. Subject to aphids. Valuable for bringing bright color to a shady area; particularly happy choice near a pool. Excellent cut flowers.

T. europaeus. To 1-2 ft. tall. Flowers yellow, 1½ in. across. Some varieties have orange flowers.

T. ledebouri. To 2 ft. tall. Flowers gold-orange, 2 in. across. The variety 'Golden Queen' reaches 4 ft., has 4-in.-wide flowers.

TROPAEOLUM. NASTURTIUM. Perennial, generally grown as annual. Distinctive appearance, rapid growth, and easy culture are three of nasturtiums' many strong points. Less conspicuous, but odd and pretty, is the closely related canary bird flower.

T. majus. GARDEN NASTURTIUM. Two main kinds: climbing ones trail over the ground or climb to 6 ft. by coiling leaf stalks; dwarf kinds are compact, up to 15 in. tall. Both have round, shield-shaped bright green leaves on long stalks. Flower colors range through maroon, red-brown, orange, yellow, and red to creamy white. Flowers are broad and have a long spur, refreshing fragrance. Young leaves, flowers, and unripe seedpods have a peppery flavor like watercress, may be used in salads.

Easy in most well drained soils in sun; best in sandy soil. Sow early spring. Grows and blooms quickly, often reseeds itself. Has become naturalized in some California beach areas. Needs no feeding in average soils.

Climbing or trailing kinds will cover fences, banks, stumps, rocks. Use dwarf kinds for bedding, to cover fading bulb foliage, quick flower color in ground or in pots. Good cut flowers.

In the dwarf forms (most sold) you can get seeds of mixed colors in several strains, or a few separate colors including cherry rose, mahogany, gold. There are also both single and double flowered forms.

T. peregrinum. CANARY BIRD FLOWER. Climbs to 10-15 ft. Leaves deeply 5-lobed. Flowers ¾-1 in. across, canary yellow, frilled and fringed, with green curved spur. Best in light shade, moist soil.

TRUMPET CREEPER. See Campsis

TRUMPET FLOWER, YELLOW. See Steno-lobium

TRUMPET TREE, GOLDEN. See Tabebuia chrysotricha

TRUMPET VINE. See Campsis

TRUMPET VINE, BLOOD-RED. See Phae-dranthus

TRUMPET VINE, VIOLET. See Clytostoma

TRUMPET VINE, YELLOW. See Anemopaegma, Doxantha

TSUGA. HEMLOCK. Coniferous evergreen trees and shrubs. Zones 1-7, 14-17. These are mostly gigantic trees with unusually graceful foliage. Branches horizontal to drooping; needlelike leaves flattened and narrowed at the base to form distinct, short stalks. Small, medium brown cones hang down from branches. Best in acid soil, with ample moisture, high summer humidity, protection from hot sun and wind.

T. canadensis. CANADA HEMLOCK. Dense, pyramidal tree to 90 ft. tall in its native

T

Climate Zone maps pages 8-27

Climate Zone maps pages 8-27

eastern states, much smaller here. Has a tendency to grow 2 or more trunks. Outer branchlets droop gracefully. Dark green needles, white-banded beneath, about ½ in. long, mostly arranged in opposite rows on branchlets. Oval cones about ¾ in. long, on short stalks. A fine lawn tree or background planting. Can be clipped into an outstandingly beautiful hedge. One variety, 'Pendula', SARGENT WEEPING HEMLOCK, is a low, broad plant 2-3 ft. high and twice as wide, with pendulous branches; it is a good plant for large rock gardens.

T. heterophylla. WESTERN HEMLOCK. Native along coast from Alaska to northern California, inland to northern Idaho and Montana. Handsome tree with a narrow, pyramidal crown. Grows fairly fast to 125-200 ft. high. Somewhat drooping branchlets and fine-textured, dark green to yellowish green foliage give a fernlike quality. Short needles ¼-¾ in. long, in two rows; whitish bands beneath. A profusion of small 1-in. cones droop gracefully from branch tips. Needs water in dry seasons. A picturesque large conifer for background use, hedges, or screens.

T. mertensiana. MOUNTAIN HEMLOCK. Native to high mountains from Alaska south through the higher Sierra Nevada in California and to northern Idaho and Montana. Grows to 50-90 ft. high in the wild, but much less and more slowly in home gardens. Foliage blue-green with a silvery cast, with ½-1-in.-long needles growing all around stems to give branchlets a plump, tufty appearance. Cones 1½-3 in. long. Trees at timberline frequently grow in horizontal or twisted fashion. Slow-growing under lowland conditions. Thrives on a cool slope with plenty of organic matter in soil. A decorative tree for the large rock garden. Good for containers, bonsai.

TUBEROSE. See Polianthes

TUCKEROO. See Cupaniopsis

TULBAGHIA. Perennials. Zones 14-24. Many narrow leaves grow from central point to make broad clumps. Clusters of star-shaped flowers rise above clumps on long stems. Evergreen in mild climates. Frost damage at 25°, with quick recovery.

T. fragrans. Leaves to 12-14 in. long or more, an inch wide, gray-green. Flowers fragrant, lavender-pink, 20-30 on a 1½-2-ft. stalk. Blooms in winter. Good cut flower.

T. violacea. SOCIETY GARLIC. Leaves bluish green, narrow, to 12 in. long. Flowers rosy lavender, 8-20 in a cluster on 1-2-ft. stems. Some bloom most of year, with peak in spring and summer. Leaves, flower stems have onion or garlic odor if cut or crushed. Unsatisfactory cut flower for this reason (but can be used as seasoning). One form has a creamy stripe down the center of each leaf. Variety 'Silver Lace' has white-margined leaves.

TULIP. See Tulipa

TULIP, GLOBE. See Calochortus

TULIP POPPY, MEXICAN. See Hunnemannia

TULIP, STAR. See Calochortus uniflorus

TULIP TREE. See Liriodendron

TULIPA. TULIP. Bulb. All Zones. Best adapted to cold-winter climates. Tulips vary considerably in color, form, height, and general character. Some look stately and formal; others dainty and whimsical; a few are bizarre. Together, the species (the same as those growing in the wild) and hybrids provide color March-May, and plants for many different uses—in garden, in containers, and for cutting.

Use larger tulips in colonies or masses with low, spring-blooming perennials such as alyssum, arabis, aubrieta, iberis, *Phlox divaricata*; or annuals such as forget-me-not, sweet alyssum, pansies, or violas. Plant the smaller, lower-growing species in rock gardens, near paths, in raised beds, or in patio or terrace insets for close-up viewing. Tulips are superb container plants. More unusual kinds, such as Double Early, Rembrandt, and Parrot strains seem more appropriate in containers than in the garden.

Plant bulbs in October except where weather is still warm. Need sun most of the day; light shade helps prolong bloom of late-blooming kinds. Rich sandy soil is ideal, although tulips will grow in any good soil with fast drainage. Plant bulbs 2½ times as deep as they are wide, and 4-8 in. apart depending on ultimate size of plant. In the Southwest store tulip bulbs at 40°-45° for 6-8 weeks before planting in November or December (or even as late as January). Plant bulbs at least 6-8 in. deep in warmer areas to provide necessary cool root run.

Gophers, field mice, and aphids consider tulips a great delicacy. To protect from the rodents, plant bulbs in baskets of ¼-in. wire mesh. To control the aphids spray twice a month in growing season.

Tulips have been classified into many divisions. Following are the most important of these divisions, listed in approximate order of bloom:

Single Early tulips. Large single flowers of red, yellow, or white on 10-16-in. stems. Much used for growing or forcing indoors in pots. Also grown outdoors, blooming in March to mid-April. Not adapted for outdoor culture in warm winter climates. Variety 'Keizerskroon', scarlet banded yellow, a favorite since 1750.

Double Early tulips. Double peonylike flowers to 4 in. across on 6-12-in. stems. Same colors, same bloom season as Single Early tulips. In rainy areas mulch around plants or surround with ground cover to keep mud from splashing short-stemmed flowers. In colder climates effective massed in borders for early bloom. Variety 'Oranje Nassau' has orange-red flowers.

Mendel tulips. Single flowers on stems to 20 in. tall. Bloom after single and double early kinds, before Darwin tulips. Shades of white, rose, red, orange, yellow. Variety 'Krelage's Triumph', crimson red.

Triumph tulips. Single flowers on medium-height (20-in.), very sturdy stems. Bloom earlier than Darwin tulips and (like Mendel tulips) valuable in providing continuity of bloom. Variety 'Makassar', deep canary yellow.

Darwin tulips. Most popular of the late April-May-flowering tulips. Graceful, stately plants with large oval or egg-shaped flowers, square at the base, usually with stems to 30 in. tall. Clear, beautiful colors of white, cream, yellow, pink, red, mauve, lilac, purple, maroon, and near black.

The following are some of the best varieties: 'Zwanenburg', pure white; 'Golden Age', golden yellow; 'Clara Butt', salmon pink; 'Farneombe Sanders', red; 'Bleu Aimable', bluish heliotrope; 'Insurpassable', lilac; 'Queen of the Night', velvet maroon, almost black.

Darwin Hybrids. Spectacular group bred from Darwin tulips and the huge, brilliant species *T. fosteriana*. Bloom before Darwins; have enormous, brightly colored flowers on 24-28-in. stems. Most are in the scarlet-orange-red range; some have contrasting eyes or penciling; some measure 7 in. across. Variety 'Holland's Glory', orange-scarlet with black base.

Breeder tulips. Large oval to globular flowers on stems to 35 in. tall. May-blooming. Unusual colors include orange, bronze, purplish, mahogany—often overlaid with flush of contrasting shade. Called Breeders because Dutch growers once grew them primarily to breed the much admired "broken" (variegated) tulips. Variety 'Bacchus', bright purple.

Lily-flowered tulips. Once included in Cottage division; now separate group. Flowers long and narrow, with long, pointed segments. Graceful, slender-stemmed, fine in the garden (where they blend well with other flowers) or for cutting. Stems 20-26 in. tall. May-blooming. Full range of tulip colors. Variety 'Mariette', rose-pink.

Cottage tulips. (Often called May-flowering tulips.) About the same size and height as Darwins. Flower form variable, long oval to egg-shaped to vase-shaped, often with pointed segments. May-blooming. Variety 'Dido', orange-red, edged bright orange.

Rembrandt tulips. "Broken" (variegated) Darwin tulips. Scarlet striped white, white flamed lilac purple, white edged red are characteristic patterns. Variety 'American Flag', scarlet, with white stripes.

Bizarre tulips. "Broken" Breeder or Cottage tulips. Flowers have a yellow background marked bronze, brown, maroon, or purple.

Bybloems (Bijbloemens). "Broken" Breeder or Cottage tulips with white background marked rose, lilac, or purple.

Parrot tulips. May-flowering tulips with large, long, deeply fringed and ruffled blooms striped and feathered in various colors. Many have descriptive names like 'Blue Parrot', 'Red Parrot'. Good in containers, unusual cut flowers.

Double Late tulips. (Often called peony-flowered.) Large, heavy blooms like peonies. They range from 18-22 in. tall; flowers may be damaged by rain or wind in exposed locations. Variety 'Mt. Tacoma', pure white.

Seven divisions include varieties and hybrids of *T. batalinii*, *T. eichleri*, *T. fosteriana*, *T. greigii*, *T. kaufmanniana*, and *T. marjolettii*, and another division that includes all other species. Most important:

Hybrids and varieties of *T. fosteriana*, including the huge, fiery red variety 'Red Emperor' ('Mme. Lefeber'), 16 in. tall.

Varieties of *T. greigii* and its hybrids with *T. kaufmanniana*, 7-14 in. tall, with big flowers usually red-orange; leaves usually strongly marked with brown or purplish.

Varieties and hybrids of *T. kaufmanniana*, 5-10 in. tall, very early blooming, in white, pink, orange, and red, often with markings, some with leaves patterned brown.

Three fairly new novelty groups include: Fringed tulips, variations from Single Early, Double Early, and Darwin tulips, finely fringed on edges of segments; Viridiflora tulips, 10-20 in. tall, flowers edged or blended green with other colors—white, yellow, rose, red, or buff; and Multiflowered, 3-6 flowers on each 20-27-in. stem, flowers white, yellow, pink and red, May blooming.

Most species tulips—wild tulips—are low growing and early blooming, but there are exceptions. Generally best in rock gardens or wild gardens where plantings can remain undisturbed for many years.

Following are outstanding species:

T. acuminata. Flowers have long, twisted, spidery segments of red and yellow on 18-in. stems. May.

T. batalinii. Single, soft yellow flowers on 6-10-in. stems. Very narrow leaves. April.

T. biflora. Small flowers, off-white inside, greenish gray-purple outside, yellow at base; several blooms on each 8-in. stem. March.

T. clusiana. LADY or CANDY TULIP. Slender, medium-size flowers on 9-in. stems. Rosy red on outside, white inside. Grows well in mild-winter areas. Give sheltered position in colder areas. April-May.

T. eichleri. Big scarlet flowers with black bases margined buff on 12-in. stems. Blooms late March.

T. greigii. Scarlet flowers 6 in. across, on 10-in. stems. Foliage mottled with brown. Early-flowering.

T. kaufmanniana. WATERLILY TULIP. Medium-large creamy yellow flowers marked red on the outside and yellow at the center. Stems 6 in. tall. Very early bloom. Permanent in gardens. Many choice named varieties.

T. linifolia. Scarlet, black-based, yellow-centered flowers on 6-in. stems in late April. Handsome with *T. batalinii.*

T. praestans. Cup-shaped, orange-scarlet flowers 2-4 to a 10-12-in. stem, in early April. Variety 'Fusilier' is somewhat shorter, and has 4-6 flowers to a stem.

T. stellata chrysantha (*T. chrysantha*). Star-shaped flowers; outside segments rose

carmine shading buff at the base; inner segments pure yellow. Stems 6 in. tall. April bloom.

T. tarda (*T. dasystemon*). Each 3-in. stem has 3-6 upward facing, star-shaped flowers with golden yellow centers, white-tipped segments.

T. turkestanica. Vigorous tulip with up to 8 flowers on each slender 1-ft. stem. Flowers slender in bud, star-shaped when open, gray-green on the outside, off-white with yellow base inside. Early March bloom.

TUPELO. See Nyssa

TUPIDANTHUS calyptratus. Evergreen shrub or small tree. Zones 19-24. Grows to 20 ft. Single or multiple trunk. Leaves to 20 in. wide, divided fanwise into 7-9 leathery, glossy, bright green, stalked leaflets about 7 in. long by 2½ in. wide. Resembles the better known brassaia (schefflera), but branches from base and makes broader, denser shrub.

Needs rich, well drained soil, plenty of food and water, and a sheltered location. Best in partial shade but will take full sun in cooler coastal gardens. Can be pruned into almost any form. This is a good small tree for sheltered lanai, entryway, or patio. Splendid plant for large tubs and containers. Effective when grown against fence or wall as a triple trunked small tree.

TURNIP AND RUTABAGA. Even if you don't like turnips to eat, they are pretty to look at after you dig them and wash the soil off. Different varieties give a nice choice of colors and shapes. Colors: white, white topped with purple, creamy yellow. Shapes: globe, flattened globe. Rutabaga is a tasty kind of turnip with large, yellowish roots. It's a late-maturing crop that stores well in the ground; turnips are quick-growing and should be harvested and used as soon as they are big enough.

In cold-winter areas, plant turnips or rutabagas in April for early summer harvest, or in July or August for fall harvest. In mild-winter areas, grow as a winter crop by planting September through March.

TURRAEA obtusifolia. STAR BUSH. Evergreen shrub. Outdoors in Zones 22-24; protect from frosts in Zones 15, 16, 19-21.

Native to South Africa. Slow growth to 4-5 ft. tall, 4 ft. wide, with many drooping branchlets, some lower branches nearly prostrate. Leaves 2 in. long, dark green, glossy, polished. Many pure white flowers in loose clusters, star-shaped, with narrow petals, 1½ in. across. Long bloom season reaches peak in September, October. Temperamental: needs good drainage and either the light shade of high-branched trees or an eastern exposure without strong reflected heat. Hardy to 26°.

TWINBERRY. See Lonicera involucrata

TWINFLOWER. See Linnaea

TWINSPUR. See Diascia

UGNI molinae (*Myrtus ugni*). CHILEAN GUAVA. Evergreen shrub. Zones 14-24. Slow to moderate growth to 3-6 ft. tall. Scraggly and open in youth, it matures into a compact, rounded plant. Foliage dark green with bronze tints; leaves oval, leathery, ½ in. long, whitish beneath, with edges slightly rolled under. White, rose-tinted flowers in late spring, early summer; they are principally little brushes of stamens. Purplish or reddish ½-in. fruits follow. These have the fragrance of baking apples, and a pleasant flavor. Can be used fresh or in jams and jellies.

Sun near coast, part shade in hot areas. Neutral to acid soil. Ample water. A tidy, restrained plant for patios, terraces, near walks and paths where passers-by can pick and sample fruit, enjoy its fragrance.

ULMUS. ELM. Deciduous or partially evergreen trees. Easy to grow in any fairly good soil; will survive in most poor ones. Root systems are aggressive, and you'll have trouble growing other plants under them. Many of the larger ones are tasty to leaf beetles, bark beetles, leafhoppers, aphids, and scale, making them either time-consuming or messy or both.

U. americana. AMERICAN ELM. Zones 1-11, 14-21. Fast-growing tree which can reach 100 ft. or more with nearly equal —sometimes even greater—spread. Form stately, with stout trunk dividing into many upright main branches at some height; the outer branches are pendulous, the silhouette

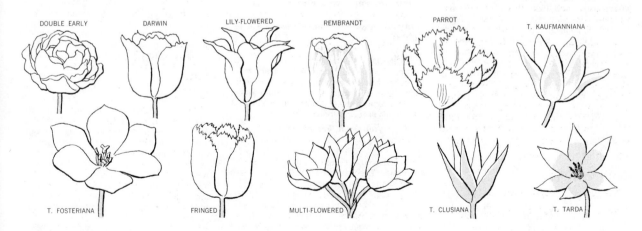

DOUBLE EARLY   DARWIN   LILY-FLOWERED   REMBRANDT   PARROT   T. KAUFMANNIANA

T. FOSTERIANA   FRINGED   MULTI-FLOWERED   T. CLUSIANA   T. TARDA

Double Early, Darwin, Lily, Rembrandt, Parrot tulips are old, familiar kinds; Fringed and Multi-flowered kinds comparative newcomers among garden divisions. Others are species (wild tulips), especially useful for naturalizing in wild garden or rock garden.

*Climate
Zone maps
pages 8-27*

vase-shaped. Rough-surfaced, toothed leaves 3-6 in. long. Leafs out very late where winters are mild. Fall color yellow. Pale green papery seeds in spring blow about, are messy.

Best in deep soil, with 70-75-ft. circle to spread in. Roots send up suckers, can make thickets; will lift pavement if crowded. Leaf and bark beetles weaken and disfigure trees; scale causes drip and sooty mildew. The only really recommendable use for such a tree is in very large gardens, out-of-the-way places, on broad boulevards unencumbered by utility lines, or in parks.

U. carpinifolia. SMOOTH-LEAFED ELM. Zones 1-11, 14-21. To 100 ft. Wide-spreading branches, weeping branchlets. Leaves 2-3½ in. long, shiny deep green above. Culture, uses, precautions same as for American elm.

U. glabra. SCOTCH ELM. Zones 1-11, 14-21. To 120 ft. tall. Non-suckering. Leaves 3-6 in. long, oval, sharply toothed, rough-surfaced, on very short stalks. Old trees sometimes seen, but scarcely grown nowadays. The variety 'Camperdownii', CAMPERDOWN ELM, has weeping branches that reach to the ground, making a tent of shade. Generally 10-20 ft. tall.

U. hollandica. DUTCH ELM. Zones 1-11, 14-21. To 100 ft. or more. Suckers freely. Name covers a number of hybrids between Scotch elm and smooth-leafed elm.

U. parvifolia. (Often sold as *U.p.* 'Sempervirens'.) CHINESE ELM, CHINESE EVERGREEN ELM. Zones 8, 9, 12-24. Evergreen or deciduous according to the winter temperatures and the tree's individual heredity. So-called evergreen elm usually sold as 'Sempervirens'; this may be evergreen most winters, lose its leaves in an unusual cold snap (new leaves come on fast). Very fast growth to 40-60 ft., with 50-70-ft. spread. Often reaches 30 ft. in 5 years. Extremely variable in form, but generally spreading, with long, arching, eventually weeping branchlets. Trunks of older trees have bark which sheds in patches somewhat like sycamore. Leaves leathery, ¾-2½ in. long, ⅓-1⅓ in. wide, oval, evenly toothed. Round fruits form in fall while leaves are still on tree.

Stake young trees until trunks will carry weight of branches. Stake and head the leading shoot higher than other shade trees to compensate for weeping. Rub or cut out small branches along trunk for first few years. Shorten overlong branches or strongly weeping branches to strengthen tree scaffolding. Older trees may need thinning to lessen chance of storm damage. Very little bothered by pests or diseases.

Good for patio shade in milder portions of West. Useful for sun screening. With careful pruning, useful as a street tree.

Varieties are 'Brea', with larger leaves, more upright habit; and 'Drake', with small leaves, weeping habit. Both are more or less evergreen.

A word of caution: Siberian elm is sometimes sold as Chinese elm. Siberian elm flowers in spring, has stiffer habit and thinner, less glossy leaves.

U. procera. ENGLISH ELM. Zones 1-11, 14-21. To 120 ft. Suckers profusely. Tall trunk with broad or tall dense crown of branches. Foliage holds dark green color later in fall than American elm. Same precautions apply to this tree as to American elm.

U. pumila. SIBERIAN ELM. All Zones. Most useful in Zones 1-3, 10, 11. To 50 ft. Leaves ¾-2 in. long, ⅓-1 in. wide, dark green, smooth. Extremely hardy and tough, enduring cold, heat, drought, and poor soil. Under worst conditions grows slowly, may even be a shrub. As a fast-growing tree, suitable for windbreaks or shelterbelts. Has brittle wood, weak crotches, and is not desirable as single garden tree. Root system troublesome in gardens, but possibly useful in holding soil in problem areas against wind or water erosion.

UMBELLULARIA californica. CALIFORNIA LAUREL, CALIFORNIA BAY, OREGON MYRTLE, PEPPERWOOD. Evergreen tree. Zones 4-10, 12-24. Native to southwestern Oregon, California Coast Ranges, lower elevations of Sierra Nevada. In wilds it varies from a huge gumdrop-shaped shrub (on windy hillsides near coast) to a tall and free-ranging tree 75 ft. high and over 100 ft. wide (in forests). Leaves are 3-5 in. long, 1 in. wide, pointed at tip, medium to deep yellow-green and glossy on top, dull light green beneath. As sure identification, crush a leaf—if it's this plant it will be powerfully aromatic. A little of the crushed fragrance is pleasant, but too much can cause headache. Leaves sometimes used as more flavorful substitute for true bay leaves (*Laurus nobilis*) in soups and stews. Tiny yellowish flowers in clusters give plant a yellowish cast in spring. They are followed by olivelike, green, inedible fruits that turn purple.

In gardens, plants tend to grow slowly (about 1 ft. a year) to 20-25 ft. high and as wide. Grows best and fastest in deep soil with ample water, but tolerates many other conditions. Will grow in deep shade and ultimately get big enough to become a shade-maker itself—casts very dense shade unless thinned. No pests or diseases except for occasional leaf chewers and scale insects. Always neat. Good for screening or tall hedges. Often forms several trunks. Good patio or street tree when thinned to one or a few trunks.

UMBRELLA PLANT. See Cyperus alternifolius

UMBRELLA TREE, TEXAS. See Melia azedarach 'Umbraculifera'

UMBU. See Phytolacca dioica

URBINIA agavoides. See Echeveria agavoides

VACCINIUM. Evergreen and deciduous shrubs. Excellent ornamental shrubs with clusters of bell-shaped flowers and colorful, edible fruit. All require acid soil and ample leaf mold, peat moss, or ground bark. Good woodland garden subjects.

V. corymbosum. See Blueberry

V. ovatum. EVERGREEN HUCKLEBERRY. Zones 4-7, 14-17. Evergreen shrub. Native Santa Barbara County north to British Columbia. Erect shrub 2-3 ft. in sun, to 8-10 ft. in shade. Young plants spreading, older plants taller than wide, compact. Leathery, lustrous, dark green leaves, ½-1¼ in. long; new growth bronzy. Flowers (March-May) white or pinkish. Berries black with whitish bloom, good in pies, jams, jellies, syrups.

Best in partial shade; will take full sun in cool-summer areas. Can be trimmed into hedge or grown in a container. Cut branches popular for arrangements.

V. parvifolium. RED HUCKLEBERRY. Zones 1-7, 14-17. Deciduous shrub. Native Sierra Nevada and northern California Coast Ranges to Alaska. Slow growth to 4-12, rarely 18 ft. Branches green, thin, giving a spreading or cascading plant with intricate, filmy winter silhouette. Leaves thin, oval, ½-¾ in. long, light green. Flowers greenish or whitish, April-May, fine for arrangements. Berries clear, bright red, showy, and delicious in jams, jellies, and pies. Needs highly acid humusy soil, partial shade.

V. vitis-idaea. LINGONBERRY. Zones 2-7, 14-17. Evergreen shrub. Slow growth to 1 ft. tall, spreading by underground runners to 3 ft. Leaves dark green, ⅓-1 in. long. Flowers clustered, white or pinkish, May. Edible red berries sour, something like tiny cranberries, esteemed for preserves, syrups. Handsome little plants for small-scale ground cover, informal edging around larger acid-soil plantings. With ample water, will take full sun in cool-summer areas. *V. v. minus,* MOUNTAIN CRANBERRY, is smaller, with leaves ⅛-½ in. long.

VALERIANA officinalis. VALERIAN, GARDEN HELIOTROPE. Perennial herb. All Zones. Tall straight stems grow to about 4 ft. high. The bulk of leaves remain fairly close to the ground. They are light green, in pairs that are further divided into 8-10 pairs of narrow leaflets. Tiny flowers are white, pink, or lavender-blue, in rounded clusters at ends of stems. Plant spreads and can become invasive. Roots are strong smelling.

Valerian has no herbal uses in the modern world. When it was known as all-heal and St. George's herb, it was used to treat ailments of the heart and brain.

True heliotrope is another plant entirely. In similar manner, another plant (*Centranthus ruber*) often goes by the name valerian. Both of these plants are more common than *Valeriana officinalis*.

Plant in sun or part shade. Start new plants from seeds or divisions. Grow in mixed herb or flower borders but don't allow it to crowd other plants. Use cut flowers in arrangements.

V. rubra. See Centranthus

VALLOTA speciosa. SCARBOROUGH LILY. Bulb. Zones 16, 17, 23, 24 outdoors; anywhere in containers. Native to South Africa. Strap-shaped, evergreen leaves 1-2 ft. long. Clusters of bright orange-vermilion, funnel-shaped, 2½-3-in.-wide flowers on 2-ft. stalks. Bloom summer and early fall. White-flowered form rarely available. Survives out of doors where frosts are very light and infrequent; succeeds even in competition with tree roots. Excellent container plant. Plant June-July or just after flowering. Set bulbs with tips just below surface. Use smallest pots possible; repot or divide only when absolutely necessary; blooms best when roots crowded. Fertilize monthly during active growth. Water regularly except during semi-dormant period in winter and spring, but never let plant dry out completely.

VANCOUVERIA. Deciduous and evergreen perennials. These close relatives of *Epimedium* have the same uses in the garden.

Climate Zone maps pages 8-27

Leaves divided into numerous leaflets. Flowers in late spring, early summer. Attractive ground cover for tree-shaded beds. Cut foliage attractive in bouquets.

V. chrysantha. Zones 5, 6, 14-17. Evergreen. To 8-16 in. tall, native to Siskiyou Mountains. Bronzed, gray-green leaves, 1½ in. long and wide. Small yellow flowers 4-15 to the stalk, each flower ½ in. across.

V. hexandra. Zones 4-6, 14-17. Deciduous. To 4-16 in. tall, native to coastal forests from northern California to Washington. Leaflets 1-2½ in. long, light green; fresh appearance all summer. Flower stalks usually 3-flowered, white flowers to ½ in. across, drooping, petals and sepals sharply bent backward.

V. planipetala (*V. parviflora*). INSIDE-OUT FLOWER. Zones 4-6, 14-17. Evergreen, sometimes deciduous in cold-winter areas. To 2 ft. in height. Light to medium green leaflets, shallowly lobed, 1½ in. long and wide. Flowers white, even smaller than on *V. hexandra*, but with 25-50 flowers in the cluster.

VANDA. Epiphytic orchids. Greenhouse or indoors. Beautiful orchids, but difficult to flower in coastal fog belts where light is limited. Plants grow erect, with leaves arranged opposite each other up the stem. Flowers grow on stalk formed in the leaf joints.

Plant in osmunda fiber, tree fern fiber, or ground bark. Support stem against stake of tree fern stem about ⅔ height of plant to provide anchor for aerial roots. Temperatures shouldn't drop below 60° at night, can rise to almost any height during day provided that humidity is kept high and air

Flowers of Vanda orchids come in many colors; V. caerulea is pale to dark blue.

circulates freely. Water very lightly during winter. They need plenty of light all year, but especially from November to February in order to set flower buds.

V. caerulea. India. Large 3-4-in. flowers varying in color from pale to dark blue on 1-2-ft.-long stems in late summer, early fall. Plants 1-2 ft. high with rigid, dark green 6-10-in.-long leaves.

V. teres. Burma. The flower so frequently used in making leis; often flown in from Hawaii. Sepals white tinged rose, petals deep rose, side lobes of lip yellow, lower lobe rose lined and spotted with yellow. Flowers 3-4 in. across, 2 to 5 on stalk

from May to September. Cylindrical, slightly tapered leaves clothe slender 2-7-ft. climbing stems. Needs decided winter rest and much light.

VELTHEIMIA viridifolia. Bulb. Zones 23, 24 outdoors; anywhere in containers as house plant or summer patio plant. Native to South Africa. Unique and beautiful plant with clump of broad, shining, deep green, wavy-margined leaves 1 ft. long, 3 in. wide. Beautiful even without bloom. Heavy cluster of pale rose, green-tipped, tubular, drooping flowers on 12-in., stout, brown-marked stem, resemble red-hot poker (*Kniphofia*). Blooms in winter or early spring. Set bulbs with upper ⅓ above surface. Grow cool and keep barely moist until roots start to form. Increase watering, light, and warmth as growth begins. Fertilize every 2 weeks through growing season. Dry off as foliage ripens in summer; resume watering in September when new growth begins. Outdoors, protect from hot sun and wind.

VELVET PLANT. See Gynura

VERBASCUM. MULLEIN. Perennials. All Zones. Stately, sun-loving, summer-blooming. Broad leaves closely set on stem. Shallow-dished flowers in straight spikes. A large group, some of them weedy. They self-sow freely.

V. blattaria. MOTH MULLEIN. Low clumps of smooth, dark green, cut or toothed leaves. Flower spikes 1½-2½ ft. high with pale yellow or white blooms, purple stamens. Flowers open with morning light.

V. olympicum. Stems to 5 ft. high. Large leaves, 2 ft. or more long, white, with soft, downy hairs. Bright yellow 1-in. flowers clustered in many long spikes.

V. phoeniceum. PURPLE MULLEIN. Stems 2-4 ft. high. Leaves smooth, only hairy on underside. Purple flowers in slender spikes half the height of the plant or more.

VERBENA. Perennials, some grown as annuals. They need sun and heat in order to thrive, and are drought resistant. Set 2 ft. apart for ground cover; growth is fast. Species listed below adjust effectively to planting in parking strips, along sides of driveways, and on dry banks, walls, and rock crevices where they display their colors all summer.

V. hybrida (*V. hortensis*). GARDEN VERBENA. Perennial usually grown as an annual. Many-branched plants 6-12 in. high and spreading 1½-3 ft. Oblong, 2-4-in.-long leaves are bright green or gray-green, with toothed margins. Flowers in flat compact clusters, 2-3 in. wide. Colors include white, pink, bright red, purple, blue, and combinations. Variety 'Amethyst' is a good sky blue; 'Miss Susie' is a good double salmon-pink. Subject to mildew—there will be less chance of it if you water deeply and not too often. If used as a perennial, prune severely in winter or early spring. Good ground cover in Zones 12, 13 if Bermuda grass can be kept out of it.

V. peruviana (*V. chamaedryfolia*). Perennial, often grown as an annual. Zones 8-24. Spreads rapidly, forms a very flat mat. (Planted 2 ft. apart, can make solid cover in a season.) Leaves are neat, small, closely-set. Flat-topped flower clusters on slender stems lavishly cover foliage. In original

form, corolla tube is white, spreading lobes rich scarlet. Hybrids spread somewhat more slowly, have slightly larger leaves and stouter stems, and are available in several colors: 'Appleblossom'; 'Cherry Pink'; 'Princess Gloria' in salmon tones; many purplish and red varieties; and a very fine pure white. Especially popular in southern California and in desert areas.

V. rigida (*V. venosa*). Perennial. All Zones. Spreading plants 10-20 in. tall. Leaves rough, dark green, 2-4 in. long, strongly toothed. Lilac to purple-blue flowers in cylindrical clusters on tall, stiff stems summer and fall. Takes considerable drought; useful in low-maintenance gardens. Can be grown as an annual; blooms in 4 months from seed.

V. tenera maonettii. Creeping perennial. Zones 8-24. Leaves cut to midrib and lobes cut again. Flat clusters of pink flowers with distinct white margins.

VERBENA, LEMON. See Aloysia

VERBENA, SAND. See Abronia

VERONICA. SPEEDWELL. Perennials (for shrubby plants sold as *Veronica*, see *Hebe*). All Zones. Handsome plants ranging from 4 in. to 2½ ft. in height. Small flowers, (¼-½ in. across) are massed to display effectively the white, rose, pink, pale or deep blue color. Use in sunny borders and rock gardens.

V. holophylla. Many stems to 24 in. high, densely clothed with dark green, very glossy leaves. Long stalks of rich deep blue flowers show above foliage mass.

V. hybrids. These include a number of midsummer-blooming, upright, bushy perennials ranging from 10 to 18 in. high. Choice varieties: 'Barcarole', to 10 in. tall,

Tight, erect spikes of Veronica hybrids come in shades of blue and pink, white.

rose-pink flowers; 'Crater Lake Blue', to 10 in. tall, bright blue flower spikes; 'Icicle', 15-18 in. tall, white flower spikes.

V. longifolia subsessilis. Clumps of upright stems to 2 ft. tall topped by close-flowered spikes of deep blue flowers about ½ in. across in midsummer. Stems are

V

Climate Zone maps pages 8-27

leafy and rather closely set with narrow pointed leaves.

V. pectinata. Forms prostrate mats that spread by creeping stems which root at the joints. Roundish, ½-in.-long leaves with scallop-toothed or deeply cut edges. Flowers profuse, deep blue with white center, in 5-6-in. spikes among the leaves. Good as a rock plant or in wall crevices.

V. prostrata (*V. rupestris*). Tufted, hairy stems, some of which are prostrate. Leaves ½-¾ in. long. Flower stems to 8 in. high topped by short cluster of pale blue flowers.

V. repens. Shining green, ½-in.-long leaves clothe prostrate stems, give mosslike effect. Flowers ¼ in. wide, lavender to white in few-flowered clusters in spring. Good cover for small bulbs.

V. saturejoides. Many tufted stems spread by creeping roots. Roundish, ½-in.-long leaves are closely overlapping on stems. Dark blue flowers in short, compact spikes appear in May. A fine rock plant.

V. spicata. Much like *V. longifolia subsessilis*, but less robust and with shorter flower spikes. A miniature variety, 'Nana', grows 6 in. high, with violet-blue flowers June-July.

VETCH, CROWN. See Coronilla

VETCH, HORSESHOE. See Hippocrepis

VIBURNUM. Deciduous or evergreen shrubs, rarely small trees. Large and diverse group of plants with clustered, often fragrant flowers and clusters of 1-seeded, often brilliantly colored fruits much liked by birds. They tend to fall into groups determined by landscape use.

Evergreen viburnums used principally as foliage plants are *V. cinnamomifolium, V. davidii, V. japonicum, V. propinquum,* and *V. rhytidophyllum.*

Evergreen viburnums used as foliage and flowering plants are *V. odoratissimum, V. suspensum,* and *V. tinus.*

Partially deciduous viburnums grown for flowers are *V. burkwoodii* and *V. macrocephalum.* They are nearly evergreen in mild climates and have showy flowers.

Deciduous viburnums grown for fragrant flowers are *V. bitchiuense, V. bodnantense, V. carlcephalum, V. carlesii, V.* 'Carlotta', *V. chenaultii, V. farreri,* and *V. juddii.*

Deciduous viburnums for showy flowers, fall leaf color include *V. opulus* (also has showy fruit), *V. o.* 'Roseum', *V. plicatum, V. p. tomentosum,* and *V. trilobum.*

Deciduous viburnums for fruit color are *V. dilatatum, V. ichangense,* and *V. wrightii.*

Viburnums, with few exceptions noted in the descriptions, tolerate alkaline and acid soils. They do well in heavy rich soils with ample moisture. Many have unusually wide range in climate adaptability; note *V. burkwoodii* and *V. tinus* 'Robustum' for examples. They grow in sun or shade. Most evergreen kinds look better with some protection from the sun where summers are hot and long. Prune to shape to prevent legginess; some evergreen kinds can be sheared. Aphids, thrips, spider mites, and scale likely to be a problem. Use an all-purpose insecticide spray in early spring as at 2-week intervals. Keep sulfur sprays off viburnum foliage.

V. bitchiuense. Deciduous shrub. Zones 4-9, 14-24. To 10 ft. Leaves oval, 1½-3½ in. long, downy. Flowers (May) pink aging white, very fragrant. Fruit black, not showy. Somewhat more open habit than *V. carlesii.*

V. bodnantense. Deciduous shrub. Zones 5-9, 14-24. To 10 ft. or more. Oval leaves 1½-4 in. long are deeply veined, turn dark scarlet in fall. Flowers deep pink fading paler, very fragrant, in loose clusters October-April. Fruit red, not showy. This plant is a hybrid and there are several varieties. Best known is 'Dawn' ('Pink Dawn'). Flower buds freeze in coldest Northwest winters.

V. burkwoodii. Deciduous shrub in coldest areas, nearly evergreen elsewhere. Zones 1-12, 14-24. To 6-12 ft. tall, 4-5 ft. wide. Leaves dark green, glossy above, white hairy beneath, to 3½ in. long. Purplish in cold weather. Flowers in dense 4-in. clusters, pink in bud, opening white, very fragrant, February-March. Fruit blue-black, not showy. Early growth straggly, mature plants dense. Can be trained as espalier.

V. carlcephalum. FRAGRANT SNOWBALL. Deciduous shrub. Zones 1-11, 14-24. To 6-7 ft. tall, 4-5 ft. wide. Leaves dull grayish green, downy beneath, 2-3½ in. long. Flowers white, fragrant, in dense 4-5-in. clusters in spring, early summer. No fruits. Showy as common snowball, but has added fragrance.

V. carlesii. KOREAN SPICE VIBURNUM. Deciduous shrub. Zones 1-11, 14-24. To 4-8 ft. tall, 4-5 ft. broad. Leaves like those of *V. carlcephalum.* Flowers pink in bud opening white, in 2-3-in.-wide clusters,

sweetly fragrant, March-May. Loose, open habit. Best in part shade summer, sun in spring, winter.

V. 'Carlotta'. Deciduous shrub. Zones 1-11, 14-24. Like a bigger-flowered *V. carlesii,* with a different fragrance. Dense clusters of waxy flowers.

V. chenaultii. Deciduous shrub. Zones 2-12, 14-24. To 4-6 ft. tall, 3-4 ft. broad. Leaves and flowers much like those of *V. burkwoodii,* plant more compact, more deciduous than the latter.

V. cinnamomifolium. Evergreen shrub. Zones 5-9, 14-24. To 10-20 ft. tall, equally wide. Leaves 3-6 in. long, 1-3 in. wide, leathery, glossy dark green, strongly 3-veined. Flowers pink in bud opening white, individually tiny, in flattish clusters 6 in. across, April. Faintly honey-scented. Fruits shiny blue-black, small. Looks like a much-magnified *V. davidii.* Use in screens, background. Best in acid soil with plenty of water.

V. davidii. Evergreen shrub. Zones 4-9, 14-24. To 1-3 ft. tall, 3-4 ft. wide. Leaves dark green, deeply veined, to 6 in. long. Flower clusters to 3 in. wide, white, from dull pinkish red buds. Not showy. Fruits metallic turquoise blue. For abundant berry production set out more than one plant.

Use as foundation shrub, in foreground plantings, with ferns, azaleas, other acid soil plants in part shade. Extremely valuable in Northwest, cooler California gardens.

V. dilatatum. LINDEN VIBURNUM. Deciduous shrub. Zones 1-9, 14-16. To 10 ft. tall, broad, compact. Leaves nearly round, 2-5 in. long, gray-green. Flowers tiny, creamy white, in 5-in.-wide clusters in early summer. Showy bright red fruits produced best where summers are warm; they ripen in September, hang on into winter.

V. farreri (*V. fragrans*). Deciduous shrub. Zones 5-9, 14-24. To 10-15 ft. tall, and as wide. Leaves oval, heavily veined, smooth green, 1½-3 in. long. Turn soft russet red in fall. Flowers white to pink, in 2-in. clusters, fragrant. Bloom November-March. Blossoms will stand to 20°-22°, freeze in colder temperatures. Fruit bright red. Prune to prevent leggy growth. *V. f.* 'Album' (*V. f.* 'Candidissimum') has pure white flowers. *V. f.* 'Nanum' is lower-growing (to 2 ft.), with pink flowers.

V. ichangense. Deciduous shrub. Zones 4-9, 14-20. To 6 ft. tall, with oval, long, pointed leaves 1½-2½ in. long. Profuse

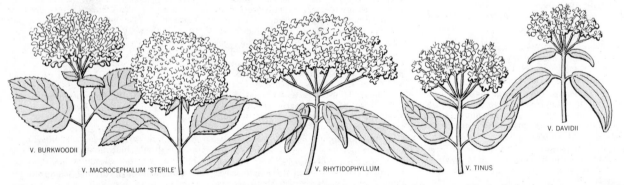

Viburnum macrocephalum 'Sterile' has showy white flower clusters; flowers of V. burkwoodii are sweetly fragrant. Although V. tinus has light fragrance, it is grown principally for handsome evergreen foliage, as are V. davidii, V. rhytidophyllum.

Climate Zone maps pages 8-27

clusters of white, fragrant flowers in late spring. Heavy crop of bright red fruits in fall, early winter. Leggy, open shrub best grown in borders for fruit display.

V. japonicum. Evergreen shrub or small tree. Zones 5-9, 14-24. To 10-20 ft. tall. Leaves leathery, glossy dark green, to 6 in. long. Sparse bloom; flowers in spring in 4-in. clusters, white, fragrant. Red fruit is sparse but very attractive. Big, bulky shrub or small tree for background plantings. Best with some shade in warmer areas. Keep aphids under control.

V. juddii. Deciduous shrub. Zones 1-12, 14-24. To 4-8 ft. tall. Hybrid between *V. carlesii*, *V. bitchiuense*. More spreading and bushy than *V. carlesii*, otherwise similar to it.

V. lantana. WAYFARING-TREE. Deciduous shrub or small tree. Zones 1-12, 14-20. To 8-15 ft. tall. Leaves broadly oval, to 5 in. long, downy on both sides; turn red in fall. Flowers tiny, white, in 2-4-in. clusters. May or June. Fruits bright scarlet turning black, showy. Use in woodland or background plantings. Will take dryish conditions.

V. macrocephalum 'Sterile'. CHINESE SNOWBALL. Deciduous shrub in coldest areas, nearly evergreen elsewhere. Zones 1-9, 14-24. To 12-20 ft. tall, with broad, rounded habit. Leaves oval to oblong, dull green, 2-4 in. long. Big rounded flower clusters to 6-8 in., composed of sterile flowers. Blooms April-May. No fruit. Spectacular bloom clusters; plant good for espaliers, display.

V. odoratissimum. SWEET VIBURNUM. Evergreen shrub (briefly deciduous in colder winter areas). Risky in Zones 5, 6, reliable in Zones 8, 9, 14-24. To 10-20 ft. tall, broader than tall. Leaves bright green, 3-8 in. long, with glossy, varnished-looking surface. Conical 3-6-in. clusters of white, lightly fragrant flowers, May. Fruit red, ripening black. Use as big screen or single plant.

V. opulus. EUROPEAN CRANBERRY BUSH. Deciduous shrub. Zones 1-9, 14-24. To 10-20 ft. Lobed, maple-shaped leaves 2-4 in. long and wider are dark green, turn red in fall. Flower clusters 2-4 in. across, white, rimmed with ¾-in.-wide sterile white flowers in "lace cap" effect. May. Large, red, showy fruits. Needs careful spraying to control aphids.

V. o. 'Nanum'. Dwarf form of the above. To 2 ft. tall, 2 ft. wide. Needs no trimming as a low hedge. Can take poor, wet soils. No flowers, fruit.

V. o. 'Roseum' (*V. o.* 'Sterile'). COMMON SNOWBALL. To 10-15 ft. Resembles *V. opulus* except that flower clusters resemble snowballs, 2-2½ in. through and composed entirely of sterile flowers (so no fruit).

V. plicatum (*V. tomentosum* 'Sterile'). JAPANESE SNOWBALL. Deciduous shrub. Zones 1-9, 14-24. To 15 ft. tall and as wide. Oval, dull dark green, strongly veined leaves 3-6 in. long. Leaves turn purplish red in fall. Snowball clusters of white sterile flowers 2-3 in. across, borne in opposite rows along horizontal branches. May. Less subject to aphids than *V. opulus*. Horizontal branching pattern, fall color, flowers all attractive.

V. p. tomentosum. DOUBLEFILE VIBURNUM. Resembles the plant above, but flat flower clusters are 2-4 in. wide, edged with sterile 1-1½-in.-wide flowers in lace cap effect. Fruits red, showy, not always profuse. *V. p. t.* 'Mariesii' has larger sterile flowers.

V. propinquum. Evergreen shrub. Zones 5-9, 14-24. To 4 ft. tall. Leaves narrowish oval, 3-veined, 2-3½ in. long, dark glossy green. New growth bronzy. Greenish white flowers in clusters 1½-3 in. wide. Fruit blue-black, small. Resembles a bushier *V. davidii* with twiggier outline, smaller leaves.

V. rhytidophyllum. LEATHERLEAF VIBURNUM. Evergreen shrub. Zones 2-9, 14-24. Narrow, upright shrub to 6-15 ft. tall, fast growing in colder areas, slow in Zones 18-24. Leaves narrowish, to 4-10 in. long, deep green and wrinkled above, densely fuzzy underneath. Flowers off-white, in clusters 4-8 in. across, in spring. Fruit scarlet, turning black. Cold-hardy, but tattered-looking where cold winds blow. Some think it striking, others merely coarse. Two hybrids (neither significantly different from species): *V. rhytidocarpum* and *V. rhytidophylloides* 'Willowwood'.

V. suspensum. SANDANKWA VIBURNUM. Evergreen shrub. Zones 8-24. To 8-10 ft. tall and as broad. Leaves oval, 2-4 in. long, leathery, glossy, deep green above, paler beneath. Flowers white, in 2-4-in., loose clusters in early spring. Fragrance objectionable to some people. Fruit red turning black, not long lasting. Takes sun or considerable shade. Serviceable screen, hedge, with dense foliage. Watch for thrips, spider mites, aphids.

V. tinus. LAURUSTINUS. Evergreen shrub or small, narrow tree. Zones 4-12, 14-23. To 6-12 ft. tall, half as wide. Leaves dark green, oval, leathery, slightly rolled under at edges, 2-3 in. long. New stems wine red. Tight clusters of pink buds open to white flowers November-spring. Lightly fragrant. Fruits bright metallic blue, lasting through summer. Dense foliage right to ground makes it a good plant for screens, hedges, clipped topiary shapes. Mildews near ocean.

V. t. 'Dwarf'. Similar to above, but grows only 3-5 ft. tall, equally wide. Low screens, hedges, foundation plantings.

V. t. 'Lucidum'. SHINING LAURUSTINUS. Zones 4-9, 14-24. Leaves larger than *V. tinus*; plant less hardy, but more resistant to mildew near coast.

V. t. 'Robustum'. ROUNDLEAF LAURUSTINUS. Zones 4-9, 14-24. Leaves coarser, rougher than in *V. tinus*, less pink in flowers. More resistant to mildew. Makes an excellent, small, narrow tree.

V. t. 'Variegatum'. Zones 4-9, 14-23. Like *V. tinus*, except that leaves are variegated with white and pale yellow.

V. trilobum. CRANBERRY BUSH. Deciduous shrub. Zones 1-11, 14-20. To 10-15 ft. tall. Leaves much like those of *V. opulus*; turn red in fall. Lace cap flowers and fruit almost identical to those of *V. opulus*. Less susceptible to aphid damage than *V. opulus*.

V. wrightii. Deciduous shrub. Zones 4-9, 14-17. To 6-10 ft. tall, with narrow, erect habit. Leaves smooth, bright green, oval, 2-5 in. long, 1-2½ in wide. Flowers small, white, in 2-4-in.-wide clusters, May. Fruit (most valuable feature) showy, bright red, lasting many months.

VINCA. PERIWINKLE, MYRTLE. Evergreen perennials. Trailing habit; extensively used as ground covers, for pattern plantings, and for rough slopes and otherwise unused areas.

V. major. Zones 5-24. Long, trailing stems root as they spread, carry many 1-3-in., somewhat broad-based, oval, dark green, glossy leaves (white-variegated form also common). Short flowering branches with lavender-blue flowers 1-2 in. across the flat spreading lobes. Will mound up 6-12 in. possibly to 2 ft. high. A tough plant, quite easy to grow. Needs shade and some moisture to look its best, but will take sun if watered generously. If used as ground cover, shear close to ground occasionally to bring on fresh new growth.

V. minor. DWARF PERIWINKLE. All Zones. A perfect miniature of *V. major*, except leaves are more often oblong, have shorter stalks, are more closely spaced. Also requires more care—2 or 3 good soakings per month and feeding several times a year. In desert, grow only in shade. Lavender-blue flowers an inch across; also forms with white, wine red, and deeper blue flowers.

V. rosea. See Catharanthus roseus

VIOLA. VIOLET, PANSY. Perennials; some treated as annuals. Botanically speaking, violas, pansies, and violets are all perennials belonging to the genus *Viola*. Pansies and violas, however, are generally treated as annuals, especially in mild-winter areas.

All three grow best in rich, moist soil. Plant violas and pansies in full sun in coastal areas, in partial shade in warmer sections. Violets need shade from hot afternoon sun; in desert and other hot-summer climates, plant in full shade.

Violas and pansies are invaluable for winter and spring color in mild regions, from spring through summer in cooler areas. They provide mass color in borders and edgings, as ground covers for spring flowering bulbs, and in containers outdoors. Pansies also give colorful displays in pots and boxes. Sweet violets are notorious hosts to spider mites. That's why many nurseries don't grow them.

V. cornuta. VIOLA, TUFTED PANSY. All Zones. Tufted plants 6-8 in. high. Smooth, wavy-toothed, ovalish leaves. Purple, pansy-like flowers about 1½ in. across, with a slender spur. Newer strains and varieties have larger flowers with shorter spurs, in solid colors of purple, blue, yellow, apricot, ruby red, and white. Crystal strain has especially large flowers in clear colors.

In mild-winter climates, sow seed of violas in late summer, set out plants in fall for color from late winter or early spring to summer. In cold regions, sow seed in September or early spring; transplant September-sown seedlings to coldframe, keep there over winter, set plants outside in spring. Named varieties of violas such as 'Maggie Mott' and 'Pride of Victoria' also increased by division or cuttings.

V. hederacea. AUSTRALIAN VIOLET. Zones 8, 9, 14-24. Tufted, spreads by stolons. Leaves kidney-shaped. Flowers ¼-¾ in. across, nearly spurless, white, or blue fading to white at petal tips. Summer bloom; plant goes dormant at about 30°. Use as ground cover.

V. odorata. SWEET VIOLET. All Zones. The violet of song and story. Tufted, long runners root at joints. Leaves dark green, heart-shaped, toothed on margins. Flowers fragrant, short-spurred, deep violet, bluish rose, or white. Large, deep blue 'Royal Robe' is widely used. 'Marie Louise' has fragrant double white and bluish lavender flowers; 'Royal Elk' single, fragrant, long-stemmed violet-colored flowers; 'Charm' grows in clumps, has small white flowers; 'Rosina' is pink-flowered.

Remove runners and shear rank growth in late fall for better spring flower display. For heavy bloom, feed in very early spring, before flowering, with complete fertilizer.

V. priceana. CONFEDERATE VIOLET. All Zones. Stemless, with sturdy rootstock. Leaves somewhat heart-shaped, to 5 in. wide. Flowers ½-¾ in. across, white, heavily veined with violet blue, flat-faced like pansies. Self-sows readily; best in woodland garden. Good ground cover among rhododendrons.

V. tricolor. JOHNNY-JUMP-UP. Annual or short-lived perennial. To 6-12 in. tall. Tufted habit. Purple and yellow flowers resemble miniature pansies. Color forms available in blue or in a mix including yellow, lavender, mauve. Spring bloom. Self-sows profusely.

V. tricolor hortensis. PANSY. Excellent strains with flowers 2-4 in. across, in white, blue, mahogany red, rose, yellow, apricot, purple; also bicolors. Petals striped or blotched. Plants grow to about 8 in. high. F_1 and F_2 hybrids more free-flowering, heat tolerant.

Sow pansy seed from mid-July to mid-August. In mild-winter areas, set out plants in fall for bloom from late winter or early spring to summer. In cold sections, transplant seedlings into a coldframe, set out plants in spring; or sow seed indoors in January or February, plant outdoors in spring. Or, plant nursery plants in spring. Pansies need rich, cool, moist soil with protection from hottest sun. To prolong bloom, pick flowers (with some foliage) regularly, remove faded blooms before they set seed. In warmer climates, plants get ragged by midsummer, should be removed.

VIOLET. See Viola

VIOLET, AFRICAN. See Saintpaulia

VIOLET, DOGS TOOTH. See Erythronium dens-canis

VIOLET, SWEET. See Viola odorata

VIRGILIA divaricata. KEURBOOM. Evergreen tree. Zones 18-24. Native to South Africa. Very fast growth to 30 ft. Plants often bloom at 10 ft. and 2 years from seed. Spreading, rather rounded habit. Leaves 4-8 in. long, divided into 1-in. leaflets in the manner of locust. Springtime flowers pink, fragrant, sweet pea-shaped, in hanging clusters. A pretty flowering tree for quick effects or to give height to shrubbery. Plant out of strong wind. Good garden soil and ample water. Protect young plants from frost; older ones can take 25°. Not long-lived; 15 years is about the maximum expectancy.

VISCARIA. See Silene coeli-rosa

VITEX. CHASTE TREE. Deciduous and evergreen shrubs or trees. Two species sold in the West. Both have divided leaves and clustered flowers.

V. agnus-castus. CHASTE TREE. Deciduous shrub or small tree. Zones 4-24. Growth slow in cold climates, fast in warmer areas. Size varies from 6 ft. in Northwest to 25 ft. in low desert. Habit broad and spreading, usually with multiple trunks. Leaves divided fanwise into 5-7 narrow, 2-6-in.-long leaflets that are dark green above, gray beneath. Conspicuous 7-in. spikes of lavender-blue flowers in summer and fall.

Tolerates many types of soils, but requires plenty of summer heat for richly colored, profuse bloom. In rich, moist soils it grows luxuriantly, but has paler flowers. Good for summer flower color in shrub border. Trained high, a good small shade tree. Varieties are: 'Alba', white flowers; 'Latifolia', (often sold as *V. macrophylla*) sturdy, with large leaflets; and 'Rosea', with pinkish flowers. Combines well with smaller-leafed gray plants and with such boldly colored big flowering shrubs as *Poinciana gilliesii, Spartium junceum,* or red, pink, and white crape myrtle.

V. lucens. NEW ZEALAND CHASTE TREE. Evergreen tree. Zones 16, 17, 22-24. Slow to moderate growth to 40-60 ft. Leaves with 3-5 shining, glossy, corrugated-looking, roundish, 5-in.-long leaflets. Pink winter buds open to lavender-pink 1-in. flowers in loose clusters. Fruit bright red, resembling a small cherry. Needs deep, rich soil, ample water, and protection from frost while young. Luxuriant near coast; tolerates sea breezes.

VRIESIA. See Tillandsia

WAHLENBERGIA saxicola. (Often sold as *W. tasmanica*.) Perennial. Zones 4-9, 14-17. A small, tufted plant, resembling one of the smaller campanulas and closely related to them. Has narrow, spoon-shaped leaves in tiny rosettes which multiply to make flat mats of bright green. In late spring and early summer, the ½-in. blue flowers stand above the mat singly on 3-in. stems. Sun or light shade. Pretty rock garden item.

WAKE ROBIN. See Trillium

WALLFLOWER, SIBERIAN. See Erysimum asperum

WALNUT (*Juglans*). Deciduous trees. Usually large and spreading, with leaves divided into leaflets. Oval or round nuts in fleshy husks. English walnut (*J. regia*) is a well known orchard tree in many parts of the West; the American native species are sometimes planted as shade trees with an incidental bonus of edible nuts or are used as understock for grafting English walnut. English and California black walnut trees are notorious as hosts to aphids. The pests and their honeydew exudation are so inevitable that you should not plant either tree where branches will arch over a patio or automobile parking place.

J. californica. SOUTHERN CALIFORNIA BLACK WALNUT. Zones 18-24. Native to southern California. Treelike shrub or small tree 15-30 ft., usually with several stems from the ground. Leaves 6-12 in., with 9-19 leaflets to 2¼ in. long. Roundish, ¾-in. nuts. Not commercially grown, but worth saving if it grows as a native. Takes drought and poor soil.

J. cinerea. BUTTERNUT. Zones 1-9, 14-17. Native to eastern U. S. To 50-60 ft., with a broad, spreading head. Resembles black walnut (*J. nigra*), but is smaller; leaves have fewer leaflets; nuts are oval or elongated rather than round. Flavor good, but shells thick and hard.

J. hindsii. CALIFORNIA BLACK WALNUT. Zones 5-9, 14-20. Native to scattered localities in northern California. Tree 30-60 ft. tall, with single trunk and broad crown. Leaves have 15-19, 3-5-in. leaflets. Widely used as rootstock for English walnut in California; resistant to oak root fungus (*Armillaria*).

J. major (*J. rupestris major*). NOGAL, ARIZONA WALNUT. Zones 10, 12-13. Native to Arizona, New Mexico, northern Mexico. Broad tree to 50 ft. Leaves have 9-13 leaflets. Round, small, thick-shelled nuts in husks that dry on tree. Takes desert heat and wind, needs deep soil, some water.

J. nigra. BLACK WALNUT. Zones 1-9, 14-21. Native to eastern U.S. High-branched tree grows to 150 ft. high (usually not over 100 ft. in the West) with round crown, furrowed blackish brown bark. Leaves with 15-23 leaflets, each 2½-5 in. long. Nuts 1-1½ in. across, thick-shelled but with rich flavor. Improved varieties (scarce) with thinner shells are 'Thomas', 'Stabler', and 'Ohio'. Big, hardy shade tree for big places. Don't plant near vegetable or flower gardens, rhododendrons or azaleas. Black walnut inhibits their growth, either through root competition or by a substance that inhibits growth of other plants. Long dormant season.

J. regia. ENGLISH WALNUT. Zones 4-9, 14-23; some varieties in Zones 1-3. Native to southwest Asia, southeast Europe. To 60 ft. high, with an equal spread, fast growing, especially when young. Smooth gray bark on the trunk and heavy horizontal or upward-angled branches. Leaves with 5-7 leaflets, rarely more, 3-6 in. long. The tree is hardy to –5°, but certain varieties are injured by late and early frosts in colder regions. Strains from the Carpathian mountains of eastern Europe are hardy in all but the coldest mountain areas.

English walnut should not be planted as a landscape tree except on very large lots. It's out of leaf a long time, messy when in leaf (drip and sooty mildew from aphid exudations), and messy in fruit (husks can stain). It needs deep soil and deep watering. Nevertheless many owners of subdivision homes in former walnut orchards will want to keep existing trees for shade.

To thrive, these need deep soil moisture and they need to have bases of trunks kept dry to prevent fungus attack and rot. Deep, slow irrigation in basins is ideal; where tree must grow with lawn sprinkling, keep base of trunk dry by digging away earth down to level of first roots, replacing it with coarse gravel or rock. Or pave area near trunk with brick or stone on sand. Keep plantings out under drip line where feeder roots grow.

Established plants take some drought, but in dry summer areas need deep, regular watering in summer for top-quality nuts. Old plants need pruning only to remove dead wood or correct shape. Young plants grow fast, should be trained to make a central leading shoot and branch high enough for comfortable foot traffic. Shorten overlong side branches.

Climate Zone maps pages 8-27

Spray for aphids, scale insects, codling moths, spider mites. Walnut husk fly attacks husks, making them adhere to and disfigure nuts. Control with repeated malathion sprays.

Walnut husks open in fall, dropping nuts to ground. Hasten drop by knocking nuts from tree. Pick up nuts immediately. Remove any adhering husks. Dry in a single layer spread out in airy shade—until kernels become brittle, then store.

In Zones 1-3 grow Carpathian or Hardy Persian walnuts. In Zones 4-7, 'Adams', 'Franquette', and 'Mayette' bloom late enough to escape spring frosts, yield high-quality nuts. Gardeners in Zones 8, 9 can grow 'Carmelo' (bears huge nuts), 'Drummond', 'Eureka', 'Hartley', or 'Payne'. Best varieties for Zones 14-16 are 'Carmelo', 'Concord', 'Franquette', 'Hartley', 'Mayette', 'Payne', or 'Wasson'. In Zones 18-20 grow 'Drummond', 'Payne', or 'Placentia'. In Zones 21-23, best choice is 'Placentia'.

WANDERING JEW. See Tradescantia fluminensis, Zebrina

WANDFLOWER. See Galax

WASHINGTONIA. Palms. Zones 8-24. Native to California, Arizona, northern Mexico. Fan-shaped leaves. These two are the most widely planted palms in California.

W. filifera. CALIFORNIA FAN PALM. Fast grower to 60 ft. In native stands in Southwest deserts, it always grows near springs or other moist spots. Takes desert heat and some drought, but thrives on moisture in well drained soil. Long-stalked leaves stand well apart in open crown. As leaves mature, they bend down to form a petticoat of thatch which develops in straight lines, tapering inward toward trunk at lowest edge of petticoat. Trunk much more robust than that of its Mexican cousin, even though cousin's name is "robusta". Hardy to 22°.

Use young trees in containers. In landscape can serve as street or parkway planting, in groves, or in large gardens as single trees or in groups.

Washingtonia robusta (right), is less robust-looking than W. filifera (left).

W. robusta. MEXICAN FAN PALM. Taller (to 100 ft.) more slender, more widely sold than the California fan palm. Leaf stalks are shorter, with a distinguishing reddish streak on the undersides. More compact crown, less smooth thatch. Very fast growing. Old plants take on a natural curvature; young ones started at an angle will grow upright to produce a bend. Hardy to 24°. Takes poor soil or drought, but grows faster with good conditions.

WATERCRESS. This small perennial plant grows naturally in running streams. You can plant seed in flats or pots and transplant seedlings to the moist banks, where they will grow rapidly. Or insert cuttings of watercress from the market into wet soil in or near the stream; these root readily. It can also be grown in a wet place in the garden, but requires some shade in warm inland gardens. Or, grow it in pots of soil placed in a tub of water; the water should be changed at least weekly by running a hose slowly into the tub.

WATERMELON. These need a long growing season, more heat than most other melons, and more space than other vine crops—space "hills" (circles of seed) 8 ft. by 8 ft. Other than that, culture is as described under Melon. If you garden in a commercial watermelon growing area—one of the hot-summer agricultural valleys in the coastal states or Arizona—choose any variety that suits your fancy. If your summers are short or cool (Zones 1, 4-6, 15-17, 22-24) choose one of the fast-maturing ("early") varieties. Those listed in catalogs and on seed packets at 70-75 days to harvest are best.

WATSONIA. Deciduous and evergreen perennials growing from corms. All Zones (lift and store like gladiolus in cold-winter climates). Native to South Africa. Flowers

Watsonias differ from gladiolus in having smaller, more numerous flowers on stems.

are smaller, generally more tubular than gladiolus, on taller, branched stems. They grow in fall and winter and hence are of limited use where winters are severe. All are good cut flowers. Plant late summer or early fall; plants produce foliage in autumn. Full sun. Stake tall stems if grown in pots. In mild climates they can remain undisturbed for many years. Lift and divide overcrowded clumps in summer after bloom, divide, and replant as quickly as possible.

Of about 70 species the following are best known:

W. beatricis. Evergreen. Leaves 30 in. long; July-August flowers 3 in. long, bright apricot red, on somewhat branched, 3½-ft. stems.

W. rosea. Deciduous. Blooms late spring, early summer. Rose pink to rose red 2½-in. flowers in spikelike clusters on 4-6-ft. branched stems. Many excellent large-flowered hybrids in pink, white, lavender, red. *W. r. ardernei* (often listed as *W. ardernei*), pure white.

WATTLE. See Acacia

WAXFLOWER, GERALDTON. See Chamaelaucium

WAX PLANT. See Hoya

WAYFARING-TREE. See Viburnum lantana

WEEPING WILLOW. See Salix babylonica

WEIGELA. Deciduous shrubs. Zones 1-11, 14-17. Valuable for voluminous flower display late in spring season (May-June in Northwest, earlier in California). Funnel-shaped flowers form singly or in short clusters all along previous season's shoots. When weigelas finish blooming their charm fades—they aren't especially attractive out of bloom. Most are rather coarse-leafed and stiff. They become rangy unless pruned carefully.

After flowering, prune branches that have bloomed back to unflowered side branches. Leave only 1 or 2 of these to each stem. Cut some of the oldest stems to the ground. Thin new suckers to a few of the most vigorous.

Use as backgrounds for flower borders, as summer screens, in mixed shrub borders. Can grow in full sun to part shade.

Many garden varieties are complex hybrids of four species; names are often mixed in nursery trade.

W. 'Bristol Ruby'. To 6-7 ft. tall, nearly as wide. Ruby red flowers in late spring, some repeat bloom midsummer and fall.

W. 'Bristol Snowflake'. Resembles 'Bristol Ruby', but has white flowers.

W. florida *(W. rosea).* Fast growth to 8-10 ft. tall. Flowers pink to rose red, 1 in. long, in May and June.

W. f. 'Variegata'. Bright green foliage variegated with cream. Popular and showy.

W. middendorffiana. Dense, broad shrub to 3-4 ft. tall. Leaves 2-3 in. long, 1-1½ in. wide, wrinkled, dark green. Flowers (April, May) sulfur yellow marked orange, an inch long and as wide, clustered at ends of branches. Best in cool, moist place; less rugged than other weigelas.

W. 'Newport Red'. (Also sold as *W.* 'Vaniceki', 'Cardinal', 'Rhode Island Red'.) To 6 ft. tall, with brilliant red flowers 1-1½ in. across in May-June.

WESTRINGIA rosmariniformis. Evergreen shrub. Zones 15-17, 19-24. Native to Australia. Spreading, rather loose growth to 3-6 ft. tall, half again as wide. Leaves medium green to gray-green above, white below, slightly finer, filmier in texture than rosemary. Small white flowers February through spring in colder areas, all year in milder climates.

Needs light, well drained soil in sun. Little to average water. Good near coast; very wind tolerant. Effective on sunny banks and in borders with lavender; charming with *Podocarpus gracilior.*

WHITE CUP. See Nierembergia repens

W

WHITE IRONBARK. See Eucalyptus leucoxylon

WHITETHORN, MOUNTAIN. See Ceanothus cordulatus

WIGANDIA caracasana. Treelike, woody perennial. Zones 17, 22-24. Fast growth to 10-25 ft. or more. Spreads by underground stems. Stems permanent, leaves evergreen in mildest areas. Stems die back, leaves drop at 30°; young plants may die at this temperature. Established plants root-hardy to 25°. Foliage very coarse; leaves 1½-2 ft. long, broadly oval (sometimes lobed), covered with stinging prickles. Flowers (early spring) lavender-blue, ¾ in. across, in long, large, curving clusters.

Takes almost any soil, little or much water. Because of size and coarseness, best used with big plants, bold structures, boulders. Can bring look of tropical foliage to dry hillsides. Must be sprayed to control caterpillars, keep leaves unmarred.

WILGA. See Geijera

WILLOW. See Salix

WILLOW, AUSTRALIAN. See Geijera

WILLOW, DESERT. See Chilopsis

WILLOW MYRTLE, AUSTRALIAN. See Agonis flexuosa

WINDFLOWER. See Anemone

WINEBERRY, NEW ZEALAND. See Aristotelia

WINGNUT, CHINESE. See Pterocarya

WINTER CREEPER, BIGLEAF. See Euonymus fortunei radicans 'Vegeta'

WINTER CREEPER, COMMON. See Euonymus fortunei radicans

WINTER CREEPER, PURPLE LEAF. See Euonymus fortunei 'Colorata'

WINTER HAZEL. See Corylopsis

WINTER'S BARK. See Drimys

WINTERGREEN. See Gaultheria procumbens

WINTERSWEET. See Chimonanthus

WINTERSWEET, AFRICAN. See Acokanthera spectabilis

WIRE VINE. See Muehlenbeckia

WISHBONE FLOWER. See Torenia

WISTERIA. Deciduous vine. All Zones (but some flower buds damaged in cold winters in coldest parts of Zone 1). Twining, woody vines of great size, long life, and exceptional beauty in flower. So adaptable that it can be grown as a tree, a shrub, or a vine.

To get off to a good start, buy a grafted or cutting-grown wisteria; seedlings may not bloom for many years. Keep suckers pulled, or they may take over. Wisterias are not fussy about soil, but they need good drainage, ample water during bloom or growth. In alkaline soil, watch for chlorosis and treat with iron chelates or iron sulfate.

Pruning and training are important for bloom production and control of plant's size, shape. Let newly set plants grow to establish a framework. Remove stems that interfere with framework, pinch back side stems and long streamers, rub off buds that develop on trunk. Remember that main stem will become a good-sized trunk, and that the weight of a mature vine is considerable. Give firm support, and tie developing stems where you want them.

Tree wisterias can be bought ready-trained; or you can train your own. Remove all but one main stem, and stake this one securely. Tie stem to stake at frequent intervals; use soft ties to prevent binding. When plant has reached height at which you wish head to form, pinch or prune out tip to force branching. Shorten branches to beef them up. Pinch back long streamers, rub off all buds that form below head. Replace stakes and ties as needed.

Wisterias can be trained as big shrubs or multi-stem, small, semi-weeping trees; permit well spaced branches to form the framework, shorten side branches, and nip long streamers. Unsupported plants make vigorous bank cover.

Young plants should be well fed and watered; blooming-size, established plants flower better with less food and water. Prune blooming plants every winter, cutting back or thinning out side shoots from main or structural stems and shortening back to 2-3 buds the flower-producing spurs that grow from these shoots. You'll have no trouble recognizing the fat flower buds on these spurs.

In summer cut back long streamers before they tangle up in the main body of the vine; save those you want to use to extend height or length of vine and tie them to support—eaves, wall, trellis, arbor. If old plants grow rampantly but fail to bloom, prune roots by cutting vertically with a spade.

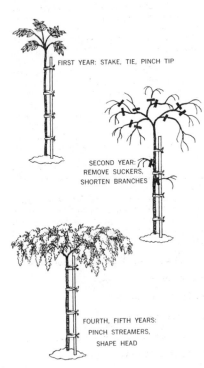

FIRST YEAR: STAKE, TIE, PINCH TIP

SECOND YEAR: REMOVE SUCKERS, SHORTEN BRANCHES

FOURTH, FIFTH YEARS: PINCH STREAMERS. SHAPE HEAD

Training a wisteria to tree form consists mostly of staking, controlling growth.

W. floribunda. (Often sold as *W. multijuga.*) JAPANESE WISTERIA. Leaves 12-16 in. long, divided into 15-19 leaflets. Violet or violet-blue, fragrant flowers in 18-in. clusters appear with leaves in April-May. Flowers begin to open at top of cluster, gradually open toward bottom, prolonging bloom season but making less spectacular burst of color than Chinese wisteria. Long clusters give extreme beauty of line. Many varieties obtainable: 'Alba' has white flowers; 'Geisha', bluest flowers, in clusters of moderate length; 'Issai', blue-purple, in 12 in. clusters, often repeats bloom in midsummer; 'Longissima' ('Macrobotrys'), very long (1½-3-ft.) clusters of violet flowers; 'Longissima Alba', white flowers in 2-ft. clusters; 'Rosea', pink flowers in 15-18-in. clusters; 'Royal Purple', violet purple, in clusters to 2 ft.

Japanese wisteria blooms best in full sun.

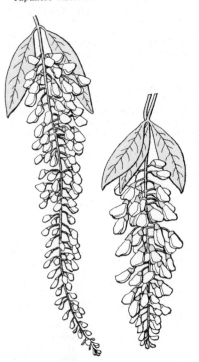

Long clusters of Japanese wisteria (left); Chinese opens whole cluster at once.

W. sinensis. CHINESE WISTERIA. Most widely planted throughout West. Leaves divided into 7-13 leaflets. Plants bloom before leaves expand in April-May. Flower clusters shorter (to 12 in.) than those of Japanese wisteria, but make quite a show by opening nearly the full length of the cluster at one time. Violet-blue. Slightly fragrant. Will bloom in considerable shade. *W. s.* 'Alba' is the white flowering form.

W. venusta. (Often sold as *W. v.* 'Alba'.) SILKY WISTERIA. Leaves have silky hairs. Individual flowers white, very large, long-stalked, in short, heavy clusters that open all at once. Very profuse bloom when leaves begin to break in April. *W. v.* 'Violacea' has fragrant, purple-blue flowers. Older plants (especially in tree form) remarkably profuse in bloom.

WISTERIA TREE, SCARLET. See Daubentonia

WITCH HAZEL. See Hamamelis

WONGA-WONGA VINE. See Pandorea pandorana

WOODBINE. See Lonicera periclymenum

WOODWARDIA. CHAIN FERN. Large, strong-growing ferns. The only common species is the native giant chain fern.

W. fimbriata. (Often sold as *W. chamissoi* or *W. radicans*.) GIANT CHAIN FERN. Zones 4-9, 14-24. Native British Columbia to Mexico, always in moist places. The largest native fern, it can reach 9 ft. tall in wet coastal forests. Fronds twice cut, rather coarse in texture, with strong upright or spreading silhouette. Excellent near pool or brook, against a shaded wall, in woodland gardens. Slow to establish, ultimately withstands neglect.

W. orientalis. Zones 17, 22-24. Native to Japan, Formosa. Broad, arching, drooping fronds to 8 ft. long, of leathery texture and quite red when immature, deep green later. Produces many plantlets on fronds. Stunning in shaded raised beds, where its fronds will cascade; or massed at woodland edge. Hardy to 26°.

W. radicans. EUROPEAN CHAIN FERN. Zones 15-17, 19-24. Southern Europe to China. Resembles *W. fimbriata* but more arching and drooping, the fronds broader at the base. Forms bulblets at tips of fronds; these root while attached to plant. To 3 ft. tall, fronds 4-6 ft. long, 1½-2 ft. wide.

WOOLFLOWER, CHINESE. See Celosia argentea 'Childsii'

WOOLLY BLUE CURLS. See Trichostema

WORMWOOD. See Artemisia

XANTHOCERAS sorbifolium. HYACINTH SHRUB. Deciduous. Zones 1-10, 14-17. Slow to moderate growth to 8-10, rarely 25 ft. tall, usually wider than high. Sometimes a multi-stem tree with spreading trunks. Leaves much like mountain ash, 5-8 in. long, with 9-17 narrow, bright green leaflets. Showy in bloom—April-May. Upright spikelike flower clusters 6-10 in. long, dense, with many crinkled inch-wide white flowers. These have yellow centers that age to rose. Shorter clusters on short side branches. Seeds marble-size, black, in leathery capsules. Average soil, good drainage. Takes heat, cold, wind. Use in big shrub borders, or as single plant in a lawn.

XANTHORRHEA. GRASSTREE. Perennials. Zones 17, 20-24. Native to Australia. Dense tufts of narrow, long, grasslike leaves radiate out from top of thick, woody, very slow growing stem. Flowers white, in a dense, narrow spike on a tall stem. Drought resistant. Best used with yuccas, century plants, succulents in dry, loose, sandy soil.

X. preissii. BLACKBOY. Stem slow growing, but in age may reach 15 ft. Leaves 2-4 ft. long, about ⅛ in. wide. Flower spike 1-3 ft. long, on a stem of equal length.

X. quadrangulata. Trunk several feet high. Leaves 1½ ft. long. Spike and its stem may reach 12-15 ft.

XANTHOSOMA. Cormlike tubers. Zone 24. Tender to half-hardy. Tropical foliage plants related to *Alocasia*. All have big arrow-shaped leaves on long stalks. Flowers

clustered on a spike surrounded by a calla-like spathe, usually greenish or yellowish and more curious than attractive. Rich soil, ample water. Use with ferns, begonias, schefflera. Protect from hard frosts.

X. sagittaefolium. Trunklike stem to 3 ft. Dark green leaves 3 ft. long on 3 ft. stems. Spathes greenish white, 7-9 in. long.

X. violaceum. Stemless, forming clumps by offsets. Leaves to 2 ft. long, 18 in. wide, dark green above, lighter beneath, purplish veins and margin, powdery appearance. Leaf stalks 2½ ft., purple, with a heavy, waxy, bluish or grayish cast. Spathes yellowish white, large.

XERANTHEMUM annuum. COMMON IMMORTELLE. Annual. To 2½ ft. tall. An everlasting flower; fluffy heads of papery bracts up to 1½ in. across in pink, lavender, white, shades of violet-purple. Scant foliage is silvery green. Sow seed in spring in place in full sun. Accepts almost any soil. Cut flowers dried for winter bouquets.

XYLOSMA congestum (*X. senticosum*). Evergreen or deciduous shrub or small tree. Zones 8-24. Usually a loose, graceful, spreading shrub 8-10 ft. tall and as wide or wider. Height easily controlled. Leaves shiny, yellowish green, long-pointed oval in shape, clean and attractive. New growth bronzy. Flowers insignificant, rarely seen.

Left alone, plants develop an angular main stem that takes its time zigzagging upward. Meanwhile side branches grow long and graceful, arching or drooping, sometimes lying on the ground. Easily trained as espalier. If shrub is staked and side growth pruned, can be made into a 15-30-ft. spreading tree.

Adaptable to most soils; heat tolerant; established plants survive with little water but look better with adequate water, moderate feeding. Best growth in full sun or filtered shade. Spray as necessary to control occasional scale or red spider mites. Apply iron chelates or iron sulfate for chlorosis.

One of the handsomest, easiest, and most versatile of the all-foliage, landscape structure plants. Unattractive appearance in nursery cans (especially in winter, when plants may be nearly bare of leaves) and slow start in the ground may discourage the gardener. Plants actually are hardy to 10°, but may lose many (or all) leaves in sharp frosts. Plant normally sheds many old leaves in April when new growth begins. Well established plants usually evergreen except in coldest seasons, and new leaves come on fast.

Use as single or multiple trunk tree, arching shrub, ground or bank cover (prune out erect growth), espalier on wall or fence, clipped or unclipped hedge (twine long branches together to fill in gaps faster).

YANGTAO. See Actinidia chinensis

YARROW. See Achillea

YATE. See Eucalyptus

YAUPON. See Ilex vomitoria

YELLOW BELLS. See Stenolobium

YELLOW-ELDER. See Stenolobium

YELLOW-EYED GRASS. See Sisyrinchium californicum

YELLOW MESSMATE. See Eucalyptus cloeziana

YELLOW WOOD. See Cladrastis

YERBA BUENA. See Satureja douglasii

YESTERDAY-TODAY-AND-TOMORROW. See Brunfelsia floribunda

YEW. See Taxus

YEW, KOREAN. See Cephalotaxus

YUCCA. Evergreen perennials, shrubs, trees. Yuccas grow over much of North America, and hardiness depends on species. All have clusters of tough, sword-shaped leaves and large clusters of white or whitish flowers. Some are stemless while others reach tree size. Best in full sun in well drained soil. Most take considerable drought when established—many are true desert plants. Most will accept garden watering.

Group with agaves, cactus, succulents in desert gardens or grow with various softer leafed tropical foliage plants. Taller kinds make striking silhouettes, and even stemless species make important and vertical effects when in bloom. Some have sharp-pointed leaves; keep these away from walks, terraces, other well traveled areas.

Y. aloifolia. SPANISH BAYONET. Zones 7-24. Native southern U.S. Slow growth to 10 ft. or more, trunk either single or branched, or sprawling in picturesque effect. Sharp-pointed leaves to 2½ ft. long and 2 in. wide densely clothe stems. Leaves are dark green; in *Y. a.* 'Variegata' they are marked yellow or white. Flowers white sometimes tinged purple, to 4 in. across in dense, erect clusters to 2 ft. tall. Summer bloom.

Y. australis (*Y. filifera*). Zones 16, 17, 19-24. Native to Mexico. Tree 20-50 ft. tall; trunk 2-5 ft. thick, swollen at base. Leaves 1-1½ ft. long, 1-1½ in. wide. Flowers (May-June) white, in dense, hanging clusters 4-5 ft. long, 15-18 in. thick.

Y. baccata. DATIL YUCCA. All Zones. Native to deserts of southern California, Nevada, to Colorado and Texas. Single stemless rosettes or sometimes in clumps with short, leaning trunks to 3 ft. Leaves 2 ft. long, 2 in. wide. Flowers (May-June) fleshy, red-brown outside, white inside, in a dense cluster 2 ft. long. Fleshy fruits were eaten by Indians.

Y. brevifolia. JOSHUA TREE. Zones 8-24. Native to deserts southern California, Nevada. Utah, Arizona. Tree of slow growth to 15-30 ft. with heavy trunk, few, heavy branches. Leaves clustered near ends of branches, short, broad, sword-shaped. Old, dead leaves hang on a long time. Flowers (February-April) greenish white, in dense, heavy, foot-long clusters.

Collected plants sometimes available; nursery plants very slow to make trunks. Best in dry, well drained soil in desert gardens. Difficult under average garden conditions.

Y. elata. SOAPTREE YUCCA. Zones 7-24. Native to Arizona-west Texas and northern Mexico. Slow growth to 6-20 ft. with single or branched trunk. Leaves to 4 ft. long, ½ in. wide. White summer flowers in very tall spikes.

Y. elephantipes (*Y. gigantea*). GIANT YUCCA. Zones 16, 17, 19-24. Native to Mexico. Fast growing (to 2 ft. a year), eventually 15-30 ft. tall, usually with several

Y

Climate Zone maps pages 8-27

trunks. Leaves 4 ft. long, 3 in. wide, dark rich green, not spine-tipped. Striking silhouette alone or combined with other big scale foliage plants; out of scale in smaller gardens. Large spikes of creamy white flowers in spring. Does best in good, well drained soil with ample water.

Y. filamentosa. ADAM'S NEEDLE. All Zones. Native to southeastern U.S. Much like *Y. flaccida*, but with stiffer, narrower leaves, narrower flower clusters.

Y. flaccida. All Zones. Native southeastern U.S. Leaves to 2½ ft. long, 1 in. wide, with long, loose fibers at edges of leaves. Flowers white, in tall branching clusters to 4-7 ft. or more in height. Lightly fragrant in the evening. One of hardiest, most widely planted in colder regions.

Y. glauca. SMALL SOAPWEED. All Zones. Native Texas, New Mexico to Montana, South Dakota. Stemless or short-stemmed. Leaves 1-2½ ft. long. Summer flowers greenish white in tall, narrow clusters.

Y. gloriosa. SPANISH DAGGER, SOFT-TIP YUCCA. Zones 7-24. Much like *Y. aloifolia*, generally with multiple trunks, to 10 ft. tall. Blooms late summer. Leaf points will not penetrate skin. Good green color blends well with lush, tropical-looking plants. Easy garden plant, but over-watering may produce black areas on leaf margins. There is a variegated form.

Y. harrimaniae. All Zones. Native to Colorado and the Southwest. Short stemmed or stemless; clumps single or clustered. Leaves yellowish or bluish green, 4-18 in. long, ½-1½ in. wide. Summer flowers greenish white, 2-2½ in. across, in erect, unbranched clusters 1-3 ft. tall. May be slow to reach blooming age in coldest climates.

Y. recurvifolia (*Y. pendula*). Zones 7-24. Native southeastern U.S. Single, unbranching trunk to 6-10 ft. tall, or lightly branched in age. Can be cut back to keep a single trunk. Spreads by offsets to make large groups. Leaves 2-3 ft. long, 2 in. wide, beautiful blue-gray-green, spine-tipped,

sharply bent downward. Leaf tips bend to touch, are not dangerous. Less stiff and metallic-looking than most yuccas. Flower (in June) white, in a loose, open cluster 3-5 ft. tall. Easy to grow under all garden conditions.

Y. schidigera (*Y. mohavensis*). Zones 10-24. Native to deserts of California, Nevada, Arizona, Baja California. Trunk 3-12 ft. tall, single or branched. Leaves 2-3 ft. long, 1-2½ in. wide, yellowish green. Flowers (April-May) in 2-ft. clusters, creamy or purple-tinted.

Y. schottii (*Y. macrocarpa*). Zones 7-24. Native to Arizona, New Mexico, northern Mexico. Treelike with unbranched or branched trunk 6-20 ft. tall. Leaves gray-green to yellow-green, 1½-3 ft. long, 1½ in. wide, tipped with sharp spines. Summer flowers white, 1-2 in. long, in branched clusters 1-3 ft. long.

Y. torreyi. TORREY YUCCA. Zones 7-24. Native to west Texas. Trunk to 10-15 ft., usually not branched. Leaves to 3 ft. long, stiff, sharp-pointed. White summer flowers in dense, heavy, fat-looking clusters partially hidden by leaves.

Y. whipplei. OUR LORD'S CANDLE. Zones 5-24. Native to southern California mountains, California coast, Baja California. Stemless, with dense cluster of rigid, gray-green leaves 1-1¾ ft. long. These are needle-tipped; don't plant where people can walk into them.

Flowering stems to 6-14 ft. long. Drooping, bell-shaped, 1-2-in. creamy white blossoms in large, branched spikes 3-6 ft. long. Plants die after blooming and producing seed. New plants come from seeds or offsets.

ZANTEDESCHIA. CALLA. Rhizome. Zones 5, 6, 8, 9, 14-24. Native to South Africa. Basal clumps of long-stalked, shining, rich green, arrow- or lance-shaped leaves, sometimes spotted white. Flower bract surrounds a central spike that is tightly covered with tiny true flowers.

Common calla tolerates many soils. Full sun near coast, partial shade in hot-summer areas. Thrives on heavy watering, even grows in bogs. Nearly evergreen in mild areas, deciduous where winters are cold. Set rhizomes 4-6 in. deep, 1-2 ft. apart.

Golden, pink, and spotted callas need slightly acid soil, moderate water with drainage, and a resting season. Plant 2 in. deep, 12 in. apart. In mild climates they survive in well drained, open ground beds. If drainage is poor or frosts heavy, dry off gradually in late summer, dig, and store at 40°-50° in dry soil, sawdust, or peat moss. To grow in pots, set 2 in. deep (1 rhizome to a 6-in. pot), water sparingly until leaves appear. Then water freely, feed weekly with mild solution of complete fertilizer. Reduce watering after bloom to dry off plants, then withhold entirely until new growth begins.

Z. aethiopica. COMMON CALLA. Forms large clump of leaves 18 in. long, 10 in. wide. Pure white or creamy white 8-in.-long bracts on 3-ft. stems appear almost continuously in mild climates. Variety 'Godefreyana' smaller than species, flowers very heavily. 'Hercules' larger than species, has big bracts that open flat, curve backward. 'Childsiana' is 12-in. tall. 'Minor' 18 in., bracts 4 in. long.

Z. albo-maculata. SPOTTED CALLA. Grows to 2 ft. Leaves spotted white. Bracts 4-5 in. long, creamy yellow or white with purplish crimson blotch at base. Spring-summer bloom.

Z. elliottiana. GOLDEN CALLA. To 18-24 in., with bright green, white spotted leaves 10 in. long by 6 in. wide. Flower bracts 4-5 in. long, changing from greenish yellow to rich golden yellow. June-July.

Z. rehmannii. RED OR PINK CALLA. To 12-18 in., with narrow, lance-shaped, unspotted green leaves 1 ft. long. Pink or rosy pink bracts to 4 in. long. Blooms May. 'Superba' deeper pink, improved variety, generally sold rather than species. Hybrids of this and other callas available; flowers range through pinks and yellows to orange and buff tones, with some purplish and lavender tones on yellow grounds.

ZANTHOXYLUM piperitum. JAPAN PEPPER. Deciduous shrub or small tree. Zones 6-9, 14-17. Dense, to 20 ft. Leaves 3-6 in. long, divided into 7-11, 2-in.-long, oval leaflets. Main leaf stalk prickly. The form sometimes seen in California nurseries has yellow main leaf stalk, yellow blotches at base of each leaflet. Flowers inconspicuous, green. Small black aromatic fruits ground and used as seasoning in Japan.

Ordinary garden soil. Full sun. Moderate water.

ZAUSCHNERIA. CALIFORNIA FUCHSIA, HUMMINGBIRD FLOWER. Perennials or subshrubs. Zones 4-9, 14-24. These California natives can take dry, hot summers and give many pretty red flowers against gray foliage from summer to fall but they never will become completely domesticated. They always grow a bit rangy, spread into other garden beds with invasive roots, go to seed and reseed themselves, and become twiggy and ungroomed through the winter. Use them in informal gardens, at summer cabins, on banks or hillsides. All have small, gray or gray-green, narrow leaves, ½-1½ in. long, and bright scarlet, trumpet-shaped flowers,

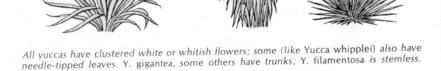

YUCCA FILAMENTOSA   Y. GIGANTEA   Y. WHIPPLEI

All yuccas have clustered white or whitish flowers; some (like Yucca whipplei) also have needle-tipped leaves. Y. gigantea, some others have trunks; Y. filamentosa is stemless.

Climate Zone maps pages 8-27

1½-2 in. long. The flowers attract hummingbirds.

Z. californica. Stems upright or somewhat arching, 1-2 ft. tall. Plants sometimes shrubby at base. Evergreen in mild-winter climates.

Z. cana. Stems woody at base, sprawling. Foliage dense; leaves very narrow, silvery. Evergreen in mild-winter climates.

Z. septentrionalis. (Often sold as *Z. latifolia* 'Etteri'.) Perennial. Makes mats of closely-set stems that grow about 6 in. high. Dies to ground in winter.

ZEBRA PLANT. See Calathea

ZEBRINA pendula. WANDERING JEW. Evergreen perennial. This house plant has much the same growth habit and leaf shape as *Tradescantia fluminensis,* but is not as hardy. Known mostly in its variegated forms. *Z. pendula* 'Quadricolor' has purplish green leaves with longitudinal bands of white, pink, and carmine red. When selecting a location indoors, remember that variegated plants need more light than all-green ones.

ZELKOVA serrata. SAWLEAF ZELKOVA. Deciduous tree. All Zones. A good shade tree, it grows at moderate to fast rate, eventually to 60 ft. or higher, and equally wide. Smooth gray bark like that of beech. Leaves similar to those of elm (2-3½ in. long by 1½ in. wide). Carefully train young trees to develop strong framework—head back excessively long, pendulous branches to force side growth, thin competing branches to permit full development of the strongest. Water deeply to encourage deep rooting. Very pest-free; sometimes gets red spider mites.

Fall foliage color varies from yellow to dark red to dull reddish brown.

ZENOBIA pulverulenta (*Andromeda speciosa*). Deciduous shrub. Zones 4-7, 14-17. Native southeastern U.S. Slow growth to 2-4, possibly 6 ft. Open, loose growth. Leaves pale green, 1-2 in. long, half as wide; new growth heavily dusted with bluish white powder in pearly gray effect. Flowers white, bell-shaped, ½ in. across, in loose clusters at ends of branches. Blooms June-July in Northwest. Sometimes spreads by underground stems.

Related to heaths and heathers; needs acid, uniformly moist soil, partial shade in warm exposures.

ZEPHYRANTHES. ZEPHYR FLOWER, FAIRY LILY. Bulb. All Zones. Bright green, rushlike leaves. Funnel-shaped flowers with six similarly shaped segments appear singly on hollow stems, usually in late summer or early fall, often throughout the year if kept alternately wet and dry. In the wild, flowers appear a few days after a rain (hence, often called rain lilies).

Use in rock garden or foreground of border. Good in pots. Plant late summer or early fall; set bulbs 1-2 in. deep, 3 in. apart. Full sun, although *Z. candida* takes light shade. In cold climates, plant in spring and lift in fall; or mulch heavily over winter months.

Z. ajax. Hybrid between *Z. candida* and *Z. citrina.* Free flowering, light yellow. Evergreen. Leaves to 8 in. long.

Z. candida. Rushlike evergreen leaves in large clumps. Flowers 2 in. long, glossy-textured, pure white outside, tinged rose inside; blooms in late summer, autumn.

Z. citrina. Fragrant, lemon yellow, 2-in. flowers. Narrow ridged leaves.

Z. grandiflora. Flowers 4 in. across, rose pink, look like small amaryllis; 8-in. stems. Leaves 12 in. long, appearing with flowers in late spring, early summer.

Z. hybrids. 'Alamo' has deep rose pink flowers flushed yellow. 'Apricot Queen', low growing, yellow flowers stained pink. 'Prairie Sunset', large, light yellow flowers suffused with pink, appearing after rain or a watering. 'Ruth Page' is rich pink.

ZEPHYR FLOWER. See Zephyranthes

ZINGIBER officinale. TRUE GINGER. Perennial with thick rhizomes. Zones 9, 14-24. Rhizomes are the source of ginger used in cooking. Stems 2-4 ft. tall. Narrow, bright green, glossy leaves to 1 ft. long. Flowers (rarely seen), yellowish green, with a purple lip marked yellow. Tropical in origin, ginger needs heat and humidity; shade from hottest sun. Buy roots (fresh, not dried) at a grocery store in early spring; cut into 1-2-in.-long sections with well developed growth buds. Plant jus⸱ underground in rich, moist soil. Water cautiously until top and root growth are active, then heavily. Feed once a month.

Plants are dormant in winter; rhizomes may rot in cold, wet soil. Plant with tree ferns, camellias, fuchsias, begonias. Harvest roots at any time—but allow several months for them to reach some size.

ZINNIA. Annuals. Long-time garden favorites for colorful, round flower heads in summer and early fall. Distinctly hot weather plants, they do not gain from being planted early, merely stand still until weather warms up. Subject to mildew in foggy places, or when given overhead water, and when autumn brings longer nights, more dew, and more shade. Sow seeds where plants are to grow (or set out nursery plants) in May-July. Give plants good garden soil in a sunny place. Feed and water generously but always water by soaking soil, not by overhead sprinkling.

Most garden zinnias belong to *Z. elegans,* but the other two species are grown.

Thumbelina zinnias are half the size of big 6-in. blooms of State Fair strain.

Z. angustifolia. Plants compact, 1-1½ ft. tall, leaves narrower than on common zinnias. Double strains Persian Carpet (1 ft. tall) and Old Mexico (16 in. tall) have flowers in strong shades of mahogany red, yellow, and orange, usually mixed in the same flower head. Colorful, long blooming.

Z. elegans. Plant height ranges from 1-3 ft., flower head size from less than 1 in. to 7 in. across; forms include full doubles, cactus flowered (with quilled rays), crested (cushion center surrounded by rows of broad rays); colors include white, pink, rose, red, yellow, orange, lavender, purple, and green.

Thumbelina strain blooms when 3 in. tall, and plants reach only 8 in. Tom Thumb, Cupid, and Sprite are other small-flowered kinds on larger, but still compact, plants. Large-flowered strains include State Fair, Burpeeana, Giant Cactus Flowered, Mammoth Dahlia, and F₁ Hybrid Zenith. Art Shades, Pastel Mixed, and California Giants are large flowered strains with soft, pastel colors. Pinwheel, Peppermint Stick, and Merry-Go-Round have striped, spotted, or bicolored flower heads.

Z. linearis. Compact plants to 8 in. tall. Leaves very narrow. Inch-wide flower heads orange, each ray with a paler stripe. Blooms in six weeks from seed, continues late into fall.

ZIZYPHUS jujuba. CHINESE JUJUBE. Deciduous tree. Zones 7-16, 18-24; hardy in Zones 4-6 but fruit ripens only in warmest summers. Slow to moderate growth rate to 20-30 ft. Branches spiny, gnarled, somewhat pendulous. Leaves glossy, bright green, 1-2 in. long, with 3 prominent veins. Clusters of small yellowish flowers in May-June. Shiny, reddish brown datelike fruits in fall have sweet, applelike flavor; candied and dried, they resemble dates.

Deep rooted, it takes well to desert conditions, tolerating drought, saline and alkaline soils. Grows better in good garden soil with regular, deep watering. Thrives in lawns. No serious pests, but subject to Texas root rot in deserts. Prune in winter to shape, encourage weeping habit, or reduce size. Attractive silhouette, foliage, fruit, and toughness make a good decorative tree, especially for high desert.

Fruits of seedlings are ½-1 in. long. Two cultivated varieties are 'Lang' (1½-2-in.-long fruits, bears young) and 'Li', with 2-in.-long fruits.

ZOYSIA tenuifolia. KOREAN GRASS. Zones 8-24. This zoysia is a ground cover grass—too lumpy to be called a lawn. Creeping, fine textured, makes a beautiful tapestry, especially on steep slopes. Takes full sun to medium shade. Hardy to 10° but turns brown with first frost, remains brown until early spring. Plant pieces from flats 8 in. apart.

The other species of zoysia are lawn grasses (see lawn chapter).

ZUCCHINI. See Squash

ZYGOCACTUS truncatus. Two plants have been sold under this name. For the best known of these, Christmas cactus, see *Schlumbergera bridgesii.* For the scarlet-flowered crab cactus, see *Schlumbergera truncata.*

Index

To find a plant description look up plant names in the alphabetical encyclopedia, pages 167-445.
The index that follows gives page numbers for general garden subjects only.